SIMULATION MODELING AND ANALYSIS

McGraw-Hill Series in Industrial Engineering and Management Science

Consulting Editor

James L. Riggs, *Department of Industrial Engineering, Oregon State University*

Barish and Kaplan: *Economic Analysis: For Engineering and Managerial Decision Making*
Blank: *Statistical Procedures for Engineering, Management, and Science*
Cleland Kocaoglu: *Engineering Management*
Denton: *Safety Management: Improving Performance*
Dervitsiotis: *Operations Management*
Gillet: *Introduction to Operations Research: A Computer-oriented Algorithmic Approach*
Hicks: *Introduction to Industrial Engineering and Management Science*
Huchingson: *New Horizons for Human Factors in Design*
Law and Kelton: *Simulation Modeling and Analysis*
Leherer: *White-Collar Productivity*
Love: *Inventory Control*
Niebel, Draper and Wysk: *Modern Manufacturing Process Engineering*
Polk: *Methods Analysis and Work Measurement*
Riggs and West: *Engineering Economics*
Taguchi, Elsayed and Hsiang: *Quality Engineering in Production Systems*
Riggs and West: *Essentials of Engineering Economics*
Wu and Coppins: *Linear Programming and Extensions*

SIMULATION MODELING AND ANALYSIS

Second Edition

Averill M. Law

President
Simulation Modeling and Analysis Company
Tucson, Arizona

Professor of Decision Sciences
University of Arizona

W. David Kelton

Associate Professor of Operations and Management Science
Curtis L. Carlson School of Management
University of Minnesota

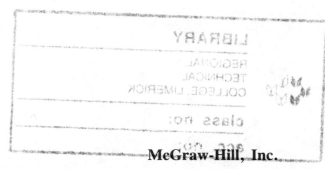
McGraw-Hill, Inc.

New York St. Louis San Francisco Auckland Bogotá Caracas Hamburg
Lisbon London Madrid Mexico Milan Montreal New Delhi Paris
San Juan São Paulo Singapore Sydney Tokyo Toronto

SIMULATION MODELING AND ANALYSIS
International Editions 1991

Exclusive rights by McGraw-Hill Book Co. - Singapore for manufacture and
export. This book cannot be re-exported from the country to which it is consigned
by McGraw-Hill.

3 4 5 6 7 8 9 0 CWP FC 9 8 7 6 5 4 3

This book was set in Times Roman.
The editors were Eric M. Munson and Margery Luhrs.
The production supervisor was Louise Karam.
The cover was designed by Ed Butler.

Library of Congress Cataloging-in-Publication Data

Law, Averill M.
      Simulation modeling and analysis/Averill M. Law, W. David
Kelton. - 2nd ed.
        p.   cm. - (McGraw-Hill series in industrial engineering and
management science)
      Includes bibliographical references and index.
      ISBN 0-07-036698-5
1. Digital computer simulation.   I. Kelton. W. David.   II. Title
III. Series.
QA76.9.C65L38   1991
003'.3 - dc20   90-42969

When ordering this title, use ISBN 0-07-100803-9

Printed in Singapore

ABOUT THE AUTHORS

Averill M. Law is President of Simulation Modeling and Analysis Company (Tucson, Arizona), and Professor of Decision Sciences at the University of Arizona. He has been a simulation consultant to such organizations as General Motors, IBM, AT&T, General Electric, 3M, Nabisco, Xerox, Kimberly-Clark, NASA, the Army, the Navy, and the Air Force. He has presented more than 160 simulation seminars in 10 countries.

He is the author (or coauthor) of four books and numerous papers on simulation, manufacturing, operations research, and statistics. His article, "Statistical Analysis of Simulation Output Data," was the first invited feature paper on simulation to appear in a major research journal. He won the 1988 Institute of Industrial Engineers' best publication award for his series of papers on the simulation of manufacturing systems. He is the codeveloper of the UniFit II software package for fitting probability distributions to observed data, and he developed a four-hour videotape on simulation with the Society for Manufacturing Engineers. Dr. Law writes a regular column on simulation for *Industrial Engineering* magazine.

He was previously Associate Professor of Industrial Enginering at the University of Wisconsin. Dr. Law has a Ph.D. in Industrial Engineering and Operations Research from the University of California at Berkeley.

W. David Kelton is Associate Professor of Operations and Management Science in the Curtis L. Carlson School of Management at the University of Minnesota, in Minneapolis, where he teaches courses on simulation, stochastic processes, statistics, and computing. He received a B.A. in Mathematics from the University of Wisconsin—Madison, an M.S. in Mathematics from Ohio University, as well as M.S. and Ph.D. degrees in Industrial Engineering from the University of Wisconsin. His research interests include the design and analysis of simulation experiments, applied stochastic processes, and statistical quality control. He serves as Associate Editor for *Operations Research* and *IIE Transactions*, and is Simulation Area Editor for the *ORSA Journal on Comput-*

ing; he is also President of The Institute for Management Sciences College on Simulation. In 1987 he served as Program Chair for the Winter Simulation Conference, and is General Chair for this conference in 1991. He has consulted with private industry, government, and nonprofit organizations on simulation and related topics.

To my wife, Steffi, and children, Heather, Adam, and Brian,
for their encouragement and understanding
during the writing of this book.
Averill M. Law

For Christie, Molly, and Anna.
W. David Kelton

CONTENTS

Chapter 9 Output Data Analysis for a Single System

Chapter 10 Comparing Alternative System Configurations

LIST OF SYMBOLS

PREFACE TO THE SECOND EDITION

While the general philosophy and organization of the First Edition have been retained, the text has been almost completely rewritten. Our primary reasons for doing such a major revision were to bring the material up to date; to improve exposition and clarity, especially for the introductory material; and to emphasize the practical utility of the more advanced techniques treated in the later chapters. There is one completely new chapter on manufacturing systems (Chap. 13), and the material on validation (formerly Chap. 10) has been moved forward (now Chap. 5) to emphasize that this activity must begin early in a simulation project. The numbers of examples, figures, and problems have been greatly expanded. A comprehensive Solutions Manual is available from the publisher.

Several specific features of the Second Edition should be mentioned. At the beginning of each chapter we suggest particular sections that we feel are fundamental for all readers. A list of symbols and abbreviations has also been added. The computer programs in Chaps. 1 and 2 have been rewritten to use FORTRAN 77, and we have added complete Pascal and C versions of the simulations in Chap. 1. (Chapter numbers henceforth refer to the Second Edition.) The material on simulation languages in Chap. 3 has been updated and now includes a discussion of animation. The review material in Chap. 4 has been expanded to make it more accessible. Chapter 5 has been updated to reflect current thinking on validation, and emphasizes practical methods. Chapter 6 has many extended examples to illustrate the difficult task of input-distribution specification. Chapter 7, on random-number generators, has been updated, and includes in App. 7A highly portable codes (in FORTRAN, Pascal, and C) for a reliable generator. Chapter 8 contains expanded explanations of variate-generation methods, emphasizing graphical aids for enhancing insight. Chapter 9 gives an updated and practically oriented discussion of output analysis. Chapters 10 through 12 have been updated and rewritten to enhance development of intuition, and include many detailed examples of the use of statistical comparison and ranking procedures, variance-reduction techniques, and experimental-design methodology. The new chapter (Chap. 13) discusses simulation applications to manufacturing systems, including relevant software and several comprehensive examples/case studies.

We have received valuable input from a large number of people and organizations in preparing this major revision. The second author received substantial support from the University of Minnesota, especially the Department of Operations and Management Science, the Carlson School of Management, and Academic Computing Services; he is also grateful to the Minnesota Supercomputer Institute for computational support. Special personal thanks go to Michael McComas and Stephen Vincent for numerous contributions throughout the book, and to Tom Schriber for his detailed reading of much of the manuscript. Knowing that we will almost surely commit grievous errors of omission, we would nonetheless like to thank the following individuals for their time and help: Joe Annino, Scott Baird, Diane Bischak, Glenn Browne, Tom Chan, John Charnes, Youngsoo Chun, Dave Goldsman, Jorge Haddock, Wali Haider, Jim Henriksen, Tom Hoffmann, Sheldon Jacobson, Walter Karplus, Pierre L'Ecuyer, Charlie Murgiano, Joe Murray, Chris Nachtsheim, Barry Nelson, Bill Nordgren, Jean O'Reilly, Dennis Pegden, Gene Polley, Steve Roberts, Ed Russell, Paul Sanchez, Bob Sargent, Bruce Schmeiser, Lee Schruben, Aarti Shanker, Murali Shanker, Marlene Smith, Mike Sullivan, Mike Thompson, Brian Unger, and Jim Wilson.

McGraw-Hill and the authors would like to thank the following reviewers for their many helpful comments and suggestions: Osman Balci, Virginia Polytechnic Institute and State University; Wafik H. Iskander, West Virginia University; Barry L. Nelson, Ohio State University; James L. Riggs, deceased; Pirooz Vakilli, Boston University; and Frank K. Wolf, Western Michigan University.

Averill M. Law
W. David Kelton

PREFACE TO THE FIRST EDITION

The goal of *Simulation Modeling and Analysis* is to give an up-to-date treatment of all the important aspects of a simulation study, including modeling, simulation languages, validation, and output data analysis. In addition, we have tried to present the material in a manner understandable to a person having only a basic familiarity with probability, statistics, and computer programming. The book does not sacrifice statistical correctness for expository convenience, but contains virtually no theorems or proofs. Technically difficult topics are placed in starred (*) sections or in an appendix to an appropriate chapter, and left for the advanced reader. (More difficult problems are also starred.) The book strives to motivate intuition about difficult topics and contains a large number of examples, figures, problems, and references for further study. There is also a solutions manual for instructors.

We feel that two of the book's major strengths are its treatment of modeling and of output data analysis. Chapters 1 and 2 show in complete detail how to build simulation models in FORTRAN of a simple queueing system, an inventory system, a time-shared computer model, a multiteller bank with jockeying, and a job-shop model. Chapter 8 contains what we believe is a complete and practical treatment of statistical analysis of simulation output data. Since lack of definitive output data analyses appears to have been a major shortcoming of most simulation studies, we feel that this chapter should enhance the practice of simulation.

We believe that *Simulation Modeling and Analysis* could serve as a textbook for the following types of courses:

1. A beginning course in simulation at the junior, senior, or first-year graduate level for engineering, business, or computer science students (Chaps. 1 through 4 and parts of Chaps. 5 through 8, 10, and 11).
2. A second, advanced course in simulation (most of Chaps. 7 through 12).
3. An introduction to simulation as part of a general course on operations research or management science (Chaps. 1 through 3).

The book should also be of interest to simulation practitioners. As a matter of fact, a large number of such practitioners from industry, government, and the military have used preliminary drafts of the manuscript while attending a seminar on simulation which has been given by the first author for the last four years.

There are a number of people and organizations that have contributed considerably to the writing of this book. Foremost among them are Dr. Thomas Varley and the Office of Naval Research, without whose research support during the past five years this book simply would not have been possible. We would also like to thank the Army Research Office for its research funding to the Mathematics Research Center at the University of Wisconsin. This support in 1980 allowed for the expeditious completion of the book. Most of the development of the simulation language SIMLIB which is discussed in Chap. 2, and almost all of the research of the statistical methods in Chap. 5 was done by Stephen Vincent, a graduate student at Wisconsin. The organization and content of Chap. 7 benefitted greatly from our having in-depth discussions with Professor Bruce Schmeiser of Purdue University. In addition, conversations with the following people positively influenced our thinking on particular chapters of the book: William Biles, Penn State University; Edward Dudewicz, Ohio State University; James Henriksen, Wolverine Software; Stephen Lavenberg, IBM; Richard Nance, Virginia Tech University; Alan Pritsker, Purdue University; Edward Russell, CACI; Robert Sargent, Syracuse University; Thomas Schriber, The University of Michigan; Edward Silver, Waterloo University; and Glenn Thomas, Kent State University. Finally, we acknowledge the following graduate students at Wisconsin who read the entire manuscript and made many valuable suggestions: Steven Kimbrough, Lloyd Koenig, Insup Lee, and Muslim Yildiz.

Averill M. Law
W. David Kelton

SIMULATION MODELING AND ANALYSIS

CHAPTER
1

BASIC
SIMULATION
MODELING

> Recommended sections for a first reading: 1.1 through 1.4, 1.7, 1.9

1.1 THE NATURE OF SIMULATION

This is a book about techniques for using computers to imitate, or *simulate*, the operations of various kinds of real-world facilities or processes. The facility or process of interest is usually called a *system*, and in order to study it scientifically we often have to make a set of assumptions about how it works. These assumptions, which usually take the form of mathematical or logical relationships, constitute a *model* that is used to try to gain some understanding of how the corresponding system behaves.

If the relationships that compose the model are simple enough, it may be possible to use mathematical methods (such as algebra, calculus, or probability theory) to obtain *exact* information on questions of interest; this is called an *analytic* solution. However, most real-world systems are too complex to allow realistic models to be evaluated analytically, and these models must be studied by means of simulation. In a *simulation* we use a computer to evaluate a model *numerically*, and data are gathered in order to *estimate* the desired true characteristics of the model.

As an example of the use of simulation, consider a manufacturing firm that is contemplating building a large extension onto one of its plants but is not sure if the potential gain in productivity would justify the construction cost. It certainly would not be cost-effective to build the extension and then remove it later if it does not work out. However, a careful simulation study could shed some light on the question by simulating the operation of the plant as it currently exists and as it *would* be *if* the plant were expanded.

Application areas for simulation are numerous and diverse. Below is a list of some particular kinds of problems for which simulation has been found to be a useful and powerful tool:

- Designing and analyzing manufacturing systems
- Evaluating hardware and software requirements for a computer system
- Evaluating a new military weapons system or tactic
- Determining ordering policies for an inventory system
- Designing communications systems and message protocols for them
- Designing and operating transportation facilities such as freeways, airports, subways, or ports
- Evaluating designs for service organizations such as hospitals, post offices, or fast-food restaurants
- Analyzing financial or economic systems

As a technique, simulation is one of the most widely used in operations research and management science. In a survey of graduates of the Department of Operations Research at Case Western Reserve University (one of the first departments of this type), Rasmussen and George (1978) found that among M.S. graduates, simulation ranked fifth among some fifteen subject areas in terms of its value after graduation (behind what they called "statistical methods," "forecasting," "systems analysis," and "information systems," all of which may arguably be outside the realm of operations research and management science). Among Ph.D. graduates, simulation tied (with linear programming) for second (behind "statistical methods"). Thomas and DaCosta (1979), in a survey of a different type, asked some 137 large firms to indicate which of fourteen techniques they used, and simulation came in second, with 84 percent of the firms responding that they used it (what they termed "statistical analysis" came in first in this survey, with 93 percent). The members of the Operations Research Division of the American Institute of Industrial Engineers were surveyed by Shannon, Long, and Buckles (1980), who reported that simulation ranked second in "familiarity" (just behind linear programming), but first in terms of utility and interest, among some twelve methodologies. Forgionne (1983) and Harpell, Lane, and Mansour (1989) also reported that simulation ranked second in utilization (again behind "statistical analysis" only) among eight tools in a survey of large corporations. All of these surveys are by now several years old, and we can assume that simulation's value and usage have since increased, due to improvements in computing power and in simulation software, as discussed below.

There have been, however, several impediments to even wider acceptance and usefulness of simulation. First, models used to study large-scale systems tend to be very complex, and writing computer programs to execute them can be an arduous task indeed. This task has been eased in recent years by the development of excellent software products that automatically provide many of the features needed to code a simulation model. A second problem with simulation of complex systems is that a large amount of computer time is often required. However, this difficulty is becoming less severe as the cost of computing continues to fall. Finally, there appears to be an unfortunate impression that simulation is just an exercise in computer programming, albeit a complicated one. Consequently, many simulation "studies" have been composed of heuristic model building, coding, and a single run of the program to obtain "the answer." We fear that this attitude, which neglects the important issue of how a properly coded model should be used to make inferences about the system of interest, has doubtless led to erroneous conclusions being drawn from many simulation studies. These questions of simulation *methodology*, which are largely independent of the software and hardware used, form an integral part of the latter chapters of this book.

In the remainder of this chapter (as well as in Chap. 2) we discuss systems and models in considerably more detail and then show how to write computer programs to simulate systems of varying degrees of complexity.

1.2 SYSTEMS, MODELS, AND SIMULATION

A *system* is defined to be a collection of entities, e.g., people or machines, that act and interact together toward the accomplishment of some logical end. [This definition was proposed by Schmidt and Taylor (1970).] In practice, what is meant by "the system" depends on the objectives of a particular study. The collection of entities that compose a system for one study might be only a subset of the overall system for another. For example, if one wants to study a bank to determine the number of tellers needed to provide adequate service for customers who want just to cash a check or make a savings deposit, the system can be defined to be that portion of the bank consisting of the tellers and the customers waiting in line or being served. If, on the other hand, the loan officer and the safety deposit boxes are to be included, the definition of the system must be expanded in an obvious way. [See also Fishman (1978, p. 3).] We define the *state* of a system to be that collection of variables necessary to describe a system at a particular time, relative to the objectives of a study. In a study of a bank, examples of possible state variables are the number of busy tellers, the number of customers in the bank, and the time of arrival of each customer in the bank.

We categorize systems to be of two types, discrete and continuous. A *discrete* system is one for which the state variables change instantaneously at separated points in time. A bank is an example of a discrete system, since state variables—e.g., the number of customers in the bank—change only when a customer arrives or when a customer finishes being served and departs. A *continuous* system is one for which the state variables change continuously with respect to time. An airplane moving through the air is an example of a continuous system, since state variables such as position and velocity can change continuously with respect to time. Few systems in practice are wholly discrete or wholly continuous, but since one type of change predominates for most systems, it will usually be possible to classify a system as being either discrete or continuous.

At some point in the lives of most systems, there is a need to study them to try to gain some insight into the relationships among various components, or to predict performance under some new conditions being considered. Figure 1.1 maps out different ways in which a system might be studied.

- *Experiment with the Actual System vs. Experiment with a Model of the System*: If it is possible (and cost-effective) to alter the system physically and then let it operate under the new conditions, it is probably desirable to do so, for in this case there is no question about whether what we study is

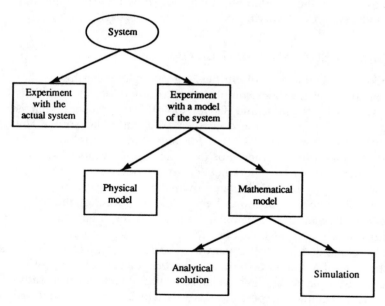

FIGURE 1.1
Ways to study a system.

relevant. However, it is rarely feasible to do this, because such an experiment would often be too costly or too disruptive to the system. For example, a bank may be contemplating reducing the number of tellers to decrease costs, but actually trying this could lead to long customer delays and alienation. More graphically, the "system" might not even exist, but we nevertheless want to study it in its various proposed alternative configurations to see how it should be built in the first place; examples of this situation might be modern flexible manufacturing facilities, or strategic nuclear weapons systems. For these reasons, it is usually necessary to build a *model* as a representation of the system and study it as a surrogate for the actual system. When using a model, there is always the question of whether it accurately reflects the system for the purposes of the decisions to be made; this question of model *validity* is taken up in detail in Chap. 5.

- *Physical Model vs. Mathematical Model*: To most people, the word "model" evokes images of clay cars in wind tunnels, cockpits disconnected from their airplanes to be used in pilot training, or miniature supertankers scurrying about in a swimming pool. These are examples of *physical* models (also called *iconic* models), and are not typical of the kinds of models that are usually of interest in operations research and systems analysis. Occasionally, however, it has been found useful to build physical models to study engineering or management systems; examples include tabletop scale models of material-handling systems, and in at least one case a full-scale physical model of a fast-food restaurant inside a warehouse, complete with full-scale, real (and presumably hungry) humans [see Swart and Donno (1981)]. But the vast majority of models built for such purposes are *mathematical*, representing a system in terms of logical and quantitative relationships that are then manipulated and changed to see how the model reacts, and thus how the system *would* react—*if* the mathematical model is a valid one. Perhaps the simplest example of a mathematical model is the familiar relation $d = rt$, where r is the rate of travel, t is the time spent traveling, and d is the distance traveled. This might provide a valid model in one instance (e.g., a space probe to another planet after it has attained its flight velocity) but a very poor model for other purposes (e.g., rush-hour commuting on congested urban freeways).

- *Analytical Solution vs. Simulation*: Once we have built a mathematical model, it must then be examined to see how it can be used to answer the questions of interest about the system it is supposed to represent. If the model is simple enough, it may be possible to work with its relationships and quantities to get an exact, *analytical* solution. In the $d = rt$ example, if we know the distance to be traveled and the velocity, then we can work with the model to get $t = d/r$ as the time that will be required. This is a very simple, closed-form solution obtainable with just paper and pencil, but some analytical solutions can become extraordinarily complex, requiring vast computing resources; inverting a large nonsparse matrix is a well-known example of a situation in which there is an analytical formula known in principle, but obtaining it numerically in a given instance is far from trivial. If an analytical solution to a mathematical model is available and is computationally efficient, it is usually desirable to study the model in this way rather than via a simulation. However, many systems are highly complex, so that valid mathematical models of them are themselves complex, precluding any possibility of an analytical solution. In this case, the model must be studied by means of *simulation*, i.e., numerically exercising the model for the inputs in question to see how they affect the output measures of performance.

While there may be an element of truth to pejorative old saws such as "method of last resort" sometimes used to describe simulation, the fact is that we are very quickly led to simulation in many situations, due to the sheer complexity of the systems of interest and of the models necessary to represent them in a valid way.

Given, then, that we have a mathematical model to be studied by means of simulation (henceforth referred to as a *simulation model*), we must then look for particular tools to do this. It is useful for this purpose to classify simulation models along three different dimensions:

- *Static vs. Dynamic Simulation Models*: A *static* simulation model is a representation of a system at a particular time, or one that may be used to represent a system in which time simply plays no role; examples of static simulations are Monte Carlo models, discussed in Sec. 1.8.3. On the other hand, a *dynamic* simulation model represents a system as it evolves over time, such as a conveyor system in a factory.

- *Deterministic vs. Stochastic Simulation Models*: If a simulation model does not contain any probabilistic (i.e., random) components, it is called *deterministic*; a complicated (and analytically intractable) system of differential equations describing a chemical reaction might be such a model. In deterministic models, the output is "determined" once the set of input quantities and relationships in the model have been specified, even though it might take a lot of computer time to evaluate what it is. Many systems, however, must be modeled as having at least some random input components, and these give rise to *stochastic* simulation models. (For an example of the danger of ignoring randomness in modeling a system, see Sec. 4.7.) Most queueing and inventory systems are modeled stochastically. Stochastic simulation models produce output that is itself random, and must therefore be treated as only an estimate of the true characteristics of the model; this is one of the main disadvantages of simulation (see Sec. 1.9) and is dealt with in Chaps. 9 through 12 of this book.

- *Continuous vs. Discrete Simulation Models*: Loosely speaking, we define *discrete* and *continuous* simulation models analogously to the way discrete and continuous systems were defined above. More precise definitions of discrete (event) simulation and continuous simulation are given in Secs. 1.3 and 1.8, respectively. It should be mentioned that a discrete model is not always used to model a discrete system and vice versa. The decision whether to use a discrete or a continuous model for a particular system depends on the specific objectives of the study. For example, a model of traffic flow on a freeway would be discrete if the characteristics and movement of individual cars are important. Alternatively, if the cars can be treated "in the aggregate," the flow of traffic can be described by differential equations in a continuous model. More discussion on this issue can be found in Sec. 5.2, and in particular in Example 5.1.

The simulation models we consider in the remainder of this book, except for those in Sec. 1.8, will be discrete, dynamic, and stochastic and will henceforth be called *discrete-event simulation models*. (Since deterministic models are a special case of stochastic models, the restriction to stochastic models involves no loss of generality.)

1.3 DISCRETE-EVENT SIMULATION

Discrete-event simulation concerns the modeling of a system as it evolves over time by a representation in which the state variables change instantaneously at separate points in time. (In more mathematical terms, we might say that the system can change at only a *countable* number of points in time.) These points in time are the ones at which an event occurs, where an *event* is defined as an instantaneous occurrence that may change the state of the system. Although discrete-event simulation could conceptually be done by hand calculations, the amount of data that must be stored and manipulated for most real-world systems dictates that discrete-event simulations be done on a digital computer. (In Sec. 1.4.2 we carry out a small hand simulation, merely to illustrate the logic involved.)

> **Example 1.1.** Consider a service facility with a single server—e.g., a one-operator barbershop or an information desk at an airport—for which we would like to estimate the (expected) average delay in queue (line) of arriving customers, where the delay in queue of a customer is the length of the time interval from the instant of his arrival at the facility to the instant he begins being served. For the objective of estimating the average delay of a customer, the state variables for a discrete-event simulation model of the facility would be the status of the server, i.e., either idle or busy, the number of customers waiting in queue to be served (if any), and the time of arrival of each person waiting in queue. The status of the server is needed to determine, upon a customer's arrival, whether the customer can be served immediately or must join the end of the queue. When the server completes serving a customer, the number of customers in the queue is used to determine whether the server will become idle or begin serving the first customer in the queue. The time of arrival of a customer is needed to compute his delay in

queue, which is the time he begins being served (which will be known) minus his time of arrival. There are two types of events for this system: the arrival of a customer and the completion of service for a customer, which results in the customer's departure. An arrival is an event since it causes the (state variable) server status to change from idle to busy or the (state variable) number of customers in the queue to increase by 1. Correspondingly, a departure is an event because it causes the server status to change from busy to idle or the number of customers in the queue to decrease by 1. We show in detail how to build a discrete-event simulation model of this single-server queueing system in Sec. 1.4.

In the above example both types of events actually changed the state of the system, but in some discrete-event simulation models events are used for purposes that do not actually effect such a change. For example, an event might be used to schedule the end of a simulation run at a particular time (see Sec. 1.4.8) or to schedule a decision about a system's operation at a particular time (see Sec. 1.5) and might not actually result in a change in the state of the system. This is why we originally said that an event *may* change the state of a system.

1.3.1   Time-Advance Mechanisms

Because of the dynamic nature of discrete-event simulation models, we must keep track of the current value of simulated time as the simulation proceeds, and we also need a mechanism to advance simulated time from one value to another. We call the variable in a simulation model that gives the current value of simulated time the *simulation clock*. The unit of time for the simulation clock is never stated explicitly when a model is written in a general-purpose language such as FORTRAN, Pascal, or C, and it is assumed to be in the same units as the input parameters. Also, there is generally no relationship between simulated time and the time needed to run a simulation on the computer.

Historically, two principal approaches have been suggested for advancing the simulation clock: *next-event time advance* and *fixed-increment time advance*. Since the first approach is used by all major simulation languages and by most people coding their model in a general-purpose language, and since the second is a special case of the first, we shall use the next-event time-advance approach for all discrete-event simulation models discussed in this book. A brief discussion of fixed-increment time advance is given in App. 1A (at the end of this chapter).

With the next-event time-advance approach, the simulation clock is initialized to zero and the times of occurrence of future events are determined. The simulation clock is then advanced to the time of occurrence of the *most imminent* (first) of these future events, at which point the state of the system is updated to account for the fact that an event has occurred, and our knowledge of the times of occurrence of future events is also updated. Then the simulation clock is advanced to the time of the (new) most imminent event, the state of the system is updated, and future event times are determined, etc. This process of advancing the simulation clock from one event time to another is continued until eventually some prespecified stopping condition is satisfied. Since all state changes occur only at event times for a discrete-event simulation model, periods of inactivity are skipped over by jumping the clock from event time to event time. (Fixed-increment time advance does not skip over these inactive periods, which can eat up a lot of computer time; see App. 1A.) It should be noted that the successive jumps of the simulation clock are generally variable (or unequal) in size.

Example 1.2 We now illustrate in detail the next-event time-advance approach for the single-server queueing system of Example 1.1. We need the following notation:

t_i = time of arrival of the ith customer ($t_0 = 0$)

$A_i = t_i - t_{i-1}$ = interarrival time between $(i - 1)$st and ith arrivals of customers

S_i = time that server actually spends serving ith customer (exclusive of customer's delay in queue)

D_i = delay in queue of ith customer

$c_i = t_i + D_i + S_i$ = time that ith customer completes service and departs

e_i = time of occurrence of ith event of any type (ith value the simulation clock takes on, excluding the value $e_0 = 0$)

Each of these defined quantities will generally be a random variable. Assume that the probability distributions of the interarrival times $A_1, A_2, \ldots$ and the service times $S_1, S_2, \ldots$ are known and have cumulative distribution functions (see Sec. 4.2) denoted by F_A and F_S, respectively. (In general, F_A and F_S would be determined by collecting data from the system of interest and then fitting distributions to these data using the techniques of Chap. 6.) At time $e_0 = 0$ the status of the server is idle, and the time t_1 of the first arrival is determined by generating A_1 from F_A (techniques for generating random observations from a specified distribution are discussed in Chap. 8) and adding it to 0. The simulation clock is then advanced from e_0 to the time of the next (first) event, $e_1 = t_1$. (See Fig. 1.2, where the curved arrows represent advancing the simulation clock.) Since the customer arriving at time t_1 finds the server idle, she immediately enters service and has a delay in queue of $D_1 = 0$ and the status of the server is changed from idle to busy. The time, c_1, when the arriving customer will complete service is computed by generating S_1 from F_S and adding it to t_1. Finally, the time of the second arrival, t_2, is computed as $t_2 = t_1 + A_2$, where A_2 is generated from F_A. If $t_2 < c_1$, as depicted in Fig. 1.2, the simulation clock is advanced from e_1 to the time of the next event, $e_2 = t_2$. (If c_1 were less than t_2, the clock would be advanced from e_1 to c_1.) Since the customer arriving at time t_2 finds the server already busy, the number of customers in the queue is increased from 0 to 1 and the time of arrival of this customer is recorded; however, his service time S_2 is not generated at this time. Also, the time of the third arrival, t_3, is computed as $t_3 = t_2 + A_3$. If $c_1 < t_3$, as depicted in the figure, the simulation clock is advanced from e_2 to the time of the next event, $e_3 = c_1$, where the customer completing service departs, the customer in the queue (i.e., the one who arrived at time t_2)

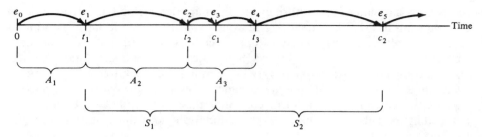

FIGURE 1.2
The next-event time-advance approach illustrated for the single-server queueing system.

begins service and his delay in queue and service-completion time are computed as $D_2 = c_1 - t_2$ and $c_2 = c_1 + S_2$ (S_2 is now generated from F_S), and the number of customers in the queue is decreased from 1 to 0. If $t_3 < c_2$, the simulation clock is advanced from e_3 to the time of the next event, $e_4 = t_3$, etc. The simulation might eventually be terminated when, say, the number of customers whose delays have been observed reaches some specified value.

1.3.2 Components and Organization of a Discrete-Event Simulation Model

Although simulation has been applied to a great diversity of real-world systems, discrete-event simulation models all share a number of common components and there is a logical organization for these components that promotes the coding, debugging, and future changing of a simulation model's computer program. In particular, the following components will be found in most discrete-event simulation models using the next-event time-advance approach:

System state: The collection of state variables necessary to describe the system at a particular time.

Simulation clock: A variable giving the current value of simulated time.

Event list: A list containing the next time when each type of event will occur.

Statistical counters: Variables used for storing statistical information about system performance.

Initialization routine: A subprogram to initialize the simulation model at time zero.

Timing routine: A subprogram that determines the next event from the event list and then advances the simulation clock to the time when that event is to occur.

Event routine: A subprogram that updates the system state when a particular type of event occurs (there is one event routine for each event type).

Library routines: A set of subprograms used to generate random observations from probability distributions that were determined as part of the simulation model.

Report generator: A subprogram that computes estimates (from the statistical counters) of the desired measures of performance and produces a report when the simulation ends.

Main program: A subprogram that invokes the timing routine to determine the next event and then transfers control to the corresponding event routine to update the system state appropriately. The main program may also check for termination and invoke the report generator when the simulation is over.

The logical relationships (flow of control) among these components is shown in Fig. 1.3. The simulation begins at time 0 with the main program invoking the initialization routine, where the simulation clock is set to zero, the system state and the statistical counters are initialized, and the event list is initialized. After control has been returned to the main program, it invokes the timing routine to determine which type of event is most imminent. If an event of type i is the next to occur, the simulation clock is advanced to the time that event type i will occur and control is returned to the main program. Then the main program invokes event routine i, where typically three types of activities occur: (1) the system state is updated to account for the fact that an event of type i has occurred; (2) information about system performance is gathered by updating the statistical counters; and (3) the times of occurrence of future events are generated and this information is added to the event list. Often it is necessary to generate random observations from probability distributions in order to determine these future event times; we will refer to such a generated observation as a *random variate*. After all processing has been completed, either in event routine i or in the main program, a check is typically made to determine (relative to some stopping condition) if the simulation should now be terminated. If it is time to terminate the simulation, the report generator is invoked from the main program to compute estimates (from the statistical counters) of the desired measures of performance and to produce a report. If it is not time for termination, control is passed back to the main program and the main program–timing routine–main program–event routine–termination check cycle is repeated until the stopping condition is eventually satisfied.

Before concluding this section, a few additional words about the system state may be in order. As mentioned in Sec. 1.2, a system is a well-defined collection of *entities*. Entities are characterized by data values called *attributes*, and these attributes are part of the system state for a discrete-event simulation model. Furthermore, entities with some common property are often grouped together in *lists* (or *files* or *sets*). For each entity there is a *record* in the list consisting of the entity's attributes, and the order in which the records are placed in the list depends on some specified rule. (See Chap. 2 for a discussion of efficient approaches for storing lists of records.) For the single-server queueing facility of Examples 1.1 and 1.2, the entities are the server and the

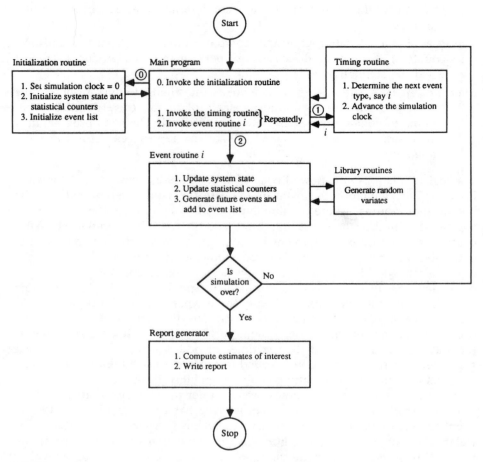

FIGURE 1.3
Flow of control for the next-event time-advance approach.

customers in the facility. The server has the attribute "server status" (busy or idle), and the customers waiting in queue have the attribute "time of arrival." (The number of customers in the queue might also be considered an attribute of the server.) Furthermore, as we shall see in Sec. 1.4, these customers in queue will be grouped together in a list.

The organization and action of a discrete-event simulation program using the next-event time-advance mechanism as depicted above is fairly typical when coding such simulations in a general-purpose programming language such as FORTRAN, Pascal, or C; it is called the *event-scheduling approach* to simulation modeling, since the times of future events are explicitly coded into the model and are scheduled to occur in the simulated future. It should be mentioned here that there is an alternative approach to simulation modeling, called the *process approach*, that instead views the simulation in terms of the individual entities involved, and the code written describes the "experience" of a "typical" entity as it "flows" through the system; coding simulations modeled from the process point of view usually requires the use of special-purpose simulation software, as discussed in Chap. 3. Even when taking the process approach, however, the simulation is actually executed behind the scenes in the event-scheduling logic as described above.

1.4 SIMULATION OF A SINGLE-SERVER QUEUEING SYSTEM

This section shows in detail how to simulate a single-server queueing system such as a one-operator barbershop. Although this system seems very simple compared with those usually of real interest, how it is simulated is actually quite representative of the operation of simulations of great complexity.

In Sec. 1.4.1 we describe the system of interest and state our objectives more precisely. We explain intuitively how to simulate this system in Sec. 1.4.2 by showing a "snapshot" of the simulated system just after each event occurs. Section 1.4.3 describes the language-independent organization and logic of the FORTRAN, Pascal, and C codes given in Secs. 1.4.4, 1.4.5, and 1.4.6. The simulation's results are discussed in Sec. 1.4.7, and Sec. 1.4.8 alters the stopping rule to another common way to end simulations. Finally, Sec. 1.4.9 briefly describes a technique for identifying and simplifying the event and variable structure of a simulation.

1.4.1 Problem Statement

Consider a single-server queueing system (see Fig. 1.4) for which the interarrival times $A_1, A_2, \ldots$ are independent, identically distributed (IID) random variables. ("Identically distributed" means that the interarrival times have the same probability distribution.) A customer who arrives and finds the server idle enters service immediately, and the service times $S_1, S_2, \ldots$ of the successive customers are IID random variables that are independent of the interarrival times. A customer who arrives and finds the server busy joins the end of a single queue. Upon completing service for a customer, the server chooses a customer from the queue (if any) in a first-in, first-out (FIFO) manner. (For a discussion of other queue disciplines and queueing systems in general, see App. 1B.)

The simulation will begin in the "empty-and-idle" state; i.e., no customers are present and the server is idle. At time 0, we will begin waiting for the arrival of the first customer, which will occur after the first interarrival time, A_1, rather than at time 0 (which would be a possibly valid, but different, modeling assumption). We wish to simulate this system until a fixed number

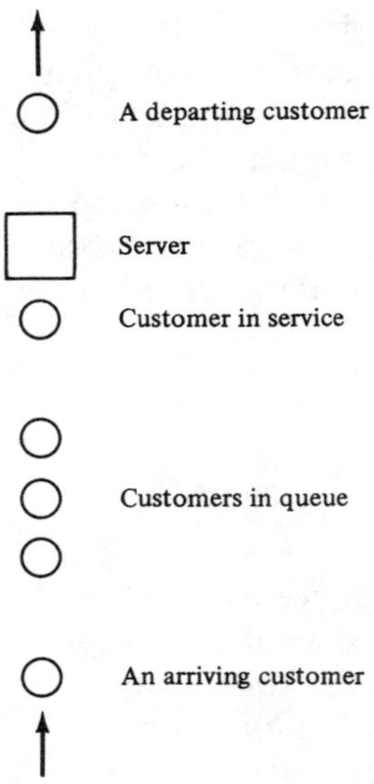

FIGURE 1.4
A single-server queueing system.

(n) of customers have completed their delays in queue; i.e., the simulation will stop when the nth customer enters service. Note that the *time* the simulation ends is thus a random variable, depending on the observed values for the interarrival and service-time random variables.

To measure the performance of this system, we will look at estimates of three quantities. First, we will estimate the expected average delay in queue of the n customers completing their delays during the simulation; we denote this quantity by $d(n)$. The word "expected" in the definition of $d(n)$ means this: On a given run of the simulation (or, for that matter, on a given run of the actual system the simulation model represents), the actual average delay observed of the n customers depends on the interarrival and service-time random variable observations that happen to have been obtained. On another run of the simulation (or on a different day for the real system) there would probably be arrivals at different times, and the service times required would also be different; this would give rise to a different value for the average of the n delays. Thus, the average delay on a given run of the simulation is properly regarded as a random variable itself. What we want to estimate, $d(n)$, is the *expected value* of this random variable. One interpretation of this is that $d(n)$ is the average of a large (actually, infinite) number of n-customer average delays. From a single run of the simulation resulting in customer delays $D_1, D_2, \ldots, D_n$, an obvious estimator of $d(n)$ is

$$\hat{d}(n) = \frac{\sum\limits_{i=1}^{n} D_i}{n}$$

which is just the average of the n D_i's that were observed in the simulation [so that $\hat{d}(n)$ could also be denoted by $\bar{D}(n)$]. (Throughout this book, a hat ($\hat{\ }$) above a symbol denotes an estimator.) It is important to note that by "delay" we do not exclude the possibility that a customer could have a delay of zero in the case of an arrival finding the system empty and idle (with this model, we know for sure that $D_1 = 0$); delays with a value of zero *are* counted in the average, since if many delays were zero this would represent a system providing very good service, and our output measure should reflect this. One reason for taking the average of the D_i's, as opposed to just looking at them individually, is that they will not have the same distribution (e.g., $D_1 = 0$, but D_2 could be positive), and the average gives us a single composite measure of all the customers' delays; in this sense, this is not the usual "average" taken in basic statistics, as the individual terms are not random observations from the same distribution. Note also that by itself, $\hat{d}(n)$ is an estimator based on a "sample" (here, a set of *complete* simulation runs) of size *1*, since we are making only a single simulation run. From elementary statistics, we know that a sample of size 1 is not worth much; we return to this issue in Chaps. 9 through 12.

While an estimate of $d(n)$ gives information about system performance from the customers' point of view, the management of such a system may want different information; indeed, since most real simulations are quite complex and may be costly to run, we usually collect many output measures of performance, describing different aspects of system behavior. One such measure for our simple model here is the expected average number of customers in the queue (but not being served), denoted by $q(n)$, where the n is necessary in the notation to indicate that this average is taken over the time period needed to observe the n delays defining our stopping rule. This is a different kind of "average" than the average delay in queue, because it is taken over (continuous) time, rather than over customers (being discrete). Thus, we need to define what is meant by this *time*-average number of customers in queue. To do this, let $Q(t)$ denote the number of customers in queue at time t, for any real number $t \geq 0$, and let $T(n)$ be the time required to observe our n delays in queue. Then for any time t between 0 and $T(n)$, $Q(t)$ is a nonnegative integer. Further, if we let p_i be the expected *proportion* (which will be between 0 and 1) of the time that $Q(t)$ is equal to i, then a reasonable definition of $q(n)$ would be

$$q(n) = \sum_{i=0}^{\infty} i p_i$$

Thus, $q(n)$ is a weighted average of the possible values i for the queue length $Q(t)$, with the weights being the expected proportion of time the queue spends at each of its possible lengths. To estimate $q(n)$ from a simulation, we simply replace the p_i's with estimates of them, and get

$$\hat{q}(n) = \sum_{i=0}^{\infty} i \hat{p}_i \tag{1.1}$$

where $\hat{p}_i$ is the *observed* (rather than expected) proportion of the time *during the simulation* that there were i customers in the queue. Computationally, however, it is easier to rewrite $\hat{q}(n)$ using some geometric considerations. If we let T_i be the *total* time during the simulation that the queue is of length i, then $T(n) = T_0 + T_1 + T_2 + \cdots$ and $\hat{p}_i = T_i/T(n)$, so that we can rewrite Eq. (1.1) above as

$$\hat{q}(n) = \frac{\sum\limits_{i=0}^{\infty} iT_i}{T(n)} \tag{1.2}$$

Figure 1.5 illustrates a possible time path, or *realization*, of $Q(t)$ for this system in the case of $n = 6$; ignore the shading for now. Arrivals occur at times 0.4, 1.6, 2.1, 3.8, 4.0, 5.6, 5.8, and 7.2. Departures (service completions) occur at times 2.4, 3.1, 3.3, 4.9, and 8.6, and the simulation ends at time $T(6) = 8.6$. Remember in looking at Fig. 1.5 that $Q(t)$ does not count the customer in service (if any), so between times 0.4 and 1.6 there is one customer in the system being served, even though the queue is empty $[Q(t) = 0]$; the same is true between times 3.1 and 3.3, between times 3.8 and 4.0, and between times 4.9 and 5.6. Between times 3.3 and 3.8, however, the system is empty of customers and the server is idle, as is obviously the case between times 0 and 0.4. To compute $\hat{q}(n)$, we must first compute the T_i's, which can be read off Fig. 1.5 as the (sometimes separated) intervals over which $Q(t)$ is equal to 0, 1,

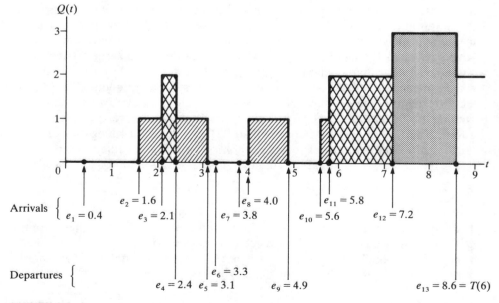

FIGURE 1.5
$Q(t)$, arrival times, and departure times for a realization of a single-server queueing system.

2, and so on:

$$T_0 = (1.6 - 0.0) + (4.0 - 3.1) + (5.6 - 4.9) = 3.2$$
$$T_1 = (2.1 - 1.6) + (3.1 - 2.4) + (4.9 - 4.0) + (5.8 - 5.6) = 2.3$$
$$T_2 = (2.4 - 2.1) + (7.2 - 5.8) = 1.7$$
$$T_3 = (8.6 - 7.2) = 1.4$$

($T_i = 0$ for $i \geq 4$, since the queue never grew to those lengths in this realization.) The numerator in Eq. (1.2) is thus

$$\sum_{i=0}^{\infty} iT_i = (0 \times 3.2) + (1 \times 2.3) + (2 \times 1.7) + (3 \times 1.4) = 9.9 \qquad (1.3)$$

and so our estimate of the time-average number in queue from this particular simulation run is $\hat{q}(6) = 9.9/8.6 = 1.15$. Now, note that each of the nonzero terms on the right-hand side of Eq. (1.3) corresponds to one of the shaded areas in Fig. 1.5: 1×2.3 is the diagonally shaded area (in four pieces), 2×1.7 is the cross-hatched area (in two pieces), and 3×1.4 is the screened area (in a single piece). In other words, the summation in the numerator of Eq. (1.2) is just the *area under the $Q(t)$ curve between the beginning and the end of the simulation*. Remembering that "area under a curve" is an integral, we can thus write

$$\sum_{i=0}^{\infty} iT_i = \int_0^{T(n)} Q(t)\, dt$$

and the estimator of $q(n)$ can then be expressed as

$$\hat{q}(n) = \frac{\int_0^{T(n)} Q(t)\, dt}{T(n)} \qquad (1.4)$$

While Eqs. (1.4) and (1.2) are equivalent expressions for $\hat{q}(n)$, Eq. (1.4) is preferable since the integral in this equation can be accumulated as simple areas of rectangles as the simulation progresses through time. It is less convenient to carry out the computations to get the summation in Eq. (1.2) explicitly. Moreover, the appearance of Eq. (1.4) suggests a continuous average of $Q(t)$, since in a rough sense, an integral can be regarded as a continuous summation.

The third and final output measure of performance for this system is a measure of how busy the server is. The expected *utilization* of the server is the expected proportion of time during the simulation [from time 0 to time $T(n)$] that the server is busy (i.e., not idle), and is thus a number between 0 and 1; denote it by $u(n)$. From a single simulation, then, our estimate of $u(n)$ is $\hat{u}(n) =$ the *observed* proportion of time during the simulation that the server is busy. Now $\hat{u}(n)$ could be computed directly from the simulation by noting the times at which the server changes status (idle to busy or vice versa) and then doing the appropriate subtractions and division. However, it is easier to look at this quantity as a continuous-time average, similar to the average queue length, by defining the "busy function"

$$B(t) = \begin{cases} 1 \text{ if the server is busy at time } t \\ 0 \text{ if the server is idle at time } t \end{cases}$$

and so $\hat{u}(n)$ could be expressed as the proportion of time that $B(t)$ is equal to 1. Figure 1.6 plots $B(t)$ for the same simulation realization as used in Fig. 1.5 for $Q(t)$. In this case, we get

$$\hat{u}(n) = \frac{(3.3 - 0.4) + (8.6 - 3.8)}{8.6} = \frac{7.7}{8.6} = 0.90 \tag{1.5}$$

indicating that the server was busy about 90 percent of the time during this simulation. Again, however, the numerator in Eq. (1.5) can be viewed as the area under the $B(t)$ function over the course of the simulation, since the height of $B(t)$ is always either 0 or 1. Thus,

$$\hat{u}(n) = \frac{\int_{0}^{T(n)} B(t)\,dt}{T(n)} \tag{1.6}$$

and we see again that $\hat{u}(n)$ is the continuous average of the $B(t)$ function, corresponding to our notion of utilization. As was the case for $\hat{q}(n)$, the reason for writing $\hat{u}(n)$ in the integral form of Eq. (1.6) is that computationally, as the simulation progresses, the integral of $B(t)$ can easily be accumulated by adding up areas of rectangles. For many simulations involving "servers" of some sort, utilization statistics are quite informative in identifying bottlenecks (utilizations

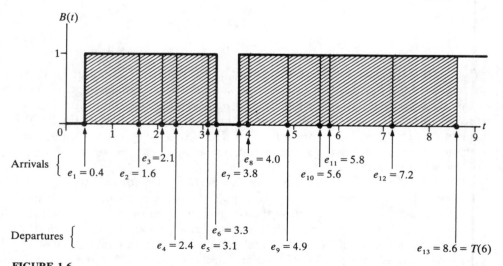

FIGURE 1.6
$B(t)$, arrival times, and departure times for a realization of a single-server queueing system (same realization as in Fig. 1.5).

near 100 percent, coupled with heavy congestion measures for the queue leading in) or excess capacity (low utilizations); this is particularly true if the "servers" are expensive items such as robots in a manufacturing system or large mainframe computers in a data-processing operation.

To recap, the three measures of performance are: the average delay in queue $\hat{d}(n)$, the time-average number of customers in queue $\hat{q}(n)$, and the proportion of time the server is busy $\hat{u}(n)$. The average delay in queue is an example of a *discrete-time statistic*, since it is defined relative to the collection of random variables $\{D_i\}$ that have a discrete "time" index, $i = 1, 2, \dots$. The time-average number in queue and the proportion of time the server is busy are examples of *continuous-time statistics*, since they are defined on the collection of random variables $\{Q(t)\}$ and $\{B(t)\}$, respectively, each of which is indexed on the continuous time parameter $t \in [0, \infty)$. (The symbol $\in$ means "contained in." Thus, in this case, t can be any nonnegative real number.) Both discrete-time and continuous-time statistics are common in simulation, and they furthermore can be other than averages. For example, we might be interested in the *maximum* of all the delays in queue observed (a discrete-time statistic), or the *proportion* of time during the simulation that the queue contained at least five customers (a continuous-time statistic).

The events for this system are the arrival of a customer and the departure of a customer (after a service completion); the state variables necessary to estimate $d(n)$, $q(n)$, and $u(n)$ are the status of the server (0 for idle and 1 for busy), the number of customers in the queue, the time of arrival of each customer currently in the queue (represented as a list), and the time of the last (i.e., most recent) event. The time of the last event, defined to be e_{i-1} if $e_{i-1} \le t < e_i$ (where t is the current time in the simulation), is needed to compute the width of the rectangles for the area accumulations in the estimates of $q(n)$ and $u(n)$.

1.4.2   Intuitive Explanation

We begin our explanation of how to simulate a single-server queueing system by showing how its simulation model would be represented inside the computer at time $e_0 = 0$ and the times $e_1, e_2, \dots, e_{13}$ at which the 13 successive events occur that are needed to observe the desired number, $n = 6$, of delays in queue. For expository convenience, we assume that the interarrival and service times of customers are

$A_1 = 0.4,\ A_2 = 1.2,\ A_3 = 0.5,\ A_4 = 1.7,\ A_5 = 0.2,\ A_6 = 1.6,\ A_7 = 0.2,\ A_8 = 1.4,\ A_9 = 1.9, \dots$

$S_1 = 2.0,\ S_2 = 0.7,\ S_3 = 0.2,\ S_4 = 1.1,\ S_5 = 3.7,\ S_6 = 0.6, \dots$

Thus, between time 0 and the time of the first arrival there is 0.4 time unit, between the arrivals of the first and second customers there are 1.2 time units, etc., and the service time required for the first customer is 2.0 time units, etc. Note that it is not necessary to declare what the time units are (minutes, hours, etc.), but only to be sure that all time quantities are expressed in the *same* units. In an actual simulation (see Secs. 1.4.4 through 1.4.6), the A_i's and the S_i's would be generated from their corresponding probability distributions, as needed, during the course of the simulation. The numerical values for the A_i's and the S_i's given above have been artificially chosen so as to generate the same simulation realization as depicted in Figs. 1.5 and 1.6 illustrating the $Q(t)$ and $B(t)$ processes.

Figure 1.7 gives a snapshot of the system itself and of a computer representation of the system at each of the times $e_0 = 0$, $e_1 = 0.4$, ..., $e_{13} = 8.6$. In the "system" pictures, the square represents the server, and circles represent customers; the numbers inside the customer circles are the times of their arrivals. In the "computer representation" pictures, the values of the variables shown are *after* all processing has been completed at that event. Our discussion will focus on how the computer representation changes at the event times.

$t = 0$:   *Initialization.* The simulation begins with the main program invoking the initialization routine. Our modeling assumption was that

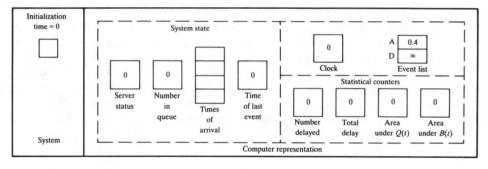

(a)

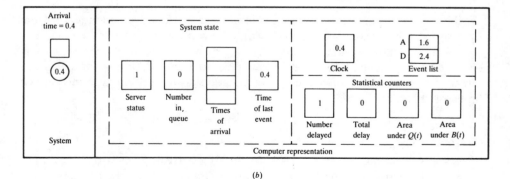

(b)

FIGURE 1.7
Snapshots of the system and of its computer representation at time 0 and at each of the thirteen succeeding event times.

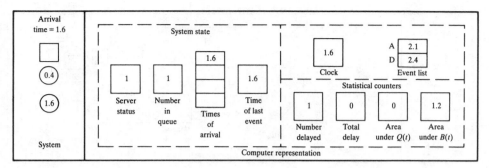

(c)

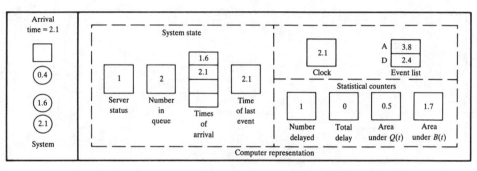

(d)

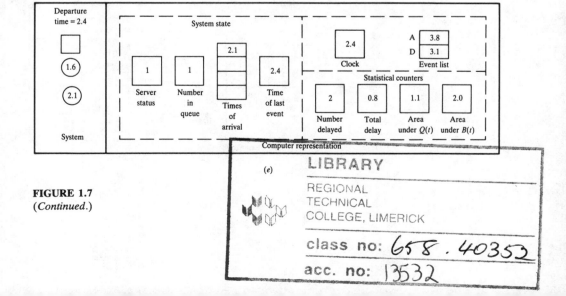

(e)

FIGURE 1.7
(*Continued.*)

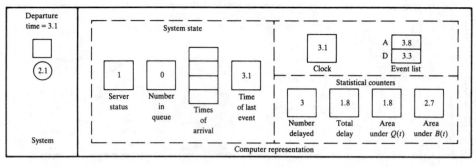

(f)

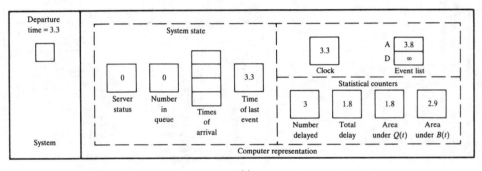

(g)

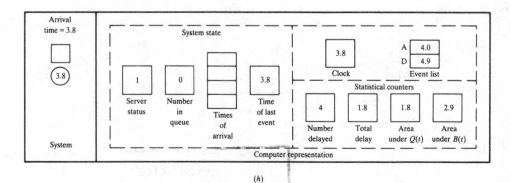

(h)

FIGURE 1.7
(*Continued.*)

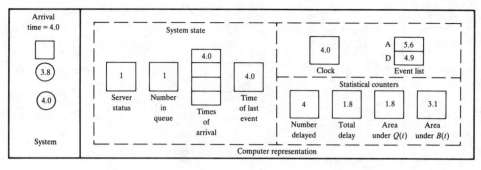

(i)

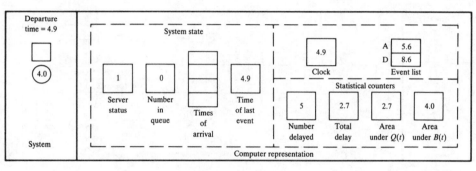

(j)

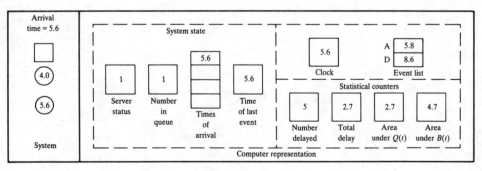

(k)

FIGURE 1.7
(*Continued.*)

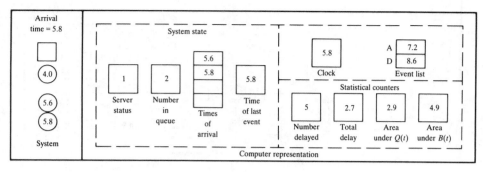

(l)

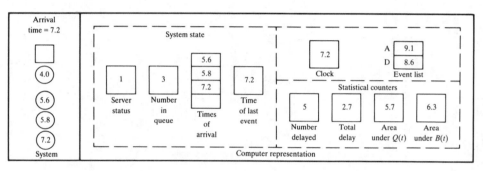

(m)

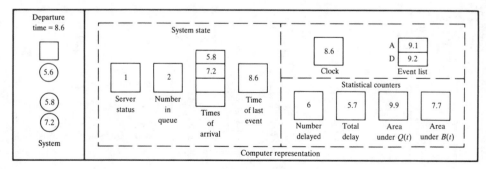

(n)

FIGURE 1.7
(*Continued.*)

initially the system is empty of customers and the server is idle, as depicted in the "system" picture of Fig. 1.7a. The model state variables are initialized to represent this: server status is zero [we use 0 to represent an idle server and 1 to represent a busy server, similar to the definition of the $B(t)$ function], and the number of customers in the queue is zero. There is a one-dimensional array to store the times of arrival of customers *currently in the queue*; this array is initially empty, and as the simulation progresses its length will grow and shrink. The time of the last (most recent) event is initialized to zero, so that at the time of the first event (when it is used), it will have its correct value. The simulation clock is set to zero, and the *event list*, giving the times of the next occurrence of each of the event types, is initialized as follows. The time of the first arrival is $0 + A_1 = 0.4$, and is denoted by "A" next to the event list. Since there is no customer in service, it does not even make sense to talk about the time of the next departure ("D" by the event list), and we know that the first event will be the initial customer arrival at time 0.4. However, the simulation progresses in general by looking at the event list and picking the smallest value from it to determine what the next event will be, so by scheduling the next departure to occur at time ∞ (or a very large number in a computer program), we effectively eliminate the departure event from consideration and force the next event to be an arrival. (This is sometimes called *poisoning* the departure event.) Finally, the four statistical counters are initialized to zero. When all initialization is done, control is returned to the main program, which then calls the timing routine to determine the next event. Since $0.4 < \infty$, the next event will be an arrival at time 0.4, and the timing routine advances the clock to this time, then passes control back to the main program with the information that the next event is to be an arrival.

$t = 0.4$:   *Arrival of customer 1.* At time 0.4, the main program passes control to the arrival routine to process the arrival of the first customer. Figure 1.7b shows the system and its computer representation *after* all changes have been made to process this arrival. Since this customer arrived to find the server idle (status equal to 0), he begins service immediately and has a delay in queue of $D_1 = 0$ (which *does* count as a delay). The server status is set to 1 to represent that the server is now busy, but the queue itself is still empty. The clock has been advanced to the current time, 0.4, and the event list is updated to reflect this customer's arrival: The next arrival will be $A_2 = 1.2$ time units from now, at time $0.4 + 1.2 = 1.6$, and the next departure (the service completion of the customer now arriving) will be $S_1 = 2.0$ time units from now, at time $0.4 + 2.0 = 2.4$. The number delayed is incremented to 1 (when this reaches $n = 6$, the simulation will end), and $D_1 = 0$ is added into the total delay (still at zero). The area under $Q(t)$ is updated by adding in the product of the *previous* value (i.e., the level it had between the last event and now) of $Q(t)$ (0 in this case) times the width of the interval of time from the last event to now, $t -$ (time of last event) $= 0.4 - 0$ in this case. Note that the time of the last event used here is its *old* value (0), before it is updated to its new value (0.4) in this event routine. Similarly, the area under $B(t)$ is updated by adding in the product of its previous value (0) times the width of the interval of time since the last event. [Look back at Figs. 1.5 and 1.6 to trace the accumulation of the areas under $Q(t)$ and $B(t)$.] Finally, the time of the last event is brought up to the current time, 0.4, and control is passed back to the main program. It invokes the timing routine, which scans the event list for the smallest value, and determines that the next event will be another arrival at time 1.6; it updates the clock to this value and passes control back to the main program with the information that the next event is an arrival.

$t = 1.6$: *Arrival of customer 2.* At this time we again enter the arrival routine, and Fig. 1.7c shows the system and its computer representation after all changes have been made to process this event. Since this customer arrives to find the server busy (status equal to 1 upon her arrival), she must queue up in the first location in the queue, her time of arrival is stored in the first location in the array, and the number-in-queue variable rises to 1. The time of the next arrival in the event list is updated to $A_3 = 0.5$ time units from now, $1.6 + 0.5 = 2.1$; the time of the next departure is not changed, since its value of 2.4 is the departure time of customer 1, who is still in service at this time. Since we are not observing the end of anyone's delay in queue, the number-delayed and total-delay variables are unchanged. The area under $Q(t)$ is increased by 0 [the previous value of $Q(t)$] times the time since the last event, $1.6 - 0.4 = 1.2$. The area under $B(t)$ is increased by 1 [the previous value of $B(t)$] times this same interval of time, 1.2. After updating the time of the last event to now, control is passed back to the main program and then to the timing routine, which determines that the next event will be an arrival at time 2.1.

$t = 2.1$: *Arrival of customer 3.* Once again the arrival routine is invoked, as depicted in Fig. 1.7d. The server stays busy, and the queue grows by one customer, whose time of arrival is stored in the queue array's second location. The next arrival is updated to $t + A_4 = 2.1 + 1.7 = 3.8$, and the next departure is still the same, as we are still waiting for the service completion of customer 1. The delay counters are unchanged, since this is not the end of anyone's delay in queue, and the two area accumulators are updated by adding in 1 [the previous values of both $Q(t)$ and $B(t)$] times the time since the last event, $2.1 - 1.6 = 0.5$. After bringing the time of the last event up to the present, we go back to the main program and invoke the timing routine, which looks at the event list to determine that the next event will be a departure at time 2.4, and updates the clock to that time.

$t = 2.4$: *Departure of customer 1.* Now the main program invokes the departure routine, and Fig. 1.7e shows the system and its representation after this occurs. The server will maintain its busy status, since customer 2 moves out of the first place in queue and into service. The queue shrinks by one, and the time-of-arrival array is moved up one place, to represent that customer 3 is now first in line. Customer 2, now entering service, will require $S_2 = 0.7$ times units, so the time of the next departure (that of customer 2) in the event list is updated to S_2 time units from now, or at time $2.4 + 0.7 = 3.1$; the time of the next arrival (that of customer 4) is unchanged, since this was scheduled earlier at the time of customer 3's arrival, and we are still waiting at this time for customer 4 to arrive. The delay statistics are updated, since at this time customer 2 is entering service and is completing her delay in queue. Here we make use of the time-of-arrival array, and compute the second delay as the current time minus the second customer's time of arrival, or $D_2 = 2.4 - 1.6 = 0.8$. (Note that the value of 1.6 was stored in the first location in the time-of-arrival array *before* it was changed, so this delay computation would have to be done before advancing the times of arrival in the array.) The area statistics are updated by adding in $2 \times (2.4 - 2.1)$ for $Q(t)$ [note that the previous value of $Q(t)$ was used], and $1 \times (2.4 - 2.1)$ for $B(t)$. The time of the last event is updated, we return to the main program, and the timing routine determines that the next event is a departure at time 3.1.

$t = 3.1$: *Departure of customer 2.* The changes at this departure are similar to those at the departure of customer 1 at time 2.4 just discussed. Note that we observe another delay in queue, and that after this event is processed the queue is again empty, but the server is still busy.

$t = 3.3$: *Departure of customer 3.* Again, the changes are similar to those in the above two departure events, with one important exception: Since the queue is now empty, the server becomes idle and we must set the next departure time in the event list to ∞, since the system now looks the same as it did at time 0 and we want to force the next event to be the arrival of customer 4.

$t = 3.8$: *Arrival of customer 4.* Since this customer arrives to find the server idle, he has a delay of zero (i.e., $D_4 = 0$) and goes right into service. Thus, the changes here are very similar to those at the arrival of the first customer at time $t = 0.4$.

The remaining six event times are depicted in Figs. 1.7i through 1.7n, and readers should work through these to be sure they understand why the variables and arrays are as they appear; it may be helpful to follow along in the plots of $Q(t)$ and $B(t)$ in Figs. 1.5 and 1.6. With the departure of customer 5 at time $t = 8.6$, customer 6 leaves the queue and enters service, at which time the number delayed reaches 6 (the specified value of n) and the simulation ends. At this point, the main program would invoke the report generator to compute the final output measures [$\hat{d}(6) = 5.7/6 = 0.95$, $\hat{q}(6) = 9.9/8.6 = 1.15$, and $\hat{u}(6) = 7.7/8.6 = 0.90$] and write them out.

A few specific comments about the above example illustrating the logic of a simulation should be made:

- Perhaps the key element in the dynamics of a simulation is the interaction between the simulation clock and the event list. The event list is maintained, and the clock jumps to the next event, as determined by scanning the event list at the end of each event's processing for the smallest (i.e., next) event time. This is how the simulation progresses through time.
- While processing an event, no "simulated" time passes. However, even though time is standing still for the model, care must be taken to process updates of the state variables and statistical counters in the appropriate order. For example, it would be incorrect to update the number in queue before updating the area-under-$Q(t)$ counter, since the height of the rectangle to be used is the *previous* value of $Q(t)$ [before the effect of the current event on $Q(t)$ has been implemented]. Similarly, it would be incorrect to update the time of the last event before updating the area accumulators. Yet another type of error would result if the queue list were changed at a departure before the delay of the first customer in queue were computed, since his time of arrival to the system would be lost.
- It is sometimes easy to overlook contingencies that seem out of the ordinary but that nevertheless must be accommodated. For example, it would be easy to forget that a departing customer could leave behind an empty queue, necessitating that the server be idled and the departure event again be eliminated from consideration. Also, termination conditions are often more involved than they might seem at first sight; in the above example, the simulation stopped in what seems to be the "usual" way, after a departure of one customer, allowing another to enter service and contribute the last delay needed, but the simulation *could* actually have ended instead with an arrival event—how?
- In some simulations it can happen that two (or more) entries in the event list are tied for smallest, and a decision rule must be incorporated to break such *time ties* (this happens with the inventory simulation considered later in Sec. 1.5). The tie-breaking rule can affect the results of the simulation, so must be chosen in accordance with how the system is to be modeled. In many simulations, however, we can ignore the possibility of ties, since the use of continuous random variables may make their occurrence an event with probability zero. In the above model, for example, if the interarrival-time or service-time distribution is continuous, then a time tie in the event list is a probability-zero event.

The above exercise is intended to illustrate the changes and data structures involved in carrying out a discrete-event simulation from the event-scheduling point of view, and contains most of the important ideas needed for more complex simulations of this type. The interarrival and service times used could have been drawn from a random-number table of some sort, constructed to reflect the desired probability distributions; this would result in what might be called a *hand simulation*, which in principle could be carried out to any length. The tedium of doing this should now be clear, so we will next turn to the use of computers (which are not easily bored) to carry out the arithmetic and bookkeeping involved in longer or more complex simulations.

1.4.3 Program Organization and Logic

In this section we set up the necessary ingredients for the programs to simulate the single-server queueing system in FORTRAN (Sec. 1.4.4), Pascal (Sec. 1.4.5), and C (Sec. 1.4.6). The organization and logic described in this section apply for all three languages, so the reader need only go through one of Secs. 1.4.4, 1.4.5, or 1.4.6, according to language preference.

There are several reasons for choosing a general-purpose language such as FORTRAN, Pascal, or C, rather than a more powerful high-level simulation language, for introducing computer simulation at this point:

- By learning to simulate in a general-purpose language, in which one must pay attention to every detail, there will be a greater understanding of how simulations actually operate, and thus less chance of conceptual errors if a switch is later made to a high-level simulation language.
- Despite the fact that there are now several very good and powerful simulation languages available (see Chap. 3), it is often necessary to write at least parts of complex simulations in a general-purpose language if the specific, detailed logic of complex systems is to be represented faithfully.
- General-purpose languages are widely available, and entire simulations are sometimes still written in this way.

It is not our purpose in this book to teach any particular simulation language in detail, although we survey several in Chap. 3. With the understanding promoted by our more general approach and by going through our simulations in this and the next chapter, the reader should find it easier to learn a specialized simulation language. Appendix 1C contains details on the particular computers and compilers used for the examples in this and the next chapter.

The single-server queueing model that we will simulate in the following three sections differs in two respects from the model used in the previous section:

- The simulation will end when $n = 1000$ delays in queue have been completed, rather than $n = 6$, in order to collect more data (and maybe to impress the reader with the patience of computers, since we have just slugged it out by hand in the $n = 6$ case in the preceding section). It is important to note that this change in the stopping rule changes the model itself, in that the output measures are defined relative to the stopping rule; hence the "n" in the notation for the quantities $d(n)$, $q(n)$, and $u(n)$ being estimated.

- The interarrival and service times will now be modeled as independent random variables from exponential distributions with mean 1 minute for the interarrival times and mean 0.5 minute for the service times. The exponential distribution with mean β (any positive real number) is continuous, with probability density function

$$f(x) = \frac{1}{\beta} e^{-x/\beta} \qquad \text{for } x \geq 0$$

(See Chaps. 4 and 6 for more information on density functions in general, and on the exponential distribution in particular.) We make this change here since it is much more common to generate input quantities (which drive the simulation) such as interarrival and service times from specified distributions than to assume that they are "known" as we did in the preceding section. The choice of the exponential distribution with the above particular values of β is essentially arbitrary, and is made primarily because it is easy to generate exponential random variates on a computer. (Actually, the assumption of exponential interarrival times is often quite realistic; assuming exponential service times, however, is seldom plausible.) Chapter 6 addresses in detail the important issue of how one chooses distribution forms and parameters for modeling simulation input random variables.

The single-server queue with exponential interarrival and service times is commonly called the *M/M/1 queue*, as discussed in App. 1B.

To simulate this model we need a way to generate random variates from an exponential distribution. The subprograms used by the FORTRAN, Pascal, and C codes all operate in the same way, which we will now develop. First, a *random-number generator* (discussed in detail in Chap. 7) is invoked to generate a variate U that is distributed (continuously) uniformly between 0 and 1; this distribution will henceforth be referred to as U(0, 1) and has probability density function

$$f(x) = \begin{cases} 1 & \text{if } 0 \leq x \leq 1 \\ 0 & \text{otherwise} \end{cases}$$

It is easy to show that the probability that a U(0, 1) random variable falls in any subinterval $[x, x + \Delta x]$ contained in the interval $[0, 1]$ is (uniformly) Δx (see Sec. 6.2.2). The U(0, 1) distribution is fundamental to simulation modeling because, as we shall see in Chap. 8, a random variate from any distribution can be generated by first generating one or more U(0, 1) random variates and then performing some kind of transformation. After obtaining U, we shall take the natural logarithm of it, multiply the result by β, and finally change the sign to return what we will show to be an exponential random variate with mean β, that is, $-\beta \ln U$.

To see why this algorithm works, recall that the (*cumulative*) *distribution function* of a random variable X is defined, for any real x, to be $F(x) = P(X \leq x)$ (Chap. 4 contains a review of basic probability theory). If X is exponential with mean β, then

$$F(x) = \int_0^x \frac{1}{\beta} e^{-t/\beta} \, dt$$

$$= 1 - e^{-x/\beta}$$

for any real $x \geq 0$, since the probability density function of the exponential distribution at the argument $t \geq 0$ is $(1/\beta)e^{-t/\beta}$. To show that our method is correct, we can try to verify that the value it returns will be less than or equal to x (any nonnegative real number), with probability $F(x)$ given above:

$$P(-\beta \ln U \leq x) = P\left(\ln U \geq -\frac{x}{\beta}\right)$$

$$= P(U \geq e^{-x/\beta})$$

$$= P(e^{-x/\beta} \leq U \leq 1)$$

$$= 1 - e^{-x/\beta}$$

The first line in the above is obtained by dividing through by $-\beta$ (recall that $\beta > 0$, so $-\beta < 0$ and the inequality reverses), the second line is obtained by exponentiating both sides (the exponential function is monotone increasing, so the inequality is preserved), the third line is just rewriting, together with knowing that U is in $[0, 1]$ anyway, and the last line follows since U is $U(0, 1)$, and the interval $[e^{-x/\beta}, 1]$ is contained within the interval $[0, 1]$. Since the last line is $F(x)$ for the exponential distribution, we have verified that our algorithm is correct. Chapter 8 discusses how to generate random variates and processes in general.

In our programs, we prefer to use a particular method for random-number generation to obtain the variate U described above, as expressed in the FORTRAN, Pascal, and C codes of Figs. 7.5 through 7.8 in App. 7A of Chap. 7. While most compilers do have some kind of built-in random-number generator, many of these are of extremely poor quality and should not be used; this issue is discussed fully in Chap. 7.

It is convenient (if not the most computationally efficient) to modularize the programs into several subprograms to clarify the logic and interactions, as discussed in general in Sec. 1.3.2. In addition to a main program, the simulation program includes routines for initialization, timing, report generation, and generating exponential random variates, as in Fig. 1.3. It also simplifies matters if we write a separate routine to update the continuous-time statistic , being the accumulated areas under the $Q(t)$ and $B(t)$ curves. The most important action, however, takes place in the routines for the events, which we number as follows:

Event description	Event type
Arrival of a customer to the system	1
Departure of a customer from the system after completing service	2

As the logic of these event routines is independent of the particular language to be used, we shall discuss it here. Figure 1.8 contains a flowchart for

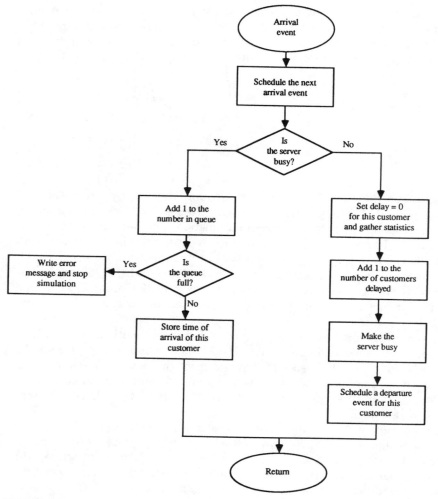

FIGURE 1.8
Flowchart for arrival routine, queueing model.

the arrival event. First, the time of the next arrival in the future is generated and placed in the event list. Then a check is made to determine whether the server is busy. If so, the number of customers in the queue is incremented by one, and we ask whether the storage space allocated to hold the queue is already full (see the code in Sec. 1.4.4, 1.4.5, or 1.4.6 for details). If the queue

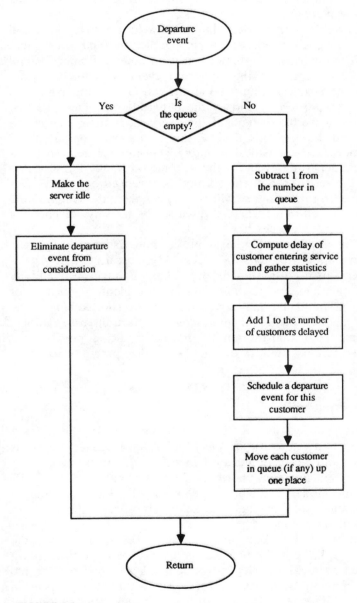

FIGURE 1.9
Flowchart for departure routine, queueing model.

is already full, an error message is produced and the simulation is stopped; if there is still room in the queue, the arriving customer's time of arrival is put at the (new) end of the queue. On the other hand, if the arriving customer finds the server idle, then this customer has a delay of zero, which *is* counted as a delay, and the number of customer delays completed is incremented by one. The server must be made busy, and the time of departure from service of the arriving customer is scheduled into the event list.

The departure event's logic is depicted in the flowchart of Fig. 1.9. Recall that this routine is invoked when a service completion (and subsequent departure) occurs. If the departing customer leaves no other customers behind in queue, the server is idled and the departure event is eliminated from consideration, since the next event must be an arrival. On the other hand, if one or more customers are left behind by the departing customer, the first customer in queue will leave the queue and enter service, so the queue length is reduced by one, and the delay in queue of this customer is computed and registered in the appropriate statistical counter. The number delayed is increased by one, and a departure event for the customer now entering service is scheduled. Finally, the rest of the queue (if any) is advanced one place. Our implementation of the list for the queue will be very simple in this chapter, and is certainly not the most efficient; Chap. 2 discusses better ways of handling lists to model such things as queues.

In the next three sections we give examples of how the above setup can be used to write simulation programs in FORTRAN, Pascal, and C. Again, only one of these sections need be studied, depending on language familiarity or preference; the logic and organization is essentially identical, except for changes dictated by a particular language's features or shortcomings. The results (which were identical across all three languages) are discussed in Sec. 1.4.7. These programs are neither the simplest nor most efficient possible, but were instead designed to illustrate how one might organize programs for more complex simulations.

1.4.4 FORTRAN Program

This section presents and describes a FORTRAN program for the $M/M/1$ queue simulation. General references on the FORTRAN language are Davis and Hoffmann (1988) and Koffman and Friedman (1987), for example.

The subroutines and functions shown in Table 1.1 make up the FORTRAN program for this model. The table also shows the FORTRAN variables used (modeling variables include state variables, statistical counters, and variables used to facilitate coding).

The code for the main program is shown in Fig. 1.10, and begins with the INCLUDE statement to bring in the lines in the file mm1.dcl, which is shown in Fig. 1.11. The action the INCLUDE statement takes is to copy the file named between the quotes (in this case, mm1.dcl) into the main program in place of the INCLUDE statement. The file mm1.dcl contains "declarations" of

TABLE 1.1
Subroutines, functions, and FORTRAN variables for the queueing model

Subprogram	Purpose
INIT	Initialization routine
TIMING	Timing routine
ARRIVE	Event routine to process type 1 events
DEPART	Event routine to process type 2 events
REPORT	Generates report when simulation ends
UPTAVG	Updates continuous-time area-accumulator statistics just before each event occurrence
EXPON(RMEAN)	Function to generate an exponential random variate with mean RMEAN
RAND(1)	Function to generate a uniform random variate between 0 and 1 (shown in Fig. 7.5)

Variable	Definition
Input parameters:	
MARRVT	Mean interarrival time ($=1.0$ here)
MSERVT	Mean service time ($=0.5$)
TOTCUS	Total number, n, of customer delays to be observed ($=1000$)
Modeling variables:	
ANIQ	Area under the number-in-queue function [$Q(t)$] so far
AUTIL	Area under the server-status function [$B(t)$] so far
BUSY	Mnemonic for server busy ($=1$)
DELAY	Delay in queue of a customer
IDLE	Mnemonic for server idle ($=0$)
MINTNE	Used by TIMING to determine which event is next
NEVNTS	Number of event types for this model, used by TIMING routine ($=2$ here)
NEXT	Event type (1 or 2 here) of the next event to occur (determined by TIMING routine)
NIQ	Number of customers currently in queue
NUMCUS	Number of customers who have completed their delays so far
QLIMIT	Number of storage locations for the queue TARRVL ($=100$)
RMEAN	Mean of the exponential random variate to be generated (used by EXPON)
SERVER	Server status (0 for idle, 1 for busy)
TARRVL(I)	Time of arrival of the customer now Ith in queue (dimensioned to have 100 places)
TIME	Simulation clock
TLEVNT	Time of the last (most recent) event
TNE(I)	Time of the next event of type I ($I = 1, 2$), part of event list
TOTDEL	Total of the delays completed so far
TSLE	Time since the last event (used by UPTAVG)
U	Random variate distributed uniformly between 0 and 1
Output variables:	
AVGDEL	Average delay in queue [$\hat{d}(n)$]
AVGNIQ	Time-average number in queue [$\hat{q}(n)$]
UTIL	Server utilization [$\hat{u}(n)$]

```fortran
*       Main program for single-server queueing system.

*       Bring in declarations file.

        INCLUDE 'mm1.dcl'

*       Open input and output files.

        OPEN (5, FILE = 'mm1.in')
        OPEN (6, FILE = 'mm1.out')

*       Specify the number of event types for the timing routine.

        NEVNTS = 2

*       Set mnemonics for server's being busy and idle.

        BUSY = 1
        IDLE = 0

*       Read input parameters.

        READ (5,*) MARRVT, MSERVT, TOTCUS

*       Write report heading and input parameters.

        WRITE (6,2010) MARRVT, MSERVT, TOTCUS
 2010 FORMAT (' Single-server queueing system'//
      &          ' Mean interarrival time',F11.3,' minutes'//
      &          ' Mean service time',F16.3,' minutes'//
      &          ' Number of customers',I14//)

*       Initialize the simulation.

        CALL INIT

*       Determine the next event.

   10 CALL TIMING

*       Update time-average statistical accumulators.

        CALL UPTAVG

*       Call the appropriate event routine.

        GO TO (20, 30), NEXT
   20     CALL ARRIVE
          GO TO 40
   30     CALL DEPART

*       If the simulation is over, call the report generator and end the
*       simulation. If not, continue the simulation.

   40 IF (NUMCUS .LT. TOTCUS) GO TO 10
      CALL REPORT

      CLOSE (5)
      CLOSE (6)

      STOP
      END
```

FIGURE 1.10
FORTRAN code for the main program, queueing model.

```
      INTEGER QLIMIT
      PARAMETER (QLIMIT = 100)
      INTEGER BUSY,IDLE,NEVNTS,NEXT,NIQ,NUMCUS,SERVER,TOTCUS
      REAL ANIQ,AUTIL,MARRVT,MSERVT,TARRVL(QLIMIT),TIME,TLEVNT,TNE(2),
     &      TOTDEL
      REAL EXPON
      COMMON /MODEL/ ANIQ,AUTIL,BUSY,IDLE,MARRVT,MSERVT,NEVNTS,NEXT,NIQ,
     &               NUMCUS,SERVER,TARRVL,TIME,TLEVNT,TNE,TOTCUS,TOTDEL
```

FIGURE 1.11
FORTRAN code for the declarations file (mm1.dcl), queueing model.

the variables and arrays to be INTEGER or REAL, the COMMON block
MODEL, and the PARAMETER value QLIMIT = 100, our guess (which may
have to be adjusted by trial and error) as to the longest the queue will ever get.
All of the statements in the file mm1.dcl must appear at the beginning of
almost all subprograms in the simulation, and using the INCLUDE statement
simply makes it easier to do this, and to make any necessary changes. The
variables in the COMMON block MODEL are those we want to be global;
i.e., variables in the block will be known and accessible to all subprograms that
contain this COMMON statement. Variables not in COMMON will be *local* to
the subprogram in which they appear. Also, we have adopted the convention
of explicitly declaring the type (REAL or INTEGER) of all variables, arrays,
and functions regardless of whether the first letter of the variable would default
to its desired type according to the FORTRAN convention. Next, the input
data file (called mm1.in) is opened and assigned to unit 5, and the file to
contain the output (called mm1.out) is opened and assigned to unit 6. (We do
not show the contents of the file mm1.in, since it is only a single line consisting
of the numbers 1.0, 0.5, and 1000, separated by any number of blanks.) The
number of event types for the simulation, NEVNTS, is initialized to 2 for this
model, and the mnemonic constants BUSY and IDLE are set to use with the
SERVER status variable, for code readability. The input parameters are then
read in free format. After writing a report heading and echoing the input
parameters (as a check that they were read correctly), the initialization routine
INIT is called. The timing routine, TIMING, is then called to determine the
event type, NEXT, of the next event to occur and to advance the simulation
clock, TIME, to its time. Before processing this event, subroutine UPTAVG is
called to update the areas under the $Q(t)$ and $B(t)$ curves, for the continuous-
time statistics; UPTAVG also brings the time of the last event, TLEVNT, up to
the present. By doing this at this time we automatically update these areas
before processing each event. Then a "computed GO TO statement," based on
NEXT, is used to pass control to the appropriate event routine. If NEXT = 1,
event routine ARRIVE is called (at statement label 20) to process the arrival
of a customer. If NEXT = 2, event routine DEPART (at statement label 30) is
called to process the departure of a customer after completing service. After
control is returned to the main program from ARRIVE or DEPART, a check
is made (at statement label 40) to see whether the number of customers who

have completed their delays, NUMCUS (which is incremented by 1 after each customer completes his or her delay), is still (strictly) less than the number of customers whose delays we want to observe, TOTCUS. If so, TIMING is called to continue the simulation. If the specified number of delays has been observed, the report generator, REPORT, is called to compute and write estimates of the desired measures of performance. Finally, the input and output files are closed (a precautionary measure that is not required on many systems), and the simulation run is terminated.

Code for subroutine INIT is given in Fig. 1.12. Note that the same declarations file, mm1.dcl, is brought in here by the INCLUDE statement. Each statement in INIT corresponds to an element of the computer representation in Fig. 1.7a. Note that the time of the first arrival, TNE(1), is determined by adding an exponential random variate with mean MARRVT, namely, EXPON(MARRVT), to the simulation clock, TIME = 0. (We explicitly used TIME in this statement, although it has a value of 0, to show the general form of a statement to determine the time of a future event.) Since no customers are present at TIME = 0, the time of the next departure, TNE(2), is set to $1.0E + 30$ (FORTRAN notation for 10^{30}), guaranteeing that the first event will be an arrival.

Subroutine TIMING is given in Fig. 1.13. The program compares TNE(1), TNE(2), . . . , TNE(NEVNTS) and sets NEXT equal to the event type whose time of occurrence is the smallest. (Note that NEVNTS is set in the main

```
      SUBROUTINE INIT
      INCLUDE 'mm1.dcl'

*     Initialize the simulation clock.

      TIME  = 0.0

*     Initialize the state variables.

      SERVER = IDLE
      NIQ    = 0
      TLEVNT = 0.0

*     Initialize the statistical counters.

      NUMCUS = 0
      TOTDEL = 0.0
      ANIQ   = 0.0
      AUTIL  = 0.0

*     Initialize event list. Since no customers are present, the
*     departure (service completion) event is eliminated from
*     consideration.

      TNE(1) = TIME + EXPON(MARRVT)
      TNE(2) = 1.0E+30

      RETURN
      END
```

FIGURE 1.12
FORTRAN code for subroutine INIT, queueing model.

```
      SUBROUTINE TIMING
      INCLUDE 'mm1.dcl'
      INTEGER I
      REAL MINTNE

      MINTNE = 1.0E+29
      NEXT   = 0

*     Determine the event type of the next event to occur.

      DO 10 I = 1, NEVNTS
         IF (TNE(I) .LT. MINTNE) THEN
            MINTNE = TNE(I)
            NEXT   = I
         END IF
   10 CONTINUE

*     Check to see whether the event list is empty.

      IF (NEXT .EQ. 0) THEN

*        The event list is empty, so stop the simulation.

         WRITE (6,2010) TIME
 2010    FORMAT (' Event list empty at time',F10.3)
         STOP

      END IF

*     The event list is not empty, so advance the simulation clock.

      TIME = MINTNE

      RETURN
      END
```

FIGURE 1.13
FORTRAN code for subroutine TIMING, queueing model.

program.) In case of ties, the lowest-numbered event type is chosen. Then the simulation clock is advanced to the time of occurrence of the chosen event type, MINTNE. The program is complicated slightly by an error check for the event list's being empty, which we define to mean that all events are scheduled to occur at TIME $= 10^{30}$. If this is ever the case (as indicated by NEXT $= 0$), an error message is produced along with the current clock time (as a possible debugging aid), and the simulation is terminated.

The code for event routine ARRIVE is in Fig. 1.14, and follows the language-independent discussion as given in Sec. 1.4.3 and in the flowchart of Fig. 1.8. Note that TIME is the time of arrival of the customer who is just now arriving, and that the queue-overflow check is made by asking whether NIQ is now greater than QLIMIT, the length for which TARRVL was dimensioned.

Event routine DEPART, whose code is shown in Fig. 1.15, is called from the main program when a service completion (and subsequent departure) occurs; the logic for it was discussed in Sec. 1.4.3, with a flowchart in Fig. 1.9. Note that if the statement TNE(2) $= 1.0E + 30$ just before the ELSE were omitted, the program would get into an infinite loop. (Why?) Advancing the

```
      SUBROUTINE ARRIVE
      INCLUDE 'mm1.dcl'
      REAL DELAY

*     Schedule next arrival.

      TNE(1) = TIME + EXPON(MARRVT)

*     Check to see whether server is busy.

      IF (SERVER .EQ. BUSY) THEN

*         Server is busy, so increment number of customers in queue.

          NIQ = NIQ + 1

*         Check to see whether an overflow condition exists.

          IF (NIQ .GT. QLIMIT) THEN

*             The queue has overflowed, so stop the simulation.

              WRITE (6,2010) TIME
 2010         FORMAT (' Overflow of the array TARRVL at time',F10.3)
              STOP

          END IF

*         There is still room in the queue, so store the time of arrival
*         of the arriving customer at the (new) end of TARRVL.

          TARRVL(NIQ) = TIME

      ELSE

*         Server is idle, so arriving customer has a delay of zero.  (The
*         following two statments are for program clarity and do not
*         affect the results of the simulation.)

          DELAY  = 0.0
          TOTDEL = TOTDEL + DELAY

*         Increment the number of customers delayed, and make server
*         busy.

          NUMCUS = NUMCUS + 1
          SERVER = BUSY

*         Schedule a departure (service completion).

          TNE(2) = TIME + EXPON(MSERVT)

      END IF

      RETURN
      END
```

FIGURE 1.14
FORTRAN code for subroutine ARRIVE, queueing model.

```
         SUBROUTINE DEPART
         INCLUDE 'mm1.dcl'
         INTEGER I
         REAL DELAY

*        Check to see whether the queue is empty.

         IF (NIQ .EQ. 0) THEN

*            The queue is empty so make the server idle and eliminate the
*            departure (service completion) event from consideration.

             SERVER = IDLE
             TNE(2) = 1.0E+30

         ELSE

*            The queue is nonempty, so decrement the number of customers in
*            queue.

             NIQ = NIQ - 1

*            Compute the delay of the customer who is beginning service and
*            update the total delay accumulator.

             DELAY  = TIME - TARRVL(1)
             TOTDEL = TOTDEL + DELAY

*            Increment the number of customers delayed, and schedule
*            departure.

             NUMCUS = NUMCUS + 1
             TNE(2) = TIME + EXPON(MSERVT)

*            Move each customer in queue (if any) up one place.

             DO 10 I = 1, NIQ
   10        TARRVL(I) = TARRVL(I + 1)

         END IF

         RETURN
         END
```

FIGURE 1.15
FORTRAN code for subroutine DEPART, queueing model.

rest of the queue (if any) one place by DO loop 10 ensures that the arrival time of the next customer entering service (after being delayed in queue) will always be stored in TARRVL(1). Note that if the queue were now empty (i.e., the customer who just left the queue and entered service had been the only one in queue), then NIQ would be equal to 0, and this DO loop would not be executed at all since the beginning value of the DO loop index, I, starts out at a value (1) that would already exceed its final value (NIQ = 0); this is a feature of FORTRAN 77 (which we use here, as detailed in App. 1C) that may not be shared by older versions of FORTRAN. (Managing the queue in this simple way, by moving the arrival times up physically, is certainly inefficient; we return to this issue in Chap. 2.) A final comment about DEPART concerns the subtraction of TARRVL(1) from the clock value, TIME, to obtain the delay in queue. If the simulation is to run for a long period of (simulated) time, both TIME and TARRVL(1) would become very large numbers in comparison with the difference between them; thus, since they are both stored as floating-point (REAL) numbers with finite accuracy, there is potentially a serious loss of precision when doing this subtraction. For this reason, it may be necessary to make both TIME and the TARRVL array DOUBLE PRECISION if we want to run this simulation out for a long period of time.

The code for subroutine REPORT, called when the termination check in the main program determines that the simulation is over, is given in Fig. 1.16. The average delay, AVGDEL, is computed by dividing the total of the delays by the number of customers whose delays were observed, and the time-average number in queue, AVGNIQ, is obtained by dividing the area under $Q(t)$, now updated to the end of the simulation (since UPTAVG is called from the main program before processing either an arrival or departure, one of which will end the simulation), by the clock value at termination. The server utilization, UTIL, is computed by dividing the area under $B(t)$ by the final clock time, and all three measures are written out. We also write out the final clock value itself, to see how long it took to observe the 1000 delays.

Subroutine UPTAVG is shown in Fig. 1.17. This subroutine is called just before processing each event (of any type) and updates the areas under the two functions needed for the continuous-time statistics; this routine is separate for coding convenience only, and is *not* an event routine. The time since the last event, TSLE, is first computed, and the time of the last event, TLEVNT, is brought up to the current time in order to be ready for the next entry into UPTAVG. Then the area under the number-in-queue function is augmented by the area of the rectangle under $Q(t)$ during the interval since the previous event, which is of width TSLE and height NIQ; remember, UPTAVG is called *before* processing an event, and state variables such as NIQ still have their previous values. The area under $B(t)$ is then augmented by the area of a

```
      SUBROUTINE REPORT
      INCLUDE 'mm1.dcl'
      REAL AVGDEL,AVGNIQ,UTIL

*     Compute and write estimates of desired measures of performance.

      AVGDEL = TOTDEL / NUMCUS
      AVGNIQ = ANIQ / TIME
      UTIL   = AUTIL / TIME
      WRITE (6,2010) AVGDEL, AVGNIQ, UTIL, TIME
 2010 FORMAT (/' Average delay in queue',F11.3,' minutes'//
     &          ' Average number in queue',F10.3//
     &          ' Server utilization',F15.3//
     &          ' Time simulation ended',F12.3,' minutes')

      RETURN
      END
```

FIGURE 1.16
FORTRAN code for subroutine REPORT, queueing model.

```
      SUBROUTINE UPTAVG
      INCLUDE 'mm1.dcl'
      REAL TSLE

*     Compute time since last event, and update last-event-time marker.

      TSLE   = TIME - TLEVNT
      TLEVNT = TIME

*     Update area under number-in-queue function.

      ANIQ   = ANIQ + NIQ * TSLE

*     Update area under server-busy indicator function.

      AUTIL  = AUTIL + SERVER * TSLE

      RETURN
      END
```

FIGURE 1.17
FORTRAN code for subroutine UPTAVG, queueing model.

rectangle of width TSLE and height SERVER; this is why it is convenient to define SERVER to be either 0 or 1. Note that this routine, like DEPART, contains a subtraction of two floating-point numbers (TIME–TLEVNT), both of which could become quite large relative to their difference if we were to run the simulation for a long time; in this case it may be necessary to declare both TIME and TLEVNT to be DOUBLE PRECISION variables.

The function EXPON, which generates an exponential random variate with mean β = RMEAN (passed into EXPON), is shown in Fig. 1.18, and follows the algorithm discussed in Sec. 1.4.3. The random-number generator RAND, used here with an INTEGER argument of 1, is discussed fully in Chap. 7, and is shown specifically in Fig. 7.5. The FORTRAN built-in function LOG returns the natural logarithm of its argument, and agrees in type with its argument.

The program described here must be combined with the random-number-generator code from Fig. 7.5. This could be done by separate compilations, followed by linking the object codes together in an installation-dependent way.

```
      REAL FUNCTION EXPON(RMEAN)
      REAL RMEAN,U
      REAL RAND

*     Generate a U(0,1) random variate.

      U = RAND(1)

*     Return an exponential random variate with mean RMEAN.

      EXPON = -RMEAN * LOG(U)

      RETURN
      END
```

FIGURE 1.18
FORTRAN code for function EXPON.

1.4.5 Pascal Program

In this section we discuss a Pascal program for the $M/M/1$ queue simulation. We follow the language conventions described by Jensen and Wirth (1985); there are also several general introductions to Pascal, such as Grogono (1984). We have taken advantage of Pascal's facility to give variables and procedures fairly long names, which should thus be self-explanatory.

The global (outer-shell) declarations are given in Fig. 1.19. The constant QLimit is set to 100, our guess (which may have to be adjusted by trial and error) as to the longest the queue will ever get. The constants Busy and Idle are defined to be used with the ServerStatus variable, for code readability. The procedures and functions for the program are declared FORWARD, since there are occasions to invoke them from more than one place; this also allows them to appear sequentially in the file, rather than in a strictly nested fashion. Note that the array Zrng, as well as the procedures and functions Randdf, Rand, Randst, and Randgt, must be declared as well in order to use the random-number generator given in Fig. 7.6.

```
PROGRAM SingleServerQ(Input, Output);

{ Global declarations for single-server queueing system. }

CONST
    QLimit = 100;   { Limit on queue length. }
    Busy   =   1;   { Mnemonics for server's being busy }
    Idle   =   0;   { and idle. }

VAR
    NextEventType, NumCustsDelayed, NumDelaysRequired, NumEvents, NumInQ,
        ServerStatus : Integer;
    AreaNumInQ, AreaServerStatus, MeanInterarrival, MeanService, Time,
        TimeLastEvent, TotalOfDelays : Real;
    TimeArrival   : ARRAY [1..QLimit] OF Real;
    TimeNextEvent : ARRAY [1..2]     OF Real;

    { The following declaration is for the random-number generator.
      Note that the name Zrng must not be used for any other purpose. }

    Zrng : ARRAY [1..100] OF Integer;

PROCEDURE Initialize;                              FORWARD;
PROCEDURE Timing;                                  FORWARD;
PROCEDURE Arrive;                                  FORWARD;
PROCEDURE Depart;                                  FORWARD;
PROCEDURE Report;                                  FORWARD;
PROCEDURE UpdateTimeAvgStats;                      FORWARD;
FUNCTION  Expon(Mean : Real) : Real;               FORWARD;

{ The following four declarations are for the random-number generator.
  }

PROCEDURE Randdf;                                          FORWARD;
FUNCTION  Rand(Stream : Integer) : Real;                   FORWARD;
PROCEDURE Randst(Zset : Integer; Stream : Integer);        FORWARD;
FUNCTION  Randgt(Stream : Integer) : Integer;              FORWARD;
```

FIGURE 1.19
Pascal code for the global declarations, queueing model.

Code for procedure Initialize is given in Fig. 1.20; this procedure is invoked before the simulation actually starts moving through time. Each statement here corresponds to an element of the computer representation in Fig. 1.7a. Note that the time of the first arrival, TimeNextEvent[1], is determined by adding an exponential random variate with mean MeanInterarrival, namely, Expon(MeanInterarrival), to the simulation clock, Time = 0. (We explicitly used Time in this statement, although it has a value of 0, to show the general form of a statement to determine the time of a future event.) Since no customers are present at Time = 0, the time of the next departure, TimeNextEvent[2], is set to 1.0E + 30 (Pascal notation for 10^{30}), guaranteeing that the first event will be an arrival.

Procedure Timing is given in Fig. 1.21, and is invoked whenever the simulation is ready to move on to whatever event should occur next. The program compares TimeNextEvent[1], TimeNextEvent[2], ..., TimeNextEvent[NumEvents] (NumEvents is the number of event types, being 2 for this model, and is set in the main program) and sets NextEventType equal to the event type whose time of occurrence is the smallest. In case of ties, the lowest-numbered event type is chosen. Then the simulation clock is advanced to the time of occurrence of the chosen event type, MinTimeNextEvent. The program is complicated slightly by an error check for the event list's being empty, which we define to mean that all events are scheduled to occur at

```
PROCEDURE Initialize;  { Initialization procedure. }

   BEGIN { Initialize }

      { Initialize the simulation clock. }

      Time := 0.0;

      { Initialize the state variables. }

      ServerStatus   := Idle;
      NumInQ         := 0;
      TimeLastEvent  := 0.0;

      { Initialize the statistical counters. }

      NumCustsDelayed  := 0;
      TotalOfDelays    := 0.0;
      AreaNumInQ       := 0.0;
      AreaServerStatus := 0.0;

      { Initialize event list.  Since no customers are present, the
        departure (service completion) event is eliminated from
        consideration. }

      TimeNextEvent[1] := Time + Expon(MeanInterarrival);
      TimeNextEvent[2] := 1.0E+30

   END; { Initialize }
```

FIGURE 1.20
Pascal code for procedure Initialize, queueing model.

```
PROCEDURE Timing;   { Timing procedure. }

   VAR
      I                  : Integer;
      MinTimeNextEvent : Real;

   BEGIN { Timing }

      MinTimeNextEvent := 1.0E+29;
      NextEventType    := 0;

      { Determine the event type of the next event to occur. }

      FOR I := 1 TO NumEvents DO BEGIN
         IF TimeNextEvent[I] < MinTimeNextEvent THEN BEGIN
            MinTimeNextEvent := TimeNextEvent[I];
            NextEventType    := I
         END
      END;

      { Check to see whether the event list is empty. }

      IF NextEventType = 0 THEN BEGIN

         { The event list is empty, so stop the simulation. }

         Writeln('Event list empty at time', Time);
         Halt

      END;

      { The event list is not empty, so advance the simulation clock. }

      Time := MinTimeNextEvent

   END; { Timing }
```

FIGURE 1.21
Pascal code for procedure Timing, queueing model.

Time $= 10^{30}$. If this is ever the case (as indicated by NextEventType $= 0$), an error message is produced along with the current clock time (as a possible debugging aid), and the simulation is terminated.

The code for event procedure Arrive is in Fig. 1.22, and follows the language-independent discussion as given in Sec. 1.4.3 and in the flowchart of Fig. 1.8. Note that Time is the time of arrival of the customer who is just now arriving, and that the queue-overflow check is made by asking whether NumInQ is now greater than QLimit, the length for which TimeArrival was dimensioned.

Event procedure Depart, whose code is shown in Fig. 1.23, is invoked from the main program when a service completion (and subsequent departure) occurs; the logic for it was discussed in Sec. 1.4.3, with the flowchart in Fig. 1.9. Note that if the statement TimeNextEvent $[2] := 1.0E + 30$ just before the first END were omitted, the program would get into an infinite loop. (Why?) Advancing the rest of the queue (if any) one place by the FOR loop near the end of the procedure ensures that the arrival time of the next customer entering service (after being delayed in queue) will always be stored in

```
PROCEDURE Arrive;   { Arrival event procedure. }

   VAR
       Delay : Real;

   BEGIN { Arrive }

       { Schedule next arrival. }

       TimeNextEvent[1] := Time + Expon(MeanInterarrival);

       { Check to see whether server is busy. }

       IF ServerStatus = Busy THEN BEGIN

           { Server is busy, so increment number of customers in queue. }

           NumInQ := NumInQ + 1;

           { Check to see whether an overflow condition exists. }

           IF NumInQ > QLimit THEN BEGIN

               { The queue has overflowed, so stop the simulation. }

               Writeln('Overflow of the array TimeArrival at time', Time);
               Halt

           END;

           { There is still room in the queue, so store the time of
             arrival of the arriving customer at the (new) end of
             TimeArrival. }

           TimeArrival[NumInQ] := Time

       END
       ELSE BEGIN

           { Server is idle, so arriving customer has a delay of zero.
             (The following two statements are for program clarity and do
             not affect the results of the simulation.) }

           Delay          := 0.0;
           TotalOfDelays := TotalOfDelays + Delay;

           { Increment the number of customers delayed, and make server
             busy. }

           NumCustsDelayed := NumCustsDelayed + 1;
           ServerStatus    := Busy;

           { Schedule a departure (service completion). }

           TimeNextEvent[2] := Time + Expon(MeanService)

       END

   END; { Arrive }
```

FIGURE 1.22
Pascal code for procedure Arrive, queueing model.

```
PROCEDURE Depart;   ( Departure event procedure. )

    VAR
        I     : Integer;
        Delay : Real;

    BEGIN ( Depart )

        ( Check to see whether the queue is empty. )

        IF NumInQ = 0 THEN BEGIN

            ( The queue is empty so make the server idle and eliminate the
              departure (service completion) event from consideration. )

            ServerStatus     := Idle;
            TimeNextEvent[2] := 1.0E+30

        END
        ELSE BEGIN

            ( The queue is nonempty, so decrement the number of customers
              in queue. )

            NumInQ := NumInQ - 1;

            ( Compute the delay of the customer who is beginning service
              and update the total delay accumulator. )

            Delay         := Time - TimeArrival[1];
            TotalOfDelays := TotalOfDelays + Delay;

            ( Increment the number of customers delayed, and schedule
              departure. )

            NumCustsDelayed  := NumCustsDelayed + 1;
            TimeNextEvent[2] := Time + Expon(MeanService);

            ( Move each customer in queue (if any) up one place. )

            FOR I := 1 TO NumInQ DO
                TimeArrival[I] := TimeArrival[I + 1]

        END

    END; ( Depart )
```

FIGURE 1.23
Pascal code for procedure Depart, queueing model.

TimeArrival[1]. Note that if the queue were now empty (i.e., the customer who just left the queue and entered service had been the only one in queue), then NumInQ would be equal to 0, and this loop would not be executed at all since the beginning value of the loop index, I, starts out at a value (1) which would already exceed its final value (NumInQ = 0). (Managing the queue in this simple way is certainly inefficient; we return to this issue in Chap. 2). A final comment about Depart concerns the subtraction of TimeArrival[1] from the clock value, Time, to obtain the delay in queue. If the simulation is to run for a long period of (simulated) time, both Time and TimeArrival[1] would become very large numbers in comparison with the difference between them;

thus, since they are both stored as floating-point (Real) numbers with finite accuracy, there is potentially a serious loss of precision when doing this subtraction. For this reason, it may be necessary to make both Time and the TimeArrival array double precision (if available) if we want to run this simulation out for a long period of time.

The code for procedure Report, invoked when the termination check in the main program determines that the simulation is over, is given in Fig. 1.24. The average delay is computed by dividing the total of the delays by the number of customers whose delays were observed, and the time-average number in queue is obtained by dividing the area under $Q(t)$, now updated to the end of the simulation (since the procedure to update the areas is called from the main program before processing either an arrival or departure, one of which will end the simulation), by the clock value at termination. The server utilization is computed by dividing the area under $B(t)$ by the final clock time, and all three measures are written out. We also write out the final clock value itself, to see how long it took to observe the 1000 delays.

Procedure UpdateTimeAvgStats is shown in Fig. 1.25. This procedure is invoked just before processing each event (of any type) and updates the areas under the two functions needed for the continuous-time statistics; this routine is separate for coding convenience only, and is *not* an event routine. The time since the last event is first computed, and the time of the last event is brought up to the current time in order to be ready for the next entry into this procedure. Then the area under the number-in-queue function is augmented by the area of the rectangle under $Q(t)$ during the interval since the previous event, which is of width TimeSinceLastEvent and of height NumInQ; remember, this procedure is invoked *before* processing an event, and state

```
PROCEDURE Report;   { Report generator procedure. }

    VAR
        AvgDelayInQ, AvgNumInQ, ServerUtilization : Real;

    BEGIN { Report }

        { Compute and write estimates of desired measures of performance.
          }

        AvgDelayInQ        := TotalOfDelays / NumCustsDelayed;
        AvgNumInQ          := AreaNumInQ / Time;
        ServerUtilization  := AreaServerStatus / Time;
        Writeln;
        Writeln('Average delay in queue', AvgDelayInQ:11:3, ' minutes');
        Writeln;
        Writeln('Average number in queue', AvgNumInQ:10:3);
        Writeln;
        Writeln('Server utilization', ServerUtilization:15:3);
        Writeln;
        Writeln('Time simulation ended', Time:12:3)

    END; { Report }
```

FIGURE 1.24
Pascal code for procedure Report, queueing model.

```
PROCEDURE UpdateTimeAvgStats;   { Update area accumulators for
                                  time-average statistics. }
   VAR
      TimeSinceLastEvent : Real;

   BEGIN { UpdateTimeAvgStats }

      { Compute time since last event, and update last-event-time
        marker. }

      TimeSinceLastEvent := Time - TimeLastEvent;
      TimeLastEvent      := Time;

      { Update area under number-in-queue function. }

      AreaNumInQ         := AreaNumInQ + NumInQ * TimeSinceLastEvent;

      { Update area under server-busy indicator function. }

      AreaServerStatus := AreaServerStatus +
                          ServerStatus * TimeSinceLastEvent

   END; { UpdateTimeAvgStats }
```

FIGURE 1.25
Pascal code for procedure UpdateTimeAvgStats, queueuing model.

variables such as NumInQ still have their previous values. The area under $B(t)$ is then augmented by the area of a rectangle of width TimeSinceLastEvent and height ServerStatus; this is why it is convenient to define ServerStatus to be either 0 or 1. Note that this procedure, like Depart, contains a subtraction of two floating-point numbers (Time − TimeLastEvent), both of which could become quite large relative to their difference if we were to run the simulation for a long time; in this case it may be necessary to declare both Time and TimeLastEvent to be double-precision variables, if available.

The function Expon, which generates an exponential random variate with mean β = Mean (passed into Expon), is shown in Fig. 1.26, and follows the algorithm discussed in Sec. 1.4.3. The random-number generator Rand, used

```
FUNCTION Expon;   { Exponential variate generation function. }
                  { Pass in Real parameter Mean giving mean, as
                    declared in FORWARD declarations earlier. }
   VAR
      U : Real;

   BEGIN { Expon }

      { Generate a U(0,1) random variate. }

      U := Rand(1);

      { Return an exponential random variate with mean Mean. }

      Expon := -Mean * Ln(U)

   END; { Expon }
```

FIGURE 1.26
Pascal code for function Expon.

```
BEGIN { SingleServerQ main program. }

    { Initialize the random-number generator. }

    Randdf;

    { Specify the number of events for the timing procedure. }

    NumEvents := 2;

    { Read input parameters. }

    Readln(MeanInterarrival, MeanService, NumDelaysRequired);

    { Write report heading and input parameters. }

    Writeln('Single-server queueing system');
    Writeln;
    Writeln('Mean interarrival time', MeanInterarrival:11:3, ' minutes');
    Writeln;
    Writeln('Mean service time', MeanService:16:3, ' minutes');
    Writeln;
    Writeln('Number of customers', NumDelaysRequired:14);
    Writeln;
    Writeln;

    { Initialize the simulation. }

    Initialize;

    { Run the simulation while more delays are still needed. }

    WHILE NumCustsDelayed < NumDelaysRequired DO BEGIN

        { Determine the next event. }

        Timing;

        { Update time-average statistical accumulators. }

        UpdateTimeAvgStats;

        { Invoke the appropriate event procedure. }

        CASE NextEventType OF
            1 : Arrive;
            2 : Depart
        END

    END;

    { Invoke the report generator and end the simulation. }

    Report

END. { SingleServerQ }
```

FIGURE 1.27
Pascal code for the main program, queueing model.

here with an Integer argument of 1, is discussed fully in Chap. 7, and is shown specifically in Fig. 7.6. The Pascal built-in function Ln returns the natural logarithm of its argument.

The code for the main program is shown in Fig. 1.27, and ties the foregoing pieces together. The random-number generator in Fig. 7.6 must be initialized by invoking Randdf. The number of event types for the simulation is initialized to 2 for this model. The input parameters are then read in. (In order to keep the code as general as possible, we assume that if input is to be from a file, it will be assigned at the operating-system level, perhaps with some kind of redirection of "standard" input; the same is true for the output.) After writing a report heading and echoing the input parameters (as a check that they were read correctly), the initialization procedure is invoked. The WHILE loop then executes the simulation as long as more customer delays are still needed to fulfill the 1000-delay stopping rule. Inside the WHILE loop, the Timing procedure is first invoked to determine the type of the next event to occur and to advance the simulation clock to its time. Before processing this event, the procedure to update the areas under the $Q(t)$ and $B(t)$ curves is invoked; by doing this at this time we automatically update these areas before processing each event. Then a CASE statement, based on NextEventType (=1 for an arrival and 2 for a departure), passes control to the appropriate event procedure. After the WHILE loop is done, the Report procedure is invoked, and the simulation ends.

As a final note, the random-number-generator procedures and functions (Randdf, Rand, Randst, and Randgt, as listed in Fig. 7.6) must be placed inside the above program between the Expon procedure and the main program. This can be done either physically with an editor, or by inserting a compiler-dependent include directive at this point to bring in the file containing the code from Fig. 7.6.

1.4.6 C Program

This section presents a C program for the $M/M/1$ queue simulation. We have chosen to write in the ANSI-standard version of the language, as described by Kernighan and Ritchie (1988), and in particular use function prototyping. We have also taken advantage of C's facility to give variables and functions fairly long names, which should thus be self-explanatory.

The external definitions are given in Fig. 1.28. The header file rand.h (listed in Fig. 7.8) is included to declare the functions for the random-number generator. The symbolic constant Q_LIMIT is set to 100, our guess (which may have to be adjusted by trial and error) as to the longest the queue will ever get. The symbolic constants BUSY and IDLE are defined to be used with the server_status variable, for code readability. File pointers *infile and *outfile are defined to allow us to open the input and output files from within the code, rather than at the operating-system level. Note also that the event list, as we have discussed it so far, will be implemented in an array called time_next_

```
/* External definitions for single-server queueing system. */

#include <stdio.h>
#include <math.h>
#include "rand.h"      /* Header file for random-number generator. */

#define Q_LIMIT 100   /* Limit on queue length. */
#define BUSY      1   /* Mnemonics for server's being busy */
#define IDLE      0   /* and idle. */

int    next_event_type, num_custs_delayed, num_delays_required,
       num_events, num_in_q, server_status;
float  area_num_in_q, area_server_status, mean_interarrival,
       mean_service, time, time_arrival[Q_LIMIT + 1],
       time_last_event, time_next_event[3], total_of_delays;
FILE   *infile, *outfile;

void   initialize(void);
void   timing(void);
void   arrive(void);
void   depart(void);
void   report(void);
void   update_time_avg_stats(void);
float  expon(float mean);
```

FIGURE 1.28
C code for the external definitions, queueing model.

event, whose 0th entry will be ignored in order to make the index agree with
the event type.

The code for the main function is shown in Fig. 1.29. The input and
output files are opened, and the number of event types for the simulation is
initialized to 2 for this model. The input parameters then are read in from the
file mm1.in, which contains a single line with the numbers 1.0, 0.5, and 1000,
separated by blanks. After writing a report heading and echoing the input
parameters (as a check that they were read correctly), the initialization
function is invoked. The "while" loop then executes the simulation as long as
more customer delays are needed to fulfill the 1000-delay stopping rule. Inside
the "while" loop, the timing function is first invoked to determine the type of
the next event to occur and to advance the simulation clock to its time. Before
processing this event, the function to update the areas under the $Q(t)$ and $B(t)$
curves is invoked; by doing this at this time we automatically update these
areas before processing each event. Then a switch statement, based on
next_event_type (=1 for an arrival and 2 for a departure), passes control to
the appropriate event function. After the "while" loop is done, the report
function is invoked, the input and output files are closed, and the simulation
ends.

Code for the initialization function is given in Fig. 1.30. Each statement
here corresponds to an element of the computer representation in Fig. 1.7a.
Note that the time of the first arrival, time_next_event[1], is determined by
adding an exponential random variate with mean mean_interarrival, namely,
expon(mean_interarrival), to the simulation clock, time = 0. (We explicitly
used "time" in this statement, although it has a value of 0, to show the general

```
main()   /* Main function. */
{
    /* Open input and output files. */

    infile  = fopen("mm1.in",  "r");
    outfile = fopen("mm1.out", "w");

    /* Specify the number of events for the timing function. */

    num_events = 2;

    /* Read input parameters. */

    fscanf(infile, "%f %f %d", &mean_interarrival, &mean_service,
           &num_delays_required);

    /* Write report heading and input parameters. */

    fprintf(outfile, "Single-server queueing system\n\n");
    fprintf(outfile, "Mean interarrival time%11.3f minutes\n\n",
            mean_interarrival);
    fprintf(outfile, "Mean service time%16.3f minutes\n\n",
            mean_service);
    fprintf(outfile, "Number of customers%14d\n\n",
            num_delays_required);

    /* Initialize the simulation. */

    initialize();

    /* Run the simulation while more delays are still needed. */

    while (num_custs_delayed < num_delays_required) {

        /* Determine the next event. */

        timing();

        /* Update time-average statistical accumulators. */

        update_time_avg_stats();

        /* Invoke the appropriate event function. */

        switch (next_event_type) {
            case 1:
                arrive();
                break;
            case 2:
                depart();
                break;
        }
    }

    /* Invoke the report generator and end the simulation. */

    report();

    fclose(infile);
    fclose(outfile);

    return 0;
}
```

FIGURE 1.29
C code for the main function, queueing model.

```
void initialize(void)   /* Initialization function. */
{
    /* Initialize the simulation clock. */

    time = 0.0;

    /* Initialize the state variables. */

    server_status    = IDLE;
    num_in_q         = 0;
    time_last_event  = 0.0;

    /* Initialize the statistical counters. */

    num_custs_delayed  = 0;
    total_of_delays    = 0.0;
    area_num_in_q      = 0.0;
    area_server_status = 0.0;

    /* Initialize event list.  Since no customers are present, the
       departure (service completion) event is eliminated from
       consideration. */

    time_next_event[1] = time + expon(mean_interarrival);
    time_next_event[2] = 1.0e+30;
}
```

FIGURE 1.30
C code for function initialize, queueing model.

form of a statement to determine the time of a future event.) Since no customers are present at time = 0, the time of the next departure, time_next_event[2], is set to 1.0e + 30 (C notation for 10^{30}), guaranteeing that the first event will be an arrival.

The timing function is given in Fig. 1.31 to compare time_next_event[1], time_next_event[2], . . . ,time_next_event[num_events] (recall that num_events was set in the main function) and set next_event_type equal to the event type whose time of occurrence is the smallest. In case of ties, the lowest-numbered event type is chosen. Then the simulation clock is advanced to the time of occurrence of the chosen event type, min_time_next_event. The program is complicated slightly by an error check for the event list's being empty, which we define to mean that all events are scheduled to occur at time = 10^{30}. If this is ever the case (as indicated by next_event_type = 0), an error message is produced along with the current clock time (as a possible debugging aid), and the simulation is terminated.

The code for event function arrive is in Fig. 1.32, and follows the language-independent discussion as given in Sec. 1.4.3 and in the flowchart of Fig. 1.8. Note that "time" is the time of arrival of the customer who is just now arriving, and that the queue-overflow check is made by asking whether num_in_q is now greater than Q_LIMIT, the length for which the array time_arrival was dimensioned.

Event function depart, whose code is shown in Fig. 1.33, is invoked from the main program when a service completion (and subsequent departure)

```
void timing(void)   /* Timing function. */
{
    int    i;
    float min_time_next_event = 1.0e+29;

    next_event_type = 0;

    /* Determine the event type of the next event to occur. */

    for (i = 1; i <= num_events; ++i) {
        if (time_next_event[i] < min_time_next_event) {
            min_time_next_event = time_next_event[i];
            next_event_type      = i;
        }
    }

    /* Check to see whether the event list is empty. */

    if (next_event_type == 0) {

        /* The event list is empty, so stop the simulation. */

        fprintf(outfile, "\nEvent list empty at time %f", time);
        exit(1);
    }

    /* The event list is not empty, so advance the simulation clock. */

    time = min_time_next_event;
}
```

FIGURE 1.31
C code for function timing, queueing model.

occurs; the logic for it was discussed in Sec. 1.4.3, with the flowchart in Fig. 1.9. Note that if the statement "time_next_event[2] = 1.0e + 30;" just before the "else" were omitted, the program would get into an infinite loop. (Why?) Advancing the rest of the queue (if any) one place by the "for" loop near the end of the function ensures that the arrival time of the next customer entering service (after being delayed in queue) will always be stored in time_arrival[1]. Note that if the queue were now empty (i.e., the customer who just left the queue and entered service had been the only one in queue), then num_in_q would be equal to 0, and this loop would not be executed at all since the beginning value of the loop index, i, starts out at a value (1) that would already exceed its final value (num_in_q = 0). (Managing the queue in this simple way is certainly inefficient, and could be improved by using pointers; we return to this issue in Chap. 2). A final comment about depart concerns the subtraction of time_arrival[1] from the clock value, time, to obtain the delay in queue. If the simulation is to run for a long period of (simulated) time, both time and time_arrival[1] would become very large numbers in comparison with the difference between them; thus, since they are both stored as floating-point (float) numbers with finite accuracy, there is potentially a serious loss of precision when doing this subtraction. For this reason, it may be necessary to make both time and the time_arrival array of type double if we are to run this simulation out for a long period of time.

```
void arrive(void)   /* Arrival event function. */
{
    float delay;

    /* Schedule next arrival. */

    time_next_event[1] = time + expon(mean_interarrival);

    /* Check to see whether server is busy. */

    if (server_status == BUSY) {

        /* Server is busy, so increment number of customers in queue.
           */

        ++num_in_q;

        /* Check to see whether an overflow condition exists. */

        if (num_in_q > Q_LIMIT) {

            /* The queue has overflowed, so stop the simulation. */

            fprintf(outfile, "\nOverflow of the array time_arrival at");
            fprintf(outfile, " time %f", time);
            exit(2);
        }

        /* There is still room in the queue, so store the time of
           arrival of the arriving customer at the (new) end of
           time_arrival. */

        time_arrival[num_in_q] = time;
    }

    else {

        /* Server is idle, so arriving customer has a delay of zero.
           (The following two statements are for program clarity and do
           not affect the results of the simulation.) */

        delay           = 0.0;
        total_of_delays += delay;

        /* Increment the number of customers delayed, and make server
           busy. */

        ++num_custs_delayed;
        server_status = BUSY;

        /* Schedule a departure (service completion). */

        time_next_event[2] = time + expon(mean_service);
    }
}
```

FIGURE 1.32
C code for function arrive, queueing model.

```
void depart(void)    /* Departure event function. */
{
    int    i;
    float delay;

    /* Check to see whether the queue is empty. */

    if (num_in_q == 0) {

        /* The queue is empty so make the server idle and eliminate the
           departure (service completion) event from consideration. */

        server_status      = IDLE;
        time_next_event[2] = 1.0e+30;
    }

    else {

        /* The queue is nonempty, so decrement the number of customers
           in queue. */

        --num_in_q;

        /* Compute the delay of the customer who is beginning service
           and update the total delay accumulator. */

        delay             = time - time_arrival[1];
        total_of_delays += delay;

        /* Increment the number of customers delayed, and schedule
           departure. */

        ++num_custs_delayed;
        time_next_event[2] = time + expon(mean_service);

        /* Move each customer in queue (if any) up one place. */

        for (i = 1; i <= num_in_q; ++i)
            time_arrival[i] = time_arrival[i + 1];
    }
}
```

FIGURE 1.33
C code for function depart, queueing model.

The code for the report function, invoked when the "while" loop in the main program is over, is given in Fig. 1.34. The average delay is computed by dividing the total of the delays by the number of customers whose delays were observed, and the time-average number in queue is obtained by dividing the area under $Q(t)$, now updated to the end of the simulation (since the function to update the areas is called from the main program before processing either an arrival or departure, one of which will end the simulation), by the clock value at termination. The server utilization is computed by dividing the area under $B(t)$ by the final clock time, and all three measures are written out directly. We also write out the final clock value itself, to see how long it took to observe the 1000 delays.

Function update_time_avg_stats is shown in Fig. 1.35. This function is invoked just before processing each event (of any type) and updates the areas

```
void report(void)   /* Report generator function. */
{
    /* Compute and write estimates of desired measures of performance.
       */

    fprintf(outfile, "\n\nAverage delay in queue%11.3f minutes\n\n",
            total_of_delays / num_custs_delayed);
    fprintf(outfile, "Average number in queue%10.3f\n\n",
            area_num_in_q / time);
    fprintf(outfile, "Server utilization%15.3f\n\n",
            area_server_status / time);
    fprintf(outfile, "Time simulation ended%12.3f", time);
}
```

FIGURE 1.34
C code for function report, queueing model.

under the two functions needed for the continuous-time statistics; this routine is separate for coding convenience only, and is *not* an event routine. The time since the last event is first computed, and then the time of the last event is brought up to the current time in order to be ready for the next entry into this function. Then the area under the number-in-queue function is augmented by the area of the rectangle under $Q(t)$ during the interval since the previous event, which is of width time_since_last_event and of height num_in_q; remember, this function is invoked *before* processing an event, and state variables such as num_in_q still have their previous values. The area under $B(t)$ is then augmented by the area of a rectangle of width time_since_last_event and height server_status; this is why it is convenient to define server_status to be either 0 or 1. Note that this function, like depart, contains a subtraction of two floating-point numbers (time − time_last_event), both of which could become quite large relative to their difference if we were to run the simulation for a long time; in this case it might be necessary to declare both time and time_last_event to be of type double.

```
void update_time_avg_stats(void)   /* Update area accumulators for
                                       time-average statistics. */
{
    float time_since_last_event;

    /* Compute time since last event, and update last-event-time
       marker. */

    time_since_last_event = time - time_last_event;
    time_last_event       = time;

    /* Update area under number-in-queue function. */

    area_num_in_q       += num_in_q * time_since_last_event;

    /* Update area under server-busy indicator function. */

    area_server_status += server_status * time_since_last_event;
}
```

FIGURE 1.35
C code for function update_time_avg_stats, queueing model.

```
float expon(float mean)   /* Exponential variate generation function.
                             */
{
    float u;

    /* Generate a U(0,1) random variate. */

    u = rand(1);

    /* Return an exponential random variate with mean "mean". */

    return -mean * log(u);
}
```

FIGURE 1.36
C code for function expon.

The function expon, which generates an exponential random variate with mean β = mean (passed into expon), is shown in Fig. 1.36, and follows the algorithm discussed in Sec. 1.4.3. The random-number generator rand, used here with an int argument of 1, is discussed fully in Chap. 7, and is shown specifically in Fig. 7.7. The C predefined function log returns the natural logarithm of its argument.

The program described here must be combined with the random-number-generator code from Fig. 7.7. This could be done by separate compilations, followed by linking the object codes together in an installation-dependent way.

1.4.7 Simulation Output and Discussion

The output (in a file named mm1.out if the FORTRAN or C program above was used) is shown in Fig. 1.37; since the same method for random-number generation was used for the programs in all three languages, they produced identical results. In this run, the average delay in queue was 0.430 minute, there was an average of 0.418 customer in the queue, and the server was busy

```
Single-server queueing system

Mean interarrival time      1.000 minutes

Mean service time           0.500 minutes

Number of customers         1000


Average delay in queue      0.430 minutes

Average number in queue     0.418

Server utilization          0.460

Time simulation ended    1027.915 minutes
```

FIGURE 1.37
Output report, queueing model.

46 percent of the time. It took 1027.915 simulated minutes to run the simulation to the completion of 1000 delays, which seems reasonable since the expected time between customer arrivals was 1 minute. (It is not a coincidence that the average delay, average number in queue, and utilization are all so close together for this model; see App. 1B.)

Note that these particular numbers in the output were determined, at root, by the numbers the random-number generator happened to come up with this time. If a different random-number generator were used, or if this one were used in another way (with another "seed" or "stream," as discussed in Chap. 7), then different numbers would have been produced in the output. Thus, these numbers are not to be regarded as "The Answers," but rather as estimates (and perhaps poor ones) of the expected quantities we want to know about, $d(n)$, $q(n)$, and $u(n)$; the statistical analysis of simulation output data is discussed in Chaps. 9 through 12. Also, the results are functions of the input parameters, in this case the mean interarrival and service times, and the $n = 1000$ stopping rule; they are also affected by the way we initialized the simulation (empty and idle).

In some simulation studies, we might want to estimate *steady-state* characteristics of the model (see Chap. 9), i.e., characteristics of a model after the simulation has been running a very long (in theory, an infinite) amount of time. For the simple $M/M/1$ queue we have been considering, it is possible to compute *analytically* the steady-state average delay in queue, the steady-state time-average number in queue, and the steady-state server utilization, all of these measures of performance being 0.5 [see, for example, Ross (1989, p. 352)]. Thus, if we wanted to determine these steady-state measures, our estimates based on the stopping rule $n = 1000$ delays were not too far off, at least in absolute terms. However, we were somewhat lucky, since $n = 1000$ was chosen arbitrarily! In practice, the choice of a stopping rule that will give good estimates of steady-state measures is quite difficult. To illustrate this point, suppose for the $M/M/1$ queue that the arrival rate of customers were increased from 1 per minute to 1.98 per minute (the mean interarrival time is now 0.505 minute), that the mean service time is unchanged, and that we wish to estimate the steady-state measures from a run of length $n = 1000$ delays, as before. We performed this simulation run and got values for the average delay, average number in queue, and server utilization of 17.404 minutes, 34.831, and 0.997, respectively. Since the true steady-state values of these measures are 49.5 minutes, 98.01, and 0.99 (respectively), it is clear that the stopping rule cannot be chosen arbitrarily. We discuss how to specify the run length for a steady-state simulation in Chap. 9.

The reader may have wondered why we did not estimate the expected average waiting time in the system of a customer, $w(n)$, rather than the expected average delay in queue, $d(n)$, where the waiting time of a customer is defined as the time interval from the instant the customer arrives to the instant the customer completes service and departs. There were two reasons. First, for many queueing systems we believe that the customer's delay in queue while waiting for other customers to be served is the most troublesome part of the customer's wait in the system. Moreover, if the queue represents part of a manufacturing system where the "customers" are actually parts waiting for service at a machine (the "server"), then the delay in queue represents a loss, whereas the time spent in service is "necessary." Our second reason for focusing on the delay in queue is one of statistical efficiency. The usual estimator of $w(n)$ would be

$$\hat{w}(n) = \frac{\sum_{i=1}^{n} W_i}{n} = \frac{\sum_{i=1}^{n} D_i}{n} + \frac{\sum_{i=1}^{n} S_i}{n} = \hat{d}(n) + \bar{S}(n) \qquad (1.7)$$

where $W_i = D_i + S_i$ is the waiting time in system of the ith customer and $\bar{S}(n)$ is the average of the n customers' service times. Since the service-time distribution would have to be known to perform a simulation in the first place, the expected or mean service time, $E(S)$, would also be known and an alternative estimator of $w(n)$ is

$$\tilde{w}(n) = \hat{d}(n) + E(S)$$

[Note that $\bar{S}(n)$ is an unbiased estimator of $E(S)$ in Eq. (1.7).] In almost all queueing simulations, $\tilde{w}(n)$ will be a more efficient (less variable) estimator of $w(n)$ than $\hat{w}(n)$ and is thus preferable (both estimators are unbiased). Therefore, if one wants an estimate of $w(n)$, estimate $d(n)$ and add the known expected service time, $E(S)$. In general, the moral is to replace estimators by their expected values whenever possible (see the discussion of indirect estimators in Sec. 11.5).

1.4.8 Alternative Stopping Rules

In the above queueing example, the simulation was terminated when the number of customers delayed became equal to 1000; the final value of the simulation clock was thus a random variable. However, for many real-world models, the simulation is to stop after some fixed amount of time, say 8 hours. Since the interarrival and service times for our example are continuous random variables, the probability of the simulation's terminating after exactly 480 minutes is 0 (neglecting the finite accuracy of a computer). Therefore, to stop the simulation at a specified time, we introduce a dummy "end-simulation" event (call it an event of type 3), which is scheduled to occur at time 480. When the time of occurrence of this event (being held in the third spot of the event list) is less than all other entries in the event list, the report generator is called and the simulation is terminated. The number of customers delayed is now a random variable.

These ideas can be implemented in the computer programs by making changes to the main program, the initialization routine, and the report generator, as described below. The reader need go through the changes for only one of the three languages, but should review carefully the corresponding code.

FORTRAN Program. Changes must be made in the main program, the declarations file (renamed mm1alt.dcl), INIT, and REPORT, as shown in Figs. 1.38 through 1.41. The only changes in TIMING, ARRIVE, DEPART, and UPTAVG are in the file name in the INCLUDE statements, and there are no changes at all in EXPON. In Figs. 1.38 and 1.39, note that we now have 3 events, that the desired simulation run length, TEND, is now an input parameter and a member of the COMMON block MODEL (TOTCUS has been removed), and that the statements after the "computed GO TO" statement have been changed. In the main program (as before), we call UPTAVG before entering an event routine, so that in particular the areas will be updated to the end of the simulation here when the type 3 event (end simulation) is next. The only change to INIT (other than the file name to INCLUDE) is the addition of the statement TNE(3) = TEND, which schedules the end of the simulation. The only change to REPORT in Fig. 1.41 is to write the number of customers delayed instead of the time the simulation ends, since in this case we know that the ending time will be 480 minutes but will not know how many customer delays will have been completed during that time.

Pascal Program. Changes must be made in the global (outer-shell) declarations, procedures Initialize and Report, and in the main program, as shown in Figs. 1.42 through 1.45; the rest of the program is unaffected. In Figs. 1.42 and 1.45, note that there are now 3 events, that the desired simulation run length, TimeEnd, is now an input parameter (NumDelaysRequired has been removed), and that the CASE statement in the main program has been changed. The only change to the initialization procedure in Fig. 1.43 is the addition of the statement TimeNextEvent[3] := TimeEnd, which schedules the end of the simulation. The only change to the Report procedure in Fig. 1.44 is to write the number of customers delayed instead of the time the simulation ends, since in this case we know that the ending time will be 480 minutes but will not know how many customer delays will have been completed during that time. To stop the simulation in the main program of Fig. 1.45, the original WHILE loop has been replaced by a REPEAT UNTIL loop, where the loop is repeated until the type of event just executed is 3 (end simulation), in which case the loop ends and the simulation stops. In the main program (as before), we invoke UpdateTimeAvgStats before entering an event procedure, so that in particular the areas will be updated to the end of the simulation here when the type 3 event (end simulation) is next.

C Program. Changes must be made in the external definitions, the main function, and in the initialize and report functions, as shown in Figs. 1.46 through 1.49; the rest of the program is unaltered. In Figs. 1.46 and 1.47, note that we now have 3 events, that the desired simulation run length, time_end, is now an input parameter (num_delays_required has been removed), and that the "switch" statement has been changed. To stop the simulation, the original "while" loop has been replaced by a "do while" loop in Fig. 1.47, where the loop keeps repeating itself as long as the type of event just executed is not 3

```
*       Main program for single-server queueing system, fixed run length.

*       Bring in declarations file.

        INCLUDE 'mm1alt.dcl'

*       Open input and output files.

        OPEN (5, FILE = 'mm1alt.in')
        OPEN (6, FILE = 'mm1alt.out')

*       Specify the number of event types for the timing routine.

        NEVNTS = 3

*       Set mnemonics for server's being busy and idle.

        BUSY = 1
        IDLE = 0

*       Read input parameters.

        READ (5,*) MARRVT, MSERVT, TEND

*       Write report heading and input parameters.

        WRITE (6,2010) MARRVT, MSERVT, TEND
 2010 FORMAT (' Single-server queueing system with fixed run length'//
      &           ' Mean interarrival time',F11.3,' minutes'//
      &           ' Mean service time',F16.3,' minutes'//
      &           ' Length of the simulation',F9.3,' minutes'//)

*       Initialize the simulation.

        CALL INIT

*       Determine the next event.

   10 CALL TIMING

*       Update time-average statistical accumulators.

        CALL UPTAVG

*       Call the appropriate event routine.

        GO TO (20, 30, 40), NEXT
   20     CALL ARRIVE
          GO TO 10
   30     CALL DEPART
          GO TO 10

*       Simulation is over; call report generator and end
*       simulation.

   40     CALL REPORT

        CLOSE (5)
        CLOSE (6)

        STOP
        END
```

FIGURE 1.38
FORTRAN code for the main program, queueing model with fixed run length.

```
      INTEGER QLIMIT
      PARAMETER (QLIMIT = 100)
      INTEGER BUSY,IDLE,NEVNTS,NEXT,NIQ,NUMCUS,SERVER
      REAL ANIQ,AUTIL,MARRVT,MSERVT,TARRVL(QLIMIT),TEND,TIME,TLEVNT,
     &      TNE(3),TOTDEL
      REAL EXPON
      COMMON /MODEL/ ANIQ,AUTIL,BUSY,IDLE,MARRVT,MSERVT,NEVNTS,NEXT,NIQ,
     &               NUMCUS,SERVER,TARRVL,TEND,TIME,TLEVNT,TNE,TOTDEL
```

FIGURE 1.39
FORTRAN code for the declarations file (mm1alt.dcl), queueing model with fixed run length.

(end simulation); after a type 3 event is chosen for execution, the loop ends and the simulation stops. In the main program (as before), we invoke update_time_avg_stats before entering an event function, so that in particular the areas will be updated to the end of the simulation here when the type 3 event (end simulation) is next. The only change to the initialization function in Fig. 1.48 is the addition of the statement time_next_event[3] = time_end, which schedules the end of the simulation. The only change to the report function in Fig. 1.49 is to write the number of customers delayed instead of the time the simulation ends, since in this case we know that the ending time will be 480 minutes but will not know how many customer delays will have been completed during that time.

```
      SUBROUTINE INIT
      INCLUDE 'mm1alt.dcl'

*     Initialize the simulation clock.

      TIME   = 0.0

*     Initialize the state variables.

      SERVER = IDLE
      NIQ    = 0
      TLEVNT = 0.0

*     Initialize the statistical counters.

      NUMCUS = 0
      TOTDEL = 0.0
      ANIQ   = 0.0
      AUTIL  = 0.0

*     Initialize event list. Since no customers are present, the
*     departure (service completion) event is eliminated from
*     consideration.  The end-simulation event (type 3) is scheduled for
*     time TEND.

      TNE(1) = TIME + EXPON(MARRVT)
      TNE(2) = 1.0E+30
      TNE(3) = TEND

      RETURN
      END
```

FIGURE 1.40
FORTRAN code for subroutine INIT, queueing model with fixed run length.

```
      SUBROUTINE REPORT
      INCLUDE 'mm1alt.dcl'
      REAL AVGDEL,AVGNIQ,UTIL

*     Compute and write estimates of desired measures of performance.

      AVGDEL = TOTDEL / NUMCUS
      AVGNIQ = ANIQ / TIME
      UTIL   = AUTIL / TIME
      WRITE (6,2010) AVGDEL, AVGNIQ, UTIL, NUMCUS
 2010 FORMAT (/' Average delay in queue',F11.3,' minutes'//
     &             ' Average number in queue',F10.3//
     &             ' Server utilization',F15.3//
     &             ' Number of delays completed',I7)

      RETURN
      END
```

FIGURE 1.41
FORTRAN code for subroutine REPORT, queueing model with fixed run length.

```
PROGRAM SingleServerQAlt(Input, Output);

{ Global declarations for single-server queueing system, fixed run
  length. }

CONST
   QLimit = 100;  { Limit on queue length. }
   Busy   =   1;  { Mnemonics for server's being busy }
   Idle   =   0;  { and idle. }

VAR
   NextEventType, NumCustsDelayed, NumEvents, NumInQ, ServerStatus :
      Integer;
   AreaNumInQ, AreaServerStatus, MeanInterarrival, MeanService, Time,
      TimeEnd, TimeLastEvent, TotalOfDelays : Real;
   TimeArrival   : ARRAY [1..QLimit] OF Real;
   TimeNextEvent : ARRAY [1..3]       OF Real;

   { The following declaration is for the random-number generator.
     Note that the name Zrng must not be used for any other purpose. }

   Zrng : ARRAY [1..100] OF Integer;

PROCEDURE Initialize;                  FORWARD;
PROCEDURE Timing;                      FORWARD;
PROCEDURE Arrive;                      FORWARD;
PROCEDURE Depart;                      FORWARD;
PROCEDURE Report;                      FORWARD;
PROCEDURE UpdateTimeAvgStats;          FORWARD;
FUNCTION  Expon(Mean : Real) : Real;   FORWARD;

{ The following four declarations are for the random-number generator.
  }

PROCEDURE Randdf;                                       FORWARD;
FUNCTION  Rand(Stream : Integer) : Real;                FORWARD;
PROCEDURE Randst(Zset : Integer; Stream : Integer);     FORWARD;
FUNCTION  Randgt(Stream : Integer) : Integer;           FORWARD;
```

FIGURE 1.42
Pascal code for the global declarations, queueing model with fixed run length.

```
PROCEDURE Initialize;   { Initialization procedure. }

    BEGIN { Initialize }

        { Initialize the simulation clock. }

        Time := 0.0;

        { Initialize the state variables. }

        ServerStatus   := Idle;
        NumInQ         := 0;
        TimeLastEvent := 0.0;

        { Initialize the statistical counters. }

        NumCustsDelayed  := 0;
        TotalOfDelays    := 0.0;
        AreaNumInQ       := 0.0;
        AreaServerStatus := 0.0;

        { Initialize event list.  Since no customers are present, the
          departure (service completion) event is eliminated from
          consideration.  The end-simulation event (type 3) is scheduled
          for time TimeEnd. }

        TimeNextEvent[1] := Time + Expon(MeanInterarrival);
        TimeNextEvent[2] := 1.0E+30;
        TimeNextEvent[3] := TimeEnd

    END; { Initialize }
```

FIGURE 1.43
Pascal code for procedure Initialize, queueing model with fixed run length.

```
PROCEDURE Report;   { Report generator procedure. }

    VAR
        AvgDelayInQ, AvgNumInQ, ServerUtilization : Real;

    BEGIN { Report }

        { Compute and write estimates of desired measures of performance.
          }

        AvgDelayInQ        := TotalOfDelays / NumCustsDelayed;
        AvgNumInQ          := AreaNumInQ / Time;
        ServerUtilization := AreaServerStatus / Time;
        Writeln;
        Writeln('Average delay in queue', AvgDelayInQ:11:3, ' minutes');
        Writeln;
        Writeln('Average number in queue', AvgNumInQ:10:3);
        Writeln;
        Writeln('Server utilization', ServerUtilization:15:3);
        Writeln;
        Writeln('Number of delays completed', NumCustsDelayed:7)

    END; { Report }
```

FIGURE 1.44
Pascal code for procedure Report, queueing model with fixed run length.

```
BEGIN { SingleServerQAlt main program. }

    { Initialize the random-number generator. }

    Randdf;

    { Specify the number of events for the timing procedure. }

    NumEvents := 3;

    { Read input parameters. }

    Readln(MeanInterarrival, MeanService, TimeEnd);

    { Write report heading and input parameters. }

    Writeln('Single-server queueing system with fixed run length');
    Writeln;
    Writeln('Mean interarrival time', MeanInterarrival:11:3, ' minutes');
    Writeln;
    Writeln('Mean service time', MeanService:16:3, ' minutes');
    Writeln;
    Writeln('Length of the simulation', TimeEnd:9:3, ' minutes');
    Writeln;
    Writeln;

    { Initialize the simulation. }

    Initialize;

    { Run the simulation until it terminates after an end-simulation
      event (type 3) occurs. }

    REPEAT

        { Determine the next event. }

        Timing;

        { Update time-average statistical accumulators. }

        UpdateTimeAvgStats;

        { Invoke the appropriate event procedure. }

        CASE NextEventType OF
            1 : Arrive;
            2 : Depart;
            3 : Report
        END

    { If the event just executed was the end-simulation event (type 3),
      end the simulation.  Otherwise, continue simulating. }

    UNTIL NextEventType = 3

END. { SingleServerQAlt }
```

FIGURE 1.45
Pascal code for the main program, queueing model with fixed run length.

```
/* External definitions for single-server queueing system, fixed run
   length. */

#include <stdio.h>
#include <math.h>
#include "rand.h"      /* Header file for random-number generator. */

#define Q_LIMIT 100    /* Limit on queue length. */
#define BUSY      1    /* Mnemonics for server's being busy */
#define IDLE      0    /* and idle. */

int   next_event_type, num_custs_delayed, num_events, num_in_q,
      server_status;
float area_num_in_q, area_server_status, mean_interarrival,
      mean_service, time, time_arrival[Q_LIMIT + 1], time_end,
      time_last_event, time_next_event[4], total_of_delays;
FILE  *infile, *outfile;

void  initialize(void);
void  timing(void);
void  arrive(void);
void  depart(void);
void  report(void);
void  update_time_avg_stats(void);
float expon(float mean);
```

FIGURE 1.46
C code for the external definitions, queueing model with fixed run length.

```
main()   /* Main function. */
{
    /* Open input and output files. */

    infile  = fopen("mm1alt.in",  "r");
    outfile = fopen("mm1alt.out", "w");

    /* Specify the number of events for the timing function. */

    num_events = 3;

    /* Read input parameters. */

    fscanf(infile, "%f %f %f", &mean_interarrival, &mean_service,
        &time_end);

    /* Write report heading and input parameters. */

    fprintf(outfile, "Single-server queueing system with fixed run");
    fprintf(outfile, " length\n\n");
    fprintf(outfile, "Mean interarrival time%11.3f minutes\n\n",
        mean_interarrival);
    fprintf(outfile, "Mean service time%16.3f minutes\n\n",
        mean_service);
    fprintf(outfile, "Length of the simulation%9.3f minutes\n\n",
        time_end);
```

FIGURE 1.47
C code for the main function, queueing model with fixed run length.

```
/* Initialize the simulation. */

initialize();

/* Run the simulation until it terminates after an end-simulation
   event (type 3) occurs. */

do {

    /* Determine the next event. */

    timing();

    /* Update time-average statistical accumulators. */

    update_time_avg_stats();

    /* Invoke the appropriate event function. */

    switch (next_event_type) {
        case 1:
            arrive();
            break;
        case 2:
            depart();
            break;
        case 3:
            report();
            break;
    }

/* If the event just executed was not the end-simulation event
   (type 3), continue simulating.  Otherwise, end the simulation.
   */

} while (next_event_type != 3);

fclose(infile);
fclose(outfile);

return 0;
}
```

FIGURE 1.47
(*Continued.*)

The output file (named mm1alt.out if either the FORTRAN or C program was run) is shown in Fig. 1.50. The number of customer delays completed was 475 in this run, which seems reasonable in a 480-minute run where customers are arriving at an average rate of 1 per minute. The same three measures of performance are again numerically close to each other, but are all somewhat less than their earlier values in the 1000-delay simulation. A possible reason for this is that the current run is roughly only half as long as the earlier one, and since the initial conditions for the simulation are empty and idle (an uncongested state), the model in this shorter run has less chance to become congested. Again, however, this is just a single run and is thus subject to perhaps considerable uncertainty; there is no easy way to assess the degree of uncertainty from only a single run.

```
void initialize(void)   /* Initialization function. */
{
    /* Initialize the simulation clock. */

    time = 0.0;

    /* Initialize the state variables. */

    server_status   = IDLE;
    num_in_q        = 0;
    time_last_event = 0.0;

    /* Initialize the statistical counters. */

    num_custs_delayed  = 0;
    total_of_delays    = 0.0;
    area_num_in_q      = 0.0;
    area_server_status = 0.0;

    /* Initialize event list.  Since no customers are present, the
       departure (service completion) event is eliminated from
       consideration.  The end-simulation event (type 3) is scheduled
       for time time_end. */

    time_next_event[1] = time + expon(mean_interarrival);
    time_next_event[2] = 1.0e+30;
    time_next_event[3] = time_end;
}
```

FIGURE 1.48
C code for function initialize, queueing model with fixed run length.

```
void report(void)   /* Report generator function. */
{
    /* Compute and write estimates of desired measures of performance.
       */

    fprintf(outfile, "\n\nAverage delay in queue%11.3f minutes\n\n",
            total_of_delays / num_custs_delayed);
    fprintf(outfile, "Average number in queue%10.3f\n\n",
            area_num_in_q / time);
    fprintf(outfile, "Server utilization%15.3f\n\n",
            area_server_status / time);
    fprintf(outfile, "Number of delays completed%7d",
            num_custs_delayed);
}
```

FIGURE 1.49
C code for function report, queueing model with fixed run length.

```
Single-server queueing system with fixed run length

Mean interarrival time        1.000 minutes

Mean service time             0.500 minutes

Length of the simulation    480.000 minutes


Average delay in queue        0.399 minutes

Average number in queue       0.394

Server utilization            0.464

Number of delays completed    475
```

FIGURE 1.50
Output report, queueing model with fixed run length.

If the queueing system being considered had actually been a one-operator barbershop open from 9 A.M. to 5 P.M., stopping the simulation after exactly 8 hours might leave a customer with hair partially cut. In such a case, we might want to close the door of the barbershop after 8 hours but continue to run the simulation until all customers present when the door closes (if any) have been served. The reader is asked in Prob. 1.10 to supply the program changes necessary to implement this stopping rule (see also Sec. 2.6).

1.4.9 Determining the Events and Variables

We defined an event in Sec. 1.3 as an instantaneous occurrence that may change the system state, and in the simple single-server queue of Sec. 1.4.1 it was not too hard to identify the events. However, the question sometimes arises, especially for complex systems, of how one determines the number and definition of events in general for a model. It may also be difficult to specify the state variables needed to keep the simulation running in the correct event sequence and to obtain the desired output measures. There is no completely general way to answer these questions, and different people may come up with different ways of representing a model in terms of events and variables, all of which may be correct. But there are some principles and techniques to help simplify the model's structure and to avoid logical errors.

Schruben (1983) presented an *event-graph* method, which was subsequently refined and extended by Sargent (1988) and Som and Sargent (1989). In this approach proposed events, each represented by a *node*, are connected by *directed arcs* (arrows) depicting how events may be scheduled from other events and from themselves. For example, in the queueing simulation of Sec. 1.4.3, the arrival event schedules another future occurrence of itself and (possibly) a departure event, and the departure event may schedule another future occurrence of itself; in addition, the arrival event must be

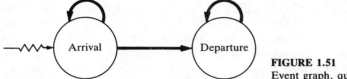

FIGURE 1.51
Event graph, queueing model.

initially scheduled in order to get the simulation going. Event graphs connect the proposed set of events (nodes) by arcs indicating the type of event scheduling that can occur. In Fig. 1.51 we show the event graph for our single-server queueing system, where the heavy smooth arrows indicate that an event at the end of the arrow *may* be scheduled from the event at the beginning of the arrow in a (possibly) *nonzero* amount of time, and the thin jagged arrow indicates that the event at its end is scheduled initially. Thus, the arrival event reschedules itself and may schedule a departure (in the case of an arrival who finds the server idle), and the departure event may reschedule itself (if a departure leaves behind someone else in queue).

For this model, it could be asked why we did not explicitly account for the act of a customer's entering service (either from the queue or upon arrival) as a separate event. This certainly happens, and it could cause the state to change (i.e., the queue length to fall by one). In fact, this could have been put in as a separate event without making the simulation incorrect, and would give rise to the event diagram in Fig. 1.52. The two thin smooth arrows each represent an event at the beginning of an arrow potentially scheduling an event at the end of the arrow without any intervening time, i.e., immediately; in this case the straight thin smooth arrow refers to a customer who arrives to an empty system and whose "enter-service" event is thus scheduled to occur immediately, and the curved thin smooth arrow represents a customer departing with a queue left behind, and so the first customer in the queue would be scheduled to enter service immediately. The number of events has now increased by one, and so we have a somewhat more complicated model. One of the uses of event graphs is to simplify a simulation's event structure by eliminating unnecessary events. There are several "rules" that allow for simplification, and one of them is that if an event node has incoming arcs that are all thin and smooth (i.e., the only way this event is scheduled is by other

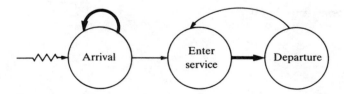

FIGURE 1.52
Event graph, queueing model with separate "enter-service" event.

events and without any intervening time), then this event can be eliminated from the model and its action built into the events that schedule it in zero time. Here, the "enter-service" event could be eliminated, and its action put partly into the arrival event (when a customer arrives to an idle server and begins service immediately) and partly into the departure event (when a customer finishes service and there is a queue from which the next customer is taken to enter service); this takes us back to the simpler event graph in Fig. 1.51. Basically, "events" that can happen only in conjunction with other events do not need to be in the model. Reducing the number of events not only simplifies model conceptualization, but may also speed its execution. Care must be taken, however, when "collapsing" events in this way to handle priorities and time ties appropriately.

Another rule has to do with initialization. The event graph is decomposed into *strongly connected* components, within each of which it is possible to "travel" from every node to every other node by following the arcs in their indicated directions. The graph in Fig. 1.51 decomposes into two strongly connected components (with a single node in each), and that in Fig. 1.52 has two strongly connected components (one of which is the arrival node by itself, and the other of which consists of the enter-service and departure nodes). The initialization rule states that in any strongly connected component of nodes that has no incoming arcs from other event nodes outside the component, there must be at least one node that is initially scheduled; if this rule were violated, it would never be possible to execute any of the events in the component. In Figs. 1.51 and 1.52, the arrival node is such a strongly connected component since it has no incoming arcs from other nodes, and so it must be initialized. Figure 1.53 shows the event graph for the queueing model of Sec. 1.4.8 with the fixed run length, for which we introduced the dummy "end simulation" event. Note that this event is itself a strongly connected component without any arcs coming in, and so it must be initialized, i.e., the end of the simulation is scheduled as part of the initialization. Failure to do so would result in erroneous termination of the simulation.

We have presented only a partial and simplified account of the event-graph technique along the lines presented by Pegden (1989, pp. 152–157).

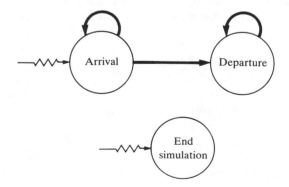

FIGURE 1.53
Event graph, queueing model with fixed run length.

There are several other features, including event-canceling relations, ways to combine similar events into one, refining the event-scheduling arcs to include conditional scheduling, and incorporating the state variables needed; see the original paper by Schruben (1983). Sargent (1988) and Som and Sargent (1989) extend and refine the technique, giving comprehensive illustrations involving a flexible manufacturing system and computer network models.

In modeling a system, the event-graph technique can be used to simplify the structure and to detect certain kinds of errors, and is especially useful in complex models involving a large number of interrelated events. Other considerations should also be kept in mind, such as continually asking why a particular state variable is needed; see Prob. 1.4.

1.5 SIMULATION OF AN INVENTORY SYSTEM

We shall now see how simulation can be used to compare alternative ordering policies for an inventory system. Many of the elements of our model are representative of those found in actual inventory systems.

1.5.1 Problem Statement

A company that sells a single product would like to decide how many items it should have in inventory for each of the next n months. The times between demands are IID exponential random variables with a mean of 0.1 month. The sizes of the demands, D, are IID random variables (independent of when the demands occur), with

$$D = \begin{cases} 1 & \text{w.p. } \frac{1}{6} \\ 2 & \text{w.p. } \frac{1}{3} \\ 3 & \text{w.p. } \frac{1}{3} \\ 4 & \text{w.p. } \frac{1}{6} \end{cases}$$

where w.p. is read "with probability."

At the beginning of each month, the company reviews the inventory level and decides how many items to order from its supplier. If the company orders Z items, it incurs a cost of $K + iZ$, where $K = \$32$ is the *setup cost* and $i = \$3$ is the *incremental cost* per item ordered. (If $Z = 0$, no cost is incurred.) When an order is placed, the time required for it to arrive (called the *delivery lag* or *lead time*) is a random variable that is distributed uniformly between 0.5 and 1 month.

The company uses a stationary (s, S) policy to decide how much to order, i.e.,

$$Z = \begin{cases} S - I & \text{if } I < s \\ 0 & \text{if } I \geq s \end{cases}$$

where I is the inventory level at the beginning of the month.

When a demand occurs, it is satisfied immediately if the inventory level is at least as large as the demand. If the demand exceeds the inventory level, the excess of demand over supply is backlogged and satisfied by future deliveries. (In this case, the new inventory level is equal to the old inventory level minus the demand size, resulting in a negative inventory level.) When an order arrives, it is first used to eliminate as much of the backlog (if any) as possible; the remainder of the order (if any) is added to the inventory.

So far we have discussed only one type of cost incurred by the inventory system, the ordering cost. However, most real inventory systems also have two additional types of costs, *holding* and *shortage* costs, which we discuss after introducing some additional notation. Let $I(t)$ be the inventory level at time t [note that $I(t)$ could be positive, negative, or zero], let $I^+(t) = \max\{I(t), 0\}$ be the number of items physically on hand in the inventory at time t [note that $I^+(t) \geq 0$], and let $I^-(t) = \max\{-I(t), 0\}$ be the backlog at time t [$I^-(t) \geq 0$ as well]. A possible realization of $I(t)$, $I^+(t)$, and $I^-(t)$ is shown in Fig. 1.54. The time points at which $I(t)$ decreases are the ones at which demands occur.

For our model, we shall assume that the company incurs a holding cost of $h = \$1$ per item per month held in (positive) inventory. The holding cost includes such costs as warehouse rental, insurance, taxes, and maintenance, as well as the opportunity cost of having capital tied up in inventory rather than invested elsewhere. We have ignored in our formulation the fact that some holding costs are still incurred when $I^+(t) = 0$. However, since our goal is to *compare* ordering policies, ignoring this factor, which after all is independent of the policy used, will not affect our assessment of which policy is best. Now, since $I^+(t)$ is the number of items held in inventory at time t, the time-average (per month) number of items held in inventory for the n-month period is

$$\bar{I}^+ = \frac{\int_0^n I^+(t)\, dt}{n}$$

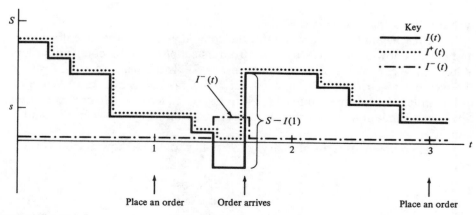

FIGURE 1.54
A realization of $I(t)$, $I^+(t)$, and $I^-(t)$ over time.

which is akin to the definition of the time-average number of customers in queue given in Sec. 1.4.1. Thus, the average holding cost per month is $h\bar{I}^+$.

Similarly, suppose that the company incurs a backlog cost of $\pi = \$5$ per item per month in backlog; this accounts for the cost of extra record keeping when a backlog exists, as well as loss of customers' goodwill. The time-average number of items in backlog is

$$\bar{I}^- = \frac{\int_0^n I^-(t)\, dt}{n}$$

so the average backlog cost per month in $\pi\bar{I}^-$.

Assume that the initial inventory level is $I(0) = 60$ and that no order is outstanding. We simulate the inventory system for $n = 120$ months and use the average total cost per month (which is the sum of the average ordering cost per month, the average holding cost per month, and the average shortage cost per month) to compare the following nine inventory policies:

s	20	20	20	20	40	40	40	60	60
S	40	60	80	100	60	80	100	80	100

We do not address here the issue of how these particular policies were chosen for consideration; statistical techniques for making such a determination are discussed in Chap. 12.

It should be noted that the state variables for a simulation model of this inventory system are the inventory level $I(t)$, the amount of an outstanding order from the company to the supplier, and the time of the last event [which is needed to compute the areas under the $I^+(t)$ and $I^-(t)$ functions].

1.5.2 Program Organization and Logic

Our model of the inventory system uses the following types of events:

Event description	Event type
Arrival of an order to the company from the supplier	1
Demand for the product from a customer	2
End of the simulation after n months	3
Inventory evaluation (and possible ordering) at the beginning of a month	4

We have chosen to make the end of the simulation event type 3 rather than type 4, since at time 120 both "end-simulation" and "inventory-evaluation" events will eventually be scheduled and we would like to execute the former event first at this time. (Since the simulation is over at time 120, there is no sense in evaluating the inventory and possibly ordering, incurring an ordering cost for an order that will never arrive.) The execution of event type 3 before event type 4 is guaranteed because the timing routines (in all three languages) give preference to the lowest-numbered event if two or more events are scheduled to occur at the same time. In general, a simulation model should be designed to process events in an appropriate order when time ties occur. An event graph (see Sec. 1.4.9) appears in Fig. 1.55.

There are three types of random variates needed to simulate this system. The interdemand times are distributed exponentially, so the same algorithm (and code) as developed in Sec. 1.4 can be used here. The demand-size random variate D must be discrete, as described above, and can be generated as follows. First divide the unit interval into the contiguous subintervals $C_1 = [0, \frac{1}{6})$, $C_2 = [\frac{1}{6}, \frac{1}{2})$, $C_3 = [\frac{1}{2}, \frac{5}{6})$, and $C_4 = [\frac{5}{6}, 1]$, and obtain a U(0, 1) random variate U from the random-number generator. If U falls in C_1, return $D = 1$; if U falls in C_2, return $D = 2$; and so on. Since the width of C_1 is $\frac{1}{6} - 0 = \frac{1}{6}$, and since U is uniformly distributed over $[0, 1]$, the probability that U falls in C_1 (and thus that we return $D = 1$) is $\frac{1}{6}$; this agrees with the desired probability that $D = 1$. Similarly, we return $D = 2$ if U falls in C_2, having probability equal to the width of C_2, $\frac{1}{2} - \frac{1}{6} = \frac{1}{3}$, as desired, and so on for the other intervals. The subprograms to generate the demand sizes all use this principle, and take as input the cutoff points defining the above subintervals, which are the *cumulative* probabilities of the distribution of D.

The delivery lags are uniformly distributed, but not over the unit interval $[0, 1]$. In general, we can generate a random variate distributed uniformly over any interval $[a, b]$ by generating a U(0, 1) random number U, and then returning $a + U(b - a)$. That this method is correct seems intuitively clear, but will be formally justified in Sec. 8.3.1.

Of the four events, only three actually involve state changes (the end-simulation event being the exception). Since their logic is language-independent, we will describe it here.

The order-arrival event is flowcharted in Fig. 1.56, and must make the changes necessary when an order (which was previously placed) arrives from the supplier. The inventory level is increased by the amount of the order, and

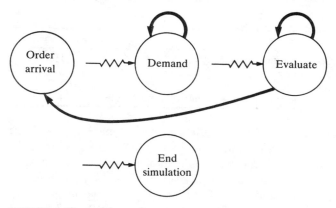

FIGURE 1.55
Event graph, inventory model.

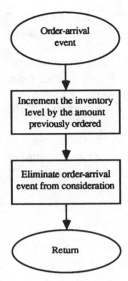

FIGURE 1.56
Flowchart for order-arrival routine, inventory model.

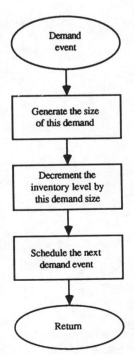

FIGURE 1.57
Flowchart for demand routine, inventory model.

the order-arrival event must be eliminated from consideration. (See Prob. 1.12 for consideration of the issue of whether there could be more than one order outstanding at a time for this model with these parameters.)

A flowchart for the demand event is given in Fig. 1.57, and processes the changes necessary to represent a demand's occurrence. First, the demand size is generated, and the inventory is decremented by this amount. Finally, the time of the next demand is scheduled into the event list. Note that this is the place where the inventory level might become negative.

The inventory-evaluation event, which takes place at the beginning of each month, is flowcharted in Fig. 1.58. If the inventory level $I(t)$ at the time of the evaluation is at least s, then no order is placed, and nothing is done except

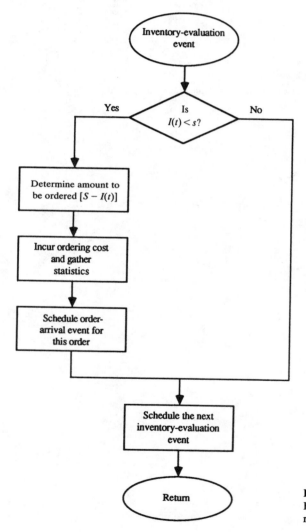

FIGURE 1.58
Flowchart for inventory-evaluation routine, inventory model.

to schedule the next evaluation into the event list. On the other hand, if $I(t) < s$, we want to place an order for $S - I(t)$ items. This is done by storing the amount of the order $[S - I(t)]$ until the order arrives, and scheduling its arrival time. In this case as well, we want to schedule the next inventory-evaluation event.

As in the single-server queueing model, it is convenient to write a separate nonevent routine to update the continuous-time statistical accumulators. For this model, however, doing so is slightly more complicated, so a flowchart for this activity appears in Fig. 1.59. The principal issue is whether we need to update the area under $I^-(t)$ or $I^+(t)$ (or neither). If the inventory level since the last event has been negative, then we have been in backlog, so the area under $I^-(t)$ only should be updated. On the other hand, if the inventory level has been positive, we need only update the area under $I^+(t)$. If the inventory level has been zero (a possibility), then neither update is needed. The code in each language for this routine also brings the variable for the time of the last event up to the present time. This routine will be invoked from the main program just after returning from the timing routine, regardless of the event type or whether the inventory level is actually changing at this point. This provides a simple (if not the most computationally efficient) way of updating integrals for continuous-time statistics.

Sections 1.5.3, 1.5.4, and 1.5.5, respectively, contain programs to simu-

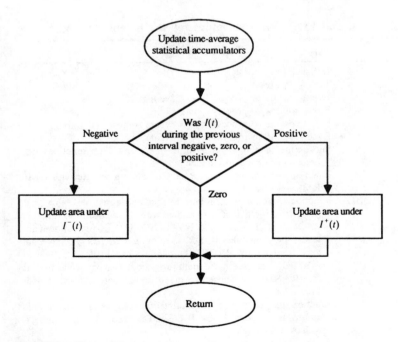

FIGURE 1.59
Flowchart for routine to update the continuous-time statistical accumulators, inventory model.

late this model in FORTRAN, Pascal, and C. As in the single-server queueing model, only one of these sections should be read, according to language preference. Neither the timing nor exponential-variate-generation subprograms will be shown, as they are the same as for the single-server queueing model in Sec. 1.4 (except for the FORTRAN version of TIMING, where the declarations file "mm1.dcl" must be changed to "inv.dcl" in the INCLUDE statement). The reader should also note the considerable similarity between the main programs of the queueing and inventory models in a given language.

1.5.3 FORTRAN Program

In addition to a main program, the model uses the subprograms and FORTRAN variables in Table 1.2.

The code for the main program is given in Fig. 1.60. After bringing in the declarations file (shown in Fig. 1.61) and declaring the local variables I and NPOLCY to be INTEGER, the input and output files are opened, and the number of events, NEVNTS, is set to 4. The input parameters (except s and S) are then read in and written out, and a report heading is produced; for each (s, S) pair the simulation will then produce in subroutine REPORT a single line of output corresponding to this heading. Then a DO loop (with foot at label 60) is begun, each iteration of which performs an entire simulation for a

TABLE 1.2
Subroutines, functions, and FORTRAN variables for the inventory model

Subprogram	Purpose
INIT	Initialization routine
TIMING	Timing routine
ORDARV	Event routine to process type 1 events
DEMAND	Event routine to process type 2 events
REPORT	Event routine to process type 3 events (report generator)
EVALU8	Event routine to process type 4 events
UPTAVG	Subroutine to update areas under $I^+(t)$ and $I^-(t)$ functions just before each event occurrence
EXPON(RMEAN)	Function to generate an exponential random variate with mean RMEAN
IRANDI(NVALUE,PROBD)	Function to generate a random integer between 1 and NVALUE (a positive integer) in accordance with the distribution function PROBD(I) $(I = 1, 2, \ldots ,$ NVALUE). If X is the random integer, the probability that X takes on a value *less than or equal to* I is given by PROBD(I). The values of NVALUE and PROBD(I) are set in the main program. (This particular format for IRANDI was chosen to make its use here consistent with Chap. 2.)
UNIFRM(A,B)	Function to generate a continuous random variate distributed uniformly between A and B (A and B are both real numbers, with $A < B$)
RAND(1)	Function to generate a uniform random variate between 0 and 1 (shown in Fig. 7.5)

TABLE 1.2
(*Continued*)

Variable	Definition
Input parameters:	
BIGS	S, second number in the specification of (s, S) inventory policy
H	h, value of unit holding cost (=1 here)
INCRMC	i, incremental cost per item ordered (=3)
INITIL	Initial inventory level (=60)
MAXLAG	Maximum delivery lag (=1.0)
MDEMDT	Mean interdemand time (=0.1)
MINLAG	Minimum delivery lag (=0.5)
NMNTHS	Length of the simulation in months (=120)
NPOLCY	Number of inventory policies being considered (=9)
NVALUE	Maximum possible demand size (=4)
PI	π, value of unit backlog cost (=5)
PROBD(I)	Probability that a demand is $\leq I$
SETUPC	K, setup cost of placing an order (=32)
SMALLS	s, first number in specification of (s, S) inventory policy
Modeling variables:	
AMINUS	Area under the $I^-(t)$ function so far
AMOUNT	Amount, Z, ordered by company from supplier
APLUS	Area under the $I^+(t)$ function so far
DSIZE	A particular demand size
INVLEV	$I(t)$, the inventory level
NEVNTS	Number of event types for model (i.e., 4)
NEXT	Event type (1, 2, 3, or 4) of the next event to occur
TIME	Simulation clock
TLEVNT	Time of the last (most recent) event
TNE(I)	Time of the next event of type I (I = 1, 2, 3, 4)
TORDC	Total ordering cost
TSLE	Time since last event
Output variables:	
ACOST	Average total cost per month
AHLDC	Average holding cost per month
AORDC	Average ordering cost per month
ASHRC	Average shortage cost per month

given (s, S) pair; the first thing done in the loop is to read the next (s, S) pair. The model is initialized by a call to INIT, and TIMING is used to determine the next event type, NEXT, and to update the simulation clock, TIME. After returning from TIMING with the next event type, a call is made to UPTAVG to update the continuous-time statistics before executing the event routine itself. A computed GO TO is then used as before to transfer control to the appropriate event routine; if the event is not the end-simulation event, control is passed back to statement 10 (the call to TIMING) and the simulation continues. If the simulation is over (NEXT = 3), REPORT is called and the simulation is ended for the current (s, S) pair.

Subroutine INIT is listed in Fig. 1.62. Observe that the first inventory evaluation is scheduled at TIME = 0 since, in general, the initial inventory

```
*       Main program for inventory system.

*       Bring in declarations file and declare local variables.

        INCLUDE 'inv.dcl'
        INTEGER I,NPOLCY

*       Open input and output files.

        OPEN (5, FILE = 'inv.in')
        OPEN (6, FILE = 'inv.out')

*       Specify the number of event types for the timing routine.

        NEVNTS = 4

*       Read input parameters.

        READ (5,*) INITIL, NMNTHS, NPOLCY, NVALUE, MDEMDT, SETUPC, INCRMC,
     &             H, PI, MINLAG, MAXLAG
        READ (5,*) (PROBD(I), I = 1, NVALUE)

*       Write report heading and input parameters.

        WRITE (6,2010) INITIL, NVALUE, (PROBD(I), I = 1, NVALUE)
 2010 FORMAT (' Single-product inventory system'//
     &          ' Initial inventory level',I24,' items'//
     &          ' Number of demand sizes',I25//
     &          ' Distribution function of demand sizes',2X,8F8.3)
        WRITE (6,2020) MDEMDT, MINLAG, MAXLAG, NMNTHS, SETUPC, INCRMC, H,
     &             PI, NPOLCY
 2020 FORMAT (/' Mean interdemand time',F26.2,' months'//
     &           ' Delivery lag range',F29.2,' to',F10.2,' months'//
     &           ' Length of the simulation',I23,' months'//
     &           ' K =',F6.1,'    i =',F6.1,'    h =',F6.1,'    pi =',F6.1//
     &           ' Number of policies',I29//
     &           10X,4(8X,'Average')/
     &           '    Policy         total cost    ordering cost',
     &           '    holding cost    shortage cost')

*       Run the simulation varying the inventory policy.

        DO 60 I = 1, NPOLCY

*           Read the inventory policy, and initialize the simulation.

            READ (5,*) SMALLS, BIGS
            CALL INIT

*           Determine the next event.

   10       CALL TIMING

*           Update time-average statistical accumulators.

            CALL UPTAVG

*           Call the appropriate event routine.

            GO TO (20, 30, 50, 40), NEXT
   20           CALL ORDARV
                GO TO 10
   30           CALL DEMAND
                GO TO 10
   40           CALL EVALU8
                GO TO 10
   50           CALL REPORT

   60   CONTINUE

        CLOSE (5)
        CLOSE (6)

        STOP
        END
```

FIGURE 1.60
FORTRAN code for the main program, inventory model.

```
      INTEGER AMOUNT,BIGS,INITIL,INVLEV,NEVNTS,NEXT,NMNTHS,NVALUE,
     &        SMALLS
      REAL AMINUS,APLUS,H,INCRMC,MAXLAG,MDEMDT,MINLAG,PI,PROBD(25),
     &        SETUPC,TIME,TLEVNT,TNE(4),TORDC
      INTEGER IRANDI
      REAL EXPON,UNIFRM
      COMMON /MODEL/ AMINUS,AMOUNT,APLUS,BIGS,H,INCRMC,INITIL,INVLEV,
     &               MAXLAG,MDEMDT,MINLAG,NEVNTS,NEXT,NMNTHS,NVALUE,PI,
     &               PROBD,SETUPC,SMALLS,TIME,TLEVNT,TNE,TORDC
```

FIGURE 1.61
FORTRAN code for the declarations file (inv.dcl), inventory model.

```
      SUBROUTINE INIT
      INCLUDE 'inv.dcl'

*     Initialize the simulation clock.

      TIME   = 0.0

*     Initialize the state variables.

      INVLEV = INITIL
      TLEVNT = 0.0

*     Initialize the statistical counters.

      TORDC  = 0.0
      APLUS  = 0.0
      AMINUS = 0.0

*     Initialize the event list. Since no order is outstanding, the
*     order-arrival event is eliminated from consideration.

      TNE(1) = 1.0E+30
      TNE(2) = TIME + EXPON(MDEMDT)
      TNE(3) = NMNTHS
      TNE(4) = 0.0

      RETURN
      END
```

FIGURE 1.62
FORTRAN code for subroutine INIT, inventory model.

```
      SUBROUTINE ORDARV
      INCLUDE 'inv.dcl'

*     Increment the inventory level by the amount ordered.

      INVLEV = INVLEV + AMOUNT

*     Since no order is now outstanding, eliminate the order-arrival
*     event from consideration.

      TNE(1) = 1.0E+30

      RETURN
      END
```

FIGURE 1.63
FORTRAN code for subroutine ORDARV, inventory model.

```
      SUBROUTINE DEMAND
      INCLUDE 'inv.dcl'
      INTEGER DSIZE

*     Generate the demand size.

      DSIZE  = IRANDI(NVALUE,PROBD)

*     Decrement the inventory level by the demand size.

      INVLEV = INVLEV - DSIZE

*     Schedule the time of the next demand.

      TNE(2) = TIME + EXPON(MDEMDT)

      RETURN
      END
```

FIGURE 1.64
FORTRAN code for subroutine DEMAND, inventory model.

level could be less than *s*. Note also that event type 1 (order arrival) is eliminated from consideration, since our modeling assumption was that there are no outstanding orders initially.

The event routines ORDARV, DEMAND, and EVALU8 are shown in Figs. 1.63 through 1.65, and correspond to the general discussion given in Sec. 1.5.2, and to the flowcharts in Figs. 1.56 through 1.58. Note that in DEMAND, the demand-size variate is generated from the function IRANDI. Also, in EVALU8, note that the variable TORDC is increased by the ordering cost for any order that might be placed here.

```
      SUBROUTINE EVALU8
      INCLUDE 'inv.dcl'

*     Check whether the inventory level is less than SMALLS.

      IF (INVLEV .LT. SMALLS) THEN

*         The inventory level is less than SMALLS, so place an order for
*         the appropriate amount.

          AMOUNT = BIGS - INVLEV
          TORDC  = TORDC + SETUPC + INCRMC * AMOUNT

*         Schedule the arrival of the order.

          TNE(1) = TIME + UNIFRM(MINLAG,MAXLAG)

      END IF

*     Regardless of the place-order decision, schedule the next
*     inventory evaluation.

      TNE(4) = TIME + 1.0

      RETURN
      END
```

FIGURE 1.65
FORTRAN code for subroutine EVALU8, inventory model.

```
        SUBROUTINE REPORT
        INCLUDE 'inv.dcl'
        REAL ACOST,AHLDC,AORDC,ASHRC

*       Compute and write estimates of desired measures of performance.

        AORDC = TORDC / NMNTHS
        AHLDC = H  * APLUS / NMNTHS
        ASHRC = PI * AMINUS / NMNTHS
        ACOST = AORDC + AHLDC + ASHRC
        WRITE (6,2010) SMALLS, BIGS, ACOST, AORDC, AHLDC, ASHRC
   2010 FORMAT (/' (',I3,',',I3,')',4F15.2)

        RETURN
        END
```

FIGURE 1.66
FORTRAN code for subroutine REPORT, inventory model.

The report generator is listed in Fig. 1.66, and computes the three components of the total cost separately, adding them together to get the average total cost per month, ACOST. The current values of s and S are written out for identification purposes, along with the average total cost and its three components (ordering, holding, and shortage costs).

Subroutine UPTAVG, which was discussed in general in Sec. 1.5.2 and flowcharted in Fig. 1.59, is shown in Fig. 1.67. Implementation is facilitated in FORTRAN by the use of an *arithmetic if* statement (a fairly old and seldom-used feature), which ends with three statement labels (10, 20, and 30 in this case) to which control is transferred if the argument (simply INVLEV here) is negative, zero, or positive, in that order. As in the single-server queueing model of Sec. 1.4, it might be necessary to make both the TIME and TLEVNT

```
        SUBROUTINE UPTAVG
        INCLUDE 'inv.dcl'
        REAL TSLE

*       Compute time since last event, and update last-event-time marker.

        TSLE   = TIME - TLEVNT
        TLEVNT = TIME


*       Determine the status of the inventory level during the previous
*       interval.  If the inventory level during the previous interval was
*       negative, update AMINUS.  If it was zero, no update is needed.  If
*       it was positive, update APLUS.

        IF (INVLEV) 10, 20, 30
    10      AMINUS = AMINUS - INVLEV * TSLE
    20      RETURN
    30      APLUS  = APLUS + INVLEV * TSLE

        RETURN
        END
```

FIGURE 1.67
FORTRAN code for subroutine UPTAVG, inventory model.

```
      INTEGER FUNCTION IRANDI(NVALUE,PROBD)
      INTEGER I,NVALUE
      REAL PROBD(1),U
      REAL RAND

*     Generate a U(0,1) random variate.

      U = RAND(1)

*     Return a random integer between 1 and NVALUE in accordance with
*     the (cumulative) distribution function PROBD.

      DO 10 I = 1, NVALUE - 1
         IF (U .LT. PROBD(I)) THEN
            IRANDI = I
            RETURN
         END IF
   10 CONTINUE
      IRANDI = NVALUE

      RETURN
      END
```

FIGURE 1.68
FORTRAN code for function IRANDI.

variables DOUBLE PRECISION to avoid severe roundoff error in their subtraction at the top of the routine if the simulation is to be run for a long period of simulated time.

The code for function IRANDI is given in Fig. 1.68, and is general in that it will generate an integer between 1 and NVALUE according to distribution function PROBD(I), provided that NVALUE and PROBD(I) ($I = 1, 2, \ldots$, NVALUE) are specified. [In our case, NVALUE = 4 and PROBD(1) = $\frac{1}{6}$, PROBD(2) = $\frac{1}{2}$, PROBD(3) = $\frac{5}{6}$, and PROBD(4) = 1, all specified to three-decimal accuracy on input.] The logic agrees with the discussion in Sec. 1.5.2; note that the input array PROBD must contain the *cumulative* distribution function rather than the probabilities that the variate takes on its possible values.

The function UNIFRM is given in Fig. 1.69, and is as described in Sec. 1.5.2.

```
      REAL FUNCTION UNIFRM(A,B)
      REAL A,B,U
      REAL RAND

*     Generate a U(0,1) random variate.

      U = RAND(1)

*     Return a U(A,B) random variate.

      UNIFRM = A + U * (B - A)

      RETURN
      END
```

FIGURE 1.69
FORTRAN code for function UNIFRM.

1.5.4 Pascal Program

The global declarations are shown in Fig. 1.70. The array ProbDistribDemand will be used to hold the cumulative probabilities for the demand sizes, and is passed into the random-integer-generation function RandomInteger. As for the queueing model, we must define the array Zrng and the four functions and procedures at the bottom of Fig. 1.70 for the random-number generator of Fig. 7.6.

Procedure Initialize appears in Fig. 1.71. Observe that the first inventory evaluation is scheduled at Time = 0 since, in general, the initial inventory level could be less than s. Note also that event type 1 (order arrival) is eliminated from consideration, since our modeling assumption was that there are no outstanding orders initially.

The event routines OrderArrival, Demand, and Evaluate are shown in Figs. 1.72 through 1.74, and correspond to the general discussion given in Sec.

```pascal
PROGRAM Inventory(Input, Output);

{ Global declarations for inventory system. }

TYPE
    DistribArray = ARRAY [1..25] OF Real;

VAR
    Amount, Bigs, DemandIndex, InitialInvLevel, InvLevel, NextEventType,
        NumEvents, NumMonths, NumPolicies, NumValuesDemand, Policy, Smalls
        : Integer;
    AreaHolding, AreaShortage, HoldingCost, IncrementalCost, Maxlag,
        MeanInterdemand, Minlag, SetupCost, ShortageCost, Time,
        TimeLastEvent, TotalOrderingCost : Real;
    ProbDistribDemand : DistribArray;
    TimeNextEvent      : ARRAY [1..4]  OF Real;

    { The following declaration is for the random-number generator.
      Note that the name Zrng must not be used for any other purpose. }

    Zrng : ARRAY [1..100] OF Integer;

PROCEDURE  Initialize;                                        FORWARD;
PROCEDURE  Timing;                                           FORWARD;
PROCEDURE  OrderArrival;                                     FORWARD;
PROCEDURE  Demand;                                           FORWARD;
PROCEDURE  Evaluate;                                         FORWARD;
PROCEDURE  Report;                                           FORWARD;
PROCEDURE  UpdateTimeAvgStats;                               FORWARD;
FUNCTION   Expon(Mean : Real) : Real;                        FORWARD;
FUNCTION   RandomInteger
               (ProbDistrib : DistribArray) : Integer;       FORWARD;
FUNCTION   Uniform(A, B : Real) : Real;                      FORWARD;

{ The following four declarations are for the random-number generator.
  }

PROCEDURE  Randdf;                                            FORWARD;
FUNCTION   Rand(Stream : Integer) : Real;                    FORWARD;
PROCEDURE  Randst(Zset : Integer; Stream : Integer);         FORWARD;
FUNCTION   Randgt(Stream : Integer) : Integer;               FORWARD;
```

FIGURE 1.70
Pascal code for the global declarations, inventory model.

```
PROCEDURE Initialize;   { Initialization procedure. }

   BEGIN { Initialize }

       { Initialize the simulation clock. }

       Time := 0.0;

       { Initialize the state variables. }

       InvLevel      := InitialInvLevel;
       TimeLastEvent := 0.0;

       { Initialize the statistical counters. }

       TotalOrderingCost := 0.0;
       AreaHolding       := 0.0;
       AreaShortage      := 0.0;

       { Initialize the event list.  Since no order is outstanding, the
         order-arrival event is eliminated from consideration. }

       TimeNextEvent[1] := 1.0E+30;
       TimeNextEvent[2] := Time + Expon(MeanInterdemand);
       TimeNextEvent[3] := NumMonths;
       TimeNextEvent[4] := 0.0

   END; { Initialize }
```

FIGURE 1.71
Pascal code for procedure Initialize, inventory model.

1.5.2, and to the flowcharts in Figs. 1.56 through 1.58. In Evaluate, note that the variable TotalOrderingCost is increased by the ordering cost for any order that might be placed here.

The report generator is listed in Fig. 1.75, and computes the three components of the total cost separately, adding them together to get the average total cost per month, AvgTotCost. The current values of s and S are written out for identification purposes, along with the average total cost and its three components (ordering, holding, and shortage costs).

```
PROCEDURE OrderArrival;   { Order arrival event procedure. }

   BEGIN { OrderArrival }

       { Increment the inventory level by the amount ordered. }

       InvLevel := InvLevel + Amount;

       { Since no order is now outstanding, eliminate the order-arrival
         event from consideration. }

       TimeNextEvent[1] := 1.0E+30

   END; { OrderArrival }
```

FIGURE 1.72
Pascal code for procedure OrderArrival, inventory model.

```
PROCEDURE Demand;   { Demand event procedure. }

   VAR
      SizeDemand : Integer;

   BEGIN { Demand }

      { Generate the demand size. }

      SizeDemand := RandomInteger(ProbDistribDemand);

      { Decrement the inventory level by the demand size. }

      InvLevel := InvLevel - SizeDemand;

      { Schedule the time of the next demand. }

      TimeNextEvent[2] := Time + Expon(MeanInterdemand)

   END; { Demand }
```

FIGURE 1.73
Pascal code for procedure Demand, inventory model.

```
PROCEDURE Evaluate;   { Inventory-evaluation event procedure. }

   BEGIN { Evaluate }

      { Check whether the inventory level is less than Smalls. }

      IF InvLevel < Smalls THEN BEGIN

         { The inventory level is less than Smalls, so place an order
           for the appropriate amount. }

         Amount            := Bigs - InvLevel;
         TotalOrderingCost := TotalOrderingCost + SetupCost +
                              IncrementalCost * Amount;

         { Schedule the arrival of the order. }

         TimeNextEvent[1] := Time + Uniform(Minlag, Maxlag)

      END;

      { Regardless of the place-order decision, schedule the next
        inventory evaluation. }

      TimeNextEvent[4] := Time + 1.0

   END; { Evaluate }
```

FIGURE 1.74
Pascal code for procedure Evaluate, inventory model.

```
PROCEDURE Report;   { Report generator procedure. }

   VAR
      AvgHoldingCost, AvgOrderingCost, AvgShortageCost, AvgTotCost :
         Real;

   BEGIN { Report }

      { Compute and write estimates of desired measures of performance.
        }

      AvgOrderingCost  := TotalOrderingCost / NumMonths;
      AvgHoldingCost   := HoldingCost * AreaHolding / NumMonths;
      AvgShortageCost  := ShortageCost * AreaShortage / NumMonths;
      AvgTotCost       := AvgOrderingCost + AvgHoldingCost +
                          AvgShortageCost;
      Writeln;
      Writeln('(', Smalls:3, ',', Bigs:3, ')', AvgTotCost:15:2,
              AvgOrderingCost:15:2, AvgHoldingCost:15:2,
              AvgShortageCost:15:2)

   END; { Report }
```

FIGURE 1.75
Pascal code for procedure Report, inventory model.

Procedure UpdateTimeAvgStats, which was discussed in general in Sec. 1.5.2 and flowcharted in Fig. 1.59, is shown in Fig. 1.76. Note that if the inventory level InvLevel is zero, neither the IF nor the ELSE IF condition is satisfied, resulting in no update at all, as desired. As in the single-server queueing model of Sec. 1.4, it might be necessary to make both the Time and TimeLastEvent variables double precision (if available) to avoid severe round-

```
PROCEDURE UpdateTimeAvgStats;   { Update area accumulators for
                                  time-average statistics. }
   VAR
      TimeSinceLastEvent : Real;

   BEGIN { UpdateTimeAvgStats }

      { Compute time since last event, and update last-event-time
        marker. }

      TimeSinceLastEvent := Time - TimeLastEvent;
      TimeLastEvent      := Time;

      { Determine the status of the inventory level during the previous
        interval. If the inventory level during the previous interval
        was negative, update AreaShortage. If it was positive, update
        AreaHolding. If it was zero, no update is needed. }

      IF InvLevel < 0 THEN
         AreaShortage := AreaShortage - InvLevel * TimeSinceLastEvent
      ELSE IF InvLevel > 0 THEN
         AreaHolding  := AreaHolding + InvLevel * TimeSinceLastEvent

   END; { UpdateTimeAvgStats }
```

FIGURE 1.76
Pascal code for procedure UpdateTimeAvgStats, inventory model.

```
FUNCTION RandomInteger;    { Random integer generation function. }
                          { Pass in Real array ProbDistrib giving
                            cumulative probability distribution
                            function, as declared in FORWARD
                            declarations earlier. }
   VAR
      I : Integer;
      U : Real;

   BEGIN { RandomInteger }

      { Generate a U(0,1) random variate. }

      U := Rand(1);

      { Return a random integer in accordance with the (cumulative)
        distribution function ProbDistrib. }

      I := 0;
      REPEAT
         I := I + 1
      UNTIL U < ProbDistrib[I];

      RandomInteger := I

   END; { RandomInteger }
```

FIGURE 1.77
Pascal code for function RandomInteger.

off error in their subtraction at the top of the routine if the simulation is to be run for a long period of simulated time.

The code for function RandomInteger is given in Fig. 1.77, and is general in that it will generate an integer according to distribution function ProbDistrib[I], provided that the values of ProbDistrib[I] are specified. (In our case, ProbDistrib[1] $= \frac{1}{6}$, ProbDistrib[2] $= \frac{1}{2}$, ProbDistrib[3] $= \frac{5}{6}$, and ProbDistrib[4] $= 1$, all specified to three-decimal accuracy on input.) The logic agrees with the discussion in Sec. 1.5.2; note that the input array ProbDistrib

```
FUNCTION Uniform;    { Uniform variate generation function. }
                     { Pass in Real parameters A and B giving left and
                       right endpoints, as declared in FORWARD
                       declarations earlier. }
   VAR
      U : Real;

   BEGIN { Uniform }

      { Generate a U(0,1) random variate. }

      U := Rand(1);

      { Return a U(A,B) random variate. }

      Uniform := A + U * (B - A)

   END; { Uniform }
```

FIGURE 1.78
Pascal code for function Uniform.

must contain the *cumulative* distribution function rather than the probabilities that the variate takes on its possible values.

The function Uniform is given in Fig. 1.78, and is as described in Sec. 1.5.2.

The code for the main program is given in Fig. 1.79. After initializing the random-number generator by invoking Randdf, the number of events is set to 4. The input parameters (except s and S) are then read in and written out, and a report heading is produced; for each (s, S) pair the simulation will then

```
BEGIN   { Inventory main program. }

  { Initialize the random-number generator. }

  Randdf;

  { Specify the number of events for the timing procedure. }

  NumEvents := 4;

  { Read input parameters. }

  Readln(InitialInvLevel, NumMonths, NumPolicies, NumValuesDemand);
  Readln(MeanInterdemand, SetupCost, IncrementalCost, HoldingCost,
         ShortageCost, Minlag, Maxlag);
  FOR DemandIndex := 1 TO NumValuesDemand DO
     Read(ProbDistribDemand[DemandIndex]);
  Readln;

  { Write report heading and input parameters. }

  Writeln('Single-product inventory system');
  Writeln;
  Writeln('Initial inventory level', InitialInvLevel:24, ' items');
  Writeln;
  Writeln('Number of demand sizes', NumValuesDemand:25);
  Writeln;
  Write   ('Distribution function of demand sizes  ');
  FOR DemandIndex := 1 TO NumValuesDemand DO
     Write(ProbDistribDemand[DemandIndex]:8:3);
  Writeln;
  Writeln;
  Writeln('Mean interdemand time', MeanInterdemand:26:2, ' months');
  Writeln;
  Writeln('Delivery lag range', Minlag:29:2, ' to', Maxlag:10:2,
          ' months');
  Writeln;
  Writeln('Length of the simulation', NumMonths:23, ' months');
  Writeln;
  Writeln('K =', SetupCost:6:1, '    i =', IncrementalCost:6:1,
          '    h =', HoldingCost:6:1, '   pi =', ShortageCost:6:1);
  Writeln;
  Writeln('Number of policies', NumPolicies:29);
  Writeln;
  Write   ('                     Average          Average');
  Writeln('          Average         Average');
  Write   ('  Policy        total cost      ordering cost');
  Writeln('  holding cost    shortage cost');
```

FIGURE 1.79
Pascal code for the main program, inventory model.

```
{ Run the simulation varying the inventory policy. }

FOR Policy := 1 TO NumPolicies DO BEGIN

    { Read the inventory policy, and initialize the simulation. }

    Readln(Smalls, Bigs);
    Initialize;

    { Run the simulation until it terminates after an end-simulation
      event (type 3) occurs. }

    REPEAT

        { Determine the next event. }

        Timing;

        { Update time-average statistical accumulators. }

        UpdateTimeAvgStats;

        { Invoke the appropriate event procedure. }

        CASE NextEventType OF
            1: OrderArrival;
            2: Demand;
            4: Evaluate;
            3: Report
        END

    { If the event just executed was the end-simulation event (type
      3), end the simulation for this (s,S) pair and go on to the next
      pair (if any).  Otherwise, continue simulating for this (s,S)
      pair. }

    UNTIL NextEventType = 3

END

END. { Inventory }
```

FIGURE 1.79
(*Continued.*)

produce in procedure Report a single line of output corresponding to this heading. Then a FOR loop is begun, each iteration of which performs an entire simulation for a given (s, S) pair; the first thing done in the loop is to read the next (s, S) pair. The model is initialized, and a REPEAT UNTIL loop is used to keep simulating until a type 3 (end-simulation) event occurs, as in Sec. 1.4.8. Inside this loop, Timing is used to determine the next event type and to update the simulation clock. After returning from Timing with the next event type, the continuous-time statistics are updated before executing the event routine itself. A CASE statement is then used as before to transfer control to the appropriate event routine. Unlike the fixed-time stopping rule of Sec. 1.4.8, when the REPEAT UNTIL loop ends here we do not stop the program, but go to the next step of the enclosing FOR loop to read in the next (s, S) pair and do a separate simulation; the entire program stops only when the FOR loop is over and there are no more (s, S) pairs to consider.

1.5.5 C Program

The external definitions are shown in Fig. 1.80. The array prob_distrib_ demand will be used to hold the cumulative probabilities for the demand sizes, and is passed into the random-integer-generation function random_integer. As for the queueing model, we must include the header file rand.h (in Fig. 7.8) for the random-number generator of Fig. 7.7.

The code for the main function is given in Fig. 1.81. After opening the input and output files, the number of events is set to 4. The input parameters (except s and S) are then read in and written out, and a report heading is produced; for each (s, S) pair the simulation will then produce in the report function a single line of output corresponding to this heading. Then a "for" loop is begun, each iteration of which performs an entire simulation for a given (s, S) pair; the first thing done in the loop is to read the next (s, S) pair. The model is initialized, and a "do while" loop is used to keep simulating as long as the type 3 (end-simulation) event does not occur, as in Sec. 1.4.8. Inside this loop, the timing function is used to determine the next event type and to update the simulation clock. After returning from timing with the next event type, the continuous-time statistics are updated before executing the event routine itself. A "switch" statement is then used as before to transfer control to the appropriate event routine. Unlike the fixed-time stopping rule of Sec. 1.4.8, when the "do while" loop ends here we do not stop the program, but go to the next step of the enclosing "for" loop to read in the next (s, S) pair and do a separate simulation; the entire program stops only when the "for" loop is over and there are no more (s, S) pairs to consider.

```
/* External definitions for inventory system. */

#include <stdio.h>
#include <math.h>
#include "rand.h"      /* Header file for random-number generator. */

int    amount, bigs, initial_inv_level, inv_level, next_event_type,
       num_events, num_months, num_values_demand, smalls;
float  area_holding, area_shortage, holding_cost, incremental_cost,
       maxlag, mean_interdemand, minlag, prob_distrib_demand[26],
       setup_cost, shortage_cost, time, time_last_event,
       time_next_event[5], total_ordering_cost;
FILE   *infile, *outfile;

void   initialize(void);
void   timing(void);
void   order_arrival(void);
void   demand(void);
void   evaluate(void);
void   report(void);
void   update_time_avg_stats(void);
float  expon(float mean);
int    random_integer(float prob_distrib []);
float  uniform(float a, float b);
```

FIGURE 1.80
C code for the external definitions, inventory model.

```
main()  /* Main function. */
{
    int i, num_policies;

    /* Open input and output files. */

    infile  = fopen("inv.in",  "r");
    outfile = fopen("inv.out", "w");

    /* Specify the number of events for the timing function. */

    num_events = 4;

    /* Read input parameters. */

    fscanf(infile, "%d %d %d %d %f %f %f %f %f %f %f",
            &initial_inv_level, &num_months, &num_policies,
            &num_values_demand, &mean_interdemand, &setup_cost,
            &incremental_cost, &holding_cost, &shortage_cost, &minlag,
            &maxlag);
    for (i = 1; i <= num_values_demand; ++i)
        fscanf(infile, "%f", &prob_distrib_demand[i]);

    /* Write report heading and input parameters. */

    fprintf(outfile, "Single-product inventory system\n\n");
    fprintf(outfile, "Initial inventory level%24d items\n\n",
            initial_inv_level);
    fprintf(outfile, "Number of demand sizes%25d\n\n",
            num_values_demand);
    fprintf(outfile, "Distribution function of demand sizes  ");
    for (i = 1; i <= num_values_demand; ++i)
        fprintf(outfile, "%8.3f", prob_distrib_demand[i]);
    fprintf(outfile, "\n\nMean interdemand time%26.2f\n\n",
            mean_interdemand);
    fprintf(outfile, "Delivery lag range%29.2f to%10.2f months\n\n",
            minlag, maxlag);
    fprintf(outfile, "Length of the simulation%23d months\n\n",
            num_months);
    fprintf(outfile, "K =%6.1f   i =%6.1f   h =%6.1f   pi =%6.1f\n\n",
            setup_cost, incremental_cost, holding_cost, shortage_cost);
    fprintf(outfile, "Number of policies%29d\n\n", num_policies);
    fprintf(outfile, "                 Average             Average");
    fprintf(outfile, "            Average\n");
    fprintf(outfile, " Policy       total cost      ordering cost");
    fprintf(outfile, " holding cost   shortage cost");

    /* Run the simulation varying the inventory policy. */

    for (i = 1; i <= num_policies; ++i) {

        /* Read the inventory policy, and initialize the simulation. */

        fscanf(infile, "%d %d", &smalls, &bigs);
        initialize();

        /* Run the simulation until it terminates after an
           end-simulation event (type 3) occurs. */

        do {

            /* Determine the next event. */

            timing();
```

FIGURE 1.81
C code for the main function, inventory model.

```
        /* Update time-average statistical accumulators. */

        update_time_avg_stats();

        /* Invoke the appropriate event function. */

        switch (next_event_type) {
            case 1:
                order_arrival();
                break;
            case 2:
                demand();
                break;
            case 4:
                evaluate();
                break;
            case 3:
                report();
                break;
        }

    /* If the event just executed was not the end-simulation event
       (type 3), continue simulating.  Otherwise, end the
       simulation for the current (s,S) pair and go on to the next
       pair (if any). */

    } while (next_event_type != 3);
}

/* End the simulations. */

fclose(infile);
fclose(outfile);

return 0;
}
```

FIGURE 1.81
(*Continued.*)

The initialization function appears in Fig. 1.82. Observe that the first inventory evaluation is scheduled at time 0 since, in general, the initial inventory level could be less than s. Note also that event type 1 (order arrival) is eliminated from consideration, since our modeling assumption was that there are no outstanding orders initially.

The event functions order_arrival, demand, and evaluate are shown in Figs. 1.83 through 1.85, and correspond to the general discussion given in Sec. 1.5.2, and to the flowcharts in Figs. 1.56 through 1.58. In evaluate, note that the variable total_ordering_cost is increased by the ordering cost for any order that might be placed here.

The report generator is listed in Fig. 1.86, and computes the three components of the total cost separately, adding them together to get the average total cost per month. The current values of s and S are written out for identification purposes, along with the average total cost and its three components (ordering, holding, and shortage costs).

Function update_time_avg_stats, which was discussed in general in Sec. 1.5.2 and flowcharted in Fig. 1.59, is shown in Fig. 1.87. Note that if the

```
void initialize(void)   /* Initialization function. */
{
    /* Initialize the simulation clock. */

    time = 0.0;

    /* Initialize the state variables. */

    inv_level       = initial_inv_level;
    time_last_event = 0.0;

    /* Initialize the statistical counters. */

    total_ordering_cost = 0.0;
    area_holding        = 0.0;
    area_shortage       = 0.0;

    /* Initialize the event list.  Since no order is outstanding, the
       order-arrival event is eliminated from consideration. */

    time_next_event[1] = 1.0e+30;
    time_next_event[2] = time + expon(mean_interdemand);
    time_next_event[3] = num_months;
    time_next_event[4] = 0.0;
}
```

FIGURE 1.82
C code for function initialize, inventory model.

```
void order_arrival(void)   /* Order arrival event function. */
{
    /* Increment the inventory level by the amount ordered. */

    inv_level += amount;

    /* Since no order is now outstanding, eliminate the order-arrival
       event from consideration. */

    time_next_event[1] = 1.0e+30;
}
```

FIGURE 1.83
C code for function order_arrival, inventory model.

```
void demand(void)   /* Demand event function. */
{
    int size_demand;

    /* Generate the demand size. */

    size_demand = random_integer(prob_distrib_demand);

    /* Decrement the inventory level by the demand size. */

    inv_level -= size_demand;

    /* Schedule the time of the next demand. */

    time_next_event[2] = time + expon(mean_interdemand);
}
```

FIGURE 1.84
C code for function demand, inventory model.

```
void evaluate(void)   /* Inventory-evaluation event function. */
{
    /* Check whether the inventory level is less than smalls. */

    if (inv_level < smalls) {

        /* The inventory level is less than smalls, so place an order
           for the appropriate amount. */

        amount                = bigs - inv_level;
        total_ordering_cost += setup_cost + incremental_cost * amount;

        /* Schedule the arrival of the order. */

        time_next_event[1] = time + uniform(minlag, maxlag);
    }

    /* Regardless of the place-order decision, schedule the next
       inventory evaluation. */

    time_next_event[4] = time + 1.0;
}
```

FIGURE 1.85
C code for function evaluate, inventory model.

```
void report(void)   /* Report generator function. */
{
    /* Compute and write estimates of desired measures of performance.
       */

    float avg_holding_cost, avg_ordering_cost, avg_shortage_cost;

    avg_ordering_cost = total_ordering_cost / num_months;
    avg_holding_cost  = holding_cost * area_holding / num_months;
    avg_shortage_cost = shortage_cost * area_shortage / num_months;
    fprintf(outfile, "\n\n(%3d,%3d)%15.2f%15.2f%15.2f%15.2f",
            smalls, bigs,
            avg_ordering_cost + avg_holding_cost + avg_shortage_cost,
            avg_ordering_cost, avg_holding_cost, avg_shortage_cost);
}
```

FIGURE 1.86
C code for function report, inventory model.

inventory level inv_level is zero, neither the "if" nor the "else if" condition is satisfied, resulting in no update at all, as desired. As in the single-server queueing model of Sec. 1.4, it might be necessary to make both the time and time_last_event variables be of type double to avoid severe roundoff error in their subtraction at the top of the routine if the simulation is to be run for a long period of simulated time.

The code for function random_integer is given in Fig. 1.88, and is general in that it will generate an integer according to distribution function prob_distrib[I], provided that the values of prob_distrib[I] are specified. (In our case, prob_distrib[1] = $\frac{1}{6}$, prob_distrib[2] = $\frac{1}{2}$, prob_distrib[3] = $\frac{5}{6}$, and prob_distrib[4] = 1, all specified to three-decimal accuracy on input.) The logic

```
void update_time_avg_stats(void)   /* Update area accumulators for
                                      time-average statistics. */
{
    float time_since_last_event;

    /* Compute time since last event, and update last-event-time
       marker. */

    time_since_last_event = time - time_last_event;
    time_last_event        = time;

    /* Determine the status of the inventory level during the previous
       interval.  If the inventory level during the previous interval
       was negative, update area_shortage.  If it was positive, update
       area_holding.  If it was zero, no update is needed. */

    if (inv_level < 0)
        area_shortage -= inv_level * time_since_last_event;
    else if (inv_level > 0)
        area_holding  += inv_level * time_since_last_event;
}
```

FIGURE 1.87
C code for function update_time_avg_stats, inventory model.

```
int random_integer(float prob_distrib[])
                            /* Random integer generation function. */
{
    int   i;
    float u;

    /* Generate a U(0,1) random variate. */

    u = rand(1);

    /* Return a random integer in accordance with the (cumulative)
       distribution function prob_distrib. */

    for (i = 1; u >= prob_distrib[i]; ++i)
        ;
    return i;
}
```

FIGURE 1.88
C code for function random_integer.

```
float uniform(float a, float b)   /* Uniform variate generation function.
                                     */
{
    float u;

    /* Generate a U(0,1) random variate. */

    u = rand(1);

    /* Return a U(a,b) random variate. */

    return a + u * (b - a);
}
```

FIGURE 1.89
C code for function uniform.

agrees with the discussion in Sec. 1.5.2; note that the input array prob_distrib must contain the *cumulative* distribution function rather than the probabilities that the variate takes on its possible values.

The function uniform is given in Fig. 1.89, and is as described in Sec. 1.5.2.

1.5.6   Simulation Output and Discussion

The simulation report (in file inv.out if either the FORTRAN or C version was used) is given in Fig. 1.90. For this model, there were some differences in the results across different languages, compilers, and computers, even though the same random-number-generator algorithm was being used; see App. 1C for details and an explanation of this discrepancy.

The three separate components of the average total cost per month were reported to see how they respond individually to changes in s and S, as a possible check on the model and the code. For example, fixing $s = 20$ and

```
Single-product inventory system

Initial inventory level                        60 items

Number of demand sizes                          4

Distribution function of demand sizes    0.167    0.500    0.833    1.000

Mean interdemand time                          0.10 months

Delivery lag range                             0.50 to      1.00 months

Length of the simulation                       120 months

K =  32.0    i =   3.0    h =   1.0    pi =   5.0

Number of policies                              9
```

Policy	Average total cost	Average ordering cost	Average holding cost	Average shortage cost
(20, 40)	126.61	99.26	9.25	18.10
(20, 60)	122.74	90.52	17.39	14.83
(20, 80)	123.86	87.36	26.24	10.26
(20,100)	125.32	81.37	36.00	7.95
(40, 60)	126.37	98.43	25.99	1.95
(40, 80)	125.46	88.40	35.92	1.14
(40,100)	132.34	84.62	46.42	1.30
(60, 80)	150.02	105.69	44.02	0.31
(60,100)	143.20	89.05	53.91	0.24

FIGURE 1.90
Output report, inventory model.

increasing S from 40 to 100 increases the holding cost steadily from $9.25 per month to $36.00 per month, while reducing shortage cost at the same time; the effect of this increase in S on the ordering cost is to reduce it, evidently since ordering up to larger values of S implies that these larger orders will be placed less frequently, thereby avoiding the fixed ordering cost more often. Similarly, fixing S at, say, 100, and increasing s from 20 to 60 leads to a decrease in shortage cost ($7.95, $1.30, $0.24) but an increase in holding cost ($36.00, $46.42, $53.91), since increases in s translate into less willingness to let the inventory level fall to low values. While we could probably have predicted the *direction* of movement of these components of cost without doing the simulation, it would not have been possible to have said much about their *magnitude* without the aid of the simulation output.

Since the overall criterion of *total* cost per month is the sum of three components that move in sometimes different directions in reaction to changes in s and S, we cannot predict even the direction of movement of this criterion without the simulation. Thus, we simply look at the values of this criterion, and it would *appear* that the $(20, 60)$ policy is the best, having an average total cost of $122.74 per month. However, in the present context where the length of the simulation is fixed (the company wants a planning horizon of 10 years), what we *really* want to estimate for each policy is the *expected* average total cost per month for the first 120 months. The numbers in Fig. 1.90 are *estimates* of these expected values, each estimate based on a sample of size 1 (simulation run or replication). Since these estimates may have large variances, the ordering of them may differ considerably from the ordering of the expected values, which is the desired information. In fact, if we reran the nine simulations using different $U(0, 1)$ random variates, the estimates obtained might differ greatly from those in Fig. 1.90. Furthermore, the ordering of the new estimates might also be different.

We conclude from the above discussion that when the simulation run length is fixed by the problem context, it will generally not be sufficient to make a single simulation run of each policy or system of interest. In Chap. 9 we address the issue of just how many runs are required to get a good estimate of a desired expected value. Chapters 10 and 12 consider related problems when we are concerned with several different expected values arising from alternative system designs.

1.6 DISTRIBUTED SIMULATION

The simulations in Secs. 1.4 and 1.5 (as well as those to be considered in Chap. 2) all operate in basically the same way. A simulation clock and event list interact to determine which event will be processed next, the clock is advanced to the time of this event, and the computer executes the event logic, which may include updating state variables, manipulating lists for queues and events, generating random numbers and random variates, and collecting statistics. This logic is executed in order of the events' simulated time of occurrence; i.e., the simulation is *sequential*. Furthermore, all work is done on a single computer.

In recent years computer technology has enabled individual computers or processors to be linked together into *parallel* or *distributed* computing environments. For example, several relatively inexpensive minicomputers (or even microcomputers) can be networked together, or a larger computer can house a number of individual processors that can work on their own as well as communicate with each other. In such an environment, it may be possible to "distribute" different parts of a computing task across individual processors operating at the same time, or in "parallel," and thus reduce the overall time to complete the task. The ability to accomplish this naturally depends on the nature of the computing task, as well as on the hardware and software available. Distributed and parallel processing is currently being investigated in many areas, such as optimization and database design; in this section we briefly discuss a few of the efforts to apply this idea to dynamic simulation. More detailed surveys, together with many references to the original sources, can be found in Chandrasekaran and Sheppard (1987) and Misra (1986).

There are many conceivable ways of splitting up a dynamic simulation to distribute its work over different processors. Perhaps the most direct approach is to allocate the distinct "support functions" (such as random-number generation, random-variate generation, event-list handling, manipulating lists and queues, and statistics collection) to different processors. The logical execution of the simulation is still sequential, as in the programs of Secs. 1.4 and 1.5, but now the "master" simulation program can delegate execution of the support functions to other processors and get on with its work. For example, when the queue list in the model of Sec. 1.4 needs updating in some way, the master simulation program sends a message to the processor handling this function concerning what is to be done, which will do it at the same time that the master simulation program goes on. Specific implementation of this idea was reported by Sheppard et al. (1985). Comfort (1984) considered in particular processing the event list in a "master–slave" arrangement of processors, since event-list processing can represent a major portion of the time to run a simulation (see Sec. 2.8).

A very different way to distribute a simulation across separate processors is to decompose the model itself into several submodels, which are then assigned to different processors for execution. For example, a manufacturing facility is often modeled as an interconnected network of queueing stations, each representing a different type of activity; see Sec. 2.7 for an example. The individual submodels (or groups of them) are assigned to different processors, each of which then goes to work simulating its piece of the model. The processors must communicate with each other whenever necessary to maintain the proper logical relationships between the submodels; in the manufacturing example, this could occur when a workpiece leaves one queueing station and goes to another station that is being simulated on a different processor. Care must be taken to maintain the correct time-ordering of actions, i.e., to *synchronize* the operation of the submodels on different processors so as to represent the model's overall actions correctly. One major advantage of this type of distributed simulation is that there is neither a (global) simulation clock nor a (complete) event list; since event-list processing in traditional simulation modeling may take up a lot of the time to run the program (see Sec. 2.8), getting rid of the event list is an attractive idea. What takes the place of the clock and event list is a system for *message passing* between the processors, where each message carries with it a "time stamp." A drawback, however, is that it is possible for *deadlock* to occur in the simulation (two processors must each wait for a message from the other before they can proceed), even if such is not possible in the real system being simulated. This causes the simulation to grind to a halt, so there must be some method of detecting and breaking deadlocks (or perhaps of avoiding them). This method of distributed simulation was developed primarily by Chandy and Misra (1979, 1981, 1983), and was surveyed in Misra (1986).

Another concept, related to the preceding discussion of distributing submodels across parallel processors, is known as *virtual time*, implemented by the *time-warp mechanism*; see Jefferson (1985). As above, each processor simulates its own piece of the model forward in time, but does *not* wait to receive messages from other processors that may be moving along at different rates; this waiting is necessary in the above message-passing approach. If a submodel being simulated on a particular processor does receive a message that should have been received in its past (and thus potentially affecting its actions from that point in time on), a *rollback* occurs for the receiving submodel, whereby its time reverts to the (earlier) time of the incoming message. For example, if submodel B has been simulated up to time 87 and a message from submodel A comes in that was supposed to have been received at time 61, the clock for submodel B is rolled back to 61, and the simulation of submodel B between times 61 and 87 is canceled since it might have been done incorrectly without knowing the contents of the time 61 message. Part of this canceled work may have been sending messages to other submodels, each of which is nullified by sending a corresponding *antimessage*; the antimessages may themselves generate secondary rollbacks at their destination submodels, and so on. It seems unfortunate that the work done between times 61 and 87 is lost, and that we must incur the extra overhead associated with executing the rollback; however, all processors are busily simulating at all times (except during a rollback), rather than sitting idly waiting for messages before proceeding "correctly" through time in a forward way. In a stochastic simulation, whether a rollback will be necessary is uncertain, so the time-warp mechanism has been called a "game of chance," with the downside being the overhead in extra memory and processing for possible rollbacks but the upside being the possibility that rollbacks will be rare and that all processors will keep moving forward at all times. Furthermore, with the time-warp mechanism, deadlocks are avoided.

Development and evaluation of distributed processing in simulation is currently an active area of research. It does seem clear, however, that how well (or even whether) a particular method will work may depend on the model's structure and parameters, as well as on the computing environment available. For example, if a model can be decomposed into submodels that are only weakly related (e.g., a network of queues in which customers only rarely move from one queue to another), then either of the model-based schemes discussed above for distributing the simulation may be expected to show more promise. For specific investigations into the efficacy of distributed simulation, see Lavenberg, Muntz, and Samadi (1983), Comfort (1984), and Heidelberger (1988); the last of these papers considers the impact of distributed simulation on statistical (rather than run-time) efficiency, with mixed results.

Martin Marietta Corporation used distributed simulation with an extremely complex simulation related to the Strategic Defense Initiative program. Seven "super" minicomputers were linked together by message passing in order to make the overall simulation model execute in real time, which was necessary for this man-in-the-loop application.

1.7 STEPS IN A SIMULATION STUDY

Now that we have looked in some detail at the inner workings of discrete-event simulations, we should step back and recognize that detailed modeling and coding are just part of an overall simulation effort to understand or design a complex system, and that attention must be paid to a variety of other concerns, ranging from statistical experimental design to budget and personnel management. Figure 1.91 shows the steps that will compose a typical, sound simulation study and the relationships among them [see also Banks and Carson (1984, p. 12), Law and McComas (1990) Shannon (1975, p. 23), and Gordon (1978, p. 52)]. The number beside the symbol representing each step refers to the more detailed discussion of that step below. Not all studies will necessarily contain all these steps and in the order stated; some studies may contain steps that do not fit neatly into the diagram. Moreover, a simulation study is not a simple sequential process. As one proceeds with a study and a better understanding of the system of interest is obtained, it is often desirable to go back to a previous step. For example, new insights about the system obtained during the study may necessitate reformulating the problem to be solved.

1. *Formulate problem and plan the study.* Every study must begin with a clear statement of the study's overall objectives and specific issues to be addressed; without such a statement there is little hope for success. The alternative system designs to be studied should be delineated (if possible), and criteria for evaluating the efficacy of these alternatives should be given. The overall study should be planned in terms of the number of people, the cost, and the time required for each aspect of the study.

2. *Collect data and define a model.* Information and data should be collected on the system of interest (if it exists) and used to specify operating procedures and probability distributions for the random variables used in the model (see Chap. 6). For example, in modeling a bank, one might

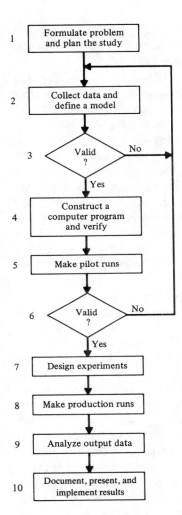

FIGURE 1.91
Steps in a simulation study.

collect interarrival times and service times and use these data to specify interarrival-time and service-time distributions for use in the model. If possible, data on the performance of the system, e.g., delays in queue of customers in a bank, should be collected for validation purposes in step 6. The construction of a mathematical and logical model of a real system for a given objective is still as much an art as it is a science. Although there are few firm rules on how one should go about the modeling process, one point on which most authors agree is that it is always a good idea to start with a model that is only moderately detailed, which can later be made more sophisticated if necessary. A model should contain only enough detail to capture the essence of the system for the purposes for which the model is intended; it is not necessary to have a one-to-one correspondence between elements of the model and elements of the system. A model with excessive detail may be too expensive to program and to execute. A good discussion of the art of modeling can be found in Shannon (1975).

3. *Valid?* Although we believe that validation (see Chap. 5) is something that should be done throughout the entire simulation study (rather than after the model has been built and only if there is time and money still remaining), there are several points in the study where validation is particularly appropriate. One such point is during step 3. In building the model, it is imperative for the modelers to involve people in the study who are intimately familiar with the operations of the actual system. It is also advisable for the modelers to interact with the decision maker (or the model's intended user) on a regular basis. This will increase the actual validity of the model, and the credibility (or perceived validity) of the model to the decision maker will also be increased (see Sec. 5.5.1 for further discussion). In addition, the adequacy of the probability distributions specified for generating input random variates should be tested using goodness-of-fit tests (see Sec. 6.6).

4. *Construct a computer program and verify.* The simulation modeler must decide whether to program the model in a general-purpose language such as FORTRAN, Pascal, or C (Chaps. 1 and 2) or in a specially designed simulation language such as GPSS, SIMAN, SIMSCRIPT II.5, or SLAM II (Chap. 3). A general-purpose language will probably already be known and available on the modeler's computer. It may also lead to shorter execution times. On the other hand, by providing many of the features needed in programming a model, a simulation language may reduce the required programming time significantly. Chapter 8 discusses techniques for generating random variates on a computer with a specified probability distribution. This capability may be needed in programming a model, depending on the language used. Chapter 7 discusses the related topic of generating $U(0, 1)$ random variates (often called *random numbers*), which are the basis for generating all other types of random variates in Chap. 8. Techniques for verifying or debugging a computer program are discussed in Sec. 5.3.

5. *Make pilot runs.* Pilot runs of the verified model are made for validation purposes in step 6.

6. *Valid?* Pilot runs can be used to test the sensitivity of the model's output to small changes in an input parameter. If the output changes greatly, a better estimate of the input parameter must be obtained (see Sec. 5.5.2 for further discussion of this and other uses of sensitivity analyses). If a system similar to the one of interest currently exists, output data from pilot runs for a model of the *existing* system can be compared with those from the actual existing system (collected in step 2). If the agreement is "good," the "validated" model is modified so that it represents the system of interest; we would hope that this modification is not too extensive. (See Secs. 5.5 and 5.6 for further discussion of this idea.)

7. *Design experiments*. It must be decided what system designs to simulate if, as is sometimes the case in practice, there are more alternatives than one can reasonably simulate. Often the complete decision cannot be made at this time. Instead, using output data from the production runs (from step 8) of certain selected system designs and also techniques discussed in Chap. 12, the analyst can decide which additional systems to simulate. For each system design to be simulated, decisions have to be made on such issues as initial conditions for the simulation run(s), the length of the warmup period (if any), the length of the simulation run(s), and the number of independent simulation runs (replications) to make for each alternative. These issues are discussed in Chap. 9. When designing and making the production runs, it is sometimes possible to use certain *variance-reduction techniques* to give results with greater statistical precision (the variances of the estimators are decreased) at little or no additional cost. These techniques are discussed in Chap. 11. (A review of basic probability and statistics is given in Chap. 4.)

8. *Make production runs*. Production runs are made to provide performance data on the system designs of interest.

9. *Analyze output data*. Statistical techniques are used to analyze the output data from the production runs. Typical goals are to construct a confidence interval for a measure of performance for one particular system design (see Chap. 9) or to decide which simulated system is best relative to some specified measure of performance (see Chap. 10).

10. *Document, present, and implement results*. Because simulation models are often used for more than one application, it is important to document the assumptions that went into the model as well as the computer program itself. Finally, a simulation study whose results are never implemented is most likely a failure. Furthermore, results from highly credible models are much more likely to be used.

1.8 OTHER TYPES OF SIMULATION

Although the emphasis in this book is on discrete-event simulation, several other types of simulation are of considerable importance. Our goal here is to explain these other types of simulation briefly and to contrast them with discrete-event simulation. In particular, we shall discuss continuous, combined discrete-continuous, and Monte Carlo simulations.

1.8.1 Continuous Simulation

Continuous simulation concerns the modeling over time of a system by a representation in which the state variables change continuously with respect to time. Typically, continuous simulation models involve differential equations that give relationships for the rates of change of the state variables with time. If the differential equations are particularly simple, they can be solved analytically to give the values of the state variables for all values of time as a function of the values of the state variables at time 0. For most continuous models analytic solutions are not possible, however, and numerical-analysis techniques, e.g., Runge-Kutta integration, are used to integrate the differential equations numerically, given specific values for the state variables at time 0.

Several languages, such as ACSL and CSSL-IV [see Pratt (1987)], have been specifically designed for building continuous simulation models. In addition, the discrete-event simulation languages SIMAN [see Pegden (1989)], SIMSCRIPT II.5 [see Fayek (1988)], and SLAM II [see Pritsker (1986)] also have continuous modeling capabilities. These three languages have the added advantage of allowing both discrete and continuous components simultaneously in one model (see Sec. 1.8.2). Readers interested in applications of continuous simulation may wish to consult the journal *Simulation*.

> **Example 1.3.** We now consider a continuous model of competition between two populations. Biological models of this type, which are called *predator–prey* (or *parasite–host*) models, have been considered by many authors, including Braun (1975, p. 583) and Gordon (1978, p. 103). An environment consists of two populations, predators and prey, which interact with each other. The prey are passive, but the predators depend on the prey as their source of food. [For example, the predators might be sharks and the prey might be food fish; see Braun (1975).] Let $x(t)$ and $y(t)$ denote, respectively, the numbers of individuals in the prey and predator populations at time t. Suppose that there is an ample supply of food for the prey and, in the absence of predators, that their rate of growth is $rx(t)$ for some positive r. (We can think of r as the natural birth rate minus the natural death rate.) Because of the interaction between predators and prey, it is reasonable to assume that the death rate of the prey due to interaction is proportional to the product of the two population sizes, $x(t)y(t)$. Therefore, the overall rate of change of the prey population, dx/dt, is given by
>
> $$\frac{dx}{dt} = rx(t) - ax(t)y(t) \tag{1.8}$$
>
> where a is a positive constant of proportionality. Since the predators depend on the prey for their very existence, the rate of change of the predators in the absence of prey is $-sy(t)$ for some positive s. Furthermore, the interaction between the two populations causes the predator population to increase at a rate that is also proportional to $x(t)y(t)$. Thus, the overall rate of change of the predator population, dy/dt, is
>
> $$\frac{dy}{dt} = -sy(t) + bx(t)y(t) \tag{1.9}$$
>
> where b is a positive constant. Given initial conditions $x(0) > 0$ and $y(0) > 0$, the solution of the model given by Eqs. (1.8) and (1.9) has the interesting property that $x(t) > 0$ and $y(t) > 0$ for all $t \geq 0$ [see Braun (1975)]. Thus, the prey population can never be completely extinguished by the predators. The solution $\{x(t), y(t)\}$ is also a periodic function of time. That is, there is a $T > 0$ such that $x(t + nT) = x(t)$ and $y(t + nT) = y(t)$ for all positive integers n. This result is not unexpected. As the predator population increases, the prey population decreases.

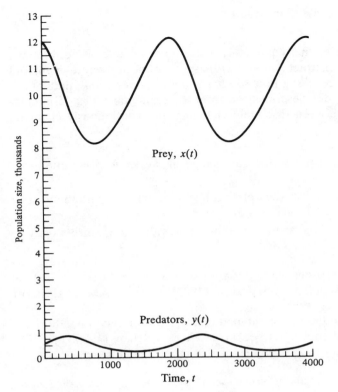

FIGURE 1.92
Numerical solution of a predator–prey model.

This causes a decrease in the rate of increase of the predators, which eventually results in a decrease in the number of predators. This in turn causes the number of prey to increase, etc.

Consider the particular values $r = 0.001$, $a = 2 \times 10^{-6}$, $s = 0.01$, $b = 10^{-6}$ and the initial population sizes $x(0) = 12,000$ and $y(0) = 600$. Figure 1.92 is a numerical solution of Eqs. (1.8) and (1.9) resulting from using a computer package designed to solve systems of differential equations numerically (not explicitly a continuous simulation language).

Note that the above example was completely deterministic; i.e., it contained no random components. It is possible, however, for a continuous simulation model to embody uncertainty; in Example 1.3 there could have been random terms added to Eqs. (1.8) and (1.9) that might depend on time in some way, or the constant factors could be modeled as quantities that change their value randomly at certain points in time.

1.8.2 Combined Discrete-Continuous Simulation

Since some systems are neither completely discrete nor completely continuous, the need may arise to construct a model with aspects of both discrete-event and continuous simulation, resulting in a *combined discrete-continuous* simulation. Pritsker (1986, pp. 61–62) describes the three fundamental types of interactions that can occur between discretely changing and continuously changing state variables:

- A discrete event may cause a discrete change in the value of a continuous state variable.
- A discrete event may cause the relationship governing a continuous state variable to change at a particular time.
- A continuous state variable achieving a threshold value may cause a discrete event to occur or to be scheduled.

Combined discrete-continuous simulation models can be built in SIMAN [Pegden (1989)], SIMSCRIPT II.5 [Fayek (1988)], and SLAM II [Pritsker (1986)].

The following example of a combined discrete-continuous simulation is a brief description of a model described in detail by Pritsker (1986, pp. 354–364), who also provides other examples of this type of simulation.

Example 1.4. Tankers carrying crude oil arrive at a single unloading dock, supplying a storage tank that in turn feeds a refinery through a pipeline. An unloading tanker delivers oil to the storage tank at a specified constant rate. (Tankers that arrive when the dock is busy form a queue.) The storage tank supplies oil to the refinery at a different specified rate. The dock is open from 6 A.M. to midnight, and, because of safety considerations, unloading of tankers ceases when the dock is closed.

The discrete events for this (simplified) model are the arrival of a tanker for unloading, closing the dock at midnight, and opening the dock at 6 A.M. The levels of oil in the unloading tanker and in the storage tank are given by continuous state variables whose rates of change are described by differential equations [see Pritsker (1986, pp. 354–364) for details]. Unloading the tanker is considered complete when the level of oil in the tanker is less than 5 percent of its capacity, but unloading must be temporarily stopped if the level of oil in the storage tank reaches its capacity. Unloading can be resumed when the level of oil in the tank decreases to 80 percent of its capacity. If the level of oil in the tank ever falls below 5000 barrels, the refinery must be shut down temporarily. In order to avoid frequent startups and shutdowns of the refinery, the tank does not resume supplying oil to the refinery until the tank once again contains 50,000 barrels. Each of the five events concerning the levels of oil, e.g., the level of oil in the tanker falling below 5 percent of the tanker's capacity, is what Pritsker calls a *state event*. Unlike discrete events, state events are not scheduled but occur when a continuous state variable crosses a threshold.

1.8.3 Monte Carlo Simulation

We define *Monte Carlo* simulation to be a scheme employing random numbers, that is, U(0, 1) random variates, which is used for solving certain stochastic or deterministic problems where the passage of time plays no substantive role. Thus, Monte Carlo simulations are generally static rather than dynamic. The reader should note that although some authors define Monte Carlo simulation to be *any* simulation involving the use of random numbers, our definition is more restrictive. The name "Monte Carlo" simulation or method originated during World War II, when this approach was applied to problems related to the development of the atomic bomb. For a more detailed discussion of Monte Carlo simulation, see Hammersley and Handscomb (1964), Halton (1970), Rubinstein (1981), and Morgan (1984).

Example 1.5. Suppose that we want to evaluate the integral

$$I = \int_a^b g(x)\, dx$$

where $g(x)$ is a real-valued function that is not analytically integrable. (In practice, Monte Carlo simulation would probably not be used to evaluate a single integral, since there are more efficient numerical-analysis techniques for this purpose. It is more likely to be used on a multiple-integral problem with an ill-behaved integrand.) To see how this *deterministic* problem can be approached by Monte Carlo simulation, let Y be the random variable $(b - a)g(X)$, where X is a continuous random variable distributed uniformly on $[a, b]$ [denoted by U(a, b)]. Then the expected value of Y is

$$E(Y) = E[(b - a)g(X)]$$

$$= (b - a)E[g(X)]$$

$$= (b - a)\int_a^b g(x)f_X(x)\, dx$$

$$= (b - a)\frac{\int_a^b g(x)\, dx}{(b - a)}$$

$$= I$$

where $f_X(x) = 1/(b - a)$ is the probability density function of a U(a, b) random variable (see Sec. 6.2.2). [For justification of the third equality, see, for example, Ross (1989, p. 43).] Thus, the problem of evaluating the integral has been reduced to one of estimating the expected value $E(Y)$. In particular, we shall estimate $E(Y) = I$ by the sample mean

$$\overline{Y}(n) = \frac{\sum_{i=1}^{n} Y_i}{n} = (b - a)\frac{\sum_{i=1}^{n} g(X_i)}{n}$$

where $X_1, X_2, \ldots, X_n$ are IID U(a, b) random variables. {It is instructive to think of $\overline{Y}(n)$ as an estimate of the area of the rectangle that has a base of length

TABLE 1.3
$\overline{Y}(n)$ for various values of n resulting from applying Monte Carlo simulation to the estimation of the integral $\int_0^{\pi} \sin x \, dx = 2$

n	10	20	40	80	160
$\overline{Y}(n)$	2.213	1.951	1.948	1.989	1.993

$(b - a)$ and a height $I/(b - a)$, which is the continuous average of $g(x)$ over $[a, b]$.} Furthermore, it can be shown that $E[\overline{Y}(n)] = I$, that is, $\overline{Y}(n)$ is an unbiased estimator of I, and $\text{Var}[\overline{Y}(n)] = \text{Var}(Y)/n$ (see Sec. 4.4). Assuming that $\text{Var}(Y)$ is finite, it follows that $\overline{Y}(n)$ will be arbitrarily close to I for sufficiently large n (with probability 1) (see Sec. 4.6).

To illustrate the above scheme numerically, suppose that we would like to evaluate the integral

$$I = \int_0^{\pi} \sin x \, dx$$

which can be shown by elementary calculus to have a value of 2. Table 1.3 shows the results of applying Monte Carlo simulation to the estimation of this integral for various values of n.

Monte Carlo simulation is now widely used to solve certain problems in statistics that are not analytically tractable. For example, it has been applied to estimate the critical values or the power of a new hypothesis test. Determining the critical values for the Kolmogorov-Smirnov test for normality, discussed in Sec. 6.6, is such an application. The advanced reader might also enjoy perusing the technical journals *Communications in Statistics* (Part B, Simulation and Computation), *Journal of Statistical Computation and Simulation*, and *Technometrics*, all of which contain many examples of this type of Monte Carlo simulation.

Finally, it should be mentioned that the procedures discussed in Sec. 9.4 can be used to determine the sample size, n, required to obtain a specified precision in a Monte Carlo simulation study.

1.9 ADVANTAGES, DISADVANTAGES, AND PITFALLS OF SIMULATION

We conclude this introductory chapter by listing some good and bad characteristics of simulation (as opposed to other methods of studying systems), and by noting some common mistakes made in simulation studies that can impair or even ruin a simulation project. This subject was also discussed to some extent in Sec. 1.2, but now that we have worked through some simulation examples, it may be possible to be more specific.

As mentioned in Sec. 1.2, simulation is a widely used and increasingly popular method for studying complex systems. Some possible advantages of simulation that may account for its widespread appeal are the following.

- Most complex, real-world systems with stochastic elements cannot be accurately described by a mathematical model that can be evaluated *analytically*. Thus, a simulation is often the only type of investigation possible.
- Simulation allows one to estimate the performance of an existing system under some projected set of operating conditions.
- Alternative proposed system designs (or alternative operating policies for a single system) can be compared via simulation to see which best meets a specified requirement.
- In a simulation we can maintain much better control over experimental conditions than would generally be possible when experimenting with the system itself (see Chap. 11).
- Simulation allows us to study a system with a long time frame—e.g., an economic system—in compressed time, or alternatively to study the detailed workings of a system in expanded time.

Simulation is not without its drawbacks. Some disadvantages are as follows.

- Each run of a *stochastic* simulation model produces only *estimates* of a model's true characteristics for a particular set of input parameters. Thus, several independent runs of the model will probably be required for each set of input parameters to be studied (see Chap. 9). For this reason, simulation models are generally not as good at optimization as they are at comparing a fixed number of specified alternative system designs. On the other hand, an analytic model, *if appropriate*, can often easily produce the *exact* true characteristics of that model for a variety of sets of input parameters. Thus, if a "valid" analytic model is available or can easily be developed, it will generally be preferable to a simulation model.
- Simulation models are often expensive and time-consuming to develop.
- The large volume of numbers produced by a simulation study or the persuasive impact of a realistic animation (see Sec. 3.4.2) often creates a tendency to place greater confidence in a study's results than is justified. If a model is not a "valid" representation of a system under study, the simulation results, no matter how impressive they appear, will provide little useful information about the actual system.

When deciding whether or not a simulation study is appropriate in a given situation, we can only advise that these advantages and drawbacks be kept in mind and that all other relevant facets of one's particular situation be brought to bear as well. Finally, it should be noted that in some studies both simulation and analytic models might be useful. In particular, simulation can be used to check the validity of assumptions needed in an analytic model. On the other hand, an analytic model can suggest reasonable alternatives to investigate in a simulation study.

Assuming that the decision has been prudently made to use the simulation tool, we have found that there are several pitfalls along the way to successful completion of a simulation study [see also Solomon (1983, p. 10) and Law and McComas (1989)]:

- Failure to have a well-defined set of objectives at the beginning of the simulation study
- Inappropriate level of model detail
- Failure to communicate with management on a regular basis throughout the course of the simulation study
- Treating a simulation study as if it were primarily a complicated exercise in computer programming
- Failure to have people with operations-research and statistical training on the modeling team
- Obliviously using commercial simulation software that may contain errors or whose complex macro statements may not be well documented and may not implement the modeling logic desired
- Reliance on simulators that make simulation accessible to "anyone" (see Sec. 3.3.1)
- Misuse of animation
- Failure to account correctly for sources of randomness in the actual system
- Using arbitrary distributions (e.g., normal or uniform) as input to the simulation
- Analyzing the output data from one simulation run using statistical formulas that assume independence
- Making a single replication of a particular system design and treating the output statistics as the "true answers"
- Comparing alternative system designs on the basis of one replication for each design
- Using wrong measures of performance

We will have more to say about what *to* do (rather than what *not* to do) concerning some of the above potential stumbling blocks in the later chapters of this book.

APPENDIX 1A
FIXED-INCREMENT TIME ADVANCE

As mentioned in Sec. 1.3.1, the second principal approach for advancing the simulation clock in a discrete-event simulation model is called *fixed-increment time advance*. With this approach, the simulation clock is advanced in increments of exactly Δt time units for some appropriate choice of Δt. After each update of the clock, a check is made to determine if any events should have occurred during the previous interval of length Δt. If one or more events were scheduled to have occurred during this interval, these events are considered to occur at the *end* of the interval and the system state (and statistical counters) are updated accordingly. The fixed-increment time-advance approach is illustrated in Fig. 1.93, where the curved arrows represent the advancing of the simulation clock and e_i $(i = 1, 2, \ldots)$ is the *actual* time of occurrence of the ith event of any type (*not* the ith value of the simulation clock). In the time interval $[0, \Delta t)$, an event occurs at time e_1 but is considered to occur at time Δt by the model. No events occur in the interval $[\Delta t, 2\Delta t)$, but the model checks to determine that this is the case. Events occur at the times e_2 and e_3 in the interval $[2\Delta t, 3\Delta t)$, but both events are considered to occur at time $3\Delta t$, etc. A set of rules must be built into the model to decide in what order to process events when two or more events are considered to occur at the same time by the model. Two disadvantages of fixed-increment time advance are the errors introduced by processing events at the end of the interval in which they occur and the necessity of deciding which event to process first when events that are not simultaneous in reality are treated as such by the model. These problems can be made less severe by making Δt smaller, but this increases the amount of checking for event occurrences that must be done and results in an increase in execution time. Because of these considerations, fixed-increment time advance is generally not used for discrete-event simulation models when the times between successive events can vary greatly.

The primary use of this approach appears to be for systems where it can reasonably be assumed that all events *actually* occur at one of the times $n\Delta t$ $(n = 0, 1, 2, \ldots)$ for an appropriately chosen Δt. For example, data in economic systems are often available only on an annual basis, and it is natural in a simulation model to advance the simulation clock in increments of 1 year. [See Naylor (1971) for a discussion of simulation of economic systems. See also Sec. 4.3 for discussion of an inventory system that can be simulated, without loss of accuracy, by fixed-increment time advance.]

It should be noted that fixed-increment time advance can be realized when using the next-event time-advance approach by artificially scheduling "events" to occur every Δt time units.

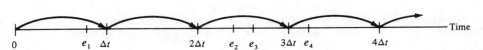

FIGURE 1.93
An illustration of fixed-increment time advance.

APPENDIX 1B
A PRIMER ON QUEUEING SYSTEMS

A *queueing system* consists of one or more servers that provide service of some kind to arriving customers. Customers who arrive to find all servers busy (generally) join one or more *queues* (or lines) in front of the servers, hence the name "queueing" system.

Historically, a large proportion of all discrete-event simulation studies have involved the modeling of a real-world queueing system, or at least some component of the system being simulated was a queueing system. Thus, we believe that it is important for the student of simulation to have at least a basic understanding of the components of a queueing system, standard notation for queueing systems, and measures of performance that are often used to indicate the quality of service being provided by a queueing system. Some examples of real-world queueing systems that have often been simulated are given in Table 1.4. For additional information on queueing systems in general, see Gross and Harris (1985) and Kleinrock (1975). Chandy and Sauer (1981) and Kleinrock (1976) are recommended for those interested in queueing models of computer systems.

1B.1   Components of a Queueing System

A queueing system is characterized by three components: arrival process, service mechanism, and queue discipline. Specifying the *arrival process* for a queueing system consists of describing how customers arrive to the system. Let A_i be the interarrival time between the arrivals of the $(i-1)$st and ith customers (see Sec. 1.3). If $A_1, A_2, \ldots$ are assumed to be IID random variables, we shall denote the *mean* (or expected) *interarrival time* by $E(A)$ and call $\lambda = 1/E(A)$ the *arrival rate* of customers.

The *service mechanism* for a queueing system is articulated by specifying the number of servers (denoted by s), whether each server has its own queue

TABLE 1.4
Examples of queueing systems

System	Servers	Customers
Bank	Tellers	Customers
Hospital	Doctors, nurses, beds	Patients
Computer system	Central processing unit, input/output devices	Jobs
Manufacturing line	Workers, machines	Items being manufactured
Airport	Runways, gates, security check-in stations	Airplanes, travelers
Communication system	Lines, circuits, operators	Calls, callers, messages

or there is one queue feeding all servers, and the probability distribution of customers' service times. Let S_i be the service time of the ith arriving customer. If $S_1, S_2, \ldots$ are IID random variables, we shall denote the *mean service time* of a customer by $E(S)$ and call $\omega = 1/E(S)$ the *service rate* of a server.

The *queue discipline* of a queueing system refers to the rule that a server uses to choose the next customer from the queue (if any) when the server completes the service of the current customer. Commonly used queue disciplines include:

FIFO: Customers are served in a first-in, first-out manner.

LIFO: Customers are served in a last-in, first-out manner (see Prob. 2.17).

Priority: Customers are served in order of their importance (see Prob. 2.22) or on the basis of their service requirements (see Probs. 1.24, 2.20, and 2.21).

1B.2 Notation for Queueing Systems

Certain queueing systems occur so often in practice that standard notations have been developed for them. In particular, consider the queueing system shown in Fig. 1.94, which has the following characteristics:

1. s servers in parallel and one FIFO queue feeding all servers.
2. $A_1, A_2, \ldots$ are IID random variables.
3. $S_1, S_2, \ldots$ are IID random variables.
4. The A_i's and S_i's are independent.

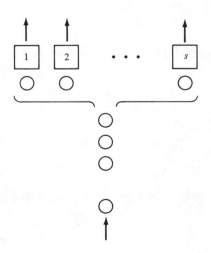

FIGURE 1.94
A *GI/G/s* queue.

We call such a system a *GI/G/s* queue, where *GI* (general independent) refers to the distribution of the A_i's and *G* (general) refers to the distribution of the S_i's. If specific distributions are given for the A_i's and the S_i's (as is always the case for simulation), symbols denoting these distributions are used in place of *GI* and *G*. The symbol *M* is used for the exponential distribution because of the Markovian, i.e., memoryless, property of the exponential distribution (see Prob. 4.26), the symbol E_k for a *k*-Erlang distribution (if *X* is a *k*-Erlang random variable, then $X = \sum_{i=1}^{k} Y_i$, where the Y_i's are IID exponential random variables), and *D* for deterministic (or constant) times. Thus, a single-server queueing system with exponential interarrival times and service times and a FIFO queue discipline is called an *M/M/1* queue.

For any *GI/G/s* queue, we shall call the quantity $\rho = \lambda/(s\omega)$ the *utilization factor* of the queueing system ($s\omega$ is the service rate of the system when all servers are busy). It is a measure of how heavily the resources of a queueing system are utilized.

1B.3   Measures of Performance for Queueing Systems

There are many possible measures of performance for queueing systems. We now describe four such measures that are usually used in the mathematical study of queueing systems. The reader should not infer from our choices that these measures are necessarily the most relevant or important in practice (see Chap. 9 for further discussion). As a matter of fact, for some real-world systems these measures may not even be well defined; i.e., they may not exist.

Let

D_i = delay in queue of *i*th customer

$W_i = D_i + S_i$ = waiting time in system of *i*th customer

$Q(t)$ = number of customers in queue at time *t*

$L(t)$ = number of customers in system at time *t* [$Q(t)$ plus number of customers being served at time *t*]

Then the measures

$$d = \lim_{n \to \infty} \frac{\sum_{i=1}^{n} D_i}{n} \qquad \text{w.p. } 1$$

and

$$w = \lim_{n \to \infty} \frac{\sum_{i=1}^{n} W_i}{n} \qquad \text{w.p. } 1$$

(if they exist) are called the *steady-state average delay* and the *steady-state average waiting time*. Similarly, the measures

$$Q = \lim_{T \to \infty} \frac{\int_0^T Q(t)\, dt}{T} \qquad \text{w.p. } 1$$

and
$$L = \lim_{T \to \infty} \frac{\int_0^T L(t)\,dt}{T} \qquad \text{w.p. 1}$$

(if they exist) are called the *steady-state time-average number in queue* and the *steady-state time-average number in system*. Here and throughout this book, the qualifier "w.p. 1" (with probability 1) is given for mathematical correctness and has little practical significance. For example, suppose that $\sum_{i=1}^n D_i/n \to d$ as $n \to \infty$ (w.p. 1) for some queueing system. This means that if one performs a very large (an infinite) number of experiments, then in virtually every experiment $\sum_{i=1}^n D_i/n$ converges to the finite quantity d. Note that $\rho < 1$ is a necessary condition for d, w, Q, and L to exist for a $GI/G/s$ queue.

Among the most general and useful results for queueing systems are the *conservation equations*

$$Q = \lambda d \qquad \text{and} \qquad L = \lambda w$$

These equations hold for every queueing system for which d and w exist [see Stidham (1974)]. (Section 11.5 gives a simulation application of these relationships.) Another equation of considerable practical value is given by

$$w = d + E(S)$$

(see Sec. 1.4.7 and also Sec. 11.5 for further discussion).

It should be mentioned that the measures of performance discussed above can be analytically computed for $M/M/s$ queues ($s \geq 1$), $M/G/1$ queues for any distribution G, and for certain other queueing systems. In general, the interarrival-time distribution, the service-time distribution, or both must be exponential (or a variant of exponential, such as k-Erlang) for analytic solutions to be possible [see Gross and Harris (1985) or Kleinrock (1975, 1976)].

One interesting (and instructive) example of such an analytical solution is the steady-state average delay in queue for an $M/G/1$ queue, given by

$$d = \frac{\lambda\{\text{Var}(S) + [E(S)]^2\}}{2[1 - \lambda E(S)]}$$

where $\text{Var}(S)$ denotes the variance of the service-time distribution [see, for example, Ross (1989, p. 376) for a derivation of this formula]. Thus, we can see that if $E(S)$ is large, then congestion (here measured by d) will be larger; this is certainly to be expected. The formula also brings out the perhaps less obvious fact that congestion also increases if the *variability* of the service-time distribution is large, even if the mean service time stays the same; intuitively, this is because a highly variable service-time random variable will have a greater chance of taking on a large value (since it must be positive), which means that the (single) server will be tied up for a long time, causing the queue to build up.

APPENDIX 1C
NOTES ON THE COMPUTERS AND COMPILERS USED

The example simulation programs written in general-purpose languages in this and the next chapter have been run on several different computer systems and compilers, in an attempt to make them as general and portable as possible. There may still be some machine or compiler dependence, however, for example in input/output conventions. We have tried to obey standards for versions of the languages, where they exist.

All the FORTRAN programs shown in this book are in ANSI-Standard FORTRAN 77, with the exception of the INCLUDE statements found in the code and used to bring an external file into the source code at the point of their appearance. Moreover, these programs have all run in the following environments:

- IBM PC with IBM Professional FORTRAN (Version 1.00)
- IBM PS/2 Model 50Z with Microsoft FORTRAN (Version 4.01)
- Apple Macintosh SE with Absoft FORTRAN (Version 2.4)
- VAX 8650 running the VMS 5.2 operating system with VAX FORTRAN (Version 5.0)
- Encore Multimax 320 running the UMAX 4.3 operating system (a version of UNIX) with UMAX FORTRAN (f77)
- Cray-2 running the UNICOS 5.0.7 operating system (a version of UNIX System V) with Cray FORTRAN 77 (cft77, release 3.0)

(The Absoft FORTRAN compiler on the Macintosh SE has a problem with ENTRY points, necessitating changes in RAND and references to it, as detailed in App. 7A.) For the IBM PC Professional FORTRAN, VAX FORTRAN, UMAX FORTRAN, and on the Cray-2, no changes at all are necessary from the code shown in this book, i.e., the INCLUDE statements work as shown. For the IBM PS/2 with Microsoft FORTRAN, the form of the INCLUDE statements must be changed to

$INCLUDE:'filename'

where the filename is mm1.dcl or mm1alt.dcl, etc., and the $ is in position 1. For Absoft FORTRAN on the Macintosh SE, the INCLUDE statements are the same as in the text except that the single quotes around the file name to be included must be removed.

The Pascal programs in this chapter have been run in the following environments:

- VAX 8650 running the VMS 5.2 operating system with VAX Pascal (Version 3.5)

- Cray-2 running the UNICOS 5.0.7 operating system (a version of UNIX System V) with Cray Pascal (4.0)

We did not run the Pascal programs on any microcomputers, since we did not have compilers available that support 32-bit integers, a requirement for the random-number generator of Fig. 7.6.

The C programs in this chapter have been run in the following environments:

- IBM PS/2 Model 50Z with Borland Turbo C (Version 1.5)
- Apple Macintosh IIcx with THINK C 4.0 (the names of the built-in functions rand and time in the ANSI library had to be changed to avoid conflicts with our use of these names)
- VAX 8650 running the VMS 5.2 operating system with VAX C (Version 2.4)
- Cray-2 running the UNICOS 5.0.7 operating system (a version of UNIX System V) with the Cray Standard C compiler (scc, release 1.0)

As noted in Sec. 1.4.6, we have used the ANSI-standard version of C, the most important feature of which is complete function prototyping. This prototyping could be removed from our programs to be run on compilers that do not support it.

The results did differ in some cases for a given model run in different languages, with different compilers, or on different machines, due to inaccuracies in floating-point operations. This can matter if, for example, at some point two events are scheduled to be very close together, and roundoff error could result in different sequencing. In particular, representing the simulation clock as a floating-point number, as we have done, can lead to variable results in many ways. In the inventory simulation of Sec. 1.5, for instance, there are actually nine separate simulation runs made, and a particular demand event [whose interdemand time was generated by a particular $U(0, 1)$ random number] occurred near the end of run 2 on one machine, but at the beginning of run 3 on another machine due to different floating-point roundoff errors in the simulation clock; from this point on, the results differed. The numerical output shown in all cases (in this and the following chapter) was produced on an IBM PC with IBM Professional FORTRAN.

PROBLEMS

1.1. Describe what you think would be the most effective way to study each of the following systems, in terms of the possibilities in Fig. 1.1, and discuss why:
   (*a*) A small section of an existing factory
   (*b*) A freeway interchange that has experienced severe congestion
   (*c*) An emergency room in an existing hospital
   (*d*) A pizza-delivery operation
   (*e*) The shuttle-bus operation for a rental-car agency at an airport
   (*f*) A battlefield-communication system

1.2. For each of the systems in Prob. 1.1, suppose that it has been decided to make a study via a simulation model. Discuss whether the simulation should be static or dynamic, deterministic or stochastic, and continuous or discrete.

1.3. For the single-server queueing system in Sec. 1.4, define $L(t)$ to be the *total* number of customers in the system at time t (including the queue and the customer in service at time t, if any).
  (*a*) Is it true that $L(t) = Q(t) + 1$? Why or why not?
  (*b*) For the same realization considered for the hand simulation in Sec. 1.4.2, make a plot of $L(t)$ vs. t (similar to Figs. 1.5 and 1.6) between times 0 and $T(6)$.
  (*c*) From your plot in part (*b*), compute $\hat{\ell}(6) =$ the time-average number of customers in the system during the time interval $[0, T(6)]$. What is $\hat{\ell}(6)$ estimating?
  (*d*) Augment Fig. 1.7 to indicate how $\hat{\ell}(6)$ is computed during the course of the simulation.

1.4. For the single-server queue of Sec. 1.4, suppose that we did not want to estimate the expected average delay in queue; the model's structure and parameters remain the same. Does this change the state variables? If so, how?

1.5. For the single-server queue of Sec. 1.4, let $W_i =$ the *total* time in the system of the ith customer to finish service, which includes the time in queue plus the time in service of this customer. For the same realization considered for the hand simulation in Sec. 1.4.2, compute $\hat{w}(m) =$ the average time in system of the first m customers to exit the system, for $m = 5$; do this by augmenting Fig. 1.7 appropriately. How does this change the state variables, if at all?

1.6. From Fig. 1.5, it is clear that the maximum length of the queue was 3. Write a general expression for this quantity (for the n-delay stopping rule) and augment Fig. 1.7 so that it can be computed systematically during the simulation.

1.7. Modify the code for the single-server queue in Sec. 1.4.4, 1.4.5, or 1.4.6 to compute and write in addition the following measures of performance:
  (*a*) The time-average number in the system (see Prob. 1.3)
  (*b*) The average total time in the system (see Prob. 1.5)
  (*c*) The maximum queue length (see Prob. 1.6)
  (*d*) The maximum delay in queue
  (*e*) The maximum time in the system
  (*f*) The proportion of customers having a delay in queue in excess of 1 minute.
  Run this program using the random-number generator given in App. 7A.

1.8. The algorithm in Sec. 1.4.3 for generating an exponential random variate with mean β was to return $-\beta \ln U$, where U is a $U(0, 1)$ random variate. This algorithm could validly be changed to return $-\beta \ln(1 - U)$. Why?

1.9. Run the single-server queueing simulation of Sec. 1.4.4, 1.4.5, or 1.4.6 ten times by placing a loop around most of the main program, beginning just before the initialization and ending just after invoking the report generator. Discuss the results. (This is called *replicating* the simulation ten times independently.)

1.10. For the single-server queueing simulation of Sec. 1.4, suppose that the facility opens its doors at 9 A.M. (call this time 0) and closes its doors at 5 P.M., but operates until all customers present (in service or in queue) at 5 P.M. have been served. Change the code to reflect this stopping rule, and estimate the same performance measures as before.

1.11. For the single-server queueing system of Sec. 1.4, suppose that there is room in the queue for only two customers, and that a customer arriving to find that the queue is full just goes away (this is called *balking*). Simulate this system for a stopping rule of exactly 480 minutes, and estimate the same quantities as in Sec. 1.4, as well as the expected number of customers who balk.

1.12. Consider the inventory simulation of Sec. 1.5.

(*a*) For this model with these parameters, there can never be more than one order outstanding (i.e., previously ordered but not yet delivered) at a time. Why?

(*b*) Describe specifically what changes would have to be made if the delivery lag were uniformly distributed between 0.5 and 6.0 months (rather than between 0.5 and 1.0 month); no other changes to the model are being considered. Should ordering decisions be based only on the inventory level $I(t)$?

1.13. Modify the inventory simulation of Sec. 1.5 so that it makes five replications of each (s, S) policy; see Prob. 1.9. Discuss the results. Which inventory policy is best? Are you sure?

1.14. A service facility consists of two servers in series (tandem), each with its own FIFO queue (see Fig. 1.95). A customer completing service at server 1 proceeds to server 2, while a customer completing service at server 2 leaves the facility. Assume that the interarrival times of customers to server 1 are IID exponential random variables with mean 1 minute. Service times of customers at server 1 are IID exponential random variables with mean 0.7 minute, and at server 2 are IID exponential random variables with mean 0.9 minute. Run the simulation for exactly 1000 minutes and estimate for each server the expected average delay in queue of a customer, the expected time-average number of customers in queue, and the expected utilization.

1.15. In Prob. 1.14, suppose that there is a travel time from the exit from server 1 to the arrival to queue 2 (or to server 2). Assume that this travel time is distributed uniformly between 0 and 2 minutes. Modify the simulation and rerun it under the same conditions to obtain the same performance measures. What is the required dimension (i.e., length) of the event list?

1.16. In Prob. 1.14, suppose that no queueing is allowed for server 2. That is, if a customer completing service at server 1 sees that server 2 is idle, she proceeds directly to server 2, as before. However, a customer completing service at server 1 when server 2 is busy with another customer must stay at server 1 until server 2 gets done; this is called *blocking*. While a customer is blocked from entering server 2, she receives no additional service from server 1, but prevents server 1 from taking the first customer, if any, from queue 1. Furthermore, "fresh" customers continue to arrive to queue 1 during a period of blocking. Compute the same six performance measures as in Prob. 1.14.

1.17. For the inventory system of Sec. 1.5, suppose that if the inventory level $I(t)$ at the beginning of a month is less than zero, the company places an *express order* to its

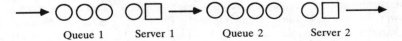

Queue 1   Server 1   Queue 2   Server 2

FIGURE 1.95
A tandem queueing system.

supplier. (If $0 \leq I(t) < s$, the company still places a normal order.) An express order for Z items costs the company $48 + 4Z$ dollars, but the delivery lag is now uniformly distributed on $[0.25, 0.50]$ month. Run the simulation for all nine policies and estimate the expected average total cost per month, the expected proportion of time that there is a backlog, that is, $I(t) < 0$, and the expected number of express orders placed. Is express ordering worth it?

1.18. For the inventory simulation of Sec. 1.5, suppose that the inventory is *perishable*, having a shelf life distributed uniformly between 1.5 and 2.5 months. That is, if an item has a shelf life of ℓ months, then ℓ months after it is placed in inventory it spoils and is of no value to the company. (Note that different items in an order from the supplier will have different shelf lives.) The company discovers that an item is spoiled only upon examination before a sale. If an item is determined to be spoiled, it is discarded and the next item in the inventory is examined. Assume that items in the inventory are processed in a FIFO manner. Repeat the nine simulation runs and observe the same costs as before. Also compute the proportion of items taken out of the inventory that are discarded due to being spoiled.

1.19. Consider a service facility with s (where $s \geq 1$) parallel servers. Assume that interarrival times of customers are IID exponential random variables with mean $E(A)$ and that service times of customers (regardless of the server) are IID exponential random variables with mean $E(S)$. If a customer arrives and finds an idle server, the customer begins service immediately, choosing the leftmost (lowest-numbered) idle server if there are several available. Otherwise, the customer joins the tail of a *single* FIFO queue that supplies customers to all the servers. (This is called an $M/M/s$ queue; see App. 1B.) Write a general program to simulate this system that will estimate the expected average delay in queue, the expected time-average number in queue, and the expected utilization of each of the servers, based on a stopping rule of n delays having been completed. The quantities s, $E(A)$, $E(S)$, and n should be input parameters. Run the model for $s = 5$, $E(A) = 1$, $E(S) = 4$, and $n = 1000$.

1.20. Repeat Prob. 1.19, but now assume that an arriving customer finding more than one idle server chooses among them with equal probability. For example, if $s = 5$ and a customer arrives to find servers 1, 3, 4, and 5 idle, he chooses each of these servers with probability 0.25.

1.21. Customers arrive to a bank consisting of three tellers in parallel.

(*a*) If there is a single FIFO queue feeding all tellers, what is the required dimension (i.e., length) of the event list for a simulation model of this system?

(*b*) If each teller has his own FIFO queue and if a customer can *jockey* (i.e., jump) from one queue to another (see Sec. 2.6 for the jockeying rules), what is the required dimension of the event list? Assume that jockeying takes no time.

(*c*) Repeat part (*b*) if jockeying takes 3 seconds.

Assume in all three parts that no events are required to terminate the simulation.

1.22. A manufacturing system contains m machines, each subject to randomly occurring breakdowns. A machine runs for an amount of time that is an exponential random variable with mean 8 hours before breaking down. There are s (where s is a fixed, positive integer) repairmen to fix broken machines, and it takes one repairman an exponential amount of time with mean 2 hours to complete the repair of one machine; no more than one repairman can be assigned to work on a broken machine even if there are other idle repairmen. If more than s machines are broken down at a given time, they form a FIFO "repair" queue and wait for the first available repairman. Further, a repairman works on a broken machine until it is fixed, regardless of what else is happening in the system. Assume that it costs the system $50 for each hour that each machine is broken down and $10 an hour to employ each repairman. (The repairmen are paid an hourly wage regardless of whether they are actually working.) Assume that $m = 5$, but write general code to accommodate a value of m as high as 20 by changing an input parameter. Simulate the system for exactly 800 hours for each of the employment policies $s = 1, 2, \ldots, 5$ to determine which policy results in the smallest expected average cost per hour. Assume that at time 0 all machines have just been "freshly" repaired.

1.23. For the facility of Prob. 1.10, suppose that the server normally takes a 30-minute lunch break at the first time after 12 noon that the facility is empty. If, however, the server has not gone to lunch by 1 P.M., the server will go after completing the customer in service at 1 P.M. (Assume in this case that all customers in the queue at 1 P.M. will wait until the server returns.) If a customer arrives while the server is at lunch, the customer *may* leave immediately without being served; this is called *balking*. Assume that whether such a customer balks depends on the amount of time remaining before the server's return. (The server posts his time of return from lunch.) In particular, a customer who arrives during lunch will balk with the following probabilities:

Time remaining before server's return (minutes)	Probability of a customer's balking
[20, 30)	0.75
[10, 20)	0.50
[0, 10)	0.25

(The random-integer-generation method discussed in Sec. 1.5.2 can be used to determine whether a customer balks. For a simpler approach, see Sec. 8.4.1.) Run the simulation and estimate the same measures of performance as before. (Note that the server is not busy when at lunch and that the time-average number in queue is computed including data from the lunch break.) In addition, estimate the expected number of customers who balk.

1.24. For the single-server queueing facility of Sec. 1.4, suppose that a customer's service time is known at the instant of arrival. Upon completing service to a customer, the server chooses from the queue (if any) the customer with the smallest service time. Run the simulation until 1000 customers have completed their delays and estimate the expected average delay in queue, the expected time-average number in queue, and the expected proportion of customers whose delay in queue is greater than 1 minute. (This priority queue discipline is called *shortest job first.*)

1.25. For the tandem queue of Prob. 1.14, suppose that with probability 0.2, a customer completing service at server 2 is *dissatisfied* with her overall service and must be completely served over again (at least once) by both servers. Define the delay in queue of a customer (in a particular queue) to be the total delay in that queue for all of that customer's passes through the facility. Simulate the facility for each of the following cases (estimate the same measures as before):

(a) Dissatisfied customers join the tail of queue 1.

(b) Dissatisfied customers join the head of queue 1.

1.26. A service facility consists of two type A servers and one type B server (not necessarily in the psychological sense). Assume that customers arrive at the facility with interarrival times that are IID exponential random variables with a mean of 1 minute. Upon arrival, a customer is determined to be either a type 1 customer or a type 2 customer, with respective probabilities of 0.75 and 0.25. A type 1 customer can be served by any server but will choose a type A server if one is available. Service times for type 1 customers are IID exponential random variables with a mean of 0.8 minute, regardless of the type of server. Type 1 customers who find all servers busy join a single FIFO queue *for type 1 customers*. A type 2 customer requires service from *both* a type A server *and* the type B server *simultaneously*. Service times for type 2 customers are uniformly distributed between 0.5 and 0.7 minute. Type 2 customers who arrive to find both type A servers busy *or* the type B server busy join a single FIFO queue *for type 2 customers*. Upon completion of service of *any* customer, preference is given to a type 2 customer if one is present and if both a type A and the type B server are then idle. Otherwise, preference is given to a type 1 customer. Simulate the facility for exactly 1000 minutes and estimate the expected average delay in queue and the expected time-average number in queue for each type of customer. Also estimate the expected proportion of time that each server spends on each type of customer.

1.27. A supermarket has two checkout stations, regular and express, with a single checker per station; see Fig. 1.96. Regular customers have exponential interarrival times with mean 2.1 minutes and have exponential service times with mean 2.0 minutes. Express customers have exponential interarrival times with mean 1.1 minutes and exponential service times with mean 0.9 minute. The arrival processes of the two types of customers are independent of each other. A regular customer arriving to find at least one checker idle begins service immediately, choosing the regular checker if both are idle; regular customers arriving to find both checkers busy join the end of the regular queue. Similarly, an express customer arriving to find an idle checker goes right into service, choosing the express checker if both are idle; express customers arriving to find both checkers busy join the end of the express queue, even if it is longer than the regular queue. When either checker finishes serving a customer, he takes the next customer from his queue, if any, and if his queue is empty but the other one is not, he takes the first customer from the other queue. If both queues are empty the checker becomes idle. Note that the mean service time of a customer is determined by the

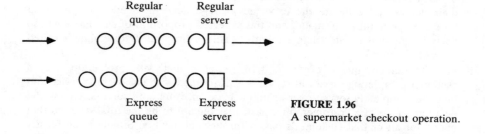

Regular queue   Regular server

Express queue   Express server

FIGURE 1.96
A supermarket checkout operation.

customer type, and not by whether the checker is the regular or express one. Initially, the system is empty and idle and the simulation is to run for exactly 8 hours. Compute the average delay in each queue, the time-average number in each queue, and the utilization of each checker. What recommendations would you have for further study or improvement of this system? (On June 21, 1983, the Cleveland *Plain Dealer*, in a story entitled "Fast Checkout Wins over Low Food Prices," reported that "Supermarket shoppers think fast checkout counters are more important than attractive prices, according to a survey [by] the Food Marketing Institute.... The biggest group of shoppers, 39 percent, replied 'fast checkouts,'... and 28 percent said good or low prices... [reflecting] growing irritation at having to stand in line to pay the cashier.")

1.28. A one-pump gas station is always open and has two types of customers. A police car arrives every 30 minutes (exactly), with the first police car arriving at time 15 minutes. Regular (nonpolice) cars have exponential interarrival times with mean 5.6 minutes, with the first regular car arriving at time 0. Service times at the pump for all cars are exponential with mean 4.8 minutes. A car arriving to find the pump idle goes right into service, and regular cars arriving to find the pump busy join the end of a single queue. A police car arriving to find the pump busy, however, goes to the front of the line, ahead of any regular cars in line. [If there are already other police cars at the front of the line, assume that an arriving police car gets in line ahead of them as well. (How could this happen?)] Initially the system is empty and idle, and the simulation is to run until exactly 500 cars (of any type) have completed their delays in queue. Estimate the expected average delay in queue for each type of car separately, the expected time-average number of cars (of either type) in queue, and the expected utilization of the pump.

1.29. Of interest in telephony are models of the following type. Between two large cities, A and B, are a fixed number, n, of long-distance lines or circuits. Each line can operate in either direction (i.e., can carry calls originating in A or B) but can carry only one call at a time; see Fig. 1.97. If a person in A or B wants to place a call to the other city and a line is open (i.e., idle), the call goes through immediately on one of the open lines. If all n lines are busy, the person gets a recording saying that she must hang up and try later; there are no facilities for queueing for the next open line, so these *blocked* callers just go away. The times between attempted calls from A to B are exponential with mean 10 seconds, and the times between attempted calls from B to A are exponential with mean 12 seconds. The length of a conversation is exponential with mean 4 minutes, regardless of the city of origin. Initially all lines are open, and the simulation is to run for 12 hours; compute the time-average number of lines that are busy, the time-average proportion of lines that are busy, the total number of attempted calls (from either city), the number of calls that are blocked, and the proportion

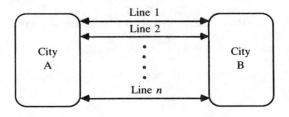

FIGURE 1.97
A long-distance telephone system.

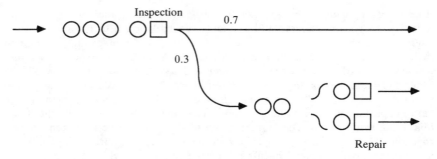

FIGURE 1.98
A bus maintenance depot.

of calls that are blocked. Determine approximately how many lines would be needed so that no more than 5 percent of the attempted calls will be blocked.

1.30. City busses arrive to the maintenance facility with exponential interarrival times with mean 2 hours. The facility consists of a single inspection station and two identical repair stations; see Fig. 1.98. Every bus is inspected, and inspection times are distributed uniformly between 15 minutes and 1.05 hours; the inspection station is fed by a single FIFO queue. Historically, 30 percent of the busses have been found during inspection to need some repair. The two parallel repair stations are fed by a single FIFO queue, and repairs are distributed uniformly between 2.1 hours and 4.5 hours. Run the simulation for 160 hours and compute the average delay in each queue, the average length of each queue, the utilization of the inspection station, and the utilization of the repair station (defined to be half of the time-average number of busy repair stations, since there are two stations). Replicate the simulation five times. Suppose that the arrival rate of busses quadrupled, i.e., the mean interarrival time decreased to 30 minutes. Would the facility be able to handle it? Can you answer this question without simulation?

REFERENCES

Banks, J., and J. S. Carson: *Discrete-Event System Simulation*, Prentice-Hall, Englewood Cliffs, N.J. (1984).

Braun, M.: *Differential Equations and Their Applications*, Applied Mathematical Sciences, Vol. 15, Springer-Verlag, New York (1975).

Chandrasekaran, U., and S. Sheppard: Discrete Event Distributed Simulation—A Survey, *Proc. Conference on Methodology and Validation*, Orlando, Fla., pp. 32–37 (1987).

Chandy, K. M., and J. Misra: Distributed Simulation: A Case Study in Design and Verification of Distributed Programs, *IEEE Trans. Software Eng.*, SE-5: 440–452 (1979).

Chandy, K.M., and J. Misra: Asynchronous Distributed Simulation via a Sequence of Parallel Computations, *Commun. Assoc. Comput. Mach.*, 24: 198–206 (1981).

Chandy, K.M., and J. Misra: Distributed Deadlock Detection, *Assoc. Comput. Mach. Trans. Computer Systems*, 1: 144–156 (1983).

Chandy, K. M., and C. H. Sauer: *Computer Systems Performance Analysis*, Prentice-Hall, Englewood Cliffs, N.J. (1981).

Comfort, J. C.: The Simulation of a Master-Slave Event-Set Processor, *Simulation*, *42*: 117–124 (1984).

Davis, G. B., and T. R. Hoffmann: *FORTRAN 77: A Structured, Disciplined Style*, 3d ed., McGraw-Hill, New York (1988).

Fayek, A.-M. M.: *Introduction to Combined Discrete-Continuous Simulation Using PC SIMSCRIPT II.5*, CACI Products Company, La Jolla, Calif. (1988).

Fishman, G. S.: *Principles of Discrete Event Simulation*, John Wiley, New York (1978).

Forgionne, G. A.: Corporate Management Science Activities: An Update, *Interfaces*, *13:3*: 20–23 (1983).

Gordon, G.: *System Simulation*, 2d ed., Prentice-Hall, Englewood Cliffs, N.J. (1978).

Grogono, P.: *Programming in Pascal*, 2d ed., Addison-Wesley, Reading, Mass. (1984).

Gross, D., and C. M. Harris: *Fundamentals of Queueing Theory*, 2d ed., John Wiley, New York (1985).

Halton, J. H.: A Retrospective and Prospective Survey of the Monte Carlo Method, *SIAM Rev.*, *12*: 1–63 (1970).

Hammersley, J. M., and D. C. Handscomb: *Monte Carlo Methods*, Methuen, London (1964).

Harpell, J. L., M. S. Lane, and A. H. Mansour: Operations Research in Practice: A Longitudinal Study, *Interfaces*, *19:3*: 65–74 (1989).

Heidelberger, P.: Discrete Event Simulations and Parallel Processing: Statistical Properties, *SIAM J. Statist. Comput.*, *9*: 1114–1132 (1988).

Jefferson, D. R.: Virtual Time, *Assoc. Comput. Mach. Trans. Programming Languages and Systems*, *7*: 404–425 (1985).

Jensen, K., and N. Wirth (revised by A. B. Mickel and J. F. Miner): *Pascal User Manual and Report*, 3d ed., Springer-Verlag, New York (1985).

Kernighan, B. W., and D. M. Ritchie: *The C Programming Language*, 2d ed., Prentice-Hall, Englewood Cliffs, N.J. (1988).

Kleinrock, L.: *Queueing Systems, Vol. I, Theory*, John Wiley, New York (1975).

Kleinrock, L.: *Queueing Systems, Vol. II, Computer Applications*, John Wiley, New York (1976).

Koffman, E. B., and F. L. Friedman: *Problem Solving and Structured Programming in FORTRAN 77*, 3d ed., Addison-Wesley, Reading, Mass. (1987).

Lavenberg, S., R. Muntz, and B. Samadi: Performance Analysis of a Rollback Method for Distributed Simulation, *Performance '83* (A. K. Agrawala and S. K. Tripathi, eds.): 117–132 (1983).

Law, A. M., and M. G. McComas: Pitfalls to Avoid in the Simulation of Manufacturing Systems, *Ind. Eng.*, *21*: 28–31 (May 1989).

Law, A. M., and M. G. McComas: Secrets of Successful Simulation Studies, *Ind. Eng.*, *22*: 47–48, 51–53, 72 (May 1990).

Misra, J.: Distributed Discrete-Event Simulation, *Computing Surveys*, *18*: 39–65 (1986).

Morgan, B. J. T.: *Elements of Simulation*, Chapman & Hall, London (1984).

Naylor, T. H.: *Computer Simulation Experiments with Models of Economic Systems*, John Wiley, New York (1971).

Pegden, C. D.: *Introduction to SIMAN* (January 1989 version), Systems Modeling Corp., Sewickley, Pa. (1989).

Pratt, C. A.: Catalog of Simulation Software, *Simulation*, *49*: 165–181 (1987).

Pritsker, A. A. B.: *Introduction to Simulation and SLAM II*, 3d ed., Systems Publishing Corp., West Lafayette, Ind. (1986).

Rasmussen, J. J., and T. George: After 25 Years: A Survey of Operations Research Alumni, Case Western Reserve University, *Interfaces*, *8:3*: 48–52 (1978).

Ross, S. M.: *Introduction to Probability Models*, 4th ed., Academic Press, San Diego, Calif. (1989).

Rubinstein, R. Y.: *Simulation and the Monte Carlo Method*, John Wiley, New York (1981).

Sargent, R. G.: Event Graph Modelling for Simulation with an Application to Flexible Manufacturing Systems, *Management Sci.*, *34*: 1231–1251 (1988).

Schmidt, J. W., and R. E. Taylor: *Simulation and Analysis of Industrial Systems*, Richard D. Irwin, Homewood, Ill. (1970).

Schruben, L.: Simulation Modeling with Event Graphs, *Commun. Assoc. Comput. Mach.*, *26*: 957–963 (1983).

Shannon, R. E.: *Systems Simulation: The Art and Science*, Prentice-Hall, Englewood Cliffs, N.J. (1975).

Shannon, R. E., S. S. Long, and B. P. Buckles: Operations Research Methodologies in Industrial Engineering, *AIIE Trans.*, *12*: 364–367 (1980).

Sheppard, S., R. E. Young, U. Chandrasekaran, and M. Krishnamurthi: Three Mechanisms for Distributing Simulation, *Proc. 12th Conference of the NSF Production Research and Technology Program*, Madison, Wis., pp. 67–70 (1985).

Solomon, S. L.: *Simulation of Waiting-Line Systems*, Prentice-Hall, Englewood Cliffs, N.J. (1983).

Som, T. K., and R. G. Sargent: A Formal Development of Event Graphs as an Aid to Structured and Efficient Simulation Programs, *ORSA J. Comput.*, *1*: 107–125 (1989).

Stidham, S: A Last Word on $L = \lambda w$, *Operations Res.*, *22*: 417–421 (1974).

Swart, W., and L. Donno: Simulation Modeling Improves Operations, Planning, and Productivity for Fast Food Restaurants, *Interfaces*, *11:6*: 35–47 (1981).

Thomas, G., and J. DaCosta: A Sample Survey of Corporate Operations Research, *Interfaces*, *9:4*: 102–111 (1979).

CHAPTER 2

MODELING
COMPLEX
SYSTEMS

Recommended sections for a first reading: 2.1 through 2.5

2.1 INTRODUCTION

In Chap. 1 we looked at simulation modeling in general, and then modeled and coded two specific systems. Those systems were very simple, and it was possible to program them directly in a general-purpose language, without using any special simulation software or support programs (other than a random-number generator). Most real-world systems, however, are quite complex, and coding them without supporting software can be a difficult and time-consuming task.

In this chapter we first discuss an activity that takes place in most simulations, *list processing*. A group of FORTRAN support routines, SIMLIB, is then introduced, which takes care of some standard list-processing tasks as well as several other common simulation chores, such as processing the event list, accumulating statistics, generating random numbers and observations from a few distributions, and writing out results. SIMLIB is then used in four example simulations, the first of which is just the single-server queueing system from Sec. 1.4 (included to illustrate the use of SIMLIB on a familiar model); the last three examples are of somewhat greater complexity.

Our purpose in this chapter is to illustrate how more complex systems can be modeled, and to show how list processing and the SIMLIB utility routines can aid in their programming. Our intention in using a package such as SIMLIB is purely pedagogical, allowing the reader to move quickly into modeling more complex systems and to appreciate how real simulation languages handle lists and other data. We do not mean to imply that SIMLIB is as comprehensive or efficient, or in any other way comparable, to the modern commercial simulation languages discussed in Chap. 3; in fact, the complete source code for SIMLIB is given in App. 2A and Fig. 7.5.

2.2 LIST PROCESSING IN SIMULATION

The simulation models considered in Chap. 1 were really quite simple in that they contained either one or no *lists* of *records* other than the event list. Furthermore, the records in these lists consisted of a single *attribute* and were always processed in a FIFO manner. In the queueing example, there was a FIFO list containing the records of all customers waiting in queue, and each customer record consisted of a single attribute, the time of arrival. In the inventory example there were no lists other than the event list. However, most complex simulations require many lists, each of which may contain a large number of records, consisting in turn of possibly many attributes each. Furthermore, it is often necessary to process these lists in a manner other than FIFO. For example, in some models one must be able to remove that record in a list with the smallest value for a specified attribute (other than the time the record was placed in the list). If this large amount of information is not stored and manipulated efficiently, the model may require so much execution time or so many storage locations that the simulation study would not be feasible.

In Sec. 2.2.1 we discuss two approaches to storing lists of records in a computer, sequential and linked allocation, and then explain why the latter approach is preferable for complex simulations. In Sec. 2.2.2 we present a treatment of linked storage allocation that is sufficient for the development of a simple FORTRAN-based simulation "language," SIMLIB, in Sec. 2.3. This language, which can be completely mastered in just a few hours of study, provides considerable insight into the nature of the special-purpose simulation languages discussed in Chap. 3, which require much more time to learn. More important, SIMLIB provides a vehicle for explaining how to simulate systems that are considerably more complicated than those discussed in Chap. 1.

2.2.1 Approaches to Storing Lists in a Computer

There are two principal approaches to storing lists of records in a computer. In the *sequential-allocation* approach, used in Chap. 1, the records in a list are put into physically adjacent storage locations, one record after another. This was the approach taken in Sec. 1.4 with the list of arrival times for customers in the queue.

In the *linked-allocation* approach, each record in a list contains its usual attributes and, in addition, *pointers* (or *links*) giving the *logical* relationship of the record to other records in the list. Records in a list that follow each other logically need not be stored in physically adjacent locations. A detailed discussion of linked allocation is given in Sec. 2.2.2. Linked allocation of lists has several advantages for simulation modeling:

- The time required to process certain kinds of lists can be significantly reduced. For the queueing example of Sec. 1.4, every time a customer completed service (and left a nonempty queue behind) we had to move each entry in the arrival-time array up one storage location; this would be quite inefficient if the queue were long, in which case the array would contain a large number of records. As we shall see in Example 2.1, linked allocation expedites processing of such arrays.
- For simulation models where the event list contains a large number of event records simultaneously, we can speed up event-list processing considerably; see Example 2.2 and Sec. 2.8 for further discussion.
- For some simulation models, the amount of computer memory required for storage can be reduced; see the discussion at the end of Sec. 2.2.2.
- Linked allocation provides a general framework that allows one to store and manipulate many lists simultaneously with ease, whereby records in different lists may be processed in different ways. This generality is one of the reasons for the use of the linked-allocation approach by all major simulation languages.

2.2.2 Linked Storage Allocation

In this section we present a discussion of linked storage allocation sufficient for development of the simple FORTRAN-based simulation "language" SIMLIB, described in the next section. For a more complete and general discussion of list-processing principles, see, for example, Knuth (1974, chap. 2).

Suppose that a list of records is to be stored in an array, that the rows of the array correspond to the records, and that the columns of the array correspond to the attributes (or data fields) that make up the records. For the queueing simulation of Sec. 1.4, each customer waiting in the queue had a record in the arrival-time list, and each record consisted of a single attribute, the corresponding customer's time of arrival. In general, a customer's record might have additional attributes such as age, a priority number, service requirement, etc.

A list of records is called *doubly linked* if each record has associated with it a predecessor link and a successor link. The *successor link* (or *forward pointer*) for a particular record gives the *physical* row number in the array of the record that *logically* succeeds the specified record. If no record succeeds the specified record, the successor link is set to zero. The *predecessor link* (or *backward pointer*) for a particular record gives the physical row number in the array of the record that logically precedes the specified record. If no record precedes the specified record, the predecessor link is set to zero. The number of the physical row in the array that contains the record that is logically first in the list is identified by a *head pointer*, which is set to zero when the list contains no records. The physical row number of the record that is logically last in the list is identified by a *tail pointer*, which is set to zero when the list is empty.

At any given time a list will probably occupy only a subset of the rows of the array in which it is physically stored. The "empty" rows of the array that are available for future use are linked together in a *list of available space* (LAS). The LAS is usually processed in a LIFO (last-in, first-out) manner: this means that when a row is needed to store an additional record, it is taken from the head of the LAS; and when a row is no longer needed to store a record, it is returned to the head of the LAS. Since all operations are done at the head of the LAS, it requires neither a tail pointer nor predecessor links. (We call such a list *singly linked*.) At time 0 in a simulation, all rows in the array are members of the LAS, the successor link of row i is set to $i + 1$ (except for that of the last row, which is set to 0), all predecessor links are set to 0, and the head of the LAS is set to 1. (The predecessor link for a particular row is set to a positive integer only when that row is occupied by a record.)

Example 2.1. For the queueing simulation of Sec. 1.4, consider the list containing the customers waiting in queue to be served. Each record in this list has the single attribute, "time of arrival." Suppose that at time 25 in the simulation there are three customers in queue, with times of arrival 10, 15, 25, and that these records are stored in (physical) rows 2, 3, and 1 of an array with 5 rows and 1 column. (To make the figures below manageable, we assume that there will never be more than five customers in queue at any time.) Rows 4 and 5 are members of the LAS. The situation is depicted in Fig. 2.1. Note that the head pointer of the list is equal to 2, the successor link for the record in row 2 is equal to 3, the predecessor link for the record in row 3 is equal to 2, etc.

Suppose that the next event in the simulation (after time 25) is the arrival of a customer at time 40 and that we would like to add an appropriate record to the list, which is to be processed in a FIFO manner. Since the head pointer for the LAS is equal to 4, the record for the arriving customer will be placed in physical row 4 of the array and the head pointer of the LAS is now set to 5, which is the value of the successor link for row 4. Since the new record will be added to the tail of the list and the tail pointer for the list is now equal to 1, the successor link for the record in row 1 is set to 4, the predecessor link for the new record, i.e., the one in (physical) row 4, is set to 1, the successor link for the new record is set to 0, and the tail pointer for the list is set to 4. The state of both lists after these changes have been made is shown in Fig. 2.2.

Suppose that the next event in the simulation (after time 40) is the service completion at time 50 of the customer who was being served (at least since time 25) and that we want to remove the record of the customer at the head of the list so that this customer can begin service. Since the head pointer for the list is equal to 2 and the successor link for the record in (physical) row 2 is equal to 3, the

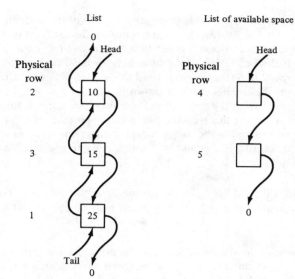

FIGURE 2.1
State of the lists for the queueing
simulation at time 25.

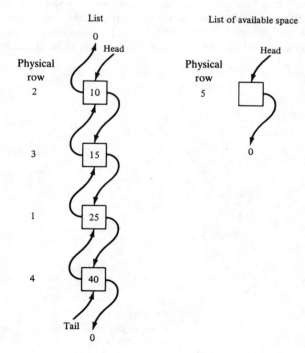

FIGURE 2.2
State of the lists for the queueing
simulation at time 40.

time of arrival of the record in row 2 is used to compute the delay of the customer who will enter service (this delay is 50–10), the head pointer for the list is set to 3, the predecessor link for the record in row 3 is set to 0, and row 2 (which is no longer needed) is placed at the head of the LAS by setting its head pointer to 2 and the successor link for row 2 to 5 (the previous head of the LAS). The state of both lists after these changes have been made is shown in Fig. 2.3.

Thus, removing a record from the head of the list always requires setting only four links or pointers. Contrast this with the brute-force approach of Chap. 1, which requires moving each record in the (sequential) list up by one location. If the list contained, say, 100 records, this would be a much more time-consuming task than with the linked-list approach.

While storing a queue as a linked list as in the above example seems fairly natural, the next example illustrates how the event list can also be processed as a linked list.

Example 2.2. For the inventory simulation of Sec. 1.5, the event list was stored in an array with each of the four event types having a dedicated physical location. If an event was not currently scheduled to occur, its entry in the list was set to ∞ (represented as 10^{30} in the computer). However, for many complex simulations written in a general-purpose language and for simulations using the special-purpose simulation languages described in Chap. 3, the event list is stored as a linked list ranked in increasing order on event time. Now, events having an event time of ∞ are simply not included in the event list. Moreover, since the event list is kept ranked in increasing order on the event times (attribute 1), the next event to occur will always be at the head of the list, so we need only remove this record to determine the next event time (attribute 1) and its type (attribute 2). For instance, suppose that the event list for the inventory simulation is to be stored in

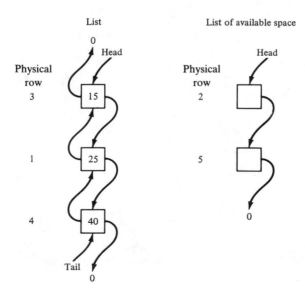

FIGURE 2.3
State of the lists for the queueing simulation at time 50.

an array of 4 rows and 2 columns, column 1 being for the attribute "event time" and column 2 being for the attribute "event type," i.e., 1, 2, 3, or 4. Suppose that at time 0 we know that the first demand for the product (event type 2) will occur at time 0.25, the first inventory evaluation (event type 4) will occur immediately at time 0, the simulation will end (event type 3) at time 120, and there is no outstanding order scheduled to arrive (event type 1). The state of the event list and the LAS just after initialization at time 0 is shown in Fig. 2.4. Note that event type 1 is not included in the event list, and that event type 2 is in (physical) row 1 of the array since it was the first event record to be placed in the event list.

To determine the next (first) event to occur at time 0, the first record is removed from the event list, the simulation clock is updated to the first attribute of this record, i.e., the clock is set to 0, the event type of the next event to occur is set to the second attribute of this record, i.e., is set to 4, and row 3, which contained this record, is placed at the head of the LAS. Since the next event type is 4, an inventory-evaluation event will occur next (at time 0). Suppose that an order is placed at time 0 and that it will arrive from the supplier at time 0.6. To place this order-arrival event in the event list, first 0.6 and 1 are placed in columns 1 and 2, respectively, of row 3 (the head of the LAS), and then this new record is added to the event list by logically proceeding down the event list (using the successor links) until the correct location is found. In particular, attribute 1 of the new record (0.6) is first compared with attribute 1 of the record in row 1 (0.25). Since $0.6 > 0.25$, the new record should be farther down the event list. Next, 0.6 is compared with attribute 1 of the record in row 2 (120). (Note that the successor link of the record in row 1 is equal to 2.) Since $0.6 < 120$, the new record is logically placed between the records in physical rows 1 and 2 by adjusting the

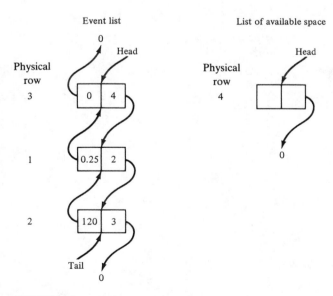

FIGURE 2.4
State of the lists for the inventory simulation just after initialization at time 0.

successor and predecessor links for the three records. After this has been done, another inventory-evaluation event is scheduled at time 1 and placed in the event list in a manner similar to that for the order-arrival event. The state of both lists after all processing has been done at time 0 is shown in Fig. 2.5.

In the above discussion, a single list was stored in an array where the empty rows were members of the LAS, but we could just as well store many different lists simultaneously in the same physical array. There is a single LAS, and the beginning and end of each list are identified by separate head and tail pointers. This approach can lead to significant savings in storage space for some applications. For example, suppose that a simulation requires 20 lists, each containing up to 100 records of 10 attributes each. Using the sequential storage method (as in Chap. 1), 20 arrays with 100 rows and 10 columns each would be required, for a total storage requirement of 20,000 locations. Suppose, however, that at any given time an average of only 25 percent of all available rows are actually being used. Then an alternative approach might be to store all 20 lists in one array consisting of 1000 rows and 10 columns. This approach would require 10,000 locations for the array plus an additional 2040 locations for the links and pointers, for a total of 12,040 storage locations.

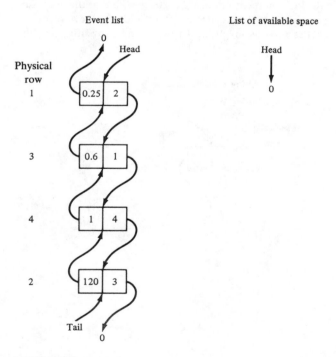

FIGURE 2.5
State of the lists for the inventory simulation after all processing has been done at time 0.

Furthermore, at a particular point in a simulation, some lists may be occupying more than their fair share of the available rows without causing an overflow condition.

The simple simulation language SIMLIB, developed in the next section, stores all lists (including the event list) in a single master array.

2.3 A SIMPLE SIMULATION LANGUAGE, SIMLIB

In this section we describe an easy-to-understand FORTRAN-based simulation "language," SIMLIB, which implements the concept of linked storage allocation presented in Sec. 2.2.2. The language makes it easy to file a record in a list (the record may be filed first in the list, last in the list, or so that the list is kept ranked in increasing or decreasing order on a specified attribute), to remove a record from a list (either the first record or the last record in the list may be removed), to process the event list, to compute discrete-time statistics on a variable of interest (e.g., the average delay in queue in a queueing system), to compute continuous-time statistics on a variable of interest (e.g., the time-average number of items in an inventory system), to generate the random variates used in the examples of Chap. 1, and to provide "standard" output if desired. Although SIMLIB provides many of the important features found in special-purpose simulation languages (see Chap. 3), it is designed for neither completeness nor computational efficiency. Our reasons for presenting it here are to provide some insight into the operation of simulation languages and, more important, to provide a vehicle for understanding how to simulate systems that are much more complicated than those in Chap. 1.

The heart of SIMLIB is the REAL storage array MASTER, which has 1000 rows and 10 columns. In this array one can store up to 1000 records, each with up to 10 attributes, in up to 25 different lists. However, list 25 is always reserved for the event list. Furthermore, attribute 1 for the event list is always the time that the event is to occur, and attribute 2 is always the event type. The user has at his or her disposal the following variables, which are contained in the COMMON block labeled SIMLIB (and in the following order):

LDECR	A mnemonic for the option of keeping a list ranked in decreasing order according to the attribute specified in the LRANK array for the list. (LDECR is simply an INTEGER variable set to the constant 4 in the SIMLIB initialization routine, INITLK; see the discussion of routine FILE below.)
LEVENT	A mnemonic for the number of the event list, 25, set to 25 in INITLK.
LFIRST	A mnemonic for the option of filing or removing a record at the beginning of a list, set to 1 in INITLK.
LINCR	A mnemonic for the option of keeping a list ranked in increasing order according to the attribute specified in the LRANK array, set to 3 in INITLK.
LLAST	A mnemonic for the option of filing or removing a record at the end of a list, set to 2 in INITLK.

LRANK(LIST) The attribute number, if any, according to which the records in list LIST are to be ranked (in increasing or decreasing order) by subroutine FILE. For example, if list 4 is to be kept so that the records are arranged in order according to attribute 2, then the statement LRANK(4) = 2 would have to be executed before using FILE to file a record in list 4; one of the arguments in subroutine FILE controls whether the order is increasing or decreasing. Typically, LRANK(LIST) is set by the user in the main program. If list LIST is not ranked (i.e., records are inserted only at the end or the beginning), then LRANK(LIST) need not be set at all. Note that LRANK(25) is set to 1 in the SIMLIB initialization routine INITLK, since attribute 1 of the event list (list 25) is always the event time, and we wish to keep the event list ranked in order of the event times.

LSIZE(LIST) The current number of records in list LIST, which is automatically updated by SIMLIB. The user should not need to alter the value of LSIZE(LIST), but only query its value if appropriate. For example, if list 3 has been set up to represent a queue, then LSIZE(3) will always be the number in this queue, so that we can tell if it is empty by asking if LSIZE(3) is equal to 0.

MAXATR The maximum number of attributes for any record in any list in the simulation model. If MAXATR is not set in the main program by the user, a default value of 10 is used; MAXATR cannot be more than 10. (Setting MAXATR to a value less than 10, if possible, will result in faster program execution.)

NEXT The type of the next event, determined by SIMLIB routine TIMING (see the discussion of routine TIMING below).

TIME The simulation clock, updated by SIMLIB routine TIMING (see the discussion of routine TIMING below).

TRNSFR A real array of length 10 used for transferring data into and out of the lists used in the simulation, where TRNSFR(I) refers to attribute I of a record. TRNSFR is also used by SIMLIB as a place to transfer to the user the values of certain summary statistics.

The variables and arrays in the COMMON block SIMLIB are used or set by the user during the simulation, and thus the statements

```
      INTEGER LDECR,LEVENT,LFIRST,LINCR,LLAST,LRANK(25),LSIZE(25),
     &        MAXATR,NEXT
      REAL TIME,TRNSFR(10)
      COMMON /SIMLIB/ LDECR,LEVENT,LFIRST,LINCR,LLAST,LRANK,LSIZE,
     &                MAXATR,NEXT,TIME,TRNSFR
```

must appear at the beginning of every user-written subroutine in which access to these SIMLIB variables is required. Note that these statements must appear *exactly* as above, since that is the way they appear in the SIMLIB routines; in particular, the order of the variables and arrays in the COMMON statement must be the same as above, and the arrays must be dimensioned the same size as shown. SIMLIB also uses another COMMON block, labeled LLISTS, for internal transfer of data that are not relevant to the user, such as the list pointers; for this reason, the user may not have a COMMON block labeled LLISTS.

In addition to the array MASTER and the variables in the COMMON block SIMLIB, there are some 15 subroutines and functions, each designed to perform a frequently occurring simulation activity:

INITLK. This subroutine, to be called from the main program by the user at the beginning of each simulation run, initializes the successor and predecessor links as well as the head and tail pointers for each list, sets the list mnemonics described above, initializes the simulation clock to 0, sets LRANK(25) to 1 to keep the event list ranked on event times, and sets MAXATR to a default value of 10. Also, the statistical accumulators for routines SAMPST and TIMEST (see their discussion below) are set to 0. Finally, INITLK defines the output unit number for SIMLIB error messages to be unit 6; this could be changed by the user simply by changing the statement IOUT = 6 at the bottom of INITLK to reflect the desired unit number.

FILE (OPTION, LIST). This subroutine places the attributes of a record that the user has placed in the TRNSFR array into list LIST in a location controlled by the INTEGER variable OPTION. That is, when FILE is called, TRNSFR(I) is placed in list LIST as the I*th* attribute of the new record, for I = 1, . . . , MAXATR. The following options are available:

OPTION	Action
1 (or LFIRST)	File the record in TRNSFR before the first record currently in list LIST.
2 (or LLAST)	File the record in TRNSFR after the last record currently in list LIST.
3 (or LINCR)	File the record in TRNSFR into list LIST so that the list is kept ranked in increasing order on attribute LRANK(LIST), which must have been given a value previously. [If two records have the same value of attribute LRANK(LIST), the rule is FIFO.]
4 (or LDECR)	File the record in TRNSFR into list LIST so that the list is kept ranked in decreasing order on attribute LRANK(LIST), which must have been given a value previously. [If two records have the same value of attribute LRANK(LIST), the rule is FIFO.]

Thus, CALL FILE(1, 3) would file TRNSFR(1), . . . , TRNSFR(MAXATR) into list 3, with this becoming the first record in the list; CALL FILE(LFIRST, 3) would do the same thing. If we want list 2 to be kept ranked in decreasing order according to attribute 4 of the records in that list, then we could execute CALL FILE(LDECR, 2), making sure that we had set LRANK(2) = 4 previously, probably in the main program. Finally, we could schedule an event into the event list by executing CALL FILE(LINCR, LEVENT) after setting (at least) TRNSFR(1) to the time of occurrence of this event, and TRNSFR(2) to the type of this event.

REMOVE (OPTION, LIST). A call to this subroutine removes a record from list LIST, and copies it (i.e., its attributes) into the TRNSFR array. The INTEGER variable OPTION determines which record is removed:

OPTION	Action
1 (or LFIRST)	Remove the first record from list LIST and place it in the TRNSFR array.
2 (or LLAST)	Remove the last record from list LIST and place it in the TRNSFR array.

After calling REMOVE, the elements of TRNSFR, now being equal to those in the record just removed, are typically used for some purpose in the simulation. For example, CALL REMOVE(2, 1) removes the last record in list 1 and places it in the TRNSFR array; CALL REMOVE(LLAST, 1) does the same thing.

TIMING. This subroutine, called by the user from the main program, accomplishes what the TIMING routines of Chap. 1 did, except now TIMING is an internal SIMLIB routine, and it uses the list structure of the event list exactly as described in Example 2.2. The type of the next event, NEXT (a SIMLIB variable in the common block SIMLIB), is determined, and the clock, TIME, is updated to the current time. Actually, TIMING simply calls RE-MOVE to remove the first record from list 25, the event list; since the event list is kept in increasing order on the event time, we know that this will be the next event to occur. Thus, attributes 1 through MAXATR of the first event record are placed in TRNSFR, and can be used if desired. In particular, it is sometimes advantageous to make use of attributes *other* than 1 and 2 in event records; see Secs. 2.6 and 2.7, as well as Prob. 2.3.

CANCEL (ETYPE). This routine cancels (removes) the first event in the event list with event type ETYPE (a REAL value), and places the attributes of the canceled event in the TRNSFR array. If the event list does not have an event of type ETYPE, no action is taken by CANCEL. Note that ETYPE must be REAL; thus, CALL CANCEL(2.0) would remove the first type 2 event (if any), while CALL CANCEL(2) would lead to an error on most computers.

SAMPST (VALUE, VARIBL). This subroutine accumulates and summarizes discrete-time data, such as customer delays in queue. There is provision for up to 20 different "SAMPST variables," maintained and summarized separately, and indexed by the INTEGER variable VARIBL. For example, a model could involve three separate queues, and SAMPST variables 1, 2, and 3 could be used to accumulate and summarize customer delays in each of these queues, separately. There are three different "typical" uses of SAMPST:

> *During the simulation*: Each time a new value of SAMPST variable VARIBL is observed (e.g., the end of a delay in queue), its value is placed in the REAL variable VALUE, and SAMPST is called. For instance, if we have defined SAMPST variable 2 to be the delays in queue 2 of a model, we could execute CALL SAMPST(DELAY2, 2) after

having placed the desired delay in the REAL variable DELAY2. SAMPST internally maintains separate registers for each variable, in which statistics are accumulated to produce the output described below.

At the end of the simulation: SAMPST can be called with the *negative* of the variable VARIBL desired, to produce summary statistics that are placed into the TRNSFR array as follows:

I	TRNSFR(I)
1	Mean (average) of the values of variable VARIBL observed
2	Number of values of variable VARIBL observed
3	Maximum value of variable VARIBL observed
4	Minimum value of variable VARIBL observed

For example, executing CALL SAMPST(0.0, −2) would place the summary statistics on SAMPST variable 2 in the TRNSFR array, as described above; the desired summary statistics would then typically be written out by the user, or perhaps used in some other way. Note that in this use of SAMPST, the value of VALUE is ignored. (A technicality: If no values for variable VARIBL were observed, the mean, maximum, and minimum are undefined. In this case, SAMPST returns the mean as 0, the maximum as -10^{30}, and the minimum as 10^{30}.)

To reset all SAMPST variable accumulators: The accumulators for all SAMPST variables are reinitialized to zero, as at the start of the simulation, by executing CALL SAMPST(0.0, 0); note that this was done in INITLK at time 0. This capability would be useful *during* a simulation if we wanted to start observing data only after the simulation had "warmed up" for some time, as described in Sec. 9.5.1; see also Prob. 2.7.

TIMEST (VALUE, VARIBL). This subroutine is similar to SAMPST, but operates instead on *continuous*-time data, such as the number-in-queue function; see Sec. 1.4.1. Again, the INTEGER variable VARIBL refers to one of up to 20 separate "TIMEST variables" on which data are accumulated and summarized when desired. For example, TIMEST variables 1, 2, and 3 could refer to the number of customers in queues 1, 2, and 3, respectively. As with SAMPST, there are three "typical" usages:

During the simulation: Each time TIMEST variable VARIBL attains a new value, we must execute CALL TIMEST(VALUE, VARIBL), where the REAL variable VALUE contains the *new* (i.e., *after* the change) value of TIMEST variable VARIBL. For example, if the length of queue 2 changes as a result of an arrival or departure to the (REAL) value Q2, we could execute CALL TIMEST(Q2, 2) to do the proper accumulation.

The accumulators for TIMEST are initialized in INITLK under the assumption that all continuous-time functions being tracked by TIMEST are initially zero; this can be overridden by executing CALL TIMEST (VALUE, VARIBL) just after the call to INITLK, where VALUE contains the desired (nonzero) initial value of TIMEST variable VARIBL. (This would be done for each desired TIMEST variable.)

At the end of the simulation: TIMEST can be called with the *negative* of the variable VARIBL desired, to produce summary statistics that are placed into the TRNSFR array as follows:

I	TRNSFR(I)
1	Time-average of the values of variable VARIBL observed, *updated to the time of this call*
2	Maximum value of variable VARIBL observed up to the time of this call
3	Minimum value of variable VARIBL observed up to the time of this call

For example, executing CALL TIMEST(0.0, −2) would place the summary statistics on TIMEST variable 2 in the TRNSFR array, as described above; the desired summary statistics might then be written out by the user.

To reset all TIMEST variable accumulators: The accumulators for all TIMEST variables are reinitialized to zero, as at the start of the simulation, by executing CALL TIMEST(0.0, 0); note that this assumes that all TIMEST variables should have the value 0, which can be overridden by immediately executing CALL TIMEST(VALUE, VARIBL) to initialize TIMEST variable VARIBL to the value VALUE.

FILEST(LIST). This routine, typically called only at the end of a simulation run, provides summary data on the number of records in list LIST, placing them into the TRNSFR array in a manner similar to TIMEST, as follows:

I	TRNSFR(I)
1	Time-average number of records in list LIST, *updated to the time of this call*
2	Maximum number of records in list LIST, up to the time of this call
3	Minimum number of records in list LIST, up to the time of this call

SIMLIB treats the number of records in a list as a continuous-time function whose value may rise or fall only at the times of events, so that it is sensible to speak of the time-average number of records in a list, etc. SIMLIB automatically tracks each list in this way, and can produce these statistics when FILEST is called. Who cares about the history of list lengths? This capability turns out to be quite convenient, since the number of records in a list often has some physical meaning. For example, a queue will usually be represented in a simulation by a list, and the number of records in that list is thus identical to the number of customers in the queue; hence, the time-average and maximum number of customers in the queue are simply the time average and maximum of the number of records in the list. Another example is a list being used to represent a server, where the list will have one record in it if the server is busy and will be empty if the server is idle; the server utilization is thus the time-average number of records in this list, since the only possibilities for its length are 0 and 1. In this way, we can often (but not always) avoid explicitly tracking a continuous-time function via TIMEST. However, TIMEST should probably be used instead of FILEST if the corresponding list is set up merely for convenience in statistics collection, especially when the function being tracked rises or falls by increments other than 1 (e.g., the inventory level in the model of Sec. 1.5), due to the overhead in filing and removing many dummy records. Moreover, TIMEST would have to be used instead of FILEST if the function being tracked can take on noninteger values. [Internally, SIMLIB treats the number of records in list LIST as TIMEST variable $20 + \text{LIST}$, so that there are actually 45 TIMEST variables, but only the first 20 are accessible to the user. FILEST then simply calls TIMEST with $\text{VARIBL} = -(20 + \text{LIST})$ to get statistics on list LIST.]

OUTSAM (UNIT, LOWVAR, HIVAR). If desired, this subroutine may be called to produce the summary statistics on SAMPST variables LOWVAR through HIVAR (inclusively) and write them to unit UNIT; all three arguments are INTEGER. This produces a "standard" output format (which fits within an 80-character line), and obviates the need for the *final* call to SAMPST (but *not* the calls during the course of the simulation) and also eliminates the need for WRITE statements, formatting, etc. The disadvantage of using OUTSAM is that the annotation and layout of the output cannot be controlled or customized. For example, CALL OUTSAM(6, 1, 3) would write summary statistics to unit 6 on SAMPST variables 1, 2, and 3; CALL OUTSAM(21, 4, 4) would write summary statistics to unit 21 on SAMPST variable 4. In the SIMLIB simulations later in this chapter, we show examples of using (and ignoring) the standard-output option.

OUTTIM (UNIT, LOWVAR, HIVAR). Similar to OUTSAM, this optional routine may be used to produce standard output on unit UNIT for TIMEST variables LOWVAR through HIVAR. All three arguments are INTEGER.

OUTFIL (UNIT, LOWFIL, HIFIL). This routine uses FILEST to produce summary statistics on the number of records in files LOWFIL through HIFIL, written out to unit UNIT; all three arguments are INTEGER.

EXPON (RMEAN, ISTRM). This is a function subprogram that returns in its name an observation from an exponential distribution with mean RMEAN, a REAL number. The INTEGER argument ISTRM is the user-specified "stream" number, discussed more fully in Sec. 7.1 and App. 7A. For now, we can think of the stream number as a separate, independent random-number generator (or list of random numbers) to be used for the purpose of generating the desired observations from the exponential distribution. It is generally a good idea to "dedicate" a random-number stream to a particular source of randomness in a simulation, such as stream 1 for interarrivals and stream 2 for service times, etc., to facilitate the use of *variance-reduction techniques* (see Chap. 11). These techniques can often provide a great improvement in the statistical precision of simulations. Furthermore, using dedicated streams can facilitate program verification (debugging). Except for the stream specification, this is the same routine used in Sec. 1.4.4 for generating observations from an exponential distribution. There are 100 separate streams available in SIMLIB; i.e., ISTRM must be an INTEGER between 1 and 100 inclusively, and the length of each stream is 100,000 random numbers.

IRANDI (NVALUE, PROBD, ISTRM). This function generates an INTEGER value between 1 and NVALUE (an INTEGER) inclusively, in accordance with the (cumulative) distribution function contained in the REAL array PROBD; the INTEGER variable or constant ISTRM specifies the random-number stream to be used. The REAL array PROBD must be dimensioned by the user to have at least NVALUE places, and must be filled with the desired *cumulative* distribution function; i.e., PROBD(I) should be the probability that the random variable is *less than or equal to* I, for $I = 1, 2, \ldots$, NVALUE. Except for the random-number stream specification, this is the same routine used for the inventory model in Sec. 1.5.3.

UNIFRM (A, B, ISTRM). This function returns in its name an observation from a (continuous) uniform distribution between A and B (REAL variables or constants, with $A < B$). As before, ISTRM is the stream choice.

RAND (ISTRM). This is the random-number generator used by SIMLIB, a function returning in its name a number uniformly distributed between 0 and 1, using stream ISTRM; its code is given in Fig. 7.5 of App. 7A, instead of in App. 2A.

This completes the description of SIMLIB, but before proceeding with concrete examples of its use, we conclude this section with an overview of how SIMLIB's components are used together in a simulation. It is still up to the user to write a FORTRAN main program and event routines, but the SIMLIB routines will make the coding much easier. First, we must determine the events and decide what lists will be used for what purpose; the numbering of lists and their attributes is in large measure arbitrary, but it is essential to be consistent. Also, any SAMPST and TIMEST variables to be used must be defined. The COMMON block SIMLIB must be placed in every routine in which access to SIMLIB is desired, usually meaning every routine as well as the main program. There will also probably be a user-defined COMMON block MODEL (say) needed to pass things such as input parameters between the routines. In the main program, the following activities take place, roughly in the order listed:

1. Read and echo-print the input parameters.
2. Call INITLK to initialize the SIMLIB variables.
3. (If necessary) Set LRANK(LIST) to the attribute number on which list LIST is to be ranked, for all lists that need to be kept in some sort of order according to the value of a particular attribute. (If no lists other than the event list are to be ranked, then this step is skipped.)
4. Set MAXATR to the maximum number of attributes used in any list. Note that MAXATR must be at least 2, since the records in the event list have at least two attributes. If this is skipped, MAXATR defaults to 10 and the simulation will run correctly, but setting MAXATR to a smaller value will make the simulation faster, since it avoids repeated copying of unused attributes into and out of the lists.
5. (If necessary) Call TIMEST to initialize any TIMEST variables that are not to be zero initially.
6. Initialize the event list by setting TRNSFR(1) and TRNSFR(2) (at least), and then executing CALL FILE(LINCR, LEVENT) for each event to be scheduled at time 0. Events that cannot occur are simply not placed in the event list.
7. Call TIMING to determine NEXT, the type of the next event to occur.
8. Transfer control to the appropriate event routine (user-written, but using SIMLIB variables and routines where possible), as determined by NEXT; this is typically done by a computed GO TO statement, routing control to one of several CALL statements to the event routines, as was done in Chap. 1.
9. When the simulation ends, call a report generator (user-written), which in turn will call SAMPST, TIMEST, or FILEST and then write out the desired summary statistics. Alternatively, the report generator could call OUTSAM, OUTTIM, or OUTFIL to write out the summary statistics in standard format.

While the simulation is running, lists are maintained by using FILE and REMOVE, together with the TRNSFR array to transfer the data in the attributes of records into and out of lists. SAMPST and TIMEST are used when needed to gather statistics on variables of interest.

A final note on SIMLIB's capabilities concerns error checking. While no software package can detect all errors and suggest how to fix them, there are special opportunities to do some of this in simulation programs, as discussed in Chap. 1. SIMLIB contains several such error checks, and will write out a message (to unit 6, unless the variable IOUT is changed in SIMLIB routine INITLK) indicating the nature of the error and the clock value when it occurred. For example, SIMLIB routine TIMING checks for a "time reversal," i.e., an attempt to schedule an event at a time earlier than the present. Also, there are checks for illegal list numbers, illegal variable numbers, etc., as well as checks for overflowing the list structure (which could happen if the *total* number of records in all of the lists exceeds 1000 at some point), and for attempting to remove a record from a list that is empty.

In Secs. 2.4 through 2.7 we show how to use SIMLIB to simulate systems of varying complexity.

2.4 SINGLE-SERVER QUEUEING SIMULATION WITH SIMLIB

2.4.1 Problem Statement

In this section we show how to simulate the single-server queueing system from Sec. 1.4 using SIMLIB. The model is exactly the same, so that we can concentrate on the use of SIMLIB without having to worry about the structure of a new model. We will use the 1000-delay stopping rule, as originally described in Sec. 1.4.3.

2.4.2 SIMLIB Program

The first step is to identify the events; they are the same as before—an arrival is a type 1 event and a departure (service completion) is a type 2 event. Next, we must define the SIMLIB lists and the attributes in their records. It is important to write this down, as it will be referenced while developing the program:

List	Attribute 1	Attribute 2
1, queue	Time of arrival to queue	—
2, server	—	—
25, event list	Event time	Event type

Note that list 1 (representing the queue) is quite similar to the array TARRVL used in Sec. 1.4.4, except that we are now taking advantage of SIMLIB's list-processing capabilities; list 1 has only a single attribute. List 2 represents the server, and will either be empty (if the server is idle) or will contain a single record (if the server is busy); a record in list 2 when the server is busy is a "dummy" record, in that it has no actual attributes. The purpose for defining such a list is to allow the use of FILEST at the end of the simulation to get the server utilization. Also, we can tell whether the server is busy by asking whether LSIZE(2) is equal to 1. This usage of a dummy list is convenient in that the SERVER status variable is eliminated, and we need not use TIMEST during and at the end of the simulation to get the utilization; however, it is not the most computationally efficient approach, since all the machinery of the linked lists is invoked whenever the server changes status, rather than simply altering the value of a SERVER status variable. (This is a good example of the trade-off between computation time and analyst's time in coding a model.) Finally, list 25 is the event list, with attribute 1 being event time and attribute 2 being event type; this is required in all SIMLIB programs, but for some models we could use additional attributes for the event records in list 25.

Next, we should identify all SAMPST and TIMEST variables used. Our only SAMPST variable is as follows:

SAMPST variable number	Meaning
1	Delays in queue

Since we can obtain both the number-in-queue and utilization statistics using FILEST (or OUTFIL if standard output is acceptable), we do not need any TIMEST variables for this model. Finally, we allocate separate random-number streams for generating the interarrival and service times, as follows:

Stream	Purpose
1	Interarrival times
2	Service times

The subprograms and variables are given in Table 2.1. Note that we need neither a timing routine nor the EXPON function, since these capabilities are in SIMLIB. Also, there are far fewer variables needed, since SIMLIB maintains most of the data internally. We do not need any of our own output variables, since the standard output report feature will be used in REPORT to write the desired performance measures directly.

Figure 2.6 shows the main program, which must still be written by the user. The declarations file mm1smlb.dcl, shown in Fig. 2.7, is brought in first

TABLE 2.1
Subprograms and FORTRAN variables for the queueing model with SIMLIB

Subprogram	Purpose
INIT	Initialization routine
ARRIVE	Processes type 1 events
DEPART	Processes type 2 events
REPORT	Generates report when simulation ends

Variable	Definition
Input parameters:	
MARRVT	Mean interarrival time (=1.0 here)
MSERVT	Mean service time (=0.5)
TOTCUS	Total number, n, of customer delays to be observed (=1000)
Modeling variables:	
DELAY	Delay in queue of a customer
NUMCUS	Number of customers who have completed their delays so far
QUEUE	Number of the list for the queue (=1)
SERVER	Number of the list for the server (=2)

```
*       Main program for single-server queueing system using SIMLIB.

*       Bring in declarations file.

        INCLUDE 'mm1smlb.dcl'

*       Open input and output files.

        OPEN (5, FILE = 'mm1smlb.in')
        OPEN (6, FILE = 'mm1smlb.out')

*       Read input parameters.

        READ (5,*) MARRVT, MSERVT, TOTCUS

*       Write report heading and input parameters.

        WRITE (6,2010) MARRVT, MSERVT, TOTCUS
 2010   FORMAT (' Single-server queueing system using SIMLIB'//
       &        ' Mean interarrival time',F11.3,' minutes'//
       &        ' Mean service time',F16.3,' minutes'//
       &        ' Number of customers',I14//)

*       Initialize SIMLIB.

        CALL INITLK

*       Set the maximum number of attributes per record.

        MAXATR = 2

*       Define the list numbers for the queue and the server.

        QUEUE  = 1
        SERVER = 2

*       Initialize the simulation model.

        CALL INIT

*       Determine the next event.

     10 CALL TIMING

*       Call the appropriate event routine.

        GO TO (20, 30), NEXT
     20     CALL ARRIVE
           GO TO 40
     30     CALL DEPART

*       If the simulation is over, call the report generator and end the
*       simulation. If not, continue the simulation.

     40 IF (NUMCUS .LT. TOTCUS) GO TO 10
        CALL REPORT

        CLOSE (5)
        CLOSE (6)

        STOP
        END
```

FIGURE 2.6
FORTRAN code for the main program, queueing model with SIMLIB.

```
      INTEGER NUMCUS,QUEUE,SERVER,TOTCUS
      REAL MARRVT,MSERVT
      REAL EXPON
      COMMON /MODEL/ MARRVT,MSERVT,NUMCUS,QUEUE,SERVER,TOTCUS

      INTEGER LDECR,LEVENT,LFIRST,LINCR,LLAST,LRANK(25),LSIZE(25),
     &        MAXATR,NEXT
      REAL TIME,TRNSFR(10)
      COMMON /SIMLIB/ LDECR,LEVENT,LFIRST,LINCR,LLAST,LRANK,LSIZE,
     &                MAXATR,NEXT,TIME,TRNSFR
```

FIGURE 2.7
FORTRAN code for the declarations file (mm1smlb.dcl), queueing model with SIMLIB.

via the INCLUDE statement. Note that the declarations file now contains the COMMON block SIMLIB, exactly as given in Sec. 2.3, as well as the INTEGER, REAL, and MODEL common statements; COMMON block MODEL contains only the user-defined (non-SIMLIB) variables needed, which are now far fewer in number. The main program then opens the input and output files, and reads and echo-prints the input parameters. SIMLIB is initialized with the call to INITLK, after which the maximum number of attributes is set to 2, corresponding to an event record (which has the largest number of attributes per record). We are not using any ranked lists (other than the event list), so we do not need to set anything in the LRANK array; also, both of the continuous-time functions (queue length and server status) are initially zero, so we need not override their default values. The variables QUEUE and SERVER are set to the correct list numbers; using these mnemonics is not necessary, but it makes the code more readable (and general) than using the list numbers themselves when referring to the lists. The user-written initialization routine INIT is then called, and the rest of the main program is similar to Fig. 1.10 for the non-SIMLIB version of this model, except that we need not update continuous-time statistical accumulators since SIMLIB takes care of that internally.

INIT is shown in Fig. 2.8, and begins by setting the NUMCUS counter to zero for the number of delays observed. Next, the first arrival event is

```
      SUBROUTINE INIT
      INCLUDE 'mm1smlb.dcl'

*     Initialize the non-SIMLIB statistical counter.

      NUMCUS = 0

*     Initialize event list. Since no customers are present, the
*     departure (service completion) event is not scheduled.

      TRNSFR(1) = TIME + EXPON(MARRVT,1)
      TRNSFR(2) = 1.0
      CALL FILE(LINCR,LEVENT)

      RETURN
      END
```

FIGURE 2.8
FORTRAN code for subroutine INIT, queueing model with SIMLIB.

scheduled by filling the TRNSFR array's first location with the event time (generated from SIMLIB routine EXPON, using random-number stream 1 for interarrival times), and the second location with the event type (1). This event record is then filed in the event list (list number LEVENT = 25), and in increasing order according to the first attribute (OPTION = LINCR = 3); recall that LRANK(25) is set to attribute 1 in the SIMLIB initialization routine INITLK. In Chap. 1 we had to set the time of "impossible" events to infinity (actually, 10^{30}), but now we simply leave them out of the event list, ensuring that they cannot happen next. Thus, we just do not schedule a departure event at all here.

Figure 2.9 shows the code for event routine ARRIVE, which begins as usual by bringing in the declarations file. The first action is to schedule the next

```
        SUBROUTINE ARRIVE
        INCLUDE 'mm1smlb.dcl'

*       Schedule next arrival.

        TRNSFR(1) = TIME + EXPON(MARRVT,1)
        TRNSFR(2) = 1.0
        CALL FILE(LINCR,LEVENT)

*       Check to see whether server is busy (i.e., list SERVER contains a
*       record).

        IF (LSIZE(SERVER) .EQ. 1) THEN

*           Server is busy, so store time of arrival of arriving customer
*           at end of list QUEUE.

            TRNSFR(1) = TIME
            CALL FILE(LLAST,QUEUE)

        ELSE

*           Server is idle, so start service on arriving customer, who has
*           a delay of zero. (The following statement IS necessary here.)

            CALL SAMPST(0.0,1)

*           Increment the number of customers delayed.

            NUMCUS = NUMCUS + 1

*           Make server busy by filing a dummy record in list SERVER.

            CALL FILE(LFIRST,SERVER)

*           Schedule a departure (service completion).

            TRNSFR(1) = TIME + EXPON(MSERVT,2)
            TRNSFR(2) = 2.0
            CALL FILE(LINCR,LEVENT)

        END IF

        RETURN
        END
```

FIGURE 2.9
FORTRAN code for subroutine ARRIVE, queueing model with SIMLIB.

arrival, in a manner similar to that in INIT. We then check to see whether the server is busy, by asking whether the server list (list SERVER = 2) contains a (dummy) record; this is done by checking whether the SIMLIB variable LSIZE(SERVER) is equal to 1. If so, the arriving customer must join the queue, which is done by placing the time of arrival (now) into the first location of the TRNSFR array, and by filing this record at the end (OPTION = LLAST = 2) of the queue list (LIST = QUEUE = 1). Note that we do not have an explicit check for overflow of the queue here; an overflow *could* occur in a SIMLIB list, but SIMLIB checks for this automatically and would write out an error message to this effect and stop the simulation. On the other hand, if the server is idle, the customer experiences a delay of zero, which is noted by the call to SAMPST; this call *is* necessary even though the delay is zero, since SAMPST will also increment the number of observations by one. NUMCUS is incremented since a delay is being observed, and a departure event is scheduled into the event list; note that we are dedicating stream 2 here to service times.

Event routine DEPART, in Fig. 2.10, checks whether the queue is empty, by looking at the length of the queue list, held by SIMLIB in LSIZE(QUEUE). If so, the server is made idle by removing the (dummy)

```
      SUBROUTINE DEPART
      INCLUDE 'mm1smlb.dcl'
      REAL DELAY

*     Check to see whether the queue is empty.

      IF(LSIZE(QUEUE) .EQ. 0) THEN

*         The queue is empty, so make the server idle and leave the
*         departure (service completion) event out of the event list. (It
*         is currently not in the event list, having just been removed by
*         TIMING before coming here.)

          CALL REMOVE(LFIRST,SERVER)

      ELSE

*         The queue is nonempty, so remove the first customer from the
*         queue, compute and register delay, increment the number of
*         customers delayed, and schedule departure.

          CALL REMOVE(LFIRST,QUEUE)
          DELAY = TIME - TRNSFR(1)
          CALL SAMPST(DELAY,1)
          NUMCUS = NUMCUS + 1
          TRNSFR(1) = TIME + EXPON(MSERVT,2)
          TRNSFR(2) = 2.0
          CALL FILE(LINCR,LEVENT)

      END IF

      RETURN
      END
```

FIGURE 2.10
FORTRAN code for subroutine DEPART, queueing model with SIMLIB.

```
        SUBROUTINE REPORT
        INCLUDE 'mm1smlb.dcl'

*       Get and write out estimates of desired measures of performance.

        WRITE (6,2010)
 2010   FORMAT (/' Delays in queue, in minutes:')
        CALL OUTSAM(6,1,1)
        WRITE (6,2020)
 2020   FORMAT (///' Queue length (1) and server utilization (2):')
        CALL OUTFIL(6,1,2)
        WRITE (6,2030) TIME
 2030   FORMAT (///' Time simulation ended:',F12.3,' minutes')

        RETURN
        END
```

FIGURE 2.11
FORTRAN code for subroutine REPORT, queueing model with SIMLIB.

record from the SERVER list, the only action needed; note that we are removing the first record in the list, but we could also have removed the last one since there is only one record there. On the other hand, if there is a queue, the first customer is removed from it, and that customer's time of arrival is placed in TRNSFR(1) by REMOVE. The delay is computed and tallied in SAMPST, and the number of delays observed is incremented; as in the examples in Chap. 1, if the simulation were to be run for a long amount of simulated time, it might be necessary to make both TIME and the TRNSFR array DOUBLE PRECISION to avoid loss of precision in the subtraction to compute DELAY. Finally, the service completion of this customer is scheduled by filing the appropriate event record in the event list. Note that we need no longer move the queue up, since this is done internally by SIMLIB, using linked storage allocation as discussed in Example 2.1.

The report generator is shown in Fig. 2.11, and uses the standard output generators OUTSAM for the delay-in-queue measure and OUTFIL for the number-in-queue and utilization measures. Note that we write out brief headers before calling the standard output generators to make the report a little more readable.

2.4.3 Simulation Output and Discussion

The output file (mm1smlb.out) is given in Fig. 2.12 and shows the format of the standard output. Note that scientific notation is used for the data to avoid the possibility of overflowing the field widths. We get all aspects of the output measures, i.e., average, maximum, and minimum for all measures, as well as the count for the discrete-time variables used by SAMPST. We also write out the final clock value, as a check.

An important point to note is that these results are *not* the same as those in Fig. 1.37 for the non-SIMLIB version of this same model; in fact, they are quite a bit different, with the average delay in queue changing from 0.430 in

```
Single-server queueing system using SIMLIB

Mean interarrival time        1.000 minutes

Mean service time             0.500 minutes

Number of customers           1000
```

```
Delays in queue, in minutes:
```

SAMPST Variable Number	Average	Number of Values	Maximum	Minimum
1	0.5248728E+00	0.1000000E+04	0.5633087E+01	0.0000000E+00

```
Queue length (1) and server utilization (2):
```

File Number	Time Average	Maximum	Minimum
1	0.5400774E+00	0.8000000E+01	0.0000000E+00
2	0.5106926E+00	0.1000000E+01	0.0000000E+00

```
Time simulation ended:     971.847 minutes
```

FIGURE 2.12
Output report, queueing model with SIMLIB.

Chap. 1 to 0.525 here, a difference of some 22 percent. The reason for this is that we are now using the concept of "dedicating" a random-number stream to a particular source of randomness, while in Chap. 1 we used the same random-number stream (number 1) for everything. Both programs are correct, and this graphically illustrates the need for careful statistical analysis of simulation output data, as discussed in Chaps. 9 through 12.

While using SIMLIB did simplify the coding of this model considerably, the value of such a package becomes more apparent in complex models with richer list structures. Such models are considered next, in Secs. 2.5 through 2.7.

2.5 TIME-SHARED COMPUTER MODEL

In this section we use SIMLIB to simulate a model of a time-shared computer facility considered by Adiri and Avi-Itzhak (1969).

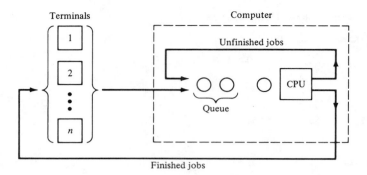

FIGURE 2.13
Time-shared computer model.

2.5.1 Problem Statement

A company has a computer system consisting of a single central processing unit (CPU) and n terminals, as shown in Fig. 2.13. The operator of each terminal "thinks" for an amount of time that is an exponential random variable with mean 25 seconds and then sends a job to the CPU with a service time distributed exponentially with mean 0.8 second. Arriving jobs join a single queue in front of the CPU but are served in a *round-robin* rather than FIFO manner. That is, the CPU allocates to each job a maximum service *quantum* of length $q = 0.1$ second. If the (remaining) service time of a job, s, is no more than q, the CPU spends s seconds, plus a fixed "swap" time of $\tau = 0.015$ second, processing the job, which then returns to its terminal. If $s > q$, the CPU spends $q + \tau$ seconds processing the job, which then joins the end of the queue, and its remaining service time is decremented by q seconds. This process is repeated until the job's service is eventually completed, at which point it returns to its terminal, whose operator begins another think time.

Let R_i be the *response time* of the ith job to finish service, which is defined as the time elapsing between the instant the job leaves its terminal and the instant it is finished being processed at the CPU. For each of the cases $n = 10, 20, \ldots, 80$, we use SIMLIB to simulate the computer system for 1000 job completions and estimate the expected average response time of these jobs, the expected time-average number of jobs waiting in queue, and the expected utilization of the CPU. Assume that all terminals are in the think state at time 0. The company would like to know how many terminals it can have on its system and still provide users with an average response time of no more than 30 seconds.

2.5.2 SIMLIB Program

The events for this model are:

Event description	Event type
Arrival of a job to the CPU from a terminal, at the end of a think time	1
End of a CPU run, when a job either completes its service requirement or has received the maximum processing quantum q	2
End of the simulation	3

Note that we have defined an "end-simulation" event, even though the stopping rule for this model is not a fixed point in simulated time. The end-simulation event is scheduled at the time the 1000th response time is observed, and is scheduled to occur immediately, i.e., at that time. Clearly, there are other ways in which this stopping rule could be implemented, as discussed below.

An event graph (see Sec. 1.4.9) for this model is shown in Fig. 2.14. The n separate initializations of the arrival (i.e., end-think-time) event refer to the fact that each of the n terminals will be initially scheduled to have such an event. Note also that the arrival and end-CPU-run events can potentially schedule each other; an arrival can schedule the end of a CPU run if the arriving job finds the CPU idle, and an end-CPU-run event can schedule an arrival if the job exiting the CPU is finished and returns to its terminal. Also, an end-CPU-run event can schedule itself in the case of a job's leaving the CPU before its total processing is finished. Finally, note that the end-simulation event can only be scheduled from the end-CPU-run event in zero time, in the case that a finished job leaves the CPU and supplies the last (1000th) response time required; as discussed in Sec. 1.4.9, an event having incoming arcs that are all thin and smooth (representing a scheduling of the event in zero time from the event from which the thin smooth arrow emanates) can be eliminated from the model and its action incorporated elsewhere. Problem 2.2 deals with this issue for this model.

Three lists of records will be used, one corresponding to the jobs in queue (list 1), one for the job being served by the CPU (list 2), and one for the event list (list 25, as usual). These lists have the following attributes:

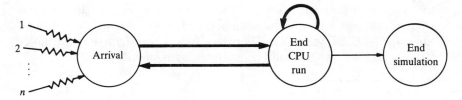

FIGURE 2.14
Event graph, computer model.

List	Attribute 1	Attribute 2
1, queue	Time of arrival of job to computer	Remaining service time
2, CPU	Time of arrival of job to computer	Remaining service time
25, event list	Event time	Event type

As in Sec. 2.4, we are using a list to represent a server (list 2 for the CPU), thereby facilitating estimation of the CPU utilization via FILEST at the end of the simulation. Here, however, this "server" list's attributes are *not* dummies; they carry necessary information about the job, since it may have to revisit the CPU several times, and its time of arrival and remaining service time must be carried along for it to be processed correctly. Note also that we have "matched up" the attributes in lists 1 and 2, so that transferring a record between these lists can be done simply by calls to REMOVE and FILE without having to rearrange the attributes in the TRNSFR array. Finally, we are not explicitly keeping track of the terminal of origin for a job, so that when its processing is complete in the computer we do not know what terminal to send it back to in order for its next think time to begin. This would certainly not do in reality, since the terminal operators would be getting each others' output back, but in the *simulation* we need not represent the ownership of each job by a particular terminal since we want only overall (i.e., over all terminals) performance measures for the response times. Furthermore, all the terminals are probabilistically identical, as the think-time and CPU-time distributions are the same. Problem 2.3 asks that the model be enriched by collecting separate response-time statistics for each terminal, and allowing the terminal characteristics to vary; any of these changes would require that the terminal of origin of a job be carried along with it while it is inside the computer.

Since there is only a single discrete-time statistic of interest (the response times), we need only a single SAMPST variable:

SAMPST variable number	Meaning
1	Response times

For each of the continuous-time statistics desired (number in queue and CPU utilization) there is a corresponding list whose length represents the desired quantity, so we can again obtain the output via FILEST, and we do not need any of our own TIMEST variables. There are two types of random variables for this model, and we use the following stream assignments:

Stream	Purpose
1	Think times
2	Service times

Table 2.2 contains the subprograms (in addition to the main program) and the variables used. Note that there is not a separate initialization routine, since there is little required to initialize this model (beyond what SIMLIB does in INITLK), so this activity was simply built into the main program. Also, we have written a nonevent subroutine, START, to process a particular activity that may occur when either a type 1 or a type 2 event occurs; thus, the same block of code need not be repeated. As in Sec. 2.4, we use mnemonic variables for the queue and CPU lists. For this model, we chose not to use the standard output option, since we are really doing eight separate simulations and would like to arrange the data in a customized table, with one line per simulation. Also, we wish to get only the mean of the output performance measures rather than all of the characteristics (maximum, etc.).

The main program is shown in Fig. 2.15. As usual, the declarations file (tscomp.dcl, listed in Fig. 2.16) is brought in first, the input and output files are opened, and the input parameters are read and echo-printed; the FORMAT statement also supplies a heading for the custom output table. After setting the

TABLE 2.2
Subprograms and FORTRAN variables for computer model

Subprogram	Purpose
ARRIVE	Processes type 1 events
START	Removes a job from the queue and places it in the CPU to start service (*not* an event routine)
ENDRUN	Processes type 2 events
REPORT	Generates report (called when the simulation ends)

Variable	Definition
Input parameters:	
INCREM	Increment in number of terminals (=10 here)
MAXTER	Maximum number of terminals (=80)
MINTER	Minimum number of terminals (=10)
MSERVT	Mean service time (=0.8 second)
MTHINK	Mean think time (=25 seconds)
QUANTM	Quantum (=0.1 second)
SWAP	Swap time (=0.015 second)
TOTJOB	Total number of response times to be observed (=1000)
Modeling variables:	
CPU	Number of the list for the CPU (=2)
NTERML	Number of terminals for the current simulation
NUMJOB	Number of response times observed so far
QUEUE	Number of the list for the queue (=1)
RESPTM	Response time of a job
RUNTIM	Amount of time to process a job during a single particular pass through the CPU
Output variables:	
AVGNIQ	Average number in queue
ARESPT	Average response time
UTIL	Utilization of the CPU

```
*      Main program for time-shared computer model.
*      Bring in declarations file.
       INCLUDE 'tscomp.dcl'
*      Open input and output files.
       OPEN (5, FILE = 'tscomp.in')
       OPEN (6, FILE = 'tscomp.out')
*      Read input parameters.
       READ (5,*) MINTER, MAXTER, INCREM, TOTJOB, MTHINK, MSERVT, QUANTM,
     &            SWAP
*      Write report heading and input parameters.
       WRITE (6,2010) MINTER, MAXTER, INCREM, MTHINK, MSERVT, QUANTM,
     &                SWAP, TOTJOB
 2010  FORMAT (' Time-shared computer model'//
     &          ' Number of terminals',I9,' to',I4,' by',I4//
     &          ' Mean think time',F13.3,' seconds'//
     &          ' Mean service time',F11.3,' seconds'//
     &          ' Quantum',F21.3,' seconds'//
     &          ' Swap time',F19.3,' seconds'//
     &          ' Number of jobs processed',I12///
     &          ' Number of',6X,'Average',9X,'Average',7X,'Utilization'/
     &          ' terminals   response time  number in queue     of CPU')
*      Define the list numbers for the queue and CPU.
       QUEUE  = 1
       CPU    = 2
*      Run the simulation varying the number of terminals.
       DO 60 NTERML = MINTER, MAXTER, INCREM
*          Initialize SIMLIB.
           CALL INITLK
*          Set the maximum number of attributes per record.
           MAXATR = 2
*          Initialize the non-SIMLIB statistical counter.
           NUMJOB = 0
*          Schedule the first arrival to the CPU from each terminal.
           DO 10 TERMNL  = 1, NTERML
               TRNSFR(1)  = EXPON(MTHINK,1)
               TRNSFR(2)  = 1.0
               CALL FILE(LINCR,LEVENT)
 10        CONTINUE
*          Determine the next event.
 20        CALL TIMING
*          Call the appropriate event routine.
           GO TO (30, 40, 50), NEXT
 30            CALL ARRIVE
               GO TO 20
 40            CALL ENDRUN
               GO TO 20
 50            CALL REPORT
 60    CONTINUE
       CLOSE (5)
       CLOSE (6)
       STOP
       END
```

FIGURE 2.15
FORTRAN code for the main program, computer model.

```
INTEGER CPU,INCREM,MAXTER,MINTER,NTERML,NUMJOB,QUEUE,TERMNL,TOTJOB
REAL MSERVT,MTHINK,QUANTM,SWAP
REAL EXPON
COMMON /MODEL/ CPU,MSERVT,MTHINK,NTERML,NUMJOB,QUANTM,QUEUE,SWAP,
&              TOTJOB

INTEGER LDECR,LEVENT,LFIRST,LINCR,LLAST,LRANK(25),LSIZE(25),
&        MAXATR,NEXT
REAL TIME,TRNSFR(10)
COMMON /SIMLIB/ LDECR,LEVENT,LFIRST,LINCR,LLAST,LRANK,LSIZE,
&               MAXATR,NEXT,TIME,TRNSFR
```

FIGURE 2.16
FORTRAN code for the declarations file (tscomp.dcl), computer model.

mnemonic values for the queue and CPU lists, a DO loop (with foot at statement 60) sets the number of terminals (NTERML) to each of the desired values, beginning with MINTER and stopping with MAXTER; the third variable in the DO statement, INCREM, is the amount by which the DO index NTERML is incremented, which we specify here rather than taking the default value of 1. Within loop 60, then, an entire simulation is run, including initialization and result-writing. The first step in doing this is to initialize SIMLIB by calling INITLK, after which the maximum number of attributes is set to two. The number of jobs whose response times have been observed is then set to zero. Loop 10 generates end-think-time (i.e., arrival) events for each terminal and files them in the event list; note that we will then have NTERML events, all of type 1, in the event list together, each one representing a particular terminal. The rest of the main program then executes the simulation by calling TIMING and passing control to the appropriate event routine, in the usual fashion. Note that the end-simulation event (type 3) is not scheduled initially, but will be scheduled in ENDRUN at the time of the 1000th response-time completion, to occur at that time, whereupon the main program will transfer control to the report generator to end the current simulation.

The arrival event is flowcharted in Fig. 2.17 and the code is in Fig. 2.18. While in the computer (i.e., in the queue or in the CPU), each job has its own record with attributes as described earlier. Since this event represents a job's arrival to the computer at the end of a think time, its attributes must be defined now, so the time of arrival is stored in the first attribute and the total service requirement is generated and stored in the second attribute. The record for this newly arrived job is then placed at the end of the queue. It could be, however, that the CPU is actually idle [i.e., the number of records in list CPU, LSIZE(CPU), is equal to zero], in which case START is called to take this job out of the queue (it would be the only one there) and place it in the CPU to begin its processing. Implicit in the logic of this routine is that a job arriving to the computer and finding the CPU idle cannot just go right in, but must first enter the queue and then be removed immediately; this is really a physical assumption that does matter, since there is a swap time incurred whenever a

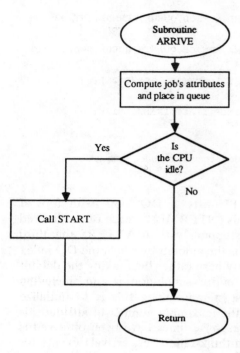

FIGURE 2.17
Flowchart for arrival routine, computer model.

job leaves the queue and enters the CPU, as executed by subroutine START to be discussed next.

The *nonevent* subroutine START is flowcharted in Fig. 2.19 and its code is in Fig. 2.20. This routine is designed to be called from ARRIVE, as just discussed, or from ENDRUN; thus, it must be general enough to handle either case. The purpose of the routine is to take the first job out of the queue, place

```
        SUBROUTINE ARRIVE
        INCLUDE 'tscomp.dcl'

*       Place the arriving job at the end of the queue.
*       Note that the following attributes are stored for each job record
*           1. Time of arrival to the computer.
*           2. The (remaining) CPU service time required (here equal to
*              the total service time since the job is just arriving).

        TRNSFR(1) = TIME
        TRNSFR(2) = EXPON(MSERVT,2)
        CALL FILE(LLAST,QUEUE)

*       If the CPU is idle, start a CPU run.

        IF (LSIZE(CPU) .EQ. 0) CALL START

        RETURN
        END
```

FIGURE 2.18
FORTRAN code for subroutine ARRIVE, computer model.

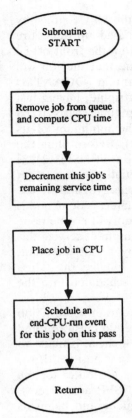

FIGURE 2.19
Flowchart for subroutine START, computer model.

```
      SUBROUTINE START
      INCLUDE 'tscomp.dcl'
      REAL RUNTIM

*     Remove the first job from the queue.
      CALL REMOVE(LFIRST,QUEUE)

*     Determine CPU time for this pass, including swap time. (MIN is a
*     FORTRAN function returning the minimum of its arguments.)
      RUNTIM = MIN(QUANTM,TRNSFR(2)) + SWAP

*     Decrement remaining CPU time by a full quantum. (If less than a
*     full quantum is needed, this attribute becomes negative. This
*     indicates that the job, after exiting the CPU for the current
*     pass, will be done and is to be sent back to its terminal.)
      TRNSFR(2) = TRNSFR(2) - QUANTM

*     Place job into the CPU.
      CALL FILE(LFIRST,CPU)

*     Schedule the end of the CPU run.
      TRNSFR(1) = TIME + RUNTIM
      TRNSFR(2) = 2.0
      CALL FILE(LINCR,LEVENT)

      RETURN
      END
```

FIGURE 2.20
FORTRAN code for subroutine START, computer model.

it in the CPU, and schedule the time when it will leave the CPU, either by virtue of being completely done or by virtue of having used up an entire quantum. The first thing to do is thus to remove the job from the front of the queue, which is done by calling REMOVE. Next, the time that the job will occupy the CPU is computed, being the smaller of a quantum (QUANTM) and the remaining service time [held in the job's second attribute, having just been placed in TRNSFR(2) by REMOVE], plus a swap time. MIN is an intrinsic FORTRAN function that returns in its name the minimum of its arguments (with type agreeing with that of the arguments). Before filing the job's record in the CPU list, its remaining service time [in TRNSFR(2)] is decremented by a full quantum, even if it needs only a partial quantum to get done; in this case the second attribute of the job becomes negative, and we use this condition as a flag that the job, when leaving the CPU later, is done and is to be sent back to its terminal. On the other hand, if the job will not be done after this pass through the CPU, it will be getting a full quantum of service this time, and its second attribute should be decremented by a full quantum, correctly representing the remaining service time needed. Finally, the job is placed in the CPU list, and the end of this CPU pass is scheduled into the event list.

Event routine ENDRUN is called from the main program when a job completes a pass through the CPU; it is flowcharted and listed in Figs. 2.21 and 2.22. The job is first removed from the CPU, after which a check is made to see if it still needs more CPU time, i.e., if its second attribute is positive. If so, it is simply put back at the end of the queue (note that the attributes for the queue and CPU lists match up, so that the contents of TRNSFR are correct), and START is called to remove the first job from the queue and begin its processing. On the other hand, if the job coming out of the CPU is finished, its response time is computed as TIME − TRNSFR(1) and registered by SAMPST; as before, for long simulations, both TIME and TRNSFR might have to be made DOUBLE PRECISION to avoid loss of precision in this subtraction. The end of its next think time is scheduled, and the number of response times observed is incremented. Then, a check is made to see whether this response time was the last one required; if so, an end-simulation event (type 3) is scheduled to occur immediately, by giving it an event time of now (TIME) and forcing it to the top of the event list (OPTION = LFIRST, instead of the usual LINCR in event-list filing). Note that this forcing to the top is redundant in this case since the first attribute is the present time, but it is slightly more efficient since FILE will not have to do any searching for the record's correct location; in other models, however, this forcing might be required if another event could be scheduled at this same time. In this way, the TIMING routine will pick off the end-simulation event immediately (i.e., without the passage of any simulated time), and the main program will call REPORT to end the simulation. If, however, the simulation is not over, a call to START is made, provided that the queue is not empty; otherwise, no action is taken and the simulation simply continues.

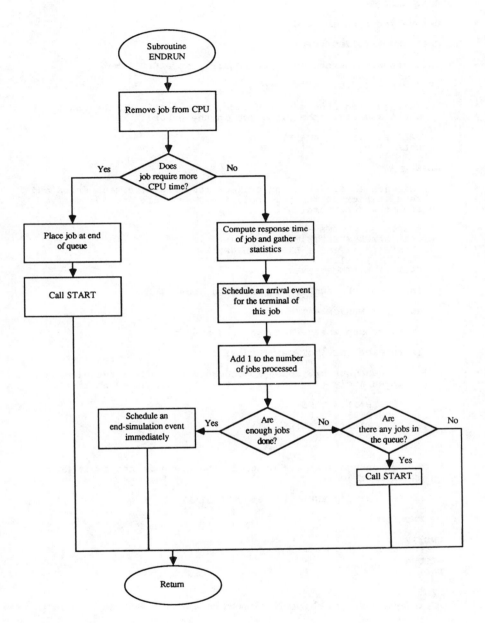

FIGURE 2.21
Flowchart for end-CPU-run routine, computer model.

```
          SUBROUTINE ENDRUN
          INCLUDE 'tscomp.dcl'
          REAL RESPTM

*         Remove job from the CPU.

          CALL REMOVE(LFIRST,CPU)

*         Check to see whether this job requires more CPU time.

          IF (TRNSFR(2) .GT. 0.0) THEN

*             This job requires more CPU time, so place it at the end of the
*             queue and start the first job in the queue.

              CALL FILE(LLAST,QUEUE)
              CALL START

          ELSE

*             This job is finished, so collect response-time statistics and
*             send it back to its terminal, i.e., schedule another arrival
*             from the same terminal.

              RESPTM    = TIME - TRNSFR(1)
              CALL SAMPST(RESPTM,1)
              TRNSFR(1) = TIME + EXPON(MTHINK,1)
              TRNSFR(2) = 1.0
              CALL FILE(LINCR,LEVENT)

*             Increment the number of completed jobs.

              NUMJOB = NUMJOB + 1

*             Check to see whether enough jobs are done.

              IF (NUMJOB .GE. TOTJOB) THEN

*                 Enough jobs are done, so schedule the end of the simulation
*                 immediately (forcing it to the head of the event list).

                  TRNSFR(1) = TIME
                  TRNSFR(2) = 3.0
                  CALL FILE(LFIRST,LEVENT)

              ELSE

*                 Not enough jobs are done; if the queue is not empty, start
*                 another job.

                  IF (LSIZE(QUEUE) .GT. 0) CALL START

              END IF

          END IF

          RETURN
          END
```

FIGURE 2.22
FORTRAN code for subroutine ENDRUN, computer model.

```
      SUBROUTINE REPORT
      INCLUDE 'tscomp.dcl'
      REAL ARESPT,AVGNIQ,UTIL
*     Get and write estimates of desired measures of performance.
      CALL SAMPST(0.0,-1)
      ARESPT = TRNSFR(1)
      CALL FILEST(1)
      AVGNIQ = TRNSFR(1)
      CALL FILEST(2)
      UTIL = TRNSFR(1)
      WRITE (6,2010) NTERML, ARESPT, AVGNIQ, UTIL
 2010 FORMAT(/I6,3F16.3)

      RETURN
      END
```

FIGURE 2.23
FORTRAN code for subroutine REPORT, computer model.

The report generator is listed in Fig. 2.23, and uses SAMPST and FILEST directly to get the desired statistics, then writes them out in accordance with the header produced by the WRITE statement in the main program. Note that we must copy the desired average statistics from the TRNSFR array into the local variables ARESPT, AVGNIQ, and UTIL to avoid overwriting their values, since TRNSFR(1) is used to hold each of them.

2.5.3 Simulation Output and Discussion

The output file, tscomp.out, is shown in Fig. 2.24. As expected, congestion in the computer gets worse as the number of terminals rises, as measured by the

```
Time-shared computer model

Number of terminals        10 to  80 by  10

Mean think time        25.000 seconds

Mean service time       0.800 seconds

Quantum                 0.100 seconds

Swap time               0.015 seconds

Number of jobs processed     1000
```

Number of terminals	Average response time	Average number in queue	Utilization of CPU
10	1.324	0.156	0.358
20	2.165	0.929	0.658
30	5.505	4.453	0.914
40	12.698	12.904	0.998
50	24.593	23.871	0.998
60	31.712	32.958	1.000
70	42.310	42.666	0.999
80	47.547	51.158	1.000

FIGURE 2.24
Output report, computer model.

average response time, average queue length, and CPU utilization. In particular, it appears that this system could bear about 60 terminals before the average response time degrades to a value much worse than 30 seconds. At this level, we see that the average queue length would be around 30 jobs, which could be useful for determining the amount of disk space needed to hold these jobs (the maximum queue length might have been a better piece of information for this purpose); further, the CPU would be busy nearly all the time with such a system. Our usual caveat applies to these conclusions, however: The output data on which they are based resulted from just a single run of the system (of somewhat arbitrary length), and are thus of unknown accuracy.

2.6 MULTITELLER BANK WITH JOCKEYING

We now use SIMLIB to simulate a multiteller bank where the customers are allowed to jockey (move) from one queue to another if it seems to be to their advantage. This model also illustrates how to deal with another common stopping rule for a simulation.

2.6.1 Problem Statement

A bank with five tellers opens its doors at 9 A.M. and closes its doors at 5 P.M., but operates until all customers in the bank by 5 P.M. have been served. Assume that the interarrival times of customers are IID exponential random variables with mean 1 minute and that the service times of customers are IID exponential random variables with mean 4.5 minutes.

Each teller has a separate queue. An arriving customer joins the shortest queue, choosing the leftmost shortest queue in case of ties. Let n_i be the total number of customers in front of teller i (in service plus in queue) at a particular instant. If the completion of a customer's service at teller i causes $n_j > n_i + 1$ for some other teller j, then the customer from the tail of queue j jockeys to the tail of queue i. (If there are two or more such customers, the one from the closest, leftmost queue jockeys.) If teller i is idle, the jockeying customer begins service at teller i; see Fig. 2.25.

The bank's management is concerned with operating costs as well as the quality of service currently being provided to customers, and is thinking of changing the number of tellers. For each of the cases $n = 4, 5, 6$. and 7 tellers,

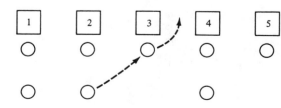

FIGURE 2.25
The customer being served by teller $i = 3$ completes service, causing the customer from the tail of queue $j = 2$ to jockey.

we use SIMLIB to simulate the bank and estimate the expected time-average total number of customers in queue, the expected average delay in queue, and the expected maximum delay in queue. In all cases we assume that no customers are present when the bank opens.

2.6.2   SIMLIB Program

The events for this model are:

Event description	Event type
Arrival of a customer to the bank	1
Departure of a customer upon completion of his or her service	2
Bank closes its doors at 5 P.M.	3

An event graph for this model is given in Fig. 2.26. It is identical to that for the single-server queue with fixed run length (see Fig. 1.53), except that the "end-simulation" event has been replaced by the "close-doors" event. Even though these two events fit into the event diagram in the same way, the action they must take is quite different.

This model requires $2n + 1$ lists of records, where n is the number of tellers for a particular simulation run. Lists 1 through n contain the records of the customers waiting in the respective queues. Lists $n + 1$ through $2n$ are used to indicate whether or not the tellers are busy. If list $n + i$ (where $i = 1, 2, \ldots, n$) contains one record, teller i is busy; if it contains no records, teller i is idle. Finally, list 25 is the event list, as usual. The attributes for all these lists are as follows:

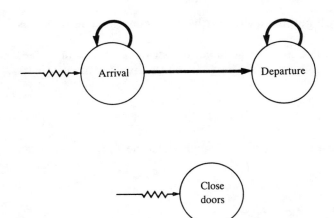

FIGURE 2.26
Event graph, bank model.

List	Attribute 1	Attribute 2	Attribute 3
1 through n, queues	Time of arrival to queue	—	—
$n + 1$ through $2n$, tellers	—	—	—
25, event list	Event time	Event type	Teller number if event type $= 2$

Here again we are using separate lists for the servers in the model; in this case the only reason for doing so is to represent the busy/idle status of the servers, since no meaningful information is stored in the attributes of the records in these lists, and we are not asking for server utilization statistics. Note also that we are taking advantage of the opportunity to store more than just the event time and type in the records in the event list. The reason for this is that, in the case of a departure event (type 2), we need to know the teller number from which the departure will occur in order to manage the queues and the jockeying rules correctly.

The statistics collection in this model is somewhat different. Since there are several different queues, a customer may experience his or her delay (the time elapsing between arrival to the system and commencement of service at *some* server) in several different queues, due to the possibility of jockeying. The customer carries along the time of arrival (in attribute 1 of the queue lists) regardless of what queue he or she may be in, so that the delay can be computed when service begins. Thus, we simply lump all the customer delays together into a single SAMPST variable:

SAMPST variable number	Meaning
1	Delay in queue (or queues)

By using SAMPST, we will automatically get the maximum delay in queue as well.

We also want to get the time-average *total* number of customers in queue, which will be computed as follows. If we let $Q_i(t)$ be the number of customers in queue i at time t, for $i = 1, 2, \ldots, n$, then

$$Q(t) = \sum_{i=1}^{n} Q_i(t) \qquad (2.1)$$

is the total number of customers in all the queues at time t. Thus, what we want to compute is

$$\hat{q} = \frac{\int_0^T Q(t)\, dt}{T} \qquad (2.2)$$

where T is the time the simulation ends (as determined by the stopping rule described above). However, if we substitute Eq. (2.1) into Eq. (2.2) and use the linearity of integrals, we get

$$\hat{q} = \hat{q}_1 + \hat{q}_2 + \cdots + \hat{q}_n$$

where

$$\hat{q}_i = \frac{\int_0^T Q_i(t)\, dt}{T}$$

is simply the time-average number of customers in queue i. All this really says is that the average of the sum of the individual queue lengths is the sum of their average lengths. Thus, we can use FILEST (applied to the lists for the individual queues) at the end of the simulation to obtain the $\hat{q}_i$'s, and then just add them together to get $\hat{q}$. To be sure, $\hat{q}$ could be obtained directly by defining a TIMEST variable corresponding to $Q(t)$, incrementing it upon each arrival and decrementing it with the commencement of each service, but we have to keep the queue lists anyway, so the above approach is preferred. (Problem 2.4 considers an extension of this model where we want to know the *maximum* total number of customers in the queues, as well as the above statistics; the question addressed there concerns whether the maximum of the total is equal to the total of the maxima.)

There are two types of random variables in this model, interarrival times. and service times. We use the following stream assignments:

Stream	Purpose
1	Interarrival times
2	Service times

The program for this model consists of a main program and the subroutines in Table 2.3, as well as the variables listed there. For two of the subroutines, it turns out to be useful to pass arguments representing teller numbers. For this model, we chose not to use mnemonics for list numbers, since they are already indexed by variable names, as will be seen in the code. Finally, we will use a combination of standard output reporting (for the delay-in-queue statistics) and our own printing (for the queue-length statistics), so that we need an output variable for the latter quantity only.

The main program is shown in Fig. 2.27, with the declarations file in Fig. 2.28. As in the computer model, there is a DO loop around most of the main program (after the input is taken care of), now with the DO index (NUMTEL) representing the number of tellers (n) for the current model variant. SIMLIB is initialized as usual by calling INITLK, and MAXATR is set to 3 in this case. The first arrival is scheduled, and the close-doors event (type 3) is also placed

TABLE 2.3
Subprograms and FORTRAN variables for bank model

Subprogram	Purpose
ARRIVE	Processes type 1 events
DEPART(ITEL)	Processes type 2 events, where ITEL (INTEGER-valued) is the number of the teller completing service
JOCKEY(ITEL)	Jockeys a customer from one queue to another, where ITEL (INTEGER-valued) is the number of the teller completing a service (JOCKEY is called from DEPART and is *not* an event routine)
REPORT	Generates report and is called from the main program when the simulation ends (at *or after* 5 P.M.)

Variable	Definition
Input parameters:	
LENGTH	Amount of time (in hours) the bank's doors are open (=8 here)
MARRVT	Mean interarrival time (=1 minute)
MAXTEL	Maximum number of tellers (=7)
MINTEL	Minimum number of tellers (=4)
MSERVT	Mean service time (=4.5 minutes)
Modeling variables:	
CHOICE	Number of queue an arriving customer will join
DELAY	Delay in queue of a customer
DIS	Absolute value of the difference between ITEL and the number of the queue from which a customer might jockey
INDEX	Number of list corresponding to teller TELLER
INDEXI	Number of list corresponding to teller ITEL
INDEXJ	Number of list corresponding to teller JTEL
ITEL	Number of the teller completing a service, or his or her queue
JTEL	Number of a queue from which jockeying might occur
JUMPER	Number of a queue from which a customer wants to jockey
MINDIS	Minimum distance between queue ITEL and the queue from which a customer wants to jockey
NI	Number of customers facing teller ITEL
NJ	Number of customers facing teller JTEL
NUMTEL	Number of tellers for a particular simulation run
SHORT	Number of customers in the shortest queue upon a customer's arrival
TELLER	Number of a teller or his or her queue
Output variable:	
AVGNIQ	Average total number of customers in all the queues

in the event list; we must be careful to decide on and use a consistent time unit throughout the code, in this case minutes. TIMING is called, and control is passed to ARRIVE or DEPART if the event type is 1 or 2, respectively. Note that for a departure, we pass to DEPART the INTEGER argument ITEL, which is set to TRNSFR(3); this will contain the number of the teller who is completing service, since TIMING has just filled the TRNSFR array with the entire event record, and for a type 2 event this record contains in its third attribute the desired teller number. For the close-doors event, SIMLIB routine

```
*      Main program for multiteller bank.

*      Bring in declarations file.

       INCLUDE 'mtbank.dcl'
       INTEGER ITEL

*      Open input and output files.

       OPEN (5, FILE = 'mtbank.in')
       OPEN (6, FILE = 'mtbank.out')

*      Read input parameters.

       READ (5,*) MINTEL, MAXTEL, MARRVT, MSERVT, LENGTH

*      Write report heading and input parameters.

       WRITE (6,2010) MINTEL, MAXTEL, MARRVT, MSERVT, LENGTH
 2010 FORMAT (' Multiteller bank with separate queues & jockeying'//
      &        ' Number of tellers',I16,' to',I3//
      &        ' Mean interarrival time',F11.3,' minutes'//
      &        ' Mean service time',F16.3,' minutes'//
      &        ' Bank closes after',F16.3,' hours'/)

*      Run the simulation varying the number of tellers.

       DO 60 NUMTEL = MINTEL, MAXTEL

*          Initialize SIMLIB.

           CALL INITLK

*          Set the maximum number of attributes per record.

           MAXATR = 3

*          Schedule the first arrival.

           TRNSFR(1) = EXPON(MARRVT,1)
           TRNSFR(2) = 1.0
           CALL FILE(LINCR,LEVENT)

*          Schedule the bank closing.  (Note need for consistency of
*          units.)

           TRNSFR(1) = 60.0 * LENGTH
           TRNSFR(2) = 3.0
           CALL FILE(LINCR,LEVENT)

*          Determine the next event.

    10     CALL TIMING

*          Call the appropriate event routine.

           GO TO (20, 30, 40), NEXT
    20         CALL ARRIVE
               GO TO 10
    30         ITEL = TRNSFR(3)
               CALL DEPART(ITEL)
               GO TO 50
```

FIGURE 2.27
FORTRAN code for the main program, bank model.

```
*              The close-doors event is accomplished by simply cancelling
*              the next arrival, thereby cutting off all future arrivals
*              as well.
   40          CALL CANCEL(1.0)

*          If the bank is closed and no customers are present, end the
*          simulation.
   50      IF (LSIZE(LEVENT) .GT. 0) GO TO 10
           CALL REPORT

   60 CONTINUE

      CLOSE (5)
      CLOSE (6)

      STOP
      END
```

FIGURE 2.27
(*Continued.*)

CANCEL is used to cancel the arrival event scheduled at that time, thereby preventing this customer, who would have been the first customer to arrive after 5 P.M., from arriving. Since an arrival is scheduled only by the previous arrival, this "chokes off" the arrival stream, and no further arrivals can occur. After doing this, a check is made to see whether the event list is empty; if so, all tellers must be idle (i.e., no departure events are scheduled), and this simulation ends after calling REPORT. If the event list is not empty, the simulation is allowed to continue until all customers in the bank have been served. If the event list is ever empty after a service completion occurs, it must be after 5 P.M. (otherwise there would be arrival and close-doors events in the event list) and there are no further service completions scheduled, so the bank is empty and this simulation ends after calling REPORT.

A flowchart and listing for the ARRIVE event routine are given in Figs. 2.29 and 2.30. The subroutine begins by scheduling the next arrival event. Then a DO loop (with foot at statement 10) is entered that runs over the teller numbers, and each server is looked at in turn (list numbers INDEX $= n + 1$, $n + 2, \ldots, 2n$) to see whether they are idle [i.e., whether LSIZE(INDEX) is

```
      INTEGER MAXTEL,MINTEL,NUMTEL
      REAL LENGTH,MARRVT,MSERVT
      REAL EXPON
      COMMON /MODEL/ MARRVT,MSERVT,NUMTEL

      INTEGER LDECR,LEVENT,LFIRST,LINCR,LLAST,LRANK(25),LSIZE(25),
     &        MAXATR,NEXT
      REAL TIME,TRNSFR(10)
      COMMON /SIMLIB/ LDECR,LEVENT,LFIRST,LINCR,LLAST,LRANK,LSIZE,
     &                MAXATR,NEXT,TIME,TRNSFR
```

FIGURE 2.28
FORTRAN code for the declarations file (mtbank.dcl), bank model.

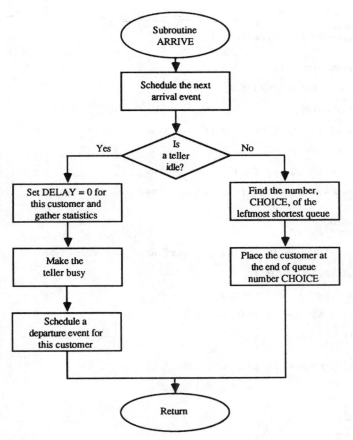

FIGURE 2.29
Flowchart for arrival routine, bank model.

0]. As soon as an idle server is found, the customer's delay of zero is registered in SAMPST, the teller is made busy by filing a dummy record in that teller's list, and this customer's service-completion event is scheduled. Then, the RETURN statement transfers control back to the main program, and neither the rest of the routine nor the rest of loop 10 (if any) is executed. The rest of the routine refers to the case when all tellers are busy, and the remainder of loop 10 refers to other, higher-numbered tellers, at whom we don't want to look in any case due to the preference for the lowest-numbered idle teller. If loop 10 is completed, then all tellers are busy, and loop 20 searches across the queues to find the shortest one, choosing the lowest-numbered one if there is a tie. This tie-breaking rule is implemented by the strict inequality (".LT.") in the IF statement in loop 20, meaning that in the left-to-right search, a new choice of the queue would be taken only if the new queue is strictly shorter

```
      SUBROUTINE ARRIVE
      INCLUDE 'mtbank.dcl'
      INTEGER CHOICE,INDEX,SHORT,TELLER
      REAL DELAY

*     Schedule the next arrival.

      TRNSFR(1) = TIME + EXPON(MARRVT,1)
      TRNSFR(2) = 1.0
      CALL FILE(LINCR,LEVENT)

*     If a teller is idle, start service on the arriving customer.

      DO 10 TELLER = 1, NUMTEL
         INDEX = NUMTEL + TELLER
         IF (LSIZE(INDEX) .EQ. 0) THEN

*            Teller number TELLER is idle, so customer has a delay of
*            zero.

             DELAY = 0.0
             CALL SAMPST(DELAY,1)

*            Make teller number TELLER busy (attributes are irrelevant).

             CALL FILE(LFIRST,INDEX)

*            Schedule a service completion.

             TRNSFR(1) = TIME + EXPON(MSERVT,2)
             TRNSFR(2) = 2.0
             TRNSFR(3) = TELLER
             CALL FILE(LINCR,LEVENT)

*            Return control to the main program.

             RETURN

         END IF

   10 CONTINUE

*     All tellers are busy, so find the shortest queue (leftmost
*     shortest in case of ties).

      SHORT  = LSIZE(1)
      CHOICE = 1
      DO 20 TELLER = 2, NUMTEL
         IF (LSIZE(TELLER) .LT. SHORT) THEN
            SHORT  = LSIZE(TELLER)
            CHOICE = TELLER
         END IF
   20 CONTINUE

*     Place the customer at the end of the shortest queue.

      TRNSFR(1) = TIME
      CALL FILE(LLAST,CHOICE)

      RETURN
      END
```

FIGURE 2.30
FORTRAN code for subroutine ARRIVE, bank model.

than the earlier choice. After finishing loop 20, the INTEGER variable CHOICE will contain the queue number chosen, and the arriving customer is put at the end of that queue, with the time of arrival being the only attribute needed.

Event subroutine DEPART, with the flowchart and listing given in Figs. 2.31 and 2.32, is called from the main program when a customer completes service; the INTEGER argument ITEL passed into DEPART is the number of the teller who is completing a service. If the queue for this teller is empty, the teller is made idle (by removing the dummy record from the corresponding list) and subroutine JOCKEY is called to determine whether a customer from another queue can jockey into service at teller number ITEL, who was just idled. On the other hand, if the queue for this teller is not empty, the first customer is removed, his or her delay is computed and registered, and the

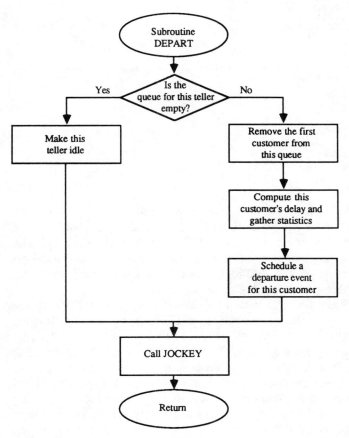

FIGURE 2.31
Flowchart for departure routine, bank model.

```
      SUBROUTINE DEPART(ITEL)
      INCLUDE 'mtbank.dcl'
      INTEGER INDEXI,ITEL
      REAL DELAY

*     Check to see whether the queue for teller ITEL is empty.

      IF (LSIZE(ITEL) .EQ. 0) THEN

*         The queue is empty, so make the teller idle.

          INDEXI = NUMTEL + ITEL
          CALL REMOVE(LFIRST,INDEXI)

      ELSE

*         The queue is not empty, so start service on a customer.

          CALL REMOVE(LFIRST,ITEL)
          DELAY = TIME - TRNSFR(1)
          CALL SAMPST(DELAY,1)
          TRNSFR(1) = TIME + EXPON(MSERVT,2)
          TRNSFR(2) = 2.0
          TRNSFR(3) = ITEL
          CALL FILE(LINCR,LEVENT)

      END IF

*     Let a customer from the end of another queue jockey to the end of
*     this queue, if possible.

      CALL JOCKEY(ITEL)

      RETURN
      END
```

FIGURE 2.32
FORTRAN code for subroutine DEPART, bank model.

service-completion event is scheduled; for long simulations, TIME and TRNSFR might have to be made DOUBLE PRECISION to avoid loss of precision in the subtraction to calculate DELAY. In any case, we must invoke JOCKEY to see if any customers from *other* queues want to jockey into this queue. (Note that no customers should jockey after an arrival occurs, since this would not decrease their expected time to departure.)

Subroutine JOCKEY is called with an INTEGER argument ITEL to see if a customer can jockey to the queue for teller ITEL from another (longer) queue, or possibly right into service at teller ITEL if he was just idled; its flowchart and code are in Figs. 2.33 and 2.34. JUMPER will be the INTEGER variable holding the queue number of the jockeying customer, if any; it is set to zero initially and is made positive only if such a customer is found. MINDIS is the (absolute) distance (in numbers of queues) of a potential jockeyer to the destination queue, and is set to a large number initially, since we want to scan for the minimum such distance. NI is set to the number of customers facing teller ITEL, that is, $NI = n_i$ for $i = ITEL$. Loop 10 examines the queues (JTEL) to see if any of them satisfy the jockeying requirements, represented

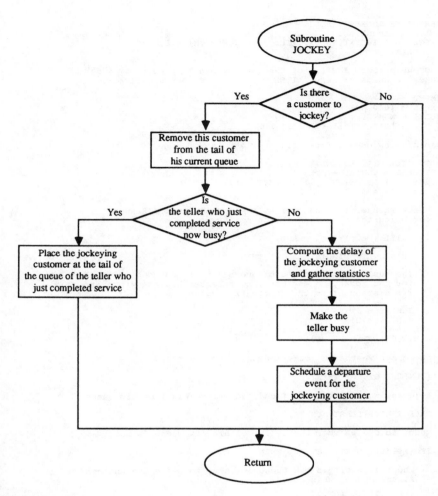

FIGURE 2.33
Flowchart for subroutine JOCKEY, bank model.

here by the conditions that JTEL ≠ ITEL (since a customer would not jockey
to his or her own queue) and $NJ > NI + 1$, where NJ is the number of
customers facing teller JTEL, that is, $NJ = n_j$ for $j = $ JTEL. If both of these
conditions are satisfied, then the customer at the end of queue number JTEL
would like to jockey, and this customer will (temporarily, perhaps) be issued a
jockeying pass if she is strictly closer to the target queue than earlier customers
who would also like to jockey (i.e., if DIS, the number of queues this would-be
jockeyer is away, is strictly less than the distance of the earlier closest would-be
jockeyer). Note that in the case of two closest would-be jockeyers (one on the
left and one on the right), we would jockey the one from the left since the one

```
      SUBROUTINE JOCKEY(ITEL)
      INCLUDE 'mtbank.dcl'
      INTEGER DIS,INDEXI,INDEXJ,ITEL,JTEL,JUMPER,MINDIS,NI,NJ
      REAL DELAY

*     Find the number, JUMPER, of the queue whose last customer will
*     jockey to queue or server ITEL, if there is such a customer.

      JUMPER = 0
      MINDIS = 1000
      INDEXI = NUMTEL + ITEL
      NI     = LSIZE(ITEL) + LSIZE(INDEXI)

*     Scan all the queues from left to right.

      DO 10 JTEL = 1, NUMTEL
         INDEXJ = NUMTEL + JTEL
         NJ     = LSIZE(JTEL) + LSIZE(INDEXJ)
         DIS    = ABS(ITEL - JTEL)

*        Check whether the customer at the end of queue JTEL qualifies
*        for being the jockeying choice so far.

         IF (JTEL .NE. ITEL    .AND.
     &       NJ   .GT. NI + 1  .AND.
     &       DIS  .LT. MINDIS        ) THEN

*           The customer at the end of queue JTEL is our choice so far
*           for the jockeying customer, so remember his queue number and
*           its distance from the destination queue.

            JUMPER = JTEL
            MINDIS = DIS
         END IF
   10 CONTINUE

*     Check to see whether a jockeying customer was found.

      IF (JUMPER .GT. 0) THEN

*        A jockeying customer was found, so remove him from his queue.

         CALL REMOVE(LLAST,JUMPER)

*        Check to see whether the teller of his new queue is busy.

         IF (LSIZE(INDEXI) .GT. 0) THEN

*           The teller of his new queue is busy, so place the customer
*           at the end of this queue.
            CALL FILE(LLAST,ITEL)

         ELSE

*           The teller of his new queue is idle, so tally the jockeying
*           customer's delay, make the teller busy, and start service.

            DELAY = TIME - TRNSFR(1)
            CALL SAMPST(DELAY,1)
            CALL FILE(LFIRST,INDEXI)
            TRNSFR(1) = TIME + EXPON(MSERVT,2)
            TRNSFR(2) = 2.0
            TRNSFR(3) = ITEL
            CALL FILE(LINCR,LEVENT)

         END IF

      END IF

      RETURN
      END
```

FIGURE 2.34
FORTRAN code for subroutine JOCKEY, bank model.

```
      SUBROUTINE REPORT
      INCLUDE 'mtbank.dcl'
      INTEGER TELLER
      REAL AVGNIQ

*     Compute and write out estimates of desired measures of system
*     performance.

      AVGNIQ = 0.0
      DO 10 TELLER = 1, NUMTEL
         CALL FILEST(TELLER)
         AVGNIQ = AVGNIQ + TRNSFR(1)
   10 CONTINUE
      WRITE (6,2010) NUMTEL, AVGNIQ
 2010 FORMAT (////' With',I2,' tellers, average number in queue =',F10.3
     &             //' Delays in queue, in minutes:')
      CALL OUTSAM(6,1,1)

      RETURN
      END
```

FIGURE 2.35
FORTRAN code for subroutine REPORT, bank model.

on the right would have to have been *strictly* closer. When loop 10 ends, JUMPER will be zero if the other queue lengths were such that nobody wants to jockey, in which case control is passed back to the main program and no action is taken. If, however, JUMPER is positive, then it is equal to the queue number from which a customer will jockey; that customer is removed from the end of his queue. A check is then made to see whether the teller who just finished service is busy (with the customer who was first in this teller's queue), in which case the jockeying customer just joins the end of his new queue. If this teller is idle, however, the jockeying customer jockeys right into service, so his delay is computed and registered, the server is made busy again, and the jockeying customer's service completion is scheduled.

The code for the report generator is in Fig. 2.35, and starts with a loop to add up the average numbers in the separate queues to get the average total number in queue, as explained earlier; this is then written out together with the number of tellers in this model variant. Finally, the standard output report generator is called for SAMPST variable 1, to write out the average and maximum of the customer delays in queue(s).

2.6.3 Simulation Output and Discussion

Figure 2.36 contains the results (in file mtbank.out) of the simulation. Compared with the current policy of five tellers, a reduction to four tellers would seem to carry a heavy penalty in terms of customer service quality, in terms of both delays in queue as well as the queue lengths. In the other direction, adding a sixth teller would bring a substantial improvement in customer service and average queue lengths; whether this is economically advisable would depend on how management values this improvement in customer service with

```
Multiteller bank with separate queues & jockeying

Number of tellers              4 to  7

Mean interarrival time         1.000 minutes

Mean service time              4.500 minutes

Bank closes after              8.000 hours


With 4 tellers, average number in queue =     51.319

Delays in queue, in minutes:
```

SAMPST Variable Number	Average	Number of Values	Maximum	Minimum
1	0.6322289E+02	0.5010000E+03	0.1563631E+03	0.0000000E+00

```
With 5 tellers, average number in queue =     2,441

Delays in queue, in minutes:
```

SAMPST Variable Number	Average	Number of Values	Maximum	Minimum
1	0.2481493E+01	0.4830000E+03	0.2188733E+02	0.0000000E+00

```
With 6 tellers, average number in queue =     0.718

Delays in queue, in minutes:
```

SAMPST Variable Number	Average	Number of Values	Maximum	Minimum
1	0.7637553E+00	0.4670000E+03	0.1651025E+02	0.0000000E+00

```
With 7 tellers, average number in queue =     0.179

Delays in queue, in minutes:
```

SAMPST Variable Number	Average	Number of Values	Maximum	Minimum
1	0.1761804E+00	0.4930000E+03	0.6971222E+01	0.0000000E+00

FIGURE 2.36
Output report, bank model.

respect to the cost of the extra teller. It seems unlikely in this example that adding a seventh teller could be justified, since the service gains do not appear great relative to the six-teller system. Note also that we know how many customers were served during the day in each system variant, being the number of delays observed. There is little variation in this quantity across the system variants, since the arrival rate is constant and the lobby has unlimited space.

Problems 2.4(b) and 2.4(c) embellish this model by adding new output measures (a measure of server utilization and the maximum total number of customers in the queues), and Prob. 2.4(d) further enhances the model by considering the realistic possibility of a limit on the size of the bank's lobby to hold the customers in the queue.

2.7 JOB-SHOP MODEL

In this section, we use SIMLIB to simulate a model of a manufacturing facility. This example, the most complex one we have considered, illustrates how simulation can be used to identify bottlenecks in a production process. For comparison purposes, the reader may be interested in a coding of this model in the GPSS/H simulation language in Schriber (1990, sec. 13.23); see Sec. 3.5.1 for some general information on GPSS/H.

2.7.1 Problem Statement

A manufacturing shop consists of five groups of machines, and at present groups $1, 2, \ldots, 5$ consist of 3, 2, 4, 3, and 1 identical machines, respectively (see Fig. 2.37). (In effect, the shop is a network of five multiserver queues.) Assume that jobs arrive at the shop with interarrival times that are IID exponential random variables with mean 0.25 hour. There are three types of jobs, and arriving jobs are of type 1, 2, 3, with respective probabilities 0.3, 0.5, and 0.2. Job types 1, 2, 3 require 4, 3, 5 tasks to be done, respectively, and each task must be done at a specified machine group and in a prescribed order. The routings for the different job types are:

Job type	Machine groups in routing
1	3, 1, 2, 5
2	4, 1, 3
3	2, 5, 1, 4, 3

Thus, type 2 jobs first have a task done at machine group 4, then have a task done at group 1, and finally have a task done at group 3.

If a job arrives at a particular machine group and finds all machines in that group already busy, the job joins a single FIFO queue at that machine group. The time to perform a task at a particular machine is an independent

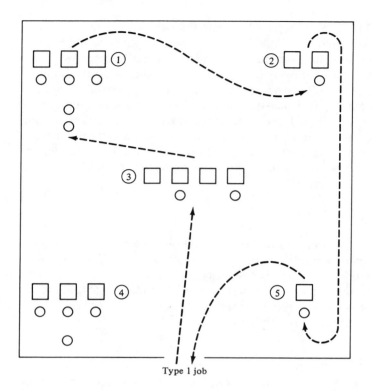

FIGURE 2.37
Manufacturing shop with five machine groups, showing the route of type 1 jobs.

2-Erlang random variable whose mean depends on the job type and the group to which the machine belongs. (If X is a 2-Erlang random variable with mean r, then $X = Y_1 + Y_2$, where Y_1 and Y_2 are independent exponential random variables each with mean $r/2$. Alternatively, X is known as a *gamma* random variable with shape parameter 2 and scale parameter $r/2$. See Sec. 6.2.2 for further details.) We chose the 2-Erlang distribution to represent service times because experience has shown that if one collects data on the time to perform some task, the histogram of these data will often have a shape similar to that of the density function for an Erlang distribution. The mean service time for each job type and each task are:

Job type	Mean service times for successive tasks, hours
1	0.50, 0.60, 0.85, 0.50
2	1.10, 0.80, 0.75
3	1.20, 0.25, 0.70, 0.90, 1.00

Thus, a type 2 job requires a mean service time of 1.10 hours at machine group 4 (the group where its first task will be done).

Assuming no loss of continuity between successive days' operations of the shop, we simulate the shop for 365 eight-hour days and estimate the expected average total delay in queue (exclusive of service times) for each job type and the expected overall average job total delay. We use the true probabilities 0.3, 0.5, 0.2 in computing the latter quantity. In addition, we estimate the expected average number in queue, the expected utilization (using SIMLIB routine TIMEST), and the expected average delay in queue for each machine group.

Suppose that all machines cost approximately the same amount and the shop has the opportunity to purchase one new machine with an eye toward efficiency improvement. We will use the results of the above simulation to decide what additional simulation runs should be made. (Each of these new runs will involve a total of 14 machines, being one more than the original number.) From these additional runs, we will use the overall average job total delay to help decide what type of machine the shop should purchase.

2.7.2 SIMLIB Program

The events for this model are quite straightforward:

Event description	Event type
Arrival of a job to the shop	1
Departure of a job from a particular machine group	2
End of the simulation	3

Note that for this model, the departure event refers to a job's departing from *any* machine group on its route, so does not represent the job's leaving the shop unless the departure is from the final machine group on its route. An event graph for this model is given in Fig. 2.38.

We will use the following list structure:

List	Attribute 1	Attribute 2	Attribute 3	Attribute 4
1 through 5, queues	Time of arrival to machine group	Job type	Task number	—
25, event list	Event time	Event type	Job type	Task number

The "time of arrival" in attribute 1 of the queue lists refers to the arrival time to the machine group for *that* list, rather than the arrival time to the shop. The "task number" of a job represents how far along it is on its route, and will be equal to 1 for the first task, 2 for the second task, and so on; for example, task

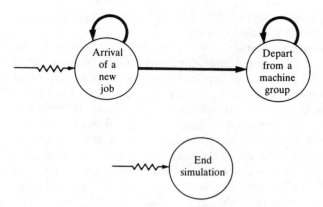

FIGURE 2.38
Event graph, job-shop model.

number 2 for a job of type 3 refers to its processing at machine group 5. Thus, the machine group for a job can be determined by knowing the job type and task number.

The delays of the jobs in the queues are used in different ways in this model, so the SAMPST variable structure is richer. We want the average delay in queue for each machine group (regardless of job type), and SAMPST variables 1 through 5 will be used for this. Also, we want to find the average delay in all the queues visited by each job type (regardless of machine group), for which SAMPST variables 6 through 8 will be used:

SAMPST variable number	Meaning
1	Delay in queue at machine group 1
2	Delay in queue at machine group 2
3	Delay in queue at machine group 3
4	Delay in queue at machine group 4
5	Delay in queue at machine group 5
6	Delay in queues for job type 1
7	Delay in queues for job type 2
8	Delay in queues for job type 3

Thus, each delay in each queue will be registered into two different SAMPST variables, one for the machine group and another for the job type.

For the continuous-time statistics we use FILEST as before, and will now use TIMEST as well. Since we have a list for each queue, we can easily get the time-average number in each of the queues by using FILEST. We also want to observe the utilization of each machine group; since there may be more than one machine in a group, this is defined as the time-average number of machines that are busy in the group, divided by the total number of machines in the group. To find the average number of busy machines in a group, we will keep our own (i.e., non-SIMLIB) array NBUSY(I), which we will maintain as the number of machines currently busy in group I, and TIMEST will be called whenever this changes value for any machine group. Thus, we have the following TIMEST variables:

TIMEST variable number	Meaning
1	Number of machines busy in group 1
2	Number of machines busy in group 2
3	Number of machines busy in group 3
4	Number of machines busy in group 4
5	Number of machines busy in group 5

For this model, there are three types of random variables needed, to which we assign the following streams:

Stream	Purpose
1	Interarrival times
2	Job types
3	Service times

Stream 3 is used to generate the service times of all jobs, regardless of type; in some simulations we might want to dedicate a separate stream to generate the service times of each job type or at each machine group in order to control the exact characteristics of each job or each machine group.

As usual, there is a main program, which together with the subprograms in Table 2.4 use the indicated variables and arrays. Subroutine ARRIVE serves both as an event routine to process type 1 events (where a value of 1 is passed in for the argument NEW), and as a "utility" nonevent routine in the case of a job leaving one machine group and "arriving" at the next group along its route, where NEW = 2 is passed in. For the output variable AJDEL(I), the "total" delay in queue refers to the fact that this is the average delay in *all* the queues along the route for type I jobs. The overall average job total delay, OAJDEL, is a weighted average of the AJDEL(I) values, with the weights' being the *true* probabilities of occurrence for the job types; this provides a more precise (i.e., less variable) estimate than if we simply averaged all the total job delays regardless of job type.

The main program, which is of the usual form, is in Fig. 2.39, and the declarations file is given in Fig. 2.40.

Subroutine ARRIVE, flowcharted and listed in Figs. 2.41 and 2.42, begins by checking NEW to determine whether it is being used as an event routine to process a new arrival to the shop (NEW = 1), or whether it is being used as the last part of a machine-group-departure event to process an existing job's arrival at the next group along its route (NEW = 2). If this is a new arrival, the next arrival is scheduled and the job type of this new arrival is

TABLE 2.4
Subprograms and FORTRAN variables for job-shop model

Subprogram	Purpose
ARRIVE(NEW)	Processes arrival of a job, where NEW = 1 if this is a new job arriving to the shop (type 1 event) and NEW = 2 if the job has been routed after completing service at another machine group (NEW is an INTEGER)
DEPART	Processes type 2 events
REPORT	Generates report, called when the simulation ends
ERLANG(M, RMEAN, ISTRM)	Generates an M-Erlang random variable (M is a positive INTEGER) with mean RMEAN (REAL-valued) using stream ISTRM

Variable	Definition
Input parameters:	
LENGTH	Length of the simulation, in 8-hour days (=365 here)
MARRVT	Mean interarrival time of jobs, in hours (=0.25)
MSERVT(I, J)	Mean service time of task J for job type I, in hours
NGROUP	Number of machine groups (=5)
NMACHS(I)	Number of machines in group I
NTASKS(I)	Number of tasks for job type I
NTYPES	Number of job types (=3)
PROBD(I)	Probability of a job type $\leq$ I
ROUTE(I, J)	Number of the machine group for task J of job type I
Modeling variables:	
DELAY	Delay in queue of a job at a machine group
GROUP	Machine group of a job
INDEX	Number of SAMPST variable for delays for a job type
JOBTQ	Job type of a job leaving queue and entering service at a machine group
JOBTYP	Job type of a job
M	Number of exponential random variables composing the Erlang random variable (used in ERLANG)
MEXP	Mean of the component exponential random variables (used in ERLANG)
NBUSY(I)	Number of machines in group I that are busy
NEW	(See discussion of event routine ARRIVE above)
RMEAN	Mean of the Erlang random variate to be generated (used in ERLANG)
SUM	Distribution function value for a particular job type (used in subroutine REPORT)
TASK	Current task number of a job [$1 \leq$ TASK $\leq$ NTASKS(I) for job type I]
TASKQ	Current task number of a job leaving the queue and entering service at a machine group
Output variables:	
AJDEL(I)	Average total delay in queue for job type I
AMDEL(I)	Average delay in queue at machine group I
AUTIL(I)	Average utilization of the machines in group I
AVGNIQ(I)	Average number in queue at machine group I
OAJDEL	Overall average job delay in queue

```
*      Main program for job-shop model.

*      Bring in declarations file.

       INCLUDE 'jobshop.dcl'
       INTEGER I,J

*      Open input and output files.

       OPEN (5, FILE = 'jobshop.in')
       OPEN (6, FILE = 'jobshop.out')

*      Read input parameters.

       READ (5,*) NGROUP, NTYPES, MARRVT, LENGTH
       READ (5,*) (NMACHS(I), I = 1, NGROUP)
       READ (5,*) (NTASKS(I), I = 1, NTYPES)
       DO 10 I = 1, NTYPES
           READ (5,*) (ROUTE(I,J),  J = 1, NTASKS(I))
           READ (5,*) (MSERVT(I,J), J = 1, NTASKS(I))
   10 CONTINUE
       READ (5,*) (PROBD(I), I = 1, NTYPES)

*      Write report heading and input parameters.

       WRITE (6,2010) NGROUP, (NMACHS(I), I = 1, NGROUP)
 2010 FORMAT (' Job-shop model'//
      &          ' Number of machine groups',I20//
      &          ' Number of machines in each group',7X,8I5)
       WRITE (6,2020) NTYPES, (NTASKS(I), I = 1, NTYPES)
 2020 FORMAT (/' Number of job types',I25//
      &          ' Number of tasks for each job type',6X,8I5)
       WRITE (6,2030) (PROBD(I), I = 1, NTYPES)
 2030 FORMAT (/' Distribution function of job types',2X,8F8.3)
       WRITE (6,2040) MARRVT, LENGTH
 2040 FORMAT (/' Mean interarrival time of jobs',F14.2,' hours'//
      &          ' Length of the simulation',F20.1,' eight-hour days'///
      &          ' Job type      Machine groups on route')
       DO 20 I = 1, NTYPES
   20 WRITE (6,2050) I, (ROUTE(I,J), J = 1, NTASKS(I))
 2050 FORMAT (/I5,8X,8I5)
       WRITE (6,2060)
 2060 FORMAT (//' Job type      Mean service time (in hours) for ',
      &          'successive tasks')
       DO 30 I = 1, NTYPES
   30 WRITE (6,2070) I, (MSERVT(I,J), J = 1, NTASKS(I))
 2070 FORMAT (/I5,5X,8F8.2)

*      Initialize all machines in all groups to the idle state.

       DO 40 I = 1, NGROUP
   40 NBUSY(I) = 0

*      Initialize SIMLIB.

       CALL INITLK

*      Set the maximum number of attributes per record.

       MAXATR = 4
```

FIGURE 2.39
FORTRAN code for the main program, job-shop model.

```
*       Schedule the arrival of the first job.

        TRNSFR(1) = EXPON(MARRVT,1)
        TRNSFR(2) = 1.0
        CALL FILE(LINCR,LEVENT)

*       Schedule the end of the simulation.

        TRNSFR(1) = 8.0 * LENGTH
        TRNSFR(2) = 3.0
        CALL FILE(LINCR,LEVENT)

*       Determine the next event.

     50 CALL TIMING

*       Call the appropriate event routine.

        GO TO (60, 70, 80), NEXT
     60     CALL ARRIVE(1)
            GO TO 50
     70     CALL DEPART
            GO TO 50
     80     CALL REPORT

        CLOSE (5)
        CLOSE (6)

        STOP
        END
```

FIGURE 2.39
(*Continued*.)

generated as a random integer between 1 and 3, using IRANDI; finally, the task number for this new job is initialized to 1. Regardless of whether the job is new, the routine continues by determining the machine group of the arrival from its job type and task number, by a lookup in the array ROUTE. For an existing job (NEW = 2), DEPART would have set JOBTYP and TASK, as we will see below. Then a check is made to see whether all the machines in the group are busy. If so, the job is just put at the end of the group's queue. If not, the job has a zero delay here (registered in SAMPST for the machine group and for the job type), a machine in this group is made busy, and this is noted in

```
      INTEGER JOBTYP,NBUSY(5),NGROUP,NMACHS(5),NTASKS(5),NTYPES,
     &        ROUTE(5,5),TASK
      REAL LENGTH,MARRVT,MSERVT(5,5),PROBD(3)
      INTEGER IRANDI
      REAL ERLANG,EXPON
      COMMON /MODEL/ JOBTYP,LENGTH,MARRVT,MSERVT,NBUSY,NGROUP,NMACHS,
     &               NTASKS,NTYPES,PROBD,ROUTE,TASK

      INTEGER LDECR,LEVENT,LFIRST,LINCR,LLAST,LRANK(25),LSIZE(25),
     &        MAXATR,NEXT
      REAL TIME,TRNSFR(10)
      COMMON /SIMLIB/ LDECR,LEVENT,LFIRST,LINCR,LLAST,LRANK,LSIZE,
     &                MAXATR,NEXT,TIME,TRNSFR
```

FIGURE 2.40
FORTRAN code for the declarations file (jobshop.dcl), job-shop model.

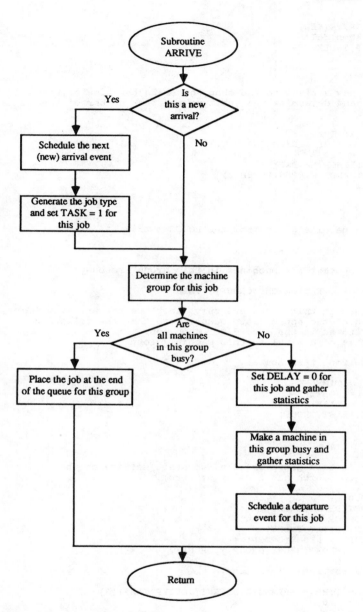

FIGURE 2.41
Flowchart for arrival routine, job-shop model.

```fortran
      SUBROUTINE ARRIVE(NEW)
      INCLUDE 'jobshop.dcl'
      INTEGER GROUP,INDEX,NEW
      REAL DELAY


*     If this is a new arrival to the shop, generate the time of the
*     next arrival and determine the job type and task number of the
*     arriving job.

      IF (NEW .EQ. 1) THEN
         TRNSFR(1) = TIME + EXPON(MARRVT,1)
         TRNSFR(2) = 1.0
         CALL FILE(LINCR,LEVENT)
         JOBTYP = IRANDI(NTYPES,PROBD,2)
         TASK    = 1
      END IF


*     Determine the machine group from the ROUTE matrix.

      GROUP = ROUTE(JOBTYP,TASK)

*     Check to see whether all machines in this group are busy.

      IF (NBUSY(GROUP) .EQ. NMACHS(GROUP)) THEN

*        All machines in this group are busy, so place the arriving job
*        at the end of the appropriate queue. Note that the following
*        data are stored in the record for each job:
*                 1. Time of arrival to this machine group.
*                 2. Job type.
*                 3. Current task number.

         TRNSFR(1) = TIME
         TRNSFR(2) = JOBTYP
         TRNSFR(3) = TASK
         CALL FILE(LLAST,GROUP)

      ELSE


*        A machine in this group is idle, so start service on the
*        arriving job (which has a delay of zero).

         DELAY = 0.0
         CALL SAMPST(DELAY,GROUP)
         INDEX = NGROUP + JOBTYP
         CALL SAMPST(DELAY,INDEX)
         NBUSY(GROUP) = NBUSY(GROUP) + 1
         CALL TIMEST(FLOAT(NBUSY(GROUP)),GROUP)

*        Schedule a service completion.

         TRNSFR(1) = TIME + ERLANG(2,MSERVT(JOBTYP,TASK),3)
         TRNSFR(2) = 2.0
         TRNSFR(3) = JOBTYP
         TRNSFR(4) = TASK
         CALL FILE(LINCR,LEVENT)

      END IF

      RETURN
      END
```

FIGURE 2.42
FORTRAN code for subroutine ARRIVE, job-shop model.

the appropriate TIMEST variable. The intrinsic FORTRAN function FLOAT is used to transform the INTEGER value in the NBUSY array into a REAL number, as required for input to TIMEST. Finally, this job's exit from this machine group is scheduled.

A flowchart and listing for subroutine DEPART are given in Figs. 2.43 and 2.44. The job type, JOBTYP, and task number, TASK, of the departing

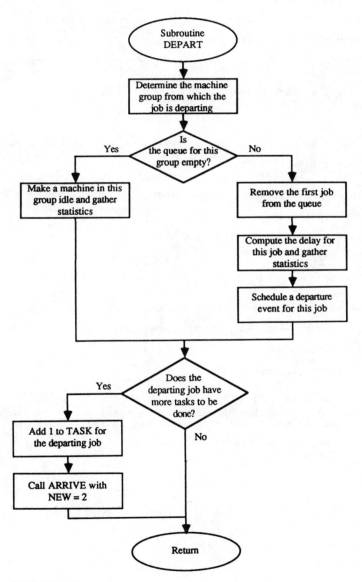

FIGURE 2.43
Flowchart for departure routine, job-shop model.

```
        SUBROUTINE DEPART
        INCLUDE 'jobshop.dcl'
        INTEGER GROUP,INDEX,JOBTQ,TASKQ
        REAL DELAY

*       Determine the machine group from which the job is departing.

        JOBTYP = TRNSFR(3)
        TASK   = TRNSFR(4)
        GROUP  = ROUTE(JOBTYP,TASK)

*       Check to see whether the queue for this machine group is empty.

        IF (LSIZE(GROUP) .EQ. 0) THEN

*           The queue for this machine group is empty, so make a machine in
*           this group idle.

            NBUSY(GROUP) = NBUSY(GROUP) - 1
            CALL TIMEST(FLOAT(NBUSY(GROUP)),GROUP)

        ELSE

*           The queue is not empty, so start service on first job in queue.

            CALL REMOVE(LFIRST,GROUP)
            DELAY = TIME - TRNSFR(1)

*           Tally this delay for this machine group.

            CALL SAMPST(DELAY,GROUP)

*           Tally this same delay for this job type.

            JOBTQ = TRNSFR(2)
            TASKQ = TRNSFR(3)
            INDEX = NGROUP + JOBTQ
            CALL SAMPST(DELAY,INDEX)

*           Schedule end of service for this job at this machine group.

            TRNSFR(1) = TIME + ERLANG(2,MSERVT(JOBTQ,TASKQ),3)
            TRNSFR(2) = 2.0
            TRNSFR(3) = JOBTQ
            TRNSFR(4) = TASKQ
            CALL FILE(LINCR,LEVENT)

        END IF

*       If the current departing job has one or more tasks yet to be done,
*       send the job to the next machine group on its route.

        IF (TASK .LT. NTASKS(JOBTYP)) THEN
            TASK = TASK + 1
            CALL ARRIVE(2)
        END IF

        RETURN
        END
```

FIGURE 2.44
FORTRAN code for subroutine DEPART, job-shop model.

job are obtained from the departure event record, which was placed in the TRNSFR array by TIMING, and the machine group GROUP from which this job is leaving is then looked up in the routing matrix. If the queue for this group is empty, a machine in the group is idled, and TIMEST is notified. If there is a queue, the first job is removed from it (having job type JOBTQ and task number TASKQ, to maintain its distinction from the earlier job that is leaving this group), its delay is registered in the two appropriate SAMPST variables, and its departure from this group is scheduled; again, for long simulations TIME and TRNSFR might have to be DOUBLE PRECISION to avoid excessive roundoff error in the subtraction for the delay calculation.

```
      SUBROUTINE REPORT
      INCLUDE 'jobshop.dcl'
      INTEGER I,INDEX
      REAL AJDEL(5),AMDEL(5),AUTIL(5),AVGNIQ(5),OAJDEL,SUM

*     Compute the average total delay in queue for each job type and the
*     overall average job delay.

      OAJDEL    = 0.0
      SUM       = 0.0
      DO 10 I = 1, NTYPES
         INDEX = NGROUP + I
         CALL SAMPST(0.0,-INDEX)
         AJDEL(I) = TRNSFR(1) * NTASKS(I)
         OAJDEL   = OAJDEL + (PROBD(I) - SUM) * AJDEL(I)
         SUM      = PROBD(I)
   10 CONTINUE

*     Compute the average number in queue, the average utilization, and
*     the average delay in queue for each machine group.

      DO 20 I = 1, NGROUP
         CALL SAMPST(0.0,-I)
         AMDEL(I) = TRNSFR(1)
         CALL FILEST(I)
         AVGNIQ(I) = TRNSFR(1)
         CALL TIMEST(0.0,-I)
         AUTIL(I) = TRNSFR(1) / NMACHS(I)
   20 CONTINUE
      WRITE (6,2010)
 2010 FORMAT (///' Job type      Average total delay in queue')
      DO 30 I = 1, NTYPES
   30 WRITE (6,2020) I, AJDEL(I)
 2020 FORMAT (/I5,F27.3)
      WRITE (6,2030) OAJDEL
 2030 FORMAT (/' Overall average job total delay =',F10.3
     &        ////' Machine      Average number         Average',7X,
     &             'Average delay'/
     &        '  group      number in queue      utilization',5X,
     &        '   in queue')
      DO 40 I = 1, NGROUP
   40 WRITE (6,2040) I, AVGNIQ(I), AUTIL(I), AMDEL(I)
 2040 FORMAT (/I5,3F17.3)

      RETURN
      END
```

FIGURE 2.45
FORTRAN code for subroutine REPORT, job-shop model.

Finally, if the job leaving this group still has more tasks to be done, its task number is incremented and it is sent on its way to the next group on its route by calling ARRIVE, now with NEW set to 2 to indicate that this is not a newly arrived job.

The code for the report generator is in Fig. 2.45. The first DO loop (with foot at 10) computes the average total delay in queue for each job type, then weights them by the probabilities for the job types and adds them up to get the overall average job total delay, OAJDEL. For each job type I, note that after calling SAMPST we multiply TRNSFR(1) (the average value) by the number of tasks for job type I, NTASKS(I), since SAMPST was called for each job of this type that left the system NTASKS(I) times rather than once, so that the denominator used by SAMPST to compute the average is NTASKS(I) times too large. Also, we must take successive differences in the PROBD array to recover the probabilities of the job types' occurring, since PROBD contains the *cumulative* probabilities. [A technicality: The above multiplication of TRNSFR(1) by NTASKS(I) in loop 10 is slightly incorrect. Since there will be some jobs left in the system at the end of the simulation that have not experienced their delays in all the queues, they should not have had *any* of their delays registered in SAMPST. However, since this simulation is $365 \times 8 = 2920$ hours long and since there are 4 job arrivals expected each hour, there will be an expected 11,680 job arrivals, so this error is likely to be minor. See Prob. 2.5 for an alternative way of collecting the total delays in queue by job type, which avoids this difficulty.]

The function to generate an M-Erlang random variable is in Fig. 2.46, and follows the physical model for the Erlang distribution described earlier. Note that we must divide the desired expectation of the final Erlang random variable by M to determine the expectation of the component exponential random variables. Also, the user-specified stream number, ISTRM, is taken as input here and simply passed through to the random-number generator RAND.

```
      REAL FUNCTION ERLANG(M,RMEAN,ISTRM)
      INTEGER I,M,ISTRM
      REAL MEXP,RMEAN
      REAL EXPON

*     Generate an M-Erlang random variate with mean RMEAN using stream
*     ISTRM.

      MEXP = RMEAN / M
      ERLANG = 0.0
      DO 10 I = 1, M
   10 ERLANG = ERLANG + EXPON(MEXP,ISTRM)

      RETURN
      END
```

FIGURE 2.46
FORTRAN code for function ERLANG, job-shop model.

2.7.3 Simulation Output and Discussion

Figure 2.47 shows the output file (jobshop.out) for this simulation. Weighted by job type, the average time spent by jobs waiting in the queues was almost 11 hours; this is not the average time in the shop, since it does not include processing times at the machine groups (see Prob. 2.6).

```
Job-shop model

Number of machine groups                5

Number of machines in each group        3    2    4    3    1

Number of job types                     3

Number of tasks for each job type       4    3    5

Distribution function of job types    0.300  0.800  1.000

Mean interarrival time of jobs        0.25 hours

Length of the simulation              365.0 eight-hour days
```

Job type	Machine groups on route				
1	3	1	2	5	
2	4	1	3		
3	2	5	1	4	3

Job type	Mean service time (in hours) for successive tasks				
1	0.50	0.60	0.85	0.50	
2	1.10	0.80	0.75		
3	1.20	0.25	0.70	0.90	1.00

Job type	Average total delay in queue
1	10.022
2	9.403
3	15.808

```
Overall average job total delay =    10.870
```

Machine group	Average number number in queue	Average utilization	Average delay in queue
1	12.310	0.969	3.055
2	11.404	0.978	5.677
3	0.711	0.719	0.177
4	17.098	0.961	6.110
5	2.095	0.797	1.043

FIGURE 2.47
Output report, job-shop model.

TABLE 2.5
Estimated expected overall average job total delays for current and proposed machine configurations

Number of machines in groups	Overall average job total delay, in hours
3, 2, 4, 3, 1 (current configuration)	10.9
4, 2, 4, 3, 1 (add a machine to group 1)	8.1
3, 3, 4, 3, 1 (add a machine to group 2)	7.6
3, 2, 4, 4, 1 (add a machine to group 4)	7.5

Looking at the statistics by machine group, it appears that the bottlenecks are at machine groups 1, 2, and 4, although the order of their apparent severity depends on whether we look at average number in queue, utilization, or average delay in queue. Thus, we made three additional runs, adding a machine to each of these groups (machine groups 3 and 5 appear to be comparatively uncongested, so we did not consider them for a new machine) to see which type of new machine would have the greatest impact on the shop's efficiency. Using the overall average job total delay as a single measure of performance, the results from these additional simulations are in Table 2.5. From simply looking at these numbers, we see that a machine should apparently be added to group 4 to achieve the greatest reduction in overall average job total delay. As usual, however, this conclusion is rather tentative, since we have only a single simulation run of each model variant; this is especially true in this case, since the results for the three new machine configurations are really much too close to call.

2.8 EFFICIENT EVENT-LIST MANIPULATION

Common to all of the dynamic simulations we have considered in this and the preceding chapter is the need to schedule future events in some way, and to determine which of the events scheduled should occur next. We have looked at two different ways to handle the event list. In Chap. 1 it was stored sequentially, with the storage index number being the event type, and the next-event determination was made by searching the event list from top to bottom for the smallest event time. Then in Chap. 2, armed with SIMLIB's ability to handle linked lists, we have stored the event list as a doubly linked list ranked in increasing order on the event-time attribute while using another attribute for the event type; it was easy to determine the next event since it was always on top of the event list. Placing the event record on the list, however, was more work, since it involved searching for the correct location. In either case, a search of the event list is required, either when taking the event off the list or when putting it on.

The need for some sort of event-list processing in dynamic simulations has led a number of researchers to investigate whether other methods might be faster, at least for some types of simulations. For complex simulations involving a large number of events, much of the computer time required to perform the simulation can be expended on event-list processing. Comfort (1981) reported that for one example class of models, the number of instructions required to process the event list can comprise as much as 40 percent of the total number of instructions for the whole simulation. McCormack (1979) and McCormack and Sargent (1981) provide additional evidence that the choice of event-processing algorithm can have a great impact on simulation execution time. Henriksen (1983) used the term "spectacular failure" to describe the performance (in the case of one example model) of the simple top-to-bottom search to insert event records into the event list; Reeves (1984) suggested that ". . . it may be thought scandalous" to continue to use this method of storing and managing the event list.

One way to improve the SIMLIB method of searching for the correct location of the new event record would be to use a more efficient search technique. One well-known search algorithm, known as *binary search*, would introduce another pointer for the event list (in addition to the head and tail pointers), which would always point to the middle record of the event list, or one of the two middle records if the list has an even number of records. When a new event record is to be placed on the list, the record at (or adjacent to) the middle pointer is first examined to determine whether the new record should be placed in the first half or in the second half of the event list. The appropriate half of the list is then searched sequentially to determine the new record's location. (Strictly speaking, the term "binary search" would imply that the chosen half-list would itself be split into two quarter-lists, the appropriate one of which would be split again, etc. If the event list is stored as a linked list, however, this would involve maintaining many additional pointers to identify all of these split points.) For simulations in which the event list can become very long (such as the time-shared computer model of Sec. 2.5 with a very large number of terminals), such a method could make a real difference in overall computation time. (See Prob. 2.35.)

There are many other algorithms for event-list processing, some involving data structures other than linked lists (trees, heaps, etc.). Comfort (1979) provides a taxonomy of event-list-management techniques and Henriksen (1983) gives a good tutorial on some of these, as well as references to the literature; more recent general discussions are provided by Devroye (1986, pp. 735–748), Jones et al. (1986), Kingston (1986), and Brown (1988), all of which cite additional references.

The choice of the best event-list-handling algorithm may depend on the type of simulation, the parameters and distributions used, and other factors that influence how the events are distributed in the event list. For example, in a simulation for which the time elapsing between when an event is scheduled (i.e., put on the event list) and when it occurs (i.e., taken off the event list) is more or less the same for all events, the events will tend to be inserted toward the end of the list in a linked-list data structure; in this case, it could be advantageous to search the event list from bottom to top, since in most cases the search would end quickly. Most modern simulation languages (see Chap. 3) use efficient event-list-processing algorithms; see Henriksen (1983).

APPENDIX 2A
FORTRAN CODE FOR SIMLIB

The FORTRAN code for the subroutines and functions composing SIMLIB are given in Figs. 2.48 through 2.61. In subroutine TIMEST in Fig. 2.54, a subtraction occurs at statement label 200 involving the simulation clock (TIME) and the time of the last event [TLVC(VARIBL)]; for long simulations, both could become very large relative to their difference, so might have to be made DOUBLE PRECISION to avoid loss of precision in this subtraction. The random-number generator RAND included in SIMLIB is not shown here, but is given in Fig. 7.5. Most of the SIMLIB subroutines contain the common block LLISTS, which consists of the following variables:

Variable	Definition
HEAD(LIST)	Head pointer for list LIST (LIST = 1, 2, . . . , 25)
IOUT	Output unit number for SIMLIB error messages (set to 6 by INITLK)
LINKPR(I)	Predecessor link for row I of array MASTER (I = 1, 2, . . . , 1000)
LINKSR(I)	Successor link for row I of array MASTER (I = 1, 2, . . . , 1000)
MASTER(I, J)	Value (REAL) of the entry in the I*th* row and J*th* column of array MASTER (I = 1, 2, . . . , 1000 and J = 1, 2, . . . , 10)
NAR	Next available row in array MASTER, i.e., head of the list of available space
TAIL(LIST)	Tail pointer for list LIST (LIST = 1, 2, . . . , 25)

```
      SUBROUTINE INITLK

      INTEGER HEAD(25),IOUT,LINKPR(1000),LINKSR(1000),LIST,NAR,ROW,
     &        TAIL(25)
      REAL MASTER(1000,10)
      COMMON /LLISTS/ HEAD,IOUT,LINKPR,LINKSR,MASTER,NAR,TAIL

      INTEGER LDECR,LEVENT,LFIRST,LINCR,LLAST,LRANK(25),LSIZE(25),
     &        MAXATR,NEXT
      REAL TIME,TRNSFR(10)
      COMMON /SIMLIB/ LDECR,LEVENT,LFIRST,LINCR,LLAST,LRANK,LSIZE,
     &                MAXATR,NEXT,TIME,TRNSFR

*     Ensure integrity of variables in COMMON block LLISTS, which
*     appears for the first time in a subprogram.

      SAVE

*     Initialize links.

      DO 10 ROW = 1, 1000
         LINKPR(ROW) = 0
   10 LINKSR(ROW) = ROW + 1
      LINKSR(1000) = 0
```

FIGURE 2.48
SIMLIB routine INITLK.

```
*      Initialize list attributes.

       DO 20 LIST = 1, 25
          HEAD(LIST)  = 0
          TAIL(LIST)  = 0
          LSIZE(LIST) = 0
   20 LRANK(LIST) = 0

*      Initialize mnemonics for record location in lists.

       LFIRST = 1
       LLAST  = 2
       LINCR  = 3
       LDECR  = 4

*      Initialize mnemonic for event list number.

       LEVENT = 25

*      Initialize system attributes.

       TIME           = 0.0
       NAR            = 1
       LRANK(LEVENT)  = 1
       MAXATR         = 10

*      Initialize statistical routines.

       CALL SAMPST(0.0,0)
       CALL TIMEST(0.0,0)

*      Initialize output unit number for SIMLIB error messages.

       IOUT = 6

       RETURN
       END
```

FIGURE 2.48
(*Continued.*)

```
       SUBROUTINE FILE(OPTION,LIST)

       INTEGER AHEAD,BEHIND,HEAD(25),IHEAD,IOUT,ITAIL,ITEM,LINKPR(1000),
      &        LINKSR(1000),LIST,NAR,OPTION,ROW,TAIL(25)
       REAL MASTER(1000,10),SIZE
       COMMON /LLISTS/ HEAD,IOUT,LINKPR,LINKSR,MASTER,NAR,TAIL

       INTEGER LDECR,LEVENT,LFIRST,LINCR,LLAST,LRANK(25),LSIZE(25),
      &        MAXATR,NEXT
       REAL TIME,TRNSFR(10)
       COMMON /SIMLIB/ LDECR,LEVENT,LFIRST,LINCR,LLAST,LRANK,LSIZE,
      &                MAXATR,NEXT,TIME,TRNSFR

*      If the master storage array is full, stop the simulation.

       IF (NAR .EQ. 0) THEN
          WRITE (IOUT,10) TIME
   10     FORMAT (' From SIMLIB: MASTER storage array overflow at time',
      &           F10.3)
          STOP
       END IF
```

FIGURE 2.49
SIMLIB routine FILE.

```
*     If the list value is improper, stop the simulation.

      IF (LIST .LT. 1 .OR. LIST .GT. 25) THEN
         WRITE (IOUT,20) LIST, TIME
   20    FORMAT (' From SIMLIB:',I10,
     &               ' is an improper value for FILE LIST at time ',F10.3)
         STOP
      END IF

*     Increment the list size.

      LSIZE(LIST) = LSIZE(LIST) + 1

*     If the option value is improper, stop the simulation.

      IF (OPTION .LT. 1 .OR. OPTION .GT. 4) THEN
         WRITE (IOUT,30) OPTION, TIME
   30    FORMAT (' From SIMLIB:',I10,
     &               ' is an improper value for FILE OPTION at time ',F10.3)
         STOP
      END IF

*     File according to the desired option.

      GO TO (300, 200, 100, 100), OPTION

*     List is ranked. Determine item on which list is to be ranked.

  100 ITEM = LRANK(LIST)

*     If an invalid item has been specified, stop the simulation.

      IF (ITEM .LT. 1 .OR. ITEM .GT. MAXATR) THEN
         WRITE (IOUT,110) ITEM, LIST
  110    FORMAT (' From SIMLIB:',I10,
     &               ' is an improper value for ranking attribute of list',
     &            I3)
         STOP
      END IF

*     If this is not the first record in this list, continue.

      IF (LSIZE(LIST) .EQ. 1) GO TO 400

*     Search the list for the proper location.

      ROW = HEAD(LIST)
  120 IF (OPTION .EQ. 4) GO TO 130

*     Rank the list in increasing order.

      IF (TRNSFR(ITEM) .GE. MASTER(ROW,ITEM)) GO TO 150

*     The correct location has been found.

      GO TO 140

*     Rank the list in decreasing order.

  130 IF (TRNSFR(ITEM) .LE. MASTER(ROW,ITEM)) GO TO 150
```

FIGURE 2.49
(*Continued.*)

```
*      Correct location found. Insert before last record examined.

  140 IF (ROW .EQ. HEAD(LIST)) GO TO 300

*      Insert in proper location between preceding, succeeding records.

      AHEAD = LINKSR(BEHIND)
      ROW   = NAR
      NAR   = LINKSR(ROW)
      IF (NAR .GT. 0) LINKPR(NAR) = 0
      LINKPR(ROW)    = BEHIND
      LINKSR(BEHIND) = ROW
      LINKPR(AHEAD)  = ROW
      LINKSR(ROW)    = AHEAD

*      Go to transfer the data.

      GO TO 500

*      Continue searching, consider the next row.

  150 BEHIND = ROW
      ROW    = LINKSR(BEHIND)

*      If last row considered was not the tail of the list, continue.

      IF (TAIL(LIST) .NE. BEHIND) GO TO 120

*      Insert after the last record in the list.

  200 IF (LSIZE(LIST) .EQ. 1) GO TO 400
      ROW = NAR
      NAR = LINKSR(ROW)
      IF (NAR .GT. 0) LINKPR(NAR) = 0
      ITAIL         = TAIL(LIST)
      LINKPR(ROW)   = ITAIL
      LINKSR(ITAIL) = ROW
      LINKSR(ROW)   = 0
      TAIL(LIST)    = ROW

*      Go to transfer the data.

      GO TO 500

*      Insert before the first record in the list.

  300 IF (LSIZE(LIST) .EQ. 1) GO TO 400
      ROW = NAR
      NAR = LINKSR(ROW)
      IF (NAR .GT. 0) LINKPR(NAR) = 0
      IHEAD         = HEAD(LIST)
      LINKPR(IHEAD) = ROW
      LINKSR(ROW)   = IHEAD
      LINKPR(ROW)   = 0
      HEAD(LIST)    = ROW

*      Go to transfer the data.

      GO TO 500
```

FIGURE 2.49
(*Continued.*)

```
*       Insert the first record in the list.

   400 ROW = NAR
       NAR = LINKSR(ROW)
       IF (NAR .GT. 0) LINKPR(NAR) = 0
       LINKSR(ROW) = 0
       HEAD(LIST)  = ROW
       TAIL(LIST)  = ROW

*       Transfer the data.

   500 DO 510 ITEM = 1, MAXATR
   510 MASTER(ROW,ITEM) = TRNSFR(ITEM)

*       Update the area under the number-in-list curve.

       CALL TIMEST(FLOAT(LSIZE(LIST)),20 + LIST)

       RETURN
       END
```

FIGURE 2.49
(*Continued.*)

```
       SUBROUTINE REMOVE(OPTION,LIST)

       INTEGER HEAD(25),IHEAD,IOUT,ITAIL,ITEM,LINKPR(1000),LINKSR(1000),
      &        LIST,NAR,OPTION,ROW,TAIL(25)
       REAL MASTER(1000,10),SIZE
       COMMON /LLISTS/ HEAD,IOUT,LINKPR,LINKSR,MASTER,NAR,TAIL

       INTEGER LDECR,LEVENT,LFIRST,LINCR,LLAST,LRANK(25),LSIZE(25),
      &        MAXATR,NEXT
       REAL TIME,TRNSFR(10)
       COMMON /SIMLIB/ LDECR,LEVENT,LFIRST,LINCR,LLAST,LRANK,LSIZE,
      &                MAXATR,NEXT,TIME,TRNSFR

*       If the list value is improper, stop the simulation.

       IF (LIST .LT. 1 .OR. LIST .GT. 25) THEN
           WRITE (IOUT,10) LIST, TIME
    10     FORMAT (' From SIMLIB:',I10,
      &            ' is an improper value for REMOVE LIST at time ',F10.3)
           STOP
       END IF

*       If the list is empty, stop the simulation.

       IF (LSIZE(LIST) .LE. 0) THEN
           WRITE (IOUT,20) LIST, TIME
    20     FORMAT (' From SIMLIB: underflow of list ',I2,
      &            ' at time ',F10.3)
           STOP
       END IF

*       Decrement the list size.

       LSIZE(LIST) = LSIZE(LIST) - 1
```

FIGURE 2.50
SIMLIB routine REMOVE.

```
*      If the option value is improper, stop the simulation.

       IF (OPTION .NE. 1 .AND. OPTION .NE. 2) THEN
           WRITE (IOUT,30) OPTION, TIME
   30      FORMAT (' From SIMLIB:',I10,
       &             ' is improper value for REMOVE OPTION at time ',F10.3)
           STOP
       END IF


*      If there is more than one record in the list, continue.

       IF (LSIZE(LIST) .EQ. 0) GO TO 300


*      Remove according to the desired option.

       GO TO (100, 200), OPTION


*      Remove the first record in the list.

  100 ROW           = HEAD(LIST)
      IHEAD         = LINKSR(ROW)
      LINKPR(IHEAD) = 0
      HEAD(LIST)    = IHEAD

*      Go to transfer the data.

       GO TO 400

*      Remove the last record in the list.

  200 ROW           = TAIL(LIST)
      ITAIL         = LINKPR(ROW)
      LINKSR(ITAIL) = 0
      TAIL(LIST)    = ITAIL

*      Go to transfer the data.

       GO TO 400


*      Remove the only record in the list.

  300 ROW        = HEAD(LIST)
      HEAD(LIST) = 0
      TAIL(LIST) = 0


*      Transfer the data.

  400 LINKSR(ROW) = NAR
      LINKPR(ROW) = 0
      NAR         = ROW
      DO 410 ITEM = 1, MAXATR
  410 TRNSFR(ITEM) = MASTER(ROW,ITEM)


*      Update the area under the number-in-list curve.

       CALL TIMEST(FLOAT(LSIZE(LIST)),20 + LIST)

       RETURN
       END
```

FIGURE 2.50
(*Continued.*)

```
      SUBROUTINE TIMING

      INTEGER HEAD(25),IOUT,LINKPR(1000),LINKSR(1000),NAR,TAIL(25)
      REAL MASTER(1000,10)
      COMMON /LLISTS/ HEAD,IOUT,LINKPR,LINKSR,MASTER,NAR,TAIL

      INTEGER LDECR,LEVENT,LFIRST,LINCR,LLAST,LRANK(25),LSIZE(25),
     &        MAXATR,NEXT
      REAL TIME,TRNSFR(10)
      COMMON /SIMLIB/ LDECR,LEVENT,LFIRST,LINCR,LLAST,LRANK,LSIZE,
     &                MAXATR,NEXT,TIME,TRNSFR

*     Remove the first event from the event list.

      CALL REMOVE(LFIRST,LEVENT)

*     Check for a time reversal.

      IF (TRNSFR(1) .LT. TIME) THEN
          WRITE (IOUT,10) TRNSFR(2), TRNSFR(1), TIME
   10     FORMAT (' From SIMLIB: Attempt to schedule an event of type ',
     &            F3.0/' at time ',F10.3,' when the clock is ',F10.3)
          STOP
      END IF

*     Advance the simulation clock.

      TIME = TRNSFR(1)
      NEXT = TRNSFR(2)

      RETURN
      END
```

FIGURE 2.51
SIMLIB routine TIMING.

```
      SUBROUTINE CANCEL(ETYPE)

      INTEGER AHEAD,BEHIND,HEAD(25),IOUT,ITEM,LINKPR(1000),LINKSR(1000),
     &        NAR,ROW,TAIL(25)
      REAL ETYPE,HIGH,LOW,MASTER(1000,10),SIZE,VALUE
      COMMON /LLISTS/ HEAD,IOUT,LINKPR,LINKSR,MASTER,NAR,TAIL

      INTEGER LDECR,LEVENT,LFIRST,LINCR,LLAST,LRANK(25),LSIZE(25),
     &        MAXATR,NEXT
      REAL TIME,TRNSFR(10)
      COMMON /SIMLIB/ LDECR,LEVENT,LFIRST,LINCR,LLAST,LRANK,LSIZE,
     &                MAXATR,NEXT,TIME,TRNSFR

*     Search the event list.

      IF (LSIZE(LEVENT) .EQ. 0) RETURN
      ROW    = HEAD(LEVENT)
      LOW    = ETYPE - 0.1
      HIGH   = ETYPE + 0.1
   10 VALUE = MASTER(ROW,2)
      IF (LOW .LT. VALUE .AND. HIGH .GT. VALUE) GO TO 20
```

FIGURE 2.52
SIMLIB routine CANCEL.

```
*      Go to the next event.

       IF (ROW .EQ. TAIL(LEVENT)) RETURN
       ROW = LINKSR(ROW)
       GO TO 10

*      Cancel this event.

   20 IF (ROW .NE. HEAD(LEVENT)) GO TO 30

*      Remove the first event in the event list.

       CALL REMOVE(LFIRST,LEVENT)
       RETURN

   30 IF (ROW .NE. TAIL(LEVENT)) GO TO 40

*      Remove the last event in the event list.

       CALL REMOVE(LLAST,LEVENT)
       RETURN

*      Remove this event which is somewhere in the middle of event list.

   40 AHEAD           = LINKSR(ROW)
      BEHIND          = LINKPR(ROW)
      LINKSR(BEHIND)  = AHEAD
      LINKPR(AHEAD)   = BEHIND
      LINKSR(ROW)     = NAR
      LINKPR(ROW)     = 0
      NAR             = ROW
      LSIZE(LEVENT)   = LSIZE(LEVENT) - 1

*      Place the attributes of the canceled event in the TRNSFR array.

       DO 50 ITEM = 1, MAXATR
   50 TRNSFR(ITEM) = MASTER(ROW,ITEM)

*      Update the area under the number-in-list curve.

       CALL TIMEST(FLOAT(LSIZE(LEVENT)),45)

       RETURN
       END
```

FIGURE 2.52
(*Continued.*)

```
       SUBROUTINE SAMPST(VALUE,VARIBL)

       INTEGER HEAD(25),IOUT,IVAR,LINKPR(1000),LINKSR(1000),NAR,NOBS(20),
      &        TAIL(25),VARIBL
       REAL MASTER(1000,10),MAX(20),MIN(20),SUM(20),VALUE
       COMMON /LLISTS/ HEAD,IOUT,LINKPR,LINKSR,MASTER,NAR,TAIL

       INTEGER LDECR,LEVENT,LFIRST,LINCR,LLAST,LRANK(25),LSIZE(25),
      &        MAXATR,NEXT
       REAL TIME,TRNSFR(10)
       COMMON /SIMLIB/ LDECR,LEVENT,LFIRST,LINCR,LLAST,LRANK,LSIZE,
      &                MAXATR,NEXT,TIME,TRNSFR
```

FIGURE 2.53
SIMLIB routine SAMPST.

```
*      Force saving of local accumulator arrays between calls.

       SAVE MAX,MIN,NOBS,SUM

*      If the variable number is improper, stop the simulation.

       IF (VARIBL .LT. -20 .OR. VARIBL .GT. 20) THEN
           WRITE (IOUT,10) VARIBL, TIME
   10      FORMAT (' From SIMLIB:',I10,
       &              ' is improper value for SAMPST variable at time ',
       &            F10.3)
           STOP
       END IF

*      Execute the desired option.

       IF (VARIBL) 300, 100, 200

*      Initialize the routine.

  100 DO 110 IVAR = 1, 20
          SUM(IVAR)  = 0.0
          MAX(IVAR)  = -1.0E+30
          MIN(IVAR)  = 1.0E+30
  110 NOBS(IVAR) = 0
      RETURN

*      Collect data.

  200 SUM(VARIBL) = SUM(VARIBL) + VALUE
      IF (VALUE .GT. MAX(VARIBL)) MAX(VARIBL) = VALUE
      IF (VALUE .LT. MIN(VARIBL)) MIN(VARIBL) = VALUE
      NOBS(VARIBL) = NOBS(VARIBL) + 1
      RETURN

*      Report the results.

  300 IVAR       = -VARIBL
      TRNSFR(1) = 0.0
      TRNSFR(2) = NOBS(IVAR)
      TRNSFR(3) = MAX(IVAR)
      TRNSFR(4) = MIN(IVAR)
      IF (NOBS(IVAR) .EQ. 0) RETURN
      TRNSFR(1) = SUM(IVAR) / TRNSFR(2)

      RETURN
      END
```

FIGURE 2.53
(*Continued.*)

```
       SUBROUTINE TIMEST(VALUE,VARIBL)

       INTEGER HEAD(25),IOUT,IVAR,LINKPR(1000),LINKSR(1000),NAR,TAIL(25),
      &         VARIBL
       REAL AREA(45),MASTER(1000,10),MAX(45),MIN(45),PREVAL(45),TLVC(45),
      &      VALUE,TRESET
       COMMON /LLISTS/ HEAD,IOUT,LINKPR,LINKSR,MASTER,NAR,TAIL
```

FIGURE 2.54
SIMLIB routine TIMEST.

```
      INTEGER LDECR,LEVENT,LFIRST,LINCR,LLAST,LRANK(25),LSIZE(25),
     &        MAXATR,NEXT
      REAL TIME,TRNSFR(10)
      COMMON /SIMLIB/ LDECR,LEVENT,LFIRST,LINCR,LLAST,LRANK,LSIZE,
     &                MAXATR,NEXT,TIME,TRNSFR


*     Force saving of local accumulator arrays between calls.


      SAVE AREA,MAX,MIN,PREVAL,TLVC


*     If the variable value is improper, stop the simulation.


      IF (VARIBL .LT. -45 .OR. VARIBL .GT. 45) THEN
         WRITE (IOUT,10) VARIBL, TIME
   10    FORMAT (' From SIMLIB:',I10,
     &           ' is improper value for TIMEST variable at time ',
     &           F10.3)
         STOP
      END IF


*     Execute the desired option.

      IF (VARIBL) 300, 100, 200

*     Initialize the routine.

  100 DO 110 IVAR = 1, 45
         AREA(IVAR)   = 0.0
         MAX(IVAR)    = -1.0E+30
         MIN(IVAR)    = 1.0E+30
         PREVAL(IVAR) = 0.0
  110 TLVC(IVAR)      = TIME
      TRESET = TIME
      RETURN

*     Collect data.


  200 AREA(VARIBL) = AREA(VARIBL) + (TIME - TLVC(VARIBL))*PREVAL(VARIBL)
      IF (VALUE .GT. MAX(VARIBL)) MAX(VARIBL) = VALUE
      IF (VALUE .LT. MIN(VARIBL)) MIN(VARIBL) = VALUE
      PREVAL(VARIBL) = VALUE
      TLVC(VARIBL) = TIME
      RETURN


*     Report the results.

  300 IVAR       = -VARIBL
      AREA(IVAR) = AREA(IVAR) + (TIME - TLVC(IVAR)) * PREVAL(IVAR)
      TLVC(IVAR) = TIME
      TRNSFR(1)  = AREA(IVAR) / (TIME - TRESET)
      TRNSFR(2)  = MAX(IVAR)
      TRNSFR(3)  = MIN(IVAR)

      RETURN
      END
```

FIGURE 2.54
(*Continued.*)

```
      SUBROUTINE FILEST(LIST)

      INTEGER ILIST,LIST

      INTEGER LDECR,LEVENT,LFIRST,LINCR,LLAST,LRANK(25),LSIZE(25),
     &        MAXATR,NEXT
      REAL TIME,TRNSFR(10)
      COMMON /SIMLIB/ LDECR,LEVENT,LFIRST,LINCR,LLAST,LRANK,LSIZE,
     &                MAXATR,NEXT,TIME,TRNSFR

*     Compute summary statistics for the list.

      ILIST = -(20 + LIST)
      CALL TIMEST(0.0,ILIST)

      RETURN
      END
```

FIGURE 2.55
SIMLIB routine FILEST.

```
      SUBROUTINE OUTSAM(UNIT,LOWVAR,HIVAR)

      INTEGER HIVAR,I,IVAR,LOWVAR,UNIT

      INTEGER LDECR,LEVENT,LFIRST,LINCR,LLAST,LRANK(25),LSIZE(25),
     &        MAXATR,NEXT
      REAL TIME,TRNSFR(10)
      COMMON /SIMLIB/ LDECR,LEVENT,LFIRST,LINCR,LLAST,LRANK,LSIZE,
     &                MAXATR,NEXT,TIME,TRNSFR

*     Write header.

      WRITE (UNIT,10)
   10 FORMAT (/'  SAMPST ',24X,'Number'/
     &         ' Variable',26X,'of'/
     &         '  Number ',6X,'Average',11X,'Values',10X,'Maximum',
     &        10X,'Minimum'/1X,76('_'))

*     Loop for desired SAMPST variable range.

      DO 20 IVAR = LOWVAR, HIVAR

*        Obtain and write summary statistics on SAMPST variable IVAR.

         CALL SAMPST(0.0,-IVAR)
   20 WRITE (UNIT,30) IVAR, (TRNSFR(I), I = 1, 4)
   30 FORMAT (/3X,I3,3X,4(1X,E15.7,1X))
      WRITE (UNIT,40)
   40 FORMAT (1X,76('_'))

      RETURN
      END
```

FIGURE 2.56
SIMLIB routine OUTSAM.

```
      SUBROUTINE OUTTIM(UNIT,LOWVAR,HIVAR)

      INTEGER HIVAR,I,IVAR,LOWVAR,UNIT

      INTEGER LDECR,LEVENT,LFIRST,LINCR,LLAST,LRANK(25),LSIZE(25),
     &        MAXATR,NEXT
      REAL TIME,TRNSFR(10)
      COMMON /SIMLIB/ LDECR,LEVENT,LFIRST,LINCR,LLAST,LRANK,LSIZE,
     &                MAXATR,NEXT,TIME,TRNSFR

*     Write header.

      WRITE (UNIT,10)
   10 FORMAT (/'  TIMEST '/
     &        ' Variable',7X,'Time'/
     &        ' Number ',6X,'Average',10X,'Maximum',10X,'Minimum'/
     &        1X,59('_'))

*     Loop for desired TIMEST variable range.

      DO 20 IVAR = LOWVAR, HIVAR

*        Obtain and write summary statistics on TIMEST variable IVAR.

         CALL TIMEST(0.0,-IVAR)
   20 WRITE (UNIT,30) IVAR, (TRNSFR(I), I = 1, 3)
   30 FORMAT (/3X,I3,3X,3(1X,E15.7,1X))
      WRITE (UNIT,40)
   40 FORMAT (1X,59('_'))

      RETURN
      END
```

FIGURE 2.57
SIMLIB routine OUTTIM.

```
      SUBROUTINE OUTFIL(UNIT,LOWFIL,HIFIL)

      INTEGER HIFIL,I,IFIL,LOWFIL,UNIT

      INTEGER LDECR,LEVENT,LFIRST,LINCR,LLAST,LRANK(25),LSIZE(25),
     &        MAXATR,NEXT
      REAL TIME,TRNSFR(10)
      COMMON /SIMLIB/ LDECR,LEVENT,LFIRST,LINCR,LLAST,LRANK,LSIZE,
     &                MAXATR,NEXT,TIME,TRNSFR

*     Write header.

      WRITE (UNIT,10)
   10 FORMAT (/'   File ',8X,'Time'/
     &        ' Number',7X,'Average',10X,'Maximum',10X,'Minimum'/
     &        1X,59('_'))

*     Loop for desired file number range.

      DO 20 IFIL = LOWFIL, HIFIL

*        Obtain and write summary statistics on file IFIL.

         CALL FILEST(IFIL)
   20 WRITE (UNIT,30) IFIL, (TRNSFR(I), I = 1, 3)
   30 FORMAT (/3X,I3,3X,3(1X,E15.7,1X))
      WRITE (UNIT,40)
   40 FORMAT (1X,59('_'))

      RETURN
      END
```

FIGURE 2.58
SIMLIB routine OUTFIL.

```
      REAL FUNCTION EXPON(RMEAN,ISTRM)

      INTEGER ISTRM
      REAL RMEAN,U
      REAL RAND

*     Generate a U(0,1) random variate from stream ISTRM.

      U = RAND(ISTRM)

*     Generate an exponential random variate with mean RMEAN.

      EXPON = -RMEAN * LOG(U)
      RETURN
      END
```

FIGURE 2.59
SIMLIB routine EXPON.

```
      INTEGER FUNCTION IRANDI(NVALUE,PROBD,ISTRM)

      INTEGER I,ISTRM,NVALUE
      REAL PROBD(1),U
      REAL RAND

*     Generate a U(0,1) random variate from stream ISTRM.

      U = RAND(ISTRM)

*     Generate a random integer between 1 and NVALUE in accordance with
*     the (cumulative) distribution function PROBD.

      DO 10 I = 1, NVALUE - 1
         IF (U .LT. PROBD(I)) THEN
            IRANDI = I
            RETURN
         END IF
   10 CONTINUE
      IRANDI = NVALUE

      RETURN
      END
```

FIGURE 2.60
SIMLIB routine IRANDI.

```
      REAL FUNCTION UNIFRM(A,B,ISTRM)

      INTEGER ISTRM
      REAL A,B,U
      REAL RAND

*     Generate a U(0,1) random variate from stream ISTRM.

      U = RAND(ISTRM)

*     Generate a U(A,B) random variate.

      UNIFRM = A + U * (B - A)
      RETURN
      END
```

FIGURE 2.61
SIMLIB routine UNIFRM.

PROBLEMS

The following problems are to be done using SIMLIB wherever possible.

2.1. For the single-server queue with SIMLIB in Sec. 2.4, replace the dummy list for the server with a variable of your own representing the server status (busy or idle), and use TIMEST instead of FILEST to get the server utilization. If possible on your machine, time the original and modified versions of the simulation as a comparison.

2.2. For the time-shared computer model of Sec. 2.5, combine the end-simulation event with the end-run event. Redraw the event diagram, and alter and run the program with this simplified event structure.

2.3. For the time-shared computer model of Sec. 2.5, suppose that we want to collect the average response time for each terminal individually, as well as overall. Alter the simulation to do this, and run for the case of $n = 10$ terminals only. (*Hint*: You will have to add another attribute to represent a job's terminal of origin, and you will need to define additional SAMPST variables as well.)

2.4. For the multiteller bank model of Sec. 2.6, suppose that we want to know the maximum number of customers that are ever waiting in the queues. Do the following parts in order, i.e., with each part building on the previous ones.

(*a*) Explain why this cannot be obtained by adding up the maxima of the individual queues.

(*b*) Modify the program to collect this statistic, and write it out. Run for each of the cases of $n = 4$, 5, 6, and 7 tellers.

(*c*) Add to this an additional output measure, being the utilization of the servers. Since there are multiple servers, the utilization is defined here as the time-average number of servers busy, divided by the number of servers. Note that this will be a number between 0 and 1.

(*d*) Now suppose that the bank's lobby is large enough to hold only 25 customers in the queues (total). If a customer arrives to find that there are already a total of 25 customers in the queues, he or she just goes away, and the business is lost; this is called *balking* and is clearly unfortunate. Change the program to reflect balking, where the capacity of 25 should be read in as an input parameter. In addition to all the other output measures, observe the number of customers who balk during the course of the simulation.

2.5. In the job-shop model of Sec. 2.7, correct the minor error described in the report generator regarding the collection of the total job delay in queue by job type. To do this, add an attribute to each job representing the cumulative delay in queue so far. When the job leaves the system, tally this value in SAMPST. Rerun the simulation for this alternative approach in the "current configuration" of the number of machines in each group.

2.6. For the job-shop model of Sec. 2.7, estimate the expected overall average job time in system, being the weighted average of the expected times in system (delays in queue plus processing times) for the three job types, using the probabilities of occurrence of the job types as the weights. (*Hint*: You won't need a computer to do this.)

2.7. For the original configuration of the job shop of Sec. 2.7, run the model for 100 eight-hour days but use only the data from the last 90 days to estimate the quantities of interest. In effect, the state of the system at time 10 days represents the initial conditions for the simulation. The idea of "warming up" the model before beginning data collection is a common simulation practice, discussed in Sec. 9.5.1. (You may want to look at the code for SIMLIB routine TIMEST in Fig. 2.54, paying special attention to the variable TRESET, to understand how the continuous-time statistics will be computed.)

2.8. For the job-shop model of Sec. 2.7, suggest a different definition of the attributes that would simplify the model's coding.

2.9. Do Prob. 1.15, except use SIMLIB. Use stream 1 for interarrival times, stream 2 for service times at server 1, stream 3 for service times at server 2, and stream 4 for the travel times.

2.10. Do Prob. 1.22, except use SIMLIB. Use stream 1 for the machine up times and stream 2 for the repair times.

2.11. Do Prob. 1.24, except use SIMLIB. Use stream 1 for interarrival times and stream 2 for service times. Note how much easier this model is to simulate with the list-processing tools.

2.12. Do Prob. 1.26, except use SIMLIB. Use stream 1 for interarrival times, stream 2 for determining the customer type, stream 3 for service times of type 1 customers, and stream 4 for service times of type 2 customers.

2.13. Do Prob. 1.27, except use SIMLIB. Use streams 1 and 2 for interarrival times and service times, respectively, for regular customers, and streams 3 and 4 for interarrival times and service times, respectively, of express customers.

2.14. Do Prob. 1.28, except use SIMLIB. Use stream 1 for interarrival times for regular cars and stream 2 for service times for all cars.

2.15. Do Prob. 1.30, except use SIMLIB. Use stream 1 for interarrival times, stream 2 for inspection times, stream 3 to decide whether a bus needs repair, and stream 4 for repair times.

2.16. For the inventory example of Sec. 1.5, suppose that the delivery lag is distributed uniformly between 1 and 3 months, so there could be between 0 and 3 outstanding orders at a time. Thus, the company bases its ordering decision at the beginning of each month on the sum of the (net) inventory level [denoted by $I(t)$ in Sec. 1.5] and the inventory on order; this sum could be positive, zero, or negative. For each of the nine inventory policies, run the model for 120 months and estimate the expected average total cost per month and the expected proportion of time there is a backlog. Note that holding and shortage costs are still based on the net inventory level. Use stream 1 for interdemand times, stream 2 for demand sizes, and stream 3 for delivery lags.

2.17. Problem 1.18 described a modification of the inventory system of Sec. 1.5 in which the items were perishable. Do this problem using SIMLIB, and in addition consider the case of LIFO (as well as FIFO) processing of the items in inventory. Use the same stream assignments as in Prob. 2.16, and in addition use stream 4 for the shelf lives.

2.18. For the time-shared computer model of Sec. 2.5, suppose that instead of processing jobs in the queue in a round-robin manner, the CPU chooses the job from the queue that has made the fewest number of previous passes through the CPU. In case of ties, the rule is FIFO. (This is equivalent to using the time of arrival to the queue to break ties.) Run the model with $n = 60$ terminals for 1000 job completions.

2.19. Ships arrive at a harbor with interarrival times that are IID exponential random variables with a mean of 1.25 days. The harbor has a dock with two berths and two cranes for unloading the ships; ships arriving when both berths are occupied join a FIFO queue. The time for one crane to unload a ship is distributed uniformly between 0.5 and 1.5 days. If only one ship is in the harbor, both cranes unload the ship and the (remaining) unloading time is cut in half. When two ships are in the harbor, one crane works on each ship. If both cranes are unloading one ship when a second ship arrives, one of the cranes immediately begins serving the second ship and the remaining service time of the first ship is doubled. Assuming that no ships are in the harbor at time 0, run the simulation for 90 days and compute the minimum, maximum, and average time that ships are in the harbor (which includes their time in berth). Also estimate the expected utilization of each berth and of the cranes. Use stream 1 for the interarrival times and stream 2 for the unloading times. [This problem is a paraphrasing of an example in Russell (1976, p. 134).]

2.20. Jobs arrive at a single-CPU computer facility with interarrival times that are IID exponential random variables with mean 1 minute. Each job specifies upon its arrival the maximum amount of processing time it requires, and the maximum times for successive jobs are IID exponential random variables with mean 1.1 minutes. However, if m is the specified maximum processing time for a particular job, the actual processing time is distributed uniformly between $0.55m$ and $1.05m$. The CPU will never process a job for more than its specified maximum; a job whose required processing time exceeds its specified maximum leaves the facility without completing service. Simulate the computer facility until 1000 jobs have left the CPU if (a) jobs in the queue are processed in a FIFO manner, and (b) jobs in the queue are ranked in increasing order of their specified maximum processing time. For each case, compute the average and maximum delay in queue of jobs, the proportion of jobs that are delayed in queue more than 5 minutes, and the maximum number of jobs ever in queue. Use stream 1 for the interarrival times, stream 2 for the maximum processing times, and stream 3 for the actual processing times. Which operating policy would you recommend?

2.21. In a quarry, trucks deliver ore from three shovels to a single crusher. Trucks are assigned to specific shovels, so that a truck will always return to its assigned shovel after dumping a load at the crusher. Two different truck sizes are in use, 20 and 50 tons. The size of the truck affects its loading time at the shovel, travel time to the crusher, dumping time at the crusher, and return-trip time from the crusher back to its shovel, as follows (all times are in minutes):

	20-ton truck	50-ton truck
Load	Exponentially distributed with mean 5	Exponentially distributed with mean 10
Travel	Constant 2.5	Constant 3
Dump	Exponentially distributed with mean 2	Exponentially distributed with mean 4
Return	Constant 1.5	Constant 2

To each shovel is assigned two 20-ton trucks and one 50-ton truck. The shovel queues are all FIFO, and the crusher queue is ranked in decreasing order of truck size, the rule's being FIFO in case of ties. Assume that at time 0 all trucks are at their respective shovels, with the 50-ton trucks just beginning to be loaded. Run the simulation model for 8 hours and estimate the expected time-average number in queue for each shovel and for the crusher. Also estimate the expected utilizations of all four pieces of equipment. Use streams 1 and 2 for the loading times of the 20-ton and 50-ton trucks, respectively, and streams 3 and 4 for the dumping times of the 20-ton and 50-ton trucks, respectively. [This problem is taken from Pritsker (1986, pp. 153–158).]

2.22. A batch-job computer facility with a single CPU opens its doors at 7 A.M. and closes its doors at midnight, but operates until all jobs present at midnight have been processed. Assume that jobs arrive at the facility with interarrival times that are exponentially distributed with mean 1.91 minutes. Jobs request either express (class 4), normal (class 3), deferred (class 2), or convenience (class 1) service, and the classes occur with respective probabilities 0.05, 0.50, 0.30, and 0.15. When the CPU is idle, it will process the highest-class (priority) job present, the rule's being FIFO within a class. The times required for the CPU to process class 4, 3, 2, and 1 jobs are 3-Erlang random variables (see Sec. 2.7) with respective means 0.25, 1.00, 1.50, and 3.00 minutes. Simulate the computer facility for each of the following cases:

(*a*) A job being processed by the CPU is not preempted by an arriving job of a higher class.

(*b*) If a job of class i is being processed and a job of class j (where $j > i$) arrives, the arriving job preempts the job being processed. The preempted job joins the queue and takes the highest priority in its class, and only its remaining service time needs to be completed at some future time.

Estimate for each class the expected time-average number of jobs in queue and the expected average delay in queue. Also estimate the expected proportion of time that the CPU is busy and the expected proportion of CPU busy time spent on each class. Note that it is convenient to have one list for each class's queue and also an input parameter that is set to 0 for case (*a*) and 1 for case (*b*). Use stream 1 for the interarrival times, stream 2 for the job-class determination, and streams 3, 4, 5, and 6 for the processing times for classes 4, 3, 2, and 1, respectively.

2.23. A port in Africa loads tankers with crude oil for overwater shipment, and the port has facilities for loading as many as three tankers simultaneously. The tankers, which arrive at the port every 11 ± 7 hours, are of three different types. (All times given as a "±" range in this problem are distributed uniformly over the range.) The relative frequency of the various types and their loading-time requirements are:

Type	Relative frequency	Loading time, hours
1	0.25	18 ± 2
2	0.25	24 ± 4
3	0.50	36 ± 4

There is one tug at the port. Tankers of all types require the services of a tug to move from the harbor into a berth and later to move out of a berth into the harbor. When the tug is available, any berthing or deberthing activity takes about an hour. It takes the tug 0.25 hour to travel from the harbor to the berths, or vice versa, when not pulling a tanker. When the tug finishes a berthing activity, it will deberth the first tanker in the deberthing queue if this queue is not empty. If the deberthing queue is empty but the harbor queue is not, the tug will travel to the harbor and begin berthing the first tanker in the harbor queue. (If both queues are empty, the tug will remain idle at the berths.) When the tug finishes a deberthing activity, it will berth the first tanker in the harbor queue if this queue is not empty and a berth is available. Otherwise, the tug will travel to the berths, and if the deberthing queue is not empty, will begin deberthing the first tanker in the queue. If the deberthing queue is empty, the tug will remain idle at the berths.

The situation is further complicated due to the fact that the area experiences frequent storms that last 4 ± 2 hours. The time between the end of one storm and the onset of the next is an exponential random variable with mean 48 hours. The tug will not start a new activity when a storm is in progress but will always finish an activity already in progress. (The berths will operate during a storm.) If the tug is traveling from the berths to the harbor without a tanker when a storm begins, it will turn around and head for the berths.

Run the simulation model for a 1-year period (8760 hours) and estimate:

(a) The expected proportion of time the tug is idle, is traveling without a tanker, and is engaged in either a berthing or deberthing activity.

(b) The expected proportion of time each berth is unoccupied, is occupied but not loading, and is loading.

(c) The expected time-average number of tankers in the deberthing queue and in the harbor queue.

(d) The expected average in-port residence time of each type of tanker.

Use stream 1 for interarrivals, stream 2 to determine the type of a tanker, stream 3 for loading times, stream 4 for the duration of a storm, and stream 5 for the time between the end of one storm and the start of the next.

A shipper considering bidding on a contract to transport oil from the port to the United Kingdom has determined that five tankers of a particular type would have to be committed to this task to meet contract specifications. These tankers would require 21 ± 3 hours to load oil at the port. After loading and deberthing, they would travel to the United Kingdom, offload the oil, return to the port for reloading, etc. The round-trip travel time, including offloading, is estimated to be 240 ± 24 hours. Rerun the simulation and estimate, in addition, the expected average in-port residence time of the proposed additional tankers. Assume that at time 0 the five additional tankers are in the harbor queue. Use the same stream assignments as before, and in addition use stream 6 for the oil-loading times at the port and stream 7 for the round-trip travel times for these new tankers. [This problem is an embellishment of one in Schriber (1974, p. 329).]

2.24. In Prob. 2.23, suppose that the tug has a two-way radio giving it the position and status of each tanker in the port. As a result, the tug changes its operating policies, as follows. If the tug is traveling from the harbor to the berths without a tanker and is less than halfway there when a new tanker arrives, it will turn around and go pick up the new tanker. If the tug is traveling from the berths to the harbor without a tanker and is less than halfway there when a tanker completes its loading, it will turn around and go pick up the loaded tanker. Run the simulation with the same parameters and stream assignments as before, under this new operating policy.

2.25. In Prob. 2.24, suppose in addition that if the tug is traveling from the harbor to the berths without a tanker and the deberthing queue is empty when a new tanker arrives, it will turn around and go pick up the new tanker, regardless of its position. Run the simulation with the same parameters and stream assignments as before, under this operating policy.

2.26. Two-piece suits are processed by a dry cleaner as follows. Suits arrive with exponential interarrival times having mean 10 minutes, and are all initially served by server 1, perhaps after a wait in a FIFO queue; see Fig. 2.62. Upon completion

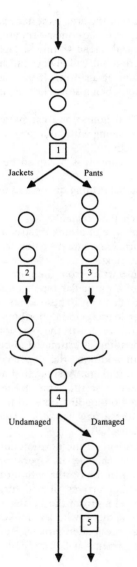

FIGURE 2.62
A dry-cleaning operation.

of service at server 1, one piece of the suit (the jacket) goes to server 2, and the other part (the pants) to server 3. During service at server 2, the jacket has a probability of 0.05 of being damaged, and while at server 3 the probability of a pair of pants' being damaged is 0.10. Upon leaving server 2, the jackets go into a queue for server 4; upon leaving server 3, the pants go into a different queue for server 4. Server 4 matches and reassembles suit parts, initiating this when he is idle and two parts from the same suit are available. If both parts of the reassembled suit are undamaged, the suit is returned to the customer. If either (or both) of the parts are damaged, the suit goes to customer relations (server 5). Assume that all service times are exponential, with the following means (in minutes), and use the indicated stream assignments:

Server number	Mean service time, in minutes	Stream
1	6	1
2	4	2
3	5	3
4	5 (undamaged)	4
4	8 (damaged)	5
5	12	6

In addition, use stream 7 for interarrival times, and streams 8 and 9 for determining whether the pieces are damaged at servers 2 and 3, respectively. The system is initially empty and idle, and runs for exactly 12 hours. Observe the average and maximum time in the system for each type of outcome (damaged or not), separately, the average and maximum length of each queue, and the utilization of each server. What would happen if the arrival rate were to double (i.e., the interarrival-time mean were 5 minutes instead of 10 minutes)? In this case, if you could place another person anywhere in the system to help out with one of the 5 tasks, where should it be?

2.27. A queueing system has two servers (A and B) in series, and two types of customers (1 and 2). Customers arriving to the system have their types determined immediately upon their arrival. An arriving customer is classified as type 1 with probability 0.6. However, an arriving customer may *balk*, i.e., may not actually join the system, if the queue for server A is too long. Specifically, assume that if an arriving customer finds m ($m \geq 0$) other customers already in the queue for A, he will join the system with probability $1/(m + 1)$, regardless of the type (1 or 2) of customer he may be. Thus, for example, an arrival finding nobody else in the queue for A (i.e., $m = 0$) will join the system for sure [probability = $1/(0 + 1) = 1$], whereas an arrival finding 5 others in the queue for A will join the system with probability $1/6$. All customers are served by A. (If A is busy when a customer arrives, the customer joins a FIFO queue.) Upon completing service at A, type 1 customers leave the system, while type 2 customers are served by B. (If B is busy, type 2 customers wait in a FIFO queue.) Compute the average *total* time each type of customer spends in the *system*, as well as the number of balks. Also compute the time-average and maximum length of each queue, and both server utilizations. Assume that all interarrival and service times are exponentially distributed, with the following parameters:

- Mean interarrival time (for any customer type) = 1 minute

- Mean service time at server A (regardless of customer type) = 0.8 minute

- Mean service time at server B = 1.2 minutes

Initially the system is empty and idle, and is to run until 1000 customers (of either type) have left the system. Use stream 1 for determining the customer type, stream 2 for deciding whether a customer balks, stream 3 for interarrivals, stream 4 for service times at A (of both customer types), and stream 5 for service times at B.

2.28. An antiquated computer operates in a batch multiprocessing mode, meaning that it starts many (up to a fixed maximum of $k = 4$) jobs at a time, runs them simultaneously, but cannot start any new jobs until all the jobs in a batch are done. Within a batch, each job has its own completion time, and leaves the CPU when it finishes. There are three priority classes, with jobs of class 1 being the highest priority and class 3 jobs being the lowest priority. When the CPU finishes the last job in a batch, it first looks for jobs in the class 1 queue and takes as many as possible from it, up to a maximum of k. If there were fewer than k jobs in the class 1 queue, as many jobs as possible from the class 2 queue are taken to bring the total of class 1 and class 2 jobs to no more than the maximum batch size, k. If still more room is left in the batch, the CPU moves on to the class 3 queue. If the total number of jobs waiting in all the queues is less than k, the CPU takes them all and begins running this partially full batch; it cannot begin any jobs that subsequently arrive until it finishes all of its current batch. If no jobs at all are waiting in the queues, the CPU becomes idle, and the next arriving job will start the CPU running with a batch of size 1. Note that when a batch begins running, there may be jobs of many different classes running together in the same batch.

Within a class queue, the order of jobs taken is to be *either* FIFO or shortest job first (SJF); the simulation is to be written to handle either queue discipline by changing only an input parameter. (Thus, a job's service requirement should be generated when it arrives, and stored alongside its time of arrival in the queue. For FIFO, this would not really be necessary, but it simplifies the general programming.) The service requirement of a class i job is distributed uniformly between constants $a(i)$ and $b(i)$ minutes. Each class has its own separate arrival process, i.e., the interarrival time between two successive class i jobs is exponentially distributed with mean $r(i)$ minutes. Thus, at any given point in the simulation, there should be three separate arrivals scheduled, one for each class. If a job arrives to find the CPU busy, it joins the queue for its class in the appropriate place, depending on whether the FIFO or SJF option is in force. A job arriving to find the CPU idle begins service immediately; this would be a batch of size 1. The parameters are as follows:

i	$r(i)$	$a(i)$	$b(i)$
1	0.2	0.05	0.11
2	1.6	0.94	1.83
3	5.4	4.00	8.00

Initially the system is empty and idle, and the simulation is to run for exactly 720 minutes. For each queue, compute the average, minimum, and maximum delay, as well as the time-average and maximum length. Also, compute the utilization of the CPU, defined here as the proportion of time it is busy regardless of the number of jobs running. Finally, compute the time-average number of jobs running in the CPU (where 0 jobs are considered running when the CPU is idle). Use streams 1, 2, and 3 for the interarrival times of jobs of class 1, 2, and 3, respectively, and streams 4, 5, and 6 for their respective service requirements. Suppose that a hardware upgrade could increase k to 6. Would this be worth it?

2.29. Consider a queueing system with a fixed number $n = 5$ of parallel servers fed by a single queue. Customers arrive with interarrival times that are exponentially distributed with mean 5 (all times are in minutes). An arriving customer finding an idle server will go directly into service, choosing the leftmost idle server if there are several, while an arrival finding all servers busy joins the end of the queue. When a customer (initially) enters service, her service requirement is distributed uniformly between $a = 2$ and $b = 2.8$, but upon completion of her initial service, she may be "dissatisfied" with her service, which occurs with probability $p = 0.2$. If the service was satisfactory, the customer simply leaves the system, but if her service was not satisfactory, she will require further service. The determination as to whether a service was satisfactory is to be made when the service is completed. If an unsatisfactory service is completed and there are no other customers waiting in the queue, the dissatisfied customer immediately begins another service time at her same server. On the other hand, if there is a queue when an unsatisfactory service is completed, the dissatisfied customer must join the queue (according to one of two options, described below), and the server takes the first person from the queue to serve next. Each time a customer *reenters* service, her service time and probability of being dissatisfied are lower; specifically, a customer who has *already* had i (unsatisfactory) services has a next service time that is distributed uniformly between $a/(i + 1)$ and $b/(i + 1)$, and her probability of being dissatisfied with this next service is $p/(i + 1)$. Theoretically, there is no upper limit on the number of times a given customer will have to be served to be finally satisfied.

There are two possible rules concerning what to do with a dissatisfied customer when other people are waiting in queue; the program is to be written so that respecifying a single input parameter will change the rule from (i) to (ii):

(i) A customer who has just finished an unsatisfactory service joins the end of the queue.

(ii) A customer who has just finished an unsatisfactory service rejoins the queue so that the next person taken from the (front of the) queue will be the customer who has already had the largest number of services; the rule is FIFO in case of ties. This rule is in the interest of both equity and efficiency, since customers with a long history of unsatisfactory service tend to require shorter service and also tend to be more likely to be satisfied with their next service.

Initially the system is empty and idle, and the simulation is to run for exactly 480 minutes. Compute the average and maximum total time in system [including all the delay(s) in queue and service time(s) of a customer], and the number of satisfied customers who leave the system during the simulation. Also compute the average and maximum length of the queue, and the time-average and maximum number of servers that were busy. Use stream 1 for interarrivals, stream 2 for all service times, and stream 3 to determine whether each service was satisfactory.

2.30. The student-center cafeteria at Big State University is trying to improve its service during the lunch rush from 11:30 A.M. to 1:00 P.M. Customers arrive together in groups of size 1, 2, 3, and 4, with respective probabilities 0.5, 0.3, 0.1, and 0.1. Interarrival times between groups are exponentially distributed with mean 30 seconds. Initially, the system is empty and idle, and is to run for the 90-minute period. Each arriving customer, whether alone or part of a group, takes one of three routes through the cafeteria (groups in general split up after they arrive):

- Hot-food service, then drinks, then cashier
- Specialty-sandwich bar, then drinks, then cashier
- Drinks (only), then cashier

The probabilities of these routes are respectively 0.80, 0.15, and 0.05; see Fig. 2.63. At the hot-food counter and the specialty-sandwich bar, customers are served one at a time (although there might actually be one or two workers present, as discussed below). The drinks stand is self-service, and assume that nobody ever has to queue up here; this is equivalent to thinking of the drinks stand as having infinitely many servers. There are either two or three cashiers (see below), each having his own queue, and there is no jockeying; customers arriving to the cashiers simply choose the shortest queue. All queues in the model are FIFO.

In Fig. 2.63, ST stands for service time at a station, and ACT stands for the accumulated (future) cashier time due to having visited a station; the notation $\sim U(a, b)$ means that the corresponding quantity is distributed uniformly between a and b seconds. For example, a route 1 customer goes first to the hot-food station, joins the queue there if necessary, receives service there that is uniformly distributed between 50 and 120 seconds, "stores away" part of a (future) cashier time that is uniformly distributed between 20 and 40 seconds, then spends an amount of time uniformly distributed between 5 seconds and 20 seconds getting a drink, and accumulates an additional amount of (future) cashier time distributed uniformly between 5 seconds and 10 seconds. Thus, his service requirement at a cashier will be the sum of the $U(20, 40)$ and $U(5, 10)$ random variates he "picked up" at the hot-food and drinks stations.

Report the following measures of system performance:

- The average and maximum delay in queue for hot food, specialty sandwiches, and cashiers (regardless of which cashier)
- The time-average and maximum number in queue for hot food and specialty sandwiches (separately), and the time-average and maximum total number in all cashier queues
- The average and maximum total delay in all the queues for each of the three types of customers (separately)
- The overall average total delay for all customers, found by weighting their individual average total delays by their respective probabilities of occurrence
- The time-average and maximum total number of customers in the entire system (for reporting to the fire marshall)

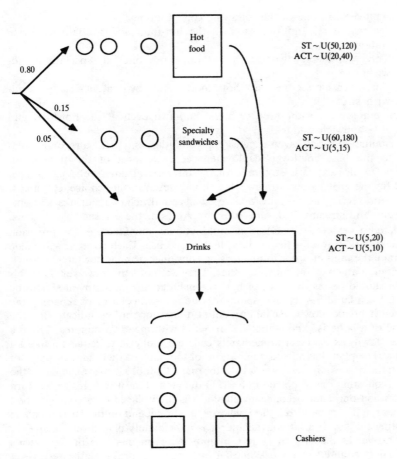

FIGURE 2.63
The BSU cafeteria.

There are several questions about the system's operation. For security reasons, there must be at least two cashiers, and the maximum number of cashiers is three. Also, there must be at least one person working at each of the hot-food and specialty-sandwich stations. Thus, the minimum number of employees is four; run this as the "base-case" model. Then, consider adding employees, in several ways:

(a) Five employees, with the additional person used in one of the following ways:
    (i) As a third cashier.
    (ii) To help at the hot-food station. In this case, customers are still served one at a time, but their service time is cut in half, being distributed uniformly between 25 seconds and 60 seconds.
    (iii) To help at the specialty-sandwich bar, meaning that service is still one at a time, but distributed uniformly between 30 seconds and 90 seconds.

(*b*) Six employees, in one of the following configurations:
  (i) Two cashiers, and two each at the hot-food and specialty-sandwich stations.
  (ii) Three cashiers, two at hot food, and one at specialty sandwiches.
  (iii) Three cashiers, one at hot food, and two at specialty sandwiches.
(*c*) Seven employees, with three cashiers, and two each at the hot-food and specialty-sandwich stations.

Run the simulation for all seven expansion possibilities, and make a recommendation as to the best employee deployment at each level of the number of employees. In all cases, use stream 1 for the interarrival times between groups, stream 2 for the group sizes, stream 3 for an individual's route choice, streams 4, 5, and 6 for service at the hot-food, specialty-sandwich, and drinks stations, respectively, and streams 7, 8, and 9 for the ACTs at these respective stations.

2.31. Consolidated Corkscrews (CC) is a multinational manufacturer of precision carbon-steel corkscrews for heavy-duty, high-speed use. Each corkscrew is made on a metal lathe, and in order to meet rising consumer demand for their product, CC is planning a new plant with six lathes. They are not sure, however, how this new plant should be constructed, or how the maintenance department should be equipped. Each lathe has its own operator, who is also in charge of repairing the lathe when it breaks down. Reliability data on lathe operation indicate that the "up" time of a lathe is exponentially distributed with mean 75 minutes. When a lathe goes down, its operator immediately calls the tool crib to request a tool kit for repairs. The plant has a fixed number, m, of tool kits, so there may or may not be a kit in the crib when an operator calls for one. If a tool kit is not available, the operator requesting one is placed in a FIFO queue and must wait his or her turn for a kit; when one later becomes available, it is then placed on a conveyor belt and arrives t_i minutes later to lathe i, where t_i might depend on the lathe number, i, requesting the kit. If a kit is available, it is immediately placed on a conveyor belt and arrives at the broken lathe t_i minutes later; in this case the operator's queue delay is counted as zero. When an operator of a broken lathe receives a tool kit, he or she begins repair, which takes an amount of time distributed as a 3-Erlang random variable with mean 15 minutes. When the repair is complete, the lathe is brought back up and the tool kit is sent back to the tool crib, where it arrives t_i minutes later, if it is sent back from lathe i. Initially, assume that all lathes are up and have just been "freshly repaired," and that all m tool kits are in the crib. CC wants to know about the projected operation of the plant over a continuous 24-hour day by looking at:

• The proportion of time that each of the six lathes is down
• The time-average number of lathes that are down
• The time-average number of tool kits sitting idle in the crib
• The average delay in queue of operators requesting a tool kit

There are two major questions to be addressed:

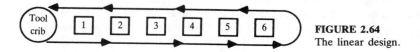

FIGURE 2.64
The linear design.

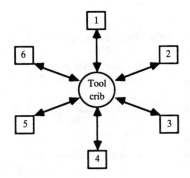

FIGURE 2.65
The circular design.

(a) How should the plant be laid out? Two layouts are under consideration:

  (i) In the linear design (see Fig. 2.64), the lathes are placed in a straight line with the tool crib at the left end, and a single conveyor belt for the tool kits can reach all lathes. In this case, $t_i = 2i$ minutes, for $i = 1, 2, \ldots, 6$.

  (ii) In the circular design, the lathes are placed around the tool crib (see Fig. 2.65), and each lathe has its own conveyor belt to the crib; here, $t_i = 3$ for all lathe numbers i. This is a more expensive design, but results in shorter travel times for the kits.

(b) How many tool kits should there be? As tool kits are quite expensive, CC does not want to purchase more than necessary.

Carry out the necessary simulations and advise CC on questions (a) and (b). In all cases, use stream 1 for the lathe-up times, and stream 2 for repair times.

2.32. The engines on jet aircraft must be periodically inspected and, if necessary, repaired. An inspection/repair facility at a large airport handles some seven different types of jets, as described in the table below. The times between successive arrivals of planes of type i (where $i = 1, 2, \ldots, 7$) are exponentially distributed with mean $a(i)$, as given in the table; all times are in days. There are n parallel service stations, each of which sequentially handles the inspection and repair of all the engines on a plane, but can deal with only one engine at a time. For example, a B707 has four engines, so when it enters service, each engine must undergo a complete inspection and repair process (as described below) before the next engine on this plane can begin service, and all four engines must be inspected and (if necessary) repaired before the plane leaves the service station. Each service station is capable of dealing with any type of plane. As usual, a plane arriving to find an idle service station goes directly into service, while an arriving plane finding all service stations occupied must join a single queue.

i	Plane type	Number of engines	$a(i)$	$A(i)$	$B(i)$	$p(i)$	$r(i)$	$c(i)$
1	B707	4	8.1	0.7	2.1	0.30	2.1	2.1
2	B727	3	2.9	0.9	1.8	0.26	1.8	1.7
3	B737	2	3.6	0.8	1.6	0.18	1.6	1.0
4	B747*	4	8.4	1.9	2.8	0.12	3.1	3.9
5	DC8	4	10.9	0.7	2.2	0.36	2.2	1.4
6	DC9	2	6.7	0.9	1.7	0.14	1.7	1.1
7	DC10*	3	3.0	1.6	2.0	0.21	2.8	3.7

Two of the seven types of planes are classified as widebody (denoted by a $*$ in the above table), while the other five are classified as regular. Two disciplines for the queue are of interest:
(i)   Simple FIFO with all plane types mixed together in the same queue
(ii) Nonpreemptive priority given to widebody jets, with the rule being FIFO within the widebody and regular classifications
For each engine on a plane (independently), the following process takes place (i denotes the plane type):

- The engine is initially inspected, taking an amount of time distributed uniformly between $A(i)$ and $B(i)$.

- A decision is made as to whether repair is needed; the probability that repair is needed is $p(i)$. If no repair is needed, inspection of the jet's next engine begins, or if this was the last engine, the jet leaves the facility.

- If repair is needed, it is carried out, taking an amount of time distributed as a 2-Erlang random variable with mean $r(i)$.

- After repair, another inspection is done, taking an amount of time distributed uniformly between $A(i)/2$ and $B(i)/2$ (i.e., half as long as the initial inspection, since tear-down is already done). The probability that the engine needs further repair is $p(i)/2$.

- If the initial repair was successful, the engine is done. If the engine still fails inspection, it requires further repair, taking an amount of time distributed as 2-Erlang with mean $r(i)/2$, after which it is inspected again, taking an amount of time distributed uniformly between $A(i)/2$ and $B(i)/2$; it fails this inspection with probability $p(i)/2$, and would need yet more repair, which would take a 2-Erlang amount of time with mean $r(i)/2$. This procedure continues until the engine finally passes inspection. The mean repair time stays at $r(i)/2$, the probability of failure stays at $p(i)/2$, and the inspection times stay between $A(i)/2$ and $B(i)/2$.

A cost of $c(i)$ (measured in tens of thousands of dollars) is incurred for every (full) day a type i plane is down, i.e., is in queue or in service. The general idea is to study how the total (summed across all plane types) average daily downtime cost depends on the number of service stations, n. Initially the system is empty and idle, and the simulation is to run for 365 round-the-clock days. Observe the average delay in queue for each plane type and the overall average delay in queue for all plane types, the time-average number of planes in queue, the time-average number of planes down for each plane type separately, and the total average daily downtime cost for all planes added together. Try various values of n to get a feel for the system's behavior. Recommend a choice for n, as well as which of the queue disciplines (i) or (ii) above appears to lead to the most cost-effective operation. Use streams 1 through 7 for the interarrival times of plane types $i = 1$ through $i = 7$, respectively, streams 8 through 14 for their respective inspection times (first or subsequent), streams 15 through 21 to determine whether they need (additional) repair, and streams 22 through 28 for their repair times (first or subsequent).

As an alternative to the above layout, consider separating entirely the service of the widebody and regular jets. That is, take n_2 of the n stations and

$(n_1 + n_2 = n)$

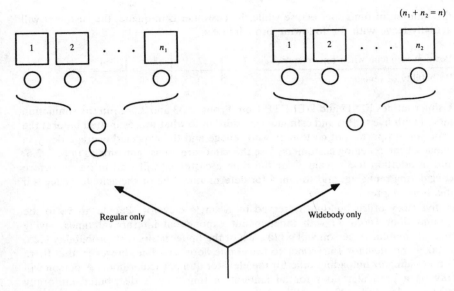

FIGURE 2.66
Alternative layout for the aircraft-repair facility.

send all the widebody jets there (with a single queue of widebodies feeding all n_2 stations), and the remaining $n_1 = n - n_2$ stations are for regular jets only; see Fig. 2.66. Do you think that this alternative layout would be better? Why? Use the same parameters and stream assignments as above.

2.33. Write a FORTRAN function FIND to find the physical row number in the array MASTER that contains the (logically) first record with a value VALUE (a real-valued representation of an integer, for example, 5.0) for attribute ITEM (ITEM = 1, 2, . . . , MAXATR) in list LIST (LIST = 1, 2, . . . , 25). To determine the desired row, a statement of the form ROW = FIND(ITEM, VALUE, LIST) is executed. In addition, copy the record that has been found into the TRNSFR array. If no record is found, set FIND equal to −1.

2.34. Write a FORTRAN subroutine DELETE to delete the record from list LIST (LIST = 1, 2, . . . , 25), which is in (physical) row ROW (ROW = 1, 2, . . . , 1000) of the array MASTER. To delete the desired record, a statement of the form CALL DELETE(ROW, LIST) is executed. If there is an error condition, write out an error message and stop the simulation. Also, update the statistics for list LIST by calling TIMEST (see the code for REMOVE in App. 2A).

2.35. Write a FORTRAN subroutine INSERT to insert a new event record into the event list using the middle-pointer algorithm discussed in Sec. 2.8. If two event records have the same event time, give preference to the event with the lowest-numbered event type.

2.36. For the bank model in Sec. 2.6, suppose that after a customer has waited in queue a certain amount of time, the customer *may* leave without being served; this is called *reneging*. Assume that the amount of time a customer will wait in queue before considering reneging is distributed uniformly between 5 and 10 minutes; if this amount of time does elapse while the customer is in queue, the customer will actually leave with the following probabilities:

Position in queue when time elapses	1	2	3	≥4
Probability of reneging	0	0.25	0.50	1

Using routines FIND and DELETE from Probs. 2.33 and 2.34, run the simulation model with five tellers and estimate (in addition to what was estimated before) the expected proportion of customers who renege and the expected average delay in queue of the reneging customers. Use the same stream assignments as in Sec. 2.6, and in addition use stream 3 for the time a customer will wait in queue before considering reneging, and stream 4 for determining if he or she actually reneges if this time elapses.

2.37. A five-story office building is served by a single elevator. People arrive to the ground floor (floor 1) with independent exponential interarrival times having mean 1 minute. A person will go to each of the upper floors with probability 0.25. It takes the elevator 15 seconds to travel one floor. Assume, however, that there is no loading or unloading time for the elevator at a particular floor. A person will stay on a particular floor for an amount of time that is distributed uniformly between 15 and 120 minutes. When a person leaves floor i (where $i = 2, 3, \ldots, 5$), he or she will go to floor 1 with probability 0.7, and will go to each of the other three floors with probability 0.1. The elevator can carry six people, and starts on floor 1. If there is not room to get all people waiting at a particular floor on the arriving elevator, the excess remain in queue. A person coming down to floor 1 departs from the building immediately. The following control logic also applies to the elevator:

- When the elevator is going up, it will continue in that direction if a current passenger wants to go to a higher floor or if a person on a higher floor wants to get on the elevator.
- When the elevator is going down, it will continue in that direction if it has at least one passenger or if there is a waiting passenger at a lower floor.
- If the elevator is at floor i (where $i = 2, 3, 4$) and going up (down), then it will not immediately pick up a person who wants to go down (up) at that floor.
- When the elevator is idle, its home base is floor 1.
- The elevator decides at each floor what floor it will go to next. It will not change directions between floors.

Use the following random-number stream assignments:

1, interarrival times of people to the building
2, next-floor determination (generate upon arrival at origin floor)
3, length of stay on a particular floor (generate upon arrival at floor)

Run a simulation for 20 hours and gather statistics on:
(*a*) Average delay in queue in each direction (if appropriate), for each floor
(*b*) Average of individual delays in queue over all floors and all people

(c) Proportion of time that the elevator is moving with people, moving empty, and is idle (on floor 1)

(d) Average and maximum number in the elevator

(e) Proportion of people who cannot get on the elevator since it is full, for each floor

Rerun the simulation if the home base for the elevator is floor 3. Which home base gives the smallest average delay [output statistic (b)]?

2.38. Coal trains arrive to an unloading facility with independent exponential interarrival times with mean 10 hours. If a train arrives and finds the system idle, the train is unloaded immediately. Unloading times for the train are independent and distributed uniformly between 3.5 and 4.5 hours. If a train arrives to a busy system, it joins a FIFO queue.

The situation is complicated by what the railroad calls "hogging out." In particular, a train crew can work for only 12 hours, and a train cannot be unloaded without a crew present. When a train arrives, the remaining crew time (out of 12 hours) is independent and distributed uniformly between 6 and 11 hours. When a crew's 12 hours expire, it leaves immediately and a replacement crew is called. The amount of time between when a replacement crew is called and when it actually arrives is independent and distributed uniformly between 2.5 and 3.5 hours.

If a train is being unloaded when its crew hogs out, unloading is suspended until a replacement crew arrives. If a train is in queue when its crew hogs out, the train cannot leave the queue until its replacement crew arrives. Thus, the unloading equipment can be idle with one or more trains in queue.

Run the simulation for 720 hours (30 days) and gather statistics on:

(a) Average and maximum time a train spends in the system

(b) Proportion of time unloading equipment is busy, idle, and hogged out

(c) Average and maximum number of trains in queue

(d) Proportion of trains that hog out 0, 1, and 2 times

Note that if a train is in queue when its crew hogs out, the record for this train must be accessed. (This train may be anywhere in the queue.) Use the FORTRAN function FIND from Prob. 2.33.

2.39. Consider a car-rental system as shown in Fig. 2.67, with all distances given in miles. People arrive at location i (where $i = 1, 2, 3$) with independent exponential interarrival times at respective rates of 14, 10, and 24 per hour. Each location has a FIFO queue with unlimited capacity. There is one bus with a capacity of 20 people and a speed of 30 miles per hour. The bus is initially at location 3 (car rental), and leaves immediately in a counterclockwise direction. All people arriving at a terminal want to go to the car rental. All people arriving at the car rental want to go to terminals 1 and 2 with respective probabilities 0.583 and 0.417. When a bus arrives at a location, the following rules apply:

- People are first unloaded in a FIFO manner. The time to unload one person is distributed uniformly between 16 and 24 seconds.
- People are then loaded on the bus up to its capacity, with a loading time per person that is distributed uniformly between 15 and 25 seconds.
- The bus always spends at least 5 minutes at each location. If no loading or unloading is in process after 5 minutes, the bus will leave immediately.

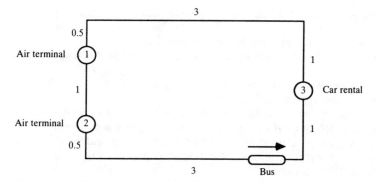

FIGURE 2.67
A car-rental system.

Run a simulation for 80 hours and gather statistics on:

(*a*) Average and maximum number in each queue
(*b*) Average and maximum delay in each queue
(*c*) Average and maximum number on the bus
(*d*) Average, maximum, and minimum time the bus is stopped at each location
(*e*) Average, maximum, and minimum time for the bus to make a loop (departure from the car rental to the next such departure)
(*f*) Average, maximum, and minimum time a person is in the system by arrival location

Use the following random-number stream assignments:

i, interarrival times at location *i* (where $i = 1, 2, 3$)
4, unloading times
5, loading times
6, determining destination of an arrival at the car rental

REFERENCES

Adiri, I., and B. Avi-Itzhak: A Time-Sharing Queue with a Finite Number of Customers, *J. Assoc. Comput. Mach.*, *16*: 315–323 (1969).

Brown, R.: Calendar Queues: A Fast O(1) Priority Queue Implementation for the Simulation Event Set Problem, *Commun. Assoc. Comput. Mach.*, *31*: 1220–1227 (1988).

Comfort, J. C.: A Taxonomy and Analysis of Event Set Management Algorithms for Discrete Event Simulation, *Proc. 12th Annual Simulation Symposium*, pp. 115–146 (1979).

Comfort, J. C.: The Simulation of a Microprocessor-Based Event Set Processor, *Proc. 14th Annual Simulation Symposium*, pp. 17–33 (1981).

Devroye, L.: *Non-Uniform Random Variate Generation*, Springer-Verlag, New York (1986).

Henriksen, J. O.: Event List Management—A Tutorial, *Proc. 1983 Winter Simulation Conference*, Washington, D.C., pp. 543–551 (1983).

Jones, D. W., J. O. Henriksen, C. D. Pegden, R. G. Sargent, R. M. O'Keefe, and B. W. Unger: Implementations of Time (Panel), *Proc. 1986 Winter Simulation Conference*, Washington, D.C., pp. 409–416 (1986).

Kingston, J. H.: Analysis of Henriksen's Algorithm for the Simulation Event Set, *SIAM J. Comput.*, *15*: 887–902 (1986).

Knuth, D. E.: *The Art of Computer Programming*, Vol. 1: Fundamental Algorithms, 2d ed., Addison-Wesley, Reading, Mass. (1974).

McCormack, W. M.: Analysis of Future Event Set Algorithms for Discrete Event Simulation, Ph.D. Dissertation, Syracuse University, Syracuse, N.Y. (1979).

McCormack, W. M., and R. G. Sargent: Analysis of Future Event Set Algorithms for Discrete Event Simulation, *Commun. Assoc. Comput. Mach.*, *24*: 801–812 (1981).

Pritsker, A. A. B.: *Introduction to Simulation and SLAM II*, 3d ed., Systems Publishing, West Lafayette, Ind. (1986).

Reeves, C. M.: Complexity Analyses of Event Set Algorithms, *The Computer Journal*, *27*: 72–79 (1984).

Russell, E. C.: *Simulation and SIMSCRIPT II.5*, CACI, Inc., Los Angeles (1976).

Schriber, T. J.: *Simulation Using GPSS*, John Wiley, New York (1974).

Schriber, T. J.: *An Introduction to Simulation Using GPSS/H*, John Wiley, New York (1990).

CHAPTER
3

SIMULATION SOFTWARE

Recommended sections for a first reading: 3.1 through 3.4

3.1 INTRODUCTION

In studying the simulation examples in Chaps. 1 and 2, the reader probably noticed several features needed in programming most discrete-event simulation models, including:

- Generating random numbers, that is, random values from the $U(0, 1)$ probability distribution
- Generating random values from a specified probability distribution (e.g., exponential)
- Advancing simulated time
- Determining the next event from the event list and passing control to the appropriate block of code
- Adding records to, or deleting records from, a list
- Collecting and analyzing data
- Reporting the results
- Detecting error conditions

As a matter of fact, it is the commonality of these and other features to most simulation programs that led to the development of special-purpose simulation languages. Furthermore, we believe that the improvement, standardization, and greater availability of these languages has been one of the major factors in the increased popularity of simulation in recent years.

We discuss in Sec. 3.2 the relative merits of using a simulation language rather than a general-purpose language such as FORTRAN or C for programming simulation models. Most simulation languages in use today employ one of two modeling approaches or orientations. These two orientations, called the *event-scheduling* and the *process* approaches, are discussed in Sec. 3.3. Desirable features for simulation software, including animation, are described in Sec. 3.4. In Secs. 3.5 through 3.8 we present brief descriptions of GPSS, SIMAN, SIMSCRIPT II.5, and SLAM II, which are probably the most widely used simulation languages in the United States. A simulation model of the $M/M/1$ queue (see Sec. 1.4.3) is also given in each language. These languages are compared in Sec. 3.9, followed by a discussion of other simulation software (e.g., application-oriented simulators) in Sec. 3.10.

3.2   COMPARISON OF SIMULATION LANGUAGES WITH GENERAL-PURPOSE LANGUAGES

One of the most important decisions a modeler or analyst must make in performing a simulation study is the choice of a language. An inappropriate choice may in itself cause a simulation project to be unsuccessful if it cannot be completed on time. The following are some advantages of programming a simulation model in a simulation language rather than in a general-purpose language, e.g., FORTRAN, C, Pascal, or BASIC:

- Simulation languages automatically provide most of the features needed in programming a simulation model (see Secs. 3.1 and 3.4), resulting in a significant decrease in programming time.
- They provide a natural framework for simulation modeling. Their basic building blocks are more closely akin to simulation than are those in a language like FORTRAN.
- Simulation models are generally easier to change when written in a simulation language.
- Most simulation languages provide dynamic storage allocation during execution.
- They provide better error detection because many potential types of errors have been identified and are checked for automatically. Since fewer lines of code have to be written, the chance of making an error will probably be smaller. (Conversely, errors in a new version of a simulation language itself may be difficult for a user to find.)

On the other hand, many simulation models (particularly for defense-related applications) are still written in a general-purpose language. Some advantages of such a choice are as follows:

- Most modelers already know a general-purpose language, but this is often not the case with a simulation language.
- FORTRAN or BASIC is available on virtually every computer, but a particular simulation language may not be accessible on the computer that the analyst wants to use.
- An *efficiently* written FORTRAN or C program may require less execution time than the corresponding program written in a simulation language. This is because a simulation language is designed to model a wide variety of systems with one set of building blocks, whereas a FORTRAN program can be tailored to the particular application. This consideration has, however, become less important with the availability of relatively inexpensive, high-speed microcomputers and engineering work stations.
- General-purpose languages may allow greater programming flexibility than certain simulation languages.
- Software cost may be lower (but not necessarily project cost).

Although there are clear advantages to using both types of languages, we believe, in general, that a modeler would be prudent to give serious consideration to using a simulation language. If such a decision has indeed been made, the criteria discussed in Secs. 3.4 and 3.9 may be helpful in deciding which particular simulation language to choose.

3.3 CLASSIFICATION OF SIMULATION SOFTWARE

In this section we discuss various aspects of simulation software, including two different ways in which it can be classified.

3.3.1 Simulation Languages vs. Simulators

There are currently two major classes of simulation software: languages and simulators. A *simulation language* is a computer package that is general in nature but may have special features for certain types of applications. For example, SIMAN and SLAM II have manufacturing modules for conveyors and automated guided vehicles. A model is developed in a simulation language by writing a program using the language's modeling constructs. The major strength of most languages is their ability to model almost any kind of system, regardless of the system's operating procedures or control logic. Possible drawbacks of simulation languages are the need for programming expertise and the possibly long coding and debugging time associated with modeling complex systems (relative to simulators, if applicable).

A *simulator* is a computer package that allows one to simulate a system contained in a *specific* class of systems with little or no programming. For example, there are currently simulators available for certain types of manufacturing, computer, and communication systems. The particular system of interest (in the domain of the package) is typically selected for simulation by the use of menus and graphics, without the need for programming. The major advantage of a simulator is that "program" development time may be considerably less than that for a simulation language. This may be very important given the tight time constraints in many business environments. Another advantage is that most simulators have modeling constructs related specifically to the components of the target class of systems, which is particularly desirable for operational personnel. Also, people without programming experience or who use simulation only occasionally (e.g., a manufacturing engineer in a factory) often prefer simulators because of their ease of use. The major drawback of many simulators is that they are limited to modeling only those system configurations allowed by their standard features. This difficulty can be somewhat overcome if the simulator has "programming-like" commands to model complex decision logic; most of the model would still be developed using menus and graphics. (This capability might be available in the simulator itself or in external routines called by the simulator.) Simulators are currently most often used for *high-level analyses*, where the system is modeled at an aggregate level without including details of the control logic.

3.3.2 Modeling Approaches

Almost all simulation languages use one of two basic approaches to discrete-event simulation modeling; these approaches are also used by modelers using a general-purpose language. In the *event-scheduling approach*, used in the programs in Chaps. 1 and 2, a system is modeled by identifying its characteristic events and then writing a set of event routines that give a detailed description of the state changes taking place at the time of each event. The simulation evolves over time by executing the events in increasing order of their time of occurrence. Here a basic property of an event routine is that no simulated time passes during its execution. The event-scheduling approach is available in SIMAN, SIMSCRIPT II.5, and SLAM II.

A *process* is a time-ordered sequence of interrelated events separated by passages of time, which describes the entire experience of an "entity" as it flows through a "system." The process corresponding to an entity arriving to and being served at a single server is shown in Fig. 3.1. A system or simulation model may have several different types of processes. Corresponding to each process in the model, there is a process "routine" that describes the entire history of its "process entity" as it moves through the corresponding process. A process "routine" explicitly contains the passage of simulated time and generally has multiple entry points.

To illustrate the nature of the *process approach* more succinctly, Fig. 3.2 gives a flowchart for a prototype customer-process routine in the case of a

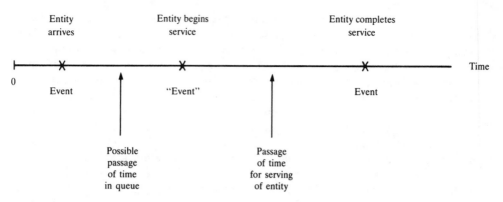

FIGURE 3.1
Process describing the flow of an entity through a system.

single-server queueing system. (This process routine describes the entire experience of a customer as it progresses through the system.) Unlike an event routine, this process routine has multiple entry points at blocks 1, 5, and 9. Entry into this routine at block 1 corresponds to the arrival event for a customer entity that is the most imminent event in the event list. At block 1 an arrival event record is placed in the event list for the *next* customer entity to arrive. (This next customer entity will arrive at a time equal to the time the *current* customer entity arrives plus an interarrival time.) To determine whether the customer entity currently arriving can begin service, a check is made (at block 2) to see whether the server is idle. If the server is busy, this customer entity is placed at the end of the queue (block 3) and made to wait (at block 4) until selected for service at some undetermined time in the future. (This is called a *conditional wait.*) Control is then returned to the "timing routine" to determine what customer entity's event is the most imminent *now*. (If we think of a flowchart like the one in Fig. 3.2 as existing for each customer entity in the system, control will next be passed to the appropriate entry point for the flowchart corresponding to the most imminent event for some other customer.) When this customer entity (the one made to wait at block 4) is activated at some point in the future (when it is first in queue and another customer completes service and makes the server idle), it is removed from the queue *at block 5* and begins service immediately, thereby making the server busy (block 6). A customer entity arriving to find the server idle also begins service immediately (at block 6); in either case, we are now at block 7. There the departure time for the customer beginning service is determined, and a corresponding event record is placed in the event list. This customer entity is then made to wait (at block 8) until its service has been completed. (This is an *unconditional wait*, since its activation time is known.) Control is returned to the timing routine to determine what customer entity will be processed next. When the customer made to wait at block 8 is activated at the end of its

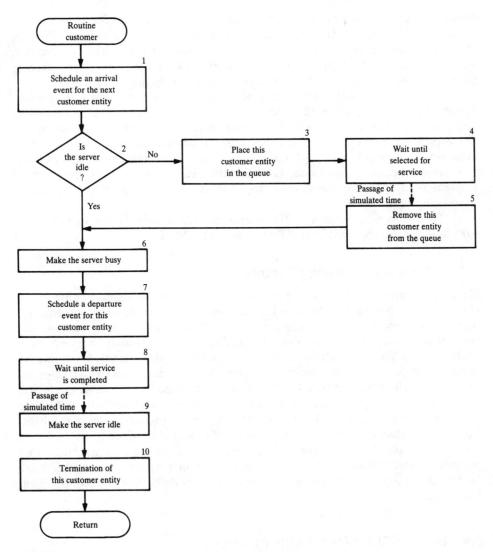

FIGURE 3.2
Prototype customer-process routine for a single-server queueing system.

service, it makes the server idle *at block 9* (allowing the first customer in the queue to become active immediately), and then this customer is removed from the system at block 10. [A more detailed explanation of the process approach in the context of SIMSCRIPT II.5 may be found in Law and Larmey (1984).]

A simulation using the process approach also evolves over time by executing the events in increasing order of their time of occurrence. Internally, the two approaches to simulation are very similar (e.g., both approaches use a simulation clock, an event list, a timing routine, etc.). They differ mainly in the language constructs that they make available to model a system. Process statements are more "macro" in nature and automatically translate certain situations commonly occurring in a simulation model, e.g., customers arriving to a queueing system, into the corresponding event logic.

The process approach has several advantages over the event-scheduling approach. For many types of systems the process approach is more natural in some sense, since one process routine describes the entire experience of the corresponding process entity. Furthermore, a process simulation model of a system usually requires fewer lines of code than the comparable program using the event-scheduling approach. On the other hand, the process approach as implemented in some simulation languages is less flexible than the event-scheduling approach.

The process approach is the major modeling orientation in GPSS/H, GPSS/PC, SIMAN, SIMSCRIPT II.5, and SLAM II.

3.3.3   Common Modeling Elements

There are a number of modeling elements common to the simulation packages (languages or simulators) discussed in this chapter. An *entity* (or *transaction*) is a person or object that arrives to a system, is "serviced" in some manner, and then usually departs. Examples of entities are a customer arriving to a barbershop, a part in a factory, and a message for a communication system. An *attribute* (or *parameter*) is a piece of information that describes or characterizes an entity, such as haircut type for a customer, due date for a part, or the length of a message. A *queue* (or *file* or *set*) is a collection of entities with some common characteristic, such as parts waiting to be processed on a machine. Entities in a queue may be processed in a FIFO or LIFO manner, or based on the value of some entity attribute. A *resource* is a person or "machine" that provides service to an entity while it is present in a system. Examples are a barber, a worker or machine in a factory, and a node or link in a communication system.

3.4   DESIRABLE SOFTWARE FEATURES

In Sec. 3.1 we discussed some basic features or capabilities needed in programming a simulation model. We now continue this discussion by presenting a number of additional features that should be available in a contemporary simulation package, with these features being grouped into five categories. [See Law and Haider (1989), and also the discussion of material-handling modules in Sec. 13.3.]

3.4.1   General Features

Perhaps the most important feature for a simulation package to have is *modeling flexibility*, because no two systems are exactly the same. If the simulation package does not have the necessary capabilities for a particular application then the system must be approximated, resulting in a model with unknown validity. Entities should have *general attributes* (e.g., due date, message length, etc.), which can be appropriately changed; this capability is generally available in simulation languages but is less common in simulators.

Ease of model development is another very important feature, due to the short time frame for many projects. The accuracy and speed of the modeling process will be increased if the package has good *debugging aids*, such as an interactive debugger, on-line input error checking, and on-line help.

Fast model execution speed is particularly important for very large models (e.g., certain military applications) and when the simulation model is to be run on a microcomputer. For a complicated simulation model of a 40-machine food-packaging plant, it took 7 hours to simulate 2 weeks of production on a 16-megahertz microcomputer.

The *maximum model size* allowed by the simulation package may be an important factor when the model is to be executed on a microcomputer. For some packages, the maximum model size is currently less than 100 K bytes. This potential difficulty will become less important as many vendors are beginning to offer versions with extended model sizes.

It is also desirable for a simulation package to be available for a number of different computer classes (i.e., microcomputer, work station, and minicomputer/mainframe), and for the software to be *compatible across these classes*. Thus, for example, a model could be developed on a microcomputer and then uploaded to a minicomputer or mainframe for execution of the production runs.

Finally, in some applications (e.g., steel manufacturing) it is convenient for the software to have capabilities for *combined discrete-continuous simulation* (see Sec. 1.8.2).

3.4.2 Animation

Easy-to-use animation is one of the main reasons for the increased popularity of simulation modeling. In an *animation*, key elements of a system (e.g., machines and parts) are represented on a CRT by icons that change shape, color, or position when there is a change of state in the simulation. Thus, a system can be seen graphically to change over time. Most contemporary animation packages operate in a *concurrent mode*, where the animation is displayed while the simulation is actually running (perhaps slowed down to allow for visual comprehension). On the other hand, some animation packages function in a *playback mode*, where the animation is displayed after the simulation is completed from state changes recorded in a disk file. Several examples of animation and graphics are given in color Plate 1.

The major reason for the popularity of animation is its ability to communicate the essence of a simulation model (or of simulation itself) to managers and other key project personnel, greatly increasing the model's credibility. Other potential benefits of animation are:

- Debugging a simulation computer program
- Showing that a simulation model is *not* valid
- Suggesting improved operational procedures or control logic for a system
- Understanding the dynamic behavior of a system
- Training operational personnel

Animation also has certain shortcomings or disadvantages. In particular, it is not a substitute for a careful statistical analysis of the simulation output data. One cannot conclude that a system is "well defined" by watching an animation for a "short" period of time since, if the simulation were run for a longer period of time, a crucial piece of equipment might fail and cause a major system bottleneck. Animating a simulation model increases model development time, and simulation packages with an animation capability are often considerably more expensive. Finally, only part of a simulation model's logic can actually be seen in an animation; thus, a "correct" animation is no guarantee of a valid or debugged model.

There are a number of desirable features for an animation package. First and foremost, since animation is primarily a communication tool, it is important for it to look realistic (particularly for presentations to high-level managers). The user should be able to *create high-resolution icons* using bit-mapped rather than character graphics. There should be *smooth movement of icons* across the computer screen, rather than "jumpy" or "pulsating" movement. It should be possible to *store icons in a library* for use in a future model, and the library should come with *standard icons* to facilitate animation development. The animation should be *easy to develop*, relying more on menus and graphics that on programming. There should be the capability for *multiple-screen layout*, since some models will not "fit" on a single standard computer screen. Additional animation features are discussed in Law and Haider (1989).

A useful graphical companion to animation is dynamic presentation-quality graphics, where histograms, level meters, dials, etc., are updated as the simulation progresses through time.

3.4.3   Statistical Capabilities

Since most real-world systems exhibit some sort of random behavior, a simulation package must contain good statistical capabilities that should actually be used. In general, each source of system randomness (interarrival times, service times, machine operating times, etc.) needs to be modeled by a probability distribution, *not* just its mean (see Sec. 4.7). A simulation package should contain a wide variety of *standard distributions* (e.g., exponential, gamma, and triangular), should be able to use *distributions based on observed system data* (see Sec. 6.2.4), and should contain a *multiple-stream random-number generator* to facilitate comparing alternative system designs (see Secs. 7.1 and 11.2).

Since random samples from the input probability distributions "drive" a simulation model through time, simulation output data (e.g., daily throughputs in a factory) are also random and appropriate statistical techniques must be used to design and interpret the simulation runs. A simulation package should contain a single *command* to make *independent replications* of the model automatically, with each replication using different random numbers, starting in the same initial state, and resetting the statistical counters to zero. We should be able to specify a *warmup period* (at the end of which statistical counters are reset to zero) and to construct *confidence intervals* for desired measures of performance (e.g., mean daily throughput) in order to determine the statistical precision of the simulation results.

3.4.4   Customer Support

Most users of simulation software require some level of ongoing support from the vendor. First, the software vendor should present *public seminars* on the use of the software on a regular basis. Also, the vendor should provide timely *technical support* for specific modeling problems encountered by the user. (A toll-free phone number is desirable.) *Good documentation*, including a well-written textbook, a user's manual, and numerous detailed examples, is important for software use as well as initial installation. *Free software trials* and *demo disks* are helpful to the prospective user in evaluating the software for their particular needs.

3.4.5   Output Reports

A simulation package should provide time-saving *standard reports* for commonly occurring performance statistics (e.g., utilizations, queue sizes and delays, and throughput), but should also allow *tailored reports* to be developed easily. For example, standard reports are often not suitable for management presentations. Furthermore, it is often of interest to obtain (static) *presentation-quality graphical displays* [e.g., histograms, bar charts, pie charts, or time plots of important variables (see Sec. 9.8)] and to have *access to the individual model output observations* (rather than just the usual summary statistics) so that additional analyses can be performed. For example, one might want to export the output observations (e.g., daily throughputs) to a graphics package, a spreadsheet, or a statistics package.

3.5   GPSS

GPSS (General-Purpose Simulation System) is a process-oriented simulation language [see, for example, Gordon (1975) and Schriber (1974)] that is well suited for queueing systems. Originally developed by Geoffrey Gordon at the IBM Corporation in 1961, it evolved through a number of versions, with the most recent IBM version being GPSS V. In the 1960s and 1970s, GPSS was a very popular simulation language, probably due to the queueing nature of many simulation models, IBM's strong influence on the computer industry, and GPSS's being taught in many university simulation courses. IBM stopped enhancing and actively supporting GPSS in 1972, with the void eventually being filled by the introduction of GPSS/H and GPSS/PC by other vendors. These improved versions of GPSS are described in the following sections.

3.5.1 GPSS/H

GPSS/H [see Banks, Carson, and Sy (1989) and Schriber (1990)] was developed by James Henriksen in 1977 and is marketed by Wolverine Software (Annandale, Virginia). GPSS/H is a compiled language, compared with the interpretive approach of GPSS V, and is reported to run, on the average, five times faster [see Abed, Barta, and McRoberts (1985)]. It has a number of other significant enhancements relative to GPSS V, including a real-valued clock, ability to read and write external files, tailored output reports, improved control statements (e.g., DO loops and IF-THEN-ELSE logic), mathematical functions, and a limited number of routines for generating random values from probability distributions. Because of these capabilities and the basic nature of GPSS statements, most GPSS/H models do not require the use of external routines (in FORTRAN or other languages). The random-number generator has also been improved, allowing for an essentially unlimited number of nonoverlapping streams. PROOF [see Brunner and Henriksen (1989)] is a playback-oriented animation package that is marketed by Wolverine Software. It has several interesting features, such as the ability to change quickly from a plan (top) view to an isometric view and the capability to be used with simulation packages developed by several different vendors.

The GPSS/H language consists of more than 60 standard statements, many of which have a corresponding pictorial representation (called a *block*) that is intended to be suggestive of the operation performed by the statement. Building a GPSS model can be thought of as combining a set of standard blocks into a block diagram that represents the path taken by a typical entity as it progresses through the system. After the block-diagram model has been constructed, it is translated by the user into the corresponding set of GPSS statements for execution on the computer. However, the block diagram itself may be useful in explaining the nature of the model to a manager, who may not be familiar with any programming language. Customers or entities that require service of some kind from the system of interest are called *transactions* in GPSS, and their attributes are called *parameters*. The servers or resources that provide the service required by the transactions are called *facilities* or *storages*, corresponding to a single server or a group of parallel servers, respectively.

3.5.2 Simulation of the $M/M/1$ Queue

A block diagram and a statement listing for a GPSS/H program of the $M/M/1$ queue (see Sec. 1.4.3) are given in Figs. 3.3 and 3.4, respectively. (The

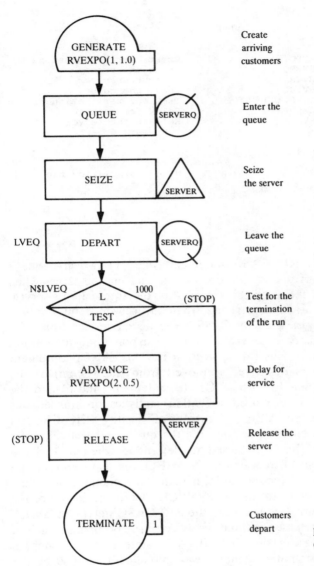

FIGURE 3.3
GPSS/H block diagram, queueing model.

program was provided by Professor Thomas Schriber of The University of Michigan.) In Fig. 3.4, statements with an asterisk (*) in column 1 are comments. Also, in lines 5 through 16 the words after position 37 are comments. Line numbers are not part of the program.

The SIMULATE statement (line 4 of the program) is a control statement necessary for program execution. The GENERATE statement (line 5) creates transactions representing customers with exponential (RVEXPO) interarrival times having mean 1.0 and using random-number stream 1. The SEIZE

```
 1     *
 2     *          SIMULATION OF THE M/M/1 QUEUE
 3     *
 4                SIMULATE
 5                GENERATE    RVEXPO(1,1.0)       Create arriving customers
 6                QUEUE       SERVERQ             Enter the queue
 7                SEIZE       SERVER              Seize the server
 8     LVEQ       DEPART      SERVERQ             Leave the queue
 9                TEST L      N$LVEQ,1000,STOP    Test for termination of the run
10                ADVANCE     RVEXPO(2,0.5)       Delay for service
11     STOP       RELEASE     SERVER              Release the server
12                TERMINATE   1                   Customers depart
13     *
14     *          CONTROL STATEMENTS
15     *
16                START       1000                Make 1 simulation run
17                END
```

FIGURE 3.4
GPSS/H program, queueing model.

statement (line 7) and the RELEASE statement (line 11), which define a *facility* called SERVER, correspond to a transaction's seizing the server when it is (or becomes) idle and releasing the server after the transaction's service has been completed. (Transactions arriving when the server is busy join a queue that is automatically defined by GPSS.) The actual service time of a transaction, which is in this case generated from an exponential distribution with mean 0.5 (using stream 2), is experienced at the ADVANCE statement (line 10). The transaction is destroyed (removed from the system) at the TERMINATE statement (line 12). The QUEUE statement (line 6) and the DEPART statement (line 8) are used to gather statistics on transactions waiting in the queue (called SERVERQ) "in front of" facility SERVER, and correspond to a customer's entering and leaving the queue, respectively.

The TEST statement (line 9) is used to determine when to end the simulation run. If the number of transactions, N$LVEQ, that have entered the DEPART block labeled LVEQ (equivalently, have left the queue) is less than 1000, the transaction proceeds to the ADVANCE statement in a normal manner. Otherwise, the transaction is sent to the RELEASE statement labeled STOP, where the server is released without a service time's occurring. Each of the 1000 transactions that enter the TERMINATE statement decrement a counter by 1. Since the termination counter was initially set to 1000 by the START (control) statement (line 16), the 1000th transaction's decrementing the counter reduces the counter value to 0 and results in the termination of the simulation.

The GPSS/H standard output report for this program is given in Fig. 3.5. Note that the average delay is 0.614 (see "AVERAGE TIME/UNIT" for queue SERVERQ). Also, the time-average number in queue (see "AVER-AGE CONTENTS" for queue SERVERQ) and server utilization (see "...TOTAL TIME" for facility SERVER) are 0.605 and 0.516, respectively. Server utilization is *automatically* provided when a facility (e.g., SERVER) is

RELATIVE CLOCK: 1014.1565   ABSOLUTE CLOCK: 1014.1565

BLOCK	CURRENT	TOTAL
1		1000
2		1000
3		1000
LVEQ		1000
5		1000
6		999
STOP		1000
8		1000

FACILITY	--AVG-UTIL-DURING-- TOTAL TIME	AVAIL TIME	UNAVL TIME	ENTRIES	AVERAGE TIME/XACT	CURRENT STATUS	PERCENT AVAIL	SEIZING XACT	PREEMPTING XACT
SERVER	0.516			1000	0.523	AVAIL	AVAIL		

QUEUE	MAXIMUM CONTENTS	AVERAGE CONTENTS	TOTAL ENTRIES	ZERO ENTRIES	PERCENT ZEROS	AVERAGE TIME/UNIT	$AVERAGE TIME/UNIT	QTABLE NUMBER	CURRENT CONTENTS
SERVERQ	8	0.605	1000	454	45.4	0.614	1.124		0

RANDOM STREAM	ANTITHETIC VARIATES	INITIAL POSITION	CURRENT POSITION	SAMPLE COUNT	CHI-SQUARE UNIFORMITY
1	OFF	100000	101001	1001	0.71
2	OFF	200000	200999	999	0.69

FIGURE 3.5
GPSS/H standard output report, queueing model.

defined by the SEIZE and RELEASE statements. The other two statistics result from the use of the QUEUE and DEPART statements.

3.5.3 GPSS/PC

GPSS/PC [see Minuteman (1988)] is a simulation language designed specifically for use on the IBM PC and compatibles. It was developed by Springer Cox in 1984 and is marketed by Minuteman Software (Stow, Massachusetts). It has several nice debugging features, including on-line input error checking, on-line help, and the ability to see transactions flowing through the block diagram graphically. Because GPSS/PC is not a compiler, changes made to a model are seen "immediately," without waiting for the program to be recompiled. There are also useful graphical displays for facilities, storages, and histograms, which are updated *dynamically* during the execution of the simulation. GPSS/PC comes standard with concurrent character-graphics animation. An optional three-dimensional, bit-mapped graphics animation capability is also available for use in a playback mode. On the other hand, it has limited facilities for generating random values from probability distributions. One is more likely to need external routines in GPSS/PC than in GPSS/H to perform complex decision logic or produce tailored reports. Also, GPSS/PC is not completely compatible with minicomputer and mainframe versions of GPSS. GPSS/PC has the same *basic* modeling elements (e.g., transactions and facilities) as GPSS/H.

3.6 SIMAN/Cinema

SIMAN (SIMulation ANalysis) is a simulation language in which one can build a process-oriented model, an event-oriented model, or a combination of the two [see Pegden, Sadowski, and Shannon (1990)]. In a typical application, most of the simulation model is developed using the process orientation. Complicated decision logic, which is impossible or inconvenient in the process approach, can be coded in event routines and then called from the process model. SIMAN was developed by Dennis Pegden in 1982 and is distributed by Systems Modeling Corporation (Sewickley, Pennsylvania). SIMAN gained quick acceptance because it was the first major simulation language to be available for microcomputers and also because of its special features for manufacturing, including work stations, transporters (e.g., a fork-lift truck), conveyors, and automated guided vehicles. Cinema is a simulation language that contains all of the features of SIMAN and, in addition, the capability to produce high-quality animation. The latest releases of these languages are called SIMAN IV and Cinema IV.

A SIMAN *process* simulation model is broken into two distinct parts, a model frame and an experimental frame, which are kept is separate files. In the *model frame*, modeling constructs called *blocks* are used to describe the logic by which the model's entities and resources interact dynamically. Each block has a corresponding pictorial representation, and these symbols can be combined into a linear top-down *block diagram*, which graphically describes the flow of entities through the system. Some analysts prefer to construct a block diagram before coding the actual model-frame statements.

In the *experimental frame*, modeling constructs called *elements* are used to specify the particular parameter values (e.g., mean service time) for the present simulation run(s), to define resource types and quantities, and to delineate the output statistics desired. This model/experiment dichotomy may allow the analyst to make two distinct runs of the simulation, perhaps differing only in some parameter value, without recompiling the model frame.

The SIMAN Output Processor allows one to perform certain statistical procedures such as confidence intervals and hypothesis tests on the output data produced by simulation runs from the same or different system configurations. Additionally, it can be used to produce presentation-quality graphical displays such as time plots of variables, histograms, and bar charts. Furthermore, the analyst can choose the desired output data treatments *after* the simulation runs have been made.

SIMAN is available for all major classes of computers. However, with the microcomputer version, it is possible to use an interactive graphical preprocessor called BLOCKS to build the (process-orientation) block diagram. The diagram is then automatically translated into the statement model for execution on the computer. A similar program called ELEMENTS can be used to develop the experimental frame. This capability can increase the speed and accuracy of the model-development process.

The major modeling building blocks in SIMAN are entities (with attributes), queues (or files), and resources.

3.6.1   Simulation of the $M/M/1$ Queue

This section shows how to simulate the $M/M/1$ queue considered in Sec. 1.4.3 using the process orientation of SIMAN. A block diagram is given in Fig. 3.6 and the corresponding model-frame statements are given in Fig. 3.7, where the line numbers are for expository purposes and are not part of the program. The CREATE block (line 2) places new customers in the system with exponential $[EX(1, 1)]$ interarrival times, with the first "1" in the parentheses specifying that the mean interarrival time is given by parameter set 1 (see the "1.0" in line 5 of the experimental frame in Fig. 3.8) and the second "1" giving the random-number stream. The modifier MARK(1) stores the time of arrival of a customer in its attribute 1 for later use.

When a customer actually arrives to the system, it temporarily passes through the QUEUE block (line 3) and attempts to seize the resource SERVER (line 4), which is defined in line 4 of the experimental frame. By default, there is one unit of SERVER available. If the server is available, the customer has its zero delay in queue computed and recorded by the TALLY block in line 5 (as the current time minus its time of arrival in attribute 1) and

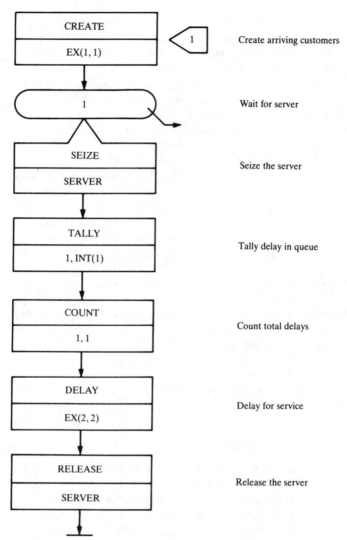

FIGURE 3.6
SIMAN block diagram, queueing model.

```
1   BEGIN;
2           CREATE,,EX(1,1):EX(1,1):MARK(1);        Create arriving customers
3           QUEUE,1;                                 Wait for server
4           SEIZE:SERVER;                            Seize server
5           TALLY:1,INT(1);                          Tally delay in queue
6           COUNT:1,1;                               Count total delays
7           DELAY:EX(2,2);                           Delay for service
8           RELEASE:SERVER:DISPOSE;                  Release server
9   END;
```

FIGURE 3.7
SIMAN model frame, queueing model.

```
 1   BEGIN;
 2   PROJECT,M M 1 QUEUE,A. LAW,7/12/89;
 3   DISCRETE,100,1,1;
 4   RESOURCES:1,SERVER;
 5   PARAMETERS:1,1.0:
 6             2,0.5;
 7   TALLIES:1,DELAY IN QUEUE;
 8   COUNTER:1,CUSTOMER DELAYS,1000;
 9   DSTAT:1,NQ(1),NUMBER IN QUEUE:
10         2,NR(1),SERVER UTIL.;
11   REPLICATE,1;
12   END;
```

FIGURE 3.8
SIMAN experimental frame, queueing model.

the COUNT block (line 6) adds one to counter 1 to indicate that one more delay has been observed. When this counter reaches 1000 delays, as specified by the COUNTER element in line 8 of Fig. 3.8, the simulation terminates. The customer actually experiences its service time at the DELAY block (line 7); in this case, service times are exponentially distributed with the mean of 0.5 given by parameter set 2 (see line 6 in Fig. 3.8) and are generated using random-number stream 2. [If the server is busy when the above customer arrives, the customer is placed at the end of the queue (file 1) in line 3.] When the customer completes its service, it releases the resource SERVER (line 8) and is removed from the system by the DISPOSE modifier. If there are any customers in the queue, then the first of these is removed, seizes the server (line 4), has its positive delay computed in line 5, etc.

The PROJECT element (line 2) of the experimental frame states the project name, the analyst, and the date. The DISCRETE element (line 3) specifies the computer storage requirements for the model, here being 100 entities (customers) simultaneously in the model, a maximum of 1 attribute for any entity, and 1 queue (file) for the model. The elements in lines 4 through 6 have been explained above. The TALLIES element (line 7) places a label of "DELAY IN QUEUE" on the discrete-time statistics produced by the TALLY block in line 5 of the model frame. The DSTAT element (lines 9 and 10) computes continuous-time statistics (e.g., the time average and the maximum) for the number in queue 1 [NQ(1)] and for the number of busy units of resource 1, NR(1); these functions are referred to as DSTAT variables 1 and 2, respectively. Thus, for example, the time average of variable 2 will be the server utilization. The REPLICATE element (line 11) specifies that one replication of the simulation is to be made. A more general form of this statement can be used to specify multiple replications, a simulation run length, and a warmup period.

The simulation results are given in Fig. 3.9. Note that the average delay in queue is 0.49558 (see "Tally Variables"). Also, the time-average number in queue and server utilization (computed by the DSTAT element) are 0.50658 and 0.51872, respectively (see "Discrete Change Variables"). The "Standard Deviation" results in the output report are not reliable, in general, since they are based on formulas that assume independent output data, which will not be satisfied in practice (see Sec. 4.4).

```
                      SIMAN Summary Report

                      Run Number    1 of  1

Project:   M M 1 QUEUE
Analyst:   A. LAW
Date   :    7/12/1989

Run ended at time     .9783E+03


                          Tally Variables
                          ---------------

Number Identifier       Average    Standard  Minimum    Maximum    Number
                                   Deviation  Value      Value      of Obs.
-------------------------------------------------------------------------------

    1  DELAY IN QUEUE      .49558     .80138    .00000    4.04199       1000


                      Discrete Change Variables
                      -------------------------

Number Identifier       Average    Standard  Minimum    Maximum    Time
                                   Deviation  Value      Value      Period
-------------------------------------------------------------------------------

    1  NUMBER IN QUEUE     .50658    1.14931    .00000   10.00000     978.28
    2  SERVER UTIL.        .51872     .49965    .00000    1.00000     978.28


                               Counters
                               --------

Number Identifier       Count    Limit
-------------------------------------------
    1  CUSTOMER DELAYS    1000     1000
```

FIGURE 3.9
SIMAN output report, queueing model.

Observe that the output statistics for GPSS/H and SIMAN are somewhat different due to differences in the random-number generators used (see also Secs. 3.7 and 3.8). This points out the importance of proper design and analysis of simulation runs, as discussed in Chap. 9.

3.7 SIMSCRIPT II.5

SIMSCRIPT II.5 is a process-oriented or event-oriented simulation language [see Law and Larmey (1984) and Russell (1983)]; however, because of the generality of the process approach in SIMSCRIPT, the use of the event-scheduling approach is not necessary. SIMSCRIPT was developed by Harry Markowitz and others at the Rand Corporation in 1962. It evolved through a number of versions, with the latest one, SIMSCRIPT II.5, being marketed by CACI Products Company (La Jolla, California).

SIMSCRIPT II.5 is actually a general programming language containing the capabilities for building discrete-event, continuous, or combined simulation models. (It has the programming features of FORTRAN, ALGOL, and PL/I.) Furthermore, its English-like and free-form syntax make SIMSCRIPT II.5 simulation programs easy to read and almost self-documenting. Because of its general process approach, its sophisticated data structures, and its powerful control statements, SIMSCRIPT II.5 is often used for large, complex simulation models, particularly when the system is not queueing-oriented. For example, most military combat models have been written either in SIMSCRIPT II.5 or FORTRAN.

SIMSCRIPT II.5 is available for microcomputers, work stations, and minicomputers/mainframes. The IBM PC and compatibles version is embedded in the SIMLAB package, which is an interactive, multitasking programming environment for facilitating the use of SIMSCRIPT. It contains an editor, the SIMSCRIPT II.5 compiler, a debugger, and on-line help.

The microcomputer and work station versions include the SIMGRAPHICS animation and graphics package. It can be used to produce both dynamic and static presentation-quality graphics, such as histograms, pie and bar charts, level meters and dials, and time plots of variables. Animations of the simulation output are also constructed using SIMGRAPHICS. Finally, SIMGRAPHICS can be used to produce interactive graphical "front ends" (or forms) for entering model input data. An input form may include such graphical elements as menubars (with pull-down menus), text or data "boxes," and "buttons" that are clicked on with a mouse to select an alternative. The graphical model front end allows one to make a certain set of modifications to the model without programming, which facilitates model use by people who are not programming experts.

The major modeling elements of the process part of SIMSCRIPT II.5 are processes (or process entities), resources, and sets (similar to queues). A process entity flows through its corresponding process and may have attributes. To construct a simulation model in SIMSCRIPT II.5, the analyst must write a preamble, a main program, and a process routine corresponding to each process. The *preamble*, which does not contain any executable statements, is used to define the building blocks for the simulation, such as processes and resources. It is also used to define global variables, the basic unit of time for the simulation clock, and the desired output statistics. In the latter case, the TALLY and ACCUMULATE statements are used to specify discrete-time and continuous-time statistics, respectively. The main program is where the execution of a SIMSCRIPT program begins. This routine is used to read input parameters for the simulation, to specify the number of available units for each resource, and to place the "initial" event records (called *process notices*) into the event list using the ACTIVATE statement. The simulation actually begins by executing the START SIMULATION statement, which is actually just a call to the timing routine. The timing routine is part of the SIMSCRIPT II.5 language and does not have to be written by the modeler.

3.7.1 Simulation of the $M/M/1$ Queue

This section shows how to simulate the $M/M/1$ queue of Sec. 1.4.3 using the process orientation of SIMSCRIPT II.5. (The line numbers in Figs. 3.10 through 3.14 are for expository purposes and are not part of the actual program.) The preamble is given in Fig. 3.10. Three types of processes, ARRIVAL.GENERATOR, CUSTOMER, and REPORT, are defined in line 3. Process (routine) CUSTOMER describes the flow of a typical customer as it moves through the system. On the other hand, process (routine) ARRIVAL.GENERATOR creates new customers, and process (routine) REPORT is used to print the final report at the end of the simulation after 1000 delays in queue have been completed. Similarly, SERVER is defined to be a resource in line 5, and has the two associated sets, Q.SERVER (customers in queue for SERVER) and X.SERVER (customers executing on SERVER), automatically specified. The three quantities in lines 7 and 8 are defined to be *global* real variables. (If a variable is not defined in the preamble, it is a local variable. Also, all variables are by default real, regardless of the letter they begin with.) The desired simulation run length in delays, TOT.DELAYS, is defined to be a global integer variable in line 10. In line 12, MINUTES is defined (in effect) to be the basic unit of time for internal program calculations; the default is days. The TALLY statement (lines 14 and 15) is used to obtain discrete-time statistics for the variable DELAY.IN.QUEUE. In particular, NUM.DELAYS will be the number of delays observed (i.e., the number of times that a statement with DELAY.IN.QUEUE on the left-hand side of an equal sign is executed), and AVG.DELAY.IN.QUEUE will be the sample mean of these delays. The ACCUMULATE statement (line 17) is used to compute continuous-time statistics on the system-defined variable N.Q.SER-

```
 1    PREAMBLE
 2
 3       PROCESSES INCLUDE ARRIVAL.GENERATOR, CUSTOMER, AND REPORT
 4
 5       RESOURCES INCLUDE SERVER
 6
 7       DEFINE DELAY.IN.QUEUE, MEAN.INTERARRIVAL.TIME, AND
 8          MEAN.SERVICE.TIME AS REAL VARIABLES
 9
10       DEFINE TOT.DELAYS AS AN INTEGER VARIABLE
11
12       DEFINE MINUTES TO MEAN UNITS
13
14       TALLY AVG.DELAY.IN.QUEUE AS THE AVERAGE AND NUM.DELAYS AS
15          THE NUMBER OF DELAY.IN.QUEUE
16
17       ACCUMULATE AVG.NUMBER.IN.QUEUE AS THE AVERAGE OF N.Q.SERVER
18
19       ACCUMULATE UTIL.SERVER AS THE AVERAGE OF N.X.SERVER
20
21    END
```

FIGURE 3.10
SIMSCRIPT II.5 preamble, queueing model.

VER, which is the number of customers in the set Q.SERVER at a particular point in time. The quantity AVG.NUMBER.IN.QUEUE will be the time average of N.Q.SERVER over the length of the simulation. The system-defined variable N.X.SERVER in line 19 is the number of customers in the set X.SERVER at a particular point in time, which can be 1 or 0 in our case. Thus, if we use the ACCUMULATE statement to compute the time average of this variable over the length of the simulation, we obtain the proportion of time UTIL.SERVER that the server is busy.

The main program is listed in Fig. 3.11. In line 3, a free-format READ statement is used to read in the input parameters MEAN.INTERARRIVAL. TIME (=1.0), MEAN.SERVICE.TIME (=0.5), and TOT.DELAYS (=1000). The CREATE statement (line 5) specifies that there is one type of the resource SERVER. (Each type of a resource is fed by a single queue.) In line 6 the number of available units of the first (and in this case only) type of resource SERVER, namely, U.SERVER(1), is set to 1. The ACTIVATE statement (line 8) places an ARRIVAL.GENERATOR process notice into the event list with an event time (called an *activation time*) of "NOW." Time "NOW" means that the process notice has an activation time equal to the current value of simulated time, TIME.V (=0 in this instance), and that this process notice is placed "first" in the event list. This process notice is used to initialize the ARRIVAL.GENERATOR process routine at time 0. The START SIMULA-TION statement (line 10) calls the timing routine and begins the execution of the simulation. The timing routine will remove the first process notice from the event list, which in this case will be the one corresponding to the ARRIVAL.GENERATOR process.

The ARRIVAL.GENERATOR process routine is listed in Fig. 3.12. [We will not explain its exact operation here; see Law and Larmey (1984, pp. 2–12) for details.] It is used to cause new customers to arrive to the system with exponential interarrival times having mean MEAN.INTERARRIVAL.TIME minutes using random-number stream 1 (line 5). At the time instant that a particular customer is to arrive, the ARRIVAL.GENERATOR routine places a CUSTOMER process notice in the event list with an activation time of NOW (line 6). This causes the timing routine to call the CUSTOMER process

```
 1   MAIN
 2
 3       READ MEAN.INTERARRIVAL.TIME, MEAN.SERVICE.TIME, AND TOT.DELAYS
 4
 5       CREATE EVERY SERVER(1)
 6       LET U.SERVER(1) = 1
 7
 8       ACTIVATE AN ARRIVAL.GENERATOR NOW
 9
10       START SIMULATION
11
12   END
```

FIGURE 3.11
SIMSCRIPT II.5 main program, queueing model.

```
1   PROCESS ARRIVAL.GENERATOR
2
3      WHILE TIME.V >= 0.0
4      DO
5         WAIT EXPONENTIAL.F(MEAN.INTERARRIVAL.TIME,1) MINUTES
6         ACTIVATE A CUSTOMER NOW
7      LOOP
8
9   END
```

FIGURE 3.12
SIMSCRIPT II.5 process routine ARRIVAL.GENERATOR, queueing model.

routine immediately in order to process the newly arriving customer. The SIMSCRIPT II.5 ARRIVAL.GENERATOR routine corresponds to the CREATE statement in SIMAN and SLAM II and to the GENERATE statement in GPSS.

The process routine for process CUSTOMER is given in Fig. 3.13, and is called each time a process notice for a customer process entity is removed from the event list, corresponding to the arrival of a new customer. [This routine is also called in several other situations, such as when a customer departs; see Law and Larmey (1984) for details.] The DEFINE statement in line 3 specifies that TIME.OF.ARRIVAL is a local real variable (associated with each customer). The time of arrival of the currently arriving customer is set to the current value of the simulation clock, TIME.V, in line 5. The customer then requests one unit of the resource SERVER(1) in line 6. If the server is already busy serving another customer entity, the arriving customer joins the queue Q.SERVER(1) and waits to be served at some point in the future. If the server is idle, the delay in queue of the arriving customer is set to 0 in line 7 and a check for termination of the simulation run is made in lines 8 through 10 (to be discussed below). The server then *works* on the service request of the customer (line 11), whose service duration is generated from an exponential distribution with mean MEAN.SERVICE.TIME minutes using stream 2. After this customer's service has been completed, the customer *relinquishes* the server in line

```
1    PROCESS CUSTOMER
2
3       DEFINE TIME.OF.ARRIVAL AS A REAL VARIABLE
4
5       LET TIME.OF.ARRIVAL = TIME.V
6       REQUEST 1 SERVER(1)
7       LET DELAY.IN.QUEUE = TIME.V - TIME.OF.ARRIVAL
8       IF NUM.DELAYS = TOT.DELAYS
9          ACTIVATE A REPORT NOW
10      ALWAYS
11      WORK EXPONENTIAL.F(MEAN.SERVICE.TIME,2) MINUTES
12      RELINQUISH 1 SERVER(1)
13
14   END
```

FIGURE 3.13
SIMSCRIPT II.5 process routine CUSTOMER, queueing model.

12 and is then removed from the system. If any customers are in Q.SERVER(1) when the server becomes available, the first customer is removed and experiences a positive delay in queue in line 7, etc.

Lines 8 through 10 of process routine CUSTOMER are used to determine when to terminate the simulation run. If NUM.DELAYS (defined in the preamble) is equal to TOT.DELAYS (=1000), then a REPORT process notice is placed in the event list with an activation time of NOW. Control is then returned to the timing routine, which immediately calls the REPORT process routine to terminate the simulation run.

The REPORT process routine is listed in Fig. 3.14, and is called by the timing routine when 1000 customer delays have been completed. The PRINT statement (line 3), which contains no variables, specifies that the five lines following this statement (the first three of which are blank) are printed out exactly as shown. The PRINT statement in lines 9 and 10 says that the three specified variables will be printed out in eight lines exactly as shown. The formats for the three variables are given by the three successive asterisk groups. Thus, the format for MEAN.INTERARRIVAL.TIME is "**.**," which means that the corresponding printed value will be real-valued, have two places to the right of the decimal point, etc. The PRINT statement in lines 19 and 20 is similar. Note, however, that the resource type is specified explicitly in

```
1    PROCESS REPORT
2
3        PRINT 5 LINES THUS


SIMULATION OF THE M/M/1 QUEUE

9        PRINT 8 LINES WITH MEAN.INTERARRIVAL.TIME, MEAN.SERVICE.TIME,
10           AND TOT.DELAYS THUS

MEAN INTERARRIVAL TIME        **.**

MEAN SERVICE TIME             **.**

NUMBER OF CUSTOMERS           *****

19       PRINT 8 LINES WITH AVG.DELAY.IN.QUEUE, AVG.NUMBER.IN.QUEUE(1),
20           AND UTIL.SERVER(1) THUS

AVERAGE DELAY IN QUEUE        ***.**

AVERAGE NUMBER IN QUEUE       ***.**

SERVER UTILIZATION             *.**

29       STOP
30
31   END
```

FIGURE 3.14
SIMSCRIPT II.5 process routine REPORT, queueing model.

```
SIMULATION OF THE M/M/1 QUEUE


MEAN INTERARRIVAL TIME        1.00

MEAN SERVICE TIME              .50

NUMBER OF CUSTOMERS           1000


AVERAGE DELAY IN QUEUE         .43

AVERAGE NUMBER IN QUEUE        .43

SERVER UTILIZATION             .50
```

FIGURE 3.15
SIMSCRIPT II.5 output report, queueing model.

the output. For example, AVG.NUMBER.IN.QUEUE(1) is the time average of Q.SERVER(1). Finally, execution of the STOP statement (line 29) will terminate the simulation, as desired.

The SIMSCRIPT II.5 output report, as printed by process routine REPORT, is given in Fig. 3.15.

3.8   SLAM II AND RELATED SOFTWARE

SLAM II (Simulation Language for Alternative Modeling) is a simulation language in which one can build a process-oriented model, an event-oriented model, or a combination of the two [see Pritsker (1986)]. In a typical application, most of the simulation model is developed using the process orientation. Complicated decision logic, which is impossible or inconvenient in the process approach, is coded in event routines and then called from the process model. SLAM was developed by Dennis Pegden and Alan Pritsker in 1979 and is distributed by the Pritsker Corporation (Indianapolis, Indiana).

The building of a process model often begins with the analyst developing a graphical network diagram for the system. This diagram is constructed by combining a standard set of symbols, called *nodes* and *branches*, into an interconnected *network* that represents the flow of an entity through its corresponding process. A node may correspond, for example, to the creation of entities or to a queue, while a branch may correspond to the passage of time (e.g., a service time). The network model of the system is then translated into an equivalent set of SLAM II program statements for execution on the computer. The program statements could also be coded directly, without a network diagram.

SLAM II is available in several different forms, depending on the computer platform and whether an animation capability is desired. The basic SLAM II language is available for all computer classes, but does not include animation. SLAMSYSTEM is a microcomputer version of SLAM II that is integrated with Microsoft Windows. It provides animation, presentation-quality graphics (e.g., time plots of variables, histograms, bar charts, and pie charts), and a user-friendly environment. SLAM II/TESS is available for engineering work stations, minicomputers, and mainframes. It has animation and graphics capabilities similar to SLAMSYSTEM and, in addition, contains an integrated database for model input/output and enhanced statistical features such as confidence intervals.

With SLAMSYSTEM or SLAM II/TESS, one can graphically build the SLAM II network diagram on a CRT, which is then automatically translated into the corresponding program statements for execution by SLAM II. This feature can increase the speed and accuracy of the modeling process.

There is a Material Handling Extension to SLAM II that allows one to simulate automated guided vehicle systems, cranes, and automated storage and retrieval systems.

A SLAM II process simulation model is coded in a single integrated subprogram. Discrete-time statistics (e.g., average and maximum delay) are obtained in SLAM II using the COLCT node. On the other hand, continuous-time statistics on queues (e.g., average length) and resources (e.g., utilization) are provided *automatically*. The major modeling elements in SLAM II are entities (with attributes), files (or queues), and resources.

3.8.1 Simulation of the $M/M/1$ Queue

This section presents a SLAM process model for the $M/M/1$ queue of Sec. 1.4.3. The network diagram and statement model are given in Figs. 3.16 and 3.17, respectively; the line numbers in Fig. 3.17 are for expository purposes and are not part of the program. The GEN (general) control statement in line 1 states the analyst, the project name, the date, the number of runs (i.e., 1), and the number of columns for output reports (i.e., 72), respectively. (The successive commas represent accepted defaults.) The LIMITS control statement (line 2) declares that the model will contain 1 file (queue), a maximum of 1 attribute per entity, and that no more than 100 entities will be present in the model simultaneously. The NETWORK and END statements in lines 4 and 17 signify the start and end of the process (network) model.

The RESOURCE block in line 6 defines a resource named SERVER with a capacity of 1 unit as specified in the parentheses. The second "1" states that when the SERVER is available, it will serve the first customer in file 1 (see line 9) next. (Lines beginning with semicolons are comments.) The CREATE node (line 8) places new customers in the system with interarrival times $2, 3, \ldots$ being exponentially (EXPON) distributed with a mean of 1.0 and using random-number stream 1. The first 1 after the right parenthesis states that the first interarrival time is exactly 1. (The CREATE node in SLAM II does not allow the first interarrival time to be a random variable; this difficulty could be overcome by adding two additional lines of code.) The next 1 places the time of arrival of each arriving entity in its attribute 1. The AWAIT node (line 9) corresponds to the resource SERVER and its preceding queue. If a

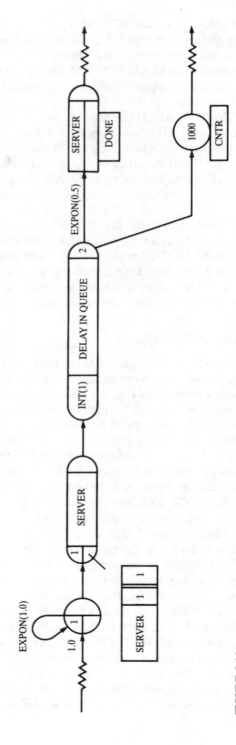

FIGURE 3.16
SLAM II network diagram, queueing model.

260

```
1    GEN,A. LAW,M M 1 QUEUE,7/13/1989,1,,,,,,72;
2    LIM,1,1,100;
3    ;
4    NETWORK;
4    ;
6              RESOURCE/SERVER(1),1;              Define the resource server
7    ;
8              CREATE,EXPON(1.0,1),1,1;           Create arriving customers
9              AWAIT(1),SERVER;                   Wait for/seize server
10             COLCT,INT(1),DELAY IN QUEUE,,2;    Collect delay in queue
11             ACTIVITY,EXPON(0.5,2),,DONE;       Delay for service
12             ACTIVITY,,,CNTR;                   Send "dummy" entity to counter
13   DONE      FREE,SERVER;                       Release server
14             TERM;                              Customers depart
15   ;
16   CNTR      TERM,1000;                         End simulation after 1000 delays
17             END;
18   ;
19   INIT;
20   FIN;
```

FIGURE 3.17
SLAM II program, queueing model.

customer arrives and the SERVER is available, the customer seizes the server immediately and moves to the next line of the program. Otherwise, the customer is placed last in the FIFO queue (file 1). The COLCT node (line 10) computes and records the delay in queue of each customer as the current time minus its time of arrival in attribute 1. Strictly speaking, it is not needed here to compute the average delay in queue, since this will be done automatically by the AWAIT node. However, the COLCT node is needed in general to obtain discrete-time statistics (e.g., maximum delay in queue) and is included here to illustrate its use. The 2 at the end of this line creates a duplicate copy of the entity, with one entity's being routed to line 11 and the other to line 12 (to be discussed after line 14). The entity arriving to line 11 corresponds to the actual customer moving through the system. The ACTIVITY branch there is where the customer actually experiences its service time, which is generated from an exponential distribution with mean 0.5 using stream 2. When the customer's service is completed, the entity is routed to the statement labeled DONE (line 13). At this line, the FREE node causes the entity to release the server and to move on to line 14 for removal from the system (termination). If there are any customers in the queue (file 1), then the first of these is removed and seizes the server in line 9, etc.

The "dummy" entity arriving to line 12 is used to terminate the simulation in the appropriate manner. It is immediately sent to the TERMINATE node in line 16 (labeled CNTR), which adds one to a counter to indicate that one more delay has been observed. When this counter reaches 1000 delays, the simulation is terminated.

The simulation results are given in Fig. 3.18. Note that the average delay in queue is 0.608 (see "STATISTICS FOR VARIABLES BASED ON OB-SERVATION"), as computed by the COLCT node. (See also "AVERAGE

S L A M   I I   S U M M A R Y   R E P O R T

SIMULATION PROJECT M M 1 QUEUE   BY A. LAW

DATE 7/13/1989   RUN NUMBER   1 OF   1

CURRENT TIME   .9171E+03
STATISTICAL ARRAYS CLEARED AT TIME   .0000E+00

STATISTICS FOR VARIABLES BASED ON OBSERVATION

	MEAN VALUE	STANDARD DEVIATION	COEFF. OF VARIATION	MINIMUM VALUE	MAXIMUM VALUE	NO.OF OBS
DELAY IN QUEUE	.608E+00	.100E+01	.165E+01	.000E+00	.589E+01	1000

FILE STATISTICS

FILE NUMBER	LABEL/TYPE	AVERAGE LENGTH	STANDARD DEVIATION	MAXIMUM LENGTH	CURRENT LENGTH	AVERAGE WAIT TIME
1	AWAIT	.662	1.354	9	0	.608
2	CALENDAR	1.555	.497	3	2	.285

RESOURCE STATISTICS

RESOURCE NUMBER	RESOURCE LABEL	CURRENT CAPACITY	AVERAGE UTIL	STANDARD DEVIATION	MAXIMUM UTIL	CURRENT UTIL
1	SERVER	1	.55	.497	1	1

RESOURCE NUMBER	RESOURCE LABEL	CURRENT AVAILABLE	AVERAGE AVAILABLE	MINIMUM AVAILABLE	MAXIMUM AVAILABLE
1	SERVER	0	.4452	0	1

FIGURE 3.18
SLAM II output report, queueing model.

WAIT TIME" for file number 1.) In addition, the time-average number in queue (see "AVERAGE LENGTH" for file number 1) and server utilization (see "AVERAGE UTIL" for resource number 1) are 0.662 and 0.55, respectively. These statistics are automatically computed and written out when the AWAIT node is used. The "STANDARD DEVIATION" results in the output report are not reliable, in general, since they are based on formulas that assume independent output data, which will not be satisfied in practice (see Sec. 4.4).

3.9 COMPARISON OF SIMULATION LANGUAGES

In this section we briefly discuss and compare the simulation languages presented in Secs. 3.5 through 3.8. These languages actually have very similar basic modeling constructs, due to language cross-fertilization over the years. This can be seen in Table 3.1, where we show the GPSS (H or PC), SIMAN/Cinema, SIMSCRIPT II.5, and SLAM II/SLAMSYSTEM language statements for creating new entities, for entities to seize and release resources, for a passage of time (e.g., a service time), and for collecting discrete-time and continuous-time statistics.

Many simulations have a queueing orientation, and GPSS and the process parts of SIMAN and SLAM II have modeling constructs well suited for these types of problems. SIMAN and SLAM II also have constructs for the more basic event-scheduling approach. This should allow them to model *conveniently* a somewhat larger class of non-queueing-oriented systems than GPSS. On the other hand, there is some indication that GPSS/H has the fastest compilation and execution times [see Abed, Barta, and McRoberts (1985)].

SIMSCRIPT II.5 has the most general process approach of the major simulation languages; thus, virtually any system can be modeled without using the event-scheduling approach. However, because of its general structure, it

TABLE 3.1
Implementation of basic simulation capabilities

Feature	GPSS (H or PC)	SIMAN/ Cinema	SIMSCRIPT II.5	SLAM II/ SLAMSYSTEM
	Language			
Create new entities	GENERATE	CREATE	ACTIVATE	CREATE
Seize and release a resource	SEIZE/ RELEASE	SEIZE/ RELEASE	REQUEST/ RELINQUISH	AWAIT/ FREE
Passage of time (e.g., a service time)	ADVANCE	DELAY	WORK, WAIT	ACTIVITY
Discrete-time statistics	QUEUE/ DEPART, TABULATE	TALLY	TALLY	COLCT[a]
Continuous-time statistics	QUEUE/ DEPART, ENTER/ LEAVE, TABULATE[a]	DSTAT	ACCUMULATE	TIMST[a]

[a] Some statistics provided automatically.

TABLE 3.2
Comparison of the simulation languages

Feature	Language					
	GPSS/H	GPSS/PC	SIMAN/ Cinema	SIMSCRIPT II.5	SLAM II	SLAMSYSTEM
Event (E) or process (P) orientation	P	P	E, P	E, P	E, P	E, P
Available for which computer classes?	MICRO,[a] WORK,[b] MIN/MAIN[c]	MICRO	MICRO, WORK, MIN/MAIN	MICRO, WORK, MIN/MAIN	MICRO, WORK, MIN/MAIN	MICRO
Animation for which computer classes?	MICRO	MICRO	(MICRO, WORK)[d]	MICRO, WORK	(WORK, MIN/MAIN)[e]	MICRO
Graphical model input	No	No	Yes[f]	No	Yes[e]	Yes
Combined discrete-continuous simulation	No	Yes	Yes	Yes	Yes	Yes
Number of random-number streams	Essentially unlimited	Essentially unlimited	10[g]	10[g]	10[g]	10
Standard probability distributions[h]	Ex, N, T, U	U	Be, Er, Ex, Ga, L, N, P, T, U, W	Be, Bi, Er, Ex, Ga, L, N, P, T, U, W	Be, Er, Ex, Ga, L, N, P, T, U, W	Be, Er, Ex, Ga, L, N, P, T, U, W
Single command for automatic multiple replications	No	No	Yes	No	Yes	Yes
Confidence-interval procedures[i]	None	R, BM	R, BM, STS	None	(R, BM)[e]	None

[a] Microcomputer.
[b] Work station.
[c] Minicomputer/mainframe.
[d] Cinema only.
[e] Using SLAM II/TESS.
[f] Microcomputer only.
[g] Extendable.
[h] Abbreviations: Be, beta; Bi, binomial; Er, Erlang; Ex, exponential; Ga, gamma; L, lognormal; N, normal; P, Poisson; T, triangular; U, uniform; W, Weibull.
[i] Abbreviations: R, replication; BM, batch means; STS, standardized time series.

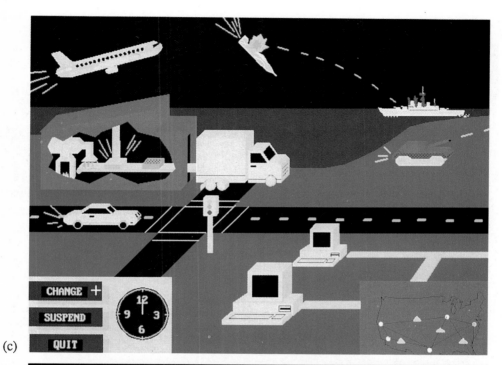

(c)

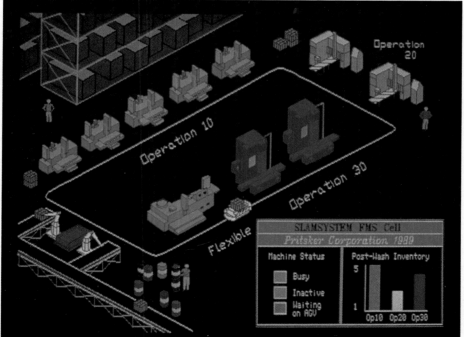

(d)

PLATE I
(*Continued.*)

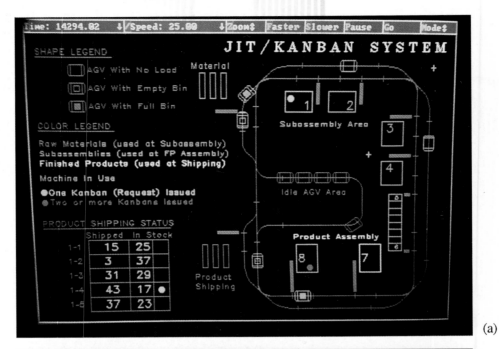

(a)

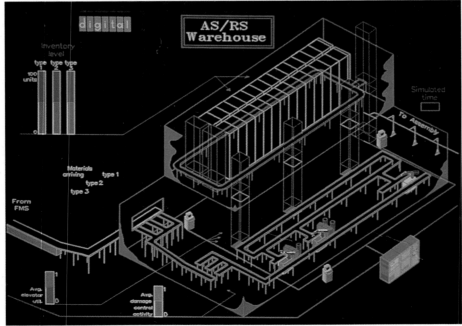

(b)

PLATE I

Examples of animation and graphics: (*a*) GPSS/H; (*b*) SIMAN/Cinema; (*c*) SIMSCRIPT II.5;
(*d*) SLAM II.

may require more lines of code than GPSS, SIMAN, or SLAM II for "standard" queueing problems. For "complicated" simulation models (particularly those that are large or non-queueing-oriented), SIMSCRIPT II.5 is an attractive choice because it is a general programming language with sophisticated control statements and data structures.

In Sec. 3.4 we discussed a number of features to consider when selecting simulation software. There are two levels at which such a decision could be made. At the first level, an organization must decide what languages or simulators to purchase (or lease) for its general use. The reader should be aware that there is no simulation package that is convenient and appropriate for *all* applications. Thus, organizations that do a large amount of simulation may want to consider having several simulation packages, to be used for different types of applications and by people with different backgrounds. At the second level, an analyst must decide what simulation software to use for a particular study.

Many important simulation software features are quite subjective in nature (e.g., ease of model development and vendor technical support) and, thus, will not be used to compare the simulation languages discussed above. As an alternative, we present in Table 3.2 a comparison of the simulation languages based on nine quantitative features or factors. This list is *not exhaustive*, and whether a feature is important could depend on the particular application. For example, most simulation studies do not require capabilities for combined discrete-continuous simulation. In Table 3.2 a simulation language is said to have a particular feature if it is part of the software usually distributed by the vendor.

Note in Table 3.2 that SIMSCRIPT II.5 does not explicitly provide automatic multiple replications and confidence intervals. However, this capability (including replication and batch-means confidence intervals) is available from CACI in free, optional software [see Law (1979)]. Also, multiple replications can easily be obtained in GPSS/H using a DO loop.

Some additional information on the above simulation languages is given in Banks and Carson (1985). In particular, they provide GPSS/H, SIMAN, SIMSCRIPT II.5, and SLAM II programs for a simple manufacturing system.

3.10 ADDITIONAL SIMULATION SOFTWARE

In addition to the simulation languages discussed in the previous sections, there are several others of note, namely, INSIGHT [SysTech (1985)], PCModel [White (1988)], and SIMPLE_1 [Sierra (1989)]. In addition, MODSIM II [Belanger et al. (1989)] and SIM++ [Jade (1989)] are recently introduced simulation languages based on object-oriented programming that promote greater simulation software reusability and will also run on parallel processors.

A large number of simulation packages have been developed specifically for manufacturing applications, including AutoMod II, ProModel, SIMFAC-

TORY II.5, WITNESS, and XCELL+; these products are described in Sec. 13.3.

NETWORK II.5 is a simulator for computer systems and local-area networks [see Cheung, Dimitriadis, and Karplus (1987) and CACI (1988a)]. Its basic building blocks are processing elements (e.g., a CPU), transfer devices (e.g., a bus), storage devices (e.g., a disk drive), and software modules. COMNET II.5, on the other hand, is a simulator for wide-area telecommunication networks [CACI (1988b)]. Its building blocks are the network topology (nodes and their connecting links), network traffic (source, destination, and size of messages), and network operations (strategies for choosing message routes). Both simulators are distributed by CACI Products Company.

REFERENCES

Abed, S. Y., T. A. Barta, and K. L. McRoberts: A Quantitative Comparison of Three Simulation Languages: GPSS/H, SLAM, SIMSCRIPT, *Comput. Ind. Eng.*, 9: 45–66 (1985).

Banks, J., and J. S. Carson: Process-Interaction Simulation Languages, *Simulation*, 44: 225–235 (1985).

Banks, J., J. S. Carson, and J. N. Sy: *Getting Started with GPSS/H*, Wolverine Software Corporation, Annandale, Va. (1989).

Belanger, R. F., B. Donovan, K. L. Morse, S. V. Rice, and D. B. Rockower: *MODSIM II Reference Manual*, CACI Products Company, La Jolla, Calif. (1989).

Brunner, D. T., and J. O. Henriksen: A General Purpose Animator, *Proc. 1989 Winter Simulation Conference*, Washington, D.C., pp. 155–163 (1989).

CACI Products Company: *NETWORK II.5 User's Manual*, La Jolla, Calif. (1988a).

CACI Products Company: *COMNET II.5 User's Manual*, La Jolla, Calif. (1988b).

Cheung, S., S. Dimitriadis, and W. J. Karplus: *Introduction to Simulation Using NETWORK II.5*, CACI Products Company, La Jolla, Calif. (1987).

Gordon, G.: *The Application of GPSS V to Discrete System Simulation*, Prentice-Hall, Englewood Cliffs, N.J. (1975).

Jade Simulations International Corporation: *SIM++ Release 2.0*, Calgary, Alberta (1989).

Law, A. M.: *Statistical Analysis of Simulation Output Data with SIMSCRIPT II.5*, CACI Products Company, La Jolla, Calif. (1979).

Law, A. M., and S. W. Haider: Selecting Simulation Software for Manufacturing Applications: Practical Guidelines & Software Survey, *Ind. Eng.*, 31: 33–46 (May 1989).

Law, A. M., and C. S. Larmey: *Introduction to Simulation Using SIMSCRIPT II.5*, CACI Products Company, La Jolla, Calif. (1984).

Minuteman Software: *GPSS/PC Reference Manual*, Stow, Mass. (1988).

Pegden, C. D., R. P. Sadowski, and R. E. Shannon: *Introduction to Simulation Using SIMAN*, Systems Modeling Corporation, Sewickley, Pa. (1990).

Pritsker, A. A. B.: *Introduction to Simulation and SLAM II*, 3d ed., Halsted, New York (1986).

Russell, E. C.: *Building Simulation Models with SIMSCRIPT II.5*, CACI Products Company, La Jolla, Calif. (1983).

Schriber, T. J.: *Simulation Using GPSS*, John Wiley, New York (1974).

Schriber, T. J.: *An Introduction to Simulation Using GPSS/H*, John Wiley, New York (1990).

Sierra Simulations & Software: *SIMPLE_1 Version 4 Reference Manual*, Canaan, N.H. (1989).

SysTech, Inc.: *INSIGHT User's Manual*, Indianapolis, Ind. (1985).

White, D. A.: *PCModel User's Guide*, Simulation Software Systems, San Jose, Calif. (1988).

REVIEW OF BASIC PROBABILITY AND STATISTICS

Recommended sections for a first reading: 4.1 through 4.7

4.1 INTRODUCTION

The completion of a successful simulation study involves much more than constructing a flowchart of the system under study, translating the flowchart into a computer language, and then making one or a few replications of each proposed system configuration. The use of probability and statistics is such an integral part of a simulation study that every simulation modeling team should include at least one person who is thoroughly trained in such techniques. In particular, probability and statistics are needed to understand how to model a probabilistic system (see Sec. 4.7), validate the simulation model (Chap. 5), choose the input probability distributions (Chap. 6), generate random samples from these distributions (Chaps. 7 and 8), perform statistical analyses of the simulation output data (Chaps. 9 and 10), and design the simulation experiments (Chaps. 11 and 12).

In this chapter we establish a statistical notation used throughout the book and review some basic probability and statistics particularly relevant to simulation. We also point out the potential dangers of applying classical statistical techniques based on independent observations to simulation output data, which are rarely, if ever, independent.

4.2 RANDOM VARIABLES AND THEIR PROPERTIES

An *experiment* is a process whose outcome is not known with certainty. The set of all possible outcomes of an experiment is called the *sample space* and is denoted by S. The outcomes themselves are called the *sample points* in the sample space.

Example 4.1. If the experiment consists of flipping a coin, then

$$S = \{H, T\}$$

where the symbol $\{\ \ \}$ means the "set consisting of," and "H" and "T" mean that the outcome is a head and a tail, respectively.

Example 4.2. If the experiment consists of tossing a die, then

$$S = \{1, 2, \ldots, 6\}$$

where the outcome i means that i appeared on the die, $i = 1, 2, \ldots, 6$.

A *random variable* is a function (or rule) that assigns a real number (any number greater than $-\infty$ and less than ∞) to each point in the sample space S.

Example 4.3. Consider the experiment of rolling a pair of dice. Then

$$S = \{(1, 1), (1, 2), \ldots, (6, 6)\}$$

where (i, j) means that i and j appeared on the first and second die, respectively. If X is the random variable corresponding to the sum of the two dice, then X assigns the value 7 to the outcome $(4, 3)$.

Example 4.4. Consider the experiment of flipping two coins. If X is the random variable corresponding to the number of heads that occur, then X assigns the value 1 to either the outcome (H, T) or the outcome (T, H).

In general, we will denote random variables by capital letters such as X, Y, Z and the values that random variables take on by lowercase letters such as x, y, z.

The *distribution function* (sometimes called the *cumulative* distribution function) $F(x)$ of the random variable X is defined for each real number x as follows:

$$F(x) = P(X \leq x) \qquad \text{for } -\infty < x < \infty$$

where $P(X \leq x)$ means the probability associated with the event $\{X \leq x\}$. [See Ross (1989, chap. 1) for a discussion of events and probabilities.] Thus, $F(x)$ is the probability that, when the experiment is done, the random variable X will have taken on a value no larger than the number x.

A distribution function $F(x)$ has the following properties:

1. $0 \leq F(x) \leq 1$ for all x.
2. $F(x)$ is nondecreasing [i.e., if $x_1 < x_2$, then $F(x_1) \leq F(x_2)$].
3. $\lim\limits_{x \to \infty} F(x) = 1$ and $\lim\limits_{x \to -\infty} F(x) = 0$ (since X takes on only finite values).

A random variable X is said to be *discrete* if it can take on at most a countable number of values, say, $x_1, x_2, \ldots$. ("Countable" means that the set of possible values can be put into a one-to-one correspondence with the set of positive integers. An example of an uncountable set is all real numbers between 0 and 1.) Thus, a random variable that takes on only a finite number of values $x_1, x_2, \ldots, x_n$ is discrete. The probability that the discrete random variable X takes on the value x_i is given by

$$p(x_i) = P(X = x_i) \qquad \text{for } i = 1, 2, \ldots$$

and we must have

$$\sum_{i=1}^{\infty} p(x_i) = 1$$

where the summation means add together $p(x_1)$, $p(x_2)$, ... All probability statements about X can (at least in principle) be computed from $p(x)$, which is called the *probability mass function* for the discrete random variable X. If $I = [a, b]$, where a and b are real numbers such that $a \leq b$, then

$$P(X \in I) = \sum_{a \leq x_i \leq b} p(x_i)$$

where the symbol $\in$ means "contained in" and the summation means add together $p(x_i)$ for all x_i such that $a \leq x_i \leq b$. The distribution function $F(x)$ for the discrete random variable X is given by

$$F(x) = \sum_{x_i \leq x} p(x_i) \qquad \text{for all } -\infty < x < \infty$$

Example 4.5. For the inventory example of Sec. 1.5, the size of the demand for the product is a discrete random variable X that takes on the values 1, 2, 3, 4 with respective probabilities $\frac{1}{6}, \frac{1}{3}, \frac{1}{3}, \frac{1}{6}$. The probability mass function and the distribution function for X are given in Figs. 4.1 and 4.2. Furthermore,

$$P(2 \leq X \leq 3) = p(2) + p(3) = \tfrac{1}{3} + \tfrac{1}{3} = \tfrac{2}{3}$$

Example 4.6. A manufacturing system produces parts that must then be inspected for quality. Suppose that 90 percent of the inspected parts are good (denoted by 1) and 10 percent are bad and must be scrapped (denoted by 0). If X denotes the outcome of inspecting a part, then X is a discrete random variable with $p(0) = 0.1$ and $p(1) = 0.9$. (See the discussion of the Bernoulli random variable in Sec. 6.2.3.)

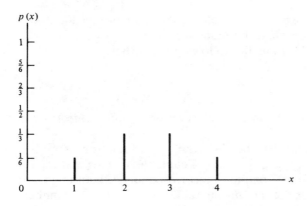

FIGURE 4.1
$p(x)$ for the demand-size random variable X.

We now consider random variables that can take on an uncountably infinite number of different values (e.g., all nonnegative real numbers). A random variable X is said to be *continuous* if there exists a nonnegative function $f(x)$ such that for any set of real numbers B (e.g., B could be all real numbers between 1 and 2),

$$P(X \in B) = \int_B f(x)\, dx \quad \text{and} \quad \int_{-\infty}^{\infty} f(x)\, dx = 1$$

[Thus, the total area under $f(x)$ is 1. Also, if X is a nonnegative random variable, as is often the case in simulation applications, the second range of integration is from 0 to ∞.] All probability statements about X can (in principle) be computed from $f(x)$, which is called the *probability density function* for the continuous random variable X.

For a discrete random variable X, $p(x)$ is the actual probability associated with the value x. However, $f(x)$ is *not* the probability that a continuous random variable X equals x. For any real number x,

$$P(X = x) = P(X \in [x, x]) = \int_x^x f(y)\, dy = 0$$

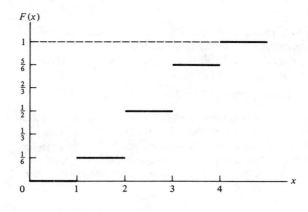

FIGURE 4.2
$F(x)$ for the demand-size random variable X.

Since the probability associated with each value x is zero, we now give an interpretation to $f(x)$. If x is any number and $\Delta x > 0$, then

$$P(X \in [x, x + \Delta x]) = \int_{x}^{x + \Delta x} f(y)\, dy$$

which is the area under $f(x)$ between x and $x + \Delta x$ as shown in Fig. 4.3. It follows that a continuous random variable X is more likely to fall in an interval above which $f(x)$ is "large" than in an interval of the same width above which $f(x)$ is "small."

The distribution function $F(x)$ for a continuous random variable X is given by

$$F(x) = P(X \in [-\infty, x]) = \int_{-\infty}^{x} f(y)\, dy \qquad \text{for all } -\infty < x < \infty$$

Thus (under some mild technical assumptions), $f(x) = F'(x)$ [the derivative of $F(x)$]. Furthermore, if $I = [a, b]$ for any real numbers a and b such that $a < b$, then

$$P(X \in I) = \int_{a}^{b} f(y)\, dy = F(b) - F(a)$$

where the last equality is an application of the *fundamental theorem of calculus*, since $F'(x) = f(x)$.

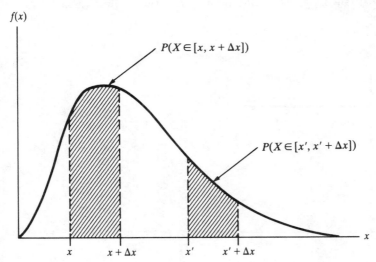

FIGURE 4.3
Interpretation of the probability density function $f(x)$.

Example 4.7. A uniform random variable on the interval $[0, 1]$ has the following probability density function:

$$f(x) = \begin{cases} 1 & \text{if } 0 \le x \le 1 \\ 0 & \text{otherwise} \end{cases}$$

Furthermore, if $0 \le x \le 1$, then

$$F(x) = \int_0^x f(y)\, dy = \int_0^x 1\, dy = x$$

[What is $F(x)$ if $x < 0$ or if $x > 1$?] Plots of $f(x)$ and $F(x)$ are given in Figs. 4.4 and 4.5, respectively.

Finally, if $0 \le x < x + \Delta x \le 1$, then

$$P(X \in [x, x + \Delta x]) = \int_x^{x+\Delta x} f(y)\, dy$$

$$= F(x + \Delta x) - F(x)$$

$$= (x + \Delta x) - x$$

$$= \Delta x$$

It follows that a uniform random variable is equally likely to fall in any interval of length Δx between 0 and 1, which justifies the name "uniform." The uniform random variable is fundamental to simulation, since it is the basis for generating any random quantity on a computer (see Chaps. 7 and 8).

Example 4.8. In Chap. 1 the exponential random variable was used for interarrival and service times in the queueing example and for interdemand times in the inventory example. The probability density function and distribution function for an exponential random variable with mean β are given in Figs. 4.6 and 4.7.

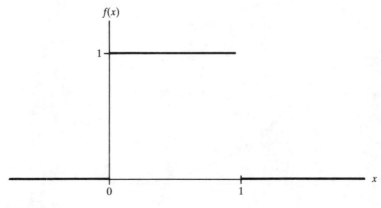

FIGURE 4.4
$f(x)$ for a uniform random variable on $[0, 1]$.

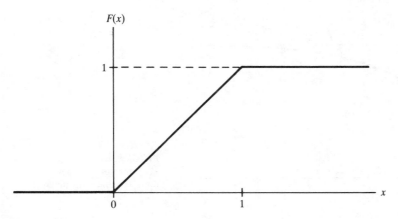

FIGURE 4.5
$F(x)$ for a uniform random variable on $[0, 1]$.

So far in this chapter we have considered only one random variable at a time, but in a simulation one must usually deal with n (a positive integer) random variables $X_1, X_2, \ldots, X_n$ simultaneously. For example, in the queueing model of Sec 1.4, we were interested in the (input) service-time random variables $S_1, S_2, \ldots, S_n$ and the (output) delay random variables $D_1, D_2, \ldots, D_n$. In the discussion that follows, we will assume for expository convenience that $n = 2$ and that the two random variables in question are X and Y.

If X and Y are discrete random variables, then let

$$p(x, y) = P(X = x, Y = y) \qquad \text{for all } x, y$$

where $p(x, y)$ is called the *joint probability mass function* of X and Y. In this case, X and Y are *independent* if

$$p(x, y) = p_X(x)p_Y(y) \qquad \text{for all } x, y$$

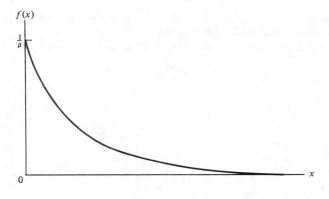

FIGURE 4.6
$f(x)$ for an exponential random variable with mean β.

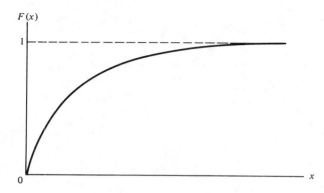

FIGURE 4.7
$F(x)$ for an exponential random variable with mean β.

where

$$p_X(x) = \sum_{\text{all } y} p(x, y)$$

$$p_Y(y) = \sum_{\text{all } x} p(x, y)$$

are the (marginal) probability mass functions of X and Y.

Example 4.9. Suppose that X and Y are jointly discrete random variables with

$$p(x, y) = \begin{cases} \dfrac{xy}{27} & \text{for } x = 1, 2 \text{ and } y = 2, 3, 4 \\ 0 & \text{otherwise} \end{cases}$$

Then

$$p_X(x) = \sum_{y=2}^{4} \frac{xy}{27} = \frac{x}{3} \qquad \text{for } x = 1, 2$$

$$p_Y(y) = \sum_{x=1}^{2} \frac{xy}{27} = \frac{y}{9} \qquad \text{for } y = 2, 3, 4$$

Since $p(x, y) = xy/27 = p_X(x)p_Y(y)$ for all x, y, the random variables X and Y are independent.

Example 4.10. Suppose that 2 cards are dealt from a deck of 52 without replacement. Let the random variables X and Y be the number of aces and kings that occur, both of which have possible values of $0, 1, 2$. It can be shown that

$$p_X(1) = p_Y(1) = 2\left(\frac{4}{52}\right)\left(\frac{48}{51}\right)$$

and

$$p(1, 1) = 2\left(\frac{4}{52}\right)\left(\frac{4}{51}\right)$$

Since

$$p(1, 1) = 2\left(\frac{4}{52}\right)\left(\frac{4}{51}\right) \neq 4\left(\frac{4}{52}\right)^2\left(\frac{48}{51}\right)^2$$

it follows that X and Y are *not* independent (see Prob. 4.5).

The random variables X and Y are *jointly continuous* if there exists a nonnegative function $f(x, y)$, called the *joint probability density function* of X and Y, such that for all sets of real numbers A and B,

$$P(X \in A, Y \in B) = \int_B \int_A f(x, y) \, dx \, dy$$

In this case, X and Y are *independent* if

$$f(x, y) = f_X(x)f_Y(y) \qquad \text{for all } x, y$$

where

$$f_X(x) = \int_{-\infty}^{\infty} f(x, y) \, dy$$

$$f_Y(y) = \int_{-\infty}^{\infty} f(x, y) \, dx$$

are the (marginal) probability density functions of X and Y.

Example 4.11. Suppose that X and Y are jointly continuous random variables with

$$f(x, y) = \begin{cases} 24xy & \text{for } x \geq 0, \ y \geq 0, \text{ and } x + y \leq 1 \\ 0 & \text{otherwise} \end{cases}$$

Then

$$f_X(x) = \int_0^{1-x} 24xy \, dy = 12xy^2 \Big|_0^{1-x} = 12x(1-x)^2 \qquad \text{for } 0 \leq x \leq 1$$

$$f_Y(y) = \int_0^{1-y} 24xy \, dx = 12yx^2 \Big|_0^{1-y} = 12y(1-y)^2 \qquad \text{for } 0 \leq y \leq 1$$

Since

$$f\left(\frac{1}{2}, \frac{1}{2}\right) = 6 \neq \left(\frac{3}{2}\right)^2 = f_X\left(\frac{1}{2}\right)f_Y\left(\frac{1}{2}\right)$$

X and Y are not independent.

Intuitively, the random variables X and Y (whether discrete or continuous) are independent if knowing the value that one random variable takes on tells us nothing about the distribution of the other. Also, if X and Y are not independent, we say that they are *dependent*.

We now consider once again the case of n random variables $X_1, X_2, \ldots, X_n$, and discuss some characteristics of the single random variable X_i and also some measures of the dependence that may exist between two random variables X_i and X_j.

The *mean* or *expected value* of the random variable X_i (where $i = 1, 2, \ldots, n$) will be denoted by μ_i or $E(X_i)$ and is defined by

$$\mu_i = \begin{cases} \displaystyle\sum_{j=1}^{\infty} x_j p_{X_i}(x_j) & \text{if } X_i \text{ is discrete} \\[2em] \displaystyle\int_{-\infty}^{\infty} x f_{X_i}(x) \, dx & \text{if } X_i \text{ is continuous} \end{cases}$$

The mean is one measure of central tendency in the sense that it is the center of gravity [see, for example, Billingsley et al. (1986, pp. 42–43)].

Example 4.12. For the demand-size random variable in Example 4.5, the mean is given by

$$\mu = 1\left(\frac{1}{6}\right) + 2\left(\frac{1}{3}\right) + 3\left(\frac{1}{3}\right) + 4\left(\frac{1}{6}\right) = \frac{5}{2}$$

Example 4.13. For the uniform random variable in Example 4.7, the mean is given by

$$\mu = \int_0^1 xf(x)\, dx = \int_0^1 x\, dx = \frac{1}{2}$$

Let c or c_i denote a constant (real number). Then the following are important properties of means:

1. $E(cX) = cE(X)$.
2. $E(\sum_{i=1}^{n} c_i X_i) = \sum_{i=1}^{n} c_i E(X_i)$ *even if the X_i's are dependent.*

The *median* $x_{0.5}$ of the random variable X_i, which is an alternative measure of central tendency, is defined to be the smallest value of x such that $F_X(x) \geq 0.5$. If X_i is a continuous random variable, then $F(x_{0.5}) = 0.5$, as shown in Fig. 4.8. The median may be a better measure of central tendency than the

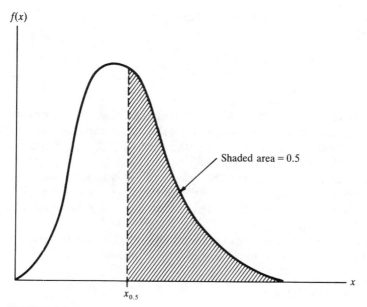

FIGURE 4.8
The median $x_{0.5}$ for a continuous random variable.

mean when X_i can take on very large or very small values, since extreme values can greatly affect the mean even if they are very unlikely to occur; such is not the case with the median.

Example 4.14. Consider a discrete random variable X that takes on each of the values $1, 2, 3, 4, 5$ with probability 0.2. Clearly, the mean and median of X are 3. Consider now a random variable Y that takes on each of the values $1, 2, 3, 4, 100$ with probability 0.2. The mean and median of Y are 22 and 3, respectively. Note that the median is insensitive to the change in the distribution.

The *variance* of the random variable X_i will be denoted by σ_i^2 or $\text{Var}(X_i)$ and is defined by

$$\sigma_i^2 = E[(X_i - \mu_i)^2] = E(X_i^2) - \mu_i^2$$

The variance is a measure of the dispersion of a random variable about its mean, as seen in Fig. 4.9. The larger the variance, the more likely the random variable is to take on values far from its mean.

Example 4.15. For the demand-size random variable in Example 4.5, the variance is computed as follows:

$$E(X^2) = 1^2\left(\frac{1}{6}\right) + 2^2\left(\frac{1}{3}\right) + 3^2\left(\frac{1}{3}\right) + 4^2\left(\frac{1}{6}\right) = \frac{43}{6}$$

$$\text{Var}(X) = E(X^2) - \mu^2 = \frac{43}{6} - \left(\frac{5}{2}\right)^2 = \frac{11}{12}$$

Example 4.16. For the uniform random variable in Example 4.7, the variance is computed as

$$E(X^2) = \int_0^1 x^2 f(x)\, dx = \int_0^1 x^2\, dx = \frac{1}{3}$$

$$\text{Var}(X) = E(X^2) - \mu^2 = \frac{1}{3} - \left(\frac{1}{2}\right)^2 = \frac{1}{12}$$

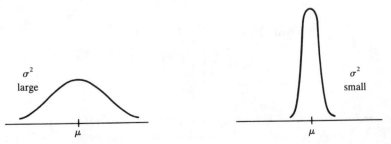

FIGURE 4.9
Density functions for continuous random variables with large and small variances.

The variance has the following properties:

1. $\text{Var}(X) \geq 0$.
2. $\text{Var}(cX) = c^2 \, \text{Var}(X)$.
3. $\text{Var}(\Sigma_{i=1}^n X_i) = \Sigma_{i=1}^n \text{Var}(X_i)$ if the X_i's are independent (or uncorrelated, as discussed below).

The *standard deviation* of the random variable X_i is defined to be $\sigma_i = \sqrt{\sigma_i^2}$.

We now consider measures of dependence between two random variables. The *covariance* between the random variables X_i and X_j (where $i = 1, 2, \ldots, n; j = 1, 2, \ldots, n$), which is a measure of their (linear) dependence, will be denoted by C_{ij} or $\text{Cov}(X_i, X_j)$ and is defined by

$$C_{ij} = E[(X_i - \mu_i)(X_j - \mu_j)] = E(X_i X_j) - \mu_i \mu_j \qquad (4.1)$$

Note that covariances are symmetric, that is, $C_{ij} = C_{ji}$, and that if $i = j$, then $C_{ij} = C_{ii} = \sigma_i^2$.

Example 4.17. For the jointly continuous random variables X and Y in Example 4.11, the covariance is computed as

$$E(XY) = \int_0^1 \int_0^{1-x} xy f(x, y) \, dy \, dx$$

$$= \int_0^1 x^2 \left[\int_0^{1-x} 24y^2 \, dy \right] dx$$

$$= \int_0^1 8x^2(1 - x)^3 \, dx$$

$$= \frac{2}{15}$$

$$E(X) = \int_0^1 x f_X(x) \, dx = \int_0^1 12x^2(1 - x)^2 \, dx = \frac{2}{5}$$

$$E(Y) = \int_0^1 y f_Y(y) \, dy = \int_0^1 12y^2(1 - y)^2 \, dy = \frac{2}{5}$$

Therefore,

$$\text{Cov}(X, Y) = E(XY) - E(X)E(Y)$$

$$= \frac{2}{15} - \left(\frac{2}{5}\right)\left(\frac{2}{5}\right)$$

$$= -\frac{2}{75}$$

If $C_{ij} = 0$, the random variables X_i and X_j are said to be *uncorrelated*. It is easy to show that if X_i and X_j are independent random variables, then $C_{ij} = 0$ (see Prob. 4.8). In general, though, the converse is not true (see Prob. 4.9). However, if X_i and X_j are jointly normally distributed random variables with $C_{ij} = 0$, then they are also independent (see Prob. 4.10).

We now give two definitions that will shed some light on the significance of the covariance C_{ij}. If $C_{ij} > 0$, then X_i and X_j are said to be *positively correlated*. In this case, $X_i > \mu_i$ and $X_j > \mu_j$ tend to occur together, and $X_i < \mu_i$ and $X_j < \mu_j$ also tend to occur together [see Eq. (4.1)]. Thus, for positively correlated random variables, if one is large, the other is likely to be large also. If $C_{ij} < 0$, then X_i and X_j are said to be *negatively correlated*. In this case, $X_i > \mu_i$ and $X_j < \mu_j$ tend to occur together, and $X_i < \mu_i$ and $X_j > \mu_j$ also tend to occur together. Thus, for negatively correlated random variables, if one is large, the other is likely to be small. We give examples of positively and negatively correlated random variables in the next section.

If $X_1, X_2, \ldots, X_n$ are simulation output data (for example, X_i might be the delay D_i for the queueing example of Sec. 1.4), we shall often need to know not only the mean μ_i and variance σ_i^2 for $i = 1, 2, \ldots, n$, but also a measure of the dependence between X_i and X_j for $i \neq j$. However, the difficulty with using C_{ij} as a measure of dependence between X_i and X_j is that it is not dimensionless, which makes its interpretation troublesome. (If X_i and X_j are in units of minutes, say, then C_{ij} is in units of minutes squared.) As a result, we use the *correlation* ρ_{ij}, defined by

$$\rho_{ij} = \frac{C_{ij}}{\sqrt{\sigma_i^2 \sigma_j^2}} \qquad \begin{matrix} i = 1, 2, \ldots, n \\ j = 1, 2, \ldots, n \end{matrix} \qquad (4.2)$$

as our primary measure of the (linear) dependence (see Prob. 4.11) between X_i and X_j. [We shall also denote the correlation between X_i and X_j by $\mathrm{Cor}(X_i, X_j)$.] Since the denominator in Eq. (4.2) is positive, it is clear that ρ_{ij} has the same sign as C_{ij}. Furthermore, it can be shown that $-1 \leq \rho_{ij} \leq 1$ for all i and j (see Prob. 4.12). If ρ_{ij} is close to $+1$, then X_i and X_j are highly positively correlated. On the other hand, if ρ_{ij} is close to -1, then X_i and X_j are highly negatively correlated.

Example 4.18. For the random variables in Example 4.11, it can be shown that $\mathrm{Var}(X) = \mathrm{Var}(Y) = \frac{1}{25}$. Therefore,

$$\mathrm{Cor}(X, Y) = \frac{\mathrm{Cov}(X, Y)}{\sqrt{\mathrm{Var}(X)\,\mathrm{Var}(Y)}} = \frac{-\frac{2}{75}}{\frac{1}{25}} = -\frac{2}{3}$$

4.3. SIMULATION OUTPUT DATA AND STOCHASTIC PROCESSES

Since most simulation models use random variables as input, the simulation output data are themselves random and care must be taken in drawing conclusions about the model's true characteristics, e.g., the (expected) average delay in the queueing example of Sec. 1.4. In this and the next three sections we lay the groundwork for a careful treatment of output data analysis in Chaps. 9 and 10.

A *stochastic process* is a collection of random variables ordered over time, which are all defined on a common sample space. The set of all possible values that these random variables can take on is called the *state space*. If the collection is $X_1, X_2, \ldots$, then we have a *discrete-time* stochastic process. If the collection is $\{X(t), t \geq 0\}$, then we have a *continuous-time* stochastic process.

Example 4.19. Consider a single-server queueing system, e.g., the $M/M/1$ queue, with IID interarrival times $A_1, A_2, \ldots$, IID service times $S_1, S_2, \ldots$, and customers served in a FIFO manner. Relative to the experiment of generating the random variates $A_1, A_2, \ldots$ and $S_1, S_2, \ldots$, one can define the discrete-time stochastic process of delays in queue $D_1, D_2, \ldots$ as follows (see Prob. 4.14):

$$D_1 = 0$$

$$D_{i+1} = \max\{D_i + S_i - A_{i+1}, 0\} \qquad \text{for } i = 1, 2, \ldots$$

Thus, the simulation maps the input random variables (i.e., the A_i's and the S_i's) into the output stochastic process $D_1, D_2, \ldots$ of interest. Here, the state space is the set of nonnegative real numbers.

Example 4.20. For the queueing system of Example 4.19, let $Q(t)$ be the number of customers in the queue at time t. Then $\{Q(t), t \geq 0\}$ is a continuous-time stochastic process with state space $\{0, 1, 2, \ldots\}$.

Example 4.21. For the inventory system of Sec. 1.5, let C_i be the total cost (i.e., the sum of the ordering, holding, and shortage costs) in month i. Then $C_1, C_2, \ldots$ is a discrete-time stochastic process with state space the nonnegative real numbers.

In order to draw inferences about an underlying stochastic process from a set of simulation output data, one must sometimes make assumptions about the stochastic process that may not be strictly true in practice. (Without such assumptions, however, statistical analysis of the output data may not be possible.) An example of this is to assume that a stochastic process is covariance stationary, a property that we now define. A discrete-time stochastic process $X_1, X_2, \ldots$ is said to be *covariance stationary* if

$$\mu_i = \mu \qquad \text{for } i = 1, 2, \ldots \text{ and } -\infty < \mu < \infty$$

$$\sigma_i^2 = \sigma^2 \qquad \text{for } i = 1, 2, \ldots \text{ and } \sigma^2 < \infty$$

and $C_{i,i+j} = \text{Cov}(X_i, X_{i+j})$ is independent of i for $j = 1, 2, \ldots$.

Thus, for a covariance-stationary process the mean and variance are stationary over time (the common mean and variance are denoted by μ and σ^2, respectively) and the covariance between two observations X_i and X_{i+j} depends only on the separation j (sometimes called the *lag*) and not on the actual time values i and $i + j$. (It is also possible to define a covariance-stationary continuous-time stochastic process $\{X_t, t \geq 0\}$ in an analogous way.)

For a covariance-stationary process, we denote the covariance and correlation between X_i and X_{i+j} by C_j and ρ_j, respectively, where

$$\rho_j = \frac{C_{i,i+j}}{\sqrt{\sigma_i^2 \sigma_{i+j}^2}} = \frac{C_j}{\sigma^2} = \frac{C_j}{C_0} \qquad \text{for } j = 0, 1, 2, \ldots$$

Example 4.22. Consider the output process $D_1, D_2, \ldots$ for a covariance-stationary (see App. 4A for a discussion of this technical detail) $M/M/1$ queue with $\rho = \lambda/\omega < 1$ (recall that λ is the arrival rate and ω is the service rate). From results in Daley (1968), one can compute ρ_j, which we plot in Fig. 4.10 for $\rho = 0.5$ and 0.9. (Do not confuse ρ_j and ρ.) Note that the correlations ρ_j are positive and monotonically decrease to zero as j increases. In particular, $\rho_1 = 0.99$ for $\rho = 0.9$ and $\rho_1 = 0.78$ for $\rho = 0.5$. Furthermore, the convergence of ρ_j to zero is considerably slower for $\rho = 0.9$; in fact, ρ_{50} is (amazingly) 0.69. (In general, our experience indicates that output processes for queueing systems are positively correlated.)

Example 4.23. Consider an (s, S) inventory system with zero delivery lag and backlogging. (For this inventory system, which is a simpler version of the one considered in Sec. 1.5, it is possible to compute the desired correlations analytically.) Let I_i, J_i, and Q_i denote, respectively, the amount of inventory on hand before ordering, the amount of inventory on hand after ordering, and the demand, each in month i. Assume that Q_i has a Poisson distribution (see Sec. 6.2.3 for further discussion) with a mean of 25; that is,

$$p(x) = P(Q_i = x) = \frac{e^{-25}(25)^x}{x!} \qquad \text{for } x = 0, 1, 2, \ldots$$

If $I_i < s$, we order $S - I_i$ items ($J_i = S$) and incur a cost $K + i(S - I_i)$, where $K = 32$ and $i = 3$. If $I_i \geq s$, no order is placed ($J_i = I_i$) and no ordering cost is incurred. After J_i has been determined, the demand Q_i occurs. If $J_i - Q_i \geq 0$, a holding cost $h(J_i - Q_i)$ is incurred, where $h = 1$. If $J_i - Q_i < 0$, a shortage cost $\pi(Q_i - J_i)$ is incurred, where $\pi = 5$. In either case, $I_{i+1} = J_i - Q_i$. Let C_i be the total cost in month i and assume that $s = 17$, $S = 57$, and $I_1 = S$. From results in Wagner (1969, p. A19), one can compute ρ_j for the output process $C_1, C_2, \ldots$, which we plot in Fig. 4.11. (See App. 4A for discussion of a technical detail.) Note that ρ_2 is positive, since for this particular system one tends to order every other

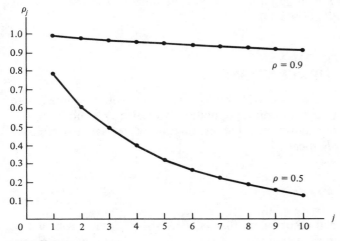

FIGURE 4.10
Correlation function ρ_j of the process $D_1, D_2, \ldots$ for the $M/M/1$ queue.

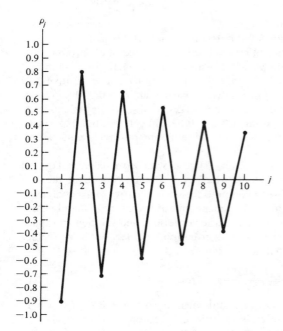

FIGURE 4.11
Correlation function ρ_j of the process $C_1, C_2, \ldots$ for an (s, S) inventory system.

month, incurring a large cost each time. On the other hand, ρ_1 is negative, because if one orders in a particular month (large cost), then it is likely that no order will be placed the next month (small cost).

If $X_1, X_2, \ldots$ is a stochastic process beginning at time zero in a simulation, then it is quite likely *not* to be covariance stationary (see App. 4A). However, for *some* simulations $X_{k+1}, X_{k+2}, \ldots$ will be approximately covariance stationary if k is large enough, where the number k is the length of the *warmup period* (see Sec. 9.5.1).

4.4 ESTIMATION OF MEANS, VARIANCES, AND CORRELATIONS

Suppose that $X_1, X_2, \ldots, X_n$ are IID random variables (observations) with finite population mean μ and finite population variance σ^2 and that our primary objective is to estimate μ; the estimation of σ^2 is of secondary interest. Then the *sample mean*

$$\bar{X}(n) = \frac{\sum\limits_{i=1}^{n} X_i}{n} \tag{4.3}$$

is an unbiased (point) estimator of μ; that is, $E[\bar{X}(n)] = \mu$ (see Prob. 4.16). [Intuitively, $\bar{X}(n)$ an unbiased estimator of μ means that if we perform a very large number of independent experiments each resulting in an $\bar{X}(n)$, the average of the $\bar{X}(n)$'s will be μ.] Similarly, the *sample variance*

$$S^2(n) = \frac{\sum_{i=1}^{n} [X_i - \bar{X}(n)]^2}{n-1} \tag{4.4}$$

is an unbiased estimator of σ^2, since $E[S^2(n)] = \sigma^2$ (see Prob. 4.16). Note that the estimators $\bar{X}(n)$ and $S^2(n)$ are sometimes denoted by $\hat{\mu}$ and $\hat{\sigma}^2$, respectively.

The difficulty with using $\bar{X}(n)$ as an estimator of μ without any additional information is that we have no way of assessing how close $\bar{X}(n)$ is to μ. Because $\bar{X}(n)$ is a random variable with variance $\text{Var}[\bar{X}(n)]$, on one experiment $\bar{X}(n)$ may be close to μ while on another $\bar{X}(n)$ may differ from μ by a large amount. (See Fig. 4.12, where the X_i's are assumed to be continuous random variables.) The usual way to assess the precision of $\bar{X}(n)$ as an estimator of μ is to construct a confidence interval for μ, which we discuss in the next section. However, the first step in constructing a confidence interval is to estimate $\text{Var}[\bar{X}(n)]$. Since

$$\text{Var}[\bar{X}(n)] = \text{Var}\left(\frac{1}{n} \sum_{i=1}^{n} X_i\right)$$

$$= \frac{1}{n^2} \text{Var}\left(\sum_{i=1}^{n} X_i\right)$$

$$= \frac{1}{n^2} \sum_{i=1}^{n} \text{Var}(X_i) \qquad \text{(because the } X_i\text{'s are independent)}$$

$$= \frac{1}{n^2} n\sigma^2 = \frac{\sigma^2}{n} \tag{4.5}$$

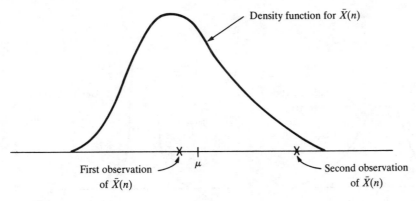

FIGURE 4.12
Two observations of the random variable $\bar{X}(n)$.

it is clear that, in general, the bigger the sample size n, the closer $\bar{X}(n)$ should be to μ (see Fig. 4.13). Furthermore, an unbiased estimator of $\text{Var}[\bar{X}(n)]$ is obtained by replacing σ^2 in Eq. (4.5) by $S^2(n)$, resulting in

$$\widehat{\text{Var}}[\bar{X}(n)] = \frac{S^2(n)}{n} = \frac{\sum\limits_{i=1}^{n} [X_i - \bar{X}(n)]^2}{n(n-1)}$$

Observe that the expression for $\widehat{\text{Var}}[\bar{X}(n)]$ has both an n and an $n-1$ in the denominator when it is rewritten in terms of the X_i's and $\bar{X}(n)$.

Finally, note that if the X_i's are independent, they are uncorrelated, and thus $\rho_j = 0$ for $j = 1, 2, \ldots, n-1$.

It has been our experience that simulation output data are always corre-lated. (If there are simulations with independent output data, we have never seen one.) Thus, the above discussion about IID observations is not *directly* applicable to analyzing simulation output data. In order to understand the dangers of treating simulation output data as if they were independent, we shall use the covariance-stationary model discussed in the last section. In particular, assume that the random variables $X_1, X_2, \ldots, X_n$ are from a covariance-stationary stochastic process. Then it is still true that the sample mean $\bar{X}(n)$ is an unbiased estimator of μ; however, the sample variance $S^2(n)$ is no longer an unbiased estimator of σ^2. In fact, it can be shown [see Anderson (1971, p. 448)] that

$$E[S^2(n)] = \sigma^2 \left[1 - 2 \frac{\sum\limits_{j=1}^{n-1} (1 - j/n)\rho_j}{n-1} \right] \tag{4.6}$$

Thus, if $\rho_j > 0$ (positive correlation), as is very often the case in practice, $S^2(n)$ will have a negative bias: $E[S^2(n)] < \sigma^2$. This is important because several of the major simulation languages (see Chap. 3) use $S^2(n)$ to estimate the variance of a set of simulation output data, which can lead to serious errors in analysis.

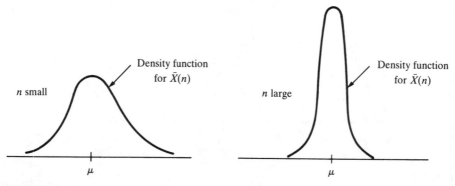

FIGURE 4.13
Distributions of $\bar{X}(n)$ for small and large n.

Let us now consider the problem of estimating the variance of the sample mean $\text{Var}[\bar{X}(n)]$ (which will be used to construct a confidence interval for μ in the next section), when $X_1, X_2, \ldots, X_n$ are from a covariance-stationary process. It can be shown (see Prob. 4.17) that

$$\text{Var}[\bar{X}(n)] = \sigma^2 \frac{\left[1 + 2 \sum_{j=1}^{n-1} (1 - j/n)\rho_j\right]}{n} \tag{4.7}$$

Thus, if one estimates $\text{Var}[\bar{X}(n)]$ from $S^2(n)/n$ (the correct expression in the IID case), which has often been done historically, there are two sources of error: the bias in $S^2(n)$ as an estimator of σ^2 and the negligence of the correlation terms in Eq. (4.7). As a matter of fact, if we combine Eq. (4.6) and Eq. (4.7), we get

$$E\left[\frac{S^2(n)}{n}\right] = \frac{[n/a(n)] - 1}{n - 1} \text{Var}[\bar{X}(n)] \tag{4.8}$$

where $a(n)$ denotes the quantity in square brackets in Eq. (4.7). If $\rho_j > 0$, then $a(n) > 1$ and $E[S^2(n)/n] < \text{Var}[\bar{X}(n)]$.

Example 4.24. Suppose that we have the data $D_1, D_2, \ldots, D_{10}$ from the process of delays $D_1, D_2, \ldots$ for a covariance-stationary $M/M/1$ queue with $\rho = 0.9$. Then, substituting the true correlations ρ_j (where $j = 1, 2, \ldots, 9$) into Eqs. (4.6) and (4.8), we get

$$E[S^2(10)] = 0.0328\sigma^2$$

and

$$E\left[\frac{S^2(10)}{10}\right] = 0.0034 \, \text{Var}[\bar{D}(10)]$$

where

$$\sigma^2 = \text{Var}(D_i), \quad \bar{D}(10) = \frac{\sum_{i=1}^{10} D_i}{10}, \quad \text{and} \quad S^2(10) = \frac{\sum_{i=1}^{10} [D_i - \bar{D}(10)]^2}{9}$$

Thus, on the average $S^2(10)/10$ will be a gross underestimate of $\text{Var}[\bar{D}(10)]$, and we are likely to be overly optimistic about the closeness of $\bar{D}(10)$ to $\mu = E(D_i)$.

Sometimes one is interested in estimating the ρ_j's (or C_j's) from the data $X_1, X_2, \ldots, X_n$. (For example, estimates of the ρ_j's might be substituted into Eq. (4.7) to obtain a better estimate of $\text{Var}[\bar{X}(n)]$; see Sec. 9.5.3 for an application.) If this is the case, ρ_j (for $j = 1, 2, \ldots, n - 1$) can be estimated as follows:

$$\hat{\rho}_j = \frac{\hat{C}_j}{S^2(n)}, \quad \hat{C}_j = \frac{\sum_{i=1}^{n-j} [X_i - \bar{X}(n)][X_{i+j} - \bar{X}(n)]}{n - j} \tag{4.9}$$

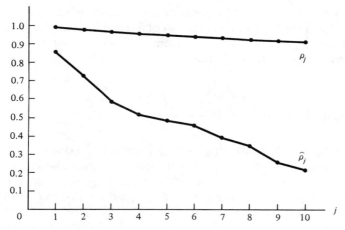

FIGURE 4.14
ρ_j and $\hat{\rho}_j$ of the process $D_1, D_2, \ldots$ for the $M/M/1$ queue with $\rho = 0.9$.

[Other estimators of ρ_j are also used. For example, one could replace the $n - j$ in the denominator of $\hat{C}_j$ by n.] The difficulty with the estimator $\hat{\rho}_j$ (or any other estimator of ρ_j) is that it is biased, it has a large variance unless n is very large, and it is correlated with other correlation estimators; that is, $\text{Cov}(\hat{\rho}_j, \hat{\rho}_k) \neq 0$. (In particular, $\hat{\rho}_{n-1}$ will be a poor estimator of ρ_{n-1} since it is based on the single product $[X_1 - \bar{X}(n)][X_n - \bar{X}(n)]$.) Thus, in general, "good" estimates of the ρ_j's will be difficult to obtain unless n is very large and j is small relative to n.

Example 4.25. Suppose we have the data $D_1, D_2, \ldots, D_{100}$ from the process considered in Example 4.24. In Fig. 4.14 we plot $\hat{\rho}_j$ [as computed from Eq. (4.9)] and ρ_j for $j = 1, 2, \ldots, 10$. Note the poor quality of the correlation estimates.

It should be noted that correlation estimates will not necessarily be zero when the X_i's are independent, since the estimator $\hat{\rho}_j$ is a random variable.

We have seen that simulation output data are correlated, and thus that formulas from classical statistics based on IID observations cannot be used directly for estimating variances. However, we shall see in Chap. 9 that it is often possible to group simulation output data into new "observations" to which the formulas based on IID observations *can* be applied. Thus, the formulas in this and the next two sections based on IID observations are *indirectly* applicable to analyzing simulation output data.

4.5 CONFIDENCE INTERVALS AND HYPOTHESIS TESTS FOR THE MEAN

Let $X_1, X_2, \ldots, X_n$ be IID random variables with finite mean μ and finite variance σ^2. (Also assume that $\sigma^2 > 0$, so that the X_i's are not degenerate random variables.) In this section we discuss how to construct a confidence interval for μ and also the complementary problem of testing the hypothesis that $\mu = \mu_0$.

We begin with a statement of the most important result in probability theory, the classical central limit theorem. Let Z_n be the random variable $[\bar{X}(n) - \mu]/\sqrt{\sigma^2/n}$ and let $F_n(z)$ be the distribution function of Z_n for a sample size of n; that is, $F_n(z) = P(Z_n \leq z)$. [Note that μ and σ^2/n are the mean and variance of $\bar{X}(n)$, respectively.] Then the *central limit theorem* is as follows [see Chung (1974, p. 169) for a proof].

Theorem 4.1. $F_n(z) \rightarrow \Phi(z)$ as $n \rightarrow \infty$, where $\Phi(z)$, the distribution function of a normal random variable with $\mu = 0$ and $\sigma^2 = 1$ (henceforth called a *standard normal random variable*; see Sec. 6.2.2), is given by

$$\Phi(z) = \frac{1}{\sqrt{2\pi}} \int_{-\infty}^{z} e^{-y^2/2} \, dy \qquad \text{for } -\infty < z < \infty$$

The theorem says, in effect, that if n is "sufficiently large," the random variable Z_n will be approximately distributed as a standard normal random variable, regardless of the distribution of the X_i's. It can also be shown for large n that the sample mean $\bar{X}(n)$ is approximately distributed as a normal random variable with mean μ and variance σ^2/n.

The difficulty with using the above results in practice is that the variance σ^2 is generally unknown. However, since the sample variance $S^2(n)$ converges to σ^2 as n gets large, it can be shown that Theorem 4.1 remains true if we replace σ^2 by $S^2(n)$ in the expression for Z_n. With this change the theorem says that if n is sufficiently large, the random variable $t_n = [\bar{X}(n) - \mu]/\sqrt{S^2(n)/n}$ is approximately distributed as a standard normal random variable. It follows for large n that

$$P\left(-z_{1-\alpha/2} \leq \frac{\bar{X}(n) - \mu}{\sqrt{S^2(n)/n}} \leq z_{1-\alpha/2}\right)$$

$$= P\left(\bar{X}(n) - z_{1-\alpha/2}\sqrt{\frac{S^2(n)}{n}} \leq \mu \leq \bar{X}(n) + z_{1-\alpha/2}\sqrt{\frac{S^2(n)}{n}}\right)$$

$$\approx 1 - \alpha \qquad (4.10)$$

where the symbol $\approx$ means "approximately equal" and $z_{1-\alpha/2}$ (for $0 < \alpha < 1$) is the upper $1 - \alpha/2$ critical point for a standard normal random variable (see Fig. 4.15 and the last line of Table T.1 of the Appendix at the back of the book). Therefore, if n is sufficiently large, an approximate $100(1 - \alpha)$ percent confidence interval for μ is given by

$$\bar{X}(n) \pm z_{1-\alpha/2}\sqrt{\frac{S^2(n)}{n}} \qquad (4.11)$$

For a given set of data $X_1, X_2, \ldots, X_n$, the lower confidence-interval endpoint $l(n, \alpha) = \bar{X}(n) - z_{1-\alpha/2}\sqrt{S^2(n)/n}$ and the upper confidence-interval endpoint

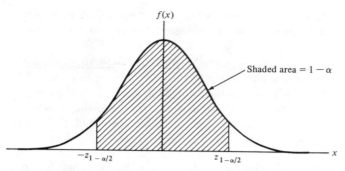

FIGURE 4.15
Density function for the standard normal distribution.

$u(n, \alpha) = \bar{X}(n) + z_{1-\alpha/2}\sqrt{S^2(n)/n}$ are just numbers (actually, specific realizations of random variables) and the confidence interval $[l(n, \alpha), u(n, \alpha)]$ either contains μ or does not contain μ. Thus, there is nothing probabilistic about the single confidence interval $[l(n, \alpha), u(n, \alpha)]$ *after* the data have been obtained and the interval's endpoints have been given numerical values. The correct interpretation to give to the confidence interval (4.11) is as follows [see (4.10)]: If one constructs a very large number of independent $100(1 - \alpha)$ percent confidence intervals each based on n observations, where n is sufficiently large, the proportion of these confidence intervals that contain (cover) μ should be $1 - \alpha$. We call this proportion the *coverage* for the confidence interval.

The difficulty in using (4.11) to construct a confidence interval for μ is in knowing what "n sufficiently large" means. It turns out that the more skewed (i.e., nonsymmetric) the distribution of the X_i's, the larger the value of n needed for the distribution of t_n to be closely approximated by $\Phi(z)$. (See the discussion later in this section.) If n is chosen too small, the actual coverage of a desired $100(1 - \alpha)$ percent confidence interval will generally be less than $1 - \alpha$. This is why the confidence interval given by (4.11) is stated to be only approximate.

In light of the above discussion, we now develop an alternative confidence-interval expression. If the X_i's are *normal* random variables, the random variable $t_n = [\bar{X}(n) - \mu]/\sqrt{S^2(n)/n}$ has a t distribution with $n - 1$ degrees of freedom (df) [see, for example, Hogg and Craig (1970, p. 195)] and an *exact* (for any $n \geq 2$) $100(1 - \alpha)$ percent confidence interval for μ is given by

$$\bar{X}(n) \pm t_{n-1,1-\alpha/2}\sqrt{\frac{S^2(n)}{n}} \tag{4.12}$$

where $t_{n-1,1-\alpha/2}$ is the upper $1 - \alpha/2$ critical point for the t distribution with $n - 1$ df. These critical points are given in Table T.1 of the Appendix at the back of the book. Plots of the density functions for the t distribution with 4 df and for the standard normal distribution are given in Fig. 4.16. Note that the t

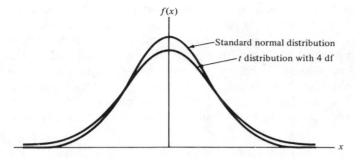

FIGURE 4.16
Density functions for the t distribution with 4 df and for the standard normal distribution.

distribution is less peaked and has longer tails than the normal distribution. We call (4.12) the *t confidence interval*.

The quantity that we add to and subtract from $\bar{X}(n)$ in (4.12) to construct the confidence interval is called the *half-length* of the confidence interval. It is a measure of how precisely we know μ. It can be shown that if we increase the sample size from n to $4n$ in (4.12), then the half-length is decreased by a factor of approximately 2 (see Prob. 4.20).

In practice, the distribution of the X_i's will rarely be normal, and the confidence interval given by (4.12) will also be approximate in terms of coverage. Since $t_{n-1,1-\alpha/2} > z_{1-\alpha/2}$, the confidence interval given by (4.12) will be larger than the one given by (4.11) and will generally have coverage closer to the desired level $1 - \alpha$. For this reason, we recommend using (4.12) to construct a confidence interval for μ. Note that $t_{n-1,1-\alpha/2} \to z_{1-\alpha/2}$ as $n \to \infty$; in particular, $t_{40,0.95}$ differs from $z_{0.95}$ by less than 3 percent. However, in most of our applications of (4.12) in Chaps. 9, 10, and 12, n will be small enough for the difference between (4.11) and (4.12) to be appreciable.

Example 4.26. Suppose that the 10 observations 1.20, 1.50, 1.68, 1.89, 0.95, 1.49, 1.58, 1.55, 0.50, and 1.09 are from a normal distribution with unknown mean μ and that our objective is to construct a 90 percent confidence interval for μ. From these data we get

$$\bar{X}(10) = 1.34 \quad \text{and} \quad S^2(10) = 0.17$$

which results in the following confidence interval for μ:

$$\bar{X}(10) \pm t_{9,0.95} \sqrt{\frac{S^2(10)}{10}} = 1.34 \pm 1.83 \sqrt{\frac{0.17}{10}} = 1.34 \pm 0.24$$

Note that (4.12) was used to construct the confidence interval and that $t_{9,0.95}$ was taken from Table T.1. Therefore, subject to the interpretation stated above, we claim with 90 percent confidence that μ is in the interval $[1.10, 1.58]$.

We now discuss how the coverage of the confidence interval given by (4.12) is affected by the distribution of the X_i's. In Table 4.1 we give estimated coverages for 90 percent confidence intervals based on 500 independent experiments for each of the sample sizes $n = 5$, 10, 20, and 40 and each of the distributions normal, exponential, chi square with 1 df (a standard normal random variable squared; see the discussion of the gamma distribution in Sec. 6.2.2), lognormal (e^Y, where Y is a standard normal random variable; see Sec. 6.2.2), and a hyperexponential distribution whose distribution function is given by

$$F(x) = 0.9F_1(x) + 0.1F_2(x)$$

where $F_1(x)$ and $F_2(x)$ are the distribution functions of exponential random variables with means 0.5 and 5.5, respectively. For example, the table entry for the exponential distribution and $n = 10$ was obtained as follows. Ten observations were generated from an exponential distribution with a *known* mean μ, a 90 percent confidence interval was constructed using (4.12), and it was determined whether the interval contained μ. (This constituted one experiment.) Then the whole procedure was repeated 500 times, and 0.878 is the proportion of the 500 confidence intervals that contained μ. Note that the coverage for the normal distribution and $n = 10$ is 0.902 rather than the expected 0.900, since the table is based on 500 rather than an infinite number of experiments.

Observe from the table that for a particular distribution, coverage generally gets closer to 0.90 as n gets larger, which follows from the central limit theorem (see Prob. 4.22). (The results for the exponential distribution would also probably follow this behavior if the number of experiments were larger.) Notice also that for a particular n, coverage decreases as the skewness of the distribution gets larger, where skewness is defined by

$$\nu = \frac{E[(X - \mu)^3]}{(\sigma^2)^{3/2}} \qquad (-\infty < \nu < \infty)$$

The skewness, which is a measure of symmetry, is equal to 0 for a symmetric distribution such as the normal. We conclude from the table that the larger the skewness of the distribution in question, the larger the sample size needed to obtain satisfactory (close to 0.90) coverage.

TABLE 4.1
Estimated coverages based on 500 experiments

Distribution	Skewness ν	$n = 5$	$n = 10$	$n = 20$	$n = 40$
Normal	0.00	0.910	0.902	0.898	0.900
Exponential	2.00	0.854	0.878	0.870	0.890
Chi square	2.83	0.810	0.830	0.848	0.890
Lognormal	6.18	0.758	0.768	0.842	0.852
Hyperexponential	6.43	0.584	0.586	0.682	0.774

Assume that $X_1, X_2, \ldots, X_n$ are normally distributed (or are approximately so) and that we would like to test the null hypothesis H_0 that $\mu = \mu_0$, where μ_0 is a fixed, hypothesized value for μ. Intuitively, we would expect that if $|\bar{X}(n) - \mu_0|$ is large [recall that $\bar{X}(n)$ is the point estimator for μ], H_0 is not likely to be true. However, in order to develop a test with known statistical properties, we need a statistic (a function of the X_i's) whose distribution is known when H_0 is true. It follows from the above discussion that if H_0 is true, the statistic $t_n = [\bar{X}(n) - \mu_0]/\sqrt{S^2(n)/n}$ will have a t distribution with $n - 1$ df. Therefore, consistent with our intuitive discussion above, the form of our (two-tailed) hypothesis test for $\mu = \mu_0$ is

$$\text{If } |t_n| \begin{cases} > t_{n-1,1-\alpha/2} & \text{reject } H_0 \\ \leq t_{n-1,1-\alpha/2} & \text{``accept'' } H_0 \end{cases} \tag{4.13}$$

The portion of the real line that corresponds to rejection of H_0, namely, the set of all x such that $|x| > t_{n-1,1-\alpha/2}$, is called the *critical region* for the test, and the probability that the statistic t_n falls in the critical region given that H_0 is true, which is clearly equal to α, is called the *level* (or size) of the test. Typically, an experimenter will choose the level equal to 0.05 or 0.10. We call the hypothesis test given by (4.13) the *t test*.

When one performs a hypothesis test, two types of errors can be made. If one rejects H_0 when in fact it is true, this is called a *Type I error*. The probability of a Type I error is equal to the level α and is thus under the experimenter's control. If one accepts H_0 when it is false, this is called a *Type II error*. For a fixed level α and sample size n, the probability of a *Type II error*, which we denote by β, depends on what is actually true (as compared to H_0) and may be unknown. We call $\delta = 1 - \beta$ the *power* of the test, and it is equal to the probability of rejecting H_0 when it is false. (Clearly, a test with high power is desirable.) If α is fixed, the power of a test can be increased only by increasing n. Since the power of a test may be low and unknown to us, we shall henceforth say that we "fail to reject H_0" (instead of "accept H_0") when the statistic t_n does not lie in the critical region. (When H_0 is not rejected, we generally do not know with any certainty whether H_0 is true or whether H_0 is false, since our test might not be powerful enough to detect any difference between H_0 and what is actually true.)

Example 4.27. For the data of Example 4.26, suppose that we would like to test the null hypothesis H_0 that $\mu = 1$ at level $\alpha = 0.10$. Since

$$t_{10} = \frac{\bar{X}(10) - 1}{\sqrt{S^2(10)/10}} = \frac{0.34}{\sqrt{0.17/10}} = 2.65 > 1.83 = t_{9,0.95}$$

we reject H_0.

Example 4.28. For the null hypothesis H_0 that $\mu = 1$ in Example 4.27, we can estimate the power of the test when, in fact, the X_i's have a normal distribution with mean $\mu = 1.5$ and standard deviation $\sigma = 1$. We generated randomly 1000 independent observations of the statistic

$t_{10} = [\bar{X}(10) - 1]/\sqrt{S^2(10)/10}$ under the assumption that $\mu = 1.5$ and $\sigma = 1$ (the X_i's were, of course, normal). For 447 out of the 1000 observations, $|t_{10}| > 1.83$ and, therefore, the estimated power is $\hat{\delta} = 0.447$. Thus, if $\mu = 1.5$ and $\sigma = 1$, we will only reject the null hypothesis $\mu = 1$ approximately 45 percent of the time for a test at level $\alpha = 0.10$. To see what effect the standard deviation σ has on the power of the test, we generated 1000 observations of t_{10} when $\mu = 1.5$ and $\sigma = 0.75$ and also 1000 observations of t_{10} when $\mu = 1.5$ and $\sigma = 0.5$ (all X_i's were normal). The estimated powers were $\hat{\delta} = 0.619$ and $\hat{\delta} = 0.900$, respectively. It is not surprising that the power is apparently a decreasing function of σ, since we would expect to distinguish better between the true mean 1.5 and the hypothesized mean 1 when σ is small. [Note that in the case of normal sampling, as in this example, the power of the test can actually be computed exactly, obviating the need for simulation as done here; see advanced texts on statistics such as Bickel and Doksum (1977) with reference to the *noncentral t* distribution.]

It should be mentioned that there is an intimate relationship between the confidence interval given by (4.12) and the hypothesis test given by (4.13). In particular, rejection of the null hypothesis H_0 that $\mu = \mu_0$ is equivalent to μ_0 not being contained in the confidence interval for μ.

4.6   THE STRONG LAW OF LARGE NUMBERS

The second most important result in probability theory (after the central limit theorem) is arguably the strong law of large numbers. Let $X_1, X_2, \ldots, X_n$ be IID random variables with finite mean μ. Then the *strong law of large numbers* is as follows [see Chung (1974, p. 126) for a proof].

Theorem 4.2. $\bar{X}(n) \to \mu$ w.p. 1 as $n \to \infty$.

The theorem says, in effect, that if one performs an infinite number of experiments each resulting in an $\bar{X}(n)$ and n is sufficiently large, then $\bar{X}(n)$ will be arbitrarily close to μ for almost all of the experiments.

Example 4.29. Suppose that $X_1, X_2, \ldots$ are IID normal variables with $\mu = 1$ and $\sigma^2 = 0.01$. Figure 4.17 plots the values of $\bar{X}(n)$ for various n that resulted from sampling from this distribution. Note that $\bar{X}(n)$ differed from μ by less than 1 percent for $n \geq 28$.

4.7.   THE DANGER OF REPLACING A PROBABILITY DISTRIBUTION BY ITS MEAN

Simulation analysts have sometimes replaced an input probability distribution by its mean in their simulation models. This practice may be caused by a lack of understanding on the part of the analyst or by lack of information on the actual form of the distribution (e.g., only an estimate of the mean of the distribution is available). The following example illustrates the danger of this practice.

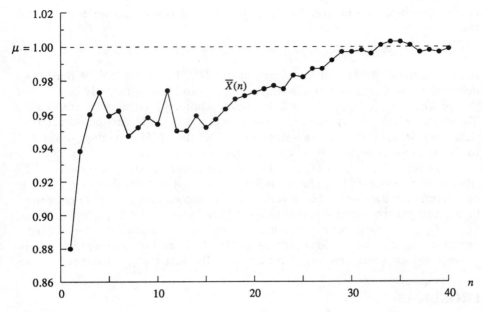

FIGURE 4.17
$\bar{X}(n)$ for various values of n when the X_i's are normal random variables with $\mu = 1$ and $\sigma^2 = 0.01$.

Example 4.30. Consider a manufacturing system consisting of a single machine tool. Suppose that "raw" parts arrive to the machine with exponential interarrival times having a mean of 1 minute and that processing times at the machine are exponentially distributed with a mean of 0.99 minute. Thus, this system is an $M/M/1$ queue with utilization factor $\rho = 0.99$. Furthermore, it can be shown that the average delay in queue of a part in the long run is 98.01 minutes [see App. 1B or Gross and Harris (1985, p. 77)]. On the other hand, if we replace each distribution by its corresponding mean (i.e., if customers arrive at times 1 minute, 2 minutes, ... and if each part has a processing time of exactly 0.99 minute), then no part is ever delayed in the queue. In general, the variances as well as the means of the input distributions determine the output measures for queueing-type systems, as noted at the end of App. 1B.

APPENDIX 4A
COMMENTS ON COVARIANCE-STATIONARY PROCESSES

Consider the process $\{D_i, i \geq 1\}$ for the $M/M/1$ queue when no customers are present at time 0. Clearly, $D_1 = 0$, but $P(D_i > 0) > 0$ for $i = 2, 3, \ldots$. Therefore, $E(D_1) = 0$ and $E(D_i) > 0$ for $i = 2, 3, \ldots$, which implies that $\{D_i, i \geq 1\}$

is *not* covariance stationary. However, if $\rho < 1$, it can be shown for all $x \geq 0$ that

$$P(D_i \leq x) \to (1 - \rho) + \rho[1 - e^{-(\omega - \lambda)x}] \qquad \text{as } i \to \infty \qquad (4.14)$$

It follows from (4.14) and the equation for D_{i+1} in Example 4.19 that if we delete the first k observations from $D_1, D_2, \ldots$ and k is sufficiently large, then the process $D_{k+1}, D_{k+2}, \ldots$ will be (approximately) covariance stationary. Therefore, when we say "consider the process $\{D_i, i \geq 1\}$ for the covariance-stationary $M/M/1$ queue," we mean that we let the $M/M/1$ queue "warm up" for some amount of time before observing the first delay.

Consider the process $\{C_i, i \geq 1\}$ for the inventory system of Example 4.23 when $I_1 = S$. Since $P(I_i = S) \neq 1$ for $i = 2, 3, \ldots$, it follows that $\{C_i, i \geq 1\}$ is not covariance stationary. However, it can be shown that $P(C_i \leq x)$ converges to a limiting distribution function as $i \to \infty$ [see Wagner (1969, p. A48)]. Thus, $C_{k+1}, C_{k+2}, \ldots$ will be (approximately) covariance stationary for k large. Furthermore, the correlations plotted in Fig. 4.11 are for an inventory system warmed up for some amount of time before the first cost is observed.

PROBLEMS

4.1. Suppose that X is a discrete random variable with probability mass function given by

$$p(1) = \frac{1}{10}, \qquad p(2) = \frac{3}{10}, \qquad p(3) = \frac{2}{10}, \qquad p(4) = \frac{3}{10}, \qquad \text{and}$$

$$p(5) = \frac{1}{10}$$

(a) Plot $p(x)$.
(b) Compute and plot $F(x)$.
(c) Compute $P(1.4 \leq X \leq 4.2)$, $E(X)$, and $\text{Var}(X)$.

4.2. Suppose that X is a continuous random variable with probability density function given by

$$f(x) = x^2 + \frac{2}{3}x + \frac{1}{3} \qquad \text{for } 0 \leq x \leq c$$

(a) What must be the value of c?
Assuming this value for c, do the following:
(b) Plot $f(x)$.
(c) Compute and plot $F(x)$.
(d) Compute $P(\frac{1}{3} \leq X \leq \frac{2}{3})$, $E(X)$, and $\text{Var}(X)$.

4.3. Suppose that X and Y are jointly discrete random variables with

$$p(x, y) = \begin{cases} \dfrac{2}{n(n+1)} & \text{for } x = 1, 2, \ldots, n \text{ and} \\ & \qquad\quad y = 1, 2, \ldots, x \\ 0 & \text{otherwise} \end{cases}$$

Compute $p_X(x)$ and $p_Y(y)$ and determine whether X and Y are independent.

4.4. Suppose that X and Y are jointly discrete random variables with

$$p(x, y) = \begin{cases} \dfrac{x + y}{30} & \text{for } x = 0, 1, 2 \text{ and} \\ & \quad\ y = 0, 1, 2, 3 \\ 0 & \text{otherwise} \end{cases}$$

(a) Compute and plot $p_X(x)$ and $p_Y(y)$.
(b) Are X and Y independent?
(c) Compute and plot $F_X(x)$ and $F_Y(y)$.
(d) Compute $E(X)$, $\text{Var}(X)$, $E(Y)$, $\text{Var}(Y)$, $\text{Cov}(X, Y)$, and $\text{Cor}(X, Y)$.

4.5. Are the random variables X and Y in Example 4.10 independent if the sampling of the two cards is done *with* replacement?

4.6. Suppose that X and Y are jointly continuous random variables with

$$f(x, y) = \begin{cases} 32x^3y^7 & \text{if } 0 \le x \le 1 \text{ and} \\ & \quad\ 0 \le y \le 1 \\ 0 & \text{otherwise} \end{cases}$$

Compute $f_X(x)$ and $f_Y(y)$ and determine whether X and Y are independent.

4.7. Suppose that X and Y are jointly continuous random variables with

$$f(x, y) = \begin{cases} y - x & \text{for } 0 < x < 1 \text{ and} \\ & \quad\ 1 < y < 2 \\ 0 & \text{otherwise} \end{cases}$$

(a) Compute and plot $f_X(x)$ and $f_Y(y)$.
(b) Are X and Y independent?
(c) Compute $F_X(x)$ and $F_Y(y)$.
(d) Compute $E(X)$, $\text{Var}(X)$, $E(Y)$, $\text{Var}(Y)$, $\text{Cov}(X, Y)$, and $\text{Cor}(X, Y)$.

4.8. If X and Y are jointly continuous random variables with joint probability density function $f(x, y)$ and X and Y are independent, show that $\text{Cov}(X, Y) = 0$. Therefore, X and Y being independent implies that $E(XY) = E(X)E(Y)$.

4.9. Suppose that X is a discrete random variable with $p_X(x) = 0.25$ for $x = -2, -1, 1, 2$. Let Y also be a discrete random variable such that $Y = X^2$. Clearly, X and Y are not independent. However, show that $\text{Cov}(X, Y) = 0$. Therefore, uncorrelated random variables are not necessarily independent.

4.10. Suppose that X_1 and X_2 are jointly normally distributed random variables with joint probability density function

$$f_{X_1, X_2}(x_1, x_2) = \frac{1}{2\pi\sqrt{\sigma_1^2\sigma_2^2(1 - \rho_{12}^2)}}\, e^{-q/2} \quad \begin{array}{l} \text{for } -\infty < x_1 < \infty \\ \text{and } -\infty < x_2 < \infty \end{array}$$

where

$$q = \frac{1}{1 - \rho_{12}^2}\left[\frac{(x_1 - \mu_1)^2}{\sigma_1^2} - 2\rho_{12}\frac{(x_1 - \mu_1)(x_2 - \mu_2)}{\sqrt{\sigma_1^2\sigma_2^2}} + \frac{(x_2 - \mu_2)^2}{\sigma_2^2}\right]$$

If $\rho_{12} = 0$, show that X_1 and X_2 are independent.

4.11. Suppose that X and Y are random variables such that $Y = aX + b$ and a, b are constants. Show that

$$\text{Cor}(X, Y) = \begin{cases} +1 & \text{if } a > 0 \\ -1 & \text{if } a < 0 \end{cases}$$

This is why the correlation is said to be a measure of *linear* dependence.

4.12. If X_1 and X_2 are random variables, then $E(X_1^2)E(X_2^2) \geq [E(X_1X_2)]^2$ by *Schwarz's inequality*. Use this fact to show that $-1 \leq \rho_{12} \leq 1$.

4.13. For any random variables X_1, X_2 and any numbers a_1, a_2, show that $\text{Var}(a_1X_1 + a_2X_2) = a_1^2 \text{Var}(X_1) + 2a_1a_2 \text{Cov}(X_1, X_2) + a_2^2 \text{Var}(X_2)$.

4.14. Justify the equation for D_{i+1} in Example 4.19.

4.15. Using the equation for D_{i+1} in Example 4.19 write a FORTRAN, Pascal, or C program requiring approximately 15 lines of code to simulate the $M/M/1$ queue with a mean interarrival time of 1 and a mean service time of 0.5. Run the program until 1000 D_i's have been observed and compute $\bar{D}(1000)$. The program should not require a simulation clock, an event list, or a timing routine.

4.16. Using the fact that $E(\sum_{i=1}^{n} a_iX_i) = \sum_{i=1}^{n} a_iE(X_i)$ for any random variables X_1, X_2, ... , X_n and any numbers a_1, a_2, ... , a_n, show that if X_1, X_2, ... , X_n are IID random variables with mean μ and variance σ^2, then $E[\bar{X}(n)] = \mu$ and $E[S^2(n)] = \sigma^2$. Show that the first result still holds if the X_i's are dependent.

4.17. Show that Eq. (4.7) is correct.

4.18. If X_1, X_2, ... , X_n are IID random variables with mean μ and variance σ^2, then compute $\text{Cov}[\bar{X}(n), S^2(n)]$. When will this covariance be equal to 0?

4.19. Show that the equality of the two probability statements in Eq. (4.10) is correct.

4.20. For the confidence interval given by (4.12), show that if we increase the sample size from n to $4n$, then the half-length is decreased by a factor of approximately 2.

4.21. Explain why the 90 percent confidence interval in Example 4.26 contained only 5 of the 10 observations.

4.22. For the confidence interval given by (4.12), show that the coverage approaches $1 - \alpha$ as $n \to \infty$.

4.23. Suppose that 7.3, 6.1, 3.8, 8.4, 6.9, 7.1, 5.3, 8.2, 4.9, and 5.8 are 10 observations from a distribution (not highly skewed) with unknown mean μ. Compute $\bar{X}(10)$, $S^2(10)$, and an approximate 95 percent confidence interval for μ.

4.24. For the data in Prob. 4.23, test the null hypothesis H_0: $\mu = 6$ at level $\alpha = 0.05$.

4.25. Suppose that X and Y are random variables with unknown covariance $\text{Cov}(X, Y)$. If the pairs X_i, Y_i (for $i = 1, 2, \ldots, n$) are independent observations of X, Y, then show that

$$\widehat{\text{Cov}}(X, Y) = \frac{\sum_{i=1}^{n} [X_i - \bar{X}(n)][Y_i - \bar{Y}(n)]}{n - 1}$$

is an unbiased estimator of $\text{Cov}(X, Y)$.

4.26. A random variable X is said to have the *memoryless property* if

$$P(X > t + s \mid X > t) = P(X > s) \qquad \text{for all } t, s > 0$$

[The conditional probability $P(X > t + s \mid X > t)$ is the probability of the event $\{X > t + s\}$ occurring given that the event $\{X > t\}$ has occurred; see Ross (1989), chap. 3).] Show that the exponential distribution has the memoryless property.

4.27. A geometric distribution with parameter p $(0 < p < 1)$ has probability mass function

$$p(x) = p(1 - p)^x \qquad \text{for } x = 0, 1, 2, \ldots$$

Show that this distribution has the memoryless property.

REFERENCES

Anderson, T. W.: *The Statistical Analysis of Time Series*, John Wiley, New York (1971).

Bickel, P. J., and K. A. Doksum: *Mathematical Statistics*: *Basic Ideas and Selected Topics*, Holden-Day, San Francisco (1977).

Billingsley, P., D. J. Croft, D. V. Huntsberger, and C. J. Watson: *Statistical Inference for Management and Economics*, 3d ed., Allyn & Bacon, Boston (1986).

Chung, K. L.: *A Course in Probability Theory*, 2d ed., Academic Press, New York (1974).

Daley, D. J.: The Serial Correlation Coefficients of Waiting Times in a Stationary Single Server Queue, *J. Austr. Math. Soc.*, *8*: 683–699 (1968).

Gross, D., and C. M. Harris: *Fundamentals of Queueing Theory*, 2d ed., John Wiley, New York (1985).

Hogg, R. V., and A. F. Craig: *Introduction to Mathematical Statistics*, 3d ed., Macmillan, New York (1970).

Ross, S. M.: *Introduction to Probability Models*, 4th ed., Academic Press, San Diego (1989).

Wagner, H. M.: *Principles of Operations Research*, Prentice-Hall, Englewood Cliffs, N.J. (1969).

CHAPTER

5

BUILDING VALID AND CREDIBLE SIMULATION MODELS

Recommended sections for a first reading: 5.1 through 5.5, 5.6.1

5.1 INTRODUCTION AND DEFINITIONS

One of the most difficult problems facing a simulation analyst is that of trying to determine whether a simulation model is an accurate representation of the actual system being studied, i.e., whether the model is *valid*. If a model is not valid, then any conclusions derived from the model will be of doubtful value.

In this chapter we present a discussion of most major practical validation techniques. Information for this survey came not only from existing papers and books on validation, but is also based on conversations with hundreds of simulation practitioners. The reader should keep in mind, however, that validation in practice will typically employ a subset of the major validation techniques presented here and, in addition, special methods developed for the application at hand. [Important works on validation include Balci (1987), Banks and Carson (1984), Carson (1986), Feltner and Weiner (1985), Gass (1983), Gass and Thompson (1980), Naylor and Finger (1967), Sargent (1988), Schellenberger (1974), Shannon (1975), and Van Horn (1971). Furthermore, a comprehensive bibliography on validation is given by Balci and Sargent (1984b).]

We begin by defining the important terms used in this chapter, including verification, validation, and credibility. *Verification* is determining that a simulation computer program performs as intended, i.e., debugging the computer program. Thus, verification checks the translation of the *conceptual simulation model* (e.g., flowcharts and assumptions) into a correctly working program. Although verification is simple in concept, debugging a large-scale simulation model is a difficult and arduous task. *Validation* is concerned with determining whether the conceptual simulation model (as opposed to the computer program) is an accurate representation of the system under study. If a model is "valid," then the decisions made with the model should be similar to those that would be made by physically experimenting with the system (if this were possible). [Fishman and Kiviat (1968) appear to be the first ones to have given definitions similar to these.] When a simulation model and its results are accepted by the manager/client as being valid, and are used as an aid in making decisions, we call the model *credible* [see Carson (1986)]. Although credibility has not been discussed a great deal in the simulation literature, it is probably as important as validation in terms of actual implementation of simulation results. The importance of model credibility is the major reason for the widespread interest in animating simulation output (see Sec. 3.4.2), since animation is an effective way for an analyst to communicate the essence of a model to the manager. Furthermore, many of the ideas discussed in this chapter are designed to enhance both model validity and credibility.

The timing and relationships of validation, verification, and establishing credibility are given in Fig. 5.1. The rectangles represent states of the model or the system of interest, the solid horizontal arrows correspond to the actions necessary to move from one state to another, and the curved dashed arrows show where the three major concepts are most prominently employed. The numbers below each solid arrow correspond to the steps in a sound simulation study as discussed in Sec. 1.7. We have not attempted to illustrate feedback arcs in the figure.

Validation should be contrasted with *output analysis* (the subject of Chap. 9), which is concerned with determining (estimating) a simulation *model's* (not

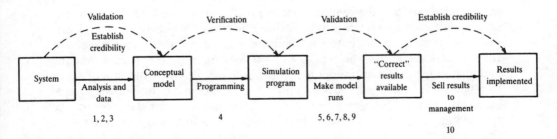

FIGURE 5.1
Timing and relationships of validation, verification, and establishing credibility.

necessarily the system's) true measures of performance. Thus, output analysis is essentially a statistical problem involving such issues as run length and the required number of replications.

5.2 SOME PRINCIPLES OF VALID SIMULATION MODELING

A simulation practitioner must determine what aspects of a complex real-world system actually need to be incorporated into the simulation model, and what aspects can safely be ignored. It is generally not necessary to have a one-to-one correspondence between each element of the system and each element of the model. Modeling each aspect of the system will seldom be required to make effective decisions, and will also be infeasible due to time, money, or computer constraints.

> **Example 5.1.** A dog food manufacturer had a consulting company build a simulation model of its manufacturing line, which produced 1 million cans a day at a constant rate. Because each can of food was represented by a separate entity in the model, the model was very expensive to run and, thus, not very useful. A few years later the model was rewritten treating the manufacturing process as a "continuous flow" (see Sec. 1.2). The new model produced accurate results and executed in a small fraction of the time necessary for the original model.

We now present some general guidelines for determining the level of detail required by a simulation model.

- Carefully define the issues to be investigated, the measures of performance for evaluation, the manner in which the model is to be used, and the alternative system configurations of interest at the beginning of the study. Models are not universally valid, but are designed for specific purposes. If the issues of interest have not been specified, then it is impossible to determine the appropriate level of model detail. Since some models can accurately estimate one measure of performance but not another, it is also important to specify the measures of interest. For example, a simple model of a manufacturing system might accurately predict throughput (e.g., parts per day) but be inadequate for determining the required floor space for work-in-process (see Example 13.4). The end user of the model and the anticipated frequency of model use affect how user-friendly the model needs to be and how quickly it must execute. A good understanding of the system configurations to be simulated will help avoid a major rewrite of the simulation program at a future date. Finally, it is important to understand the manager's (or client's) needs. A great model for the wrong problem will never be used. Problem formulation should probably be done at a meeting with all of the project's key people present; see the discussion of the structured walk-through of a conceptual model in Sec. 5.5.1.

- Use "experts" and sensitivity analyses to help determine the level of model detail. People who are familiar with systems similar to the one of interest are asked what components of the proposed system are likely to be most important and, thus, need to be carefully modeled. Sensitivity analyses (see Sec. 5.5.2) can be used to determine which parameters, distributions, or subsystems will have the greatest impact on the desired measures of performance. Given a limited amount of time for model development, one should obviously concentrate on the most important factors.

- A mistake often made by beginning modelers is to include an excessive amount of model detail. As a result, we recommend starting with a "moderately detailed" model, which can later be embellished if needed. The adequacy of a particular model is determined in part by presenting the model to experts and managers. Regular interaction with these people also maintains their interest in the simulation study.

- Do not have more detail in a model than is necessary to address the issues of interest, subject to the proviso that the model must have enough detail to be credible. Thus, it may sometimes be necessary to include things in a model that are not strictly required for model validity, due to credibility concerns.

- The level of model detail should be consistent with the type of data that are available. A model used to design a new manufacturing system will generally be less detailed than one used to fine-tune an existing system, since little or no data will be available for a proposed system.

- In some simulation studies, time and money constraints are a major factor in determining the amount of model detail.

- If the number of factors (aspects of interest) for the study is large, then use a "coarse" simulation model or an analytic model to identify the important factors before developing a detailed simulation model [see Haider, Noller, and Robey (1986)].

The manager of the system of interest should be aware that a successful simulation study will require a commitment of his or her time and resources. In particular, the manager must be personally involved during problem formulation and during the model-building process itself. This increases model validity, credibility, and the likelihood that the model will actually be used in the decision-making process. Simulation studies also require use of an organization's technical personnel for some period of time. If the study is done in-house, then several company personnel may be required full-time for several months. These people often have other jobs such as being responsible for the day-to-day operations of a manufacturing line. Even if the study is done by a consultant, company personnel must be involved in the modeling process and may also be needed to collect data.

5.3 VERIFICATION OF SIMULATION COMPUTER PROGRAMS

In this section we discuss eight possible techniques that can be used to debug the computer program of a simulation model [see also Bryan and Natrella (1985)]. Some of these techniques may be used to debug any computer program, while others we believe to be unique to simulation modeling.

Technique 1. In developing a simulation model, write and debug the computer program in modules or subprograms. By way of example, for a 10,000-statement simulation model it would be poor programming practice to write the entire program before attempting any debugging. When this large, untested program is finally run, it almost certainly will not execute, and determining the location of the errors in the program will be extremely difficult. Instead, the simulation model's main program and a few of the key subprograms should be written and debugged first, perhaps representing the other required subprograms as "dummies" or "stubs." Then, additional subprograms or levels of detail should be added and debugged successively, until a model is developed that satisfactorily represents the system under study. In general, it is always better to start with a "moderately detailed" model, which is gradually made as complex as needed, than to develop "immediately" a complex model, which may turn out to be more detailed than necessary and excessively expensive to run (see Sec. 5.5.2 for further discussion).

> **Example 5.2.** For the multiteller bank with jockeying considered in Sec. 2.6, a good programming approach would be first to write and debug the computer program without letting customers jockey from queue to queue.

Technique 2. It is advisable when developing large simulation models to have more than one person read the computer program, since the writer of a particular subprogram may get into a mental rut and thus not be a good critic. In some organizations, this idea is implemented formally and is called a "structured walk-through." For example, all members of the modeling team, e.g., systems analysts, programmers, etc., are assembled in a room and each is given a copy of a particular set of subprograms to be debugged. Then the subprograms' developer goes through the computer code but does not proceed from one statement to another until everyone is convinced that a statement is correct.

Technique 3. Run the simulation under a variety of settings of the input parameters and check to see that the output is reasonable. In some cases, certain simple measures of performance may be computed exactly and used for comparison. (See the case study in Sec. 13.6.)

Example 5.3. For many queueing systems with s servers in parallel, it can be shown that the long-run average utilization of the servers is $\rho = \lambda/(s\omega)$ (see App. 1B for notation). Thus, if the average utilization from a simulation run is close to the utilization factor ρ, there is some indication that the program may be working correctly.

Technique 4. One of the most powerful techniques that can be used to debug a discrete-event simulation program is a "trace." In a *trace*, the state of the simulated system, i.e., the contents of the event list, the state variables, certain statistical counters, etc., is printed out just after each event occurs and compared with hand calculations to see if the program is operating as intended. In performing a trace it is desirable to evaluate each possible program path and also the program's ability to deal with "extreme" conditions. Sometimes such a thorough evaluation may require that special (perhaps deterministic) input data be prepared for the model. All of the major simulation languages used in the United States explicitly provide the capability to perform traces.

A batch-mode trace produces a large volume of output, which must be checked event by event for errors. Unfortunately, some key information may be omitted from the trace (not having been requested by the analyst) or, worse yet, a particular error may not occur in the "short" debugging simulation run. Either difficulty will require that the simulation be rerun. As a result, it is usually preferable to use an interactive debugger to find programming errors.

An *interactive debugger* allows an analyst to stop the simulation at a selected point in time, and to examine and possibly change the values of certain variables. This latter capability can be used to "force" the occurrence of certain types of errors. Most modern simulation languages have an interactive debugger.

Example 5.4. Table 5.1 shows a trace for the intuitive explanation of the single-server queue in Sec. 1.4.2. The first row of the table is a snapshot of the system just after initialization at time 0, the second row is a snapshot of the system just after the first event (an arrival) has occurred, etc.

Technique 5. The model should be run, when possible, under simplifying assumptions for which its true characteristics are known or can easily be computed.

Example 5.5. For the job-shop model presented in Sec. 2.7 it is not possible to compute the desired system characteristics analytically. Therefore, one must resort to simulation. In order to debug the simulation model, one could first run the general model of Sec. 2.7.2 with one machine group, one machine in that group, and only type 1 jobs (which have an arrival rate of $0.3/0.25 = 1.2$ jobs per hour). The resulting model is known as the $M/E_2/1$ queue and has known transient and steady-state characteristics [see Kelton (1985) and Gross and Harris (1985, p. 268)]. Table 5.2 gives the theoretical values of the steady-state average number in queue, average utilization, and average delay in queue and also estimates of these quantities from a simulation run of length 2000 eight-hour days.

TABLE 5.1
Partial trace for the single-server queue considered in Sec. 1.4.2

Event	Clock	Server status	Number in queue	Times of arrival	Event list		Number of customers delayed	Total delay	Area under number-in-queue function	Area under busy function
					Arrive	Depart				
Initialization	0	0	0		0.4	∞	0	0	0	0
Arrival	0.4	1	0		1.6	2.4	1	0	0	0
Arrival	1.6	1	1	1.6	2.1	2.4	1	0	0	1.2
Arrival	2.1	1	2	1.6, 2.1	3.8	2.4	1	0	0.5	1.7
Departure	2.4	1	1	2.1	3.8	3.1	2	0.8	1.1	2.0
Departure	3.1	1	0		3.8	3.3	3	1.8	1.8	2.7
Departure	3.3	0	0		3.8	∞	3	1.8	1.8	2.9

TABLE 5.2
Theoretical values (T) and simulation estimates (S) for a simplified job-shop model ($M/E_2/1$ queue)

Average number in queue		Average utilization		Average delay in queue	
T	S	T	S	T	S
0.676	0.685	0.600	0.604	0.563	0.565

Since the estimates are very close to the true values, we have some degree of confidence that the computer program is correct.

A more definitive test of the program can be achieved by running the general model of Sec. 2.7.2 with the original number of machine groups (5), the original number of machines in each group (3, 2, 4, 3, 1), only type 1 jobs, and with exponential service times (with the same mean as the corresponding 2-Erlang service time) at each machine group. The resulting model is, in effect, four multiserver queues in series, with the first queue an $M/M/3$, the second an $M/M/2$, etc. [The interdeparture times from an $M/M/s$ queue (s is the number of servers) that has been in operation for a long time are IID exponential random variables; see Gross and Harris (1985, p. 221).] Furthermore, steady-state characteristics are known for the $M/M/s$ queue [see Gross and Harris (1985, p. 84)]. Table 5.3 gives, for each machine group, the theoretical values of the steady-state average number in queue, average utilization, and average delay in queue and also estimates of these quantities from a simulation run of length 2000 eight-hour days. Once again the simulation estimates are quite close to the theoretical values, which gives increased confidence in the program.

Technique 6. With some types of simulation models, it may be helpful to observe an animation of the simulation output (see Sec. 3.4.2).

Example 5.6. A simulation model of a network of automobile traffic intersections was developed, supposedly debugged, and used for some time to study such issues as the effect of various light-sequencing policies. However, when the simulated

TABLE 5.3
Theoretical values (T) and simulation estimates (S) for a simplified job-shop model (four multiserver queues in series)

Machine group	Average number in queue		Average utilization		Average delay in queue	
	T	S	T	S	T	S
3	0.001	0.001	0.150	0.149	0.001	0.001
1	0.012	0.012	0.240	0.238	0.010	0.010
2	0.359	0.350	0.510	0.508	0.299	0.292
5	0.900	0.902	0.600	0.601	0.750	0.752

flow of traffic was animated on a graphics terminal, it was found that simulated cars were actually colliding in the intersections; subsequent inspection of the computer program revealed several undetected errors.

Technique 7. Write out the sample mean and sample variance for each simulation input probability distribution and compare them with the desired (e.g., historical) mean and variance. This suggests that values are being correctly generated from these distributions.

> **Example 5.7.** The parameters of a gamma distribution are defined differently in various simulation packages and books. Thus, this technique would be valuable here.

Technique 8. Use a simulation package to reduce the required number of lines of code. On the other hand, care must be taken when using a simulation package (particularly a recently released one), since it may contain errors of a subtle nature. Also, simulation packages contain powerful macro statements, which may not be well documented.

5.4 GENERAL PERSPECTIVES ON VALIDATION

We now describe some general perspectives on validation. They should not be thought of as definitive recommendations on how to validate a simulation model, but rather as somewhat philosophical considerations to be kept in mind when contemplating how to validate a model of a real-world system.

1. Experimentation with a simulation model is a surrogate for actually experimenting with an existing or proposed system. Thus, an idealistic goal in validation is to ensure that the simulation model is good enough so that it can be used to make decisions about the system similar to those that would be made if it *were* feasible and cost-effective to experiment with the system itself.
2. The ease or difficulty of the validation process depends on the complexity of the system being modeled and on whether a version of the system currently exists. For example, a model of a neighborhood bank would be relatively easy to validate since it could be closely observed. On the other hand, a model of the effectiveness of a naval weapons system in the year 2025 would be virtually impossible to validate completely, since the location of the battle and the nature of the enemy weapons would be unknown.
3. A simulation model of a complex system can only be an *approximation* to the actual system, regardless of how much effort is put into developing the model. There is no such thing as an absolutely valid model. The more time (and hence money) is spent on model development, the more valid the model should be in general. However, the most valid model is not necessari-

ly the most cost-effective one. For example, increasing the validity of a model beyond a certain level may be quite expensive, since extensive data collection may be required.

4. A simulation model should always be developed for a particular set of purposes. Indeed, a model that is valid for one purpose may not be valid for another. For example, consider a company that builds a simulation model of its computer system. Since simulation models are generally better at comparing alternatives than at determining absolute answers, a particular model of the computer system might be sufficiently valid to compare, in a relative sense, three proposed job-scheduling policies. However, it might not be valid enough to determine quite as precisely the average response of the computer under a particular scheduling policy when the arrival rate of jobs is hypothesized to increase by 50 percent.

5. A logbook of the simulation model's asssumptions should be updated on a regular basis, and eventually turned into a final report. This report should be given to all attendees at the structured walk-through of the conceptual simulation model, which is described in Sec. 5.5.1. It is also useful after the project has been completed to determine the model's validity for other potential applications. Note, in general, that it is not sufficient to write down the model's assumptions at the end of the project, since many of them may have been forgotten. See National Bureau of Standards (1981) and Gass et al. (1981) for further discussion of model documentation.

6. A simulation model should be validated relative to those measures of performance that will actually be used for decision making. For example, if a manufacturing manager will choose among different system designs based primarily on system throughput, then the simulation model's ability to predict throughput accurately should be determined. Other measures such as work-in-process may not be important.

7. Validation is not something to be attempted after the simulation model has already been developed, and only if there is time and money still remaining. Instead, model development and validation should be done hand-in-hand throughout the entire simulation study. (Our experience indicates that this recommendation is seldom followed.)

8. It is generally impossible to perform a formal statistical validation between model output data and the corresponding system (if it exists) output data, due to the nature of these data. (See Sec. 5.5.3 for further discussion.)

5.5 A THREE-STEP APPROACH FOR DEVELOPING VALID AND CREDIBLE SIMULATION MODELS

One of the important papers in the validation literature is that of Naylor and Finger (1967), where a three-step approach is given for "validating" a simulation model [see also Van Horn (1971)]. Here we augment their approach by giving specific recommendations and examples of how to carry out each step.

Their approach will not guarantee an absolutely valid model, but it will make the model more representative of the real system and also more credible.

5.5.1 Develop a Model with High Face Validity

The primary objective during the first step is to develop a model with high *face validity*, i.e., a model that, on the surface, seems reasonable to people who are knowledgeable about the system under study. In order to develop such a model, the simulation modelers should make use of all existing information, including the following.

Conversations with System "Experts." A simulation model is not an abstraction developed by an analyst working in isolation; the modeler should work closely with people who are intimately familiar with the system. There will rarely be one person or document that contains all the information needed to build the model. Therefore, the analyst will have to be resourceful in order to obtain all of the required information. The process of bringing all of the system information together in one place is often valuable in its own right even if a simulation is never performed.

> **Example 5.8.** In modeling a manufacturing system, the modelers should obtain information from such sources as machine operators, manufacturing and industrial engineers, managers, vendors, and blueprints.

Observations of the System. If a system similar to the one of interest exists, then data should be obtained from it for use in building the model. These data may be available from historical records or may have to be collected during a time study. Care must be taken to ensure that the data are correct (e.g., contain no recording errors), are in the right format, and are representative of what is being modeled. For example, the data collected during a military field test (see Sec. 5.5.3) may not be representative of actual combat conditions due to differences in troop behavior and lack of battlefield smoke (see also Prob. 5.1). Schellenberger (1974) discusses this and also aspects of data validity.

> **Example 5.9.** If one is modeling a multiteller bank with jockeying (see Sec. 2.6), then interarrival times are collected and used to fit a theoretical interarrival-time distribution, service times are collected and used to fit a theoretical service-time distribution, and the bank is observed in order to construct a model of how people jockey from one line to another.

Existing Theory. For example, if one is modeling a service system such as a bank and the arrival rate of customers is constant over some time period, theory tells us that the interarrival times of customers are quite likely to be IID exponential random variables; in other words, customers arrive in accordance with a Poisson process (see Sec. 6.10.1).

Relevant Results from Similar Simulation Models. For example, if one is building a simulation model of a military ground encounter, then results from similar studies should be sought out and used, if possible.

Experience/Intuition. It will often be necessary to use one's experience or intuition to hypothesize how certain components of a complex system operate, particularly if the system does not currently exist in some form. It is hoped that these hypotheses can be substantiated during the later steps of the validation process.

We now discuss two of the most important ideas in this chapter, whose use will increase considerably the likelihood that the completed model will actually be used in the decision-making process. *First, it is extremely important for the modeler to interact with the manager/client on a regular basis throughout the course of the simulation study.* This approach has the following benefits:

- Often when a simulation study is first initiated, there is not a clear idea of the problem to be solved. Thus, as the study proceeds and the nature of the problem becomes clearer, this information should be conveyed to the manager, who may reformulate the study's objectives. The greatest model for the wrong problem is clearly invalid!
- The manager's interest and involvement in the study are maintained.
- The manager's knowledge of the system contributes to the actual validity of the model.
- The model is more credible, since the manager understands and accepts the model's assumptions. As a matter of fact, it is extremely desirable to have the manager (and other important personnel) "sign off" on key model assumptions. This may cause the manager to say to himself "Of course, it's a good model, since I (helped) developed it."

Another very important idea for validity/credibility enhancement is for the modelers to perform a structured walk-through of the conceptual model (prior to the beginning of coding) before an audience of all key people. This meeting helps ensure that the model's assumptions are correct, complete, and consistent (i.e., that "local" information obtained from different people is not contradictory). The structured walk-through should be performed before coding begins to avoid significant reprogramming if major problems are discovered at the meeting.

Example 5.10. We performed a structured walk-through in doing a simulation study for a Fortune 500 manufacturing company (see Sec. 13.6). There were nine people at the meeting, including two modelers and seven people from the client organization. The client personnel included the foreman of the machine operators, two people from the planning department, three engineers of different types, and a manager. Each person at the meeting received a report containing a set of approximately 160 tentative model assumptions. (This report was obtained from the model logbook discussed in Sec. 5.4.) Each of the 160 assumptions was presented and discussed, with the whole process taking five and a half hours. The process resulted in several erroneous assumptions being discovered and corrected, a few new assumptions being added, and some level-of-detail issues being resolved. Furthermore, at the end of the meeting, all nine people collectively felt that *they* had a valid model!

5.5.2 Test the Assumptions of the Model Empirically

The goal of the second step of validation is to test quantitatively the assumptions made during the initial stages of model development. We now give some examples of techniques that can be used for this purpose, all of which are generally applicable.

If a theoretical probability distribution has been fitted to some observed data and used as input to the simulation model, the adequacy of the fit can be assessed by the graphical plots and goodness-of-fit tests discussed in Chap. 6.

As stated in Sec. 5.5.1, it is important to use representative data in building a model; however, it is equally important to exercise care when structuring these data. For example, if several sets of data have been observed for the "same" random phenomenon, then the correctness of merging these data can be determined by the Kruskal-Wallis test of homogeneity of populations (see Sec. 6.11). If the data sets are homogeneous, they can be merged and used for some purpose in the simulation model.

> **Example 5.11.** For the manufacturing system described in the case study of Sec. 13.6, time-to-failure and repair-time data were collected for two "identical" machines made by the same vendor. However, the Kruskal-Wallis test showed that both distributions were, in fact, different for the two machines. Thus, each machine had its own time-to-failure and repair-time distributions in the simulation.

One of the most useful tools during the second step of validation is *sensitivity analysis*. This can be used to determine if the simulation output changes significantly when the value of an input parameter is changed, when an input probability distribution is changed, or when the level of detail for a subsystem is changed. If the output is sensitive to some aspect of the model, then that aspect must be modeled carefully.

> **Example 5.12.** In a simulation study of a new system, suppose that the value of a parameter is estimated to be 0.75 as a result of conversations with experts. The importance of this parameter can be determined by running the simulation with 0.75 and, in addition, by running it with each of the values 0.70 and 0.80. If the three simulation runs produce approximately the same results, then the output is not sensitive to the choice of the parameter over the range 0.70 to 0.80. Otherwise, a better specification of the parameter is needed.

Example 5.13. For a simulation model of a cigarette filter rod manufacturing line [see Carson et al. (1981b)], the modelers needed to decide what the basic entity flowing through the process would be. A single filter rod was first used as the basic entity, but this resulted in excessive computer execution time. Then, a sensitivity analysis was performed and it was found that using 100 filter rods as the entity produced virtually the same results, while reducing the execution time considerably.

Example 5.14. We developed on a minicomputer a simulation model of the assembly and test areas for a personal computer manufacturing company. Later the company management decided that they wanted the model to run on their own computers, but the memory requirements of the model were too great. As a result, we were forced to simplify greatly the model of the assembly area to save computer memory. We ran the simplified simulation model (the model of the test area was unchanged) and found that it produced virtually the same results as the original model for the performance measures of primary interest (e.g., overall throughput). Thus, a large amount of detail was not necessary for the assembly line.

When performing a sensitivity analysis, it is important to use the method of common random numbers (see Sec. 11.2) to control the randomness in the simulation. Otherwise, the effect of changing one aspect of the model may be confounded with other changes (e.g., different random values from some input distribution) that inadvertently occur.

If one is trying to determine the sensitivity of the simulation output to changes in two or more factors of interest, then statistical experimental design (see Chap. 12) may be used for this purpose. The effect of each factor can be formally estimated and, if the number of factors is not too large, interactions between factors can also be detected.

5.5.3 Determine How Representative the Simulation Output Data Are

The most definitive test of a simulation model's validity is establishing that its output data closely resemble the output data that would be expected from the actual (proposed) system. If a system similar to the proposed one now exists, then a simulation model of the existing system is developed and its output data are compared to those from the existing system itself. If the two sets of data compare "favorably," then the model of the *existing* system is considered "valid." (The accuracy required from the model will depend on its intended use and the utility function of the manager.) The model is then modified so that it represents the proposed system. The greater the commonality between the existing and proposed systems, the greater our confidence in the model of the proposed system. There is no completely definitive approach for validating the model of the proposed system. If there were, there might be no need for a simulation model in the first place.

There is often an opportunity to apply the above validation idea qualitatively. For example, suppose that we are simulating a manufacturing system and the goal is to determine the effect of replacing a human worker by a robot or to determine the effect of implementing a new production-scheduling policy. In both cases there is an existing system that has much in common with the proposed system. In some simulation studies, however, there may not be an existing system. For example, certain proposed military weapons systems may not have an existing counterpart.

Some managers might balk at the idea of first building a simulation model of an existing system, since it may seem on the surface to waste time and money. However, if a model is not validated, then any results produced by it are of doubtful value, regardless of how little the model costs. The following are some additional reasons why building a model of the existing system may be worthwhile:

- A model of the existing system may suggest improvements to the system.
- If this modeling effort is successful, the credibility of the study is increased [see, for example, Carson (1986)].
- A model of the existing system is often needed to compare the existing and proposed systems (which is usually desired), since little data may be available from the existing system. (See Chap. 10 for a discussion of statistical techniques for comparing systems.)

A number of statistical tests have been suggested in the validation literature for comparing the output data from a simulation model with those from the corresponding real-world system [see, for example, Shannon (1975, p. 208)]. However, the comparison is not as simple as it might appear, since the output processes of almost all real-world systems and simulations are *nonstationary* (the distributions of the successive observations change over time) and *autocorrelated* (the observations in the process are correlated with each other). Thus, classical statistical tests based on IID observations are not *directly* applicable. Furthermore, we question whether hypothesis tests, as compared with constructing confidence intervals for differences, are even the appropriate statistical approach. Since the model is only an approximation to the actual system, a null hypothesis that the system and model are the "same" is clearly false. We believe that it is more useful to ask whether or not the differences between the system and the model are significant enough to affect any conclusions derived from the model. For a discussion of statistical procedures that can be used to compare system and model output data, see Sec. 5.6.

In addition to statistical procedures, one can use a *Turing test* [see Turing (1950) and Carson (1986)] to compare the output data from the model to those from the system. People knowledgeable about the system (e.g., managers or engineers) are asked to examine one or more sets of system data as well as one or more sets of model data without knowing which sets are which. Each data set should be presented on a separate piece of paper using exactly the same format. If these "experts" can differentiate between the system and model data, their explanation of how they were able to do so is used to improve the model.

> **Example 5.15.** Schruben (1980) reports the use of a Turing test in a simulation study of an automobile component factory. Data from the factory and from the simulation were put on time-study forms and reviewed at a meeting by three managers, three industrial engineers, and two factory workers. The inability of these people to agree on which data were real and which were simulated led to immediate acceptance of the simulation model.

If there is not an existing system similar to the proposed system or if there is an existing system but no definitive output data, then it is still worthwhile to have system experts review the simulation output data for reasonableness. (Care must be taken in performing this exercise, since if one knew exactly what output to expect, there would be no need for a model.) An animation may also be an effective way for experts to evaluate the validity of a simulation model.

> **Example 5.16.** The above idea was put to good use by the developers of the ISEM simulation model of the U.S. Air Force Manpower and Personnel System. (This model was designed to provide Air Force policy analysts with a system-wide view of the effects of various proposed personnel policies.) The model was run under the baseline personnel policy, and the results were shown to Air Force analysts and decision makers, who subsequently identified some discrepancies between model and perceived system behavior. This information was used to improve the model, and after several additional evaluations and improvements, a model was obtained that appeared to approximate current Air Force policy closely. This exercise improved not only the validity of the model, but also its credibility.

If the decisions to be made with a simulation model are of particularly great importance, field tests are sometimes used (primarily by the military) to obtain system output data from a version of the proposed system (or a subsystem) for validation purposes. For example, suppose some military organization is thinking of purchasing a weapons system for which it is infeasible or too expensive to perform a complete set of evaluational tests. As an alternative, a simulation model of the system is developed, and then a prototype of the actual system is field-tested on a military reservation for one or more specified scenarios. If the model and system output data compare closely for each of the specified scenarios, the "validated" simulation model is used to evaluate the system for scenarios for which system field tests are not possible. For further discussion of field tests, see Shannon (1975, p. 231).

Up to now we have discussed validating a simulation model relative to past or present system output data; however, a perhaps more definitive test of a model is to establish its ability to predict *future* system behavior. Since models often evolve over time and are used for multiple applications, there is often an opportunity for such *prospective* validation. For example, if a model is used to decide which version of a proposed system to build, then after the system has been built and sufficient time has elapsed for output data to be collected, these data can be compared with the predictions of the model. If there is reasonable agreement, we have increased confidence in the "validity" of the model. On the other hand, discrepancies between the two data sets should be used to update the model. Regardless of the accuracy of a model's past predictions, a model should be carefully scrutinized before each new application, since a change in purpose or the passage of time may have invalidated some aspect of the existing model. This once again points out the need for good documentation of the model.

Suppose that we compare the output data from an existing system to those from a simulation model of that system and find significant discrepancies. If these discrepancies or other information objectively suggest how to improve the model, then these changes should be made and the simulation rerun. If the new simulation output data compare favorably with the system output data, then the model can be considered "valid."

Suppose instead that there are major discrepancies between the system and model output data, but that changes are made to the model, somewhat without justification (e.g., "correction factors" are added), and the resulting output data are again compared with the system output data. This procedure, which we call *calibration* of a model, is continued until the two data sets agree closely. However, we must ask whether this procedure produces a valid model for the system, in general, or whether the model is only representative of the particular set of input data. To answer this question (in effect, to validate the model), one can use a completely independent set of system input and output data. The calibrated model might be driven by the second set of input data (in a manner similar to that described in Sec. 5.6.1) and the resulting model output data compared with the second set of system output data. This idea of using one set of data for calibration and another independent set for validation is fairly common in economics and the biological sciences. In particular, it was used by the Crown Zellerbach Corporation in developing a simulation model of tree growth. Here the system data were available from the U.S. Forest Service.

5.6 STATISTICAL PROCEDURES FOR COMPARING REAL-WORLD OBSERVATIONS AND SIMULATION OUTPUT DATA

Suppose that $R_1, R_2, \ldots, R_k$ are observations from a real-world system and that $M_1, M_2, \ldots, M_l$ are output data from a corresponding simulation model (see Example 5.17). We would like to compare the two data sets in some way to determine whether the model is an accurate representation of the real-world system. The first approach that comes to mind is to use one of the classical statistical tests (t, Mann-Whitney, two-sample chi-square, two-sample Kolmogorov-Smirnov, etc.) to determine whether the underlying distributions of the two data sets can be safely regarded as being the same. [For a good discussion of these tests, which assume IID data, see Breiman (1973).] However, as pointed out above, the output processes of almost all real-world systems and simulations are nonstationary and autocorrelated, and thus none of these tests is *directly* applicable. In Secs. 5.6.1 through 5.6.3 we discuss, respectively, inspection, confidence-interval, and time-series approaches to this comparison problem.

5.6.1 Inspection Approach

The approach that seems to be used by most simulation practitioners who attempt the third step of the suggested validation procedure is to compute one or more statistics from the real-world observations and corresponding statistics from the model output data, and then compare the two sets of statistics without the use of a formal statistical procedure. Examples of statistics that might be used for this purpose are the sample mean, the sample variance (see Sec. 4.4 for a discussion of the danger in using the sample variance), the sample correlation function, and "histograms." (The word histogram is put in quotation marks because histograms are usually derived from IID data.) The difficulty with this inspection approach, which is graphically illustrated below in Example 5.17, is that each statistic is essentially a sample of size 1 from some underlying population, making this idea particularly vulnerable to the inherent randomness of the observations from both the real system and the simulation model.

Example 5.17. In order to illustrate the danger of using inspection, suppose that the real-world system of interest is the $M/M/1$ queue with $\rho = 0.6$ and that the corresponding simulation model is the $M/M/1$ queue with $\rho = 0.5$. Suppose that the output process of interest is $D_1, D_2, \ldots$ (where D_i is the delay in queue of the ith customer) and let

$$X = \frac{\sum_{i=1}^{200} D_i}{200} \qquad \text{for the system}$$

and

$$Y = \frac{\sum_{i=1}^{200} D_i}{200} \qquad \text{for the model}$$

(Thus, the number of observations for the system, k, and for the model, l, are both equal to 200.) We shall attempt to determine how good a representation the model is for the system for comparing an estimate for $\mu_Y = E(Y) = 0.49$ [the expected average delay of the first 200 customers for the model; see Heathcote and Winer (1969) for a discussion of how to compute $E(Y)$] with an estimate of $\mu_X = E(X) = 0.87$. Table 5.4 gives the results of three independent simulation experiments, each corresponding to a possible application of the inspection

TABLE 5.4
Results for three experiments with the inspection approach

Experiment	$\hat{\mu}_X$	$\hat{\mu}_Y$	$\hat{\mu}_X - \hat{\mu}_Y$
1	0.90	0.70	0.20
2	0.70	0.71	-0.01
3	1.08	0.35	0.73

approach. For each experiment, $\hat{\mu}_X$ and $\hat{\mu}_Y$ represent the sample mean of the 200 delays for the system and model, respectively, and $\hat{\mu}_X - \hat{\mu}_Y$ is an estimate of $\mu_X - \mu_Y = 0.38$, which is what we are really trying to estimate. Note that $\hat{\mu}_X - \hat{\mu}_Y$ varies greatly from experiment to experiment. Also observe for experiment 2 that $\hat{\mu}_X - \hat{\mu}_Y = -0.01$, which would tend to lead one to think that the model is a good representation for the system. However, we believe that the model is really a poor representation for the system for purposes of estimation of the expected average delay in the real-world system, since μ_Y is nearly 44 percent smaller than μ_X.

Because of the inherent danger in using the *basic inspection approach* presented above, we now describe a better approach for comparing system and model output data if the system data are complete enough and in the right format. In particular, it is recommended that the system and model be compared by driving the model with historical system input data (e.g., actual observed interarrival times and service times), rather than samples from the input probability distributions, and then comparing the model and system outputs; see Fig. 5.2. (The system outputs are those corresponding to the historical system input data.) Thus, the system and the model experience *exactly the same observations* from the input random variables, which should result in a statistically more precise comparison. We call this idea the *correlated inspection approach*, since it generally results in comparable model and system statistics being positively correlated.

Example 5.18. In order to illustrate the benefits of the correlated inspection approach, suppose that the system is the five-teller bank of Sec. 2.6 with jockeying and that the model is the same bank but without jockeying (i.e., customers never leave the line they originally join). Assume, however, that the mean service time is now 4 minutes. Let

$$X = \text{average delay in queue for the system}$$

and

$$Y = \text{average delay in queue for the model}$$

We will attempt to determine the accuracy of the model by comparing an estimate of the expected average delay for the model $\mu_Y = E(Y)$ with an estimate of the expected average delay for the system $\mu_X = E(X)$. Table 5.5 gives the results

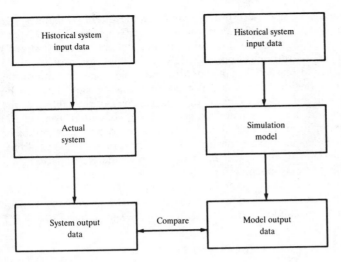

FIGURE 5.2
The correlated inspection approach.

from the first 10 of 500 independent experiments, each corresponding to a possible application of the correlated inspection approach. There X_j and Y_j are the average delay for the system and for the model in the jth experiment, respectively, and $X_j - Y_j$ is an estimate of $\mu_X - \mu_Y$, which is what we are really trying to estimate. (Note that X_j and Y_j use exactly the same interarrival times and service times; they differ only in the jockeying rule employed.) Also given in the table are Y'_j, which is the average delay for the model in the jth experiment

TABLE 5.5
Results for the first 10 of 500 experiments with the correlated and basic inspection approaches, and a summary for all 500

Experiment j	X_j	Y_j	Y'_j	$X_j - Y_j$	$X_j - Y'_j$
1	3.06	3.81	2.62	−0.75	0.44
2	2.79	3.37	2.05	−0.58	0.74
3	2.21	2.61	4.56	−0.40	−2.35
4	2.54	3.59	1.86	−1.05	0.68
5	9.27	11.02	2.41	−1.75	6.86
6	3.09	3.75	1.85	−0.66	1.24
7	2.50	2.84	1.13	−0.34	1.37
8	0.31	0.71	3.12	−0.40	−2.81
9	3.17	3.94	5.09	−0.77	−1.92
10	0.98	1.18	1.25	−0.20	−0.27
Sample mean of all 500	2.10	2.85	2.70	−0.75	−0.60
Sample variance of all 500	2.02	2.28	2.12	0.08	4.08

when *different* random numbers are used to generate the interarrival times and service times, and $X_j - Y'_j$, whose mean is also $\mu_X - \mu_Y$. (Note that X_j and Y'_j are based on different realizations of the same input probability distributions.) Comparing Y'_j and X_j corresponds approximately to an application of the basic inspection approach. (In an actual application of the basic inspection approach, the input probability distributions would not be known and would have to be estimated from system input data.) Finally, the last two rows of the table give the usual sample mean and sample variance for each column computed from *all 500* experiments. Observe from the table that $X_j - Y_j$ is a much better estimator of $\mu_X - \mu_Y$ than $X_j - Y'_j$, since it has a considerably smaller variance (0.08 vs. 4.08). Thus, the difference $X - Y$ for a particular application of the correlated inspection approach is likely to be much closer to $\mu_X - \mu_Y$ than the difference $X - Y'$ for a particular application of the basic inspection approach.

We now explain more clearly why $\text{Var}(X - Y)$ is less than $\text{Var}(X - Y')$. In particular, if A and B are random variables, then it can be shown (see Prob. 4.13) that

$$\text{Var}(A - B) = \text{Var}(A) + \text{Var}(B) - 2\,\text{Cov}(A, B)$$

In the case of the basic inspection approach, $A = X$, $B = Y'$, $\text{Cov}(X, Y') = 0$ (the estimated value was 0.03; see Prob. 4.25), and

$$\text{Var}(X - Y') = \text{Var}(X) + \text{Var}(Y')$$

For the correlated inspection approach, $A = X$, $B = Y$, $\widehat{\text{Cov}}(X, Y) = 2.11$ [$\widehat{\text{Cor}}(X, Y) = 0.99$], and

$$\text{Var}(X - Y) = \text{Var}(X) + \text{Var}(Y) - 2\,\text{Cov}(X, Y)$$
$$= \text{Var}(X) + \text{Var}(Y') - 2\,\text{Cov}(X, Y)$$
$$< \text{Var}(X - Y')$$

The idea of comparing a model and the corresponding system under the same statistical conditions is similar to the use of the variance-reduction technique known as common random numbers in simulation (see Sec. 11.2) and the use of "blocking" in statistical experimental design. It should be mentioned, however, that we do not recommend using historical system input data to drive a model for the purpose of making *production* runs (see Sec. 6.1).

Example 5.19. The correlated inspection approach was used to help validate a simulation model of a cigarette manufacturing process at Brown & Williamson Tobacco Company [see Carson (1986) and Carson et al. (1981a) for details]. The manufacturing system basically consists of a cigarette maker, a reservoir (buffer) for cigarettes, a packer, and a cartoner. The maker and packer are subject to frequent product-induced failures such as the cigarette paper tearing. The major objective of the study was to determine the optimal capacity of the reservoir, which helps lessen the effect of the above failures.

The existing system was observed over a 4-hour period, and operating-time (before failure) and repair-time data were collected for the maker and packer, as well as the total cigarette production. These operating times and repair times were used to drive the simulation model for a 4-hour simulation run, and the total model cigarette production was observed. The fact that the model production differed from the actual production by only 1 percent helped convince management of the model's validity.

In summary, we believe that the inspection approach may provide valuable insight into the adequacy of a simulation model for some simulation studies (particularly if the correlated approach can be used). As a matter of fact, for some studies it may be the only feasible approach because of severe limitations on the amount of data available on the operation of the real system. However, as Example 5.17 shows, extreme care must be used in interpreting the results of this approach (especially with the basic version).

5.6.2   Confidence-Interval Approach Based on Independent Data

We now describe a more reliable approach for comparing a model with the corresponding system for the situation where it is possible to collect a potentially large amount of data from both the model and the system. This might be the case, for example, when the system is an existing computer facility from which a large amount of data can be readily obtained. This approach will not, however, be feasible for most military and manufacturing situations due to the paucity of real-world data.

In the spirit of terminating simulations (see Secs. 9.3 and 9.4, and Chap. 10), suppose we collect m independent sets of data from the system and n independent sets of data from the model. Let X_j be the average of the observations in the jth set of system data, and let Y_j be the average of the observations in the jth set of model data. The X_j's are IID random variables (assuming that the m sets of system data are homogeneous) with mean $\mu_X = E(X_j)$, and the Y_j's are IID random variables (assuming that the n data sets for the model were produced by independent replications) with mean $\mu_Y = E(Y_j)$. We shall attempt to compare the model with the system by constructing a confidence interval for $\zeta = \mu_X - \mu_Y$. We believe that constructing a confidence interval for ζ is preferable to testing the null hypothesis $H_0: \mu_X = \mu_Y$ for the following reasons:

- Since the model is only an approximation to the system, H_0 will clearly be false in almost all cases.
- A confidence interval provides more information than the corresponding hypothesis test. If the hypothesis test indicates that $\mu_X \neq \mu_Y$, then the confidence interval will provide this information and also give an indication of the magnitude by which μ_X differs from μ_Y.

Constructing a confidence interval for ζ is a special case of the problem of comparing two systems by means of a confidence interval discussed in Sec.

10.2. Thus, we may construct a confidence interval for ζ by using either the paired-t approach or the Welch approach. (In the notation of Sec. 10.2, $n_1 = m$, $n_2 = n$, $X_{1j} = X_j$, and $X_{2j} = Y_j$.) The paired-t approach requires $m = n$ but allows X_j to be correlated with Y_j, which would be the case if the idea underlying the correlated inspection approach is used (see Sec. 5.6.1). The Welch approach can be used for any values of $m \geq 2$ and $n \geq 2$ but requires that the X_j's be independent of the Y_j's.

Suppose that we have constructed a $100(1 - \alpha)$ percent confidence interval for ζ by using either the paired-t or Welch approach, and let $l(\alpha)$ and $u(\alpha)$ be the corresponding lower and upper confidence-interval endpoints, respectively. If $0 \notin [l(\alpha), u(\alpha)]$, then the observed difference between μ_X and μ_Y, $\bar{X}(m) - \bar{Y}(n)$, is said to be *statistically significant* at level α. This is equivalent to rejecting the null hypothesis H_0: $\mu_X = \mu_Y$ in favor of the two-sided alternative hypothesis H_1: $\mu_X \neq \mu_Y$ at the same level α. If $0 \in [l(\alpha), u(\alpha)]$, any observed difference between μ_X and μ_Y is not statistically significant at level α and might be explained by sampling fluctuation. Even if the observed difference between μ_X and μ_Y is statistically significant, this need not mean that the model is, for practical purposes, an "invalid" representation of the system. For example, if $\zeta = 1$ but $\mu_X = 1000$ and $\mu_Y = 999$, then the difference that exists between the model and the system is probably of no practical consequence. We shall say that the difference between a model and a system is *practically significant* if the "magnitude" of the difference is large enough to invalidate any inferences about the system that would be derived from the model. Clearly, the decision as to whether the difference between a model and a system is practically significant is a subjective one, depending on such factors as the purpose of the model and the utility function of the person who is going to use the model.

If the length of the confidence interval for ζ is not small enough to decide practical significance, it will be necessary to obtain additional X_j's or Y_j's. It should be noted, however, that for the Welch approach it is not possible to make the confidence interval arbitrarily small by adding only X_j's or only Y_j's. Thus, if the number of sets of system data, m, cannot be increased, it may not be possible to determine practical significance by making more and more replications of the model.

Example 5.20. Suppose that X_j and Y_j are defined as in Example 5.18, and that we would like to construct a 90 percent confidence interval for $\zeta = \mu_X - \mu_Y$ using the paired-t approach to determine whether the model (no jockeying) is an accurate representation of the system (jockeying). Letting $W_j = X_j - Y_j$ and $m = n = 10$, we obtained from the first 10 rows of Table 5.5 the following:

$$\bar{W}(10) = \bar{X}(10) - \bar{Y}(10) = 2.99 - 3.68 = -0.69$$

(point estimate for ζ)

$$\widehat{\text{Var}[\bar{W}(10)]} = \frac{\sum\limits_{j=1}^{10} [W_j - \bar{W}(10)]^2}{(10)(9)} = 0.02$$

and the 90 percent confidence interval for ζ is

$$\bar{W}(10) \pm t_{9,0.95}\sqrt{\widehat{\text{Var}[\bar{W}(10)]}} = -0.69 \pm 0.26$$

or $[-0.95, -0.43]$. Since the interval does not contain 0, the observed difference between μ_X and μ_Y is statistically significant. It remains to decide the practical significance of such a difference.

Balci and Sargent (1984a) present a confidence-interval methodology that allows one to perform a trade-off analysis among sample sizes (m and n), the confidence level (e.g., 90 percent), and the confidence-interval half-length. Their approach is also applicable when several measures of performance are being used to validate the model [see also Balci and Sargent (1981, 1983)].

Two difficulties with the above replication approach are that it may require a large amount of data (each set of output data produces only one "observation") and that it provides no information about the autocorrelation structures of the two output processes (if of interest).

5.6.3 Time-Series Approaches

In this section we briefly discuss three time-series approaches for comparing model output data with system output data. [A *time series* is a finite realization of a stochastic process. For example, the delays $D_1, D_2, \ldots, D_{200}$ from a queueing model (see Example 5.17) or system form a time series.] These approaches require only one set of each type of output data and may also yield information on the autocorrelation structures of the two output processes. Thus, the two difficulties of the replication approach mentioned above are not present here. There are, however, other difficulties.

The *spectral-analysis* approach [see Fishman and Kiviat (1967) and Naylor (1971, p. 247)] proceeds by computing the sample spectrum, i.e., the Fourier cosine transformation of the estimated autocovariance function, of each output process and then using existing theory to construct a confidence interval for the difference of the logarithms of the two spectra. This confidence interval can potentially be used to assess the degree of similarity of the two autocorrelation functions. Two drawbacks of this approach are that it requires an output process to be covariance stationary (an assumption generally not satisfied in practice), and that a high level of mathematical sophistication is required in order to apply it. The method can also be quite expensive in terms of computer time or storage.

Spectral analysis is a nonparametric approach in that it makes no assumptions about the distributions of the observations in the time series. Hsu and Hunter (1977) suggest an alternative approach, which consists of fitting a parametric time-series model [see Box and Jenkins (1976)] to each set of output data and then applying a hypothesis test to see whether the two models appear to be the same.

Chen and Sargent (1987) give a method for constructing a confidence interval for the difference between the steady-state mean of a system and the corresponding steady-state mean of the simulation model, based on Schruben's standardized time-series approach (see Sec. 9.5.3). An attractive feature of the method, as compared to the approach in Sec. 5.6.2, is that only one set of output data is needed from the system and one set from the model. The method does, however, require that the two sets of output data be independent and satisfy certain other assumptions.

PROBLEMS

5.1. As stated in Sec. 5.5.1, care must be taken that data collected on a system are representative of what one actually wants to model. Discuss this potential problem with regard to a study that will involve observing the efficiency of workers on an assembly line for the purpose of building a simulation model. (The phenomenon you have identified is called the *Hawthorne effect*.)

5.2. Discuss why validating a model of a computer system might be easier than validating a military combat model. Assume that the computer system of interest is similar to an existing one.

5.3. If one constructs a confidence interval for $\zeta = \mu_X - \mu_Y$ using the confidence-interval approach of Sec. 5.6.2, which of the following outcomes are possible?

	Statistically significant	Practically significant
(a)	Yes	Yes
(b)	Yes	No
(c)	Yes	?
(d)	No	Yes
(e)	No	No
(f)	No	?

5.4. Use the Welch approach with $m = 5$ and $n = 10$ to construct a 90 percent confidence interval for $\zeta = \mu_X - \mu_Y$ given the following data:

X_j's: 0.92, 0.91, 0.57, 0.86, 0.90

Y_j's: 0.28, 0.32, 0.48, 0.49, 0.70, 0.51, 0.39, 0.28, 0.45, 0.57

Is the confidence interval statistically significant?

5.5. Suppose that one is simulating a single-server queueing system (see Sec. 1.4) with exponential interarrival times and would like to perform a sensitivity analysis to determine the effect of using gamma vs. lognormal (see Sec. 6.2.2) service times. Discuss how you would use the method of common random numbers (see Sec. 11.2) to make the analysis more statistically precise. What relationship does your method have to the correlated inspection approach?

5.6. Repeat the analysis of Example 5.20 if the Y_j's are replaced by the Y_j''s from Table 5.5. Comment on the efficacy of the two confidence intervals.

REFERENCES

Balci, O.: Credibility Assessment of Simulation Results: The State of the Art, *Proc. Conference on Methodology and Validation*, Orlando, Fla., pp. 19–25 (1987).

Balci, O., and R. G. Sargent: A Methodology for Cost-Risk Analysis in the Statistical Validation of Simulation Models, *Commun. Assoc. Comput. Mach.*, *24*: 190–197 (1981).

Balci, O., and R. G. Sargent: Validation of Multivariate Response Trace-Driven Simulation Models, *Performance 83, Proc. 9th International Symposium on Computer Performance Modelling, Measurement, and Evaluation*, A. K. Agrawada and S. K. Tripathi, eds., North Holland, Amsterdam, pp. 309–323 (1983).

Balci, O., and R. G. Sargent: Validation of Simulation Models Via Simultaneous Confidence Intervals, *Am. J. Math. Management Sci.*, *4*: 375–406 (1984a).

Balci, O., and R. G. Sargent: A Bibliography on the Credibility Assessment and Validation of Simulation and Mathematical Models, *Simuletter*, *15*: 15–27 (1984b).

Banks, J., and J. S. Carson: *Discrete-Event System Simulation*, Prentice-Hall, Englewood Cliffs, N.J. (1984).

Box, G. E. P., and G. M. Jenkins: *Time Series Analysis: Forecasting and Control*, rev. ed., Holden-Day, San Francisco (1976).

Breiman, L.: *Statistics: With a View Toward Applications*, Houghton Mifflin, Boston (1973).

Bryan, O. F., Jr., and M. C. Natrella: Testing Large-Scale Simulations: *Byte*, *10*: 183–194 (October 1985).

Carson J. S.: Convincing Users of Model's Validity Is Challenging Aspect of Modeler's Job, *Ind. Eng.*, *18*: 74–85 (June 1986).

Carson, J. S., N. Wilson, D. Caroll, and C. H. Wysocki: A Discrete Simulation Model of a Cigarette Fabrication Process, *Proc. Twelfth Modeling and Simulation Conference*, University of Pittsburgh, pp. 683–689 (1981a).

Carson, J. S., N. Wilson, D. Carroll, and C. H. Wysocki: Simulation of a Filter Rod Manufacturing Process, *Proc. 1981 Winter Simulation Conference*, Atlanta, Ga., pp. 535–541 (1981b).

Chen, B.-C., and R. G. Sargent: Using Standardized Time Series to Estimate the Difference between Two Stationary Stochastic Processes, *Operations Res.*, *35*: 428–436 (1987).

Feltner, C. E., and S. A. Weiner: Models, Myths and Mysteries in Manufacturing, *Ind. Eng.*, *17*: 66–76 (July 1985).

Fishman, G. S., and P. J. Kiviat: The Analysis of Simulation-Generated Time Series, *Management Sci.*, *13*: 525–557 (1967).

Fishman, G. S., and P. J. Kiviat: The Statistics of Discrete-Event Simulation, *Simulation*, *10*: 185–195 (1968).

Gass, S. I.: Decision-Aiding Models: Validation, Assessment, and Related Issues in Policy Analysis, *Operations Res.*, *31*: 603–631 (1983).

Gass, S. I., K. L. Hoffman, R. H. F. Jackson, L. S. Joel, and P. B. Saunders: Documentation for a Model: A Hierarchical Approach, *Commun. Assoc. Comput. Mach.*, *24*: 728–733 (1981).

Gass, S. I., and B. W. Thompson: Guidelines for Model Evaluation: An Abridged Version of the U.S. General Accounting Office Exposure Draft, *Operations Res.*, *28*: 431–439 (1980).

Gross, D., and C. M. Harris: *Fundamentals of Queueing Theory*, 2d ed., John Wiley, New York (1985).

Haider, S. W., D. G. Noller, and T. B. Robey: Experiences with Analytic and Simulation Modeling for a Factory of the Future Project at IBM, *Proc. 1986 Winter Simulation Conference*, Washington, D.C., pp. 641–648 (1986).

Heathcote, C. R., and P. Winer: An Approximation to the Moments of Waiting Times, *Operations Res.*, *17*: 175–186 (1969).

Hsu, D. A., and J. S. Hunter: Analysis of Simulation-Generated Responses Using Autoregressive Models, *Management Sci.*, *24*: 181–190 (1977).

Kelton, W. D.: Transient Exponential-Erlang Queues and Steady-State Simulation, *Commun. Assoc. Comput. Mach.*, *28*: 741–749 (1985).

National Bureau of Standards: *Computer Model Documentation Guide*, Natl. Bur. Std. Spec. Publ. 500-73, Washington, D.C. (1981).

Naylor, T. H.: *Computer Simulation Experiments with Models of Economic Systems*, John Wiley, New York (1971).

Naylor, T. H., and J. M. Finger: Verification of Computer Simulation Models, *Management Sci.*, *14*: 92–101 (1967).

Sargent, R. G.: A Tutorial on Validation and Verification of Simulation Models, *Proc. 1988 Winter Simulation Conference*, San Diego, Calif., pp. 33–39 (1988).

Schellenberger, R. E.: Criteria for Assessing Model Validity for Managerial Purposes, *Decision Sci.*, *5*: 644–653 (1974).

Schruben, L. W.: Establishing the Credibility of Simulations, *Simulation*, *34*: 101–105 (1980).

Shannon, R. E.: *Systems Simulation: The Art and Science*, Prentice-Hall, Englewood Cliffs, N.J. (1975).

Turing, A.M.: Computing Machinery and Intelligence, *Mind*, *59*: 433–460 (1950).

Van Horn, R. L.: Validation of Simulation Results, *Management Sci.*, *17*: 247–258 (1971).

CHAPTER
6

SELECTING
INPUT
PROBABILITY
DISTRIBUTIONS

Recommended sections for a first reading: 6.1, 6.2, 6.4 through 6.7, 6.9

6.1 INTRODUCTION

In order to carry out a simulation using random inputs such as interarrival times or demand sizes, we have to specify their probability distributions. For example, in the simulation of the single-server queueing system in Sec. 1.4.3, the interarrival times were taken to be IID exponential random variables with a mean of 1 minute; the demand sizes in the inventory simulation of Sec. 1.5 were specified to be 1, 2, 3, or 4 items with respective probabilities $\frac{1}{6}, \frac{1}{3}, \frac{1}{3}$, and $\frac{1}{6}$. Then, given that the input random variables to a simulation model follow particular distributions, the simulation proceeds through time by generating random values from these distributions. Chapters 7 and 8 discuss methods for generating random values from various distributions and processes. Our concern in this chapter is with how the analyst might go about specifying these input probability distributions.

Almost all real systems contain one or more sources of randomness, as illustrated in Table 6.1. Furthermore, we have seen in Sec. 4.7 that it is generally necessary to represent each source of system randomness by a

TABLE 6.1
Sources of randomness for common simulation applications

Type of system	Sources of randomness
Manufacturing	Processing times, machine operating times before a downtime, machine repair times
Computer	Interarrival times of jobs, job types, processing requirements of jobs
Communication	Interarrival times of messages, message types, message lengths
Defense-related	Arrival times and payloads of missiles or airplanes, outcome of an engagement, miss distances for munitions

probability distribution (rather than just its mean) in the simulation model. The following example shows that failure to choose the "correct" distribution can also affect the accuracy of a model's results, sometimes drastically.

> **Example 6.1.** A single-server queueing system (e.g., a single machine in a factory) has exponential interarrival times with a mean of 1 minute. Suppose that 200 service times are available from the system, but their underlying probability distribution is unknown. Using an approach to be discussed in Sec. 6.5, we "fit" the "best" exponential, gamma, Weibull, lognormal, and normal distributions (see Sec. 6.2.2 for a discussion of these distributions) to the observed service-time data. (In the case of the exponential distribution, we chose the mean β so that the resulting distribution most closely "resembled" the available data.) We then made 100 independent simulation runs (i.e., different random numbers were used for each run, as discussed in Sec. 7.2) of the queueing system using *each* of the five fitted distributions. Each of the 500 simulation runs was continued until 1000 delays in queue were collected. A summary of the results from these simulation runs is given in Table 6.2. Note in column 2 of the table that the average of the 100,000 delays is given for each of the service-time distributions. As we will see in Sec. 6.7, the Weibull distribution actually provides the best model for the service-time data. Thus, the average delay for the real system should be close to 4.36 minutes. On the other hand, the average delays for the normal and lognormal distributions are 6.04 and 7.19 minutes, respectively, corresponding to

TABLE 6.2
Simulation results for the five service-time distributions (in minutes where appropriate)

Service-time distribution	Average delay in queue	Average number in queue	Proportion of delays ≥ 20
Exponential	6.71	6.78	0.064
Gamma	4.54	4.60	0.019
Weibull	4.36	4.41	0.013
Lognormal	7.19	7.30	0.078
Normal	6.04	6.13	0.045

model output errors of 39 percent and 65 percent. This is particularly surprising for the lognormal distribution, since it has the same general shape (i.e., skewed to the right) as the Weibull distribution. However, it turns out that the lognormal distribution has a "thicker" right tail, which allows larger service times and delays to occur. The relative differences between the "tail probabilities" in column 4 of the table are even more significant. The choice of probability distributions can evidently have a large impact on the simulation output and, potentially, on the quality of the decisions made with the simulation results.

If it is possible to collect data on an input random variable of interest, these data can be used in one of the following approaches to specify a distribution (in increasing order of desirability):

1. The data values themselves are used directly in the simulation. For example, if the data represent service times, then one of the data values is used whenever a service time is needed in the simulation. This is sometimes called a *trace-driven simulation*.
2. The data values themselves are used to define an *empirical* distribution function (see Sec. 6.2.4) in some way. If these data represent service times, we would sample from this distribution when a service time is needed in the simulation.
3. Standard techniques of statistical inference are used to "fit" a *theoretical* distribution form (see Example 6.1), e.g., exponential or Poisson, to the data and to perform hypothesis tests to determine the goodness of fit. If a particular theoretical distribution with certain values for its parameters is a good model for the service-time data, then we would sample from this distribution when a service time is needed in the simulation.

Two drawbacks of approach 1 are that the simulation can only reproduce what has happened historically and that there is seldom enough data to make all the desired simulation runs. Approach 2 avoids these shortcomings since, at least for continuous data, any value between the minimum and maximum observed data points can be generated (see Sec. 8.3.12). Thus, approach 2 is generally preferable to approach 1. It should be mentioned, however, that approach 1 is recommended for *model validation* when comparing model output for an existing system with the corresponding output for the system itself. (See the discussion of the correlated inspection approach in Sec. 5.6.1.)

If a theoretical distribution can be found that fits the observed data reasonably well (approach 3), then this will generally be preferable to using an empirical distribution (approach 2) for the following reasons:

- An empirical distribution function may have certain "irregularities," particularly if only a small number of data values is available. A theoretical distribution, on the other hand, "smooths out" the data and may provide information on the overall underlying distribution.

- If empirical distributions are used in the *usual* way (see Sec. 6.2.4), it is not possible to generate values outside the range of the observed data in the simulation (see Sec. 8.3.12). This is unfortunate, since many measures of performance for simulated systems depend heavily on the probability of an "extreme" event's occurring, e.g., generation of a very large service time. With a fitted theoretical distribution, on the other hand, values outside the range of the observed data can be generated.

- There may be a compelling physical reason in some situations for using a certain theoretical distribution form as a model for a particular input random variable. Even when we are fortunate enough to have this kind of information, it is a good idea to use observed data to provide empirical support for the use of this particular distribution.

- A theoretical distribution is a compact way of representing a set of data values. Conversely, if n data values are available from a continuous distribution, then $2n$ values (data and corresponding cumulative probabilities) must be entered and stored in the computer to represent an empirical distribution in many simulation languages. Thus, use of an empirical distribution will be cumbersome if the data set is large.

There are definitely situations for which no theoretical distribution will provide an adequate fit for the observed data. In these cases we recommend using an empirical distribution. It should also be mentioned that a fourth approach for using observed data to specify a distribution has been proposed by several authors [see, for example, Swain, Venkatraman, and Wilson (1988)]. This approach involves using a general four-parameter family of distributions (e.g., the Johnson translation system) to model all sources of system randomness.

The remainder of this chapter discusses various topics related to the selection of input distributions. Section 6.2 discusses how theoretical distributions are parameterized, provides a compendium of relevant facts on most of the commonly used continuous and discrete distributions, and discusses how empirical distributions can be specified. In Sec. 6.3 we present techniques for determining whether the data are independent observations from some underlying distribution, which is a requirement of many of the statistical procedures in this chapter. Sections 6.4 through 6.6 discuss the three basic activities in specifying a theoretical distribution on the basis of observed data; a comprehensive example illustrating these methods is given in Sec. 6.7. It should be mentioned, however, that choosing a distribution is not necessarily a strictly sequential procedure. Based on the results from one activity, it may be necessary to go back to an earlier activity. In Sec. 6.8 we discuss how certain of the theoretical continuous distributions, e.g., gamma, Weibull, and lognormal, can be "shifted" away from 0 to make them better fit our observed data in some cases. Section 6.9 discusses possible methods for specifying input distributions when no data are available. Several useful probabilistic models for describing the manner in which "customers" arrive to a system are given in Sec. 6.10, while Sec. 6.11 presents techniques for determining whether observations from different sources can be "pooled."

Most of the graphical plots and goodness-of-fit tests presented in this chapter were developed using the UniFit II distribution-fitting package [see Law and Vincent (1990)].

6.2 USEFUL PROBABILITY DISTRIBUTIONS

The purpose of this section is to discuss a variety of distributions that have been found useful in simulation modeling and to provide a unified listing of relevant properties of these distributions [see also Hastings and Peacock (1975)]. Section 6.2.1 provides a short discussion of common methods by which continuous distributions are defined, or parameterized. Then, Secs. 6.2.2 and 6.2.3 contain compilations of several continuous and discrete distributions. Finally, Sec. 6.2.4 suggests how the data themselves can be used directly to define an empirical distribution.

6.2.1 Parameterization of Continuous Distributions

For a given family of continuous distributions, e.g., normal or gamma, there are usually several alternative ways to define, or *parameterize*, the probability density function. However, if the parameters are defined correctly, they can be classified, on the basis of their physical or geometric interpretation, as being one of three basic types: location, scale, or shape parameters.

A *location parameter* γ specifies an abscissa (x axis) location point of a distribution's range of values; usually γ is the midpoint (e.g., the mean μ for a normal distribution) or lower endpoint (see Sec. 6.8) of the distribution's range. (In the latter case, location parameters are sometimes called *shift parameters*.) As γ changes, the associated distribution merely shifts left or right without otherwise changing. A *scale parameter* β determines the scale (or unit) of measurement of the values in the range of the distribution. A change in β compresses or expands the associated distribution without altering its basic form. A *shape parameter* α determines, distinct from location and scale, the basic form or shape of a distribution within the general family of distributions of interest. A change in α generally alters a distribution's properties (e.g., skewness) more fundamentally than a change in location or scale. Some distributions, e.g., exponential and normal, do not have a shape parameter, while others may have several (the beta distribution has two).

6.2.2 Continuous Distributions

Table 6.3 gives information relevant to simulation modeling applications for 10 continuous distributions. Possible applications are given first to indicate some (certainly not all) uses of the distribution [see Hahn and Shapiro (1967) and

TABLE 6.3
Continuous distributions

Uniform	U(a,b)
Possible applications	Used as a "first" model for a quantity that is felt to be randomly varying between a and b but about which little else is known. The $U(0,1)$ distribution is essential in generating random values from all other distributions (see Chaps. 7 and 8)
Density (see Fig. 6.1)	$f(x) = \begin{cases} \dfrac{1}{b-a} & \text{if } a \le x \le b \\ 0 & \text{otherwise} \end{cases}$
Distribution	$F(x) = \begin{cases} 0 & \text{if } x < a \\ \dfrac{x-a}{b-a} & \text{if } a \le x \le b \\ 1 & \text{if } b < x \end{cases}$
Parameters	a and b real numbers with $a < b$; a is a location parameter, $b - a$ is a scale parameter
Range	$[a,b]$
Mean	$\dfrac{a+b}{2}$
Variance	$\dfrac{(b-a)^2}{12}$
Mode	Does not uniquely exist
MLE	$\hat{a} = \min\limits_{1 \le i \le n} X_i, \quad \hat{b} = \max\limits_{1 \le i \le n} X_i$
Comments	1. The $U(0,1)$ distribution is a special case of the beta distribution (when $\alpha_1 = \alpha_2 = 1$)
	2. If $X \sim U(0,1)$ and $[x, x + \Delta x]$ is a subinterval of $[0,1]$ with $\Delta x \ge 0$,

$$P(X \in [x, x + \Delta x]) = \int_x^{x+\Delta x} 1\,dy = (x + \Delta x) - x = \Delta x$$

which justifies the name "uniform"

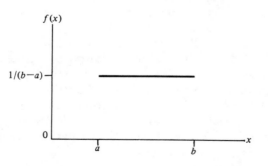

FIGURE 6.1
$U(a,b)$ density function.

Exponential	expo(β)
Possible applications	Interarrival times of "customers" to a system that occur at a constant rate
Density (see Fig. 6.2)	$f(x) = \begin{cases} \dfrac{1}{\beta} e^{-x/\beta} & \text{if } x \ge 0 \\ 0 & \text{otherwise} \end{cases}$

TABLE 6.3 (*continued*)

Exponential	expo(β)

Distribution	$F(x) = \begin{cases} 1 - e^{-x/\beta} & \text{if } x \geq 0 \\ 0 & \text{otherwise} \end{cases}$
Parameter	Scale parameter $\beta > 0$
Range	$[0, \infty)$
Mean	β
Variance	β^2
Mode	0
MLE	$\hat{\beta} = \bar{X}(n)$
Comments	1. The expo(β) distribution is a special case of both the gamma and Weibull distributions (for shape parameter $\alpha = 1$ and scale parameter β in both cases)
	2. If $X_1, X_2, \ldots, X_m$ are independent expo(β) random variables, then $X_1 + X_2 + \cdots + X_m \sim$ gamma(m, β), also called the m-*Erlang distribution*
	3. The exponential distribution is the only continuous distribution with the memoryless property (see Prob. 4.26)

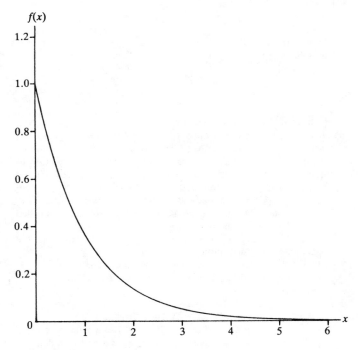

FIGURE 6.2
expo(1) density function.

Gamma	gamma(α, β)

Possible applications	Time to complete some task, e.g., customer service or machine repair

TABLE 6.3 (*continued*)

Gamma	gamma(α, β)

Density (see Fig. 6.3)

$$f(x) = \begin{cases} \dfrac{\beta^{-\alpha} x^{\alpha-1} e^{-x/\beta}}{\Gamma(\alpha)} & \text{if } x > 0 \\ 0 & \text{otherwise} \end{cases}$$

where $\Gamma(\alpha)$ is the *gamma function*, defined by $\Gamma(z) = \int_0^\infty t^{z-1} e^{-t}\, dt$ for any real number $z > 0$. Some properties of the gamma function: $\Gamma(z+1) = z\Gamma(z)$ for any $z > 0$, $\Gamma(k+1) = k!$ for any nonnegative integer k, $\Gamma(k + \frac{1}{2}) = \sqrt{\pi} \cdot 1 \cdot 3 \cdot 5 \cdots (2k-1)/2^k$ for any positive integer k, $\Gamma(1/2) = \sqrt{\pi}$

Distribution
If α is not an integer, there is no closed form. If α is a positive integer, then

$$F(x) = \begin{cases} 1 - e^{-x/\beta} \sum_{j=0}^{\alpha-1} \dfrac{(x/\beta)^j}{j!} & \text{if } x > 0 \\ 0 & \text{otherwise} \end{cases}$$

Parameters | Shape parameter $\alpha > 0$, scale parameter $\beta > 0$
Range | $[0, \infty)$
Mean | $\alpha\beta$
Variance | $\alpha\beta^2$
Mode | $\beta(\alpha - 1)$ if $\alpha \geq 1$, 0 if $\alpha < 1$
MLE | The following two equations must be satisfied:

$$\ln \hat{\beta} + \Psi(\hat{\alpha}) = \frac{\sum_{i=1}^{n} \ln X_i}{n}, \qquad \hat{\alpha}\hat{\beta} = \bar{X}(n)$$

which could be solved numerically. [$\Psi(\hat{\alpha}) = \Gamma'(\hat{\alpha})/\Gamma(\hat{\alpha})$ and is called the *digamma function*; Γ' denotes the derivative of Γ.] Alternatively, approximations to $\hat{\alpha}$ and $\hat{\beta}$ can be obtained by letting $T = [\ln \bar{X}(n) - \sum_{i=1}^{n} \ln X_i/n]^{-1}$, using Table 6.19 (see App. 6A) to obtain $\hat{\alpha}$ as a function of T, and letting $\hat{\beta} = \bar{X}(n)/\hat{\alpha}$. [See Choi and Wette (1969) for the derivation of this procedure and of Table 6.19]

Comments
1. The expo(β) and gamma$(1, \beta)$ distributions are the same
2. For a positive integer m, the gamma(m, β) distribution is called the m-Erlang(β) distribution
3. The chi-square distribution with k df is the same as the gamma$(k/2, 2)$ distribution
4. If $X_1, X_2, \ldots, X_m$ are independent random variables with $X_i \sim$ gamma(α_i, β), then $X_1 + X_2 + \cdots + X_m \sim$ gamma$(\alpha_1 + \alpha_2 + \cdots + \alpha_m, \beta)$
5. If X_1 and X_2 are independent random variables with $X_i \sim$ gamma(α_i, β), then $X_1/(X_1 + X_2) \sim$ beta(α_1, α_2)
6. $X \sim$ gamma(α, β) if and only if $Y = 1/X$ has a Pearson type V distribution with shape and scale parameters α and $1/\beta$, denoted PT5$(\alpha, 1/\beta)$
7.

$$\lim_{x \to 0} f(x) = \begin{cases} \infty & \text{if } \alpha < 1 \\ \dfrac{1}{\beta} & \text{if } \alpha = 1 \\ 0 & \text{if } \alpha > 1 \end{cases}$$

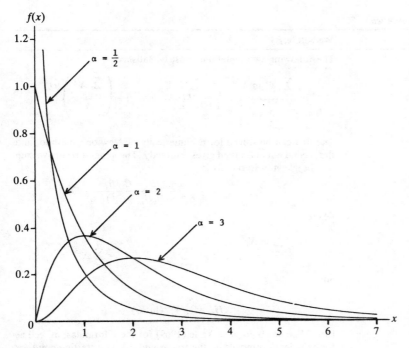

FIGURE 6.3
gamma(α,1) density functions.

TABLE 6.3 (*continued*)

Weibull	Weibull(α, β)
Possible applications	Time to complete some task (density takes on shapes similar to gamma densities), time to failure of a piece of equipment
Density (see Fig. 6.4)	$f(x) = \begin{cases} \alpha\beta^{-\alpha}x^{\alpha-1}e^{-(x/\beta)^{\alpha}} & \text{if } x>0 \\ 0 & \text{otherwise} \end{cases}$
Distribution	$F(x) = \begin{cases} 1 - e^{-(x/\beta)^{\alpha}} & \text{if } x>0 \\ 0 & \text{otherwise} \end{cases}$
Parameters Range	Shape parameter $\alpha > 0$, scale parameter $\beta > 0$ [0,∞)
Mean	$\dfrac{\beta}{\alpha}\Gamma\left(\dfrac{1}{\alpha}\right)$
Variance	$\dfrac{\beta^2}{\alpha}\left\{2\Gamma\left(\dfrac{2}{\alpha}\right) - \dfrac{1}{\alpha}\left[\Gamma\left(\dfrac{1}{\alpha}\right)\right]^2\right\}$
Mode	$\begin{cases} \beta\left(\dfrac{\alpha-1}{\alpha}\right)^{1/\alpha} & \text{if } \alpha \geq 1 \\ 0 & \text{if } \alpha < 1 \end{cases}$

TABLE 6.3 (*continued*)

Weibull	Weibull(α, β)
MLE	The following two equations must be satisfied:

$$\frac{\sum_{i=1}^{n} X_i^{\hat{\alpha}} \ln X_i}{\sum_{i=1}^{n} X_i^{\hat{\alpha}}} - \frac{1}{\hat{\alpha}} = \frac{\sum_{i=1}^{n} \ln X_i}{n}, \qquad \hat{\beta} = \left(\frac{\sum_{i=1}^{n} X_i^{\hat{\alpha}}}{n} \right)^{1/\hat{\alpha}}$$

The first can be solved for $\hat{\alpha}$ numerically by Newton's method, and the second equation then gives $\hat{\beta}$ directly. The general recursive step for the Newton iterations is

$$\hat{\alpha}_{k+1} = \hat{\alpha}_k + \frac{A + 1/\hat{\alpha}_k - C_k/B_k}{1/\hat{\alpha}_k^2 + (B_k H_k - C_k^2)/B_k^2}$$

where

$$A = \frac{\sum_{i=1}^{n} \ln X_i}{n}, \qquad B_k = \sum_{i=1}^{n} X_i^{\hat{\alpha}_k}, \qquad C_k = \sum_{i=1}^{n} X_i^{\hat{\alpha}_k} \ln X_i$$

and

$$H_k = \sum_{i=1}^{n} X_i^{\hat{\alpha}_k} (\ln X_i)^2$$

[See Thoman, Bain, and Antle (1969) for these formulas, as well as for confidence intervals on the true α and β.] As a starting point for the iterations, the estimate

$$\hat{\alpha}_0 = \left\{ \frac{\frac{6}{\pi^2} \left[\sum_{i=1}^{n} (\ln X_i)^2 - \left(\sum_{i=1}^{n} \ln X_i \right)^2 / n \right]}{n - 1} \right\}^{-1/2}$$

[due to Menon (1963) and suggested in Thoman, Bain, and Antle (1969)] may be used. With this choice of $\hat{\alpha}_0$, it was reported in Thoman, Bain, and Antle (1969) that an average of only 3.5 Newton iterations were needed to achieve four-place accuracy.

Comments	1. The expo(β) and Weibull($1, \beta$) distributions are the same

2. $X \sim$ Weibull(α, β) if and only if $X^{\alpha} \sim$ expo(β^{α}) (see Prob. 6.2)
3. The (natural) logarithm of a Weibull random variable has a distribution known as the *extreme-value* or *Gumbel distribution* [see Law and Vincent (1990), Lawless (1982), and Prob. 8.1(*b*)]
4. The Weibull($2, \beta$) distribution is also called a *Rayleigh distribution* with parameter β, denoted Rayleigh(β). If Y and Z are independent normal random variables with mean 0 and variance β^2 (see the normal distribution), then $X = (Y^2 + Z^2)^{1/2} \sim$ Rayleigh($2^{1/2}\beta$)
5. As $\alpha \to \infty$, the Weibull distribution becomes degenerate at β. Thus, Weibull densities for large α have a sharp peak at the mode
6.

$$\lim_{x \to 0} f(x) = \begin{cases} \infty & \text{if } \alpha < 1 \\ \dfrac{1}{\beta} & \text{if } \alpha = 1 \\ 0 & \text{if } \alpha > 1 \end{cases}$$

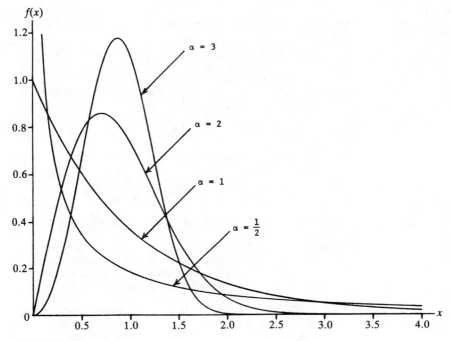

FIGURE 6.4
Weibull(α,1) density functions.

TABLE 6.3 (*continued*)

Normal	$N(\mu,\sigma^2)$
Possible applications	Errors of various types, e.g., in the impact point of a bomb; quantities that are the sum of a large number of other quantities (by virtue of central limit theorems)
Density (see Fig. 6.5)	$f(x) = \dfrac{1}{\sqrt{2\pi\sigma^2}}\, e^{-(x-\mu)^2/2\sigma^2}$ for all real numbers x
Distribution	No closed form
Parameters	Location parameter $\mu \in (-\infty,\infty)$, scale parameter $\sigma > 0$
Range	$(-\infty,\infty)$
Mean	μ
Variance	σ^2
Mode	μ
MLE	$\hat{\mu} = \bar{X}(n)$, $\hat{\sigma} = \left[\dfrac{n-1}{n}\, S^2(n)\right]^{1/2}$
Comments	1. If two jointly distributed normal random variables are uncorrelated, they are also independent. For distributions other than normal, this implication is not true in general

TABLE 6.3 (*continued*)

Normal	$N(\mu,\sigma^2)$

2. Suppose that the joint distribution of $X_1, X_2, \ldots, X_m$ is multivariate normal and let $\mu_i = E(X_i)$ and $C_{ij} = \text{Cov}(X_i, X_j)$. Then for any real numbers $a, b_1, b_2, \ldots, b_m$, the random variable $a + b_1 X_1 + b_2 X_2 + \cdots + b_m X_m$ has a normal distribution with mean $\mu = a + \sum_{i=1}^m b_i \mu_i$ and variance

$$\sigma^2 = \sum_{i=1}^m \sum_{j=1}^m b_i b_j C_{ij}$$

Note that we need *not* assume independence of the X_i's. If the X_i's *are* independent, then

$$\sigma^2 = \sum_{i=1}^m b_i^2 \text{Var}(X_i)$$

3. The $N(0,1)$ distribution is often called the *standard* or *unit normal distribution*
4. If $X_1, X_2, \ldots, X_k$ are independent standard normal random variables, then $X_1^2 + X_2^2 + \cdots + X_k^2$ has a chi-square distribution with k df, which is also the gamma$(k/2,2)$ distribution
5. If $X \sim N(\mu,\sigma^2)$, then e^X has the *lognormal distribution* with parameters μ and σ, denoted $LN(\mu,\sigma^2)$
6. If $X \sim N(0,1)$, if Y has a chi-square distribution with k df, and if X and Y are independent, then $X/\sqrt{Y/k}$ has a t distribution with k df (sometimes called *Student's t distribution*)
7. If the normal distribution is used to represent a nonnegative quantity (e.g., time), then its density should be truncated at $x = 0$ (see Sec. 6.8)
8. As $\sigma \to 0$, the normal distribution becomes degenerate at μ

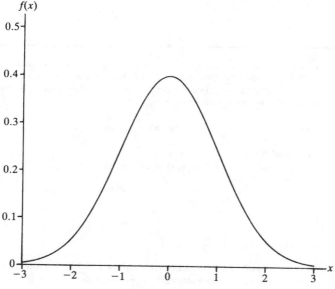

FIGURE 6.5
$N(0,1)$ density function.

TABLE 6.3 (*continued*)

Lognormal	$\mathbf{LN(\mu,\sigma^2)}$

Possible applications
: Time to perform some task [density takes on shapes similar to gamma(α,β) and Weibull(α,β) densities for $\alpha > 1$, but can have a large "spike" close to $x = 0$ that is often useful]; quantities that are the product of a large number of other quantities (by virtue of central limit theorems)

Density (see Fig. 6.6)
: $$f(x) = \begin{cases} \dfrac{1}{x\sqrt{2\pi\sigma^2}} \exp\dfrac{-(\ln x - \mu)^2}{2\sigma^2} & \text{if } x > 0 \\ 0 & \text{otherwise} \end{cases}$$

Distribution
: No closed form

Parameters
: Shape parameter $\sigma > 0$, scale parameter $\mu \in (-\infty,\infty)$

Range
: $[0,\infty)$

Mean
: $e^{\mu+\sigma^2/2}$

Variance
: $e^{2\mu+\sigma^2}(e^{\sigma^2} - 1)$

Mode
: $e^{\mu-\sigma^2}$

MLE
: $$\hat{\mu} = \frac{\sum\limits_{i=1}^{n} \ln X_i}{n}, \qquad \hat{\sigma} = \left[\frac{\sum\limits_{i=1}^{n} (\ln X_i - \hat{\mu})^2}{n}\right]^{1/2}$$

Comments
: 1. $X \sim \text{LN}(\mu,\sigma^2)$ if and only if $\ln X \sim \text{N}(\mu,\sigma^2)$. Thus, if one has data $X_1, X_2, \ldots, X_n$ that are thought to be lognormal, the logarithms of the data points, $\ln X_1, \ln X_2, \ldots, \ln X_n$, can be treated as normally distributed data for purposes of hypothesizing a distribution, parameter estimation, and goodness-of-fit testing
  2. As $\sigma \to 0$, the lognormal distribution becomes degenerate at e^μ. Thus, lognormal densities for small σ have a sharp peak at the mode
  3. $\lim\limits_{x\to 0} f(x) = 0$, regardless of the parameter values

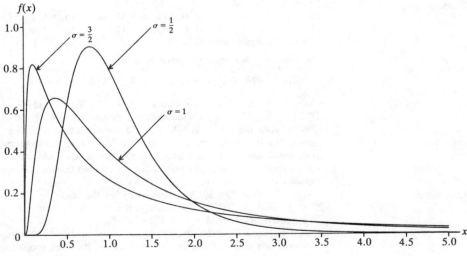

FIGURE 6.6
LN$(0,\sigma^2)$ density functions.

TABLE 6.3 (*continued*)

Beta	beta(α_1, α_2)

Possible applications	Used as a rough model in the absence of data (see Sec. 6.9); distribution of a random proportion, such as the proportion of defective items in a shipment; time to complete a task, e.g., in a PERT network

Density (see Fig. 6.7)

$$f(x) = \begin{cases} \dfrac{x^{\alpha_1-1}(1-x)^{\alpha_2-1}}{B(\alpha_1,\alpha_2)} & \text{if } 0 < x < 1 \\ 0 & \text{otherwise} \end{cases}$$

where $B(\alpha_1, \alpha_2)$ is the *beta function*, defined by

$$B(z_1, z_2) = \int_0^1 t^{z_1-1}(1-t)^{z_2-1}\, dt$$

for any real numbers $z_1 > 0$ and $z_2 > 0$. Some properties of the beta function:

$$B(z_1, z_2) = B(z_2, z_1), \qquad B(z_1, z_2) = \frac{\Gamma(z_1)\Gamma(z_2)}{\Gamma(z_1 + z_2)}$$

Distribution	No closed form, in general. If either α_1 or α_2 is a positive integer, a binomial expansion can be used to obtain $F(x)$, which will be a polynomial in x, and the powers of x will be, in general, positive real numbers ranging from 0 through $\alpha_1 + \alpha_2 - 1$
Parameters	Shape parameters $\alpha_1 > 0$ and $\alpha_2 > 0$
Range	$[0,1]$
Mean	$\dfrac{\alpha_1}{\alpha_1 + \alpha_2}$
Variance	$\dfrac{\alpha_1 \alpha_2}{(\alpha_1 + \alpha_2)^2(\alpha_1 + \alpha_2 + 1)}$

Mode

$$\begin{cases} \dfrac{\alpha_1 - 1}{\alpha_1 + \alpha_2 - 2} & \text{if } \alpha_1 > 1, \alpha_2 > 1 \\ 0 \text{ and } 1 & \text{if } \alpha_1 < 1, \alpha_2 < 1 \\ 0 & \text{if } (\alpha_1 < 1, \alpha_2 \geq 1) \text{ or if } (\alpha_1 = 1, \alpha_2 > 1) \\ 1 & \text{if } (\alpha_1 \geq 1, \alpha_2 < 1) \text{ or if } (\alpha_1 > 1, \alpha_2 = 1) \\ \text{does not uniquely exist} & \text{if } \alpha_1 = \alpha_2 = 1 \end{cases}$$

MLE

The following two equations must be satisfied:

$$\Psi(\hat{\alpha}_1) - \Psi(\hat{\alpha}_1 + \hat{\alpha}_2) = \ln G_1, \qquad \Psi(\hat{\alpha}_2) - \Psi(\hat{\alpha}_1 + \hat{\alpha}_2) = \ln G_2$$

where Ψ is the digamma function, $G_1 = (\prod_{i=1}^n X_i)^{1/n}$, and $G_2 = [\prod_{i=1}^n (1 - X_i)]^{1/n}$ [see Gnanadesikan, Pinkham, and Hughes (1967)]; note that $G_1 + G_2 \leq 1$. These equations could be solved numerically [see Beckman and Tietjen (1978)], or approximations to $\hat{\alpha}_1$ and $\hat{\alpha}_2$ can be obtained from Table 6.20 (see App. 6A), which was computed for particular (G_1, G_2) pairs by modifications of the methods in Beckman and Tietjen (1978)

Comments

1. The U(0,1) and beta(1,1) distributions are the same
2. If X_1 and X_2 are independent random variables with $X_i \sim$ gamma(α_i, β), then $X_1/(X_1 + X_2) \sim$ beta(α_1, α_2)
3. A beta random variable X on $[0,1]$ can be rescaled and relocated to obtain a beta random variable on $[a,b]$ of the same shape by the transformation $a + (b - a)X$

TABLE 6.3 (*continued*)

Beta	beta(α_1, α_2)

4. $X \sim \text{beta}(\alpha_1, \alpha_2)$ if and only if $1 - X \sim \text{beta}(\alpha_2, \alpha_1)$
5. $X \sim \text{beta}(\alpha_1, \alpha_2)$ if and only if $Y = X/(1 - X)$ has a Pearson type VI distribution with shape parameters α_1, α_2 and scale parameter 1, denoted $\text{PT6}(\alpha_1, \alpha_2, 1)$
6. The beta(1,2) density is a left triangle, and the beta(2,1) density is a right triangle
7.

$$\lim_{x \to 0} f(x) = \begin{cases} \infty & \text{if } \alpha_1 < 1 \\ \alpha_2 & \text{if } \alpha_1 = 1 \\ 0 & \text{if } \alpha_1 > 1 \end{cases}, \qquad \lim_{x \to 1} f(x) = \begin{cases} \infty & \text{if } \alpha_2 < 1 \\ \alpha_1 & \text{if } \alpha_2 = 1 \\ 0 & \text{if } \alpha_2 > 1 \end{cases}$$

8. The density is symmetric about $x = \frac{1}{2}$ if and only if $\alpha_1 = \alpha_2$. Also, the mean and the mode are equal if and only if $\alpha_1 = \alpha_2$

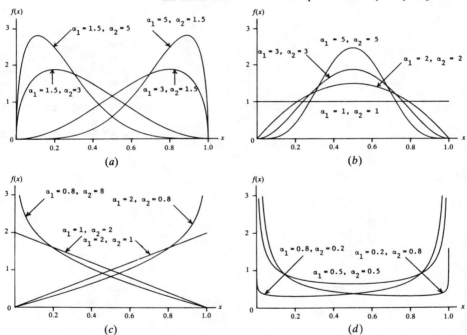

FIGURE 6.7
beta(α_1, α_2) density functions.

Pearson type V	PT5(α, β)
Possible applications	Time to perform some task (density takes on shapes similar to lognormal, but can have a larger "spike" close to $x = 0$)
Density (see Fig. 6.8)	$f(x) = \begin{cases} \dfrac{x^{-(\alpha+1)} e^{-\beta/x}}{\beta^{-\alpha} \Gamma(\alpha)} & \text{if } x > 0 \\ 0 & \text{otherwise} \end{cases}$

TABLE 6.3 (*continued*)

Pearson type V	PT5(α, β)

Distribution

$$F(x) = \begin{cases} 1 - F_G\left(\dfrac{1}{x}\right) & \text{if } x > 0 \\ 0 & \text{otherwise} \end{cases}$$

where $F_G(x)$ is the distribution function of a gamma$(\alpha, 1/\beta)$ random variable

Parameters   Shape parameter $\alpha > 0$, scale parameter $\beta > 0$

Range $[0, \infty)$

Mean $\dfrac{\beta}{\alpha - 1}$ for $\alpha > 1$

Variance $\dfrac{\beta^2}{(\alpha - 1)^2(\alpha - 2)}$ for $\alpha > 2$

Mode $\dfrac{\beta}{\alpha + 1}$

MLE   If one has data $X_1, X_2, \ldots, X_n$, then fit a gamma(α_G, β_G) distribution to $1/X_1, 1/X_2, \ldots, 1/X_n$, resulting in the maximum-likelihood estimators $\hat{\alpha}_G$ and $\hat{\beta}_G$. Then the maximum-likelihood estimators for the PT5(α, β) are $\hat{\alpha} = \hat{\alpha}_G$ and $\hat{\beta} = 1/\hat{\beta}_G$ (see comment 1 below)

Comments
1. $X \sim \text{PT5}(\alpha, \beta)$ if and only if $Y = 1/X \sim \text{gamma}(\alpha, 1/\beta)$. Thus, the Pearson type V distribution is sometimes called the *inverted gamma distribution*
2. Note that the mean and variance exist only for certain values of the shape parameter

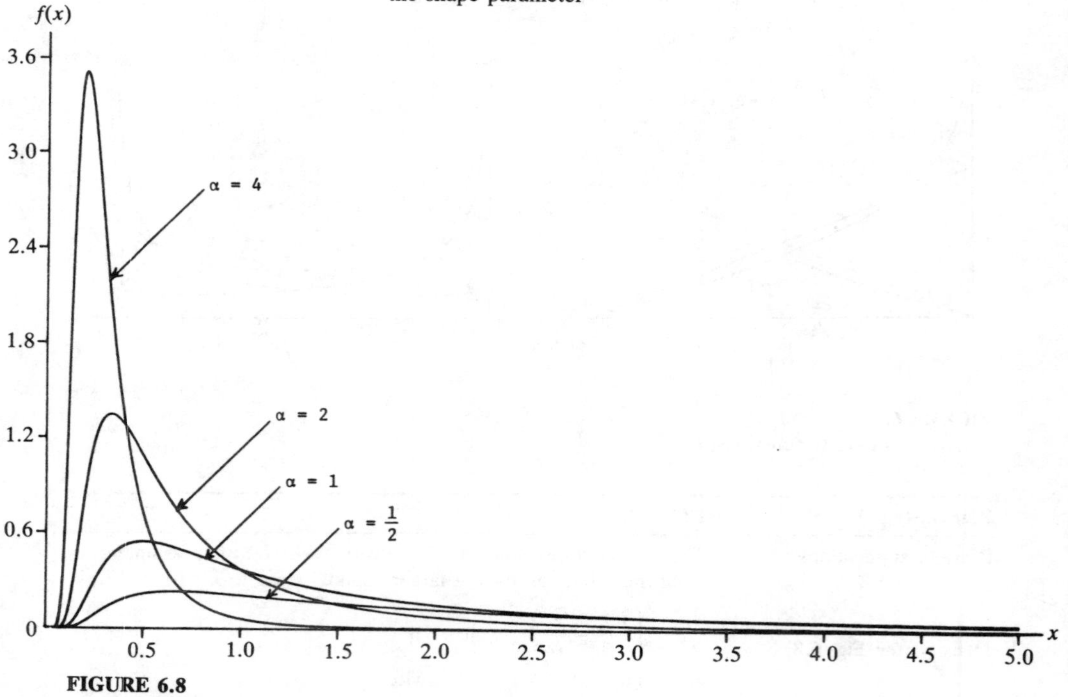

FIGURE 6.8
PT5$(\alpha, 1)$ density functions.

TABLE 6.3 (*continued*)

Pearson type VI	**PT6($\alpha_1, \alpha_2, \beta$)**

Possible applications	Time to perform some task
Density (see Fig. 6.9)	$f(x) = \begin{cases} \dfrac{(x/\beta)^{\alpha_1 - 1}}{\beta B(\alpha_1, \alpha_2)[1 + (x/\beta)]^{\alpha_1 + \alpha_2}} & \text{if } x > 0 \\ 0 & \text{otherwise} \end{cases}$
Distribution	$F(x) = \begin{cases} F_B\left(\dfrac{x}{x + \beta}\right) & \text{if } x > 0 \\ 0 & \text{otherwise} \end{cases}$
	where $F_B(x)$ is the distribution function of a beta(α_1, α_2) random variable
Parameters	Shape parameters $\alpha_1 > 0$ and $\alpha_2 > 0$, scale parameter $\beta > 0$
Range	$[0, \infty)$
Mean	$\dfrac{\beta \alpha_1}{\alpha_2 - 1}$ for $\alpha_2 > 1$
Variance	$\dfrac{\beta^2 \alpha_1 (\alpha_1 + \alpha_2 - 1)}{(\alpha_2 - 1)^2 (\alpha_2 - 2)}$ for $\alpha_2 > 2$
Mode	$\begin{cases} \dfrac{\beta(\alpha_1 - 1)}{\alpha_2 + 1} & \text{if } \alpha_1 \geq 1 \\ 0 & \text{otherwise} \end{cases}$
MLE	If one has data $X_1, X_2, \ldots, X_n$ that are thought to be PT6($\alpha_1, \alpha_2, 1$), then fit a beta(α_1, α_2) distribution to $X_i/(1 + X_i)$ for $i = 1, 2, \ldots, n$, resulting in the maximum-likelihood estimators $\hat{\alpha}_1$ and $\hat{\alpha}_2$. Then the maximum-likelihood estimators for the PT6($\alpha_1, \alpha_2, 1$) (note that $\beta = 1$) distribution are also $\hat{\alpha}_1$ and $\hat{\alpha}_2$ (see comment 1 below)
Comments	1. $X \sim$ PT6($\alpha_1, \alpha_2, 1$) if and only if $Y = X/(1 + X) \sim$ beta(α_1, α_2)
	2. If X_1 and X_2 are independent random variables with $X_i \sim$ gamma(α_i, β), then $Y = X_1/X_2 \sim$ PT6($\alpha_1, \alpha_2, \beta$) (see Prob. 6.3)
	3. Note that the mean and variance exist only for certain values of the shape parameter α_2

Triangular	**triang(a, b, c)**

Possible applications	Used as a rough model in the absence of data (see Sec. 6.9)
Density (see Fig. 6.10)	$f(x) = \begin{cases} \dfrac{2(x - a)}{(b - a)(c - a)} & \text{if } a \leq x \leq c \\ \dfrac{2(b - x)}{(b - a)(b - c)} & \text{if } c < x \leq b \\ 0 & \text{otherwise} \end{cases}$
Distribution	$F(x) = \begin{cases} 0 & \text{if } x < a \\ \dfrac{(x - a)^2}{(b - a)(c - a)} & \text{if } a \leq x \leq c \\ 1 - \dfrac{(b - x)^2}{(b - a)(b - c)} & \text{if } c < x \leq b \\ 1 & \text{if } b < x \end{cases}$
Parameters	a, b, and c real numbers with $a < c < b$. a is a location parameter, $b - a$ is a scale parameter, c is a shape parameter
Range	$[a, b]$

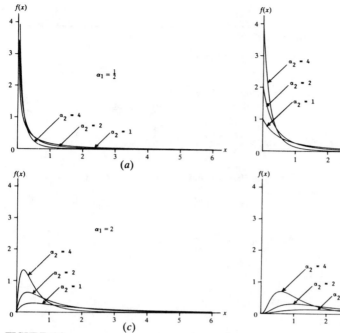

FIGURE 6.9
PT6($\alpha_1,\alpha_2,1$) density functions.

TABLE 6.3 (*continued*)

Triangular	triang(a,b,c)
Mean	$\dfrac{a + b + c}{3}$
Variance	$\dfrac{a^2 + b^2 + c^2 - ab - ac - bc}{18}$
Mode	c
MLE	Our use of the triangular distribution, as described in Sec. 6.9, is as a rough model when there are no data. Thus, MLEs are not relevant
Comment	The limiting cases as $c \to b$ and $c \to a$ are called the *right triangular* and *left triangular distributions*, respectively, and are discussed in Prob. 8.7. For $a = 0$ and $b = 1$, both the left and right triangular distributions are special cases of the beta distribution

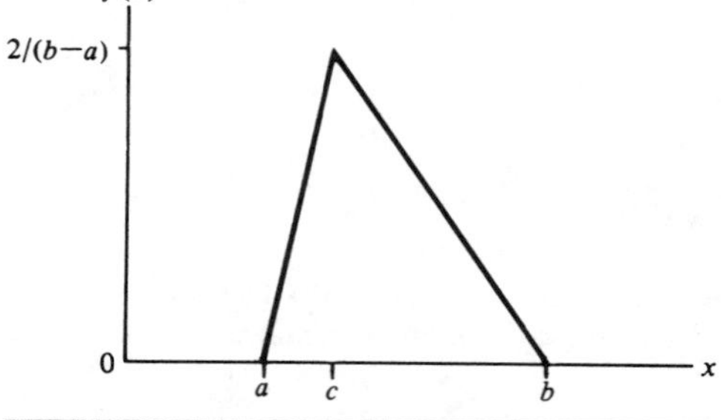

FIGURE 6.10
triang(a,b,c) density functions.

Lawless (1982) for other applications]. Then the density function and distribution function (if it exists in simple closed form) are listed. Next is a short description of the parameters, including their possible values. The range indicates the interval where the associated random variable can take on values. Also listed are the mean (expected value), variance, and mode, i.e., the value at which the density function is maximized. MLE refers to the maximum-likelihood estimator(s) of the parameter(s), treated later in Sec. 6.5. General comments include relationships of the distribution under study to other distributions. Graphs are given of the density functions for each distribution. The notation following the name of each distribution is our abbreviation for that distribution, which includes the parameters. The symbol $\sim$ is read "is distributed as."

Note that we have included the less familiar Pearson type V and Pearson type VI distributions, because we have found that these distributions often provide a better fit to data sets whose histograms are skewed to the right (see Fig. 6.19) than standard distributions such as gamma, Weibull, and lognormal.

6.2.3 Discrete Distributions

The descriptions of the six discrete distributions in Table 6.4 follow the same pattern as for the continuous distributions in Table 6.3.

TABLE 6.4
Discrete distributions

Bernoulli	Bernoulli(p)
Possible applications	Random occurrence with two possible outcomes; used to generate other discrete random variates, e.g., binomial, geometric, and negative binomial
Mass (see Fig. 6.11)	$p(x) = \begin{cases} 1-p & \text{if } x=0 \\ p & \text{if } x=1 \\ 0 & \text{otherwise} \end{cases}$
Distribution	$F(x) = \begin{cases} 0 & \text{if } x<0 \\ 1-p & \text{if } 0 \le x<1 \\ 1 & \text{if } 1 \le x \end{cases}$
Parameter	$p \in (0,1)$
Range	$\{0,1\}$
Mean	p
Variance	$p(1-p)$
Mode	$\begin{cases} 0 & \text{if } p<\frac{1}{2} \\ 0 \text{ and } 1 & \text{if } p=\frac{1}{2} \\ 1 & \text{if } p>\frac{1}{2} \end{cases}$
MLE	$\hat{p} = \bar{X}(n)$
Comments	1. A Bernoulli(p) random variable X can be thought of as the outcome of an experiment that either "fails" or "succeeds." If the probability of success is p, and we let $X=0$ if the experiment

TABLE 6.4 (*continued*)

Bernoulli	Bernoulli(p)

fails and $X = 1$ if it succeeds, then $X \sim$ Bernoulli(p). Such an experiment, often called a *Bernoulli trial*, provides a convenient way of relating several other discrete distributions to the Bernoulli distribution

2. If t is a positive integer and $X_1, X_2, \ldots, X_t$ are independent Bernoulli(p) random variables, $X_1 + X_2 + \cdots + X_t$ has the binomial distribution with parameters t and p. Thus, a binomial random variable can be thought of as the number of successes in a fixed number of independent Bernoulli trials

3. Suppose we begin making independent replications of a Bernoulli trial with probability p of success on each trial. Then the number of failures *before* observing the first success has a geometric distribution with parameter p. For a positive integer s, the number of failures before observing the sth success has a negative binomial distribution with parameters s and p

4. The Bernoulli(p) distribution is a special case of the binomial distribution (with $t = 1$ and the same value for p)

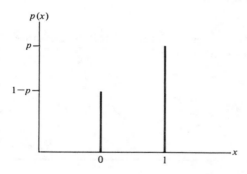

FIGURE 6.11
Bernoulli(p) mass function ($p > 0.5$ here).

Discrete uniform	DU(i, j)
Possible applications	Random occurrence with several possible outcomes, each of which is equally likely; used as a "first" model for a quantity that is varying among the integers i through j but about which little else is known

Mass (see Fig. 6.12)

$$p(x) = \begin{cases} \dfrac{1}{j - i + 1} & \text{if } x \in \{i, i+1, \ldots, j\} \\ 0 & \text{otherwise} \end{cases}$$

Distribution

$$F(x) = \begin{cases} 0 & \text{if } x < i \\ \dfrac{\lfloor x \rfloor - i + 1}{j - i + 1} & \text{if } i \leq x \leq j \\ 1 & \text{if } j < x \end{cases}$$

where $\lfloor x \rfloor$ denotes the largest integer $\leq x$

Parameters $\quad$ i and j integers with $i \leq j$; i is a location parameter, $j - i$ is a scale parameter

Range $\quad$ $\{i, i+1, \ldots, j\}$

TABLE 6.4 (*continued*)

Discrete uniform	DU(i, j)
Mean	$\dfrac{i + j}{2}$
Variance	$\dfrac{(j - i + 1)^2 - 1}{12}$
Mode	Does not uniquely exist
MLE	$\hat{i} = \min_{1 \leq k \leq n} X_k, \qquad \hat{j} = \max_{1 \leq k \leq n} X_k$
Comment	The DU$(0,1)$ and Bernoulli$(\frac{1}{2})$ distributions are the same

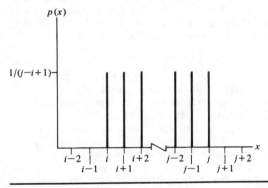

FIGURE 6.12
DU(i, j) mass function.

Binomial	bin(t, p)
Possible applications	Number of successes in t independent Bernoulli trials with probability p of success on each trial; number of "defective" items in a batch of size t; number of items in a batch (e.g., a group of people) of random size; number of items demanded from an inventory
Mass (see Fig. 6.13)	$p(x) = \begin{cases} \dbinom{t}{x} p^x (1 - p)^{t - x} & \text{if } x \in \{0, 1, \ldots, t\} \\ 0 & \text{otherwise} \end{cases}$ where $\dbinom{t}{x}$ is the *binomial coefficient*, defined by $$\binom{t}{x} = \frac{t!}{x!(t - x)!}$$
Distribution	$F(x) = \begin{cases} 0 & \text{if } x < 0 \\ \displaystyle\sum_{i=0}^{\lfloor x \rfloor} \dbinom{t}{i} p^i (1 - p)^{t - i} & \text{if } 0 \leq x \leq t \\ 1 & \text{if } t < x \end{cases}$
Parameters	t a positive integer, $p \in (0,1)$
Range	$\{0, 1, \ldots, t\}$
Mean	tp
Variance	$tp(1 - p)$
Mode	$\begin{cases} p(t + 1) - 1 \text{ and } p(t + 1) & \text{if } p(t + 1) \text{ is an integer} \\ \lfloor p(t + 1) \rfloor & \text{otherwise} \end{cases}$
MLE	If t is known, then $\hat{p} = \bar{X}(n)/t$. If both t and p are unknown, then $\hat{t}$ and $\hat{p}$ exist if and only if $\bar{X}(n) > (n - 1)S^2(n)/n = V(n)$. Then the

TABLE 6.4 (*continued*)

Binomial	bin(t, p)

following approach could be taken. Let $M = \max\limits_{1 \le i \le n} X_i$, and for $k = 0, 1, \ldots, M$, let f_k be the number of X_i's $\ge k$. Then it can be shown that $\hat{t}$ and $\hat{p}$ are the values for t and p that maximize the function

$$g(t, p) = \sum_{k=1}^{M} f_k \ln (t - k + 1) + nt \ln (1 - p) + n\bar{X}(n) \ln \frac{p}{1 - p}$$

subject to the constraints that $t \in \{M, M+1, \ldots\}$ and $0 < p < 1$. It is easy to see that for a fixed value of t, say t_0, the value of p that maximizes $g(t_0, p)$ is $\bar{X}(n)/t_0$, so $\hat{t}$ and $\hat{p}$ are the values of t and $\bar{X}(n)/t$ that lead to the largest value of $g[t, \bar{X}(n)/t]$ for $t \in \{M, M+1, \ldots, M'\}$, where M' is given by [see DeRiggi (1983)]

$$M' = \left\lfloor \frac{\bar{X}(n)(M - 1)}{1 - [V(n)/\bar{X}(n)]} \right\rfloor$$

Note also that $g[t, \bar{X}(n)/t]$ is a unimodal function of t

Comments
1. If $Y_1, Y_2, \ldots, Y_t$ are independent Bernoulli(p) random variables, then $Y_1 + Y_2 + \cdots + Y_t \sim \text{bin}(t, p)$
2. If $X_1, X_2, \ldots, X_m$ are independent random variables and $X_i \sim \text{bin}(t_i, p)$, then $X_1 + X_2 + \cdots + X_m \sim \text{bin}(t_1 + t_2 + \cdots + t_m, p)$
3. The bin(t, p) distribution is symmetric if and only if $p = \frac{1}{2}$
4. $X \sim \text{bin}(t, p)$ if and only if $t - X \sim \text{bin}(t, 1 - p)$
5. The bin($1, p$) and Bernoulli(p) distributions are the same

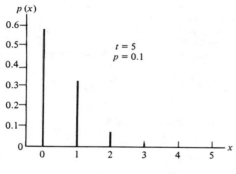

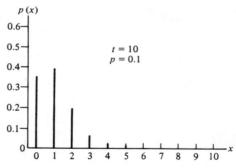

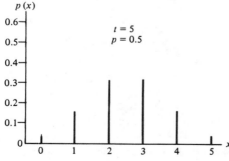

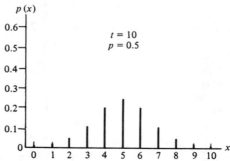

FIGURE 6.13
bin(t, p) mass functions.

TABLE 6.4 (*continued*)

Geometric	geom(*p*)

Possible applications	Number of failures before the first success in a sequence of independent Bernoulli trials with probability *p* of success on each trial; number of items inspected before encountering the first defective item; number of items in a batch of random size; number of items demanded from an inventory
Mass (see Fig. 6.14)	$p(x) = \begin{cases} p(1-p)^x & \text{if } x \in \{0, 1, \ldots\} \\ 0 & \text{otherwise} \end{cases}$
Distribution	$F(x) = \begin{cases} 1 - (1-p)^{\lfloor x \rfloor + 1} & \text{if } x \geq 0 \\ 0 & \text{otherwise} \end{cases}$
Parameter	$p \in (0,1)$
Range	$\{0, 1, \ldots\}$
Mean	$\dfrac{1-p}{p}$
Variance	$\dfrac{1-p}{p^2}$
Mode	0
MLE	$\hat{p} = \dfrac{1}{\bar{X}(n) + 1}$
Comments	1. If $Y_1, Y_2, \ldots$ is a sequence of independent Bernoulli(*p*) random variables and $X = \min\{i : Y_i = 1\} - 1$, then $X \sim \text{geom}(p)$. 2. If $X_1, X_2, \ldots, X_s$ are independent geom(*p*) random variables, then $X_1 + X_2 + \cdots + X_s$ has a negative binomial distribution with parameters *s* and *p* 3. The geometric distribution is the discrete analog of the exponential distribution, in the sense that it is the only discrete distribution with the memoryless property (see Prob. 4.27) 4. The geom(*p*) distribution is a special case of the negative binomial distribution (with $s = 1$ and the same value for *p*)

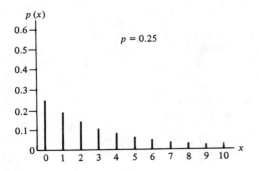
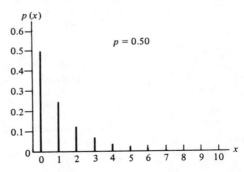

FIGURE 6.14
geom(*p*) mass functions.

TABLE 6.4 (*continued*)

Negative binomial	negbin(s, p)

Possible applications	Number of failures before the sth success in a sequence of indepen- dent Bernoulli trials with probability p of success on each trial; number of good items inspected before encountering the sth defec- tive item; number of items in a batch of random size; number of items demanded from an inventory
Mass (see Fig. 6.15)	$$p(x) = \begin{cases} \binom{s+x-1}{x} p^s (1-p)^x & \text{if } x \in \{0, 1, \ldots\} \\ 0 & \text{otherwise} \end{cases}$$
Distribution	$$F(x) = \begin{cases} \sum_{i=0}^{\lfloor x \rfloor} \binom{s+i-1}{i} p^s (1-p)^i & \text{if } x \geq 0 \\ 0 & \text{otherwise} \end{cases}$$
Parameters Range	s a positive integer, $p \in (0,1)$ $\{0, 1, \ldots\}$
Mean	$\dfrac{s(1-p)}{p}$
Variance	$\dfrac{s(1-p)}{p^2}$
Mode	Let $y = [s(1-p)-1]/p$; then $$\text{Mode} = \begin{cases} y \text{ and } y+1 & \text{if } y \text{ is an integer} \\ \lfloor y \rfloor + 1 & \text{otherwise} \end{cases}$$
MLE	If s is known, then $\hat{p} = s/[\bar{X}(n) + s]$. If both s and p are unknown, then $\hat{s}$ and $\hat{p}$ exist if and only if $V(n) = (n-1)S^2(n)/n > \bar{X}(n)$. Let $M = \max_{1 \leq i \leq n} X_i$, and for $k = 0, 1, \ldots, M$, let f_k be the number of X_i's $\geq k$. Then we can show that $\hat{s}$ and $\hat{p}$ are the values for s and p that maximize the function $$h(s,p) = \sum_{k=1}^{M} f_k \ln(s+k-1) + ns \ln p + n\bar{X}(n) \ln(1-p)$$ subject to the constraints that $s \in \{1, 2, \ldots\}$ and $0 < p < 1$. For a fixed value of s, say s_0, the value of p that maximizes $h(s_0,p)$ is $s_0/[\bar{X}(n) + s_0]$, so that we could examine $h(1, 1/[\bar{X}(n) + 1])$, $h(2, 2/[\bar{X}(n) + 2]), \ldots$ Then $\hat{s}$ and $\hat{p}$ are chosen to be the values of s and $s/[\bar{X}(n) + s]$ that lead to the biggest observed value of $h(s, s/[\bar{X}(n) + s])$. However, since $h(s,s/[\bar{X}(n) + s])$ is a unimodal function of s [see Levin and Reeds (1977)], it is clear when to terminate the search
Comments	1. If $Y_1, Y_2, \ldots, Y_s$ are independent geom(p) random variables, then $Y_1 + Y_2 + \cdots + Y_s \sim$ negbin(s, p) 2. If $Y_1, Y_2, \ldots$ is a sequence of independent Bernoulli(p) random variables and $X = \min\{i: \Sigma_{j=1}^{i} Y_j = s\} - s$, then $X \sim$ negbin(s, p) 3. If $X_1, X_2, \ldots, X_m$ are independent random variables and $X_i \sim$ negbin(s_i, p), then $X_1 + X_2 + \cdots + X_m \sim$ negbin$(s_1 + s_2 + \cdots + s_m, p)$ 4. The negbin$(1, p)$ and geom(p) distributions are the same

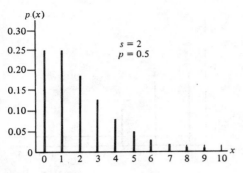

FIGURE 6.15
negbin(s, p) mass functions.

TABLE 6.4 (*continued*)

Poisson	Poisson(λ)
Possible applications	Number of events that occur in an interval of time when the events are occuring at a constant rate (see Sec. 6.10); number of items in a batch of random size; number of items demanded from an inventory

Mass (see Fig. 6.16)

$$p(x) = \begin{cases} \dfrac{e^{-\lambda}\lambda^x}{x!} & \text{if } x \in \{0, 1, \ldots\} \\ 0 & \text{otherwise} \end{cases}$$

Distribution

$$F(x) = \begin{cases} 0 & \text{if } x < 0 \\ e^{-\lambda} \displaystyle\sum_{i=0}^{\lfloor x \rfloor} \dfrac{\lambda^i}{i!} & \text{if } 0 \le x \end{cases}$$

Parameter	$\lambda > 0$
Range	$\{0, 1, \ldots\}$
Mean	λ
Variance	λ

Mode

$$\begin{cases} \lambda - 1 \text{ and } \lambda & \text{if } \lambda \text{ is an integer} \\ \lfloor \lambda \rfloor & \text{otherwise} \end{cases}$$

MLE $\quad \hat{\lambda} = \bar{X}(n)$

Comments
1. Let $Y_1, Y_2, \ldots$ be a sequence of nonnegative IID random variables, and let $X = \max\{i: \Sigma_{j=1}^{i} Y_j \le 1\}$. Then the distribution of the Y_i's is expo($1/\lambda$) if and only if $X \sim$ Poisson(λ). Also, if $X' = \max\{i: \Sigma_{j=1}^{i} Y_j \le \lambda\}$, then the Y_i's are expo(1) if and only if $X' \sim$ Poisson(λ) (see also Sec. 6.10)
2. If $X_1, X_2, \ldots, X_m$ are independent random variables and $X_i \sim$ Poisson(λ_i), then $X_1 + X_2 + \cdots + X_m \sim$ Poisson($\lambda_1 + \lambda_2 + \cdots + \lambda_m$)

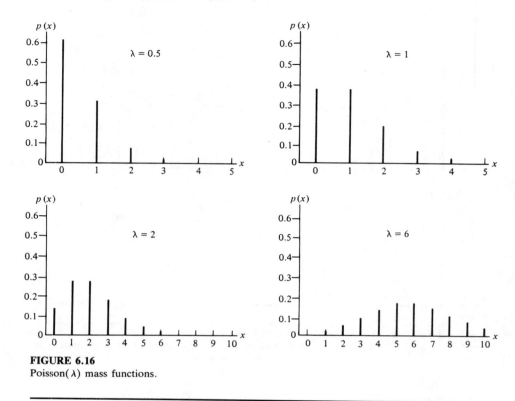

FIGURE 6.16
Poisson(λ) mass functions.

6.2.4 Empirical Distributions

In some situations we might want to use the observed data themselves to specify directly (in some sense) a distribution, called an *empirical distribution*, from which random values are generated during the simulation, rather than fitting a theoretical distribution to the data. For example, it could happen that we simply cannot find a theoretical distribution that fits the data adequately (see Secs. 6.4 through 6.6). This section explores ways of specifying empirical distributions.

For continuous random variables, the type of empirical distribution that can be defined depends on whether we have the actual values of the individual original observations $X_1, X_2, \ldots, X_n$ rather than only the *number* of X_i's that fall into each of several specified intervals. (The latter case is called *grouped data* or *data in the form of a histogram.*) If the original data are available, we can define a continuous, piecewise-linear distribution function F by first sorting the X_i's into increasing order. Let $X_{(i)}$ denote the ith smallest of the X_j's, so that $X_{(1)} \leq X_{(2)} \leq \cdots \leq X_{(n)}$. Then F is given by

$$F(x) = \begin{cases} 0 & \text{if } x < X_{(1)} \\ \dfrac{i-1}{n-1} + \dfrac{x - X_{(i)}}{(n-1)(X_{(i+1)} - X_{(i)})} & \begin{aligned} &\text{if } X_{(i)} \leq x < X_{(i+1)} \\ &\quad \text{for } i = 1, 2, \ldots, n-1 \end{aligned} \\ 1 & \text{if } X_{(n)} \leq x \end{cases}$$

Figure 6.17 gives an illustration for $n = 6$. Note that $F(x)$ rises most rapidly over those ranges of x in which the X_i's are most densely distributed, as desired. Also, for each i, $F(X_{(i)}) = (i-1)/(n-1)$, which is approximately (for large n) the proportion of the X_j's that are *less than* $X_{(i)}$; this is also the way we would like a *continuous* distribution function to behave. (See Prob. 6.5 for a discussion of other ways to define F.) However, one clear disadvantage of specifying this particular empirical distribution is that random values generated from it during a simulation run can never be less than $X_{(1)}$ or greater than $X_{(n)}$ (see Sec. 8.3.12). Also, the mean of $F(x)$ is not equal to the sample mean $\bar{X}(n)$ of the X_i's (see Prob. 6.6).

If, on the other hand, the data are grouped, a different approach must be taken since we do not know the values of the individual X_i's. Suppose that the n X_i's are grouped into k adjacent intervals $[a_0, a_1)$, $[a_1, a_2)$, $\ldots$, $[a_{k-1}, a_k)$, so that the jth interval contains n_j observations, where $n_1 + n_2 + \cdots + n_k = n$. (Often the a_j's will be equally spaced, but we need not make this assumption.) A reasonable piecewise-linear empirical distribution function G could be specified by first letting $G(a_0) = 0$ and $G(a_j) = (n_1 + n_2 + \cdots + n_j)/n$ for $j = 1, 2, \ldots, k$. Then, interpolating linearly between the a_j's, we define

$$G(x) = \begin{cases} 0 & \text{if } x < a_0 \\ G(a_{j-1}) + \dfrac{x - a_{j-1}}{a_j - a_{j-1}} [G(a_j) - G(a_{j-1})] & \begin{aligned} &\text{if } a_{j-1} \leq x < a_j \\ &\quad \text{for } j = 1, 2, \ldots, k \end{aligned} \\ 1 & \text{if } a_k \leq x \end{cases}$$

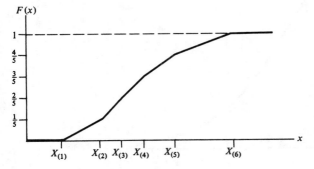

FIGURE 6.17
Continuous, piecewise-linear empirical distribution function from original data.

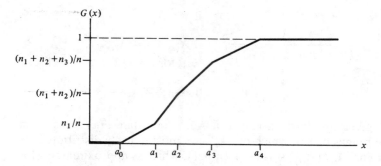

FIGURE 6.18
Continuous, piecewise-linear empirical distribution function from grouped data.

Figure 6.18 illustrates this specification of an empirical distribution for $k = 4$. In this case, $G(a_j)$ is the proportion of the X_i's that are less than a_j, and $G(x)$ rises most rapidly over ranges of x where the observations are most dense. The random values generated from this distribution, however, will still be bounded both below (by a_0) and above (by a_k); see Sec. 8.3.12.

In practice, many continuous distributions are skewed to the right and have a density with a shape similar to that in Fig. 6.19. Thus, if the sample size n is not very large, we are likely to have few, if any, observations from the right tail of the true underlying distribution (since these tail probabilities are usually small). Moreover, the above empirical distributions do not allow random values to be generated beyond the largest observation. On the other

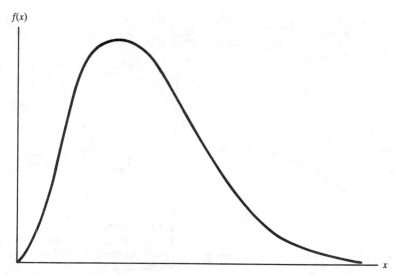

FIGURE 6.19
Typical density function experienced in practice.

hand, very large generated values can have a significant impact on the disposition of a simulation run. For example, a large service time can cause considerable congestion in a queueing-type system. As a result, Bratley, Fox, and Schrage (1987, pp. 131–133, 150–151) suggest appending an exponential distribution to the right side of the empirical distribution, which allows values larger than $X_{(n)}$ to be generated.

For discrete data, it is quite simple to define an empirical distribution, provided that the original data values $X_1, X_2 \ldots, X_n$ are available. For each possible value x, an empirical mass function $p(x)$ can be defined to be the proportion of the X_i's that are equal to x. For grouped discrete data we could define a mass function such that the *sum* of the $p(x)$'s over all possible values of x in an interval is equal to the proportion of the X_i's in that interval. How the individual $p(x)$'s are allocated for the possible values of x within an interval is essentially arbitrary.

6.3 TECHNIQUES FOR ASSESSING SAMPLE INDEPENDENCE

An important assumption made by many of the statistical techniques discussed in this chapter is that the observations $X_1, X_2, \ldots, X_n$ are an *independent* (or *random*) sample from some underlying distribution. For example, maximum-likelihood estimation (see Sec. 6.5) and chi-square tests (see Sec. 6.6.2) assume independence. If the assumption of independence is not satisfied, then these statistical techniques may not be valid. However, even when the data are not independent, heuristic techniques such as histograms can still be used.

It is sometimes the case that observations collected over time are dependent. For example, suppose that $X_1, X_2, \ldots$ represent hourly temperatures in a certain city starting at noon on a particular day. We would not expect these data to be independent, since hourly temperatures close together in time should be positively correlated. As a second example, consider the single-server queueing system in Sec. 1.4. Let $X_1, X_2, \ldots$ be the delays in queue of the successive customers arriving to the system. If the arrival rate of customers is close to the service rate, the system will be congested and the X_i's will be highly positively correlated (see Sec. 4.3).

We now describe two graphical techniques for informally assessing whether the data $X_1, X_2, \ldots, X_n$ (listed in time order of collection) are independent. The *correlation plot* is a graph of the sample correlation $\hat{\rho}_j$ (see Sec. 4.4) for $j = 1, 2, \ldots, l$ (l a positive integer). The sample correlation $\hat{\rho}_j$ is an estimate of the true correlation, ρ_j, between two observations that are j observations apart in time. (Note that $-1 \le \rho_j \le 1$.) If the observations $X_1, X_2, \ldots, X_n$ are independent, then $\rho_j = 0$ for $j = 1, 2, \ldots, n - 1$. However, the $\hat{\rho}_j$'s will not be exactly zero even when the X_i's are independent, since $\hat{\rho}_j$ is an observation of a random variable whose mean is not equal to 0 (see Sec. 4.4). If the $\hat{\rho}_j$'s differ from 0 by a significant amount, then this is strong evidence that the X_i's are not independent.

The *scatter diagram* of the observations $X_1, X_2, \ldots, X_n$ is a plot of the pairs (X_i, X_{i+1}) for $i = 1, 2, \ldots, n-1$. Suppose for simplicity that the X_i's are nonnegative. If the X_i's are independent, one would expect the points (X_i, X_{i+1}) to be scattered randomly throughout the first quadrant of the (X_i, X_{i+1}) plane. The nature of the scattering will, however, depend on the underlying distributions of the X_i's. If the X_i's are positively correlated, then the points will tend to lie along a line with positive slope in the first quadrant. If the X_i's are negatively correlated, then the points will tend to lie along a line with negative slope in the first quadrant.

Example 6.2. In Figs. 6.20 and 6.21 we give the correlation plot and scatter diagram for 100 *independent* observations from an exponential distribution with a mean of 1. Note in Fig. 6.20 that the sample correlations are close to 0, but have absolute values as large as 0.16. The scattering of the points in Fig. 6.21 substantiates the independence of the exponential data.

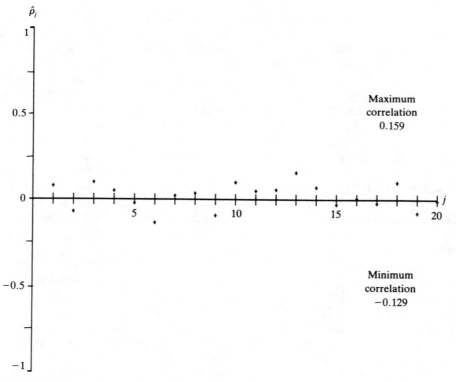

FIGURE 6.20
Correlation plot for independent exponential data.

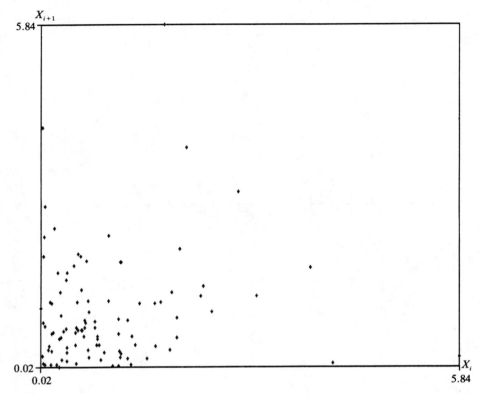

FIGURE 6.21
Scatter diagram for independent exponential data.

Example 6.3. In Figs. 6.22 and 6.23 we present the correlation plot and scatter diagram for 100 delays in queue from an $M/M/1$ queueing system (see Sec. 1.4.3) with utilization factor $\rho = 0.8$. Note that the $\hat{\rho}_j$'s are large for small values of j and that the points in the scatter diagram tend to lie along a line with positive slope. These facts are consistent with our statement that delays in queue are positively correlated.

There are also several nonparametric (i.e., no assumptions are made about the distributions of the X_i's) statistical tests that can be used to test formally whether $X_1, X_2, \ldots, X_n$ are independent. Bartels (1982) proposes a rank version of von Neumann's ratio as a test statistic for independence, and provides the necessary critical values to carry out the test. However, one potential drawback is that the test assumes that there are no "ties" in the data, where a tie means $X_i = X_j$ for $i \neq j$. This requirement will generally not be met for discrete data, and may not even be satisfied for continuous data if they are recorded with only a few decimal places of accuracy. (See the interarrival times

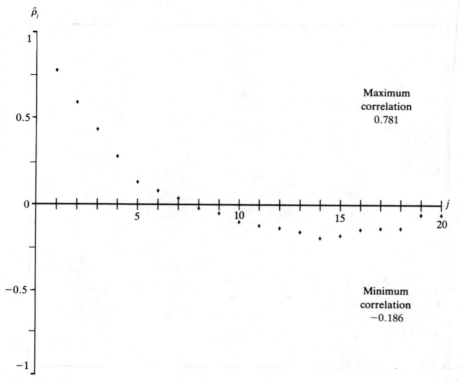

FIGURE 6.22
Correlation plot for correlated queueing data.

in Table 6.7.) Bartels states that his critical values may still be reasonably accurate if the number of ties is small.

There are several versions of the runs test [see, for example, Sec. 7.4.1 and Gibbons (1985)], which can also be used to assess the independence of the X_i's. They should have less difficulty with ties than the rank von Neumann test, since runs tests require only that $X_i \neq X_{i+1}$ for $i = 1, 2, \ldots, n-1$. On the other hand, Bartels showed empirically that the rank von Neumann test is considerably more powerful than one of the runs test against certain types of alternatives to the X_i's being independent.

6.4 ACTIVITY I: HYPOTHESIZING FAMILIES OF DISTRIBUTIONS

The first step in selecting a particular input distribution is to decide what general families—e.g., exponential, normal, or Poisson—appear to be appropriate on the basis of their shapes, without worrying (yet) about the specific parameter values for these families. This section describes some general

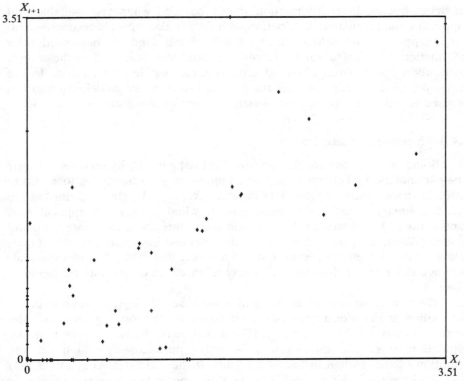

FIGURE 6.23
Scatter diagram for correlated queueing data.

techniques that can be used to *hypothesize* families of distributions that might be representative of a simulation input random variable.

In some situations, use can be made of *prior knowledge* about a certain random variable's role in a system to select a modeling distribution or at least rule out some distributions; this is done on theoretical grounds and does not require any data at all. For example, if we feel that customers arrive to a service facility one at a time, at a constant rate, and so that the numbers of customers arriving in disjoint time intervals are independent, there are theoretical reasons (see Sec. 6.10.1) for postulating that the interarrival times are IID exponential random variables. Recall also that several discrete distributions—binomial, geometric, and negative binomial—were developed from a physical model. Often the range of a distribution rules it out as a modeling distribution. Service times, for example, should not be generated directly from a normal distribution (at least in principle), since a random value from *any* normal distribution can be negative. The proportion of defective items in a large batch should not be assumed to have a gamma distribution, since proportions must be between 0 and 1, whereas gamma random variables have no upper bound. Prior information should be used whenever available, but supporting the postulated distribution with data is also strongly recommended.

In practice, we seldom have enough of this kind of theoretical prior information to select a single distribution, and the task of hypothesizing a distribution family from observed data is somewhat less structured. In the remainder of this section, we discuss various *heuristics*, or guidelines, that can be used to help one choose appropriate families of distributions.

6.4.1 Summary Statistics

Some distributions are characterized at least partially by functions of their *true* parameters. In Table 6.5 we give a number of such functions, formulas to estimate these functions from IID data $X_1, X_2, \ldots, X_n$ (these estimates are called *summary statistics*), an indication of whether they are applicable to continuous (C) or discrete (D) data, and comments about their interpretation or use. (We have included the sample minimum and maximum because of their utility, even though they may not be a direct function of a distribution's parameters.) Further discussion of many of these functions may be found in Chap. 4.

These functions might be used in some cases to suggest an appropriate distribution family. For a symmetric continuous distribution (e.g., normal), the mean μ is equal to the median $x_{0.5}$. (For a symmetric discrete distribution, the population mean and median may be only approximately equal; see the definition of the median in Sec. 4.2.) Thus, if the estimates $\bar{X}(n)$ and $\hat{x}_{0.5}(n)$ are "almost equal," this is some indication that the underlying distribution may be symmetric. One should keep in mind that $\bar{X}(n)$ and $\hat{x}_{0.5}(n)$ are observations of random variables and, thus, their relationship does not necessarily provide definitive information about the true relationship between μ and $x_{0.5}$.

The *coefficient of variation* cv can sometimes provide useful information about the form of a continuous distribution. In particular, cv $= 1$ for the exponential distribution, regardless of the scale parameter β. Thus, $\widehat{cv}(n)$ being close to 1 suggests that the underlying distribution is exponential. For the gamma and Weibull distributions, cv is greater than, equal to, or less than 1 when the shape parameter α is less than, equal to, or greater than 1, respectively. Furthermore, these distributions will have a shape similar to the density function in Fig. 6.19 when $\alpha > 1$, which implies that cv < 1. On the other hand, the lognormal distribution always has a density with a shape similar to that in Fig. 6.19, but its cv can be any positive real number. Thus, if the underlying distribution (observed histogram) has this shape and $\widehat{cv}(n) > 1$, the lognormal may be a better model than either the gamma or Weibull. For the remainder of the distributions in Table 6.3, the cv is not particularly useful. [In fact, cv is not even well defined for distributions such as U$(-c,c)$ (for $c > 0$) or N$(0,\sigma^2)$, since the mean μ is zero.]

For a discrete distribution, the *lexis ratio* τ plays the same role that the coefficient of variation does for a continuous distribution. We have found the

TABLE 6.5
Useful summary statistics

Function	Sample estimate (summary statistic)	Continuous (C) or discrete (D)	Comments
Minimum, maximum	$X_{(1)}, X_{(n)}$	C, D	$[X_{(1)}, X_{(n)}]$ is a rough estimate of range
Mean μ	$\bar{X}(n)$	C, D	Measure of central tendency
Median $x_{0.5}$	$\hat{x}_{0.5}(n) = \begin{cases} X_{((n+1)/2)} & \text{if } n \text{ is odd} \\ [X_{(n/2)} + X_{((n/2)+1)}]/2 & \text{if } n \text{ is even} \end{cases}$	C, D	Alternative measure of central tendency
Variance σ^2	$S^2(n)$	C, D	Measure of variability
Coefficient of variation, $cv = \sqrt{\sigma^2}/\mu$	$\widehat{cv}(n) = \dfrac{\sqrt{S^2(n)}}{\bar{X}(n)}$	C	Alternative measure of variability
Lexis ratio, $\tau = \sigma^2/\mu$	$\hat{\tau}(n) = \dfrac{S^2(n)}{\bar{X}(n)}$	D	Alternative measure of variability
Skewness, $\nu = E[(X - \mu)^3]/(\sigma^2)^{3/2}$	$\hat{\nu}(n) = \dfrac{\sum_{i=1}^{n} [X_i - \bar{X}(n)]^3/n}{[S^2(n)]^{3/2}}$	C, D	Measure of symmetry

lexis ratio to be very useful in discriminating among the Poisson, binomial, and negative binomial distributions, since $\tau = 1$, $\tau < 1$, and $\tau > 1$, respectively, for these distributions. (Note that the geometric distribution is a special case of the negative binomial.)

The *skewness* ν is a measure of the symmetry of a distribution. For symmetric distributions like the normal, $\nu = 0$. If $\nu > 0$ (e.g., $\nu = 2$ for the exponential distribution), the distribution is skewed to the right; if $\nu < 0$, the distribution is skewed to the left. Thus, the estimated skewness $\hat{\nu}(n)$ can be used to ascertain the shape of the underlying distribution. Our experience indicates that many distributions encountered in practice are skewed to the right and, furthermore, that $|\hat{\nu}(n)|$ is somewhat less than $|\nu|$ for most samples [see Johnson and Lowe (1979)].

It is possible to define another function of a distribution's parameters, called the *kurtosis*, which is a measure of the "tail weight" of a distribution [see, for example, Kendall, Stuart, and Ord (1987, pp. 107–108)]. However, we have not found the kurtosis to be very useful for discriminating among distributions.

6.4.2 Histograms and Line Graphs

For a continuous data set, a histogram is essentially a graphical estimate (see the discussion below) of the plot of the density function corresponding to the distribution of our data $X_1, X_2, \ldots, X_n$. Density functions, as shown in Figs. 6.1 through 6.9, tend to have recognizable shapes in many cases. Therefore, a graphical estimate of a density should provide a good clue to the distributions that might be tried as a model for the data.

To make a *histogram*, we break up the range of values covered by the data into k disjoint adjacent intervals $[b_0, b_1), [b_1, b_2), \ldots, [b_{k-1}, b_k)$. All the intervals should be the same width, say, $\Delta b = b_j - b_{j-1}$, which might necessitate throwing out a few extremely large or small X_i's to avoid getting an unwieldy-looking histogram plot. (Discarded data should be noted on the histogram plot itself in some way.) For $j = 1, 2, \ldots, k$, let h_j be the *proportion* of the X_i's that are in the jth interval $[b_{j-1}, b_j)$. Finally, we define the function

$$h(x) = \begin{cases} 0 & \text{if } x < b_0 \\ h_j & \text{if } b_{j-1} \le x < b_j \\ 0 & \text{if } b_k \le x \end{cases} \quad \text{for } j = 1, 2, \ldots, k$$

which we plot as a function of x. (See Example 6.4 below for an illustration of a histogram.) The plot of h, which is piecewise-constant, is then compared with plots of densities of various distributions on the basis of shape alone (location and scale differences are ignored) to see what distributions have densities that resemble the histogram h.

To see why the shape of h should resemble the true density f of the data, let X be a random variable with density f, so that X is distributed as the X_i's.

Then, for any fixed j ($j = 1, 2, \ldots, k$),

$$P(b_{j-1} \leq X < b_j) = \int_{b_{j-1}}^{b_j} f(x) \, dx = \Delta b \, f(y)$$

for some number $y \in (b_{j-1}, b_j)$. (The first equation is by the definition of a continuous random variable, and the second follows from the mean-value theorem of calculus.) On the other hand, the probability that X falls in the jth interval is approximated by h_j, which is the value of $h(y)$. Therefore,

$$h(y) = h_j \approx \Delta b \, f(y)$$

so that $h(y)$ is roughly proportional to $f(y)$; that is, h and f have roughly the same shape. (Actually, an *estimate* of f is obtained by dividing the function h by the constant Δb.)

Histograms are applicable to any continuous distribution and provide a readily interpreted visual synopsis of the data. Furthermore, it is easy to "eyeball" a histogram in reference to certain density functions. There are, however, certain difficulties. Most vexing is the absence of a definitive guide for choosing the number of intervals k (or, equivalently, their width Δb).

Several rules-of-thumb have been suggested for choosing the number of intervals k {e.g., Sturges' rule [see Hoaglin, Mosteller, and Tukey (1983, pp. 23–24)] and a normal approximation due to Scott (1979)}. The best known of these guidelines is probably Sturges' rule, which says that k should be chosen according to the following formula:

$$k = \lfloor 1 + \log_2 n \rfloor = \lfloor 1 + 3.322 \log_{10} n \rfloor$$

However, in general, we do not believe that such rules are very useful (see Example 6.4). We recommend trying several different values of Δb and choosing one that gives a "smooth" histogram with a shape similar to the density function of one of the standard distributions. This is clearly a matter of some subjectivity and represents the major problem in using histograms. If Δb is chosen too small, the histogram will have a "ragged" shape since the variances of the h_j's will be large. If Δb is chosen too large, then the histogram will have a "block-like" shape, and the true shape of the underlying density will be masked since the data have been overaggregated. In particular, a large spike in the density function near $x = 0$ or elsewhere (see Fig. 6.8) could be missed if Δb is too large.

As we have noted, a histogram is an estimate (except for rescaling) of the density function. There are many other ways in which the density function can be estimated from data, some of which are quite sophisticated. We refer the interested reader to the survey paper of Wegman (1982, pp. 309–315) and the book by Silverman (1986).

The probability mass function corresponding to a discrete data set can be estimated in a natural way using a *line graph*. For each possible value x_j that can be assumed by the data, let h_j be the proportion of the X_i's that are equal to x_j. Vertical lines of height h_j are plotted vs. x_j, and this is compared with the mass functions of the discrete distributions in Sec. 6.2.3 on the basis of shape.

The justification for line graphs stems from the fact that h_j (which is a random variable) is an unbiased estimator of $p(x_j)$, where $p(x)$ is the true (unknown) mass function of the data (see Prob. 6.7). Line graphs are quite similar to histograms in their construction, interpretation, and use, but they are more appealing because we need not make any arbitrary subjective decisions about interval width and placement.

There are certain situations where the histogram (or line graph) will have several local modes (or "humps"), in which case none of the standard distributions discussed in Sec. 6.2 will provide an adequate representation. In Fig. 6.24 we give such an example, which might represent (continuous) times to repair some machine collected over a 1-year period. There are two types of breakdowns for the machine. Most of the breakdowns are minor and the corresponding repair time is relatively small; this case corresponds to the left hump in Fig. 6.24. A small proportion of the breakdowns are major and have large repair times, since spare parts need to be ordered. This results in the right hump in Fig. 6.24. If the observed repair times can be separated into these two cases (corresponding to minor and major repairs), with p_j being the proportion of observations for case j ($j = 1, 2$), then a density $f_j(x)$ is fit to the class j observations ($j = 1, 2$) using the methods discussed in Sec. 6.4 through 6.6. Thus, the overall repair-time density $f(x)$ is given by

$$f(x) = p_1 f_1(x) + p_2 f_2(x)$$

and random repair times can be generated from $f(x)$ during a simulation using the composition technique (see Sec. 8.2.2). See Prob. 6.8 for an alternative method for modeling a histogram with several modes.

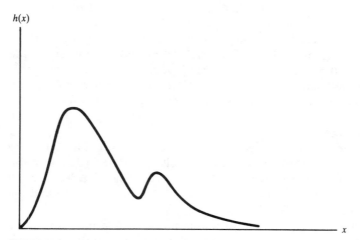

FIGURE 6.24
Histogram corresponding to a density function with two local modes.

6.4.3 Quantile Summaries and Box Plots

The *quantile summary* [see, for example, Tukey (1970)] is a synopsis of the sample that is useful for determining whether the underlying probability density function or probability mass function is symmetric or skewed to the right or to the left. It is applicable to either continuous or discrete data sets; however, for expository convenience we will explain it only for the continuous case.

Suppose that $F(x)$ is the distribution function for a continuous random variable. Suppose further that $F(x)$ is continuous and strictly increasing when $0 < F(x) < 1$. [This means that if $x_1 < x_2$ and $0 < F(x_1) \le F(x_2) < 1$, then in fact $F(x_1) < F(x_2)$.] For $0 < q < 1$, the *q-quantile* of $F(x)$ is that number x_q such that $F(x_q) = q$. If F^{-1} denotes the inverse of $F(x)$, then $x_q = F^{-1}(q)$. $\{F^{-1}$ is that function such that $F[F^{-1}(x)] = F^{-1}[F(x)] = x$.$\}$ Here we are particularly interested in the median $x_{0.5}$, the lower and upper quartiles $x_{0.25}$ and $x_{0.75}$, and the lower and upper octiles $x_{0.125}$ and $x_{0.875}$. A quantile summary for the sample $X_1, X_2, \ldots, X_n$ has a form that is given in Table 6.6.

In Table 6.6, if the "depth" subscript l (l is equal to i, j, or k) is halfway between the integers m and $m' = m + 1$, then $X_{(l)}$ is defined to be the average of $X_{(m)}$ and $X_{(m')}$. The value $X_{(i)}$ is an estimate of the median, $X_{(j)}$ and $X_{(n-j+1)}$ are estimates of the quartiles, and $X_{(k)}$ and $X_{(n-k+1)}$ are estimates of the octiles. If the underlying distribution of the X_i's is symmetric, then the four midpoints should be approximately equal. On the other hand, if the underlying distribution of the X_i's is skewed to the right (left), then the four midpoints (from the top to the bottom of the table) should be increasing (decreasing).

A *box plot* is a graphical representation of the quantile summary (see Fig. 6.26). Fifty percent of the observations fall within the horizontal boundaries of the box $[x_{0.25}, x_{0.75}]$.

The following two examples illustrate the use of the techniques discussed in Sec. 6.4.

Example 6.4. A simulation model was developed for a drive-up banking facility, and data were collected on the arrival pattern for cars. Over a fixed 90-minute interval, 220 cars arrived, and we noted the (continuous) interarrival time X_i (in minutes) between cars i and $i + 1$, for $i = 1, 2, \ldots, 219$. Table 6.7 lists these

TABLE 6.6
Structure of the quantile summary for the sample $X_1, X_2, \ldots, X_n$

Quantile	Depth	Sample value(s)		Midpoint
Median	$i = (n + 1)/2$	$X_{(i)}$		$X_{(i)}$
Quartiles	$j = (\lfloor i \rfloor + 1)/2$	$X_{(j)}$	$X_{(n-j+1)}$	$[X_{(j)} + X_{(n-j+1)}]/2$
Octiles	$k = (\lfloor j \rfloor + 1)/2$	$X_{(k)}$	$X_{(n-k+1)}$	$[X_{(k)} + X_{(n-k+1)}]/2$
Extremes	1	$X_{(1)}$	$X_{(n)}$	$[X_{(1)} + X_{(n)}]/2$

TABLE 6.7
$n = 219$ interarrival times (minutes) sorted into increasing order

0.01	0.06	0.12	0.23	0.38	0.53	0.88
0.01	0.07	0.12	0.23	0.38	0.53	0.88
0.01	0.07	0.12	0.24	0.38	0.54	0.90
0.01	0.07	0.13	0.25	0.39	0.54	0.93
0.01	0.07	0.13	0.25	0.40	0.55	0.93
0.01	0.07	0.14	0.25	0.40	0.55	0.95
0.01	0.07	0.14	0.25	0.41	0.56	0.97
0.01	0.07	0.14	0.25	0.41	0.57	1.03
0.02	0.07	0.14	0.26	0.43	0.57	1.05
0.02	0.07	0.15	0.26	0.43	0.60	1.05
0.03	0.07	0.15	0.26	0.43	0.61	1.06
0.03	0.08	0.15	0.26	0.44	0.61	1.09
0.03	0.08	0.15	0.26	0.45	0.63	1.10
0.04	0.08	0.15	0.27	0.45	0.63	1.11
0.04	0.08	0.15	0.28	0.46	0.64	1.12
0.04	0.09	0.17	0.28	0.47	0.65	1.17
0.04	0.09	0.18	0.29	0.47	0.65	1.18
0.04	0.10	0.19	0.29	0.47	0.65	1.24
0.04	0.10	0.19	0.30	0.48	0.69	1.24
0.05	0.10	0.19	0.31	0.49	0.69	1.28
0.05	0.10	0.20	0.31	0.49	0.70	1.33
0.05	0.10	0.21	0.32	0.49	0.72	1.38
0.05	0.10	0.21	0.35	0.49	0.72	1.44
0.05	0.10	0.21	0.35	0.49	0.72	1.51
0.05	0.10	0.21	0.35	0.50	0.74	1.72
0.05	0.10	0.21	0.36	0.50	0.75	1.83
0.05	0.11	0.22	0.36	0.50	0.76	1.96
0.05	0.11	0.22	0.36	0.51	0.77	
0.05	0.11	0.22	0.37	0.51	0.79	
0.06	0.11	0.23	0.37	0.51	0.84	
0.06	0.11	0.23	0.38	0.52	0.86	
0.06	0.12	0.23	0.38	0.52	0.87	

$n = 219$ interarrival times after they have been sorted into increasing order. The number of cars arriving in the six consecutive 15-minute intervals were counted and found to be approximately equal, suggesting that the arrival rate is somewhat constant over *this* 90-minute interval. Furthermore, cars arrive one at a time, and there is no reason to believe that the numbers of arrivals in disjoint intervals are not independent. Thus, on theoretical grounds we postulate that the interarrival times are exponential. To substantiate this hypothesis, we first look at the summary statistics given in Table 6.8. Since $\bar{X}(219) = 0.399 > 0.270 = \hat{x}_{0.5}(219)$ and $\hat{\nu}(219) = 1.458$, this suggests that the underlying distribution is skewed to the right, rather than symmetric. Furthermore, $\widehat{cv}(219) = 0.953$, which is close to the theoretical value of 1 for the exponential distribution. Next we made three different histograms of the data using $b_0 = 0$ in each case and $\Delta b = 0.050, 0.075,$ and 0.100, as shown in Fig. 6.25. The smoothest-looking histogram appears to be for $\Delta b = 0.100$, and its shape resembles that of an exponential density. (Note that Sturges' rule gives $k = 8$ and $\Delta b = 0.250$, resulting in an overaggregation of the

TABLE 6.8
Summary statistics for the
interarrival-time data

Summary statistic	Value
Minimum	0.010
Maximum	1.960
Mean	0.399
Median	0.270
Variance	0.144
Coefficient of variation	0.953
Skewness	1.458

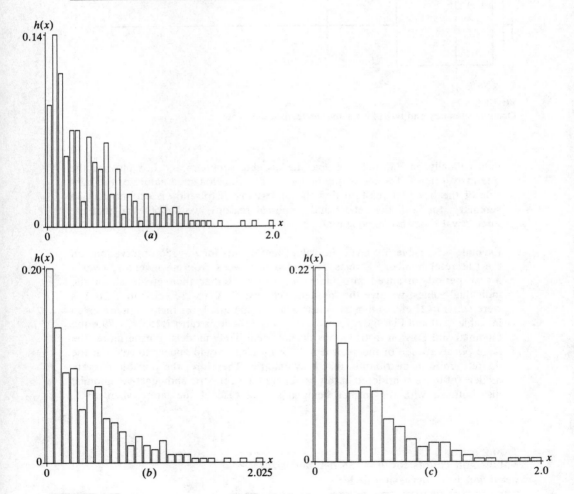

FIGURE 6.25
Histograms of the interarrival-time data in Table 6.7: (*a*) $\Delta b = 0.050$; (*b*) $\Delta b = 0.075$; (*c*) $\Delta b = 0.100$.

Quantile	Depth	Sample value(s)		Midpoint
Median	110		0.270	0.270
Quartiles	55.5	0.100	0.545	0.323
Octiles	28	0.050	0.870	0.460
Extremes	1	0.010	1.960	0.985

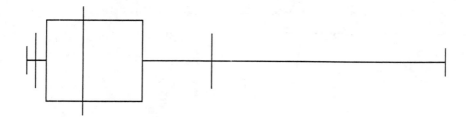

FIGURE 6.26
Quantile summary and box plot for the interarrival-time data.

data.) Finally, in Fig. 6.26 we give the quantile summary and box plot for the interarrival times. The increasing midpoints and the elongated nature of the right side of the box plot reaffirm that the underlying distribution is exponential. In summary, for both theoretical and empirical reasons, we hypothesize that the interarrival times are exponential.

Example 6.5. Table 6.9 gives the values and counts for $n = 156$ observations on the (discrete) number of items demanded in a week from an inventory over a 3-year period, arranged into increasing order. Rather than giving all of the individual values, we give the frequency counts; 59 X_i's were equal to 0, 26 X_i's were equal to 1, etc. Summary statistics and a line graph for these data are given in Table 6.10 and Fig. 6.27, respectively. Since the lexis ratio $\hat{\tau}(156) = 2.795$, the binomial and Poisson distributions do not seem likely models. Furthermore, the large positive value of the skewness $\hat{\nu}(156) = 1.655$ would appear to rule out the discrete uniform distribution that is symmetric. Therefore, the possible discrete models (of those considered in this book) are the geometric and negative binomial distributions, with the former being a special case of the latter when $s = 1$.

TABLE 6.9
Values and counts for $n = 156$ demand sizes arranged into increasing order

0(59),	1(26),	2(24),	3(18),	4(12),
5(5),	6(4),	7(3),	9(3),	11(2)

TABLE 6.10
Summary statistics for the
demand-size data

Summary statistic	Value
Minimum	0.000
Maximum	11.000
Mean	1.891
Median	1.000
Variance	5.285
Lexis ratio	2.795
Skewness	1.655

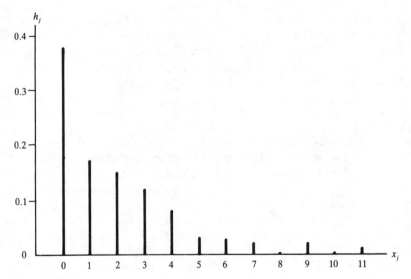

FIGURE 6.27
Line graph of the demand-size data in Table 6.9.

However, based on the monotonically decreasing line graph in Fig. 6.27 (and the mass functions in Fig. 6.14), we hypothesize that the demand data are from a geometric distribution.

6.5 ACTIVITY II: ESTIMATION OF PARAMETERS

After one or more candidate families of distributions have been hypothesized in Activity I, we must somehow specify the values of their parameters in order to have completely specified distributions for possible use in the simulation. Our IID data $X_1, X_2, \ldots, X_n$ were used to help us hypothesize distributions, and these same data can also be used to estimate their parameters. When data are used directly in this way to specify a numerical value for an unknown parameter, we say that we are *estimating* that parameter from the data.

An *estimator* is a numerical function of the data. There are many ways to specify the form of an estimator for a particular parameter of a given distribution, and many alternative ways to evaluate the quality of an estimator. We shall consider explicitly only one type, *maximum-likelihood estimators* (MLEs), for three reasons: (1) MLEs have several desirable properties often not enjoyed by alternative methods of estimation, e.g., least-squares estimators, unbiased estimators, and the method of moments; (2) the use of MLEs turns out to be important in justifying the chi-square goodness-of-fit test (see Sec. 6.6.2); and (3) the central idea of maximum-likelihood estimation has a strong intuitive appeal.

The basis for MLEs is most easily understood in the discrete case. Suppose that we have hypothesized a discrete distribution for our data that has one unknown parameter θ. Let $p_\theta(x)$ denote the probability mass function for this distribution, so that the parameter θ is part of the notation. *Given that we have already observed* the IID data $X_1, X_2, \ldots, X_n$, we define the *likelihood function $L(\theta)$* as follows:

$$L(\theta) = p_\theta(X_1)p_\theta(X_2)\cdots p_\theta(X_n)$$

$L(\theta)$, which is just the joint probability mass function since the data are independent (see Sec. 4.2), gives the probability (likelihood) of obtaining our observed data if θ is the value of the unknown parameter. Then, the MLE of the unknown value of θ, which we denote by $\hat{\theta}$, is defined to be the value of θ that maximizes $L(\theta)$; that is, $L(\hat{\theta}) \geq L(\theta)$ for all possible values of θ. Thus, $\hat{\theta}$ "best explains" the data we have collected. In the continuous case, MLEs do not have quite as simple an intuitive explanation, since the probability that a continuous random variable *equals* any fixed number is always 0 [see Prob. 6.26 and Breiman (1973, pp. 67–68) for intuitive justification of MLEs in the continuous case]. Nevertheless, MLEs for continuous distributions are defined analogously to the discrete case. If $f_\theta(x)$ denotes the hypothesized density function (again we assume that there is only one unknown parameter θ), the likelihood function is given by

$$L(\theta) = f_\theta(X_1)f_\theta(X_2)\cdots f_\theta(X_n)$$

The MLE $\hat{\theta}$ of θ is defined to be the value of θ that maximizes $L(\theta)$ over all permissible values of θ. The following two examples show how to compute MLEs for the distributions hypothesized earlier in Examples 6.4 and 6.5.

Example 6.6. For the exponential distribution, $\theta = \beta$ $(\beta > 0)$ and $f_\beta(x) = (1/\beta)e^{-x/\beta}$ for $x \geq 0$. The likelihood function is

$$L(\beta) = \left(\frac{1}{\beta}\ e^{-X_1/\beta}\right)\left(\frac{1}{\beta}\ e^{-X_2/\beta}\right)\cdots\left(\frac{1}{\beta}\ e^{-X_n/\beta}\right)$$

$$= \beta^{-n}\exp\left(-\frac{1}{\beta}\sum_{i=1}^{n}X_i\right)$$

and we seek the value of β that maximizes $L(\beta)$ over all $\beta > 0$. This task is more easily accomplished if, instead of working directly with $L(\beta)$, we work with its logarithm. Thus, we define the *log-likelihood function* as

$$l(\beta) = \ln L(\beta) = -n \ln \beta - \frac{1}{\beta} \sum_{i=1}^{n} X_i$$

Since the logarithm function is strictly increasing, maximizing $L(\beta)$ is equivalent to maximizing $l(\beta)$, which is much easier; that is, $\hat{\beta}$ maximizes $L(\beta)$ if and only if $\hat{\beta}$ maximizes $l(\beta)$. Standard differential calculus can be used to maximize $l(\beta)$ by setting its derivative to zero and solving for β. That is,

$$\frac{dl}{d\beta} = \frac{-n}{\beta} + \frac{1}{\beta^2} \sum_{i=1}^{n} X_i$$

which equals zero if and only if $\beta = \sum_{i=1}^{n} X_i/n = \bar{X}(n)$. To make sure that $\beta = \bar{X}(n)$ is a maximizer of $l(\beta)$ (as opposed to a minimizer or an inflection point), a sufficient (but not necessary) condition is that $d^2l/d\beta^2$, evaluated at $\beta = \bar{X}(n)$, be negative. But

$$\frac{d^2l}{d\beta^2} = \frac{n}{\beta^2} - \frac{2}{\beta^3} \sum_{i=1}^{n} X_i$$

which is easily seen to be negative when $\beta = \bar{X}(n)$ since the X_i's are positive. Thus, the MLE of β is $\hat{\beta} = \bar{X}(n)$. Notice that the MLE is quite natural here, since β is the mean of the hypothesized distribution and the MLE is the *sample* mean. For the data of Example 6.4, $\hat{\beta} = \bar{X}(219) = 0.399$.

Example 6.7. The discrete data of Example 6.5 were hypothesized to come from a geometric distribution. Here $\theta = p$ $(0 < p < 1)$ and $p_p(x) = p(1 - p)^x$ for $x = 0, 1, \ldots$. The likelihood function is

$$L(p) = p^n(1 - p)^{\sum_{i=1}^{n} X_i}$$

which is again amenable to the logarithmic transformation to obtain

$$l(p) = \ln L(p) = n \ln p + \sum_{i=1}^{n} X_i \ln (1 - p)$$

Differentiating $l(p)$, we get

$$\frac{dl}{dp} = \frac{n}{p} - \frac{\sum_{i=1}^{n} X_i}{1 - p}$$

which equals zero if and only if $p = 1/[\bar{X}(n) + 1]$. To make sure that this is a maximizer, note that

$$\frac{d^2l}{dp^2} = -\frac{n}{p^2} - \frac{\sum_{i=1}^{n} X_i}{(1 - p)^2} < 0$$

for any valid p. Thus, the MLE of p is $\hat{p} = 1/[\bar{X}(n) + 1]$, which is intuitively appealing (see Prob. 6.9). For the demand-size data of Example 6.5, $\hat{p} = 0.346$.

The above two examples illustrate two important practical tools for deriving MLEs, namely, the use of the log-likelihood function and setting its derivative (with respect to the parameter being estimated) equal to zero to find the MLE. While these tools are often useful in finding MLEs, the reader should be cautioned against assuming that finding a MLE is always a simple matter of setting a derivative to zero and solving easily for $\hat{\theta}$. For some distributions, neither the log-likelihood function nor differentiation is useful; probably the best-known example is the uniform distribution (see Prob. 6.10). For other distributions, both tools are useful, but solving $dl/d\theta = 0$ cannot be accomplished by simple algebra, and numerical methods must be used; the gamma, Weibull, and beta distributions are (multiparameter) examples of this general situation. We refer the reader to Breiman (1973, pp. 65–84) for examples of techniques used to find MLEs for a variety of distributions.

We have said that MLEs have several desirable statistical properties, some of which are as follows [see Breiman (1973, pp. 85–88) and Kendall and Stuart (1979, chap. 18)]:

1. For most of the common distributions, the MLE is unique; that is, $L(\hat{\theta})$ is *strictly* greater than $L(\theta)$ for any other value of θ.
2. Although MLEs need not be unbiased, in general, the asymptotic distribution (as $n \to \infty$) of $\hat{\theta}$ has mean equal to θ (see property 4 below).
3. MLEs are *invariant*; that is, if $\phi = h(\theta)$ for some function h, then the MLE of ϕ is $h(\hat{\theta})$. (Unbiasedness is not invariant.) For example, the variance of an expo(β) random variable is β^2, so the MLE of this variance is $[\bar{X}(n)]^2$.
4. MLEs are asymptotically normally distributed; that is, $\sqrt{n}(\hat{\theta} - \theta) \xrightarrow{\mathscr{D}} N(0, \delta(\theta))$, where $\delta(\theta) = -n/E(d^2l/d\theta^2)$ (the expectation is with respect to X_i, assuming that X_i has the hypothesized distribution) and $\xrightarrow{\mathscr{D}}$ denotes convergence in distribution. Furthermore, if $\tilde{\theta}$ is any other estimator such that $\sqrt{n}(\tilde{\theta} - \theta) \xrightarrow{\mathscr{D}} N(0, \sigma^2)$, then $\delta(\theta) \leq \sigma^2$. (Thus, MLEs are called *best asymptotically normal*.)
5. MLEs are *strongly consistent*; that is, $\lim_{n \to \infty} \hat{\theta} = \theta$ (w.p. 1).

The proofs of these and other properties sometimes require additional mild "regularity" assumptions; see Kendall and Stuart (1979).

Property 4 is of special interest, since it allows us to establish an approximate confidence interval for θ. If we define $\delta(\theta)$ as in property 4 above, it can be shown that

$$\frac{\hat{\theta} - \theta}{\sqrt{\delta(\hat{\theta})/n}} \xrightarrow{\mathscr{D}} N(0,1)$$

as $n \to \infty$. Thus, for large n an approximate $100(1 - \alpha)$ percent confidence interval for θ is

$$\hat{\theta} \pm z_{1-\alpha/2}\sqrt{\frac{\delta(\hat{\theta})}{n}} \tag{6.1}$$

Example 6.8. Construct a 90 percent confidence interval for the parameter p of the geometric distribution and specialize it to the data of Example 6.5. It is easy to show that

$$E\left[\frac{d^2l}{dp^2}\right] = -\frac{n}{p^2} - \frac{n(1-p)/p}{(1-p)^2} = -\frac{n}{p^2(1-p)}$$

so that $\delta(p) = p^2(1-p)$ and, for large n, an approximate 90 percent confidence interval for p is given by

$$\hat{p} \pm 1.645 \sqrt{\frac{\hat{p}^2(1-\hat{p})}{n}}$$

For the data of Example 6.5, we get 0.346 ± 0.037.

This suggests a way of checking how sensitive a simulation output measure of performance is to a particular input parameter. The simulation could be run for θ set at, say, the left endpoint, the center ($\hat{\theta}$), and the right endpoint of the confidence interval in (6.1). If the measure of performance appeared to be insensitive to values of θ in this range, we could feel confident that we have an adequate estimate of θ for our purposes. On the other hand, if the simulation seemed to be sensitive to θ, we might seek a better estimate of θ; this would usually entail collecting more data.

So far, we have explicitly treated only distributions with a single unknown parameter. If a distribution has several parameters, we can define MLEs of these parameters in a natural way. For instance, the gamma distribution has two parameters (α and β), and the likelihood function is defined to be

$$L(\alpha, \beta) = \frac{\beta^{-n\alpha}\left(\prod_{i=1}^{n} X_i\right)^{\alpha-1} \exp\left(-\frac{1}{\beta}\sum_{i=1}^{n} X_i\right)}{[\Gamma(\alpha)]^n}$$

The MLEs $\hat{\alpha}$ and $\hat{\beta}$ of the unknown values of α and β are defined to be the values of α and β that (jointly) maximize $L(\alpha, \beta)$. [Finding $\hat{\alpha}$ and $\hat{\beta}$ usually proceeds by letting $l(\alpha, \beta) = \ln L(\alpha, \beta)$ and trying to solve the equations $\partial l/\partial \alpha = 0$ and $\partial l/\partial \beta = 0$ simultaneously for α and β.] Analogs of the properties of MLEs listed above also hold in this multiparameter case. Unfortunately, the process of finding MLEs when there are several parameters is usually quite difficult. (The normal distribution is a notable exception.)

For each of the distributions in Secs. 6.2.2 (except for the triangular distribution) and 6.2.3, we listed either formulas for the MLEs or a method for obtaining them numerically. For the gamma MLEs, Table 6.19 can be used with standard linear interpolation. For the beta MLEs, Table 6.20 can be used; one could either simply pick $(\hat{\alpha}_1, \hat{\alpha}_2)$ corresponding to the closest table values of G_1 and G_2 or devise a scheme for two-dimensional interpolation.

6.6   ACTIVITY III: DETERMINING HOW REPRESENTATIVE THE FITTED DISTRIBUTIONS ARE

After determining one or more probability distributions that might fit our observed data in Activities I and II, we must now closely examine these distributions to see how well they represent the true underlying distribution for our data. If several of these distributions are "representative," we must also determine which distribution provides the best fit. In general, none of our fitted distributions will probably be *exactly* correct. What we are really trying to do is determine a distribution that is accurate enough for the intended purposes of the model.

In this section we discuss both heuristic procedures and goodness-of-fit hypothesis tests for determining the "quality" of fitted distributions.

6.6.1   Heuristic Procedures

We will discuss four heuristic or graphical procedures for comparing fitted distributions with the true underlying distribution; several additional techniques can be found in Law and Vincent (1990).

Frequency Comparisons. For continuous data, a *frequency comparison* is a graphical comparison of a histogram of the data with the density function $\hat{f}(x)$ of a fitted distribution. Let $[b_0, b_1)$, $[b_1, b_2)$, ..., $[b_{k-1}, b_k)$ be a set of k histogram intervals each with width $\Delta b = b_j - b_{j-1}$. Let h_j be the *observed* proportion of the X_i's in the jth interval $[b_{j-1}, b_j)$ and let r_j be the *expected* proportion of the n observations that would fall in the jth interval if the fitted distribution were in fact the true one, i.e., r_j is given by (see Prob. 6.13)

$$r_j = \int_{b_{j-1}}^{b_j} \hat{f}(x)\, dx \tag{6.2}$$

Then the frequency comparison is made by plotting both h_j and r_j in the jth histogram interval for $j = 1, 2, \ldots, k$.

For discrete data, a *frequency comparison* is a graphical comparison of a line graph of the data with the mass function $\hat{p}(x)$ of a fitted distribution. Let h_j be the observed proportion of the X_i's that are equal to x_j and let r_j be the expected proportion of the n observations that would be equal to x_j if the fitted distribution were in fact the true one, i.e., $r_j = \hat{p}(x_j)$. Then the frequency comparison is made by plotting both h_j and r_j vs. x_j for all relevant values of x_j.

In either case, if the fitted distribution is a good representation for the true underlying distribution of the data (and if the sample size n is sufficiently large), then r_j and h_j should closely agree.

For continuous data, an alternative comparison can be made by plotting $\Delta b\, \hat{f}(x)$ over the histogram $h(x)$ and looking for similarities. [Recall that the area under $h(x)$ is Δb.]

Example 6.9. For the interarrival-time data of Example 6.4, we hypothesized an exponential distribution and obtained the MLE $\hat{\beta} = 0.399$ in Example 6.6. Thus, the density of the fitted distribution is

$$\hat{f}(x) = \begin{cases} 2.506e^{-x/0.399} & \text{if } x \geq 0 \\ 0 & \text{otherwise} \end{cases}$$

For the histogram in Fig. 6.25(c) with $\Delta b = 0.1$ and $k = 20$, the expected proportion, r_j, in the interval $[b_{j-1}, b_j)$ is given by

$$r_j = \int_{b_{j-1}}^{b_j} \hat{f}(x)\, dx = e^{-b_{j-1}/0.399} - e^{-b_j/0.399} = 0.285e^{-0.251j}$$

since $b_j = (\Delta b)j = 0.1j$ for $j = 1, 2, \ldots, 20$ in this case. The frequency comparison is given in Fig. 6.28, where the h_j's are represented by wide, hollow rectangles and the r_j's by narrow, solid rectangles. In general, the agreement between the h_j's and r_j's seems good.

Example 6.10. The demand-size data of Example 6.5 were hypothesized to have come from a geometric distribution, and the MLE of the parameter p was found

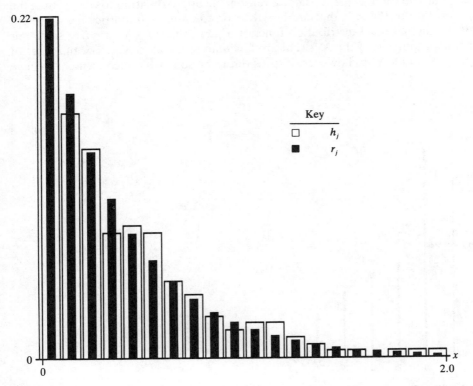

FIGURE 6.28
Frequency comparison for the fitted exponential distribution and the interarrival-time data.

in Example 6.7 to be $\hat{p} = 0.346$. Thus, the mass function of the fitted distribution is

$$p(x) = \begin{cases} 0.346(0.654)^x & \text{if } x = 0, 1, 2, \ldots \\ 0 & \text{otherwise} \end{cases}$$

For the line graph in Fig. 6.27, $r_j = \hat{p}(x_j) = \hat{p}(j-1)$ for $j = 1, 2, \ldots, 12$, and the frequency comparison is given in Fig. 6.29, where the h_j's are represented by the heights of the vertical lines and the r_j's by the crosses on these lines. Once again, the agreeement is good except possibly for $x_2 = 1$.

Probability Plots. A probability plot can be thought of as a graphical comparison of an estimate of the true distribution function of our data $X_1, X_2, \ldots, X_n$ with the distribution function of one of the fitted distributions. There are many kinds (and uses) of probability plots, only two of which we describe here; see Barnett (1975), Hahn and Shapiro (1967), and Wilk and Gnanadesikan (1968) for additional discussions.

As in Sec. 6.2.4, let $X_{(i)}$ be the ith smallest of the X_j's, sometimes called the *ith order statistic* of the X_j's. Recall that the distribution function F of a random variable X is defined so that for any x, $F(x) = P(X \le x)$. If X has the same distribution as the X_j data, a reasonable approximation to $F(x)$ is thus the proportion of the X_j's that are less than or equal to x. In particular, we might define an empirical distribution function $\tilde{F}_n(x)$ so that $\tilde{F}_n(X_{(i)}) = i/n$, since this is the proportion of the X_j's that are less than or equal to $X_{(i)}$. For purposes of probability plotting, however, it turns out to be somewhat inconvenient to have

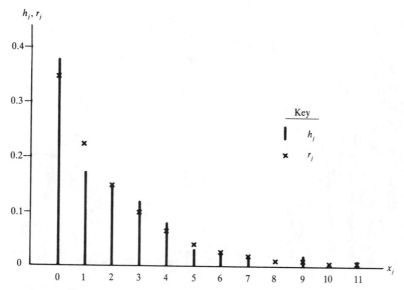

FIGURE 6.29
Frequency comparison for the fitted geometric distribution and the demand-size data.

$\tilde{F}_n(X_{(n)}) = 1$, that is, to have an empirical distribution function that is equal to 1 for a finite value of x (see Prob. 6.14). We therefore make a small adjustment and define

$$\tilde{F}_n(X_{(i)}) = \frac{i - 0.5}{n}$$

for $i = 1, 2, \ldots, n$. [Clearly, for moderately large n, this adjustment is quite small. Other adjustments have been suggested, such as $i/(n+1)$.] A straightforward procedure would then be to plot the n points $(X_{(1)}, 0.5/n)$, $(X_{(2)}, 1.5/n), \ldots, (X_{(n)}, (n-0.5)/n)$, compare this result with plots of the distribution functions of several of the distributions being considered as a model for the data, and look for similarities. However, distribution functions generally do not have as characteristic an appearance as density or mass functions. In fact, many distribution functions have some sort of an "S" shape, and eyeballing for differences or similarities in shapes between S-shaped curves is somewhat perplexing. Most of us, however, *can* recognize whether or not a set of plotted points appears to lie more or less along a *straight* line, and probability-plotting techniques reduce the problem of comparing distribution functions to one of looking for a straight line.

Let $q_i = (i - 0.5)/n$ for $i = 1, 2, \ldots, n$, so that $0 < q_i < 1$. For any *continuous* data set (see Prob. 6.15), a *quantile–quantile* (Q–Q) *plot* (see Sec. 6.4.3 for the definition of a quantile) is a graph of the q_i-quantile of a fitted (model) distribution function $\hat{F}(x)$, namely, $x_{q_i}^M = \hat{F}^{-1}(q_i)$, vs. the q_i-quantile of the sample distribution function $\tilde{F}_n(x)$, namely, $x_{q_i}^S = \tilde{F}_n^{-1}(q_i) = X_{(i)}$, for $i = 1, 2, \ldots, n$. The definition of a Q–Q plot is illustrated in Fig. 6.30, where we have represented $\tilde{F}_n(x)$ as a smooth curve for convenience. Corresponding to each ordinate value q are the two quantiles x_q^M and x_q^S.

If $\hat{F}(x)$ is the same distribution as the true underlying distribution $F(x)$, and if the sample size n is large, then $\hat{F}(x)$ and $\tilde{F}_n(x)$ will be close together and the Q–Q plot will be approximately linear with an intercept of 0 and a slope of 1. Even if $\hat{F}(x)$ is the correct distribution, there will be departures from linearity for small to moderate sample sizes.

A *probability–probability* (P–P) *plot* is a graph of the model probability $\hat{F}(X_{(i)})$ vs. the sample probability $\tilde{F}_n(X_{(i)}) = q_i$, for $i = 1, 2, \ldots, n$; it is valid for both continuous and discrete data sets. This definition is also illustrated in Fig. 6.30. Corresponding to each abscissa value p are the two probabilities $\hat{F}(p)$ and $\tilde{F}_n(p)$. If $\hat{F}(x)$ and $\tilde{F}_n(x)$ are close together, then the P–P plot will also be approximately linear with an intercept of 0 and a slope of 1.

The Q–Q plot will amplify differences that exist between the tails of the model distribution function $\hat{F}(x)$ and the tails of the sample distribution function $\tilde{F}_n(x)$, whereas the P–P plot will amplify differences between the middle of $\hat{F}(x)$ and the middle of $\tilde{F}_n(x)$. The difference between the right tails of the distribution functions in Fig. 6.31 is amplified by the Q–Q plot but not the P–P plot. On the other hand, the difference between the "middles" of the two distribution functions in Fig. 6.32 is amplified by the P–P plot.

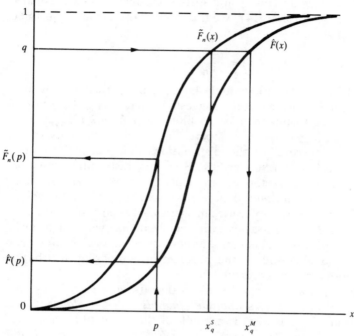

FIGURE 6.30
Definitions of Q–Q and P–P plots.

The above formulations of Q–Q and P–P plots implicitly assumed that the X_i's were distinct (no ties); this certainly will not always be the case. To modify the definitions when the X_i's may not be distinct, let $Y_1, Y_2, \ldots, Y_l$ be the distinct values in the sample $X_1, X_2, \ldots, X_n$ arranged in increasing order, where $l \le n$. (If the X_i's are distinct, then $Y_i = X_{(i)}$ for $i = 1, 2, \ldots, n$.) Let q'_i be defined by

$$q'_i = (\text{proportion of } X_j\text{'s} \le Y_i) - \frac{0.5}{n}$$

In other words, $q'_i = \tilde{F}_n(Y_i)$. Then q'_i replaces q_i and Y_i replaces $X_{(i)}$ in the definitions of Q–Q and P–P plots.

The construction of a Q–Q plot requires the calculation of the model quantile $\hat{F}^{-1}(q_i)$. For the uniform, exponential, and Weibull distributions, there is no problem, since a closed-form expression for $\hat{F}^{-1}$ is available. For the other continuous distributions, we give in Table 6.11 either a transformation for addressing the problem or a reference to a numerical approximation for $\hat{F}^{-1}$. Also given in Table 6.11 are similar prescriptions for computing the model probability $\hat{F}(X_{(i)})$, which is required for a P–P plot. Functions for

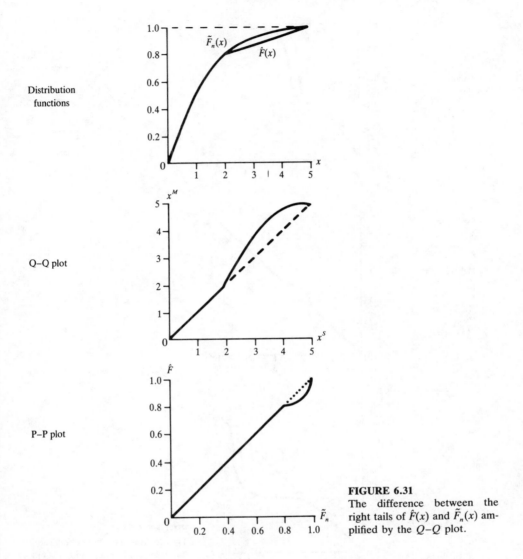

Distribution functions

Q–Q plot

P–P plot

FIGURE 6.31
The difference between the right tails of $\hat{F}(x)$ and $\tilde{F}_n(x)$ amplified by the Q–Q plot.

computing $\hat{F}$ or $\hat{F}^{-1}$ are also available in Chapter 17 of the IMSL Statistical Library (1987), and the UniFit II statistical package [Law and Vincent (1990)] performs Q–Q and P–P plots automatically; see also Kennedy and Gentle (1980, chap. 5).

Example 6.11. A Q–Q plot for the fitted exponential distribution and the interarrival-time data is given in Fig. 6.33. The plot is fairly linear except for large values of q_i'. This is not uncommon, since the Q–Q plot will amplify small differences between $\hat{F}(x)$ and $\tilde{F}_n(x)$ when they are both close to 1. The corre-

Distribution
functions

Q–Q plot

P–P plot

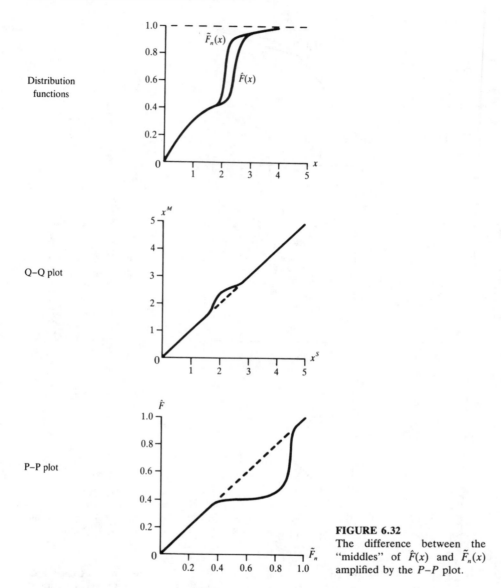

FIGURE 6.32
The difference between the "middles" of $\hat{F}(x)$ and $\tilde{F}_n(x)$ amplified by the P–P plot.

sponding P–P plot is given in Fig. 6.34. Its linearity indicates that the middle of the fitted exponential agrees closely with the middle of the true underlying distribution.

Example 6.12. The P–P plot for the fitted geometric distribution and the demand-size data is given in Fig. 6.35. Once again we find the P–P plot to be reasonably linear, indicating agreement between the geometric and true distributions.

TABLE 6.11
Approaches for computing $\hat{F}$ or $\hat{F}^{-1}$ for certain mathematically intractable distributions

	$\hat{F}$	$\hat{F}^{-1}$
Gamma	See Bhattacharjee (1970)	See Best and Roberts (1975)
Normal	See Milton and Hotchkiss (1969)	See Odeh and Evans (1974)
Lognormal	Fit a normal distribution to $Y_i = \ln X_i$ for $i = 1, 2, \ldots, n$; see Sec. 6.2.2	Same as $\hat{F}$
Beta	See Bosten and Battiste (1974)	See Cran, Martin, and Thomas (1977)
Pearson type V	Fit a gamma distribution to $Y_i = 1/X_i$ for $i = 1, 2, \ldots, n$; see Sec. 6.2.2	Same as $\hat{F}$
Pearson type VI	Fit a beta distribution to $Y_i = X_i/(1 + X_i)$ for $i = 1, 2, \ldots, n$; see Sec. 6.2.2	Same as $\hat{F}$

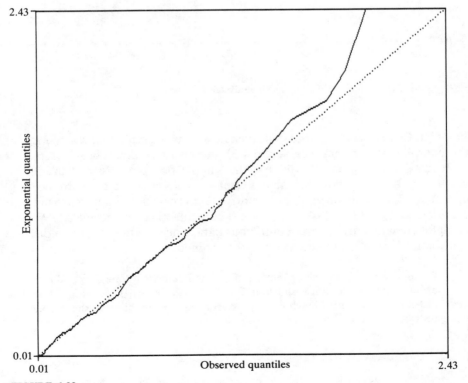

FIGURE 6.33
Q–Q plot for exponential distribution and interarrival-time data.

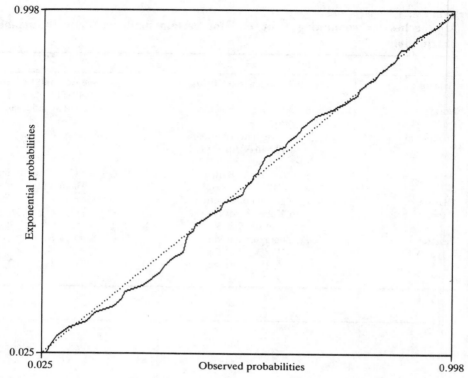

FIGURE 6.34
$P-P$ plot for exponential distribution and interarrival-time data.

Box-Plot Comparisons. A *box-plot comparison* is a graphical presentation of the box plot of our data (see Sec. 6.4.3) and also of a theoretical box plot of each fitted distribution. Recall that the sample box plot displays the 0.125, 0.250, 0.500, 0.750, and 0.875 quantiles of the data and also the extremes $X_{(1)}$ and $X_{(n)}$. For a theoretical box plot, the lower and upper extremes are represented by the $1/(2n)$ and $1 - [1/(2n)]$ quantiles, respectively. We use box-plot comparisons only for continuous data, since the quantiles of a discrete distribution are not, in general, uniquely defined.

> **Example 6.13.** A box-plot comparison for the interarrival-time data and the fitted exponential distribution is shown in Fig. 6.36. The (internal) quantiles of the two distributions seem to match closely, supporting the suitability of the exponential distribution.

6.6.2   Goodness-of-Fit Tests

A *goodness-of-fit test* is a statistical hypothesis test (see Sec. 4.5) that is used to assess formally whether the observations $X_1, X_2, \ldots, X_n$ are an independent

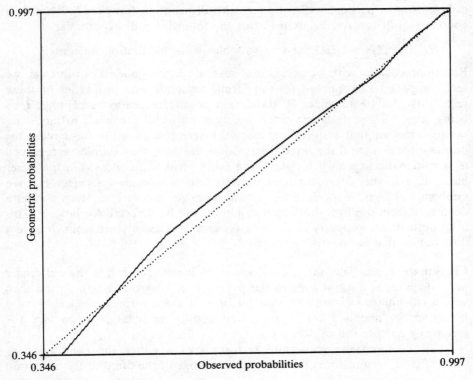

FIGURE 6.35
P–P plot for geometric distribution and demand-size data.

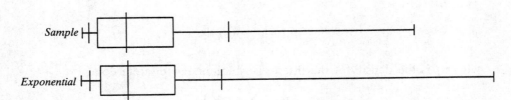

FIGURE 6.36
Box-plot comparison for interarrival-time data and fitted exponential distribution.

sample from a particular distribution with distribution function $\hat{F}$. That is, a goodness-of-fit test can be used to test the following null hypothesis:

H_0: The X_i's are IID random variables with distribution function $\hat{F}$.

Before proceeding with a discussion of several specific goodness-of-fit tests, we feel compelled to comment on the formal structure and properties of these tests. First, failure to reject H_0 should *not* be interpreted as "accepting H_0 as being true." These tests are often not very powerful for small to moderate sample sizes n; that is, they are not very sensitive to subtle disagreements between the data and the fitted distribution. Instead, they should be regarded as a systematic approach for detecting fairly gross differences. On the other hand, if n is very large, then these tests will almost always reject H_0 [see Gibbons (1985, p. 76)]. Since H_0 is virtually never *exactly* true, even a minute departure from the hypothesized distribution will be detected for large n. This is an unfortunate property of these tests, since it is usually sufficient to have a distribution that is "nearly" correct.

Chi-Square Tests. The oldest goodness-of-fit hypothesis test is the *chi-square test*, which dates back at least to the paper of K. Pearson (1900). As we shall see, a chi-square test may be thought of as a more formal comparison of a histogram or line graph with the fitted density or mass function (see the frequency comparison in Sec. 6.6.1).

To compute the chi-square test statistic in either the continuous or discrete case, we must first divide the entire range of the fitted distribution into k adjacent intervals $[a_0, a_1), [a_1, a_2), \ldots, [a_{k-1}, a_k)$, where it could be that $a_0 = -\infty$, in which case the first interval is $(-\infty, a_1)$, or $a_k = +\infty$, or both. Then we tally

$$N_j = \text{number of } X_i\text{'s in the } j\text{th interval } [a_{j-1}, a_j)$$

for $j = 1, 2, \ldots, k$. (Note that $\sum_{j=1}^{k} N_j = n$.) Next, we compute the expected *proportion* p_j of the X_i's that would fall in the jth interval if we were sampling from the fitted distribution. In the continuous case,

$$p_j = \int_{a_{j-1}}^{a_j} \hat{f}(x) \, dx$$

where $\hat{f}$ is the density of the fitted distribution. For discrete data,

$$p_j = \sum_{a_{j-1} \le x_i < a_j} \hat{p}(x_i)$$

where $\hat{p}$ is the mass function of the fitted distribution. Finally, the test statistic is

$$\chi^2 = \sum_{j=1}^{k} \frac{(N_j - np_j)^2}{np_j}$$

Since np_j is the expected number of the n X_i's that would fall in the jth interval if H_0 were true (see Prob. 6.17), we would expect χ^2 to be small if the fit is good. Therefore, we reject H_0 if χ^2 is too large. The precise form of the test depends on whether or not we have estimated any of the parameters of the fitted distribution from our data.

First, suppose that all parameters of the fitted distribution are known; i.e., we specified the fitted distribution without making use of the data in any way. [This all-parameters-known case might appear to be of little practical use, but there are at least two applications for it in simulation: (1) in the Poisson-process test (later in this section), we test to see whether times of arrival can be regarded as being IID $U(0,T)$ random variables, where T is a constant independent of the data; and (2) in empirical testing of random-number generators (Sec. 7.4.1), we test for a $U(0,1)$ distribution.] Then if H_0 is true, χ^2 converges in distribution (as $n \rightarrow \infty$) to a chi-square distribution with $k-1$ df, which is the same as the gamma$((k-1)/2, 2)$ distribution. Thus, for large n, a test with *approximate* level α is obtained by rejecting H_0 if $\chi^2 > \chi^2_{k-1,1-\alpha}$ (see Fig. 6.37), where $\chi^2_{k-1,1-\alpha}$ is the upper $1-\alpha$ critical point for a chi-square distribution with $k-1$ df. (Values for $\chi^2_{k-1,1-\alpha}$ can be found in

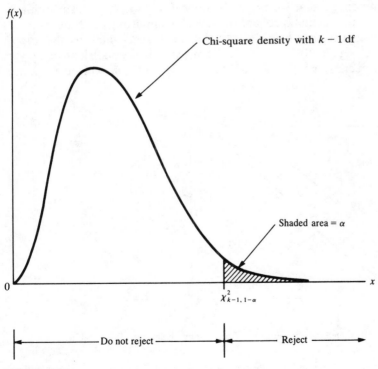

FIGURE 6.37
The chi-square test when all parameters are known.

Table T.2 at the end of the book.) Note that the chi-square test is only *valid*, i.e., is of level α, asymptotically as $n \to \infty$.

Second, suppose that in order to specify the fitted distribution we had to estimate m parameters $(m \geq 1)$ from the data. When MLEs are used, Chernoff and Lehmann (1954) showed that if H_0 is true, then as $n \to \infty$ the distribution function of χ^2 converges to a distribution function that lies *between* the distribution functions of chi-square distributions with $k - 1$ and $k - m - 1$ df. (See Fig. 6.38, where F_{k-1} and F_{k-m-1} represent the distribution functions of chi-square distributions with $k - 1$ and $k - m - 1$ df, respectively, and the dotted distribution function is the one to which the distribution function of χ^2 converges as $n \to \infty$.) If we let $\chi^2_{1-\alpha}$ be the upper $1 - \alpha$ critical point of the asymptotic distribution of χ^2, then

$$\chi^2_{k-m-1,1-\alpha} \leq \chi^2_{1-\alpha} \leq \chi^2_{k-1,1-\alpha}$$

as shown in Fig. 6.38; unfortunately, the value of $\chi^2_{1-\alpha}$ will not be known in general. It is clear that we should reject H_0 if $\chi^2 > \chi^2_{k-1,1-\alpha}$ and we should not reject H_0 if $\chi^2 < \chi^2_{k-m-1,1-\alpha}$; an ambiguous situation occurs when

$$\chi^2_{k-m-1,1-\alpha} \leq \chi^2 \leq \chi^2_{k-1,1-\alpha}$$

It is often recommended that we reject H_0 only if $\chi^2 > \chi^2_{k-1,1-\alpha}$, since this is *conservative*; i.e., the actual probability α' of committing a Type I error [rejecting H_0 when it is true (see Sec. 4.5)] is at *least* as small as the *stated* probability α (see Fig. 6.38). This choice, however, will entail loss of power (probability of rejecting a false H_0) of the test. Usually, m will be no more

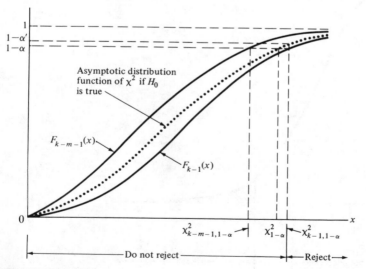

FIGURE 6.38
The chi-square test when m parameters are estimated by their MLEs.

than 2, and if k is fairly large, the difference between $\chi^2_{k-m-1,1-\alpha}$ and $\chi^2_{k-1,1-\alpha}$ will not be too great. Thus, we reject H_0 if (and only if) $\chi^2 > \chi^2_{k-1,1-\alpha}$, as in the all-parameters-known case. The rejection region for χ^2 is indicated in Fig. 6.38.

The most troublesome aspect of carrying out a chi-square test is choosing the number and size of the intervals. This is a difficult problem, and no definitive prescription can be given that is guaranteed to produce good results in terms of validity (actual level of the test close to the desired level α) and high power for all hypothesized distributions and all sample sizes. There are, however, a few guidelines that are often followed. First, some of the ambiguity in interval selection is eliminated if the intervals are chosen so that $p_1 = p_2 = \cdots = p_k$, which is called the *equiprobable approach*. In the continuous case, this might be inconvenient to do for some distributions since the distribution function of the fitted distribution must be inverted (see Example 6.14 below). Furthermore, for discrete distributions, we will generally be able to make the p_j's only approximately equal (see Example 6.15).

We now discuss how to choose the intervals to ensure "validity" of the test. Let $a = \min_{1 \le j \le k} np_j$ and let $y(5)$ be the number of np_j's less than 5. Based on extensive theoretical and empirical investigations (for the all-parameters-known case), Yarnold (1970) states that the chi-square test will be approximately valid if $k \ge 3$ and $a \ge 5y(5)/k$. For equiprobable intervals, these conditions will be satisfied if $k \ge 3$ and $np_j \ge 5$ for all j.

We now turn our attention to the power of the chi-square test. A test is said to be *unbiased* if it is more likely to reject H_0 when it is false than when it is true or, in other words, power is greater than the probability of a Type I error. A test without this property would certainly be undesirable. It can be shown that the chi-square test is always unbiased for the equiprobable approach [see Kendall and Stuart (1979, pp. 455–461)]. If the np_j's are not equal (and many are small), it is possible to obtain a valid test that is highly biased [see Haberman (1988)].

In general, there is no rule for choosing the intervals so that high power is obtained for all alternative distributions. For a particular null distribution, a fixed sample size n, and the equiprobable approach, Kallenberg, Oosterhoff, and Schriever (1985) showed empirically that power is an increasing function of the number of intervals k for some alternative distributions, and a decreasing function of k for other alternative distributions. Surprisingly, they also found in certain cases that the power was greater when the np_j's were smaller in the tails (see Prob. 6.18).

In the absence of a definitive guideline for choosing the intervals, we recommend the equiprobable approach and $np_j \ge 5$ for all j in the continuous case. This guarantees a valid and unbiased test. In the discrete case, we suggest making the np_j's approximately equal and all at least 5. The lack of a clear prescription for interval selection is the major drawback of the chi-square test. In some situations entirely different conclusions can be reached from the *same* data set depending on how the intervals are specified. The chi-square test nevertheless remains in wide use, since it can be applied to any hypothesized distribution; as we shall see below, other goodness-of-fit tests do not enjoy such a wide range of applicability.

Example 6.14. We now use a chi-square test to compare the $n = 219$ interarrival times of Table 6.7 with the fitted exponential distribution having distribution function $\hat{F}(x) = 1 - e^{-x/0.399}$ for $x \geq 0$. If we form, say, $k = 20$ intervals with $p_j = 1/k = 0.05$ for $j = 1, 2, \ldots, 20$, then $np_j = (219)(0.05) = 10.950$, so that this satisfies the guidelines that the intervals be chosen with equal p_j's and $np_j \geq 5$. In this case, it is easy to find the a_j's, since $\hat{F}$ can be inverted. That is, we set $a_0 = 0$ and $a_{20} = \infty$, and for $j = 1, 2, \ldots, 19$ we want a_j to satisfy $\hat{F}(a_j) = j/20$; this is equivalent to setting $a_j = -0.399 \ln (1 - j/20)$ for $j = 1, 2, \ldots, 19$ since $a_j = \hat{F}^{-1}(j/20)$. (For continuous distributions such as the normal, gamma, and beta, the inverse of the distribution function does not have a simple closed form. In these cases, however, F^{-1} can be evaluated by numerical methods; consult the references given in Table 6.11.) The computations for the test are given in Table 6.12, and the value of the test statistic is $\chi^2 = 22.188$. Referring to Table T.2, we see that $\chi^2_{19,0.90} = 27.204$, which is not exceeded by χ^2, so we would not reject H_0 at the $\alpha = 0.10$ level. (Note that we would also not reject H_0 for certain larger values of α such as 0.25.) Thus, this test gives us no reason to conclude that our data are poorly fitted by the expo(0.399) distribution.

TABLE 6.12
A chi-square goodness-of-fit test for the interarrival-time data

j	Interval	N_j	np_j	$\dfrac{(N_j - np_j)^2}{np_j}$
1	$[0, 0.020)$	8	10.950	0.795
2	$[0.020, 0.042)$	11	10.950	0.000
3	$[0.042, 0.065)$	14	10.950	0.850
4	$[0.065, 0.089)$	14	10.950	0.850
5	$[0.089, 0.115)$	16	10.950	2.329
6	$[0.115, 0.142)$	10	10.950	0.082
7	$[0.142, 0.172)$	7	10.950	1.425
8	$[0.172, 0.204)$	5	10.950	3.233
9	$[0.204, 0.239)$	13	10.950	0.384
10	$[0.239, 0.277)$	12	10.950	0.101
11	$[0.277, 0.319)$	7	10.950	1.425
12	$[0.319, 0.366)$	7	10.950	1.425
13	$[0.366, 0.419)$	12	10.950	0.101
14	$[0.419, 0.480)$	10	10.950	0.082
15	$[0.480, 0.553)$	20	10.950	7.480
16	$[0.553, 0.642)$	9	10.950	0.347
17	$[0.642, 0.757)$	11	10.950	0.000
18	$[0.757, 0.919)$	9	10.950	0.347
19	$[0.919, 1.195)$	14	10.950	0.850
20	$[1.195, \infty)$	10	10.950	0.082
				$\chi^2 = 22.188$

Example 6.15. As an illustration of the chi-square test in the discrete case, we test how well the fitted geom(0.346) distribution agrees with the demand-size data of Table 6.9. As is usually the case for discrete distributions, we cannot make the p_j's exactly equal, but by grouping together adjacent points on which the mass function $\hat{p}(x)$ is defined (here, the nonnegative integers), we can define intervals that make the p_j's roughly the same. One way to do this is to note that the mode of the fitted distribution is 0; thus, $\hat{p}(0) = 0.346$ is the largest value of the mass function. The large value for the mode limits our choice of intervals and we end up with the three intervals given in Table 6.13, where the calculations for the chi-square test are also presented. In particular, $\chi^2 = 1.930$, which is less than the critical value $\chi^2_{2,0.90} = 4.605$. Thus, we would not reject H_0 at the $\alpha = 0.10$ level, and we have no reason to believe that the demand-size data are not fitted well by a geom(0.346) distribution.

Kolmogorov-Smirnov Tests. As we just saw, chi-square tests can be thought of as a more formal comparison of a histogram or line graph of the data with the density or mass function of the fitted distribution. We also identified a real difficulty in using a chi-square test in the continuous case, namely, that of deciding how to specify the intervals. *Kolmogorov-Smirnov* (K-S) *tests* for goodness of fit, on the other hand, compare an empirical *distribution* function with the *distribution* function $\hat{F}$ of the hypothesized distribution. As we shall see, K-S tests do not require us to group our data in any way, so no information is lost; this also eliminates the troublesome problem of interval specification. Another advantage of K-S tests is that they are valid (exactly) for any sample size n (in the all-parameters-known case), whereas chi-square tests are valid only in an asymptotic sense. Finally, K-S tests tend to be more powerful than chi-square tests against many alternative distributions; see, for example, Stephens (1974).

Nevertheless, K-S tests do have some drawbacks, at least at present. Most seriously, their range of applicability is more limited than that for chi-square tests. First, for discrete data, the required critical values are not readily available and must be computed using a complicated set of formulas [see Conover (1980, pp. 350–352) and Gleser (1985)]. These authors state that the required calculations can only be done easily on a computer for sample sizes of $n \leq 50$. [See also Pettitt and Stephens (1977).] Second, the *original*

TABLE 6.13
A chi-square goodness-of-fit test for the demand-size data

j	Interval	N_j	np_j	$\dfrac{(N_j - np_j)^2}{np_j}$
1	$\{0\}$	59	53.960	0.471
2	$\{1, 2\}$	50	58.382	1.203
3	$\{3, 4, \ldots\}$	47	43.658	0.256
				$\chi^2 = 1.930$

form of the K-S test is valid only if *all* the parameters of the hypothesized distribution are *known* and the distribution is continuous; i.e., the parameters cannot have been estimated from the data. In recent years, the K-S test has been extended to allow for estimation of the parameters in the cases of normal (lognormal), exponential, and Weibull distributions. Although the K-S test in its original (all-parameters-known) form has often been applied directly for any continuous distribution with estimated parameters and for discrete distributions, this will, in fact, produce a conservative test [see Conover (1980, pp. 347, 357)]. That is, the probability of a Type I error will be smaller than specified.

To define the K-S statistic, we must first define an empirical distribution function. As we have already seen in this chapter, there are several different reasonable ways to do this. For the K-S test, we define an empirical distribution function $F_n(x)$ from our data $X_1, X_2, \ldots, X_n$ as

$$F_n(x) = \frac{\text{number of } X_i\text{'s} \leq x}{n}$$

for all real numbers x. Thus, $F_n(x)$ is a (right-continuous) step function such that $F_n(X_{(i)}) = i/n$ for $i = 1, 2, \ldots, n$ (see Prob. 6.19). If $\hat{F}(x)$ is the fitted distribution function, a natural assessment of goodness of fit is some kind of measure of the closeness between the functions F_n and $\hat{F}$. The K-S test statistic D_n is simply the *largest* (vertical) distance between $F_n(x)$ and $\hat{F}(x)$ *for all values of x* and is defined formally by

$$D_n = \sup_x \{|F_n(x) - \hat{F}(x)|\}$$

[The "sup" of a set of numbers A is the smallest value that is greater than or equal to all members of A. The "sup" is used here instead of the more familiar "max" since, in some cases, the maximum may not be well defined. For example, if $A = (0,1)$, there is no maximum but the "sup" is 1.] D_n can be computed by calculating

$$D_n^+ = \max_{1 \leq i \leq n} \left\{ \frac{i}{n} - \hat{F}(X_{(i)}) \right\}, \quad D_n^- = \max_{1 \leq i \leq n} \left\{ \hat{F}(X_{(i)}) - \frac{i-1}{n} \right\}$$

and finally letting

$$D_n = \max\{D_n^+, D_n^-\}$$

An example is given in Fig. 6.39 for $n = 4$, where $D_n = D_n^+$. [*Beware!* Incorrect computational formulas are often given for D_n. In particular, one sometimes sees

$$D_n' = \max_{1 \leq i \leq n} \left\{ \left| \frac{i}{n} - \hat{F}(X_{(i)}) \right| \right\}$$

as a "formula" for D_n. For the situation of Fig. 6.39, it *is* true that $D_n' = D_n$. Consider, however, Fig. 6.40, where $D_n' = \hat{F}(X_{(2)}) - \frac{2}{4}$ but the correct value for D_n is $\hat{F}(X_{(2)}) - \frac{1}{4}$, which occurs *just before* $x = X_{(2)}$. Clearly, $D_n' \neq D_n$ in this

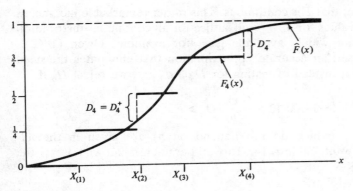

FIGURE 6.39
Geometric meaning of the K-S test statistic D_n for $n = 4$.

case.] Direct computation of D_n^+ and D_n^- requires sorting the data to obtain the $X_{(i)}$'s. For moderate values of n (up to several hundred), sorting can be done quickly by simple methods. If n is large, however, even sophisticated sorting methods become expensive (computing time is proportional to $n \ln n$). Gonzalez, Sahni, and Franta (1977) provide an algorithm for computing D_n^+ and D_n^- without sorting; their algorithm's computation time is proportional to n.

Clearly, a large value of D_n indicates a poor fit, so that the form of the test is to reject the null hypothesis H_0 if D_n exceeds some constant $d_{n,1-\alpha}$, where α is the specified level of the test. The numerical value of the critical point $d_{n,1-\alpha}$ depends on how the hypothesized distribution was specified, and we must distinguish several cases.

Case 1. If *all parameters of $\hat{F}$ are known*, i.e., none of the parameters of $\hat{F}$ is estimated in any way from the data, the distribution of D_n does not depend on

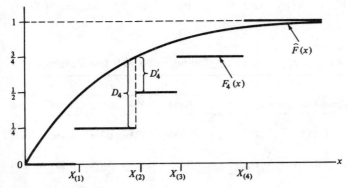

FIGURE 6.40
An example where the K-S test statistic D_n is not equal to D_n'.

$\hat{F}$, assuming (of course) that $\hat{F}$ is continuous. This rather remarkable fact means that a single table of values for $d_{n,1-\alpha}$ will suffice for all continuous distribution forms; these tables are widely available [see, for example, Owen (1962)]. Stephens (1974) devised an accurate approximation that eliminates the need for all but a tiny table; instead of testing for $D_n > d_{n,1-\alpha}$, we reject H_0 if

$$\left(\sqrt{n} + 0.12 + \frac{0.11}{\sqrt{n}}\right) D_n > c_{1-\alpha}$$

where values for $c_{1-\alpha}$ (which do not depend on n) are given in the all-parameters-known row of Table 6.14. This all-parameters-known case is the original form of the K-S test.

Case 2. Suppose that the hypothesized distribution is $N(\mu, \sigma^2)$ with both μ and σ^2 unknown. We can estimate μ and σ^2 by $\bar{X}(n)$ and $S^2(n)$, respectively, and define the distribution function $\hat{F}$ to be that of the $N(\bar{X}(n), S^2(n))$ distribution; i.e., let $\hat{F}(x) = \Phi\{[x - \bar{X}(n)]/\sqrt{S^2(n)}\}$, where Φ is the distribution function of the standard normal distribution. Using this $\hat{F}$ (which *has* estimated parameters), D_n is computed in the same way, but different critical points must be used. Lilliefors (1967) estimated (via Monte Carlo simulation) the critical points of D_n as a function of n and $1 - \alpha$. Stephens (1974) performed further Monte Carlo simulations and provided an accurate approximation that obviates the need for large tables; namely, we reject H_0 if

$$\left(\sqrt{n} - 0.01 + \frac{0.85}{\sqrt{n}}\right) D_n > c'_{1-\alpha}$$

where values for $c'_{1-\alpha}$ are given in the $N(\bar{X}(n), S^2(n))$ row of Table 6.14. (This case includes a K-S test for the lognormal distribution if the X_i's are the *logarithms* of the basic data points we have hypothesized to have a lognormal distribution; see Sec. 6.2.2.)

Case 3. Suppose the hypothesized distribution is $\text{expo}(\beta)$ with β unknown. β is estimated by its MLE $\bar{X}(n)$, and we define $\hat{F}$ to be the $\text{expo}(\bar{X}(n))$

TABLE 6.14
Modified critical values $c_{1-\alpha}$, $c'_{1-\alpha}$, and $c''_{1-\alpha}$ for adjusted K-S test statistics

Case	Adjusted test statistic	$1 - \alpha$				
		0.850	0.900	0.950	0.975	0.990
All parameters known	$\left(\sqrt{n} + 0.12 + \frac{0.11}{\sqrt{n}}\right) D_n$	1.138	1.224	1.358	1.480	1.628
$N(\bar{X}(n), S^2(n))$	$\left(\sqrt{n} - 0.01 + \frac{0.85}{\sqrt{n}}\right) D_n$	0.775	0.819	0.895	0.955	1.035
$\text{expo}(\bar{X}(n))$	$\left(D_n - \frac{0.2}{n}\right)\left(\sqrt{n} + 0.26 + \frac{0.5}{\sqrt{n}}\right)$	0.926	0.990	1.094	1.190	1.308

distribution function; that is, $\hat{F}(x) = 1 - e^{-x/\bar{X}(n)}$ for $x \geq 0$. In this case, critical points for D_n were originally estimated by Lilliefors (1969) in a Monte Carlo study, and exact tables were later obtained by Durbin (1975) [see also Margolin and Maurer (1976)]. Stephens' (1974) approximation in this case is to reject H_0 if

$$\left(D_n - \frac{0.2}{n}\right)\left(\sqrt{n} + 0.26 + \frac{0.5}{\sqrt{n}}\right) > c''_{1-\alpha}$$

where $c''_{1-\alpha}$ can be found in the expo($\bar{X}(n)$) row of Table 6.14.

Case 4. Suppose the hypothesized distribution is Weibull with both shape parameter α and scale parameter β unknown; we estimate these parameters by their respective MLEs $\hat{\alpha}$ and $\hat{\beta}$. (See the discussion of the Weibull MLEs in Sec. 6.2.2.) $\hat{F}$ is taken to be the Weibull($\hat{\alpha},\hat{\beta}$) distribution function, $\hat{F}(x) = 1 - \exp[-(x/\hat{\beta})^{\hat{\alpha}}]$ for $x \geq 0$, and D_n is computed in the usual fashion. Then H_0 is rejected if the adjusted K-S statistic $\sqrt{n}D_n$ is greater than the modified critical value $c^*_{1-\alpha}$ [see Chandra, Singpurwalla, and Stephens (1981)] given in Table 6.15. Note that critical values are available only for certain sample sizes n, and that the critical values for $n = 50$ and ∞ (an extremely large sample size) are, fortunately, very similar. [Critical values for other n less than 50 are given by Littell, McClave, and Offen (1979).]

> **Example 6.16.** In example 6.14 we used a chi-square test to check the goodness of fit of the fitted expo(0.399) distribution for the interarrival-time data of Table 6.7. We can also apply a K-S test with $\hat{F}(x) = 1 - e^{-x/0.399}$ for $x \geq 0$, by using Case 3 above. Using the formulas for D_{219}^+ and D_{219}^-, we found that $D_{219} = 0.047$, so that the adjusted test statistic is
>
> $$\left(D_{219} - \frac{0.2}{219}\right)\left(\sqrt{219} + 0.26 + \frac{0.5}{\sqrt{219}}\right) = 0.696$$
>
> Since 0.696 is less than $0.990 = c''_{0.90}$ (from the last row of Table 6.14), we do not reject H_0 at the $\alpha = 0.10$ level.

TABLE 6.15
Modified critical values $c^*_{1-\alpha}$ for the K-S test for the Weibull distribution

n	$1 - \alpha$			
	0.900	**0.950**	**0.975**	**0.990**
10	0.760	0.819	0.880	0.944
20	0.779	0.843	0.907	0.973
50	0.790	0.856	0.922	0.988
∞	0.803	0.874	0.939	1.007

Anderson-Darling Tests.* One possible drawback of K-S tests is that they give the same weight to the difference $|F_n(x) - \hat{F}(x)|$ for every value of x, whereas many distributions of interest differ primarily in their tails. The *Anderson-Darling* (A-D) *test* [see Anderson and Darling (1954)], on the other hand, is designed to detect discrepancies in the tails and has higher power than the K-S test against many alternative distributions [see Stephens (1974)]. The A-D statistic A_n^2 is defined by

$$A_n^2 = n \int_{-\infty}^{\infty} [F_n(x) - \hat{F}(x)]^2 \psi(x) \hat{f}(x)\, dx$$

where the *weight function* $\psi(x) = 1/\{\hat{F}(x)[1 - \hat{F}(x)]\}$. Thus, A_n^2 is just the weighted average of the squared differences $[F_n(x) - \hat{F}(x)]^2$ and the weights are the largest for $\hat{F}(x)$ close to 1 (right tail) and $\hat{F}(x)$ close to 0 (left tail). If we let $Z_i = \hat{F}(X_{(i)})$ for $i = 1, 2, \ldots, n$, then it can be shown that

$$A_n^2 = \left(-\left\{\sum_{i=1}^{n} (2i - 1)[\ln Z_i + \ln (1 - Z_{n+1-i})]\right\}/n\right) - n$$

which is the form of the statistic used for actual computations. Since A_n^2 is a "weighted distance," the form of the test is to reject the null hypothesis H_0 if A_n^2 exceeds some critical value $a_{n,1-\alpha}$, where α is the level of the test.

Critical values $a_{n,1-\alpha}$ are available for the A-D test for the same four continuous distributions [see Stephens (1974, 1976, 1977)] as for the K-S test. [See Gleser (1985) for a discussion of the discrete case.] Furthermore, $\hat{F}(x)$ is computed in the same manner as before; see Example 6.17 below. Performance of the A-D test is facilitated by the use of adjusted test statistics (except for the all-parameters-known case) and modified critical values, which are given in Table 6.16. If the adjusted test statistic is greater than the modified critical value, then H_0 is rejected.

TABLE 6.16
Modified critical values for adjusted A-D test statistics

Case	Adjusted test statistic	1 − α			
		0.900	**0.950**	**0.975**	**0.990**
All parameters known	A_n^2 for $n \geq 5$	1.933	2.492	3.070	3.857
$N(\bar{X}(n), S^2(n))$	$\left(1 + \dfrac{4}{n} - \dfrac{25}{n^2}\right) A_n^2$	0.632	0.751	0.870	1.029
$\text{expo}(\bar{X}(n))$	$\left(1 + \dfrac{0.6}{n}\right) A_n^2$	1.070	1.326	1.587	1.943
Weibull$(\hat{\alpha}, \hat{\beta})$	$\left(1 + \dfrac{0.2}{\sqrt{n}}\right) A_n^2$	0.637	0.757	0.877	1.038

---

*Skip this section on the first reading.

Example 6.17. We can use case 3 of the A-D test to see whether the fitted exponential distribution $\hat{F}(x) = 1 - e^{-x/0.399}$ provides a good model for the inter-arrival-time data at level $\alpha = 0.10$. We found that $A_{219}^2 = 0.558$, so that the adjusted test statistic is

$$\left(1 + \frac{0.6}{219}\right) A_{219}^2 = 0.560$$

Since 0.560 is less than the modified critical value 1.070 (from the third row of Table 6.16), we do not reject H_0 at level 0.10.

Poisson-Process Tests.* Suppose that we observe a Poisson process (see Sec. 6.10.1 below) for a *fixed* interval of time $[0, T]$, where T is a constant that is decided upon before we start our observation. Let n be the number of events we observe in the interval $[0, T]$, and let t_i be the time of the ith event for $i = 1, 2, \ldots, n$. {Thus, $0 \le t_1 \le t_2 \le \cdots \le t_n \le T$. If $t_n < T$, then no events occurred in the interval $(t_n, T]$.} Then the joint distribution of $t_1, t_2, \ldots, t_n$ is related to the $U(0, T)$ distribution in the following way. Assume that $Y_1, Y_2, \ldots, Y_n$ (the same n as above) are IID random variables with the $U(0, T)$ distribution, and let $Y_{(1)}, Y_{(2)}, \ldots, Y_{(n)}$ be their corresponding order statistics (see Sec. 6.2.4). Then a property of the Poisson process is that $t_1, t_2, \ldots, t_n$ have the same joint distribution as $Y_{(1)}, Y_{(2)}, \ldots, Y_{(n)}$. [See Ross (1989, p. 224) for a proof.]

One way of interpreting this property is that if someone simply showed us the *values* of $t_1, t_2, \ldots, t_n$ without telling us that t_i was obtained as the time of the ith event in some sequence of events, it would appear (in a statistical sense) that these n numbers had been obtained by taking a sample of n IID random values from the $U(0, T)$ distribution and then sorting them into increasing order. Alternatively, one could think of this property as saying that if we consider $t_1, t_2, \ldots, t_n$ as unordered random variables, they are IID with the $U(0, T)$ distribution. This is why we sometimes see a Poisson process described as one in which events occur "at random," since the instants at which events occur are uniformly distributed over time.

In any case, this property provides us with a different way of testing the null hypothesis that an observed sequence of events was generated by a Poisson process. (We have already seen one way this hypothesis can be tested, namely, testing whether the interevent times appear to be IID exponential random variables; see Sec. 6.10.1 and Examples 6.14, 6.16, and 6.17.) We simply test whether the event times $t_1, t_2, \ldots, t_n$ appear to be IID $U(0, T)$ random variables using any applicable testing procedure.

Example 6.18. The interarrival-time data of Table 6.7 were collected over a fixed 90-minute period, and $n = 220$ arrivals were recorded during this interval. (It was decided beforehand to start observing the process at exactly 5 P.M., rather than at

---

*Skip this section on the first reading.

the first time after 5:00 when an arrival happened to take place. Also, data collection terminated promptly at 6:30 P.M., regardless of any arrivals that occurred later. It is important for the validity of this test that the data collection be designed in this way, i.e., independent of the actual event times.) The times of arrivals were $t_1 = 1.53$, $t_2 = 1.98$, ..., $t_{220} = 88.91$ (in minutes after 5 P.M.). To test whether these numbers can be regarded as being independent with the U(0,90) distribution, we used the *all-parameters-known* cases of the chi-square and K-S tests. [The density and distribution function of the fitted distribution are, respectively, $\hat{f}(x) = 1/90$ and $\hat{F}(x) = x/90$, for $0 \leq x \leq 90$. Note also that our "data" points are already sorted, conveniently.] We carried out a chi-square test with the $k = 17$ equal-sized intervals $[0, 5.294)$, $[5.294, 10.588)$, ..., $[84.706, 90]$, so that $np_j = 220/17 = 12.941$ for $j = 1, 2, ..., 17$. The resulting value of χ^2 was 13.827, and since $\chi^2_{16,0.90} = 23.542$, we cannot reject the null hypothesis that the arrivals occurred in accordance with a Poisson process at level 0.10. The K-S test resulted in $D_{220} = 0.045$, and the value of the adjusted test statistic from the all-parameters-known row of Table 6.14 is thus 0.673. Since this is well below $c_{0.90} = 1.224$, once again we cannot reject the null hypothesis at level 0.10.

6.7 AN EXTENDED EXAMPLE

In this section we will investigate which of the continuous probability distributions of Sec. 6.2.2, if any, provides the best model for the $n = 200$ service times of Example 6.1. However, for expository convenience we will limit our analyses to the exponential, gamma, Weibull, lognormal, and normal distributions.

In Table 6.17 we present the summary statistics for the service times and in Fig. 6.41 is a corresponding histogram based on $k = 11$ intervals of width $\Delta b = 0.2$. The shape of the histogram strongly suggests that the true underlying distribution is skewed to the right. This is supported by $\bar{X}(200) = 0.888 > 0.849 = \hat{x}_{0.5}(200)$, $\hat{\nu}(200) = 0.506 > 0$, and the shape of the box plot (see Figure 6.45). Furthermore, $\widehat{cv}(200) = 0.515$ makes it fairly unlikely that the true distribution could be an exponential, which has a coefficient of variation of 1.

TABLE 6.17
Summary statistics for the service-time data

Summary statistic	Value
Minimum	0.054
Maximum	2.131
Mean	0.888
Median	0.849
Variance	0.210
Coefficient of variation	0.515
Skewness	0.506

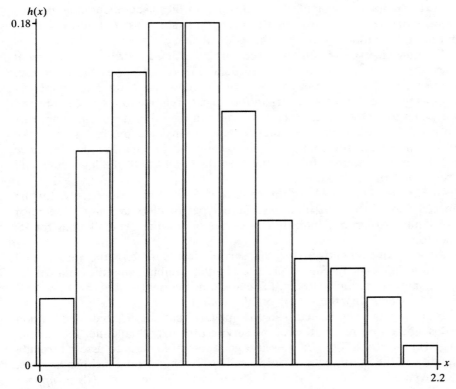

FIGURE 6.41
Histogram of the service-time data with $\Delta b = 0.2$.

Since the densities of the gamma, Weibull, and lognormal distributions can all take on shapes similar to that of the histogram, we propose them as candidate distributions.

In order to have a particular distribution for use in a simulation model, we must determine the parameters for the three proposed distributions. In Table 6.18 we give the MLEs of the parameters for the hypothesized models.

TABLE 6.18
MLEs for the three proposed distributions

Distribution	Shape parameter	Scale parameter
Gamma	3.251	0.273
Weibull	2.045	1.003
Lognormal	0.625	−0.280

Note that gamma and Weibull distributions with these shape parameters have an appearance similar to that of the histogram (see Figs. 6.3 and 6.4); the lognormal distribution always has this general shape.

We now assess how well our three particular fitted distributions represent the actual distribution of the observed data. Figure 6.42 gives the frequency comparisons for the lognormal and Weibull distributions. Note that the lognormal "density" rises up from the origin too quickly relative to the histogram and also appears to be too thick in the right tail. On the other hand, there appears to be good agreement between the Weibull density and the histogram. (We have not shown the frequency comparison for the gamma distribution, since the quality of the gamma "fit" lies between the "bad fit" of the lognormal and the "good fit" of the Weibull.)

In Figs. 6.43 and 6.44 are the Q–Q and P–P plots, respectively, for the lognormal and Weibull distributions. Both types of plots are more linear for the Weibull distribution, indicating a better fit for the Weibull than for its competitors.

A box-plot comparison for the service-time data and the three fitted distributions appears in Fig. 6.45. Clearly the Weibull quantiles match the sample quantiles the most closely. (The arrow at the right end of the lognormal box plot indicates that the plot is off the scale.)

Based on the above heuristics, it appears that the Weibull distribution provides a better representation of the service-time data than either the gamma or lognormal distribution. We now use goodness-of-fit tests to assess formally the quality of the Weibull representation. We first performed a chi-square test for the Weibull distribution with $k = 25$ equiprobable intervals (thus, $np_j = 8$ for all j), resulting in a statistic value of $\chi^2 = 22.250$. Since $22.250 < 33.196 = \chi^2_{24,0.90}$, we cannot reject the Weibull null hypothesis at level $\alpha = 0.10$.

We computed the K-S statistic for the Weibull distribution and obtained $D_{200} = 0.030$. Since the adjusted K-S statistic $\sqrt{200}D_{200} = 0.428$ is much less than the modified critical value $c^*_{0.90}$ (for $n = 50$ or ∞) from Table 6.15, we cannot reject the Weibull distribution at level $\alpha = 0.10$. It should be mentioned that the K-S statistic D_{200}, which is a measure of goodness of fit, was equal to 0.052 and 0.084 for the gamma and lognormal distributions, respectively.

The A-D statistic for the Weibull distribution is $A^2_{200} = 0.264$. Since the adjusted A-D statistic $(1 + 0.2/\sqrt{200})A^2_{200} = 0.268$ is less than the modified critical value 0.637 for level $\alpha = 0.10$ from the last row of Table 6.16, we cannot reject the Weibull distribution at this level. (The A-D statistic A^2_{200} was equal to 0.521 and 2.076 for the gamma and lognormal distributions, respectively.)

In summary, there is no reason to believe based on the above heuristics and tests that the Weibull distribution does not provide a good model for the service-time data.

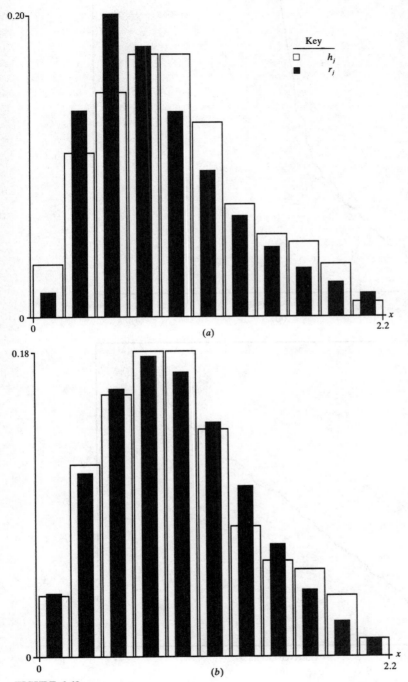

FIGURE 6.42
Frequency comparisons for the service-time data: (*a*) lognormal; (*b*) Weibull.

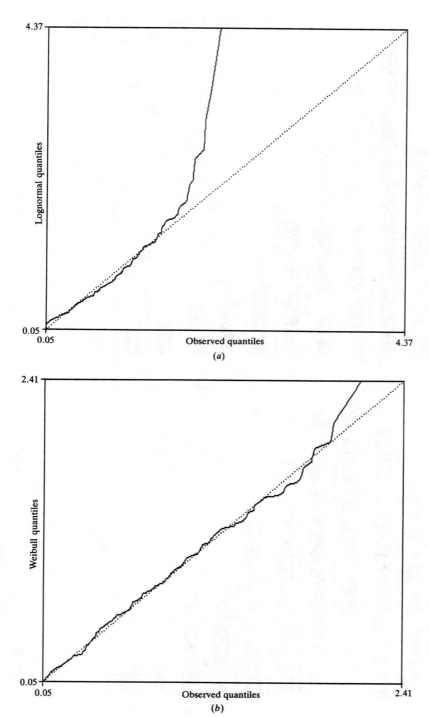

FIGURE 6.43

$Q-Q$ plots for the service-time data: (a) lognormal; (b) Weibull.

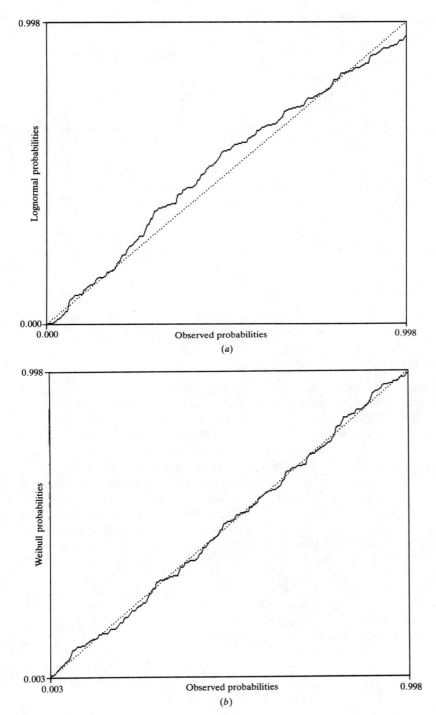

FIGURE 6.44
P–P plots for the service-time data: (a) lognormal; (b) Weibull.

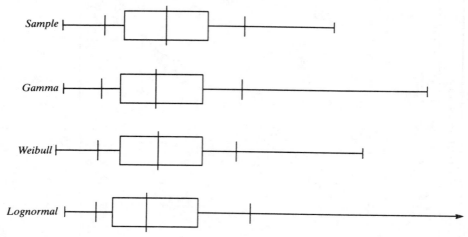

FIGURE 6.45
Box-plot comparison for the service-time data.

6.8 SHIFTED AND TRUNCATED DISTRIBUTIONS

The exponential, gamma, Weibull, lognormal, Pearson type V, and Pearson type VI distributions, discussed in Sec. 6.2.2, had range $[0, \infty)$. Thus, if the random variable X has any of these distributions, it can take on arbitrarily small positive values. However, it is frequently the case in practice that if X represents the time to complete some task (such as customer service), it is simply impossible for X to be less than some fixed positive number. For example, in a bank it is probably not possible to serve anyone in less than, say, 30 seconds; this will be reflected in the service-time data we might collect on the bank's operation. Thus, in reality $P(X < 30$ seconds$) = 0$; however, for a fitted gamma distribution, for instance, there is a *positive* probability of generating a random value that is less than 30 seconds. Thus, it would appear that a modification of these distribution forms would provide a more realistic model and might result in a better fit *in some cases*.

   This change can be effected by *shifting* the distribution some distance to the right. What this really amounts to is generalizing the density function of the distribution in question to include a location parameter (see Sec. 6.2.1). For example, the gamma distribution shifted to the right by an amount $\gamma > 0$ has density

$$f(x) = \begin{cases} \dfrac{\beta^{-\alpha}(x - \gamma)^{\alpha-1}e^{-(x-\gamma)/\beta}}{\Gamma(\alpha)} & \text{if } x > \gamma \\ 0 & \text{otherwise} \end{cases}$$

which has the same shape and scale parameters as the gamma(α, β) distribution but is shifted γ units to the right. (This is often called the *three-parameter gamma distribution*.) Shifted versions of the other distributions discussed above are defined similarly, by replacing x by $x - \gamma$ in the density functions and their domains of definition. The range of these shifted distributions is $[\gamma, \infty)$.

With these shifted distributions, we then have to estimate γ as well as the other parameters. In theory, this can be done by finding the MLE for γ in addition to the MLEs for the original parameters. For the shifted exponential, $\hat{\gamma}$ and $\hat{\beta}$ are relatively easy to find (see Prob. 6.12). However, finding MLEs for the three-parameter distributions is considerably more problematic. For example, in the case of the gamma, Weibull, and lognormal distributions, it is known that (global) MLEs are not well defined [see Cheng and Amin (1983), Cohen and Whitten (1980), and Zanakis (1979a)]. That is, the likelihood function L can be made infinite by choosing $\hat{\gamma} = X_{(1)}$ (the smallest observation in the sample), which results in inadmissible values for the other parameters. Harter and Moore (1966) have suggested the alternative of seeking a local, as opposed to global, maximum point of L. However, this approach may be ill-defined (e.g., the gamma and Weibull distributions with shape parameter $\alpha < 1$) or it may experience numerical difficulties.

Cheng and Amin (1983) introduced a new method, called *maximum product of spacing (MPS) estimation*, which can be used to estimate the three parameters of the distributions discussed above. They show that MPS estimation is well defined in certain situations where MLE estimation fails. In practice, MPS estimation requires solving three equations in three unknowns using a numerical procedure such as Newton-Raphson iteration.

A simple approach to the three-parameter estimation problem is first to estimate the location parameter γ by

$$\tilde{\gamma} = \frac{X_{(1)}X_{(n)} - X_{(k)}^2}{X_{(1)} + X_{(n)} - 2X_{(k)}}$$

where k is the smallest integer in $\{2, 3, \ldots, n - 1\}$ such that $X_{(k)} > X_{(1)}$ [see Dubey (1967)]. It can be shown that $\tilde{\gamma} < X_{(1)}$ if and only if $X_{(k)} < [X_{(1)} + X_{(n)}]/2$, which is very likely to occur; see Prob. 6.23. [Zanakis (1979b) has shown empirically the accuracy of $\tilde{\gamma}$ for the Weibull distribution.] Given the value $\tilde{\gamma}$, we next define X_i' as follows:

$$X_i' = X_i - \tilde{\gamma} \geq 0 \qquad \text{for } i = 1, 2, \ldots, n$$

Finally, MLE estimators of the scale and shape parameters are obtained by applying the usual two-parameter MLE procedures to the observations $X_1', X_2', \ldots, X_n'$.

Example 6.19. In Fig. 6.46, we give a histogram (with $\Delta b = 0.1$) of the time (in hours) to unload $n = 808$ coal trains, each consisting of approximately 110 cars.

(Figure 6.46 is actually a frequency comparison.) The shape of the histogram suggests that a fitted distribution would require a positive location parameter. Since $X_{(1)} = 3.37$, $X_{(2)} = 3.68$, and $X_{(808)} = 6.32$, we get $\tilde{\gamma} = 3.329$. The values $X'_i = X_i - 3.329$ for $i = 1, 2, \ldots, 808$ were then used to obtain the MLEs $\hat{\alpha} = 16.504$ and $\hat{\beta} = 0.079$ for the gamma distribution, whose expected proportions r_j are also given in Fig. 6.46. In general, the agreement between the shifted gamma density function and the histogram seems quite good.

Generating random values from shifted distributions is very easy given the ability to generate from the original unshifted distribution; see Prob. 8.15.

There are situations where a fitted distribution provides a good model for observed data, in general, but there is system information that says that no value can be larger than, say, the positive number l. If the range of the fitted distribution is $[0,\infty)$, then this is incompatible with the limit l. In this case, it might be worthwhile to use instead a truncated density function f^*. If f is the original density function, let $a(l) = \int_0^l f(x)\, dx$ which is less than 1 for finite

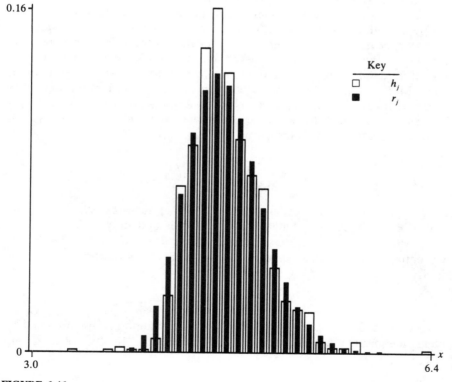

FIGURE 6.46
Frequency comparison for train unloading times and the fitted gamma distribution.

values of $l > 0$. Then the truncated density function, with range $[0,l)$, is given by

$$f^*(x) = \begin{cases} f(x)/a(l) & \text{if } 0 \leq x \leq l \\ 0 & \text{otherwise} \end{cases}$$

Techniques for generating random values from f^* are discussed in Sec. 8.2.1 and Prob. 8.3.

> **Example 6.20.** If a gamma distribution is found to provide a good model for service times in a bank, then the density function might be truncated from above at $l = 6$ hours, if this is the length of a work day.

An alternative approach to modeling a random variable with range $[0,l]$ is to use a beta distribution on the interval $[0,l]$ (see Sec. 6.2.2).

6.9 SELECTING A DISTRIBUTION IN THE ABSENCE OF DATA

In some simulation studies it may not be possible to collect data on the random variables of interest, so the techniques of Secs. 6.4 through 6.6 are not applicable to the problem of selecting corresponding probability distributions. For example, if the system being studied does not currently exist in some form, collecting data from the system is obviously not possible. This difficulty can also occur for existing systems, if the number of required probability distributions is large and the time available for the simulation study prohibits the necessary data collection and analysis. In this section we discuss two heuristic procedures for choosing a distribution in the absence of data, which we have found are used by many simulation practitioners.

Let us assume that the random quantity of interest is a continuous random variable X. It will also be useful to think of this random variable as being the time to perform some task, e.g., the time required to repair a piece of equipment when it fails. The first step in using either heuristic approach is to identify an interval $[a,b]$ (where a and b are real numbers such that $a < b$) in which it is felt that X will lie with probability close to 1; that is, $P(X < a$ or $X > b) \approx 0$. In order to obtain *subjective* estimates of a and b, "experts" are asked for their most optimistic and pessimistic estimates, respectively, of the time to perform the task. Once an interval $[a,b]$ has been identified subjectively, the next step is to place a probability density function on $[a,b]$ that is thought to be representative of X.

In the triangular approach, the experts are also asked for their subjective estimate of the most likely time to perform the task. This most likely value c is the mode of the distribution of X. Given a, b, and c, the random variable X is then considered to have a triangular distribution (see Sec. 6.2.2) on the interval $[a,b]$ with mode c. A graph of a triangular density function is given in Fig.

6.10. Furthermore, an algorithm for generating a triangular random variate is given in Sec. 8.3.11.

One difficulty with this triangular approach is that it requires subjective estimates of the absolute minimum and maximum possible values a and b, which can be problematic. For example, is the value b the maximum over the next 3 months or the maximum over a lifetime? As a result, it may be desirable in some cases to consider alternative triangular distributions discussed in Keefer and Bodily (1983), which require subjective estimates of the 0.05 and 0.95 quantiles rather than a and b. It is probably easier, for example, to estimate that value which is exceeded only 5 percent of the time than to estimate the absolute maximum b.

A second approach to placing a density function on $[a,b]$ is to assume that the random variable X has a beta distribution (see Sec. 6.2.2) on this interval with shape parameters α_1 and α_2. This approach offers more modeling flexibility because of the variety of shapes the beta density function can assume (see Fig. 6.7). On the other hand, it is not clear how to choose the parameters α_1 and α_2 so as to specify the distribution completely. We can suggest several possible ideas. If one is willing to assume that X is equally likely to take on any value between a and b, choose $\alpha_1 = \alpha_2 = 1$, which results in the U(a,b) distribution (see Fig. 6.7). (This model might be used if very little is known about the random variable X other than its range $[a,b]$.) An alternative idea, which we feel is generally more realistic, is to assume that the density function of X is skewed to the right. (Our experience with real-world data indicates that density functions corresponding to the time to perform some task often have this shape.) This density shape corresponds to $\alpha_2 > \alpha_1 > 1$ in the beta distribution (see Fig. 6.7). Furthermore, such a beta distribution has a mean μ and a mode c, given by

$$\mu = a + \frac{\alpha_1(b-a)}{\alpha_1 + \alpha_2} \quad \text{and} \quad c = a + \frac{(\alpha_1 - 1)(b-a)}{\alpha_1 + \alpha_2 - 2}$$

Given subjective estimates of μ and c, these equations can be solved to obtain the following estimates of α_1 and α_2:

$$\tilde{\alpha}_1 = \frac{(\mu - a)(2c - a - b)}{(c - \mu)(b - a)} \quad \text{and} \quad \tilde{\alpha}_2 = \frac{(b - \mu)\tilde{\alpha}_1}{\mu - a}$$

Note, however, that μ must be greater than c for the density to be skewed to the right; if $\mu < c$, it will be skewed to the left. [Keefer and Bodily (1983) suggest alternative ways of specifying the parameters of a beta distribution.] Algorithms for generating a beta random variate are given in Sec. 8.3.8.

6.10 MODELS OF ARRIVAL PROCESSES

In many simulations we need to generate a sequence of random points in time, $0 = t_0 \le t_1 \le t_2 \le \cdots$, such that the ith event of some kind occurs at time t_i

($i = 1, 2, \ldots$) and the distribution of the event times $\{t_i\}$ follows some specified form. Let $N(t) = \max\{i : t_i \le t\}$ be the number of events to occur at or before time t for $t \ge 0$. We call the stochastic process $\{N(t), t \ge 0\}$ an *arrival process* since, for our purposes, the events of interest are usually arrivals of customers to a service facility of some kind. In what follows, we call $A_i = t_i - t_{i-1}$ (where $i = 1, 2, \ldots$) the *interarrival time* between the $(i - 1)$st and ith customers.

In Sec. 6.10.1 we discuss the Poisson process, which is an arrival process for which the A_i's are IID exponential random variables. The Poisson process is the most commonly used model for the arrival process of customers to a queueing system. Section 6.10.2 discusses the nonstationary Poisson process, which is often used as a model of the arrival process to a system when the arrival rate varies with time. Finally, in Sec. 6.10.3 we describe an approach to modeling arrival processes where each event is really the arrival of a "batch" of customers.

A general reference for this section is Çinlar (1975, chap. 4).

6.10.1 Poisson Processes

In this section we define a Poisson process, state some of its important properties, and in the course of doing so explain why the interarrival times for many real-world systems closely resemble IID exponential random variables.

The stochastic process $\{N(t), t \ge 0\}$ is said to be a *Poisson process* if:

1. Customers arrive one at a time.
2. $N(t + s) - N(t)$ (the number of arrivals in the time interval $(t, t + s]$) is independent of $\{N(u), 0 \le u \le t\}$.
3. The distribution of $N(t + s) - N(t)$ is independent of t for all $t, s \ge 0$.

Properties 1 and 2 are characteristic of many actual arrival processes. Property 1 would not hold if customers arrived in batches; see Sec. 6.10.3. Property 2 says that the number of arrivals in the interval $(t, t + s]$ is independent of the number of arrivals in the earlier time interval $[0, t]$ and also of the times at which these arrivals occur. This property could be violated if, for example, a large number of arrivals in $[0, t]$ caused some customers arriving in $(t, t + s]$ to balk, i.e., to go away immediately without being served, because they find the system highly congested. Property 3, on the other hand, will be violated by most real-life arrival processes since it implies that the arrival rate of customers does not depend on the time of day, etc. If, however, the time period of interest for the system is relatively short, say, a 1- or 2-hour period of peak demand, we have found that for many systems (but certainly not all) the arrival rate is reasonably constant over this interval and the Poisson process is a good model for the process during this interval. (See Theorem 6.2 below and then Example 6.4.)

The following theorem, proved in Çinlar (1975, pp. 74–76), explains where the Poisson process gets its name.

Theorem 6.1. If $\{N(t), t \geq 0\}$ is a Poisson process, then the number of arrivals in any time interval of length s is a Poisson random variable with parameter λs (where λ is a positive real number). That is,

$$P[N(t + s) - N(t) = k] = \frac{e^{-\lambda s}(\lambda s)^k}{k!} \qquad \begin{array}{l} \text{for } k = 0, 1, 2, \ldots \\ \text{and } t, s \geq 0 \end{array}$$

Therefore, $E[N(s)] = \lambda s$ (see Sec. 6.2.3) and, in particular, $E[N(1)] = \lambda$. Thus, λ is the expected number of arrivals in any interval of length 1. We also call λ the *arrival rate* of the process.

We now see that the interarrival times for a Poisson process are IID exponential random variables; see Çinlar (1975, pp. 79–80).

Theorem 6.2. If $\{N(t), t \geq 0\}$ is a Poisson process with rate λ, then its corresponding interarrival times $A_1, A_2, \ldots$ are IID exponential random variables with mean $1/\lambda$.

This result together with our above discussion explains why we have found that interarrival times during a restricted time period are often approximately IID exponential random variables. For example, recall that the interarrival times of cars for the drive-up bank of Example 6.4 were found to be approximately exponential during a 90-minute period.

The converse of Theorem 6.2 is also true. Namely, if the interarrival times $A_1, A_2, \ldots$ for an arrival process $\{N(t), t \geq 0\}$ are IID exponential random variables with mean $1/\lambda$, then $\{N(t), t \geq 0\}$ is a Poisson process with rate λ [Çinlar (1975, p. 80)].

6.10.2 Nonstationary Poisson Processes

Let $\lambda(t)$ be the arrival rate of customers to some system at time t. [See below for some insight into the meaning of $\lambda(t)$.] If customers arrive at the system in accordance with a Poisson process with rate λ, then $\lambda(t) = \lambda$ for all $t \geq 0$. However, for many real-world systems, $\lambda(t)$ is actually a function of t. For example, the arrival rate of customers to a fast-food restaurant will be larger during the noon rush hour than in the middle of the afternoon. Also, traffic on a freeway will be heavier during the morning and evening rush hours. If the arrival rate $\lambda(t)$ does in fact change with time, then the interarrival times $A_1, A_2, \ldots$ are *not* identically distributed; thus, it is not appropriate to fit a single probability distribution to the A_i's using the techniques discussed in Secs. 6.4 through 6.6. In this section we discuss a commonly used model for arrival processes with time-varying arrival rates.

The stochastic process $\{N(t), t \geq 0\}$ is said to be a *nonstationary Poisson process* if:

1. Customers arrive one at a time.
2. $N(t + s) - N(t)$ is independent of $\{N(u), 0 \leq u \leq t\}$.

Thus, for a nonstationary Poisson process, customers must still arrive one at a time, and the numbers of arrivals in disjoint intervals are independent, but now the arrival rate $\lambda(t)$ is allowed to be a function of time.

Let $\Lambda(t) = E[N(t)]$ for all $t \geq 0$. If $\Lambda(t)$ is differentiable for a particular value of t, we formally define $\lambda(t)$ as

$$\lambda(t) = \frac{d}{dt} \Lambda(t)$$

Intuitively, $\lambda(t)$ will be large in intervals for which the expected number of arrivals is large. We call $\Lambda(t)$ and $\lambda(t)$ the *expectation function* and the *rate function*, respectively, for the nonstationary Poisson process.

The following theorem shows that the number of arrivals in the interval $(t, t + s]$ for a nonstationary Poisson process is a Poisson random variable whose parameter depends on *both* t and s.

Theorem 6.3. If $\{N(t), t \geq 0\}$ is a nonstationary Poisson process with continuous expectation function $\Lambda(t)$, then

$$P[N(t + s) - N(t) = k] = \frac{e^{-b(t,s)}[b(t,s)]^k}{k!} \qquad \begin{array}{l} \text{for } k = 0, 1, 2, \ldots \\ \text{and } t, s \geq 0 \end{array}$$

where $b(t,s) = \Lambda(t + s) - \Lambda(t) = \int_t^{t+s} \lambda(y)\, dy$, the last equality holding if $d\Lambda(t)/dt$ is bounded on $[t, t + s]$ and if $d\Lambda(t)/dt$ exists and is continuous for all but finitely many points in $[t, t + s]$ (see Prob. 6.25).

We have not yet addressed the question of how to estimate $\lambda(t)$ [or $\Lambda(t)$] from a set of observations on an arrival process of interest. The following example gives a heuristic but practical approach. [For a discussion of alternative approaches, see, for example, Lewis and Shedler (1976) and Kao and Chang (1988).]

Example 6.21. A simulation model was developed for a xerographic copy shop, and data were collected on the times of arrivals of customers between 11 A.M. and 1 P.M. for eight different days. From observing the characteristics of the arriving customers, it was felt that properties 1 and 2 for the nonstationary Poisson process were applicable and, in addition, that $\lambda(t)$ varied over the 2-hour interval. To obtain an estimate of $\lambda(t)$, the 2-hour interval was divided into the following 12 subintervals:

[11:00, 11:10), [11:10, 11:20), . . . , [12:40, 12:50), [12:50, 1:00)

For each day, the number of arrivals in each of these subintervals was determined. Then, for each subinterval, the average number of arrivals in that subinterval over the 8 days was computed. These 12 averages are estimates of the expected number of arrivals in the corresponding subintervals. Finally, for each subinterval, the average number of arrivals in that subinterval was divided by the subinterval length, 10 minutes, to obtain an estimate of the arrival rate for that subinterval. The estimated arrival rate $\hat{\lambda}(t)$ (in customers per minute) is plotted in Fig. 6.47. Note that the estimated arrival rate varies substantially over the 2-hour period.

One might legitimately ask how we decided on these subintervals of length 10 minutes. Actually, we computed estimates of $\lambda(t)$ in the above manner for subintervals of length 5, 10, and 15 minutes. The estimate of $\lambda(t)$ based on subintervals of length 5 minutes was rejected because it was felt that the corresponding plot of $\hat{\lambda}(t)$ was too ragged; i.e., a subinterval length of 5 minutes was too small. On the other hand, the estimate of $\lambda(t)$ based on subintervals of length 15 minutes was not chosen because the corresponding plot of $\hat{\lambda}(t)$ seemed too "smooth," meaning that information on the true nature of $\lambda(t)$ was being lost. In general, the problem of choosing a subinterval length here is similar to that of choosing the interval width for a histogram (see Sec. 6.4.2).

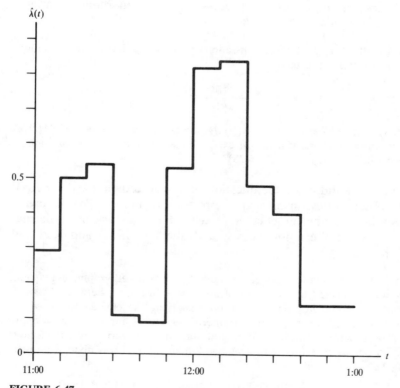

FIGURE 6.47
Plot of the estimated rate function $\hat{\lambda}(t)$ in customers per minute for the arrival process to a copy shop between 11 A.M. and 1 P.M.

6.10.3 Batch Arrivals

For some real-world systems, customers arrive in *batches*, or groups, so that property 1 of the Poisson process and of the nonstationary Poisson process is violated. For example, people arriving at a sporting event or at a cafeteria often come in batches. We now consider how one might model such an arrival process.

Let $N(t)$ now be the number of *batches* of individual customers that have arrived by time t. By applying the techniques discussed previously in this chapter to the times of arrivals of the successive batches, we can develop a model for the process $\{N(t), t \geq 0\}$. For example, if the interarrival times of batches appear to be approximately IID exponential random variables, $\{N(t), t \geq 0\}$ can be modeled as a Poisson process. Next, we fit a discrete distribution to the sizes of the successive batches; the batch sizes will be positive integers. Thus, for the original arrival process, it is assumed that batches of customers arrive in accordance with the arrival process $\{N(t), t \geq 0\}$ and that the number of customers in each batch is a random variable with the fitted discrete distribution.

The above informal discussion can be made more precise. If $X(t)$ is the total number of individual customers to arrive by time t, and if B_i is the number of customers in the ith batch, then $X(t)$ is given by

$$X(t) = \sum_{i=1}^{N(t)} B_i \qquad \text{for } t \geq 0$$

If the B_i's are assumed to be IID random variables that are also independent of $\{N(t), t \geq 0\}$, and if $\{N(t), t \geq 0\}$ is a Poisson process, then the stochastic process $\{X(t), t \geq 0\}$ is said to be a *compound Poisson process*.

6.11 ASSESSING THE HOMOGENEITY OF DIFFERENT DATA SETS

Sometimes an analyst collects k sets of observations on a random phenomenon independently and would like to know whether these data sets are homogeneous and can thus be merged. For example, it might be of interest to know whether service times of customers in a bank collected on different days are homogeneous. If they are, then the service times from the different days can be merged and the combined sample used to find *the* service-time distribution. Otherwise, more than one service-time distribution is needed. In this section, we discuss the Kruskal-Wallis hypothesis test for homogeneity. It is a nonparametric test since no assumptions are made about the distributions of the data.

Suppose that we have k independent samples of possibly different sizes, and that the samples themselves are independent. Denote the ith sample of size n_i by $X_{i1}, X_{i2}, \ldots, X_{in_i}$ for $i = 1, 2, \ldots, k$, and let n denote the total number of observations,

$$n = \sum_{i=1}^{k} n_i$$

Then we would like to test the null hypothesis

H_0: All of the population distribution functions are identical
against the alternative hypothesis

H_1: At least one of the populations tends to yield larger observations
than at least one of the other populations

To construct the Kruskal-Wallis (K-W) statistic, assign rank 1 to the smallest of the n observations, rank 2 to the second smallest, and so on to the largest of the n observations, which receives rank n. Let $R(X_{ij})$ represent the rank assigned to X_{ij} and let R_i be the sum of the ranks assigned to the ith sample, that is,

$$R_i = \sum_{j=1}^{n_i} R(X_{ij}) \qquad \text{for } i = 1, 2, \ldots, k$$

Then the K-W test statistic T is defined as

$$T = \frac{12}{n(n+1)} \sum_{i=1}^{k} \frac{R_i^2}{n_i} - 3(n+1)$$

We reject the null hypothesis H_0 at level α if $T > \chi^2_{k-1,1-\alpha}$, where $\chi^2_{k-1,1-\alpha}$ is the upper $1 - \alpha$ critical value for a chi-square distribution with $k - 1$ degrees of freedom. The above expression for T assumes that no two observations are equal. If this is not the case, then a different expression for T must be used [see Conover (1980, pp. 229–231)].

Example 6.22. A simulation model was developed for the hub operations of an overnight air-delivery service for the purpose of determining the amount of unloading equipment required. The model included provision for the fact that planes may arrive before or after their scheduled arrival times. Data were available on the actual times of arrival for two different incoming flight numbers (each corresponding to a different origin city) for 57 different days. (Each flight number arrives once a day, 5 days a week.) Let X_{ij} be the scheduled time of arrival minus the actual time of arrival (in minutes) for day j and flight number i, for $j = 1, 2, \ldots, 57$ and $i = 1, 2$. If $X_{ij} < 0$, then flight number i was late on day j. We want to perform a K-W test to determine whether the X_{1j}'s and X_{2j}'s are homogeneous, i.e., whether the arrival patterns for the two flight numbers are similar. We computed the K-W statistic and obtained $T = 4.317$, which is greater than the critical value $2.706 = \chi^2_{1,0.90}$. Therefore, we rejected the null hypothesis at level $\alpha = 0.10$ and the arrival patterns for the two flight numbers had to be modeled separately. The observed differences were to a large extent due to different weather conditions in the two origin cities.

TABLE 6.19
$\hat{\alpha}$ as a function of T, gamma distribution

T	$\hat{\alpha}$	T	$\hat{\alpha}$	T	$\hat{\alpha}$	T	$\hat{\alpha}$
0.01	0.010	1.40	0.827	5.00	2.655	13.00	6.662
0.02	0.019	1.50	0.879	5.20	2.755	13.50	6.912
0.03	0.027	1.60	0.931	5.40	2.856	14.00	7.163
0.04	0.036	1.70	0.983	5.60	2.956	14.50	7.413
0.05	0.044	1.80	1.035	5.80	3.057	15.00	7.663
0.06	0.052	1.90	1.086	6.00	3.157	15.50	7.913
0.07	0.060	2.00	1.138	6.20	3.257	16.00	8.163
0.08	0.068	2.10	1.189	6.40	3.357	16.50	8.413
0.09	0.076	2.20	1.240	6.60	3.458	17.00	8.663
0.10	0.083	2.30	1.291	6.80	3.558	17.50	8.913
0.11	0.090	2.40	1.342	7.00	3.658	18.00	9.163
0.12	0.098	2.50	1.393	7.20	3.759	18.50	9.414
0.13	0.105	2.60	1.444	7.40	3.859	19.00	9.664
0.14	0.112	2.70	1.495	7.60	3.959	19.50	9.914
0.15	0.119	2.80	1.546	7.80	4.059	20.00	10.164
0.16	0.126	2.90	1.596	8.00	4.159	20.50	10.414
0.17	0.133	3.00	1.647	8.20	4.260	21.00	10.664
0.18	0.140	3.10	1.698	8.40	4.360	21.50	10.914
0.19	0.147	3.20	1.748	8.60	4.460	22.00	11.164
0.20	0.153	3.30	1.799	8.80	4.560	22.50	11.414
0.30	0.218	3.40	1.849	9.00	4.660	23.00	11.664
0.40	0.279	3.50	1.900	9.20	4.760	23.50	11.914
0.50	0.338	3.60	1.950	9.40	4.860	24.00	12.164
0.60	0.396	3.70	2.001	9.60	4.961	24.50	12.414
0.70	0.452	3.80	2.051	9.80	5.061	25.00	12.664
0.80	0.507	3.90	2.101	10.00	5.161	30.00	15.165
0.90	0.562	4.00	2.152	10.50	5.411	35.00	17.665
1.00	0.616	4.20	2.253	11.00	5.661	40.00	20.165
1.10	0.669	4.40	2.353	11.50	5.912	45.00	22.665
1.20	0.722	4.60	2.454	12.00	6.162	50.00	25.166
1.30	0.775	4.80	2.554	12.50	6.412		

TABLE 6.20
$\hat{\alpha}_1$ and $\hat{\alpha}_2$ as functions of G_1 and G_2, beta distribution
If $G_1 \leq G_2$, use the first line of labels; if $G_2 \leq G_1$, use the second line of labels

G_1 G_2	G_2 G_1	$\hat{\alpha}_1$ $\hat{\alpha}_2$	$\hat{\alpha}_2$ $\hat{\alpha}_1$	G_1 G_2	G_2 G_1	$\hat{\alpha}_1$ $\hat{\alpha}_2$	$\hat{\alpha}_2$ $\hat{\alpha}_1$
0.01	0.01	0.112	0.112	0.15	0.35	0.405	0.563
0.01	0.05	0.126	0.157	0.15	0.40	0.432	0.653
0.01	0.10	0.135	0.192	0.15	0.45	0.464	0.762
0.01	0.15	0.141	0.223	0.15	0.50	0.502	0.903

TABLE 6.20 (*continued*)

G_1 G_2	G_2 G_1	$\hat{\alpha}_1$ $\hat{\alpha}_2$	$\hat{\alpha}_2$ $\hat{\alpha}_1$	G_1 G_2	G_2 G_1	$\hat{\alpha}_1$ $\hat{\alpha}_2$	$\hat{\alpha}_2$ $\hat{\alpha}_1$
0.01	0.20	0.147	0.254	0.15	0.55	0.550	1.090
0.01	0.25	0.152	0.285	0.15	0.60	0.612	1.353
0.01	0.30	0.157	0.318	0.15	0.65	0.701	1.752
0.01	0.35	0.163	0.354	0.15	0.70	0.842	2.429
0.01	0.40	0.168	0.395	0.15	0.75	1.111	3.810
0.01	0.45	0.173	0.441	0.15	0.80	1.884	8.026
0.01	0.50	0.179	0.495	0.15	0.84	7.908	42.014
0.01	0.55	0.185	0.559	0.20	0.20	0.395	0.395
0.01	0.60	0.192	0.639	0.20	0.25	0.424	0.461
0.01	0.65	0.200	0.741	0.20	0.30	0.456	0.537
0.01	0.70	0.210	0.877	0.20	0.35	0.491	0.626
0.01	0.75	0.221	1.072	0.20	0.40	0.531	0.735
0.01	0.80	0.237	1.376	0.20	0.45	0.579	0.873
0.01	0.85	0.259	1.920	0.20	0.50	0.640	1.057
0.01	0.90	0.299	3.162	0.20	0.55	0.720	1.314
0.01	0.95	0.407	8.232	0.20	0.60	0.834	1.701
0.01	0.98	0.850	42.126	0.20	0.65	1.016	2.352
0.05	0.05	0.180	0.180	0.20	0.70	1.367	3.669
0.05	0.10	0.195	0.223	0.20	0.75	2.388	7.654
0.05	0.15	0.207	0.263	0.20	0.79	10.407	39.649
0.05	0.20	0.217	0.302	0.25	0.25	0.500	0.500
0.05	0.25	0.228	0.343	0.25	0.30	0.543	0.588
0.05	0.30	0.238	0.387	0.25	0.35	0.592	0.695
0.05	0.35	0.248	0.437	0.25	0.40	0.651	0.830
0.05	0.40	0.259	0.494	0.25	0.45	0.724	1.007
0.05	0.45	0.271	0.560	0.25	0.50	0.822	1.254
0.05	0.50	0.284	0.640	0.25	0.55	0.962	1.624
0.05	0.55	0.299	0.739	0.25	0.60	1.186	2.243
0.05	0.60	0.317	0.867	0.25	0.65	1.620	3.486
0.05	0.65	0.338	1.037	0.25	0.70	2.889	7.230
0.05	0.70	0.366	1.280	0.25	0.74	12.905	37.229
0.05	0.75	0.403	1.655	0.30	0.30	0.647	0.647
0.05	0.80	0.461	2.305	0.30	0.35	0.717	0.777
0.05	0.85	0.566	3.682	0.30	0.40	0.804	0.947
0.05	0.90	0.849	8.130	0.30	0.45	0.920	1.182
0.05	0.94	2.898	45.901	0.30	0.50	1.086	1.532
0.10	0.10	0.245	0.245	0.30	0.55	1.352	2.115
0.10	0.15	0.262	0.291	0.30	0.60	1.869	3.280
0.10	0.20	0.278	0.337	0.30	0.65	3.387	6.779
0.10	0.25	0.294	0.386	0.30	0.69	15.402	34.780
0.10	0.30	0.310	0.441	0.35	0.35	0.879	0.879
0.10	0.35	0.327	0.503	0.35	0.40	1.013	1.101
0.10	0.40	0.345	0.576	0.35	0.45	1.205	1.430
0.10	0.45	0.365	0.663	0.35	0.50	1.514	1.975
0.10	0.50	0.389	0.770	0.35	0.55	2.115	3.060
0.10	0.55	0.417	0.909	0.35	0.60	3.883	6.313
0.10	0.60	0.451	1.093	0.35	0.64	17.897	32.315
0.10	0.65	0.497	1.356	0.40	0.40	1.320	1.320
0.10	0.70	0.560	1.756	0.40	0.45	1.673	1.827
0.10	0.75	0.660	2.443	0.40	0.50	2.358	2.832

TABLE 6.20 (*continued*)

G_1 G_2	G_2 G_1	$\hat{\alpha}_1$ $\hat{\alpha}_2$	$\hat{\alpha}_2$ $\hat{\alpha}_1$	G_1 G_2	G_2 G_1	$\hat{\alpha}_1$ $\hat{\alpha}_2$	$\hat{\alpha}_2$ $\hat{\alpha}_1$
0.10	0.80	0.846	3.864	0.40	0.55	4.376	5.837
0.10	0.85	1.374	8.277	0.40	0.59	20.391	29.841
0.10	0.89	5.406	44.239	0.45	0.45	2.597	2.597
0.15	0.15	0.314	0.314	0.45	0.50	4.867	5.354
0.15	0.20	0.335	0.367	0.45	0.54	22.882	27.359
0.15	0.25	0.357	0.424	0.49	0.49	12.620	12.620
0.15	0.30	0.380	0.489	0.49	0.50	24.873	25.371

PROBLEMS

6.1. Suppose that a man's job is to install 98 rivets in the right wing of an airplane under construction. If the random variable T is the total time required for one airplane, then what is the approximate distribution of T?

6.2. Prove comment 2 for the Weibull distribution in Table 6.3.

6.3. Prove comment 2 for the Pearson type VI distribution in Table 6.3.

6.4. Consider a four-parameter Pearson type VI distribution with shape parameters α_1, α_2, scale parameter β, and location parameter γ. If $\alpha_1 = 1$, $\gamma = \beta = c > 0$, then the resulting density is

$$f(x) = \alpha_2 x^{-(\alpha_2+1)} c^{\alpha_2} \qquad \text{for } x > c$$

which is the density function of a *Pareto distribution* with parameters c and α_2, denoted Pareto(c,α_2). Show that $X \sim \text{Pareto}(c,\alpha_2)$ if and only if $Y = \ln X \sim$ expo($\ln c$, $1/\alpha_2$), an exponential distribution with location parameter $\ln c$ and scale parameter $1/\alpha_2$.

6.5. For the empirical distribution given by $F(x)$ in Sec. 6.2.4, discuss the merit of defining $F(X_{(i)}) = i/n$ for $i = 1, 2, \ldots, n$, which seems like an intuitive definition. In this case, how would you define $F(x)$ for $0 \le x < X_{(1)}$?

6.6. Compute the expectation of the empirical distribution given by $F(x)$ in Sec. 6.2.4.

6.7. For discrete distributions, prove that the line graph (Sec. 6.4.2) is an unbiased estimator of the (unknown) mass function; i.e., show that $E(h_j) = p(x_j)$ for all j. *Hint:* For j fixed, define

$$Y_i = \begin{cases} 1 & \text{if } X_i = x_j \\ 0 & \text{otherwise} \end{cases} \qquad \text{for } i = 1, 2, \ldots, n$$

6.8. Suppose that the histogram of your observed data has several local modes (see Fig. 6.24), but that it is not possible to break the data into natural groups with a different probability distribution fitting each group. Describe an alternative approach for modeling your data.

6.9. For a geometric distribution with parameter p, explain why the MLE $\hat{p} = 1/[\bar{X}(n) + 1]$ is intuitive.

6.10. For each of the following distributions, derive formulas for the MLEs of the indicated parameters. Assume that we have IID data $X_1, X_2, \ldots, X_n$ from the distribution in question.

   (*a*) U($0,b$), MLE for b

   (*b*) U($a,0$), MLE for a

(c) U(a,b), joint MLEs for a and b
(d) N(μ,σ^2), joint MLEs for μ and σ
(e) LN(μ,σ^2), joint MLEs for μ and σ
(f) Bernoulli(p), MLE for p
(g) DU(i, j), joint MLEs for i and j
(h) bin(t,p), MLE for p assuming that t is known
(i) negbin(s,p), MLE for p assuming that s is known
(j) U($\theta - 0.5, \theta + 0.5$), MLE for θ

6.11. For a Poisson distribution with parameter λ, derive an approximate $100(1 - \alpha)$ percent confidence interval for λ given the data $X_1, X_2, \ldots, X_n$. Use the asymptotic normality of the MLE $\hat{\lambda}$.

6.12. Consider the shifted (two-parameter) exponential distribution, which has density function

$$f(x) = \begin{cases} \dfrac{1}{\beta} e^{-(x-\gamma)/\beta} & \text{if } x \geq \gamma \\ 0 & \text{otherwise} \end{cases}$$

for $\beta > 0$ and any real number γ. Given a sample $X_1, X_2, \ldots, X_n$ of IID random values from this distribution, find formulas for the joint MLEs $\hat{\gamma}$ and $\hat{\beta}$. *Hint:* Remember that γ cannot exceed any X_i.

6.13. For a frequency comparison, show that r_j as given by (6.2) is actually the expected proportion of the n observations that would fall in the jth interval if the fitted distribution were in fact the true one.

6.14. For Q–Q plots, why it is inconvenient to have an empirical distribution function $\tilde{F}_n(x)$ such that $\tilde{F}_n(X_{(n)}) = 1$?

6.15. What difficulty arises when you try to define a Q–Q plot for a discrete distribution?

6.16. Suppose that the true distribution function $F(x)$ and the fitted distribution function $\hat{F}(x)$ are the same. For what distribution $F(x)$ will the Q–Q and P–P plots be essentially the same if the sample size n is large?

6.17. Suppose that the random variable M_j is the number of the n X_i's that would fall in the jth interval $[a_{j-1}, a_j)$ for a chi-square test if the fitted distribution were in fact the true one. What is the distribution of M_j, and what is its mean?

6.18. For the chi-square test, explain intuitively why Kallenberg, Oosterhoff, and Schriever (1985) found in certain cases that power was greater when the np_j's were smaller in the tails rather than all being equal.

6.19. Let $F_n(x)$ be the empirical distribution function used for the K-S test. Show that $F_n(x) \to F(x)$ as $n \to \infty$ (w.p. 1) for all x, where $F(x)$ is the true underlying distribution function.

6.20. Assume that the data in Table 6.21 are independent observations on service times (in minutes) at a single-server queueing system. Use all appropriate techniques from Secs. 6.4 through 6.6 to hypothesize a distribution form, estimate its parameter(s) (using MLE estimation), and evaluate goodness of fit.

6.21. Suppose that the data in Table 6.22 are independent observations on deviations from the desired diameter of ball bearings produced by a new high-speed machine. Use all appropriate techniques from Secs. 6.4 through 6.6 to hypothesize a distribution form, estimate its parameter(s) (using MLE estimation), and evaluate goodness of fit.

6.22. Assume that the number of items demanded per day from an inventory on

TABLE 6.21
Service-time data

0.02	4.04	0.37	4.85	8.22	3.14	2.19
1.39	4.85	2.66	2.39	1.04	1.95	1.65
5.02	4.75	0.99	4.06	3.27	2.13	1.52
3.04	16.44	2.83	5.03	2.66	2.54	3.67
3.45	6.71	4.45	11.51	2.14	1.58	5.49
1.85	1.92	3.78	2.57	7.23	3.19	0.71
0.83	2.28	7.66	1.99	3.43	6.88	3.46
4.39	2.50	6.03	10.29	3.07	7.12	3.26
4.39	3.34	3.41	4.73	7.98	0.94	8.52
7.78	3.79	1.16	5.00	0.86	7.02	4.95
2.66	6.03	4.21	4.19	5.08	3.29	3.57
3.37	2.80	2.82	1.03	5.16	3.35	
5.83	5.97	4.56	4.05	5.79	2.34	
0.72	2.10	7.15	6.64	1.36	10.79	
0.89	2.82	5.08	2.12	0.51	3.23	
3.43	3.47	2.07	2.93	4.46	2.08	
4.33	3.09	0.84	5.12	6.36	1.15	

different days are IID random variables and that the data in Table 6.23 are those demand sizes on 76 different days. Use all appropriate techniques from Secs. 6.4 through 6.6 to hypothesize a distribution form, estimate its parameter(s) (using MLE estimation), and evaluate goodness of fit.

6.23. For the location parameter estimator $\tilde{\gamma}$ in Sec. 6.8, show that $\tilde{\gamma} < X_{(1)}$ if and only if $X_{(k)} < [X_{(1)} + X_{(n)}]/2$.

TABLE 6.22
Data on errors in the diameter of ball bearings

2.31	0.94	1.55	1.10	1.68	−0.16	0.48
1.49	1.20	1.48	0.85	3.21	1.71	4.01
2.10	0.26	1.97	1.09	2.72	1.18	0.28
0.30	1.40	0.59	1.99	2.14	1.59	1.50
0.48	2.12	1.15	2.54	0.70	1.63	1.47
1.71	1.41	0.95	1.55	1.28	0.44	−1.72
0.19	2.73	0.45	0.49	1.23	2.44	−1.62
0.00	1.33	−0.51	1.62	0.06	2.20	1.87
0.66	0.26	2.36	2.40	1.00	2.30	1.74
−1.27	3.11	1.03	0.59	1.37	1.30	0.78
1.01	0.99	0.24	2.18	2.24	0.22	1.01
−0.54	0.24	2.66	1.14	1.06	1.09	1.63
1.70	1.35	1.00	1.21	1.75	3.27	1.62
2.58	0.60	0.19	1.43	2.21	0.49	0.46
0.56	1.17	2.28	2.02	1.71	1.08	2.08
0.38	1.12	0.01	1.82	1.96	0.77	1.70
0.77	2.79	0.31	1.11	1.69	1.23	2.05
2.29	0.17	−0.12	2.69	1.78	2.26	0.02
1.55	0.44	0.89	1.51	−0.67	1.06	−0.05
0.27	0.78	0.60	1.06	2.29	1.13	1.85
1.62	1.50	0.21	2.04	1.26	1.98	1.50
0.94	0.17	1.90	1.64	1.12	0.89	0.49

TABLE 6.23
Demand-size data

2	7	1	3	6	1	3
2	0	1	5	11	5	3
2	8	1	7	4	8	4
4	0	2	20	0	2	5
1	6	12	7	0	5	11
8	6	2	0	4	2	4
8	10	6	6	5	2	6
3	6	5	0	1	3	1
0	2	1	8	5	6	1
0	1	9	4	1	4	2
2	1	1	2	1	4	

6.24. Let $LN(\gamma,\mu,\sigma^2)$ denote the shifted (three-parameter) lognormal distribution, which has density

$$f(x) = \begin{cases} \dfrac{1}{(x-\gamma)\sqrt{2\pi\sigma^2}} \exp \dfrac{-[\ln(x-\gamma)-\mu]^2}{2\sigma^2} & \text{if } x > \gamma \\ 0 & \text{otherwise} \end{cases}$$

for $\sigma > 0$ and any real numbers γ and μ. [Thus, $LN(0,\mu,\sigma^2)$ is the original $LN(\mu,\sigma^2)$ distribution.]

(a) Verify that $X \sim LN(\gamma,\mu,\sigma^2)$ if and only if $X - \gamma \sim LN(\mu,\sigma^2)$.

(b) Show that for a fixed, known value of γ, the MLEs of μ and σ in the $LN(\gamma,\mu,\sigma^2)$ distribution are

$$\hat{\mu} = \frac{\sum\limits_{i=1}^{n} \ln(X_i - \gamma)}{n} \quad \text{and} \quad \hat{\sigma} = \left\{ \frac{\sum\limits_{i=1}^{n} [\ln(X_i - \gamma) - \hat{\mu}]^2}{n} \right\}^{1/2}$$

i.e., we simply shift the data by an amount $-\gamma$ and then treat them as being (unshifted) lognormal data.

6.25. For Theorem 6.3 in Sec. 6.10.2, explain intuitively why the expected number of arrivals in the interval $(t, t+s]$, $b(t, s)$, should be equal to $\int_t^{t+s} \lambda(y)\, dy$.

6.26. Provide an intuitive motivation for the definition of MLEs in the continuous case (see Sec. 6.5) by going through steps (a) through (c) below. As before, the observed data are $X_1, X_2, \ldots, X_n$, and are IID realizations of a random variable X with density f_θ. Bear in mind that the X_i's have already been observed, so are to be regarded as fixed numbers rather than variables.

(a) Let ε be a small (but strictly positive) real number, and define the phrase "getting a value of X near X_i" to be the event $\{X_i - \varepsilon < X < X_i + \varepsilon\}$. Use the mean-value theorem from calculus to argue that $P(\text{getting a value of } X$ near $X_i) \approx 2\varepsilon f_\theta(X_i)$, for any $i = 1, 2, \ldots, n$.

(b) Define the phrase "getting a sample of n IID values of X near the observed data" to be the event (getting a value of X near X_1, getting a value of X near $X_2, \ldots$, getting a value of X near X_n). Show that $P(\text{getting a sample of } n$ IID values of X near the observed data) $\approx (2\varepsilon)^n f_\theta(X_1) f_\theta(X_2) \cdots f_\theta(X_n)$, and note that this is *proportional* to the likelihood function $L(\theta)$.

(c) Argue that the MLE $\hat{\theta}$ is the value of θ that maximizes the approximate probability of getting a sample of n IID values of X near the observed data, and in this sense "best explains" the data that were actually observed.

REFERENCES

Anderson, T W., and D. A. Darling: A Test of Goodness of Fit, *J. Am. Statist. Assoc.*, *49*: 765–769 (1954).

Barnett, V.: Probability Plotting Methods and Order Statistics, *Appl. Statist.*, *24*: 95–108 (1975).

Bartels, R.: The Rank Version of von Neumann's Ratio Test for Randomness, *J. Am. Statist. Assoc.*, *77*: 40–46 (1982).

Beckman, R. J., and G. L. Tietjen: Maximum Likelihood Estimation for the Beta Distribution, *J. Statist. Comput. Simul.*, *7*: 253–258 (1978).

Best, D. J., and D. E. Roberts: The Percentage Points of the χ^2 Distribution, *Appl. Statist.*, *24*: 385–388 (1975).

Bhattacharjee, G. P.: Algorithm AS32: The Incomplete Gamma Integral, *Appl. Statist.*, *19*: 285–287 (1970).

Bosten, N. E., and E. L. Battiste: Remark on Algorithm 179, *Commun. Assoc. Comput. Mach.*, *17*: 156–157 (1974).

Bratley, P., B. L. Fox, and L. E. Schrage: *A Guide to Simulation*, 2d ed., Springer-Verlag, New York (1987).

Breiman, L.: *Statistics: With a View toward Applications*, Houghton Mifflin, Boston (1973).

Chandra, M., N. D. Singpurwalla, and M. A. Stephens: Kolmogorov Statistics for Tests of Fit for the Extreme-Value and Weibull Distributions, *J. Am. Statist. Assoc.*, *76*: 729–731 (1981).

Cheng, R. C. H., and N. A. K. Amin: Estimating Parameters in Continuous Univariate Distributions with a Shifted Origin, *J. Roy. Statist. Soc. B*, *45*: 394–403 (1983).

Chernoff, H., and E. L. Lehmann: The Use of Maximum Likelihood Estimates in χ^2 Tests for Goodness of Fit, *Ann. Math. Statist.*, *25*: 579–586 (1954).

Choi, S. C., and R. Wette: Maximum Likelihood Estimation of the Parameters of the Gamma Distribution and Their Bias, *Technometrics*, *11*: 683–690 (1969).

Çinlar, E.: *Introduction to Stochastic Processes*, Prentice-Hall, Englewood Cliffs, N.J. (1975).

Cohen, A. C., and B. J. Whitten: Estimation in the Three-Parameter Lognormal Distribution, *J. Am. Statist. Assoc.*, *75*: 399–404 (1980).

Conover, W. J.: *Practical Nonparametric Statistics*, 2d ed., John Wiley, New York (1980).

Cran, G. W., K. J. Martin, and G. E. Thomas: A Remark on Algorithms AS63: The Incomplete Beta Integral, AS64: Inverse of the Incomplete Beta Function Ratio, *Appl. Statist.*, *26*: 111–114 (1977).

DeRiggi, D. F.: Unimodality of Likelihood Functions for the Binomial Distribution, *J. Am. Statist. Assoc.*, *78*: 181–183 (1983).

Dubey, S. D.: On Some Permissible Estimators of the Location Parameter of the Weibull and Certain Other Distributions, *Technometrics*, *9*: 293–307 (1967).

Durbin, J.: Kolmogorov-Smirnov Tests When Parameters Are Estimated with Applications to Tests of Exponentiality and Tests on Spacings, *Biometrika*, *62*: 5–22 (1975).

Gibbons, J. D.: *Nonparametric Methods for Quantitative Analysis*, 2d ed., American Sciences Press, Columbus, Ohio (1985).

Gleser, L. J.: Exact Power of Goodness-of-Fit Tests of Kolmogorov Type for Discontinuous Distributions, *J. Am. Statist. Assoc.*, *80*: 954–958 (1985).

Gnanadesikan, R., R. S. Pinkham, and L. P. Hughes: Maximum Likelihood Estimation of the Parameters of the Beta Distribution from Smallest Order Statistics, *Technometrics*, *9*: 607–620 (1967).

Gonzalez, T., S. Sahni, and W. R. Franta: An Efficient Algorithm for the Kolmogorov-Smirnov and Lilliefors Tests, *Assoc. Comput. Mach. Trans. Math. Software*, *3*: 60–64 (1977).

Haberman, S. J.: A Warning on the Use of Chi-Squared Statistics with Frequency Tables with Small Expected Cell Counts, *J. Am. Statist. Assoc.*, *83*: 555–560 (1988).

Hahn, G. J., and S. S. Shapiro: *Statistical Models in Engineering*, John Wiley, New York (1967).

Harter, H. L., and A. H. Moore: Local Maximum-Likelihood Estimation of the Parameters of Three-Parameter Log-Normal Populations from Complete and Censored Samples, *J. Am. Statist. Assoc.*, *61*: 842–851 (1966).

Hastings, N. A. J., and J. B. Peacock: *Statistical Distributions*, John Wiley, New York (1975).

Hoaglin, D. C., F. Mosteller, and J. W. Tukey, *Understanding Robust and Exploratory Data Analysis*, John Wiley, New York (1983).

IMSL, Inc.: *User's Manual: Stat/Library*, Vol. 3, IMSL, Houston, Tex. (1987).

Johnson, M. E., and V. W. Lowe, Jr.: Bounds on the Sample Skewness and Kurtosis, *Technometrics*, *21*: 377–378 (1979).

Kallenberg, W. C. M., J. Oosterhoff, and B. F. Schriever: The Number of Classes in Chi-Squared Goodness-of-Fit Tests, *J. Am. Statist. Assoc.*, *80*: 959–968 (1985).

Kao, E. P. C., and S.-L. Chang: Modeling Time-Dependent Arrivals to Service Systems: A Case in Using a Piecewise-Polynomial Rate Function in a Nonhomogeneous Poisson Process, *Management Sci.*, *34*: 1367–1379 (1988).

Keefer, D. L., and S. E. Bodily: Three-Point Approximations for Continuous Random Variables, *Management Sci.*, *29*: 595–609 (1983).

Kendall, M. G., and A. Stuart: *The Advanced Theory of Statistics*, Vol. 2, 4th ed., Griffin, London (1979).

Kendall, M. G., A. Stuart, and J. K. Ord: *The Advanced Theory of Statistics*, Vol. 1, 5th ed., Oxford University Press, New York (1987).

Kennedy, W. J., Jr., and J. E. Gentle: *Statistical Computing*, Marcel Dekker, New York (1980).

Law, A. M., and S. G. Vincent: *UniFit II User's Guide*, Simulation Modeling and Analysis Company, Tucson, Ariz. (1990).

Lawless, J. F.: *Statistical Models for Lifetime Data*, John Wiley, New York (1982).

Levin, B., and J. Reeds: Compound Multinomial Likelihood Functions Are Unimodal: Proof of a Conjecture of I. J. Good, *Ann. Statist.*, *5*: 79–87 (1977).

Lewis, P. A. W., and G. S. Shedler: Statistical Analysis of Non-Stationary Series of Events in a Data Base System, *IBM J. Res. Dev.*, *20*: 465–482 (1976).

Lilliefors, H. W.: On the Kolmogorov-Smirnov Test for Normality with Mean and Variance Unknown, *J. Am. Statist. Assoc.*, *62*: 399–402 (1967).

Lilliefors, H. W.: On the Kolmogorov-Smirnov Test for the Exponential Distribution with Mean Unknown, *J. Am. Statist Assoc.*, *64*: 387–389 (1969).

Littell, R. C., J. T. McClave, and W. W. Offen: Goodness-of-Fit Tests for the Two Parameter Weibull Distribution, *Commun. Statist.*, *B8*: 257–269 (1979).

Margolin, B. H., and W. Maurer: Tests of the Kolmogorov-Smirnov Type for Exponential Data with Unknown Scale, and Related Problems, *Biometrika*, *63*: 149–160 (1976).

Menon, M. V.: Estimation of the Shape and Scale Parameters of the Weibull Distribution, *Technometrics*, *5*: 175–182 (1963).

Milton, R. C., and R. Hotchkiss: Computer Evaluation of the Normal and Inverse Normal Distribution Functions, *Technometrics*, *11*: 817–822 (1969).

Odeh, R. E., and J. O. Evans: The Percentage Points of the Normal Distribution, *Appl. Statist.*, *23*: 96–97 (1974).

Owen, D. B.: *Handbook of Statistical Tables*, Addison-Wesley, Reading, Mass. (1962).

Pearson, K.: On a Criterion That a Given System of Deviations from the Probable in the Case of a Correlated System of Variables Is Such That It Can Be Reasonably Supposed to Have Arisen in Random Sampling, *Phil. Mag.* (5), *50*: 157–175 (1900).

Pettitt, A. N., and M. A. Stephens: The Kolmogorov-Smirnov Goodness-of-Fit Statistic with Discrete and Grouped Data, *Technometrics*, *19*: 205–210 (1977).

Ross, S. M.: *Introduction to Probability Models*, 4th ed., Academic Press, San Diego (1989).

Scott, D. W., On Optimal and Data-Based Histograms, *Biometrika*, *66*: 605–610 (1979).

Silverman, B. W.: *Density Estimation for Statistics and Data Analysis*, Chapman & Hall, London (1986).

Stephens, M. A.: EDF Statistics for Goodness of Fit and Some Comparisons, *J. Am. Statist. Assoc.*, *69*: 730–737 (1974).

Stephens, M. A.: Asymptotic Results for Goodness-of-Fit Statistics with Unknown Parameters, *Ann. Statist.*, *4*: 357–369 (1976).

Stephens, M. A.: Goodness of Fit for the Extreme Value Distribution, *Biometrika*, *64*: 583–588 (1977).

Swain, J. J., S. Venkatraman, and J. R. Wilson: Least-Squares Estimation of Distribution Functions in Johnson's Translation System, *J. Statist. Comput. Simul.*, *29*: 271–297 (1988).

Thoman, D. R., L. J. Bain, and C. E. Antle: Inferences on the Parameters of the Weibull Distribution, *Technometrics*, *11*: 445–460 (1969).

Tukey, J. W.: *Exploratory Data Analysis*, Addison-Wesley, Reading, Mass. (1970).

Wegman, E. J.: Density Estimation, in *Encyclopedia of Statistical Sciences*, Vol. 2, N. L. Johnson and S. Kotz, eds., pp. 309–315, John Wiley, New York (1982).

Wilk, M. B., and R. Gnanadesikan: Probability Plotting Methods for the Analysis of Data, *Biometrika*, *55*: 1–17 (1968).

Yarnold, J. K.: The Minimum Expectation in χ^2 Goodness-of-Fit Tests and the Accuracy of Approximations for the Null Distribution, *J. Am. Statist. Assoc.*, *65*: 864–886 (1970).

Zanakis, S. H.: Extended Pattern Search with Transformations for the Three-Parameter Weibull MLE Problem, *Management Sci.*, *25*: 1149–1161 (1979a).

Zanakis, S. H.: A Simulation Study of Some Simple Estimators for the Three-Parameter Weibull Distribution, *J. Statist. Comput. Simul.*, *9*: 101–116 (1979b).

CHAPTER
7

RANDOM-NUMBER
GENERATORS

Recommended sections for a first reading: 7.1, 7.2, 7.4.1, 7.4.3, 7.5, 7.6

7.1 INTRODUCTION

A simulation of any system or process in which there are inherently random components requires a method of generating or obtaining numbers that are *random*, in some sense. For example, the queueing and inventory models of Chaps. 1 and 2 required interarrival times, service times, demand sizes, etc., that were "drawn" from some specified distribution, such as exponential or Erlang. In this and the next chapter, we discuss how random values can be conveniently and efficiently generated from a desired probability distribution for use in executing simulation models. So as to avoid speaking of "generating random variables," which would not be strictly correct since a random variable is defined in mathematical probability theory as a function satisfying certain conditions, we will adopt more precise terminology and speak of "generating random *variates*."

This entire chapter is devoted to methods of generating random variates from the uniform distribution on the interval [0,1]; this distribution was denoted by U(0,1) in Chap. 6. Random variates generated from the U(0,1) distribution will be called *random numbers*. Although this is the simplest continuous distribution of all, it is extremely important that we be able to

420

obtain such independent random numbers. This prominent role of the U(0,1) distribution stems from the fact that random variates from all other distributions (normal, gamma, binomial, etc.) and realizations of various random processes (e.g., a nonstationary Poisson process) can be obtained by transforming IID random numbers in a way determined by the desired distribution or process. This chapter discusses ways to obtain independent random numbers, and the following chapter treats methods of transforming them to obtain variates from other distributions, and realizations of various processes.

The methodology of generating random numbers has a long and interesting history; see Hull and Dobell (1962), Morgan (1984, pp. 51–56), and Dudewicz (1975) for entertaining accounts. The earliest methods were essentially carried out by hand, such as casting lots (Matthew 27:35), throwing dice, dealing out cards, or drawing numbered balls from a "well-stirred urn." Many lotteries are still operated in this way, as is well known by American males who were of draft age in the late 1960s and early 1970s. In the early twentieth century, statisticians joined gamblers in their interest in random numbers, and mechanized devices were built to generate random numbers more quickly; in the late 1930s, Kendall and Babington-Smith (1938) used a rapidly spinning disk to prepare a table of 100,000 random digits. Some time later, electric circuits based on randomly pulsating vacuum tubes were developed that delivered random digits at rates of up to 50 per second. One such random-number machine, the Electronic Random Number Indicator Equipment (ERNIE) was used by the British General Post Office to pick the winners in the Premium Savings Bond lottery [see Thomson (1959)]. Another electronic device was used by the Rand Corporation (1955) to generate a table of a million random digits. Many other schemes have been contrived, such as picking numbers "randomly" out of phone books or census reports, or using digits in an expansion of π to 100,000 decimal places. There is evidently still interest in building and testing physical random-number "machines"; for example, Miyatake et al. (1983) describe a device based on counting gamma rays.

As computers (and simulation) became more widely used, increasing attention was paid to methods of random-number generation compatible with the way computers work. One possibility would be to hook up an electronic random-number machine, such as ERNIE, directly to the computer. This has several disadvantages, chiefly that we could not reproduce a previously generated random-number stream exactly. (The desirability of being able to do this is discussed later in this section.) Another alternative would be to read in a table, such as the Rand Corporation table, but this would entail either large memory requirements or a lot of time for relatively slow input operations. (Also, it is not at all uncommon for a modern large-scale simulation to use far more than a million random *numbers*, each of which would require several individual random *digits*.) Therefore, research in the 1940s and 1950s turned to *numerical* or *arithmetic* ways to generate "random" numbers. These methods are sequential, with each new number being determined by one or several of its predecessors according to a fixed mathematical formula. The first such arithmetic generator, proposed by von Neumann and Metropolis in the 1940s, is the famous *midsquare method*, an example of which follows.

> **Example 7.1.** Start with a four-digit positive integer Z_0 and square it to obtain an integer with up to eight digits; if necessary, append zeros to the left to make it exactly eight digits. Take the *middle four* digits of this eight-digit number as the next four-digit number, Z_1. Place a decimal point at the left of Z_1 to obtain the first "U(0,1) random number," U_1. Then let Z_2 be the middle four digits of Z_1^2 and let U_2 be Z_2 with a decimal point at the left, and so on. Table 7.1 lists the first few Z_i's and U_i's for $Z_0 = 7182$ (the first four digits to the right of the decimal point in the number e).

Intuitively the midsquare method seems to provide a good scrambling of one number to obtain the next, and so we might think that such a haphazard rule would provide a fairly good way of generating random numbers. In fact, it does not work very well at all. One serious problem (among others) is that it has a strong tendency to degenerate fairly rapidly to zero, where it will stay forever. (Continue Table 7.1 for just a few more steps, or try $Z_0 = 1009$, the first four digits from the Rand Corporation tables.) This illustrates the danger in assuming that a good random-number generator will always be obtained by doing something strange and nefarious to one number to obtain the next.

A more fundamental objection to the midsquare method is that it is not "random" at all, in the sense of being unpredictable. Indeed, if we know one number, the next is completely determined since the rule to obtain it is fixed; actually, when Z_0 is specified, the *whole sequence* of Z_i's and U_i's is determined. This objection applies to all arithmetic generators (the only kind we consider in the rest of this chapter), and arguing about it usually leads one quickly into mystical discussions about the true nature of truly random numbers. (Sometimes arithmetic generators are called *pseudorandom*, an awkward term that we avoid, even though it is probably more accurate.) Indeed, in an oft-quoted quip, John von Neumann (1951) declared that:

TABLE 7.1
The midsquare method

i	Z_i	U_i	Z_i^2
0	7,182	—	51,581,124
1	5,811	0.5811	33,767,721
2	7,677	0.7677	58,936,329
3	9,363	0.9363	87,665,769
4	6,657	0.6657	44,315,649
5	3,156	0.3156	09,960,336
.	.	.	.
.	.	.	.
.	.	.	.

Any one who considers arithmetical methods of producing random digits is, of course, in a state of sin. For, as has been pointed out several times, there is no such thing as a random number—there are only methods to produce random numbers, and a strict arithmetic procedure of course is not such a method. . . . We are here dealing with mere "cooking recipes" for making digits. . . .

It is seldom stated, however, that von Neumann goes on in the same paragraph to say, less gloomily, that these "recipes"

. . . probably . . . can not be justified, but should merely be judged by their results. Some statistical study of the digits generated by a given recipe should be made, but exhaustive tests are impractical. If the digits work well on one problem, they seem usually to be successful with others of the same type.

This more practical attitude was shared by Lehmer (1951), who developed the most widely used class of techniques for random-number generation (discussed in Sec. 7.2); he viewed the idea of an arithmetic random-number generator as

. . . a vague notion embodying the idea of a sequence in which each term is unpredictable to the uninitiated and whose digits pass a certain number of tests traditional with statisticians and depending somewhat on the use to which the sequence is to be put.

More formal definitions of "randomness" in an axiomatic sense are cited by Ripley (1987, p. 19); Niederreiter (1978a) argues that statistical randomness may not even be desirable, and that other properties of the generated numbers, such as "evenness" of the distribution of points, are more important in some applications, such as Monte Carlo integration. We agree with most writers that arithmetic generators, if designed carefully, can produce numbers that *appear* to be independent draws from the U(0,1) distribution, in that they pass a series of statistical tests (see Sec. 7.4). This is a useful definition of "random numbers," to which we subscribe.

A "good" arithmetic random-number generator should possess several properties:

1. Above all, the numbers produced should appear to be distributed uniformly on [0,1] and should not exhibit any correlation with each other; otherwise, the simulation's results may be completely invalid.
2. From a practical standpoint, we would naturally like the generator to be fast and avoid the need for a lot of storage.
3. We would like to be able to reproduce a given stream of random numbers exactly, for at least two reasons. First, this can sometimes make debugging or verification of the computer program easier. More important, we might want to use *identical* random numbers in simulating different systems in order to obtain a more precise comparison; Sec. 11.2 discusses this in detail.

4. There should be provision in the generator for producing several separate "streams" of random numbers. As we shall see, a stream is simply a subsegment of the numbers produced by the generator, with one stream beginning where the previous stream ends. We can think of the different streams as being separate and independent generators (provided that we do not use up a whole stream, typically set to be of length 100,000 or more). Thus, the user can "dedicate" a particular stream to a particular source of randomness in the simulation. We did this, for example, in the single-server queueing model of Sec. 2.4, where stream 1 was used for generating interarrival times and stream 2 for generating service times. Using separate streams for separate purposes facilitates reproducibility and comparability of simulation results. While this idea has obvious intuitive appeal, there is probabilistic foundation in support of it as well, as discussed in Sec. 11.2. Further advantages of having streams available are discussed in other parts of Chap. 11.

Most of the commonly used generators are quite fast, require very little storage, and can easily reproduce a given sequence of random numbers, so that points 2 and 3 above are almost universally met. Furthermore, many generators now have the facility for multiple streams in some way, especially those generators included in most modern simulation languages, satisfying point 4. Unfortunately, there are many generators (including several in actual use and supplied with some computer systems) that fail to satisfy the uniformity and independence criteria of point 1 above, which are absolutely necessary if one hopes to obtain correct simulation results. The abundance of such statistically unacceptable generators is illustrated by the very title of the paper by Sawitzki (1985). Park and Miller (1988) report several instances of published generators' displaying very poor performance, including one that can even repeat the same "random" number forever.

In Sec. 7.2 we discuss the most popular kind of generator, while Sec. 7.3 mentions some alternative methods. Section 7.4 discusses how one can test a given random-number generator for the desired statistical properties. Sections 7.5 and 7.6 describe random-number generation on microcomputers and the generators used by certain simulation languages. Finally, App. 7A contains portable computer code for an acceptable generator in three languages.

The subject of random-number generators is a complicated one, involving such disparate disciplines as abstract algebra and number theory on the one hand and systems programming and computer hardware engineering on the other; see Sowey (1986) and Nance and Overstreet (1972) for extensive bibliographies, and L'Ecuyer (1990) for a research survey. Its importance, however, should be clear, since random-number generators lie at the very heart of a stochastic simulation.

7.2 LINEAR CONGRUENTIAL GENERATORS

The great majority of random-number generators in use today are *linear congruential generators* (LCGs), introduced by Lehmer (1951). A sequence of integers $Z_1, Z_2, \ldots$ is defined by the recursive formula

$$Z_i = (aZ_{i-1} + c)(\mathrm{mod}\ m) \tag{7.1}$$

where m (the *modulus*), a (the *multiplier*), c (the *increment*), and Z_0 (the *seed* or *starting value*) are nonnegative integers. Thus, Eq. (7.1) says that to obtain Z_i, divide $aZ_{i-1} + c$ by m and let Z_i be the *remainder* of this division. Therefore, $0 \le Z_i \le m - 1$, and to obtain the desired random numbers U_i (for $i = 1, 2, \ldots$) on [0,1], we let $U_i = Z_i/m$. We shall concentrate our attention for the most part on the Z_i's, although the precise nature of the division of Z_i by m should be paid attention to due to differences in the way various computers and compilers handle floating-point arithmetic, as noted by Fishman (1978, pp. 348–349) and by Marse and Roberts (1983). In addition to nonnegativity, the integers m, a, c, and Z_0 should satisfy $0 < m$, $a < m$, $c < m$, and $Z_0 < m$.

Immediately, two objections could be raised against LCGs. The first objection is one common to all (pseudo) random-number generators, namely, that the Z_i's defined by Eq. (7.1) are not really random at all. In fact, one can show by mathematical induction that for $i = 1, 2, \ldots$,

$$Z_i = \left[a^i Z_0 + \frac{c(a^i - 1)}{a - 1} \right](\mathrm{mod}\ m)$$

so that *every* Z_i is completely determined by m, a, c, and Z_0. However, by careful choice of these four parameters we try to induce behavior in the Z_i's that makes the corresponding U_i's *appear* to be IID U(0,1) random variates when subjected to a variety of tests (see Sec. 7.4).

The second objection to LCGs might be that the U_i's can take on only the rational values $0, 1/m, 2/m, \ldots, (m - 1)/m$; in fact, the U_i's might actually take on only a fraction of these values, depending on the specification of the constants m, a, c, and Z_0, as well as on the nature of the floating-point division by m. Thus there is no possibility of getting a value of U_i between, say, $0.1/m$ and $0.9/m$, whereas this *should* occur with probability $0.8/m > 0$. As we shall see, the modulus m is usually chosen to be very large, say 10^9 or more, so that the points in [0, 1] where the U_i's can fall are very dense; for $m \ge 10^9$, there are at least a billion possible values. While this should provide an accurate approximation to the true continuous U(0,1) distribution sufficient for most purposes, Monahan (1985) points out that "With the plummeting cost of computation comes the possibility of an astronomical number of replications" and thus the restriction of the U_i's to the discrete fractions could introduce appreciable inaccuracy in simulation estimates; he proposes ways to measure the error due to this effect, and recommends alternative ways to transform pseudorandom integers to the (continuous) interval [0, 1].

Example 7.2. Consider the LCG defined by $m = 16$, $a = 5$, $c = 3$, and $Z_0 = 7$. Table 7.2 gives Z_i and U_i (to three decimal places) for $i = 1, 2, \ldots, 19$. Note that $Z_{17} = Z_1 = 6$, $Z_{18} = Z_2 = 1$, and so on. That is, from $i = 17$ through 32, we shall obtain *exactly* the same values of Z_i (and hence U_i) that we did from $i = 1$ through 16, and in *exactly* the same order. (We do not seriously suggest that anyone use this generator since m is so small; it only illustrates the arithmetic of LCGs.)

TABLE 7.2
The LCG $Z_i = (5Z_{i-1} + 3)$ (mod 16) with $Z_0 = 7$

i	Z_i	U_i	i	Z_i	U_i	i	Z_i	U_i	i	Z_i	U_i
0	7	—	5	10	0.625	10	9	0.563	15	4	0.250
1	6	0.375	6	5	0.313	11	0	0.000	16	7	0.438
2	1	0.063	7	12	0.750	12	3	0.188	17	6	0.375
3	8	0.500	8	15	0.938	13	2	0.125	18	1	0.063
4	11	0.688	9	14	0.875	14	13	0.813	19	8	0.500

The "looping" behavior of the LCG in Example 7.2 in inevitable. By the definition in Eq. (7.1), whenever Z_i takes on a value it has had previously, exactly the same sequence of values is generated, and this cycle repeats itself endlessly. The length of a cycle is called the *period* of a generator. For LCGs, Z_i depends *only* on the previous integer Z_{i-1}, and since $0 \le Z_i \le m-1$, it is clear that the period is at most m; if it is in fact m, the LCG is said to have *full period*. (The LCG in Example 7.2 has full period.) Clearly, if a generator is full-period, any choice of the initial seed Z_0 from $\{0, 1, \ldots, m-1\}$ will produce the entire cycle in some order. If, however, a generator has less than full period, the cycle length could in fact depend on the particular value of Z_0 chosen, in which case we should really refer to the period of the *seed* for this generator.

Since large-scale simulation projects can use hundreds of thousands of random numbers, it is manifestly desirable to have LCGs with long periods. Furthermore, it is comforting to have full-period LCGs, since we are assured that every integer between 0 and $m-1$ will occur exactly once in each cycle, which should contribute to the uniformity of the U_i's. (Even full-period LCGs, however, can exhibit nonuniform behavior in segments within a cycle. For example, if we generate only $m/2$ consecutive Z_i's, they may leave large gaps in the sequence $0, 1, \ldots, m-1$ of possible values.) Thus, it is useful to know how to choose m, a, and c so that the corresponding LCG will have full period. The following theorem, proved by Hull and Dobell (1962), gives such a characterization.

Theorem 7.1. The LCG defined in Eq. (7.1) has full period if and only if the following three conditions hold:
(a) The only positive integer that (exactly) divides both m and c is 1.
(b) If q is a prime number (divisible by only itself and 1) that divides m, then q divides $a - 1$.
(c) If 4 divides m, then 4 divides $a - 1$.

[Condition (a) in Theorem 7.1 is often stated as "c is relatively prime to m."]
Obtaining a full (or at least a long) period is just one desirable property for a good LCG; as indicated in Sec. 7.1, we also want good statistical

properties (such as apparent independence), computational and storage efficiency, reproducibility, and facilities for separate streams. Reproducibility is simple, for we must only remember the initial seed used, Z_0, and initiate the generator with this value again to obtain the same sequence of U_i's exactly. Also, we can easily resume generating the Z_i's at any point in the sequence by saving the final Z_i obtained previously and using it as the new seed; this is a common way to obtain nonoverlapping, "independent" sequences of random numbers.

Streams are typically set up in a LCG by simply specifying the initial seed for each stream. For example, if we want streams of length 100,000 each, we would set Z_0 for the first stream to some value, then use Z_{100000} as the seed for the second stream, Z_{200000} as the seed for the third stream, and so on. Thus, we see that the streams are actually nonoverlapping adjacent subsequences of *the single* sequence of random numbers being generated; if we were to use more than 100,000 random numbers from one stream in the above example, we would be encroaching on the beginning of the next stream, which might already have been used for something else, resulting in unwanted correlation.

In the remainder of this section we consider the choice of parameters for obtaining good LCGs and identify some notably poor LCGs that may still be in use. Because of condition (a) in Theorem 7.1, LCGs tend to behave differently for $c > 0$ (called *mixed* LCGs) than for $c = 0$ (called *multiplicative* LCGs).

7.2.1 Mixed Generators

For $c > 0$, condition (a) of Theorem 7.1 is possible, so we might be able to obtain full period m. We first discuss the choice of m.

For a large period and high density of the U_i's on $[0, 1]$, we want m to be large. Furthermore, dividing by m to obtain the remainder in Eq. (7.1) is a relatively slow arithmetic operation, and it would be desirable to avoid having to do this division explicitly. A choice of m that is good in all these respects is $m = 2^b$, where b is the number of bits (*binary digits*) in a word on the computer being used that are available for actual data storage. For example, IBM mainframe computers have 32-bit words, the leftmost bit being a sign bit, so $b = 31$; the same is true for DEC VAX minicomputers. Although many microcomputers in current use have 16-bit words, FORTRAN and C compilers for them often carry out integer arithmetic as though the words *were* 32 bits, so $b = 31$ again. If b is reasonably large, say, $b \geq 31$, then $m \geq 2^{31} > 2.1$ billion. Furthermore, choosing $m = 2^b$ *does* allow us to avoid explicit division by m on most computers by taking advantage of *integer overflow*. The largest integer that can be represented is $2^b - 1$, and any attempt to store a larger integer W (with, say, $h > b$ binary digits) will result in loss of the left (most significant) $h - b$ binary digits of this oversized integer. What remains in the retained b bits is precisely $W \pmod{2^b}$. The following example illustrates modulo division by overflow for $m = 2^b$.

Example 7.3. Suppose that the LCG of Example 7.2 is implemented on a mythical computer with $b = 4$ bits per word available for data storage; $m = 16 = 2^b$, conveniently. How can overflow be used to obtain $Z_7 = 12$ from $Z_6 = 5$? Now $5Z_6 + 3 = 28$, which in binary representation is 11100. Since our 4-bit computer can store only four binary digits, the leftmost digit of the binary number 11100 is dropped, leaving the binary number 1100, which is the binary representation of $12 = Z_7$.

We caution the reader to check out exactly how integer overflow is handled; e.g., the sign bit might be turned on in the operation, necessitating an adjustment that could depend on the computer's architecture, the format for representing integers, and the language being used.

Thus, $m = 2^b$ would appear to be a good choice for the modulus. With this choice, Theorem 7.1 says that we shall obtain full period if c is odd and $a - 1$ is divisible by 4; with such a full-period generator, Z_0 can be any integer between 0 and $m - 1$ without affecting the generator's period. We next consider the choice of the multiplier a.

Early work on LCGs emphasized efficiency in effecting the multiplication of Z_{i-1} by a, which led to multipliers of the form

$$a = 2^l + 1 \tag{7.2}$$

for some positive integer l. Then

$$aZ_{i-1} = 2^l Z_{i-1} + Z_{i-1}$$

so that aZ_{i-1} can be obtained by "shifting" the binary representation of Z_{i-1} to the left by l bits and adding Z_{i-1}. Thus, the explicit multiplication can be replaced by the shift-and-add operations. However, more recent work has indicated that multipliers of the form in Eq. (7.2) should be avoided, since they result in generators with poor statistical properties [Knuth (1981, p. 23)].

How, then, should one choose a and c when $m = 2^b$ to obtain a good mixed LCG? Tentatively, we might address this question by suggesting that consideration be given to not using a mixed LCG; the simpler and better-understood multiplicative LCGs (treated in Sec. 7.2.2) have generally performed as well as mixed LCGs and in fact are more widely used. Nevertheless, we can identify two mixed LCGs (both with modulus $m = 2^b$) that have been suggested as providing adequate performance. For $b = 35$ (e.g., UNIVAC machines), Coveyou and MacPherson (1967) tested the generator defined by $a = 5^{15}$ and $c = 1$, with favorable results. For $b = 31$ (e.g., IBM and DEC VAX mainframes and minicomputers, as well as many microcomputers with modern compilers, as discussed in Sec. 7.2.2), Kobayashi (1978, p. 240) proposed the generator defined by $a = 314,159,269$ and $c = 453,806,245$.

7.2.2 Multiplicative Generators

Multiplicative LCGs are advantageous in that the addition of c is not needed, but they cannot have full period since condition (a) of Theorem 7.1 cannot be satisfied (because, for example, m is positive and divides both m and $c = 0$). As we shall see, however, it is possible to obtain period $m - 1$ if m and a are chosen carefully. Multiplicative LCGs came before mixed LCGs historically and have been studied more intensively. The majority of LCGs in use today *are* multiplicative, since the improvement in performance hoped for in the more recent mixed LCGs has not been demonstrated conclusively; many researchers on random-number generators have thus chosen to stick with the original multiplicative LCGs.

As with mixed generators, it is still computationally efficient to choose $m = 2^b$ and thus avoid explicit division. However, it can be shown [see, for example, Knuth (1981, p. 19)] that in this case the period is at most 2^{b-2}, that is, only *one-fourth* of the integers 0 through $m - 1$ can be obtained as values for the Z_i's. (In fact, the period is 2^{b-2} if Z_0 is odd and a is of the form $8k + 3$ or $8k + 5$ for some $k = 0, 1, \ldots$.) Furthermore, we generally shall not know *where* these $m/4$ integers will fall; i.e., there might be unacceptably large gaps in the Z_i's obtained. Additionally, if we choose a to be of the form $2^l + j$ (so that the multiplication of Z_{i-1} by a is replaced by a shift and j adds), poor statistical properties can be induced. The generator usually known as RANDU is of this form ($m = 2^{31}$, $a = 2^{16} + 3 = 65,539$, $c = 0$) and has been shown to have very undesirable statistical properties (see Sec. 7.4); use of RANDU should therefore be avoided. Even if one does not choose $a = 2^l + j$, using $m = 2^b$ in multiplicative LCGs is probably not a good idea, if only because of the shorter period of $m/4$ and the resulting possibility of gaps.

Because of these difficulties associated with choosing $m = 2^b$ in multiplicative LCGs, attention was paid to finding other ways of specifying m. Such a method, which has proved to be quite successful, was reported by Hutchinson (1966), who attributed the idea to Lehmer. Instead of letting $m = 2^b$, it was proposed that m be the largest prime number that is less than 2^b. For example, in the case of $b = 31$, the largest prime that is less than 2^{31} is, very agreeably, $2^{31} - 1 = 2,147,483,647$. Now for m prime, it can be shown that the period is $m - 1$ if a is a *primitive element modulo m*; that is, the smallest integer l for which $a^l - 1$ is divisible by m is $l = m - 1$; see Knuth (1981, p. 19). With m and a chosen in this way, we obtain each integer $1, 2, \ldots, m - 1$ exactly once in each cycle, so that Z_0 can be any integer from 1 through $m - 1$ and a period of $m - 1$ will still result. These are called *prime modulus multiplicative LCGs* (PMMLCGs).

Two issues immediately arise concerning PMMLCGs: (1) How does one obtain a primitive element modulo m? Although Knuth (1981, p. 20) gives some characterizations, the task is quite complicated from a computational standpoint. We shall, in essence, finesse this point by referring the reader to the end of this section, where we explicitly give some "tried-and-true" PMMLCGs. (2) Since we are not choosing $m = 2^b$, we can no longer use the overflow mechanism directly to effect the division modulo m. A technique for avoiding explicit division in this case, which also uses a type of overflow, was given by Payne, Rabung, and Bogyo (1969) and has been called *simulated division*. [See also Fishman (1973, pp. 179–180; 1978, p. 357), Schrage (1979), and Marse and Roberts (1983).] For PMMLCGs, m is of the form $2^b - q$ for some positive integer q. To obtain $Z_i = (aZ_{i-1}) \pmod{2^b - q}$ from Z_{i-1}, let $Z_i' = (aZ_{i-1}) \pmod{2^b}$, which can be obtained by overflow without division. If k is the largest integer that is less than or equal to $aZ_{i-1}/2^b$, then

$$Z_i = \begin{cases} Z_i' + kq & \text{if } Z_i' + kq < 2^b - q \\ Z_i' + kq - (2^b - q) & \text{if } Z_i' + kq \geq 2^b - q \end{cases}$$

Marse and Roberts' portable FORTRAN generator, which we discuss below, uses simulated division. [See L'Ecuyer (1988) for an alternative technique to accomplish this.]

We close this section by giving examples of specific PMMLCGs with modulus $m^* = 2^{31} - 1$, together with multipliers that are primitive elements modulo m^*, which have performed well. The case of $b = 31$ is of special importance, since it includes many computers and compilers in current use. Moreover, using a machine with a word length longer than 32 bits certainly does not preclude using generators with modulus $2^{31} - 1$. Although a period of $2^{31} - 2$ may seem small in comparison with some older or larger mainframe computers with longer word length, it can be put into perspective by noting that at the rate of 1000 random numbers per second, a cycle would not be completed for more than 3 weeks.

For these reasons, considerable work has been directed toward identifying good multipliers a for PMMLCGs with modulus m^*; the search has been restricted to values of a that are primitive elements modulo m^*, to get a period of $m^* - 1$. Hoaglin (1976) studied the performance of 50 such multipliers using the spectral and lattice tests (see Sec. 7.4.2 below), and identified several good values of a, as well as several poor choices. In a definitive set of papers, Fishman and Moore (1981, 1982, 1986) evaluated *all* the multipliers a that are primitive elements modulo m^*, numbering some 534 million, by means of both empirical and theoretical tests (see Sec. 7.4 below); they identified several multipliers that appear to perform very well according to a number of fairly stringent criteria.

Two particular values of the multiplier a that have been widely used for the modulus m^* are $a_1 = 7^5 = 16,807$, and $a_2 = 630,360,016$, both of which are primitive elements modulo m^* (although neither was found by Fishman and Moore to be among the best). The multiplier a_1 was originally suggested by Lewis, Goodman, and Miller (1969), who also provided an IBM assembly-language code that uses explicit hardware division rather than simulated division; a_1 is also used in the LLRANDOM package of Learmonth and Lewis (1973), and as the default multiplier in IMSL's (1987) generator RNUN. Schrage (1979) also used a_1 in a clever FORTRAN implementation using simulated division; his code should work on any computer with a FORTRAN compiler that correctly computes and stores INTEGER values inclusively between $-2^{31} + 1$ and $2^{31} - 1$, covering virtually all cases (including most microcomputers). Schrage also gave a DOUBLE PRECISION version for use if this range of INTEGERs is not available. The importance of Schrage's code was that it provided a reasonably good and *portable* random-number generator; i.e., it can be implemented in FORTRAN on nearly any computer. Park and Miller (1988) provide several Pascal codes using a_1, some of which are valid even without the range of integers required by Schrage's code, if floating-point arithmetic is used instead.

The multiplier a_2, suggested originally by Payne, Rabung, and Bogyo (1969), was found by Fishman and Moore to yield statistical performance much better than does a_1, and Marse and Roberts (1983) provided a highly portable FORTRAN routine (which will work under the same INTEGER-arithmetic conditions required by Schrage's implementation) for this case; we give the code for it in App. 7A, together with Pascal and C versions. This is the generator we used for all the examples in Chaps. 1 and 2, and is the one built into the SIMLIB package in Chap. 2. The Marse-Roberts code takes additional care in converting the integers Z_i to the U_i's on $[0, 1]$ to avoid distortion and machine-dependent variation due to the method of computing and storing floating-point numbers; their code as given in App. 7A.1 will produce the same single-precision U_i's on any machine carrying at least 23 bits for the unsigned floating-point mantissa, a condition satisfied in nearly all implementations of FORTRAN, again including most microcomputers. (Schrage's code, while producing the same sequence of Z_i's on any machine for which it can be used, may not produce exactly the same sequence of U_i's on each such machine, due to its direct division of Z_i by m^* to get U_i.) Although the Marse-Roberts code appears to be only about half as fast as Schrage's code, the statistical superiority of a_2 over a_1 argues for its use; as Marse and Roberts further point out, generating random numbers may actually consume only a small fraction (they reported typical values of 2 to 3 percent in the INSIGHT simulation language) of the total execution time for a complex, large-scale, dynamic simulation. If speed in random-number generation is critical, however, Schrage's code might be considered instead. Note that one cannot simply plug larger multipliers into the Schrage or Marse-Roberts codes, due to overflow difficulties that would ensue. For most cases, we feel comfortable in recommending use of the PMMLCG with $m = m^* = 2^{31} - 1$ and $a = a_2 = 630,360,016$, in one of the implementations in App. 7A, as it provides a well-tested, acceptable generator that should work properly (and consistently) on virtually any computer apt to be used for serious simulation.

7.3 OTHER KINDS OF GENERATORS

Although LCGs are by far the most widely used and best understood kind of random-number generator, there are many alternative types. (We have already seen one alternative in Sec. 7.1, the midsquare method, which is not recommended.) Most of these other generators have been developed in an attempt to obtain longer periods and better statistical properties. Often, however, a simple LCG with carefully chosen parameters can perform nearly as well as (sometimes better than) these more complicated alternatives. Our treatment in this section is not meant to be an exhaustive compendium of all kinds of generators, but only to indicate some of the main alternatives to LCGs.

7.3.1 More General Congruences

LCGs can be thought of as a special case of generators defined by

$$Z_i = g(Z_{i-1}, Z_{i-2}, \ldots)(\text{mod } m) \tag{7.3}$$

where g is a fixed deterministic function of previous Z_j's. As with LCGs, the Z_i's defined by Eq. (7.3) lie between 0 and $m - 1$, and the U(0,1) random numbers are given by $U_i = Z_i/m$. [For LCGs, the function g is, of course, $g(Z_{i-1}, Z_{i-2}, \ldots) = aZ_{i-1} + c$.] Here we simply mention a few of these kinds of generators and refer the reader to Knuth (1981, pp. 25–33) for a more detailed discussion.

One obvious generalization of LCGs would be to let $g(Z_{i-1}, Z_{i-2}, \ldots) = a'Z_{i-1}^2 + aZ_{i-1} + c$, which produces a *quadratic* congruential generator. A special case that has received some attention is when $a' = a = 1$, $c = 0$, and m is a power of 2; although this particular generator turns out to be a close relative of the midsquare method (see Sec. 7.1), it has better statistical properties. Since Z_i still depends only on Z_{i-1} (and not on earlier Z_j's), and since $0 \le Z_i \le m - 1$, the period of quadratic congruential generators is at most m, as for LCGs.

A different choice of the function g is to maintain linearity but to use earlier Z_j's; this gives rise to generators defined by

$$g(Z_{i-1}, Z_{i-2}, \ldots) = a_1 Z_{i-1} + a_2 Z_{i-2} + \cdots + a_q Z_{i-q} \tag{7.4}$$

where $a_1, a_2, \ldots, a_q$ are constants. Huge periods (as high as $m^q - 1$) then become possible if the parameters are chosen properly. L'Ecuyer and Blouin (1988) investigate such generators, and include a generalization of the spectral test (see Sec. 7.4.2) for their evaluation; they also identify several specific generators of this type that perform well, and give a portable implementation. Additional attention to generators with g of the form in Eq. (7.4) used in Eq. (7.3) has focused on g's defined as $Z_{i-1} + Z_{i-q}$, which includes the old Fibonacci generator,

$$Z_i = (Z_{i-1} + Z_{i-2})(\text{mod } m)$$

This generator tends to have a period in excess of m but is completely unacceptable from a statistical standpoint; see Prob. 7.12.

A generalization of LCGs along a different line was proposed by Haas (1987), who suggested that in the basic LCG of Eq. (7.1) we change both the multiplier a and the increment c according to congruential formulas before generating each new Z_i. Statistical tests of this type of generator (see Sec. 7.4.1) appeared favorable, and portable FORTRAN code was given. His analysis indicated that we can readily obtain enormous periods, such as 800 trillion in one example.

7.3.2 Composite Generators

Several researchers have developed methods that take two or more *separate* generators (usually two or three different LCGs) and combine them in some way to generate the final random numbers. It is hoped that this *composite* generator will exhibit better statistical behavior than any of the simple generators composing it. In fact, Brown and Solomon (1979) show that, in a certain abstract sense, the numbers from the composite generator are at least as close to "true" uniformity as any of the component generators. The disadvantage in using a composite generator is, of course, that the cost of obtaining each U_i is more than that of using one of the simple generators alone.

The best known of the composite generators uses a second LCG to *shuffle* the output from the first LCG; it was developed by MacLaren and Marsaglia (1965) and extended by Marsaglia and Bray (1968), Grosenbaugh (1969), and Nance and Overstreet (1975). Initially, a vector $\mathbf{V} = (V_1, V_2, \ldots, V_k)$ is filled sequentially with the first k U_i's from the first LCG ($k = 128$ was originally suggested). Then the second LCG is used to generate a random integer I distributed uniformly on the integers $1, 2, \ldots, k$ (see Sec. 8.4.2), and V_I is returned as the first U(0,1) variate; the first LCG then replaces this Ith location in $\mathbf{V}$ with its next U_i, and the second LCG randomly chooses the next returned random number from this updated $\mathbf{V}$, etc. Shuffling has a natural intuitive appeal, especially since we would expect it to break up any correlation and greatly extend the period. Indeed, MacLaren and Marsaglia obtained a shuffling generator with very good statistical behavior even though the two individual LCGs were quite poor. In a subsequent evaluation of shuffling, Nance and Overstreet (1978) confirm that shuffling one bad LCG by another bad LCG can result in a good composite generator, e.g., by extending the period when used on computers with short word lengths, but that little is accomplished by shuffling a good LCG; in addition, they found that a vector of length $k = 2$ works as well as much larger vectors.

Several variations on this shuffling scheme have been considered; Bays and Durham (1976) and Gebhardt (1967) propose shuffling a generator by itself rather than by another generator. [The IMSL (1987) generators offer self-shuffling as an option.] Atkinson (1980) also reported that simply applying a *fixed* permutation (rather than a random shuffling) of the output of LCGs "... removes the effect of all but the worst generators, and very appreciably alleviates the damage that even a dreadful generator can cause."

Despite these apparent advantages of rearranging a simple generator's output in some way, there is not as much known about shuffled generators; for example, one cannot jump into an arbitrary point of a shuffled generator's output sequence without generating all the intermediate values, whereas this is possible for LCGs [e.g., see the routine NXSEED in Marse and Roberts (1983) and in App. 7A.4].

Another way to combine two generators is discussed and evaluated by L'Ecuyer (1988). In simplified form, the idea is to let $\{Z_{1i}\}$ and $\{Z_{2i}\}$ denote the integer sequences generated by two different LCGs with different moduli, then let $Z_i = (Z_{1i} - Z_{2i})$ (mod m) for some integer m, and finally set $U_i = Z_i/m$. This idea could clearly be extended to more than two generators, and has several advantages; the period is very long (at least 10^{18} in one example given by L'Ecuyer), the multipliers in each of the component generators can be small (thus promoting portability and usability on virtually any micro-computer), the resulting generator is quite fast, and the statistical properties of these generators also appear to be very good. L'Ecuyer and Côté (1990) describe a portable software package to implement these types of generators.

Wichmann and Hill (1982) proposed the following idea for combining three generators, again striving for long period, portability, speed, and usability on small computers (as well as statistical adequacy). If U_{1i}, U_{2i}, and U_{3i} are the ith random numbers produced by three separate generators, then let U_i be the fractional part (i.e., ignore any digits to the left of the decimal point) of $U_{1i} + U_{2i} + U_{3i}$; see Prob. 7.13 for the underlying motivation. This indeed produces a very long period [although not as long as claimed in the original paper; see Wichmann and Hill (1984)], and is highly portable and efficient. It was later pointed out by McLeod (1985), however, that their code may have numerical difficulties in some computer architectures. Zeisel (1986) subsequently showed that this generator is identical to a multiplicative LCG, but that this equivalent LCG has an enormous modulus and multiplier; thus, the Wichmann-Hill generator turned out to be a way to implement a multiplicative LCG with very large parameters on even the smallest computers.

There are many conceivable ways to combine individual random-number generators, some of which we have reviewed above. Others are discussed by Kennedy and Gentle (1980, pp. 162–165), Ripley (1987, pp. 42–43), and Bratley, Fox, and Schrage (1987, pp. 203–205).

7.3.3 Tausworthe and Related Generators

Several interesting kinds of generators have been developed on the basis of a paper by Tausworthe (1965). These generators, which are related to crypto-graphic methods, operate directly with bits to form random numbers.

Define a sequence $b_1, b_2, \ldots$ of binary digits by the recurrence

$$b_i = (c_1 b_{i-1} + c_2 b_{i-2} + \cdots + c_q b_{i-q})(\text{mod } 2) \tag{7.5}$$

where $c_1, c_2, \ldots, c_q$ are constants that are either 0 or 1. Note the similarity of the recurrence for b_i with Eq. (7.4); the maximum period here is $2^q - 1$. In essentially all applications of Tausworthe generators, only two of the c_j coefficients are nonzero, in which case Eq. (7.5) becomes

$$b_i = (b_{i-r} + b_{i-q})(\text{mod } 2) \tag{7.6}$$

for integers r and q satisfying $0 < r < q$. Execution of Eq. (7.6) is expedited by noting that addition modulo 2 is equivalent to the *exclusive or* instruction on bits; that is, Eq. (7.6) can be expressed as

$$b_i = \begin{cases} 0 & \text{if } b_{i-r} = b_{i-q} \\ 1 & \text{if } b_{i-r} \neq b_{i-q} \end{cases}$$

To initialize the $\{b_i\}$ sequence, the first q b_i's must be specified somehow; this is akin to specifying the seed Z_0 for LCGs.

Example 7.4. Let $r = 3$ and $q = 5$ in Eq. (7.6), and let $b_1 = b_2 = \cdots = b_5 = 1$. [This example is given by Lewis and Payne (1973).] Thus, for $i \geq 6$, b_i is the "exclusive or" of b_{i-3} with b_{i-5}. The first 42 b_i's are then

$$111110001101110101000010010110011111000110$$

Note that the period (of the bits) is $31 = 2^q - 1$.

Kennedy and Gentle (1980, pp. 150–163) discuss further implementation issues for Tausworthe generators, including the "feedback-shift-register" technique; see also Payne (1970) for a FORTRAN code.

With this sequence $\{b_i\}$ so defined, the question arises: How should it be transformed into U(0,1) random numbers? One natural possibility is to string together l consecutive b_i's to form an l-bit binary integer between 0 and $2^l - 1$, which is then divided by 2^l. (In Example 7.4, choosing $l = 4$ results in the sequence of random numbers $\frac{15}{16}, \frac{8}{16}, \frac{13}{16}, \frac{13}{16}, \frac{4}{16}, \frac{2}{16}, \frac{5}{16}, \frac{9}{16}, \frac{15}{16}, \frac{1}{16}, \ldots$) However, l would have to be no more than the word size of the computer. There is disagreement over how well this works, so another possibility would be to use l consecutive bits for the first integer, then *skip* some number of the following b_i's, then use the next l bits for the second integer, etc. A much more sophisticated bit-selection algorithm was given by Lewis and Payne (1973) and further studied by Bright and Enison (1979). The important question of how r and q are specified is also treated by Tausworthe (1965), Tootill, Robinson, and Adams (1971), and Tootill, Robinson, and Eagle (1973). These papers also discuss various tests of several particular Tausworthe generators.

Tausworthe generators offer a number of potential advantages over LCGs. They are essentially independent of the computer used and its word size, and one can readily obtain periods of almost unthinkable length (such as $2^{521} - 1 > 10^{156}$, or more). Furthermore, they have appealing theoretical properties [see Tausworthe (1965), Tootill, Robinson, and Eagle (1973), Kennedy and Gentle (1980, pp. 151–152), Fushimi and Tezuka (1983), and Fushimi (1988)]. For these reasons, Johnson (1987, pp. 41–42) recommends them as the basis for generating multivariate random vectors. However, empirical evidence on Tausworthe generators may be inconclusive [see Tootill, Robinson, and Adams (1971)]. Furthermore, actual use of Tausworthe generators does not appear to be particularly widespread. For example, the GPSS/H simulation language recently switched from a Tausworthe generator to a LCG in order to facilitate stream management [Henriksen (1988)].

The essential ingredient in Tausworthe generators is a sequence of bits generated in some way. A different method for doing this, also with applications to cryptography, was proposed by Blum, Blum, and Shub (1986). Let p and q be large prime numbers, with $p - 3$ and $q - 3$ each divisible by 4. These determine a modulus $m = pq$, from which a sequence of integers $\{X_i\}$ is generated by the quadratic congruential recurrence relation $X_i = X_{i-1}^2 \pmod{m}$. The bit sequence is then defined by $b_i = $ the *parity* (rightmost bit) of X_i, being 0 if X_i is even and 1 otherwise. Blum, Blum and Shub (1986) show that this bit sequence is practically unpredictable in the sense that discovering nonrandomness (e.g., filling in a missing bit accurately) is computationally equivalent to factoring m into pq, a problem that is generally believed to require vast computer resources. Such theoretical support for a generator is certainly appealing, and this method has attracted considerable attention, including a *New York Times* article [Gleick (1988)] with the hopeful title "The Quest for True Randomness Finally Appears Successful." At this writing, these generators are still being studied; L'Ecuyer and Proulx (1989) evaluate some practical issues in their implementation.

Finally, we note that Reif and Tygar (1988) analyzed a method for simultaneously generating multiple random bit sequences in a parallel-processing environment.

7.4 TESTING RANDOM-NUMBER GENERATORS

As we have seen in Secs. 7.1 through 7.3, all random-number generators currently used in computer simulation are actually completely deterministic. Thus, we can only hope that the U_i's generated *appear* as if they *were* IID U(0,1) random variates. In this section we discuss several tests to which a random-number generator can be subjected to ascertain how well the generated U_i's do (or can) resemble values of true IID U(0,1) random variates.

Most computers have a "canned" random-number generator as part of the available software. Before such a generator is actually used in a simulation, we strongly recommend that one identify exactly what kind of generator it is and what its numerical parameters are. Unless a generator is one of the "good" ones identified (and tested) somewhere in the literature (or is one of the specific generators recommended above), the responsible analyst should subject it (at least) to the empirical tests discussed below.

There are two quite different kinds of tests, which we discuss separately in Secs. 7.4.1 and 7.4.2. *Empirical* tests are the usual kinds of statistical tests and are based on the actual U_i's produced by a generator. *Theoretical* tests are not tests in the statistical sense, but use the numerical parameters of a generator to assess it globally without actually generating any U_i's at all.

7.4.1 Empirical Tests

Perhaps the most direct way to test a generator is to *use* it to generate some U_i's, which are then examined statistically to see how closely they resemble

IID $U(0,1)$ random variates. We discuss four such empirical tests; several others are treated in Banks and Carson (1984, pp. 267–287), Fishman (1978, pp. 371–386), and Knuth (1981, pp. 38–73).

The first test is designed to check whether the U_i's appear to be uniformly distributed between 0 and 1, and it is a special case of a test we have seen before (in Sec. 6.6.2), the chi-square test with all parameters known. We divide $[0, 1]$ into k subintervals of equal length and generate $U_1, U_2, \ldots, U_n$. (As a general rule, k should be at least 100 here, and n/k should be at least 5.) For $j = 1, 2, \ldots, k$, let f_j be the number of the U_i's that are in the jth subinterval, and let

$$\chi^2 = \frac{k}{n} \sum_{j=1}^{k} \left(f_j - \frac{n}{k} \right)^2$$

Then for large n, χ^2 will have an approximate chi-square distribution with $k - 1$ df under the null hypothesis that the U_i's are IID $U(0,1)$ random variables. Thus, we reject this hypothesis at level α if $\chi^2 > \chi^2_{k-1,1-\alpha}$, where $\chi^2_{k-1,1-\alpha}$ is the upper $1 - \alpha$ critical point of the chi-square distribution with $k - 1$ df. (For the large values of k likely to be encountered here, we can use the approximation

$$\chi^2_{k-1,1-\alpha} \approx (k-1)\left\{ 1 - \frac{2}{9(k-1)} + z_{1-\alpha}\sqrt{2/[9(k-1)]} \right\}^3$$

where $z_{1-\alpha}$ is the upper $1 - \alpha$ critical point of the $N(0,1)$ distribution.)

Example 7.5. We applied the chi-square test of uniformity to the PMMLCG $Z_i = 630,360,016 \, Z_{i-1} \pmod{2^{31} - 1}$, as implemented in App. 7A, using stream 1 with the default seed. We took $k = 2^{12} = 4096$ (so that the most significant 12 bits of the U_i's are being examined for uniformity) and let $n = 2^{15} = 32,768$. We obtained $\chi^2 = 4141.0$; using the above approximation for the critical point, $\chi^2_{4095,0.90} \approx 4211.4$, so the null hypothesis of uniformity is not rejected at level $\alpha = 0.10$. Therefore, *these particular* 32,768 U_i's produced by this generator do not behave in a way that is significantly different from what would be expected from truly IID $U(0,1)$ random variables, so far as this chi-square test can ascertain.

Our second empirical test, the *serial test*, is really just a generalization of the chi-square test to higher dimensions. If the U_i's were really IID $U(0,1)$ random variates, the nonoverlapping d-tuples

$$\mathbf{U}_1 = (U_1, U_2, \ldots, U_d), \mathbf{U}_2 = (U_{d+1}, U_{d+2}, \ldots, U_{2d}), \ldots$$

should be IID random *vectors* distributed uniformly on the d-dimensional unit hypercube, $[0,1]^d$. Divide $[0,1]$ into k subintervals of equal size and generate $\mathbf{U}_1, \mathbf{U}_2, \ldots, \mathbf{U}_n$ (requiring nd U_i's). Let $f_{j_1 j_2 \cdots j_d}$ be the number of $\mathbf{U}_i$'s having first component in subinterval j_1, second component in subinterval j_2, etc. (It is easier to tally the $f_{j_1 j_2 \cdots j_d}$'s than might be expected; see Prob. 7.7) If we let

$$\chi^2(d) = \frac{k^d}{n} \sum_{j_1=1}^{k} \sum_{j_2=1}^{k} \cdots \sum_{j_d=1}^{k} \left(f_{j_1 j_2 \cdots j_d} - \frac{n}{k^d} \right)^2$$

then $\chi^2(d)$ will have an approximate chi-square distribution with $k^d - 1$ df. (Again, it is advisable to have $n/k^d \geq 5$.) The test for d-dimensional uniformity is carried out exactly as for the one-dimensional chi-square test above.

Example 7.6. For $d = 2$, we tested the null hypothesis that the pairs (U_1, U_2), $(U_3, U_4), \ldots, (U_{2n-1}, U_{2n})$ are IID random vectors distributed uniformly over the unit square. We used the generator in App. 7A, but starting with stream 2, and generated $n = 32,768$ pairs of U_i's. We took $k = 64$, so that the degrees of freedom were again $4095 = 64^2 - 1$ and the level $\alpha = 0.10$ critical value was the same, 4211.4. The value of $\chi^2(2)$ was 4016.5, indicating acceptable uniformity in two dimensions for the first two-thirds of stream 2 (recall that the streams are of length 100,000 U_i's, and we used $2n = 65,536$ of them here). For $d = 3$, we used stream 3, took $k = 16$ (keeping the degrees of freedom as $4095 = 16^3 - 1$ and the level $\alpha = 0.10$ critical value at 4211.4), and generated $n = 32,768$ nonoverlapping *triples of U_i's*. $\chi^2(3)$ was 4174.5, again indicating acceptable uniformity in three dimensions.

Why should we care about this kind of uniformity in *higher* dimensions? If the individual U_i's are correlated, the distribution of the d-vectors $\mathbf{U}_i$ will deviate from d-dimensional uniformity; thus, the serial test provides an indirect check on the assumption that the individual U_i's are independent. For example, if adjacent U_i's tend to be postitively correlated, the pairs (U_i, U_{i+1}) will tend to cluster around the southwest-northeast diagonal in the unit square, and $\chi^2(2)$ should pick this up. Finally, it should be apparent that the serial test for $d > 3$ could be quite costly because of the large storage requirements needed to tally the k^d values of $f_{j_1 j_2 \cdots j_d}$. (Choosing $k = 16$ in Example 7.6 when $d = 3$ is probably not a sufficiently fine division of $[0,1]$.)

The third empirical test we consider, the *runs* (or *runs-up*) *test*, is a more direct test of the independence assumption. (In fact, it is a test of independence *only*; i.e., we are not testing for uniformity in particular.) We examine the U_i sequence (or, equivalently, the Z_i sequence) for unbroken subsequences of maximal length within which the U_i's increase monotonically; such a subsequence is called a *run up*. For example, consider the following sequence $U_1, U_2, \ldots, U_{10}$: 0.86, 0.11, 0.23, 0.03, 0.13, 0.06, 0.55, 0.64, 0.87, 0.10. The sequence starts with a run up of length 1 (0.86), followed by a run up of length 2 (0.11, 0.23), then another run up of length 2 (0.03, 0.13), then a run up of length 4 (0.06, 0.55, 0.64, 0.87), and finally another run up of length 1 (0.10). From a sequence of n U_i's, we count the number of runs up of length 1, 2, 3, 4, 5, and ≥ 6, and then define

$$r_i = \begin{cases} \text{number of runs up of length } i & \text{for } i = 1, 2, \ldots, 5 \\ \text{number of runs up of length} \geq 6 & \text{for } i = 6 \end{cases}$$

(See Prob. 7.8 for an algorithm to tally the r_i's. For the 10 U_i's above, $r_1 = 2$, $r_2 = 2$, $r_3 = 0$, $r_4 = 1$, $r_5 = 0$, and $r_6 = 0$.) The test statistic is then

$$R = \frac{1}{n} \sum_{i=1}^{6} \sum_{j=1}^{6} a_{ij}(r_i - nb_i)(r_j - nb_j)$$

where a_{ij} is the (i, j)th element of the matrix

$$\begin{bmatrix} 4,529.4 & 9,044.9 & 13,568 & 18,091 & 22,615 & 27,892 \\ 9,044.9 & 18,097 & 27,139 & 36,187 & 45,234 & 55,789 \\ 13,568 & 27,139 & 40,721 & 54,281 & 67,852 & 83,685 \\ 18,091 & 36,187 & 54,281 & 72,414 & 90,470 & 111,580 \\ 22,615 & 45,234 & 67,852 & 90,470 & 113,262 & 139,476 \\ 27,892 & 55,789 & 83,685 & 111,580 & 139,476 & 172,860 \end{bmatrix}$$

and the b_i's are given by

$$(b_1, b_2, \ldots, b_6) = \left(\frac{1}{6}, \frac{5}{24}, \frac{11}{120}, \frac{19}{720}, \frac{29}{5040}, \frac{1}{840} \right)$$

[See Knuth (1981, pp. 65–68) for derivation of these constants.* The a_{ij}'s given above are accurate to five significant digits.] For large n (Knuth recommends $n \geq 4000$), R will have an approximate chi-square distribution with 6 df, under the null hypothesis that the U_i's are IID random variables.

> **Example 7.7.** We subjected stream 4 of the generator in App. 7A to the runs-up test, using $n = 5000$, and obtained $(r_1, r_2, \ldots, r_6) = (808, 1026, 448, 139, 43, 4)$, leading to a value of $R = 9.3$. Since $\chi^2_{6,0.90} = 10.6$, we do not reject the hypothesis of independence at level $\alpha = 0.10$.

The runs-up test can be reversed in the obvious way to obtain a runs-down test; the a_{ij} and b_i constants are the same. Grafton (1981) gives FORTRAN programs for the runs-up and runs-down tests. There are several other kinds of runs tests, such as counting runs up or down in the same sequence, or simply counting the number of runs without regard to their length; we refer the reader to Banks and Carson (1984, pp. 273–281) and Fishman (1978, pp. 373–376), for example. Recall as well our discussion of runs tests in Sec. 6.3. Since runs tests look solely for independence (and not specifically for uniformity), it would probably be a good idea to apply a runs test *before* performing the chi-square or serial tests, since the last two tests implicitly assume independence. Knuth feels that the runs test is more powerful than the chi-square tests, in the sense that many generators pass the chi-square and serial tests but fail the runs tests; his explanation is that LCGs with small multipliers and increments tend to generate longer runs than would be expected for truly IID U_i's.

The final type of empirical test we consider is a direct way to assess whether the generated U_i's exhibit discernible correlation: Simply compute an estimate of the correlation at lags $j = 1, 2, \ldots, l$ for some value of l. Recall from Sec. 4.3 that the correlation at lag j in a sequence $X_1, X_2, \ldots$ of random

---

* Knuth, D. E., *The Art of Computer Programming*, Vol. 2, 2d ed., 1981, Addison-Wesley Publishing Company, Inc. Reprinted with permission.

variables is defined as $\rho_j = C_j/C_0$, where

$$C_j = \text{Cov}(X_i, X_{i+j}) = E(X_i X_{i+j}) - E(X_i)E(X_{i+j})$$

is the covariance between entries in the sequence separated by j; note that $C_0 = \text{Var}(X_i)$. (It is assumed here that the process is covariance-stationary; see Sec. 4.3.) In our case, we are interested in $X_i = U_i$, and under the hypothesis that the U_i's are uniformly distributed on $[0,1]$, we have $E(U_i) = \frac{1}{2}$ and $\text{Var}(U_i) = \frac{1}{12}$, so that $C_j = E(U_i U_{i+j}) - \frac{1}{4}$ and $C_0 = \frac{1}{12}$; thus, $\rho_j = 12E(U_i U_{i+j}) - 3$ in this case. From a sequence $U_1, U_2, \ldots, U_n$ of generated values, an estimate of ρ_j can thus be obtained by estimating $E(U_i U_{i+j})$ directly from U_1, U_{1+j}, U_{1+2j}, etc., to obtain

$$\hat{\rho}_j = \frac{12}{h+1} \sum_{k=0}^{h} U_{1+kj} U_{1+(k+1)j} - 3$$

where $h = \lfloor (n-1)/j \rfloor - 1$. Under the further assumption that the U_i's are independent, it turns out [see, for example, Banks and Carson (1984, p. 282)] that

$$\text{Var}(\hat{\rho}_j) = \frac{13h + 7}{(h+1)^2}$$

Under the null hypothesis that $\rho_j = 0$ and assuming that n is large, it can be shown that the test statistic

$$A_j = \frac{\hat{\rho}_j}{\sqrt{\text{Var}(\hat{\rho}_j)}}$$

has an approximate standard normal distribution. This provides a test of zero lag j correlation at level α, by rejecting this hypothesis if $|A_j| > z_{1-\alpha/2}$. The test should probably be carried out for several values of j, since it could be, for instance, that there is no appreciable correlation at lags 1 or 2, but there is dependence between the U_i's at lag 3, due to some anomaly of the generator.

> **Example 7.8.** We tested streams 5 through 10 of the generator in App. 7A for correlation at lags 1 through 6, respectively, taking $n = 5000$ in each case; i.e., we tested stream 5 for lag 1 correlation, stream 6 for lag 2 correlation, etc. The values of $A_1, A_2, \ldots, A_6$ were 0.90, -1.03, -0.12, -1.32, 0.39, and 0.76, respectively, none of which is significantly different from 0 in comparison with the $N(0,1)$ distribution, at level $\alpha = 0.10$ (or smaller). Thus, the first 5000 values in these streams do not exhibit observable autocorrelation at these lags.

Note that, as stated, this test specifically tests for lag j correlation starting with U_1; we could also test for lag j correlation by starting with U_2 (using U_2, U_{2+j}, U_{2+2j} in the definition of $\hat{\rho}_j$), and so on for other starting values in the sequence.

As mentioned above, these are just four of many possible empirical tests. For example, the Kolmogorov-Smirnov test discussed in Sec. 6.6.2 (for the case with all parameters known) could be applied instead of the chi-square test for one-dimensional uniformity. Several empirical tests have been developed around the idea that the generator in question be used to simulate a relatively simple stochastic system with *known* (population) performance measures that the simulation estimates. The simulated results are compared in some way with the known exact "answers," perhaps by means of a chi-square test. A simple application of this idea is in Prob. 7.10; Rudolph and Hawkins (1976) test several generators by using them to simulate Markov processes. A comprehensive package called TESTRAND was developed by Dudewicz and Ralley (1981), consisting of some 20 different generators and 14 tests. In conclusion, we feel that as many empirical tests should be performed as are practicable.

Lest the reader be left with the impression that the empirical tests we have presented in this section have no discriminative power at all, we subjected the infamous generator RANDU [defined by $Z_i = 65,539 Z_{i-1} \pmod{2^{31}}$], with seed $Z_0 = 123,456,789$, to the same tests as reported for the generator in App. 7A in Examples 7.5 through 7.8. The test statistics were as follows:

Chi-square test:	χ^2	$= 4,202.0$
Serial tests:	$\chi^2(2) =$	$4,202.3$
	$\chi^2(3) =$	$16,252.3$
Runs up test:	R	$= 6.3$
Correlation tests:	All A_j's were insignificant	

While uniformity appears acceptable on [0,1] and the unit square, note the enormous value of the three-dimensional serial test statistic, indicating a severe problem for this generator in terms of uniformity on the unit cube. RANDU is a fatally flawed generator, due primarily to its utter failure in three dimensions; we shall see why in Sec. 7.4.2 below. Unfortunately, RANDU can frequently be found as a built-in, intrinsic function. *Under no circumstances should RANDU ever be used*, especially with the availability of highly reliable and portable codes for demonstrably acceptable generators, such as the Marse-Roberts code given in App. 7A.

One potential disadvantage of empirical tests is that they are only *local*; i.e., only that segment of a cycle (for LCGs, for example) that was actually used to generate the U_i's for the test is examined, so we cannot say anything about how the generator might perform in other segments of the cycle. On the other hand, this local nature of empirical tests can be advantageous, since it might allow us to examine the actual random numbers that will be used later in a simulation. (Often we can calculate ahead of time how many random numbers will be used in a simulation, or at least get a conservative estimate, by analyzing the model's operation and the techniques used for generating the necessary random variates.) Then this entire random-number stream can be tested empirically, one would hope without excessive cost. (The tests in Examples 7.5 through 7.8 were all done together in a single FORTRAN program that took about 10 seconds on a DEC VAX 8650). A more global empirical test could be performed by replicating an entire test several times and statistically comparing the observed values of the test statistics against the distribution under the null hypothesis; Fishman (1978, pp. 371–372) suggests this approach. For example, the runs-up test of Example 7.7 could be done, say, 100 times using 100 separate random-number streams from the same generator, each of length 5000. This would result in 100 independent values for R, which could then be compared with the chi-square distribution with 6 df using, for example, the K-S test with all parameters known. Fishman's approach could be used to identify "bad" segments within a cycle of a LCG; this was done for the PMMLCG with $m = 2^{31} - 1$ and $a = 630,360,016$, and a "bad" segment was indeed discovered and eliminated from use in SIMSCRIPT II.5 [see Fishman (1973, p. 183)]. Also, GPSS/H [Henriksen (1988)], as part of its standard output, produces results for chi-square tests of uniformity on the random numbers that were actually used in the simulation. However, we would expect that even a "perfect" random-number generator would occasionally produce an "unacceptable" test statistic; in fact this *ought* to happen with probability $\alpha =$ the level of the test being done. Thus, it can be argued that such hand-picking of segments to avoid "bad" ones is in fact a poor idea.

7.4.2 Theoretical Tests

We now briefly discuss theoretical tests for LCGs. Since these tests are quite sophisticated and mathematically complex, we shall describe them only qualitatively; for detailed accounts see Fishman (1978, pp. 358–371) or Knuth (1981, pp. 75–110). As mentioned earlier, theoretical tests do not require that we generate any U_i's at all but are *a priori*, in that they indicate how well a LCG *can* perform by looking at its defining constants m, a, and c. Theoretical tests also differ from empirical tests in that they are *global*; i.e., a LCG's behavior over its *entire* cycle is examined. As we mentioned at the end of Sec. 7.4.1, it is debatable whether local or global tests are preferable; global tests have a natural appeal but do not generally indicate how well a specific segment of a cycle will behave.

For LCGs and for Tausworthe generators, it is sometimes possible to compute the "sample" mean, variance, and correlations over an entire cycle directly from the constants m, a, c, and Z_0 defining the generator. Many of these results are quoted by Kennedy and Gentle (1980, pp. 139–143). For example, in a full-period LCG, the average of the U_i's, taken over an entire cycle, is $1/2 - 1/(2m)$, which is seen to be very close to the desired $1/2$ if m is one of the large values (in the billions) typically used; see Prob. 7.14. Similarly, we can compute the "sample" variance of the U_i's over a full cycle, and get $1/12 - 1/(12m^2)$, which is close to $1/12$, the variance of the U(0,1) distribution. Kennedy and Gentle also discuss "sample" correlations for LCGs. Although such formulas may seem comforting, they can be misleading; for example, the result for the full-period LCG "sample" lag 1 correlation suggests that, to minimize this value, a be chosen close to $\sqrt{m}$, which turns out to be a poor choice from the standpoint of other important statistical considerations. Niederreiter (1977, 1978b) provides rigorous investigations into the independence properties of LCGs.

The best-known theoretical tests are based on the rather upsetting observation by Marsaglia (1968) that "random numbers fall mainly in the planes." That is, if $U_1, U_2, \ldots$ is a sequence of random numbers generated by a LCG, the overlapping d-tuples $(U_1, U_2, \ldots, U_d)$, $(U_2, U_3, \ldots, U_{d+1})$, $\ldots$ will all fall in a relatively small number of $(d-1)$-dimensional hyperplanes passing through the d-dimensional unit hypercube $[0,1]^d$. For example, if $d = 2$, the pairs (U_1, U_2), (U_2, U_3), $\ldots$ will be arranged in a "crystalline" or "lattice" fashion along several different families of parallel lines going through the unit square. (The lines within a family are parallel to each other, but lines from different families are not parallel.) Figure 7.1 displays all the pairs (U_i, U_{i+1}) for the full-period generator defined by $Z_i = (37Z_{i-1} + 1) \pmod{64}$. While the apparent regularity certainly does not seem very "random," it may not be too disturbing since the pairs seem to fill up the unit square fairly well, or at least

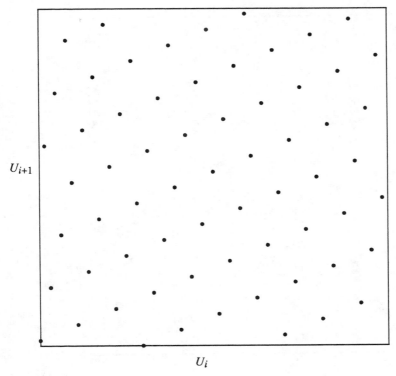

FIGURE 7.1
Two-dimensional lattice structure for the full-period LCG with $m = 64$, $a = 37$, and $c = 1$.

as well as could be expected with such a tiny modulus. However, by simply changing the multiplier a from 37 to 21 (which still yields a full-period generator), we get the pairs plotted in Fig. 7.2, which are definitely anxiety-provoking, since there are large areas of the unit square where we can never realize a pair of U_i's; a simulation using such a generator would almost certainly produce invalid results. Ripley (1987, pp. 23–40) and L'Ecuyer (1987, 1988) give several interesting plots of this type for various generators. In three dimensions, the triples (U_i, U_{i+1}, U_{i+2}) from the generator of Fig. 7.1 appear in Fig. 7.3, viewed from a particular point outside the unit cube; the planes cutting through the cube are clear. A real example of this problem concerns the generator RANDU ($m = 2^{31}$, $a = 2^{16} + 3 = 65,539$, $c = 0$), which produces triples of U_i's (of which there are some half-billion across a period, allowing for overlaps) that all fall on *only 15* parallel planes passing through the unit cube; Fig. 7.4 illustrates this for 2000 triples, clearly showing the 15 planes. This explains the horrific performance of RANDU on the three-dimensional serial test noted at the end of Sec. 7.4.1.

Both the *spectral test* [developed originally by Coveyou and MacPherson (1967)] and the *lattice test* [proposed independently by Beyer, Roof, and

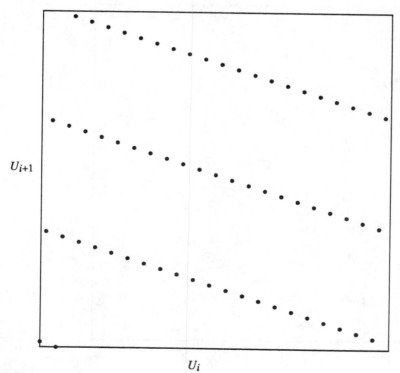

FIGURE 7.2
Two-dimensional lattice structure for the full-period LCG with $m = 64$, $a = 21$, and $c = 1$.

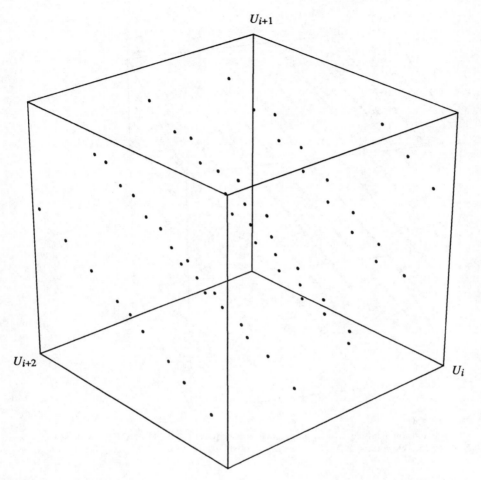

FIGURE 7.3
Three-dimensional lattice structure for the full-period LCG with $m = 64$, $a = 37$, and $c = 1$.

Williamson (1971) and by Marsaglia (1972)] are aimed at identifying how densely the d-tuples of U_i's from a particular LCG *can* fill up $[0,1]^d$. By "can fill up," we mean that since all the possible d-tuples are constrained to lie on families of parallel planes, they cannot fall in any of the space between adjacent planes in the same family. If two such planes are far apart, then the generator will leave large gaps in this space and thus perform poorly; these two tests measure, in different ways, the size of such gaps. If one or both of them indicates that there are large gaps in $[0,1]^d$ that cannot contain any d-tuples, we have evidence that the LCG being tested will exhibit poor behavior, at least in d dimensions. For example, the generator in Fig. 7.1 would fare better under the spectral and lattice tests in two dimensions than that in Fig. 7.2 (although

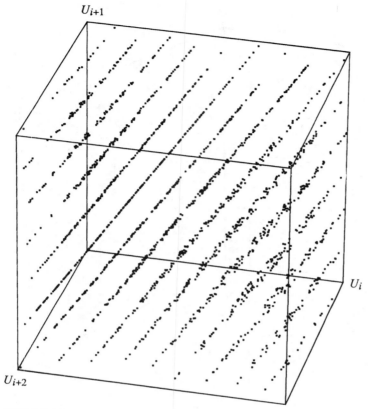

FIGURE 7.4
Three-dimensional lattice structure for 2000 triples from the LCG RANDU with $m = 2^{31}$, $a = 2^{16} + 3 = 65,539$, and $c = 0$.

neither is a serious generator); RANDU, as one would suspect from looking at Fig. 7.4, fails miserably in three dimensions. Usually these tests are applied separately for each dimension from $d = 2$ to as high as $d = 10$. As exemplified in Hoaglin (1976), Coveyou and MacPherson (1967), and Fishman and Moore (1986), a given LCG might pass nicely in some dimensions but fail in others. Thus, one should interpret the results of these two tests in light of the proposed use of the LCG. The information obtained from both of these tests is often similar, as noted by Ripley (1983). Hoaglin and King (1978) and Atkinson (1980) argue that the original version of the spectral test should be applied only to full-period LCGs (implying, in light of Theorem 7.1, that only mixed generators be considered); Atkinson modifies the test for the case of multiplicative generators (which cannot have full period). Hopkins (1983) gives a FORTRAN program for carrying out the spectral test; see also Hill (1985) for a comment on Hopkins' code.

7.4.3   Some General Observations on Testing

The number, variety, and range of complexity of tests for random-number generators are truly bewildering. To make matters worse, there has been (and probably always will be) considerable controversy over which tests are best, whether theoretical tests are really more definitive than empirical tests, and so on. Indeed, no amount of testing can ever absolutely convince everyone that some particular generator is absolutely "the best." One piece of advice that is often offered, however, is that a random-number generator should be tested in a way that is consistent with its intended use. This would entail, for example, examining the behavior of pairs of U_i's (perhaps with the two-dimensional serial test) if random numbers are naturally used in pairs in the simulation itself. In a broader sense, this advice would imply that one should be more careful in choosing and testing a random-number generator if the simulation in which it will be used is very costly, requires high-precision results, or is a particularly critical component of a larger study.

7.5   RANDOM-NUMBER GENERATION ON MICROCOMPUTERS

The rapid advance of microcomputer capabilities in recent years has been accompanied by increased use of such machines for simulation. Due to their relatively low price and essentially zero cost of operation, micros may be almost exclusively "dedicated" to simulation. Random-number generation on microprocessors, however, presents special challenges due to the short word length typically encountered; while 8-bit processors are probably mostly gone in terms of simulation and scientific computing, 16-bit processors are still common. Unfortunately, vendors of microcomputer hardware and software have not always been aware of the subtleties of random-number generation, resulting in some perfectly awful generators being supplied (and no doubt used, regrettably); Modianos, Scott, and Cornwell (1984) and Park and Miller (1988) studied several such cases. Furthermore, some published work on implementation of LCGs for microcomputers may propose generators of questionable statistical performance or weak theoretical foundation, as pointed out by L'Ecuyer (1988).

Thus, care should be exercised when using random-number generators on microcomputers. As mentioned earlier in the chapter, many microcomputers currently being used for simulation have available high-level language compilers allowing for representation of integers as though a 32-bit word were available. We have implemented the Marse and Roberts (1983) generator successfully in FORTRAN (Fig. 7.5) and C (Figs. 7.7 and 7.8) on several microcomputers; see App. 7A for details. Further, it should be possible to use good composite generators as discussed in Sec. 7.3.2, where each component generator involves only relatively small integer calculations, and thus is workable on short-word-length machines; Wichmann and Hill (1987) discuss such a scheme in a paper published in the popular press for microcomputing. Specific generators, with code, for microcomputers are given by Park and Miller (1988), Thesen (1985), and Thesen, Sun, and Wang (1984). L'Ecuyer (1987, 1988) provides a very good class of composite generators, with Pascal code, for use on microcomputers with word lengths as short as 16 bits.

As noted in Chap. 3, most simulation languages now have versions available that will run on popular microcomputers. The designers of these languages have usually taken care to use acceptable random-number generators, so that they generally can be relied upon to produce valid results on microcomputers as well as on mainframes.

7.6 GENERATORS USED BY SIMULATION LANGUAGES

We close this chapter by describing the generators used in some of the major simulation languages, as of the time of this writing. In each, a PMMLCG was used with modulus $m = 2^{31} - 1$, and with a variety of multipliers a, all of which are primitive roots modulo $2^{31} - 1$, so that a period of $2^{31} - 2$ results. The values for a in several languages are given in Table 7.3, together with an indication of the facilities for separate streams. The multipliers used by SIMAN, SLAM II, and SIMSCRIPT II.5 were discussed in Sec. 7.2.2, and those used by GPSS/H and GPSS/PC were found to be among the best in the studies of Fishman and Moore (1981, 1982, 1986). Also, the generators used by related products are usually the same as in the basic language: SIMFACTORY II.5 uses the SIMSCRIPT II.5 generator, and XCELL+ uses the SLAM II generator, etc. In all cases, the generators used are reliable, and have been chosen with care. In terms of the number of streams, both GPSS/H and GPSS/PC allow the user to select any starting point for the random-number generator, so that the number of streams is limited only by the inherent cycle length; most languages, however, have a default of 10 streams, which may not be entirely adequate for some applications.

TABLE 7.3
Multipliers used by some simulation languages

Language	Multiplier	Number of streams
GPSS/H	742,938,285	Essentially unlimited
GPSS/PC	397,204,094	Essentially unlimited
SIMAN	16,807	10 (extendable)
SIMSCRIPT II.5	630,360,016	10 (extendable)
SLAM II	16,807	10 (extendable)

APPENDIX 7A
PORTABLE COMPUTER CODES

Here we present computer codes in FORTRAN, Pascal, and C to implement the PMMLCG defined by modulus $m = m^* = 2^{31} - 1 = 2,147,483,647$ and multiplier $a = a_2 = 630,360,016$, discussed at the end of Sec. 7.2.2. These codes are all based closely on the FORTRAN code of Marse and Roberts (1983), and require that integers between $-m^*$ and m^* be represented and computed correctly, which is often (but not always) the case in implementations of these languages on most machines, including microcomputers. A FORTRAN function NXSEED, from Marse and Roberts, is also shown, which returns the starting seed for any of the streams, assuming that all streams are of length 100,000.

If this range of integers is not available, there are several implementations of the generator with this same modulus m^* but with the (less desirable) multiplier $a_1 = 16,807$ instead; see Schrage (1979) for a DOUBLE PRECISION FORTRAN version, and Park and Miller (1988) for several Pascal implementations. As these codes use floating-point rather than integer arithmetic, they are naturally slower. More appealing in this case is the 16-bit Pascal code in L'Ecuyer (1988), which implements a composite generator, as discussed in Sec. 7.3.2.

7A.1 FORTRAN

Figure 7.5 presents the FORTRAN code of Marse and Roberts (1983), modified slightly to provide for seed management via ENTRY points, as well

```
      REAL FUNCTION RAND(ISTRM)
*       Prime modulus multiplicative linear congruential generator
*       Z(I) = (630360016 * Z(I - 1)) (MOD(2**31 - 1)), based on Marse
*       and Roberts' portable random-number generator UNIRAN.  Multiple
*       (100) streams are supported, with seeds spaced 100,000 apart.
*       Throughout, input argument ISTRM must be an INTEGER giving the
*       desired stream number.
*
*       Usage: (Three options)
*
*       1. To obtain the next U(0,1) random number from stream ISTRM,
*          execute
*              U = RAND(ISTRM)
*          The REAL variable U will contain the next random number.
*
*       2. To set the seed for stream ISTRM to a desired value IZSET,
*          execute
*              CALL RANDST(IZSET,ISTRM)
```

FIGURE 7.5
FORTRAN code for the PMMLCG with $m = 2^{31} - 1$ and $a = 630,360,016$ from Marse and Roberts (1983).

```
*          where IZSET must be an INTEGER constant or variable set to the
*          desired seed, a number between 1 and 2147483646 (inclusive).
*          Default seeds for all 100 streams are given in the code.
*
*       3. To get the current (most recently used) integer in the
*          sequence being generated for stream ISTRM into the INTEGER
*          variable IZGET, execute
*             IZGET = IRANDG(ISTRM)

        INTEGER B2E15,B2E16,HI15,HI31,ISTRM,IZGET,IZSET,LOW15,LOWPRD,
     &          MODLUS,MULT1,MULT2,OVFLOW,ZI,ZRNG(100)
        INTEGER IRANDG,RANDST

*       Force saving of ZRNG between calls.

        SAVE ZRNG

*       Define the constants.

        DATA MULT1,MULT2/24112,26143/
        DATA B2E15,B2E16,MODLUS/32768,65536,2147483647/

*       Set the default seeds for all 100 streams.

        DATA ZRNG/1973272912, 281629770,  20006270,1280689831,2096730329,
     &            1933576050, 913566091, 246780520,1363774876, 604901985,
     &            1511192140,1259851944, 824064364, 150493284, 242708531,
     &              75253171,1964472944,1202299975, 233217322,1911216000,
     &             726370533, 403498145, 993232223,1103205531, 762430696,
     &            1922803170,1385516923,  76271663, 413682397, 726466604,
     &             336157058,1432650381,1120463904, 595778810, 877722890,
     &            1046574445,  68911991,2088367019, 748545416, 622401386,
     &            2122378830, 640690903,1774806513,2132545692,2079249579,
     &              78130110, 852776735,1187867272,1351423507,1645973084,
     &            1997049139, 922510944,2045512870, 898585771, 243649545,
     &            1004818771, 773686062, 403188473, 372279877,1901633463,
     &             498067494,2087759558, 493157915, 597104727,1530940798,
     &            1814496276, 536444882,1663153658, 855503735,  67784357,
     &            1432404475, 619691088, 119025595, 880802310, 176192644,
     &            1116780070, 277854671,1366580350,1142483975,2026948561,
     &            1053920743, 786262391,1792203830,1494667770,1923011392,
     &            1433700034,1244184613,1147297105, 539712780,1545929719,
     &             190641742,1645390429, 264907697, 620389253,1502074852,
     &             927711160, 364849192,2049576050, 638580085, 547070247/

*       Generate the next random number.

        ZI      = ZRNG(ISTRM)
        HI15    = ZI / B2E16
        LOWPRD  = (ZI - HI15 * B2E16) * MULT1
        LOW15   = LOWPRD / B2E16
        HI31    = HI15 * MULT1 + LOW15
        OVFLOW  = HI31 / B2E15
        ZI      = (((LOWPRD - LOW15 * B2E16) - MODLUS) +
     &            (HI31 - OVFLOW * B2E15) * B2E16) + OVFLOW
        IF (ZI .LT. 0) ZI = ZI + MODLUS
        HI15    = ZI / B2E16
        LOWPRD  = (ZI - HI15 * B2E16) * MULT2
        LOW15   = LOWPRD / B2E16
        HI31    = HI15 * MULT2 + LOW15
        OVFLOW  = HI31 / B2E15
        ZI      = (((LOWPRD - LOW15 * B2E16) - MODLUS) +
     &            (HI31 - OVFLOW * B2E15) * B2E16) + OVFLOW
        IF (ZI .LT. 0) ZI = ZI + MODLUS
        ZRNG(ISTRM) = ZI
        RAND    = (2 * (ZI / 256) + 1) / 16777216.0
        RETURN
```

FIGURE 7.5
(*Continued.*)

```
*      Set the current ZRNG for stream ISTRM to IZSET.

       ENTRY RANDST(IZSET,ISTRM)
       ZRNG(ISTRM) = IZSET
       RETURN

*      Return the current ZRNG for stream ISTRM.

       ENTRY IRANDG(ISTRM)
       IRANDG = ZRNG(ISTRM)
       RETURN

       END
```

FIGURE 7.5
(*Continued.*)

as built-in default seeds for 100 streams spaced 100,000 apart. The comments in the code detail its use. We have tested this program on the following microcomputers and compilers: an IBM PC with IBM Professional FORTRAN (Version 1.0), an IBM PS/2 Model 50Z with Microsoft FORTRAN (Version 4.01), and an Apple Macintosh SE with Absoft FORTRAN (Version 2.4, with one difficulty noted below). It has also been used on the following machines: a DEC VAX 8650 with VAX FORTRAN, an Encore Multimax 320 with UMAX FORTRAN, and a Cray-2 with the cft77 compiler. The Absoft compiler used for the Macintosh has a deficiency in its implementation of ENTRY points, resulting in the need to change the first line of the code to REAL FUNCTION RAND(DUMMY, ISTRM) and the final ENTRY point to ENTRY IRANDG(DUMMY, ISTRM), with a corresponding change in usage, e.g., U = RAND(DUMMY, 1), etc.. The code in Fig. 7.5 was used in the FORTRAN examples in Chap. 1, as well as in all the examples of Chap. 2.

7A.2 Pascal

Figure 7.6 gives a Pascal code for this generator, consisting of some four separate procedures; the comments give specific instructions for its use. In this particular implementation, the procedure Randdf must be invoked *before* using the generator Rand to initialize the seeds for the 100 streams. Also, it is required to add the VAR declaration for Zrng noted in the comments (Zrng

```
{ Prime modulus multiplicative linear congruential generator
  Z[I] = (630360016 * Z[I - 1]) (MOD 2147483647), based on Marse and
  Roberts' portable FORTRAN random-number generator UNIRAN.  Multiple
  (100) streams are supported, with seeds spaced 100,000 apart.
  Throughout, input argument Stream must be an Integer giving the
  desired stream number.  The initialization procedure Randdf described
  below must be invoked before using the generator, in order to set the
  seeds for the 100 predefined streams.
```

FIGURE 7.6
Pascal code for the PMMLCG with $m = 2^{31} - 1$ and $a = 630{,}360{,}016$ based on Marse and Roberts (1983).

The following declarations must appear in the program using this generator:

```
VAR
    Zrng : ARRAY [1..100] OF Integer;

PROCEDURE Randdf;                                        FORWARD;
FUNCTION  Rand(Stream : Integer) : Real;                 FORWARD;
PROCEDURE Randst(Zset : Integer; Stream : Integer);      FORWARD;
FUNCTION  Randgt(Stream : Integer) : Integer;            FORWARD;
```

Note that the name Zrng is thus reserved and cannot be used for any other purpose.

Usage: (Four procedures)

1. Before using the generator, it is required to initialize the routines by executing
       Randdf;
   This sets the initial seed values for all 100 streams in the array Zrng.

2. To obtain the next U(0,1) random number from stream Stream, execute
       U := Rand(Stream)
   The Real variable U will contain the next random number.

3. To set the seed for stream Stream to a desired value Zset, execute
       Randst(Zset, Stream)
   where Zset must be an Integer constant or variable set to the desired seed, a number between 1 and 2147483646 (inclusive). Seeds for all 100 streams are given in the code, and must be initialized by invoking Randdf.

4. To get the current (most recently used) integer in the sequence being generated for stream Stream into the Integer variable Zget, execute
       Zget = Randgt(Stream);
}

```
PROCEDURE Randdf;

  BEGIN { Randdf }

    { Set the seeds for all 100 streams. }

       Zrng[ 1]:=1973272912; Zrng[ 2]:= 281629770; Zrng[ 3]:=  20006270;
       Zrng[ 4]:=1280689831; Zrng[ 5]:=2096730329; Zrng[ 6]:=1933576050;
       Zrng[ 7]:= 913566091; Zrng[ 8]:= 246780520; Zrng[ 9]:=1363774876;
       Zrng[10]:= 604901985; Zrng[11]:=1511192140; Zrng[12]:=1259851944;
       Zrng[13]:= 824064364; Zrng[14]:= 150493284; Zrng[15]:= 242708531;
       Zrng[16]:=  75253171; Zrng[17]:=1964472944; Zrng[18]:=1202299975;
       Zrng[19]:= 233217322; Zrng[20]:=1911216000; Zrng[21]:= 726370533;
       Zrng[22]:= 403498145; Zrng[23]:= 993232223; Zrng[24]:=1103205531;
       Zrng[25]:= 762430696; Zrng[26]:=1922803170; Zrng[27]:=1385516923;
       Zrng[28]:=  76271663; Zrng[29]:= 413682397; Zrng[30]:= 726466604;
       Zrng[31]:= 336157058; Zrng[32]:=1432650381; Zrng[33]:=1120463904;
       Zrng[34]:= 595778810; Zrng[35]:= 877722890; Zrng[36]:=1046574445;
       Zrng[37]:=  68911991; Zrng[38]:=2088367019; Zrng[39]:= 748545416;
       Zrng[40]:= 622401386; Zrng[41]:=2122378830; Zrng[42]:= 640690903;
       Zrng[43]:=1774806513; Zrng[44]:=2132545692; Zrng[45]:=2079249579;
       Zrng[46]:=  78130110; Zrng[47]:= 852776735; Zrng[48]:=1187867272;
       Zrng[49]:=1351423507; Zrng[50]:=1645973084; Zrng[51]:=1997049139;
       Zrng[52]:= 922510944; Zrng[53]:=2045512870; Zrng[54]:= 898585771;
```

FIGURE 7.6
(*Continued.*)

```
      Zrng[55]:= 243649545;  Zrng[56]:=1004818771;  Zrng[57]:= 773686062;
      Zrng[58]:= 403188473;  Zrng[59]:= 372279877;  Zrng[60]:=1901633463;
      Zrng[61]:= 498067494;  Zrng[62]:=2087759558;  Zrng[63]:= 493157915;
      Zrng[64]:= 597104727;  Zrng[65]:=1530940798;  Zrng[66]:=1814496276;
      Zrng[67]:= 536444882;  Zrng[68]:=1663153658;  Zrng[69]:= 855503735;
      Zrng[70]:=  67784357;  Zrng[71]:=1432404475;  Zrng[72]:= 619691088;
      Zrng[73]:= 119025595;  Zrng[74]:= 880802310;  Zrng[75]:= 176192644;
      Zrng[76]:=1116780070;  Zrng[77]:= 277854671;  Zrng[78]:=1366580350;
      Zrng[79]:=1142483975;  Zrng[80]:=2026948561;  Zrng[81]:=1053920743;
      Zrng[82]:= 786262391;  Zrng[83]:=1792203830;  Zrng[84]:=1494667717;
      Zrng[85]:=1923011392;  Zrng[86]:=1433700034;  Zrng[87]:=1244184613;
      Zrng[88]:=1147297105;  Zrng[89]:= 539712780;  Zrng[90]:=1545929719;
      Zrng[91]:= 190641742;  Zrng[92]:=1645390429;  Zrng[93]:= 264907697;
      Zrng[94]:= 620389253;  Zrng[95]:=1502402852;  Zrng[96]:= 927711160;
      Zrng[97]:= 364849192;  Zrng[98]:=2049576050;  Zrng[99]:= 638580085;
      Zrng[100]:= 547070247

END; { Randdf }

FUNCTION Rand; { Generate the next random number. }

   { Define the constants. }
   CONST
      B2E15  =         32768;
      B2E16  =         65536;
      Modlus = 2147483647;
      Mult1  =         24112;
      Mult2  =         26143;

   VAR
      Hi15, Hi31, Low15, Lowprd, Ovflow, Zi : Integer;

   BEGIN { Rand }

      { Generate the next random number. }

      Zi       := Zrng[Stream];
      Hi15     := Zi DIV B2E16;
      Lowprd   := (Zi - Hi15 * B2E16) * Mult1;
      Low15    := Lowprd DIV B2E16;
      Hi31     := Hi15 * Mult1 + Low15;
      Ovflow   := Hi31 DIV B2E15;
      Zi       := (((Lowprd - Low15 * B2E16) - Modlus) +
                    (Hi31 - Ovflow * B2E15) * B2E16) + Ovflow;
      IF Zi < 0 THEN Zi := Zi + Modlus;
      Hi15     := Zi DIV B2E16;
      Lowprd   := (Zi - Hi15 * B2E16) * Mult2;
      Low15    := Lowprd DIV B2E16;
      Hi31     := Hi15 * Mult2 + Low15;
      Ovflow   := Hi31 DIV B2E15;
      Zi       := (((Lowprd - Low15 * B2E16) - Modlus) +
                    (Hi31 - Ovflow * B2E15) * B2E16) + Ovflow;
      IF Zi < 0 THEN Zi := Zi + Modlus;
      Zrng[Stream] := Zi;
      Rand     := (2 * (Zi DIV 256) + 1) / 16777216.0

   END; { Rand }

PROCEDURE Randst;

   BEGIN { Randst }

      { Set the current Zrng for stream Stream to Zset. }

      Zrng[Stream] := Zset

   END; { Randst }
```

FIGURE 7.6
(*Continued.*)

```
FUNCTION Randgt;

    BEGIN { Randgt }

        { Return the current Zrng for stream Stream. }

        Randgt := Zrng[Stream]

    END; { Randgt }
```

FIGURE 7.6
(*Continued.*)

thus becomes a reserved word from the user's point of view), and the PROCEDURE and FUNCTION FORWARD declarations for Randdf, Rand, Randst, and Randgt. These four procedures would then have to be placed inside the Pascal program for the simulation, either physically with an editor or with a compiler-dependent "include" directive. We have used this code on a DEC VAX 8650 with VAX Pascal, and on a Cray-2 with UNICOS Pascal. It was used for the Pascal examples in Chap. 1.

7A.3 C

Figure 7.7 gives code for an ANSI C (i.e., using function prototyping) version of this generator, in three functions, as detailed in the comments. Figure 7.8

```
/* Prime modulus multiplicative linear congruential generator
   Z[i] = (630360016 * Z[i-1]) (mod(pow(2,31) - 1)), based on Marse and
   Roberts' portable FORTRAN random-number generator UNIRAN.  Multiple
   (100) streams are supported, with seeds spaced 100,000 apart.
   Throughout, input argument "stream" must be an int giving the
   desired stream number.  The header file rand.h must be included in
   the calling program (#include "rand.h") before using these
   functions.

   Usage: (Three functions)

   1. To obtain the next U(0,1) random number from stream "stream,"
      execute
           u = rand(stream);
      where rand is a float function.  The float variable u will
      contain the next random number.

   2. To set the seed for stream "stream" to a desired value zset,
      execute
              randst(zset, stream);
      where randst is a void function and zset must be a long set to
      the desired seed, a number between 1 and 2147483646 (inclusive).
      Default seeds for all 100 streams are given in the code.

   3. To get the current (most recently used) integer in the sequence
      being generated for stream "stream" into the long variable zget,
      execute
           zget = randgt(stream);
      where randgt is a long function.
*/
```

FIGURE 7.7
C code for the PMMLCG with $m = 2^{31} - 1$ and $a = 630,360,016$ based on Marse and Roberts (1983).

```
/* Define the constants. */

#define MODLUS 2147483647
#define MULT1       24112
#define MULT2       26143

/* Set the default seeds for all 100 streams. */

static long zrng[] =
{          0,
 1973272912, 281629770,  20006270,1280689831,2096730329,1933576050,
  913566091, 246780520,1363774876,  604901985,1511192140,1259851944,
  824064364, 150493284, 242708531,  75253171,1964472944,1202299975,
  233217322,1911216000, 726370533, 403498145, 993232223,1103205531,
  762430696,1922803170,1385516923,  76271663, 413682397, 726466604,
  336157058,1432650381,1120463904, 595778810, 877722890,1046574445,
   68911991,2088367019, 748545416, 622401386,2122378830, 640690903,
 1774806513,2132545692,2079249579,  78130110, 852776735,1187867272,
 1351423507,1645973084,1997049139, 922510944,2045512870, 898585771,
  243649545,1004818771, 773686062, 403188473, 372279877,1901633463,
  498067494,2087759558, 493157915, 597104727,1530940798,1814496276,
  536444882,1663153658, 855503735,  67784357,1432404475, 619691088,
  119025595, 880802310, 176192644,1116780070, 277854671,1366580350,
 1142483975,2026948561,1053920743, 786262391,1792203830,1494667770,
 1923011392,1433700034,1244184613,1147297105, 539712780,1545929719,
  190641742,1645390429, 264907697, 620389253,1502074852, 927711160,
  364849192,2049576050, 638580085, 547070247 };

/* Generate the next random number. */

float rand(int stream)
{
    long zi, lowprd, hi31;

    zi     = zrng[stream];
    lowprd = (zi & 65535) * MULT1;
    hi31   = (zi >> 16) * MULT1 + (lowprd >> 16);
    zi     = ((lowprd & 65535) - MODLUS) +
             ((hi31 & 32767) << 16) + (hi31 >> 15);
    if (zi < 0) zi += MODLUS;
    lowprd = (zi & 65535) * MULT2;
    hi31   = (zi >> 16) * MULT2 + (lowprd >> 16);
    zi     = ((lowprd & 65535) - MODLUS) +
             ((hi31 & 32767) << 16) + (hi31 >> 15);
    if (zi < 0) zi += MODLUS;
    zrng[stream] = zi;
    return ((zi >> 7 | 1) + 1)/ 16777216.0;
}

/* Set the current zrng for stream "stream" to zset. */

void randst (long zset, int stream)
{
    zrng[stream] = zset;
}

/* Return the current zrng for stream "stream". */

long randgt (int stream)
{
    return zrng[stream];
}
```

FIGURE 7.7
(*Continued.*)

```
/* The following 3 declarations are for use of the random-number
   generator rand and the associated functions randst and randgt for
   seed management.  This file (named rand.h) should be included in any
   program using these functions by executing
        #include "rand.h"
   before referencing the functions.
*/

float rand(int stream);
void randst(long zset, int stream);
long randgt(int stream);
```

FIGURE 7.8
C header file (rand.h) to accompany the C code in Fig. 7.7.

also gives a header file (rand.h) that the user must #include to declare the
functions. We have used this code on an IBM PS/2 with Turbo C (Version
1.5), on an Apple Macintosh IIcx with THINK C 4.0 (the name of the built-in
function rand in the ANSI library had to be changed to avoid conflict with our
use of this name), and on a DEC VAX 8650 with VAX C; it was used for the C
examples in Chap. 1. At this writing, some C compilers do not yet support the
ANSI function prototyping, so this code could be modified to work under
"old" C by removing the prototyping.

7A.4 Obtaining Initial Seeds for the Streams

Figure 7.9 gives the FORTRAN function NXSEED from Marse and Roberts
(1983), which takes as input the desired INTEGER stream number ISTRM
and returns in its name the seed for this stream; it is assumed that the streams
are adjacent blocks of length 100,000 random numbers each. Thus, for

```
        INTEGER FUNCTION NXSEED(ISTRM)

*       Function from Marse and Roberts to return in its name the beginning
*       seed for stream ISTRM in the generator of Figs. 7.5, 7.6, and 7.7.
*       All streams are assumed to be of length 100,000 random numbers.

*       Usage:  To get the beginning seed for stream ISTRM into INTEGER
*       variable ISEED, execute
*            ISEED = NXSEED(ISTRM)
*       Input argument ISTRM is an INTEGER between 1 and 21,474.

        INTEGER I,SEED,ISTRM
        DOUBLE PRECISION Z
        Z = 1973272912
        DO 10 I = 1, ISTRM
           Z = DMOD( 715.D0*Z, 2147483647.D0)
           Z = DMOD(1058.D0*Z, 2147483647.D0)
           Z = DMOD(1385.D0*Z, 2147483647.D0)
10      CONTINUE
        NXSEED = IDINT(Z)
        RETURN
        END
```

FIGURE 7.9
FORTRAN function NXSEED returning the beginning seed for any of the possible streams (of
length 100,000) for the generator in Figs. 7.5, 7.6, and 7.7, from Marse and Roberts (1983).

example, NXSEED(3) returns the value 20,006,270. It is assumed that the seed for stream 1 is 1,973,272,912. Since the cycle length is $2^{31} - 1 = 2,147,483,647$, there are 21,474 of these streams, and NXSEED finds the beginning seed for any one of them. As written, NXSEED determines the beginning seeds for each of streams $1, 2, \ldots,$ ISTRM but returns only the last of these; it could, of course, be rewritten to return them all in an INTEGER vector in the argument list.

PROBLEMS

7.1. For the LCG of Example 7.2, find Z_{500} using only pencil and paper.

7.2. For the following multiplicative LCGs, compute Z_i for enough values of $i \geq 1$ to cover an entire cycle:

(a) $Z_i = (11\ Z_{i-1})(\bmod\ 16), Z_0 = 1$
(b) $Z_i = (11\ Z_{i-1})(\bmod\ 16), Z_0 = 2$
(c) $Z_i = (2\ Z_{i-1})(\bmod\ 13), Z_0 = 1$
(d) $Z_i = (3\ Z_{i-1})(\bmod\ 13), Z_0 = 1$

Note that (a) and (b) have m of the form 2^b; (c) is a PMMLCG, for which $a = 2$ is a primitive element modulo $m = 13$.

7.3. Without actually computing any Z_i's, determine which of the following mixed LCGs have full period:

(a) $Z_i = (13\ Z_{i-1} + 13)(\bmod\ 16)$
(b) $Z_i = (12\ Z_{i-1} + 13)(\bmod\ 16)$
(c) $Z_i = (13\ Z_{i-1} + 12)(\bmod\ 16)$
(d) $Z_i = (Z_{i-1} + 12)(\bmod\ 13)$

7.4. For the four mixed LCGs in Prob. 7.3, compute Z_i for enough values of $i \geq 1$ to cover an entire cycle; let $Z_0 = 1$ in each case. Comment on the results.

7.5. (a) Implement the PMMLCG $Z_i = 630,360,016\ Z_{i-1}\ (\bmod\ 2^{31} - 1)$ on your computer using the Marse-Roberts code in one of the languages from App. 7A.

(b) Repeat the empirical tests of Examples 7.5 through 7.8 with this generator and compare your results with those given in the examples.

7.6. Use the multiplicative LCG in part (a) of Prob. 7.2 to shuffle the output from the mixed LCG in part (d) of Prob. 7.3, using a vector **V** of length 2. Let the seed for both LCGs be 1 and list the first 100 values of **V**, I, and V_I. Identity the period and comment generally on the results.

7.7. For the chi-square test of uniformity, verify the following algorithm for computing $f_1, f_2, \ldots, f_k$:

```
Set f_j =0 for j=1, 2, . . . , k
For i=1, . . . , n do
    Generate U_i
    Set J =⌈kU_i⌉
    Replace f_J by f_J +1
End do
```

(For a real number x, $\lceil x \rceil$ denotes the smallest integer that is greater than or equal to x.) Generalize this algorithm to compute the test statistic for a general d-dimensional serial test.

7.8. Show that the following algorithm correctly computes $r_1, r_2, \ldots, r_6$ for the runs-up test, from the generated numbers $U_1, U_2, \ldots, U_n$:

```
Set r_j =0 for j=1, . . . , 6
Generate U_1, set A=U_1, and set J=1
For i=2, . . . , n do
    Generate U_i and set B=U_i
    If A ≥ B then
        Set J=min(J,6)
        Replace r_J by r_J+1
        Set J=1
    Else
        Replace J by J+1
    End if
    Replace A by B
End do
Set J=min(J,6)
Replace r_J by r_J+1
```

7.9. Subject the canned random-number generator on your computer to the chi-square test, two- and three-dimensional serial tests, the runs-up test, and correlation tests at lags $1, 2, \ldots, 5$. Use the same values for n, k, and α that were used in Examples 7.5 through 7.8. (If your generator does not pass these tests, we suggest that you exercise caution in using it until you can obtain more information on it, either from the literature or from your own further testing.)

7.10. A general approach to testing a random-number generator empirically is to use it to simulate a *simple* stochastic model and obtain estimates of *known* parameters; a standard test is then used to compare the estimate(s) against the known parameter(s). For example, we know that in throwing two fair dice independently, the sum of the two outcomes will be $2, 3, \ldots, 12$ with respective probabilities $\frac{1}{36}, \frac{1}{18}, \frac{1}{12}, \frac{1}{9}, \frac{5}{36}, \frac{1}{6}, \frac{5}{36}, \frac{1}{9}, \frac{1}{12}, \frac{1}{18}$, and $\frac{1}{36}$. Simulate 1000 independent throws of a pair of independent fair dice and compare the observed proportion of 1s, 2s, $\ldots$, 12s with the known probabilities, using an appropriate test from Chap. 6. Use the canned generator on your computer or one of the generators in App. 7A.

7.11. For the LCG in part (d) of Prob. 7.3, plot the pairs $(U_1, U_2), (U_2, U_3), \ldots$ and observe the lattice structure obtained. Note that this LCG has full period.

7.12. Consider the Fibonacci generator discussed in Sec. 7.3.1.
  (a) Show that this generator can never produce the following arrangement of three consecutive output values: $U_{i-2} < U_i < U_{i-1}$.
  (b) Show that the arrangement in (a) should occur with probability $\frac{1}{6}$ for a "perfect" random-number generator.
  This points out a gross defect in the generator, as noted by Bratley, Fox and Schrage (1987), who credit U. Dieter with having noticed this.

7.13. Suppose that $U_1, U_2, \ldots, U_k$ are IID $U(0,1)$ random variables. Show that the fractional part (i.e., ignoring anything to the left of the decimal point) of $U_1 + U_2 + \cdots + U_k$ is also uniformly distributed on the interval $[0,1]$. [This property motivated the composite generator of Wichmann and Hill (1982).]

7.14. Show that the average of the U_i's taken over an entire cycle of a full-period LCG is $1/2 - 1/(2m)$. [*Hint:* for a positive integer k, *Euler's formula* states that $1 + 2 + \cdots + k = k(k+1)/2$.]

REFERENCES

Atkinson, A. C.: Tests of Pseudo-random Numbers, *Appl. Statist.*, *29*: 164–171 (1980).

Banks, J., and J. S. Carson: *Discrete-Event System Simulation*, Prentice-Hall, Englewood Cliffs, N.J. (1984).

Bays, C., and S. D. Durham: Improving a Poor Random Number Generator, *Assoc. Comput. Mach. Trans. Math. Soft.*, *2*: 59–64 (1976).

Beyer, W. A., R. B. Roof, and D. Williamson: The Lattice Structure of Multiplicative Congruential Pseudo-random Vectors, *Math. Comput.*, *25*: 345–363 (1971).

Blum, L., M. Blum, and M. Shub: A Simple Unpredictable Pseudo-random Number Generator, *SIAM J. Comput.*, *15*: 364–383 (1986).

Bratley, P., B. L. Fox, and L. E. Schrage: *A Guide to Simulation*, 2d ed., Springer-Verlag, New York (1987).

Bright, H. S., and R. L. Enison: Quasi-random Number Sequences from a Long-Period TLP Generator with Remarks on Application to Cryptography, *Comp. Surveys*, *11*: 357–370 (1979).

Brown, M., and H. Solomon: On Combining Pseudorandom Number Generators, *Annals Statist.*, *7*: 691–695 (1979).

Coveyou, R. R., and R. D. MacPherson: Fourier Analysis of Uniform Random Number Generators, *J. Assoc. Comput. Mach.*, *14*: 100–119 (1967).

Dudewicz, E. J.: Random Numbers: The Need, the History, the Generators, in *Statistical Distributions in Scientific Work 2*, G. P. Patil, S. Kotz, and J. K. Ord, eds., D. Reidel, Dordrecht, The Netherlands, pp. 25–36 (1975). [Also reprinted in *Modern Design and Analysis of Discrete-Event Computer Simulations*, E. J. Dudewicz and Z. A. Karian, eds., IEEE Computer Society, pp. 2–10 (1985).]

Dudewicz, E. J., and T. G. Ralley: *The Handbook of Random Number Generation and Testing with TESTRAND Computer Code*, American Sciences Press, Columbus, Ohio (1981).

Fishman, G. S.: *Concepts and Methods in Discrete Event Digital Simulation*, John Wiley, New York (1973).

Fishman, G. S.: *Principles of Discrete Event Simulation*, John Wiley, New York (1978).

Fishman, G. S., and L. R. Moore: In Search of Correlation in Multiplicative Congruential Generators with Modulus $2^{31} - 1$, in *Computer Science and Statistics: Proceedings of the 13th Symposium on the Interface*, W. F. Eddy, ed., Springer-Verlag, New York (1981).

Fishman, G. S., and L. R. Moore: A Statistical Evaluation of Multiplicative Congruential Random Number Generators with Modulus $2^{31} - 1$, *J. Am. Statist. Assoc.*, *77*: 129–136 (1982).

Fishman, G. S., and L. R. Moore: An Exhaustive Analysis of Multiplicative Congruential Random Number Generators with Modulus $2^{31} - 1$, *SIAM J. Sci. Stat. Comput.*, *7*: 24–45 (1986).

Fushimi, M.: Designing a Uniform Random Number Generator Whose Subsequences Are *k*-Distributed, *SIAM J. Comput.*, *17*: 89–99 (1988).

Fushimi, M., and S. Tezuka: The *k*-Distribution of Generalized Feedback Shift Register Pseudo-random Numbers, *Commun. Assoc. Comput. Mach.*, *26*: 516–523 (1983).

Gebhardt, F.: Generating Pseudo-random Numbers by Shuffling a Fibonacci Sequence, *Math. Comput.*, *21*: 708–709 (1967).

Gleick, J.: The Quest for True Randomness Finally Appears Successful, *The New York Times*, Tuesday, April 19, 1988, pp. C1 and C8.

Grafton, R. G. T.: The Runs-up and Runs-down Tests, *Appl. Statist.*, *30*: 81–85 (1981).

Grosenbaugh, L. R.: More on Fortran Random Number Generators, *Commun. Assoc. Comput. Mach.*, *12*: 639 (1969).

Haas, A.: The Multiple Prime Random Number Generator, *Assoc. Comput. Mach. Trans. Math. Software*, *13*: 368–381 (1987).

Henriksen, J. O.: *GPSS/H User's Manual*, Wolverine Software Corp., Annandale, Va. (1988).

Hill, I. D.: A Remark on AS 193: A Revised Algorithm for the Spectral Test, *Appl. Statist.*, *34*: 102–103 (1985).

Hoaglin, D. C.: Theoretical Properties of Congruential Random-Number Generators: An Empirical View, *Harvard Univ. Dept. Statist. Mem.* NS-340, Cambridge, Mass. (1976).

Hoaglin, D. C., and M. L. King: A Remark on AS 98: The Spectral Test for the Evaluation of Congruential Pseudo-random Generators, *Appl. Statist.*, *27*: 375–377 (1978).

Hopkins, T. R.: A Revised Algorithm for the Spectral Test, *Appl. Statist.*, *32*: 328–335 (1983).

Hull, T. E., and A. R. Dobell: Random Number Generators, *SIAM Rev.*, *4*: 230–254 (1962).

Hutchinson, D. W.: A New Uniform Pseudorandom Number Generator, *Commun. Assoc. Comput. Mach.*, *9*: 432–433 (1966).

IMSL, Inc.: *User's Manual: Stat/Library*, Vol. 3, IMSL, Houston, Tex. (1987).

Johnson, M. E.: *Multivariate Statistical Simulation*, John Wiley, New York (1987).

Kendall, M. G., and B. Babington-Smith: Randomness and Random Sampling Numbers, *J. Roy. Statist. Soc.*, *101A*: 147–166 (1938).

Kennedy, W. J., Jr., and J. E. Gentle: *Statistical Computing*, Marcel Dekker, New York (1980).

Knuth, D. E.: *The Art of Computer Programming*, Vol. 2, 2d ed., Addison-Wesley, Reading, Mass. (1981).

Kobayashi, H.: *Modeling and Analysis: An Introduction to System Performance Evaluation Methodology*, Addison-Wesley, Reading, Mass. (1978).

Learmonth, G. P., and P. A. W. Lewis: Naval Postgraduate School Random Number Generator Package LLRANDOM, Naval Postgraduate School, Monterey, Calif. (1973).

L'Ecuyer, P.: A Portable Random Number Generator for 16-Bit Computers, in *Modeling and Simulation on Microcomputers 1987*, The Society for Computer Simulation, La Jolla, Calif., pp. 45–49 (1987).

L'Ecuyer, P.: Efficient and Portable Combined Random Number Generators, *Commun. Assoc. Comput. Mach.*, *31*: 742–749 and 774 (1988).

L'Ecuyer, P.: Random Numbers for Simulation, *Commun. Assoc. Comput. Mach.*, *33*: (1990).

L'Ecuyer, P., and F. Blouin: Linear Congruential Generators of Order $k > 1$, *Proc. 1988 Winter Simulation Conference*, San Diego, Calif., pp. 432–439 (1988).

L'Ecuyer, P., and S. Côté: Implementing a Random Number Package with Splitting Facilities, *Assoc. Comput. Mach. Trans. Math. Software*, *16*: (1990).

L'Ecuyer, P., and R. Proulx: About Polynomial-Time "Unpredictable" Generators, *Proc. 1989 Winter Simulation Conference*, Washington, D.C., pp. 467–476 (1989).

Lehmer, D. H.: Mathematical Methods in Large-Scale Computing Units, *Ann. Comput. Lab. Harvard Univ.*, *26*: 141–146 (1951).

Lewis, P. A. W., A. S. Goodman, and J. M. Miller: A Pseudo-random Number Generator for the System/360, *IBM Syst. J.*, *8*: 136–146 (1969).

Lewis, T. G., and W. H. Payne: Generalized Feedback Shift Register Pseudorandom Number Algorithm, *J. Assoc. Comput. Mach.*, *20*: 456–468 (1973).

MacLaren, M. D., and G. Marsaglia: Uniform Random Number Generators, *J. Assoc. Comput. Mach.*, *12*: 83–89 (1965).

Marsaglia, G.: Random Numbers Fall Mainly in the Planes, *Natl. Acad. Sci. Proc.*, *61*: 25–28 (1968).

Marsaglia, G.: The Structure of Linear Congruential Sequences, in *Applications of Number Theory to Numerical Analysis*, S. K. Zaremba, ed., Academic Press, New York, pp. 249–285 (1972).

Marsaglia, G., and T. A. Bray: One-Line Random Number Generators and Their Use in Combinations, *Commun. Assoc. Comput. Mach.*, *11*: 757–759 (1968).

Marse, K., and S. D. Roberts: Implementing a Portable FORTRAN Uniform (0,1) Generator, *Simulation*, *41*: 135–139 (1983).

McLeod, I.: A Remark on AS 183. An Efficient and Portable Pseudo-random Number Generator, *Appl. Statist.*, *34*: 198–200 (1985).

Miyatake, O., M. Ichimura, Y. Yoshizawa, and H. Inoue: Mathematical Analysis of Random Number Generator Using Gamma-Rays I, *Math. Jap.*, *28*: 399–414 (1983).

Modianos, D. T., R. C. Scott, and L. W. Cornwell: Random Number Generation on Microcomputers, *Interfaces*, *14*: 81–87 (1984).

Monahan, J. F.: Accuracy in Random Number Generation, *Math. Comput.*, *45*: 559–568 (1985).

Morgan, B. J. T.: *Elements of Simulation*, Chapman & Hall, London (1984).

Nance, R. E., and C. Overstreet, Jr.: A Bibliography on Random Number Generation, *Comp. Rev.*, *13*: 495–508 (1972).

Nance, R. E., and C. Overstreet, Jr.: Implementation of Fortran Random Number Generators on Computers with One's Complement Arithmetic, *J. Statist. Comput. Simul.*, *4*: 235–243 (1975).

Nance, R. E., and C. Overstreet, Jr.: Some Experimental Observations on the Behavior of Composite Random Number Generators, *Operations Res.*, *26*: 915–935 (1978).

Niederreiter, H.: Pseudo-random Numbers and Optimal Coefficients, *Adv. Math.*, *26*: 99–181 (1977).

Niederreiter, H.: Quasi-Monte Carlo Methods and Pseudo-random Numbers, *Bull. Am. Math. Soc.*, *84*: 957–1041 (1978a).

Niederreiter, H.: The Serial Test for Linear Congruential Pseudo-random Numbers, *Bull. Am. Math. Soc.*, *84*: 273–274 (1978b).

Park, S. K., and K. W. Miller: Random Number Generators: Good Ones Are Hard to Find, *Commun. Assoc. Comput. Mach.*, *31*: 1192–1201 (1988).

Payne, W. H.: Fortran Tausworthe Pseudorandom Number Generator, *Commun. Assoc. Comput. Mach.*, *13*: 57 (1970).

Payne, W. H., J. R. Rabung, and T. P. Bogyo: Coding the Lehmer Pseudorandom Number Generator, *Commun. Assoc. Comput. Mach.*, *12*: 85–86 (1969).

Rand Corporation: *A Million Random Digits with 100,000 Normal Deviates*, Free Press, Glencoe, Ill. (1955).

Reif, J. H., and J. D. Tygar: Efficient Parallel Pseudorandom Number Generation, *SIAM J. Comput.*, *17*: 404–411 (1988).

Ripley, B. D.: The Lattice Structure of Pseudo-random Number Generators, *Proc. Roy. Soc. London*, *A389*: 197–204 (1983).

Ripley, B. D.: *Stochastic Simulation*, John Wiley, New York (1987).

Rudolph, E., and D. M. Hawkins: Random Number Generators in Cyclic Queueing Applications, *J. Statist. Comput. Simul.*, *5*: 65–71 (1976).

Sawitzki, G.: Another Random Number Generator Which Should Be Avoided, *Statistical Software Newsletter*, *11*: 81–82 (1985).

Schrage, L.: A More Portable Random Number Generator, *Assoc. Comput. Mach. Trans. Math. Software*, *5*: 132–138 (1979).

Sowey, E. R.: A Third Classified Bibliography on Random Number Generation and Testing, *J. Roy. Statist. Soc.*, *A149*: 83–107 (1986).

Tausworthe, R. C.: Random Numbers Generated by Linear Recurrence Modulo Two, *Math. Comput.*, *19*: 201–209 (1965).

Thesen, A.: An Efficient Generator of Uniformly Distributed Random Variates between Zero and One, *Simulation*, *44*: 17–22 (1985).

Thesen, A., Z. Sun, and T. Wang: Some Efficient Random Number Generators for Microcomputers, *Proc. 1984 Winter Simulation Conference*, Dallas, Texas, pp. 187–196 (1984).

Thomson, W. E.: ERNIE—A Mathematical and Statistical Analysis, *J. Roy. Statist. Soc.*, *122A*: 301–324 (1959).

Tootill, J. P. R., W. D. Robinson, and A. G. Adams: The Runs up-and-down Performance of Tausworthe Pseudo-random Number Generators, *J. Assoc. Comput. Mach.*, *18*: 381–399 (1971).

Tootill, J. P. R., W. D. Robinson, and D. J. Eagle: An Asymptotically Random Tausworthe Sequence, *J. Assoc. Comput. Mach.*, *20*: 469–481 (1973).

von Neumann, J. (Summarized by G. E. Forsythe): Various Techniques Used in Connection with Random Digits, *Natl. Bur. Std. Appl. Math. Ser.*, *12*: 36–38 (1951).

Wichmann, B. A., and I. D. Hill: An Efficient and Portable Pseudo-random Number Generator, *Appl. Statist.*, *31*: 188–190 (1982).

Wichmann, B. A., and I. D. Hill: Correction to "An Efficient and Portable Pseudo-random Number Generator," *Appl. Statist.*, *33*: 123 (1984).

Wichmann, B. A., and I. D. Hill: Building a Random-Number Generator, *BYTE*, pp. 127–128 (March 1987).

Zeisel, H.: A Remark on AS 183. An Efficient and Portable Pseudo-random Number Generator, *Appl. Statist.*, *35*: 89 (1986).

CHAPTER
8

GENERATING
RANDOM
VARIATES

Recommended sections for a first reading: 8.1 and 8.2

8.1 INTRODUCTION

A simulation that has any random aspects at all must involve sampling, or *generating* random variates from probability distributions. As in Chap. 7, we use the phrase "generating a random variate" to refer to the activity of obtaining an observation on (or a realization of) a random variable from the desired distribution. These distributions are often specified as a result of fitting some appropriate distributional form, e.g., exponential, gamma, or Poisson, to observed data, as discussed in Chap. 6. In this chapter we assume that a distribution has already been specified somehow (including the values of the parameters), and we address the issue of how we can generate random variates with this distribution in order to run the simulation model. For example, the queueing-type models discussed in Sec. 1.4 and Chap. 2 required generation of interarrival and service times to drive the simulation through time, and the inventory model of Sec. 1.5 needed randomly generated demand sizes at the times when a demand occurred.

As we shall see in this chapter, the basic ingredient needed for *every* method of generating random variates from *any* distribution or random process is a source of IID $U(0,1)$ random variates. For this reason, it is essential that a statistically reliable $U(0,1)$ random-number generator be available. Most computer installations and simulation languages have a convenient random-number generator, but some of them (especially the older ones) do not perform adequately (see Chap. 7). Without an acceptable random-number generator it is impossible to generate random variates correctly from any distribution. In the rest of this chapter, we therefore assume that a good source of random numbers is available.

There are usually several alternative algorithms that can be used for generating random variates from a given distribution, and several factors should be considered when choosing which algorithm to use in a particular simulation study. Unfortunately, these different factors often conflict with each other, so the analyst's judgment of which algorithm to use must involve a number of trade-offs. All we can do here is raise some of the pertinent questions.

The first issue is *exactness*. We feel that, if possible, one should use an algorithm that results in random variates with exactly the desired distribution, within the unavoidable external limitations of machine accuracy and exactness of the $U(0,1)$ random-number generator. Efficient and exact algorithms are now available for most of the commonly used distributions, obviating the need to consider any older, approximate methods. [Many of these approximations, e.g., the well-known technique of obtaining a "normal" random variate as 6 less than the sum of 12 $U(0,1)$ random variates, are based on the central limit theorem.] On the other hand, the practitioner may argue that a specified distribution is really only an approximation to reality anyway, so that an approximate generation method should suffice; since this depends on the situation and is often difficult to quantify, we would still prefer to use an exact method.

Given that we have a choice, then, of alternative exact algorithms, we would like to use one that is *efficient*, in terms of both storage space and execution time. Some algorithms require *storage* of a large number of constants or of large tables, which could prove troublesome. As for execution time, there are really two factors. Obviously, we hope that we can accomplish the generation of each random variate in a small amount of time; this is called the *marginal execution time*. Second, some algorithms have to do some initial computing to specify constants or tables that depend on the particular distribution and parameters; the time required to do this is called the *setup time*. In most simulations, we shall be generating a large number of random variates from a given distribution, so that marginal execution time is likely to be more important than setup time. If the parameters of a distribution change often or randomly during the course of the simulation, however, setup time could become an important consideration.

A somewhat subjective issue in choosing an algorithm is its overall *complexity*, including conceptual as well as implementational factors. One must ask whether the potential gain in efficiency that might be experienced by using a more complicated algorithm is worth the extra effort to understand and implement it. This issue should be considered relative to the purpose in implementing a method for random-variate generation; a more efficient but more complex algorithm might be appropriate for use as permanent software but not for a "one-time" simulation model.

Finally, there are a few issues of a more technical nature. Some algorithms rely on a source of random variates from distributions other than $U(0,1)$, which is undesirable, other things being equal. Another technical issue is that a given algorithm may be efficient for some parameter values but costly for others. We would like to have algorithms that are efficient for all parameter values (sometimes called *robustness* of the algorithm). One last technical point is relevant if we want to use certain kinds of variance-reduction techniques in order to obtain better (less variable) estimates (see Chap. 11 and also Chaps. 10 and 12). Two commonly used variance-reduction techniques (common random numbers and antithetic variates) require synchronization of the basic $U(0,1)$ input random variates used in the simulation of the system(s) under study, and this synchronization is more easily accomplished for certain types of random-variate generation algorithms. In particular, the general inverse-transform approach can be very helpful in facilitating the desired synchronization and variance reduction; Sec. 8.2.1 treats this point more precisely.

There is a large literature on the subject of random-variate generation, and several good comprehensive treatments are available. The most complete and up-to-date reference is Devroye (1986), an in-depth and rigorous book of some 843 pages devoted entirely to topics in variate generation; another full book on the subject is Dagpunar (1988). Kennedy and Gentle (1980, pp. 176–264) also provide a detailed discussion, together with many references. Johnson (1987) provides an entire book on modeling with and generating from multivariate distributions; we discuss some of this material in Sec. 8.5. A number of general tutorial papers on random-variate generation have also been written [Schmeiser (1980b), Leemis and Schmeiser (1985), and Ripley (1983)], which typically include long reference lists. In addition, surveys of more specialized topics have been made, such as Schmeiser and Lal (1980a) on multivariate modeling and generation, and Kachitvichyanukul (1983) and Schmeiser (1983) on generating random variates from discrete distributions. Finally, there are several extensive bibliographies on the subject; see Sowey (1986) and the references therein. Several computer packages include good facilities for generating random variates from a wide range of distributions, notably the IMSL FORTRAN routines [IMSL (1987, chap. 18)].

Our chapter on this subject is organized as follows. In Sec. 8.2 we survey the most important general approaches for random-variate generation, including examples and discussions of the relative merits of the various approaches. Sections 8.3 and 8.4 then present algorithms for generating random variates from particular continuous and discrete distributions that have been found useful in simulation. Finally, Secs. 8.5 and 8.6 discuss two more specialized topics, generating correlated random variates and generating realizations of both stationary and nonstationary arrival processes.

8.2 GENERAL APPROACHES TO GENERATING RANDOM VARIATES

There are many techniques for generating random variates, and the particular algorithm used must, of course, depend on the distribution from which we wish to generate; however, nearly all these techniques can be classified according to their theoretical basis. In this section we discuss these general approaches.

8.2.1 Inverse Transform

Suppose that we wish to generate a random variate X that is continuous (see Sec. 4.2) and has distribution function F that is continuous and strictly increasing when $0 < F(x) < 1$. [This means that if $x_1 < x_2$ and $0 < F(x_1) \le F(x_2) < 1$, then in fact $F(x_1) < F(x_2)$.] Let F^{-1} denote the inverse of the function F. Then an algorithm for generating a random variate X having distribution function F is as follows (recall that $\sim$ is read "is distributed as"):

1. Generate $U \sim U(0,1)$.
2. Return $X = F^{-1}(U)$.

Note that $F^{-1}(U)$ will always be defined, since $0 \le U \le 1$ and the range of F is [0,1]. Figure 8.1 illustrates the algorithm graphically, where the random variable corresponding to this distribution function can take on either positive or negative values; the particular value of U determines which will be the case. In the figure, the random number U_1 results in the positive random variate X_1, while the random number U_2 leads to the negative variate X_2.

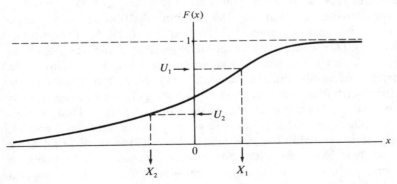

FIGURE 8.1
Inverse-transform method for continuous random variables.

To show that the value X returned by the above algorithm, called the general *inverse-transform method*, has the desired distribution F, we must show that for any real number x, $P(X \leq x) = F(x)$. Since F is invertible, we have

$$P(X \leq x) = P(F^{-1}(U) \leq x) = P(U \leq F(x)) = F(x)$$

where the last equality follows since $U \sim U(0,1)$ and $0 \leq F(x) \leq 1$. (See the discussion of the uniform distribution in Sec. 6.2.2.)

Example 8.1. Let X have the exponential distribution with mean β (see Sec. 6.2.2). The distribution function is

$$F(x) = \begin{cases} 1 - e^{-x/\beta} & \text{if } x \geq 0 \\ 0 & \text{otherwise} \end{cases}$$

so to find F^{-1}, we set $u = F(x)$ and solve for x to obtain

$$F^{-1}(u) = -\beta \ln (1 - u)$$

Thus, to generate the desired random variate we first generate a $U \sim U(0,1)$ and then let $X = -\beta \ln U$. [It is possible in this case to use U instead of $1 - U$, since $1 - U$ and U have the same $U(0,1)$ distribution. This saves a subtraction.]

In the above example, we replaced $1 - U$ by U for the sake of a perhaps minor gain in efficiency. However, replacing $1 - U$ by U in situations like this results in negative correlation of the X's with the U's, rather than positive correlation. Also, it is not true that wherever a "$1 - U$" appears in a variate-generation algorithm it can be replaced by a "U," as illustrated in Sec. 8.3.11.

The inverse-transform method's validity in the continuous case was demonstrated mathematically above, but there is also a strong intuitive appeal. The density function $f(x)$ of a continuous random variable may be interpreted as the relative chance of observing variates on different parts of the range; on regions of the x axis above which $f(x)$ is high we expect to observe a lot of variates, and where $f(x)$ is low we should find only a few. For example, Fig. 8.2b shows the density function for the Weibull distribution with shape parameter $\alpha = 1.5$ and scale parameter $\beta = 6$ (see Sec. 6.2.2 for definition of this distribution), and we would expect that many generated variates would fall between, say, $x = 2$ and $x = 5$, but not many between 13 and 16. Figure 8.2a shows the corresponding distribution function, $F(x)$. Since the density is the derivative of the distribution function [that is, $f(x) = F'(x)$], we can view $f(x)$ as the "slope function" of $F(x)$; that is, $f(x)$ is the slope of F at x. Thus, F rises most steeply for values of x where $f(x)$ is large (e.g., for x between 2 and 5), and, conversely, F is relatively flat in regions where $f(x)$ is small (e.g., for x between 13 and 16). Now, the inverse-transform method says to take the random number U, which should be evenly (uniformly) spread on the interval $[0,1]$ on the vertical axis of the plot for $F(x)$, and "read across and down." More U's will hit the steep parts of $F(x)$ than the flat parts, thus concentrating the X's under those regions where $F(x)$ is steep—which are precisely those regions where $f(x)$ is high. The interval $[0.25, 0.30]$ on the vertical axis in Fig.

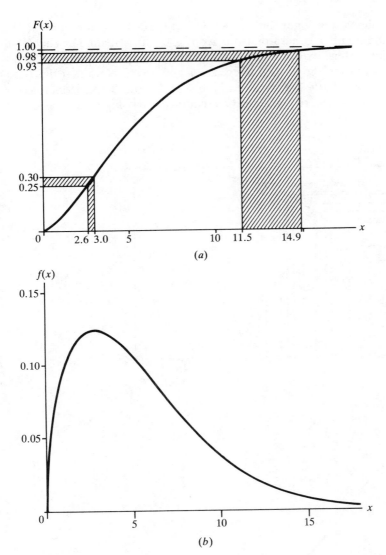

FIGURE 8.2
(a) Intervals for U and X, inverse transform for Weibull(1.5, 6) distribution; (b) density for Weibull(1.5, 6) distribution.

8.2a should contain about 5 percent of the U's, which lead to X's in the relatively narrow region [2.6, 3.0] on the x axis; thus, about 5 percent of the X's will be in this region. On the other hand, the interval [0.93, 0.98] on the vertical axis, which is of the same size as [0.25, 0.30] and thus contains about 5 percent of the U's as well, leads to X's in the large interval [11.5, 14.9] on the x axis; here we will also find about 5 percent of the X's, but spread out over a much larger interval.

Figure 8.3 shows the algorithm in action, with 50 X's being generated (using the random-number generator from App. 7A with stream 1). The U's are plotted on the vertical axis of Fig. 8.3a, and the X's corresponding to them are obtained by following the dashed lines across and down. Note that the U's on the vertical axis are fairly evenly spread, but the X's on the horizontal axis are indeed more dense where the density function $f(x)$ is high, and become

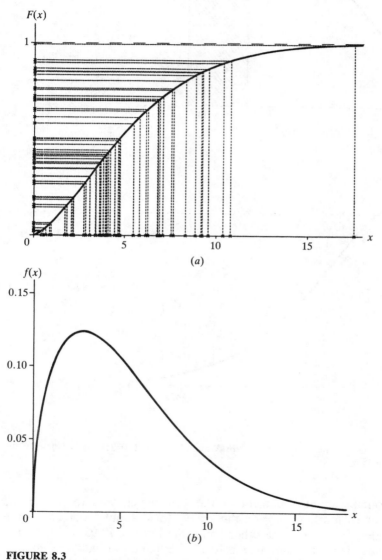

FIGURE 8.3
(a) Sample of 50 U's and X's, inverse transform for Weibull(1.5, 6) distribution; (b) density for Weibull(1.5, 6) distribution.

more spread out where $f(x)$ is low. Thus, the inverse-transform method essentially deforms the uniform distribution of the U's to result in a distribution of the X's in accordance with the desired density.

The inverse-transform method can also be used when X is discrete. Here the distribution function is

$$F(x) = (X \leq x) = \sum_{x_i \leq x} p(x_i)$$

where $p(x_i)$ is the probability mass function

$$p(x_i) = P(X = x_i)$$

(We assume that X can take on only the values $x_1, x_2, \ldots$ where $x_1 < x_2 < \cdots$.) Then the algorithm is as follows:

1. Generate $U \sim U(0,1)$.
2. Determine the smallest positive integer I such that $U \leq F(x_I)$, and return $X = x_I$.

Figure 8.4 illustrates the method, where we generate $X = x_4$ in this case. Although this algorithm might not seem related to the inverse-transform method for continuous random variates, the similarity between Figs. 8.1 and 8.4 is apparent.

To verify that the discrete inverse-transform method is valid, we need to show that $P(X = x_i) = p(x_i)$ for all i. For $i = 1$, we get $X = x_1$ if and only if $U \leq F(x_1) = p(x_1)$, since we have arranged the x_i's in increasing order. Since $U \sim U(0,1)$, $P(X = x_1) = p(x_1)$, as desired. For $i \geq 2$, the algorithm sets $X = x_i$ if and only if $F(x_{i-1}) < U \leq F(x_i)$, since the i chosen by the algorithm is the

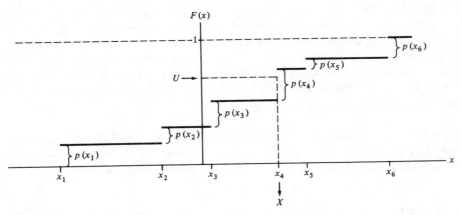

FIGURE 8.4
Inverse-transform method for discrete random variables.

smallest positive integer such that $U \le F(x_i)$. Further, since $U \sim U(0,1)$ and $0 \le F(x_{i-1}) < F(x_i) \le 1$,

$$P(X = x_i) = P[F(x_{i-1}) < U \le F(x_i)] = F(x_i) - F(x_{i-1}) = p(x_i)$$

Example 8.2. Recall the inventory example of Sec. 1.5, where the demand-size random variable X is discrete, taking on the values 1, 2, 3, 4 with respective probabilities $\frac{1}{6}, \frac{1}{3}, \frac{1}{3}, \frac{1}{6}$; the distribution function F is given in Fig. 4.2. To generate an X, first generate $U \sim U(0,1)$ and set X to either 1, 2, 3, or 4, depending on the subinterval in [0,1] into which U falls. If $U \le \frac{1}{6}$, then let $X = 1$; if $\frac{1}{6} < U \le \frac{1}{2}$, let $X = 2$; if $\frac{1}{2} < U \le \frac{5}{6}$, let $X = 3$; finally, if $\frac{5}{6} < U$, let $X = 4$.

Although both Fig. 8.4 and Example 8.2 deal with discrete random variables taking on only finitely many values, the discrete inverse-transform method can also be used directly as stated to generate random variates with an infinite range, e.g., the Poisson, geometric, or negative binomial.

The discrete inverse-transform method, when written as in Example 8.2, is really quite intuitive. We split the unit interval into contiguous subintervals of width $p(x_1)$, $p(x_2)$, ... and assign X according to whichever of these subintervals contains the generated U. For example, U will fall in the second subinterval with probability $p(x_2)$, in which case we let $X = x_2$. The efficiency of the algorithm will depend on how we look for the subinterval that contains a given U. The simplest approach would be to start at the left and move up; first check whether $U \le p(x_1)$, in which case we return $X = x_1$. If $U > p(x_1)$, check whether $U \le p(x_1) + p(x_2)$, in which case we return $X = x_2$, etc. The number of comparisons needed to determine a value for X is thus dependent on U and the $p(x_i)$'s. If, for example, the first several $p(x_i)$'s are very small, the probability is high that we will have to do a large number of comparisons before the algorithm terminates. This suggests that we might be well advised to perform this search in a more sophisticated manner, using appropriate sorting and searching techniques from the computer science literature [see, for example, Knuth (1973)]. One simple improvement would be first to check whether U lies in the widest subinterval, since this would be the single most likely case. If not, we would check the second widest subinterval, etc. This method would be particularly useful when some $p(x_i)$ values are considerably greater than others and there are many x_i's; see Prob. 8.2 for more on this idea. See also Chen and Asau (1974) and Fishman and Moore (1984) for very efficient search methods using the idea of *indexing*.

Generalization, Advantages, and Disadvantages of the Inverse-Transform Method. Both the continuous and discrete versions of the inverse-transform method can be combined, at least formally, into the more general form

$$X = \min\{x: F(x) \ge U\}$$

which has the added advantage of being valid for distributions that are *mixed*, i.e., having both continuous and discrete components, as well as for continuous distribution functions with flat spots. To check that the above is valid in the continuous case, note in Fig. 8.1 that the set $\{x: F(x) \geq U_1\}$ is the interval $[X_1, \infty)$, which has minimum X_1. In the discrete case, we see in Fig. 8.4 that $\{x: F(x) \geq U\} = [x_4, \infty)$, which has minimum x_4. Figure 8.5 shows a mixed distribution with two jump discontinuities and a flat spot; in this case the associated random variable X should satisfy $P(X = x_1) = u_1' - u_1$ (jump at x_1), $P(X = x_2) = u_2' - u_2$ (jump at x_2), and $P(x_0 \leq X \leq x_0') = 0$ (flat spot between x_0 and x_0'). For the continuous component, note that

$$X = \min\{x: F(x) \geq U_C\} = \min[X_C, \infty) = X_C$$

as expected. For the jump discontinuity at x_1, we get, for $u_1 \leq U_1 \leq u_1'$,

$$X = \min\{x: F(x) \geq U_1\} = \min[x_1, \infty) = x_1$$

which will occur with probability $u_1' - u_1$, as desired; the jump at x_2 is similar. For the flat spot, we will generate a variate X in (x_0, x_0') only if we generate a random number U that is *equal* to u_0; as U represents a continuous random variable, this occurs with probability 0, although in practice the finite accuracy of the generated random number U could in principle result in $U = u_0$. Thus, this more general statement of the inverse-transform method handles any continuous, discrete, or mixed distribution. How it is acutally implemented, though, will of course depend heavily on the distribution desired.

Let us now consider some general advantages and disadvantages of the inverse-transform method in both the continuous and discrete cases. One possible impediment to use of the method in the continuous case is the need to

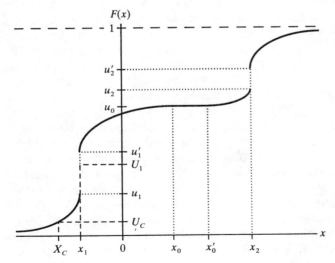

FIGURE 8.5
Inverse-transform method for a mixed distribution.

evaluate $F^{-1}(U)$. Since we might not be able to write a formula for F^{-1} in closed form for the desired distribution, e.g., the normal and gamma distributions, simple use of the method, as in Example 8.1, might not be possible. However, even if F^{-1} does not have a simple closed-form expression, we might be able to use numerical methods, e.g., a power-series expansion, to evaluate F^{-1}. (See, for example, the discussion in Sec. 8.3 concerning the generation of gamma, normal, and beta random variates.) These numerical methods can yield arbitrary accuracy, so in particular can match the accuracy inherent in machine roundoff error; in this sense, they are exact for all practical purposes. However, Devroye (1986, pp. 31–35) points out that it may be difficult to specify an acceptable stopping rule for some distributions, especially those whose range is infinite. Kennedy and Gentle (1980, chap. 5) provide a comprehensive survey of numerical methods for computing distribution functions and their inverses; see also Abramowitz and Stegun (1964, chap. 26). The IMSL library [IMSL (1987, chap. 17)] includes FORTRAN routines to compute most of the common distribution functions and their inverses, using carefully chosen algorithms. As an alternative to approximating F^{-1} numerically, Marsaglia (1984) proposes that a function g be found that is "close" to F^{-1} and is easy to evaluate; then X is generated as $g(Y)$, where Y has a particular distribution that is "close" to U(0,1).

A second potential disadvantage is that for a given distribution the inverse-transform method may not be the fastest way to generate the corresponding random variate; in Secs. 8.3 and 8.4 we discuss the efficiency of alternative algorithms for each distribution considered.

Despite these possible drawbacks, there are some important advantages in using the inverse-transform method. The first is to facilitate variance-reduction techniques (see Chap. 11) that rely on inducing correlation between random variates; examples of such techniques are common random numbers and antithetic variates. If F_1 and F_2 are two distribution functions, then $X_1 = F_1^{-1}(U_1)$ and $X_2 = F_2^{-1}(U_2)$ will be random variates with respective distribution functions F_1 and F_2, where U_1 and U_2 are random numbers. If U_1 and U_2 are independent, then of course X_1 and X_2 will be independent as well. However, if we let $U_2 = U_1$, then the correlation between X_1 and X_2 is maximized, and taking $U_2 = 1 - U_1$ (which, recall, is also distributed uniformly over [0,1]) makes the correlation between X_1 and X_2 as negative as possible. Thus, the inverse-transform method induces the strongest correlation (of either sign) between the generated random variates, which we hope will propagate through the simulation model to induce the strongest possible correlation in the output, thereby contributing to the success of the variance-reduction technique. [It is possible, however, to induce correlation in random variates generated by methods other than the inverse-transform method; see Schmeiser and Kachitvichyanukul (1986)]. On a more pragmatic level, inverse transform eases application of variance-reduction techniques since we always need exactly one random number to produce one value of the desired X. (Other methods to be discussed later may require several random numbers to obtain a single value of X, or the number of random numbers might itself be random, as in the acceptance-rejection method.) This observation is important since proper implementation of many variance-reduction techniques requires some sort of synchronization of the input random numbers between different simulation runs. If the inverse-transform technique is used, synchronization is easier to achieve.

The second advantage concerns ease of generating from truncated distributions (see Sec. 6.8). In the continuous case, suppose that we have a density f with corresponding distribution function F. For $a < b$ (with the possibility that $a = -\infty$ or $b = +\infty$), we define the *truncated density*

$$f^*(x) = \begin{cases} \dfrac{f(x)}{F(b) - F(a)} & \text{if } a \le x \le b \\ 0 & \text{otherwise} \end{cases}$$

which has corresponding *truncated distribution function*

$$F^*(x) = \begin{cases} 0 & \text{if } x < a \\ \dfrac{F(x) - F(a)}{F(b) - F(a)} & \text{if } a \le x \le b \\ 1 & \text{if } b < x \end{cases}$$

(The discrete case is analogous.) Then an algorithm for generating an X having distribution function F^* is as follows:

1. Generate $U \sim U(0,1)$.
2. Let $V = F(a) + [F(b) - F(a)]U$.
3. Return $X = F^{-1}(V)$.

We leave it as an exercise (Prob. 8.3) to show that the X defined by this algorithm indeed has distribution function F^*. Note that the inverse-transform idea is really used twice: first in step 2 to distribute V uniformly between $F(a)$ and $F(b)$ and then in step 3 to obtain X. (See Prob. 8.3 for another way to generate X and Prob. 8.4 for a different type of truncation, which results in a distribution function that is *not* the same as F^*.)

Finally, the inverse-transform method can be quite useful for generating order statistics. Suppose that $Y_1, Y_2, \ldots, Y_n$ are IID with common distribution function F and that for $i = 1, 2, \ldots, n$, $Y_{(i)}$ denotes the ith smallest of the Y_j's. Recall from Chap. 6 that $Y_{(i)}$ is called the ith order statistic from a sample of size n. [Order statistics have been useful in simulation when one is concerned with the reliability, or *lifetime*, of some system having components subject to failure. If Y_j is the lifetime of the jth component, then $Y_{(1)}$ is the lifetime of a system consisting of n such components connected in series and $Y_{(n)}$ is the lifetime of the system if the components are connected in parallel.] One direct way of generating $X = Y_{(i)}$ is first to generate n IID variates $Y_1, Y_2, \ldots, Y_n$

with distribution function F, then sort them into increasing order, and finally set X to the ith value of the Y_j's after sorting. This method, however, requires generating n separate variates with distribution function F and then sorting them, which can be very slow if n is large. As an alternative, we can use the following algorithm to generate $X = Y_{(i)}$:

1. Generate $V \sim \text{beta}(i, n - i + 1)$.
2. Return $X = F^{-1}(V)$.

The validity of this algorithm is established in Prob. 8.5. Note that step 1 requires generating from a beta distribution, which we discuss below in Sec. 8.3.8. No sorting is required, and we need to evaluate F^{-1} only once; this is particularly advantageous if n is large or evaluating F^{-1} is slow. Two important special cases are generating either the minimum or maximum of the n Y_j's, where step 1 becomes particularly simple. For the minimum, $i = 1$, and V in step 1 can be defined by $V = 1 - U^{1/n}$, where $U \sim U(0,1)$. For the maximum, $i = n$, and we can set $V = U^{1/n}$ in step 1. (See Prob. 8.5 for verification in these two special cases.) For more on generating order statistics, see Ramberg and Tadikamalla (1978), Schmeiser (1978a, 1978b), and Schucany (1972).

8.2.2 Composition

The *composition* technique applies when the distribution function F from which we wish to generate can be expressed as a convex combination of other distribution functions $F_1, F_2, \ldots$. We would hope to be able to sample from the F_j's more easily than from the original F.

Specifically, we assume that for all x, $F(x)$ can be written as

$$F(x) = \sum_{j=1}^{\infty} p_j F_j(x)$$

where $p_j \geq 0$, $\sum_{j=1}^{\infty} p_j = 1$, and each F_j is a distribution function. (Although we have written this combination as an infinite sum, there may be a k such that $p_k > 0$ but $p_j = 0$ for $j > k$, in which case the sum is actually finite.) Equivalently, if X has density f that can be written as

$$f(x) = \sum_{j=1}^{\infty} p_j f_j(x)$$

where the f_j's are other densities, the method of composition still applies; the discrete case is analogous. The general composition algorithm, then, is as follows:

1. Generate a positive random integer J such that

$$P(J = j) = p_j \quad \text{for} \quad j = 1, 2, \ldots$$

2. Return X with distribution function F_J.

Step 1 can be thought of as choosing the distribution function F_j with probability p_j and could be accomplished, for example, by the discrete inverse-transform method. Given that $J = j$, generating X in step 2 should be done, of course, independently of J. By conditioning on the value of J generated in step 1, we can easily see that the X returned by the algorithm will have distribution function F [see, for example, Ross (1989, chap. 3)]:

$$P(X \le x) = \sum_{j=1}^{\infty} P(X \le x \mid J = j)P(J = j) = \sum_{j=1}^{\infty} F_j(x)p_j = F(x)$$

Sometimes we can give a geometric interpretation to the composition method. For a continuous random variable X with density f, for example, we might be able to divide the area under f into regions of areas $p_1, p_2, \ldots$, corresponding to the decomposition of f into its convex-combination representation. Then we can think of step 1 as choosing a region and step 2 as generating from the distribution corresponding to the chosen region. The following two examples allow this kind of geometric interpretation.

Example 8.3. The *double-exponential* (or *Laplace*) *distribution* has density $f(x) = 0.5e^{-|x|}$ for all real x; this density is plotted in Fig. 8.6. From the plot we see that except for the normalizing factor 0.5, $f(x)$ is two exponential densities placed back to back; this suggests the use of composition. Indeed, we can express the density as

$$f(x) = 0.5e^x I_{(-\infty,0)}(x) + 0.5e^{-x} I_{[0,\infty)}(x)$$

where I_A denotes the *indicator function* of the set A, defined by

$$I_A(x) = \begin{cases} 1 & \text{if } x \in A \\ 0 & \text{otherwise} \end{cases}$$

Thus, $f(x)$ is a convex combination of $f_1(x) = e^x I_{(-\infty,0)}(x)$ and $f_2(x) = e^{-x} I_{[0,\infty)}(x)$, both of which are densities, and $p_1 = p_2 = 0.5$. Therefore, we can generate an X with density f by composition. First generate U_1 and U_2 as IID U(0,1). If $U_1 \le 0.5$, return $X = \ln U_2$. On the other hand, if $U_1 > 0.5$, return $X = -\ln U_2$. Note that we are essentially generating an exponential random variate with mean 1 and then changing its sign with probability 0.5. Alternatively, we are generating from the left half of the density in Fig. 8.6 with probability equal to the corresponding area (0.5) and from the right half with probability 0.5.

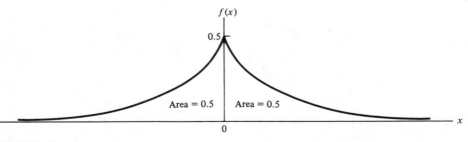

FIGURE 8.6
Double-exponential density.

Note that in Example 8.3, step 2 of the general composition algorithm was accomplished by means of the inverse-transform method for exponential random variates; this illustrates how different general approaches for generating random variates might be combined. Also, we see that *two* random numbers are required to generate a single X in this example; in general, we shall need *at least two* random numbers to use the composition method. (The reader may find it interesting to compare Example 8.3 with the inverse-transform method for generating a double-exponential random variate; see Prob. 8.6.)

In Example 8.3 we obtained the representation for f by dividing the area below the density with a vertical line, namely, the ordinate axis. In the following example, we make a horizontal division instead.

Example 8.4. For $0 < a < 1$, the *right-trapezoidal distribution* has density

$$f(x) = \begin{cases} a + 2(1-a)x & \text{if } 0 \le x \le 1 \\ 0 & \text{otherwise} \end{cases}$$

(see Fig. 8.7). As suggested by the dashed lines, we can think of dividing the area under f into a rectangle having area a and a right triangle with area $1 - a$. Now $f(x)$ can be decomposed as

$$f(x) = aI_{[0,1]}(x) + (1-a)2xI_{[0,1]}(x)$$

so that $f_1(x) = I_{[0,1]}(x)$, which is simply the U(0,1) density, and $f_2(x) = 2xI_{[0,1]}(x)$ is a right-triangular density. Clearly, $p_1 = a$ and $p_2 = 1 - a$. The composition method thus calls for generating $U_1 \sim$ U(0,1) and checking whether $U_1 \le a$. If so, generate an independent $U_2 \sim$ U(0,1), and return $X = U_2$. If $U_1 > a$, however, we must generate from the right-triangular distribution. This can be accomplished either by generating $U_2 \sim$ U(0,1) and returning $X = \sqrt{U_2}$, or by generating U_2 and U_3 distributed as IID U(0,1) and returning $X = \max\{U_2, U_3\}$ (see Prob. 8.7). Since the time to take a square root is probably greater than that required to generate an extra U(0,1) random variate *and* perform a comparison, the latter method would appear to be a faster way of generating an X with density f_2.

Again, the reader is encouraged to develop the inverse-transform method for generating a random variate from the right-trapezoidal distribution in

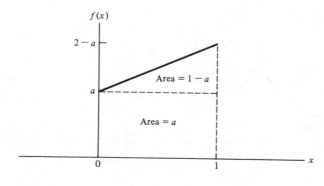

FIGURE 8.7
Right-trapezoidal density.

Example 8.4. Note that especially if a is large, the composition method will be faster than the inverse transform, since the latter *always* requires that a square root be taken, while it is quite likely (with probability a) that the former will simply return $X = U_2 \sim U(0,1)$. This increase in speed must be played off by the analyst against the possible disadvantage of having to generate two or three random numbers to obtain one value of X. Trapezoidal distributions like that in Example 8.4 play an important role in the efficient methods developed by Schmeiser and Lal (1980b) for generating gamma random variates and for beta generation in Schmeiser and Babu (1980).

Composition methods (also called "mixture" methods) are further analyzed by Peterson and Kronmal (1982), who show as well that many specific variate-generation methods can actually be expressed as a composition of some sort. An interesting technique that is related closely to composition, the *acceptance-complement method*, was proposed by Kronmal and Peterson (1981, 1982); Devroye (1986, pp. 75–81) further discusses this and associated methods.

8.2.3 Convolution

For several important distributions, the desired random variable X can be expressed as a sum of other random variables that are IID and can be generated more readily than direct generation of X. We assume that there are IID random variables $Y_1, Y_2, \ldots, Y_m$ (for fixed m) such that $Y_1 + Y_2 \cdots + Y_m$ has the same distribution as X; hence we write

$$X = Y_1 + Y_2 + \cdots + Y_m$$

The name of this method, *convolution*, comes from terminology in stochastic processes, where the distribution of X is called the *m-fold convolution* of the distribution of a Y_j. The reader should take care not to confuse this situation with the method of composition. Here we assume that the *random variable X* can be represented as a sum of other *random variables*, whereas the assumption behind the method of composition is that the *distribution function* of X is a (weighted) sum of other *distribution functions*; the two situations are fundamentally different.

The algorithm for generating the desired random variate X is quite intuitive (let F be the distribution function of X and G be the distribution function of a Y_j):

1. Generate $Y_1, Y_2, \ldots, Y_m$ IID each with distribution function G.
2. Return $X = Y_1 + Y_2 + \cdots + Y_m$.

To demonstrate the validity of this algorithm, recall that we assumed that X and $Y_1 + Y_2 + \cdots + Y_m$ have the same distribution function, namely, F. Thus,

$$P(X \le x) = P(Y_1 + Y_2 + \cdots + Y_m \le x) = F(x)$$

Example 8.5. The m-Erlang random variable X with mean β can be defined as the sum of m IID exponential random variables with common mean β/m. Thus, to generate X, we can first generate $Y_1, Y_2, \ldots, Y_m$ as IID exponential with mean β/m (see Example 8.1), then return $X = Y_1 + Y_2 + \cdots + Y_m$. (See Sec. 8.3.3 for an improvement in efficiency of this algorithm.)

The convolution method, when it can be used, is very simple, provided that we can generate the required Y_j's easily. However, depending on the particular parameters of the distribution of X, it may not be the most efficient way. For example, to generate an m-Erlang random variate by the convolution method (as in Example 8.5) when m is large could be very slow. In this case it would be better to recall that the m-Erlang distribution is a special case of the gamma distribution (see Sec. 6.2.2) and use a general method for generating gamma random variates (see Sec. 8.3.4).

Convolution is really an example of a more general idea, that of transforming some intermediate random variates into a final variate that has the desired distribution; the transformation with convolution is just adding, and the intermediate variates are IID. There are many other ways to transform intermediate variates, some of which are discussed in Sec. 8.2.5, as well as in Secs. 8.3 and 8.4.

8.2.4 Acceptance-Rejection

The three general approaches for generating random variates discussed so far (inverse transform, composition, and convolution) might be called *direct* in the sense that they deal directly with the distribution or random variable desired. The *acceptance-rejection method* is less direct in its approach and can be useful when the direct methods fail or are inefficient. Our discussion is for the continuous case, where we want to generate X having distribution function F and density f; the discrete case is exactly analogous and is treated in Prob. 8.9. The underlying idea dates back at least to von Neumann (1951).

The acceptance-rejection method requires that we specify a function t that *majorizes* the density f; that is, $t(x) \geq f(x)$ for all x. Now t will not, in general, be a density since

$$ c = \int_{-\infty}^{\infty} t(x)\, dx \geq \int_{-\infty}^{\infty} f(x)\, dx = 1 $$

but the function $r(x) = t(x)/c$ clearly *is* a density. (We assume that t is such that $c < \infty$.) We must be able to generate (easily and quickly, we hope) a random variate Y having density r. The general algorithm follows:

1. Generate Y having density r.
2. Generate $U \sim U(0,1)$, independent of Y.
3. If $U \leq f(Y)/t(Y)$, return $X = Y$. Otherwise, go back to step 1 and try again.

The algorithm continues looping back to step 1 until finally we generate a (Y,U) pair in steps 1 and 2 for which $U \leq f(Y)/t(Y)$, when we "accept" the value Y for X. Since demonstrating the validity of this algorithm is more complicated than for the three previous methods, we refer the reader to App. 8A for a proof.

Example 8.6. The beta(4,3) distribution (on the unit interval) has density

$$f(x) = \begin{cases} 60x^3(1-x)^2 & \text{if } 0 \leq x \leq 1 \\ 0 & \text{otherwise} \end{cases}$$

[Since the distribution function $F(x)$ is a sixth-degree polynomial, the inverse-transform approach would not be simple, involving numerical methods to find polynomial roots.] By standard differential calculus, i.e., setting $df/dx = 0$, we see that the maximum value of $f(x)$ occurs at $x = 0.6$, where $f(0.6) = 2.0736$ (exactly). Thus, if we define

$$t(x) = \begin{cases} 2.0736 & \text{if } 0 \leq x \leq 1 \\ 0 & \text{otherwise} \end{cases}$$

then t majorizes f. Next, $c = \int_0^1 2.0736 \, dx = 2.0736$, so that $r(x)$ is just the U(0,1) density. The functions f, t, and r are shown in Fig. 8.8. The algorithm first

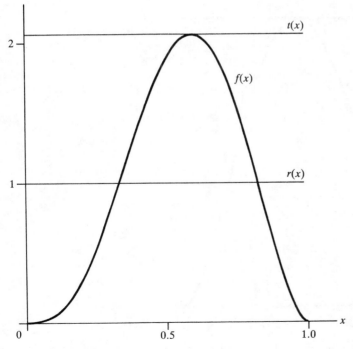

FIGURE 8.8
$f(x)$, $t(x)$, and $r(x)$ for the acceptance-rejection method, beta(4,3) distribution.

generates Y and U as IID U(0,1) random variates in steps 1 and 2; then in step 3 we check whether

$$U \leq \frac{60 Y^3 (1 - Y)^2}{2.0736}$$

If so, we return $X = Y$; otherwise, we reject Y and go back to step 1.

Note that in the preceding example, X is bounded on an interval (the unit interval in this case), and so we were able to choose t to be constant over this interval, which in turn led to r's being a uniform density. The acceptance-rejection method is often stated *only* for such bounded random variables X and *only* for this uniform choice of r; our treatment is more general.

The acceptance-rejection algorithm above seems curious to say the least, and the proof of its validity in App. 8A adds little insight. There is, however, a natural intuition to the method. Figure 8.9 presents again the $f(x)$ and $t(x)$ curves from Example 8.6, and in addition shows the algorithm in action. We generated 50 X's from the beta(4,3) distribution by acceptance-rejection (using stream 2 of the random-number generator in App. 7A), which are marked by crosses on the x axis. On the $t(x)$ curve at the top of the graph we also mark

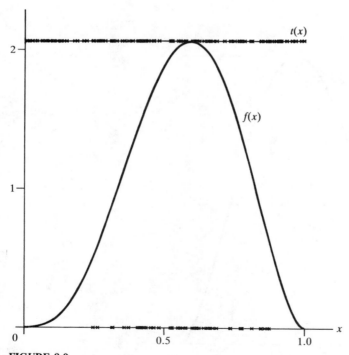

FIGURE 8.9
Sample of 50 X's (on horizontal axis) and the required Y's [on the $t(x)$ line], acceptance-rejection method for beta(4,3) distribution.

the location of all the Y's generated in step 1 of the algorithm, regardless of whether they ended up being accepted as X's; 50 of these Y's were accepted and made it down to the x axis. The uniformity of the Y's on the $t(x)$ curve is evident, and the higher concentration of the X's on the x axis where $f(x)$ is high is also clear. For those Y's falling in regions where $f(x)$ is low (e.g., x near 0 or 1), $f(Y)/t(Y)$ is small, and as this is the probability of accepting Y as an X, most of such Y's will be rejected. This can be seen in Fig. 8.9 for small (near 0) and large (near 1) values of Y where $f(x)$ is small. On the other hand, Y values where $f(x)$ is high (e.g., near $x = 0.6$) will probably be kept, since $f(Y)/t(Y)$ is nearly 1; thus, most of the Y's around $x = 0.6$ are accepted as X's and make it down to the x axis. In this way, the algorithm "thins out" the Y's from the $r(x)$ density where $t(x)$ is much larger than $f(x)$, but retains most of the Y's where $t(x)$ is only a little higher than $f(x)$. The result is that the concentration of the Y's from $r(x)$ is altered to agree with the desired density $f(x)$.

The principle of acceptance-rejection is quite general, and looking at the above algorithm in a slightly different way clarifies how it can be extended to generation of random points in higher-dimensional spaces; this is important, for example, in Monte Carlo estimation of multiple integrals (see Sec. 1.8.3). The acceptance condition in step 3 of the algorithm can obviously be restated as $Ut(Y) \leq f(Y)$, which means geometrically that Y will be accepted as an X if the point $(Y, Ut(Y))$ falls under the curve for the density f. Figure 8.10 shows this for the same Y values as in Fig. 8.9, with the dots being the points $(Y, Ut(Y))$ and the 50 accepted values of X again being marked by crosses on the x axis. By accepting the Y values for those $(Y, Ut(Y))$ points falling under the $f(x)$ curve, it is intuitive that the accepted X's will be more dense on the x axis where $f(x)$ is high, since it is more likely that the uniformly distributed dots will be under $f(x)$ there. While in this particular example the rectangular nature of the region under $t(x)$ makes the uniformity of the points $(Y, Ut(Y))$ clear, the same is true for regions of any shape, and in any dimension. The challenge is to find a way of efficiently generating points uniformly in an arbitrary non-rectangular region; Smith (1984) discusses this, and proposes a more efficient alternative to acceptance-rejection in high-dimensional spaces.

Although acceptance-rejection generates a value of X with the desired distribution regardless of the choice of the majorizing function t, this choice will play an important role in its efficiency in two ways. First, since step 1 requires generating Y with density $t(x)/c$, we want to choose t so that this can be accomplished rapidly. (The uniform t chosen in Example 8.6 certainly satisfies this wish.) Second, we hope that the probability of rejection in step 3 can be made small, since we have to start all over if this rejection occurs. In App. 8A we show that on any given iteration through the algorithm, the probability of acceptance in step 3 is $1/c$; we therefore would like to choose t so that c is small. Thus, we want to find a t that fits closely above f, bringing c closer to 1, its lower bound. Intuitively, a t that is only a little above f leads to a density r that will be close to f, so that the Y values generated from r in step 1 are from a distribution that is almost correct and so we should accept most of

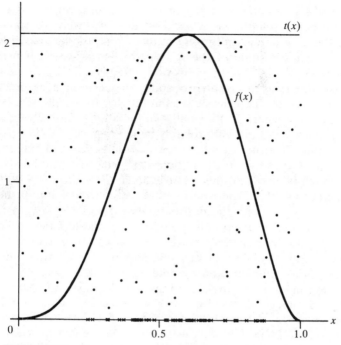

FIGURE 8.10
Sample of 50 X's (on horizontal axis) and the required $(Y, Ut(Y))$ pairs, acceptance-rejection method for beta(4,3) distribution.

them. (From this standpoint, then, we see that the uniform choice of t in Example 8.6 might not be so wise after all, since it does not fit down on top of f very snugly. Since $c = 2.0736$, the probability of acceptance is only about 0.48, being lower than we might like.) These two goals, ease of generation from $t(x)/c$ and a small value of c, may well conflict with each other, so the choice of t is by no means obvious and deserves care. Considerable research has been aimed at identifying good choices for t for a given distribution; see, for example, Ahrens and Dieter (1972, 1974), Atkinson (1979b), Atkinson and Whittaker (1976), Schmeiser (1980a, 1980b), Schmeiser and Babu (1980), Schmeiser and Lal (1980b), Schmeiser and Shalaby (1980), and Tadikamalla (1978). One popular method of finding a suitable t is *first* to specify $r(x)$ to be some common density, e.g., a normal or double exponential, then find the smallest c such that $t(x) = cr(x) \geq f(x)$ for all x.

Example 8.7. Consider once again the beta(4,3) distribution from Example 8.6, but now with a more elaborate majorizing function in an attempt to raise the probability of acceptance without unduly burdening the generation of Y's from $r(x)$; we do this along the lines of Schmeiser and Shalaby (1980). For this density, there are two *inflection points* [i.e., values of x above which $f(x)$ switches from convex to concave, or vice versa], which can be found by solving $f''(x) = 0$ for those values of x between 0 and 1; the solutions are $x = 0.36$ and $x = 0.84$ (to two decimals). Checking the signs of $f''(x)$ on the three regions of $[0,1]$ created by these two inflection points, we find that $f(x)$ is convex on $[0, 0.36]$, concave on $[0.36, 0.84]$, and again convex on $[0.84, 1]$. By the definition of convexity, a line from the point $(0, 0)$ to the point $(0.36, f(0.36))$ will lie above $f(x)$; similarly, the line connecting $(0.84, f(0.84))$ with the point $(1, 0)$ will be above $f(x)$. Over the concave region, we simply place a horizontal line at height 2.0736, the maximum of $f(x)$. This leads to the piecewise-linear majorizing function $t(x)$ shown in Fig. 8.11; adding up the areas of the two triangles and the rectangle, we get $c = 1.28$, so that the probability of acceptance on a given pass through the algorithm is 0.78, being considerably better than the 0.48 acceptance probability when using the simple uniform majorizing function in Example 8.6. However, it now becomes more difficult to generate values from the density $r(x)$, which is plotted in Fig. 8.12; this is a typical trade-off in specifying a majorizing function. As suggested in Fig. 8.12, generating from $r(x)$ can be done using composition, dividing the area under $r(x)$ into three regions, each corresponding to a density from which generation is easy; see Prob. 8.16. Thus, we would really be combining three

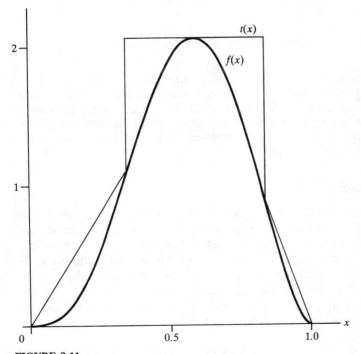

FIGURE 8.11
$f(x)$ and piecewise-linear majorizing function $t(x)$, acceptance-rejection method for beta(4,3) distribution.

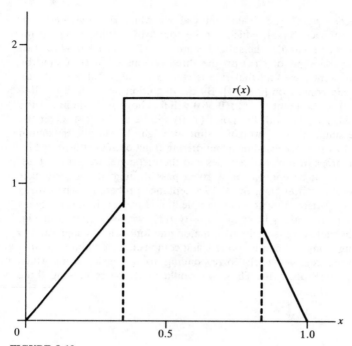

FIGURE 8.12
$r(x)$ corresponding to the piecewise-linear majorizing function $t(x)$ in Fig. 8.11.

different generation techniques here: inverse transform [for the component densities of $r(x)$], composition [for $r(x)$], and finally acceptance-rejection [for $f(x)$]. In comparison with Example 8.6, whether the higher acceptance probability justifies the increased work to generate a Y is not clear, and may depend on several factors, such as the particular parameters, code efficiency, as well as the language, compiler, and hardware.

8.2.5 Special Properties

Although most methods for generating random variates can be classified into one of the four approaches discussed so far in Sec. 8.2, some techniques simply rely on some *special property* of the desired distribution function F or the random variable X. Frequently, the special property will take the form of representing X in terms of other random variables that are more easily generated; in this sense the method of convolution is a "special" special property. Since there is no general form for these techniques, we shall merely give examples of the kinds of things that can be done.

Example 8.8. If $Y \sim N(0,1)$ (the standard normal distribution), then Y^2 has a chi-square distribution with 1 df. [We write $X \sim \chi_k^2$ to mean that X has a chi-square distribution with k df.] Thus, to generate $X \sim \chi_1^2$, generate $Y \sim N(0,1)$ (see Sec. 8.3.6), and return $X = Y^2$.

Example 8.9. If $Z_1, Z_2, \ldots, Z_k$ are IID χ_1^2 random variables, then $X = Z_1 + Z_2 + \cdots + Z_k \sim \chi_k^2$. Thus, to generate $X \sim \chi_k^2$, first generate $Y_1, Y_2, \ldots, Y_k$ as IID N(0,1) random variates, and then return $X = Y_1^2 + Y_2^2 + \cdots + Y_k^2$ (see Example 8.8). Since for large k this may be quite slow, we might want to exploit the fact that the χ_k^2 distribution is a gamma distribution with shape parameter $\alpha = k/2$ and scale parameter $\beta = 2$. Then X can be obtained directly from the gamma-generation methods discussed in Sec. 8.3.4.

Example 8.10. If $Y \sim N(0,1)$, $Z \sim \chi_k^2$, and Y and Z are independent, then $X = Y/\sqrt{Z/k}$ is said to have *Student's t distribution* with k df, which we denote $X \sim t_k$. Thus, to generate $X \sim t_k$, we generate $Y \sim N(0,1)$ and $Z \sim \chi_k^2$ independently of Y (see Example 8.9), and return $X = Y/\sqrt{Z/k}$.

Example 8.11. If $Z_1 \sim \chi_{k_1}^2$, $Z_2 \sim \chi_{k_2}^2$, and Z_1 and Z_2 are independent, then

$$X = \frac{Z_1/k_1}{Z_2/k_2}$$

is said to have an *F distribution* with (k_1, k_2) df, denoted $X \sim F_{k_1,k_2}$. We thus generate $Z_1 \sim \chi_{k_1}^2$ and $Z_2 \sim \chi_{k_2}^2$ independently, and return $X = (Z_1/k_1)/(Z_2/k_2)$.

Although Examples 8.8 through 8.11 all have to do with normal-theory random variables, these kinds of observations can be used to generate random variates that may not have anything at all to do with the normal distribution. (For example, see the discussion of the beta distribution in Sec. 8.3.8.)

8.3 GENERATING CONTINUOUS RANDOM VARIATES

In this section we discuss particular algorithms for generating random variates from several commonly occurring continuous distributions; Sec. 8.4 contains a similar treatment for discrete random variates. Although there may be several different algorithms for generating from a given distribution, we explicitly present only one technique in each case and provide references for other algorithms that may be better in some sense, e.g., in terms of speed at the expense of increased setup cost and greater complexity. In deciding which algorithm to present, we have tried to choose those that are simple to describe and implement, and are reasonably efficient as well. We also give only exact (up to machine accuracy) methods, as opposed to approximations. If speed is critically important, however, we urge the reader to pursue the various references given for the desired distribution. For definitions of density functions, mass functions, and distribution functions, see Secs. 6.2.2. and 6.2.3.

8.3.1 Uniform

The distribution function of a U(a,b) random variable is easily inverted by solving $u = F(x)$ for x to obtain, for $0 \le u \le 1$,

$$x = F^{-1}(u) = a + (b - a)u$$

Thus, we can use the inverse-transform method to generate X:

1. Generate $U \sim U(0,1)$.
2. Return $X = a + (b - a)U$.

If many X values are to be generated, the constant $b - a$ should, of course, be computed beforehand and stored for use in the algorithm.

8.3.2 Exponential

The exponential random variable with mean $\beta > 0$ was considered in Example 8.1, where we derived the following inverse-transform algorithm:

1. Generate $U \sim U(0,1)$.
2. Return $X = -\beta \ln U$.

[Recall that the U in step 2 would be $1 - U$ instead if we want a literal version of $X = F^{-1}(U)$ in order to make the correlation between the X's and U's positive.] This is certainly a simple technique and has all the advantages of the inverse-transform method discussed in Sec. 8.2.1. It is also reasonably fast, with most of the computing time's being taken up in evaluating the logarithm. In the experiments of Ahrens and Dieter (1972), this method was the fastest of the four algorithms considered if programming in FORTRAN, with some 72 percent of the time taken up by the logarithm evaluation. If one is willing to program in assembly language, however, there are other methods that avoid the logarithm and are faster, although considerably more complex and involving various amounts of preliminary setup; see von Neumann (1951), Marsaglia (1961), and MacLaren, Marsaglia, and Bray (1964). We refer the interested reader to Ahrens and Dieter (1972) and to Fishman (1978, pp. 402–410) for further discussion.

8.3.3 *m*-Erlang

As discussed in Example 8.5, if X is an m-Erlang random variable with mean β, we can write $X = Y_1 + Y_2 + \cdots + Y_m$, where the Y_i's are IID exponential random variables, each with mean β/m. This led to the convolution algorithm described in Example 8.5. Its efficiency can be improved, however, as follows. If we use the inverse-transform method of Sec. 8.3.2 to generate the exponential Y_i's [$Y_i = (-\beta/m) \ln U_i$, where $U_1, U_2, \ldots, U_m$ are IID $U(0,1)$ random variates], then

$$X = \sum_{i=1}^{m} Y_i = \sum_{i=1}^{m} \frac{-\beta}{m} \ln U_i = \frac{-\beta}{m} \ln \left(\prod_{i=1}^{m} U_i \right)$$

so that we need to evaluate only one logarithm (rather than m logarithms).

Then the statement of the algorithm is as follows:

1. Generate $U_1, U_2, \ldots, U_m$ as IID $U(0,1)$.

2. Return $X = \dfrac{-\beta}{m} \ln\left(\prod\limits_{i=1}^{m} U_i\right)$.

(Again, one should compute β/m beforehand and store it for repeated use.) This algorithm is really a combination of the composition and inverse-transform methods.

Since we must generate m random numbers and perform m multiplications, the execution time of the algorithm is approximately proportional to m. Therefore, one might look for an alternative method when m is large. Fortunately, the m-Erlang distribution is a special case of the gamma distribution (with shape parameter α equal to the integer m), so that we can use one of the methods for generating gamma random variates here as well (see Sec. 8.3.4 for discussion of gamma generation). The precise threshold for m beyond which one should switch to general gamma generation will depend on the method used for generating a gamma random variate as well as on languages, compilers, and hardware; preliminary experimentation in one's particular situation might prove worthwhile. [For the gamma generator of Sec. 8.3.4 in the case $\alpha > 1$, timing experiments in Cheng (1977) indicate that using his general gamma generator becomes faster than the above m-Erlang algorithm for $m \geq 10$, approximately.] Another potential problem with using the above algorithm, especially for large m, is that $\prod_{i=1}^{m} U_i$ might get close to zero, which could lead to numerical difficulties when its logarithm is taken.

8.3.4 Gamma

General gamma random variates are more complicated to generate than the three types of random variates considered so far in this section, since the distribution function has no simple closed form for which we could try to find an inverse. First note that given $X \sim \text{gamma}(\alpha,1)$, we can obtain, for any $\beta > 0$, a gamma(α,β) random variate X' by letting $X' = \beta X$, so that it is sufficient to restrict attention to generating from the gamma$(\alpha,1)$ distribution. Furthermore, recall that the gamma$(1,1)$ distribution is just the exponential distribution with mean 1, so that we need consider only $0 < \alpha < 1$ and $\alpha > 1$. Since the available algorithms for generating gamma random variates are for the most part valid in only one of these ranges of α, we shall discuss them separately. [Tadikamalla and Johnson (1981) provide a comprehensive review of gamma variate generation methods that were available at that time.]

We first consider the case $0 < \alpha < 1$. (Note that if $\alpha = 0.5$, we have a rescaled χ_1^2 distribution and X can be easily generated using Example 8.8; the algorithm stated below is nevertheless valid for $\alpha = 0.5$.) Atkinson and Pearce (1976) tested three alternative algorithms for this case, and we present one of them, due to Ahrens and Dieter (1974). [The algorithm of Forsythe (1972) was usually the fastest in the comparisons in Atkinson and Pearce (1976), but it is considerably more complicated.] This algorithm, denoted GS in Ahrens and Dieter (1974), is an acceptance-rejection technique, with majorizing function

$$
t(x) = \begin{cases} 0 & \text{if } x \le 0 \\ \dfrac{x^{\alpha-1}}{\Gamma(\alpha)} & \text{if } 0 < x \le 1 \\ \dfrac{e^{-x}}{\Gamma(\alpha)} & \text{if } 1 < x \end{cases}
$$

Thus, $c = \int_0^\infty t(x)\, dx = b/[\alpha\Gamma(\alpha)]$, where $b = (e + \alpha)/e > 1$, which yields the density $r(x) = t(x)/c$ as

$$
r(x) = \begin{cases} 0 & \text{if } x \le 0 \\ \dfrac{\alpha x^{\alpha-1}}{b} & \text{if } 0 < x \le 1 \\ \dfrac{\alpha e^{-x}}{b} & \text{if } 1 < x \end{cases}
$$

Generating a random variate Y with density $r(x)$ can be done by the inverse-transform method; the distribution function corresponding to r is

$$
R(x) = \int_0^x r(y)\, dy = \begin{cases} \dfrac{x^\alpha}{b} & \text{if } 0 \le x \le 1 \\ 1 - \dfrac{\alpha e^{-x}}{b} & \text{if } 1 < x \end{cases}
$$

which can be inverted to obtain

$$
R^{-1}(u) = \begin{cases} (bu)^{1/\alpha} & \text{if } u \le \dfrac{1}{b} \\ -\ln \dfrac{b(1-u)}{\alpha} & \text{otherwise} \end{cases}
$$

Thus, to generate Y with density r, we first generate $U_1 \sim U(0,1)$. If $U_1 \le 1/b$, we set $Y = (bU_1)^{1/\alpha}$; in this case, $Y \le 1$. Otherwise, if $U_1 > 1/b$, set $Y = -\ln[b(1-U_1)/\alpha]$, which will be greater than 1. Noting that

$$
\frac{f(Y)}{t(Y)} = \begin{cases} e^{-Y} & \text{if } 0 \le Y \le 1 \\ Y^{\alpha-1} & \text{if } 1 < Y \end{cases}
$$

we obtain the final algorithm [$b = (e + \alpha)/e$ must be computed beforehand]:

1. Generate $U_1 \sim U(0,1)$, and let $P = bU_1$. If $P > 1$, go to step 3. Otherwise, proceed to step 2.
2. Let $Y = P^{1/\alpha}$, and generate $U_2 \sim U(0,1)$. If $U_2 \le e^{-Y}$, return $X = Y$. Otherwise, go back to step 1.
3. Let $Y = -\ln[(b - P)/\alpha]$ and generate $U_2 \sim U(0,1)$. If $U_2 \le Y^{\alpha-1}$, return $X = Y$. Otherwise, go back to step 1.

We now consider the case $\alpha > 1$, where there are several good algorithms. In view of timing experiments by Schmeiser and Lal (1980b) and Cheng and Feast (1979), we will present a modified acceptance-rejection method due to Cheng (1977), who calls this the GB algorithm. This algorithm has a "capped" execution time; i.e., its execution time is bounded as $\alpha \to \infty$ and in fact appears to become faster as α grows. (The modification of the general acceptance-rejection method consists of adding a faster pretest for acceptance.) To obtain a majorizing function $t(x)$, first let $\lambda = \sqrt{2\alpha - 1}$, $\mu = \alpha^\lambda$, and $c = 4\alpha^\alpha e^{-\alpha} / [\lambda \Gamma(\alpha)]$. Then define $t(x) = cr(x)$, where

$$r(x) = \begin{cases} \dfrac{\lambda \mu x^{\lambda - 1}}{(\mu + x^\lambda)^2} & \text{if } x > 0 \\ 0 & \text{otherwise} \end{cases}$$

The distribution function corresponding to the density $r(x)$ is

$$R(x) = \begin{cases} \dfrac{x^\lambda}{\mu + x^\lambda} & \text{if } x \geq 0 \\ 0 & \text{otherwise} \end{cases}$$

which is easily inverted to obtain

$$R^{-1}(u) = \left(\frac{\mu u}{1 - u} \right)^{1/\lambda} \qquad \text{for } 0 < u < 1$$

To verify that $t(x)$ indeed majorizes $f(x)$, see Cheng (1977). Note that this is an example of obtaining a majorizing function by first specifying a known distribution [this $R(x)$ is known as the *log logistic* distribution function] and then rescaling the density $r(x)$ to majorize $f(x)$. Thus, we use the inverse-transform method to generate Y with density r. After adding an advantageous pretest for acceptance and streamlining for computational efficiency, Cheng (1977) recommends the following algorithm (the prespecified constants are $a = 1/\sqrt{2\alpha - 1}$, $b = \alpha - \ln 4$, $q = \alpha + 1/a$, $\theta = 4.5$, and $d = 1 + \ln \theta$):

1. Generate U_1 and U_2 as IID $U(0, 1)$.
2. Let $V = a \ln [U_1/(1 - U_1)]$, $Y = \alpha e^V$, $Z = U_1^2 U_2$, and $W = b + qV - Y$.
3. If $W + d - \theta Z \geq 0$, return $X = Y$. Otherwise, proceed to step 4.
4. If $W \geq \ln Z$, return $X = Y$. Otherwise, go back to step 1.

Step 3 is the added pretest, which (if passed) avoids computing the logarithm in the regular acceptance-rejection test in step 4. (If step 3 were removed, the algorithm would still be valid and would just be the literal acceptance-rejection method.)

As mentioned above, there are several other good algorithms that could be used when $\alpha > 1$. Schmeiser and Lal (1980b) present another acceptance-rejection method with $t(x)$ piecewise linear in the "body" of $f(x)$ and exponential in the tails; their algorithm was roughly twice as fast as the one we chose to present above, for α ranging from 1.0001 through 1000. However, their algorithm is more complicated and requires additional time to set up the necessary constants for a given value of α. This is typical of the trade-offs the analyst must consider in choosing among alternative variate-generation algorithms.

Finally, we consider direct use of the inverse-transform method to generate gamma random variates. Since neither the gamma distribution function nor its inverse has a simple closed form, we must resort to numerical methods. Best and Roberts (1975) give a numerical procedure for inverting the distribution function of a chi-square random variable with degrees of freedom that need not be an integer, so is applicable for gamma generation for any $\alpha > 0$. [If $Y \sim \chi_\nu^2$, where $\nu > 0$ need not be an integer, then $Y \sim \text{gamma}(\nu/2, 2)$. If we want $X \sim \text{gamma}(\alpha, 1)$, first generate $Y \sim \chi_{2\alpha}^2$, and then return $X = Y/2$.] A FORTRAN subroutine for the procedure is also provided in Best and Roberts (1975). IMSL (1987, pp. 921–922) also contains a FORTRAN routine CHIIN to invert the chi-square distribution function.

8.3.5 Weibull

The Weibull distribution function is easily inverted to obtain

$$F^{-1}(u) = \beta[-\ln(1-u)]^{1/\alpha}$$

which leads to the following inverse-transform algorithm:

1. Generate $U \sim U(0,1)$.
2. Return $X = \beta(-\ln U)^{1/\alpha}$.

Again we are exploiting the fact that U and $1 - U$ have the same $U(0,1)$ distribution, so that in step 2, U should be replaced by $1 - U$ if the literal inverse-transform method is desired. This algorithm can also be justified by noting that if Y has an exponential distribution with mean β^α, then $Y^{1/\alpha} \sim$ Weibull(α, β); see Sec. 6.2.2.

8.3.6 Normal

First note that given $X \sim N(0,1)$, we can obtain $X' \sim N(\mu, \sigma^2)$ by setting $X' = \mu + \sigma X$, so that we can restrict attention to generating standard normal random variates. Efficiency is important, since the normal density has often been used to provide majorizing functions for acceptance-rejection generation of random variates from other distributions, e.g., Ahrens and Dieter's (1974) gamma and beta generators. Normal random variates can also be transformed directly into random variates from other distributions, e.g., the lognormal. Also, statisticians seeking to estimate empirically, in a Monte Carlo study, the null distribution of a test statistic for normality will need an efficient source of normal random variates. [See, for example, Filliben (1975), Lilliefors (1967), or Shapiro and Wilk (1965).]

One of the early methods for generating $N(0,1)$ random variates, due to Box and Muller (1958), is evidently still in wide use despite the availability of much faster algorithms. It does have the advantage, however, of maintaining a one-to-one correspondence between the random numbers used and the $N(0,1)$ random variates produced; it may thus prove useful for maintaining synchronization in the use of common random numbers or antithetic variates as a variance-reduction technique (see Secs. 11.2 and 11.3). The method simply says to generate U_1 and U_2 as IID $U(0,1)$, then set $X_1 = \sqrt{-2 \ln U_1} \cos 2\pi U_2$ and $X_2 = \sqrt{-2 \ln U_1} \sin 2\pi U_2$. Then X_1 and X_2 are IID $N(0,1)$ random variates. Since we obtain the desired random variates in pairs, we could, on odd-numbered calls to the subprogram, actually compute X_1 and X_2 as just described, but return only X_1, saving X_2 for immediate return on the next (even-numbered) call. Thus, we use *two* random numbers to produce *two* $N(0,1)$ random variates. While this method is valid in principle, i.e., if U_1 and U_2 are truly IID $U(0,1)$ random variables, there is a serious difficulty if U_1 and U_2 are actually adjacent random numbers produced by a linear congruential generator (see Sec. 7.2), as they might be in practice. Due to the fact that U_2 would depend on U_1 according to the recursion in Eq. (7.1) in Sec. 7.2, it can be shown that the generated variates X_1 and X_2 must fall on a spiral in (X_1, X_2) space, rather than being truly independently normally distributed; see, for example, Bratley, Fox, and Schrage (1987, pp. 223–224). Thus, the Box-Muller method should not be used with a single stream of a linear congruential generator; it might be possible to use separate streams or a composite generator instead, e.g., a shuffling generator (see Sec. 7.3.2), but one of the methods described below for normal variate generation should probably be used instead.

An improvement to the Box and Muller method, which eliminates the trigonometric calculations and was described in Marsaglia and Bray (1964), has become known as the *polar method*. It relies on a special property of the normal distribution and was found by Atkinson and Pearce (1976) to be between 9 and 31 percent faster in FORTRAN programming than the Box and Muller method, depending on the machine used. [Ahrens and Dieter (1972) experienced a 27 percent reduction in time.] The polar method, which also generates $N(0,1)$ random variates in pairs, is as follows:

1. Generate U_1 and U_2 as IID $U(0,1)$, let $V_i = 2U_i - 1$ for $i = 1, 2$, and let $W = V_1^2 + V_2^2$.

2. If $W > 1$, go back to step 1. Otherwise, let $Y = \sqrt{(-2 \ln W)/W}$, $X_1 = V_1 Y$, and $X_2 = V_2 Y$. Then X_1 and X_2 are IID $N(0,1)$ random variates.

Since a "rejection" of U_1 and U_2 can occur in step 2 (with probability $1 - \pi/4$, by Prob. 8.12), the polar method will require a random number of $U(0,1)$ random variates to generate each pair of $N(0,1)$ random variates. More recently, a very fast algorithm for generating $N(0,1)$ random variates was developed by Kinderman and Ramage (1976), which is more complicated but required 30 percent less time than the polar method in their FORTRAN experiments.

For direct use of the inverse-transform method in normal generation, one must use a numerical method, since neither the normal distribution function nor its inverse has a simple closed-form expression. Such a method, complete with a FORTRAN subroutine for implementation, is given by Odeh and Evans (1974). Also, the FORTRAN routine ANORIN in the IMSL (1987, pp. 911–912) library inverts the standard normal distribution function.

8.3.7   Lognormal

A special property of the lognormal distribution, namely, that if $Y \sim N(\mu, \sigma^2)$ then $e^Y \sim LN(\mu, \sigma^2)$, is used to obtain the following algorithm:

1. Generate $Y \sim N(\mu, \sigma^2)$.
2. Return $X = e^Y$.

To accomplish step 1, any method discussed in Sec. 8.3.6 for normal generation can be used.

Note that μ and σ^2 are *not* the mean and variance of the $LN(\mu, \sigma^2)$ distribution. In fact, if $X \sim LN(\mu, \sigma^2)$ and we let $\mu_l = E(X)$ and $\sigma_l^2 = \text{Var}(X)$, then $\mu_l = e^{\mu + \sigma^2/2}$ and $\sigma_l^2 = e^{2\mu + \sigma^2}(e^{\sigma^2} - 1)$. Thus, if we want to generate a lognormal random variate with *given* mean μ_l and variance σ_l^2, we should solve for μ and σ^2 in terms of μ_l and σ_l^2 first, *before* generating the desired random variates. The formulas are easily obtained as $\mu = \ln(\mu_l^2/\sqrt{\sigma_l^2 + \mu_l^2})$ and $\sigma^2 = \ln[(\sigma_l^2 + \mu_l^2)/\mu_l^2]$.

8.3.8   Beta

First note that we can obtain $X' \sim \text{beta}(\alpha_1, \alpha_2)$ on the interval $[a,b]$ for $a < b$ by setting $X' = a + (b - a)X$, where $X \sim \text{beta}(\alpha_1, \alpha_2)$ on the interval $[0,1]$, so that it is sufficient to consider only the latter case, which we henceforth call *the* beta(α_1, α_2) distribution.

Some properties of the beta(α_1, α_2) distribution for certain (α_1, α_2) combinations facilitate generating beta random variates. First, if $X \sim \text{beta}(\alpha_1, \alpha_2)$, then $1 - X \sim \text{beta}(\alpha_2, \alpha_1)$, so that we can readily generate a beta(α_2, α_1) random variate if we can obtain a beta(α_1, α_2) random variate easily. One such situation occurs when either α_1 or α_2 is equal to 1. If $\alpha_2 = 1$, for example, then for $0 \leq x \leq 1$ we have $f(x) = \alpha_1 x^{\alpha_1 - 1}$, so the distribution function is $F(x) = x^{\alpha_1}$, and we can easily generate $X \sim \text{beta}(\alpha_1, 1)$ by the inverse-transform method, i.e., by returning $X = U^{1/\alpha_1}$, for $U \sim U(0,1)$. Finally, the beta$(1,1)$ distribution is simply $U(0,1)$.

A general method for generating a beta(α_1, α_2) random variate for any $\alpha_1 > 0$ and $\alpha_2 > 0$ is a result of the fact that if $Y_1 \sim \text{gamma}(\alpha_1, 1)$, $Y_2 \sim$

gamma$(\alpha_2,1)$, and Y_1 and Y_2 are independent, then $Y_1/(Y_1 + Y_2) \sim$ beta(α_1,α_2). This leads to the following algorithm:

1. Generate $Y_1 \sim$ gamma$(\alpha_1,1)$ and $Y_2 \sim$ gamma$(\alpha_2,1)$ independent of Y_1.
2. Return $X = Y_1/(Y_1 + Y_2)$.

Generating the two gamma random variates Y_1 and Y_2 can be done by any appropriate algorithm for gamma generation (see Sec. 8.3.4), so that we must take care to check whether α_1 and α_2 are less than or greater than 1.

This method is quite convenient, in that it is essentially done provided that we have gamma$(\alpha,1)$ generators for all $\alpha > 0$; its efficiency will, of course, depend on the speed of the chosen gamma generators. There are, however, considerably faster (and more complicated, as usual) algorithms for generating from the beta distribution directly. For $\alpha_1 > 1$ and $\alpha_2 > 1$, Schmeiser and Babu (1980) present a very fast acceptance-rejection method, where the majorizing function is piecewise linear over the center of $f(x)$ and exponential over the tails; a fast acceptance pretest is specified by a piecewise-linear function $b(x)$ that minorizes (i.e., is always below) $f(x)$. If $\alpha_1 < 1$ or $\alpha_2 < 1$ (or both), algorithms for generating beta(α_1,α_2) random variates directly are given by Atkinson and Whittaker (1976, 1979), Cheng (1978), and Jöhnk (1964). Cheng's (1978) method BA is quite simple and is valid as well for any $\alpha_1 > 0$, $\alpha_2 > 0$ combination; the same is true for the algorithms of Atkinson (1979a) and Jöhnk (1964).

The inverse-transform method for generating beta random variates must rely on numerical methods, as was the case for the gamma and normal distributions. Cran, Martin, and Thomas (1977) give such a method with a FORTRAN program, and the IMSL (1987, pp. 925–926) FORTRAN routine for this task is called BETIN.

8.3.9 Pearson Type V

As noted in Sec. 6.2.2, $X \sim$ PT5(α,β) if and only if $1/X \sim$ gamma$(\alpha, 1/\beta)$, which leads to the following special-property algorithm:

1. Generate $Y \sim$ gamma$(\alpha, 1/\beta)$.
2. Return $X = 1/Y$.

Any method from Sec. 8.3.4 for gamma generation could be used, taking care to note whether $\alpha < 1$, $\alpha = 1$, or $\alpha > 1$. To use the inverse-transform method, we note from Sec. 6.2.2 that the PT5(α,β) distribution function is $F(x) = 1 - F_G(1/x)$ for $x > 0$, where F_G is the gamma$(\alpha, 1/\beta)$ distribution function. Setting $F(X) = U$ thus leads to $X = 1/F_G^{-1}(1 - U)$ as the literal inverse-transform method, or to $X = 1/F_G^{-1}(U)$ if we want to exploit the fact that $1 - U$ and U have the same U$(0,1)$ distribution. In any case, we would generally have to use a numerical method to evaluate F_G^{-1}, as discussed in Sec. 8.3.4.

8.3.10 Pearson Type VI

From Sec. 6.2.2, we note that if Y_1 and Y_2 are independent random variables with $Y_i \sim \text{gamma}(\alpha_i, \beta)$, then $Y_1/Y_2 \sim \text{PT6}(\alpha_1, \alpha_2, \beta)$; this leads directly to:

1. Generate $Y_1 \sim \text{gamma}(\alpha_1, \beta)$ and $Y_2 \sim \text{gamma}(\alpha_2, \beta)$ independent of Y_1.
2. Return $X = Y_1/Y_2$.

Any method from Sec. 8.3.4 for gamma generation could be used, noticing whether $\alpha < 1$, $\alpha = 1$, or $\alpha > 1$. To use the inverse-transform method, note from Sec. 6.2.2 that the $\text{PT6}(\alpha_1, \alpha_2, \beta)$ distribution function is $F(x) = F_B(x/(x + \beta))$ for $x > 0$, where F_B is the beta(α_1, α_2) distribution function. Setting $F(X) = U$ thus leads to $X = \beta F_B^{-1}(U)/[1 - F_B^{-1}(U)]$, where $F_B^{-1}(U)$ would generally have to be evaluated by a numerical method, as discussed in Sec. 8.3.8.

8.3.11 Triangular

First notice that, if we have $X \sim \text{triang}(0, 1, (c - a)/(b - a))$, then $X' = a + (b - a)X \sim \text{triang}(a, b, c)$, so we can restrict attention to triang$(0,1,c)$ random variables, where $0 < c < 1$. (For the limiting cases $c = 0$ or $c = 1$, giving rise to a left or right triangle, see Prob. 8.7.) The distribution function is easily inverted to obtain, for $0 \le u \le 1$,

$$F^{-1}(u) = \begin{cases} \sqrt{cu} & \text{if } 0 \le u \le c \\ 1 - \sqrt{(1 - c)(1 - u)} & \text{if } c < u \le 1 \end{cases}$$

Therefore, we can state the following inverse-transform algorithm for generating $X \sim \text{triang}(0,1,c)$:

1. Generate $U \sim \text{U}(0,1)$.
2. If $U \le c$, return $X = \sqrt{cU}$. Otherwise, return $X = 1 - \sqrt{(1 - c)(1 - U)}$.

(Note that if $U > c$ in step 2, we *cannot* replace the $1 - U$ in the formula for X by U. Why?) For an alternative method of generating a triangular random variate (by composition), see Prob. 8.13.

8.3.12 Empirical Distributions

In this section we give algorithms for generating random variates from the continuous empirical distribution functions F and G defined in Sec. 6.2.4. In both cases, the inverse-transform approach can be used.

First suppose that we have the original individual observations, which we use to define the empirical distribution function $F(x)$ given in Sec. 6.2.4 (see also Fig. 6.17). Although an inverse-transform algorithm might at first appear to involve some kind of a search, the fact that the "corners" of F occur precisely at levels $0, 1/(n - 1), 2/(n - 1), \ldots, (n - 2)/(n - 1)$, and 1 allows us to avoid an explicit search. We leave it to the reader to verify that the following algorithm *is* the inverse-transform method:

1. Generate $U \sim U(0,1)$, let $P = (n-1)U$, and let $I = \lfloor P \rfloor + 1$.
2. Return $X = X_{(I)} + (P - I + 1)(X_{(I+1)} - X_{(I)})$.

Note that the $X_{(i)}$'s must be stored and that storing a separate array containing the values of $X_{(I+1)} - X_{(I)}$ would eliminate a subtraction in step 2. Also, the values of X generated will always be between $X_{(1)}$ and $X_{(n)}$; this limitation is a possible disadvantage of specifying an empirical distribution in this way. The lack of a search makes the marginal execution time of this algorithm essentially independent of n, although large n entails more storage and setup time for sorting the X_i's.

Now suppose that our data are grouped; that is, we have k adjacent intervals $[a_0,a_1)$, $[a_1,a_2)$, $\ldots$, $[a_{k-1},a_k]$, and the jth interval contains n_j observations, with $n_1 + n_2 + \cdots + n_k = n$. In this case, we defined an empirical distribution function $G(x)$ in Sec. 6.2.4 (see also Fig. 6.18), and the following inverse-transform algorithm generates a random variate with this distribution:

1. Generate $U \sim U(0,1)$.
2. Find the nonnegative integer J $(0 \leq J \leq k-1)$ such that $G(a_J) \leq U < G(a_{J+1})$, and return $X = a_J + [U - G(a_J)](a_{J+1} - a_J)/[G(a_{J+1}) - G(a_J)]$.

Note that the J found in step 2 satisfies $G(a_J) < G(a_{J+1})$, so that no X can be generated in an interval for which $n_j = 0$. (Also, it is clear that $a_0 \leq X \leq a_k$.) Determining J in step 2 could be done by a straightforward left-to-right search or by a search starting with the value of j for which $G(a_{j+1}) - G(a_j)$ is largest, then next largest, etc. As an alternative that avoids the search entirely (at the expense of extra storage), we could initially define a vector $(m_1,m_2,\ldots,m_n)$ by setting the first n_1 m_i's to 0, the next n_2 m_i's to 1, etc., with the last n_k m_i's being set to $k-1$. (If some n_j is 0, no m_i's are set to $j-1$. For example, if $k \geq 3$ and $n_1 > 0$, $n_2 = 0$, and $n_3 > 0$, the first n_1 m_i's are set to 0 and the *next* n_3 m_i's are set to 2.) Then the value of J in step 2 can be determined by setting $L = \lfloor nU \rfloor + 1$ and letting $J = m_L$. Whether or not this is worthwhile depends on the particular characteristics of the data and on the importance of any computational speed that might be gained relative to the extra storage and programming effort. Finally, Chen and Asau (1974) give another method for determining J in step 2, based on preliminary calculations that reduce the range of search for a given U; it requires only 10 extra memory locations. (Their treatment is for a discrete empirical distribution function but can also be applied to the present case.)

The empirical/exponential distribution mentioned briefly in Sec. 6.2.4 can also be inverted so that the inverse-transform method can be used; an explicit algorithm is given in Bratley, Fox, and Schrage (1987, p. 151).

8.4 GENERATING DISCRETE RANDOM VARIATES

This section discusses particular algorithms for generating random variates from various discrete distributions that might be useful in a simulation study. As in Sec. 8.3, we usually present for each distribution one algorithm that is fairly simple to implement and reasonably efficient. References will be made to alternative algorithms that might be faster, usually at the expense of greater complexity.

The discrete inverse-transform method, as described in Sec. 8.2.1, can be used for any discrete distribution, whether the range of possible values is finite or (countably) infinite. Many of the algorithms presented in this section *are* the discrete inverse-transform method, although in some cases this fact is very well disguised due to the particular way the required search is performed, which often takes advantage of the special form of the probability mass function. As was the case for continuous random variates, however, the inverse-transform method may not be the most efficient way to generate a random variate from a given distribution.

One other general approach should be mentioned here, which can be used for generating *any* discrete random variate having a *finite* range of values. This is the *alias method*, developed by Walker (1977) and refined by Kronmal and Peterson (1979); it is very general and efficient, but it does require some initial setup as well as extra storage. We discuss the alias method in more detail in Sec. 8.4.3, but the reader should keep in mind that it is applicable to *any* discrete distribution with a finite range (such as the binomial). For an infinite range, the alias method can be used indirectly in conjunction with the general composition approach (see Sec. 8.2.2); this is also discussed in Sec. 8.4.3.

In addition to the alias method, there are some other general discrete-variate generation ideas; see, for example, Shanthikumar (1985), and Peterson and Kronmal (1983).

A final comment concerns the apparent loss of generality in considering below only distributions that have range $S_n = \{0,1,2,...,n\}$ or $S = \{0,1,2,...\}$, which may appear to be more restrictive than our original definition of a discrete random variable having general range $T_n = \{x_1,x_2,...,x_n\}$ or $T = \{x_1,x_2,...\}$. However, no generality is actually lost. If we really want a random variate X with mass function $p(x_i)$ and general range T_n (or T), we can first generate a random variate I with range S_{n-1} (or S) such that $P(I = i - 1) = p(x_i)$ for $i = 1, 2, \ldots, n$ (or $i = 1,2,...$). Then the random variate $X = x_{I+1}$ is returned and has the desired distribution. (Given I, x_{I+1} could be determined from a stored table of the x_i's, or from a formula that computes x_i as a function of i.)

8.4.1 Bernoulli

The following algorithm is quite intuitive and is equivalent to the inverse-transform method (if the roles of U and $1 - U$ are reversed):

1. Generate $U \sim U(0,1)$.
2. If $U \leq p$, return $X = 1$. Otherwise, return $X = 0$.

8.4.2 Discrete Uniform

Again, the straightforward intuitive algorithm given below is (exactly) the inverse-transform method:

1. Generate $U \sim U(0,1)$.
2. Return $X = i + \lfloor (j - i + 1)U \rfloor$.

Note that no search is required. The constant $j - i + 1$ should, of course, be computed ahead of time and stored.

8.4.3 Arbitrary Discrete Distribution

Consider the very general situation where we have *any* probability mass function $p(0)$, $p(1)$, $p(2)$, ... on the nonnegative integers S, and we want to generate a discrete random variate X with the corresponding distribution. The $p(i)$'s could have been specified theoretically by some distributional form or empirically from a data set directly. The case of finite range S_n is included here by setting $p(i) = 0$ for all $i \geq n + 1$. (Note that this formulation includes *every* special discrete distribution form.)

The direct inverse-transform method, for either the finite- or infinite-range case, is as follows (define the empty sum to be 0):

1. Generate $U \sim U(0,1)$.
2. Return the nonnegative integer $X = I$ satisfying

$$\sum_{j=0}^{I-1} p(j) \leq U < \sum_{j=0}^{I} p(j)$$

Note that this algorithm will never return a value $X = i$ for which $p(i) = 0$, since the strict inequality between the two summations in step 2 would be impossible. Step 2 does require a search, which may be time-consuming. As an alternative, we could initially sort the $p(i)$'s into decreasing order so that the search would be likely to terminate after a smaller number of comparisons; see Prob. 8.2 for an example.

Due to the generality of the present situation, we present three other methods that are useful when the desired random variable has *finite* range S_n. The first of these methods assumes that each $p(i)$ is exactly equal to a q-place decimal; for exposition we take the case $q = 2$, so that $p(i)$ is of the form $0.01k_i$ for some integer $k_i \in \{0,1,\ldots,100\}$ ($i = 0,1,\ldots,n$), and $\sum_{i=0}^{n} k_i = 100$. We initialize a vector $(m_1, m_2, \ldots, m_{100})$ by setting the first k_0 m_j's to 0, the next k_1 m_j's to 1, etc., and the last k_n m_j's to n. (If $k_i = 0$ for some i, no m_j's are set to i.)

Then an algorithm for generating the desired random variate X is as follows:

1. Generate $J \sim \mathrm{DU}(1,100)$.
2. Return $X = m_J$.

(See Sec. 8.4.2 to accomplish step 1.) Note that this method requires 10^q extra storage locations and an array reference in step 2; it *is*, however, the inverse-transform method provided that J is generated by the algorithm in Sec. 8.4.2. If three or four decimal places are needed to specify the $p(i)$'s exactly, the value 100 in step 1 would be replaced by 1000 or 10,000, respectively, and the storage requirements would also grow by one or two orders of magnitude. Even if the $p(i)$'s are not *exactly* q-place decimals for some small value of q, the analyst might be able to obtain sufficient accuracy by rounding the $p(i)$'s to the nearest hundredth or thousandth; this is an attractive alternative especially when the $p(i)$'s are proportions obtained directly from data, and may not be accurate beyond two or three decimal places anyway. When rounding the $p(i)$'s, however, it is important to remember that they must sum exactly to 1.

The above idea is certainly fast, but it could require large tables if we need high precision in the probabilities. Marsaglia (1963) proposed another kind of table-based algorithm requiring less storage and only slightly more time. For example, consider the distribution

$$p(0) = 0.15, \quad p(1) = 0.20, \quad p(2) = 0.37, \quad p(3) = 0.28$$

Then the idea of the preceding paragraph would require a vector of length 100 to store 15 0's, 20 1's, 37 2's, and 28 3's. Instead, define *two* vectors—one for the "tenths" place and the other for the "hundredths" place. To fill up the tenths vector, look only at the tenths place in the probabilities, and put in that many copies of the associated i (for $i = 0, 1, 2, 3$), so we would take one 0, two 1's, three 2's, and two 3's to get

$$0\,1\,1\,2\,2\,2\,3\,3$$

Similarly, the hundredths vector is

$$0\,0\,0\,0\,0\,2\,2\,2\,2\,2\,2\,3\,3\,3\,3\,3\,3\,3\,3$$

corresponding to the hundredths place in the probabilities; thus, there are 28 storage locations in all (as opposed to 100 for the earlier table method). To generate an X, pick the tenths vector with probability equal to one-tenth the sum of the digits in the probabilities' tenths places, i.e., with probability

$$\frac{1 + 2 + 3 + 2}{10} = 0.8$$

and then choose one of the eight members of the tenths vector at random (equiprobably) as the returned X. On the other hand, we choose the hundredths vector with probability equal to $1/100$ of the sum of the digits in the hundredths' place in the original probabilities, i.e., with probability

$$\frac{5 + 0 + 7 + 8}{100} = 0.20$$

and then choose one of the 20 entries in the hundredths vector at random to return as the value of X. It is easy to see that this method is valid; for example,

$$P(X = 2) = P(X = 2 | \text{choose tenths vector}) \, P(\text{choose tenths vector})$$

$$+ \, P(X = 2 | \text{choose hundredths vector}) \, P(\text{choose hundredths vector})$$

$$= \tfrac{3}{8}(0.8) + \tfrac{7}{20}(0.20)$$

$$= 0.37$$

as required. The storage advantage of Marsaglia's tables becomes more marked as the number of decimal places in the probabilities increases; in his original example there were three-place decimals, so the direct table method of the preceding paragraph would require 1000 storage locations; the three vectors (tenths, hundredths, and thousandths) in this example required only 91 locations.

The third attractive technique to use when X has range S_n is the alias method mentioned earlier. The method requires that we initally calculate two arrays of length $n + 1$ each, from the given $p(i)$'s. The first array contains what are called the *cutoff values* $F_i \in [0,1]$ for $i = 0, 1, \ldots, n$, and the second array gives the *aliases* $L_i \in S_n$ for $i = 0, 1, \ldots, n$; two algorithms for computing valid cutoff values and aliases from the $p(i)$'s are given in App. 8B. (The cutoff values and aliases are not unique, and indeed the two algorithms in App. 8B may produce different results for the same distribution; both will result in a valid variate-generation algorithm, however.) Then the alias method is as follows:

1. Generate $I \sim DU(0,n)$ and $U \sim U(0,1)$ independent of I.
2. If $U \leq F_I$, return $X = I$. Otherwise, return $X = L_I$.

Thus, step 2 involves a kind of "rejection," but upon rejecting I we need *not* start over but only return I's alias, L_I, rather than I itself. The cutoff values are seen to be the probabilities with which we return I rather than its alias. There is only one comparison needed to generate each X, and we need exactly two random numbers for each X if I is generated as in Sec. 8.4.2. (See Prob. 8.17 for a way to accomplish step 1 with only *one* random number.) Although the setup is not complicated, storing the cutoffs and aliases does require $2(n + 1)$ extra storage locations; Kronmal and Peterson (1979) discuss a way to cut the storage in half (see Prob. 8.18). In any case, storage is of order n, which is regarded as the principal weakness of the alias method if n could be very large.

Example 8.12. Consider a random variable on $S_3 = \{0,1,2,3\}$ with probability mass function $p(0) = 0.1$, $p(1) = 0.4$, $p(2) = 0.2$, and $p(3) = 0.3$. Applying the first algorithm in App. 8B leads to the following setup:

i	0	1	2	3
$p(i)$	0.1	0.4	0.2	0.3
F_i	0.4	0.0	0.8	0.0
L_i	1	1	3	3

For instance, if step 1 of the algorithm produces $I = 2$, the probability is $F_2 = 0.8$ that we would keep $X = I = 2$, and with probability $1 - F_2 = 0.2$ we would return $X = L_2 = 3$ instead. Thus, since 2 is not the alias of anything else (i.e., none of the other L_i's is equal to 2), the algorithm returns $X = 2$ if and only if $I = 2$ in step 1 and $U \leq 0.8$ in step 2, so that

$$P(X = 2) = P(I = 2 \text{ and } U \leq 0.8)$$
$$= P(I = 2)P(U \leq 0.8)$$
$$= 0.25 \times 0.8$$
$$= 0.2$$

which is equal to $p(2)$, as desired. (The second equality in the above follows since U and I are generated independently.) On the other hand, the algorithm can return $X = 3$ in two different (and mutually exclusive) ways: If $I = 3$, then since $F_3 = 0$ we will always return $X = L_3 = 3$; and if $I = 2$ we will return $X = L_2 = 3$ with probability $1 - F_2 = 0.2$. Thus,

$$P(X = 3) = P(I = 3) + P(I = 2 \text{ and } U > F_2)$$
$$= 0.25 + (0.25 \times 0.2)$$
$$= 0.3$$

which is $p(3)$. The reader is encouraged to verify that the algorithm is correct for $i = 0$ and 1 as well. Figure 8.13 illustrates the method's rationale. Figure 8.13a shows bars whose (total) height is $1/(n + 1) = 0.25$, and thus is the probability mass function of I generated in step 1. The shaded areas in the bars represent the probability mass that is moved by the method, and the number in each shaded area is the value L_i that will be returned as X. Thus, if step 1 generates $I = 0$, there is a probability of $1 - F_0 = 0.6$ that this I will be changed into its alias, $L_0 = 1$, for the returned X; the shaded area in the bar above 0 is of height $0.6 \times 0.25 = 0.15$, or 60 percent of that bar. Similarly, the fraction $1 - F_2 = 0.2$ of the 0.25-high bar (resulting in a shaded area of height $0.2 \times 0.25 = 0.05$) above 2 represents the chance that a generated $I = 2$ will be changed into $X = L_2 = 3$. Note that the entire bars above 1 and 3 are shaded, since F_1 and F_3 are both zero; however, the indicated values are their own aliases, so they do not really get moved. Figure 8.13b shows the probability mass function of the returned X after the shaded areas (probabilities) are moved to their destination values, and it is seen to equal the desired probabilities $p(i)$.

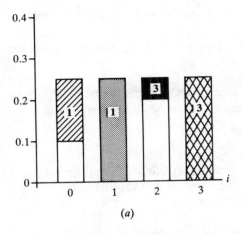

(a)

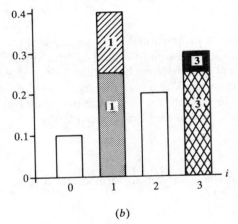

(b)

FIGURE 8.13
Setup for the alias method in Example 8.12.

Although the alias method is limited to discrete random variables with a finite range, it can be used indirectly for discrete distributions with an infinite range, such as the geometric, negative binomial, or Poisson, by combining it with the general composition method. For example, if X can be any nonnegative integer, we can examine the $p(i)$'s to find an n such that $q = \sum_{i=0}^{n} p(i)$ is close to 1, so that the probability is high that $X \in S_n$. Since for any i we can write

$$p(i) = q\left[\frac{p(i)}{q} I_{S_n}(i)\right] + (1-q)\left\{\frac{p(i)}{1-q}[1 - I_{S_n}(i)]\right\}$$

we obtain the following general algorithm:

1. Generate $U \sim U(0,1)$. If $U \leq q$, go to step 2. Otherwise, go to step 3.

2. Use the alias method to return X on S_n with probability mass function $p(i)/q$ for $i = 0, 1, \ldots, n$.
3. Use any other method to return X on $\{n+1, n+2,\ldots\}$ with probability mass function $p(i)/(1-q)$ for $i = n+1, n+2, \ldots$.

In step 3, we could use the inverse-transform method, for example. Since n was chosen to make q close to 1, we would expect to avoid step 3 most of the time.

8.4.4 Binomial

To generate a bin(t, p) random variate, recall from Sec. 6.2.3 that the sum of t IID Bernoulli(p) random variables has the bin(t, p) distribution. This relation leads to the following convolution algorithm:

1. Generate $Y_1, Y_2, \ldots, Y_t$ as IID Bernoulli(p) random variates.
2. Return $X = Y_1 + Y_2 + \cdots + Y_t$.

Since the execution time of this algorithm is proportional to t, we might want to look for an alternative if t is large. One possibility would be the direct inverse-transform method with an efficient search. Another alternative is the alias method (see Sec. 8.4.3), since the range of X is finite. Finally, algorithms specific to the binomial distribution that are efficient for large t are discussed by Ahrens and Dieter (1974) and Kachitvichyanukul and Schmeiser (1988).

8.4.5 Geometric

The following algorithm is equivalent to the inverse-transform method if we replace U by $1 - U$ in step 2 (see Prob. 8.14):

1. Generate $U \sim U(0,1)$.
2. Return $X = \lfloor \ln U / \ln(1-p) \rfloor$.

The constant $\ln(1-p)$ should, of course, be computed beforehand. If p is near 0, $\ln(1-p)$ will also be near zero, so that double-precision arithmetic should be considered to avoid excessive roundoff error in the division in step 2. For p near 1, $\ln(1-p)$ will be a large negative number, which also could cause numerical difficulties; fortunately, for large p it is more efficient to use an altogether different algorithm based on the relationship between geometric and Bernoulli random variables described in Sec. 6.2.3 (see Prob. 8.14).

8.4.6 Negative Binomial

The relation between the negbin(s, p) and geom(p) distributions in Sec. 6.2.3 leads to the following convolution algorithm:

1. Generate $Y_1, Y_2, \ldots, Y_s$ as IID geom(p) random variates.
2. Return $X = Y_1 + Y_2 + \cdots + Y_s$.

This is simple, but its execution time is proportional to s. For large s, consideration might be given to an alternative method discussed in Fishman (1978), which makes use of a special relationship between the negative binomial, gamma, and Poisson distributions; its efficiency depends on the ability to generate rapidly from the gamma and Poisson distributions. Other alternatives are discussed in Ahrens and Dieter (1974).

8.4.7 Poisson

Our algorithm for generating Poisson(λ) random variates is based essentially on the relationship between the Poisson(λ) and expo($1/\lambda$) distributions stated in Sec. 6.2.3. The algorithm is as follows:

1. Let $a = e^{-\lambda}$, $b = 1$, and $i = 0$.
2. Generate $U_{i+1} \sim U(0,1)$ and replace b by bU_{i+1}. If $b < a$, return $X = i$. Otherwise, go to step 3.
3. Replace i by $i + 1$ and go back to step 2.

The algorithm is justified by noting that $X = i$ if and only if

$$\sum_{j=1}^{i} Y_j \leq 1 < \sum_{j=1}^{i+1} Y_j$$

where $Y_j = (-1/\lambda) \ln U_j \sim$ expo($1/\lambda$) and the Y_j's are independent. That is, $X = \max\{i : \sum_{j=1}^{i} Y_j \leq 1\}$, so that $X \sim$ Poisson(λ) by the first comment in the description of the Poisson distribution in Table 6.4.

Unfortunately, this algorithm becomes slow as λ increases, since a large λ means that $a = e^{-\lambda}$ is smaller, requiring more executions of step 2 to bring the cumulative product of the U_{i+1}'s down under a. [In fact, since X is 1 less than the number of U_{i+1}'s required, the expected number of executions of step 2 is $E(X) + 1 = \lambda + 1$, so that execution time grows with λ in an essentially linear fashion.] One alternative would be to use the alias method in concert with the composition approach (since the range of X is infinite), as described in Sec. 8.4.3. Another possibility would be the inverse-transform method with an efficient search. Atkinson (1979b, 1979c) examined several such search procedures and reported that an indexed search similar to the method of Chen and Asau (1974), discussed earlier in Sec. 8.3.12, performed well. (This search procedure, called PQM by Atkinson, requires a small amount of setup and extra storage but is still quite simple to implement.) Other fast methods of generating Poisson variates are given by Devroye (1981) and by Schmeiser and Kachitvichyanukul (1981).

8.5 GENERATING CORRELATED RANDOM VARIATES

So far in this chapter we have really considered generation of only a single random variate at a time from various *univariate distributions*. Applying one of these algorithms repeatedly with independent sets of random numbers produces a sequence of IID random variates from the desired distribution. In some simulation models, however, we may want to generate a random *vector* $\mathbf{X} = (X_1, X_2, \ldots, X_k)^T$ from a specified *joint* (or *multivariate*) *distribution*, where the individual components of the vector might not be independent. (A^T denotes the transpose of a vector or matrix A.) Even if we cannot specify the exact, full joint distribution of $X_1, X_2, \ldots, X_n$, we might want to generate them so that the individual X_i's have specified univariate distributions (called the *marginal distributions* of the X_i's) and so that the correlations, ρ_{ij}, between X_i and X_j are specified by the modeler. In this section we give examples of methods for generating such correlated random variates in some specific cases. There are several other problems related to generating correlated random variates that we do not discuss explicitly, e.g., simulating autoregressive processes and generating from a multivariate exponential distribution; we refer the reader to Johnson (1987), Johnson, Wang, and Ramberg (1984), Fishman (1973, 1978), Mitchell and Paulson (1979), and Marshall and Olkin (1967).

It is easy to think of models where correlated random variates would be appropriate. For example, consider a maintenance shop that can be modeled as a tandem queue with two service stations. At the first station, incoming items are inspected, and any defects are marked for repair at the second station. Since a badly damaged item would require more time for *both* inspection *and* repair, we would expect the two service times for a given item to be positively correlated. Mitchell, Paulson, and Beswick (1977) found that ignoring this correlation in modeling a system can lead to serious inaccuracies in the results of a simulation, underscoring the need to be able to generate correlated random variates.

8.5.1 Using Conditional Distributions

Suppose that we have a fully specified joint distribution function $F_{X_1, X_2, \ldots, X_n}(x_1, x_2, \ldots, x_n)$ from which we would like to generate a random vector $\mathbf{X} = (X_1, X_2, \ldots, X_n)^T$. Also assume that for $k = 2, 3, \ldots, n$ we can obtain the *conditional distribution* of X_k given that $X_i = x_i$ for $i = 1, 2, \ldots, k-1$; denote the conditional distribution function by $F_k(x_k \mid x_1, x_2, \ldots, x_{k-1})$. [See any probability text, such as Mood, Graybill, and Boes (1974, chap. IV) or Ross (1989, chap. 3) for a discussion of conditional distributions.] In addition, let $F_{X_i}(x_i)$ be the marginal distribution function of X_i for $i = 1, 2, \ldots, n$. Then a general algorithm for generating a random vector $\mathbf{X}$ with joint distribution function $F_{X_1, X_2, \ldots, X_n}$ is as follows:

1. Generate X_1 with distribution function F_{X_1}.
2. Generate X_2 with distribution function $F_2(\cdot \mid X_1)$.
3. Generate X_3 with distribution function $F_3(\cdot \mid X_1, X_2)$.

$\vdots$

n. Generate X_n with distribution function $F_n(\cdot \mid X_1, X_2, \ldots, X_{n-1})$.
$n+1$. Return $\mathbf{X} = (X_1, X_2, \ldots, X_n)^T$.

Note that in steps 2 through n the conditional distributions used are those with the previously generated X_i's; for example, if x_1 is the value generated for X_1 in step 1, the conditional distribution function used in step 2 is $F_2(\cdot \mid x_1)$, etc. Proof of the validity of this algorithm relies on the definition of conditional distributions and is left to the reader.

As general as this approach may be, its practical utility is probably quite limited. Not only is specification of the entire joint distribution required, but also derivation of all the required marginal and conditional distributions must be carried out. Such a level of detail is probably rarely obtainable in a complicated simulation.

8.5.2   Multivariate Normal and Multivariate Lognormal

The n-dimensional multivariate normal distribution with mean vector $\boldsymbol{\mu} = (\mu_1, \mu_2, \ldots, \mu_n)^T$ and covariance matrix Σ, where the (i,j)th entry is σ_{ij}, has joint density function

$$f(\mathbf{x}) = (2\pi)^{-n/2} |\Sigma|^{-1/2} \exp\left[\frac{-(\mathbf{x} - \boldsymbol{\mu})^T \Sigma^{-1} (\mathbf{x} - \boldsymbol{\mu})}{2} \right]$$

where $\mathbf{x} = (x_1, x_2, \ldots, x_n)^T$ is any point in n-dimensional real space and $|\Sigma|$ is the determinant of Σ. We denote this joint distribution as $N_n(\boldsymbol{\mu}, \Sigma)$ and note that if $\mathbf{X} = (X_1, X_2, \ldots, X_n)^T \sim N_n(\boldsymbol{\mu}, \Sigma)$, then $E(X_i) = \mu_i$ and $\text{Cov}(X_i, X_j) = \sigma_{ij} = \sigma_{ji}$; that is, Σ is symmetric and is positive definite.

Although the conditional-distribution approach of Sec. 8.5.1 can be applied, a simpler method due to Scheuer and Stoller (1962) is available, which uses a special property of the multivariate normal distribution. Since Σ is symmetric and positive definite, we can factor it uniquely as $\Sigma = CC^T$, where the $n \times n$ matrix C is lower triangular. [See, for example, Fishman (1973, p. 217) for an algorithm to compute C; the IMSL (1987, pp. 1144–1146) FORTRAN routine CHFAC also does this factorization.] If c_{ij} is the (i,j)th element of C, an algorithm for generating the desired multivariate normal vector $\mathbf{X}$ is as follows:

1. Generate $Z_1, Z_2, \ldots, Z_n$ as IID $N(0,1)$ random variates.
2. For $i = 1, 2, \ldots, n$, let $X_i = \mu_i + \Sigma_{j=1}^{i} c_{ij} Z_j$ and return $\mathbf{X} = (X_1, X_2, \ldots, X_n)^T$.

To accomplish the univariate normal generation in step 1, see Sec. 8.3.6. In matrix notation, if we let $\mathbf{Z} = (Z_1, Z_2, ..., Z_n)^T$, the algorithm is just $\mathbf{X} = \boldsymbol{\mu} + \mathbf{CZ}$; note the similarity with the transformation $X' = \mu + \sigma X$ for generating $X' \sim N(\mu, \sigma^2)$ given $X \sim N(0,1)$.

For a discussion of generating a random vector from a multivariate lognormal distribution, see Johnson and Ramberg (1978).

8.5.3 Correlated Gamma Random Variates

We now come to a case where we cannot write the entire joint distribution but only specify the marginal distributions (gamma) and the correlations between the component random variables of the $\mathbf{X}$ vector. Indeed, there is not even agreement about what the "multivariate gamma" distribution should be. Unlike the multivariate normal case, specification of the marginal distributions and the correlation matrix does *not* completely determine the joint distribution here.

The problem, then, is as follows. For a given set of shape parameters $\alpha_1, \alpha_2, ..., \alpha_n$, scale parameters $\beta_1, \beta_2, ..., \beta_n$, and correlations $\rho_{ij}(i = 1, 2, ..., n; \; j = 1, 2, ..., n)$ we want to generate a random vector $\mathbf{X} = (X_1, X_2, ..., X_n)^T$ so that $X_i \sim \text{gamma}(\alpha_i, \beta_i)$ and $\text{Cor}(X_i, X_j) = \rho_{ij}$. An immediate difficulty is that not all ρ_{ij} values between -1 and $+1$ are theoretically consistent with a given set of α_i's; that is, the α_i's place a limitation on the possible ρ_{ij}'s [see Schmeiser and Lal (1982)]. The next difficulty is that, even for a set of α_i's and ρ_{ij}'s that *are* theoretically possible, there might not be an algorithm that will do the job. For this reason, we must be content at present with generating correlated gamma random variates in some restricted cases.

One situation in which there *is* a simple algorithm is the bivariate case, $n = 2$. A further restriction is that $\rho = \rho_{12} \geq 0$, that is, positive correlation, and yet another restriction is that $\rho \leq \min\{\alpha_1, \alpha_2\}/\sqrt{\alpha_1 \alpha_2}$. Nevertheless, this does include many useful situations, especially when α_1 and α_2 are close together. (If $\alpha_1 = \alpha_2$, the upper bound on ρ is removed.) Notice that any two positively correlated exponential random variates are included by setting $\alpha_1 = \alpha_2 = 1$. The algorithm, using a general technique developed by Arnold (1967), relies on a special property of gamma distributions:

1. Generate $Y_1 \sim \text{gamma}(\alpha_1 - \rho\sqrt{\alpha_1 \alpha_2}, 1)$.
2. Generate $Y_2 \sim \text{gamma}(\alpha_2 - \rho\sqrt{\alpha_1 \alpha_2}, 1)$, independent of Y_1.
3. Generate $Y_3 \sim \text{gamma}(\rho\sqrt{\alpha_1 \alpha_2}, 1)$, independent of Y_1 and Y_2.
4. Return $X_1 = \beta_1(Y_1 + Y_3)$ and $X_2 = \beta_2(Y_2 + Y_3)$.

This technique is known as *trivariate reduction*, since the three random variates Y_1, Y_2, and Y_3 are "reduced" to the two final random variates X_1 and X_2. Note that the algorithm does not control the joint distribution of X_1 and X_2; this point is addressed by Schmeiser and Lal (1982).

Correlated gamma random variates can also be generated in some less restrictive cases. Schmeiser and Lal (1982) give algorithms for generating bivariate gamma random vectors with any theoretically possible correlation, either positive or negative. Ronning (1977) treats the general multivariate case ($n \geq 2$) but again restricts consideration to certain positive correlations. Lewis (1983) gives a method for generating negatively correlated gamma variates that have the same shape and scale parameters.

8.6 GENERATING ARRIVAL PROCESSES

In this section, we show how to generate the times of arrival $t_1, t_2, \ldots$ for the arrival processes discussed in Sec. 6.10.

8.6.1 Poisson Processes

The (stationary) Poisson process with rate $\lambda > 0$, discussed in Sec. 6.10.1, has the property that the interarrival times $A_i = t_i - t_{i-1}$ (where $i = 1,2,\ldots$) are IID exponential random variables with common mean $1/\lambda$. Thus, we can generate the t_i's recursively, as follows (assume that t_{i-1} has been determined and we want to generate the next arrival time, t_i):

1. Generate $U \sim U(0,1)$ independent of any previous random variates.
2. Return $t_i = t_{i-1} - (1/\lambda) \ln U$.

The recursion starts by computing t_1 (recall that $t_0 = 0$).

This algorithm can be easily modified to generate any arrival process where the interarrival times are IID random variables, whether or not they are exponential. Step 2 would just add an independently generated interarrival time to t_{i-1} in order to get t_i; the form of step 2 as given above is simply a special case for exponential interarrival times.

8.6.2 Nonstationary Poisson Processes

We now discuss how to generate arrival times that follow a nonstationary Poisson process (see Sec. 6.10.2).

It is tempting to modify the algorithm of Sec. 8.6.1 to generate t_i given t_{i-1} by substituting $\lambda(t_{i-1})$ in step 2 for λ. However, this would be incorrect, as can be seen from Fig. 8.14. (This figure might represent traffic arrival rates at an intersection over a 24-hour day.) If $t_{i-1} = 5$, for example, this erroneous "algorithm" would tend to generate a large interarrival time before t_i, since $\lambda(5)$ is low compared with $\lambda(t)$ for t between 6 and 9. Thus, we would miss this upcoming rise in the arrival rate and would not generate the high traffic density associated with the morning rush; indeed, if t_i turned out to be 11, we would miss the morning rush altogether. Kaminsky and Rumpf (1977) illustrate the danger in using other more sophisticated approximations.

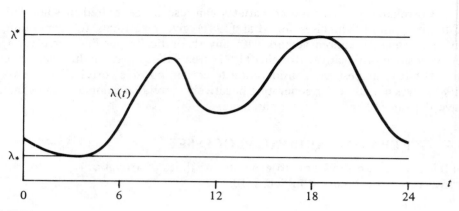

FIGURE 8.14
Nonstationary Poisson process.

Care must be taken, then, to generate a nonstationary Poisson process in a valid way. A general and simple method proposed by Lewis and Shedler (1979), known as *thinning*, can be used. We present a special case of the thinning algorithm that works when $\lambda^* = \max_t\{\lambda(t)\}$ is finite. Briefly, we generate a stationary Poisson process with constant rate λ^* and arrival times $\{t_i^*\}$ (using, for example, the algorithm of Sec. 8.6.1), then "thin out" the t_i^*'s by throwing away (rejecting) each t_i^* as an arrival with probability $1 - \lambda(t_i^*)/\lambda^*$. Thus, we are more likely to accept t_i^* as an arrival if $\lambda(t_i^*)$ is high, yielding the desired property that arrivals will occur more frequently in intervals for which $\lambda(t)$ is high. An equivalent algorithm, in a more convenient recursive form, is as follows (again we assume that t_{i-1} has been validly generated and we want to generate the next arrival time t_i):

1. Set $t = t_{i-1}$.
2. Generate U_1 and U_2 as IID U(0,1) independent of any previous random variates.
3. Replace t by $t - (1/\lambda^*) \ln U_1$.
4. If $U_2 \leq \lambda(t)/\lambda^*$, return $t_i = t$. Otherwise, go back to step 2.

(Once again the algorithm is started by computing t_1.) If the evaluation of $\lambda(t)$ is slow [which might be the case if, for example, $\lambda(t)$ is a complicated function involving exponential and trigonometric calculations], computation time might be saved in step 4 by adding an acceptance pretest; i.e., the current value for t is automatically accepted as the next arrival time if $U_2 \leq \lambda_*/\lambda^*$, where $\lambda_* = \min_t\{\lambda(t)\}$. This would be useful especially when $\lambda(t)$ is fairly flat.

> **Example 8.13.** Recall Example 6.21, where $\lambda(t)$ was specified empirically from data to be the piecewise-constant function plotted in Fig. 6.47. This rate function is plotted again in Fig. 8.15, along with $\lambda_* = 0.09$ and $\lambda^* = 0.84$ as indicated.

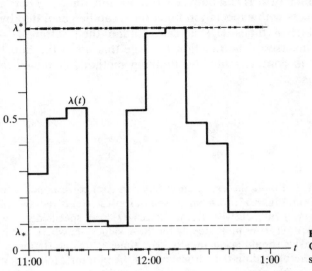

FIGURE 8.15
Generating a nonstationary Poisson process by thinning.

Values of $\{t_i^*\}$ from the stationary Poisson process at rate λ^* were generated (using stream 3 of the random-number generator in App. 7A), and are marked by the crosses on the λ^* line; these indeed appear to be distributed uniformly along the line, as would be expected. The t_i^*'s were then thinned out, as specified by the algorithm, and the "accepted" arrivals are marked with crosses on the t axis. As desired, these actual arrivals are few and far between when $\lambda(t)$ is low (e.g., between 11:30 and 11:50), since most of the t_i^*'s were thinned out. On the other hand, most t_i^*'s were retained as actual arrivals during peak arrival periods (e.g., 12:00 to 12:20). Note the similarity between Fig. 8.15 and Fig. 8.9, which exemplifies another "thinning" idea, the acceptance-rejection method for random-variate generation.

Although the thinning algorithm is simple, it might be inefficient in some cases. For example, if $\lambda(t)$ is relatively low except for a few high and narrow peaks, λ^* will be a lot larger than $\lambda(t)$ most of the time, resulting in thinning out most of the t_i^*'s. In such cases, a more general thinning algorithm with a nonconstant λ^* curve could be used [see Lewis and Shedler (1979)].

There is a different and older method, treated, for example, by Çinlar (1975, pp. 94–101), and is the analog of the inverse-transform method of random-variate generation, just as the thinning algorithm is analogous to the acceptance-rejection method for variate generation. Recall from Sec. 6.10.2 that the expectation function is

$$\Lambda(t) = \int_0^t \lambda(y)\, dy$$

which will always be a continuous function of t, since it is an indefinite integral;

$\Lambda(t)$ is the expected number of arrivals between time 0 and time t. Then a nonstationary Poisson process with expectation function Λ can be generated by first generating Poisson arrival times $\{t_i'\}$ at rate 1, and then setting $t_i = \Lambda^{-1}(t_i')$, where Λ^{-1} is the inverse of the function Λ. Note that *all* of the rate 1 arrival times t_i' are used, in contrast with the thinning method. A recursive version of this algorithm is:

1. Generate $U \sim U(0,1)$.
2. Set $t_i' = t_{i-1}' - \ln U$.
3. Return $t_i = \Lambda^{-1}(t_i')$.

> **Example 8.14.** Figure 8.16*a* plots the expectation function $\Lambda(t)$ corresponding to the rate function $\lambda(t)$ from Fig. 8.15; for comparison purposes, $\lambda(t)$ is redrawn in Fig. 8.16*b*. Note that $\Lambda(t)$ in piecewise linear, since $\lambda(t)$ was specified to be piecewise constant. Also, $\Lambda(t)$ rises most steeply for those values of t where $\lambda(t)$ is highest, i.e., where arrivals should occur rapidly. The times t_i' for the stationary rate 1 Poisson process are plotted on the vertical axis of the plot for $\Lambda(t)$, and do appear to be fairly uniformly spread. Following the dashed lines across to $\Lambda(t)$ and down (i.e., taking Λ^{-1} of the t_i''s) leads to the actual arrival times t_i, marked on the t axis of the plot. The concentration of the t_i's where $\lambda(t)$ is high [and $\Lambda(t)$ is steep, thus "catching" many t_i''s] seems evident, such as between 12:00 and 12:20, and the spreading out of the t_i's during the low-arrival period of 11:30 to 11:50 is also clear. Thus, applying Λ^{-1} to the uniformly spread t_i''s on the vertical axis has the effect of deforming their uniformity to agree with the nonstationarity of the arrival process, just as applying F^{-1} to the uniform U's in the inverse-transform variate-generation algorithm deformed them to agree with the density f. Indeed, there is a strong similarity between Figs. 8.16 and 8.3.

This second algorithm for generating a nonstationary Poisson process does, however, require inversion of Λ, which could be difficult. (In Example 8.14, this could be accomplished easily by a short search and linear interpolation, since Λ was piecewise linear.) This must be traded off against the "wasting" of generated t_i^*'s in the thinning algorithm. For more on comparison of these and other methods, see Lewis and Shedler (1979). Klein and Roberts (1984) give an efficient and explicit algorithm for the case of a piecewise-linear *rate* function λ, in which case the expectation function Λ is piecewise quadratic.

8.6.3 Batch Arrivals

Consider an arrival process where the ith batch of customers arrives at time t_i and the number of customers in this batch is a discrete random variable B_i. Assume that the B_i's are IID and, in addition, are independent of the t_i's. Then a general recursive algorithm for generating this arrival process is as follows:

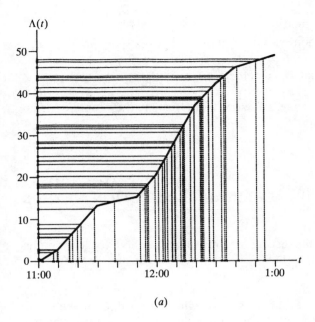

(a)

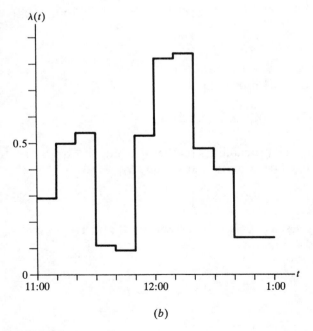

(b)

FIGURE 8.16
Generating a nonstationary Poisson process by inverting the expectation function: (a) $\Lambda(t)$ and generated arrival times; (b) $\lambda(t)$.

1. Generate the next arrival time t_i.

2. Generate the discrete random variate B_i independently of any previous B_j's and also independently of $t_1, t_2, \ldots, t_i$.

3. Return the information that B_i customers are arriving at time t_i.

Note that the arrival times $\{t_i\}$ are arbitrary; in particular, they could be from a nonstationary Poisson process.

APPENDIX 8A

VALIDITY OF THE ACCEPTANCE-REJECTION METHOD

We demonstrate here that the acceptance-rejection method for continuous random variables (Sec. 8.2.4) is valid by showing that for any x, $P(X \leq x) = \int_{-\infty}^{x} f(y)\, dy$.

Let A denote the event that acceptance occurs in step 3 of the algorithm. Now X is defined only on the event (or set) A, which is a *subset* of the entire space on which Y and U (of steps 1 and 2) are defined. Thus, *unconditional* probability statements about X alone are really *conditional* probability statements (conditioned on A) about Y and U. Since, given that A occurs we have $X = Y$, we can write

$$P(X \leq x) = P(Y \leq x \,|\, A) \tag{8.1}$$

We shall evaluate the right side of Eq. (8.1) directly.

By the definition of conditional probability,

$$P(Y \leq x \,|\, A) = \frac{P(A, Y \leq x)}{P(A)} \tag{8.2}$$

We shall solve explicitly for the two probabilities on the right side of Eq. (8.2). To do this, it will be convenient first to note that for any y,

$$P(A \,|\, Y = y) = P\left[U \leq \frac{f(y)}{t(y)} \right] = \frac{f(y)}{t(y)} \tag{8.3}$$

where the first equality follows since U is independent of Y and the second equality since $U \sim U(0,1)$ and $f(y) \leq t(y)$.

We now use Eq. (8.3) to show that

$$
\begin{aligned}
P(A, Y \leq x) &= \int_{-\infty}^{x} P(A, Y \leq x \,|\, Y = y) r(y)\, dy \\
&= \int_{-\infty}^{x} P(A \,|\, Y = y) \frac{t(y)}{c}\, dy \\
&= \frac{1}{c} \int_{-\infty}^{x} f(y)\, dy
\end{aligned}
\tag{8.4}
$$

Next, we note that $P(A) = \int_{-\infty}^{\infty} P(A \mid Y = y) r(y)\, dy = 1/c$ [by Eq. (8.3) and the fact that f is a density, so integrates to 1]. This, together with Eqs. (8.4), (8.2), and (8.1), yields the desired result.

APPENDIX 8B
SETUP FOR THE ALIAS METHOD

There are at least two different algorithms for computing the cutoff values F_i and the aliases L_i in the setup for the alias method in Sec. 8.4.3; they do not in general lead to the same sets of cutoff values and aliases for a given distribution, but both will be valid. Originally, Walker (1977) gave the following algorithm in an explicit FORTRAN program:

1. Set $L_i = i$, $F_i = 0$, and $b_i = p(i) - 1/(n+1)$, for $i = 0, 1, \ldots, n$.
2. For $i = 0, 1, \ldots, n$, do the following steps:
   a. Let $c = \min\{b_0, b_1, \ldots, b_n\}$ and let k be the index of this minimal b_j. (Ties can be broken arbitrarily.)
   b. Let $d = \max\{b_0, b_1, \ldots, b_n\}$ and let m be the index of this maximal b_j. (Ties can be broken arbitrarily.)
   c. If $\sum_{j=0}^{n} |b_j| < \epsilon$, stop the algorithm.
   d. Let $L_k = m$, $F_k = 1 + c(n+1)$, $b_k = 0$, and $b_m = c + d$.

Note that if the condition in step 2c is satisfied at some point, the rest of the range of i in step 2 will not be completed. This condition in step 2c should theoretically be for equality of the summation to 0, but insisting on this could cause numerical difficulties in floating-point arithmetic; in the above, ϵ is a small positive number such as 10^{-5}.

While the above algorithm is easy to implement in any programming language, Kronmal and Peterson (1979) gave a more efficient algorithm using set operations:

1. Set $F_i = (n+1)\, p(i)$ for $i = 0, 1, \ldots, n$.
2. Define the sets $G = \{i: F_i \geq 1\}$ and $S = \{i: F_i < 1\}$.
3. Do the following steps until S becomes empty:
   a. Remove an element k from G and remove an element m from S.
   b. Set $L_m = k$ and replace F_k by $F_k - 1 + F_m$.
   c. If $F_k < 1$, put k into S; otherwise, put k back into G.

This algorithm will leave at least one L_i undefined, but the corresponding F_i values will be equal to 1, so these aliases will never be used in the variate-generation algorithm. Implementing the sets G and S in this second algorithm could be accomplished in many ways, such as a simple push/pop stack, by using a linked-list structure like SIMLIB in Chap. 2, or directly in a language such as Pascal with facilities for set operations.

The second algorithm is more efficient, since in the first algorithm steps 2a and 2b each require a search of $n + 1$ elements, while no such search is required in the second algorithm; this could be important if n is large. However, we should note that numerical difficulties can occur in the second algorithm if the $p(i)$'s do not sum *exactly* to 1; this could occur if, for instance, the $p(i)$'s are proportions corresponding to frequency counts from data, complete with roundoff error. We experienced failure of the second algorithm (using several different set implementations) when the sum of the $p(i)$'s differed from 1 by as little as 10^{-5}.

PROBLEMS

8.1. Give algorithms for generating random variates with the following densities:
   (a) Cauchy

$$f(x) = \left\{ \pi\beta \left[1 + \left(\frac{x - \alpha}{\beta} \right)^2 \right] \right\}^{-1} \qquad \text{where } -\infty < \alpha < \infty, \quad \beta > 0, \quad -\infty < x < \infty$$

   (b) Gumbel (or extreme value)

$$f(x) = \frac{1}{\beta} \exp\left[-e^{-(x-\alpha)/\beta} - (x - \alpha)/\beta \right] \qquad \text{where } -\infty < \alpha < \infty, \quad \beta > 0$$

$$-\infty < x < \infty$$

   (c) Logistic

$$f(x) = \frac{(1/\beta)e^{-(x-\alpha)/\beta}}{(1 + e^{-(x-\alpha)/\beta})^2} \qquad \text{where } -\infty < \alpha < \infty, \quad \beta > 0, \quad -\infty < x < \infty$$

   (d) Pareto

$$f(x) = \frac{\alpha_2 c^{\alpha_2}}{x^{\alpha_2 + 1}} \qquad \text{where } c > 0, \quad \alpha_2 > 0, \quad x > c$$

   For $\alpha = 0$ and $\beta = 1$ in each of (a), (b), and (c), use your algorithms to generate IID random variates $X_1, X_2, \ldots, X_{5000}$ and write out $\bar{X}(n) = \sum_{i=1}^{n} X_i/n$ for $n = 50, 100, 150, \ldots, 5000$ to verify empirically the strong law of large numbers (Sec. 4.6), i.e., that $\bar{X}(n)$ converges to $E(X_i)$ (if it exists); do the same for (d) with $c = 1$ and $\alpha_2 = 2$.

8.2. Let X be discrete with probability mass function $p(1) = 0.05$, $p(2) = 0.05$, $p(3) = 0.1$, $p(4) = 0.1$, $p(5) = 0.6$, and $p(6) = 0.1$, and for $i = 1, 2, \ldots, 6$, let $q(i) = p(1) + p(2) + \cdots + p(i)$. Convince yourself that the following algorithm is explicitly the discrete inverse-transform method with a simple left-to-right search:

1. Generate $U \sim U(0,1)$ and set $i = 1$.
2. If $U \leq q(i)$, return $X = i$. Otherwise, go to step 3.
3. Replace i by $i + 1$ and go back to step 2.

Let N be the number of times step 2 is executed (so that N is also the number of comparisons). Show that N has the same distribution as X, so $E(N) = E(X) = 4.45$. This algorithm can be represented as in Fig. 8.17a, where the circled numbers are the values to which X is set if U falls in the interval directly below them and the search is left-to-right.

Alternatively, we could first sort the $p(i)$'s into decreasing order and form a *coding vector* $i'(i)$, as follows. Let $q'(1) = 0.6$, $q'(2) = 0.7$, $q'(3) = 0.8$, $q'(4) = 0.9$, $q'(5) = 0.95$, and $q'(6) = 1$; also let $i'(1) = 5$, $i'(2) = 3$, $i'(3) = 4$, $i'(4) = 6$, $i'(5) = 1$, and $i'(6) = 2$. Show that the following algorithm is valid:

1'. Generate $U \sim U(0,1)$ and set $i = 1$.
2'. If $U \le q'(i)$, return $X = i'(i)$. Otherwise, go to step 3'.
3'. Replace i by $i + 1$ and go back to step 2'.

If N' is the number of comparisons for this second algorithm, show that $E(N') = 2.05$, which is less than half of $E(N)$. This saving in marginal execution time will depend on the particular distribution and must be weighed against the extra setup time and storage for the coding vector $i'(i)$. This second algorithm can be represented as in Fig. 8.17b.

8.3. Recall the truncated distribution function F^* and the algorithm for generating from it, as given in Sec. 8.2.1.
 (*a*) Show that the algorithm stated in Sec. 8.2.1 is valid when F is continuous and strictly increasing.
 (*b*) Show that the following algorithm is also valid for generating X with distribution function F^* (assume again that F is continuous and strictly increasing):

1. Generate $U \sim U(0,1)$.
2. If $F(a) \le U \le F(b)$, return $X = F^{-1}(U)$. Otherwise, go back to step 1.

Which algorithm do you think is "better"? In what sense? Under what conditions?

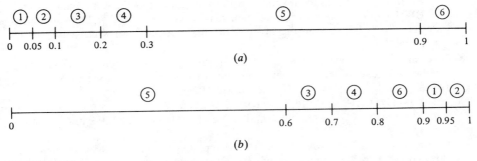

(*a*)

(*b*)

FIGURE 8.17
Representation of the two algorithms in Prob. 8.2.

8.4. A truncation of a distribution function F can be defined differently from the F^* of Sec. 8.2.1. Again for $a < b$, define the distribution function

$$\tilde{F}(x) = \begin{cases} 0 & \text{if } x < a \\ F(x) & \text{if } a \le x < b \\ 1 & \text{if } b \le x \end{cases}$$

Find a method for generating from the distribution function $\tilde{F}$, assuming that we already have a method for generating from F. Demonstrate the validity of your algorithm.

8.5. Show that the algorithm in Sec. 8.2.1 for generating the ith order statistic is valid when F is strictly increasing. [*Hint:* Use the fact that if $U_1, U_2, \ldots, U_n$ are IID $U(0,1)$, then $U_{(i)} \sim \text{beta}(i, n - i + 1)$.] Verify directly that for $i = 1$ and $i = n$ it is valid to let $V = 1 - U^{1/n}$ and $V = U^{1/n}$, respectively.

8.6. Derive the inverse-transform algorithm for the double-exponential distribution of Example 8.3 and compare it with the composition algorithm as given in the example. Which would you prefer?

8.7. For $a < b$, the *right-triangular distribution* has density function

$$f_R(x) = \begin{cases} \dfrac{2(x - a)}{(b - a)^2} & \text{if } a \le x \le b \\ 0 & \text{otherwise} \end{cases}$$

and the *left-triangular distribution* has density function

$$f_L(x) = \begin{cases} \dfrac{2(b - x)}{(b - a)^2} & \text{if } a \le x \le b \\ 0 & \text{otherwise} \end{cases}$$

These distributions are denoted by $\text{RT}(a,b)$ and $\text{LT}(a,b)$, respectively.
(*a*) Show that if $X \sim \text{RT}(0,1)$, then $X' = a + (b - a)X \sim \text{RT}(a,b)$; verify the same relation between $\text{LT}(0,1)$ and $\text{LT}(a,b)$. Thus it is sufficient to generate from $\text{RT}(0,1)$ and $\text{LT}(0,1)$.
(*b*) Show that if $X \sim \text{RT}(0,1)$, then $1 - X \sim \text{LT}(0,1)$. Thus it is enough to restrict our attention further to generating from $\text{RT}(0,1)$.
(*c*) Derive the inverse-transform algorithm for generating from $\text{RT}(0,1)$. Despite the result in (*b*), also derive the inverse-transform algorithm for generating directly from $\text{LT}(0,1)$.
(*d*) As an alternative to the inverse-transform method, show that if U_1 and U_2 are IID $U(0,1)$ random variables, then $\max\{U_1, U_2\} \sim \text{RT}(0,1)$. Do you think that this is better than the inverse-transform method? In what sense? (See Example 8.4.)

8.8. In each of the following cases, give an algorithm that uses exactly *one* random number for generating a random variate with the same distribution as X.
(*a*) $X = \min\{U_1, U_2\}$, where U_1 and U_2 are IID $U(0,1)$.
(*b*) $X = \max\{U_1, U_2\}$, where U_1 and U_2 are IID $U(0,1)$.
(*c*) $X = \min\{Y_1, Y_2\}$, where Y_1 and Y_2 and IID exponential with common mean β.

Compare (*a*) and (*b*) with Prob. 8.7. Compare your one-U algorithms in (*a*) through (*c*) with the direct ones of actually generating the U_i's or Y_i's and then taking the minimum or maximum.

8.9. The general acceptance-rejection method of Sec. 8.2.4 has the following discrete analog. Let X be discrete with probability mass function $p(x_i)$ for $i = 0, \pm 1, \pm 2, \ldots$, let the majorizing function be $t(x_i) \geq p(x_i)$ for all i, let $c = \sum_{i=-\infty}^{\infty} t(x_i)$, and let $r(x_i) = t(x_i)/c$ for $i = 0, \pm 1, \pm 2, \ldots$.

1'. Generate Y having probability mass function r.
2'. Generate $U \sim U(0,1)$, independent of Y.
3'. If $U \leq p(Y)/t(Y)$, return $X = Y$. Otherwise, go back to step 1' and try again.

Show that this algorithm is valid by following steps similar to those in App. 8A. What considerations are important in choosing the function $t(x_i)$?

8.10. For the general acceptance-rejection method (either continuous, as in Sec. 8.2.4, or discrete, as in Prob. 8.9) find the distribution of the number of (Y,U) pairs that are rejected before acceptance occurs. What is the expected number of rejections?

8.11. Give inverse-transform, composition, and acceptance-rejection algorithms for generating from each of the following densities. Discuss which algorithm is preferable for each density. (First plot the densities.)
(*a*)

$$f(x) = \begin{cases} \dfrac{3x^2}{2} & \text{if } -1 \leq x \leq 1 \\ 0 & \text{otherwise} \end{cases}$$

(*b*) For $0 < a < \frac{1}{2}$,

$$f(x) = \begin{cases} 0 & \text{if } x \leq 0 \\ \dfrac{x}{a(1-a)} & \text{if } 0 \leq x \leq a \\ \dfrac{1}{1-a} & \text{if } a \leq x \leq 1-a \\ \dfrac{1-x}{a(1-a)} & \text{if } 1-a \leq x \leq 1 \\ 0 & \text{if } 1 \leq x \end{cases}$$

8.12. Recall the polar method of Sec. 8.3.6 for generating $N(0,1)$ random variates. Show that the probability of "acceptance" of W in step 2 is $\pi/4$ and find the distribution of the number of "rejections" of W before "acceptance" finally occurs. What is the expected number of executions of step 1?

8.13. Give a composition algorithm for generating from the $\text{triang}(0,1,c)$ distribution $(0 < c < 1)$ of Sec. 8.3.11. Compare it with the inverse-transform algorithm in Sec. 8.3.11. (*Hint:* See Prob. 8.7.)

8.14. (*a*) Demonstrate the validity of the algorithm given in Sec. 8.4.5 for generating from the $\text{geom}(p)$ distribution. (*Hint:* For a real number x and an integer i, $\lfloor x \rfloor = i$ if and only if $i \leq x < i + 1$.) Also verify (with $1 - U$ in place of U) that this *is* the inverse-transform algorithm.
(*b*) Show that the following algorithm is also valid for generating $X \sim \text{geom}(p)$:

1. Let $i = 0$.

2. Generate $U \sim U(0,1)$ independent of any previously generated $U(0,1)$ random variates.

3. If $U \leq p$, return $X = i$. Otherwise, replace i by $i + 1$ and go back to step 2.

Note that if p is large (close to 1), this algorithm is an attractive alternative to the one given in Sec. 8.4.5, since no logarithms are required and early termination is likely.

8.15. Recall the shifted exponential, gamma, Weibull, lognormal, and Pearson types V and VI distributions discussed in Sec. 6.8. Assuming the ability to generate random variates from the original (unshifted) versions of these distributions, give a general algorithm for generating random variates from the shifted versions. (Assume that the shift parameter γ is specified.)

8.16. Give an explicit algorithm for generating a variate Y from the density $r(x)$ in Example 8.7; $r(x)$ is plotted in Fig. 8.12. (See also Prob. 8.7.)

8.17. The alias method, as stated in Sec. 8.4.3, requires generating at least two $U(0,1)$ random numbers—one to generate I in step 1, and the other to determine whether I or its alias is returned in step 2. Show that the following version of the alias method, which requires only one random number, is also valid:

1. Generate $U \sim U(0,1)$.

2. Let $V = (n + 1)U$, $I = \lfloor V \rfloor$, and $U' = V - I$.

3. If $U' \leq F_I$, return $X = I$. Otherwise, return $X = L_I$.

[*Hint:* What is the joint distribution of I and U'? Although this "trick" does reduce the number of random numbers generated, it is probably not a good idea, since it depends on the low-order (least significant) bits of $V - I$ being "random," which may be doubtful for many (pseudo) random-number generators.]

8.18. The setup algorithms in App. 8B for the alias method produce cutoff values F_i that could actually be equal to 1; this will occur for at least one i if the second algorithm is used.

(*a*) Find a way to alter the cutoff and alias values so that every F_i will be strictly less than 1.

(*b*) With the F_i's all being strictly less than 1, find a way to reduce the storage requirements from $2(n + 1)$ to $n + 1$ by combining the L_i and F_i arrays into a single array of length $n + 1$. Restate the alias algorithm from Sec. 8.4.3 so that it works with this one-array method of holding the aliases and cutoff values.

REFERENCES

Abramowitz, M., and I. A. Stegun, eds.: *Handbook of Mathematical Functions with Formulas, Graphs, and Mathematical Tables*, National Bureau of Standards, Washington, D.C. (1964).

Ahrens, J. H., and U. Dieter: Computer Methods for Sampling from the Exponential and Normal Distributions, *Commun. Assoc. Comput. Mach.*, 15: 873–882 (1972).

Ahrens, J. H., and U. Dieter: Computer Methods for Sampling from Gamma, Beta, Poisson, and Binomial Distributions, *Computing*, 12: 223–246 (1974).

Arnold, B. C.: A Note on Multivariate Distributions with Specified Marginals, *J. Am. Statist. Assoc.*, *62*: 1460–1461 (1967).

Atkinson, A. C.: A Family of Switching Algorithms for the Computer Generation of Beta Random Variables, *Biometrika*, *66*: 141–145 (1979a).

Atkinson, A. C.: The Computer Generation of Poisson Random Variables, *Appl. Statist.*, *28*: 29–35 (1979b).

Atkinson, A. C.: Recent Developments in the Computer Generation of Poisson Random Variables, *Appl. Statist.*, *28*: 260–263 (1979c).

Atkinson, A. C., and M. C. Pearce: The Computer Generation of Beta, Gamma, and Normal Random Variables, *J. Roy. Statist. Soc.*, *A139*: 431–448 (1976).

Atkinson, A. C., and J. Whittaker: A Switching Algorithm for the Generation of Beta Random Variables with at Least One Parameter Less Than 1, *J. Roy. Statist. Soc.*, *A139*: 462–467 (1976).

Atkinson, A. C., and J. Whittaker: The Generation of Beta Random Variables with One Parameter Greater Than and One Parameter Less Than 1, *Appl. Statist.*, *28*: 90–93 (1979).

Best, D. J., and D. E. Roberts: The Percentage Points of the χ^2 Distribution, *Appl. Statist.*, *24*: 385–388 (1975).

Box, G. E. P., and M. E. Muller: A Note on the Generation of Random Normal Deviates, *Ann. Math. Statist.*, *29*: 610–611 (1958).

Bratley, P., B. L. Fox, and L. E. Schrage: *A Guide to Simulation*, 2d ed., Springer-Verlag, New York (1987).

Chen, H., and Y. Asau: On Generating Random Variates from an Empirical Distribution, *AIIE Trans.*, *6*: 163–166 (1974).

Cheng, R. C. H.: The Generation of Gamma Variables with Non-integral Shape Parameter, *Appl. Statist.*, *26*: 71–75 (1977).

Cheng, R. C. H.: Generating Beta Variates with Nonintegral Shape Parameters, *Commun. Assoc. Comput. Mach.*, *21*: 317–322 (1978).

Cheng, R. C. H., and G. M. Feast: Some Simple Gamma Variate Generators, *Appl. Statist.*, *28*: 290–295 (1979).

Çinlar, E.: *Introduction to Stochastic Processes*, Prentice-Hall, Englewood Cliffs, N.J. (1975).

Cran, G. W., K. J. Martin, and G. E. Thomas: A Remark on Algorithm AS63: The Incomplete Beta Integral, AS64: Inverse of the Incomplete Beta Function Ratio, *Appl. Statist.*, *26*: 111–114 (1977).

Dagpunar, J.: *Principles of Random Variate Generation*, Clarendon Press, Oxford (1988).

Devroye, L.: The Computer Generation of Poisson Random Variables, *Computing*, *26*: 197–207 (1981).

Devroye, L.: *Non-Uniform Random Variate Generation*, Springer-Verlag, New York (1986).

Filliben, J. J.: The Probability Plot Correlation Coefficient Test for Normality, *Technometrics*, *17*: 111–117 (1975).

Fishman, G. S.: *Concepts and Methods in Discrete Event Digital Simulation*, John Wiley, New York (1973).

Fishman, G. S.: *Principles of Discrete Event Simulation*, John Wiley, New York (1978).

Fishman, G. S., and L. R. Moore: Sampling from a Discrete Distribution while Preserving Monotonicity, *Am. Statistician*, *38*: 219–223 (1984).

Forsythe, G. E.: von Neumann's Comparison Method for Random Sampling from the Normal and Other Distributions, *Math. Comput.*, *26*: 817–826 (1972).

IMSL, Inc.: *User's Manual: Stat/Library*, Vol. 3, IMSL, Houston, Tex. (1987).

Jöhnk, M. D.: Erzeugung von Betaverteilten und Gammaverteilten Zufallszahlen, *Metrika*, *8*: 5–15 (1964).

Johnson, M. E.: *Multivariate Statistical Simulation*, John Wiley, New York (1987).

Johnson, M. E., and J. S. Ramberg: Transformations of the Multivariate Normal Distribution with Applications to Simulation, Los Alamos Sci. Lab. Tech. Rep. LA-UR-77-2595, Los Alamos, N.M. (1978).

Johnson, M. E., C. Wang, and J. S. Ramberg: Generation of Continuous Multivariate Distributions for Statistical Applications, *Am. J. Math. and Management Sci.*, *4*: 96–119 (1984).

Kachitvichyanukul, V.: Discrete Univariate Random Variate Generation, *Proc. 1983 Winter Simulation Conference*, Washington, D.C., pp. 179–187 (1983).

Kachitvichyanukul, V., and B. W. Schmeiser: Binomial Random Variate Generation, *Commun. Assoc. Comput. Mach.*, *31*: 216–222 (1988).

Kaminsky, F. C., and D. L. Rumpf: Simulating Nonstationary Poisson Processes: A Comparison of Alternatives including the Correct Approach, *Simulation*, *29*: 17–20 (1977).

Kennedy, W. J., Jr., and J. E. Gentle: *Statistical Computing*, Marcel Dekker, New York (1980).

Kinderman, A. J., and J. G. Ramage: Computer Generation of Normal Random Variables, *J. Am. Statist. Assoc.*, *71*: 893–896 (1976).

Klein, R. W., and S. D. Roberts: A Time-Varying Poisson Arrival Process Generator, *Simulation*, *43*: 193–195 (1984).

Knuth, D. E.: *The Art of Computer Programming, Vol. 3: Sorting and Searching*, Addison-Wesley, Reading, Mass. (1973).

Kronmal, R. A., and A. V. Peterson, Jr.: On the Alias Method for Generating Random Variables from a Discrete Distribution, *Am. Statistician*, *33*: 214–218 (1979).

Kronmal, R. A., and A. V. Peterson, Jr.: A Variant of the Acceptance-Rejection Method for Computer Generation of Random Variables, *J. Am. Statist. Assoc.*, *76*: 446–451 (1981).

Kronmal, R. A., and A. V. Peterson, Jr.: Corrigenda, *J. Am. Statist. Assoc.*, *77*: 954 (1982).

Leemis, L., and B. W. Schmeiser: Random Variate Generation for Monte Carlo Experiments, *IEEE Trans. Reliability*, *R-34*: 81–85 (1985).

Lewis, P. A. W.: Generating Negatively Correlated Gamma Variates Using the Beta-Gamma Transformation, *Proc. 1983 Winter Simulation Conference*, Washington, D.C., pp. 175–176 (1983).

Lewis, P. A. W., and G. S. Shedler: Simulation of Nonhomogeneous Poisson Process by Thinning, *Nav. Res. Logist. Quart.*, *26*: 403–413 (1979).

Lilliefors, H. W.: On the Kolmogorov-Smirnov Test for Normality with Mean and Variance Unknown, *J. Am. Statist. Assoc.*, *62*: 399–402 (1967).

MacLaren, M. D., G. Marsaglia, and T. A. Bray: A Fast Procedure for Generating Exponential Random Variables, *Commun. Assoc. Comput. Mach.*, *7*: 298–300 (1964).

Marsaglia, G.: Generating Exponential Random Variables, *Ann. Math. Statist.*, *32*: 899–902 (1961).

Marsaglia, G.: Generating Discrete Random Variables in a Computer, *Commun. Assoc. Comput. Mach.*, *6*: 37–38 (1963).

Marsaglia, G.: The Exact-Approximation Method for Generating Random Variables in a Computer, *J. Am. Statist. Assoc.*, *79*: 218–221 (1984).

Marsaglia, G., and T. A. Bray: A Convenient Method for Generating Normal Variables, *SIAM Rev.*, *6*: 260–264 (1964).

Marshall, A. W., and I. Olkin: A Multivariate Exponential Distribution, *J. Am. Statist. Assoc.*, *62*: 30–44 (1967).

Mitchell, C. R., and A. S. Paulson: $M/M/1$ Queues with Interdependent Arrival and Service Processes, *Nav. Res. Logist. Quart.*, *26*: 47–56 (1979).

Mitchell, C. R., A. S. Paulson, and C. A. Beswick: The Effect of Correlated Exponential Service Times on Single Server Tandem Queues, *Nav. Res. Logist. Quart.*, *24*: 95–112 (1977).

Mood, A. M., F. A. Graybill, and D. C. Boes: *Introduction to the Theory of Statistics*, 3d ed., McGraw-Hill, New York (1974).

Odeh, R. E., and J. O. Evans: The Percentage Points of the Normal Distribution, *Appl. Statist.*, *23*: 96–97 (1974).

Peterson, A. V., Jr., and R. A. Kronmal: On Mixture Methods for the Computer Generation of Random Variables, *Am. Statistician*, *36*: 184–191 (1982).

Peterson, A. V., Jr., and R. A. Kronmal: Analytic Comparison of Three General-Purpose Methods for the Computer Generation of Discrete Random Variables, *Appl. Statist.*, *32*: 276–286 (1983).

Ramberg, J. S., and P. R. Tadikamalla: On the Generation of Subsets of Order Statistics, *J. Statist. Comput. Simul.*, *6*: 239–241 (1978).

Ripley, B. D.: Computer Generation of Random Variables: A Tutorial, *Int. Statist. Rev., 51*: 301–319 (1983).

Ronning, G.: A Simple Scheme for Generating Multivariate Gamma Distributions with Non-negative Covariance Matrix, *Technometrics, 19*: 179–183 (1977).

Ross, S. M.: *Introduction to Probability Models*, 4th ed., Academic Press, San Diego (1989).

Scheuer, E. M., and D. S. Stoller: On the Generation of Normal Random Vectors, *Technometrics, 4*: 278–281 (1962).

Schmeiser, B. W.: Generation of the Maximum (Minimum) Value in Digital Computer Simulation, *J. Statist. Comput. Simul., 8*: 103–115 (1978a).

Schmeiser, B. W.: The Generation of Order Statistics in Digital Computer Simulation: A Survey, *Proc. 1978 Winter Simulation Conference*, Miami, Florida, pp. 137–140 (1978b).

Schmeiser, B. W.: Generation of Variates from Distribution Tails, *Operations Res., 28*: 1012–1017 (1980a).

Schmeiser, B. W.: Random Variate Generation: A Survey, *Proc. 1980 Winter Simulation Conference*, Orlando, Florida, pp. 79–104 (1980b).

Schmeiser, B. W.: Recent Advances in Generating Observations from Discrete Random Variables, *Proc. 15th Symposium on the Interface of Computer Science and Statistics*, North-Holland, pp. 154–160 (1983).

Schmeiser, B. W., and A. J. G. Babu: Beta Variate Generation via Exponential Majorizing Functions, *Operations Res., 28*: 917–926 (1980).

Schmeiser, B. W., and V. Kachitvichyanukul: Poisson Random Variate Generation, School of Industrial Engineering Research Memorandum 81–4, Purdue Univ., West Lafayette, Indiana (1981).

Schmeiser, B. W., and V. Kachitvichyanukul: Correlation Induction without the Inverse Transformation, *Proc. 1986 Winter Simulation Conference*, Washington D.C., pp. 266–274 (1986).

Schmeiser, B. W., and R. Lal: Multivariate Modeling in Simulation: A Survey, *ASQC Tech. Conf. Trans.*, pp. 252–261 (1980a).

Schmeiser, B. W., and R. Lal: Squeeze Methods for Generating Gamma Variates, *J. Am. Statist. Assoc., 75*: 679–682 (1980b).

Schmeiser, B. W., and R. Lal: Bivariate Gamma Random Vectors, *Operations Res., 30*: 355–374 (1982).

Schmeiser, B. W., and M. A. Shalaby: Acceptance/Rejection Methods for Beta Variate Generation, *J. Am. Statist. Assoc., 75*: 673–678 (1980).

Schucany, W. R.: Order Statistics in Simulation, *J. Statist. Comput. Simul., 1*: 281–286 (1972).

Shanthikumar, J. G.: Discrete Random Variate Generation Using Uniformization, *Eur. J. Operations Res., 21*: 387–398 (1985).

Shapiro, S. S., and M. B. Wilk: An Analysis of Variance Test for Normality (Complete Samples), *Biometrika, 52*: 591–611 (1965).

Smith, R. L.: Efficient Monte Carlo Procedures for Generating Points Uniformly Distributed over Bounded Regions, *Operations Res., 32*: 1296–1308 (1984).

Sowey, E. R.: A Third Classified Bibliography on Random Number Generation and Testing, *J. Roy. Statist. Soc., A149*: 83–107 (1986).

Tadikamalla, P. R.: Computer Generation of Gamma Random Variables—II, *Commun. Assoc. Comput. Mach., 21*: 925–928 (1978).

Tadikamalla, P. R., and M. E. Johnson: A Complete Guide to Gamma Variate Generation, *Am. J. Math. Management Sci., 1*: 78–95 (1981).

von Neumann, J.: Various Techniques Used in Connection with Random Digits, *Natl. Bur. Std. Math. Ser., 12*: 36–38 (1951).

Walker, A. J.: An Efficient Method for Generating Discrete Random Variables with General Distributions, *Assoc. Comput. Mach. Trans. Math. Software, 3*: 253–256 (1977).

CHAPTER
9

OUTPUT DATA ANALYSIS FOR A SINGLE SYSTEM

Recommended sections for a first reading: 9.1 through 9.3, 9.4.1, 9.4.3, 9.5.1, 9.5.2, 9.8

9.1 INTRODUCTION

In many simulation studies a great deal of time and money is spent on model development and programming, but little effort is made to analyze the simulation output data appropriately. As a matter of fact, a very common mode of operation is to make a single simulation run of somewhat arbitrary length and then to treat the resulting simulation estimates as the "true" model characteristics. Since random samples from probability distributions are typically used to drive a simulation model through time, these estimates are just particular realizations of random variables that may have large variances. As a result, these estimates could, in a particular simulation run, differ greatly from the corresponding true characteristics for the model. The net effect is, of course, that there could be a significant probability of making erroneous inferences about the system under study.

Historically, there are several reasons why output data analyses have not been conducted in an appropriate manner. First, users often have the unfortunate impression that simulation is just an exercise in computer programming,

522

albeit a complicated one. Consequently, many simulation "studies" begin with heuristic model building and coding, and end with a single run of the program to produce "the answers." In fact, however, a simulation is a computer-based statistical sampling experiment. Thus, if the results of a simulation study are to have any meaning, appropriate statistical techniques must be used to design and analyze the simulation experiments. A second reason for inadequate statistical analyses is that the output processes of virtually all simulations are nonstationary and autocorrelated (see Sec. 5.5.3). Thus, classical statistical techniques based on IID observations are not directly applicable. At present, there are still several output-analysis problems for which there is no completely accepted solution, and the methods that are available are often complicated to apply. Another impediment to obtaining precise estimates of a model's true parameters or characteristics is the cost of the computer time needed to collect the necessary amount of simulation output data. Indeed, there are situations where an appropriate statistical procedure is available, but the cost of collecting the quantity of data dictated by the procedure is prohibitive. This latter difficulty is becoming less severe since many analysts now have their own high-speed microcomputers or engineering work stations. These computers are relatively inexpensive to buy and can be run overnight or on weekends to produce large amounts of simulation output data, at essentially zero marginal cost.

We now describe more precisely the random nature of simulation output. Let $Y_1, Y_2, \ldots$ be an output stochastic process (see Sec. 4.3) from a *single* simulation run. For example, Y_i might be the throughput (production) in the ith hour for a manufacturing system. The Y_i's are random variables that will. in general, be neither independent nor identically distributed. Thus, most of the formulas of Chap. 4, which assume independence [e.g., the confidence interval given by (4.12)], do not apply *directly*.

Let $y_{11}, y_{12}, \ldots, y_{1m}$ be a realization of the random variables $Y_1, Y_2, \ldots, Y_m$ resulting from making a simulation run of length m observations using the random numbers $u_{11}, u_{12}, \ldots$. (The ith random number used in the jth run is denoted u_{ji}.) If we run the simulation with a different set of random numbers $u_{21}, u_{22}, \ldots$, then we will obtain a different realization $y_{21}, y_{22}, \ldots, y_{2m}$ of the random variables $Y_1, Y_2, \ldots, Y_m$. (The two realizations are not the same since the different random numbers used in the two runs produce different samples from the input probability distributions.) In general, suppose that we make n independent replications (runs) of the simulation (i.e., different random numbers are used for each replication, the statistical counters are reset at the beginning of each replication, and each replication uses the same initial conditions; see Sec. 9.4.3) of length m, resulting in the observations:

$$
\begin{array}{cccc}
y_{11}, & \ldots, & y_{1i}, & \ldots, & y_{1m} \\
y_{21}, & \ldots, & y_{2i}, & \ldots, & y_{2m} \\
\vdots & & \vdots & & \vdots \\
y_{n1}, & \ldots, & y_{ni}, & \ldots, & y_{nm}
\end{array}
$$

The observations from a particular replication (row) are clearly not IID. However, note that $y_{1i}, y_{2i}, \ldots, y_{ni}$ (from the ith column) are IID observations of the random variable Y_i, for $i = 1, 2, \ldots, m$. This *independence across runs* (see Prob. 9.1) is the key to the relatively simple output-data-analysis methods described in later sections of this chapter. Then, roughly speaking, the goal of output analysis is to use the observations y_{ji} ($i = 1, 2, \ldots, m$; $j = 1, 2, \ldots, n$) to draw inferences about the (distributions of the) random variables $Y_1, Y_2, \ldots, Y_m$. For example, $\bar{y}_i(n) = \sum_{j=1}^{n} y_{ji}/n$ is an unbiased estimate of $E(Y_i)$.

> **Example 9.1.** Consider a bank with five tellers and one queue, which opens its doors at 9 A.M., closes its doors at 5 P.M., but stays open until all customers in the bank at 5 P.M. have been served. Assume that customers arrive in accordance with a Poisson process at rate 1 per minute (i.e., IID exponential interarrival times with mean 1 minute), that service times are IID exponential random variables with mean 4 minutes, and that customers are served in a FIFO manner. Table 9.1 shows several typical output statistics from 10 independent replications of a simulation of the bank, assuming that no customers are present initially. Note that results from various replications can be quite different. Thus, one run clearly does not produce "the answers."

Our goal in this chapter is to discuss methods for statistical analysis of simulation output data and to present the material with a practical focus that should be accessible to a reader having a basic understanding of probability and statistics. (Reviewing Chap. 4 might be advisable before reading this chapter.) We will discuss what we believe are all the important methods for output analysis; however, the emphasis will be on statistical procedures that are relatively easy to understand and implement, have been shown to perform well in practice, and have applicability to real-world problems.

TABLE 9.1
Results for 10 independent replications of the bank model

Replication	Number served	Finish time (hours)	Average delay in queue (minutes)	Average queue length	Proportion of customers delayed < 5 minutes
1	484	8.12	1.53	1.52	0.917
2	475	8.14	1.66	1.62	0.916
3	484	8.19	1.24	1.23	0.952
4	483	8.03	2.34	2.34	0.822
5	455	8.03	2.00	1.89	0.840
6	461	8.32	1.69	1.56	0.866
7	451	8.09	2.69	2.50	0.783
8	486	8.19	2.86	2.83	0.782
9	502	8.15	1.70	1.74	0.873
10	475	8.24	2.60	2.50	0.779

In Secs. 9.2 and 9.3 we discuss types of simulations with regard to output analysis, and also measures of performance or parameters θ for each type. Sections 9.4 through 9.6 show how to get a point estimator $\hat{\theta}$ and confidence interval for each type of parameter θ, with the confidence interval typically requiring an estimate of the variance of $\hat{\theta}$, namely, $\widehat{\text{Var}}(\hat{\theta})$. Each of the analysis methods discussed may suffer from one or both of the following problems:

1. $\hat{\theta}$ is not an unbiased estimator of θ, that is, $E(\hat{\theta}) \neq \theta$; see, for example, Sec. 9.5.2
2. $\widehat{\text{Var}}(\hat{\theta})$ is not an unbiased estimator of $\text{Var}(\hat{\theta})$; see, for example, Sec. 9.5.3

Section 9.7 extends the above analyses to confidence-interval construction for several different parameters simultaneously. Finally, in Sec. 9.8 we show how time plots of important variables may provide insight into a system's dynamic behavior.

We will not attempt to give every reference on the subject of output data analysis, since a very comprehensive set of references was given in the survey paper by Law (1983). Also see the book chapter by Welch (1983).

9.2 TRANSIENT AND STEADY-STATE BEHAVIOR OF A STOCHASTIC PROCESS

Consider the output stochastic process $Y_1, Y_2, \ldots$. Let $F_i(y|I) = P(Y_i \leq y|I)$ for $i = 1, 2, \ldots$, where y is a real number and I represents the initial conditions used to start the simulation at time 0. [The conditional probability $P(Y_i \leq y|I)$ is the probability that the event $\{Y_i \leq y\}$ occurs *given* the initial conditions I.] For a manufacturing system, I might specify the number of jobs present, and whether each machine is busy or idle, at time 0. We call $F_i(y|I)$ the *transient distribution* of the output process at (discrete) time i for initial conditions I. Note that $F_i(y|I)$ will, in general, be different for each value of i and each set of initial conditions I. The density functions for the transient distributions corresponding to the random variables $Y_{i_1}, Y_{i_2}, Y_{i_3}$, and Y_{i_4} are shown in Fig. 9.1 for a particular set of initial conditions I and increasing time indices i_1, i_2, i_3, and i_4, where it is assumed that the random variable Y_{i_j} has density function $f_{Y_{i_j}}$. The density $f_{Y_{i_j}}$ specifies how the random variable Y_{i_j} can vary from one replication to another.

For fixed y and I, the probabilities $F_1(y|I), F_2(y|I), \ldots$ are just a sequence of numbers. If $F_i(y|I) \rightarrow F(y)$ as $i \rightarrow \infty$ for all y and for any initial conditions I, then $F(y)$ is called the *steady-state distribution* of the output process $Y_1, Y_2, \ldots$. Strictly speaking, the steady-state distribution $F(y)$ is only obtained in the limit as $i \rightarrow \infty$. In practice, however, there will often be a finite time index, say, $k + 1$, such that the distributions from this point on will be approximately the same as each other; "steady state" is figuratively said to start at time $k + 1$ as shown in Fig. 9.1. Note that steady state does *not* mean

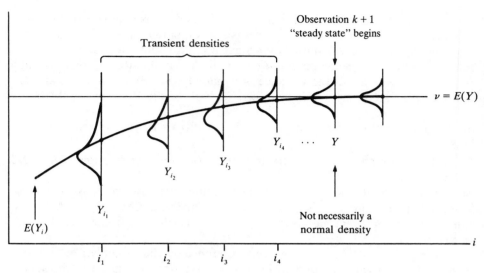

FIGURE 9.1
Transient and steady-state density functions for a particular stochastic process $Y_1, Y_2, \ldots$ and initial conditions I.

that the random variables $Y_{k+1}, Y_{k+2}, \ldots$ will all take on the same value in a particular simulation run; rather, it means that they will all have approximately the same *distribution*. Furthermore, these random variables will not be independent, but will approximately constitute a covariance-stationary stochastic process (see Sec. 4.3). See Welch (1983) for an excellent discussion of transient and steady-state distributions.

The steady-state distribution $F(y)$ does not depend on the initial conditions I; however, the rate of convergence of the transient distributions $F_i(y|I)$ to $F(y)$ does, as the following example shows.

Example 9.2. Consider the stochastic process $D_1, D_2, \ldots$ for the $M/M/1$ queue with $\rho = 0.9$ ($\lambda = 1$, $\omega = 10/9$), where D_i is the delay in queue of the ith customer. In Fig. 9.2 we plot the convergence of the transient mean $E(D_i)$ to the steady-state mean $d = E(D) = 8.1$ as i gets large for various values of number in system at time 0, s. (The random variable D has the steady-state delay in queue distribution.) Note that the convergence of $E(D_i)$ to d is, surprisingly, much faster for $s = 15$ than for $s = 0$ (see Prob. 9.11). The values for $E(D_i)$ were derived in Kelton and Law (1985); see also Kelton (1985) and Murray and Kelton (1988). The distribution function of D is given by (4.14) in App. 4A.

Example 9.3. Consider the stochastic process $C_1, C_2, \ldots$ for the inventory problem of Example 4.23, where C_i is the total cost in the ith month. In Fig. 9.3 we plot the convergence of $E(C_i)$ to the steady-state mean $c = E(C) = 112.11$ [see Wagner (1969, p. A19)] as i gets large for an initial inventory level of 57. Note that the convergence is clearly not monotone.

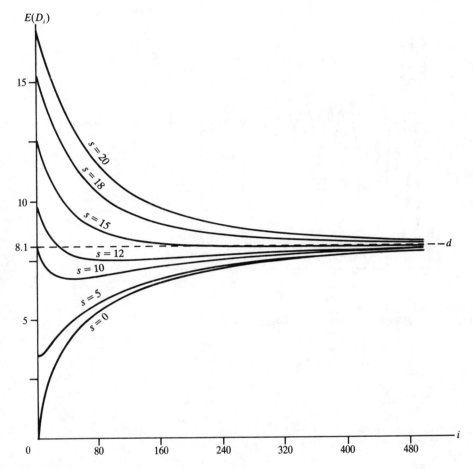

FIGURE 9.2
$E(D_i)$ as a function of i and the number in system at time 0, s, for the $M/M/1$ queue with $\rho = 0.9$.

In Examples 9.2 and 9.3 we plotted the convergence of the *expected value* $E(Y_i)$ to the steady-state mean $E(Y)$. It should be remembered, however, that the entire *distribution* of Y_i is also converging to the distribution of Y as i gets large.

9.3 TYPES OF SIMULATIONS WITH REGARD TO OUTPUT ANALYSIS

The options available in designing and analyzing simulation experiments depend on the type of simulation at hand, as depicted in Fig. 9.4. Simulations may be either terminating or nonterminating, depending on whether there is an obvious way for determining run length. Furthermore, measures of perfor-

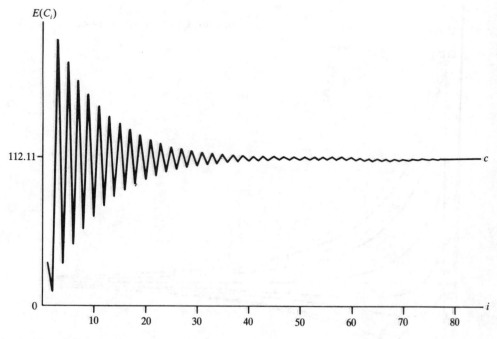

FIGURE 9.3
$E(C_i)$ as a function of i for the (s,S) inventory system.

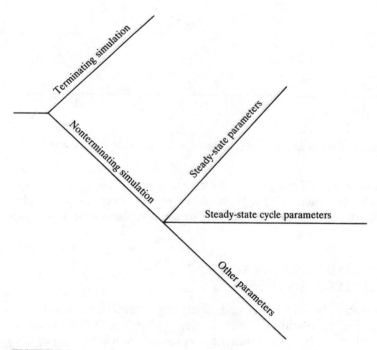

FIGURE 9.4
Types of simulations with regard to output analysis.

mance or parameters for nonterminating simulations may be of several types, as shown in the figure. These concepts are defined more precisely below.

A *terminating simulation* is one for which there is a "natural" event E that specifies the length of each run (replication). Since different runs use independent random numbers and the same initialization rule, this implies that comparable random variables from the different runs are IID (see Sec. 9.4). The event E often occurs at a time point beyond which no useful information is obtained or at a time point when the system is "cleaned out." It is specified before any runs are made, and the time of occurrence of E for a particular run may be a random variable. Since the *initial conditions for a terminating simulation generally affect the desired measures of performance*, these conditions should be representative of those for the actual system (see Sec. 9.4.3).

Example 9.4. A retail/commercial establishment, e.g., a bank, closes each evening. If the establishment is open from 9 to 5, the objective of a simulation might be to estimate some measure of the quality of customer service over the period beginning at 9 A.M. and ending when the last customer who entered before the doors closed at 5 P.M. has been served. In this case $E = \{$at least 8 hours of simulated time have elapsed and the system is empty$\}$, and the initial conditions for the simulation are the number of customers present at time 0 (see Sec. 9.4.3).

Example 9.5. Consider a military ground confrontation between a blue force and a red force. Relative to some initial force strengths, the goal of a simulation might be to determine the (final) force strengths when the battle ends. In this case $E = \{$either the blue force or the red force has "won" the battle$\}$. An example of a condition that would end the battle is one side losing 30 percent of its force, since this side would no longer be considered viable. The choice of initial conditions, e.g., the number of troops and tanks for each force, for the simulation is generally not a problem here, since they are specified by the military scenario under consideration.

Example 9.6. An aerospace manufacturer receives a contract to produce 100 airplanes, which must be delivered within 18 months. The company would like to simulate various manufacturing configurations to see which one can meet the delivery deadline at least cost. In this case $E = \{$100 airplanes have been completed$\}$.

Example 9.7. Consider a manufacturing company that operates 16 hours a day (two shifts) with work in process carrying over from one day to the next. Would this qualify as a terminating simulation with $E = \{$16 hours of simulated time have elapsed$\}$? No, since this manufacturing operation is essentially a continuous process, with the ending conditions for one day being the initial conditions for the next day.

Example 9.8. A company that sells a single product would like to decide how many items to have in inventory during a planning horizon of 120 months (see Sec. 1.5). Given some initial inventory level, the objective might be to determine how much to order each month so as to minimize the expected average cost per month of operating the inventory system. In this case $E = \{$120 months have been simulated$\}$, and the simulation is initialized with the current inventory level.

A *nonterminating simulation* is one for which there is no natural event E to specify the length of a run. A measure of performance for such a simulation is said to be a *steady-state parameter* if it is a characteristic of the steady-state distribution of some output stochastic process $Y_1, Y_2, \ldots$. In Fig. 9.1, if the random variable Y has the steady-state distribution, then we might be interested in estimating the steady-state mean $\nu = E(Y)$.

Example 9.9. Consider a company that is going to build a new manufacturing system and would like to determine the long-run (steady-state) mean hourly throughput of their system after it has been running long enough for the workers to know their jobs and for mechanical difficulties to have been worked out. Assume that:

(a) The system will operate 16 hours a day for 5 days a week.
(b) There is negligible loss of production at the end of one shift or at the beginning of the next shift (see Prob. 9.3).
(c) There are no breaks (e.g., lunch) that shut down production at specified times each day.

This system could be simulated by "pasting together" 16-hour days, thus ignoring the system idle time at the end of each day and on the weekend. Let N_i be the number of parts manufactured in the ith hour. If the stochastic process $N_1, N_2, \ldots$ has a steady-state distribution with corresponding random variable N, then we are interested in estimating the mean $\nu = E(N)$ (see Prob. 9.4).

It should be mentioned that stochastic processes for most *real* systems do not have steady-state distributions, since the characteristics of the system change over time. For example, in a manufacturing system the production-scheduling rules and the facility layout (e.g., number and location of machines) may change from time to time. On the other hand, a simulation model (which is an abstraction of reality) may have steady-state distributions, since characteristics of the *model* are often assumed not to change over time.

If, in Example 9.9, the manufacturing company wanted to know the time required for the system to go from startup to operating in a "normal" manner, this would be a terminating simulation with terminating event $E = \{$simulated system is running "normally"$\}$ (if such can be defined). Thus, a simulation for a particular system might be either terminating or nonterminating, depending on the objectives of the simulation study.

Example 9.10. Consider a simulation model for a computer (or communication) system that does not currently exist. Since there are typically no representative data available on the arrival mechanism for jobs, it is common to assume that jobs arrive in accordance with a Poisson process with *constant* rate equal to the *predicted* arrival rate of jobs during the period of peak loading. (When the system is actually built, the arrival rate will vary as a function of time and the period of peak loading may be relatively short.) Since the state of the system during "normal operation" is unknown, initial conditions must be chosen somewhat arbitrarily (e.g., no jobs present at time 0). Then the goal is to run the simulation long enough so that the arbitrary choice of initial conditions is no longer having a significant effect on the estimated measures of performance (e.g., mean response time for a job).

In performing the above steady-state analysis of the proposed computer system, we are essentially trying to determine how the system will respond to a peak load of infinite duration. If, however, the peak period in the actual system is short or if the arrival rate before the peak period is considerably lower than the peak rate, our analysis may overestimate the congestion level during the peak period in the system. This might result in purchasing a computer configuration that is more powerful than actually needed.

Consider a stochastic process $Y_1, Y_2, \ldots$ for a nonterminating simulation that does not have a steady-state distribution. Suppose that we divide the time axis into equal-length, contiguous time intervals called *cycles*. (For example, in a manufacturing system a cycle might be an 8-hour shift.) Let Y_i^C be a random variable defined on the ith cycle, and assume that $Y_1^C, Y_2^C, \ldots$ are comparable. Suppose that the process $Y_1^C, Y_2^C, \ldots$ has a steady-state distribution F^C and that $Y^C \sim F^C$. Then a measure of performance is said to be a *steady-state cycle parameter* if it is a characteristic of Y^C such as the mean $\nu^C = E(Y^C)$. Thus, a steady-state cycle parameter is just a steady-state parameter of the appropriate cycle process $Y_1^C, Y_2^C, \ldots$.

Example 9.11. Suppose for the manufacturing system in Example 9.9 that there is a half-hour lunch break at the beginning of the fifth hour in each 8-hour shift. Then the process of hourly throughputs $N_1, N_2, \ldots$ has no steady-state distribution (see Prob. 9.6). Let N_i^C be the average hourly throughput in the ith 8-hour shift (cycle). Then we might be interested in estimating the steady-state expected average hourly throughput over a cycle, $\nu^C = E(N^C)$, which is a steady-state cycle parameter.

Example 9.12. Consider a national long-distance telephone company for which one must dial a local phone number to gain access to the system. Suppose that the arrival rate of calls to the system varies with the time of day and day of the week, but assume that the pattern of arrival rates is identical from week to week. Let D_i be the delay experienced by the ith arriving call between dialing the local phone number and actually gaining access to the system, at which time the desired long-distance number can be entered. The stochastic process $D_1, D_2, \ldots$ does not have a steady-state distribution. Let D_i^C be the average delay over the ith week. Then we might be interested in estimating the steady-state expected average delay over a week, $\nu^C = E(D^C)$.

For a nonterminating simulation, suppose that the stochastic process $Y_1, Y_2, \ldots$ does not have a steady-state distribution, and that there is no appropriate cycle definition such that the corresponding process $Y_1^C, Y_2^C, \ldots$ has a steady-state distribution. This can occur, for example, if the parameters for the model continue to change over time. In Example 9.12, if the arrival rate of calls changes from week to week and from year to year, then steady-state (cycle) parameters will probably not be well defined. In these cases, however, there will typically be a fixed amount of data describing how input parameters change over time. This provides, in effect, a terminating event E for the simulation and, thus, the analysis techniques for terminating simulations in Sec. 9.4 are appropriate. This is why we do not treat this situation as a separate case later in the chapter. Measures of performance or parameters for such simulations usually change over time and are included in the category "other parameters" in Fig. 9.4.

> **Example 9.13.** Consider a manufacturing system for microcomputers consisting of an assembly line and a test area. There is a 3-month build schedule available from marketing, which describes the types and numbers of computers to be produced each week. The schedule changes from week to week because of changing sales and the introduction of new computers. In this case, weekly or monthly through-puts do not have steady-state distributions. We therefore perform a terminating simulation of length 3 months and estimate the actual mean throughput for each week.

9.4 STATISTICAL ANALYSIS FOR TERMINATING SIMULATIONS

Suppose that we make n independent replications of a terminating simulation, where each replication is terminated by the event E and is begun with the "same" initial conditions (see Sec. 9.4.3). The independence of replications is accomplished by using different random numbers for each replication. (For a discussion of how this can easily be accomplished if the n replications are made in more than one execution, see Sec. 7.2.) Assume for simplicity that there is a single measure of performance of interest. (This assumption is dropped in Sec. 9.7.) Let X_j be a random variable defined on the jth replication for $j = 1, 2, \ldots, n$; it is assumed that the X_j's are comparable for different replications. Then the X_j's are IID random variables. For the bank of Examples 9.1 and 9.4, X_j might be the average delay $\sum_{i=1}^{N} D_i / N$ over a day from the jth replication, where N (a random variable) is the number of customers served in a day. For the combat model of Example 9.5, X_j might be the number of red tanks destroyed on the jth replication. Finally, for the inventory system of Example 9.8, X_j could be the average cost $\sum_{i=1}^{120} C_i / 120$ from the jth replication.

9.4.1 Estimating Means

Suppose that we would like to obtain a point estimate and confidence interval for the mean $\mu = E(X)$, where X is random variable defined on a replication as described above. Make n independent replications of the simulation and let $X_1, X_2, \ldots, X_n$ be the resulting IID random variables. Then, by substituting the X_j's into (4.3) and (4.12), we get that $\bar{X}(n)$ is an unbiased point estimator for μ, and an approximate $100(1 - \alpha)$ percent $(0 < \alpha < 1)$ confidence interval for μ is given by

$$\bar{X}(n) \pm t_{n-1,1-\alpha/2}\sqrt{\frac{S^2(n)}{n}} \tag{9.1}$$

where the sample variance $S^2(n)$ is given by Eq. (4.4). We will call the confidence interval based on (9.1) the *fixed-sample-size procedure*.

Example 9.14. For the bank of Example 9.1, suppose that we want to obtain a point estimate and an approximate 90 percent confidence interval for the expected average delay of a customer over a day, which is given by

$$E(X) = E\left(\frac{\sum\limits_{i=1}^{N} D_i}{N}\right)$$

(Note that we estimate the expected *average* delay, since each delay has, in general, a different mean.) From the 10 replications given in Table 9.1 we obtained

$$\bar{X}(10) = 2.03 , \qquad S^2(10) = 0.31$$

and

$$\bar{X}(10) \pm t_{9,0.95}\sqrt{\frac{S^2(10)}{10}} = 2.03 \pm 0.32$$

Thus, subject to the correct interpretation to be given to confidence intervals (see Sec. 4.5), we can claim with approximately 90 percent confidence that $E(X)$ is contained in the interval $[1.71, 2.35]$ minutes.

Example. 9.15. For the inventory system of Sec. 1.5 and Example 9.8, suppose that we want to obtain a point estimate and an approximate 90 percent confidence interval for the expected average cost over the 120-month planning horizon, which is given by

$$E(X) = E\left(\frac{\sum\limits_{i=1}^{120} C_i}{120}\right)$$

We made 10 independent replications and obtained the following X_j's:

129.35	127.11	124.03	122.13	120.44
118.39	130.17	129.77	125.52	133.75

which resulted in

$$\bar{X}(10) = 126.07 , \qquad S^2(10) = 23.55$$

and the 90 percent confidence interval

$$126.07 \pm 2.81 \qquad \text{or, alternatively,} \qquad [123.26, 128.88]$$

Note that the estimated coefficient of variation (see Table 6.5), a measure of variability, is 0.04 for the inventory system and 0.27 for the bank model. Thus the X_j's for the bank model are inherently more variable than those for the inventory system.

Example 9.16. For the bank of Example 9.1, suppose that we would like to obtain a point estimate and an approximate 90 percent confidence interval for the expected proportion of customers with a delay less than 5 minutes over a day, which is given by

$$E(X) = E\left(\frac{\sum_{i=1}^{N} I_i(0,5)}{N}\right)$$

where the *indicator function* $I_i(0,5)$ is defined as

$$I_i(0,5) = \begin{cases} 1 & \text{if } D_i < 5 \\ 0 & \text{otherwise} \end{cases}$$

for $i = 1, 2, \ldots, N$. From the last column of Table 9.1, we obtained

$$\bar{X}(10) = 0.853, \qquad S^2(10) = 0.004$$

and the 90 percent confidence interval

$$0.853 \pm 0.036 \qquad \text{or} \qquad [0.817, 0.889]$$

The correctness of the confidence interval given by (9.1) (in terms of having coverage close to $1 - \alpha$) depends on the assumption that the X_j's are normal random variables; this is why we called the confidence intervals in Examples 9.14, 9.15, and 9.16 *approximate* 90 percent confidence intervals. Since this assumption will rarely be satisfied in practice, we now use several simple stochastic models with *known* means to investigate empirically the robustness of the confidence interval to departures from normality. Our goal is to provide the simulation practitioner with some guidance as to how well the confidence interval will perform, in terms of coverage, in practice.

We first made 500 independent simulation experiments for the $M/M/1$ queue with $\rho = 0.9$. For each experiment we considered $n = 5, 10, 20, 40$, and for each n we used (9.1) to construct an approximate 90 percent confidence interval for

$$d(25|s = 0) = E\left(\frac{\sum_{i=1}^{25} D_i}{25}\,\bigg|\,s = 0\right) = 2.12$$

where s is the number of customers present at time 0 [see Heathcote and Winer (1969) and Example 9.2]. Table 9.2 gives the proportion, $\hat{p}$, of the 500 confidence intervals that covered the true $d(25|s = 0)$, a 90 percent confidence interval for the true coverage p [the proportion of a very large number of confidence intervals that would cover $d(25|s = 0)$], and the average value of the confidence-interval half-length [that is, $t_{n-1,1-\alpha/2}\sqrt{S^2(n)/n}$] divided by the point estimate $\bar{X}(n)$ over the 500 experiments, which is a measure of the precision of the confidence interval; see below for further discussion. The 90 percent confidence interval for the true coverage is computed from

$$\hat{p} \pm z_{0.95}\sqrt{\frac{\hat{p}(1-\hat{p})}{500}}$$

TABLE 9.2
Fixed-sample-size results for $d(25|s=0)=2.12$ based on 500 experiments, $M/M/1$ queue with $\rho=0.9$

n	Estimated coverage	Average of (confidence interval half-length)/$\bar{X}(n)$
5	0.880 ± 0.024	0.67
10	0.864 ± 0.025	0.44
20	0.886 ± 0.023	0.30
40	0.914 ± 0.021	0.21

and is based on the fact that $(\hat{p}-p)/\sqrt{\hat{p}(1-\hat{p})/500}$ is approximately distributed as a standard normal random variable [e.g., Hogg and Craig (1970, p. 187)].

From Table 9.2 it can be seen that 86.4 percent of the 500 confidence intervals based on $n=10$ replications covered $d(25|s=0)$, and we know with approximately 90 percent confidence that the true coverage for $n=10$ is between 0.839 and 0.889. Considering that a simulation model is always just an approximation to the corresponding real-world system, we believe that the estimated coverages presented in Table 9.2 are close enough to the desired 0.9 to be useful. Note also from the last column of the table that four times as many replications are required to increase the precision of the confidence interval by a factor of approximately 2. This is not surprising since there is a $\sqrt{n}$ in the denominator of the expression for the confidence-interval half-length in (9.1).

To show that the confidence interval given by (9.1) does not always produce coverages close to $1-\alpha$, we considered a second example. A reliability model consisting of three components will function as long as component 1 works and either component 2 or 3 works. If G is the time to failure of the whole system and G_i is the time to failure of component i (where $i=1,2,3$), then $G=\min\{G_1,\max\{G_2,G_3\}\}$. We further assume that the G_i's are independent random variables and that each G_i has a Weibull distribution with shape parameter 0.5 and scale parameter 1 (see Sec. 6.2.2). This particular Weibull distribution is extremely skewed and nonnormal. Once again we performed 500 independent simulation experiments; for each experiment we considered $n=5$, 10, 20, 40, and for each n we used (9.1) to construct a 90 percent confidence interval for $E(G|\text{all components new})=0.78$ (which was calculated by analytic reasoning). The results from these experiments are given in Table 9.3. Note that for small values of n there is significant coverage degradation. Also, as n gets large, the coverage appears to be approaching 0.9, as guaranteed by the central limit theorem.

We can see from Tables 9.2 and 9.3 that the coverage actually obtained from the confidence interval given by (9.1) depends on the simulation model under consideration (actually, on the distribution of the resulting X_j's) and also on the sample size n. It is therefore natural to ask why the confidence interval

TABLE 9.3
Fixed-sample-size results for $E(G|\text{all components new}) = 0.78$ based on 500 experiments, reliability model

n	Estimated coverage	Average of (confidence interval half-length)$/\bar{X}(n)$
5	0.708 ± 0.033	1.16
10	0.750 ± 0.032	0.82
20	0.800 ± 0.029	0.60
40	0.840 ± 0.027	0.44

worked better for the $M/M/1$ queue than it did for the reliability model. Two possible reasons come to mind. First, an X_j for the queueing system is actually an average of 25 individual delays, while an X_j for the reliability model is computed from the three individual times to failure by a formula involving a minimum and a maximum. There are central limit theorems for certain types of correlated data which state that averages of these data become approximately normally distributed as the number of points in the average gets large. (See Sec. 9.5.3 for further discussion.) We therefore expect that if X_j is the average of a large number of individual points (even though correlated), the degradation in coverage of the confidence interval may not be severe. Our experience indicates that many real-world simulations produce X_j's of this type. A second reason is that the delays for the queueing system are themselves more normal-like than are the times to failure for the reliability model. In fact, recall that the distribution of the times to failure of the individual components was purposely chosen to be extremely nonnormal.

Obtaining a Specified Precision. One disadvantage of the fixed-sample-size procedure based on n replications is that the analyst has no control over the confidence-interval half-length [or the precision of $\bar{X}(n)$]; for fixed n, the half-length will depend on $\text{Var}(X)$, the population variance of the X_j's. In what follows we discuss procedures for determining the number of replications required to estimate the mean $\mu = E(X)$ with a specified error or precision.

We begin by defining two ways of measuring the error in the estimate $\bar{X}$. (The dependence on n is suppressed, since the number of replications may be a random variable.) If the estimate $\bar{X}$ is such that $|\bar{X} - \mu| = \beta$, then we say that $\bar{X}$ has an *absolute error* of β. If we make replications of a simulation until the half-length of the $100(1 - \alpha)$ percent confidence interval given by (9.1) is less than or equal to β (where $\beta > 0$), then

$$1 - \alpha \approx P(\bar{X} - \text{half-length} \leq \mu \leq \bar{X} + \text{half-length})$$
$$= P(|\bar{X} - \mu| \leq \text{half-length})$$
$$\leq P(|\bar{X} - \mu| \leq \beta)$$

[If A and B are events with A being a subset of B, then $P(A) \leq P(B)$.] Thus, $\bar{X}$ has an absolute error of at most β with a probability of approximately $1 - \alpha$. In other words, if we construct 100 independent 90 percent confidence intervals using the above stopping rule, we would expect $\bar{X}$ to have an absolute error of at most β in about 90 out of the 100 cases; in about 10 cases the absolute error would be greater than β.

Suppose that we have constructed a confidence interval for μ based on a fixed number of replications n. If we assume that our estimate $S^2(n)$ of the population variance will not change (appreciably) as the number of replications increases, an *approximate* expression for the total number of replications, $n_a^*(\beta)$, required to obtain an absolute error of β is given by

$$n_a^*(\beta) = \min\left\{ i \geq n: t_{i-1,1-\alpha/2}\sqrt{\frac{S^2(n)}{i}} \leq \beta \right\} \tag{9.2}$$

(The colon ":" is read "such that.") We can determine $n_a^*(\beta)$ by iteratively increasing i by 1 until a value of i is obtained for which $t_{i-1,1-\alpha/2}\sqrt{S^2(n)/i} \leq \beta$. [Alternatively, $n_a^*(\beta)$ can be approximated as the smallest integer i satisfying $i \geq S^2(n)(z_{1-\alpha/2}/\beta)^2$.] If $n_a^*(\beta) > n$ and if we make $n_a^*(\beta) - n$ additional replications of the simulation, then the estimate $\bar{X}$ based on all $n_a^*(\beta)$ replications should have an absolute error of approximately β. The accuracy of Eq. (9.2) depends on how close the variance estimate $S^2(n)$ is to $\text{Var}(X)$.

Example 9.17. For the bank of Example 9.14, suppose that we would like to estimate the expected average delay with an absolute error of 0.25 minute and a confidence level of 90 percent. From the 10 available replications, we get

$$n_a^*(0.25) = \min\left\{ i \geq 10: t_{i-1,0.95}\sqrt{\frac{0.31}{i}} \leq 0.25 \right\} = 16$$

We now discuss another way of measuring the error in $\bar{X}$. If the estimate $\bar{X}$ is such that $|\bar{X} - \mu|/|\mu| = \gamma$, then we say that $\bar{X}$ has a *relative error* of γ, or that the *percentage error* in $\bar{X}$ is 100γ percent. Suppose that we make replications of a simulation until the half-length of the confidence interval given by (9.1), divided by $|\bar{X}|$, is less than or equal to γ $(0 < \gamma < 1)$. This ratio is an estimate of the actual relative error. Then

$$
\begin{aligned}
1 - \alpha &\approx P(|\bar{X} - \mu|/|\bar{X}| \leq \text{half-length}/|\bar{X}|) \\
&\leq P(|\bar{X} - \mu| \leq \gamma|\bar{X}|) && [(\text{half-length}/|\bar{X}|) \leq \gamma] \\
&= P(|\bar{X} - \mu| \leq \gamma|\bar{X} - \mu + \mu|) && (\text{add, subtract } \mu) \\
&\leq P(|\bar{X} - \mu| \leq \gamma(|\bar{X} - \mu| + |\mu|)) && (\text{triangle inequality}) \\
&= P((1 - \gamma)|\bar{X} - \mu| \leq \gamma|\mu|) && (\text{algebra}) \\
&= P(|\bar{X} - \mu|/|\mu| \leq \gamma/(1 - \gamma)) && (\text{algebra})
\end{aligned}
$$

Thus, $\bar{X}$ has a relative error of at most $\gamma/(1 - \gamma)$ with a probability of approximately $1 - \alpha$. In other words, if we construct 100 independent 90 percent confidence intervals using the above stopping rule, we would expect $\bar{X}$ to have a relative error of at most $\gamma/(1 - \gamma)$ in about 90 of the 100 cases; in about 10 cases the relative error would be greater than $\gamma/(1 - \gamma)$. Note that we get a relative error of $\gamma/(1 - \gamma)$ rather than the desired γ, since we *estimate* $|\mu|$ by $|\bar{X}|$.

Suppose once again that we have constructed a confidence interval for μ based on a fixed number of replications n. If we assume that our estimates of both the population mean and population variance will not change (appreciably) as the number of replications increases, an *approximate* expression for the number of replications, $n_r^*(\gamma)$, required to obtain a relative error of γ is given by

$$n_r^*(\gamma) = \min\left\{ i \geq n: \frac{t_{i-1,1-\alpha/2}\sqrt{S^2(n)/i}}{|\bar{X}(n)|} \leq \gamma' \right\} \tag{9.3}$$

where $\gamma' = \gamma/(1 + \gamma)$ is the "adjusted" relative error needed to get an *actual* relative error of γ. {Again, $n_r^*(\gamma)$ is approximated as the smallest integer i satisfying $i \geq S^2(n)[z_{1-\alpha/2}/\gamma'\bar{X}(n)]^2$.} If $n_r^*(\gamma) > n$ and if we make $n_r^*(\gamma) - n$ additional replications of the simulation, then the estimate $\bar{X}$ based on all $n_r^*(\gamma)$ replications should have a relative error of approximately γ.

Example 9.18. For the bank of Example 9.14, suppose that we would like to estimate the expected average delay with a relative error of 0.10 and a confidence level of 90 percent. From the 10 available replications, we get

$$n_r^*(0.10) = \min\left\{ i \geq 10: \frac{t_{i-1,0.95}\sqrt{0.31/i}}{2.03} \leq 0.09 \right\} = 27$$

where $\gamma' = 0.1/(1 + 0.1) = 0.09$.

The difficulty with using Eq. (9.3) directly to obtain an estimate $\bar{X}$ with a relative error of γ is that $\bar{X}(n)$ and $S^2(n)$ may not be precise estimates of their corresponding population parameters. If $n_r^*(\gamma)$ is greater than the number of replications actually required, then a significant number of unnecessary replications may be made, resulting in a waste of computer resources. Conversely, if $n_r^*(\gamma)$ is too small, then an estimate $\bar{X}$ based on $n_r^*(\gamma)$ replications may not be as precise as we think. We now present a *sequential* procedure (new replications are added one at a time) for obtaining an estimate of μ with a specified relative error that takes only as many replications as are actually needed. The procedure assumes that $X_1, X_2, \ldots$ is a sequence of IID random variables that need not be normal.

The specific objective of the procedure is to obtain an estimate of μ with a relative error of γ $(0 < \gamma < 1)$ and a confidence level of $100(1 - \alpha)$ percent. Choose an initial number of replications $n_0 \geq 2$ and let

$$\delta(n, \alpha) = t_{n-1,1-\alpha/2}\sqrt{\frac{S^2(n)}{n}}$$

be the usual confidence-interval half-length. Then the sequential procedure is as follows:

0. Make n_0 replications of the simulation and set $n = n_0$.

1. Compute $\bar{X}(n)$ and $\delta(n,\alpha)$ from $X_1, X_2, \ldots, X_n$.

2. If $\delta(n,\alpha)/|\bar{X}(n)| \leq \gamma'$, use $\bar{X}(n)$ as the point estimate for μ and stop. Equivalently,

$$I(\alpha,\gamma) = [\bar{X}(n) - \delta(n,\alpha),\ \bar{X}(n) + \delta(n,\alpha)] \tag{9.4}$$

is an approximate $100(1 - \alpha)$ percent confidence interval for μ with the desired precision. Otherwise, replace n by $n + 1$, make an additional replication of the simulation, and go to step 1.

Note that the procedure computes a new estimate of $\text{Var}(X)$ after *each* replication is obtained, and that the total number of replications required by the procedure is a random variable.

> **Example 9.19.** For the bank of Example 9.14, suppose that we would like to obtain an estimate of the expected average delay with a relative error of $\gamma = 0.1$ and a confidence level of 90 percent. Using the previous $n_0 = 10$ replications as a starting point, we obtained
>
> $$\text{number of replications at termination} = 74$$
> $$\bar{X}(74) = 1.76, \qquad S^2(74) = 0.67$$
> $$90 \text{ percent confidence interval: } [1.60, 1.92]$$
>
> Note that the number of replications actually required, 74, is considerably larger than the 27 predicted in Example 9.18, due mostly to the imprecise variance estimate based on 10 replications.

Although the sequential procedure described above is intuitively appealing, the question naturally arises as to how well it performs in terms of producing a confidence interval with coverage close to the desired $1 - \alpha$. In Law, Kelton, and Koenig (1981), it is shown that if $\mu \neq 0$ [and $0 < \text{Var}(X) < \infty$], then the coverage of the confidence interval given by Eq. (9.4) will be arbitrarily close to $1 - \alpha$, provided the desired relative error is sufficiently close to 0. Based on sampling from a large number of stochastic models and probability distributions (including the $M/M/1$ queue and the above reliability model) for which the true values of μ are known, our recommendation is to use the sequential procedure with $n_0 \geq 10$ and $\gamma \leq 0.15$. It was found that if these recommendations are followed, the estimated coverage (based on 500 independent experiments for each model) for a desired 90 percent confidence interval was never less than 0.864.

Analogous to the sequential procedure described above is a sequential procedure due to Chow and Robbins (1965) for constructing a $100(1 - \alpha)$ percent confidence interval for μ with a small absolute error β. Furthermore, it can be shown that the coverage actually produced by the procedure will be arbitrarily close to $1 - \alpha$ provided the desired absolute error β is sufficiently close to 0. However, since the meaning of "*absolute error* sufficiently small" is extremely model-dependent, and since the coverage results in Law (1980) indicate that the procedure is very sensitive to the choice of β, we do not recommend the use of the Chow and Robbins procedure in general.

Recommended Use of the Procedures. We now make our recommendations on the use of the fixed-sample-size and sequential procedures for terminating simulations. If one is performing an exploratory experiment where the precision of the confidence interval may not be overwhelmingly important, we recommend using the fixed-sample-size procedure. However, if the X_j's are highly nonnormal and the number of replications n is too small, the actual coverage of the constructed confidence interval may be somewhat lower than desired.

From an exploratory experiment consisting of n replications, one can estimate the cost per replication and the population variance of the X_j's, and then obtain from Eq. (9.2) a *rough estimate* of the number of replications, $n_a^*(\beta)$, required to estimate μ with a desired absolute error β. Alternatively, one can obtain from Eq. (9.3) a *rough estimate* of the number of replications, $n_r^*(\gamma)$, required to estimate μ with a desired relative error γ. Sometimes the choice of β or γ may have to be tempered by the cost associated with the required number of replications. If it is finally decided to construct a confidence interval with a small relative error γ, we recommend use of the sequential procedure with $\gamma \leq 0.15$ and $n_0 \geq 10$. If one wants a confidence interval with a relative error γ greater than 0.15, we recommend several successive applications of the fixed-sample-size approach. In particular, one might estimate $n_r^*(\gamma)$, collect, say $[n_r^*(\gamma) - n]/2$ more replications, and then use (9.1) to construct a confidence interval based on the existing $[n + n_r^*(\gamma)]/2$ replications. If the estimated relative error of the resulting confidence interval is still greater than γ', then $n_r^*(\gamma)$ can be reestimated based on a new variance estimate, and some portion of the necessary additional replications may be collected, etc. To construct a confidence interval with a small absolute error β, we once again recommend several successive applications of the fixed-sample-size approach. It should be mentioned that all of the statistical analyses [except the calculation of $n_a^*(\beta)$] for terminating simulations thus far discussed can be performed in SIMSCRIPT II.5 using an optional library routine called STAT.R [see Law (1979)].

Regardless of the cost per replication, we recommend always making at least three to five replications of a stochastic simulation to assess the variability of the X_j's. If this is not possible due to time or cost considerations, then the simulation study should probably not be done at all.

9.4.2 Estimating Other Measures of Performance

In this section we discuss estimating measures of performance other than means. As the following example shows, comparing two or more systems by some sort of mean system response may result in misleading conclusions.

Example 9.20. Consider the bank of Example 9.14, where the utilization factor $\rho = \lambda/(5\omega) = 0.8$. We compare the policy of having one queue for each teller (and jockeying) with the policy of having one queue feed all tellers on the basis of *expected average delay in queue* (see Example 9.14) and *expected time-average number of customers in queue*, which is defined by

$$E\left[\frac{\int_0^T Q(t)\,dt}{T}\right]$$

where $Q(t)$ is the number of customers in queue at time t and T is the bank's operating time ($T \geq 8$ hours). Table 9.4 gives the results of making one simulation run of each policy. [These simulation runs were performed so that the time of arrival of the ith customer ($i = 1, 2, \ldots, N$) was identical for both policies and so that the service time of the ith customer to begin service ($i = 1, 2, \ldots, N$) was the same for both policies.] Thus, on the basis of "average system response," it would appear that the two policies are equivalent. However, this is clearly not the case. Since customers need not be served in the order of their arrival with the multiqueue policy, we would expect this policy to result in greater variability of a customer's delay. Table 9.5 gives estimates, computed from the same two simulation runs used above, of the expected proportion of customers with a delay in the interval [0,5) (in minutes), the expected proportion of customers with a delay in [5,10), ..., the expected proportion of customers with a delay in [40,45) for both policies. (We did not estimate variances from these runs since, as pointed out in Sec. 4.4, variance estimates computed from correlated simulation output data are highly biased.) Observe from Table 9.5 that a customer is more likely to have a large delay with the multiqueue policy than with the single-queue policy. In particular, if 480 customers arrive in a day, then 33 and 6 of them would be expected to have delays greater than or equal to 20 minutes for the five-queue and one-queue policies, respectively. (For larger values of ρ, the differences between the two policies would be even greater.) This observation together with the greater equitability of the single-queue policy has probably led many organizations, e.g., banks and airlines, to adopt this policy.

We conclude from the above example that comparing alternative systems or policies on the basis of average system behavior alone can sometimes result in misleading conclusions and, furthermore, that proportions can be a useful measure of system performance. In Example 9.16 we showed how to obtain a point estimate and a confidence interval for an expected proportion. In this

TABLE 9.4
Simulation results for the two bank policies: averages

Measure of performance	Estimates	
	Five queues	One queue
Expected operating time, hours	8.14	8.14
Expected average delay, minutes	5.57	5.57
Expected average number in queue	5.52	5.52

TABLE 9.5
Simulation results for the two bank policies:
proportions

Interval (minutes)	Estimates of expected proportions of delays in interval	
	Five queues	One queue
[0,5)	0.626	0.597
[5,10)	0.182	0.188
[10,15)	0.076	0.107
[15,20)	0.047	0.095
[20,25)	0.031	0.013
[25,30)	0.020	0
[30,35)	0.015	0
[35,40)	0.003	0
[40,45)	0	0

section we show how to perform similar analyses for probabilities and quantiles in the context of terminating simulations.

Let X be a random variable defined on a replication as described in Sec. 9.4.1. Suppose that we would like to estimate the probability $p = P(X \in B)$, where B is a set of real numbers. (For example, B could be the interval $[20,\infty)$ in Example 9.20.) Make n independent replications and let $X_1, X_2, \ldots, X_n$ be the resulting IID random variables. Let S be the number of X_j's that fall in the set B. Then S has a binomial distribution (see Sec. 6.2.3) with parameters n and p, and an unbiased point estimator for p is given by

$$\hat{p} = \frac{S}{n}$$

Furthermore, a confidence interval for p may be constructed using procedures described in Welch (1983, pp. 285–287) and Conover (1980, pp. 99–104) (see also Prob. 9.9).

Example 9.21. For the bank of Example 9.14, suppose that we would like to get a point estimate for

$$p = P(X \le 15) \qquad \text{where } X = \max_{0 \le t \le T} Q(t)$$

In this case $B = [0,15]$. We made 100 independent replications of the bank simulation and obtained $\hat{p} = 0.77$. Thus, for approximately 77 out of every 100 days, we expect the maximum queue length during a day to be less than or equal to 15 customers.

Suppose now that we would like to estimate the q-quantile ($100q$th percentile) x_q of the distribution of the random variable X (see Sec. 6.4.3 for the definition). For example, the 0.5-quantile is the median. If $X_{(1)}, X_{(2)}, \ldots, X_{(n)}$ are the order statistics corresponding to the X_j's from n

independent replications, then a point estimator for x_q is the sample q-quantile $\hat{x}_q$, which is given by

$$\hat{x}_q = \begin{cases} X_{(nq)} & \text{if } nq \text{ is an integer} \\ X_{(\lfloor nq+1 \rfloor)} & \text{otherwise} \end{cases}$$

A confidence interval for x_q can also be obtained; see Welch [1983, pp. 287–288) and Conover (1980, pp. 111–116).

> **Example 9.22.** For the bank of Example 9.14, suppose that we would like to decide how large a lobby is needed to accommodate customers waiting in the queue. If we let X be the maximum queue length as defined in Example 9.21, then we might want to build a lobby large enough to hold $x_{0.95}$ customers, the 0.95-quantile of X. From the 100 replications in the previous example, we obtained $\hat{x}_{0.95} = X_{(95)} = 20$. Thus, if the lobby has room for 20 customers, this will be sufficient for approximately 95 out of every 100 days. Note also that $\hat{x}_{0.99} = X_{(99)} = 23$.

The interested reader may also want to consult Conover (1980, pp. 117–121) for a discussion of *tolerance limits*, which is an interval that contains a specified proportion of the *values* of the random variable X (and does so with a certain prescribed confidence level).

9.4.3 Choosing Initial Conditions

As stated in Sec. 9.3, the measures of performance for a terminating simulation depend explicitly on the state of the system at time 0; thus, care must be taken in choosing appropriate initial conditions. Let us illustrate this potential problem by means of an example. Suppose that we would like to estimate the expected average delay of all customers who arrive and complete their delays between 12 noon and 1 P.M. (the busiest period) in a bank. Since the bank will probably be quite congested at noon, starting the simulation then with no customers present (the usual initial conditions for a queueing simulation) will cause our estimate of expected average delay to be biased low. We now discuss two heuristic approaches to this problem, the first of which appears to be used widely (see Sec. 9.5.1).

For the first approach, let us assume that the bank opens at 9 A.M. with no customers present. Then we can start the simulation at 9 A.M. with no customers present and run it for 4 simulated hours. In estimating the desired expected average delay, we use only the delays of those customers who arrive and complete their delays between noon and 1 P.M. The evolution of the simulation between 9 A.M. and noon (the "warmup period") determines the appropriate conditions for the simulation at noon. A disadvantage of this approach is that 3 hours of simulated time are not used directly in the estimate. As a result, one might compromise and start the simulation at some other time, say 11 A.M., with no customers present. However, there is no guarantee that the conditions in the simulation at noon will be representative of the actual conditions in the bank at noon. This approach can be carried out in SIMLIB (see Chap. 2) by reinitializing the statistical counters for subroutines SAMPST, TIMEST, and FILEST (see Prob. 2.7) at noon.

An alternative approach is to collect data on the number of customers present in the bank at noon for several different days. Let $\hat{p}_i$ be the proportion of these days that i customers ($i = 0, 1, \ldots$) are present at noon. Then we simulate the bank from noon to 1 P.M. with the number of customers present at noon being randomly chosen from the distribution $\{\hat{p}_i\}$. (All customers who are being served at noon might be assumed to be just beginning their services. Starting all services fresh at noon results in an approximation to the actual situation in the bank, since the customers who are in the process of being served at noon would have partially completed their services. However, the effect of this approximation should be negligible for a simulation of length 1 hour.)

If more than one simulation run from noon to 1 P.M. is desired, then a different sample from $\{\hat{p}_i\}$ is drawn for each run. The X_j's that result from these runs are still IID, since the initial conditions for each run are chosen independently from the same distribution.

9.5 STATISTICAL ANALYSIS FOR STEADY-STATE PARAMETERS

Let $Y_1, Y_2, \ldots$ be an output stochastic process from a single run of a nonterminating simulation. Suppose that $P(Y_i \leq y) = F_i(y) \to F(y) = P(Y \leq y)$ as $i \to \infty$, where Y is the steady-state random variable of interest with distribution function F. (We have suppressed in our notation the dependence of F_i on the initial conditions I.) Then ϕ is a steady-state parameter if it is a characteristic of Y such as $E(Y)$, $P(Y \leq y)$, or a quantile of Y. One difficulty in estimating ϕ is that the distribution function of Y_i (for $i = 1, 2, \ldots$) is different from F, since it will generally not be possible to choose I to be representative of "steady-state behavior." This causes an estimator of ϕ based on the observations $Y_1, Y_2, \ldots, Y_m$ not to be "representative." For example, the sample mean $\bar{Y}(m)$ will be a biased estimator of $\nu = E(Y)$ for all finite values of m. The problem we have just described is called the *problem of the initial transient* or the *startup problem* in the simulation literature.

Example 9.23. To illustrate the startup problem more succinctly, consider the process of delays $D_1, D_2, \ldots$ for the $M/M/1$ queue with $\rho < 1$ (see Example 9.2). From queueing theory, it is possible to show that

$$P(D_i \leq y) \to P(D \leq y) = (1 - \rho) + \rho[1 - e^{-(\omega - \lambda)y}] \qquad \text{as } i \to \infty$$

If the number of customers s present at time 0 is 0, then $D_1 = 0$ and $E(D_i) \neq E(D) = d$ for any i. On the other hand, if s is chosen in accordance with the steady-state number in system distribution [see, for example, Gross and Harris (1985, p. 65)], then for all i, $P(D_i \leq y) = P(D \leq y)$ and $E(D_i) = d$ (see Prob. 9.11). Thus, there is no initial transient in this case.

In practice, the steady-state distribution will not be known exactly and the above initialization technique will not be possible. Techniques for dealing with the startup problem in practice are discussed in the next section.

9.5.1 The Problem of the Initial Transient

Suppose that we want to estimate the steady-state mean $\nu = E(Y)$, which is also generally defined by

$$\nu = \lim_{i \to \infty} E(Y_i)$$

Thus, the transient means converge to the steady-state mean. The most serious consequence of the problem of the initial transient is probably that $E[\bar{Y}(m)] \neq \nu$ for any m [see Law (1983, pp. 1010–1012) for further discussion]. The technique most often suggested for dealing with this problem is called *warming up the model* or *initial-data deletion*. The idea is to delete some number of observations from the beginning of a run and to use only the remaining observations to estimate ν. For example, given the observations $Y_1, Y_2, \ldots, Y_m$, it is often suggested to use

$$\bar{Y}(m,l) = \frac{\displaystyle\sum_{i=l+1}^{m} Y_i}{m - l}$$

$(1 \le l \le m - 1)$ rather than $\bar{Y}(m)$ as an estimator of ν. In general, one would expect $\bar{Y}(m,l)$ to be less biased than $\bar{Y}(m)$, since the observations near the "beginning" of the simulation may not be very representative of steady-state behavior due to the choice of initial conditions. For example, this is true for the process $D_1, D_2, \ldots$ in the case of an $M/M/1$ queue with $s = 0$, since $E(D_i)$ increases monotonically to d as $i \to \infty$ (see Fig. 9.2).

The question naturally arises as to how to choose the *warmup period* (or deletion amount) l. We would like to pick l (and m) such that $E[\bar{Y}(m,l)] \approx \nu$. If l and m are chosen too small, then $E[\bar{Y}(m,l)]$ may be significantly different from ν. On the other hand, if l is chosen larger than necessary, then $\bar{Y}(m,l)$ will probably have an unnecessarily large variance. There have been a number of methods suggested in the literature for choosing l. However, Gafarian, Ancker, and Morisaku (1978) found that none of the methods available at that time performed well in practice. Kelton and Law (1983) developed an algorithm for choosing l (and m) that worked well {that is, $E[\bar{Y}(m,l)] \approx \nu$} for a wide variety of stochastic models. However, a theoretical limitation of the procedure is that it basically makes the assumption that $E(Y_i)$ is a monotone function of i.

The simplest and most general technique for determining l is a graphical procedure due to Welch (1981, 1983). Its specific goal is to determine a time index l such that $E(Y_i) \approx \nu$ for $i > l$, where l is the warmup period. [This is equivalent to determining when the transient mean curve $E(Y_i)$ (for $i =$

1, 2, . . .) "flattens out" at level v; see Fig. 9.1.] In general, it is very difficult to determine l from a single replication due to the inherent variability of the process $Y_1, Y_2, \ldots$ (see Fig. 9.7, below). As a result, Welch's procedure is based on making n independent replications of the simulation and employing the following four steps:

1. Make n replications of the simulation ($n \geq 5$), each of length m (where m is large). Let Y_{ji} be the ith observation from the jth replication ($j = 1, 2, \ldots, n; i = 1, 2, \ldots, m$), as shown in Fig. 9.5.
2. Let $\bar{Y}_i = \sum_{j=1}^{n} Y_{ji}/n$ for $i = 1, 2, \ldots, m$ (see Fig. 9.5). The averaged process $\bar{Y}_1, \bar{Y}_2, \ldots$ has means $E(\bar{Y}_i) = E(Y_i)$ and variances $\text{Var}(\bar{Y}_i) = \text{Var}(Y_i)/n$ (see Prob. 9.12). Thus, the averaged process has the same transient mean curve as the original process, but its plot has only $(1/n)$th the variance.
3. To smooth out the high-frequency oscillations in $\bar{Y}_1, \bar{Y}_2, \ldots$ (but leave the low-frequency oscillations or long-run trend of interest), we further define the moving average $\bar{Y}_i(w)$ (where w is the *window* and is a positive integer such that $w \leq \lfloor m/2 \rfloor$) as follows:

$$
\bar{Y}_i(w) = \begin{cases} \dfrac{\displaystyle\sum_{s=-w}^{w} \bar{Y}_{i+s}}{2w + 1} & \text{if } i = w + 1, \ldots, m - w \\[4mm] \dfrac{\displaystyle\sum_{s=-(i-1)}^{i-1} \bar{Y}_{i+s}}{2i - 1} & \text{if } i = 1, \ldots, w \end{cases}
$$

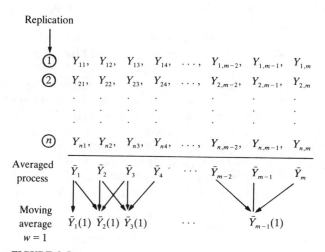

FIGURE 9.5

Averaged process and moving average with $w = 1$ based on n replications of length m.

Thus, if i is not too close to the beginning of the replications, then $\bar{Y}_i(w)$ is just the simple average of $2w + 1$ observations of the averaged process centered at observation i (see Fig. 9.5). It is called a moving average since i moves through time.

4. Plot $\bar{Y}_i(w)$ for $i = 1, 2, \ldots, m - w$ and choose l to be that value of i beyond which $\bar{Y}_1(w), \bar{Y}_2(w), \ldots$ appears to have converged. See Welch (1983, p. 292) for an aid in determining convergence.

The following example illustrates the calculation of the moving average.

Example 9.24. For simplicity, assume that $m = 10$, $w = 2$, $\bar{Y}_i = i$ for $i = 1, 2, \ldots, 5$, and $\bar{Y}_i = 6$ for $i = 6, 7, \ldots, 10$. Then

$$\bar{Y}_1(2) = 1 \qquad \bar{Y}_2(2) = 2 \qquad \bar{Y}_3(2) = 3$$
$$\bar{Y}_4(2) = 4 \qquad \bar{Y}_5(2) = 4.8 \qquad \bar{Y}_6(2) = 5.4$$
$$\bar{Y}_7(2) = 5.8 \qquad \bar{Y}_8(2) = 6$$

Before giving examples of applying Welch's procedure to actual stochastic models, we make the following recommendations on choosing the parameters n, m, and w:

- Initially, make $n = 5$ or 10 replications (depending on model execution cost), with m as large as practical. In particular, m should be much larger than the anticipated value of l (see Sec. 9.5.2) and also large enough to allow infrequent events (e.g., machine breakdowns) to occur a reasonable number of times.
- Plot $\bar{Y}_i(w)$ for several values of the window w and choose the smallest value of w (if any) for which the corresponding plot is "reasonably smooth." Use this plot to determine the length of the warmup period l. [Choosing w is like choosing the interval width Δb for a histogram (see Sec. 6.4.2). If w is too small, the plot of $\bar{Y}_i(w)$ will be "ragged." If w is too large, then the $\bar{Y}_i$ observations will be overaggregated and we will not have a good idea of the shape of the transient mean curve, $E(Y_i)$ for $i = 1, 2, \ldots$.]
- If no value of w in step 3 is satisfactory, make 5 or 10 additional replications of length m. Repeat step 2 using all available replications. [For a fixed value of w, the plot of $\bar{Y}_i(w)$ will get "smoother" as the number of replications increases. Why?]

The major difficulty in applying Welch's procedure in practice is that the required number of replications, n, may be relatively large if the process $Y_1, Y_2, \ldots$ is highly variable.

Example 9.25. A small factory consists of a machining center and inspection station in series, as shown in Fig. 9.6. Unfinished parts arrive to the factory with exponential interarrival times having a mean of 1 minute. Processing times at the

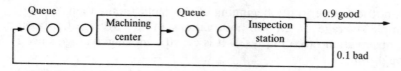

FIGURE 9.6
Small factory consisting of a machining center and an inspection station.

machine are uniform on the interval $[0.65, 0.70]$ minute, and subsequent inspection times at the inspection station are uniform on the interval $[0.75, 0.80]$ minute. Ninety percent of inspected parts are "good" and are sent to shipping; 10 percent of the parts are "bad" and are sent back to the machine for rework. (Both queues are assumed to have infinite capacity.) The machining center is subject to randomly occurring breakdowns. In particular, a new (or freshly repaired) machine will break down after an exponential amount of *calendar* time with a mean of 6 hours (see Sec. 13.4.2). Repair times are uniform on the interval $[8,12]$ minutes. Assume that the factory is initially empty and idle.

Consider the stochastic process $N_1, N_2, \ldots$, where N_i is the number of parts produced in the ith hour. Suppose that we want to determine the warmup period l so that we can eventually estimate the steady-state mean hourly throughput $\nu = E(N)$ (see Example 9.27). We made $n = 10$ independent replications of the simulation each of length $m = 160$ hours (or 20 days). In Fig. 9.7 we plot the

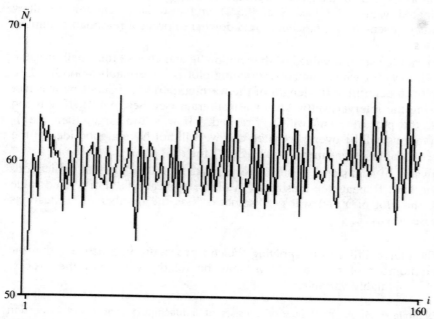

FIGURE 9.7
Averaged process for hourly throughputs, small factory.

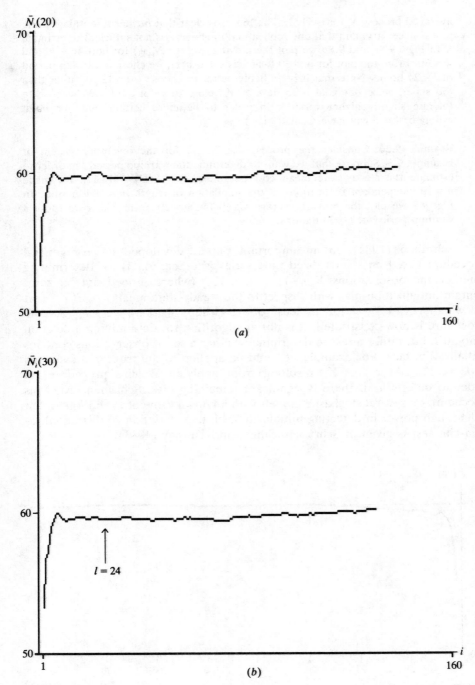

FIGURE 9.8
Moving averages for hourly throughputs, small factory: (*a*) $w = 20$; (*b*) $w = 30$.

averaged process $\bar{N}_i$ for $i = 1, 2, \ldots, 160$. It is clear that further smoothing of the plot is necessary, and that one replication, in general, is not sufficient to estimate l. In Figs. 9.8a and 9.8b we plot the moving average $\bar{N}_i(w)$ for both $w = 20$ and $w = 30$. From the plot for $w = 30$ (which is smoother), we chose a warmup period of $l = 24$ hours. Note that it is probably better to choose l too large rather than too small, since our goal is to have $E(Y_i)$ close to ν for $i > l$. (We choose to tolerate slightly higher variance in order to be more certain that our point estimator for ν will have a small bias.)

Example 9.26. Consider the process $C_1, C_2, \ldots$ for the inventory system of Example 9.3. Suppose that we want to determine the warmup period l in order to estimate the steady-state mean cost per month $c = E(C) = 112.11$. We made $n = 10$ independent replications of the simulation of length $m = 100$ months. In Fig. 9.9 we plot the moving average $\bar{C}_i(w)$ for $w = 20$, from which we chose a warmup period of $l = 30$ months.

Schruben (1982), in an important paper, developed a very general procedure based on standardized time series (see Sec. 9.5.3) for determining whether the observations $Y_{s+1}, Y_{s+2}, \ldots, Y_{s+t}$ (where s need not be zero) contain initialization bias with respect to the steady-state mean $\nu = E(Y)$, that is, whether $E(Y_i) \neq \nu$ for at least one i (where $s + 1 \leq i \leq s + t$). As the procedure is now constituted, it is not an algorithm for determining a deletion amount l, but rather a test to determine whether a set of observations contains initialization bias. For example, it could be applied to the truncated averaged process $\bar{Y}_{l+1}, \bar{Y}_{l+2}, \ldots, \bar{Y}_m$ resulting from applying Welch's procedure, in order to determine if there is significant remaining bias. Schruben tested his procedure on several stochastic models with a known value of ν, and found that it had high power in detecting initialization bias. A variation of this initialization-bias test is given in Schruben, Singh, and Tierney (1983).

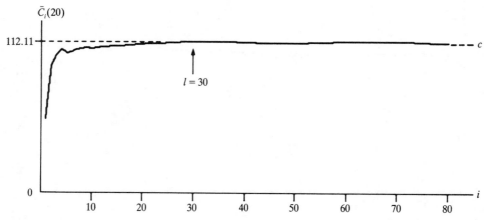

FIGURE 9.9
Moving average with $w = 20$ for monthly costs, inventory system.

In Example 9.23 we saw that initializing the $M/M/1$ queue with the steady-state number in system distribution resulted in the process $D_1, D_2, \ldots$ not having an initial transient. This suggests trying to estimate the steady-state distribution from a "pilot" run, and then independently sampling from this estimated distribution in order to determine the initial conditions for each production run. Kelton (1989) applied this idea to several queueing systems and also a computer model, where in each case the state of the system is an integer-valued random variable. He found that random initialization reduced the severity and duration of the initial transient period as compared with starting the simulation in a fixed state (e.g., no one present in a queueing system). This technique would be harder to apply, however, in the case of many real-world simulations, where the state of the system has a multivariate distribution [see Murray (1988) and Law (1983, p. 1016) for further discussion]. Glynn (1988) discusses a related method where a one-time pass through the "transient period" is used to specify the starting conditions for subsequent replications.

9.5.2 Replication/Deletion Approach for Means

Suppose that we want to estimate the steady-state mean $v = E(Y)$ of the process $Y_1, Y_2, \ldots$. There are six fundamental approaches for addressing this problem, which are discussed in this and the next section. We will for the most part, however, concentrate on one of these, the replication/deletion approach, for the following reasons:

1. If properly applied, this approach should give reasonably good statistical performance.
2. It is the easiest approach to understand and implement. (This is very important in practice due to the time constraints of many simulation projects and because many analysts do not have the statistical background necessary to use some of the more complicated analysis approaches.)
3. This approach applies to all types of output parameters (i.e., Secs. 9.4 through 9.6).
4. It can easily be used to estimate several different parameters for the same simulation model (see Sec. 9.7).
5. This approach can be used to compare different system configurations, as discussed in Chap. 10.

We now present the *replication/deletion approach* for obtaining a point estimate and confidence interval for v. The analysis is similar to that for terminating simulations except that now only those observations beyond the warmup period l in each replication are used to form the estimates. Specifically, suppose that we make n' replications of the simulation each of length m'

observations, where m' is much larger than the warmup period l determined by Welch's graphical method (see Sec. 9.5.1). Let Y_{ji} be as defined before and let X_j be given by

$$
X_j = \frac{\sum\limits_{i=l+1}^{m'} Y_{ji}}{(m'-l)} \qquad \text{for } j = 1, 2, \ldots, n'
$$

(Note that X_j uses only those observations from the jth replication corresponding to "steady state," namely, $Y_{j,l+1}, Y_{j,l+2}, \ldots, Y_{j,m'}$.) Then the X_j's are IID random variables with $E(X_j) \approx \nu$ (see Prob. 9.15), $\bar{X}(n')$ is an approximately unbiased point estimator for ν, and an approximate $100(1 - \alpha)$ percent confidence interval for ν is given by

$$
\bar{X}(n') \pm t_{n'-1,1-\alpha/2} \sqrt{\frac{S^2(n')}{n'}} \tag{9.5}
$$

where $\bar{X}(n')$ and $S^2(n')$ are computed from Eqs. (4.3) and (4.4), respectively.

One legitimate objection that might be levied against the replication/deletion approach is that it uses one set of n replications (the pilot runs) to determine the warmup period l, and then uses *only* the last $m' - l$ observations from a different set of n' replications (production runs) to perform the actual analyses. However, this is often not a problem due to the relatively low cost of computer time (see Sec. 9.1).

In some situations, it should be possible to use the initial n pilot runs of length m observations both to determine l and to construct a confidence interval. In particular, if m is substantially larger than the selected value of the warmup period l, then it is probably safe to use the "initial" runs for both purposes. Since Welch's graphical method is only approximate, a "small" number of observations beyond the warmup period l might contain significant bias relative to ν. However, if m is much larger than l, these biased observations will have little effect on the overall quality (i.e., lack of bias) of X_j (based on $m - l$ observations) or $\bar{X}(n)$. Strictly speaking, however, it is more correct statistically to base the replication/deletion approach on two independent sets of replications (see Prob. 9.16).

Example 9.27. For the manufacturing system of Example 9.25, suppose that we would like to obtain a point estimate and 90 percent confidence interval for the steady-state mean hourly throughput $\nu = E(N)$. From the $n = 10$ replications of length $m = 160$ hours used there, we specified a warmup period of $l = 24$ hours. Since $m = 160$ is much larger than $l = 24$, we will use these same replications to construct a confidence interval. Let

$$
X_j = \frac{\sum\limits_{i=25}^{160} N_{ji}}{136} \qquad \text{for } j = 1, 2, \ldots, 10
$$

Then a point estimate and 90 percent confidence interval for ν are given by

$$\hat{\nu} = \bar{X}(10) = 59.97$$

and
$$\bar{X}(10) \pm t_{9,0.95}\sqrt{\frac{0.62}{10}} = 59.97 \pm 0.46$$

Thus, in the long run we would expect the small factory to produce an average of about 60 parts per hour. Does this throughput seem reasonable? (See Prob. 9.17.)

The half-length of the replication/deletion confidence interval given by (9.5) depends on the variance of X_j, $\mathrm{Var}(X_j)$, which will be unknown when the first n replications are made. Therefore, if we make a fixed number of replications of the simulation, the resulting confidence-interval half-length may or may not be small enough for a particular purpose. We know, however, that the half-length can be decreased by a factor of approximately 2 by making four times as many replications. See also the discussion of "Obtaining a Specified Precision" in Sec. 9.4.1.

9.5.3 Other Approaches for Means

In this section we present a more comprehensive discussion of procedures for constructing a point estimate and a confidence interval for the steady-state mean $\nu = E(Y)$ of a simulation output process $Y_1, Y_2, \ldots$. The following definitions of ν are usually equivalent:

$$\nu = \lim_{i \to \infty} E(Y_i)$$

and

$$\nu = \lim_{m \to \infty} \frac{\sum_{i=1}^{m} Y_i}{m} \qquad (\text{w.p. } 1)$$

General references on this subject include Banks and Carson (1984), Bratley, Fox, and Schrage (1987), Fishman (1978), Law (1983), and Welch (1983).

Two general strategies have been suggested in the simulation literature for constructing a point estimate and confidence interval for ν:

1. *Fixed-sample-size procedures.* A single simulation run of an *arbitrary* fixed length is made, and then one of a number of available procedures is used to construct a confidence interval from the available data.
2. *Sequential procedures.* The length of a single simulation run is sequentially increased until an "acceptable" confidence interval can be constructed. There are several techniques for deciding when to stop the simulation run.

Fixed-Sample-Size Procedures. There have been six fixed-sample-size procedures suggested in the literature [see Law (1983) and Law and Kelton (1984) for surveys]. The replication/deletion approach, which was discussed in Sec. 9.5.2, is based on n independent "short" replications of length m observations.

It tends to suffer from bias in the point estimator $\hat{\nu}$ (see Sec. 9.1). The five other approaches are based on one "long" replication, and tend to have a problem with bias in the estimator $\widehat{\text{Var}}(\hat{\nu})$ of the variance of the point estimator $\hat{\nu}$. Properties of the six approaches are given in Table 9.6, and details of the five new approaches are now presented.

The method of *batch means*, like the replication/deletion approach, seeks to obtain independent observations so that the formulas of Chap. 4 can be used to obtain a confidence interval. However, since the batch-means method is based on a single long run, it has to go through the "transient period" only once. Assume that $Y_1, Y_2, \ldots$ is a covariance-stationary process (see Sec. 4.3) with $E(Y_i) = \nu$ for all i. (Alternatively, suppose that the first l observations have been deleted and we are dealing with $Y_{l+1}, Y_{l+2}, \ldots$. If ν exists, in general $Y_{l+1}, Y_{l+2}, \ldots$ will be approximately covariance stationary if l is large enough.) Suppose that we make a simulation run of length m and then divide the resulting observations $Y_1, Y_2, \ldots, Y_m$ into n batches of length k. (Assume that $m = nk$.) Thus, batch 1 consists of observations $Y_1, \ldots, Y_k$, batch 2 consists of observations $Y_{k+1}, \ldots, Y_{2k}$, etc. Let $\bar{Y}_j(k)$ (where $j = 1, 2, \ldots, n$) be the sample (or batch) mean of the k observations in the jth batch, and let $\bar{\bar{Y}}(n,k) = \sum_{j=1}^{n} \bar{Y}_j(k)/n = \sum_{i=1}^{m} Y_i/m$ be the grand sample mean. We shall use $\bar{\bar{Y}}(n,k)$ as our point estimator for ν. [The $\bar{Y}_j(k)$'s will eventually play the same role for batch means as the X_j's did for the replication/deletion approach in Sec. 9.5.2.]

If we choose the batch size k large enough, it can be shown (under relatively mild conditions) that the $\bar{Y}_j(k)$'s will be approximately uncorrelated [see Law and Carson (1979)]. Suppose that we can also choose k large enough

TABLE 9.6
Properties of steady-state estimation procedures

Approach	Number of replications	Most serious bias problem	Potential difficulties
Replication/deletion	$n(n \geq 2)$	$\hat{\nu}$	Choice of warmup period, l
Batch means	1	$\widehat{\text{Var}}(\hat{\nu})$	Choice of batch size, k, to obtain uncorrelated batch means
Autoregressive	1	$\widehat{\text{Var}}(\hat{\nu})$	Quality of autoregressive model
Spectral	1	$\widehat{\text{Var}}(\hat{\nu})$	Choice of number of covariance lags, q
Regenerative	1	$\widehat{\text{Var}}(\hat{\nu})$	Existence of cycles with "small" mean length
Standardized time series	1	$\widehat{\text{Var}}(\hat{\nu})$	Choice of batch size, k

for the $\bar{Y}_j(k)$'s to be approximately normally distributed. This is not implausible, since there are central limit theorems for certain types of correlated stochastic processes [see Anderson (1971, p. 427)]. Also, it can be shown that the sample mean of the first k delays, $\bar{D}(k)$, for the $M/M/1$ queue will be approximately normally distributed if k is large [see Law (1974)]. However, if the $\bar{Y}_j(k)$'s are both uncorrelated and jointly normally distributed, it follows from Prob. 4.10 that the $\bar{Y}_j(k)$'s are independent and normally distributed. Denote these two properties by (P1).

Since $Y_1, Y_2, \ldots$ is assumed to be covariance stationary with $E(Y_i) = \nu$, it easily follows that the $\bar{Y}_j(k)$'s have the same mean ν and the same variance [see Eq. (4.7)]. Denote these properties by (P2).

It follows from (P1) and (P2) that the $\bar{Y}_j(k)$'s are normal random variables with the same mean and variance. Since a normal random variable is completely determined by its mean and variance, it in turn follows that the $\bar{Y}_j(k)$'s are identically distributed with mean ν, which we denote by (P3). Therefore, if the batch size k is large enough, it follows from (P1) and (P3) that it is reasonable to treat the $\bar{Y}_j(k)$'s as if they were IID normal random variables with mean ν. Then a point estimate and approximate $100(1 - \alpha)$ percent confidence interval for ν is obtained by substituting $X_j = \bar{Y}_j(k)$ into Eqs. (4.3) and (4.4), and (4.12).

The major source of error for batch means is choosing the batch size k too small, which results in the $\bar{Y}_j(k)$'s possibly being highly correlated and $S^2(n)/n$ being a severely biased estimator of $\text{Var}[\bar{X}(n)] = \text{Var}[\bar{Y}(n,k)]$; see Sec. 4.4. In particular, if the Y_i's are positively correlated (as is often the case in practice), the $\bar{Y}_j(k)$'s will be too, giving a variance estimator that is biased low and a confidence interval that is too small. Thus, the confidence interval will cover ν with a probability that is lower than the desired $1 - \alpha$.

There have been several variations of batch means proposed in the literature. Meketon and Schmeiser (1984) introduced the method of *overlapping batch means*, where $\bar{Y}(n,k)$ is once again the point estimator for ν but the expression for $\widehat{\text{Var}}[\bar{Y}(n,k)]$ involves all $m - k + 1$ batch means of size k. Bischak (1988) studied the idea of *weighted batch means*, where a weight of w_i is assigned to the ith observation in a batch and the w_i's sum to 1. In the usual batch-means approach, $w_i = 1/k$ for all i. Other papers that discuss batch means, in general, are Sargent, Kang, and Goldsman (1987) and Schmeiser (1982).

Rather than attempt to achieve independence, the two methods we discuss next use estimates of the autocorrelation structure of the underlying stochastic process to obtain an estimate of the variance of the sample mean and ultimately to construct a confidence interval for ν. Assume that we have the observations $Y_1, Y_2, \ldots, Y_m$ from a single replication of the simulation and let $\bar{Y}(m) = \sum_{i=1}^{m} Y_i/m$ be our point estimator for ν. The *autoregressive method*, developed by Fishman (1971, 1973a, 1978), assumes that the process $Y_1, Y_2, \ldots$ is covariance stationary with $E(Y_i) = \nu$ and can be represented by the pth-order autoregressive model

$$\sum_{j=0}^{p} b_j (Y_{i-j} - \nu) = \epsilon_i \tag{9.6}$$

where $b_0 = 1$ and $\{\epsilon_i\}$ is a sequence of uncorrelated random variables with common mean 0 and variance σ_ϵ^2. For known autoregressive order p and

$$\sum_{j=-\infty}^{\infty} |C_j| < \infty \tag{9.7}$$

it is possible to show that $m \operatorname{Var}[\bar{Y}(m)] \to \sigma_\epsilon^2 / (\Sigma_{j=0}^{p} b_j)^2$ as $m \to \infty$. Based on estimating the covariances C_j from the observations $Y_1, \ldots, Y_m$, Fishman (1973a) gives a procedure for determining the order p and obtaining estimates $\hat{b}_j$ (where $j = 1, 2, \ldots, \hat{p}$) and $\hat{\sigma}_\epsilon^2$, where $\hat{p}$ is the estimated order. Let $\hat{b} = 1 + \Sigma_{j=1}^{\hat{p}} \hat{b}_j$. Then, for large m, an estimate of $\operatorname{Var}[\bar{Y}(m)]$ and an approximate $100(1 - \alpha)$ percent confidence interval for ν are given by

$$\widehat{\operatorname{Var}}[\bar{Y}(m)] = \frac{\hat{\sigma}_\epsilon^2}{m(\hat{b})^2}$$

and

$$\bar{Y}(m) \pm t_{\hat{f}, 1-\alpha/2} \sqrt{\widehat{\operatorname{Var}}[\bar{Y}(m)]}$$

where an expression for the estimated df $\hat{f}$ is given by

$$\hat{f} = \frac{m\hat{b}}{2 \sum_{j=0}^{\hat{p}} (\hat{p} - 2j)\hat{b}_j}$$

A major concern in using this approach is whether the autoregressive model provides a good representation for an arbitrary stochastic process. Schriber and Andrews (1984) give a generalization of the autoregressive method that allows for moving-average components as well.

The method of *spectrum analysis* also assumes that the process $Y_1, Y_2, \ldots$ is covariance stationary with $E(Y_i) = \nu$, but does not make any further assumptions such as that given by Eq. (9.6). Under this stationarity assumption, it is possible to show that

$$\operatorname{Var}[\bar{Y}(m)] = \frac{C_0 + 2 \sum_{j=1}^{m-1} (1 - j/m) C_j}{m} \tag{9.8}$$

[which is essentially the same as Eq. (4.7)], and the method of spectrum analysis uses this relationship as a starting point for estimating $\operatorname{Var}[\bar{Y}(m)]$. The name of this method is based on the fact that, provided (9.7) holds, we have $m \operatorname{Var}[\bar{Y}(m)] \to 2\pi g(0)$ as $m \to \infty$, where $g(\tau)$ is called the *spectrum* of the process at frequency τ, and is defined by the Fourier transform $g(\tau) =$

$(2\pi)^{-1} \Sigma_{j=-\infty}^{\infty} C_j \exp(-i\tau j)$ for $|\tau| \le \pi$ and $i = \sqrt{-1}$. Thus, for large m, $\text{Var}[\bar{Y}(m)] \approx 2\pi g(0)/m$ and the problem of estimating $\text{Var}[\bar{Y}(m)]$ can be viewed as that of estimating the spectrum at zero frequency.

An estimator of $\text{Var}[\bar{Y}(m)]$ that immediately presents itself is obtained by simply replacing C_j in Eq. (9.8) by an estimate $\hat{C}_j$ computed from $Y_1, Y_2, \ldots, Y_m$ and Eq. (4.9). However, for large m and j near m, C_j will generally be nearly zero, but $\hat{C}_j$ will have a large variance since it will be based on only a few observations. As a result, several authors have suggested estimators of the following form:

$$\widehat{\text{Var}}[\bar{Y}(m)] = \frac{\hat{C}_0 + 2 \sum_{j=1}^{q-1} W_q(j)\hat{C}_j}{m}$$

where q (which determines the number of $\hat{C}_j$'s in the estimator) must be specified and the weighting function $W_q(j)$ is designed to improve the sampling properties of $\widehat{\text{Var}}[\bar{Y}(m)]$. Then an approximate $100(1 - \alpha)$ percent confidence interval for ν is given by

$$\bar{Y}(m) \pm t_{f,1-\alpha/2}\sqrt{\widehat{\text{Var}}[\bar{Y}(m)]}$$

where f depends on m, q, and the choice of weighting function [see Fishman (1969, 1973a) and Law and Kelton (1984)].

This technique is complicated, requiring a fairly sophisticated background on the part of the analyst. Moreover, there is no definitive procedure for choosing the value of q. Additional discussions of spectral methods may be found in Heidelberger and Welch (1981a, 1981b, 1983).

The *regenerative method* is an altogether different approach to simulation and thus leads to different approaches to constructing a confidence interval for ν. The idea is to identify random times at which the process probabilistically "starts over," i.e., regenerates, and to use these regeneration points to obtain independent random variables to which classical statistical analysis can be applied to form point and interval estimates for ν. This method was developed simultaneously by Crane and Iglehart (1974a, 1974b, 1975) and by Fishman (1973b, 1974); we follow the presentation of the former authors.

Assume for the output process $Y_1, Y_2, \ldots$ that there is a sequence of random indices $1 \le B_1 < B_2 < \cdots$, called *regeneration points*, at which the process starts over probabilistically; i.e., the distribution of the process $\{Y_{B_j+i-1}, i = 1, 2, \ldots\}$ is the same for each $j = 1, 2, \ldots$, and the process from each B_j on is assumed to be independent of the process prior to B_j. The portion of the process between two successive B_j's is called a *regeneration cycle*, and it can be shown that successive cycles are IID replicas of each other. In particular, comparable random variables defined over the successive cycles are IID. Let $N_j = B_{j+1} - B_j$ for $j = 1, 2, \ldots$ and assume that $E(N_j) < \infty$. If $Z_j = \Sigma_{i=B_j}^{B_{j+1}-1} Y_i$, the random vectors $\mathbf{U}_j = (Z_j, N_j)^T$ (where $\mathbf{A}^T$ is the transpose of the vector **A**) are IID, and provided that $E(|Z_j|) < \infty$, the steady-state mean ν is given (see Prob. 9.21) by

$$\nu = \frac{E(Z)}{E(N)}$$

Example 9.28. Consider the output process of delays $D_1, D_2, \ldots$ for a single-server queue with IID interarrival times, IID service times, customers served in a FIFO manner, and $\rho < 1$. The indices of those customers who arrive to find the system completely empty are regeneration points (see Fig. 9.10). Let N_j be the total number of customers served in the jth cycle and let $Z_j = \sum_{i=B_j}^{B_{j+1}-1} D_i$ be the total delay of all customers served in the jth cycle. Then the steady-state mean delay d is given by $d = E(Z)/E(N)$.

Note that the indices of customers who arrive to find l customers present ($l \geq 1$ and fixed) will not, in general, be regeneration points for the process $D_1, D_2, \ldots$. This is because the distribution of the remaining service time of the customer in service will be different for successive customers who arrive to find l customers present. However, if service times are exponential random variables, these indices *are* regeneration points due to the memoryless property of the exponential distribution (see Probs. 4.26 and 9.22).

We now discuss how to obtain a point estimator and a confidence interval for ν using the regenerative method. Suppose that we simulate the process $Y_1, Y_2, \ldots$ for exactly n' regeneration cycles, resulting in the following data:

$$Z_1, Z_2, \ldots, Z_{n'}$$
$$N_1, N_2, \ldots, N_{n'}$$

Each of these sequences consists of IID random variables. In general, however, Z_j and N_j are not independent. A point estimator for ν is then given by

$$\hat{\nu}(n') = \frac{\bar{Z}(n')}{\bar{N}(n')}$$

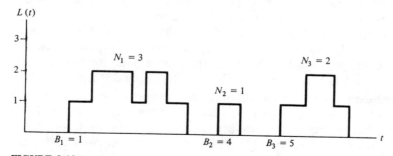

FIGURE 9.10
A realization of the number-in-system process $\{L(t), t \geq 0\}$ for a single-server queue.

Although $\bar{Z}(n')$ and $\bar{N}(n')$ are unbiased estimators of $E(Z)$ and $E(N)$, respectively, $\hat{\nu}(n')$ is *not* an unbiased estimator of ν (see App. 9A). It is true, however, that $\hat{\nu}(n')$ is a *strongly consistent estimator* of ν, that is, $\hat{\nu}(n') \rightarrow \nu$ as $n' \rightarrow \infty$ (w.p. 1); see Prob. 9.21.

Let the covariance matrix of the vector $\mathbf{U}_j = (Z_j, N_j)^T$ be

$$\Sigma = \begin{bmatrix} \sigma_{11} & \sigma_{12} \\ \sigma_{12} & \sigma_{22} \end{bmatrix}$$

for example, $\sigma_{12} = E\{[Z_j - E(Z_j)][N_j - E(N_j)]\}$, and let $V_j = Z_j - \nu N_j$. Then the V_j's are IID random variables with mean 0 and variance $\sigma_V^2 = \sigma_{11} - 2\nu\sigma_{12} + \nu^2\sigma_{22}$ (see Prob. 4.13). Therefore, if $0 < \sigma_V^2 < \infty$, it follows from the classical central limit theorem (see Theorem 4.1 in Sec. 4.5) that

$$\frac{\bar{V}(n')}{\sqrt{\sigma_V^2/n'}} \xrightarrow{\mathscr{D}} N(0,1) \qquad \text{as } n' \rightarrow \infty \tag{9.9}$$

where $\xrightarrow{\mathscr{D}}$ denotes convergence in distribution. Let

$$\hat{\Sigma}(n') = \begin{bmatrix} \hat{\sigma}_{11}(n') & \hat{\sigma}_{12}(n') \\ \hat{\sigma}_{12}(n') & \hat{\sigma}_{22}(n') \end{bmatrix} = \frac{\sum_{j=1}^{n'} [\mathbf{U}_j - \bar{\mathbf{U}}(n')][\mathbf{U}_j - \bar{\mathbf{U}}(n')]^T}{n' - 1}$$

be the estimated covariance matrix and let

$$\hat{\sigma}_V^2(n') = \hat{\sigma}_{11}(n') - 2\hat{\nu}(n')\hat{\sigma}_{12}(n') + [\hat{\nu}(n')]^2\hat{\sigma}_{22}(n')$$

be the estimate of σ_V^2 based on n' regeneration cycles. It can be shown that $\hat{\sigma}_V^2(n') \rightarrow \sigma_V^2$ as $n' \rightarrow \infty$ (w.p. 1). Consequently, we can replace σ_V^2 in (9.9) by $\hat{\sigma}_V^2(n')$ [see Chung (1974, p. 93)], and dividing through the ratio by $\bar{N}(n')$ yields

$$\frac{\hat{\nu}(n') - \nu}{\sqrt{\hat{\sigma}_V^2(n')/\{n'[\bar{N}(n')]^2\}}} \xrightarrow{\mathscr{D}} N(0,1) \qquad \text{as } n' \rightarrow \infty$$

Therefore, if the number of cycles n' is sufficiently large, an approximate (in terms of coverage) $100(1 - \alpha)$ percent confidence interval for ν is given by

$$\hat{\nu}(n') \pm \frac{z_{1-\alpha/2}\sqrt{\hat{\sigma}_V^2(n')/n'}}{\bar{N}(n')} \tag{9.10}$$

We call this regenerative approach to constructing a confidence interval for ν the *classical approach* (C). For an alternative regenerative approach to constructing a confidence interval for ν, known as the *jackknife approach* (J), see App. 9A.

The difficulty with using the regenerative method in practice is that real-world simulations may not have regeneration points, or (even if they do) the expected cycle length may be so large that only a very few cycles can be simulated [in which case the confidence interval given by (9.10) will not be valid]. For example, suppose one wants to estimate by simulation the steady-state mean total delay in queue for a network consisting of k queueing systems in series. [A customer departing from queueing system i (where $i = 1, 2, \ldots, k - 1$) proceeds to queueing system $i + 1$.] Then regeneration points for the process $D_1, D_2, \ldots$ (where D_i is the total delay of the ith customer to arrive) are the indices of those customers who arrive at the first queueing system to find the *entire* network empty. If the queueing systems composing the network are highly utilized, as is typical, regeneration points for the network will be few and far between. A more complete discussion of the regenerative method may be found in Crane and Lemoine (1977).

The *standardized time series method* [see Schruben (1983)] assumes that the process $Y_1, Y_2, \ldots$ is strictly stationary with $E(Y_i) = \nu$ for all i and is also phi-mixing. *Strictly stationary* means that the joint distribution of Y_{i_1+j}, $Y_{i_2+j}, \ldots, Y_{i_n+j}$ is independent of j for all time indices $i_1, i_2, \ldots, i_n$. (If ν exists, then, in general, $Y_{l+1}, Y_{l+2}, \ldots$ should be approximately strictly stationary if l is large enough.) Roughly speaking, $Y_1, Y_2, \ldots$ is *phi-mixing* if Y_i and Y_{i+j} become essentially independent as j becomes large [see Billingsley (1968, p. 166) for a precise definition]. Suppose that we make one simulation run of length m and divide $Y_1, Y_2, \ldots, Y_m$ into n batches of size k (where $m = nk$). Let $\bar{Y}_j(k)$ be the sample mean of the k observations in the jth batch. The grand sample mean $\bar{Y}(m)$ is the point estimator for ν. Furthermore, if m is large, then $\bar{Y}(m)$ will be approximately normally distributed with mean ν and variance τ^2/m, where

$$\tau^2 = \lim_{m \to \infty} m \operatorname{Var}[\bar{Y}(m)]$$

Let

$$A = \left(\frac{12}{k^3 - k}\right) \sum_{j=1}^{n} \left\{ \sum_{s=1}^{k} \sum_{i=1}^{s} [\bar{Y}_j(k) - Y_{i+(j-1)k}] \right\}^2$$

For a fixed number of batches n, A will be asymptotically (as $k \to \infty$) distributed as τ^2 times a chi-square random variable with n df and asymptotically independent of $\bar{Y}(m)$. Therefore, for k large, we can treat

$$\frac{[\bar{Y}(m) - \nu]/\sqrt{\tau^2/m}}{\sqrt{(A/\tau^2)/n}} = \frac{\bar{Y}(m) - \nu}{\sqrt{A/(mn)}}$$

as having a t distribution with n df, and an approximate $100(1 - \alpha)$ percent confidence interval for ν is given by

$$\bar{Y}(m) \pm t_{n,1-\alpha/2}\sqrt{A/(mn)}$$

The major source of error for standardized time series is choosing the batch size k too small [see Schruben (1983) for details]. It should be noted that this approach is based on the same underlying theory as Schruben's test for initialization bias discussed in Sec. 9.5.1. Additional references for standardized time series, including alternative confidence-interval formulations, are

Glynn and Iglehart (1990), Goldsman and Meketon (1986), Goldsman and Schruben (1984, 1990), and Sargent, Kang, and Goldsman (1987).

Since the five fixed-sample-size confidence-interval approaches presented in this section depend on assumptions that will not be strictly satisfied in an actual simulation, it is of interest to see how these approaches perform in practice. We first present the results from 400 independent simulation experiments for the $M/M/1$ queue with $\rho = 0.8$ ($\lambda = 1$ and $\omega = \frac{5}{4}$), where in each experiment our goal was to construct a 90 percent confidence interval for the steady-state mean delay $d = 3.2$ using all five procedures. Not knowing how to select definitively the total sample size m for batch means (B), autoregressive method (A), spectrum analysis (SA), and standardized times series (STS), we arbitrarily choose $m = 320, 640, 1280,$ and 2560. For the regenerative method (R), it can be shown that $E(N) = 1/(1 - p) = 5$ for the $M/M/1$ queue with $\rho = 0.8$ (see Prob. 9.25). We therefore chose the number of regeneration cycles $n' = 64, 128, 256,$ and 512 so that, on the average, all procedures used the same number of observations, that is, $m = n'E(N)$. Furthermore, we considered both the classical and jackknifed regenerative confidence intervals. For batch means and standardized time series, we chose the number of batches $n = 5, 10,$ and 20. The df f for spectrum analysis was chosen so that $f + 1 = n$, where f is related to the number of covariance estimates q in the variance expression by $q = 1.33m/f$ [see Law and Kelton (1984) for details]. Table 9.7 gives the proportion of the 400 confidence intervals that covered d for each of the 48 cases discussed above. [All results are taken from Law and Kelton (1984), except those for standardized time series, which were graciously provided by David Goldsman of Georgia Tech.] For example, in the case of $m = 320$ and $n = 5$ for batch means (i.e., each confidence interval was based on five batches of size 64), 69 percent of the 400 confidence intervals covered d, falling considerably short of the desired 90 percent. (Note that for fixed m, the estimated coverage for batch means decreases as n increases. This is because as n increases, the batch means become more correlated, resulting in a more biased estimate of the variance of the sample mean.)

We next present the results from 200 independent simulation experiments for the time-shared computer model with 35 terminals [see Law and Kelton (1984)], which was discussed in Sec. 2.5. Our objective is to construct 90 percent confidence intervals for the steady-state mean response time $r = 8.25$ [see Adiri and Avi-Itzhak (1969)]. We choose m and n as above and, since $E(N) \approx 32$ for the computer model, we took $n' = 10, 20, 40,$ and 80. Table 9.8 gives the proportion of the 200 confidence intervals that covered r for each of 36 cases (results for standardized time series were not available). Even though the computer model is physically much more complex than the $M/M/1$ queue, it can be seen from Table 9.8 that batch means with $n = 5$ produces an estimated coverage very close to 0.90 for m as small as 640. Thus, the $M/M/1$ queue with $\rho = 0.8$ is much more difficult statistically, despite its highly simple structure. These two examples illustrate that one cannot infer anything about the statistical behavior of the output data by looking at how "complex" the model's structure might be.

TABLE 9.7
Estimated coverages based on 400 experiments, $M/M/1$ queue with $\rho = 0.8$

$m(n')$	B			STS			SA			A	R	
	n			n			$f+1$				Method	
	5	10	20	5	10	20	5	10	20		C	J
320(64)	0.690	0.598	0.490	0.520	0.340	0.208	3.713	0.625	0.538	0.688	0.560	0.670
640(128)	0.723	0.708	0.588	0.628	0.485	0.318	0.760	0.735	0.645	0.723	0.683	0.728
1280(256)	0.780	0.740	0.705	0.730	0.645	0.485	0.783	0.770	0.745	0.753	0.705	0.748
2560(512)	0.798	0.803	0.753	0.798	0.725	0.598	0.833	0.808	0.773	0.755	0.745	0.763

TABLE 9.8
Estimated coverages based on 200 experiments, time-shared computer model

$m(n')$	B			SA			A	R	
	n			$f+1$				Method	
	5	10	20	5	10	20		C	J
320(10)	0.860	0.780	0.670	0.880	0.815	0.720	0.680	0.545	0.725
640(20)	0.890	0.855	0.790	0.870	0.870	0.820	0.805	0.730	0.830
1280(40)	0.910	0.885	0.880	0.910	0.910	0.905	0.890	0.830	0.865
2560(80)	0.905	0.875	0.895	0.910	0.885	0.900	0.885	0.870	0.915

From the empirical results presented in Tables 9.7 and 9.8 and also those in Law (1977) and Law and Kelton (1984), we came to the following conclusions with regard to fixed-sample-size procedures:

1. If the total sample size m (or n') is chosen too small, the actual coverages of *all* existing fixed-sample-size procedures (including replication/deletion) may be considerably lower than desired. This is really not surprising, since a steady-state parameter is defined as a limit as the length of the simulation (total number of observations) goes to infinity.

2. The "appropriate" choice of m (or n') would appear to be extremely model-dependent and thus impossible to choose arbitrarily. For the method of batch means with $n = 5$, $m = 640$ gave good results for the computer model; however, even for m as large as 2560, we did not obtain good results for the $M/M/1$ queue.

3. For m fixed, the methods of batch means, standardized time series, and spectrum analysis will achieve the best coverage for n and f small.

Sequential Procedures. We now discuss procedures that sequentially determine the length of a single simulation run needed to construct an acceptable confidence interval for the steady-state mean v. The need for such sequential procedures is evident from the fixed-sample-size results reported above. Specifically, no procedure in which the run length is fixed before the simulation begins can be relied upon to produce a confidence interval that covers v with the desired probability $1 - \alpha$, if the fixed run length is too small for the system being simulated.

In addition to the problem of coverage, an analyst might want to determine a run length large enough to obtain an estimate of v with a specified absolute error β or relative error γ (see Sec. 9.4.1). It will seldom be possible to know in advance even the order of magnitude of the run length needed to meet these goals in a given simulation problem, so some sort of procedure to increase this run length iteratively would appear to be in order.

Law and Kelton (1982) and Law (1983) surveyed the sequential procedures available at those times and found three that appeared to perform well in terms of achieved coverage. In particular, Fishman (1977) developed a procedure based on the regenerative method and an absolute-error stopping rule. Law and Kelton found that it achieved acceptable coverage for 9 out of the 10 stochastic models tested if $\beta = 0.075v$. Fishman's procedure has the disadvantage of being based on the regenerative method, which we feel limits its application to real-world problems.

Law and Carson (1979) developed a sequential procedure based on batch means and a relative-error stopping rule. Law and Kelton found that it achieved acceptable coverage for all 10 stochastic models tested if $\gamma = 0.075$. By way of example, in the case of the process $D_1, D_2, \ldots$ for the $M/M/1$ queue with $\rho = 0.8$, the estimated coverage for a nominal 90 percent confidence interval was 0.87 and the average run length when the procedure terminated was 75,648.

Heidelberger and Welch (1983) suggest a sequential procedure based on spectral methods and a relative-error stopping criterion. Based on their somewhat limited empirical results, it appears that the procedure may perform well in terms of coverage if $\gamma = 0.05$.

More recently, Duersch and Schruben (1986) proposed an interactive sequential procedure based on standardized time series and a relative-error stopping rule. The procedure is interesting, but no empirical results were provided on its performance.

If one wants to construct a confidence interval for the steady-state mean ν that is quite likely to have coverage close to $1 - \alpha$, then one of the thoroughly tested sequential procedures (with a "small" stopping criterion) discussed above is recommended. The reader should be aware, however, that these procedures are somewhat more complicated to understand and implement than, say, the replication/deletion approach of Sec. 9.5.2. They may also require large sample sizes and may not easily generalize to the common situation of multiple measures of performance (see Sec. 9.7).

9.5.4   Estimating Other Measures of Performance

As we saw in Sec. 9.4.2, the mean does not always provide us with an appropriate measure of system performance. We thus consider the estimation of steady-state parameters ϕ other than the mean $\nu = E(Y)$.

Suppose that we would like to estimate the steady-state probability $p = P(Y \in B)$, where B is a set of real numbers. By way of example, for a computer system we might want to determine the steady-state probability that the response time of a job is less than or equal to 30 seconds ($B = \{$all real numbers $\leq 30\}$). Estimating the probability p, as it turns out, is just a special case of estimating the mean ν, as we now see. Let the steady-state random variable Z be defined by

$$Z = \begin{cases} 1 & \text{if } Y \in B \\ 0 & \text{otherwise} \end{cases}$$

Then

$$P(Y \in B) = P(Z = 1) = 1 \cdot P(Z = 1) + 0 \cdot P(Z = 0)$$
$$= E(Z)$$

Thus, estimating p is equivalent to estimating the steady-state mean $E(Z)$, which has been discussed in Secs. 9.5.2 and 9.5.3. In particular, let

$$Z_i = \begin{cases} 1 & \text{if } Y_i \in B \\ 0 & \text{otherwise} \end{cases}$$

for $i = 1, 2, \ldots$, where $Y_1, Y_2, \ldots$ is the original stochastic process of interest. Then, for example, the replication/deletion approach could be applied to the output process $Z_1, Z_2, \ldots$ to obtain a point estimate and confidence interval for $E(Z) = p$. Note that the warmup period for the (binary) process $Z_1, Z_2, \ldots$ may be different from that for the original process $Y_1, Y_2, \ldots$.

Another parameter of the steady-state distribution of considerable interest is the q-quantile, y_q, which was defined in Sec. 6.4.3. That is, y_q is the value of y such that $P(Y \leq y_q) = q$, where Y is the steady-state random variable. For example, in the case of the computer system discussed above, it might be desired to estimate the 0.9-quantile of the steady-state response time distribution. Estimating quantiles is both conceptually and computationally (in terms of the number of observations required to obtain a specified precision) a more difficult problem than estimating the steady-state mean. Furthermore, most procedures for estimating quantiles are based on order statistics and require storage and sorting of the observations.

There have been several procedures proposed for estimating quantiles based on batch means, spectral, and regenerative methods [see Law (1983)]. One drawback of these procedures is that they are all based on a fixed sample size, which must be chosen somewhat arbitrarily. If this sample size is chosen too small, the coverage of the resulting confidence interval will be somewhat less than desired.

Raatikainen (1988) proposed a procedure for estimating quantiles based on the P^2 algorithm of Jain and Chlamtac (1985), which does not require storing and sorting the observations. It is a sequential procedure based on a spectral method and a relative-error stopping rule. Raatikainen tested his procedure on several stochastic models of computer systems and appeared to obtain good results in terms of coverage. The procedure is, however, difficult to implement.

9.6 STATISTICAL ANALYSIS FOR STEADY-STATE CYCLE PARAMETERS

Suppose that the output process $Y_1, Y_2, \ldots$ does not have a steady-state distribution. Assume, on the other hand, that there is an appropriate cycle definition so that the process $Y_1^C, Y_2^C, \ldots$ has a steady-state distribution F^C, where Y_i^C is the random variable defined on the ith cycle (see Sec. 9.3). If $Y^C \sim F^C$, then we are interested in estimating some characteristic of Y^C such as the mean $\nu^C = E(Y^C)$ or the probability $P(Y^C \leq y)$. Clearly, estimating a steady-state cycle parameter is just a special case of estimating a steady-state parameter, so all of the techniques of Sec. 9.5 apply, except to the *cycle* random variables Y_i^C rather than to the original Y_i's. For example, we could use Welch's method to get a warmup period and then apply the replication/deletion approach to obtain a point estimate and confidence interval for ν^C.

Example 9.29. Consider once again the small factory of Example 9.25 but suppose that there is a half-hour lunch break that starts 4 hours into each 8-hour shift. This break stops the inspection process, but unfinished parts continue to arrive and to be processed by the unmanned machine. If N_i is the throughput in the ith hour, then the process $N_1, N_2, \ldots$ does not have a steady-state distribution (see Example 9.11). We might, however, expect that it is periodic with a cycle length of 8 hours. To substantiate this, we made $n = 10$ replications of length $m = 160$ hours (20 shifts). From the plot of the averaged process $\bar{N}_i$ (where $i = 1, 2, \ldots, 160$) in Fig. 9.11, we see that the process $N_1, N_2, \ldots$ does indeed appear to have a cycle of length 8 hours.

Let N_i^C be the average production in the ith 8-hour cycle and assume that $N_1^C, N_2^C, \ldots$ has a steady-state distribution. Suppose that we want to obtain a point estimate and a 99 percent confidence interval for the steady-state expected average production over a shift, $\nu^C = E(N^C)$, using the replication/deletion approach. Let N_{ji}^C be the average production in the ith cycle of our jth available replication ($j = 1, 2, \ldots, 10; i = 1, 2, \ldots, 20$), and let $\bar{N}_i^C$ for $i = 1, 2, \ldots, 20$ be the corresponding averaged process (that is, $\bar{N}_i^C = \Sigma_{j=1}^{10} N_{ji}^C/10$), which is plotted in Fig. 9.12. We conclude from this plot that further smoothing is desirable. As a result, we plot the moving average $\bar{N}_i^C(w)$ (from Welch's procedure) for both $w = 3$ and $w = 6$ shifts in Figs. 9.13a and 9.13b. From the plot for $w = 6$ (which is smoother), we chose a warmup period of $l = 5$ shifts or 40 hours. (Compare this l with that obtained in Example 9.25.)

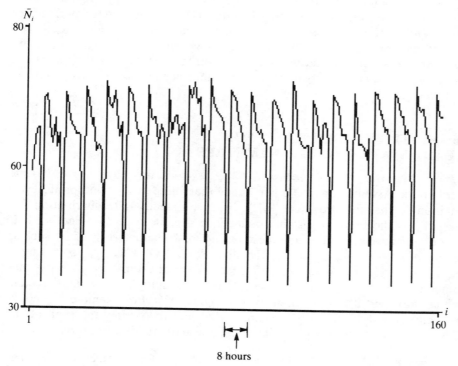

FIGURE 9.11
Averaged process for hourly throughputs, small factory with lunch breaks.

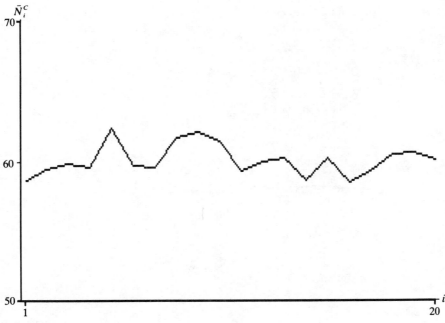

FIGURE 9.12
Averaged process for average hourly throughputs over a shift, small factory with lunch breaks.

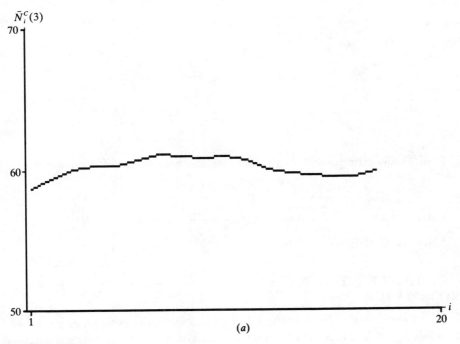

(a)

FIGURE 9.13
Moving averages for average hourly throughputs over a shift, small factory with lunch breaks: (a) $w = 3$; (b) $w = 6$.

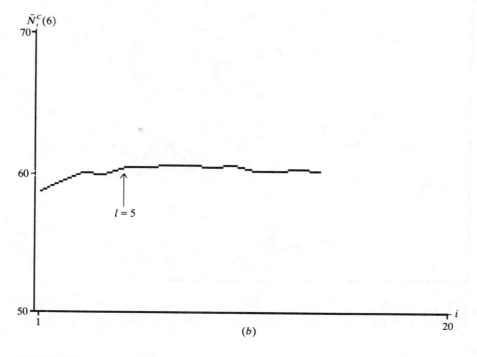

FIGURE 9.13
(*Continued.*)

Let

$$X_j^C = \frac{\displaystyle\sum_{i=6}^{20} N_{ji}^C}{15} \qquad \text{for } j = 1, 2, \ldots, 10$$

Then a point estimate and 99 percent confidence interval for ν^C are given by

$$\hat{\nu}^C = \bar{X}^C(10) = 60.24$$

and

$$\bar{X}^C(10) \pm t_{9,0.995}\sqrt{\frac{0.79}{10}} = 60.24 \pm 0.91$$

which also contains 60 (see Prob. 9.27).

9.7 MULTIPLE MEASURES OF PERFORMANCE

In Secs. 9.4 through 9.6 we presented procedures for constructing a confidence interval for a single measure of performance. However, for most real-world simulations several measures of performance are of interest simultaneously. Suppose that I_s is a $100(1 - \alpha_s)$ percent confidence interval for the measure of performance μ_s (where $s = 1, 2, \ldots, k$). (The μ_s's may all be measures of performance for a terminating simulation or may all be measures for a nonterminating simulation.) Then the probability that *all* k confidence intervals *simultaneously* contain their respective true measures satisfies (see Prob. 9.31)

$$P(\mu_s \in I_s \text{ for all } s = 1, 2, \ldots, k) \geq 1 - \sum_{s=1}^{k} \alpha_s \qquad (9.11)$$

whether or not the I_s's are independent. This result, known as the *Bonferroni inequality*, has serious implications for a simulation study. For example, suppose that one constructs 90 percent confidence intervals, that is, $\alpha_s = 0.1$ for all s, for 10 different measures of performance. Then the probability that each of the 10 confidence intervals contains its true measure can only be claimed to be greater than or equal to *zero*. Thus one cannot have much overall confidence in any conclusions drawn from such a study. The difficulty we have just described is known in the statistics literature as the *multiple-comparisons problem*.

We now describe a practical solution to the above problem when the value of k is small. If one wants the overall confidence level associated with k confidence intervals to be at least $100(1 - \alpha)$ percent, choose the α_s's so that $\sum_{s=1}^{k} \alpha_s = \alpha$. (Note that the α_s's do *not* have to be equal. Thus, α_s's corresponding to more important measures could be chosen smaller.) Therefore, one could construct ten 99 percent confidence intervals and have the overall confidence level be *at least* 90 percent. The difficulty with this solution is that the confidence intervals will be larger than they were originally if a fixed-sample-size procedure is used, or more data will be required for a specified set of k relative errors if a sequential procedure is used. For this reason, we recommend that k be no larger than about 10.

If one has a very large number of measures of performance, the only recourse available is to construct the usual 90 percent or 95 percent confidence intervals but to be aware that one or more of these confidence intervals probably does not contain its true measure.

Example 9.30. Consider the bank of Example 9.1 with five tellers and one queue. Table 9.9 gives the results of using these 10 replications of the (terminating) simulation and (9.1) to construct 96.667 percent confidence intervals for each of the measures of performance

$$E\left[\frac{\int_0^T Q(t)\, dt}{T}\right], \qquad E\left(\frac{\sum_{i=1}^{N} D_i}{N}\right), \qquad E\left[\frac{\sum_{i=1}^{N} I_i(0,5)}{N}\right]$$

so that the overall confidence level is at least 90 percent.

Example 9.31. Suppose for the small factory of Example 9.25 that we would like to obtain point estimates and confidence intervals for both the steady-state mean hourly throughput ν_N and the steady-state mean time in system of a part ν_T, with the overall confidence level being at least 90 percent. Therefore, we will make the

TABLE 9.9
Results of making 10 replications of the bank model with five tellers and one queue

Measure of performance	Point estimate	96.667% confidence interval
$E\left[\dfrac{\int_0^T Q(t)\,dt}{T}\right]$	1.97	$[1.55, 2.40]$
$E\left(\dfrac{\sum_{i=1}^N D_i}{N}\right)$	2.03	$[1.59, 2.47]$
$E\left[\dfrac{\sum_{i=1}^N I_i(0,5)}{N}\right]$	0.85	$[0.80, 0.90]$

confidence level of each individual interval 95 percent. Using the 10 replications from Example 9.27, we plotted the moving average $\bar{T}_i(w)$ $(i = 1, 2, \ldots)$ for the time-in-system process $T_1, T_2, \ldots$, in order to determine its warmup period. (Here T_i is the time in system of the ith departing part.) Since this plot was highly variable, we made an additional 10 replications of length 160 hours and used the entire 20 replications for our analysis. In Fig. 9.14a we plot the hourly throughput moving average $\bar{N}_i(w)$ for $w = 30$, and in Fig. 9.14b we plot the time-in-system moving average $\bar{T}_i(w)$ for $w = 1200$. (Note that the number of T_i observations in a 160-hour simulation run is a random variable with mean 9600. Therefore, for our analysis we used the minimum number of observations for any one of the 20 runs, which was 9407.) From Figs. 9.14a and 9.14b, we decided on warmup periods of $l_N = 24$ hours and $l_T = 2286$ times, respectively. Note, however, that 2286 times corresponds to approximately 38 hours. Since 24 and 2286 are much smaller than 160 and 9407, respectively, we will use these same replications to construct our confidence intervals.

Let

$$X_j = \frac{\sum_{i=25}^{160} N_{ji}}{136} \qquad \text{for } j = 1, 2, \ldots, 20$$

$$Y_j = \frac{\sum_{i=2287}^{9407} T_{ji}}{7121}$$

Then point estimates and 95 percent confidence intervals for v_N and v_T are given by

$$\hat{v}_N = \bar{X}(20) = 60.03 , \qquad \hat{v}_T = \bar{Y}(20) = 6.16 \text{ minutes}$$

and

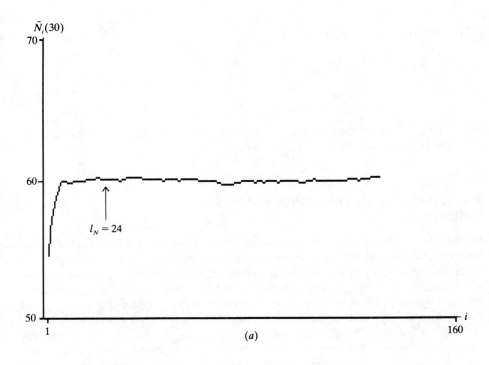

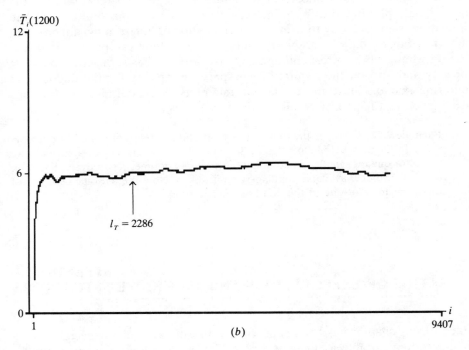

FIGURE 9.14
Moving averages for small factory: (a) $w = 30$ for hourly throughputs; (b) $w = 1200$ for times in system.

$$\bar{X}(10) \pm t_{19,0.975} \sqrt{\frac{0.70}{20}} = 60.03 \pm 0.39$$

$$\bar{Y}(10) \pm t_{19,0.975} \sqrt{\frac{0.55}{20}} = 6.16 \pm 0.35$$

Thus, we are at least 90 percent confident that ν_N and ν_T are in the intervals [59.64, 60.42] and [5.81, 6.51], respectively.

9.8 TIME PLOTS OF IMPORTANT VARIABLES

In this chapter we have seen how to construct point estimates and confidence intervals for several different measures of performance, with an emphasis on mean system response. Although these measures are clearly quite useful, there are situations where we need a better indication of how system performance changes dynamically over time. This is particularly true when characteristics of the system (e.g., number of available workers) vary as a function of time. Animation (see Sec. 3.4.2) can provide considerable insight into the short-term dynamic behavior of a system, but it does not give us an easily interpreted record of system performance over the entire length of the simulation. On the other hand, plotting one or more key variables over the duration of the simulation is an easy way to gain an understanding of long-run dynamic system behavior. For example, a graph of queue size over time can provide information on whether the corresponding server (or servers) has sufficient processing capacity and also on the required floor space or capacity for the queue. The following example illustrates the use of time plots, with additional applications being given in Chap. 13 (see also Prob. 9.28).

Example 9.32. Consider the small factory with lunch breaks discussed in Example 9.29. In Figures 9.15a and 9.15b, we plot the numbers in the machine and inspector queues sampled in 30-minute increments of time, respectively, based on the first of the 10 available simulation replications. Note the periodic behavior of the inspector plot due to the half-hour lunch break.

APPENDIX 9A
RATIOS OF EXPECTATIONS AND JACKKNIFE ESTIMATORS

Much of this chapter has been concerned with estimating the expectation of a single random variable X, namely, $E(X)$. However, as the following examples show, there are many situations in simulation where it is of interest to estimate the ratio of two expectations, such as $E(Y)/E(X)$:

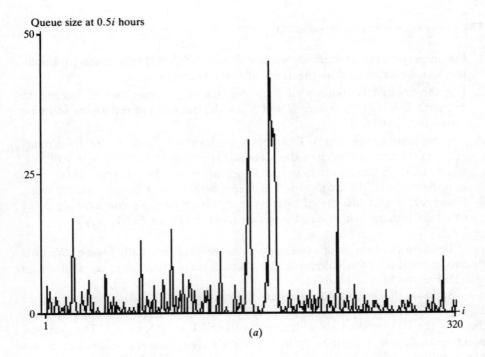

(a)

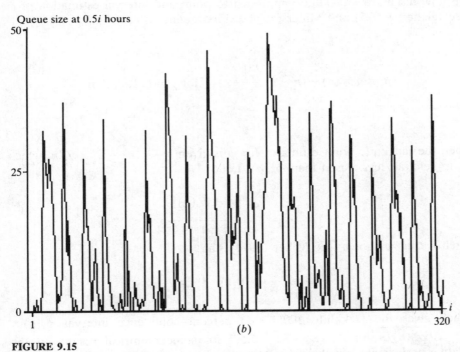

(b)

FIGURE 9.15
Time plots for number in queue in time increments of 30 minutes (run 1), small factory: (a) machine queue; (b) inspector queue.

1. For the regenerative method, we saw in Sec. 9.5.3 that steady-state parameters can be expressed as the ratio of two expectations.
2. For the combat simulation of Example 9.5, it is sometimes of interest to estimate $E(R)/E(B)$, where R and B are the numbers of red losses and blue losses in a battle.
3. For the bank simulation of Example 9.14, let $P = \sum_{i=1}^{N} D_i$ be the total delay of all customers served in a day. Then it is of interest to estimate $E(P/N)$, which can be interpreted as the expectation of the average delay of a customer where the expectation is taken with respect to all possible days. However, it may also be of interest to estimate the long-run average delay of all customers, which can be shown to be equal to $E(P)/E(N)$.

Estimators of ratios of expectations, however, are usually biased. We now discuss a method of obtaining a less biased point estimator, as well as an alternative confidence interval.

Suppose that we want to estimate the ratio $\phi = E(Y)/E(X)$ from the data $Y_1, Y_2, \ldots, Y_n$ and $X_1, X_2, \ldots, X_n$, where the X_i's are IID random variables, the Y_i's are IID random variables, and $\text{Cov}(Y_i, X_j) = 0$ for $i \neq j$. The classical point estimator of ϕ is given by $\hat{\phi}_C(n) = \bar{Y}(n)/\bar{X}(n)$; see the discussion of the regenerative method in Sec. 9.5.3 for the classical confidence interval for ϕ. We now discuss the jackknife approach to point and interval estimation of ϕ [see Iglehart (1975) and Miller (1974)]. First define

$$\theta_g = n\hat{\phi}_C(n) - (n-1)\frac{\displaystyle\sum_{\substack{j=1 \\ j \neq g}}^{n} Y_j}{\displaystyle\sum_{\substack{j=1 \\ j \neq g}}^{n} X_j} \qquad \text{for } g = 1, 2, \ldots, n$$

Then the jackknife point estimator for ϕ is given by $\hat{\phi}_J(n) = \sum_{g=1}^{n} \theta_g/n$, which is, in general, less biased than $\hat{\phi}_C(n)$. Let

$$\hat{\sigma}_J^2(n) = \frac{\displaystyle\sum_{g=1}^{n} [\theta_g - \hat{\phi}_J(n)]^2}{n-1}$$

Then it can be shown [see Miller (1974)] that

$$\frac{\hat{\phi}_J(n) - \phi}{\sqrt{\hat{\sigma}_J^2(n)/n}} \xrightarrow{\mathscr{D}} N(0,1) \qquad \text{as } n \to \infty$$

which gives the jackknife $100(1-\alpha)$ percent confidence interval $\hat{\phi}_J(n) \pm z_{1-\alpha/2}\sqrt{\hat{\sigma}_J^2(n)/n}$ for ϕ. (See Sec. 9.5.3 for some empirical results on the relative performance of the classical and jackknife confidence intervals.)

PROBLEMS

9.1. Argue heuristically that comparable output random variables from replications using different random numbers should be independent.

9.2. Consider a machine that works for an exponential amount of time having mean $1/\lambda$ before breaking down. Suppose that it takes an exponential amount of time having mean $1/\omega$ to repair the machine. Let $Y(t)$ be the state of the machine at time t for $t \geq 0$, where

$$Y(t) = \begin{cases} 1 & \text{if the machine is working at time } t \\ 0 & \text{otherwise} \end{cases}$$

Then $\{Y(t), t \geq 0\}$ is a continuous-time stochastic process. Furthermore, it can be shown that [see Ross (1989, pp. 263–265)]

$$P(Y(t) = 1 \mid Y(0) = 1) = \frac{\lambda}{\lambda + \omega} e^{-(\lambda + \omega)t} + \frac{\omega}{\lambda + \omega}$$

and

$$P(Y(t) = 1 \mid Y(0) = 0) = -\frac{\omega}{\lambda + \omega} e^{-(\lambda + \omega)t} + \frac{\omega}{\lambda + \omega}$$

Thus, the distribution of $Y(t)$ depends on both t and $Y(0)$. By letting $t \to \infty$ in these equations, compute the steady-state distribution of $Y(t)$. Does it depend on $Y(0)$?

9.3. In Example 9.9, suppose that condition (b) is violated. In particular, suppose that it takes workers 20 minutes to put their tools away at the end of a shift and it takes the new workers 20 minutes to set up their tools at the beginning of the next shift. Does $N_1, N_2, \ldots$ have a steady-state distribution?

9.4. Suppose in Example 9.9 that we would like to estimate the steady-state mean total time in system of a part. Does our approach to simulating the manufacturing system present a problem?

9.5. Why is determining the required number of tellers for a bank different from determining the hardware requirements for a computer or communication system (see Example 9.10)?

9.6. In Example 9.11, why doesn't the process of hourly throughputs $N_1, N_2, \ldots$ have a steady-state distribution?

9.7. For the following systems, state whether you think a terminating or nonterminating simulation would be more appropriate. In the terminating cases, state the terminating event E. In the nonterminating cases, would the parameter of interest be a steady-state parameter or steady-state cycle parameter?

    (a) Consider a telephone system for which an arriving call may experience a delay before obtaining a line. Suppose that the goal is to estimate the mean delay of the 100th arriving call, $E(D_{100})$.

    (b) Consider a military inventory system (see Sec. 1.5) during peacetime, which is assumed to have a long duration. Assume that system parameters (e.g., the interdemand time distribution) do not change over time and we are interested in the output process $C_1, C_2, \ldots$, where C_i is the total cost in the ith month. Suppose further that we want a measure of mean cost.

(c) Consider a manufacturing system for food products. A production schedule is issued, the system produces product for 13 days, and then the system is completely cleaned out on the fourteenth day. Then a new production schedule is issued and the 2-week cycle is repeated, etc. The goal is to estimate the mean throughput over a cycle.

(d) Consider an air freight company that provides overnight delivery of packages. Aircraft loaded with packages start arriving at the hub operations at approximately 11 P.M. The packages are unloaded and then sorted in a warehouse according to the destination zip code. Packages with similar zip codes are placed on one aircraft, and the last plane departs at approximately 5 A.M. It is desired to estimate the mean (across departing planes) amount of time that planes are late in departing.

(e) Consider a manufacturing system that operates in a similar manner 7 days a week. Suppose, however, that 6 machines operate during the first two shifts in each day, but only 4 machines operate during the third shift. Let $N_1, N_2, \ldots$ be the output process of interest, where N_i is the number of parts produced in the ith shift. We are interested in a measure of mean throughput. Does your answer depend on the relationship between the arrival rate and the service rate of an individual machine?

9.8. For the small factory of Example 9.25, suppose that the system operates 24 hours a day for 5 days and then is completely cleaned out. Thus, we have a terminating simulation of length 120 hours. Make five independent replications and construct a point estimate and 95 percent confidence interval for the mean weekly throughput. Approximately how many replications would be required to obtain an absolute error of 50? A relative error of 5 percent?

9.9. Let p be a probability of interest for a terminating simulation, as discussed in Sec. 9.4.2. Define IID random variables $Y_1, Y_2, \ldots, Y_n$ such that $\hat{p} = \bar{Y}(n)$ and use these Y_j's in Eqs. (4.3) and (4.4), and (4.12) to derive one possible confidence interval for p. Show that the variance estimate given by Eq. (4.4) can be written as $\hat{p}(1 - \hat{p})/(n - 1)$.

9.10. Consider the bank of Example 9.1. Use the data from the 10 replications in Table 9.1 to construct a point estimate for the median (i.e., 0.5-quantile) of the distribution of the average delay over a day. How does this estimate compare with the sample mean in Example 9.14?

9.11. For the $M/M/1$ queue with $\rho < 1$ of Example 9.23, suppose that the number of customers present when the first customer arrives has the following discrete distribution:

$$p(x) = (1 - \rho)\rho^x \qquad \text{for } x = 0, 1, \ldots$$

which is the steady-state distribution of the number of customers in the system. Compute the distribution function of D_1 and its mean. In this case, it can also be shown that D_i for $i \geq 2$ has this same distribution.

9.12. For Welch's procedure in Sec. 9.5.1, show that $E(\bar{Y}_i) = E(Y_i)$ and $\text{Var}(\bar{Y}_i) = \text{Var}(Y_i)/n$.

9.13. Assume that $Y_1, Y_2, \ldots$ is a covariance-stationary process and that $\rho_i < 1$ for $i \geq 1$. Show for Welch's procedure that $\text{Var}[\bar{Y}_i(w)] < \text{Var}(\bar{Y}_i)$.

9.14. Suppose that $Y_1, Y_2, \ldots$ is an output process with steady-state mean ν and that $\bar{Y}(m)$ is the usual sample mean based on m observations. Consider plotting $\bar{Y}(m)$

as a function of m and let l' be the point beyond which $\bar{Y}(m)$ does not change appreciably. Is l' a good warmup period in the sense that $E(Y_i) \approx \nu$ for $i > l'$ and also that l' is not excessively large? Why?

9.15. Consider the replication/deletion approach of Sec. 9.5.2. Show that $E(X_j) \approx \nu$. Give two reasons why the confidence interval given by (9.5) is approximate in terms of coverage.

9.16. Consider the replication/deletion approach in Sec. 9.5.2 based on using the same set of replications to determine the warmup period l and to construct a confidence interval. Are the resulting X_j's truly independent?

9.17. For the small factory of Example 9.27, what should the steady-state mean hourly throughput be if the system is well defined in the sense that $\rho < 1$ for both the machine and the inspector?

9.18. Consider a continuous-time stochastic process such as $\{Q(t), t \ge 0\}$, where $Q(t)$ is the number of customers in queue at time t. Suppose that we would like to estimate the steady-state time-average number in queue, Q (see App. 1B for one definition), using the method of batch means based on one simulation run of length m time units. Discuss two approaches for getting *exactly* m basic discrete observations $Q_1, Q_2, \ldots, Q_m$ for use in the method of batch means. The m Q_i's will be batched to form n batch means.

9.19. If $Y_1, Y_2, \ldots$ is a covariance-stationary process, show for the method of batch means that $C_i(k) = \text{Cov}[\bar{Y}_j(k), \bar{Y}_{j+i}(k)]$ is given by

$$C_i(k) = \sum_{l=-(k-1)}^{k-1} \frac{(1 - |l|/k)C_{ik+l}}{k} \qquad \text{where } C_l = \text{Cov}(Y_i, Y_{i+l})$$

9.20. Let $Y_1, Y_2, \ldots$ be a covariance-stationary process. For the method of batch means, let $\rho_i(k) = \text{Cor}[\bar{Y}_j(k), \bar{Y}_{j+i}(k)]$ and let $b(n,k)$ be such that $E\{\widehat{\text{Var}}[\bar{\bar{Y}}(n, k)]\} = b(n,k) \cdot \text{Var}[\bar{\bar{Y}}(n,k)]$. Show that $\rho_i(k) \to 0$ (for $i = 1, 2, \ldots, n-1$) as $k \to \infty$ implies that $E\{\widehat{\text{Var}}[\bar{\bar{Y}}(n, k)]\} \to \text{Var}[\bar{\bar{Y}}(n,k)]$ as $k \to \infty$. *Hint:* First show that

$$b(n,k) = \frac{\left\{ n \Big/ \left[1 + 2 \sum_{i=1}^{n-1} \left(1 - \frac{i}{n}\right) \rho_i(k) \right] \right\} - 1}{n - 1}$$

9.21. For the regenerative method, show that $\nu = E(Z)/E(N)$. [*Hint:* Observe that

$$\frac{\sum_{j=1}^{n'} Z_j}{\sum_{j=1}^{n'} N_j} = \frac{\sum_{i=1}^{M(n')} Y_i}{M(n')}$$

where n' is the number of regeneration cycles and $M(n')$ is the total number of observations (a random variable) in the n' cycles. Let $n' \to \infty$ and apply the strong law of large numbers (see Sec. 4.6) to both sides of the above equation.] Also conclude that $\hat{\nu}(n') = \bar{Z}(n')/\bar{N}(n') \to \nu$ as $n' \to \infty$ (w.p. 1), so that $\hat{\nu}(n')$ is a strongly consistent estimator of ν. (See the definitions of ν in Sec. 9.5.3.)

9.22. For the queueing system considered in Example 9.28, are the indices of those customers who depart and leave exactly l customers behind ($l \ge 0$ and fixed) regeneration points for the process $D_1, D_2, \ldots$? If not, under what circumstances would they be?

9.23. For the inventory example of Sec. 1.5, identify a sequence of regeneration points for the process $C_1, C_2, \ldots$ Repeat assuming that the interdemand times are not exponential random variables.

9.24. Suppose that $\hat{\nu}(n')$ is the (biased) regenerative point estimator for the steady-state mean ν based on simulating the process $Y_1, Y_2, \ldots$ for n' regeneration cycles. Do you think that it is advisable to have a warmup period of l cycles to reduce the point estimator bias?

9.25. Consider an $M/M/1$ queue with $\rho < 1$, and let the number of customers served in a cycle, N, be as defined in Example 9.28. By conditioning on whether the second customer arrives before or after the first customer departs, show that $E(N) = 1/(1 - \rho)$.

9.26. For Example 9.29, compute the utilization factor ρ for both the machine and the inspector. What arrival rate should be used? Is this system well defined in the sense that $\rho < 1$ in both cases?

9.27. In Example 9.29, what should be the value for ν^C if the system is well defined?

9.28. A manufacturing system consists of two machines in parallel and a single queue. Jobs arrive with exponential interarrival times at a rate of 10 per hour, and each machine has exponential processing times at a rate of 8 per hour. During the first 16 hours of each day both machines are operational, but only one machine is used during the final 8 hours.
  (a) Determine whether the system is well defined by computing the utilization factor ρ and comparing it with 1.
  (b) Let N_i be the throughput for the ith hour. Does $N_1, N_2, \ldots$ have a steady-state distribution?
  (c) Make 10 replications of the simulation of length 480 hours (20 days) each. Plot the averaged process $\bar{N}_1, \bar{N}_2, \ldots, \bar{N}_{480}$.
  (d) Let M_i be the throughput for the ith 24-hour day. Use the data from part (c) and the replication/deletion approach to construct a point estimate and 90 percent confidence interval for the steady-state mean daily throughput $\nu = E(M) = 240$.

9.29. For the system in Prob. 9.28, make one replication of length 200 days and let M_i be as previously defined. Use the M_i's and the method of batch means to construct a point estimate and a 90 percent confidence interval for $\nu = 240$ based on $n = 10$ batches and also on $n = 5$ batches.

9.30. Repeat Prob. 9.29 using standardized time series rather than batch means.

9.31. Let E_s be an event that occurs with probability $1 - \alpha_s$ for $s = 1, 2, \ldots, k$. Then prove that

$$P\left(\bigcap_{s=1}^{k} E_s\right) \geq 1 - \sum_{s=1}^{k} \alpha_s$$

where $\bigcap_{s=1}^{k} E_s$ is the intersection of the events $E_1, E_2, \ldots, E_k$. Do not assume that the E_s's are independent. [This result is called the *Bonferroni inequality*; see (9.11).] *Hint:* The proof is by mathematical induction. That is, first show that $P(E_1 \cap E_2) \geq 1 - \alpha_1 - \alpha_2$. Then show that if

$$P\left(\bigcap_{s=1}^{k-1} E_s\right) \geq 1 - \sum_{s=1}^{k-1} \alpha_s$$

is true, the desired result is also true.

REFERENCES

Adiri, I., and B. Avi-Itzhak: A Time-Sharing Queue with a Finite Number of Customers, *J. Assoc. Comput. Mach.*, 16: 315–323 (1969).

Anderson, T. W.: *The Statistical Analysis of Time Series*, John Wiley, New York (1971).

Banks, J., and J. S. Carson: *Discrete-Event System Simulation*, Prentice-Hall, Englewood Cliffs, N.J. (1984).

Billingsley, P.: *Convergence of Probability Measures*, John Wiley, New York (1968).

Bischak, D. P.: Weighted Batch Means for Improved Confidence Intervals for Steady-State Processes, Ph.D. Dissertation, Department of Industrial and Operations Engineering, University of Michigan, Ann Arbor (1988).

Bratley, P., B. L. Fox, and L. E. Schrage: *A Guide to Simulation*, 2d ed., Springer-Verlag, New York (1987).

Chow, Y. S., and H. Robbins: On the Asymptotic Theory of Fixed-Width Sequential Confidence Intervals for the Mean, *Ann. Math. Statist.*, 36: 457–462 (1965).

Chung, K. L.: *A Course in Probability Theory*, 2d ed., Academic Press, New York, 1974.

Conover, W. J.: *Practical Nonparametric Statistics*, 2d ed., John Wiley, New York (1980).

Crane, M. A., and D. L. Iglehart: Simulating Stable Stochastic Systems, I: General Multiserver Queues, *J. Assoc. Comput. Mach.*, 21: 103–113 (1974a).

Crane, M. A., and D. L. Iglehart: Simulating Stable Stochastic Systems, II: Markov Chains, *J. Assoc. Comput. Mach.*, 21: 114–123 (1974b).

Crane, M. A., and D. L. Iglehart: Simulating Stable Stochastic Systems, III: Regenerative Processes and Discrete-Event Simulations, *Operations Res.*, 23: 33–45 (1975).

Crane, M. A., and A. J. Lemoine: *An Introduction to the Regenerative Method for Simulation Analysis*, Lecture Notes in Control and Information Sciences, Vol. 4, Springer-Verlag, New York (1977).

Duersch, R. R., and L. W. Schruben: An Interactive Run Length Control for Simulations on PCs, *Proc. 1986 Winter Simulation Conference*, Washington, D.C., pp. 866–870 (1986).

Fishman, G. S.: *Spectral Methods in Econometrics*, Harvard University Press, Cambridge, Mass. (1969).

Fishman, G. S.: Estimating Sample Size in Computer Simulation Experiments, *Management Sci.*, 18: 21–38 (1971).

Fishman, G. S.: *Concepts and Methods in Discrete Event Digital Simulation*, John Wiley, New York (1973a).

Fishman, G. S.: Statistical Analysis for Queueing Simulations, *Management Sci.*, 20: 363–369 (1973b).

Fishman, G. S.: Estimation in Multiserver Queueing Simulations, *Operations Res.*, 22: 72–78 (1974).

Fishman, G. S.: Achieving Specific Accuracy in Simulation Output Analysis, *Commun. Assoc. Comput. Mach.*, 20: 310–315 (1977).

Fishman, G. S.: *Principles of Discrete Event Simulation*, John Wiley, New York (1978).

Gafarian, A. V., C. J. Ancker, Jr., and F. Morisaku: Evaluation of Commonly Used Rules for Detecting "Steady-State" in Computer Simulation, *Naval Res. Logist. Quart.*, 25: 511–529 (1978).

Glynn, P. W.: A Non-rectangular Sampling Plan for Estimating Steady-State Means, Technical Report No. 54, Department of Operations Research, Stanford University, Stanford, Calif. (1988).

Glynn, P. W., and D. L. Iglehart: The Theory of Standardized Time Series, *Math. Operations Res.*, 15: 1–16 (1990).

Goldsman, D., and M. S. Meketon: A Comparison of Several Variance Estimators, Technical Report No. J-85-12, School of Industrial and Systems Engineering, Georgia Institute of Technology, Atlanta (1986).

Goldsman, D., and L. W. Schruben: Asymptotic Properties of Some Confidence Interval Estimators for Simulation Output, *Management Sci.*, 30: 1217–1225 (1984).

Goldsman, D., and L. W. Schruben: New Confidence Interval Estimators Using Standardized Time Series, *Management Sci.*, *36*: 393–397 (1990).

Gross, D., and C. M. Harris: *Fundamentals of Queueing Theory*, 2d ed., John Wiley, New York (1985).

Heathcote, C. R., and P. Winer: An Approximation to the Moments of Waiting Times, *Operations Res.*, *17*: 175–186 (1969).

Heidelberger, P., and P. D. Welch: Adaptive Spectral Methods for Simulation Output Analysis, *IBM J. Res. Develop.*, *25*: 860–876 (1981a).

Heidelberger, P., and P. D. Welch: A Spectral Method for Confidence Interval Generation and Run Length Control in Simulations, *Commun. Assoc. Comput. Mach.*, *24*: 233–245 (1981b).

Heidelberger, P., and P. D. Welch: Simulation Run Length Control in the Presence of an Initial Transient, *Operations Res.*, *31*: 1109–1144 (1983).

Hogg, R. V., and A. T. Craig: *Introduction to Mathematical Statistics*, 3d ed., Macmillan, New York (1970).

Iglehart, D. L.: Simulating Stable Stochastic Systems, V: Comparison of Ratio Estimators, *Naval Res. Logist. Quart.*, *22*: 553–565 (1975).

Jain, R., and I. Chlamtac: The P^2 Algorithm for Dynamic Calculation of Quantiles and Histograms without Storing Observations, *Commun. Assoc. Comput. Mach.*, *28*: 1076–1085 (1985).

Kelton, W. D.: Transient Exponential-Erlang Queues and Steady-State Simulation, *Commun. Assoc. Comput. Mach.*, *28*: 741–749 (1985).

Kelton, W. D.: Random Initialization Methods in Simulation, *IIE Trans.*, *21*: 355–367 (1989).

Kelton, W. D., and A. M. Law: A New Approach for Dealing with the Startup Problem in Discrete Event Simulation, *Naval Res. Logist. Quart.*, *30*: 641–658 (1983).

Kelton, W. D., and A. M. Law: The Transient Behavior of the $M/M/s$ Queue, with Implications for Steady-State Simulation, *Operations Res.*, *33*: 378–396 (1985).

Law, A. M.: Efficient Estimators for Simulated Queueing Systems, *Univ. Calif. Operations Res. Center ORC 74–7*, Berkeley (1974).

Law, A. M.: Confidence Intervals in Discrete Event Simulation: A Comparison of Replication and Batch Means, *Naval Res. Logist. Quart.*, *24*: 667–678 (1977).

Law, A. M.: Statistical Analysis of Simulation Output Data with SIMSCRIPT II.5, CACI, Inc., Los Angeles (1979).

Law, A. M.: Statistical Analysis of the Output Data from Terminating Simulations, *Naval Res. Logist. Quart.*, *27*: 131–143 (1980).

Law, A. M.: Statistical Analysis of Simulation Output Data, *Operations Res.*, *31*: 983–1029 (1983).

Law, A. M., and J. S. Carson: A Sequential Procedure for Determining the Length of a Steady-State Simulation, *Operations Res.*, *27*: 1011–1025 (1979).

Law, A. M., and W. D. Kelton: Confidence Intervals for Steady-State Simulations, II: A Survey of Sequential Procedures, *Management Sci.*, *28*: 550–562 (1982).

Law, A. M., and W. D. Kelton: Confidence Intervals for Steady-State Simulations, I: A Survey of Fixed Sample Size Procedures, *Operations Res.*, *32*: 1221–1239 (1984).

Law, A. M., W. D. Kelton, and L. W. Koenig: Relative Width Sequential Confidence Intervals for the Mean, *Commun. Statist.*, *B10*: 29–39 (1981).

Meketon, M. S., and B. W. Schmeiser: Overlapping Batch Means: Something for Nothing?, *Proc. 1984 Winter Simulation Conference*, Dallas, pp. 227–230 (1984).

Miller, R. G.: The Jackknife—A Review, *Biometrika*, *61*: 1–15 (1974).

Murray, J. R.: Stochastic Initialization in Steady-State Simulations, Ph.D. Dissertation, Department of Industrial and Operations Engineering, University of Michigan, Ann Arbor (1988).

Murray, J. R., and W. D. Kelton: The Transient Behavior of the $M/E_k/2$ Queue and Steady-State Simulation, *Computers and Operations Res.*, *15*: 357–367 (1988).

Raatikainen, K. E. E.: Sequential Procedure for Simultaneous Estimation of Several Percentiles, Department of Computer Science, University of Helsinki, Helsinki, Finland (1988).

Ross, S. M.: *Introduction to Probability Models*, 4th ed., Academic Press, San Diego (1989).

Sargent, R. G., K. Kang, and D. Goldsman: An Investigation of Small Sample Size Behavior of Confidence Interval Estimation Procedures, Working Paper #87–005, Department of Industrial Engineering and Operations Research, Syracuse University, Syracuse, N.Y. (1987).

Schmeiser, B. W.: Batch Size Effects in the Analysis of Simulation Output, *Operations Res.*, *30*: 556–568 (1982).

Schriber, T. J., and R. W. Andrews: An ARMA-Based Confidence Interval for the Analysis of Simulation Output, *Am. J. Math. Management Sci.*, *4*: 345–373 (1984).

Schruben, L. W.: Detecting Initialization Bias in Simulation Output, *Operations Res.*, *30*: 569–590 (1982).

Schruben, L. W.: Confidence Interval Estimation Using Standardized Time Series, *Operations Res.*, *31*: 1090–1108 (1983).

Schruben, L. W., H. Singh, and L. Tierney: Optimal Tests for Initialization Bias in Simulation Output, *Operations Res.*, *31*: 1167–1178 (1983).

Wagner, H. M.: *Principles of Operations Research*, Prentice-Hall, Englewood Cliffs, N.J. (1969).

Welch, P. D.: On the Problem of the Initial Transient in Steady-State Simulation, IBM Watson Research Center, Yorktown Heights, N.Y. (1981).

Welch, P. D.: The Statistical Analysis of Simulation Results, in *The Computer Performance Modeling Handbook*, S. S. Lavenberg, ed., pp. 268–328, Academic Press, New York (1983).

CHAPTER
10

COMPARING ALTERNATIVE SYSTEM CONFIGURATIONS

Recommended sections for a first reading: 10.1 through 10.3, 10.4.1

10.1 INTRODUCTION

In Chap. 9 we saw the importance of applying appropriate statistical analyses to the output from a simulation model of a *single* system. In this chapter we discuss statistical analyses of the output from several *different* simulation models that might represent competing system designs or alternative operating policies. This is a very important subject, since the real utility of simulation lies in comparing such alternatives before implementation. As the following example illustrates, appropriate statistical methods are essential if we are to avoid making serious errors leading to fallacious conclusions and, ultimately, poor decisions. We hope that this example will demonstrate the danger inherent in making decisions based on the output from a *single* run (or replication) of each alternative system.

Example 10.1. A bank planning to install an automated teller station must choose between buying one Zippytel machine or two Klunkytel machines. Although one Zippy costs twice as much to purchase, install, and operate as one Klunky, the Zippy works twice as fast. Since the total cost to the bank is thus the same regardless of its decision, the managers would like to install the system that will provide the best service.

From available data, it appears that during a certain rush period, customers arrive one at a time according to a Poisson process with rate 1 per minute. The Zippy could provide service times that are IID exponential random variables with mean 0.9 minute. Alternatively, if two Klunkies are installed, each will yield service times that are IID exponential random variables with mean 1.8 minutes; in this case a single FIFO queue will be formed instead of two separate lines. Thus, we are comparing an $M/M/1$ queue with an $M/M/2$ queue, each with utilization factor $\rho = 0.9$, as shown in Fig. 10.1. The performance measure of interest is the expected average delay in queue of the first 100 customers, assuming that the first customer arrives to an empty and idle system; we denote these (expected) quantities by $d_Z(100)$ and $d_K(100)$ for the one-Zippy and two-Klunky cases, respectively. (The bank decided to ignore customer service times, since waiting in line is the most irritating part of the experience and customers are reasonably pacified as long as they are being served; see Prob. 10.1 for further consideration of this issue.) The bank's intrepid systems analyst decided to make a simulation run of length 100 customer delays for each system (using independent random numbers) and to use the average of the 100 delays in each case to infer whether $d_Z(100)$ or $d_K(100)$ is smaller, and thus make a recommendation.

How likely is it that the analyst will make the right recommendation? To find out, we performed 100 independent experiments of the analyst's entire scheme and noted how many times the best system would have been recommended. The best system is actually the two-Klunky installation, since $d_Z(100) = 4.13$ and $d_K(100) = 3.70$. [These values were determined from the queueing-theoretic results in Kelton and Law (1985).] Our experiment was, thus, to

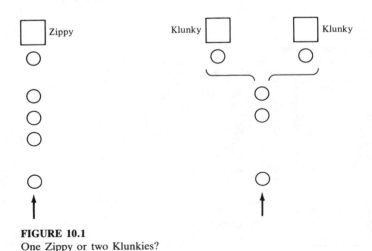

FIGURE 10.1
One Zippy or two Klunkies?

perform 100 independent pairs of independent simulations of the two systems, and average the delays in each simulation to obtain $\hat{d}_Z(100)$ and $\hat{d}_K(100)$, say, and then recommend the Zippy or Klunky system according as $\hat{d}_Z(100)$ or $\hat{d}_K(100)$ was smaller; some of the results are in Table 10.1. In only 48 of our 100 experiments was $\hat{d}_K(100) < \hat{d}_Z(100)$, so the analyst would not really appear to have any better chance of making the right decision than making the wrong one.

We have an uneasy feeling that many simulation studies are carried out in a manner similar to that described in Example 10.1. The difficulty is that the simulation output data are stochastic, so comparing the two systems on the basis of only a single run of each is a very unreliable approach.

The following example indicates how the comparison in Example 10.1 could be improved.

Example 10.2. To illuminate the problem with the one-run-of-each approach in Example 10.1, we plotted all 100 $\hat{d}_Z(100)$'s and $\hat{d}_K(100)$'s in the "$n = 1$" pair of horizontal dot plots in Fig. 10.2; each circle (solid or hollow) represents the average of the 100 delays in a single simulation, positioned according to the scale at the bottom. Even though the *expected* average delay for the two-Klunky system is smaller than that for the one-Zippy system, the distributions of the *observed* average delays overlap substantially. This accounts for the distressingly large probability of making the wrong choice noted at the end of Example 10.1.

Instead, we could make some number, n, of complete independent replications of each alternative system, and compare the systems on the basis of their averages across replications. Specifically, let X_{1j} be the average of the 100 delays in the one-Zippy system on the jth independent replication of this system, and let X_{2j} be the average of the 100 delays in the two-Klunky system on its jth replication, for $j = 1, 2, \ldots, n$. (We also made the simulations so that the X_{1j}'s and the X_{2j}'s are independent.) Then if $\bar{X}_1(n)$ and $\bar{X}_2(n)$ are the sample means of the X_{1j}'s and X_{2j}'s, respectively, we would recommend the system with the smaller $\bar{X}_i(n)$. (The method of Example 10.1 is thus a special case, taking $n = 1$.)

TABLE 10.1
Testing the analyst's decision rule

Experiment	$\hat{d}_Z(100)$	$\hat{d}_K(100)$	Recommendation	
1	3.80	4.60	Zippy	(wrong)
2	3.17	8.37	Zippy	(wrong)
3	3.96	4.18	Zippy	(wrong)
4	1.91	5.77	Zippy	(wrong)
5	1.71	2.23	Zippy	(wrong)
6	6.16	4.72	Klunky	(right)
7	5.67	1.39	Klunky	(right)
:	:	:	:	
98	8.40	9.39	Zippy	(wrong)
99	7.70	1.54	Klunky	(right)
100	4.64	1.17	Klunky	(right)

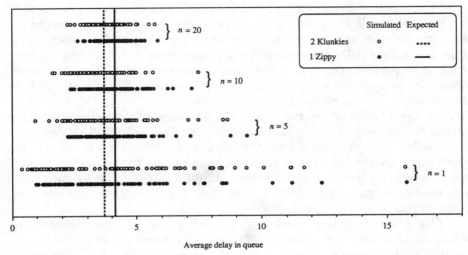

FIGURE 10.2
One Zippy vs. two Klunkies, as described in Examples 10.1 and 10.2.

Table 10.2 shows the proportion of 100 independent pairs of n-replication averages in which the one-Zippy system appeared better, i.e., would result in the wrong recommendation, for $n = 1$, 5, 10, and 20. The chance of making an error falls as n increases, but at a corresponding higher cost of simulating. The four pairs of plots in Fig. 10.2 also indicate that as n rises, the distributions of the n-replication averages (each circle represents such an average) tighten up around their expectations, but there is still considerable overlap even for $n = 20$, where the proportion of incorrect recommendations is still 0.34.

Examples 10.1 and 10.2 illustrate the need for careful design and analysis of comparative simulations. Indeed, even with $n = 20$ replications of each system design, Example 10.2 indicates that there is substantial room for error. One way of sharpening the comparison will be discussed in Sec. 11.2, and the above examples will be reworked in that context; see Example 11.2 in Sec. 11.2.4.

TABLE 10.2
Proportion of wrong recommendations in the n-replication method of Example 10.2

n	Proportion of experiments favoring the one-Zippy system
1	0.52
5	0.43
10	0.38
20	0.34

Note that both Examples 10.1 and 10.2 dealt with terminating simulations (see Secs. 9.3 and 9.4). As we shall see in this chapter, a basic requirement for using many statistical methods for comparing alternative configurations is the ability to collect IID observations with expectation equal to the desired measure of performance. For terminating simulations, this is easily accomplished by simply making independent replications; e.g., a basic unit of observation in Examples 10.1 and 10.2 was the average of the 100 delays in a single *entire* replication of the model. If we want to compare alternative systems on the basis of steady-state behavior (see Secs. 9.3 and 9.5), however, the situation becomes more complicated since we cannot easily obtain IID observations having expectation (approximately) equal to the desired steady-state measure of performance. There are different ways of dealing with steady-state comparisons, which will be discussed throughout the chapter, specifically in Secs. 10.2.4 and 10.4.4.

Our purpose in this chapter is to present several different types of comparison and selection problems that have been found useful in simulation, together with appropriate statistical procedures for their solution, and numerical examples. We assume for this chapter that the various alternative systems are simply *given*. In many situations care should be taken in choosing *which* particular system variants to simulate; see Chap. 12 for discussion of how to choose appropriate alternative systems for comparison.

In Sec. 10.2 we treat the special but important case of comparing just two systems by constructing a confidence interval for the difference between their performance measures. These ideas are extended in Sec. 10.3 to confidence-interval comparisons of more than two systems. Section 10.4 introduces some procedures for selecting the "best" of several alternative systems, as well as other goals involving choice of certain "good" subsets from among the set of all alternatives. Appendixes 10A and 10B treat certain technical issues related to the selection procedures of Sec. 10.4.

10.2 CONFIDENCE INTERVALS FOR THE DIFFERENCE BETWEEN PERFORMANCE MEASURES OF TWO SYSTEMS

Here we consider the special case of comparing two systems on the basis of some performance measure, or expected *response*. We effect this comparison by forming a confidence interval for the *difference* in the two expectations, rather than by doing a hypothesis test to see whether the observed difference is significantly different from zero. Whereas a test results in only a "reject" or "fail-to-reject" conclusion, a confidence interval gives us this information (according as the interval misses or contains zero, respectively) as well as quantifies how much the measures differ, if at all. Also, we shall take a parametric, i.e., normal-theory, approach here, even though nonparametric analogues could be used instead [see, for example, Conover (1980, pp. 223–225)]. The parametric approach is simple and familiar, and moreover should be quite robust in this context, since troublesome skewness (see Sec. 9.4.1) in the underlying distributions of the output random variables should be ameliorated upon subtraction (assuming the two output distributions are skewed in the same direction).

For $i = 1, 2$, let $X_{i1}, X_{i2}, \ldots, X_{in_i}$ be a sample of n_i IID observations from system i, and let $\mu_i = E(X_{ij})$ be the expected response of interest; we want to construct a confidence interval for $\zeta = \mu_1 - \mu_2$. Whether or not X_{1j} and X_{2j} are independent depends on how the simulations are executed, and could determine which of the two confidence-interval approaches discussed in Secs. 10.2.1 and 10.2.2 are used.

10.2.1 A Paired-t Confidence Interval

If $n_1 = n_2$ ($=n$, say), or we are willing to discard some observations from the system on which we actually have more data, we can pair X_{1j} with X_{2j} to define $Z_j = X_{1j} - X_{2j}$, for $j = 1, 2, \ldots, n$. Then the Z_j's are IID random variables and $E(Z_j) = \zeta$, the quantity for which we want to construct a confidence interval. Thus, we can let

$$\bar{Z}(n) = \frac{\sum\limits_{j=1}^{n} Z_j}{n}$$

and

$$\widehat{\text{Var}}[\bar{Z}(n)] = \frac{\sum\limits_{j=1}^{n} [Z_j - \bar{Z}(n)]^2}{n(n-1)}$$

and form the (approximate) $100(1 - \alpha)$ percent confidence interval

$$\bar{Z}(n) \pm t_{n-1, 1-\alpha/2}\sqrt{\widehat{\text{Var}}[\bar{Z}(n)]} \tag{10.1}$$

If the Z_j's are normally distributed, this confidence interval is exact, i.e., it covers ζ with probability $1 - \alpha$; otherwise, we rely on the central limit theorem (see Sec. 4.5), which implies that this coverage probability will be *near* $1 - \alpha$ for large n. An important point here is that we did *not* have to assume that X_{1j} and X_{2j} are independent; nor did we have to assume that $\text{Var}(X_{1j}) = \text{Var}(X_{2j})$. Allowing positive correlation between X_{1j} and X_{2j} can be of great importance, since this leads to a reduction in $\text{Var}(Z_j)$ (see Prob. 4.13) and thus to a smaller confidence interval. Section 11.2 discusses a method (*common random numbers*) that can often induce this positive correlation between the observations on the different systems. The confidence interval in (10.1) will be called the *paired-t confidence interval*, and in its derivation we essentially reduced the two-system problem to one involving a single sample, namely, the Z_j's. In this sense, the paired-t approach is the same as the method discussed in Sec. 9.4.1 for analysis of a single system. (Thus, the sequential confidence-interval procedures of Sec. 9.4.1 could be applied here.) It is important to note that the X_{ij}'s are random variables defined over an entire *replication*; for example, X_{1j} might be the average of the 100 delays on the jth replication of the Zippytel system of Example 10.2; it is *not* the delay of some individual customer.

> **Example 10.3.** For the inventory model of Sec. 1.5, suppose we want to compare two different (s,S) policies in terms of their effect on the expected average total cost per month for the first 120 months of operation, where we assume that the initial inventory level is 60. For the first policy $(s,S) = (20,40)$, and the second policy sets $(s,S) = (20,80)$. Here, X_{ij} is the average total cost per month of policy i on the jth independent replication. We made the runs for policy 1 and policy 2 independently of each other and made $n = n_1 = n_2 = 5$ independent replications of the model under each policy; Table 10.3 contains the results. Using the paired-t approach, we obtained $\bar{Z}(5) = 4.98$ and $\widehat{\text{Var}}[\bar{Z}(5)] = 2.44$, leading to the (approximate) 90 percent confidence interval $[1.65, 8.31]$ for $\zeta = \mu_1 - \mu_2$. Thus, with approximately 90 percent confidence, we can say that μ_1 differs from μ_2, and it furthermore appears that policy 2 is superior, since it leads to a lower average operating cost (between 1.65 and 8.31 lower, which would *not* have been evident from a hypothesis test). We must use the word "approximate" to describe the confidence level, since $n_1 = n_2 = 5$ may or may not be "large" enough for this model for the central limit theorem to have taken effect.

10.2.2 A Modified Two-Sample-t Confidence Interval

A second approach to forming a confidence interval for ζ does not pair up the observations from the two systems, but *does* require that the X_{1j}'s be independent of the X_{2j}'s. However, n_1 and n_2 can now be different.

To apply the classical two-sample-t approach [see, for example, Devore (1982, pp. 287–291)], we *must* have $\text{Var}(X_{1j}) = \text{Var}(X_{2j})$; if these variances are not equal, the two-sample-t confidence interval can exhibit serious coverage degradation. [If, however, $n_1 = n_2$, the two-sample-t approach is fairly safe even if the variances differ; see Scheffé (1970) for further discussion.] Since equality of variances is probably not a safe assumption when simulating real systems, we would recommend against using the two-sample-t approach.

TABLE 10.3
Average total cost per month for five independent replications of two inventory policies, and the differences

j	X_{1j}	X_{2j}	Z_j
1	126.97	118.21	8.76
2	124.31	120.22	4.09
3	126.68	122.45	4.23
4	122.66	122.68	−0.02
5	127.23	119.40	7.83

Instead, we shall give an old but reliable approximate solution, due to Welch (1938), to this problem of comparing two systems with unequal and unknown variances, called the *Behrens-Fisher problem* when the X_{ij}'s are normally distributed [see also Scheffé (1970)]. As usual, let

$$\bar{X}_i(n_i) = \frac{\sum_{j=1}^{n_i} X_{ij}}{n_i}$$

and

$$S_i^2(n_i) = \frac{\sum_{j=1}^{n_i} [X_{ij} - \bar{X}_i(n_i)]^2}{n_i - 1}$$

for $i = 1, 2$. Then compute the *estimated* degrees of freedom

$$\hat{f} = \frac{[S_1^2(n_1)/n_1 + S_2^2(n_2)/n_2]^2}{[S_1^2(n_1)/n_1]^2/(n_1 - 1) + [S_2^2(n_2)/n_2]^2/(n_2 - 1)}$$

and use

$$\bar{X}_1(n_1) - \bar{X}_2(n_2) \pm t_{\hat{f}, 1-\alpha/2} \sqrt{\frac{S_1^2(n_1)}{n_1} + \frac{S_2^2(n_2)}{n_2}} \qquad (10.2)$$

as an approximate $100(1 - \alpha)$ percent confidence interval for ζ. Since $\hat{f}$ will not, in general, be an integer, interpolation in the t tables will probably be necessary. The confidence interval given by (10.2), which we will call the *Welch confidence interval*, can also be used to validate a simulation model of an existing system (see Sec. 5.6.2). If "system 1" is the real-world system on which we have physically collected data and "system 2" is the corresponding simulation model from which we have simulation output data, it is likely that n_1 will be far less than n_2. Finally, if we are comparing two simulated systems and want a "small" confidence interval, a sequential procedure due to Robbins, Simons, and Starr (1967) can be used, which is efficient in the sense of minimizing the final value of $n_1 + n_2$. It is also asymptotically correct in the sense that the confidence interval will have approximately the correct coverage probability as the prespecified confidence-interval width becomes small.

Example 10.4. Since the runs for the two different inventory policies of Example 10.3 were done independently, we can apply the Welch approach to form an approximate 90 percent confidence interval for ζ; we use the same X_{ij} data as given in Table 10.3. We get $\bar{X}_1(5) = 125.57$, $\bar{X}_2(5) = 120.59$, $S_1^2(5) = 4.00$, $S_2^2(5) = 3.76$, and $\hat{f} = 7.99$. Interpolating in the t tables leads to $t_{7.99, 0.95} = 1.860$. Thus, the Welch confidence interval is $[2.66, 7.30]$.

10.2.3 Contrasting the Two Methods

Since the inventory data of Table 10.3 were collected so that $n_1 = n_2$ and the X_{1j}'s were independent of the X_{2j}'s, we could apply either the paired-t or Welch approach to construct a confidence interval for ζ. It happened that the confidence interval for the Welch approach was smaller in this case, but in general we will not know which confidence interval will be smaller.

The choice of either the paired-t or the Welch approach will usually be made according to the situation. One consideration is that using common random numbers (see Sec. 11.2) for simulating the two systems can often lead to a considerable reduction in $\text{Var}(Z_j)$ and, thus, to a much smaller confidence interval; this implies that $n_1 = n_2$ and that X_{1j} and X_{2j} will not be independent, so the paired-t approach is required. On the other hand, if $n_1 \neq n_2$ (and we want to use all the available data), the Welch approach should be used; this requires independence of the X_{1j}'s from the X_{2j}'s and so in particular would preclude the use of common random numbers.

10.2.4 Comparisons Based on Steady-State Measures of Performance

As mentioned in Sec. 10.1, the basic ingredient for most comparison techniques is a sample of IID observations with expectation equal to the performance measure on which the comparison is to be made. The examples so far in this chapter have all been terminating simulations, so such observations come naturally by simply replicating the simulation some number of times.

In other cases, however, we might want to compare two (or more) systems on the basis of a steady-state measure of performance (see Secs. 9.3 and 9.5). Here we can no longer simply replicate the models, since initialization effects may bias the output, as discussed in Sec. 9.5.1. Thus, it is more difficult to effect a valid comparison based on steady-state performance measures, and many of the concerns discussed in Sec. 9.5 arise. The following example illustrates how the replication/deletion approach for steady-state analysis, as described in Sec. 9.5.2, can be adapted to the problem of constructing a confidence interval for the difference between two steady-state means.

> **Example 10.5.** The manufacturing company in Example 9.25 is thinking of buying a new piece of inspection equipment that will reduce inspection times by 10 percent, so that they would be distributed uniformly between 0.675 minute and 0.720 minute. A simulation study could help determine whether this change will significantly reduce the *steady-state* mean time in system. Let T_{ijp} be the time in system of the pth departing part in the jth replication ($j = 1, 2, \ldots, n$) for system i ($i = 1$ and 2 for the original and proposed systems, respectively). Let l_i and m_i be the length of the warmup period and the minimum number of T_{ijp}'s in any replication, both for system i. Using the data from Example 9.31, we have $n = 20$, $l_1 = 2286$, and $m_1 = 9407$. We next make 20 replications of length 160 hours for the proposed system ($i = 2$), and the moving average $\bar{T}_{2p}(1300)$ is plotted in Fig. 10.3. From these runs and the plot, we determined that $l_2 = 2093$ and $m_2 = 9434$. Let
>
> $$X_{ij} = \frac{\displaystyle\sum_{p = l_i + 1}^{m_i} T_{ijp}}{m_i - l_i} \qquad \text{for } i = 1, 2$$

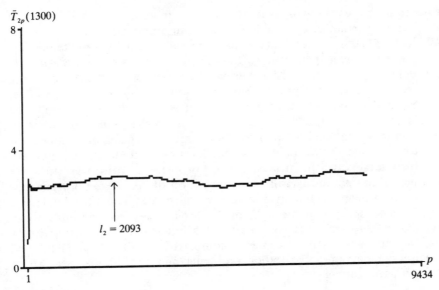

FIGURE 10.3
Time-in-system moving average ($w = 1300$) for the proposed system.

and $Z_j = X_{1j} - X_{2j}$ for $j = 1, 2, \ldots, 20$. Also, let ν_i be the steady-state mean time in system for system i. Then, from the 20 replications of each system, we used (10.1) to obtain 2.36 ± 0.31 as an approximate 90 percent confidence interval for $\nu_1 - \nu_2$. Thus, the difference between the two steady-state mean system times appears to be statistically significant, and represents a decrease of about 38 percent (3.80 vs. 6.16). (Recall that the mean inspection time was reduced by only 10 percent; explain.)

The approach used in Example 10.5 basically attempted to use the replication/deletion approach to obtain IID observations for each system with mean equal to the respective steady-state measure of performance. Several of the other single-system methods for steady-state analysis discussed in Sec. 9.5.3 could also be considered. For example, if the warmup period is long, we might want to use batch means on each alternative system as a different approach toward obtaining IID unbiased observations. Since the critical factor for success of the batch-means approach is eliminating correlation between batches, we must take care to define the batches appropriately, as discussed in Sec. 9.5.3. Another possibility would be Chen and Sargent's (1987) two-model adaptation of the standardized time-series approach (see Sec. 9.5.3).

10.3 CONFIDENCE INTERVALS FOR COMPARING MORE THAN TWO SYSTEMS

If there are just two systems to compare, the methods in Sec. 10.2 provide a way of constructing a confidence interval for the difference between their performance measures. In many studies, however, there may be more than two systems, but we can still use a confidence-interval approach.

We will be making several confidence-interval statements simultaneously, so their individual levels will have to be adjusted upward so that the *overall* confidence level of all intervals' covering their respective targets is at the desired level $1 - \alpha$. We will use the Bonferroni inequality [see (9.11) in Sec. 9.7] to ensure that the overall confidence level is *at least* $1 - \alpha$. Recall, the Bonferroni inequality implies that if we want to make some number c of confidence-interval statements, then we should make each separate interval at level $1 - \alpha/c$, so that the overall confidence level associated with all intervals' covering their targets will be at least $1 - \alpha$. For instance, if we want to make $c = 10$ intervals and get an overall confidence level of $100(1 - \alpha)$ percent $= 90$ percent, we must make each individual interval at the 99 percent level. Clearly, for large c, this implies that the individual intervals may become quite wide.

Although there are many goals that could be formulated for comparing k systems, we will focus on two problems: comparisons with a "standard," and all pairwise comparisons. For other problems and procedures, see Miller (1977) for a good survey.

10.3.1 Comparisons with a Standard

Suppose that one of the model variants is a "standard," perhaps representing the existing system or policy. If we call the standard system 1 and the other variants systems $2, 3, \ldots, k$, the goal is to construct $k - 1$ confidence intervals for the $k - 1$ differences $\mu_2 - \mu_1, \mu_3 - \mu_1, \ldots, \mu_k - \mu_1$, with overall confidence level $1 - \alpha$. Thus, we are making $c = k - 1$ individual intervals, so they should each be constructed at level $1 - \alpha/(k - 1)$. Then we can say (with a confidence level of at least $1 - \alpha$) that for all $i = 2, 3, \ldots, k$, system i differs from the standard if the interval for $\mu_i - \mu_1$ misses 0, and that system i is not significantly different from the standard if this interval contains 0.

> **Example 10.6.** Table 10.4 defines $k = 5$ different (s,S) policies for the inventory system of Sec. 1.5; policies 1 and 2 are those used in Examples 10.3 and 10.4. Suppose that policy 1, where $(s,S) = (20,40)$, is the current policy, and the other four policies are being considered as possible alternatives.

TABLE 10.4
The five alternative (s,S) inventory policies

Policy (i)	s	S
1	20	40
2	20	80
3	40	60
4	40	100
5	60	100

TABLE 10.5
Average total cost per month for five independent replications of each of the five inventory policies, with sample means and standard deviations

j	X_{1j}	X_{2j}	X_{3j}	X_{4j}	X_{5j}
1	126.97	118.21	120.77	131.64	141.09
2	124.31	120.22	129.32	137.07	143.86
3	126.68	122.45	120.61	129.91	144.30
4	122.66	122.68	123.65	129.97	141.72
5	127.23	119.40	127.34	131.08	142.61
Mean	125.57	120.59	124.34	131.93	142.72
Standard deviation	2.00	1.94	3.90	2.96	1.37

Which of these would differ from the standard? To find out, we made five independent replications of each policy, with the runs for the different policies being independent of each other as well. The individual-replication results appear in Table 10.5, along with the sample means and standard deviations (of the X_{ij}'s) for each policy. Since there are $k - 1 = 4$ intervals to construct, we made each interval at level 97.5 percent to yield an overall confidence level of at least 90 percent. Table 10.6 shows the differences in the sample means, as well as 97.5 percent confidence intervals for $\mu_i - \mu_1$, for $i = 2, 3, 4,$ and 5. For illustration, we used both the paired-t (Sec. 10.2.1) and Welch (Sec. 10.2.2) approaches to confidence-interval formation, which are both valid since the runs for the different models were independent. The asterisks indicate those intervals not containing zero, i.e., corresponding to those alternative systems that appear to differ from the standard. Note that the two approaches for forming the individual intervals may lead to different conclusions; e.g., the paired-t interval for $\mu_2 - \mu_1$ does not indicate a difference, whereas the Welch interval does. Furthermore, neither method is dominant in terms of interval smallness. At any rate, it does appear that models 4 and 5 are significantly different (actually, worse, since the output is an operating cost) than the standard, and that model 3 is not different from the standard. It is not clear from these results whether model 2 differs from the standard.

TABLE 10.6
Individual 97.5 percent confidence intervals for all comparisons with the standard system ($\mu_i - \mu_1$, $i = 2, 3, 4, 5$); * denotes a significant difference

i	$\bar{X}_i - \bar{X}_1$	Paired-t		Welch	
		Half-length	Interval	Half-length	Interval
2	−4.98	5.45	(−10.44, 0.48)	3.54	(−8.52, −1.44)*
3	−1.23	7.58	(−8.80, 6.34)	6.21	(−7.44, 4.97)
4	6.36	6.08	(0.27, 12.46)*	4.55	(1.82, 10.91)*
5	17.15	3.67	(13.48, 20.81)*	6.15	(14.07, 20.22)*

Implicit in the above example and discussion is that the individual confidence intervals have the correct probability $[1 - \alpha/(k - 1)$ in this case] of covering their respective targets. Thus, we should bear in mind the robustness concerns of Sec. 9.4.1. Also, since the Bonferroni inequality is quite general, it does not matter how the individual confidence intervals are formed; they need not result from the same number of replications of each model, nor must they be independent. For example, we could attempt to reduce the intervals' widths by making more replications of high-variance models, or by using common random numbers (Sec. 11.2) to reduce the variances of the paired differences. In addition, the above approach could be used for steady-state comparisons by using a technique for constructing individual confidence intervals for steady-state differences, as discussed in Sec. 10.2.4, with the individual confidence levels adjusted upward by the Bonferroni inequality. Finally, one can always resolve ambiguities (confidence intervals covering zero, as occurred in three of the eight intervals in Table 10.6) by making more replications (or longer runs); the rate of decrease of the intervals' widths, however, may be slow as additional simulation is done—to cut an interval in half generally requires about four times as many replications.

10.3.2 All Pairwise Comparisons

Is some studies, we might want to compare each system with every other system to detect and quantify any significant pairwise differences. For example, there may not be an existing system, and all k alternatives represent possible implementations that should be treated in the same way. One approach would be to form confidence intervals for the differences $\mu_{i_2} - \mu_{i_1}$, for all i_1 and i_2 between 1 and k, with $i_1 < i_2$. Here, there will be $k(k - 1)/2$ individual intervals, so each must be made at level $1 - \alpha/[k(k - 1)/2]$ in order to have a confidence level of at least $1 - \alpha$ for all the intervals together.

> **Example 10.7.** Now suppose that the five inventory policies in Table 10.4 are all to be compared against each other, using the data in Table 10.5. Since there are $5(5 - 1)/2 = 10$ possible pairs, we must make each individual interval at level 99 percent in order to achieve 90 percent overall confidence. Table 10.7 gives the resulting 99 percent intervals, using both the paired-t and Welch approaches, with asterisks indicating those intervals missing zero, i.e., those pairs of systems that appear to have different expected operating costs. Once again, note that the two approaches do not always agree in terms of which differences are significant, and neither approach gives intervals with uniformly smaller half-lengths. Furthermore, it is possible to arrive at apparent contradictions in the conclusions. For instance, using the Welch approach we would conclude that neither μ_1 nor μ_2 differs significantly from μ_3, so that we might (crudely) want to say something like "$\mu_1 = \mu_3 = \mu_2$" and thus think logically that "$\mu_1 = \mu_2$." But the confidence interval for $\mu_2 - \mu_1$ misses zero, indicating that we *cannot* regard μ_1 as being equal to μ_2. The problem here is that we dare not interpret the confidence-interval statements as constituting "proof" of equality or inequality; in the above

TABLE 10.7
Individual 99 percent confidence intervals for all pairwise comparisons ($\mu_{i_2} - \mu_{i_1}$ for $i_1 < i_2$); * denotes a significant difference

		Paired-t		
			i_2	
	2	3	4	5
i_1 1	-4.98 ± 7.18	-1.23 ± 9.99	6.36 ± 8.01	$17.15 \pm 4.83^*$
2		3.75 ± 9.58	$11.34 \pm 8.38^*$	$22.12 \pm 3.80^*$
3			$7.60 \pm 5.66^*$	$18.38 \pm 7.73^*$
4				$10.78 \pm 5.85^*$

		Welch		
			i_2	
	2	3	4	5
i_1 1	$-4.98 \pm 4.36^*$	-1.23 ± 7.91	$6.36 \pm 5.60^*$	$17.15 \pm 3.80^*$
2		3.75 ± 7.86	$11.34 \pm 5.88^*$	$22.12 \pm 3.72^*$
3			7.60 ± 7.67	$18.38 \pm 8.51^*$
4				$10.78 \pm 5.89^*$

discussion we just could not resolve a difference between either μ_1 or μ_2 in comparison with μ_3, but we could detect a difference between μ_1 and μ_2. Such apparent contradictions become less likely as the intervals become smaller, which could occur by making more replications of the systems or perhaps by using the method of common random numbers, discussed in Sec. 11.2.

As at the end of Sec. 10.3.1, we note the importance of ensuring the validity of the individual confidence intervals, the possibility of using common random numbers across the different models, and of taking the above approach for steady-state comparisons by using an appropriate steady-state methodology for the individual intervals.

Finally, we mention another comparison goal, that of forming simultaneous confidence intervals for the differences between the means of the k alternatives and that of the "best" alternative. Hsu (1984) provides an appropriate technique, and Gupta and Hsu (1984) describe related software. Hsu and Edwards (1983) give procedures for sequentially eliminating systems that appear inferior, retaining only those that are close to the best one. Hsu and Nelson (1988) relate these kinds of goals to the types of selection problems to be considered in Sec. 10.4, and provide several simulation examples.

10.4 RANKING AND SELECTION

In this section we consider goals that are different—and more ambitious—than simply making a comparison between several alternative systems. In Sec.

10.4.1 we describe a procedure whose goal is to select one of the k systems as being the best one, in some sense, and to control the probability that the selected system really *is* the best one. Section 10.4.2 considers a different goal, picking a subset of m of the k systems so that this selected subset contains the best system, again with a specified probability. Then in Sec. 10.4.3 we look at the problem of selecting the m best of the k systems. (The validity of these three selection procedures is considered in App. 10A.) Further problems and methods are discussed in Sec. 10.4.4, including the issue of ranking and selection based on steady-state measures of performance.

10.4.1   Selecting the Best of k Systems

As in Secs. 10.2 and 10.3, let X_{ij} be the random variable of interest from the jth replication of the ith system, and let $\mu_i = E(X_{ij})$. For this selection problem, as well as those in Secs. 10.4.2 and 10.4.3, the X_{ij}'s are all assumed to be independent of each other, i.e., the replications for a given alternative are independent, and the runs for different alternatives are also to be made independently. For example, X_{ij} could be the average total cost per month for the jth replication of policy i for the inventory model of Examples 10.6 and 10.7.

Let μ_{i_l} be the lth smallest of the μ_i's, so that $\mu_{i_1} \leq \mu_{i_2} \leq \cdots \leq \mu_{i_k}$. Our goal in this section is to select a system with the *smallest* expected response, μ_{i_1}. (If we want the *largest* mean μ_{i_k}, the signs of the X_{ij}'s and μ_i's can simply be reversed.) Let "CS" denote this event of "correct selection."

The inherent randomness of the observed X_{ij}'s implies that we can never be *absolutely* sure that we shall make the CS, but we would like to be able to prespecify the *probability* of CS. Further, if μ_{i_1} and μ_{i_2} are actually very close together, we might not care if we erroneously choose system i_2 (the one with mean μ_{i_2}), so that we want a method that avoids making a large number of replications to resolve this unimportant difference. The exact problem formulation, then, is that we want $P(\text{CS}) \geq P^*$ provided that $\mu_{i_2} - \mu_{i_1} \geq d^*$, where the minimal CS probability $P^* > 1/k$ and the "indifference" amount $d^* > 0$ are both specified by the analyst. It is natural to ask what happens if $\mu_{i_2} - \mu_{i_1} < d^*$. The procedure stated below has the nice property that, with probability at least P^*, the expected response of the *selected* system will be no larger than $\mu_{i_1} + d^*$. Thus, we are protected (with probability at least P^*) against selecting a system with mean that is more than d^* worse than that of the best system.

The statistical procedure for solving this problem, developed by Dudewicz and Dalal (1975), involves "two-stage" sampling from each of the k systems. In the first stage we make a fixed number of replications of each system, then use the resulting variance estimates to determine how many more replications from each system are necessary in a second stage of sampling in order to reach a decision. It must be assumed that the X_{ij}'s are normally distributed, but (importantly) we need *not* assume that the values of $\sigma_i^2 = \text{Var}(X_{ij})$ are known; nor do we have to assume that the σ_i^2's are the same for different i's. (Assuming known or equal variances is very unrealistic when simulating real systems.) The procedure's performance should be robust to departures from the normality assumption, especially if the X_{ij}'s are averages. (We have verified this robustness when X_{ij} is the average of a fixed number of delays in queue for an $M/M/1$ queueing system.)

In the first-stage sampling, we make $n_0 \geq 2$ replications of each of the k systems and define the first-stage sample means and variances

$$\bar{X}_i^{(1)}(n_0) = \frac{\sum\limits_{j=1}^{n_0} X_{ij}}{n_0}$$

and

$$S_i^2(n_0) = \frac{\sum\limits_{j=1}^{n_0} [X_{ij} - \bar{X}_i^{(1)}(n_0)]^2}{n_0 - 1}$$

for $i = 1, 2, \ldots, k$. Then we compute the total sample size N_i needed for system i as

$$N_i = \max\left\{ n_0 + 1, \left\lceil \frac{h_1^2 S_i^2(n_0)}{(d^*)^2} \right\rceil \right\} \tag{10.3}$$

where $\lceil x \rceil$ is the smallest integer that is greater than or equal to the real number x, and h_1 (which depends on k, P^*, and n_0) is a constant that can be obtained from Table 10.11 in App. 10B. Next, we make $N_i - n_0$ *more* replications of system i $(i = 1, 2, \ldots, k)$ and obtain the second-stage sample means

$$\bar{X}_i^{(2)}(N_i - n_0) = \frac{\sum\limits_{j=n_0+1}^{N_i} X_{ij}}{N_i - n_0}$$

Then define the weights

$$W_{i1} = \frac{n_0}{N_i} \left[1 + \sqrt{1 - \frac{N_i}{n_0}\left(1 - \frac{(N_i - n_0)(d^*)^2}{h_1^2 S_i^2(n_0)}\right)} \right]$$

and $W_{i2} = 1 - W_{i1}$, for $i = 1, 2, \ldots, k$. Finally, define the weighted sample means

$$\tilde{X}_i(N_i) = W_{i1}\bar{X}_i^{(1)}(n_0) + W_{i2}\bar{X}_i^{(2)}(N_i - n_0)$$

and select the system with the smallest $\tilde{X}_i(N_i)$. (See App. 10A for an explanation of the seemingly bizarre definition of W_{i1}.)

The choices of P^* and d^* depend on the analyst's goals and the particular systems under study; specifying them might be tempered by the computing cost of obtaining a large N_i associated with a large P^* or small d^*. However, choosing n_0 is more troublesome, and we can only say, on the basis of our experiments and various statements in the literature, that n_0 be at least 20. If n_0 is too small, we might get a poor estimate $S_i^2(n_0)$ of σ_i^2; in particular, it could be that $S_i^2(n_0)$ is much greater than σ_i^2, leading to an unnecessarily large value of N_i. On the other hand, if n_0 is too large, we could "overshoot" the necessary numbers of replications for some of the systems, which is wasteful. Table 10.11, in App. 10B, gives values of h_1 for $P^* = 0.90$ and 0.95, $n_0 = 20$ and 40, and for $k = 2, 3, \ldots, 10$. If values of h_1 are needed for other P^*, n_0, or k values, we refer the reader to Dudewicz and Dalal (1975) or Koenig and Law (1985).

> **Example 10.8.** For the inventory model of Sec. 1.5 (and Examples 10.6 and 10.7), suppose that we want to compare the $k = 5$ different (s,S) policies, as given in Table 10.4, on the basis of their corresponding expected average total costs per month for the first 120 months of operation, which we denote by μ_i for the ith policy. Our goal is to select a system with the smallest μ_i and to be $100P^* = 90$ percent sure that we have made the correct selection provided that $\mu_{i_2} - \mu_{i_1} \geq d^* = 1$. We made $n_0 = 20$ initial independent replications of each system, so that $h_1 = 2.747$ from Table 10.11. The results of the first-stage sampling are given in the $\bar{X}_i^{(1)}(20)$ and $S_i^2(20)$ columns of Table 10.8. From the $S_i^2(20)$'s, h_1, and d^*, we next computed the total sample size N_i for each system, as shown in Table 10.8. Then we made $N_i - 20$ additional replications for each policy, i.e., 90 more replications for policy 1, 41 more for policy 2, etc., and computed the second-stage sample means $\bar{X}_i^{(2)}(N_i - 20)$, as shown. Finally, we calculated the weights W_{i1} and W_{i2} for each system and the weighted sample means $\tilde{X}_i(N_i)$. Since $\tilde{X}_2(N_2)$ is the smallest weighted sample mean, we select policy 2 ($s = 20$ and $S = 80$) as being the lowest-cost configuration. Note from the $S_i^2(20)$ and N_i columns of Table 10.8 that the procedure calls for a higher value of the final N_i if the variance estimate $S_i^2(20)$ is high; this is simply reflecting the fact that we need more data on the more variable systems.

10.4.2 Selecting a Subset of Size m Containing the Best of k Systems

Now we consider a different kind of selection problem, that of selecting a subset of exactly m of the k systems (m is prespecified) so that, with probability at least P^*, the selected subset will contain a system with the smallest mean

TABLE 10.8
Selecting the best of the five inventory policies

i	$\bar{X}_i^{(1)}(20)$	$S_i^2(20)$	N_i	$\bar{X}_i^{(2)}(N_i - 20)$	W_{i1}	W_{i2}	$\tilde{X}_i(N_i)$
1	126.48	14.52	110	124.45	0.21	0.79	124.87
2	121.92	7.96	61	121.63	0.39	0.61	121.74
3	127.16	9.45	72	126.11	0.32	0.68	126.44
4	130.71	8.25	63	132.03	0.37	0.63	131.54
5	144.07	6.20	47	144.83	0.46	0.54	144.48

response μ_{i_1}. This could be a useful goal in the initial stages of a simulation study, where there may be a large number (k) of alternative systems and we would like to perform an initial screening to eliminate those that appear to be clearly inferior. Thus, we could avoid expending a large amount of computer time getting precise estimates of the behavior of these inferior systems.

We define X_{ij}, μ_i, μ_{i_l}, and σ_i^2 as in Sec. 10.4.1. Again, all X_{ij}'s are independent and normal, and for fixed i, $X_{i1}, X_{i2}, \ldots$ are IID; the σ_i^2's are unknown and need not be equal. Here, correct selection (CS) is defined to mean that the subset of size m that is selected contains a system with mean μ_{i_1} and we want $P(\text{CS}) \geq P^*$ provided that $\mu_{i_2} - \mu_{i_1} \geq d^*$; here we must have $1 \leq m \leq k - 1$, $P^* > m/k$, and $d^* > 0$. (If $\mu_{i_2} - \mu_{i_1} < d^*$, then with probability at least P^*, the subset selected will contain a system with expected response that is no larger than $\mu_{i_1} + d^*$.)

The procedure is very similar to that of Sec. 10.4.1, and has been derived by Koenig and Law (1985). We take a first-stage sample of $n_0 \geq 2$ replications from each system and define $\bar{X}_i^{(1)}(n_0)$ and $S_i^2(n_0)$ for $i = 1, 2, \ldots, k$ exactly as in Sec. 10.4.1. Next we compute the total number of replications, N_i, needed for the ith system exactly as in Eq. (10.3), except that h_1 is replaced by h_2 (which depends on m as well as on k, P^*, and n_0), as found in Table 10.12 in App. 10B. [For values of h_2 that might be needed for other P^*, n_0, k, or m values, see Koenig and Law (1985).] Then we make $N_i - n_0$ more replications, form the second-stage sample means $\bar{X}_i^{(2)}(N_i - n_0)$, weights W_{i1} and W_{i2}, and weighted sample means $\tilde{X}_i(N_i)$, exactly as in Sec. 10.4.1. Finally, we define the selected subset to consist of the m systems corresponding to the m smallest values of the $\tilde{X}_i(N_i)$'s.

Example 10.9. Consider again our five inventory systems of Example 10.8, as defined in Table 10.4. Now, however, suppose that we want to select a subset of size $m = 3$ from among the $k = 5$ systems and be assured with confidence level at least $P^* = 0.90$ that the selected subset contains the best (least-cost) system provided that $\mu_{i_2} - \mu_{i_1} \geq d^* = 1$. Again we made $n_0 = 20$ initial replications of each system (independent of those used in Example 10.8); the complete results for the subset-selection procedure are given in Table 10.9. (From Table 10.12, $h_2 = 1.243$.) The subset selected consists of policies 1, 2, and 3.

TABLE 10.9
Selecting a subset of size three containing the best of the five inventory policies

i	$\bar{X}_i^{(1)}(20)$	$S_i^2(20)$	N_i	$\bar{X}_i^{(2)}(N_i - 20)$	W_{i1}	W_{i2}	$\tilde{X}_i(N_i)$
1	124.71	17.16	27	125.64	0.80	0.20	124.89
2	121.20	12.64	21	125.69	1.01	-0.01	121.15
3	125.57	9.07	21	123.51	1.10	-0.10	125.78
4	132.39	6.22	21	133.37	1.18	-0.18	132.21
5	144.27	4.23	21	143.67	1.27	-0.27	144.43

Comparing the value of $h_2(=1.243)$ used here with that of $h_1(=2.747)$ used in Example 10.8, we see from the form of Eq. (10.3) that the more modest goal of selecting a subset of size 3 *containing* the best system requires considerably fewer replications on average than does the more ambitious goal of selecting *the* best system. (In fact, the selection problem of Sec. 10.4.1 is really just a special case of the present subset-selection problem, with $m = 1$.) This effect exemplifies what we meant at the beginning of this section by referring to this subset-selection problem as a relatively inexpensive initial "screening."

10.4.3 Selecting the *m* Best of *k* Systems

As a final type of selection problem, consider the goal of selecting a subset of specified size m $(1 \leq m \leq k - 1)$ so that with probability at least P^* the expected responses of the selected subset are equal to the m smallest expected responses $\mu_{i_1}, \mu_{i_2}, \ldots, \mu_{i_m}$. It is important to note that we are *not* saying that the m selected systems are ranked or ordered in any away among themselves, but only that the unordered *set* of m selected systems has expected responses that are the same as those of the unordered *set* of the m best systems. This particular selection goal might be useful if we want to identify several good options, since the best system might prove unacceptable for other reasons, e.g., political or environmental. The solution procedure was mentioned in Dudewicz and Dalal (1975) and developed by Koenig and Law (1985).

The setup (independence, normality, unknown and unequal variances, etc.) is exactly as in Sec. 10.4.2 except that the indifference-zone configuration and constraint on P^* must be changed. We want $P(\text{CS}) \geq P^*$ provided that $\mu_{i_{m+1}} - \mu_{i_m} \geq d^*$; CS, of course, is redefined to mean that the expected responses of the selected set are equal to those of the m best systems. (If the condition $\mu_{i_{m+1}} - \mu_{i_m} \geq d^*$ fails here, then with probability at least P^*, the expected responses of the m selected systems will not exceed $\mu_{i_m} + d^*$.) Also for this problem, we must have $P^* > m!(k-m)!/k!$. The solution procedure (including the final subset selection) here is furthermore exactly the same as that for the problem in Sec. 10.4.2, except that the constant h_2 used there must be replaced by h_3, which can be found in Table 10.13 in App. 10B. [See Koenig and Law (1985) for an algorithm to compute h_3 for other values of P^*, n_0, k, or m.] Note that the problem of Sec. 10.4.1 is also a special case, for $m = 1$.

> **Example 10.10.** Once again, we use the five inventory systems of Example 10.6 to illustrate this third selection problem. Our goal is to select the $m = 3$ best systems from the $k = 5$ systems, and we want $P(\text{CS}) \geq P^* = 0.90$ provided that $\mu_{i_4} - \mu_{i_3} \geq d^* = 1$. Making $n_0 = 20$ initial replications and carrying out the procedure, we obtained the results in Table 10.10. (For these parameters, we got $h_3 = 3.016$ from Table 10.13.) The selected subset consists of policies 1, 2, and 3, which we claim are the three best systems but not in any particular order.

TABLE 10.10
Selecting the three best of the five inventory policies

i	$\bar{X}_i^{(1)}(20)$	$S_i^2(20)$	N_i	$\bar{X}_i^{(2)}(N_i - 20)$	W_{i1}	W_{i2}	$\tilde{X}_i(N_i)$
1	123.67	11.50	105	124.86	0.21	0.79	124.60
2	120.62	8.80	81	121.75	0.29	0.71	121.42
3	125.24	7.16	66	125.13	0.36	0.64	125.17
4	132.05	6.18	57	131.26	0.41	0.59	131.58
5	144.82	3.27	30	144.24	0.71	0.29	144.65

The value of h_3 in Example 10.10 is quite a bit larger than the values of h_1 and h_2 used in Examples 10.8 and 10.9, resulting in this selection problem's calling for larger *average* values of N_i than did those of the problems in Secs. 10.4.1 and 10.4.2. (For our particular realizations, however, the N_i's of Table 10.10 are mostly *smaller* than those of Table 10.8, since the variance estimates in Table 10.10 *happened* to be mostly smaller than those in Table 10.8.) Intuitively, this is reasonable since the selection problem of this section allows us to make a considerably stronger final statement than we could for either of the previous two selection problems, so that we should expect to have to supply more supporting evidence.

10.4.4 Additional Problems and Methods

Sections 10.4.1 through 10.4.3 discussed three specific selection goals, and gave procedures to attain them. The setting was one in which IID observations that are unbiased for the respective systems' expected performance measures can be obtained, e.g., by replication in the case of a terminating simulation; the data were also assumed to be normally distributed, although violating this assumption may not prove serious.

There are, however, many other selection goals, as well as techniques to rank the alternatives. Also, work has been done on simulation-specific methods, and in particular on procedures that allow correlation between the observations taken on a given system, as would occur in a one-long-run (as opposed to replication/deletion) approach to steady-state simulation. In this section we briefly mention some of these goals and methods as they relate to simulation. More complete surveys, with many references, can be found in Dudewicz and Koo (1982), Gibbons, Olkin, and Sobel (1977), and Gupta and Panchapakesan (1979); Goldsman (1983, 1986, 1987) and Clark (1988) give surveys specifically related to simulation applications. An actual application of selection procedures is described by Gray and Goldsman (1988).

Subset Selection. The methods in Secs. 10.4.1 through 10.4.3 all used an indifference-zone approach, where the analyst prespecifies an amount d^* representing a threshold below which errors resulting from incorrect selection are deemed inconsequential. The result was the selection of a fixed, prespecified number (perhaps one) of the alternatives as "good" in some sense. Instead, Gupta (1956, 1965) developed a procedure producing a subset of *random* size that contains the best system, with prespecified probability P^*, without specifying an indifference amount (i.e., setting $d^* = 0$). Although the size of the selected subset is not controlled, this could be a useful first step in screening out those of a large number of alternatives that are clearly inferior. Gupta and Santner (1973) and Santner (1975) extended this method to allow for prespecifying the maximum size m of the selected subset, and also showed the relationship of this method to indifference-zone approaches. One limitation of these procedures in simulation is that they assume known and equal variances; Sullivan and Wilson (1989) developed a much more general restricted-subset-selection procedure that allows for unknown and unequal variances, as well as specification of an indifference amount. In all these formulations, the advantage of defining m as the *maximum* size of the selected subset, instead of insisting that *exactly m* alternatives be selected, is that far fewer than m systems could be chosen in situations where it is fairly clear that only a few of the systems are potentially the best.

Sequential-Sampling Methods. The selection techniques in Secs. 10.4.1 through 10.4.3 involved two-stage sampling, where the first stage obtained a variance estimate that was used to determine the amount of additional sampling required in the second stage. One drawback of this approach is that if the first-stage variance estimate happens to be a lot larger than the actual variance, a perhaps unnecessarily large amount of sampling in the second stage will be prescribed. Instead, multistage or sequential methods for sampling from the alternative populations have been proposed, with the aim of making the procedures more efficient, i.e., of attaining the desired selection goal with less sampling. Such methods are discussed in the surveys of Goldsman (1986, 1987). Koenig (1984) developed sequential-sampling methods related to the two-stage procedures in Koenig and Law (1985), and reduced the required total sample size by as much as 75 percent in simulations of inventory and repairman models.

Criteria Other than Expectations. The comparison and selection methods we have considered have all been based on looking at an *expected* system response, e.g., the expected average delay in queue or the expected average operating cost per month. However, in some situations other criteria may be more appropriate. Goldsman (1984a, 1984b) describes an inventory system where policy 1 results in a profit of 1000 with probability 0.001 and a profit of 0 with probability 0.999; policy 2, on the other hand, always gives profit 0.999. Thus, the expected profits from policies 1 and 2 are 1 and 0.999, respectively, so that policy 1 would be preferable on this basis. However, policy 2 will yield higher profit (0.999 instead of 0) with probability 0.999, so it could be considered preferable even though its expected profit is lower. Thus, we might reconsider what we regard as the "best" system, defining it to be the one that is the most likely to produce a "good" outcome.

Goldsman (1984a, 1984b) surveys indifference-zone methods with this goal in mind, and points out that the resulting methods are nonparametric, a desirable property when simulating real systems where we seldom know the exact form of the model's output distribution. Sequential-sampling methods have also been studied; see Bechhofer and Goldsman (1986). Chen (1988) also addresses this problem, but with a subset-selection goal instead of an indifference-zone formulation.

Correlation between Alternatives. The selection methods discussed so far assume that the observations from each alternative are independent of those from the other alternatives. In simulation, it is frequently possible to use the method of common random numbers (see Sec. 11.2) to induce positive correlation between the jth observations from each alternative system, thereby sharpening the comparison; this was mentioned in Sec. 10.3 for the confidence-interval comparison goals. In a selection problem, we might hope to reduce the sample sizes required from the alternative systems by using common random numbers across the systems or (put another way) achieve a higher-than-specified probability of correct selection by ignoring the correlation in the sample-size specification; either result would be desirable. Procedures addressing this problem have been considered by Gupta, Nagel, and Panchapakesan (1973) by viewing the data as vectors from a multivariate normal distribution. Clark and Yang (1986) proposed a simulation-specific indifference-zone selection procedure combining the Dudewicz and Dalal (1975) method with the Bonferroni inequality, and experimentally achieved good correct-selection rates with less sampling than called for by the Dudewicz-Dalal procedure alone. Yang and Nelson (1989a, 1989b) investigated the use of common random numbers in multiple-comparisons procedures and found that confidence intervals for the differences between expected responses experienced both higher coverage probability and shorter length. It is important that the common-random-numbers technique induce the desired *positive* correlation, and not "backfire" to produce *negative* correlation (see Sec. 11.2); Koenig and Law (1982) observed backfiring in testing selection procedures on inventory models, resulting in significant degradation of correct-selection probabilities.

Correlation within an Alternative. Another type of independence that we have been assuming is for the observations from a particular alternative. This poses no difficulty when the simulation is terminating, since we simply make independent replications of the model, and each replication produces an unbiased observation on the desired expected response. For a steady-state simulation, however, such unbiased independent observations do not come as easily. One approach to selection based on steady-state parameters would be to use the replication/deletion approach to produce X_{ij}'s that are independent and approximately unbiased for the steady-state mean, as done in Example 10.5. Another possibility would be to make a single long run of alternative i and then let X_{ij} be the sample mean of the observations in the jth batch within this run (see the discussion of batch means in Sec. 9.5.3); the critical issue here is how to choose the batch size so that the batch means are approximately uncorrelated. Dudewicz and Zaino (1977) developed a method to select the best system assuming that their output could be modeled as a first-order autoregressive time series. Dickinson (1983) used the steady-state method of spectrum analysis (see Sec. 9.5.3) to develop a ranking method, and Goldsman (1985) combined the standardized-time-series method of steady-state estimation (see Sec. 9.5.3) with the Dudewicz and Dalal (1975) method to arrive at a selection procedure. Iglehart (1977) developed a method based on the regenerative method (see Sec. 9.5.3) for selecting the best of k systems. Finally, Sullivan and Wilson (1989) provided a restricted-subset-selection procedure, which they call V_S, for the case of correlated observations from a model, and indicated that it performed well in several settings.

APPENDIX 10A
VALIDITY OF THE SELECTION PROCEDURES

The purpose of this appendix is to give a brief indication of how the procedures of Secs. 10.4.1 through 10.4.3 are justified and how the values for h_1, h_2, and h_3 in App. 10B were computed. For a more complete discussion, we refer the interested reader to Dudewicz and Dalal (1975), Dudewicz and Bishop (1977), Desu and Sobel (1968), and Koenig and Law (1985).

All three procedures are based on the fact that for $i = 1, 2, \ldots, k$,

$$T_i = \frac{\tilde{X}_i(N_i) - \mu_i}{d^*/h}$$

has a t distribution with $n_0 - 1$ df, where h is either h_1, h_2, or h_3 depending on which selection procedure is used; the T_i's are also independent. The rather curious form of the expressions for the weights W_{i1} and W_{i2} were chosen specifically to make $\tilde{X}_i(N_i)$ such that T_i *would* have this t distribution. [Other ways of defining W_{i1} and $\tilde{X}_i(N_i)$ also result in the T_i's having this t distribution; see Dudewicz and Dalal (1975).]

For the selection problem of Sec. 10.4.1 assume that $\mu_{i_2} - \mu_{i_1} \geq d^*$. Then correct selection occurs if and only if $\tilde{X}_{i_1}(N_{i_1})$ is the smallest of the $\tilde{X}_i(N_i)$'s (where i_1 is the index of a system with smallest expected response, μ_{i_1}). Thus if we let f and F denote the density and distribution function, respectively, of the

t distribution with $n_0 - 1$ df, we can write

$$P(\text{CS}) = P[\tilde{X}_{i_1}(N_{i_1}) < \tilde{X}_{i_l}(N_{i_l}) \text{ for } l = 2, 3, \ldots, k]$$

$$= P\left[\frac{\tilde{X}_{i_1}(N_{i_1}) - \mu_{i_1}}{d^*/h_1} \le \frac{\tilde{X}_{i_l}(N_{i_l}) - \mu_{i_l}}{d^*/h_1} + \frac{\mu_{i_l} - \mu_{i_1}}{d^*/h_1} \text{ for } l = 2, 3, \ldots, k\right]$$

$$= P\left(T_{i_l} \ge T_{i_1} - \frac{\mu_{i_l} - \mu_{i_1}}{d^*/h_1} \text{ for } l = 2, 3, \ldots, k\right)$$

$$= \int_{-\infty}^{\infty} \prod_{l=2}^{k} F\left(\frac{\mu_{i_l} - \mu_{i_1}}{d^*/h_1} - t\right) f(t) \, dt \qquad (10.4)$$

[The last line in Eq. (10.4) follows by conditioning on $T_{i_1} = t$ and by the independence of the T_i's.] Now since we assumed that $\mu_{i_2} - \mu_{i_1} \ge d^*$ and the μ_{i_l}'s are increasing with l, we know that $\mu_{i_l} - \mu_{i_1} \ge d^*$ for $l = 2, 3, \ldots, k$. Thus, since F is monotone increasing, Eq. (10.4) yields (after a change of variable in the integral)

$$P(\text{CS}) \ge \int_{-\infty}^{\infty} [F(t + h_1)]^{k-1} f(t) \, dt \qquad (10.5)$$

and equality holds in (10.5) exactly when $\mu_{i_1} + d^* = \mu_{i_2} = \cdots = \mu_{i_k}$, an arrangement of the μ_i's called the *least favorable configuration* (LFC). Table 10.11 was thus obtained by setting the integral on the right-hand side of (10.5) to P^* and solving (numerically) for h_1.

Demonstrating the validity of the subset-selection procedures of Secs. 10.4.2 and 10.4.3 is more complicated but follows a similar line of reasoning. For the procedure in Sec. 10.4.2, we can show [see Koenig and Law (1985)] ultimately that

$$P(\text{CS}) \ge (k - m)\binom{k-1}{k-m} \int_{-\infty}^{\infty} F(t + h_2)[F(t)]^{m-1}[F(-t)]^{k-m-1} f(t) \, dt$$

and we equate the right-hand side to P^* to solve for h_2, as given in Table 10.12. The LFC for this problem [in which case $P(\text{CS}) = P^*$] is the same as that for the problem in Sec. 10.4.1.

Finally, for the problem of Sec. 10.4.3, it can be shown [see Koenig and Law (1985)] that

$$P(\text{CS}) \ge m \int_{-\infty}^{\infty} [F(t + h_3)]^{k-m}[F(-t)]^{m-1} f(t) \, dt$$

and we again set the right-hand side to P^* and solve for the values of h_3 in Table 10.13. For this problem, however, the LFC occurs when $\mu_{i_1} + d^* = \cdots = \mu_{i_m} + d^* = \mu_{i_{m+1}} = \cdots = \mu_{i_k}$, when we again get $P(\text{CS}) = P^*$.

TABLE 10.11
Values of h_1 for the procedure of Sec. 10.4.1

P^*	n_0	$k = 2$	$k = 3$	$k = 4$	$k = 5$	$k = 6$	$k = 7$	$k = 8$	$k = 9$	$k = 10$
0.90	20	1.896	2.342	2.583	2.747	2.870	2.969	3.051	3.121	3.182
0.90	40	1.852	2.283	2.514	2.669	2.785	2.878	2.954	3.019	3.076
0.95	20	2.453	2.872	3.101	3.258	3.377	3.472	3.551	3.619	3.679
0.95	40	2.386	2.786	3.003	3.150	3.260	3.349	3.422	3.484	3.539

TABLE 10.12
Values of h_2 for the procedure of Sec. 10.4.2
For $m = 1$, use Table 10.11

m	$k = 3$	$k = 4$	$k = 5$	$k = 6$	$k = 7$	$k = 8$	$k = 9$	$k = 10$
				$P^* = 0.90$, $n_0 = 20$				
2	1.137	1.601	1.860	2.039	2.174	2.282	2.373	2.450
3		0.782	1.243	1.507	1.690	1.830	1.943	2.038
4			0.556	1.012	1.276	1.461	1.603	1.718
5				0.392	0.843	1.105	1.291	1.434
6					0.265	0.711	0.971	1.156
7						0.162	0.603	0.861
8							0.075	0.512
9								†
				$P^* = 0.90$, $n_0 = 40$				
2	1.114	1.570	1.825	1.999	2.131	2.237	2.324	2.399
3		0.763	1.219	1.479	1.660	1.798	1.909	2.002
4			0.541	0.991	1.251	1.434	1.575	1.688
5				0.381	0.824	1.083	1.266	1.408
6					0.257	0.693	0.950	1.133
7						0.156	0.587	0.841
8							0.072	0.497
9								†
				$P^* = 0.95$, $n_0 = 20$				
2	1.631	2.071	2.321	2.494	2.625	2.731	2.819	2.894
3		1.256	1.697	1.952	2.131	2.267	2.378	2.470
4			1.021	1.458	1.714	1.894	2.033	2.146
5				0.852	1.284	1.539	1.720	1.860
6					0.721	1.149	1.402	1.583
7						0.615	1.038	1.290
8							0.526	0.945
9								0.449
				$P^* = 0.95$, $n_0 = 40$				
2	1.591	2.023	2.267	2.435	2.563	2.665	2.750	2.823
3		1.222	1.656	1.907	2.082	2.217	2.325	2.415
4			0.990	1.420	1.672	1.850	1.987	2.098
5				0.824	1.248	1.499	1.678	1.816
6					0.695	1.114	1.363	1.541
7						0.591	1.004	1.252
8							0.505	0.913
9								0.430

† Recall that for this selection problem we must have $P^* > m/k$. [If $P^* = 0.90$, $m = 9$, and $k = 10$, we can obtain $P(\text{CS}) = P^*$ by selecting nine systems at random, without any data collection at all.]

TABLE 10.13
Values of h_3 for the procedure of Sec. 10.4.3
For $m = 1$, use Table 10.11

m	$k = 3$	$k = 4$	$k = 5$	$k = 6$	$k = 7$	$k = 8$	$k = 9$	$k = 10$
				$P^* = 0.90$, $n_0 = 20$				
2	2.342	2.779	3.016	3.177	3.299	3.396	3.477	3.546
3		2.583	3.016	3.251	3.411	3.532	3.629	3.709
4			2.747	3.177	3.411	3.571	3.691	3.787
5				2.870	3.299	3.532	3.691	3.811
6					2.969	3.396	3.629	3.787
7						3.051	3.477	3.709
8							3.121	3.546
9								3.182
				$P^* = 0.90$, $n_0 = 40$				
2	2.283	2.703	2.928	3.081	3.195	3.285	3.360	3.424
3		2.514	2.928	3.151	3.302	3.415	3.505	3.579
4			2.669	3.081	3.302	3.451	3.564	3.653
5				2.785	3.195	3.415	3.564	3.675
6					2.878	3.285	3.505	3.653
7						2.954	3.360	3.579
8							3.019	3.424
9								3.076
				$P^* = 0.95$, $n_0 = 20$				
2	2.872	3.282	3.507	3.662	3.779	3.873	3.952	4.019
3		3.101	3.507	3.731	3.885	4.001	4.094	4.172
4			3.258	3.662	3.885	4.037	4.153	4.246
5				3.377	3.779	4.001	4.153	4.269
6					3.472	3.873	4.094	4.246
7						3.551	3.952	4.172
8							3.619	4.019
9								3.679
				$P^* = 0.95$, $n_0 = 40$				
2	2.786	3.175	3.386	3.530	3.639	3.725	3.797	3.858
3		3.003	3.386	3.595	3.738	3.845	3.931	4.002
4			3.150	3.530	3.738	3.879	3.986	4.071
5				3.260	3.639	3.845	3.986	4.092
6					3.349	3.725	3.931	4.071
7						3.422	3.797	4.002
8							3.484	3.858
9								3.539

PROBLEMS

10.1. In Examples 10.1 and 10.2, what if the bank *did* want to count the service times, in addition to the delays in queue? That is, suppose that the performance measure is the expected average total time in system of the first 100 customers, instead of the expected average delay in queue. What is the "best" system in this case? Which criterion do you think is more appropriate? Discuss.

10.2. Consider the two systems of Example 10.1, with the same initial conditions and performance measures given there; let $\zeta = d_Z(100) - d_K(100)$.

(a) Make $n_1 = n_2 = 5$ independent replications of each system and construct an approximate 90 percent confidence interval for ζ. (Perform the simulations for the two systems independently of each other.) Use the paired-t approach.

(b) Make $n_1 = 5$ replications of the Zippytel system and $n_2 = 10$ replications of the Klunkytel system, and construct an approximate 90 percent confidence interval for ζ. (Again make the runs of the two systems independently.)

(c) Use the selection procedure of Sec. 10.4.1 to select the best of the $k = 2$ systems. Let $n_0 = 20$, $P^* = 0.90$, and $d^* = 0.4$.

10.3. For the time-shared computer model of Sec. 2.5, suppose that the company is considering a change in the service quantum length q in an effort to reduce the *steady-state* mean response time of a job; the values for q under consideration are 0.05, 0.10, 0.20, and 0.40. Assume that there are $n = 35$ terminals and that the other parameters and initial conditions are the same as those in Sec. 2.5. To obtain IID observations with expectation approximately equal to the steady-state mean response time of a job, it is felt that warming up the models for 50 response times is adequate, after which the next 640 response times are averaged to obtain a basic X_{ij} observation; independent replications of these 690 response times are then made as needed. Use an appropriate selection procedure from Sec. 10.4.1 through 10.4.3 with $n_0 = 20$, $P^* = 0.90$, and $d^* = 0.7$ to solve each of the following problems.

(a) Select the best of the four values for q.

(b) Select two values of q, one of which is the best.

(c) Select the best two values of q (without ordering the two selected).

10.4. For the job-shop model of Sec. 2.7, we can now carry out a better analysis for the question of deciding which machine group should be given an additional machine. (Reread Sec. 2.7.3 and note from Fig. 2.47 that, on the basis of a single replication of the existing system, machine groups 1, 2, and 4 appear to be the three most congested groups.) Use the procedure of Sec. 10.4.1 to recommend whether a machine should be added to group 1, 2, or 4, assuming that these are the only three possibilities; let $n_0 = 20$, $P^* = 0.90$, and $d^* = 1$. Use the *steady-state* expected overall average job total delay as the measure of performance; to obtain the X_{ij} observations, warm up the model for 10 eight-hour days and use the data from the next 90 days, as in Prob. 2.7. (*Beware!* This could be a case where considerations on the cost of simulating might temper the choice of d^*.) Compare your conclusions with those at the end of Sec. 2.7.3. From the moral of Example 10.1, how might this entire study be improved?

10.5. Consider the original time-shared computer model of Sec. 2.5 and the alternative processing policy described in Prob. 2.18, both with $n = 35$ terminals. Use the selection procedure of Sec. 10.4.1 with $n_0 = 20$ to recommend which processing policy results in the smallest steady-state mean response time of a job. To obtain the X_{ij}'s here, warm up the model for 50 response times, then use the average of the next 640 response times, and replicate as needed. Choose your own P^* and d^*, perhaps based on cost considerations, or your own feeling about what constitutes an "important" difference in mean response time.

10.6. For the manufacturing shop of Prob. 1.22, use the selection procedure of Sec. 10.4.2 to choose three out of the five values of s (the number of repairmen), one of which results in the smallest expected average cost per hour. Use $n_0 = 20$, $P^* = 0.90$, and $d^* = 5$.

10.7. For the four alternatives of Prob. 10.3, construct confidence intervals for all comparisons with the current ($q = 0.10$) system, using an overall confidence level of 90 percent. Make as many replications as you think are needed to get meaningful results.

10.8. For the manufacturing shop of Probs. 1.22 and 10.6, form confidence intervals for all pairwise differences of the expected average costs per hour for the five values of s; use an overall confidence level of 0.90. Replicate as needed to get meaningful results.

REFERENCES

Bechhofer, R. E., and D. Goldsman: Truncation of the Bechhofer-Kiefer-Sobel Sequential Procedure for Selecting the Multinomial Event Which Has the Largest Probability (II): Extended Tables and an Improved Procedure, *Commun. Statist.—Simulation and Computation*, *15*: 829–851 (1986).

Chen, B., and R. G. Sargent: Using Standardized Time Series to Estimate Confidence Intervals for the Difference between Two Stationary Stochastic Processes, *Operations Res.*, *35*: 428–436 (1987).

Chen, P.: On Selecting the Best of *k* Systems: An Expository Survey of Subset-Selection Multinomial Procedures, *Proc. 1988 Winter Simulation Conference*, San Diego, pp. 440–444 (1988).

Clark, G. M.: Tutorial: Analysis of Simulation Output to Compare Alternatives, *Proc. 1988 Winter Simulation Conference*, San Diego, pp. 19–24 (1988).

Clark, G. M., and W. Yang: A Bonferroni Selection Procedure When Using Common Random Numbers with Unknown Variances, *Proc. 1986 Winter Simulation Conference*, Washington, D.C., pp. 313–315 (1986).

Conover, W. J.: *Practical Nonparametric Statistics*, 2d ed., John Wiley, New York (1980).

Desu, M., and M. Sobel: A Fixed Subset-Size Approach to a Selection Problem, *Biometrika*, *55*: 401–410 (1968).

Devore, J. L.: *Probability and Statistics for Engineering and the Sciences*, Brooks/Cole, Monterey, Calif. (1982).

Dickinson, R. T.: A Multiple Ranking Procedure Adapted to Discrete Event Simulation, Ph.D. Dissertation, Department of Mechanical Engineering, University of Texas, Austin (1983).

Dudewicz, E. J., and T. A. Bishop: The Heteroscedastic Method, Ohio State University Dept. Statist. Tech. Rep. 153, Columbus (1977).

Dudewicz, E. J., and S. R. Dalal: Allocation of Observations in Ranking and Selection with Unequal Variances, *Sankhya*, *B37*: 28–78 (1975).

Dudewicz, E. J., and J. O. Koo: *The Complete Categorized Guide to Statistical Selection and Ranking Procedures*, American Sciences Press, Syracuse, N.Y. (1982).

Dudewicz, E. J., and N. A. Zaino: Allowance for Correlation in Setting Run-Length via Ranking-and-Selection Procedures, *TIMS Studies Management Sci.*, *7*: 5–61 (1977).

Gibbons, J. D., I. Olkin, and M. Sobel: *Selecting and Ordering Populations: A New Statistical Methodology*, John Wiley, New York (1977).

Goldsman, D.: Ranking and Selection in Simulation, *Proc. 1983 Winter Simulation Conference*, Washington, D.C., pp. 387–393 (1983).

Goldsman, D.: On Selecting the Best of *k* Systems: An Expository Survey of Indifference-Zone Multinomial Procedures, *Proc. 1984 Winter Simulation Conference*, Dallas, pp. 107–112 (1984a).

Goldsman, D.: A Multinomial Ranking and Selection Procedure: Simulation and Applications, *Proc. 1984 Winter Simulation Conference*, Dallas, pp. 259–264 (1984b).

Goldsman, D.: Ranking and Selection Procedures using Standardized Time Series, *Proc. 1985 Winter Simulation Conference*, San Francisco, pp. 120–123 (1985).

Goldsman, D.: Tutorial on Indifference-Zone Normal Means Ranking and Selection Procedures, *Proc. 1986 Winter Simulation Conference*, Washington, D.C., pp. 370–375 (1986).

Goldsman, D.: Ranking and Selection Tutorial: 2-Factor Normal Means Procedures, *Proc. 1987 Winter Simulation Conference*, Atlanta, pp. 52–57 (1987).

Gray, D., and D. Goldsman: Indifference-Zone Selection Procedures for Choosing the Best Airspace Configuration, *Proc. 1988 Winter Simulation Conference*, San Diego, pp. 445–450 (1988).

Gupta, S. S.: On a Decision Rule for a Problem in Ranking Means, Mimeograph Series No. 150, Institute of Statistics, University of North Carolina, Chapel Hill (1956).

Gupta, S. S.: On Some Multiple Decision (Selection and Ranking) Rules, *Technometrics*, 7: 225–245 (1965).

Gupta, S. S., and J. C. Hsu: A Computer Package for Ranking, Selection, and Multiple Comparisons with the Best, *Proc. 1984 Winter Simulation Conference*, Dallas, pp. 251–257 (1984).

Gupta, S. S., K. Nagel, and S. Panchapakesan: On the Order Statistics from Equally Correlated Normal Random Variables, *Biometrika*, 60: 403–413 (1973).

Gupta, S. S., and S. Panchapakesan: *Multiple Decision Procedures: Theory and Methodology of Selecting and Ranking Populations*, John Wiley, New York (1979).

Gupta, S. S., and T. J. Santner: On Selection and Ranking Procedures—A Restricted Subset Selection Rule, *Proc. 39th Session of the International Statistical Institute*, Vienna, Vol. 1 (1973).

Hsu, J. C.: Constrained Two-Sided Simultaneous Confidence Intervals for Multiple Comparisons with the Best, *Ann. Statist.*, 12: 1136–1144 (1984).

Hsu, J. C., and D. G. Edwards: Sequential Comparisons with the Best, *J. Am. Statist. Assoc.*, 78: 958–964 (1983).

Hsu, J. C., and B. L. Nelson: Optimization over a Finite Number of System Designs with One-Stage Sampling and Multiple Comparisons with the Best, *Proc. 1988 Winter Simulation Conference*, San Diego, pp. 451–457 (1988).

Iglehart, D. L.: Simulating Stable Stochastic Systems, VII: Selecting the Best System, *TIMS Studies Management Sci.*, 7: 37–50 (1977).

Kelton, W. D., and A. M. Law: The Transient Behavior of the $M/M/s$ Queue, with Implications for Steady-State Simulation, *Operations Res.*, 33: 378–396 (1985).

Koenig, L. W.: Subset-Selection Procedures for Normal Populations with Unknown Variances, Ph.D. Dissertation, Department of Industrial Engineering, University of Wisconsin, Madison (1984).

Koenig, L. W., and A. M. Law: A Procedure for Selecting a Subset of Size m Containing the l Best of k Independent Normal Populations, with Applications to Simulation, Technical Report 82-9, Department of Management Information Systems, University of Arizona, Tucson (1982).

Koenig, L. W., and A. M. Law: A Procedure for Selecting a Subset of Size m Containing the l Best of k Independent Normal Populations, with Applications to Simulation, *Commun. Statist.— Simulation and Computation*, 14: 719–734 (1985).

Miller, R. G., Jr.: Developments in Multiple Comparisons, 1966–1977, *J. Am. Statist. Assoc.*, 72: 779–788 (1977).

Robbins, H., G. Simons, and N. Starr: A Sequential Analogue of the Behrens-Fisher Problem, *Ann. Math. Statist.*, 38: 1384–1391 (1967).

Santner, T. J.: A Restricted Subset Selection Approach to Ranking and Selection Problems, *Ann. Statist.*, 3: 334–349 (1975).

Scheffé, H.: Practical Solutions of the Behrens-Fisher Problem, *J. Am. Statist. Assoc.*, 65: 1501–1508 (1970).

Sullivan, D. W., and J. R. Wilson: Restricted Subset Selection Procedures for Simulation, *Operations Res.*, *37*: 52–71 (1989).

Welch, B. L.: The Significance of the Difference between Two Means when the Population Variances are Unequal, *Biometrika*, *25*: 350–362 (1938).

Yang, W., and B. L. Nelson: Optimization Using Common Random Numbers, Control Variates and Multiple Comparisons with the Best, *Proc. 1989 Winter Simulation Conference*, Washington, D.C., pp. 444–449 (1989a).

Yang, W., and B. L. Nelson: Using Common Random Numbers and Control Variates in Multiple-Comparison Procedures, Ohio State University Dept. of Industrial and Systems Engineering, Tech. Rep. 1989-001, Columbus (1989b).

CHAPTER
11

VARIANCE-REDUCTION TECHNIQUES

Recommended sections for a first reading: 11.1, 11.2

11.1 INTRODUCTION

One of the points we have tried to emphasize throughout this book is that simulations driven by random inputs will produce random output. Thus, appropriate statistical techniques applied to simulation output data are imperative if the results are to be properly analyzed, interpreted, and used (see Chaps. 9, 10, and 12). Since large-scale simulations may require great amounts of computer time and storage, appropriate statistical analyses (possibly requiring multiple replications of the model, for example) can become quite costly. Sometimes the cost of even a modest statistical analysis of the output can be so high that the precision of the results, perhaps measured by confidence-interval width, will be unacceptably poor. The analyst should therefore try to use any means possible to increase the simulation's efficiency.

Of course, "efficiency" mandates careful programming to expedite execution and minimize storage requirements. In this chapter, however, we focus on *statistical* efficiency, as measured by the *variances* of the output random variables from a simulation. If we can somehow reduce the variance of an output random variable of interest (such as average delay in queue or average cost per month in an inventory system) without disturbing its expectation, we can obtain greater precision, e.g., smaller confidence intervals, for the same amount of simulating, or, alternatively, achieve a desired precision with less simulating. Sometimes such a *variance-reduction technique* (VRT), properly applied, can make the difference between an impossibly expensive simulation project and a frugal, useful one.

As we shall see, the method of applying VRTs usually depends on the particular model (or models) of interest. Therefore, a thorough understanding of the workings of the model(s) is required for proper use of VRTs. Furthermore, it is generally impossible to know beforehand how great a variance reduction might be realized, or (worse) whether the variance will be reduced at all in comparison with straightforward simulation. However, preliminary runs could be made (if affordable) to compare the results of applying a VRT with those from straightforward simulation. Finally, some VRTs themselves will increase computing cost, and this decrease in computational efficiency must be traded off against the potential gain in statistical efficiency (see Prob. 11.1). Almost all VRTs require *some* extra effort on the part of the analyst (if only to understand the technique) and this, as always, must be considered.

VRTs were developed originally in the early days of computers, to be applied in Monte Carlo simulations or distribution sampling [see Sec. 1.8.3, as well as Hammersley and Handscomb (1964) and Morgan (1984, chap. 7)]. However, many of these original VRTs have been found not to be directly applicable to simulations of complex dynamic systems.

In the remainder of this chapter we will discuss five general types of VRTs that would appear to have the most promise of successful application to a wide variety of simulations. We refer the reader to Kleijnen (1974), Bratley, Fox, and Schrage (1987, chap. 2), and Morgan (1984, chap. 7) for detailed discussions of other VRTs, such as stratified sampling and importance sampling. There is a very large literature on VRTs, and we do not attempt an exhaustive treatment here. Fortunately, there are several comprehensive surveys that provide useful ways of classifying VRTs and also contain extensive bibliographies; Wilson (1984) and Nelson (1985, 1986, 1987a, 1987c) are particularly recommended to the reader interested in going further with this subject.

11.2 COMMON RANDOM NUMBERS

The first VRT we consider, *common random numbers* (CRN), is actually different from the others in that it applies when we are comparing two or more alternative system configurations (see Chap. 10) instead of investigating a single configuration. Despite its simplicity, CRN is probably the most useful and popular VRT of all.

11.2.1 Rationale

The basic idea is that we should compare the alternative configurations "under similar experimental conditions" so that we can be more confident that any observed differences in performance are due to differences in the system configurations rather than to fluctuations of the "experimental conditions." In simulation, these "experimental conditions" are the generated random variates that are used to drive the models through simulated time. In queueing simulations, for instance, these would include interarrival times and service requirements of customers; in inventory simulations we might include inter-demand times and demand sizes. The name of this technique stems from the possibility in many situations of using the *same* basic U(0,1) random numbers (see Chap. 7) to drive each of the alternative configurations through time. As we shall see later in this section, however, certain programming techniques are often needed to facilitate proper implementation of CRN. In the terminology of classical experimental design, CRN is a form of *blocking*, i.e., "comparing like with like." CRN has also been called *correlated sampling*, *matched streams*, or *matched pairs* in some simulation contexts.

To see the rationale for CRN more clearly, consider the case of *two* alternative configurations, as in Sec. 10.2, where X_{1j} and X_{2j} are the observations from the first and second configurations on the jth independent replication, and we want to estimate $\zeta = \mu_1 - \mu_2 = E(X_{1j}) - E(X_{2j})$. If we make n replications of each system and let $Z_j = X_{1j} - X_{2j}$ for $j = 1, 2, \ldots, n$, then $E(Z_j) = \zeta$ so

$$\bar{Z}(n) = \frac{\sum\limits_{j=1}^{n} Z_j}{n}$$

is an unbiased estimator of ζ. Since the Z_j's are IID random variables,

$$\text{Var}[\bar{Z}(n)] = \frac{\text{Var}(Z_j)}{n} = \frac{\text{Var}(X_{1j}) + \text{Var}(X_{2j}) - 2\,\text{Cov}(X_{1j}, X_{2j})}{n}$$

[see Eq. (4.5) and Prob. 4.13]. If the simulations of the two different configurations are done independently, i.e., with different random numbers, X_{1j} and X_{2j} will be independent, so that $\text{Cov}(X_{1j}, X_{2j}) = 0$. On the other hand, if we could somehow do the simulations of configurations 1 and 2 so that X_{1j} and X_{2j} are *positively* correlated, then $\text{Cov}(X_{1j}, X_{2j}) > 0$, so that the variance of our estimator $\bar{Z}(n)$ is reduced. Thus, when $\bar{Z}(n)$ is observed in a particular simulation experiment, its value should be closer to ζ. CRN is a technique where we try to induce this positive correlation by using (carefully, as discussed in Sec. 11.2.3 below) the *same* random numbers to simulate all configurations. What makes this possible is the deterministic, reproducible nature of random-number generators (see Sec. 7.1); irreproducible gimmicks such as seeding the random-number generator by the square root of the computer's clock value would generally preclude the use of CRN as well as many other valuable VRTs.

11.2.2 Applicability

Unfortunately, there is no completely general proof that CRN "works," i.e., that it will always reduce the variance. Even if it does work, we usually will not know beforehand how great a reduction in variance we might experience. The efficacy of CRN depends wholly on the particular models being compared, and its use presupposes the analyst's (perhaps implicit) belief that the different models will respond "similarly" to large or small values of the random variates driving the models. For example, we would expect that smaller interarrival times for several designs of a queueing facility would result in longer delays and queues for *each* system.

There are, however, some classes of models for which CRN's success *is* guaranteed. Heidelberger and Iglehart (1979) showed this for certain types of regenerative simulations, and Bratley, Fox, and Schrage (1987, chap. 2) derive results indicating conditions under which CRN will work. See also Gal, Rubinstein, and Ziv (1984) and Rubinstein, Samorodnitsky, and Shaked (1985) for additional results of this type.

Figure 11.1 schematically illustrates the concept in principle, where the horizontal axis shows possible values of a *particular* U_k used for a *particular*

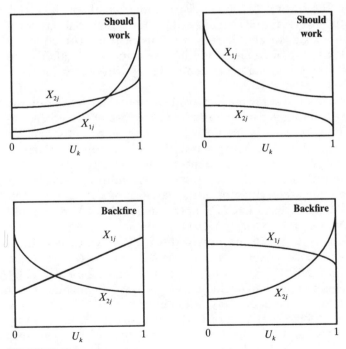

FIGURE 11.1
Model responses for CRN to work (top row) and backfire (bottom row).

purpose in both of the simulations; for instance, this U_k might be used to generate a service time. The curves indicate how the results of the simulations might react, all other things being equal, to possible values of this U_k. In either of the two situations in the top row of plots, both X_{1j} and X_{2j} react monotonically in the same direction to U_k, and we would expect CRN to induce the desired positive correlation, and thus reduce the variance. In the bottom two plots, however, X_{1j} and X_{2j} react in opposite directions to U_k, so CRN could induce negative correlation and thus "backfire," leading to $\text{Cov}(X_{1j}, X_{2j}) < 0$ and an actual *increase* in the variance. Problem 11.2 considers a specific instance of this issue.

Usually, random numbers are first used to generate variates from other distributions (see Chap. 8), which are then used to drive the simulation models. In order to give CRN the best chance of working, we should thus try first to ensure that the generated variates themselves react monotonically to the U_k's in this intermediate variate-generation step; we then must assume that the measures of performance react monotonically to the generated variates. For this reason, the inverse-transform method of variate generation (Sec. 8.2.1) is recommended, since it guarantees monotonicity of the generated input variates to the random numbers; it further provides the strongest possible positive correlation among all variate-generation methods. Since the inverse-transform method can be slow, however, for some distributions (perhaps involving numerical methods to invert the distribution function), its computational inefficiency could offset its statistical efficiency. For this reason, Schmeiser and Kachitvichyanukul (1986) developed faster non-inverse-transform methods that still induce positive correlation in the generated variates, as required for CRN to work.

If affordable, a small pilot study could provide a preliminary check on the efficacy of CRN for the alternative configurations. In the case of two configurations, make n replications of each, *using* CRN, to obtain output observations X_{1j} and X_{2j} for $j = 1, 2, \ldots, n$. Let $S_1^2(n)$ and $S_2^2(n)$ be the sample variances [using Eq. (4.4)] of the X_{1j}'s and X_{2j}'s, respectively, and let $S_Z^2(n)$ be the sample variance of the differences, $Z_j = X_{1j} - X_{2j}$; since the runs were made using CRN, $S_Z^2(n)$ is an unbiased estimator of the variance of a Z_j under CRN. Regardless of the fact that we used CRN, $S_1^2(n)$ is unbiased for $\text{Var}(X_{1j})$ and $S_2^2(n)$ is unbiased for $\text{Var}(X_{2j})$, so $S_1^2(n) + S_2^2(n)$ is an unbiased estimator of the variance of a Z_j if we *were* to make the runs without CRN. Thus, if CRN is working, we would expect to observe that $S_Z^2(n) < S_1^2(n) + S_2^2(n)$, and the difference estimates how much CRN is reducing the variance of a Z_j. Of course, any extra programming that might be necessary to implement CRN would have to be done for such a pilot study, whether or not CRN is ultimately adopted. While there are some examples of CRN's backfiring, as observed by Wright and Ramsay (1979) and Koenig and Law (1982) for inventory simulations, we feel that CRN is generally a valuable tool that should be given serious consideration by an analyst faced with the task of comparing two or more alternative configurations.

Another possible drawback to CRN is that formal statistical analyses can be complicated by the induced correlation. Adaptations for standard analysis-of-variance tests in the presence of this correlation are discussed by Heikes, Montgomery, and Rardin (1976) and by Kleijnen (1979). Further issues regarding statistical analysis in the presence of CRN-induced correlation are discussed by Nelson (1987b), who also deals with similar problems created by the antithetic-variates VRT treated in Sec. 11.3. Nozari, Arnold, and Pegden (1987) address the issue of statistical analysis in the general framework of Schruben and Margolin (1978) for correlation induction in simulation experiments. See also the discussion in Sec. 10.4.4 under the heading "Correlation between Alternatives," relating to CRN in multiple-selection procedures.

11.2.3 Synchronization

To implement CRN properly, we must match up, or *synchronize*, the random numbers across the different system configurations on a particular replication. *Ideally*, a specific random number used for a specific purpose in one configuration is used for *exactly the same* purpose in all other configurations. For instance, if a specific U_k is used in the first of two alternative queueing configurations to generate a specific service time, then it should be used in the second configuration to generate the same service time (rather than an interarrival time or some other service time) as well; otherwise, the benefit of CRN could be lost, or (worse) backfiring might occur. In particular, it is generally *not* enough just to start off the simulations of all configurations with the same seed of a random-number stream, as the following example illustrates.

Example 11.1. Recall the two competing designs for the automated teller station of Examples 10.1 and 10.2. The first configuration (one Zippytel machine) is an $M/M/1$ queue, and the second (two Klunkytels) is an $M/M/2$ queue, both with utilization factor $\rho = 0.9$. The performance measure of interest is the expected average delay in queue of the first 100 customers given that the first customer finds the system empty and idle. Thus, X_{ij} is the average delay in the $M/M/i$ queue on the jth replication, for $i = 1, 2$. In Examples 10.1 and 10.2, we generated X_{1j} and X_{2j} independently for the 100 independent replications, but we could have used CRN.

In an attempt to do so, we used a single random-number stream (see Secs. 2.3 and 7.1) to generate both interarrival and service times, and simply reset the stream's seed back to its original value before simulating the second configuration. For the $M/M/1$ case, the program logic of Sec. 1.4 was used, and the $M/M/2$ model was programmed similarly. In particular, a customer's service time was generated at the time he entered service, after any delay in queue.

In our run, the $M/M/1$ model drew 219 random numbers from the stream by the time the 100th delay was observed, while the $M/M/2$ configuration needed only 201 random numbers to complete its run. (In general, the number of random numbers required is itself a random variable, and neither configuration will always require more than the other.) Table 11.1 gives some of the actual values for the

TABLE 11.1
Random-number usage in nonsynchronized CRN for the
$M/M/1$ **queue vs. the** $M/M/2$ **queue**

k	U_k	Usage in $M/M/1$	Usage in $M/M/2$	Agree?
1	0.40	A	A	Yes
2	0.61	A	A	Yes
3	0.43	S	S	Yes
4	0.38	A	A	Yes
5	0.51	S	S	Yes
6	0.71	A	A	Yes
7	0.19	S	S	Yes
8	0.83	A	A	Yes
9	0.65	A	S	No
10	0.38	A	A	Yes
11	0.35	S	S	Yes
12	0.76	A	A	Yes
13	0.45	A	A	Yes
14	0.91	S	A	No
15	0.47	S	A	No
16	0.48	A	S	No
17	0.85	S	S	Yes
18	0.80	S	S	Yes
19	0.72	S	A	No
20	0.70	A	A	Yes
⋮	⋮	⋮	⋮	⋮
195	0.60	A	S	No
196	0.42	A	S	No
197	0.57	A	S	No
198	0.86	A	A	Yes
199	0.10	A	S	No
200	0.15	S	A	No
201	0.33	S	S	Yes
202	0.58	A		
203	0.83	A		
⋮	⋮	⋮		
218	0.34	A		
219	0.66	S		

stream of random numbers (the U_k's), and also indicates the use to which each individual U_k was put in each configuration ("A" if a random number was used to generate an interarrival time, and "S" if it was used to generate a service time). We see that the first eight random numbers happened to agree in general usage (A vs. S), but U_9 is used for an interarrival time in the first configuration but generates a service time in the second, and from then on the usage of the random numbers gets mixed up. (In general, however, synchronization could last for as few as the first four random numbers. Why?) In fact, of the 201 U_k's that were used in both configurations, only about half (102 of them, to be exact) turned out to agree in general usage. From additional runs we made, this 50 percent synchronization figure is fairly typical.

Thus, we cannot in general expect CRN to be implemented properly if we merely recycle the same random numbers without paying attention to how they are used. The poor synchronization in Example 11.1 is due in part to the particular way we programmed the simulations. We did not, however, consciously try to destroy the synchronization, but wrote code in a way that seems reasonable and is in fact correct. The issue of coding for correct synchronization is considered below and in Example 11.3, which also illustrates the statistical consequences of ignoring synchronization.

How difficult it is to maintain proper synchronization in general depends entirely on the model structure and parameters, and on the methods used to generate the random variates needed in the simulations. Several programming "tricks" could be considered to maintain synchronization in a given simulation:

- If there are multiple streams of random numbers available (see Secs. 2.3 and 7.1), or if there are several different random-number generators operating simultaneously, we could "dedicate" a stream (or generator) to producing the random numbers for each particular type of input random variate. In a queueing simulation, for instance, one stream could be dedicated to generating the interarrival times, and a different stream could be dedicated to service times. Stream dedication is generally a good idea, and most simulation languages have facility for separate random-number streams. (The number of different streams readily available, however, may not be entirely adequate for large simulations.) Moreover, since streams are usually just adjacent segments of a single random-number generator's output and thus have a particular length (often 100,000 random numbers per stream), care should be taken to avoid overlapping them when doing long simulations or when replicating intensively. A back-of-the-envelope calculation might indicate roughly how many random numbers will be used from a stream, and appropriate assignments can then be made. For example, in a simple single-server queueing simulation where about 5000 customers are expected to pass through the system, each will need an interarrival time and a service time. If the inverse-transform method (see Sec. 8.2.1) is used to generate all these variates, we would need about 5000 random numbers from each stream; if we were to replicate the simulation 30 times, we would go through some 150,000 random numbers from each stream. If the streams are 100,000 long (as usual) and we dedicated stream 1 to interarrival times and stream 2 to service times (as usual), we see that the last 50,000 random numbers for the interarrival times would actually be the same as the first 50,000 used for the service times, destroying the replications' independence:

Stream 1	Stream 2	Stream 3
$U_1 \ldots \ldots U_{100000}$	$U_{100001} \ldots \ldots U_{200000}$	$U_{200001} \ldots \ldots U_{300000}$

Interarrival Times

Service Times

The remedy is, of course, to skip some stream assignments: Keep stream 1 (and the first half of stream 2) for the interarrival times, and use, say, stream 6 (and the first half of stream 7) for the service times.

- The inverse-transform method for generating random variates (see Sec. 8.2.1) can facilitate synchronization since we always need *exactly* one random number to produce each value of the desired random variable. By contrast, the acceptance-rejection method (Sec. 8.2.4), for example, uses a *random* number of $U(0,1)$ random numbers to produce a single value of the desired random variable. The inverse-transform method, moreover, monotonically transforms the random numbers (see Sec. 11.2.2), and induces the strongest possible positive correlation between the generated variates that then serve as input to the simulations, as discussed in Sec. 8.2.1; this correlation will hopefully propagate through to the simulation output to yield the strongest variance reduction.

- It might be helpful to "waste" some random numbers at certain points in simulating some models. Problem 11.4 gives such an example.

- In some queueing simulations we could generate all of the service requirements of a customer at the time of arrival instead of when the customer actually needs them, and store them as attributes of the customer. Example 11.4 below illustrates this idea for implementing CRN for the alternative job-shop models of Sec. 2.7.3.

Even armed with such programming tricks, it may simply be impossible to attain full synchronization across all models under study. Also, the extra programming effort, computation time, or storage costs needed for full synchronization might not be worth the realized variance reduction. Thus, we might consider synchronizing *some* of the input random variates and generating others independently across the various configurations. For instance, it might be convenient to synchronize interarrival times but not service times in a complicated network of queues. In the final analysis, the benefit of using CRN and the degree to which we synchronize depend on the situation.

11.2.4 Some Examples

Since the applicability, power, and appropriate synchronization methods for CRN can be quite model-dependent, we will present several examples of its use in particular situations.

Example 11.2. We now rework the $M/M/1$ vs. $M/M/2$ comparison of Example 11.1, but this time synchronize correctly. Using separate streams to implement CRN, we estimated the effect of various degrees of synchronization in four sequences of 100 pairs of simulations each. In the first sequence, denoted "I" in Table 11.2, all runs were independent; i.e., CRN was not used at all. In the second sequence ("A" in Table 11.2), the interarrival times for the two models were generated using CRN, but we generated the service times independently.

TABLE 11.2
Statistical results of CRN for the $M/M/1$ queue vs. the $M/M/2$ queue

	I	A	S	A & S
$S^2(100)$	18.00	9.02	8.80	0.07
90% confidence-interval half-length	0.70	0.49	0.49	0.04
$\hat{p}$	0.52	0.37	0.40	0.03
$\widehat{\mathrm{Cor}}(X_{1j}, X_{2j})$	−0.17	0.33	0.44	0.995

For the third sequence ("S"), the interarrival times were independent but the service times were generated using CRN, so both systems experienced the "same" ordered sequence of arriving service demands, with those for the $M/M/2$ being exactly twice as great as those for the $M/M/1$. Finally, the fourth sequence ("A & S") was fully synchronized, matching up both interarrival and service times. We can think of these four schemes in physical terms like this:

I	Different customers (in terms of their service requirements) arrive to the two configurations, and at different times
A	Different customers arrive to the two configurations, but at the same times
S	The same customers arrive to the two configurations, but at different times
A & S	The same customers arrive at the same times to both configurations

From the 100 pairs of simulations in each of the four cases we estimated $\mathrm{Var}(Z_j)$ by the usual unbiased variance estimator $S^2(100)$, from Eq. (4.4) applied to the Z_j's. From this, the half-length of a nominal 90 percent confidence interval for ζ is $1.65\,S(100)/\sqrt{100}$. We computed as well the proportion $\hat{p}$ of the 100 pairs for which the "wrong" decision would be made, i.e., when $X_{1j} < X_{2j}$ [since $E(X_{1j}) > E(X_{2j})$, as discussed in Example 10.1]. As a more direct check on whether CRN is inducing the desired positive correlation, we also estimated the correlation between X_{1j} and X_{2j} by

$$\widehat{\mathrm{Cor}}(X_{1j}, X_{2j}) = \frac{\dfrac{1}{99} \sum_{j=1}^{100} [X_{1j} - \bar{X}_1(100)][X_{2j} - \bar{X}_2(100)]}{S_1(100)S_2(100)}$$

where $\bar{X}_i(100)$ is the sample mean of the X_{ij}'s over j, and $S_i^2(100)$ is the sample variance of the X_{ij}'s over j (see Prob. 4.25).

It is clear from Table 11.2 that the estimated variance reduction attained by full synchronization (A & S) compared with independent sampling (I) is quite potent here, being a reduction of over 99 percent, probably since the two systems are quite similar. Accordingly, the confidence-interval half-length fell from 0.70 (I) to 0.04 (A & S), a reduction of almost 95 percent. Looked at another way, let us ask how many replications of each system under independent sampling we would need in order to achieve a precision in our estimator $\bar{Z}(n)$ for ζ (perhaps measured by confidence-interval half-length) equal to that from fully synchronized CRN. If we made n_I replications of each system under independent sampling, the half-length would be approximately proportional to $\sqrt{18.00/n_I}$ (ignoring degrees of freedom); on the other hand, if we made n_C replications of each system under completely synchronized CRN, the half-length would be approximately proportional to $\sqrt{0.07/n_C}$. Equating the two square roots, we find that $n_I/n_C = 257.14$; i.e., we would need more than 250 times as many replications under independent sampling to get the same precision we would get with fully synchronized CRN.

The estimated probability of making the wrong decision is reduced from 52 percent to 3 percent (see Example 10.1). Looking at the estimated correlations, we see that fully synchronized CRN induced an extremely strong correlation between the two configurations' output measures, explaining the large reduction in variance. For the two partial synchronization schemes, we experienced weaker (but still positive) correlations, and correspondingly weaker variance reductions and only limited drops in $\hat{p}$.

The effect of CRN (completely synchronized) in this example can be expressed graphically in several ways. In Fig. 11.2a are the individual-replication

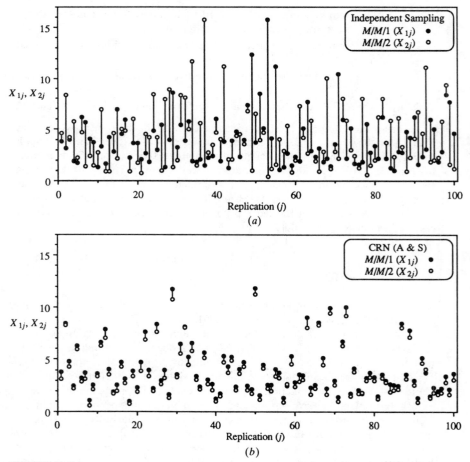

FIGURE 11.2
$M/M/1$ vs. $M/M/2$: individual replications.

results for the 100 pairs of runs under independent sampling, versus the replication number. The solid circles are the average delays in queue for the $M/M/1$ model (X_{1j}'s), and the hollow circles are for the $M/M/2$ case (X_{2j}'s); for each fixed j, X_{1j} and X_{2j} are connected by a vertical line, whose length is thus $|Z_j|$. Note in particular that there are 52 pairs for which the hollow circle ($M/M/2$) is at the top of a line and the solid circle ($M/M/1$) is at the bottom, which is the wrong order (in terms of their expectations), and corresponds to $\hat{p} = 0.52$ in the "I" column of Table 11.2. Figure 11.2*b* does likewise, but under completely synchronized CRN. The better-behaved nature of the Z_j's is apparent, with none of the very long vertical lines that appear in Fig. 11.2*a*, and with the line lengths being much more consistent within themselves. Moreover, there are only three cases in Fig. 11.2*b* where a line has the $M/M/2$ hollow circle at the top and the $M/M/1$ solid circle at the bottom, corresponding to $\hat{p} = 0.03$ in the "A & S" column of Table 11.2.

A direct way of seeing the correlation that CRN induced in this example is shown in Fig. 11.3, where we plot the pairs (X_{1j}, X_{2j}) for both independent sampling (hollow triangles) and completely synchronized CRN (solid triangles). While there is no apparent pattern in the independent pairs, we note an extremely straight (and positively sloping) alignment of the CRN pairs, corresponding to the very strong positive correlation estimate (0.995) in the "A & S" column of Table 11.2.

In the "$n = 1$" pair of dot plots at the bottom of Fig. 11.4, each square represents a Z_j, plotted according to the scale shown at the bottom, with the

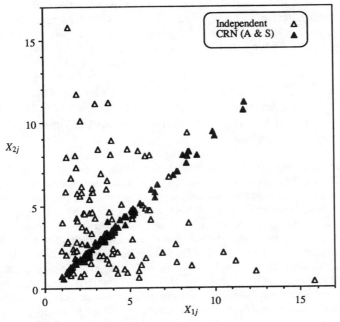

FIGURE 11.3
Correlation plot of $M/M/2$ average delays (vertical axis) vs. $M/M/1$ average delays (horizontal axis).

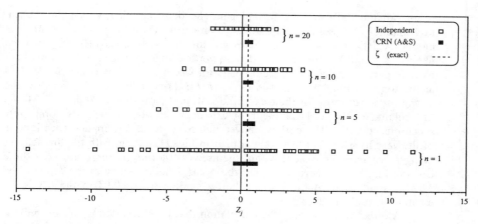

FIGURE 11.4
$M/M/1$ vs. $M/M/2$: differences.

hollow squares being the results of independent sampling, and the solid squares (which run together in the plot) being the results of fully synchronized CRN. The spread of the CRN Z_j's about their expectation (ζ) is much narrower than for the independent-sampling case. We also show in Fig. 11.4 plots of 100 observations on $\bar{Z}(n)$ for $n = 5$, 10, and 20, plotted on the same scale (these correspond to the similar cases in Fig. 10.2 in the case of independent sampling). It is striking to note that we do much better in terms of spread for CRN with $n = 1$ than we do for independent sampling for n as high as 20. Thus, CRN here gave us much better results than we could have gotten by spending more than 20 times as much with independent sampling!

Unlike Example 11.1, we implemented CRN in Example 11.2 with proper synchronization techniques, using separate streams for the two different sources of randomness. The next example illustrates the statistical importance of maintaining proper synchronization.

Example 11.3. We reran the experiments of Example 11.2, supposedly using the full "A & S" CRN, except this time we generally ignored synchronization. Our codes are all still "correct," i.e., faithfully simulate the two models, and represent programs that one could actually write, without malice aforethought to disrupt synchronization intentionally. In "Code 1" we generated service requirements upon arrival, and we used the same random-number stream throughout. As it happens, this still results in proper synchronization, as evidenced in Table 11.3. (The numbers differ from the "A & S" column of Table 11.2 since separate streams were used there.) "Code 2" of Table 11.3 uses a single stream but does not generate the service times upon arrival, waiting until a customer enters service to generate the service time; in this case, the random numbers will get mixed up in terms of their usage, as demonstrated in Example 11.1. As seen in Table 11.3, the results are really no better than the "I" case in Table 11.2, since we have lost

TABLE 11.3
Statistical results of properly (Code 1) and improperly (Codes 2 and 3) synchronized CRN for the $M/M/1$ queue vs. the $M/M/2$ queue

	Code 1	Code 2	Code 3
$S^2(100)$	0.07	16.80	12.00
90% confidence-interval half-length	0.04	0.67	0.57
$\hat{p}$	0.07	0.43	0.42
$\widehat{\text{Cor}}(X_{1j}, X_{2j})$	0.997	0.02	−0.03

the benefit (apparently nearly all) of CRN. "Code 3" is the same as Code 2, except that the next interarrival time is generated at the end of the arrival subprogram (see Sec. 1.4), representing yet another valid but nonsynchronized code; again, no benefit is seen.

The examples so far in this chapter have involved the same $M/M/1$ vs. $M/M/2$ configurations. These are very simple systems for which properly synchronized CRN is relatively easy to implement. They are also quite similar to each other, probably accounting for the dramatic variance reductions through CRN that we have seen. The next two examples involve models that are considerably more complicated, and consider as well using CRN for steady-state parameters (see Secs. 9.3 and 9.5).

Example 11.4. In the job-shop model of Sec. 2.7 recall the discussion at the end of Sec. 2.7.3. As in the last three rows of Table 2.5, let configurations 1, 2, and 3 be, respectively, the job shop obtained by adding a machine to group 1, 2, and 4, and let ν_i be the *steady-state* expected overall average job total delay in configuration i for $i = 1$, 2, and 3. Suppose that we want to estimate $\zeta_{12} = \nu_1 - \nu_2$, $\zeta_{13} = \nu_1 - \nu_3$, and $\zeta_{23} = \nu_2 - \nu_3$ by making simulations of length 100 eight-hour days of each of the three configurations but using the first 10 of these 100 days as a warmup period and collecting data on only the last 90 days (see Prob. 2.7). Let X_{ij} be the overall average job total delay over these 90 days for configuration i as observed on the jth replication, and let $Z_{12j} = X_{1j} - X_{2j}$, $Z_{13j} = X_{1j} - X_{3j}$, and $Z_{23j} = X_{2j} - X_{3j}$. We assume that the 10-day warmup period is sufficient, so that $E(Z_{i_1 i_2 j}) \approx \zeta_{i_1 i_2}$.

We made the runs of the different configurations completely independent of each other (denoted "I" in Table 11.4 below), and also used CRN across the three configurations, as follows. For each configuration, we used the same interarrival times for the jobs and made the sequence of job types the same. Further, when a job arrived at the shop and its type was determined, we immediately generated its service requirements that will be needed later as it moves along its route through the shop and stored them as additional attributes of this job. Thus, when a job entered service at a particular machine group, its service time was taken from its appropriate attribute for this station. In this way, we used synchronized CRN for all sources of randomness. Note also that in this example all types of random variates are generated at the same instant in

TABLE 11.4
CRN for the three job-shop configurations

	I	CRN	Variance reduction (%)
$S_{12}^2(10)$	6.27	1.46	77
$S_{13}^2(10)$	10.40	2.35	77
$S_{23}^2(10)$	23.08	0.87	96

simulated time (when a job arrives), so a single random-number stream could have been used for all sources of randomness.

Let $S_{i_1 i_2}^2(10)$ be the usual unbiased estimator of $\mathrm{Var}(Z_{i_1 i_2 j})$, which we computed from 10 independent replications using both independent sampling and CRN, as given in Table 11.4. Here, CRN led to variance reductions ranging from 77 percent to 96 percent, depending on which two policies are being compared. In terms of the required number of replications to achieve a desired confidence-interval half-width, we can proceed as in Example 11.2 to find that independent sampling would need 4.29 (=6.27/1.46) times as many replications as CRN to compare configurations 1 and 2, 4.43 times as many for configurations 1 and 3, and more than 26 times as many if we are interested in the difference between configurations 2 and 3.

Example 11.5. In Example 10.5 we compared two configurations of the manufacturing facility from Example 9.25. In the second configuration, the mean inspection time was smaller. We are again interested in the steady-state mean time in system of parts, so we followed the replication/deletion approach (Sec. 9.5.2) and made moving-average plots for both configurations as in Fig. 10.3. Again letting l_i and m_i be the length (in parts) of the warmup period and the minimum replication length for configuration i, we obtained $m_1 = m_2 = 9445$, $l_1 = 1929$, and $l_2 = 1796$. As in Example 10.5, we made $n = 20$ independent pairs of runs, but we now used separate streams to synchronize the random numbers for all six sources of randomness in this model [interarrival times, machine processing times, inspection times, good/bad decision, machine operating (up) times, and machine repair (down) times]. Again, we formed a 90 percent confidence interval for the difference between the steady-state mean times in system from these 20 replications, and obtained 1.98 ± 0.18; recall that in Example 10.5 the corresponding interval was 2.36 ± 0.31, from 20 replications of each configuration that were close to the same length and from which close to the same amount of initial data were deleted. Thus, CRN reduced the size of the confidence interval on the difference between the performance measures by 42 percent of its original size, corresponding to an estimated variance reduction of 66 percent. As more direct evidence that CRN is working properly, we estimated the correlation (see Example 11.2) between X_{1j} and X_{2j} to be 0.98.

The next pair of examples of CRN involves an inventory model, for which complete synchronization of all sources of randomness is not sensible; thus, we generated some inputs using properly synchronized CRN and others independently.

Example 11.6. For the inventory model (defined in Sec. 1.5) that we considered in Example 10.3, recall that (s,S) was $(20,40)$ for configuration 1, and was $(20,80)$ for configuration 2. For each configuration we can arrange for demands of the same size to occur at the same times; i.e., we use CRN (via separate streams) for the demand-size and interdemand-time sources of randomness. Due to the different values of s and S, however, orders will generally be placed at different times and for different amounts for the two policies, and so the number of orders placed will also differ under the two policies. Thus, it is not clear how we could reasonably match up the delivery-lag random variates, so we just generated them independently across the configurations.

As in Example 10.3, we made $n = 5$ independent pairs of simulations, but here with (partial) CRN as just described. We obtained $\bar{Z}(5) = 3.95$ and $\widehat{\text{Var}}[\bar{Z}(5)] = 0.27$, so that the paired-$t$ 90 percent confidence interval is $[2.84, 5.06]$. Comparing this with the independent-sampling results of Example 10.3, the estimated variance is reduced by about 89 percent, and the confidence-interval half-length is some 67 percent smaller. Thus, it would take about 45 replications of each system under independent sampling to get a confidence interval as small as the one we got from partial CRN with only 5 replications of each.

The following example illustrates how the multiple confidence-interval methods described in Sec. 10.3 can be sharpened with CRN.

Example 11.7. Consider now the five different policy configurations defined in Table 10.4. As in Example 10.6, we first regard policy 1, where $(s,S) = (20,40)$, as the standard against which the other four are to be compared. We reran the analysis of Example 10.6, again with $n = 5$ replications of each policy configuration, but now using the partial CRN sampling plan described in Example 11.6, across all five policies. Desiring overall confidence of at least 90 percent, we used the Bonferroni inequality (see Sec. 10.3) to form four individual 97.5 percent confidence intervals for $\mu_i - \mu_1$, exactly as described in Example 10.6; here, however, CRN implies that the results on a given replication (j) across the five policies are not independent, precluding use of the Welch approach to confidence-interval formation. Thus, Table 11.5 contains only the paired-t intervals corre-

TABLE 11.5
Individual 97.5 percent confidence intervals for all comparisons with the standard policy ($\mu_i - \mu_1$, $i = 2, 3, 4, 5$) using CRN; * denotes a significant difference

		Paired-t	
i	$\bar{X}_i - \bar{X}_1$	Half-length	Interval
2	-3.95	1.83	$(-5.78, -2.12)$*
3	1.02	2.65	$(-1.63, 3.68)$
4	5.94	1.41	$(4.53, 7.35)$*
5	19.69	2.28	$(17.41, 21.97)$*

TABLE 11.6
Individual 99 percent confidence intervals for all pairwise comparisons ($\mu_{i_2} - \mu_{i_1}$ for $i_1 < i_2$) using CRN; * denotes a significant difference

		Paired-t			
		i_2			
		2	**3**	**4**	**5**
i_1	1	$-3.95 \pm 2.41^*$	1.02 ± 3.49	$5.94 \pm 1.86^*$	$19.69 \pm 3.00^*$
	2		4.97 ± 5.62	$9.89 \pm 3.68^*$	$23.64 \pm 5.02^*$
	3			$4.92 \pm 2.39^*$	$18.67 \pm 1.69^*$
	4				$13.75 \pm 2.03^*$

sponding to Table 10.6. The half-lengths obtained here are all quite a bit smaller than those in Table 10.6. Moreover, comparing the paired-t approaches only, CRN enabled us to identify one more statistically significant difference (between policy 2 and the standard) than we were able to in Example 10.6.

We can also effect the all-pairwise-comparisons analysis of Sec. 10.3.2 using CRN; this was done with independent sampling in Example 10.7, with the results given in Table 10.7. Since there are now 10 individual confidence intervals, we make each at level 99 percent to attain overall confidence of at least 90 percent. The intervals resulting from CRN (again, only the paired-t approach is valid) in Table 11.6 indicate once again that CRN markedly reduced confidence-interval length in all cases except one ($i_2 = 5$, $i_1 = 2$). In this case the paired-t interval under independent sampling (22.12 ± 3.80) from Table 10.7 is smaller than the CRN interval (23.64 ± 5.02) from Table 11.6. Looking back at Table 10.7, the interval in this case was the smallest one observed, possibly due to simple sampling fluctuation, and at any rate the difference is significant both there and here. Perhaps more important, we see in Table 11.6 that 8 of the 10 CRN-based intervals miss zero (indicating a statistically significant difference between the corresponding configurations), whereas only 6 or 7 of the 10 in Table 10.7 (depending on the approach) missed zero. Thus, with no more sampling we were able to sharpen our comparisons among these policies.

11.3 ANTITHETIC VARIATES

Antithetic variates (AV) is a VRT that is applicable to simulating a *single* system, as are the rest of the VRTs in this chapter. As in CRN, we try to induce correlation between separate runs, but now we seek *negative* correlation.

The central idea, dating back at least to Hammersley and Morton (1956) in the context of Monte Carlo simulation, is to make *pairs* of runs of the model such that a "small" observation on one of the runs in a pair tends to be offset by a "large" observation on the other one; i.e., the two observations are negatively correlated. Then if we use the *average* of the two observations in the pair as a basic data point for analysis, it will tend to be closer to the common expectation μ of an observation (which we want to estimate) than it would be if the two observations in the pair were independent.

In its simplest form, AV tries to induce this negative correlation by using *complementary* random numbers to drive the two runs in a pair. That is, if U_k is a particular random number used *for a particular purpose* (e.g., to generate the ith service time) in the first run, we use $1 - U_k$ *for this same purpose* in the second run. It is valid to use $1 - U_k$ instead of simply a direct draw from the random-number generator since $U \sim U(0,1)$ implies that $1 - U \sim U(0,1)$ as well.

An important point is that the use of a U_k in one replication and its complement $1 - U_k$ in the paired replication must be synchronized, i.e., used for the same purpose; the benefit of AV could otherwise be lost, or it could even backfire. For instance, if U_k happens to be large and is used via the (literal) inverse-transform method to generate a service time, this would result in a large service time and have the effect of increasing the queue's congestion in the first run of the pair. In this case, $1 - U_k$ would be small, so if it were used erroneously to generate an interarrival time in the second run, this interarrival time would be small and would increase congestion on that run as well, which is the opposite of the intended effect. Most of the programming tricks mentioned in Sec. 11.2 for synchronizing random numbers, such as random-number stream dedication, using the inverse-transform method of variate generation wherever possible, judicious wasting of random numbers, or pregeneration, can be used here as well. Moreover, we could consider "partial" AV, generating some inputs antithetically and others independently within a pair if full synchronization proves too difficult or there does not seem to be a sensible way to use AV for all inputs (see Example 11.9 below). To be sure, then, it is *not* enough just to go through the simulation code and replace each "U" with a "$1 - U$."

As with CRN, there is a mathematical basis for AV. Suppose that we make n *pairs* of runs of the simulation resulting in observations $(X_1^{(1)}, X_1^{(2)}), \ldots, (X_n^{(1)}, X_n^{(2)})$, where $X_j^{(1)}$ is from the first run (using just the "U"s) of the jth pair, and $X_j^{(2)}$ is from the antithetic run (using the "$1 - U$"s, properly synchronized) of the jth pair. Both $X_j^{(1)}$ and $X_j^{(2)}$ are legitimate observations of the simulation model, so that $E(X_j^{(1)}) = E(X_j^{(2)}) = \mu$. Also, each pair is independent of every other pair; i.e., for $j_1 \neq j_2$, $X_{j_1}^{(l_1)}$ and $X_{j_2}^{(l_2)}$ are independent, regardless of whether l_1 and l_2 are equal. (Note that the total number of replications is thus $2n$.) For $j = 1, 2, \ldots, n$, let $X_j = (X_j^{(1)} + X_j^{(2)})/2$, and let the average of the X_j's, $\bar{X}(n)$, be the (unbiased) point estimator of $\mu = E(X_j^{(l)}) = E(X_j) = E[\bar{X}(n)]$. Then since the X_j's are IID,

$$\text{Var}[\bar{X}(n)] = \frac{\text{Var}(X_j)}{n} = \frac{\text{Var}(X_j^{(1)}) + \text{Var}(X_j^{(2)}) + 2\,\text{Cov}(X_j^{(1)}, X_j^{(2)})}{4n}$$

If the two runs within a pair were made independently, then $\text{Cov}(X_j^{(1)}, X_j^{(2)}) =$

0. On the other hand, if we could indeed induce negative correlation between $X_j^{(1)}$ and $X_j^{(2)}$, then $\text{Cov}(X_j^{(1)}, X_j^{(2)}) < 0$, which reduces $\text{Var}[\bar{X}(n)]$; this is the goal of AV.

Yet another feature that AV shares with CRN is that we cannot be completely sure that it will work, and its feasibility and efficacy are perhaps even more model-dependent than for CRN. In some cases, however, AV has been shown analytically to lead to variance reductions, although the magnitude of the reduction is not known; see Andréasson (1972), George (1977), Hammersley and Handscomb (1964), Mitchell (1973), Wilson (1979), Rubinstein, Samorodnitsky, and Shaked (1985), and Bratley, Fox, and Schrage (1987, chap. 2). In general, we cannot know beforehand how great a variance reduction might be achieved. A pilot study like that described for CRN might be useful to assess whether AV is a good idea in a specific case.

The fundamental requirement that a model should satisfy for AV to work is that its response to a random number used for a particular purpose be monotonic, in either direction. In most queueing-type models, for instance, a large random number used to generate a service time (via the literal inverse-transform method) will produce a large service time and lead to increased congestion; thus, we would expect that the response of congestion measures to random numbers used to generate service times would be monotonically increasing. Backfiring of AV could occur, for example, if a model's response were large for small U_k's, smaller for U_k's near 0.5, and then rose again for large U_k's (see Prob. 11.3). We urge the analyst to provide some kind of evidence that AV *will* work, either by arguing from "physical" properties of the model's structure or by initial experimentation. As with CRN, the inverse-transform method of generating a model's input variates is suggested in order to promote the required monotonicity by ensuring it at least in this intermediate variate-generation step. Franta (1975) gives examples of the failure of AV if other methods are used, but Schmeiser and Kachitvichyanukul (1986) develop fast non-inverse-transform methods that *do* lead to the desired negative correlation at this intermediate level.

Example 11.8. Consider the $M/M/1$ queue with $\rho = 0.9$, as in Examples 11.1 through 11.3, so that now an "observation" $X_j^{(l)}$ is the average of 100 customer delays. From the model's structure it seems reasonable to assume that large interarrival times would tend to make $X_j^{(l)}$ smaller (and vice versa), and large service times would generally result in a larger $X_j^{(l)}$. Further, if we use the method of Sec. 8.3.2 to generate the exponential interarrival-time and service-time variates, we would expect AV to work. We made $n = 100$ independent pairs of runs using both independent sampling within a pair [so $\text{Cov}(X_j^{(1)}, X_j^{(2)}) = 0$], as well as using AV, synchronizing by dedicating separate random-number streams to generating the interarrival and service times. The results are in Table 11.7, and show that AV reduced the estimated variance $S^2(100)$ of an X_j by 60 percent. If we used the 100 X_j's to form an approximate 90 percent confidence interval for μ, it would have a half-length of 0.36 under independent sampling, which would be reduced to 0.23 under AV, a reduction of 36 percent. That AV is inducing the

TABLE 11.7
Statistical results for AV in the case of the $M/M/1$ queue

	Independent	AV
$S^2(100)$	4.84	1.94
90% confidence-interval half-length	0.36	0.23
$\widehat{\text{Cor}}(X_j^{(1)}, X_j^{(2)})$	-0.07	-0.52

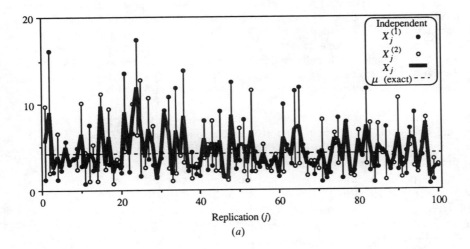

Replication (j)

(a)

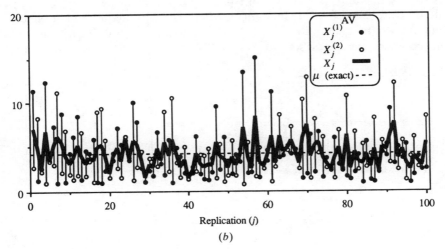

Replication (j)

(b)

FIGURE 11.5
Individual replications of the $M/M/1$ queue: (a) independent sampling; (b) AV.

desired negative correlation is confirmed by noting the estimated correlation of -0.52 between $X_j^{(1)}$ and $X_j^{(2)}$ in the AV case. Note that the extra cost of AV over independent sampling is negligible here, since AV requires almost no extra programming and only the subtraction of the random numbers from 1; both methods required 200 separate simulation runs.

Figure 11.5a shows the individual values of the independently sampled $X_j^{(1)}$'s (solid circles) and the $X_j^{(2)}$'s (hollow circles) for each j. The heavy line connects the values of X_j across j. Figure 11.5b does likewise, except for the fact that AV was used, and we see that the heavy line appears somewhat less twitchy, indicating the lower variance of the X_j's in the AV case. We can also see in Fig. 11.5b that under AV there appears to be a tendency for an $X_j^{(1)}$ on one side of the dashed line (at height μ) to be offset by an $X_j^{(2)}$ on the other side of the line, while this is less so in the independent-sampling plot in Fig. 11.5a. The lower variability of the X_j's under AV is confirmed more clearly in Fig. 11.6, where their narrower spread is evident. Finally, Fig. 11.7 gives a correlation plot of the pairs $(X_j^{(1)}, X_j^{(2)})$ under both independent sampling (hollow triangles) and AV (solid triangles). There does appear to be some negative correlation in the AV case, since the solid triangles show some tendency to slope downward.

The magnitude of the correlation induced by AV in Example 11.8 was not as strong as we observed in using CRN to compare the $M/M/1$ and $M/M/2$ queues in Example 11.2, and so the variance reduction from AV was weaker than that obtained via CRN. This is a good illustration of how a VRT's success generally depends on model characteristics. In Example 11.2 the only difference in the input variates to the two configurations (under fully synchronized CRN, called "A & S" there) was that the service times for the $M/M/2$ queue were in every case exactly twice those for the $M/M/1$ queue, and were thus *linearly* related. In the AV scheme of Example 11.8, however, the input variates for the first and second runs of a pair were not linearly related, coming basically down to using $\ln U$ vs. $\ln(1 - U)$, where U is a random number, since exponential variate generation was done by taking natural logarithms of random numbers, as described in Sec. 8.3.2. In both the CRN and AV

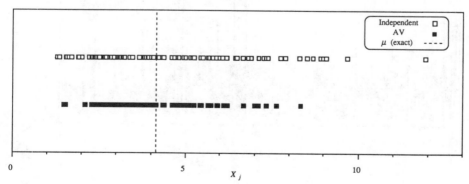

FIGURE 11.6
Within-pair averages for the $M/M/1$ queue with independent sampling and AV.

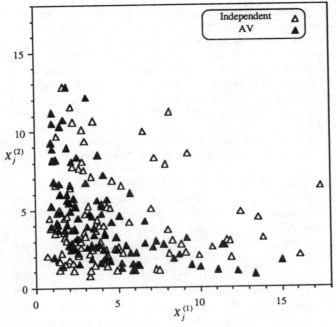

FIGURE 11.7
Correlation plot for pairs of runs of the $M/M/1$ queue with independent sampling and AV.

examples, the input variates are then transformed nonlinearly by the simulation model itself. Remembering that covariances and correlations, which figure prominently in the variance-reduction amount for both CRN and AV, measure *linear* relationships only (see Prob. 4.11), we see that the greater linearity in the CRN application of Example 11.2 evidently accounts for the stronger variance reduction than that observed in the less linear AV application of Example 11.8.

Example 11.9. In the particular case of applying AV to queueing simulations, Page (1965) suggested another type of antithetic sampling that does not involve substituting $1 - U$ for U in the second of a pair of runs. Since performance measures for queueing systems usually react to large interarrival times oppositely from the way they react to large service times, Page suggested that the random numbers used to generate the interarrival times in the first run of a pair be used instead to generate the service times in the second run, and vice versa. Implementing this idea on the $M/M/1$ model of Example 11.8, we experienced a variance reduction of 65 percent. This general method of interchanging the use of random numbers might be useful in inducing negative correlation for other types of models as well.

Our last example of AV illustrates its use in a nonqueueing model, and for which only partial synchronization is possible.

Example 11.10. Although somewhat more work is needed to see a physical rationale for response monotonicity and the potential success of AV (see Prob. 11.5), it can also be applied to the inventory model of Sec. 1.5. Take the case $(s,S) = (20,40)$, and assume the same parameters and output variables as in Example 11.6. Also as done in Example 11.6, we shall apply AV to only the interdemand times and the demand sizes, and generate the delivery lags independently between the two runs of a pair. Again we made $n = 100$ independent pairs of runs, first making $X_j^{(1)}$ and $X_j^{(2)}$ independent, and obtained 8.55 as an estimate of $Var(X_j)$, whereas the comparable variance estimate under AV was 3.26, a reduction of some 62 percent. Thus we see that an AV scheme that is only partially synchronized can still yield worthwhile variance reductions.

Due to the similarities between CRN and AV, the idea reasonably comes to mind of using them together when several alternative system configurations are to be compared. At first it would appear that we might obtain stronger variance reductions by using AV for each configuration separately and CRN across the different configurations. However, upon closer examination [see Kleijnen (1974, pp. 207–238), and Prob. 11.11] we find that if both AV and CRN work properly, i.e., induce correlations of the desired sign, certain "cross covariances" (specifically, the covariance between the first run of an antithetic pair of runs for configuration 1 and the second run of the corresponding antithetic pair for configuration 2, and vice versa) enter the relevant variance expression with the *wrong* sign, which might *increase* the variance. Thus, it is by no means clear that combining AV with CRN for comparing alternative system configurations is a good idea. Schruben and Margolin (1978) and Schruben (1979) consider in more generality the issue of random-number assignment in correlation-induction strategies for variance reduction in a variety of simulation experiments.

More general versions of AV have been developed, in terms of both the quantities to be estimated (other than expectations) as well as in the method to induce the desired negative correlation (other than using complementary random numbers); see Cheng (1982, 1984), Fishman and Huang (1983), and Wilson (1983) for specifics. A potential side benefit of AV was noted by Nelson (1990b), who showed that AV (combined with control variates, discussed in Sec. 11.4) can improve both point- and interval-estimator performance when initialization bias is present.

11.4 CONTROL VARIATES

Like CRN and AV, the method of *control variates* (CV) attempts to take advantage of correlation between certain random variables to obtain a variance reduction. Depending on the specific type of CV technique used, this correlation might arise naturally during the course of a simulation, or might be induced by using CRN in an auxiliary simulation.

In principle, at least, there is an appealing intuition to CV. Let X be an output random variable, such as the average of the first 100 customer delays in queue, and assume we want to estimate $\mu = E(X)$. Suppose that Y is another random variable involved in the simulation that is thought to be correlated with X (either positively or negatively), and that we *know* the value of $\nu = E(Y)$. For instance, Y could be the average of the service times of the first 99 customers who complete their service in the queueing model mentioned above, so we would know its expectation since we generated the service-time variates from some known input distribution. (Problem 11.12 mentions a subtle issue in this regard concerning the precise definition of Y.) It is reasonable to suspect that larger-than-average service times (i.e., $Y > \nu$) tend to lead to longer-than-average delays ($X > \mu$) and vice versa; i.e., Y is correlated with X, in this case positively. Thus if we run a simulation and notice that $Y > \nu$ (which we can tell for sure since we know ν), we might suspect that X is above its expectation μ as well (although we would not know this for sure unless the correlation between Y and X were perfect), and accordingly adjust X downward by some amount. If it turned out, on the other hand, that $Y < \nu$, we would suspect that $X < \mu$ as well and so adjust it upward instead. In this way, we use our knowledge of Y's expectation to pull X (down or up) toward *its* expectation μ, thus reducing its variability about μ from one run to the next. We call Y a *control variate* for X since it is used to adjust X, or partially "control" it.

Unlike CRN and AV, the success of CV does *not* depend on the correlation being of a particular sign. If Y and X were negatively correlated, which we might imagine if Y were the average of the first 100 generated *interarrival* times in the example of the preceding paragraph (widely separated arrivals tend to produce lower congestion levels), we would simply adjust X *upward* if $Y > \nu$ and *downward* if $Y < \nu$.

To carry out the above idea, we must quantify the amount of the upward or downward adjustment to X. It is convenient to express this amount in terms of the deviation, $Y - \nu$, of Y from its expectation. Let a be a constant (to be determined below) that has the same sign as the correlation between Y and X. In the earlier example where X is the average queueing delay and Y is the average service time, a would thus be some positive number. We use a to scale (magnify or shrink) the deviation $Y - \nu$ to arrive at an adjustment to X and thus define the "controlled" estimator

$$X_C = X - a(Y - \nu)$$

Note that if Y and X are positively correlated, so that $a > 0$, we would adjust X downward whenever $Y > \nu$ and upward when $Y < \nu$, as desired; the opposite is true when Y and X are negatively correlated, in which case $a < 0$.

Since $E(X) = \mu$ and $E(Y) = \nu$, it is clear that for any real number a, $E(X_C) = \mu$; that is, X_C is an unbiased estimator of μ that might have lower variance than X. Specifically,

$$\text{Var}(X_C) = \text{Var}(X) + a^2 \, \text{Var}(Y) - 2a \, \text{Cov}(X, Y) \tag{11.1}$$

so that X_C is less variable than X if and only if

$$2a \, \text{Cov}(X, Y) > a^2 \, \text{Var}(Y)$$

which may or may not be true, depending on the choice of Y and a. In many treatments of CV, only the special cases $a = 1$ [if we think that $\text{Cov}(X,Y) > 0$] or $a = -1$ [if we feel that $\text{Cov}(X,Y) < 0$] are considered, but this requires the more stringent condition that $|\text{Cov}(X,Y)| > \text{Var}(Y)/2$ for a variance reduction to be realized. Thus, simply setting $a = \pm 1$ places the entire burden for success upon the choice of Y; by allowing other values for a we can do better.

To find the "best" value of a for a given Y, we can view the right-hand side of Eq. (11.1) as a function $g(a)$ of a and set its derivative to zero; i.e.,

$$\frac{dg}{da} = 2a\,\text{Var}(Y) - 2\,\text{Cov}(X,Y) = 0$$

and solve for the optimal (variance-minimizing) value

$$a^* = \frac{\text{Cov}(X,Y)}{\text{Var}(Y)} \tag{11.2}$$

$[d^2g/da^2 = 2\,\text{Var}(Y)$, which is of course positive, a sufficient condition for a^* to be a minimiizer of $g(a)$, as opposed to a maximizer or an inflection point.] One of the implications of Eq. (11.2) is that if Y is strongly correlated with X, that is, $|\text{Cov}(X,Y)|$ is large, the value of a^* is increased, and so we are willing to make more drastic adjustments to X since we feel more confident about what Y's deviation from ν is telling us about what X's deviation from μ might be. Also, if Y is itself less variable, that is, $\text{Var}(Y)$ is small, we may get a larger value of a^* (and a more drastic adjustment to X) since we have more confidence in the precision of the observed value of Y itself.

Plugging a^* from Eq. (11.2) into the right-hand side of Eq. (11.1), we get that the minimum-variance *adjusted* (or *controlled*) estimator X_C^* over all choices of a has variance

$$\text{Var}(X_C^*) = \text{Var}(X) - \frac{[\text{Cov}(X,Y)]^2}{\text{Var}(Y)} = (1 - \rho_{XY}^2)\,\text{Var}(X)$$

where ρ_{XY} is the correlation between X and Y. Thus, using the optimal value a^* for a, the optimally controlled estimator X_C^* can never be more variable than the uncontrolled X, and will in fact have lower variance if Y is *at all* correlated with X. Moreover, the stronger the correlation between X and Y, the greater the variance reduction—in the extreme, as $\rho_{XY} \to \pm 1$, we see in fact that $\text{Var}(X_C^*) \to 0$. Intuitively, this says that if the correlation between Y and X were nearly perfect (± 1), we could control X almost exactly to μ every time, thereby eliminating practically all of its variance.

In practice, though, things are not quite so rosy. Depending on the source and nature of the control variate Y, we may or may not know the value of $\text{Var}(Y)$, and we will certainly not know $\text{Cov}(X,Y)$, making it impossible to find the exact value of a^*. Accordingly, several methods have been proposed to estimate a^* from simulation runs, and we next describe one of the simpler of these, due to Lavenberg, Moeller, and Welch (1982) and Lavenberg and Welch (1981), which can also be used to form a confidence interval for μ. [As stated, the method applies to terminating simulations (see Sec. 9.3) that are simply replicated, although it might be applicable to steady-state parameters by using the replication/deletion approach of Sec. 9.5.2 or by replacing the replication averages by batch means, as discussed in Sec. 9.5.3.]

The method simply replaces $\text{Cov}(X, Y)$ and $\text{Var}(Y)$ in Eq. (11.2) by their sample estimators. Suppose that we make n independent replications to obtain the n IID observations $X_1, X_2, \ldots, X_n$ on X and the n IID observations $Y_1, Y_2, \ldots, Y_n$ on Y. Let $\bar{X}(n)$ and $\bar{Y}(n)$ be the sample means of the X_j's and Y_j's, respectively, and let $S_Y^2(n)$ be the unbiased sample variance of the Y_j's. The covariance between X and Y is estimated by (see Prob. 4.25)

$$\hat{C}_{XY}(n) = \frac{\sum_{j=1}^{n} [X_j - \bar{X}(n)][Y_j - \bar{Y}(n)]}{n - 1}$$

and the estimator for a^* is then

$$\hat{a}^*(n) = \frac{\hat{C}_{XY}(n)}{S_Y^2(n)}$$

to arrive at the final point estimator for μ,

$$\overline{X_C^*}(n) = \bar{X}(n) - \hat{a}^*(n)[\bar{Y}(n) - \nu]$$

Immediately, we must note that since the constant a^* has been replaced by the random variable $\hat{a}^*(n)$, which is generally *not* independent of $\bar{Y}(n)$ (having been computed from the same simulation output data), we cannot blithely take expectations across the factors in the second term of $\overline{X_C^*}(n)$. Unfortunately, then, $\overline{X_C^*}(n)$, unlike X_C and X_C^*, will in general be biased for μ. The severity of this bias, as well as the amount of variance reduction that might be obtained from this scheme, are investigated by Lavenberg, Moeller, and Welch (1982).

Alternative estimators of a^*, based on jackknifing to reduce the bias in $\overline{X_C^*}(n)$, are discussed by Kleijnen (1974) as well as by Lavenberg, Moeller, and Welch (1982). Cheng and Feast (1980) and Bauer (1987) consider CV problems when we know the variance of the control variate. Nelson (1990a) surveys and evaluates several alternative approaches to dealing with the problem of point-estimator bias, as well as related problems.

Example 11.11. To solidify the example we have been discussing informally in this section, let X be the average delay in queue of the first 100 customers arriving to an $M/M/1$ queue that starts out empty and idle, has mean interarrival time 1 minute, and mean service time 0.9 minute; this is the same model we have used in Examples 11.1 through 11.3 and 11.8 through 11.9. As a control variate for X, let Y be the average of the 99 service times that would be needed to complete a replication of this model; since the simulation ends when the 100th service time begins, its value will have no impact on the output and so is not included in Y. Since Y is thus the average of a *fixed* number (see Prob. 11.12) of IID service times that have expectation 0.9, $\nu = E(Y) = 0.9$ as well.

We made $n = 10$ independent replications and observed the 10 X_j's and 10 corresponding Y_j's given in Table 11.8. From these data, $\bar{X}(10) = 3.78$ and $\bar{Y}(10) = 0.89$; thus, the average service time is a bit lower than its expectation $\nu = 0.9$, and the average delay in queue is also low compared to its expectation $\mu = 4.13$ (which we actually know in this artificial example), as suggested at the beginning of this section. Further, we got $S_X^2(10) = 13.33$, $S_Y^2(10) = 0.002$, and $\hat{C}_{XY}(10) = 0.07$, leading to an estimated value of 0.43 for the correlation between X and Y, confirming our feeling that they should be positively correlated. Finally, we get $\hat{a}^*(10) = 35.00$ and so $\overline{X_C^*}(10) = 4.13$, which is indeed closer to μ than is the uncontrolled estimator $\bar{X}(10) = 3.78$.

To see whether $\text{Var}[\overline{X_C^*}(10)]$ is in fact smaller than $\text{Var}[\bar{X}(10)]$, we repeated the entire 10-replication experiment of the preceding paragraph 100 times, getting 100 independent observations on both $\bar{X}(10)$ and $\overline{X_C^*}(10)$. From these data we estimated $\text{Var}[\bar{X}(10)]$ to be 0.99, whereas our estimate of $\text{Var}[\overline{X_C^*}(10)]$ was 0.66, a reduction of a third. The correlation between $\bar{X}(10)$ and $\bar{Y}(10)$ was estimated to be 0.67, which is positive, as anticipated. At the same time, we estimated from the 100 observations on $\overline{X_C^*}(10)$ that a 95 percent confidence interval for $E[\overline{X_C^*}(10)]$ is 4.18 ± 0.16, which contains μ, indicating that whatever bias in the controlled estimator was introduced by estimating a^* by $\hat{a}^*(10)$ is evidently not noticeable in this case.

In Example 11.11 we chose the average of the service times as our control variate but, as the following two examples show, the issue of what to use as a control variate is by no means clear.

Example 11.12. We repeated the experiments of Example 11.11 but used instead as a control variate Y the average of the first 100 *interarrival* times. We can be sure that there will always be at least this many and thus get a control variate based on a *fixed* number of generated interarrival times (see Prob. 11.12), so we know that $E(Y) = 1$. Carrying out a set of 100 experiments of $n = 10$ replications

TABLE 11.8
Average delays (X_j's) and average service times (Y_j's) using CV for the $M/M/1$ queue

j	X_j	Y_j
1	13.84	0.92
2	3.18	0.95
3	2.26	0.88
4	2.76	0.89
5	4.33	0.93
6	1.35	0.81
7	1.82	0.84
8	3.01	0.92
9	1.68	0.85
10	3.60	0.88

each, as described in Example 11.11, we estimated $\text{Var}[\overline{X_C^*}(10)]$ based on this control variate to be 0.89, a reduction of only 10 percent in comparison with the estimated variance of 0.99 for $\bar{X}(10)$. Thus, it appears that our original choice of the average service time as a control variate was a better idea than using the average interarrival time.

Example 11.13. Could we somehow make use of both? Let $Y^{(1)}$ be the average-service-time control variate used in Example 11.11, and let $Y^{(2)}$ be the average-interarrival-time control variate used in Example 11.12. Then, since $\text{Cov}(X, Y^{(1)})$ and $\text{Cov}(X, Y^{(2)})$ probably have opposite signs, we could perhaps incorporate information from both if we define a new control variate $Y = Y^{(1)} - Y^{(2)}$; we anticipate that $\text{Cov}(X, Y) > 0$, being supported by both $Y^{(1)}$ and $Y^{(2)}$. Indeed, when using this scheme in 100 new experiments of $n = 10$ replications each, the estimated correlation between $\bar{X}(10)$ and $\bar{Y}(10)$ was 0.77, and the estimate of the variance of the controlled estimator was 0.56, being a 43 percent reduction in variance from the 0.99 figure for the uncontrolled estimator, and better than either $Y^{(1)}$ or $Y^{(2)}$ alone. However, there was evidently some point-estimator bias introduced in this case, as a 95 percent confidence interval for $E[\overline{X_C^*}(10)]$ was 4.38 ± 0.15, which misses $\mu = 4.13$; whether or not this is worrisome depends on how one chooses to trade off bias against variance in the point estimator.

There were really two different control variates in Example 11.13 that we were able to combine in a sensible way to get a single control variate. However, why did we subtract them rather than divide one by the other? Or, why not let $Y = Y^{(1)} - 2Y^{(2)}$ instead? In complex models there will be many potential control variates available, and it could be difficult to suggest the best way to roll them all into one. Moreover, even if we could combine them in a reasonable way, we might not be using their information to our best advantage. In Example 11.13, we let *the* control variate $Y = Y^{(1)} - Y^{(2)}$, so that the controlled estimator is

$$X_C = X - a(Y - \nu)$$
$$= X - a(Y^{(1)} - \nu^{(1)}) - a(-Y^{(2)} + \nu^{(2)})$$

where $\nu^{(l)} = E(Y^{(l)})$. In this formulation, then, we are forcing both individual control variates $(Y^{(1)}$ and $-Y^{(2)})$ to enter the adjustment using the *same* coefficient, a, which may not be the best use of their information. A logical modification would be to allow the two control variates to have different weights, and redefine

$$X_C = X - a_1(Y^{(1)} - \nu^{(1)}) - a_2(Y^{(2)} - \nu^{(2)})$$

We could then find (and estimate) the weights a_1 and a_2 that minimize $\text{Var}(X_C)$, as we did before when there was just a single control variate.

This idea is easily generalized to the case where we have m control variates $Y^{(1)}, \ldots, Y^{(m)}$ with respective known expectations $\nu^{(1)}, \ldots, \nu^{(m)}$. The general (linearly) controlled estimator is

$$X_C = X - \sum_{l=1}^{m} a_l (Y^{(l)} - \nu^{(l)})$$

where the a_l's are real numbers to be determined (and estimated). Allowing for correlation not only between X and the control variates but also between the control variates themselves, we get

$$\text{Var}(X_C) = \text{Var}(X) + \sum_{l=1}^{m} a_l^2 \, \text{Var}(Y_l) - 2 \sum_{l=1}^{m} a_l \, \text{Cov}(X, Y_l)$$

$$+ 2 \sum_{l_1=2}^{m} \sum_{l_2=1}^{l_1-1} a_{l_1} a_{l_2} \, \text{Cov}(Y_{l_1}, Y_{l_2}) \tag{11.3}$$

Taking partial derivatives of the right-hand side of Eq. (11.3) with respect to each of the a_l's and equating them to zero leads to a set of m linear equations to solve for the m variance-minimizing weights (see Prob. 11.13). As in the case of a single control variate, these optimal weights must be estimated, and bias introduction in the controlled estimator is again a possibility. Lavenberg and Welch (1981) and Nelson (1990a) discuss these and related problems. The estimates of the optimal weights turn out to be identical to least-squares estimates of the coefficients in a certain linear-regression model, and so CV is sometimes referred to as *regression sampling*.

We close this section with a brief discussion of finding and selecting control variates. As we have seen, a good control variate should be strongly correlated with the output random variable X, in order to give us a lot of information about X and to make a good adjustment to it. We would also like the control variates themselves to have low variance. Finding such control variates could proceed by an analysis of the model's structure, or through initial experimentation. With these goals in mind, three general sources of control variates have been suggested:

- *Internal.* Input random variates, or simple functions of them (such as averages), are often used as control variates. All the control variates used in Examples 11.11 through 11.13 were internal. Their expectations will generally be known (see the caveat of Prob. 11.12), and a simple analysis of their role in the model could suggest how they might be correlated with the output random variable. Most important, internal control variates must be essentially generated anyway to run the simulation, so they add basically nothing to the simulation's cost; thus, they will prove worthwhile even if they do not reduce the variance greatly (see Prob. 11.1 for an economic model of the efficacy of VRTs). Detailed accounts of various kinds of internal CV applications can be found in Iglehart and Lewis (1979), Lavenberg, Moeller, and Sauer (1979), Lavenberg, Moeller, and Welch (1982), and Wilson and Pritsker (1984a, 1984b).

- *External.* Presumably, we are simulating since we cannot compute $\mu = E(X)$ analytically. Perhaps, though, if we altered the model by making some additional simplifying assumptions, we *would* be able to compute the expectation ν of the simplified model's output random variable Y. While we may be unwilling to make these simplifying assumptions in our actual model since they could materially impair the model's validity, Y could serve as a control variate for X. We would then simulate the simplified model alongside the actual model, using CRN (Sec. 11.2), and hope that Y is correlated with X, presumably positively. Unlike internal CV, this approach is *not* costless since it involves a second simulation to get the control variate; thus, the correlation between Y and X would have to be stronger for external CV to pay off than would be the case if Y were an internal CV. Examples of external CV can be found in Burt, Gaver, and Perlas (1970), Gaver and Shedler (1971), Gaver and Thompson (1973), as well as in Prob. 11.14.

- *Using multiple estimators.* In some situations we may have several unbiased estimators $X^{(1)}, \ldots, X^{(k)}$ for μ, where the $X^{(i)}$'s may or may not be independent. This might arise, for instance, when we can use the method of indirect estimation, to be discussed in Sec. 11.5. If $b_1, \ldots, b_k$ are any real numbers (not necessarily positive) that sum to 1, then

$$X_C = \sum_{i=1}^{k} b_i X^{(i)}$$

is also unbiased for μ. Since $b_1 = 1 - \Sigma_{i=2}^{k} b_i$, we can express X_C as

$$X_C = \left(1 - \sum_{i=2}^{k} b_i\right) X^{(1)} + \sum_{i=2}^{k} b_i X^{(i)}$$

$$= X^{(1)} - \sum_{i=2}^{k} b_i (X^{(1)} - X^{(i)})$$

so that we can view $Y_i = X^{(1)} - X^{(i)}$, for $i = 2, 3, \ldots, k$, as $k - 1$ control variates for $X^{(1)}$.

As can be seen from the above, there may be a very large number of possible control variates for a complex model. However, it is not necessarily a good idea to use them all, since the variance reduction they may bring is accompanied by variance contributions associated with the need to estimate the optimal a_i's. Bauer and Wilson (1989) propose a method for selecting the best subset from the available control variates, under a variety of assumptions about what we know concerning their variances and covariances. See also Rubinstein and Marcus (1985) and Venkatraman and Wilson (1986).

11.5 INDIRECT ESTIMATION

This VRT has been developed for queueing-type simulations when the quantities to be estimated are steady-state performance measures, such as d, w, Q, and L (see App. 1B). Proofs that variance reductions are obtained have been given for these kinds of models [see Law (1974, 1975), Carson and Law (1980), and Glynn and Whitt (1989)], but the idea might be applicable to other situations as well; again, initial experimentation could reveal whether worthwhile variance reductions are being experienced. The basic tools are the theoretical relations between d, w, Q, and L given in App. 1B.

Let D_i and W_i, respectively, be the delay in queue and the total wait in system of the ith customer arriving to a $GI/G/s$ queue. Thus, if S_i is the service time of the ith customer, $W_i = D_i + S_i$. Also, let $Q(t)$ and $L(t)$, respectively, be the number of customers in queue and in system at time t. From a simulation run in which a fixed number n of customers complete their service and which lasts for $T(n)$ units of simulated time, the *direct* estimators of d, w, Q, and L are, respectively,

$$\hat{d}(n) = \frac{1}{n} \sum_{i=1}^{n} D_i , \qquad \hat{w}(n) = \frac{1}{n} \sum_{i=1}^{n} W_i$$

$$\hat{Q}(n) = \frac{1}{T(n)} \int_0^{T(n)} Q(t) \, dt , \qquad \hat{L}(n) = \frac{1}{T(n)} \int_0^{T(n)} L(t) \, dt$$

Now $\hat{w}(n) = \hat{d}(n) + \bar{S}(n)$, where $\bar{S}(n) = \sum_{i=1}^{n} S_i/n$ and $E[\bar{S}(n)] = E(S)$, the known expected service time. Thus, an alternative estimator of w might be

$$\tilde{w}(n) = \hat{d}(n) + E(S)$$

i.e., we replace the estimator $\bar{S}(n)$ by its *known* (and zero-variance) expectation $E(S)$. We call $\tilde{w}(n)$ an *indirect* estimator of w, and it seems reasonable to suspect that $\tilde{w}(n)$ might be less variable than $\hat{w}(n)$, since the random term $\bar{S}(n)$ in $\hat{w}(n)$ is replaced by the fixed number $E(S)$ to obtain $\tilde{w}(n)$. For any $GI/G/s$ queue and for any n, this is indeed the case, as shown by Law (1974), although the proof is not as simple as it might seem since $\bar{S}(n)$ and $\hat{d}(n)$ are not independent. Thus, the indirect estimator $\tilde{w}(n)$ is better than the more obvious direct estimator.

The variance reduction of the previous paragraph is suggested by the *additive* relation $w = d + E(S)$, and it seems intuitive that there is no point in using the random variable $\bar{S}(n)$ in the estimator of w when we could use its expectation $E(S)$ instead, thereby avoiding an additional source of variation. What is perhaps not so intuitive is that better indirect estimators of Q and L can be obtained from the *multiplicative* relations in the two conservation equations

$$Q = \lambda d \tag{11.4}$$

$$L = \lambda w \tag{11.5}$$

where λ is the arrival rate (see App. 1B), which would again be known in a simulation. An indirect estimator of Q that Eq. (11.4) suggests is

$$\tilde{Q}(n) = \lambda \hat{d}(n)$$

and it is shown by Carson (1978) and Carson and Law (1980) that *asymptotically* [as both n and $T(n)$ become infinite] $\tilde{Q}(n)$ has smaller variance than the direct estimator $\hat{Q}(n)$. Similarly, using Eq. (11.5) and the superior indirect estimator $\tilde{w}(n)$ of w, we can show that the indirect estimator

$$\tilde{L}(n) = \lambda \tilde{w}(n) = \lambda[\hat{d}(n) + E(S)]$$

asymptotically has smaller variance than the direct estimator $\hat{L}(n)$. Thus we see that it is better to estimate w, Q, and L by simple deterministic functions of $\hat{d}(n)$ than to estimate them directly. This is one of the reasons we have emphasized estimation of the delay in queue in our examples throughout this book. Another appeal of indirect estimation is that only the delays $D_1, D_2, \ldots,$ and not W_i, $Q(t)$, or $L(t)$, need be collected during the simulation, even if we really want to estimate w, Q, or L.

Example 11.14. The exact asymptotic variance reductions obtained by estimating Q (for example) indirectly with $\tilde{Q}(n)$ rather than directly with $\hat{Q}(n)$ can be calculated for $M/G/1$ queues [see Law (1974)]. Table 11.9 gives these reductions (in percent) for exponential, 4-Erlang, and hyperexponential (see Sec. 4.5) service times, and for $\rho = 0.5$, 0.7, and 0.9.

One weakness of the above indirect-estimation technique is that as $\rho \rightarrow 1$, the variance reductions decrease to 0. This is evident in reading across each row of Table 11.9, and was shown analytically for the $M/G/1$ queue by Law (1974). But since highly congested systems are also highly variable, it is in this case that we need variance reduction the most. A more general use of indirect estimators developed by Carson (1978), which is related to techniques devised by Heidelberger (1980), does better for ρ near 1, and generally achieves stronger variance reductions. Again taking the example of estimating Q, we note that there are two estimators $\hat{Q}(n)$ and $\tilde{Q}(n)$ that could be combined to get a linear-combination estimator $Q(a_1,a_2,n) = a_1\hat{Q}(n) + a_2\tilde{Q}(n)$, where $a_1 + a_2 = 1$; it is not necessary that both a_1 and a_2 be nonnegative. Then a_1 and a_2 could be chosen to minimize $\text{Var}[Q(a_1,a_2,n)]$ subject to the constraint that $a_1 + a_2 = 1$. Note that $Q(1,0,n) = \hat{Q}(n)$ and $Q(0,1,n) = \tilde{Q}(n)$, so that this technique includes both the direct and indirect estimators as special cases; thus,

TABLE 11.9
Exact asymptotic variance reductions for indirect estimation of Q, $M/G/1$ queue

Service-time distribution	Reduction, percent		
	$\rho = 0.5$	$\rho = 0.7$	$\rho = 0.9$
Exponential	15	11	4
4-Erlang	22	17	7
Hyperexponential	4	3	2

for the optimal (a_1, a_2), $\mathrm{Var}[Q(a_1, a_2, n)] \leq \min\{\mathrm{Var}[\hat{Q}(n)], \mathrm{Var}[\tilde{Q}(n)]\}$. As with CV (Sec. 11.4), however, the optimal (a_1, a_2) must be estimated. Carson (1978) gives an asymptotically valid way to do this, based on the regenerative method, and also allows more than two alternative estimators; see the discussion on using multiple estimators in Sec. 11.4. His analytical and empirical studies indicate that variance reductions of at least 40 percent, in comparison with direct estimators, are often achieved.

11.6 CONDITIONING

The final VRT we consider, *conditioning*, shares a feature with indirect estimation in that we exploit some special property of a model to replace an *estimate* of a quantity by its *exact analytical* value. In removing this source of variability, we hope that the final output random variable will be more stable, although there is no absolute guarantee of this; again, pilot studies comparing the conditioning technique with straightforward simulation could indicate whether and to what extent the variance is being reduced. The general conditioning technique as we shall discuss it is in the same spirit as the "conditional Monte Carlo" method treated by Hammersley and Handscomb (1964).

As usual, let X be an output random variable, such as the delay in queue of a customer, whose expectation μ we want to estimate. Suppose that there is some other random variable Z such that, given any particular possible value z for Z, we can analytically compute the *conditional expectation* $E(X|Z=z)$. Note that $E(X|Z=z)$ is a (known) deterministic function of the real number z, but $E(X|Z)$ is a random variable that is this same function of the random variable Z. Then by conditioning on Z [see, e.g., Ross (1989, p. 93)], we see that $\mu = E(X) = E_Z[E(X|Z)]$ (the outer expectation is denoted E_Z since it is taken with respect to the distribution of Z), so that the random variable $E(X|Z)$ is also unbiased for μ. For instance, if Z is discrete with probability mass function $p(z) = P(Z=z)$, then

$$E_Z[E(X|Z)] = \sum_z E(X|Z=z)p(z)$$

where we assume that the $p(z)$'s are unknown. Further,

$$\mathrm{Var}_Z[E(X|Z)] = \mathrm{Var}(X) - E_Z[\mathrm{Var}(X|Z)] \leq \mathrm{Var}(X) \qquad (11.6)$$

[see Ross (1989, p. 131), for example], indicating that if we observe the random variable $E(X|Z)$ (as computed from an observation z on Z), instead of observing X directly, we will get a smaller variance. In other words, it is suggested that we simulate to get a random observation z on Z (since its distribution is not known), plug this observation into the known formula for $E(X|Z=z)$, and use *this* as a basic observation; of course, this entire scheme could then be replicated some number of times in the case of a terminating simulation.

Naturally, the trick here is specifying a random variable Z so that:

- Z can be easily and efficiently generated, since we still have to simulate it
- $E(X \mid Z = z)$ as a function of z can be computed analytically and efficiently for any possible value of z that Z can take on
- $E_Z[\text{Var}(X \mid Z)]$ is large, thus soaking up a lot of $\text{Var}(X)$ in Eq. (11.6). In words, $E_Z[\text{Var}(X \mid Z)]$ is the mean conditional variance of X over the possible values for Z, and since we have a formula for $E(X \mid Z = z)$ we never have to simulate X given Z, so we are not affected by its variance.

Since this VRT is so heavily model-dependent, our illustrations describe two successful implementations from the literature. The following example, taken from Lavenberg and Welch (1979), illustrates conditioning to obtain variance reductions in estimates of several expected delays in a queueing network.

Example 11.15. A time-shared computer model has a single CPU and 15 terminals, as well as a disk drive and a tape drive, as shown in Fig. 11.8. At each terminal sits a user who "thinks" for an exponential amount of time with mean 100 seconds, and then sends a job to the computer where it may join a FIFO queue for the CPU. Each job entering the CPU occupies it for an exponential amount of time with mean 1 second. A job leaving the CPU is finished with probability 0.20 and returns to its terminal to begin another think time; on the other hand, it may need to access the disk drive (with probability 0.72) or the tape drive (probability 0.08) instead. A job going to the disk drive potentially waits in a FIFO queue there, then occupies the drive for an exponential amount of time S_D with mean 1.39 seconds, after which it must go back to the CPU. Similarly, a job going from the CPU to the tape drive faces a FIFO queue there, uses the drive for an exponential amount of time S_T with mean 12.50 seconds, and then returns to the CPU. All think times, service times, and branching decisions are

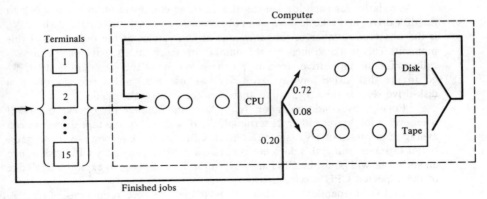

FIGURE 11.8
The time-shared computer model of Example 11.15.

independent, and all jobs are initially in the think state at their terminals. The goal is to estimate d_C, d_D, and d_T, the steady-state expected delays in queue of jobs at the CPU, disk drive, and tape drive, respectively. For this purpose, the run length was taken to be the time required for 400 jobs to be processed and sent back to their terminals.

Straightforward simulation could be used to obtain estimates of these steady-state expected delays by simply using the averages of the delays observed in each of the three queues. However, the number of observations of tape-drive delays could be quite low, since only about 8 percent of the jobs exiting the CPU go there; thus, the straightforward estimator of d_T, being based on relatively little data, could be highly variable.

We can obtain a different estimate of d_T by observing the total number N_T of jobs at the tape drive (in queue and in service) at the instant *each* job leaves the CPU, regardless of where it is going. *Given* that a job leaving the CPU *would* go to the tape drive, its expected delay in queue there *would be* $E(S_T)N_T = 12.50N_T$ seconds. (Since the job in service, if any, at the tape drive has an exponential service time, its *remaining* service time is also exponential with mean 12.50, due to the memoryless property of the exponential distribution, as described in Prob. 4.26. Conditioning is still possible for nonexponential service times but requires more information.) In this way we get an observation on tape-drive delays from *every* job leaving the CPU rather than from just the 8 percent that really go there. Moreover, we use the exact value of $E(S_T) = 12.50$ rather than draws of the random variable S_T that would be generated in a straightforward simulation. The observed values of 12.50 N_T are averaged to get an improved estimate of d_T. This approach is valid since jobs leaving the CPU "see" the same state regardless of whether they actually go to the tape drive.

In terms of our earlier general discussion, we are simulating to observe values of $Z = N_T$ whenever a job leaves the CPU, and E(delay in tape-drive queue$|N_T = z) = 12.50z$, a known deterministic function, given that $N_T = z$. However, the final output variable, the *average* delay in the tape-drive queue, is a more complicated consequence of the entire dynamic simulation, so that Eq. (11.6) does not apply overall. We still hope, though, that some of this "local" variance reduction will propagate through the model's dynamics.

Similarly, for each job leaving the CPU we could condition on its going to the disk drive, and take $1.39N_D$ as an observation on a disk-drive delay, where N_D is the observed number of jobs in queue and in service at the disk drive at this moment. This will also increase the number of observations, but not as dramatically as for the tape drive since nearly three-fourths of the jobs exiting the CPU go to the disk drive anyway. However, we use the known expectation of a disk-drive service time S_D, rather than random observations on it.

Finally, by conditioning on N_C = the total number of jobs at the CPU whenever a job leaves either its terminal, the disk drive, or the tape drive, we can average the values of $1N_C$ (since the mean CPU time is 1 second) to try to get a better estimate of d_C; this does not generate any extra imaginary CPU visits since all such jobs will go to the CPU anyway, but it does allow us to exploit knowledge of the expected CPU service time.

In 100 independent replications, estimated variance reductions of 19, 28, and 56 percent were observed in the estimates of d_C, d_D, and d_T, respectively, in comparison with straightforward simulation. As anticipated, the greatest benefit was for the tape-drive queue, where the conditioning technique led to some 12 times as many observations as observed in the straightforward simulation. Seven other versions of this model were also simulated in which second moments were estimated as well, and variance reductions from conditioning were between 9 and 86 percent, depending on the model and what was being estimated. The additional computing time in the conditioning approach was negligible.

As the preceding example shows, the conditioning VRT requires careful analysis of the model's probabilistic structure. Also, the success was evidently due not only to exploiting knowledge of an analytic formula for conditional expectations, but in addition to increasing the number of observations of a "rare" event artificially, in this case a job's going to the tape drive. These comments apply as well to the success of conditioning in the following example, due to Carter and Ignall (1975).

Example 11.16. A simulation model was developed to compare alternative policies for dispatching fire trucks in the Bronx. Certain fires are classified as "serious," since there is considerable danger that lives will be lost and property damage will be high unless the fire department is able to respond quickly with enough fire trucks. The goal of the simulation was to estimate the expected response time to a serious fire under a given dispatching policy.

Historical data indicated that about 1 of 30 fires is serious. Thus, the model would have to progress through about 30 simulated fires to get a single observation on the response time to a serious fire, which could lead to very long and expensive runs to generate enough serious fires to get a good estimate of the expected response time to them. However, the model's specific structure was such that, given the state of the system (the location of all fire trucks) at any instant, the *true* expected response time to a serious fire could be calculated analytically, should one occur at that instant. Further, the probabilistic assumptions (serious fires occur according to a Poisson process) justified conditioning on the event of a serious fire at *every* instant when the system state was observed regardless of whether a serious fire really did occur [see Wolff (1982)]. Thus, the simulation was interrupted periodically to observe the system state, the expected response time to a serious fire, given the current state, was calculated and recorded, and the simulation was resumed. The final estimator was the average of these conditional expected response times and included many more terms than the number of serious fires actually simulated.

In terms of the general discussion, the purpose of the simulation was to observe a vector Z of locations of fire trucks, and E(response time to a serious fire $|Z = z$) was analytically known as a function of z, so did not have to be estimated in the simulation. The increased frequency of the (imaginary) serious fires over that actually observed is an additional benefit of the approach.

The variance of the estimated expected response time was reduced by some 95 percent with this conditioning approach, in comparison with straightforward simulation. The conditional-expectation approach was somewhat more expensive, but even accounting for this the variance reduction was 92 percent for the same computational effort.

Note that in dynamic simulations, Eq. (11.6) applies directly only to a single random variable and may not be applicable to the simulation's overall output random variables (e.g., the average delay in queue of 1000 customers), so a variance reduction is not guaranteed.

There are several other examples of using the conditioning approach as a VRT that might be helpful. Carter and Ignall (1975) also consider an inventory model where the event on which conditioning occurs is a shortage, which seldom occurs but which has a large impact on system performance when it does happen. Burt and Garman (1971) considered simulation of stochastic PERT networks and conditioned on certain task times that are common to more than one path through the network; in their use of conditioning, the concept of artificially increasing the frequency of a rare event is not present. Further VRTs based on conditioning in stochastic network simulations are discussed by Garman (1972) and by Sigal, Pritsker, and Solberg (1979). A generalization of the method was proposed by Minh (1989) for situations where $E(X|Z = z)$ may be unknown for some values of z.

PROBLEMS

11.1. Some VRTs are nearly costless (e.g., CRN), but others could entail considerable extra cost (e.g., external CV), and this must be taken into account when deciding whether a particular VRT is worth it. Let V_0 be the appropriate variance measure with a straightforward simulation (without using a VRT) and let V_1 be the corresponding variance measure using a particular VRT. Also, let C_0 and C_1 be the costs of making a particular number of runs of a particular length with the straightforward and VRT approaches, respectively. Find conditions on V_0, V_1, C_0, and C_1 for which the VRT would be advisable.

11.2. In Sec. 11.2.2, and specifically in Fig. 11.1, we considered the question of whether CRN would induce the desired positive correlation for a given pair of alternative configurations, or whether it might backfire. Consider the following simple Monte Carlo examples, where U represents a random number:

(1) $X_{1j} = U^2$ and $X_{2j} = U^3$
(2) $X_{1j} = U^2$ and $X_{2j} = (1 - U)^3$

(a) Sketch the graphs of the responses in both examples.
(b) For each example, analytically find $\mathrm{Cov}(X_{1j}, X_{2j})$.
(c) For each example, analytically calculate $\mathrm{Var}(X_{1j} - X_{2j})$ under both independent sampling and CRN.
(d) Confirm your calculations in (b) and (c) empirically by designing and carrying out a small simulation study.

11.3. In Sec. 11.3 we discussed the conditions under which AV would work or backfire. Consider the following simple Monte Carlo examples, where U represents a random number:

(1) $X_j = U^2$
(2) $X_j = 4(U - 0.5)^2$

    (*a*) Sketch the graph of the response in both examples.
    (*b*) For each example, analytically find $\mathrm{Cov}(X_j^{(1)}, X_j^{(2)})$.
    (*c*) For each example, analytically calculate $\mathrm{Var}[(X_j^{(1)} + X_j^{(2)})/2]$ under both independent sampling and AV.
    (*d*) Confirm your calculations in (*b*) and (*c*) empirically by designing and carrying out a small simulation study.

11.4. Consider the queueing model in Fig. 11.9. Customers arrive according to a Poisson process at rate 1 per minute and face a FIFO queue for server 1, who

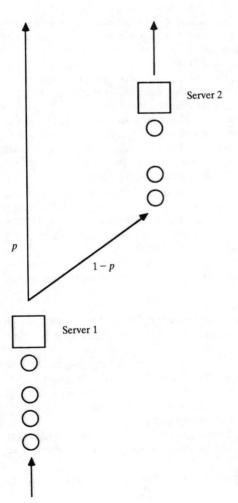

FIGURE 11.9
The queueing model of Prob. 11.4.

provides exponential service with mean 0.7 minute. Upon exiting server 1, customers leave with probability p, and go to server 2 with probability $1 - p$. Server 2 is also fed by a FIFO queue, and provides exponential service with mean 0.9 minute. All service times, interarrival times, and routing decisions are independent, the system is initially empty and idle, and it runs until 100 customers have finished their total delay in queue(s); the total delay in queues of a customer visiting server 2 is the sum of his or her delays in the two queues. The performance measure is the expected average total delay in queue(s) of the first 100 customers to complete their total delay in queue(s).

(a) Suppose there are two configurations of this system, with p being either 0.3 or 0.8. Make 10 replications of each system using both independent sampling and CRN, and compare the estimated variances of the resulting estimate of the difference between the performance measures. Take care to maintain proper synchronization when using CRN.

(b) For $p = 0.3$, make five pairs of runs using both independent sampling and AV within a pair, and compare the estimated variances of the estimated performance measure. Again, pay attention to synchronization.

11.5. Recall the inventory simulation of Sec. 1.5, as used in Example 11.10 to illustrate AV. There are three sources of randomness (interdemand times, demand sizes, and delivery lags), and three cost components (ordering, holding, and shortage). Analyze this model, as programmed in Sec. 1.5, to provide a rationale for AV. Specifically, see what the effect of a small (or large) random number would be on each of the three types of costs if it is used to generate each of the three types of input random variables. For example, suppose that a small U is used to generate an interdemand time. Would this tend to make the ordering cost generally large or small, other things being equal?

11.6. Recall the bank model of Sec. 2.6, and suppose that the bank's management would like an estimate of the effect of adding a sixth teller *and* of adding a seventh teller (in comparison with the current configuration of five tellers) that is better than the results in Fig. 2.36. Use CRN to do this, and make enough replications of the three systems to obtain what you feel are sufficiently precise estimates of the differences in the expectations of the average delays in queue. Consider generating customer service times when the customer arrives, rather than when he or she enters service.

11.7. Recall the harbor model of Prob. 2.19.

(a) Consider using AV for the model as stated originally. Specifically, which input random variates should be generated antithetically, and how could proper synchronization be maintained?

(b) Suppose that thought is being given to replacing the two existing cranes with two faster ones. Specifically, single-crane unloading times for a ship would be distributed uniformly between 0.2 and 1.0 day; everything else remains the same. Discuss proper application and implementation of CRN to compare the original system with the proposed new one.

(c) Carry out the comparative simulations, using both independent sampling and CRN, and replicate as needed to estimate the variance reduction (if any) achieved by CRN.

11.8. Discuss the use of CRN to compare job-processing policies (a) and (b) for the computer model of Prob. 2.20.

11.9. For the two priority policies in the computer model of Prob. 2.22, use CRN to sharpen the comparison between the expected average delay in queue under each policy.

11.10. Consider two $M/G/1$ queues with exponential service times in the first queue and gamma service times in the second, but with the same mean service time. Discuss problems of synchronization of the random numbers in implementing CRN to compare these two queues on the basis, say, of the expected average delay of the first 100 customers given empty and idle initial conditions. Sections 8.2.1 and 8.3.4 may be of use.

11.11. In comparing two system configurations, consider using AV and CRN together, i.e., use AV within a pair of runs of each configuration, and CRN across the configurations. To simplify things, suppose we make just one pair of runs of each configuration, shown schematically below:

	Primary		*Antithetic*
	run		*run*
Configuration 1:	$X_1^{(1)}$	$\leftarrow AV \rightarrow$	$X_1^{(2)}$
	$\uparrow$		$\uparrow$
	CRN		CRN
	$\downarrow$		$\downarrow$
Configuration 2:	$X_2^{(1)}$	$\leftarrow AV \rightarrow$	$X_2^{(2)}$

The estimator of $\zeta = E(X_1^{(l)} - X_2^{(l)})$ is $Z = (X_1^{(1)} + X_1^{(2)})/2 - (X_2^{(1)} + X_2^{(2)})/2$.

(*a*) Find an expression for Var(Z) in terms of the variances and covariances corresponding to the four runs in the above schematic.

(*b*) Assume that both CRN and AV work on their own, i.e., induce correlations of the desired signs. Does the combined scheme then work? That is, do we know that this scheme will reduce Var(Z) in comparison to independent sampling throughout? Explain.

11.12. If $Y_1, Y_2, \ldots$ is a sequence of IID random variables and N is a positive integer-valued random variable that may depend on the Y_i's in some way, then the sample mean of N Y_i's may *not* be unbiased for $\mu = E(Y_i)$. Use this fact to explain why we were careful in the CV examples in Sec. 11.4 to define the CV Y as the average of a *fixed* number of IID random variables, such as interarrival or service times, rather than letting Y be the average of all the interarrival or service times generated by the time the simulation ends.

11.13. For the general linear CV method with m control variates, the variance of the controlled estimator was given in Eq. (11.3), where the weights a_i must be specified.

(*a*) Find the optimal (i.e., variance-minimizing) weights for the cases $m = 2$ and 3.

(*b*) Assuming that the control variates are uncorrelated with each other, find the optimal weights for any m.

(*c*) For both cases (*a*) and (*b*) above, give a method for estimating the optimal weights. If we know the variances of the control variates (as we might if they are just averages of input variates), could your estimators be improved? In (*a*), what if we also know the covariances between the control variates?

11.14. Suppose that we want to estimate the expected average delay in queue of the first 100 customers in a FIFO $M/G/1$ queue where the initial conditions are empty and idle, the mean interarrival time is 1 minute, and service times have a Weibull distribution with shape parameter $\alpha = 2$ and scale parameter $\beta = 1.8/\sqrt{\pi}$ minutes. Thus, the mean service time is $\beta\Gamma[(1/\alpha) + 1] = (1.8/\sqrt{\pi})(\sqrt{\pi}/2) = 0.9$ minute (see Sec. 6.2.2), and the utilization factor is $\rho = 0.9$. (See Sec. 8.3.5 for Weibull-variate generation, which is easily done by the inverse-transform method.) As an external control variate, we could use CRN to simulate the $M/M/1$ queue for 100 customers with the same mean interarrival and service times, which is precisely the model of Example 11.11, and use the fact that the *known* expected average delay in queue for this $M/M/1$ queue is 4.13. Use the estimation technique given in Sec. 11.4 to estimate the optimal weight a^* from $n = 10$ replications, and repeat the whole process 100 times to estimate the variance reduction in comparison with straightforward simulation of this $M/G/1$ queue. Is the variance reduction worthwhile, or should the computing time needed to simulate the $M/M/1$ queue be devoted instead to making additional direct replications of this $M/G/1$ queue?

11.15. Discuss proper use of AV for the time-shared computer model of Sec. 2.5. For alternative designs of this model (such as buying a faster CPU or changing the service quantum), how could CRN be appropriately applied for making comparative simulations?

11.16. Does allowing jockeying as described in the multiteller bank of Sec. 2.6 affect customers' average delay in queue(s)? To find out, regard the original model (with jockeying) as "configuration 1" and define "configuration 2" to be this same model but without any jockeying allowed; assume five tellers in each case. Use dedicated streams to facilitate CRN—stream 1 for interarrival times and stream 2 for service times. However, it is not exactly obvious how we should generate the service times from stream 2; there are (at least) the following two possibilities:

(*a*) A customer's service time is generated when he arrives and is stored with him as an attribute. This corresponds physically to the idea of forcing the "same" customers (in terms of their service demands on the tellers) to arrive to both configurations at the same times.

(*b*) Generate a service time from stream 2 only when a customer begins service. In this case, the two configurations will not see the same customers, but the ordered sequence of service times begun for both configurations will be identical.

Carry out a simulation experiment to investigate whether (*a*) or (*b*) is a better way to implement CRN, in terms of the variance of the estimator of the difference between the expected average delay in queue(s) in the two configurations.

REFERENCES

Andréasson, I. J.: Antithetic Methods in Queueing Simulations, Roy. Inst. Technol. Dept. Comput. Sci. Tech. Rep. NA 72.58, Stockholm (1972).

Bauer, K. W.: Control Variate Selection for Multiresponse Simulation, Ph.D. Dissertation, School of Industrial Engineering, Purdue University, West Lafayette, Ind. (1987).

Bauer, K. W., and J. R. Wilson: Control-Variate Selection Criteria, Tech. Rep. SMS 89-29, School of Industrial Engineering, Purdue University, West Lafayette, Ind. (1989).

Bratley, P., B. L. Fox, and L. Schrage: *A Guide to Simulation*, 2d ed., Springer-Verlag, New York (1987).

Burt, J. M., Jr., and M. B. Garman: Conditional Monte Carlo: A Simulation Technique for Stochastic Network Analysis, *Management Sci.*, *18*: 207–217 (1971).

Burt, J. M., Jr., D. P. Gaver, and M. Perlas: Simple Stochastic Networks: Some Problems and Procedures, *Naval Res. Logist. Quart.*, *17*: 439–459 (1970).

Carson, J. S.: Variance Reduction Techniques for Simulated Queueing Processes, Univ. Wis. Dept. Ind. Eng. Tech. Rep. 78-8, Madison (1978).

Carson, J. S., and A. M. Law: Conservation Equations and Variance Reduction in Queueing Simulations, *Operations Res.*, *28*: 535–546 (1980).

Carter, G., and E. J. Ignall: Virtual Measures: A Variance Reduction Technique for Simulation, *Management Sci.*, *21*: 607–616 (1975).

Cheng, R. C. H.: The Use of Antithetic Variates in Computer Simulations, *J. Operational Res. Soc.*, *33*: 229–237 (1982).

Cheng, R. C. H.: Antithetic Variate Methods for Simulation of Processes with Peaks and Troughs, *Eur. J. Operational Res.*, *15*: 227–236 (1984).

Cheng, R. C. H., and G. M. Feast: Control Variables with Known Mean and Variance, *J. Operational Res. Soc.*, *31*: 51–56 (1980).

Fishman, G. S., and B. D. Huang: Antithetic Variates Revisited, *Commun. Assoc. Comput. Mach.*, *26*: 964–971 (1983).

Franta, W. R.: A Note on Random Variate Generators and Antithetic Sampling, *INFOR*, *13*: 112–117 (1975).

Gal, S., R. Y. Rubinstein, and A. Ziv: On the Optimality and Efficiency of Common Random Numbers, *Math. Comput. Simul.*, *26*: 502–512 (1984).

Garman, M. B.: More on Conditioned Sampling in the Simulation of Stochastic Networks, *Management Sci.*, *19*: 90–95 (1972).

Gaver, D. P., and G. S. Shedler: Control Variable Methods in the Simulation of a Model of a Multiprogrammed Computer System, *Naval Res. Logist. Quart.*, *18*: 435–450 (1971).

Gaver, D. P., and G. L. Thompson: *Programming and Probability Models*, Wadsworth, Monterey, Calif. (1973).

George, L. L.: Variance Reduction for a Replacement Process, *Simulation*, *29*: 65–74 (1977).

Glynn, P. W., and W. Whitt: Indirect Estimation Via $L = \lambda w$, *Operations Res.*, *37*: 82–103 (1989).

Hammersley, J. M., and D. C. Handscomb: *Monte Carlo Methods*, Methuen, London (1964).

Hammersley, J. M., and K. W. Morton: A New Monte Carlo Technique: Antithetic Variates, *Proc. Camb. Phil. Soc.*, *52*: 449–475 (1956).

Heidelberger, P.: Variance Reduction Techniques for the Simulation of Markov Processes, I: Multiple Estimates, *IBM J. Res. Develop.*, *24*: 570–581 (1980).

Heidelberger, P., and D. L. Iglehart: Comparing Stochastic Systems Using Regenerative Simulation with Common Random Numbers, *Adv. Appl. Prob.*, 11: 804–819 (1979).

Heikes, R. G., D. C. Montgomery, and R. L. Rardin: Using Common Random Numbers in Simulation Experiments—An Approach to Statistical Analysis, *Simulation*, 25: 81–85 (1976).

Iglehart, D. L., and P. A. W. Lewis: Regenerative Simulation with Internal Controls, *J. Assoc. Comput. Mach.*, *26*: 271–282 (1979).

Kleijnen, J. P. C.: *Statistical Techniques in Simulation*, Pt. I, Marcel Dekker, New York (1974).

Kleijnen, J. P. C.: Analysis of Simulation with Common Random Numbers: A Note on Heikes et al. (1976), *Simuletter*, *11*: 7–13 (1979).

Koenig, L. W., and A. M. Law: A Procedure for Selecting a Subset of Size *m* Containing the *l* Best of *k* Independent Normal Populations, with Applications to Simulation, Tech. Rep. 82-9, Department of Management Information Systems, University of Arizona, Tucson (1982).

Lavenberg, S. S., T. L. Moeller, and C. H. Sauer: Concomitant Control Variables Applied to the Regenerative Simulation of Queueing Systems, *Operations Res.*, *27*: 134–160 (1979).

Lavenberg, S. S., T. L. Moeller, and P. D. Welch: Statistical Results on Control Variables with Application to Queueing Network Simulation, *Operations Res.*, *30*: 182–202 (1982).

Lavenberg, S. S., and P. D. Welch: Using Conditional Expectation to Reduce Variance in Discrete Event Simulation, *Proc. 1979 Winter Simulation Conference*, San Diego, pp. 291–294 (1979).

Lavenberg, S. S., and P. D. Welch: A Perspective on the Use of Control Variables to Increase the Efficiency of Monte Carlo Simulations, *Management Sci.*, *27*: 322–335 (1981).

Law, A. M.: Efficient Estimators for Simulated Queueing Systems, Univ. Calif. Oper. Res. Cent. ORC 74-7, Berkeley (1974).

Law, A. M.: Efficient Estimators for Simulated Queueing Systems, *Management Sci.*, *22*: 30–41 (1975).

Minh, D. L.: A Variant of the Conditional Expectation Variance Reduction Technique and Its Application to the Simulation of the *GI/G/*1 Queues, *Management Sci.*, *35*: 1334–1340 (1989).

Mitchell, B.: Variance Reduction by Antithetic Variates in *GI/G/*1 Queueing Simulations, *Operations Res.*, *21*: 988–997 (1973).

Morgan, B. J. T.: *Elements of Simulation*, Chapman & Hall, London (1984).

Nelson, B. L.: A Decomposition Approach to Variance Reduction, *Proc. 1985 Winter Simulation Conference*, San Francisco, pp. 23–33 (1985).

Nelson, B. L.: Decomposition of Some Well-Known Variance Reduction Techniques, *J. Statist. Comput. Simul.*, *23*: 183–209 (1986).

Nelson, B. L.: A Perspective on Variance Reduction in Dynamic Simulation Experiments, *Commun. Statist.*, *B16*: 385–426 (1987a)

Nelson, B. L.: Some Properties of Simulation Interval Estimators under Dependence Induction, *Operations Res. Lett.*, *6*: 169–176 (1987b)

Nelson, B. L.: Variance Reduction for Simulation Practitioners, *Proc. 1987 Winter Simulation Conference*, Atlanta, pp. 43–51 (1987c).

Nelson, B. L.: Control-Variate Remedies, *Operations Res.*, *38*: (1990a).

Nelson, B. L.: Variance Reduction in the Presence of Initial-Condition Bias, *IIE Trans.*, *22*: (1990b).

Nozari, A., S. F. Arnold, and C. D. Pegden: Statistical Analysis with the Schruben and Margolin Correlation Induction Strategy, *Operations Res.*, *35*: 127–139 (1987).

Page, E. S.: On Monte Carlo Methods in Congestion Problems: II. Simulation of Queueing Systems, *Operations Res.*, *13*: 300–305 (1965).

Ross, S. M.: *Introduction to Probability Models*, 4th ed., Academic Press, San Diego (1989).

Rubinstein, R. Y., and R. Marcus: Efficiency of Multivariate Control Variates in Monte Carlo Simulation, *Operations Res.*, *33*: 661–667 (1985).

Rubinstein, R. Y., G. Samorodnitsky, and M. Shaked: Antithetic Variates, Multivariate Dependence, and Simulation of Complex Stochastic Systems, *Management Sci.*, *31*: 66–77 (1985).

Schmeiser, B. W., and V. Kachitvichyanukul: Correlation Induction without the Inverse Transform, *Proc. 1986 Winter Simulation Conference*, Washington, D.C., pp. 266–274 (1986).

Schruben, L. W.: Designing Correlation Induction Strategies for Simulation Experiments, *Current Issues in Computer Simulation*, N. R. Adam and A. Dogramici, eds., chap. 16, Academic Press, New York (1979).

Schruben, L. W., and B. H. Margolin: Pseudorandom Number Assignment in Statistically Designed Simulation and Distribution Sampling Experiments, *J. Am. Statist. Assoc.*, *73*: 504–520 (1978).

Sigal, C. E., A. A. B. Pritsker, and J. J. Solberg: The Use of Cutsets in Monte Carlo Analysis of Stochastic Networks, *Math. Comput. Simul.*, *21*: 376–384 (1979).

Venkatraman, S., and J. R. Wilson: The Efficiency of Control Variates in Multiresponse Simulation, *Operations Res. Lett.*, *5*: 37–42 (1986).

Wilson, J. R.: Proof of the Antithetic-Variates Theorem for Unbounded Functions, *Math. Proc. Camb. Phil. Soc.*, *86*: 477–479 (1979).

Wilson, J. R.: Antithetic Sampling with Multivariate Inputs, *Am. J. Math. Management Sci.*, *3*: 121–144 (1983).

Wilson, J. R.: Variance Reduction Techniques for Digital Simulation, *Am. J. Math. Management Sci.*, *4*: 277–312 (1984).

Wilson, J. R., and A. A. B. Pritsker: Variance Reduction in Queueing Simulation Using Generalized Concomitant Variables, *J. Statist. Comput. Simul.*, *19*: 129–153 (1984a).

Wilson, J. R., and A. A. B. Pritsker: Experimental Evaluation of Variance Reduction Techniques for Queueing Simulation Using Generalized Concomitant Variables, *Management Sci.*, *30*: 1459–1472 (1984b).

Wolff, R. W.: Poisson Arrivals See Time Averages, *Operations Res.*, *30*: 223–231 (1982).

Wright, R. D., and T. E. Ramsay, Jr.: On the Effectiveness of Common Random Numbers, *Management Sci.*, 25: 649–656 (1979).

CHAPTER
12

EXPERIMENTAL DESIGN AND OPTIMIZATION

Recommended sections for a first reading: 12.1 12.2, 12.3.1

12.1 INTRODUCTION

This chapter provides an introduction to the use of statistical experimental design and optimization techniques when the "experiment" is the execution of a computer simulation model. As in Chap. 10, we shall be discussing simulations of alternative system configurations and examining and comparing their results. In Chap. 10, however, we assumed that the various configurations were simply *given*, having been externally specified as *the* alternatives, perhaps based on physical constraints, contractual obligations, or political considerations. This chapter, on the other hand, deals with a situation in which there is less structure in the goal of the simulation study; we might want to find out which of possibly many parameters and structural assumptions have the greatest effect on a performance measure, or which set of model specifications appears to lead to optimal performance. For these broader (and more ambitious) objectives, we may not be able to carry out formal statistical analyses like those of Chap. 10 or make such precise probabilistic statements at the end of our analyses.

656

In experimental-design terminology, the input parameters and structural assumptions composing a model are called *factors*, and the output performance measures are called *responses*. The decision as to which parameters and structural assumptions are considered fixed aspects of a model and which are experimental factors depends on the goals of the study rather than on the inherent form of the model. Also, in simulation studies there are usually several different responses or performance measures of interest.

Factors can be either *quantitative* or *qualitative*. Quantitative factors naturally assume numerical values, while qualitative factors typically represent structural assumptions that are not naturally quantified; see Table 12.1 for some examples, and note that the distinction may not be clear for certain factors.

We can also classify factors in simulation experiments as being *controllable* or *uncontrollable*, depending on whether they represent action options to managers of the corresponding real-world system. Examples are given in Table 12.1, where a factor's controllability may depend on the particulars of the situation; it may or may not be possible to change, for instance, the buffer sizes in a factory. Usually we shall focus on controllable factors in simulation experiments, since they are most relevant to decisions that must be made about implementation of real-world systems. However, Biles (1979) pointed out that uncontrollable factors might also be of interest in simulation experiments; e.g., we might want to assess how an abrupt increase in the arrival rate of customers would affect congestion. In a mathematical-modeling activity such as simulation we do, after all, get to control *everything*, regardless of actual real-world controllability.

In simulation, *experimental design* provides a way of deciding before the runs are made which particular configurations to simulate so that the desired information can be obtained with the least amount of simulating. Carefully designed experiments are much more efficient than a "hit-or-miss" sequence of runs in which we simply try a number of alternative configurations unsystematically to see what happens. The designs we discuss in Secs. 12.2 and 12.3 are particularly useful in the early stages of experimentation, when we are pretty much in the dark about which factors are important and how they might affect the responses. As we learn more about the model's behavior (in particular, which factors really matter and how they appear to be affecting the responses), we may want to move on and become more precise in our goals; for instance, one often seeks *optimal* combinations of factor levels that maximize or minimize a response. A whole variety of techniques known as *metamodeling* and *response-surface methodologies* discussed in Sec. 12.4 can then be used to make progress toward these kinds of goals. The related topic of *gradient estimation and sensitivity*, where we try to quantify how the responses react to small changes in the quantitative factors, is mentioned in Sec. 12.5.

Although one can think of simulation experiments as just an instance of experimentation in general, there are some advantageous peculiarities about simulation that distinguish it from the usual physical industrial, laboratory, or

TABLE 12.1
Examples of factors and responses

System	Possible factors	Quantitative?	Qualitative?	Controllable?	Uncontrollable?	Possible responses
Supermarket checkout facility	Mean interarrival time	✓			✓	Delay in queue
	Mean service time	✓				Time in system
	Number of physical lanes	✓		✓?	✓?	Queue lengths
	Presence of express lanes		✓	✓		Checker utilizations
	Checker adding/removing policy	✓?	✓?	✓		Add/remove frequency
Manufacturing line	Number of machines	✓		✓?	✓?	Parts throughput
	Queue discipline		✓	✓?	✓?	Time in system
	Buffer sizes	✓		✓?	✓?	Machine utilizations
	Conveyor speeds	✓		✓?	✓?	Profitability
	Machine groupings into cells		✓	✓?	✓?	
Computer installation	Number of terminals	✓		✓?	✓?	User response times
	Disk-drive capacity	✓		✓?	✓?	CPU utilization
	CPU speed	✓		✓?	✓?	Disk utilization
	Arrival rate of jobs	✓			✓	Job throughput
	Policy for job-class specification	✓?	✓?	✓		Downtime
	Rate structure	✓?	✓?	✓		Profitability
Communication network	Message arrival rates	✓			✓	Message delays
	Message durations	✓			✓	Message throughput
	Number of nodes	✓		✓?	✓?	System reliability
	Number of links	✓		✓?	✓?	Profitability
	Protocol used		✓	✓?		
	Maintenance policy		✓	✓		
Inventory system	Mean interdemand time	✓			✓	Holding cost
	Number of items demanded	✓			✓	Shortage cost
	Lead time from supplier	✓		✓?	✓?	Ordering cost
	Reorder point	✓		✓		Profitability
	Reorder amount	✓		✓		Backlogged/lost orders
	Inventory-evaluation frequency	✓		✓?		
	Backlog vs. lost sales		✓	✓?	✓?	

agricultural experiments traditionally used as examples in the experimental-design literature:

- As mentioned earlier, we have the opportunity to control factors such as customer arrival rates that are in reality uncontrollable. Thus, we can investigate many more kinds of contingencies than we could in a physical experiment with the system.
- Another aspect of enhanced control over simulation experiments stems from the deterministic nature of random-number generators (see Chap. 7). In simulation experiments, then, we can control the basic source of variability, unlike the situation in physical experiments. Thus, we might be able to use variance-reduction techniques (Chap. 11) to sharpen our conclusions, although care must be taken to avoid potential backfiring (see the discussion following Example 12.2, as well as Prob. 12.3). Hussey, Myers, and Houck (1987) studied the effect of common random numbers and antithetic variates on certain types of experimental designs as applied to simulation.
- In most physical experiments it is prudent to randomize treatments (factor combinations) and run orders (the sequence in which the treatments are applied) to protect against systematic variation contributed by experimental conditions, such as a steady rise in ambient laboratory temperature during a sequence of biological experiments that are not thermally isolated. Randomizing in simulation experimentation, though, is not necessary, assuming that the random-number generator is working properly.

   This chapter is by no means intended to be a complete treatment of experimental design or optimization; whole books are devoted to this subject. We only hope to introduce some of the relevant topics, and illustrate how they can be used in simulation experiments. Some general texts are Box and Draper (1987), Box, Hunter, and Hunter (1978), Khuri and Cornell (1987), Montgomery (1984), and Myers (1971). References generally treating experimental design, sensitivity, and optimization in the simulation context include Hunter and Naylor (1970), Ignall (1972), Kleijnen (1975, 1977, 1982, 1987), and Rubinstein (1986).

12.2 2^k FACTORIAL DESIGNS

If a model has only one factor, the experimental design is conceptually simple: We just run the simulation at various values, or *levels*, of the factor, perhaps forming a confidence interval for the expected response at each of the factor levels. For quantitative factors, a graph of the response as a function of the factor level may be useful. In the case of terminating simulations (Sec. 9.4), we would make some number n of independent replications at each factor level. At the minimum there would be two factor levels, and we would thus need $2n$ replications; methods for reducing this effort are mentioned in Sec. 12.5.

Now suppose that there are k ($k \geq 2$) factors and we want to get an initial estimate of how each factor affects the responses. We might also like to determine whether the factors *interact* with each other, i.e., whether the effect of one factor depends on the levels of the others. One way to measure the effect of a particular factor would be to fix the levels of the *other* $k - 1$ factors at some set of values and make simulation runs for each of several levels of the factor of interest to see how the response reacts to changes in this single factor. The whole process is then repeated to examine each of the other factors, one at a time. Such a strategy turns out to be quite inefficient in terms of the number of simulation runs needed [see Box, Hunter, and Hunter (1978, pp. 312–313)] and, furthermore, does not allow us to measure any interactions; indeed, it assumes that there are no interactions.

A much more economical strategy with which we can also measure interactions, called a 2^k *factorial design*, requires that we choose just *two* levels for each factor and then calls for simulation runs at each of the 2^k possible factor-level combinations, which are sometimes called *design points*. Usually we associate a minus sign with one level of a factor and a plus sign with the other; which sign is associated with which level is arbitrary, although for quantitative factors it may be less confusing if we associate the minus sign with the lower numerical value. No general prescription can be given for how one should specify the levels. We hope that the analyst will have some intuitive feel for the model that will allow specification of reasonable values for the quantitative factors and meaningful options for the qualitative factors. The form of the experiment can be compactly represented in tabular form, as in Table 12.2 for $k = 3$. The variables R_i for $i = 1, 2, \ldots, 8$ are the values of the response when running the simulation with the ith combination of factor levels. For instance, R_6 is the response resulting from running the simulation with factors 1 and 3 at their respective "+" levels and factor 2 at its "−" level. We shall see later that writing down this array, called the *design matrix*, facilitates calculation of the factor effects and interactions.

TABLE 12.2
Design matrix for a 2^3 factorial design

Factor combination (design point)	Factor 1	Factor 2	Factor 3	Response
1	−	−	−	R_1
2	+	−	−	R_2
3	−	+	−	R_3
4	+	+	−	R_4
5	−	−	+	R_5
6	+	−	+	R_6
7	−	+	+	R_7
8	+	+	+	R_8

The *main effect* of factor j is the average *change* in the response due to moving factor j from its "$-$" level to its "$+$" level while holding all other factors fixed. This average is taken over all combinations of the other factor levels in the design. It is important to realize that a main effect is computed relative to the *current* design and factor levels only, and we cannot generally extrapolate beyond this unless other conditions (no interactions, as we shall see) are satisfied. These limitations on the interpretation of main effects are discussed later in this section as well as in Sec. 12.3.1.

For the 2^3 factorial design of Table 12.2, the main effect of factor 1 is thus

$$e_1 = \frac{(R_2 - R_1) + (R_4 - R_3) + (R_6 - R_5) + (R_8 - R_7)}{4}$$

Note that at design points 1 and 2, factors 2 and 3 remain fixed, as they do at design points 3 and 4, 5 and 6, as well as 7 and 8. The main effect of factor 2 is

$$e_2 = \frac{(R_3 - R_1) + (R_4 - R_2) + (R_7 - R_5) + (R_8 - R_6)}{4}$$

and that of factor 3 is

$$e_3 = \frac{(R_5 - R_1) + (R_6 - R_2) + (R_7 - R_3) + (R_8 - R_4)}{4}$$

Looking at Table 12.2 and the above expressions for the e_j's leads to an alternative way of defining main effects, as well as a simpler way of computing them. Namely, e_j is the *difference* between the average response when factor j is at its "$+$" level and the average response when it is at its "$-$" level. Thus, to compute e_j we simply apply the signs in the "Factor j" column to the corresponding R_i's, add them up, and divide by 2^{k-1}. (In other words, if we interpret the "$+$"'s and "$-$"'s in the design matrix as $+1$ and -1, respectively, we take the dot product of the "Factor j" column with the "Response" column and then divide by 2^{k-1}.) For example, in the 2^3 factorial design of Table 12.2,

$$e_2 = \frac{-R_1 - R_2 + R_3 + R_4 - R_5 - R_6 + R_7 + R_8}{4}$$

which is identical to the earlier expression for e_2.

The main effects measure the *average* change in the response due to a change in an individual factor, with this average being taken over all possible combinations of the other $k - 1$ factors (numbering 2^{k-1}). It could be, though, that the effect of factor j_1 depends in some way on the level of some other factor j_2, in which case these two factors are said to *interact*. We measure the degree of this interaction by the *two-factor* (or *two-way*) *interaction effect*, $e_{j_1 j_2}$, defined as *half* the difference between the average effect of factor j_1 when factor j_2 is at its "$+$" level (and all factors other than j_1 and j_2 are held constant) and the average effect of j_1 when j_2 is at its "$-$" level. ($e_{j_1 j_2}$ is also called the $j_1 \times j_2$ *interaction*.) For example, in the design of Table 12.2 we have

$$e_{12} = \frac{1}{2} \left[\frac{(R_4 - R_3) + (R_8 - R_7)}{2} - \frac{(R_2 - R_1) + (R_6 - R_5)}{2} \right]$$

$$e_{13} = \frac{1}{2} \left[\frac{(R_6 - R_5) + (R_8 - R_7)}{2} - \frac{(R_2 - R_1) + (R_4 - R_3)}{2} \right]$$

and

$$e_{23} = \frac{1}{2} \left[\frac{(R_7 - R_5) + (R_8 - R_6)}{2} - \frac{(R_3 - R_1) + (R_4 - R_2)}{2} \right]$$

As with main effects, there is an easier way to compute interaction effects, based on the design matrix. If we rearrange the above expression for e_{13}, for instance, so that the R_i's appear in increasing order of the i's, we get

$$e_{13} = \frac{R_1 - R_2 + R_3 - R_4 - R_5 + R_6 - R_7 + R_8}{4}$$

Now if we create a new column labeled "1×3" of 8 signs by "multiplying" the ith sign in the "Factor 1" column by the ith sign in the "Factor 3" column (the product of like signs is a "$+$" and the product of opposite signs is a "$-$"), we get a column of signs that gives us precisely the signs of the R_i's used to form e_{13}; as with main effects, the divisor is 2^{k-1}. Thus, the interaction effect between factors 1 and 3 can be thought of as the difference between the average response when factors 1 and 3 are at the same (both "$+$" or both "$-$") level and the average response when they are at opposite levels. (We leave it to the reader to compute e_{12} and e_{23} in this way.) Note that two-factor interaction effects are completely symmetric; for example, $e_{12} = e_{21}$, $e_{23} = e_{32}$, etc.

Although interpretation becomes more difficult, we can define and compute three- and higher-factor interaction effects, all the way up to a k-factor interaction. For example, in the 2^3 factorial design of Table 12.2, the three-factor interaction is half the difference between the average two-factor interaction effect between factors 1 and 2 when factor 3 is at its "$+$" level and the average two-factor interaction effect between factors 1 and 2 when factor 3 is at its "$-$" level. That is,

$$e_{123} = \frac{1}{2} \left[\frac{(R_8 - R_7) - (R_6 - R_5)}{2} - \frac{(R_4 - R_3) - (R_2 - R_1)}{2} \right]$$

$$= \frac{-R_1 + R_2 + R_3 - R_4 + R_5 - R_6 - R_7 + R_8}{4}$$

The second expression for e_{123} is obtained by multiplying the ith signs from the columns for factors 1, 2, and 3 in Table 12.2 and applying them to the R_i's; the denominator is once again 2^{k-1}. Three- and higher-factor interaction effects are also symmetric: $e_{123} = e_{132} = e_{213}$, etc.

In the following example we perform a 2^2 factorial experiment with the inventory model introduced in Sec. 1.5 and used in several examples in Chap. 10.

TABLE 12.3
**Coding chart for s and d in
the inventory model**

Factor	−	+
s	20	60
d	10	50

Example 12.1. It is convenient to reparameterize the inventory model of Sec. 1.5 slightly in terms of the ordering policy. Specifically, we let s be the "reorder point" as before, but instead of ordering "up to S" we will instead view our decision in terms of the *order quantity* $d = S - s$. In other words, our experimental factors are s and d and our interest is in how they affect the expected average total operating cost; of course, S would always be just $s + d$. The "low" and "high" levels we chose for these factors are given in the *coding chart* in Table 12.3. The design matrix and corresponding response variables are given in Table 12.4, together with an extra column giving the signs to be applied in computing the $s \times d$ interaction. Each R_i is the average total cost per month from a single 120-month replication; we used independent random-number streams for each separate R_i. The main effects are

$$e_s = \frac{-141.86 + 141.37 - 112.45 + 146.52}{2} = 16.79$$

and

$$e_d = \frac{-141.86 - 141.37 + 112.45 + 146.52}{2} = -12.13$$

and the $s \times d$ interaction effect is

$$e_{sd} = \frac{141.86 - 141.37 - 112.45 + 146.52}{2} = 17.28$$

Thus, the average effect of raising s from 20 to 60 was to increase the monthly cost by 16.79, and raising d from 10 to 50 decreased the monthly cost by an average of 12.13. Therefore, it appears that the smaller value of s and the larger value of d would be preferable, since lower monthly costs are desired. Since the $s \times d$ interaction is positive, there is further indication that lower costs are observed by setting s and d at opposite levels.

TABLE 12.4
**Design matrix and simulation results for the 2^2 factorial design on s and
d for the inventory model**

Factor combination (design point)	s	d	$s \times d$	Response
1	−	−	+	141.86
2	+	−	−	141.37
3	−	+	−	112.45
4	+	+	+	146.52

Since the R_i's are random variables, the effects are also random. To find out whether the effects are "real," as opposed to being explainable by random fluctuation, we must estimate their variances. Several methods could be used [see, for example, Box, Hunter, and Hunter (1978, pp. 319–322)]; a very simple approach for simulation experiments is just to replicate the *whole design* n times and obtain n independent values of each effect. These can then be used to form approximate $100(1 - \alpha)$ percent confidence intervals for the *expected* effects using the t distribution with $n - 1$ df, from (4.12). If the confidence interval for a particular effect does not contain zero, we conclude that this effect is real; otherwise we have no statistical evidence that it is actually present. As usual, larger values of n reduce confidence-interval width, making it easier to resolve that an effect is real. We must also bear in mind that *statistical* significance of an effect does not necessarily imply that its magnitude is *practically* significant.

> **Example 12.2.** We replicated the entire 2^2 factorial design of the inventory model in Example 12.1 $n = 10$ times and thus got 10 independent replicates of each of the three effects. The sample mean of the 10 main effects of s was $\bar{e}_s(10) = 17.66$ and the estimate of $\text{Var}[\bar{e}_s(10)]$ was 0.31, so that an approximate 90 percent confidence interval for $E(e_s)$ is 17.66 ± 1.02 and the main effect of s appears to be statistically significant. Similarly, an approximate 90 percent confidence interval for $E(e_d)$ is -8.73 ± 1.27 and that for $E(e_{sd})$ is 10.60 ± 1.94. Therefore, from these 10 replications, all effects appear to be real; whether the magnitudes of these *statistically* significant effects carry *practical* significance would be a matter of judgment for someone familiar with the system and its environment.

In Examples 12.1 and 12.2 we carried out the simulations across the four different factor combinations independently. Since we are dealing with four different configurations here, we could have used common random numbers (CRN) instead (see Sec. 11.2) across all four of them in an attempt to reduce the half-lengths of the confidence intervals on the expected effects. However, the situation here is not as simple as that in Sec. 11.2. If CRN in fact "works" and induces the desired positive correlations between the responses of the different configurations, certain covariances enter the expression for the variance of an effect with the wrong sign; the variance could thus increase or decrease depending on the relative magnitudes of the covariances and on which effect is involved (see Prob. 12.3). Indeed, we reran the experiment in Example 12.2 using CRN and found that the confidence-interval half-lengths for $E(e_d)$ and $E(e_{sd})$ were reduced (to 0.48 and 0.71, respectively), but that for $E(e_s)$ was increased (to 1.22). This phenomenon is an instance of the whole issue of random-number allocation in simulation raised originally by Schruben and Margolin (1978); see also Hussey, Myers, and Houck (1987).

Our last example in this section concerns a more elaborate model with a larger number of factors. It also illustrates the computational burden that can occur when applying 2^k factorial designs to mere "textbook" models, an issue we will address further in Sec. 12.3.

Example 12.3. In Example 9.25 a model of a small factory was introduced in which parts arrive for machining and then go on to be inspected; parts failing inspection are returned to the machining station for rework (see Fig. 9.6). The machine also experiences breakdowns and then must undergo repair. The model runs for 160 hours, from which the first 40 hours are deleted to allow the model to warm up to steady state. We take as our responses the average time a part spends in the system (sometimes called the *makespan*), and the average length of the queue for the inspection station, since there may be concern about having adequate floor space there. We do not consider throughput, since it will be 60 parts per hour for any well-defined system configuration. Parts arrive according to a Poisson process at rate 1 per minute, which we assume is uncontrollable and will not include in our design as an experimental factor. There are six other factors that could be controllable, as given in Table 12.5. For each factor, the "−" level is the current situation, as described in Example 9.25, and the "+" level represents what is felt would be an improvement, at least in terms of reducing the average time in system of parts. Note that in all but one case the numerical parameters at the "+" level are actually smaller than their counterparts at the "−" level, violating our earlier advice; but by coding in this way each main effect will be the consequence of the corresponding purported improvement. Factors 1 through 5 are quantitative, and the "+" level in each case constitutes a 10 percent improvement; factor 6 is qualitative and represents changing the discipline in each of the two queues from FIFO to shortest job first in terms of their actual machining or inspection times.

Table 12.6 is the complete design matrix for the 2^6 factorial design, and requires 64 different design points. We replicated this entire design $n = 5$ times to get confidence intervals on the expected effects, as in Example 12.2, so that there were in all 320 separate simulation runs for the experiment. We used the SIMAN simulation language (Sec. 3.6), and it turned out to be most convenient to use CRN across all 64 design points. The experiment was done on an IBM PS/2 Model 50Z microcomputer, and ran for about 12 hours.

Figure 12.1 plots both responses' individual replications as the small dots, so there are five of them distributed vertically over each design point. The large dots show the average of the five replications at each design point, and the horizontal lines give the overall average of each response, i.e., the average of all 320 individual-replication results. Several observations can be made directly from these graphs:

TABLE 12.5
Factor coding, small-factory model (all times are in minutes)

Factor number	Factor description	−(current)	+(improved)
1	Machining times	U(0.65,0.70)	U(0.585,0.630)
2	Inspection times	U(0.75,0.80)	U(0.675,0.720)
3	Machine uptimes	expo(360)	expo(396)
4	Machine repair times	U(8,12)	U(7.2,10.8)
5	Probability of a bad part	0.10	0.09
6	Queue disciplines (both)	FIFO	Shortest job first

TABLE 12.6
Design matrix for the 2⁶ factorial design, small-factory model

Design point	\(1\)	\(2\)	\(3\)	\(4\)	\(5\)	\(6\)
	\multicolumn{6}{c}{Factor number}					
1	−	−	−	−	−	−
2	+	−	−	−	−	−
3	−	+	−	−	−	−
4	+	+	−	−	−	−
5	−	−	+	−	−	−
6	+	−	+	−	−	−
7	−	+	+	−	−	−
8	+	+	+	−	−	−
9	−	−	−	+	−	−
10	+	−	−	+	−	−
11	−	+	−	+	−	−
12	+	+	−	+	−	−
13	−	−	+	+	−	−
14	+	−	+	+	−	−
15	−	+	+	+	−	−
16	+	+	+	+	−	−
17	−	−	−	−	+	−
18	+	−	−	−	+	−
19	−	+	−	−	+	−
20	+	+	−	−	+	−
21	−	−	+	−	+	−
22	+	−	+	−	+	−
23	−	+	+	−	+	−
24	+	+	+	−	+	−
25	−	−	−	+	+	−
26	+	−	−	+	+	−
27	−	+	−	+	+	−
28	+	+	−	+	+	−
29	−	−	+	+	+	−
30	+	−	+	+	+	−
31	−	+	+	+	+	−
32	+	+	+	+	+	−
33	−	−	−	−	−	+
34	+	−	−	−	−	+
35	−	+	−	−	−	+
36	+	+	−	−	−	+
37	−	−	+	−	−	+
38	+	−	+	−	−	+
39	−	+	+	−	−	+
40	+	+	+	−	−	+
41	−	−	−	+	−	+
42	+	−	−	+	−	+
43	−	+	−	+	−	+
44	+	+	−	+	−	+
45	−	−	+	+	−	+
46	+	−	+	+	−	+
47	−	+	+	+	−	+
48	+	+	+	+	−	+
49	−	−	−	−	+	+
50	+	−	−	−	+	+
51	−	+	−	−	+	+
52	+	+	−	−	+	+
53	−	−	+	−	+	+
54	+	−	+	−	+	+
55	−	+	+	−	+	+
56	+	+	+	−	+	+
57	−	−	−	+	+	+
58	+	−	−	+	+	+
59	−	+	−	+	+	+
60	+	+	−	+	+	+
61	−	−	+	+	+	+
62	+	−	+	+	+	+
63	−	+	+	+	+	+
64	+	+	+	+	+	+

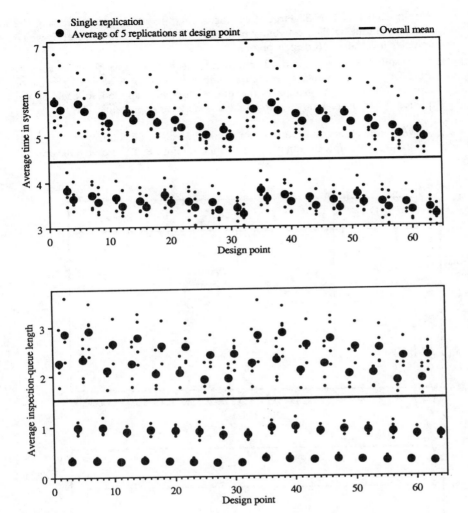

FIGURE 12.1
Experimental design for small factory: Individual-replication and average-over-replications results.

- For both responses, there is a strong and consistent pairing of the large dots—two "high" values, followed by two "low" values, then two "high" values, etc. Looking back at the design matrix in Table 12.6, we see that this pattern follows the level changes of factor 2, the inspection-time factor. What seems clear (and will be confirmed formally below with the effects computations) is that decreasing the inspection times produces a consistent and appreciable improvement in both responses.

- For both responses, within each block of 16 large dots the second eight are lower than the first eight. Factor 4 (machine repair times) is the one that changes level every eight points, so we see that improved performance could be expected from reducing machine downtimes.

- Within each block of 32 large dots, the second 16 are lower, indicating the benefit of reducing the probability of a part's failing inspection (factor 5, which switches level after 16 design points).
- The results from design points 33 through 64 seem to be a nearly exact copy of those from design points 1 through 32; the only difference between the factor settings in these two groups is the queue discipline applied to each of the queues. Thus, it appears that this factor is quite unimportant.

While the above observations are valuable, we should confirm them formally, and also attempt to quantify the effects. Figure 12.2 plots 90 percent

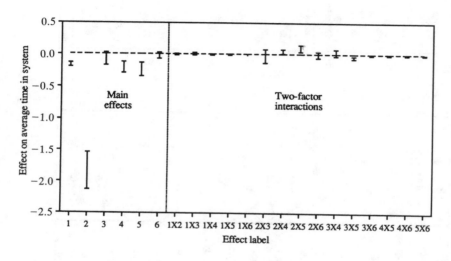

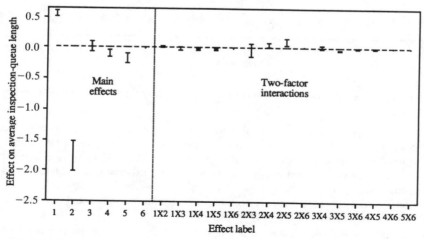

FIGURE 12.2
Experimental design for small factory: Main effects and two-factor interactions.

confidence intervals for the expected main effects and two-way interactions for both responses, obtained from the five replicates of the entire design, as described above. Although we computed three- and higher-way interactions (including the six-way interaction) as well, we do not plot them since they were all extremely close to zero. Actually, we see from Fig. 12.2 that the two-way interactions in this case are also negligible in comparison with some of the main effects.

The main effect of factor 2 (inspection times) is strongly negative for both responses, indicating that faster inspections would provide the most improvement. Beyond that, it would seem that either reducing machine repair times (factor 4) or improving quality (reducing the probability of failing inspection, factor 5) would be the next best step to take. Note the disagreement between the two responses regarding the sign of the main effect of machining times (factor 1)—reducing them would decrease the average time in system but increase the average inspection-queue length. The mean machine uptime (factor 3) appears unimportant (it is not even statistically significant), so effort should not go to improving the machine's reliability. Also, it is clear that the extra trouble associated with a shortest-job-first discipline (factor 6) in the two queues would not be worthwhile.

The next step in a study such as this could take several forms. Reducing inspection times would seem to be highly advisable, as well as perhaps making efforts to get broken machines back up more quickly and to improve quality; trying to speed up machining could shorten makespans but would at the same time increase floor-space requirements for the inspection queue. If we felt that a more detailed study of the first three factors were necessary to justify a potentially large capital investment, it is at least clear that we should forget about the queue-discipline and machine-uptime factors. This collapses the problem to four factors, eminently easing further analysis.

While factorial designs can provide valuable assistance in understanding a complicated simulation model, they do have their limitations. In order to interpret the main effects in a literal way, we must assume that the expected response can be expressed as a simple linear function of the factors, and thus in particular assume that there are no interactions. For the inventory model of Examples 12.1 and 12.2 involving the two quantitative factors s and d, if $R(s,d)$ is the response of the simulation for a particular (s,d) pair, then we are *in fact* assuming in the 2^2 factorial experiment that the *expected* response as a function of s and d takes the form

$$E[R(s,d)] = \beta_0 + \beta_s s + \beta_d d + \beta_{sd} sd \qquad (12.1)$$

for some constants β_0, β_s, β_d, and β_{sd}. Presumably this is at best an approximation, since we have gone to the trouble to do the simulation in the first place, which is certainly harder than just evaluating Eq. (12.1) for various combinations of s and d. [Note that Eq. (12.1) is a *regression model* (of the simulation model), and the least-squares estimates of β_0, β_s, β_d, and β_{sd} turn out to be just linear transformations of the overall average response, e_s, e_d, and e_{sd}; see Sec. 12.4.] But even if Eq. (12.1) *is* an accurate representation of the simulation model, literally interpreting e_s as the change in the response *in general* when moving s from its "$-$" to its "$+$" level assumes that s does not interact with d; put more succinctly, the partial derivative of Eq. (12.1) with respect to s depends on the value of d (and vice versa) unless $\beta_{sd} = 0$, that is, unless there is no interaction. So e_s cannot just be interpreted as "what happens if we increase s by 40," since the answer to this question could depend on the starting point for the increase (20 in our design) as well as on the value of d. In the inventory model of Examples 12.1 and 12.2, we *did* find strong interaction between s and d, meaning that the main effect of s or d cannot be simply interpreted as what happens to $E[R(s,d)]$ when we move s or d from its "$-$" to its "$+$" level, even within the parameter ranges considered. On the other hand, the six-factor manufacturing model of Example 12.3 did not exhibit strong interactions, so the main effects *can* be regarded as the change in the response in general that results from moving the factors one-at-a-time by an amount equal to the difference between their "$+$" and "$-$" levels. Thus, if interactions are present, we cannot just use the main effects by themselves to interpolate or extrapolate the response values for other factor levels, but should instead use the estimated version of Eq. (12.1), replete with the nonlinear cross-product term. This subject is considered further in Sec. 12.4.

12.3 COPING WITH MANY FACTORS

Our experiment with the manufacturing model of Example 12.3 involved six factors and required considerable computational effort. It is easy to imagine a more complicated version of this model in which we might be interested in dozens or even hundreds of different factors. In such a case, a full 2^k factorial design would quickly become unmanageable. For instance, $k = 11$ factors would lead to $2^{11} = 2048$ design points, and if we wanted to make $n = 5$ replications at each design point (certainly a modest sample size from a statistical viewpoint), there would be 10,240 replications in all. If each replication took, say, 1 minute of computer time (a very modest amount of time for a large simulation), we would need more than a full week of round-the-clock computing to run the experiment.

   In this section we discuss a few procedures that can be used when a large number of factors are (at least initially) present, a common situation in simulation. Section 12.3.1 describes a variation of the full 2^k factorial designs of Sec. 12.2, and in Sec. 12.3.2 we cite some literature on other types of designs that could be considered when the number of factors seems truly overwhelming. Often the hope is that we can quickly "screen out" some of the factors as being unimportant and thus forget about them in follow-up studies that pay more attention to the remaining factors that *do* matter.

12.3.1 2^{k-p} Fractional Factorial Designs

Fractional factorial designs provide a way to get good estimates of (for example) only the main effects and perhaps two-way interactions at a fraction of the computational effort required by a full 2^k factorial design. Basically, a 2^{k-p} fractional factorial design is constructed by choosing a certain subset (of size 2^{k-p}) of all the 2^k possible design points and then running the simulation for only these chosen points. Since only $1/2^p$ of the possible 2^k factor combinations are actually run, we sometimes speak of a "half fraction" if $p = 1$, an "eighth fraction" if $p = 3$, and so on. Clearly, we would like p to be large from a computational viewpoint, but a larger p may also result in less information from the experiment, as one might suspect.

The important question of *which* 2^{k-p} of the possible 2^k combinations to choose is an involved issue whose thorough explanation is best left to the experimental-design literature. We can nevertheless give a simple "cookbook" procedure to use in many situations.

To do so requires that we first discuss the idea of *confounding* in 2^{k-p} fractional factorial designs. It will turn out that in such a design we may wind up with exactly the same algebraic expression for several different effects. For instance, in a 2^{4-1} half fraction, it could be that the formulas for the main effect e_4 and the three-way interaction effect e_{123} are identical; in this case we say that the main effect of factor 4 is *confounded* with the three-way interaction effect between factors 1, 2, and 3. What this really means is that the common formula for e_4 and e_{123} is an unbiased estimator for $E(e_4) + E(e_{123})$. Now if we were willing to assume that $E(e_{123}) = 0$ or is negligible in comparison with $E(e_4)$, then e_4 is an unbiased (or nearly so) estimator of $E(e_4)$. It often happens that higher-way interactions *do* turn out to be small in comparison with main effects or perhaps two-way interactions (as we indeed noticed in Example 12.3), so such an assumption may actually be warranted. Trouble may arise, though, in cases where two-way interactions are confounded with each other; for example, the formulas for e_{12} and e_{34} could be identical, in which case this common expression is an unbiased estimator for $E(e_{12}) + E(e_{34})$ and we may feel uncomfortable assuming that either of these two-way interactions is zero. Worse, we may have a main effect confounded with a two-way interaction. In general, the larger the value of p, the more pervasive the confounding problem.

One way to quantify the overall severity of confounding is the concept of the *resolution* of a particular 2^{k-p} fractional factorial design. It is guaranteed that two effects are not confounded with each other if the sum of their "ways" is strictly less than the design's resolution; for this purpose main effects are regarded as "one-way" effects. For instance, in a resolution IV design (custom dictates that resolutions be quaintly denoted by Roman numerals), main effects are not confounded with two-way interactions $(1 + 2 < 4)$, but two-way interactions *are* confounded with each other $(2 + 2 = 4)$. Thus, assuming that three- and higher-way interactions are negligible, resolution IV designs allow us to obtain "clear" main-effects estimates but cannot provide reliable two-way interaction estimates. In simulation there could be at least two-way interactions of interest, so resolution IV designs may be inadequate. A resolution V design would, however, give us two-way interactions unconfounded with each other

$(2+2<5)$, but they would be confounded with three-way interactions; main effects are less troublesome, being confounded with nothing lower than a four-way interaction. Going the other direction, resolution III designs confound main effects with two-way interactions, so they should probably be avoided except in desperation. Notationally, the resolution is attached as a subscript: 2_{IV}^{4-1}, 2_V^{8-2}, etc.

Once we have determined the number of factors k and the desired resolution, we need to construct the design, i.e., identify p and which 2^{k-p} rows of the full 2^k factorial design matrix to use. The first step is to write a full 2^{k-p} factorial design matrix in factors $1, 2, \ldots, k-p$, as in Tables 12.2 and 12.6. The remaining p columns (for factors $k-p+1, \ldots, k$) are then determined by "multiplying" certain of the first $k-p$ columns together according to the rules given in Table 12.7 [which is excerpted from Box, Hunter, and Hunter (1978, p. 410)], where "multiplying columns" means that corresponding entries of each column are multiplied together and the product of like signs is a "$+$" while the product of different signs is a "$-$," exactly as we did in computing interactions in full designs. For example, to construct the 2_V^{8-2} design (a quarter fraction in $k=8$ factors) described in Table 12.7, we first write a full 2^6 factorial design in factors $1, 2, \ldots, 6$, and then define the column for factor 7 to be the product of columns 1, 2, 3, and 4; the column for factor 8 is the product of columns 1, 2, 5, and 6. (Note that we could have reversed the signs of either or both of columns 7 or 8, taking instead the "$-$" option in the "$\pm$" specification of Table 12.7; this flexibility could prove useful in simulation if, for instance, always taking the "$+$" option leads to model configurations that are costly to run.) The main effect of factor j is then computed as in full factorial designs: Apply the signs of the column for factor j to the corresponding numbers in the response column and add them up; this is divided, though, by 2^{k-p-1} rather than 2^{k-1}. Interactions are also computed as before: Multiply the columns for the involved factors together, apply the resulting signs to the response column, add them up, and divide by 2^{k-p-1}; when computing interactions, though, we should remember that not all of them are clear of confounding due to the limited design resolution.

A few comments before giving simulation examples of fractional factorial designs:

- That the designs defined by this procedure are actually of the indicated resolution is not immediately obvious; the interested reader is referred to the experimental-design literature. We can begin to see why, though, by looking at the definition, say, of the 2_V^{8-2} design in Table 12.7 (taking the "$+$" option for both factors 7 and 8). If we were to construct this design and then decide to compute the four-factor interaction e_{1234}, we would obviously get a formula identical to that for e_7, since this is precisely how the column for factor 7 was defined. Thus, the main effect of factor 7 is confounded with this four-way interaction, but not with a three-way interaction since four

TABLE 12.7
Rules for constructing fractional factorial designs

k	III	IV	V
		Resolution	
3	2_{III}^{3-1} $3 = \pm 12$		
4		2_{IV}^{4-1} $4 = \pm 123$	
5	2_{III}^{5-2} $4 = \pm 12$ $5 = \pm 13$		2_{V}^{5-1} $5 = \pm 1234$
6	2_{III}^{6-3} $4 = \pm 12$ $5 = \pm 13$ $6 = \pm 23$	2_{IV}^{6-2} $5 = \pm 123$ $6 = \pm 234$	
7	2_{III}^{7-4} $4 = \pm 12$ $5 = \pm 13$ $6 = \pm 23$ $7 = \pm 123$	2_{IV}^{7-3} $5 = \pm 123$ $6 = \pm 234$ $7 = \pm 134$	
8		2_{IV}^{8-4} $5 = \pm 234$ $6 = \pm 134$ $7 = \pm 123$ $8 = \pm 124$	2_{V}^{8-2} $7 = \pm 1234$ $8 = \pm 1256$
9	2_{III}^{9-5} $5 = \pm 123$ $6 = \pm 234$ $7 = \pm 134$ $8 = \pm 124$ $9 = \pm 1234$	2_{IV}^{9-4} $6 = \pm 2345$ $7 = \pm 1345$ $8 = \pm 1245$ $9 = \pm 1235$	
10	2_{III}^{10-6} $5 = \pm 123$ $6 = \pm 234$ $7 = \pm 134$ $8 = \pm 124$ $9 = \pm 1234$ $(10) = \pm 12$	2_{IV}^{10-5} $6 = \pm 1234$ $7 = \pm 1235$ $8 = \pm 1245$ $9 = \pm 1345$ $(10) = \pm 2345$	2_{V}^{10-3} $8 = \pm 1237$ $9 = \pm 2345$ $(10) = \pm 1346$
11	2_{III}^{11-7} $5 = \pm 123$ $6 = \pm 234$ $7 = \pm 134$ $8 = \pm 124$ $9 = \pm 1234$ $(10) = \pm 12$ $(11) = \pm 13$	2_{IV}^{11-6} $6 = \pm 123$ $7 = \pm 234$ $8 = \pm 345$ $9 = \pm 134$ $(10) = \pm 145$ $(11) = \pm 245$	2_{V}^{11-4} $8 = \pm 1237$ $9 = \pm 2345$ $(10) = \pm 1346$ $(11) = \pm 1234567$

separate factors were used in the definition of its column in the design matrix. All this is consistent with what is meant by a resolution V design.

- There just may not be a design of the desired resolution for a particular k (e.g., resolution IV when $k = 5$).

- In Table 12.7 the parenthesized terms (10) and (11) refer to factors 10 and 11, to avoid notational confusion with multiplying together columns of single-digit factors.

Example 12.4. Consider a generalization of the inventory model of Examples 12.1 and 12.2 in which there are two new factors. The first of these is the inventory-evaluation interval m, which is the number of months between successive evaluations of the inventory level to determine whether an order will be placed. In the original model $m = 1$, but consideration is being given to changing m to 2, that is, evaluating only at the beginning of every *other* month. The second new factor arose since the supplier has introduced an "express" delivery option. Originally, if Z items were ordered, the ordering cost was $32 + 3Z$ and the delivery lag was distributed uniformly between 0.5 and 1 month. With express delivery, the supplier will cut the delivery time in half (distributed uniformly between 0.25 and 0.5 month) but will charge $48 + 4Z$ instead. The delivery priority P is thus either "normal" or "express" and is a qualitative factor. In this generalized model, then, there are $k = 4$ factors whose levels are coded in Table 12.8.

From Table 12.7, we see that with $k = 4$ there is a resolution IV half fraction; taking the "$+$" option in the definition for column 4, we get the design matrix in Table 12.9, which also shows the responses (average total costs per month) from a single replication at each design point (using common random numbers across design points). Since the resolution is only IV, we can only really compute the main effects; they are $e_s = -2.96$, $e_d = -12.77$, $e_m = 2.85$, and $e_P = 43.55$. We replicated this design $n = 10$ times, as in Example 12.2, and formed 90 percent confidence intervals for the expected main effects:

$$E(e_s): \quad -0.61 \pm 0.86$$
$$E(e_d): -10.62 \pm 0.91$$
$$E(e_m): \quad 1.87 \pm 0.75$$
$$E(e_P): \quad 41.86 \pm 0.95$$

TABLE 12.8
Coding chart for s, d, m, and P in the generalized inventory model

Factor	$-$	$+$
s	20	60
d	10	50
m	1	2
P	Normal	Express

TABLE 12.9
Design matrix and simulation results for the 2_{IV}^{4-1} fractional factorial design on s, d, m, and P for the generalized inventory model

Factor combination (design point)	s	d	m	P	Response
1	−	−	−	−	141.86
2	+	−	−	+	183.53
3	−	+	−	+	154.20
4	+	+	−	−	147.22
5	−	−	+	+	209.34
6	+	−	+	−	123.31
7	−	+	+	−	133.02
8	+	+	+	+	172.54

As for the new factors, it does not appear to matter very much whether we evaluate the inventory each month or every other month, and the shorter delivery lags for the express-delivery option certainly do not seem to be worth the extra cost.

To see what might have been lost by doing only the half fraction described above, we carried out the other half fraction (and thus had a full 2^4 factorial design) and analyzed the results. Over 10 replications of the design, the statistically significant effects were:

$$E(e_s): \quad -2.34 \pm 0.90$$
$$E(e_d): -10.66 \pm 0.90$$
$$E(e_m): \quad 1.96 \pm 0.81$$
$$E(e_P): \quad 33.39 \pm 0.42$$
$$E(e_{sd}): \quad 18.65 \pm 1.17$$
$$E(e_{sm}): -19.43 \pm 0.68$$
$$E(e_{dm}): \quad 0.97 \pm 0.81$$
$$E(e_{dP}): \quad -2.87 \pm 0.29$$
$$E(e_{mP}): \quad -2.11 \pm 0.29$$
$$E(e_{sdm}): \quad 8.25 \pm 0.64$$
$$E(e_{dmP}): \quad 1.76 \pm 0.21$$
$$E(e_{sdmP}): \quad -0.20 \pm 0.17$$

The first thing we notice is that there *are* some important two-way interactions that were missed in the resolution IV half fraction; as noted at the end of Sec. 12.2, the presence of such interactions casts doubt on the meaning of the main effects, as estimated either from a full or fractional factorial design. Comparing the main effects of s and d here with those from the simpler model of Examples 12.1 and 12.2, we notice definite differences, which are partly accounted for by the fact that interactions are present in both cases, as well as by the fact that these are simply different models.

Beyond this, we also see from the results of the full design that there are two appreciable three-way interactions [$\bar{e}_{sdm}(10)$ and $\bar{e}_{dmP}(10)$], each of which is confounded with a main effect in this design. Specifically, the estimate $\bar{e}_s(10)$

from the half fraction estimates $E(e_s) + E(e_{dmP})$, and the estimate $\bar{e}_P(10)$ from the half fraction estimates $E(e_P) + E(e_{sdm})$. Numerically, this works out quite closely:

2_{IV}^{4-1} fractional	2^4 full
$\bar{e}_s(10) = -0.61 \approx -0.58 = -2.34 + 1.76 = \bar{e}_s(10) + \bar{e}_{dmP}(10)$	
$\bar{e}_P(10) = 41.86 \approx 41.64 = 33.39 + 8.25 = \bar{e}_P(10) + \bar{e}_{sdm}(10)$	

So in this case there was certainly some interaction information lost by doing only the half fraction, as well as some inaccuracies introduced in the main-effects estimates. However, the principal decisions from the half fraction (m doesn't matter much and express ordering isn't worth it) appear to be sound.

Example 12.5. We reconsidered the small-factory model of Example 12.3 using the 2_{IV}^{6-2} design from Table 12.7, taking the "+" options for both factors 5 and 6. Since we had already run the full 2^6 factorial design, we merely selected the appropriate 16 rows from among the 64 in Table 12.6; the chosen rows are 1, 7, 12, 14, 18, 24, 27, 29, 36, 38, 41, 47, 51, 53, 58, and 64, as the reader should confirm. From the same five replications of the design, 90 percent confidence intervals for the expected main effects (all we can estimate from a resolution IV design) are given in Table 12.10, which, in comparison with the main-effects sections of Fig. 12.2, are extremely close to their counterparts from the full design. This close agreement is not surprising in light of the results from the full design of Example 12.3, where no interactions of any importance were found; it is also consistent with the considerable redundancy noted in the individual-design-point results from the full design in Fig. 12.1. So in this case, the quarter fraction (which would have run in about 3 hours of IBM PS/2 Model 50Z time) gave us information that is every bit as good as that obtained from the 12-hour full design.

Despite their limitations, fractional factorial designs can yield useful information without the enormous computational burden of full-factorial experiments, provided that we are careful in interpreting their results. Returning to our 11-factor example in the introduction to Sec. 12.3, we could construct a 2_{IV}^{11-6} design to get at least an idea of the magnitudes of the main effects; this

TABLE 12.10
Ninety percent confidence intervals on expected main effects from the 2_{IV}^{6-2} fractional factorial design with the small-factory model

Factor number	Average time in system	Average inspection-queue length
1	-0.15 ± 0.03	0.58 ± 0.04
2	-1.83 ± 0.29	-1.76 ± 0.24
3	-0.07 ± 0.10	0.02 ± 0.09
4	-0.20 ± 0.09	-0.09 ± 0.05
5	-0.23 ± 0.10	-0.16 ± 0.07
6	-0.02 ± 0.04	-0.02 ± 0.03

would require only 32 design points rather than 2048. Using the one-minute-per-run figure, we could replicate this $n = 5$ times in 2 hours and 40 minutes of computer time, rather than the week needed for the full design.

12.3.2 Factor-Screening Strategies

When the number of factors is moderate, a fractional factorial design such as those discussed in Sec. 12.3.1 might be able to indicate which factors appear to be important and, more to the point, which factors are irrelevant and can be simply fixed at some reasonable value and omitted from further consideration. But situations arise where there are far too many factors for even a highly fractionated factorial design to be workable. For example, Haider, Noller, and Robey (1986) analyzed systems for manufacturing printed-circuit boards where there may be as many as 50 separate process steps, each of which might require several parameters for its characterization; the number of individual factors could thus grow easily into the hundreds.

Modifications of the kinds of two-level factorial designs discussed in Secs. 12.2 and 12.3.1 suitable for simulation experiments with a large number of factors are surveyed in the simulation context by Mauro (1986). Perhaps the best-known examples of this type are the *Plackett-Burman* designs, in which k factors' effects can be investigated in as few as $k + 1$ design points (rather than 2^k or 2^{k-p}), provided that $k + 1$ is divisible by 4; these designs were tabled by Plackett and Burman (1946), and are the same as 2_{III}^{k-p} fractional factorial designs when $k + 1$ is a power of 2 (such as the 2_{III}^{3-1} and 2_{III}^{7-4} designs in Table 12.7).

If the number of factors exceeds the number of design points possible, we would have to use what is called a *supersaturated design*. The construction of some supersaturated designs stems from observing that each column of the design matrix in two-level factorial designs consists of half "+" signs and the other half "−" signs, as in Tables 12.2, 12.4, and 12.6. Design matrices with this *balanced* property and an affordable number of design points can be constructed, and effects estimates would be computed from the signs in the matrix as before. For example, suppose we have $k = 120$ factors but can afford to run the simulation only 24 times (rather than the $2^{120} > 10^{36}$ design points called for by a full factorial design). One kind of supersaturated design, called a *random-balance design*, would take 12 "+" signs for factor j and sprinkle them randomly into 12 of the 24 rows of column j, and define the other 12 positions to have "−" signs; the column for each factor in the design matrix is generated in this way independently. Mauro and Smith (1984) evaluated variations and alternative analysis techniques of random-balance designs specifically in simulation applications, with encouraging results in terms of correct identification of significant factors. A flaw in random-balance designs is that the confounding patterns of the resulting effects estimates are random, and so *systematic supersaturated designs* were developed in which the signs are assigned to minimize overall measures of confounding, rather than randomly;

such designs, however, are available for only certain combinations of k and the number of affordable design points [see Mauro (1986)].

A different tack is to try to reduce the (effective) number of factors, k. Such an effort would be rewarded handsomely, since computational requirements for factor-effect investigation grow exponentially in k (2^k, 2^{k-p}, etc.). One way to accomplish this would be to *group* the factors together in some way. For example, in a manufacturing model such as an enlargement of that in Examples 12.3 and 12.5, all service-time means could be in one group, all interarrival-time means in another group, downtime means in a third group, and inspection-passing probabilities in a fourth group; a different grouping strategy could be to put those parameters associated with a particular manufacturing cell together in a group. Each group is then regarded as a single aggregate "factor," with all the individual factors inside a group set to their "+" or "−" levels together. The effects would then be interpreted accordingly as what happens when a whole group moves together between levels. Some groups may appear important while others do not, and a recursive process is used to ungroup the individual factors (at least partially) in the important groups until some subset of the original individual factors is finally identified as being important. This approach certainly can reduce the number of effective factors substantially, with an attendant dramatic decrease in computation, and it allows control of the confounding pattern among groups if a fractional design is used. Due to its recursive nature, though, the total number of simulation runs cannot be specified in advance. It may also not be obvious how the groups should be formed; a particular group may in fact contain several important individual factors, but the group as a whole could appear unimportant if some of its members' effects unexpectedly go in opposite directions and cancel each other out. For more on these *group-screening designs*, see Mauro (1984), Mauro and Burns (1984), and Mauro and Smith (1982).

The methods described so far in this section are applicable to physical experiments, and so certainly to simulation experiments as well. In a dynamic simulation, however, there are opportunities for approaches that are not possible with static models or physical experiments. One such idea, developed originally by Schruben and Cogliano (1987), is to oscillate the different input parameter values during the course of the simulation, each at a different frequency. The output process is then examined to see which input parameters' oscillation frequencies can be detected in the output. While an important factor's oscillation will produce noticeable oscillation in the output at the corresponding frequency, those of unimportant factors will not be apparent. In this way, Schruben and Cogliano were able to pick out the important factors in several test models with substantially less simulating than that required by conventional experimental-design approaches; Sanchez and Schruben (1987) present a detailed example of using this approach to identify important factors in the African-port model of Prob. 2.23. These kinds of *frequency-domain methods* are further studied by Buss (1988), Jacobson, Morrice, and Schruben (1988), Sanchez and Buss (1987), Sanchez and Sanchez (1988), Som and Sargent (1988), and Som, Sargent, and Schruben (1987).

12.4 RESPONSE SURFACES AND METAMODELS

A simulation model can be thought of as a mechanism that turns input parameters into output performance measures. In this sense, a simulation is just a *function*, which may be vector-valued or stochastic. The explicit form of this function is also unknown (and probably very complicated even if it were known), since we are going to the trouble of simulating instead of merely plugging numbers into some formula. In this section we describe methods to develop simple formulas that approximate this function. This approximate formula could then be used as a proxy for the full-blown simulation itself in order to get at least a rough idea of what would happen for a large number of input-parameter combinations. This ability is especially helpful if the simulation is very large and costly, precluding exploration of all but a few input-parameter combinations.

For example, the simulation of the inventory model of Examples 12.1 and 12.2 took as input the reorder-point parameter s and the order-size parameter d, and produced as output the average total cost per month, a random variable. We could thus is principle write

$$\text{average total cost per month} = R(s,d)$$

for some function R that is stochastic, unknown, and probably pretty messy; indeed, it is the whole simulation program itself that evaluates R for numerical input values of s and d.

To serve as a point of comparison for our use of this simple inventory model in this section, Fig. 12.3a shows a three-dimensional mesh surface of the average over 10 independent replications of simulation-generated values of $R(s,d)$ for all 420 combinations of $s = 0, 5, 10, \ldots, 100$ and $d = 5, 10, 15, \ldots, 100$. Directly below, in Fig. 12.3b, a contour map of the surface depicts the same information more quantitatively, where all (s,d) points along a given contour line would produce approximately the same average response level. These plots *numerically* characterize the response function $R(s,d)$ over this parameter range, even though we do not have an *algebraic* formula with which to characterize it. The surface in Fig. 12.3a is sometimes called a *response surface* of the simulation model, a term that is particularly apt in cases like this where there are two input factors and we can actually draw such pictures.

It is certainly nice to have a response surface like Fig. 12.3a, and we can learn a lot from it. For instance, the average total cost rises steeply as s and d both become small, evidently due to being in backlog much of the time and having to pay the fixed ordering cost frequently for such small order amounts. At the other extreme, if s and d are both too large, the holding-cost component gets out of hand. Perhaps most important, it looks as though the lowest average total monthly cost would be somewhere between \$110 and \$120 per month, which could be achieved by taking s to be around 25 and d to be about 35 or 40.

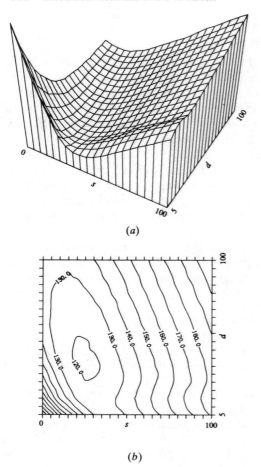

(a)

(b)

FIGURE 12.3
(a) Response-surface plot and (b) contour map from direct simulation of the inventory model.

But to generate the data for the response surface in Fig. 12.3a we had to make 4200 separate simulation replications, not the sort of thing one could do in practice with a large-scale model. Indeed, a single replication of some simulations can take hours to execute on a powerful mainframe computer, perhaps precluding even a modest fractional factorial experimental design, let alone the more or less exhaustive evaluation needed for detailed response-surface mapping. In these cases it might be worthwhile to develop a simple algebraic function relating the response to the important input factors to serve as at least a rough proxy for the full-blown simulation. In the inventory example, we would thus try to approximate the response-surface function $R(s,d)$ with a simple explicit formula involving s and d. Such a formula is in essence an algebraic model *of* the simulation model, and so is sometimes called a *metamodel*. The purpose of a metamodel is to estimate or approximate the response surface; we could then use the metamodel (instead of the actual simulation program) to learn about how the response surface *would* behave over various regions of the input-factor space, to estimate how the response *would* change at a particular point if the input factors were changed slightly, or perhaps to find approximately optimal settings of the input factors.

Often, a metamodel is specified to be a standard regression model, where the independent variables for the regression are the simulation input parameters and the dependent variable is the response of interest; we could develop several regression models if there are multiple responses. It is still necessary to carry out at least *some* simulations at different input-parameter combinations to obtain the data from which the parameters of the regression model are estimated. As with any regression model, we should be concerned with such issues as whether the functional form of the regression model is appropriate, variability, normality, heteroskedacticity, correlated errors, etc. Many of the usual techniques could be used, such as lack-of-fit tests, residual analysis for model diagnosis, etc. In using the fitted regression model, we would also have available all the usual tools, such as confidence intervals and prediction intervals.

Actually, factorial designs such as those in Secs. 12.2 and 12.3.1 are based on regression metamodels of the simulation response surface. As pointed out at the end of Sec. 12.2, the full 2^2 factorial design on the inventory model in Examples 12.1 and 12.2 assumes that the expected response surface really *does* behave like Eq. (12.1). Moreover, the usual regression least-squares estimates of the β coefficients in Eq. (12.1) are related to the effects estimates e_s, e_d, and e_{sd}, as follows. Let $\bar{s}$ and $\bar{d}$ be the mean values of s and d, respectively, in the coding chart (Table 12.3); that is, $\bar{s} = 40$ and $\bar{d} = 30$. Also let Δs and Δd be the distance between the "$-$" and "$+$" levels of the corresponding factor, so that Δs and Δd are both 40 in this case. Then we can transform s and d to fall onto -1 and $+1$ at their "$-$" and "$+$" values by defining

$$x_s = \frac{2(s - \bar{s})}{\Delta s} = \frac{s - 40}{20} \tag{12.2}$$

and

$$x_d = \frac{2(d - \bar{d})}{\Delta d} = \frac{d - 30}{20} \tag{12.3}$$

Finally, let $\bar{R}$ be the average response over all design points. With this reparameterization a regression model equivalent to Eq. (12.1) is

$$E[R(s,d)] = b_0 + b_s x_s + b_d x_d + b_{sd} x_s x_d \tag{12.4}$$

for which the least-squares estimators turn out to be

$$\hat{b}_0 = \bar{R}, \qquad \hat{b}_s = \frac{e_s}{2}, \qquad \hat{b}_d = \frac{e_d}{2}, \qquad \hat{b}_{sd} = \frac{e_{sd}}{2} \tag{12.5}$$

Note that (12.5) provides an alternative way to compute the effects estimates using any standard statistical package: Transform the independent-variable values as in Eqs. (12.2) and (12.3), fit the model (12.4), and then double the corresponding least-squares estimates using (12.5).

Example 12.6. We used the same data as in Example 12.2, being 10 independent replications at each of the four design points in the full 2^2 factorial design, transformed s and d as in Eqs. (12.2) and (12.3), and fitted the regression model in Eq. (12.4) using the Minitab statistical package [Ryan, Joiner, and Ryan (1985)]. To satisfy the basic regression assumptions so far as possible, we did not use common random numbers across the different design points. We also regarded all 40 data points as separate cases for the regression, to maximize the degrees of freedom. The least-squares estimates came out to be $\hat{b}_0 = \bar{R} = 136.48$, $\hat{b}_s = 8.83$, $\hat{b}_d = -4.37$, and $\hat{b}_{sd} = 5.30$, so that the predictive regression equation would be

$$\hat{R}(s,d) = 136.48 + 8.83x_s - 4.37x_d + 5.30x_s x_d \tag{12.6}$$

Note that $\hat{b}_s$, $\hat{b}_d$, and $\hat{b}_{sd}$ are indeed half the values of $\bar{e}_s(10)$, $\bar{e}_d(10)$, and $\bar{e}_{sd}(10)$, respectively, from Example 12.2 (up to roundoff). Using a statistical package also automatically provides us with information on the statistical significance of the fitted model (the overall F statistic for the regression) and its coefficients (the individual t ratio statistics); in this case the overall F statistic for the regression was highly significant, as were the individual t ratios for each coefficient. Thus, we can conclude, as in Example 12.2, that both main effects as well as the interaction are statistically significant.

Putting Eqs. (12.2), (12.3), and (12.5) together into the model of Eq. (12.4), we can see at last how the least-squares estimators of the β coefficients in the original regression model of Eq. (12.1) on the untransformed input parameters are related to the effects estimates:

$$\hat{\beta}_0 = \bar{R} + \frac{-e_s\bar{s}\,\Delta d - e_d\bar{d}\,\Delta s + 2e_{sd}\bar{s}\bar{d}}{\Delta s\,\Delta d} \tag{12.7}$$

$$\hat{\beta}_s = \frac{e_s\,\Delta d - 2e_{sd}\bar{d}}{\Delta s\,\Delta d} \tag{12.8}$$

$$\hat{\beta}_d = \frac{e_d\,\Delta s - 2e_{sd}\bar{s}}{\Delta s\,\Delta d} \tag{12.9}$$

$$\hat{\beta}_{sd} = \frac{2e_{sd}}{\Delta s\,\Delta d} \tag{12.10}$$

While this form of the regression model appears more complicated, it is easier to use since it is defined in terms of the original input parameters (s and d) rather than their transformations (x_s and x_d) to ± 1.

Example 12.7. Again using the data from Example 12.2, we ran a regression with the model in Eq. (12.1), using the original untransformed independent variables s and d, and obtained the fitted regression equation

$$\hat{R}(s,d) = 141.28 + 0.04s - 0.75d + 0.01sd \tag{12.11}$$

whose coefficients do agree up to roundoff with Eqs. (12.7) through (12.10) when the values of $\bar{e}_s(10)$, $\bar{e}_d(10)$, and $\bar{e}_{sd}(10)$ from Example 12.2 are plugged in.

Furthermore, putting the definitions of x_s and x_d from Eqs. (12.2) and (12.3) into the first regression equation (12.6), we do get to the second regression equation (12.11), again allowing for roundoff error. Thus, Eqs. (12.6) and (12.11) are equivalent.

The fitted equation (12.11) in Example 12.7 could be regarded as a metamodel (in terms of the original input parameters) that we might use as a proxy for the full simulation's response surface; all we would need is a pocket calculator to evaluate Eq. (12.11) for any (s,d) combination of interest. We should be careful, though, to remember that Eq. (12.11) is just an approximation to the actual simulation and may thus be inaccurate, especially far from the values of s and d that provided the data on which it is based. A metamodel, after all, is *itself* a model, and as such may or may not be valid relative to the simulation model.

Example 12.8. To get an idea of how accurate Eq. (12.11) might be as a proxy to the simulation model, we show in Fig. 12.4a a mesh surface of Eq. (12.11), below which is its corresponding contour map in Fig. 12.4b, with the design points from Table 12.3 marked as heavy dots; the ranges of s and d are the same as those in Fig. 12.3. For comparison, we also show in Fig. 12.4c the "correct" contour map obtained from the 4200 simulation runs used for the actual response surface of Fig. 12.3a, also marked with the design-point dots. Except at points near the four dots where the data were actually taken, the metamodel is not a very good approximation to the response surface.

The problem with the metamodel of Eq. (12.11) is that the four dots just do not give us enough information to predict how the surface behaves in other places. We improve things in the following example by taking simulation data over a larger portion of the region, and by enriching the model.

Example 12.9. We made five replications at the 16 combinations of $s = 20$, 40, 60, and 80, and $d = 20$, 40, 60, and 80; this required a total of 80 simulation runs of the model [twice as many as for Eq. (12.11)]. We also fit a full quadratic model to these 80 points; i.e.,

$$E[R(s,d)] = \beta_0 + \beta_s s + \beta_d d + \beta_{sd} sd + \beta_{ss} s^2 + \beta_{dd} d^2 \qquad (12.12)$$

and obtained from the regression the fitted metamodel

$$\hat{R}(s,d) = 130.63 - 0.26s - 0.53d + 0.004sd + 0.009s^2 + 0.005d^2 \quad (12.13)$$

which is shown in Figs. 12.5a and 12.5b, together with the contour map in Fig. 12.5c from the 4200-run direct simulation of the response surface, for comparison. This is certainly better than Fig. 12.4, and is actually fairly accurate within the region of the dots at which the simulation data were taken.

It does fail, however, to pick up the sharp peak for very small s and d, evidently because we did not take any data there. Figure 12.6 indicates what happened when we expanded the simulation-generated points to the edges of the region; again we made five replications at each of the 36 points, for 180 runs in

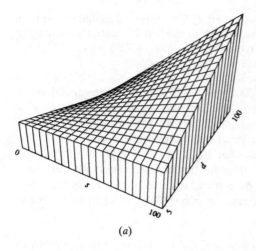

(a)

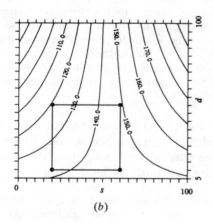

(b)

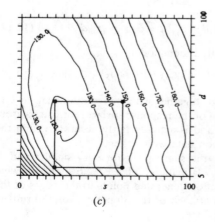

(c)

FIGURE 12.4
(a) Response-surface plot and (b) contour map of the metamodel from the 2^2 factorial design on the inventory model; (c) contour map from direct simulation.

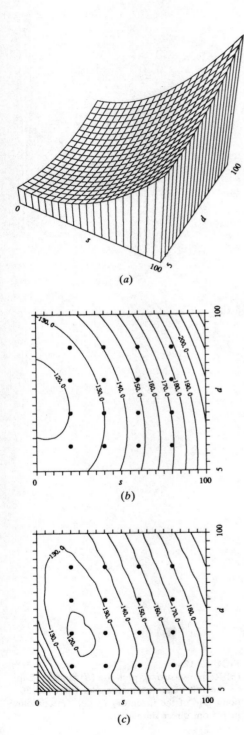

(a)

(b)

(c)

FIGURE 12.5
(a) Response-surface plot and (b) contour map of the full quadratic metamodel from the 16-point grid of the inventory model; (c) contour map from direct simulation.

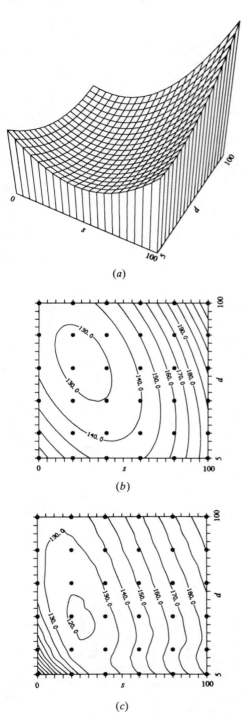

(a)

(b)

(c)

FIGURE 12.6
(a) Response-surface plot and (b) contour map of the full quadratic metamodel from the 36-point grid of the inventory model; (c) contour map from direct simulation.

all. The full-quadratic model of Eq. (12.12) as fitted to these points resulted in

$$\hat{R}(s,d) = 188.51 - 1.49s - 1.24d + 0.014sd + 0.007s^2 + 0.010d^2 \quad (12.14)$$

and is somewhat different from Eq. (12.13); the behavior of Eq. (12.14) is shown in Fig. 12.6, and does match the simulation response surface better at the extremes. Whether the extra data to obtain Eq. (12.14) instead of Eq. (12.13) is worthwhile depends on how much we care about predicting the simulation response accurately at the edges of the region.

As a final example of using metamodels on the inventory example, we address the issue of searching for optimal values of the input parameters.

Example 12.10. Going back to the 2^2 factorial design used in Examples 12.6 and 12.7, we fit a very simple linear model in s and d to the 40 data points and obtained

$$\hat{R}(s,d) = 125.37 + 0.44s - 0.22d \quad (12.15)$$

whose mesh plot and contour map are given in Figs. 12.7a and 12.7b. As an overall metamodel for the response surface, Eq. (12.15) is clearly awful, but this is not the use to which we wish to put it. Instead, we can think of Eq. (12.15) as a *local* linear approximation to the expected response surface, and ask in which direction we should move from the center of the design [i.e., the point $(\bar{s}, \bar{d})$] to decrease the metamodel's height most rapidly. (Decreasing is desirable in this example, since the response is a cost; if it were a profit we would presumably seek to increase it.) From calculus, we know that this direction of *steepest descent* is in the direction of the negative of the vector of partial derivatives for the metamodel, i.e., in the direction $(-0.44, 0.22)$ in this case. The arrow emanating from the centerpoint of the design in Fig. 12.7b indicates this direction; note that it is perpendicular to the contours of the metamodel, and that in terms of the real response surface in the bottom contour map of Fig. 12.7c, it indeed seems to indicate a good direction in which to move. We could then move along this line, picking values of s and d on it (or near it, since they must be integers in this model), running the simulation at each point, and continuing as long as the response continues to fall. When it begins to rise, we could stop, perform another 2^2 factorial design, fit another linear model, and pick a new search direction. This process could continue until we reach a point where the metamodel appears flat, i.e., the estimated coefficients of s and d are both near zero.

The procedure outlined in Example 12.10 is clearly quite crude, and is fraught with all sorts of opportunities for error, such as a completely inappropriate search direction being chosen at some point due to variability in the simulation output.

Before embarking on a potentially expensive project to optimize a simulation model, the reader is encouraged to check out some of the more advanced techniques described, for example, in the books by Box and Draper (1987), Box, Hunter, and Hunter (1978, chap. 5), Myers (1971), or Khuri and Cornell (1987). An extensive survey paper on response-surface methods in general was written by Myers, Khuri, and Carter (1989). Discussions of

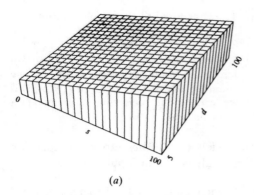

(a)

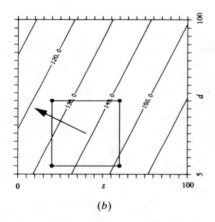

(b)

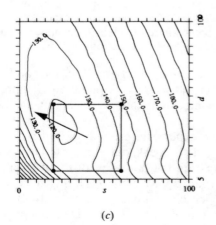

(c)

FIGURE 12.7
(a) Response-surface plot and (b) contour map of the simple linear model from the 2^2 factorial design on the inventory model; (c) contour map from direct simulation (arrows indicate search path).

optimization methods for simulation models are given by Biles and Swain (1979, 1980), Glynn (1986a), Jacobson and Schruben (1989), Meketon (1987), Safizadeh (1989,1990), Schruben (1986), and Wilson (1987). Applications are described by Bengu and Haddock (1986), Biles and Ozmen (1987), Haddock and Bengu (1987), and Smith (1973a, 1973b, 1976).

We have attempted in this section to give only an introduction to response-surface methods and metamodeling in the simulation context. This is an active area of research, and much more is possible than what we have described here. Some additional specific topics are:

- We have used only very simple designs for collecting the metamodel data, e.g., factorial or regularly spaced grids. Other designs, including "starpoints" and centerpoints, can give better estimates of the metamodel's parameters; see, for example, Myers (1971) or Khuri and Cornell (1987).
- If there are many factors, we might want to screen out any unimportant ones and exclude them from being inputs to the metamodel using, for instance, the fractional factorial designs described in Sec. 12.3.1 or some of the factor-screening strategies of Sec. 12.3.2. For an application of this, see Som, Sargent, and Schruben (1987), who give a detailed example of using the frequency-domain approach of Schruben and Cogliano (1987) to screen out unimportant factors in building a metamodel of a class of queueing systems with feedback.
- In most applications there are several output performance measures, and so we might want to build a metamodel for each one. This is discussed by Montgomery and Bettencourt (1977), as well as by Porta Nova and Wilson (1989).
- It might be possible to improve the metamodel's stability by using variance-reduction techniques (Chap. 11); see Tew and Wilson (1988) and Porta Nova and Wilson (1989).

12.5 GRADIENT ESTIMATION

One of the goals of simulation is to find out how changes in the input parameters affect the output measures of performance. If the parameters vary continuously, we are essentially asking a question about the partial derivatives of the expected response function with respect to the input parameters. The vector of these partial derivatives is called the *gradient* of the expected response function, and is of dimensionality equal to the number of input parameters considered. The gradient is interesting in its own right, since it gives the sensitivity of the simulation's expected response to small changes in the input parameters. It is also an important ingredient in many mathematical-programming methods that we might try to use to find optimal values of the input parameters, since many such methods rely on the partial derivatives to determine a direction in which to search for the optimum.

As a simple example, consider an $M/M/1$ queue operating in steady state, with arrival rate λ and service rate ω; we assume that $\rho = \lambda/\omega < 1$ (see App. 1B). For this model, the steady-state expected delay in queue of a customer is analytically known (see Sec. 1B.3 in App. 1B) and is given by

$$d(\lambda,\omega) = \frac{\lambda}{\omega^2 - \lambda\omega} \qquad (12.16)$$

where we indicate in the notation for d its dependence on λ and ω. Thus, the gradient of d is the 2-vector

$$\nabla d(\lambda,\omega) = \begin{bmatrix} \dfrac{\partial d}{\partial \lambda} \\[2mm] \dfrac{\partial d}{\partial \omega} \end{bmatrix} = \begin{bmatrix} \dfrac{1}{(\omega - \lambda)^2} \\[2mm] \dfrac{-\lambda(2\omega - \lambda)}{\omega^2(\omega - \lambda)^2} \end{bmatrix} \qquad (12.17)$$

which we could evaluate, for example, at the current values of λ and ω to see how the expected delay would change from this point.

Since in an actual simulation we would not have a formula for the expected response surface, we could not analytically find a gradient vector like Eq. (12.17). It thus becomes of interest to *estimate* the gradient for particular values of the input parameters. A direct way to do this would be to replicate the simulation n times for the current parameter values, change one of them slightly and replicate at the new point, and repeat this process for each parameter. Each partial derivative is then estimated by noting the change in the performance measure owing to the change in the corresponding parameter. If there are k parameters, this would involve $(k + 1)n$ separate simulation runs. In the spirit of Sec. 12.4, an alternative approach would be to fit a regression metamodel to the response surface and then take its partial derivatives. These are certainly simple approaches, but they do involve a potentially large number of runs.

Accordingly, several *single-run* gradient-estimation techniques have been developed; i.e., an attempt is made to estimate sensitivities from only a single run of the simulation. In the *perturbation-analysis* method, a parameter such as the service rate ω in the $M/M/1$ example above is "perturbed" slightly *during* the simulation, and an algorithm is invoked to track not only what the simulation does from this point on, but also what it *would* have done *if* the parameter had not been perturbed. This idea was originally developed for real (as opposed to simulated) systems by Ho, Eyler, and Chien (1979), and extended by several others to the simulation domain [see, for example, Ho and Cao (1983), Suri (1987), and Suri and Zazanis (1988)]. Although the ability to do this is clearly highly desirable, there have been questions concerning how widely applicable these techniques are; see Heidelberger, Cao, Zazanis, and Suri (1988).

Finally, gradient-estimation methods based on likelihood ratios have been developed by Glynn (1986b, 1987) and by Reiman and Weiss (1986). Related methods are described by Rubinstein (1986).

PROBLEMS

12.1. Recall the model of the manufacturing shop in Prob. 1.22 with five machines that are subject to breakdowns, and s repairmen. Suppose that the shop has not yet been built and that in addition to deciding how many repairmen to hire, management has the following two decisions to make:

(a) There is a higher-quality "deluxe" machine on the market that is more reliable, in that it will run for an amount of time that is an exponential random variable with mean 16 hours (rather than the 8 hours for the standard machine). However, the higher price of these deluxe machines means that it costs the shop $100 (rather than $50) for each hour that each deluxe machine is broken down. Since deluxe machines work no faster, the shop will still need five of them. Assume also that the shop cannot purchase some of each kind of machine, i.e., the machines must be either all standard or all deluxe.

(b) Instead of hiring the standard repairmen, the managers have the option of hiring a team of better-trained "expert" repairmen, who would have to be paid $15 an hour (rather than the $10 an hour for the standard repairmen) but who can repair a broken machine (regardless of whether it is standard or deluxe) in an exponential amount of time with a mean of 1.5 hours (rather than 2 hours). The repairmen hired must be either all standard or all expert.

Use the coding in Table 12.11 to perform a full 2^3 factorial experiment, replicate $n = 5$ times, and compute 90 percent confidence intervals for all expected main and interaction effects. Each simulation run is for 800 hours and begins with all five machines in working order. Make all runs independently. What are your conclusions?

12.2. For the time-shared computer model of Sec. 2.5, suppose that consideration is being given to adjusting the service quantum length q (as in Prob. 10.3) as well as to adopting the alternative processing policy discussed in Probs. 2.18 and 10.5. Perform a 2^2 factorial experiment with these two factors ($q = 0.05$ or 0.40, and the processing policy either as described originally in Sec. 2.5 or as in Prob. 2.18), running the model for 500 job completions (without warming it up), using 35 terminals with all terminals initially in the think state; make all runs independently. Replicate the design as you see fit to obtain useful estimates of the expected main and interaction effects.

12.3. Consider using common random numbers (CRN) across all four design points of the full 2^2 factorial design on the inventory model in Examples 12.1 and 12.2. Let $C_{12} = \text{Cov}(R_1, R_2)$, $C_{13} = \text{Cov}(R_1, R_3)$, etc., and assume that CRN "works," i.e., all the covariances between the R_i's are positive.

TABLE 12.11
Coding chart for the generalized machine-breakdown model

Factor	−	+
s	2	4
Machine type	Standard	Deluxe
Repairman type	Standard	Expert

(*a*) Find expressions for the variances of both main effects as well as the interaction in terms of these covariances and the variances of the R_i's. What can you conclude about whether CRN reduces the variances of the expected effects estimates?

(*b*) Suppose that we are interested primarily in getting precise estimates of the expected main effects and care less about the interaction. Suggest an alternative random-number-assignment strategy that would do this. What happens to the precision of the expected interaction estimate?

12.4. Build a regression metamodel for the average-delay-in-queue response in the $M/M/1$ queue using the code of Sec. 1.4.4, 1.4.5, or 1.4.6; use the same initial conditions and termination rules. Take as input factors the mean interarrival time and the mean service time. Evaluate the accuracy of your metamodel. Start with a simple linear model, then add cross-product and quadratic terms.

12.5. Build quadratic regression metamodels for both the average-delay-in-queue and average-number-in-queues responses for the multiteller bank model of Sec. 2.6. Take as input factors the mean service time and the number of tellers. Evaluate the accuracy of your metamodel, and use it to discuss the trade-off between increasing the number of tellers and decreasing the mean service time.

12.6. Recall the supermarket model of Prob. 1.27. Regard both of the interarrival-time means (currently 2.1 minutes for regular customers and 1.1 minutes for express customers) as factors even though they probably would not really be controllable. Take the mean service times (currently 2.0 minutes for regular customers and 0.9 minute for express customers) as two additional factors. In anticipation of an increase in business, management wants to know what would happen if traffic got heavier as a result of reducing one or both of the interarrival-time means by 10 percent from their current values. To accommodate this, service could be quickened by reducing one or both of the service-time means by 10 percent.

(*a*) Design and carry out a resolution IV fractional factorial design to investigate which of these four possible changes would have the greatest impact on the quality of customer service, as measured by the average delay in queue of all customers regardless of type; use the same run conditions as in Prob. 1.27. Replicate the design as needed to achieve acceptable precision in the expected effects estimates.

(*b*) Now carry out a full 2^4 factorial design, replicating as needed. What, if anything, was lost or obfuscated in part (*a*) by doing only the fractional factorial design?

(*c*) Compare the results of the original model [the $(-, -, -, -)$ design point] with the model with all four changes made [the $(+, +, +, +)$ design point].

(*d*) Using your information from parts (*a*) and (*b*), construct a quadratic metamodel for the response, and evaluate its accuracy.

12.7. Recall the dry-cleaning operation of Prob. 2.26, involving five servers but six service-time means since server 4 must handle two different cases (damaged or undamaged). Management is willing to make a capital investment to reduce the mean service time at one or perhaps several of these stations, but does not know where (i.e., at which server) to make the investment. Design and carry out an experiment to identify which of the six mean service times in the table in Prob. 2.26 would be best to target for reduction. Use a fractional factorial design, and the same run conditions as in Prob. 2.26. Choose a response related to customer service.

12.8. For the BSU cafeteria of Prob. 2.30, there are six service times (counting the accumulated cashier times separately) that could potentially be improved by 15 percent (i.e., both endpoints of the associated uniform distribution would be decreased by 15 percent). Where should the investment go? Use a fractional factorial experimental design with a response related to customer service.

REFERENCES

Bengu, G., and J. Haddock: A Generative Simulation-Optimization System, *Comput. Ind. Eng.*, *10*: 301–313 (1986).

Biles, W. E.: Experimental Design in Computer Simulation, *Proc. 1979 Winter Simulation Conference*, San Diego, pp. 3–9 (1979).

Biles, W. E., and H. T. Ozmen: Optimization of Simulation Responses in a Multicomputing Environment, *Proc. 1987 Winter Simulation Conference*, Atlanta, pp. 402–408 (1987).

Biles, W. E., and J. J. Swain: Mathematical Programming and the Optimization of Computer Simulations, *Math. Program. Studies*, *11*: 189–207 (1979).

Biles, W. E., and J. J. Swain: *Optimization and Industrial Experimentation*, John Wiley, New York (1980).

Box, G. E. P., and N. R. Draper: *Empirical Model-Building and Response Surfaces*, John Wiley, New York (1987).

Box, G. E. P., W. G. Hunter, and J. S. Hunter: *Statistics for Experimenters*: *An Introduction to Design*, *Data Analysis*, *and Model Building*, John Wiley, New York (1978).

Buss, A. H.: Some Extensions and Limitations of Frequency Domain Experiments, *Proc. 1988 Winter Simulation Conference*, San Diego, pp. 549–557 (1988).

Glynn, P. W.: Optimization of Stochastic Systems, *Proc. 1986 Winter Simulation Conference*, Washington, D.C., pp. 52–59 (1986a).

Glynn, P. W.: Stochastic Approximation for Monte Carlo Optimization, *Proc. 1986 Winter Simulation Conference*, Washington, D.C., pp. 356–365 (1986b).

Glynn, P. W.: Likelihood Ratio Gradient Estimation: An Overview, *Proc. 1987 Winter Simulation Conference*, Atlanta, pp. 366–375 (1987).

Haddock, J., and G. Bengu: Application of a Simulation Optimization System for a Continuous Review Inventory Model, *Proc. 1987 Winter Simulation Conference*, Atlanta, pp. 382–390 (1987).

Haider, S. W., D. G. Noller, and T. B. Robey: Experiences with Analytic and Simulation Modeling for a Factory of the Future Project at IBM, *Proc. 1986 Winter Simulation Conference*, Washington, D.C., pp. 641–648 (1986).

Heidelberger, P., X. R. Cao, M. A. Zazanis, and R. Suri: Convergence Properties of Infinitesimal Perturbation Analysis Estimates, *Management Sci.*, *34*: 1281–1302 (1988).

Ho, Y. C., and X. R. Cao: Perturbation Analysis and Optimization of Queueing Networks, *J. Optimization Theory and Applications*, *40*: 559–582 (1983).

Ho, Y. C., M. A. Eyler, and T. T. Chien: A Gradient Technique for General Buffer Storage Design in a Serial Production Line, *Int. J. Prod. Res.*, *17*: 557–580 (1979).

Hunter, J. S., and T. H. Naylor: Experimental Designs for Computer Simulation Experiments, *Management Sci.*, *16*: 422–434 (1970).

Hussey, J. R., R. H. Myers, and E. C. Houck: Correlated Simulation Experiments in First-Order Response Surface Designs, *Operations Res.*, *35*: 744–758 (1987).

Ignall, E. J.: On Experimental Designs for Computer Simulation Experiments, *Management Sci.*, *18*: 384–388 (1972).

Jacobson, S. H., D. Morrice, and L. W. Schruben: The Global Simulation Clock as the Frequency Domain Experiment Index, *Proc. 1988 Winter Simulation Conference*, San Diego, pp. 558–563 (1988).

Jacobson, S. H., and L. W. Schruben: Techniques for Simulation Response Optimization, *Operations Res. Lett.*, *8*: 1–9 (1989).

Khuri, A. I., and J. A. Cornell: *Response Surfaces*, Marcel Dekker, New York (1987).

Kleijnen, J. P. C.: *Statistical Techniques in Simulation*, part II, Marcel Dekker, New York (1975).

Kleijnen, J. P. C.: Design and Analysis of Simulations: Practical Statistical Techniques, *Simulation*, 28: 81–90 (1977).

Kleijnen, J. P. C.: Experimentation with Models: Statistical Design and Analysis Techniques, in *Progress in Modelling and Simulation*, F. E. Cellier, ed., pp. 173–185, Academic Press, London (1982).

Kleijnen, J. P. C.: Statistical Tools for Simulation Practitioners, Marcel Dekker, New York (1987).

Mauro, C. A.: On the Performance of Two-Stage Group Screening, *Technometrics*, 26: 255–264 (1984).

Mauro, C. A.: Efficient Identification of Important Factors in Large Scale Simulations, *Proc. 1986 Winter Simulation Conference*, Washington, D.C., pp. 296–305 (1986).

Mauro, C. A., and K. C. Burns: A Comparison of Random Balance and Two-Stage Group Screening Designs: A Case Study, *Commun. Statist.*, *A13*: 2625–2647 (1984).

Mauro, C. A., and D. E. Smith: The Performance of Two-Stage Group Screening in Factor Screening Experiments, *Technometrics*, 24: 325–330 (1982).

Mauro, C. A., and D. E. Smith: Factor Screening in Simulation: Evaluation of Two Strategies Based on Random Balance Sampling, *Management Sci.*, 30: 209–221 (1984).

Meketon, M. S.: Optimization in Simulation: A Survey of Recent Results, *Proc. 1987 Winter Simulation Conference*, Atlanta, pp. 58–67 (1987).

Montgomery, D. C.: *Design and Analysis of Experiments*, 2d ed., John Wiley, New York (1984).

Montgomery, D. C., and V. M. Bettencourt, Jr.: Multiple Response Surface Methods in Computer Simulation, *Simulation*, 29: 113–121 (1977).

Myers, R. H.: *Response Surface Methodology*, Allyn & Bacon, Boston (1971).

Myers, R. H., A. I. Khuri, and W. H. Carter, Jr.: Response Surface Methodology: 1966–1988, *Technometrics*, 31: 137–157 (1989).

Plackett, R. L., and J. P. Burman: The Design of Optimum Multifactor Experiments, *Biometrika*, 33: 305–325 (1946).

Porta Nova, A. M., and J. R. Wilson: Estimation of Multiresponse Simulation Metamodels Using Control Variates, *Management Sci.*, 35: 1316–1333 (1989).

Reiman, M. I., and A. Weiss: Sensitivity Analysis via Likelihood Ratios, *Proc. 1986 Winter Simulation Conference*, Washington, D.C., pp. 285–289 (1986).

Rubinstein, R. Y.: *Monte Carlo Optimization, Simulation and Sensitivity of Queueing Networks*, John Wiley, New York (1986).

Ryan, B. F., B. L. Joiner, and T. A. Ryan, Jr.: *Minitab Handbook*, 2d ed., PWS Publishers, Boston (1985).

Safizadeh, M. H.: Optimization of Simulation via Quasi-Newton Methods, Dept. of Operations and Strategic Management, Boston College (1989).

Safizadeh, M. H.: Optimization in Simulation: Current Issues and the Future Outlook, *Naval Res. Logist.*, 37 (1990).

Sanchez, P. J., and A. H. Buss: A Model for Frequency Domain Experiments, *Proc. 1987 Winter Simulation Conference*, Atlanta, pp. 424–427 (1987).

Sanchez, P. J., and S. M. Sanchez: The Design and Analysis of 2^k Factorial Experiments Using Walsh Spectral Methods, Working Paper 88-017, Systems & Industrial Engineering Dept., University of Arizona, Tucson (1988).

Sanchez, P. J., and L. W. Schruben: Simulation Factor Screening Using Frequency Domain Methods: An Illustrative Example, Working Paper 87-013, Systems & Industrial Engineering Dept., University of Arizona, Tucson (1987).

Schruben, L. W.: Simulation Optimization Using Frequency Domain Methods, *Proc. 1986 Winter Simulation Conference*, Washington, D.C., pp. 366–369 (1986).

Schruben, L. W., and V. J. Cogliano: An Experimental Procedure for Simulation Response Surface Model Identification, *Commun. Assoc. Comput. Mach.*, 30: 716–730 (1987).

Schruben, L. W., and B. H. Margolin: Pseudorandom Number Assignment in Statistically Designed Simulation and Distribution Sampling Experiments, *J. Am. Statist. Assoc.*, 73: 504–520 (1978).

Smith, D. E.: An Empirical Investigation of Optimum-Seeking in the Computer Simulation Situation, *Operations Res.*, *21*: 475–497 (1973a).

Smith, D. E.: Requirements of an "Optimizer" for Computer Simulations, *Nav. Res. Logist. Quart.*, *20*: 161–179 (1973b).

Smith, D. E.: Automatic Optimum-Seeking Program for Digital Simulation, *Simulation*, *27*: 27–31 (1976).

Som, T. K., and R. G. Sargent: Alternative Methods for Generating and Analyzing the Output Series of Frequency Domain Experiments, *Proc. 1988 Winter Simulation Conference*, San Diego, pp. 564–567 (1988).

Som, T. K., R. G. Sargent, and L. W. Schruben: Frequency Domain Metamodelling of a Feedback Queue, *Proc. 1987 Winter Simulation Conference*, Atlanta, pp. 419–423 (1987).

Suri, R.: Infinitesimal Perturbation Analysis for General Discrete Event Systems, *J. Assoc. Comput. Mach.*, *34*: 686–717 (1987).

Suri, R., and M. A. Zazanis: Perturbation Analysis Gives Strongly Consistent Estimates for the $M/G/1$ Queue, *Management Sci.*, *34*: 39–64 (1988).

Tew, J. D., and J. R. Wilson: Estimating Simulation Metamodels Using Integrated Variance Reduction Techniques, *Proc. Stat. Comput. Sec. Am. Statist. Assoc.*, pp. 23–32 (1988).

Wilson, J. R.: Future Directions in Response Surface Methodology for Simulation, *Proc. 1987 Winter Simulation Conference*, Atlanta, pp. 378–381 (1987).

CHAPTER 13

SIMULATION OF MANUFACTURING SYSTEMS

Recommended sections for a first reading: 13.1, 13.2, 13.4, 13.5

13.1 INTRODUCTION

There has been a dramatic increase in the use of simulation to design and "optimize" manufacturing and warehousing systems. Some reasons for this include the following:

- Increased competition in many industries has resulted in a greater emphasis on automation to improve productivity and quality and also to reduce costs. Since automated systems are more complex, they can typically be analyzed only by simulation.

- Computing costs have been reduced by microcomputers and engineering work stations.

- Improvements in simulation software have reduced model-development time, thereby allowing for more timely manufacturing analyses.

- The availability of animation has resulted in a greater understanding and use of simulation by engineering managers.

Example 13.1. An automobile manufacturer had used simulation to a limited extent, but not really as a regular part of doing business. Then an animated simulation package was purchased and used for both an engineering analysis and the presentation to a vice president. The manager was so impressed by the results that he mandated that all future equipment purchases and system modifications be preceded by a simulation analysis. The animation contributed to the vice president's understanding of the simulation model.

The remainder of this chapter is organized as follows. In Sec. 13.2 we discuss the types of manufacturing issues typically addressed by simulation, followed in Sec. 13.3 by a description of simulation software that is designed specifically for manufacturing applications. Modeling manufacturing-system randomness, including machine downtimes, is discussed in Sec. 13.4. Sections 13.5 and 13.6 show in considerable detail how simulation is actually used to design and analyze a manufacturing system.

General references for this chapter are Carson (1986), Conway et al. (1988), Law (1986), Law and Haider (1989), and Law and McComas (1989).

13.2 OBJECTIVES OF SIMULATION IN MANUFACTURING

Perhaps the greatest overall benefit of using simulation in a manufacturing environment is that it allows a manager or engineer to obtain a *system-wide view* of the effect of "local" changes to the manufacturing system. If a change is made at a particular work station, its impact on the performance of *this* station may be predictable. On the other hand, it may be difficult, if not impossible, to determine ahead of time the impact of this change on the performance of the *overall system*.

Example 13.2. Suppose that a work station with one machine has insufficient processing capacity to handle its work load (i.e., its processing rate is less than the arrival rate of parts). Suppose further that it has been determined that adding a second machine will alleviate the capacity shortage at this station. However, this additional machine will also increase the throughput of parts from this station. This increased throughput will, in turn, show up as increased arrival rates to downstream work stations, which may cause new capacity shortages to occur, etc.

In addition to the above general benefit of simulation, there are a number of specific potential benefits from using simulation for manufacturing analyses, including:

- Increased throughput (parts produced per unit of time)
- Reduced in-process inventories of parts
- Increased utilizations of machines or workers
- Increased on-time deliveries of products to customers

- Reduced capital requirements (land, buildings, machines, etc.) or operating expenses
- Insurance that a proposed system design will, in fact, operate as expected
- Information gathered to build the simulation model will promote a greater understanding of the system, which often produces other benefits
- A simulation model for a proposed system often causes system designers to think about certain significant issues (e.g., system control logic) long before they normally would

> **Example 13.3.** The information gathered for a simulation model of a food-packing plant showed that the control logic for the conveyor system was not implemented correctly.

Simulation has successfully addressed a number of particular manufacturing issues, which we might classify into three general categories:

The need for and the quantity of equipment and personnel

- Number and type of machines for a particular objective (e.g., production of 1000 parts per week)
- Number, type, and physical arrangement of carts (e.g., forklift trucks and automated guided vehicles), conveyors, and other support equipment (e.g., pallets and fixtures)
- Location and size of inventory buffers [see Conway et al. (1988)]
- Evaluation of a change in product volume or mix (e.g., impact of new products)
- Evaluation of the effect of a new piece of equipment (e.g., a robot) on an existing manufacturing line
- Evaluation of capital investments
- Labor-requirements planning

Performance evaluation

- Throughput analysis
- Makespan (time-in-system) analysis
- Bottleneck analysis

Evaluation of operational procedures

- Production scheduling (i.e., evaluating proposed policies for dispatching orders to the shop floor, choosing batch sizes, loading parts at a work station, and sequencing of parts through the work stations in the system)
- Policies for component-part or raw-material inventory levels

- Control strategies (e.g., for a conveyor system or an automated guided vehicle system)
- Reliability analysis (e.g., effect of preventive maintenance)
- Quality-control policies

There are several common measures of performance obtained from a simulation study of a manufacturing system, including:

- Throughput
- Time in system for parts (makespan)
- Times parts spend in queues
- Times parts spend waiting for transport
- Times parts spend in transport
- Timeliness of deliveries (e.g., proportion of late orders)
- Sizes of in-process inventories (work-in-process or queue sizes)
- Utilization of equipment and personnel (i.e., proportion of time busy)
- Proportions of time that a machine is broken, starved (waiting for parts from a previous work station), blocked (waiting for a finished part to be removed), or undergoing preventive maintenance
- Proportions of parts that are reworked or scrapped

13.3 SIMULATION SOFTWARE FOR MANUFACTURING APPLICATIONS

The simulation software requirements for manufacturing applications are not that different from those for other simulation applications, with one exception. Most modern manufacturing facilities contain material-handling systems, which are often difficult to model correctly. Therefore, in addition to the software features discussed in Chap. 3, it is desirable for simulation packages used in manufacturing to have flexible, easy-to-use material-handling modules. Important classes of material-handling systems are *forklift trucks*, *automated guided vehicle systems* (AGVS) including contention for guide paths, *transport conveyors* (equal distance between parts), *accumulating (or queueing) conveyors*, *automated storage and retrieval systems* (AS/RS), *cranes*, and *robots*. [See Davis (1986) and Henriksen and Schriber (1986) for a discussion of simulating AGVS and conveyors.]

In Chap. 3 we defined simulation languages and application-oriented simulators, and then discussed the most popular simulation languages in some detail. Simulation languages offer considerable modeling flexibility and are widely used to simulate manufacturing systems. Furthermore, some of these languages (i.e., SIMAN IV and SLAM II) provide special features for manufacturing. There are also many simulation packages (languages or simulators) designed specifically for use in a manufacturing environment. Law and Haider (1989) discuss more than 20 simulation products used in manufacturing.

We now describe AutoMod II, ProModel, SIMFACTORY II.5, WITNESS, and XCELL+, which are, at the time of this writing, important manufacturing-oriented simulation packages. For some applications, the "program" development time when using these products may be considerably less than that for a simulation language. They are also typically easier to use. On the other hand, since these products are less flexible than general-purpose simulation languages, we describe current shortcomings of each package.

AutoMod II [see AutoSimulations (1989)] is a manufacturing-oriented simulation language marketed by AutoSimulations, Inc. (Bountiful, Utah). A model is developed in AutoMod by writing a program using its modeling constructs, which are specifically oriented toward *manufacturing and material-handling systems*. AutoMod II has an impressive three-dimensional animation capability and probably the most comprehensive set of material-handling modules currently available in any simulation package. Furthermore, the layout of a material-handling system can be input graphically, which also largely defines its animation. For example, the location and size of the guide paths for an AGVS can be specified graphically.

The major modeling elements in AutoMod II are as follows:

Loads	Used to represent parts in a manufacturing system
Resources	Used to represent machines or workers that process loads
Processes	Correspond roughly to physical areas in a manufacturing system (e.g., a work station or shipping) that a load visits; the program description of the process specifies its location, the resources required to "process" a load, and the load's next process
Conveyors	Used to model transport, accumulating, or power-and-free conveyors
AGVS	Used to model AGVS, including contention for guide paths (forklift trucks can also be represented)
AS/RS	Used to model AS/RS and also bridge cranes
Kinematics	Used to model machine-tool dynamics and robots

A shortcoming of the current version of AutoMod II is that its statistical capabilities are somewhat limited. In particular, it has only a small number of input probability distributions and no easy mechanism for making multiple replications of the simulation, a fundamental requirement for simulation output analysis. It is also expensive to purchase relative to most other simulation software.

Recently, a "scaled-down" version of AutoMod II, called AutoMod[2e], was introduced by AutoSimulations, Inc. It is operated with a mouse and retains the excellent animation, conveyor (except power and free), and AGVS capabilities of AutoMod II at a fraction of the cost.

ProModel [see Production (1989)] is a manufacturing simulator marketed by Production Modeling Corporation of Utah (Orem, Utah). It is one of the most flexible simulators currently available due to its programming-like constructs and its ability to call C or Pascal routines to model complex decision logic. It is also easy to use and has good statistical capabilities, including numerous input probability distributions, machine breakdowns based on calendar time, busy time, or parts completed (see Sec. 13.4.2), and automatic multiple replications of the simulation (if desired).

The ProModel software has the following basic constructs:

Parts	Used to represent parts in manufacturing system; parts can have general attributes that can be changed
Locations	Used to model machines or buffers
Resources	Used to represent stationary or movable resources like operators, repairmen, or tools
Conveyors	Used to model transport, accumulating, or power-and-free conveyors
Transporters	Used to model forklift trucks, AGVS, cranes, and robots

The modeling shortcomings of ProModel are not currently known since it is a relatively new product; however, its animation is based on character graphics rather than on the more desirable bit-mapped graphics.

SIMFACTORY II.5 [see CACI (1990)] is a manufacturing simulator marketed by CACI Products Company (La Jolla, California). It is very easy to use and has good statistical capabilities, including a variety of input probability distributions, correct modeling of machine downtimes, automatic multiple replications of the simulation (if desired), and confidence intervals for output measures.

The basic building blocks of SIMFACTORY are:

Parts	Used to represent parts in a manufacturing system; parts *cannot* have general attributes, only priority and due-date attributes
Stations	Used to represent machines or workers that process parts
Queues	Used to store work-in-process (i.e., parts) and/or receive raw materials entering the system
Process plans	Describe the operations required to transform raw materials into finished products
Resources	"Objects" required by stations for setup or processing, or by parts for movement between stations; examples are workers, tools, fixtures, and totes
Conveyors	Used to model transport or accumulating conveyors
Transporters	Used to model forklift trucks, cranes, and *possibly* AGVS (no contention for guide paths)

A shortcoming of the current version of SIMFACTORY is that it may have inadequate modeling flexibility for certain manufacturing applications. In particular, parts currently cannot have general attributes that can change as the simulation progresses through time. [In a paper-products factory, a part could be a roll of paper with the (changing) attribute of yardage.] There is also no capability for adding programming-like statements at selected points in the model in order to deal with complex or unique decision logic. A future version of SIMFACTORY II.5 will address some of these issues.

WITNESS [see AT&T (1989)] is a manufacturing simulator marketed by AT&T ISTEL (Beachwood, Ohio). It is one of the most flexible simulators currently available due to its programming-like input/output rules and actions. For example, an output rule can be used to specify where a part is routed next after completing processing at its current machine. An action can be used to change an attribute of a part at a particular point in time. Model flexibility can be further increased by calling a FORTRAN routine to implement complex decision logic.

The WITNESS software has the following basic building blocks:

Parts	Used to represent parts in a manufacturing system; parts have general attributes that can be changed
Machines	Used to represent machines or workers that process parts
Buffers	Used to represent a queue of parts
Labor	Used to represent resources that may be required for a machine to process a part, to set up a machine, or to repair a machine; examples are workers, tools, and fixtures
Conveyors	Used to model transport or accumulating conveyors
Vehicles	Used to model AGVS (or forklift trucks)

Two current shortcomings of WITNESS are the lack of an easy mechanism for making multiple replications of a simulation and the apparent incorrect modeling of machine downtimes in the "calendar-time" approach (see Sec. 13.4.2).

XCELL+ [see Conway et al. (1987)] is a manufacturing simulator distributed by Pritsker Corporation (Indianapolis, Indiana). It is easy to learn and use, with menus being employed to place and connect predefined graphical representations of system components on a CRT. This model-building process also *automatically* defines the animation.

The basic building blocks of XCELL+ are:

Parts	Used to represent parts in a manufacturing system; parts *cannot* have general attributes
Workcenters	Used to represent machines or workers that process parts
Receiving areas	Where raw materials are received from the outside world

Shipping areas	Where completed parts are shipped to the outside world
Buffers	Used to store work-in-process
Auxiliary resources	"Objects" required by workcenters to process a part, such as workers, tools, and fixtures
Maintenance facilities	Workers used to perform maintenance on workcenters
Carriers	Used to model AGVS, forklift trucks, and power-and-free conveyors

Current shortcomings of XCELL+ are that a limited number of input probability distributions are included, there is no way to make multiple replications of a simulation, machine downtimes are based only on busy time (see Sec. 13.4.2), there is no explicit modeling of transport and accumulating conveyors, and the modeling flexibility may be inadequate for certain manufacturing applications. In particular, parts cannot have general attributes and there is no facility for adding programming-like statements to deal with complex decision logic.

Up to now in this book, we have primarily discussed using simulation to design a new manufacturing system or to improve the performance of an existing one. However, simulation is increasingly being used to support weekly scheduling decisions on the shop floor (see Sec. 13.2). FACTOR [Pritsker (1989)] is a manufacturing simulator that can access the necessary manufacturing databases and help produce production schedules. This capability will also be available in AutoMod II (see above).

13.4   MODELING SYSTEM RANDOMNESS

In Chap. 6 we presented a general discussion of how to choose input probability distributions for simulation models, and those ideas are still relevant here. We now discuss some additional topics related to modeling system randomness that are particularly germane to manufacturing systems, with our major emphasis being the representation of machine downtimes.

13.4.1   Sources of Randomness

We begin with a discussion of common sources of randomness in manufacturing systems. In particular, the following are possible examples of continuous distributions in manufacturing:

- Interarrival times of parts, jobs, or raw materials to the system
- Processing or assembly times for a part
- "Operating" times of a machine before failure or breakdown (see Sec. 13.4.2)

- Repair times for a failed or broken machine
- Setup times to change a machine over from one part type to another

Note that in some cases the above quantities might be constant. For example, processing times for an automated machine might not vary appreciably. Also, automobile engines might arrive to a final assembly area with constant inter-arrival times of 1 minute.

There are actually two other common ways in which parts "enter" a manufacturing system. In some systems (e.g., a subassembly manufacturing line), it is often assumed that there is an unlimited supply of raw parts or materials in front of the line's first machine. Thus, the rate at which parts enter the system is the effective processing rate of the first machine, i.e., accounting for downtimes, blockage, etc. Jobs or orders may also arrive to a system in accordance with a production schedule, which specifies the time of arrival, the part type, and the order size for each order. In a simulation model, the production schedule is typically read from an external file.

Histograms of observed processing (or assembly), operating (or busy), and repair times each tend to have a distinctive shape, and examples of these three types of data are given in Figs. 13.1 through 13.3. Note that the operating

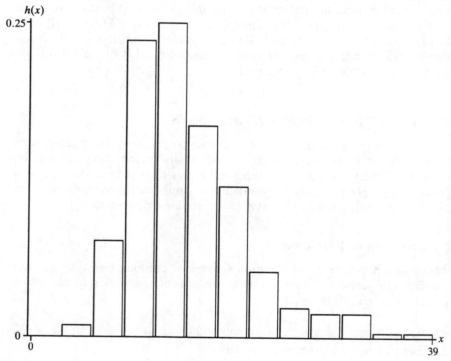

FIGURE 13.1
Histogram of assembly times for an aerospace manufacturer.

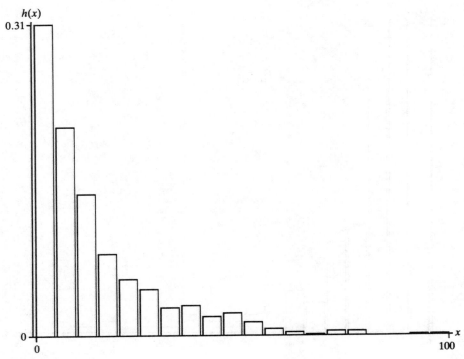

FIGURE 13.2
Histogram of machine operating (busy) times for a household-products manufacturer.

times in Fig. 13.2 have an *exponential-like shape*, with the mode (most likely value) at zero. However, the exponential distribution itself does not provide a good model for these data; see the discussion in Sec. 13.4.2. Observe also that the other two histograms have their mode at a positive value and are skewed to the right (i.e., the right tail is longer).

Discrete distributions seem, in general, to be less common than continuous distributions in manufacturing systems. However, two examples of discrete distributions are the outcome of inspecting a part (say, good or bad) and the size of an order arriving to a factory (the possible values are $1, 2, \ldots$).

13.4.2 Machine Downtimes

The most important source of randomness for many manufacturing systems is that associated with machine breakdowns or unscheduled downtime. Random downtime results from such events as actual machine failures, part jams, and broken tools. The following example illustrates the importance of modeling machine downtime correctly.

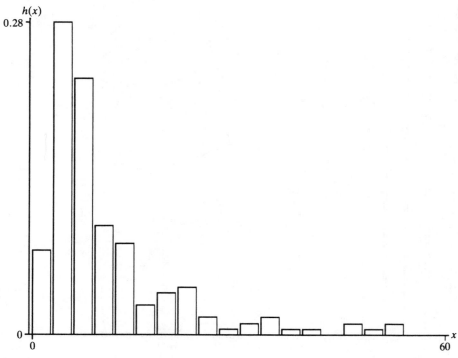

FIGURE 13.3
Histogram of machine repair times for an automobile manufacturer.

Example 13.4. A company is going to buy a new machine tool from a vendor who claims that the machine will be down 10 percent of the time. However, the vendor has no data on how long the machine will operate before breaking down or on how long it will take to repair the machine. Some simulation analysts have accounted for random breakdowns by simply reducing the machine processing rate by 10 percent. We will see, however, that this can produce results that are quite inaccurate.

Suppose that the single-machine-tool system (see, for example, Sec. 4.7) will *actually* operate according to the following assumptions *when installed* by the purchasing company:

- Jobs arrive with exponential interarrival times with a mean of 1.25 minutes.
- Processing times for a job at the machine are a constant 1 minute.
- The machine operates for an exponential amount of time with mean 540 minutes (9 hours) before breaking down.
- The repair time for the machine has a gamma distribution (shape parameter equal to 2) with mean 60 minutes (1 hour).
- The machine is, thus, broken 10 percent of the time, since the mean length of the up–down cycle is 10 hours.

In column 1 of Table 13.1 are results from five independent simulation runs of length 160 hours (20 eight-hour days) for the above system; all times are in minutes. In column 3 of the table are results from five simulation runs of length 160 hours for the machine tool system *with no breakdowns*, but with the processing (cycle) rate reduced from 1 job per minute to 0.9 job per minute, as has sometimes been the approach of simulation practitioners.

Note first that the average weekly throughput is almost identical for the two simulations. (For a system with no capacity shortages that is simulated for a *long period of time*, the average throughput for a 40-hour week must be equal to the arrival rate for a 40-hour week, which is 1920 here.) On the other hand, note that measures of performance such as average time in system for a job and maximum number of jobs in queue are vastly different for the two cases. Thus, the *deterministic* adjustment of the processing rate produces results that differ greatly from the *correct* results based on actual breakdowns of the machine.

In column 2 of Table 13.1 are results from five simulation runs of length 160 hours for the machine tool system *with breakdowns*, but with a mean operating time of 54 minutes and a mean repair time of 6 minutes; thus, the machine is still broken 10 percent of the time. Note that the average time in system and the maximum number in queue are quite different for columns 1 and 2. Therefore, when explicitly accounting for breakdowns in a simulation model, it is also important to have an accurate assessment of mean operating time and mean repair time for the actual system.

This example also shows that the required amount of model detail depends on the desired measure of performance. All three models produce accurate estimates of (expected) throughput, but this is clearly not the case for the other performance measures.

Despite the importance of modeling machine breakdowns correctly, as demonstrated by the above example, there has been little discussion of this subject in the simulation literature. Thus, we now discuss modeling random machine downtimes in some detail. Deterministic downtimes such as breaks, shift changes, and scheduled maintenance are relatively easy to model and are not treated here.

TABLE 13.1
Simulation results for the single-machine-tool system

Measure of performance	Breakdowns mean = 540 minutes	Breakdowns mean = 54 minutes	No breakdowns
Average throughput per week*	1908.8	1913.8	1914.8
Average time in system*	35.1	10.3	5.6
Maximum time in system[†]	256.7	76.1	39.1
Average number in queue*	27.2	7.3	3.6
Maximum number in queue[†]	231.0	67.0	35.0

* Average over five runs.
[†] Maximum over five runs.

A machine goes through a sequence of cycles, with the ith cycle consisting of an up ("operating") segment of length U_i followed by a down segment of length D_i. During an up segment, a machine will process parts if any are available and if the machine is not blocked. The first two up–down cycles for a machine are shown in Fig. 13.4. Let B_i and I_i be the amounts of time during U_i that the machine is busy processing parts and that the machine is idle (either starved for parts or blocked by the current finished part), respectively. Thus, $U_i = B_i + I_i$. Note that B_i and I_i may each correspond to a number of separated time segments and, thus, are not represented in Fig. 13.4.

Let W_i be the amount of time from the ith "failure" of the machine until its subsequent repair begins, and let R_i be the length of this ith repair time. Thus, $D_i = W_i + R_i$, as shown in Fig. 13.4.

We will assume for simplicity that cycles are independent of each other and are probabilistically identical. This implies that each of the six sequences of random variables defined above (e.g., $U_1, U_2, \ldots$ and $D_1, D_2, \ldots$) are IID within themselves (see Prob. 13.1). We will also assume that U_i and D_i are independent for all i (see Prob. 13.2).

We now discuss how to model machine-up segments in a simulation model assuming that "appropriate" breakdown data are available. The following two methods are widely used (see also Prob. 13.3):

Calendar Time. Assume that the uptime data $U_1, U_2, \ldots$ are available and that we can fit a standard probability distribution (e.g., exponential) F_U to these data using the techniques of Chap. 6. Alternatively, if no distribution provides a good fit, assume that an empirical distribution is used to model the U_i's. Then, starting at time 0, we generate a random value u_1 from F_U and $0 + u_1 = u_1$ is the time of the first failure of the machine in the simulation. When the machine actually fails at time u_1, note that it may either be busy or idle (see Prob. 13.18). Suppose that d_1 is determined to be the first downtime (to be discussed below) for the machine. Then the machine goes back up at time $u_1 + d_1$. (If the machine was processing a part when it failed at time u_1, then it is usually assumed that the machine finishes this part's *remaining* processing time starting at time $u_1 + d_1$.) At time $u_1 + d_1$, another value u_2 is randomly generated from F_U and the machine is up during the time interval $[u_1 + d_1, u_1 + d_1 + u_2)$. If d_2 is the second downtime, then the machine is down during the time interval $[u_1 + d_1 + u_2, u_1 + d_1 + u_2 + d_2)$, etc.

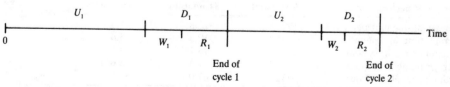

FIGURE 13.4
Up–down cycles for a machine.

There are two drawbacks of the *calendar-time approach*. First, it allows the machine to break down when it is idle, which may not be realistic. Also, assume that the machine in question is part of a larger system and has machines both upstream and downstream of it. If we simulate two different versions of the overall system using the F_U distribution to break down the specified machine (and also synchronize the downtimes), then the machine will break down at the same points in simulated (calendar) time for both simulations. However, due to different amounts of starving from the upstream machines and blocking from the downstream machines in the two simulation runs, the specified machine could have significantly less actual busy time for one configuration than for the other. This also may not be very realistic.

Busy Time. Assume that the busy-time data $B_1, B_2, \ldots$ are available and that we can fit a distribution F_B to these data. (Alternatively, an empirical distribution can be used.) Then, starting at time 0, we generate a random value b_1 from F_B. Then the machine is up until its total accumulated *busy (processing) time* reaches a value of b_1, at which point the *busy* machine fails. (For example, suppose that b_1 is equal to 60.7 minutes and each processing time is a constant 1 minute. Then the machine fails while processing its 61st part.) If f_1 is the simulated time that the machine fails for the first time ($f_1 \geq b_1$) and d_1 is the first downtime, then the machine goes back up at time $f_1 + d_1$, etc.

In general, the busy-time approach is more natural than the calendar-time approach. We would expect the next time of failure of a machine to depend more on total busy time since the last repair than on calendar time since the last repair. However, in practice, the busy-time approach may not be feasible, since uptime data $(U_1, U_2, \ldots)$ may be available but not busy-time data $(B_1, B_2, \ldots)$. In many factories, only the times that the machine fails and the times that the machine goes back up (completes repair) are recorded. Thus, the uptimes $U_1, U_2, \ldots$ may be easily computed, but the actual busy times $B_1, B_2, \ldots$ may be unknown (see Prob. 13.8). (In computing the U_i's, time intervals where the machine is off, e.g., idle shifts, should be subtracted out.) Note that if a machine is never starved or blocked, then $B_i = U_i$ and the two approaches are equivalent.

We now discuss how to model machine-down segments assuming that factory data are available. Assume first that the waiting time to repair, W_i, for the ith cycle is zero or negligible relative to the repair time R_i (for $i = 1, 2, \ldots$). Then we fit a distribution (e.g., gamma) F_D to the observed downtime data $D_1, D_2, \ldots$. Each time the machine fails, we generate a new random value from F_D and use it as the subsequent downtime (repair time).

Suppose that the W_i's may sometimes be "large," due to waiting for a repairman to arrive. If only D_i's are available (and not the W_i's and R_i's separately), as is often the case in practice, then fit a distribution F_D to the D_i's and randomly sample from F_D each time a downtime is needed in the simulation model. The reader should be aware, however, that F_D is a valid downtime distribution only for the current number of repairmen and for the maintenance requirements of the system from which the D_i's were collected.

Finally, assume that the W_i's may be significant and that the W_i's and R_i's are individually available. Then one approach is to model the waiting time for a repairman as a maintenance resource with a finite number of units and to fit a distribution F_R to the R_i's. If a repairman is available when the machine fails, the waiting time is zero unless there is a travel time, and the repair time is generated from F_R. If a repairman is not available, the broken machine joins a queue of machines waiting for a repairman, etc.

Suppose that factory data are not available to support either the calendar-time or busy-time breakdown models previously discussed. This often occurs when simulating a proposed manufacturing facility, but may also be the case for an existing plant when there is inadequate time for data collection and analysis. We now present a *tentative* model for this no-data case, which is likely to be more accurate than many of the approaches used in practice (see Example 13.4).

We will first assume that the amount of machine *busy* time, B, before a failure has a gamma distribution with shape parameter $\alpha_B = 0.7$ and scale parameter β_B to be specified. Note that the exponential distribution (gamma

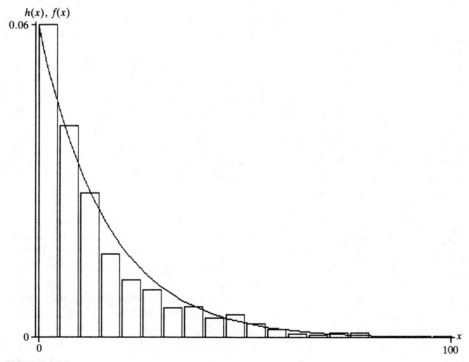

FIGURE 13.5
Histogram of machine operating (busy) times and the fitted exponential distribution.

distribution with $\alpha_B = 1.0$) does not appear, in general, to be a good model for machine busy times, even though it is often used in simulation models for this purpose.

Example 13.5. In Fig. 13.5 we show the histogram of machine operating times (actually busy times) from Fig. 13.2 with the best-fitting exponential distribution superimposed over it. It is visually clear that the exponential does not provide a very good fit for the data, since its density lies above the histogram for moderate values of x. Furthermore, it was rejected by the goodness-of-fit tests of Sec. 6.6.2.

We chose the gamma distribution because of its flexibility (i.e., its density can assume a wide variety of shapes) and because it has the general shape of many busy-time histograms when $\alpha_B \leq 1$. (The Weibull distribution could also have been used, but its mean is harder to compute.) The particular shape parameter $\alpha_B = 0.7$ for the gamma distribution was determined by fitting a gamma distribution to four different sets of busy-time data, with 0.7 being the average shape parameter obtained. In none of the four cases was the estimated shape parameter close to 1.0 (the exponential distribution). The density function for a gamma distribution with shape and scale parameters 0.7 and 1.0, respectively, is shown in Fig. 13.6.

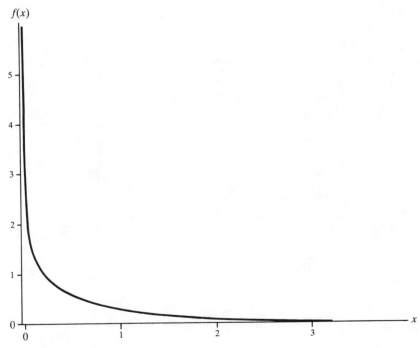

FIGURE 13.6
Gamma(0.7,1.0) distribution.

We will assume that machine downtime (or repair time) has a gamma distribution with shape parameter $\alpha_D = 1.4$ and a scale parameter β_D to be determined. This particular shape parameter was determined by fitting a gamma distribution to six different sets of downtime data, with 1.4 being the average shape parameter obtained. (The fact that $\alpha_D = 2\alpha_B$ is apparently just a coincidence.) The density function for a gamma distribution with shape and scale parameters 1.4 and 1.0, respectively, is shown in Fig. 13.7. This density function has the same general shape as downtime histograms typically experienced in practice (see Fig. 13.3).

In order to complete our model of machine downtimes in the absence of data, we need to specify the scale parameters β_B and β_D. This can be done by soliciting two pieces of information from system "experts" (e.g., engineers or vendors). We have found it convenient and typically feasible to obtain an estimate of mean downtime $\mu_D = E(D)$ and an estimate of machine efficiency e, which we now define. The *efficiency* e is defined to be the long-run proportion of potential processing time (i.e., parts present and machine not blocked) during which the machine is actually processing parts, and is given by

$$e = \frac{\mu_B}{\mu_B + \mu_D}$$

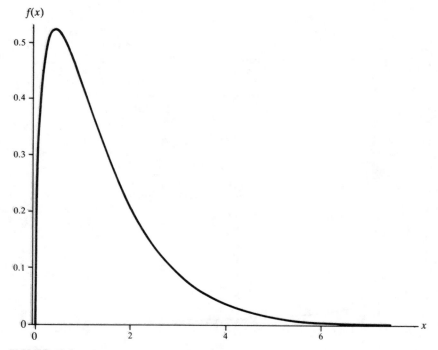

FIGURE 13.7
Gamma(1.4,1.0) distribution.

where $\mu_B = E(B)$ is the mean amount of machine busy time before a failure. If the machine is never starved or blocked, then $\mu_B = \mu_U = E(U)$ and e is the long-run proportion of time during which the machine is processing parts. Using the values of μ_D and e (and also the fact that the mean of a gamma distribution is the product of its shape and scale parameters), it is easy to show that the required scale parameters are given by

$$\beta_B = \frac{e\mu_D}{0.7(1-e)}$$

and

$$\beta_D = \frac{\mu_D}{1.4}$$

Thus, our model for machine downtimes when no data are available has been completely specified.

We have discussed above models for the breaking down and repair of machines. However, in practice there are a number of additional complications that often occur, such as multiple independent causes of machine failure. Some of these complexities are discussed in the problems at the end of the chapter.

13.5 AN EXTENDED EXAMPLE

We now illustrate how simulation can be used to improve the performance of a manufacturing system. We will simulate a number of different configurations of a system consisting of work stations and forklift trucks, with the simulation output statistics from one configuration being used to determine the next configuration to be simulated. This procedure will be continued until a system design is obtained that meets our performance requirements.

13.5.1 Problem Description and Simulation Results

A company is going to build a new manufacturing facility consisting of an input/output (or receiving/shipping) station and five work stations as shown in Fig. 13.8. The machines in a particular station are identical, but the machines in different stations are dissimilar. (This system is an embellishment of the job-shop model in Sec. 2.7.) One of the goals of the simulation study is to determine the number of machines needed in each work station. It has been decided that the distances (in feet) between the six stations will be as shown in Table 13.2 (the input/output station is numbered 6).

Assume that jobs arrive at the input/output station with interarrival times that are independent exponential random variables with a mean of 1/15 hour. Thus, 15 jobs arrive in a "typical" hour. There are three types of jobs, and jobs are of types 1, 2, and 3, with respective probabilities 0.3, 0.5, and 0.2. Job types 1, 2, and 3 require 4, 3, and 5 operations to be done, respectively, and each operation must be done at a specified work station in a prescribed order.

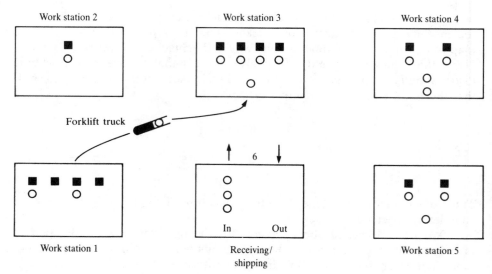

FIGURE 13.8
Layout for the manufacturing system.

Each job begins at the input/output station, travels to the work stations on its routing, and then leaves the system at the input/output station. The routings for the different job types are given in Table 13.3.

A job must be moved from one station to another by a forklift truck, which moves at a constant speed of 5 feet per second. Another goal of the simulation study is to determine the number of forklift trucks required. When a forklift becomes available, it processes requests by jobs in increasing order of the distance between the forklift and the requesting job (i.e., the rule is shortest distance first). When the forklift finishes moving a job to a work station, it remains at that station if there are no pending job requests (see Prob. 13.14).

If a job is brought to a particular work station and all machines there are already busy or blocked (see the discussion below), the job joins a single FIFO

TABLE 13.2
Distances (in feet) between the six stations

Station	1	2	3	4	5	6
1	0	150	213	336	300	150
2	150	0	150	300	336	213
3	213	150	0	150	213	150
4	336	300	150	0	150	213
5	300	336	213	150	0	150
6	150	213	150	213	150	0

TABLE 13.3
Routings for the three job types

Job type	Work stations in routing
1	3, 1, 2, 5
2	4, 1, 3
3	2, 5, 1, 4, 3

queue at that station. The time to perform an operation at a particular machine is a gamma random variable with a shape parameter of 2, whose mean depends on the job type and the work station to which the machine belongs. The mean service time for each job type and each operation is given in Table 13.4. Thus, the mean *total* service time averaged over all jobs is 0.77 hour. When a machine finishes processing a job, the job blocks that machine (i.e., the machine cannot process another job) until the job is removed by a forklift (see Prob. 13.15).

We will simulate the proposed manufacturing facility to determine how many machines are needed at each work station and how many forklift trucks are needed to achieve an expected throughput of 120 jobs per 8-hour day, which is the maximum possible. Among those system designs that can achieve the desired throughput, the best system design will be chosen on the basis of measures of performance such as average time is system, maximum input queue sizes, proportion of time each work station is busy, proportion of time transporters are moving, etc.

For each proposed system design, 10 replications of length 320 hours will be made (40 eight-hour days), with the first 64 hours of each replication being a warmup period. (See Sec. 13.5.2 for a discussion of warmup-period determination.) We will also use the method of common random numbers (see Sec. 11.2) to simulate the various system designs. This will guarantee that a particular job will arrive at the same point in time, be of the same job type, and have the same sequence of service-time values for all system designs on a particular replication. Job characteristics will, of course, be different on different replications.

To determine a starting point for our simulation runs (i.e., to determine system design 1), we will do a simple queueing-type analysis of our system. In

TABLE 13.4
Mean service time for each job type and each operation

Job type	Mean service time for successive operations (hours)
1	0.25, 0.15, 0.10, 0.30
2	0.15, 0.20, 0.30
3	0.15, 0.10, 0.35, 0.20, 0.20

TABLE 13.5
Required number of machines for each work station

Work station	Arrival rate (jobs/hour)	Service rate (jobs/hour/machine)	Required number of machines
1	15.0	4.65	$3.23 \rightarrow 4$
2	7.5	8.33	$0.90 \rightarrow 1$
3	15.0	3.77	$3.98 \rightarrow 4$
4	10.5	6.09	$1.72 \rightarrow 2$
5	7.5	4.55	$1.65 \rightarrow 2$

particular, for work station i (where $i = 1, 2, \ldots, 5$) to be well defined (have sufficient processing capacity) in the long run, its utilization factor $\rho_i = \lambda_i/(s_i \omega_i)$ (see App. 1B for notation) must be less than 1. For example, the arrival rate to station 1 is $\lambda_1 = 15$ per hour, since all jobs visit station 1. Using conditional probability [see, for example, Ross (1989, chap. 3)], the mean service time at station 1 is

$$0.3(0.15 \text{ hour}) + 0.5(0.20 \text{ hour}) + 0.2(0.35 \text{ hour}) = 0.215 \text{ hour}$$

which implies that the service rate (per machine) at station 1 is $\omega_1 = 4.65$ jobs per hour. Therefore, if we solve the equation $\rho_1 = 1$, we obtain that the required number of machines at station 1 is $s_1 = 3.23$, which we round up to 4. (What is wrong with this analysis? See Prob. 13.9.) A summary of the calculations for all five stations is given in Table 13.5, from which we see that 4, 1, 4, 2, and 2 machines are *supposedly* required for stations $1, 2, \ldots, 5$, respectively.

We can do a similar analysis for forklifts. Type 1 jobs arrive to the system at a rate of 4.5 (0.3 times 15) jobs per hour. Furthermore, the mean *travel* time for a type 1 job is 0.06 hour (along the route 6–3–1–2–5–6). Thus, 0.27 forklift will be required to move type 1 jobs. Similarly, 0.38 and 0.24 forklift will be required for type 2 and type 3 jobs, respectively. Thus, a total of 0.89 forklift is required, which we round up to 1. (What is missing from this analysis? See Prob. 13.10.) A summary of the forklift calculations is given in Table 13.6.

A summary of the 10 simulation runs for system design 1, which was specified by the above analysis, is given in Table 13.7 (all times are in hours).

TABLE 13.6
Required number of forklift trucks

Job type	Arrival rate (jobs/hour)	Mean travel time (hour/job/forklift)	Required number of forklifts
1	4.5	0.06	0.27
2	7.5	0.05	0.38
3	3.0	0.08	0.24
All			$0.89 \rightarrow 1$

TABLE 13.7
Simulation results for system design 1

Number of machines: 4, 1, 4, 2, 2
Number of forklifts: 1

Station Performance measure	1	2	3	4	5
Proportion machines busy	0.69	0.67	0.84	0.69	0.61
Proportion machines blocked	0.18	0.33	0.16	0.31	0.30
Average number in queue	1.65	342.37	121.57	224.54	2.45
Maximum number in queue	18.00	650.00	247.00	493.00	24.00

Average daily throughput: 91.60
Average time in system: 44.95
Average total time in queues: 43.85
Average total wait for transport: 0.30
Proportion forklifts moving loaded: 0.75
Proportion forklifts moving empty: 0.24

Note, for example, that the average utilization (proportion of time busy) of the four machines in station 1 (over the 10 runs) is 0.69, the time-average number of jobs in the queue feeding station 1 is 1.65, and the maximum number of jobs in this queue (over the 10 runs) is 18. More important, observe that the average daily throughput is 91.60, which is much less than the expected throughput of 120 for a well-defined system; it follows that this design must suffer from capacity shortages (i.e., machines or forklifts). The average time in system for a job is 44.95 hours (43.85 hours for *all* queues visited and 0.30 hour for *all* transporter waits), which is excessive given that the mean total service time is less than 1 hour. Note that the *total* forklift utilization is 0.99; see also Fig. 13.9, where the total number of forklift requests (busy forklifts plus jobs waiting for forklifts) is plotted in time increments of 1 hour *for replication 1*. The high forklift utilization along with the large machine-blockage proportions strongly suggest that one or more additional forklifts are needed. Finally, observe that stations 2, 3, and 4 are each either busy or blocked 100 percent of the time, and their queue statistics are quite large. (See also Fig. 13.10, where the number in queue 2 is plotted in time increments of 1 hour for the first 160 hours of replication 1.) We will therefore add a single machine to each of stations 2, 3, and 4. (We will not add a forklift at this time, although it certainly seems warranted; see system design 3.)

The results from simulating system design 2 (4, 2, 5, 3, and 2 machines for stations 1, 2, . . . , 5 and 1 forklift) are given in Table 13.8. The average daily throughput has gone from 91.60 to 105.24, but is still considerably less than that expected for a well-defined system. Likewise the average time in system has been reduced from 44.95 to 23.63 hours. Even though we added three machines to the system, the congestion level at station 5 has actually become considerably worse. In fact, station 5 is now busy or blocked 100 percent of the time. Also, the blockage proportions have increased for all

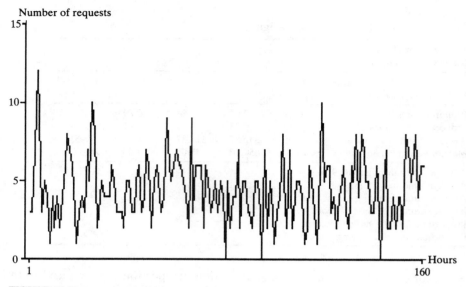

FIGURE 13.9
Total number of forklift requests in time increments of 1 hour for system design 1 (replication 1).

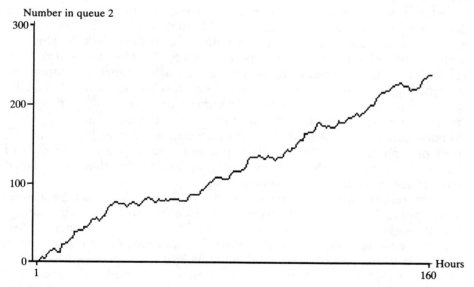

FIGURE 13.10
Number in queue 2 in time increments of 1 hour for system design 1 (replication 1).

TABLE 13.8
Simulation results for system design 2

Number of machines: 4, 2, 5, 3, 2
Number of forklifts: 1

Station	1	2	3	4	5
Performance measure					
Proportion machines busy	0.75	0.45	0.75	0.53	0.66
Proportion machines blocked	0.22	0.41	0.24	0.43	0.34
Average number in queue	19.70	1.91	63.79	9.89	275.95
Maximum number in queue	99.00	37.00	251.00	73.00	545.00

Average daily throughput: 105.24
Average time in system: 23.63
Average total time in queues: 22.38
Average total wait for transport: 0.44
Proportion forklifts moving loaded: 0.84
Proportion forklifts moving empty: 0.16

stations. This example reinforces the statement that it may not be easy to predict the effect of local changes on system-wide behavior. Since the total forklift utilization is 1.00, we now add a second forklift to the system.

The results from simulating system design 3 (4, 2, 5, 3, and 2 machines and 2 forklifts) are given in Table 13.9. The average daily throughput is now 120.40, which is not significantly different from 120 as shown in Sec. 13.5.2. *Thus, system design 3 is apparently well defined.* In addition, the average time in system has been decreased from 23.63 to 1.90 hours. Notice also that the average total utilization of the two forklifts is an acceptable 0.71 (see also Fig. 13.11), and the station blockage proportions are now small. Finally, the statistics for all five stations seem reasonable (see also Fig. 13.12), with the

TABLE 13.9
Simulation results for system design 3

Number of machines: 4, 2, 5, 3, 2
Number of forklifts: 2

Station	1	2	3	4	5
Performance measure					
Proportion machines busy	0.81	0.46	0.79	0.57	0.85
Proportion machines blocked	0.06	0.07	0.04	0.06	0.07
Average number in queue	3.86	0.26	2.02	0.50	8.58
Maximum number in queue	57.00	9.00	23.00	14.00	71.00

Average daily throughput: 120.40
Average time in system: 1.90
Average total time in queues: 1.01
Average total wait for transport: 0.07
Proportion forklifts moving loaded: 0.44
Proportion forklifts moving empty: 0.27

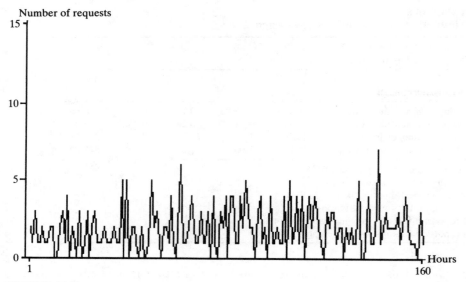

FIGURE 13.11
Total number of forklift requests in time increments of 1 hour for system design 3 (replication 1).

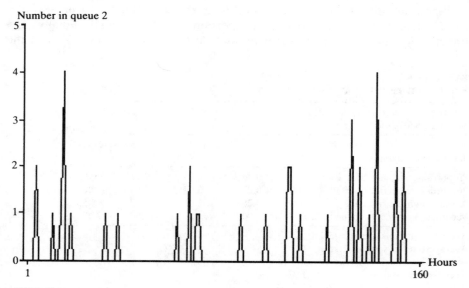

FIGURE 13.12
Number in queue 2 in time increments of 1 hour for system design 3 (replication 1).

possible exception of the maximum queue sizes for stations 1 and 5. Whether queue sizes of 57 and 71 are acceptable depends on the particular application. Since the proportions busy are definitely the largest for stations 1, 3, and 5, we now add a single machine to each of these stations.

The results for system design 4 (5, 2, 6, 3, and 3 machines and 2 forklifts) are given in Table 13.10. The throughput is essentially unchanged, but the average time in system has been reduced from 1.90 to 1.05 hours. This latter difference is statistically significant as shown in Sec. 13.5.2. The maximum queue sizes for stations 1, 3, and 5 have all been reduced, but unfortunately, so have the corresponding proportions busy. System designs 3 and 4 both appear to be well defined. The design that is preferable depends on the importance of performance measures such as the average time in system and the proportions busy; it also depends on the cost of machines and the cost of in-process storage.

We now consider another variation of system design 3. It involves, for the first time, a change in the control logic for the system. In particular, jobs waiting for the forklifts are processed in a FIFO manner, rather than shortest distance first as before. The results for system design 5 are given in Table 13.11. Average time in system has gone from 1.90 to 2.26 hours, an apparent 19 percent increase. (Histograms of time in system for system designs 3 and 5, based on all 10 runs of each, are given in Fig. 13.13.) The queue statistics for stations 1 and 5 have also increased by an appreciable amount, and the forklifts now spend more time moving empty. It takes a forklift more time to get to a waiting job, since the closest one is not generally chosen. We therefore do *not* recommend the new forklift-dispatching rule.

Finally, we discuss another variation of system design 3 (shortest-distance-first forklift-dispatching rule), where certain machines break down. In

TABLE 13.10
Simulation results for system design 4

Number of machines: 5, 2, 6, 3, 3
Number of forklifts: 2

Station	1	2	3	4	5
Performance measure					
Proportion machines busy	0.65	0.46	0.66	0.57	0.56
Proportion machines blocked	0.05	0.07	0.04	0.06	0.05
Average number in queue	0.55	0.26	0.48	0.52	0.42
Maximum number in queue	18.00	12.00	16.00	13.00	13.00

Average daily throughput: 120.46
Average time in system: 1.05
Average total time in queues: 0.15
Average total wait for transport: 0.07
Proportion forklifts moving loaded: 0.44
Proportion forklifts moving empty: 0.27

TABLE 13.11
Simulation results for system design 5

Number of machines: 4, 2, 5, 3, 2
Number of forklifts: 2
FIFO queue for forklifts

Station Performance measure	1	2	3	4	5
Proportion machines busy	0.81	0.46	0.79	0.57	0.84
Proportion machines blocked	0.08	0.08	0.06	0.08	0.09
Average number in queue	5.99	0.29	2.40	0.60	10.97
Maximum number in queue	86.00	9.00	25.00	16.00	86.00

Average daily throughput: 120.33
Average time in system: 2.26
Average total time in queues: 1.33
Average total wait for transport: 0.10
Proportion forklifts moving loaded: 0.44
Proportion forklifts moving empty: 0.31

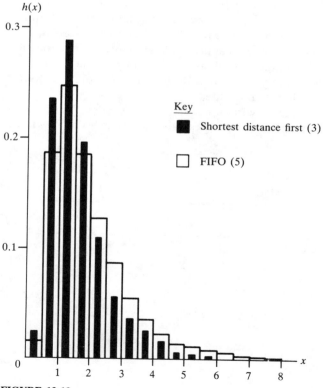

FIGURE 13.13
Histograms of time in system for system designs 3 and 5.

TABLE 13.12
Simulation results for system design 6

Number of machines: 4, 2, 5, 3, 2
Number of forklifts: 2
Machines in stations 1 and 5 have efficiencies of 0.9

Station	1	2	3	4	5
Performance measure					
Proportion machines busy	0.80	0.46	0.79	0.57	0.82
Proportion machines blocked	0.06	0.07	0.04	0.06	0.07
Proportion machines down	0.09	0.00	0.00	0.00	0.09
Average number in queue	17.95	0.27	1.90	0.46	44.23
Maximum number in queue	132.00	9.00	23.00	13.00	183.00

Average daily throughput: 118.70
Average time in system: 5.14
Average total time in queues: 4.21
Average total wait for transport: 0.07
Proportion forklifts moving loaded: 0.44
Proportion forklifts moving empty: 0.27

particular, we assume that each machine in stations 1 and 5 breaks down independently with an efficiency of 0.9 (see Sec. 13.4.2). The amount of busy time that a machine operates before failure is exponentially distributed with a mean of 4.5 hours, and repair times have a gamma distribution with a shape parameter of 2 and a mean of 0.5 hour. The simulation output for the resulting system design 6 is given in Table 13.12. The average daily throughput is now 118.70, but this is *not* significantly different from 120 (see Sec. 13.5.2). On the other hand, average time in system has gone from 1.90 to 5.14, an increase of 171 percent. The queue statistics for stations 1 and 5 are also appreciably larger. Thus, breaking down only stations 1 and 5 caused a significant degradation in system performance; breaking down all five stations would probably have an even larger impact. In summary, we have once again seen the importance of modeling machine breakdowns correctly.

13.5.2 Statistical Calculations

In this section we perform some statistical calculations related to the manufacturing system of Sec. 13.5.1. We begin by constructing a 90 percent confidence interval for the steady-state mean daily throughput for system design 3, ν_3, using the replication/deletion approach of Sec. 9.5.2. Let

$$X_j = \text{average throughput on days 9 through 40 on replication } j \text{ for } j = 1, 2, \ldots, 10$$

where the warmup period is $l = 8$ days or 64 hours. Then the desired confidence interval is

$$120.40 \pm t_{9,0.95}\sqrt{\frac{5.92}{10}} \qquad \text{or} \qquad 120.40 \pm 1.41$$

which contains 120. Similarly, we get the following 90 percent confidence interval for the steady-state mean daily throughput for system design 6, ν_6:

$$118.70 \pm t_{9,0.95}\sqrt{\frac{5.59}{10}} \qquad \text{or} \qquad 118.70 \pm 1.37$$

which also contains 120.

System designs 3 and 4 are both well defined in the sense of having steady-state mean daily throughputs that cannot be distinguished from 120. However, our estimates of the steady-state mean time in system for these system designs are 1.90 and 1.05, respectively, which *appear* to be somewhat different. To see if this difference is statistically significant, we construct a 90 percent confidence interval for $\nu_3' - \nu_4'$ using the replication/deletion approach (see Example 10.5), where ν_i' is the steady-state mean time in system for system design i (where $i = 3, 4$). We get

$$0.85 \pm t_{9,0.95}\sqrt{\frac{0.14}{10}} \qquad \text{or} \qquad 0.85 \pm 0.22$$

which does not contain 0. Thus, ν_3' is significantly different from ν_4'.

The results presented in Sec. 13.5.1 (and here) assume a warmup period of 64 hours or 8 days. This warmup period was obtained by applying Welch's procedure (Sec. 9.5.1) to the 320 hourly throughputs in each of the 10

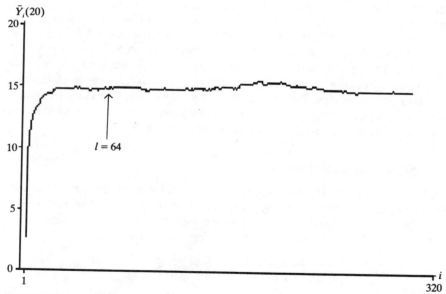

FIGURE 13.14
Moving average ($w = 20$) of hourly throughputs for system design 3.

replications for system design 3 (where Y_{ji} is the throughput in the ith hour of the jth run). The moving average $\bar{Y}_i(20)$ (using a window of $w = 20$) is plotted in Fig. 13.14, from which we obtained a warmup period of $l = 64$ hours. We performed similar analyses for system designs 4, 5, and 6, and a warmup period of 64 hours seemed adequate for these systems as well.

13.6 A SIMULATION CASE STUDY OF A METAL-PARTS MANUFACTURING FACILITY

In this section we describe the results of a successful simulation study of a manufacturing and warehousing system [see Law and McComas (1988)]. The facility described is fictitious for reasons of confidentiality, but is similar to the system actually modeled for a Fortune 500 company. The project objectives, the simulation steps, and the benefits that we describe are also very similar to the actual ones.

13.6.1 Description of the System

The manufacturing facility (see Fig. 13.15) produces several different metal parts, each requiring three distinct subassemblies. Subassemblies corresponding to a particular part are produced in large batches on one of two subassem-

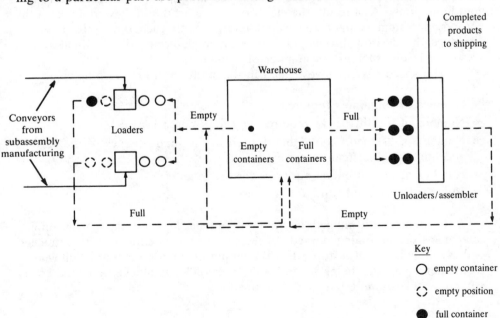

FIGURE 13.15
Layout of the system.

bly manufacturing lines, and then moved by conveyor to a loader where they are placed into empty containers. Each container holds only one type of subassembly at a time. The containers are stored in a warehouse until all three of the part subassemblies are available for assembly. Containers of the three subassemblies corresponding to a particular part are brought to an unloader/ assembler (henceforth called the assembler), where they are unloaded and assembled into the final product, which is then sent to shipping. The resulting empty containers are temporarily stored in a finite-capacity accumulating conveyor (not shown in the figure) at the back of the assembler. They are then taken to the loaders, if needed; otherwise, they are transported to the warehouse. Full and empty containers are moved by forklift trucks.

The assembler operates only 5 days a week, while the remainder of the system is in operation three shifts a day for 7 days a week. Also, the subassembly lines, the loaders, and the assembler are subject to random breakdowns.

13.6.2 Overall Objectives and Issues to Be Investigated

The subassembly lines already existed at the time of the study. However, the loaders, the warehouse, and the assembler were in the process of being designed. (They were to replace existing technology that had certain through-put limitations.) As a result, the major objectives of the study were to see if the proposed system components would interact with each other effectively to produce the desired throughput and, also, to determine the optimal system resource levels, such as the number of containers.

The specific issues investigated in the study included the following:

- Number of containers required
- Number of forklift trucks required and their control logic
- Number of "staged" containers desired in the input queues of the loaders and the assembler (cannot be exceeded)
- Number of output queue positions for the loaders
- Number of required shifts for the assembler

Containers are staged in an input queue to keep the corresponding machine from becoming starved. In the case of a starved loader, the attached subassembly line is also stopped. If the output queue for a loader is full when a container completes being loaded, then the loader is blocked and the corresponding subassembly line is also stopped.

13.6.3 Development of the Model

The study described here took 3 man-months to complete. An important part of the model-building process was the following series of meetings:

TABLE 13.13
Probability distributions for the model

Source of randomness	Distribution type
Subassembly line busy times	Empirical
Subassembly line repair times	Empirical
Subassembly line setup times	Triangular
Loader busy times	Empirical
Loader repair times	Lognormal
Assembler busy times	Weibull
Assembler repair times	Lognormal
Assembler setup times	Uniform

- Three-day initial meeting to define project objectives, delineate model assumptions, and specify data requirements
- One-day meeting (before coding) to perform a structured walk-through of the model assumptions (see Sec. 5.5.1) before an audience of the client's engineers and managers
- One-day meeting to review initial simulation results and to make changes to model assumptions

As a result of the initial meeting, the company supplied the consultants with a large amount of data that already existed in its computer databases and reports; however, a significant effort was required by both parties to get the data into a usable format. The UniFit statistical package [see Law and Vincent (1990)] was used to analyze the data and to determine the appropriate probability distribution for each source of system randomness. Highlights of their findings are given in Table 13.13. In some cases standard distributions such as lognormal or Weibull were used; in other cases, an empirical distribution (see Sec. 6.2.4) based on the actual data was necessary.

The simulation model was coded in the SIMAN (see Sec. 3.6) simulation language, although other general-purpose languages could have been used as well. SIMAN was selected because of its flexibility and material-handling features. The model consisted of approximately 2000 lines of code, 75 percent of which consisted of FORTRAN event routines. This model complexity was necessitated by a complicated set of rules (not described here) for *each* part that specify when its corresponding subassemblies are sent to the assembler.

13.6.4 Model Verification and Validation

Verification is concerned with determining if the simulation computer program is working as intended, and the initial verification efforts included the following:

- The model was coded and debugged in steps.

- An interactive debugger was used to verify that each program path was correct.
- Model output results were checked for reasonableness.
- Model summary statistics for the values generated from the input probability distributions were compared to historical data summary statistics.

In addition, two more "definitive" verification checks were performed. From the historical mean busy times and mean repair times, it was possible to compute the theoretical efficiency (see Sec. 13.4.2) for each line. These efficiencies and comparable ones produced by the simulation model (for scenario 1 in Table 13.16) are given in Table 13.14. The closeness of the efficiencies indicates that the program for the subassembly lines was probably correct.

Using the simulation efficiencies from Table 13.14 and three shifts for the assembler, it was possible to compute a theoretical efficiency of 0.643 for the assembler. On the other hand, the simulation model actually produced an assembler efficiency of 0.630. The closeness of these two efficiencies indicates that the program for the assembler is probably correct.

Validation is concerned with determining how closely the simulation model represents the actual system, and the following were some of the validation procedures performed:

- All model assumptions were reviewed and agreed upon by company personnel.
- Different data sets for the same type of randomness (e.g., subassembly busy times for the two lines) were tested for homogeneity and merged only if appropriate (see Sec. 6.11).
- All fitted probability distributions (e.g., lognormal) were tested for correctness using the techniques of Chap. 6.

It is generally impossible to validate a simulation model completely, since some part of the actual system may not currently exist. However, building a simulation model of a similar existing system and comparing model and system outputs will often be the most definitive validation technique available. In our case, the subassembly lines were already in operation, while the rest of the system was in the design phase. In Table 13.15 is a comparison for each subassembly line of the historical efficiency and the simulation efficiency. The

TABLE 13.14
Verification comparison of subassembly line efficiencies

Line	Theoretical efficiency	Simulation efficiency
1	0.732	0.741
2	0.724	0.727

TABLE 13.15
Validation comparison of subassembly line efficiencies

Line	Historical efficiency	Simulation efficiency
1	0.738	0.741
2	0.746	0.727

historical efficiencies were taken from *system output data* available in a company report and were not used in building the model. (The theoretical efficiencies in Table 13.14 were computed from historical *system input data*.) The agreement of the efficiencies in Table 13.15 indicates that the model of the subassembly lines is "valid."

13.6.5 Results of the Simulation Experiments

We first simulated seven different scenarios (system designs), which are described in Table 13.16. Each of these scenarios assumed 3000 containers and used the following company-specified priority rule for dispatching forklift trucks:

1. Take empty containers to loaders.
2. Pick up full containers from loaders.
3. Take full containers to assembler.
4. Pick up empty containers from assembler.

Five independent simulation runs were made for each scenario, with each run being 23 weeks in length and having a 3-week warmup period during which no statistics were gathered. The length of the warmup period was determined by plotting the average number of empty containers (over the five runs) in time increments of 1 hour for scenario 1, which is shown in Fig. 13.16; initially, all containers were empty. Note that this empty-container stochastic process does

TABLE 13.16
Scenarios for the initial simulation runs

Scenario	Forklift trucks	Queue sizes	Assembler shifts
1	3	2	3
2	3	2	2
3	2	2	3
4	3	1	3
5	3	3	3
6	3, 2 (weekend)	2	3
7	3	2	2 (all 7 days)

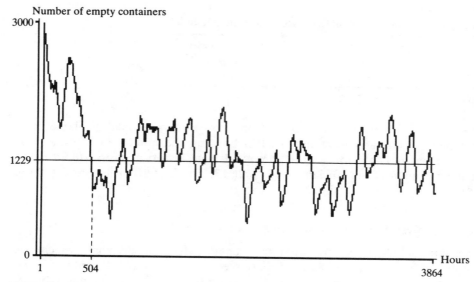

FIGURE 13.16
Average number of empty containers (over the five runs) in time increments of 1 hour for scenario 1.

not have a steady-state distribution for scenarios 1 through 6 because the assembler does not operate on weekends. What about scenario 7 (see Prob. 13.17)?

A summary (average across the five runs) of the seven sets of simulation runs appears in Table 13.17. Note that the throughput (in parts per week) for scenario 2 (two shifts) is considerably less than that for scenario 1 (three shifts). Also, scenario 2 has a high starvation proportion for the loaders. These results are due to a shortage of empty containers for scenario 2 caused by the assembler not operating enough. Observe for scenario 3 (two forklift trucks) that the throughput is again less than that for scenario 1 and, in addition, the

TABLE 13.17
Summary of simulation results for initial set of runs

Scenario	Avg. empty containers	Parts per week	Loader starved	Assembler blocked	Forklift idle
1	1229	15019	0.000	0.001	0.370
2	241	11405	0.157	0.001	0.489
3	442	13109	0.050	0.133	0.210
4	1218	14666	0.001	0.001	0.381
5	1233	15050	0.000	0.001	0.386
6	1234	15050	0.000	0.001	0.317
7	1123	15079	0.000	0.001	0.369

TABLE 13.18
Scenarios for the second set of simulation runs

Scenario	Number of containers	Forklift trucks
8	2750	3
9	2500	3
10	2250	3
11	2000	3
12	1750	3
13	3000	2*

* Dispatching rule is shortest distance first.

blockage proportion is high for the assembler. This is due to the unavailability of forklift trucks to remove empty containers from the assembler's conveyor caused by the nonoptimal priority rule (i.e., pick up at the assembler has the lowest priority); see Table 13.19. Note that queue sizes of one (scenario 4) cause a small degradation in throughput. Finally, the high forklift truck idle proportions in Table 13.17 are caused by the periods of inactivity for the loaders and the assembler.

The system description and simulation results described above were presented to approximately 20 of the company's employees including the plant manager. As a result of this meeting, it was decided to simulate the six additional scenarios described in Table 13.18. Each of these scenarios had queue sizes of 2, three assembler shifts, and the same run length and number of runs as before.

A summary of the simulation results for these scenarios (and also scenario 1 from Table 13.17) is given in Table 13.19. Note that the throughput does not change significantly when the number of containers is varied between 2250 and 3000. This can be seen more clearly in Fig. 13.17, where throughput is plotted as a function of the number of containers. Observe also that the shortest-distance-first dispatching rule (scenario 13) gives somewhat better results for two forklift trucks than the original rule (compare scenarios 13 and 3).

TABLE 13.19
Summary of simulation results for second set of runs

Scenario	Avg. empty containers	Parts per week	Loader starved	Assembler blocked	Forklift idle
1	1229	15019	0.000	0.001	0.370
8	941	14959	0.006	0.001	0.379
9	640	14798	0.014	0.001	0.384
10	402	14106	0.053	0.001	0.411
11	209	11894	0.192	0.000	0.487
12	80	8758	0.374	0.000	0.597
13	1410	14306	0.005	0.002	0.265

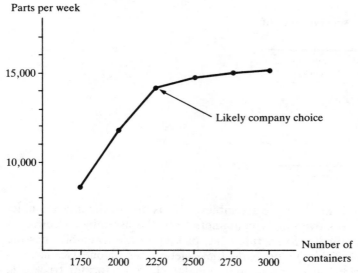

Parts per week

FIGURE 13.17
Throughput (parts per week) as a function of the number of containers.

13.6.6 Conclusions and Benefits

Based on the simulation results presented above and several conversations with the client, the following project conclusions were reached:

- The company will probably buy 2250 containers rather than the 3000 containers originally budgeted.
- Three assembler shifts (Monday through Friday) are required.
- Two or three forklift trucks are required for Monday through Friday (further investigation is needed), and two are required for Saturday and Sunday.
- Two containers should be staged in the input queues of the loaders and the assembler.
- The output queues of the loaders should have a capacity of two.
- The system can achieve the desired throughput with the above specifications.

The company received several definite benefits as a result of the simulation study. First, they gained the assurance (before building the system) that the proposed design for the loaders, warehouse, and assembler would actually meet their specified throughput requirements. If a simulation study had not been performed and if a bottleneck were discovered after system installation, the cost of retrofitting the system could have been significant.

The company will probably buy 2250 containers rather than the 3000 originally in the budget, since the throughputs for scenarios 1, 8, 9, and 10 are all sufficient for the projected product demand. Since containers cost $400 each, this is a savings of $300,000. In addition, each container occupies 20.3 square feet of floor space, and the company expects to rent floor space at a cost of $15 per square foot per year. Thus, by using 750 fewer containers, they will save $228,375 a year in floor-space rental. Therefore, the total first-year savings are $528,375.

PROBLEMS

13.1. Consider a machine with uptimes $U_1, U_2, \ldots$ and downtimes $D_1, D_2, \ldots$ as described in Sec. 13.4.2. Is it *completely* correct to assume that the U_i's and the D_i's are each IID within themselves? Why?

13.2. For the machine in Prob. 13.1, is it *completely* correct to assume that U_i and D_i are independent? Why?

13.3. Consider a machine that operates continuously until a part jams; i.e., it is never starved or blocked. Suppose that a part has a probability p of jamming independently of all other parts. What is the probability distribution of the number of parts produced before the first jam and what is its mean? Thus, if the average number of parts produced before a jam is known for an actual machine, the above model can be used to specify p for a simulation model.

13.4. Suppose that a machine will fail when either of two independent components fails. Describe how you would model breakdowns for the machine for each of the following two cases:

(*a*) The uptime of each machine is based on busy time.

(*b*) The uptime of each machine is based on calendar time.

13.5. Consider a machine that is never starved or blocked. It will fail when either component A or component B fails. These components fail independently of each other, and one component does not "age" while the other component is down. The mean busy time before failure and the mean repair (down) time for these components (in hours) are as follows:

Component	Mean busy time	Mean repair time
A	46.5	1.5
B	250.0	6.0

Compute the efficiency e of the machine.

13.6. Use a different method to compute the efficiency in Prob. 13.5 if busy time before failure and repair time are both exponentially distributed.

13.7. Consider a machine that has two types of failure. Type 1 is a minor problem, which is corrected by the machine operator with a "short" repair (down) time. A type 2 failure, on the other hand, is a major problem requiring a maintenance person and a "long" repair time. Suppose that n observations of repair time are available for the machine and n_i of them are of type i (where $i = 1, 2$), with $n_1 + n_2 = n$. Give two possible approaches for representing repair times in a simulation model. What are you implicitly assuming about the relationship between U_i and D_i (equal to R_i here)?

13.8. Consider a machine that "operates" 24 hours a day for 7 days a week. The uptimes $U_1, U_2, \ldots$ and downtimes $D_1, D_2, \ldots$ are available, but not the corresponding busy times $B_1, B_2, \ldots$. Suppose, for simplicity, that an exponential distribution fits the U_i's. The average number of parts produced per 8-hour shift is known, as well as the average processing time for parts. Assuming that the exponential distribution is also a good model for the B_i's, what mean should be used for a machine-breakdown model based on busy time?

13.9. What is missing in Sec. 13.5 from the analytic calculations to determine the number of machines for each station? *Hint:* Can a machine always process a waiting part?

13.10. What is missing in Sec. 13.5 from the analytic calculations to determine the number of forklifts?

13.11. In Fig. 13.9 the maximum number of forklift requests for system design 1 was 12, based on sampling the system state once an hour. In fact, the maximum number of requests was 20 for all possible values of time. Given this large maximum value, why do two forklifts turn out to be sufficient?

13.12. Why is the plot of Fig. 13.10 linear? Give an expression for the slope.

13.13. What would you expect a moving average for system design 1's hourly throughputs (Sec. 13.5) to look like? See Fig. 13.14 for a similar type of plot.

13.14. Simulate system design 3 in Sec. 13.5 with the change that an idle forklift has station 6 (input/output) as its home base. That is, an idle forklift will travel to station 6 to wait for its next job. Which of the two system designs is preferable?

13.15. Using simulation, determine the required number of machines for each work station and the required number of forklifts for the manufacturing system in Sec. 13.5 (original version) if each work station has an infinite-capacity output queue. Thus, no blocking occurs.

13.16. Perform a resolution IV fractional factorial design (see Sec. 12.3.1) for the manufacturing system of Sec. 13.5, using the following factors and levels:

Factor	−	+
Machines in station 1	4	5
Machines in station 2	1	2
Machines in station 3	4	5
Machines in station 4	2	3
Machines in station 5	2	3
Forklift trucks	1	2
Forklift control logic	Shortest distance first	FIFO

13.17. Does the empty-containers stochastic process discussed in Sec. 13.6.5 have a steady-state distribution for scenario 7? Why?

13.18. Consider the calendar-time approach for modeling the up segments of a machine in Sec. 13.4.2. Suppose that a machine breaks down when it is starved. (Perhaps it was idling at the time.) Do you think that the breakdown would be discovered immediately (and repair begun) or when the next part actually arrives? Assume that availability of a repairman is not an issue.

13.19. Consider a machine that is never starved or blocked. Suppose shop-floor personnel estimate that the machine has an efficiency $e = 0.9$ and typically fails twice in an 8-hour shift. What values of $E(U)$ and $E(D)$ should be used in modeling this machine?

REFERENCES

AT&T ISTEL: *WITNESS User Manual*, Version 6, Beachwood, Ohio (1989).

AutoSimulations, Inc.: *AutoMod II Users Manual*, Bountiful, Utah (1989).

CACI Products Company: *SIMFACTORY II.5 User's and Reference Manual*, Version 2.0, La Jolla, Calif. (1990).

Carson, J. S.: Convincing Users of Model's Validity Is Challenging Aspect of Modeler's Job, *Ind. Eng.*, *18*: 74–85 (June 1986).

Conway, R., W. L. Maxwell, J. O. McClain, and S. L. Worona: *User's Guide to XCELL+ Factory Modeling System*, 2d ed., Scientific Press, Redwood City, Calif. (1987).

Conway, R., W. L. Maxwell, J. O. McClain, and L. J. Thomas: The Role of Work-in-Process Inventory in Serial Production Lines, *Operations Res.*, *36*: 229–241 (1988).

Davis, D. A.: Modeling AGV Systems, *Proc. 1986 Winter Simulation Conference*, Washington, D.C., pp. 568–574 (1986).

Henriksen, J. O., and T. J. Schriber: Simplified Approaches to Modeling Accumulating and Nonaccumulating Conveyor Systems, *Proc. 1986 Winter Simulation Conference*, Washington, D.C., pp. 575–593 (1986).

Law, A. M.: Introduction to Simulation: A Powerful Tool for Analyzing Complex Manufacturing Systems, *Ind. Eng.*, *18*: 46–63 (May 1986).

Law, A. M., and S. W. Haider: Selecting Simulation Software for Manufacturing Applications: Practical Guidelines & Software Survey, *Ind. Eng.*, *31*: 33–46 (May 1989).

Law, A. M., and M. G. McComas: How Simulation Pays Off, *Manuf. Eng.*, *100*: 37–39 (February 1988).

Law, A. M., and M. G. McComas: Pitfalls to Avoid in the Simulation of Manufacturing Systems, *Ind. Eng.*, *31*: 28–31, 69 (May 1989).

Law, A. M., and S. G. Vincent: *UniFit II User's Manual*, Simulation Modeling and Analysis Company, Tucson, Arizona (1990).

Pritsker Corporation: *FACTOR Implementation Guide*, Indianapolis, Ind. (1989).

Production Modeling Corporation of Utah: *ProModel User's Manual*, Orem, Utah (1989).

Ross, S. M.: *Introduction to Probability Models*, 4th ed., Academic Press, San Diego (1989).

APPENDIX

TABLE T.1
Critical points $t_{\nu,\gamma}$ for the t distribution with ν df, and z_γ for the standard normal distribution

$\gamma = P(T_\nu \le t_{\nu,\gamma})$, where T_ν is a random variable having the t distribution with ν df; the last row, where $\nu = \infty$, gives the normal critical points satisfying $\gamma = P(Z \le z_\gamma)$, where Z is a standard normal random variable

ν	0.6000	0.7000	0.8000	0.9000	0.9333	0.9500	0.9600	0.9667	0.9750	0.9800	0.9833	0.9875	0.9900	0.9917	0.9938	0.9950
1	0.325	0.727	1.376	3.078	4.702	6.314	7.916	9.524	12.706	15.895	19.043	25.452	31.821	38.342	51.334	63.657
2	0.289	0.617	1.061	1.886	2.456	2.920	3.320	3.679	4.303	4.849	5.334	6.205	6.965	7.665	8.897	9.925
3	0.277	0.584	0.978	1.638	2.045	2.353	2.605	2.823	3.182	3.482	3.738	4.177	4.541	4.864	5.408	5.841
4	0.271	0.569	0.941	1.533	1.879	2.132	2.333	2.502	2.776	2.999	3.184	3.495	3.747	3.966	4.325	4.604
5	0.267	0.559	0.920	1.476	1.790	2.015	2.191	2.337	2.571	2.757	2.910	3.163	3.365	3.538	3.818	4.032
6	0.265	0.553	0.906	1.440	1.735	1.943	2.104	2.237	2.447	2.612	2.748	2.969	3.143	3.291	3.528	3.707
7	0.263	0.549	0.896	1.415	1.698	1.895	2.046	2.170	2.365	2.517	2.640	2.841	2.998	3.130	3.341	3.499
8	0.262	0.546	0.889	1.397	1.670	1.860	2.004	2.122	2.306	2.449	2.565	2.752	2.896	3.018	3.211	3.355
9	0.261	0.543	0.883	1.383	1.650	1.833	1.973	2.086	2.262	2.398	2.508	2.685	2.821	2.936	3.116	3.250
10	0.260	0.542	0.879	1.372	1.634	1.812	1.948	2.058	2.228	2.359	2.465	2.634	2.764	2.872	3.043	3.169
11	0.260	0.540	0.876	1.363	1.621	1.796	1.928	2.036	2.201	2.328	2.430	2.593	2.718	2.822	2.985	3.106
12	0.259	0.539	0.873	1.356	1.610	1.782	1.912	2.017	2.179	2.303	2.402	2.560	2.681	2.782	2.939	3.055
13	0.259	0.538	0.870	1.350	1.601	1.771	1.899	2.002	2.160	2.282	2.379	2.533	2.650	2.748	2.900	3.012
14	0.258	0.537	0.868	1.345	1.593	1.761	1.887	1.999	2.145	2.264	2.359	2.510	2.624	2.720	2.868	2.977
15	0.258	0.536	0.866	1.341	1.587	1.753	1.878	1.978	2.131	2.249	2.342	2.490	2.602	2.696	2.841	2.947
16	0.258	0.535	0.865	1.337	1.581	1.746	1.869	1.968	2.120	2.235	2.327	2.473	2.583	2.675	2.817	2.921
17	0.257	0.534	0.863	1.333	1.576	1.740	1.862	1.960	2.110	2.224	2.315	2.458	2.567	2.657	2.796	2.898
18	0.257	0.534	0.862	1.330	1.572	1.734	1.855	1.953	2.101	2.214	2.303	2.445	2.552	2.641	2.778	2.878
19	0.257	0.533	0.861	1.328	1.568	1.729	1.850	1.946	2.093	2.205	2.293	2.433	2.539	2.627	2.762	2.861
20	0.257	0.533	0.860	1.325	1.564	1.725	1.844	1.940	2.086	2.197	2.285	2.423	2.528	2.614	2.748	2.845
21	0.257	0.532	0.859	1.323	1.561	1.721	1.840	1.935	2.080	2.189	2.277	2.414	2.518	2.603	2.735	2.831
22	0.256	0.532	0.858	1.321	1.558	1.717	1.835	1.930	2.074	2.183	2.269	2.405	2.508	2.593	2.724	2.819
23	0.256	0.532	0.858	1.319	1.556	1.714	1.832	1.926	2.069	2.177	2.263	2.398	2.500	2.584	2.713	2.807
24	0.256	0.531	0.857	1.318	1.553	1.711	1.828	1.922	2.064	2.172	2.257	2.391	2.492	2.575	2.704	2.797
25	0.256	0.531	0.856	1.316	1.551	1.708	1.825	1.918	2.060	2.167	2.251	2.385	2.485	2.568	2.695	2.787
26	0.256	0.531	0.856	1.315	1.549	1.706	1.822	1.915	2.056	2.162	2.246	2.379	2.479	2.561	2.687	2.779
27	0.256	0.531	0.855	1.314	1.547	1.703	1.819	1.912	2.052	2.158	2.242	2.373	2.473	2.554	2.680	2.771
28	0.256	0.530	0.855	1.313	1.546	1.701	1.817	1.909	2.048	2.154	2.237	2.368	2.467	2.548	2.673	2.763
29	0.256	0.530	0.854	1.311	1.544	1.699	1.814	1.906	2.045	2.150	2.233	2.364	2.462	2.543	2.667	2.756
30	0.256	0.530	0.854	1.310	1.543	1.697	1.812	1.904	2.042	2.147	2.230	2.360	2.457	2.537	2.661	2.750
40	0.255	0.529	0.851	1.303	1.532	1.684	1.796	1.886	2.021	2.123	2.203	2.329	2.423	2.501	2.619	2.704
50	0.255	0.528	0.849	1.299	1.526	1.676	1.787	1.875	2.009	2.109	2.188	2.311	2.403	2.479	2.594	2.678
75	0.254	0.527	0.846	1.293	1.517	1.665	1.775	1.861	1.992	2.090	2.167	2.287	2.377	2.450	2.562	2.643
100	0.254	0.526	0.845	1.290	1.513	1.660	1.769	1.855	1.984	2.081	2.157	2.276	2.364	2.436	2.547	2.626
∞	0.253	0.524	0.842	1.282	1.501	1.645	1.751	1.834	1.960	2.054	2.127	2.241	2.326	2.395	2.501	2.576

TABLE T.2
Critical points $\chi^2_{\nu,\gamma}$ for the chi-square distribution with ν df

$\gamma = P(Y_\nu \leq \chi^2_{\nu,\gamma})$, where Y_ν has a chi-square distribution with ν df; for large ν, use the approximation for $\chi^2_{\nu,\gamma}$ in Sec. 7.4.1

ν	γ						
	0.250	0.500	0.750	0.900	0.950	0.975	0.990
1	0.102	0.455	1.323	2.706	3.841	5.024	6.635
2	0.575	1.386	2.773	4.605	5.991	7.378	9.210
3	1.213	2.366	4.108	6.251	7.815	9.348	11.345
4	1.923	3.357	5.385	7.779	9.488	11.143	13.277
5	2.675	4.351	6.626	9.236	11.070	12.833	15.086
6	3.455	5.348	7.841	10.645	12.592	14.449	16.812
7	4.255	6.346	9.037	12.017	14.067	16.013	18.475
8	5.071	7.344	10.219	13.362	15.507	17.535	20.090
9	5.899	8.343	11.389	14.684	16.919	19.023	21.666
10	6.737	9.342	12.549	15.987	18.307	20.483	23.209
11	7.584	10.341	13.701	17.275	19.675	21.920	24.725
12	8.438	11.340	14.845	18.549	21.026	23.337	26.217
13	9.299	12.340	15.984	19.812	22.362	24.736	27.688
14	10.165	13.339	17.117	21.064	23.685	26.119	29.141
15	11.037	14.339	18.245	22.307	24.996	27.488	30.578
16	11.912	15.338	19.369	23.542	26.296	28.845	32.000
17	12.792	16.338	20.489	24.769	27.587	30.191	33.409
18	13.675	17.338	21.605	25.989	28.869	31.526	34.805
19	14.562	18.338	22.718	27.204	30.144	32.852	36.191
20	15.452	19.337	23.828	28.412	31.410	34.170	37.566
21	16.344	20.337	24.935	29.615	32.671	35.479	38.932
22	17.240	21.337	26.039	30.813	33.924	36.781	40.289
23	18.137	22.337	27.141	32.007	35.172	38.076	41.638
24	19.037	23.337	28.241	33.196	36.415	39.364	42.980
25	19.939	24.337	29.339	34.382	37.652	40.646	44.314
26	20.843	25.336	30.435	35.563	38.885	41.923	45.642
27	21.749	26.336	31.528	36.741	40.113	43.195	46.963
28	22.657	27.336	32.620	37.916	41.337	44.461	48.278
29	23.567	28.336	33.711	39.087	42.557	45.722	49.588
30	24.478	29.336	34.800	40.256	43.773	46.979	50.892
40	33.660	39.335	45.616	51.805	55.758	59.342	63.691
50	42.942	49.335	56.334	63.167	67.505	71.420	76.154
75	66.417	74.334	82.858	91.061	96.217	100.839	106.393
100	90.133	99.334	109.141	118.498	124.342	129.561	135.807

INDEXES

AUTHOR INDEX

SUBJECT INDEX